Humankind Emerging

Humankind Emerging

NINTH EDITION

Bernard G. Campbell

James D. Loy
University of Rhode Island

Kathryn Cruz-Uribe
Northern Arizona University

Boston • New York • San Francisco
Mexico City • Montreal • Toronto • London • Madrid • Munich • Paris
Hong Kong • Singapore • Tokyo • Cape Town • Sydney

Series Editor: Jennifer Jacobson
Series Editorial Assistant: Emma Christensen
Marketing Manager: Laura Lee Manley
Editorial Production Service: Omegatype Typography, Inc.
Composition Buyer: Linda Cox
Manufacturing Buyer: Megan Cochran
Electronic Composition: Omegatype Typography, Inc.
Interior Design: Carol Somberg
Text and Photo Permissions Editor: PoYee Oster
Cover Administrator: Linda Knowles

For related titles and support materials, visit our online catalog at www.ablongman.com.

Between the time website information is gathered and then published, it is not unusual for some sites to have closed. Also, the transcription of URLs can result in typographical errors. The publisher would appreciate notification where these errors occur so that they may be corrected in subsequent editions.

Library of Congress Cataloging-in-Publication Data

Campbell, Bernard Grant.
Humankind emerging / Bernard G. Campbell, James D. Loy, Kathryn Cruz-Uribe.—9th ed.
p. cm.
Includes bibliographical references and index.
ISBN 0-205-42380-9
1. Human evolution. 2. Prehistoric peoples. 3. Physical anthropology. I. Loy, James. II. Cruz-Uribe, Kathryn. III. Title.

GN281.C36C36 2006
599.93'8-dc22

2005047672

Printed in the United States of America

Photo and Text Credits appear on pp. 517–524, which should be considered an extension of the copyright page.

Contents

Chapter 6 The South African Hominins .... page 160

Chapter 7 East Africa and the Sahel: A Multitude of Australopiths .... page 183

part three: THE EVOLUTION OF HUMANKIND

part four: MODERN HUMANITY

Preface

Humankind Emerging, first published in 1976, is one of the longest-running anthropology texts. You hold in your hands the ninth edition of this book, which generations of students have found useful in introductory anthropology, physical anthropology, and human evolution courses. The product of the collaboration between a paleoanthropologist (Bernard G. Campbell), a primatologist (James D. Loy), and an archaeologist (Kathryn Cruz-Uribe), *Humankind Emerging* treats all the subdisciplines of physical anthropology as well as several related fields but focuses mainly on paleoanthropology—the science concerned with the collection and interpretation of the fossil and cultural evidence of human evolution. Through the book's seventeen chapters, the reader learns what we know of how, when, and where humans came to exist. *Humankind Emerging* conveys the excitement of humanity's past to students who are studying physical anthropology for the first time.

In this new edition, we have made every effort to remove outdated materials and to add the latest discoveries and theories. The latter aspect of this revision has been a particular challenge, since reports of new fossils and new analyses appear constantly in scholarly journals and monographs. Nonetheless, we believe we have incorporated the main paleoanthropological developments through the latter part of 2004. Significant additions and changes to the book include the following:

- Recognition of the Plesiadapiformes as an early (archaic) semiorder of the Primates. All *primates of modern aspect,* both living and extinct, are now classified in a second semiorder, the Euprimates
- New information on the earliest stages of primate evolution, particularly the apparently stepwise evolution of grasping digits and elaborations in vision
- Descriptions of the latest theories concerning the identity, anatomy, and behavior of humankind's last ape ancestors
- A thorough taxonomic revision of the human lineage that brings this text into agreement with most modern paleoanthropological theorists. Among the major changes are these:
    - The term *hominid* is widened to include members of the human lineage as well as all great apes.
    - Living humans and their ancestors since the split from the apes are placed in the Tribe Hominini and called *hominins.*
    - Hominins are divided further into two Subtribes: Australopithecina (containing the australopiths of Africa) and Hominina (containing all living and extinct members of the genus *Homo*).
- Descriptions and analyses of the latest hominin fossil discoveries; new genera and species include *Sahelanthropus, Orrorin, Ardipithecus kadabba, Kenyanthropus,* and *Australopithecus garhi*
- Description of the new subfossil hominan species from Flores, Indonesia: *Homo floresiensis*
- Full citations of 700-plus sources throughout the text
- Thirty percent of cited sources were published in the last five years, 2000 to 2004

Finally, the following pedagogical features of *Humankind Emerging* contribute to improved teaching and learning:

- Extensive illustrations, including those of recent fossil discoveries
- A series of boxed items that describe the relevancy of physical anthropology for students' everyday lives

- "Mini-Timelines" in the Overview sections at the start of most chapters that alert students to significant fossil discoveries or other events and give their geologic age or date in history
- An extensive running glossary within the text, plus end-of-book definitions
- Lists of pertinent Internet (WWW) sites and search terms at the end of each chapter
- Supplementary reading lists at the end of each chapter and a comprehensive Bibliography of sources
- An ancillary package is available that includes an Instructor's Manual/TestBank and Computerized TestBank, all authored by Linda D. Wolfe of East Carolina University, and a dedicated web site for the discipline of anthropology, Anthropology Experience (www.anthropologyexperience.com). Visit the publisher's web site at www.ablongman.com for more information.

Humankind Emerging was originally developed from material first published in Time-Life Books' *Emergence of Man* series and *The Life Nature Library*, and this ninth edition continues to benefit from the use of certain aspects of that material. Our thanks go to the authors, editors, and consultants who worked on this edition. Many friends and colleagues were generous with their time, comments, and materials, and among them, special thanks go to Professors Alexander Black (National University of Ireland, Galway), Bruce Bourque (Bates College), Ethan Braunstein (Northern Arizona University and Mayo Clinic, Scottsdale, Arizona), Don Holly (University of Rhode Island), Jonathan Kent (Metropolitan State College of Denver), Marquisa LaVelle and Richard Pollnac (both University of Rhode Island), Bonny Sands (Northern Arizona University), Joel Schiff (Auckland University), J. Kenneth Smail (Kenyon College), H. Dieter Steklis (Rutgers University), and Marc Verhaegen (Studiecentrum Anthropologie, Putte, Belgium). Helpful comments were also forthcoming from anthropology students Nicholas Burkett, Luca Clemente, and Jen Coburn.

Several anthropologists helped especially by sharing their thoughts in careful and detailed reviews:

John Krigbaum, *University of Florida*

Amy L. Schilling, *Metropolitan State College of Denver*

Nancy E. Tatarek, *Ohio University*

Frances White, *University of Oregon*

Linda D. Wolfe, *East Carolina University*

Finally, we thank our spouses—Susan Campbell, Kent Loy, and Gene Cruz-Uribe—for their unfailing encouragement, and our editor, Jennifer Jacobson, for her support. Books are produced not by their authors alone but with the help of an enormous supporting cast. Many thanks, folks, for all your help.

Readers' feedback is invited and can be sent to jimloy@uri.edu or kathryn.cruz-uribe@nau.edu.

Bernard G. Campbell
James D. Loy
Kathryn Cruz-Uribe

Introduction

Know then thyself, presume not God to scan;
The proper study of mankind is man.
Placed on this isthmus in a middle state,
A being darkly wise, and rudely great:
With too much knowledge for the skeptic side,
With too much weakness for the Stoic's pride,
He hangs between; in doubt to act or rest;
In doubt to deem himself a God, or beast;
In doubt his mind or body to prefer;
Born but to die; and reas'ning but to err;
Alike in ignorance, his reason such,
Whether he thinks too little or too much;
Chaos of Thought and Passion, all confused;
Still by himself abused, or disabused;
Created half to rise, and half to fall;
Great Lord of all things, yet a prey to all;
Sole judge of truth, in endless error hurled;
The glory, jest, and riddle of the world!

Alexander Pope, 1688–1744.
Essay on Man, Ep. II, 1, 1–18.

These profound and brilliant lines by English poet and satirist Alexander Pope describe the paradox of human nature. Throughout history, people have been puzzled and exasperated by humankind's strange duality—half animal, half angel—and much of religious and philosophical teaching has been an attempt to understand and integrate these two sides of our being. Neither priest nor philosopher has offered us an explanation that has proved either intellectually satisfactory or (in modern jargon) operationally effective.

The writings of the wise throughout the ages have not enabled most of us to come to terms with our dual nature, however much we may have thought about these things or faced the moral dilemmas that are our inheritance. We carry the marks and needs of an animal, but we also find ourselves alienated and unsure in the natural world and in the face of our own biology. In our imagination, we travel far beyond the bounds of both our own environment and our biological nature, yet we still feel rooted to them in a way that seems to constrict the highest reaches of our humanity. Our dual natures tend to be ranged opposite each other like the earth's poles, and we find ourselves torn between them, caught in conflict.

Humanity has, quite logically, looked to the past to explain the present and in so doing has developed numerous mythological accounts of human origins. These vary widely from culture to culture, but in the Judeo-Christian tradition our duality is explained by the biblical story of a stern God who placed a perfect man and a perfect woman in paradise and then expelled them when they disobeyed His commands. This story of humankind's fall from perfection has long been used in Western cultures to account for the darker side of human nature.

Today, the sciences—particularly geology, biology, evolutionary psychology, and anthropology—have a different and naturalistic explanation to help us understand our duality. This scientific account began to be written over two centuries ago, when geologists started to accumulate both stratigraphic and fossil evidence that the world was vastly older than the few thousand years then widely believed. As this remarkable scientific deduction became generally accepted, humanity's presumably short past was stretched a thousandfold, and to the future, present, and immediate past of the historical period was added *prehistory.* Understanding this new dimension of humanity's story has become a major requirement for understanding our present.

Humankind Emerging is about this relatively newly discovered prehistoric dimension. It recounts the extraordinary story of the discovery of and the evidence for humanity's long past. It reveals to us the nature of our distant ancestors, who began the long evolutionary journey from the African forests to today's modern cities. It brings prehistory to bear upon the present-day human condition and thus gives us an entirely new way of approaching and understanding ourselves. The modern evolutionary perspective, which we owe to the nineteenth-century genius of Charles Darwin and Alfred Russel Wallace, illuminates not only the physical origins of humankind but also the light and dark sides of our behavior. But that is not all: This perspective also shows us the integrated and dynamic evolution of both behavioral aspects and their essentially interlocking relationship. The evolutionary perspective gives us profound insights into humanness and shows us that our duality arises not from two warring halves but from two interdependent aspects of an evolved whole.

This new view of human nature is just one small part of the revolution in knowledge and understanding brought about by the work of Darwin and his successors. Our past has created us and influences or determines every part of our lives. Our present condition is a consequence not just of our individual life histories, important though they may be, but of the whole history of the human species. We are, in this sense, a product both of our childhood and of our prehistory.

The theory of evolution by the Darwin/Wallace mechanism of natural selection has now been developed over more than a century as a result of an enormous amount of painstaking research. The evidence that living organisms have evolved over many millions of years is today very strong and convincing. Science builds up such hypotheses or theories on the basis of a vast range of accumulated evidence derived from experiment and observation. Each new piece of evidence has corroborated the central theory. No evidence currently known either falsifies or undermines the theory of organic evolution by natural selection.

This is a book of science that applies the Darwin/Wallace evolutionary model to the development of humankind, and as such, it advocates a *naturalistic* explanation for our physical and behavioral attributes. In so doing, it makes no claim to test (and certainly not to disprove) the existence of the Judeo–Christian God or any other deity. Gods and their creative or destructive actions are *supernaturalistic* phenomena and thus clearly outside the bounds of scientific investigation and testing. We generally agree with the idea that science and religion are both legitimate ways of knowing about the world but maintain that they have very different modes of operation and thus should be neither confused nor mixed. Only evolution provides us with a truly scientific explanation of human origins. Religion, including when it is presented in the oxymoronic guise of so-called creation science, does not do so.

Finally, we hope the following chapters will demonstrate that an evolutionary explanation of the origin of species, particularly our own, can be just as awe inspiring and full of wonder as creation myths. Indeed, this point was not lost on Charles Darwin, who in 1859 ended his book *On the Origin of Species* with these words:

> There is a grandeur in this view of life, with its several powers, having been originally breathed into a few forms or into one; and that, whilst this planet has gone cycling on according to the fixed law of gravity, from so simple a beginning endless forms most beautiful and most wonderful have been, and are being, evolved.

About the Authors

Paleoanthropologist Bernard Campbell received his Ph.D. from Cambridge University. He has taught at that institution, Harvard University, and the University of California at Los Angeles, and has conducted field work in South and East Africa and in Iran. Although retired from active teaching, Professor Campbell continues to publish widely on the evolution of human behavior and its ecological setting. Professor Campbell originally developed the text *Humankind Emerging* and guided it through six editions. (Photograph personal property of Bernard Campbell.)

James Loy (shown here with his wife Kent and two orphaned patas monkeys being hand reared) is a Professor of anthropology at the University of Rhode Island. After earning a Ph.D. from Northwestern University, Professor Loy conducted research on the sexual behavior of Old World monkeys for over twenty years. He joined the publication team of *Humankind Emerging* with its seventh edition. (Photograph personal property of James Loy.)

Kathryn Cruz-Uribe is an archaeologist specializing in the analysis of animal bones from archaeological sites. She has more than twenty years of fieldwork experience, primarily in South Africa. She received an A.B. in anthropology and art history from Middlebury College, Vermont, and her A.M. and Ph.D. in anthropology from the University of Chicago. Dr. Cruz-Uribe currently serves as Professor of Anthropology and Dean of the College of Social and Behavioral Sciences at Northern Arizona University, in Flagstaff, Arizona. (Photograph personal property of Kathryn Cruz-Uribe.)

Humankind Emerging

Chapter 1

The Search for Human Origins

A nineteenth-century caricature of Charles Darwin as a monkey.

I would not be ashamed to have a monkey for my ancestor, but I would be ashamed to be connected with a man who used great gifts to obscure the truth.

Thomas Henry Huxley, 1825–1895.
Defending Darwin's theory against the attack of Bishop Samuel Wilberforce.

Overview

Paleoanthropology the study of the *fossil* and cultural remains and other evidence of humans' *extinct* ancestors.

This is a book about **paleoanthropology**, the study of humans' physical evolution and the origins of modern behavior. Anthropologists often divide their discipline into four subfields: *Physical anthropologists* study our biology and its evolutionary development; *cultural anthropologists* focus on living humans' social and behavioral patterns; *archaeologists* are concerned with understanding people who lived in the past; and *linguistic anthropologists* study speech and language. Many practitioners of paleoanthropology consider themselves to be physical anthropologists, but some focus more on archaeology, the science of recovering and interpreting material from the past. Today, paleoanthropologists pursue the search for human origins within the Western scientific tradition, and therefore some knowledge of that tradition is necessary to understand current theories and discoveries.

Toward that end, this opening chapter describes a series of historical events and scientific developments that contributed to our modern views on evolution. Beginning with the seventeenth century—when Europeans' opinions were shaped by the biblical creation story and belief in a young earth—we will review sequentially the accumulation of geologic evidence for so-called deep time (that is, for an ancient earth); the development of Charles Darwin's theory of evolution; Gregor Mendel's research into the problem of heredity; and finally, the (relatively recent) formulation of the modern synthetic theory of evolution. The short timeline below shows the chronology of these developments.

Prescientific Theories of Human Origins

Creation Myths and Bishop Ussher's Young Earth

For thousands of years, the question of human origins has preoccupied people of all cultures. Where did we come from? What forces have shaped our bodies, behaviors, and societies? How do we fit in the natural world? This book attempts to answer these ancient questions from a modern, anthropological perspective, but for

*Mini-*TIMELINE

Years AD	Concept or Development
1930s–1940s	Modern Synthetic Theory of evolution
1880s–1920s	Mutation vs. natural selection
1900	Gregor Mendel's work rediscovered
1866	Mendel publishes his work on heredity
1859	Charles Darwin publishes his theory of evolution by natural selection
1700s and 1800s	Evidence accumulates for deep time
1600s and 1700s	Antiquarians begin to recover evidence of ancient humans
1650	Bishop Ussher publishes his date of creation

millennia, the only available answers came from the **creation myths** of the world's various cultures and religions. These prescientific myths—often beautiful, imaginative, and poetic—typically described humans as the result of supernatural and divine creative acts. The creation story told in the Bible (Genesis 1) is a particularly pertinent case in point because of the strong influence it exerted on thought in Western Europe, the geographic region destined to be the cradle of modern evolutionary theory.

Creation myth a story describing the origins, usually supernatural, of the earth and life (including humans).

According to the Genesis account, God created the earth and all of its inhabitants, including the first people, during six days of labor. Humans, created in God's own image, were then blessed, given dominion over all the other species, and directed to be fruitful and multiply. These two themes, our divine origins and earthly dominion, were stressed by the Christian church and widely accepted throughout post-Renaissance Europe (Mayr, 1982). The Bible was generally taken quite literally—to do otherwise might have meant condemning oneself to a fiery Hell—and church teachings affected the world views of people at all levels of society. Finally, on top of everything else, it was believed that God's burst of creativity had occurred rather recently and that the earth was only a few thousand years old.

The notion of a young earth was universal and supported by the Irish Archbishop James Ussher, who in 1650 AD published his calculated date for the creation of the world. Based partly on biblical references, Bishop Ussher determined that creation occurred on Sunday, October 23, 4004 BC, not quite 5,700 years before his own day! (Jenkins, 2003). Subsequently, this date was inserted as a footnote to authorized versions of the Bible, and before long it acquired the infallibility of Scripture itself. Furthermore, the validity of a young earth must have seemed assured when the Reverend John Lightfoot, who was working independently but following in Ussher's footsteps, confirmed October 23, 4004 BC as the creation date and added the detailed information that it happened at nine o'clock in the morning (Bahn, 1996). The few discoveries from nature that suggested a greater antiquity for the earth—the fossilized remains of marine shellfish collected from high mountain slopes, fossil bones unlike those from any living creature, petrified wood—were generally explained away either as the chance results of natural forces imitating life or as the remains of unlucky creatures drowned in Noah's flood.

Early Naturalists Begin to Question Human Antiquity

Ancient Bones and Tools Found Together

Even in the seventeenth century, however, there were a few brave souls in Europe who dared to challenge orthodox views. The early antiquarian Isaac de la Peyrère, for example, concluded that primitive humans had lived at a time before Adam. Unfortunately, de la Peyrère's suggestion that the world might have gone through a period of pre-Adamite existence was too audacious for the times and his book was burned publicly in 1655. Happily, by the next century, the pressure to conform to church teachings had relaxed somewhat, and in 1797, John Frere announced his discovery from Hoxne, England, of apparently ancient stone tools associated with the bones of extinct animals. Frere concluded that the stone implements (Figure 1.1; now recognized as Acheulean tools; see Chapter 11) must have been "used by a people who had not the use of metals" [and who probably lived in] "a very remote period indeed; even beyond that of the present world" (Grayson, 1983:55 and 57). Scholars still weren't ready to accept the idea of prehistoric humans, however, and although Frere's published report didn't draw the same sort of censorship as de la Peyrère's,

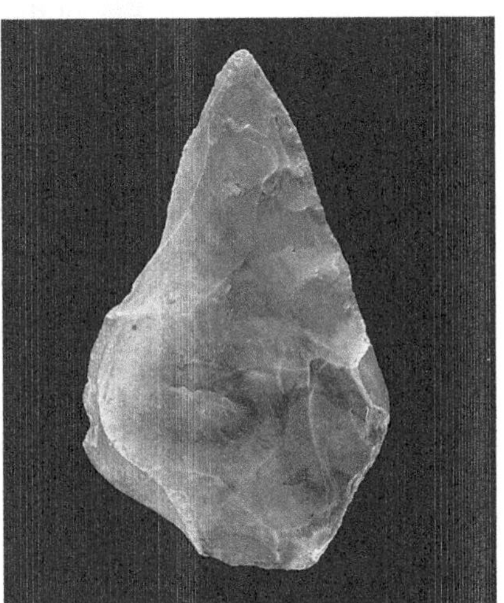

FIGURE 1.1
An example of the Acheulean stone tools recovered from Hoxne, England.

FIGURE 1.2 Excavation of the cave called Goat Hole in Wales took William Buckland many years. He described his finds in his book *Reliquiae Diluvianae* (1823), from which this figure comes. Among the finds was a human skeleton that Buckland insisted was no older than Roman times, although it has since been dated to about 25,000 years B.P. (before the present).

it did go largely ignored for more than half a century until Jacques Boucher de Perthes and others began to construct an undeniable case for ancient human life.

Boucher de Perthes was a French customs official who began in the 1830s to collect curiously chipped flints from the terraces along the Somme River—terraces that also contained the remains of extinct animals. He became convinced that his ever-growing collection of flints were tools shaped by the hands and brains of early humans (they are now classified as more examples of Acheulean tools), but in 1849, when he published his findings under the title *Antiquites Celtiques et Antediluviennes,* Boucher de Perthes gained not a single convert. Equally unappreciated was the work of the Catholic priest Father J. MacEnery. Between 1825 and 1829, MacEnery conducted excavations in a cave called Kent's Hole in southeastern England. Digging through an unbroken layer of stalagmite—and thus into quite old cave deposits—MacEnery found mammoth, rhinoceros, and cave bear bones, along with several unmistakable flint tools. Unfortunately, when he reported his find, MacEnery found himself opposed by another antiquarian cleric with a greater reputation, namely, William Buckland, Dean of Westminster. Buckland argued that MacEnery's discovery was best interpreted as the result of early but definitely post-Adamite Britons digging ovens through the stalagmite layer and then accidentally dropping some of their stone tools into the holes. MacEnery's protests fell on deaf ears, which was unfortunate, since he was right and Buckland was wrong about the evidence from Kent's Hole. And, as it turned out, Buckland's interpretation of his own discoveries at the Welsh site called Goat Hole (Figure 1.2) was just as wrong. Buckland simply was not prepared to accept any evidence of ancient human life (Grayson, 1983).

Regardless, we should not be too harsh on scholars such as Buckland who were skeptical about the accumulating proof for prehistoric human life. For one thing, contemporary procedures for site excavation and data analysis were woefully lacking in scientific rigor. This made it easy for critics to argue that chipped stone tools and extinct animal remains could have come together by accident. Furthermore, the early antiquarians were still generally laboring under the impression that the earth was only a few thousand years old—a belief that essentially precluded theories about biological or cultural histories with any time depth.

In any event, scholarly views on human prehistory changed rather abruptly in the mid-nineteenth century, and the shift was especially clear among British scholars. In 1858, the paleontologist Hugh Falconer examined Boucher de Perthes' collection of stone tools and became convinced of their authenticity. Falconer then persuaded Joseph Prestwich to examine the geology of the Somme valley—an exercise that resulted in strong proof of the commingling of chipped flint tools and extinct animals' bones on river terraces older than the modern geologic epoch. By 1863, Sir Charles Lyell, then one of England's leading geologists, was sufficiently convinced of the case for ancient humans to write a volume called *The Antiquity of Man* synthesizing the evidence (Grayson, 1983). And finally, in 1865, the naturalist and archaeologist John Lubbock proposed a classification scheme that separated the oldest and most primitive flaked implements—such as those found by Boucher de Perthes—from younger stone tools attributed to Celtic (pre-Roman) Europe. Lubbock coined the terms **Paleolithic** and **Neolithic** for the respective tool types (Bahn, 1996).

Paleolithic the Old Stone Age; the earliest stage of stone tool making, that began about 2.5 million years ago.

Neolithic the New Stone Age; a late stage of stone tool making that began about 10,000 years ago.

This shift of attitudes alone could not carry human history very far into the past, however. For 200 years, belief in Bishop Ussher's model of a young earth had firmly capped the limits of prehistory at just a few thousand years. But in fact, by the mid-nineteenth century, that model had very nearly collapsed under the weight of new geological discoveries and theories. It is to those developments that we must now turn our attention.

Geology Comes of Age: The Theory of Deep Time

Comte de Buffon

The heretical notions that the earth might be quite old (today often called the theory of **deep time**) and that it might have originated in a way different from the Genesis story actually had a few European advocates as early as the mid-eighteenth century. These scholars had to be cautious with their opinions, however, and sometimes they risked paying a high price for their theories. For example, the French naturalist Comte de Buffon suggested in his 1749 work *Histoire Naturelle* that the earth was tens of thousands of years old and had been shaped by everyday processes such as erosion by wind and water, volcanic activity, and earthquakes. For his rashness, Buffon found himself threatened with excommunication from the Catholic Church, and so he publicly retracted his views (Barber, 1980; Eisley, 1958).

Deep time the theory that the earth is billions of years old and thus has a long history of development and change.

James Hutton and the World Machine

With advances in geology, however, came increasing evidence in favor of deep time. As geologists read the accumulating "testimony of the rocks," some began to suspect that the extensive sedimentary deposits already discovered—layers of river gravels, sands, and marine limestones, sometimes dozens of feet thick and piled one on top of another—must have been laid down over long periods of time. One of the men working on this problem was the Scot James Hutton, who produced an important model of the world's formation, even though he was more of an armchair theorist than a field worker.

In 1795, Hutton published a book entitled *Theory of the Earth,* in which he described the earth as a constantly decaying and self-renewing machine. His world machine model involved ordinary geological processes operating in an endless three-stage cycle. First, Hutton wrote, terrestrial surfaces decay through weathering and erosion, with the erosional products then being carried to the sea. Second, erosional products are laid down as horizontal marine deposits, which eventually solidify into rocks. And third, sooner or later, forces within the earth cause the marine rocks to be uplifted as new continents, at which point erosion and decay come into play once again. Hutton's proof that his world machine worked relied on features such as

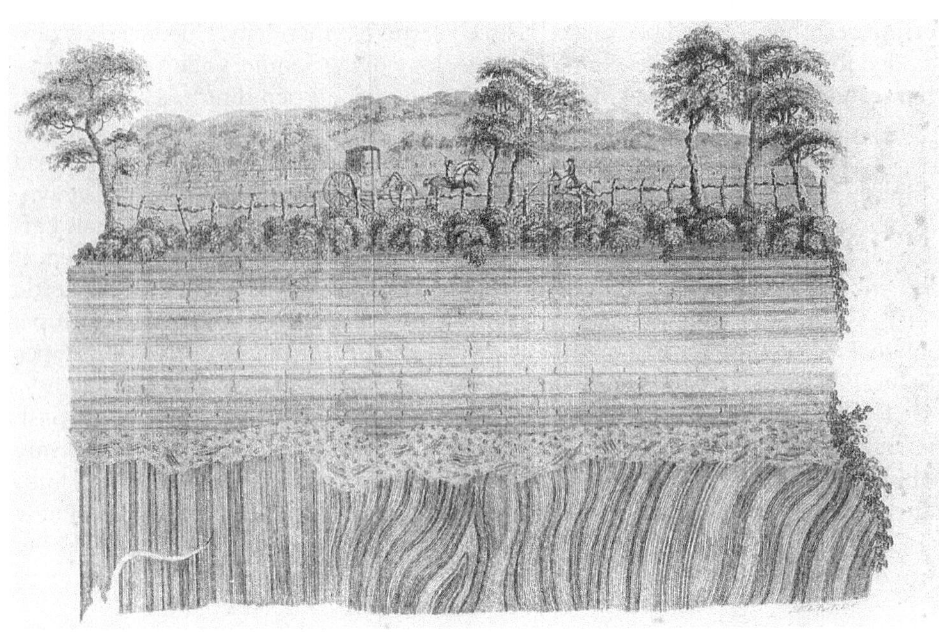

FIGURE 1.3
This engraving was published by James Hutton in 1795 in his book *Theory of the Earth*. It shows an unconformity—an ancient eroded surface—between the underlying vertical strata and the overlying horizontal strata of marine sediments at Jedburgh, Scotland. Since all these water-laid strata must have been deposited flat, it follows that the underlying sequence had arisen horizontally. Thus, we know that the lower strata were uplifted and tilted through 90 degrees. The land so formed was then eroded and produced the horizontal surface of the unconformity itself. Later the land subsided (or the seas rose), and further marine strata were deposited. Finally, the land again rose (or the sea subsided), so that the strata formed a new land surface. Thus, from this single exposure of rock, Hutton was able to deduce that the land at this place had undergone two periods of marine deposition and two periods of uplift: the first very dramatic, and the second gentle. Hutton had the genius to recognize the breathtaking significance of the sight: the immense antiquity of the earth.

the unconformity shown in Figure 1.3. Here, the deepest (and therefore oldest) rock layers have been tilted into a vertical position (in contrast to their original, horizontal layering on the sea floor) and then eroded (which bears testimony to the fact that they were high and dry at that point). Then the area was once again submerged, allowing the horizontal layers of (young) rock near the surface to be deposited. That uplift has occurred once again is obvious from the scene of present-day countryside. Hutton's view of the immensity of deep time is neatly captured in his famous closing dictum: "No vestige of a beginning—no prospect of an end" (Gould, 1987:63).

Georges Cuvier and Catastrophism

By no means was all of the geological action taking place in the British Isles. At about the same time that James Hutton was publishing his decay-and-restoration model, the French paleontologist and comparative anatomist Georges Cuvier and others were discovering the bones of ancient elephants, mammoths, whales, and other exotic and apparently long-dead species in the rocks near Paris. (Cuvier recognized each species by its members' shared physical traits. See Chapter 2 for a discussion of modern definitions of species.)

In all, Cuvier was able to show that at least 90 of the species he had recovered, as well as several genera (groups of similar species), apparently had disappeared entirely from the face of the earth. This was an extremely important discovery, because proving that extinction is a common fate of species opened the way for fossils to be used as

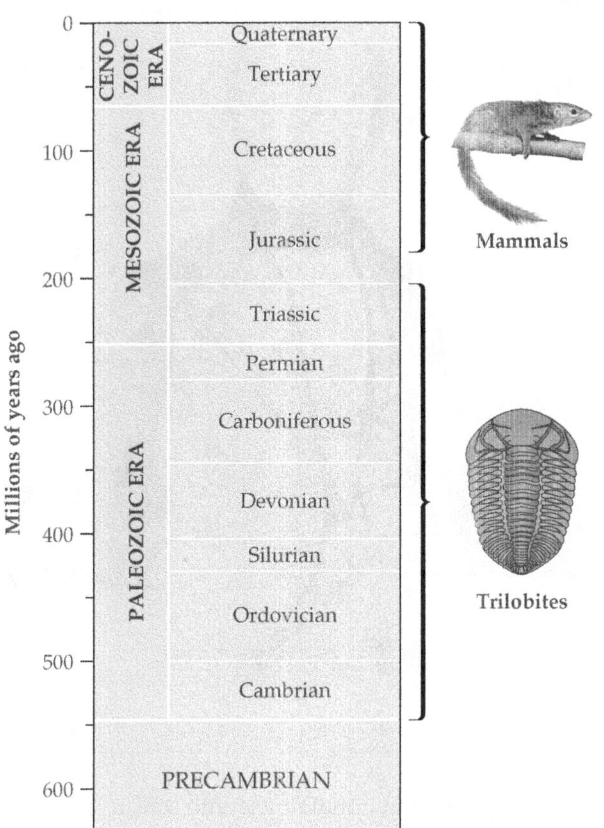

FIGURE 1.4
The use of fossils as historical markers became possible in the late 1700s and early 1800s after scientists such as Georges Cuvier proved the reality of extinction. For example, trilobites were marine arthropods that were common on the world's seafloors during the Paleozoic era. After a period of decline, trilobites disappeared completely about 253 million years ago. Thus, trilobite-bearing rock strata are easily recognized as older than those containing the fossilized remains of mammals, here represented by a shrew.

historical markers in the geologic record (Figure 1.4). But how could this massive loss of life have occurred, Cuvier wondered? What destructive forces led to extinction of the species, and what restorative forces controlled their replacement by later life forms?

In order to answer these questions, Cuvier enlisted the aid of mineralogist Alexandre Brongniart, and together they began a detailed study of the mechanisms of fossil deposition and the record of ancient environments in the Paris countryside. They studied one geologic column (sequence of rock layers) after another and found the strata to be variously filled with marine fossils, freshwater or land shells, the bones of terrestrial animals, or no fossils at all. What sense could be made of this bewildering sequence of the comings and goings of life forms?

Cuvier concluded that the history of life, in the Paris area and elsewhere, had been disrupted routinely by geologic "revolutions"—earthly convulsions related to buckling of the globe's crust as the world continued to cool down from an originally very hot state. These revolutions sometimes caused the seafloor to be raised and laid dry or, alternately, the dry land to be submerged. Such catastrophes (Cuvier's theory was dubbed **catastrophism**) were thought to have occurred suddenly and to have caused great loss of life and extinction of species over quite large areas. Following each catastrophe, Cuvier argued, devastated areas were repopulated by migrations of organisms, some entirely new for that locale, coming in from unaffected regions. Additionally, he suggested, God perhaps created a few new species after a catastrophe to help with the repopulation (Larson, 2004). Significantly, Cuvier did not see these changes in plant and animal communities as the results of **evolution** (he was strongly opposed to the evolutionary theories of his compatriot Jean Baptiste de Lamarck), but nonetheless, his work provided much new evidence in favor of deep time. For Cuvier, the world was not only ancient, but it had been shaped by a series of sudden and catastrophic shocks. On this last point, Cuvier was destined to be opposed by the gradualist model of change developed by Scottish geologist Charles Lyell (Mayr, 1982).

Catastrophism Georges Cuvier's theory that vast floods and other disasters wiped out ancient life forms again and again throughout the earth's history.

Evolution cumulative changes in the average characteristics of a *population* generally thought to occur over many generations.

FIGURE 1.5
Sir Charles Lyell in 1863. Lyell's gradualist model of change was adopted by Charles Darwin and applied to organic evolution.

Charles Lyell and Uniformitarianism

By far the most influential nineteenth century statement on the antiquity of the earth and the forces that have shaped the globe was produced by Charles Lyell (Figure 1.5), who strongly countered Cuvier's views with his own gradualist model of earthly change. His three-volume work, *Principles of Geology*, published between 1830 and 1833, synthesized the available evidence for deep time and, building on the earlier work of Hutton and others, established a theoretical position quickly named **uniformitarianism.** Although Lyell applied his uniformitarian tenets primarily to geology, the young Charles Darwin read the *Principles,* adopted Lyell's theoretical model, and later applied it to the organic world.

Uniformitarianism Charles Lyell's theory that the forces now affecting the earth—water and wind erosion, frost, volcanism—acted in a similar way in the past and that change is always gradual and nondirectional.

In the *Principles*, Lyell made four uniformitarian claims (Gould, 1987):

1. *Uniformity of law:* Through space and time, natural laws remain constant.
2. *Uniformity of process:* When possible, past phenomena should be explained as the results of processes now in operation.
3. *Uniformity of rate:* Change usually occurs slowly and steadily.
4. *Uniformity of state:* Change, although continuous, is nondirectional and nonprogressive.

Lyell's world was thus one of constant and gradual but nonprogressive change produced by processes that could be identified and understood. And although his uniformitarian model provided the vast time needed for organic evolution to produce the diversity of living species, Lyell rejected such notions. The idea of evolution was in the air during the early nineteenth century, however, primarily because of the efforts of a French scientist, Jean Baptist de Lamarck.

The Advent of Evolutionary Theories

Lamarck

The French naturalist Jean Baptiste de Monet, Chevalier de Lamarck, was a friend of Buffon and provided the first persuasive theory that could account for the process of organic evolution. In his *Philosophie Zoologique* (1809/1984) and other books, Lamarck developed his theory of the means by which animal species had been transformed. He recognized that animals and plants were finely adapted to their environments and that their relationship was dynamic, with environmental change generating biological change and adaptation. He suggested that in their daily lives, animals recognized certain needs and that through altered behavior patterns and the action of "subtle fluids" within the body, forces were generated that stimulated the development and growth of organs, even completely novel ones. Thus, the evolution of the species was a response to need, to use, or to disuse of organs, and the changes produced in each generation were inherited. This theory is sometimes described as that of the *inheritance of acquired characteristics* (Lamarck, 1809/1984; Mayr, 1982).

Although Lamarck's ideas were to be discredited, they were extremely important in the early part of the nineteenth century and had a small place in evolutionary biology until recently. The theory, however, is generally discounted because it has not been possible to prove the validity of Lamarck's main mechanism of evolutionary change: namely, that characteristics acquired during the lifetime of an individual are in fact passed on genetically to the succeeding generation.

Charles Darwin

Lyell's great work, *Principles of Geology*, was published in the early 1830s. Among its readers was a young man named Charles Darwin, who was destined to publish an even more revolutionary book, a book that combined Lyell's uniformitarianism with a valid mechanism of evolutionary change. Darwin's student life at Cambridge was undistinguished except in one respect: He was passionately interested in natural history and in collecting birds, butterflies, spiders, flowers, and even rocks—there was nothing in nature that did not fascinate him. While a student, he became a great friend of the Reverend J. S. Henslow, the professor of botany, who gave him much encouragement. Shortly after his graduation, Darwin had the opportunity to sail as a naturalist aboard one of the navy's survey ships, HMS *Beagle*, on an around-the-world cruise. The *Beagle* left England on December 27, 1831, and returned on October 2, 1836. Three-and-a-half years were spent surveying and collecting along the coasts of South America, five weeks were spent in the Galápagos Islands of Ecuador, and a year was spent returning home via Tahiti, New Zealand, Australia, and South Africa (Figure 1.6). This voyage offered Darwin a priceless opportunity to make natural history observations and collections in several foreign lands, and it gave him a brilliant panorama of the variety of organic life. One of the most important parts of the voyage for the later development of Darwin's ideas was the visit to the Galápagos or Enchanted Islands 600 miles off the coast of Ecuador (Browne, 1995; Desmond and Moore, 1991).

Soon after his arrival there, Darwin wrote that in the islands, "Both in space and time, we seem to be brought somewhere near to that great fact—that mystery of mysteries—the first appearance of new beings on this earth." Later he wrote, "It was most striking to be surrounded by new birds, new reptiles, new shells, new insects, new plants, and yet by innumerable trifling details of structure, and even by the tones of voice and plumage of the birds, to have the temperate plains of Patagonia, or the hot dry deserts of northern Chile, vividly brought before my eyes" (Darwin, 1839/1962:379 and 393). Struck by the basic similarities yet subtle differences that linked the Galápagos fauna to that of the mainland, Darwin later learned that many species differed slightly from island to island, even though many of the islands were only 50 or 60 miles apart. From an analysis of his bird collections later made by John Gould, Darwin learned that the Galápagos finches constituted distinct species on the various islands but were all obviously related. On one island, they had strong thick beaks used for cracking big nuts and seeds; on another, the beak was smaller and used for catching insects; on another, the beak was elongated

FIGURE 1.6
Charles Darwin left Devonport, England, in December 1831 and returned to Falmouth in October 1836. Out of the nearly five years spent on the voyage in HMS *Beagle*, Darwin spent more than three years in South America and its islands. The voyage was completed with visits to New Zealand, Australia, the Keeling (Cocos) Islands, the Cape of Good Hope, and St. Helena. Darwin's experience on this voyage was a rich and fertile source of observation and inspiration in the development of his ideas.

for feeding on flowers and fruit (Figure 1.7). One species used a cactus spine to probe grubs out of holes in tree trunks and branches. Clearly, the birds had found different foods on different islands and through successive generations had adapted in some manner so that they were better able to survive in their own particular environments. All this evidence was critically important in the development of Darwin's ideas (Browne, 1995; Desmond and Moore, 1991).

When, in 1859, Charles Darwin published his revolutionary book *On the Origin of Species by Means of Natural Selection,* he presented a theory that was the product

FIGURE 1.7
These four species of Galápagos finch show some of the variety of form into which the beak evolved. The far-left species is most powerfully equipped and is adapted to crack big seeds and nuts. That on the far right is adapted to feed from flowers and fruit. These species are all close relatives and all the descendants of an original South American ancestor.

FIGURE 1.8
Charles Darwin as a young man. In his *Autobiography* he wrote, "In September 1858 I set to work by the strong advice of Lyell and Hooker to prepare a volume on the transmutation of species, but was often interrupted by ill-health. . . . [The book] cost me thirteen months and ten days of hard labour." Darwin was an intermittent invalid for 40 years, but he found that invalidism had some advantages: "Even ill-health, though it annihilated several years of my life, has saved me from the distractions of society and amusement." He lived to the age of 73.

of many years of thought and observation. Darwin was encouraged to publish by seeing the work of Alfred Russel Wallace, who, working independently, had come to similar conclusions (Figures 1.8 and 1.9). Both men had traveled widely and had observed in great detail the variation that exists within animal and plant species. Members of species, they noted, are not identical but vary in size, strength, health, fertility, longevity, behavior, and many other characteristics. Darwin realized that humans use this natural variation when they selectively breed plants and animals; a breeder selects to interbreed only particular individuals possessing the desired qualities (Browne, 2002; Darwin, 1859/1964).

FIGURE 1.9
Alfred Russel Wallace was a complete contrast to Darwin in both background and character. Whereas Darwin did not need to work for a living, Wallace earned his way by collecting rare tropical plants and animals for private collectors and museums. As a result, he traveled far more widely than Darwin in both South America and Southeast Asia. Later in his life, he wrote a number of books on evolution and zoogeography.

Both Darwin and Wallace saw that a kind of *natural* selection was at work, and an understanding of the means by which selection operates in nature came to both from the same source (Darwin, 1859/1964; Raby, 2001). The first edition of *An Essay on the Principle of Population*, by English clergyman T. R. Malthus, appeared in 1798. In his book, Malthus argued that the reproductive potential of humankind far exceeds the potential increase in resources needed to nourish an expanding population. In Malthus's view, "[Human] population, when unchecked, increases in a geometrical ratio. A slight acquaintance with numbers will show the immensity of the first power in comparison of the second." And furthermore, "By that law of our nature that makes food necessary to the life of man, the effects of these two unequal powers must be kept equal. This implies a strong and constantly operating check on population from the difficulty of subsistence" (Malthus, 1798/1993:13). As a result, he argued, the size of human populations is limited by disease, famine, and war and that, in the absence of "moral restraint," such factors alone appear to check what would otherwise be a rapid growth in population" (Malthus, 1798/1993).

Both Darwin and Wallace read Malthus's essay, and remarkably, both men recorded in their diaries how they realized that in that book lay the key to understanding the evolutionary process. It was clear that what Malthus had discovered of human populations was true of populations of plants and animals: The reproductive potential vastly exceeds the rate necessary to maintain a constant population size. They realized that the individuals that do survive must be in some way better equipped to live in their environment than those that do not survive. It follows that in a naturally interbreeding population, any variation that increased the organism's ability to produce fertile offspring would most likely be preserved and passed on to future generations, while the variations that decreased that ability would most likely be eliminated.

Darwin had carried these ideas for some years; he wrote a short sketch in 1842 and a more extended *Essay* in 1844 but was not prepared to publish either. He knew he would shock the public and his family; he could hardly face the implications of his thoughts. Wallace was held back by no such inhibitions, however, and early in 1858, after he read Malthus, the idea of natural selection occurred to him. He immediately sent a short paper on the subject to Darwin. Darwin received this paper on June 18. He was quite astounded and wrote to Lyell, "I never saw a more striking coincidence; if Wallace had my MS sketch written out in 1842, he could not have made a better short abstract" (Burkhardt and Smith, 1991:107; Desmond and Moore, 1991).

The Basis of Darwin's Theory

Natural selection the principal mechanism of Darwinian *evolutionary* change, by which the individuals best adapted to the environment contribute more offspring to succeeding generations than others do. As more of such individuals' characteristics are incorporated into the *gene pool*, the characteristics of the *population* evolve.

Conspecifics members of the same *species*.

As the late zoologist Ernst Mayr showed, Darwin's theory of evolution through **natural selection,** as presented in *On the Origin of Species*, is based on five facts and three inferences (Figure 1.10). From Malthus, Darwin took the elements of organisms' potential superfecundity (Fact 1) and the limitations placed on population expansion by limited environmental resources (Fact 3). He combined these elements with the observation that most natural populations tend to remain stable in size rather than to constantly expand (Fact 2). From these three facts, Darwin (following Malthus) inferred that individual organisms (especially members of the same species) are in strong competition with one another (Inference 1). Combining this inference with the observation that individuals (including **conspecifics**) show spontaneous variations in physical and behavioral traits (Fact 4) and the observation that parents often pass their individual variations on to their offspring (Fact 5) allowed Darwin to reach a second inference: that organisms experience differential survival and reproduction based on the possession of traits that are adaptive in their particular environment (Inference 2; this is the statement that we recognize as natural selection). Finally, Darwin argued that through the action of natural selection over many generations, a species could slowly but surely *evolve* (Inference 3) (Mayr, 1991).

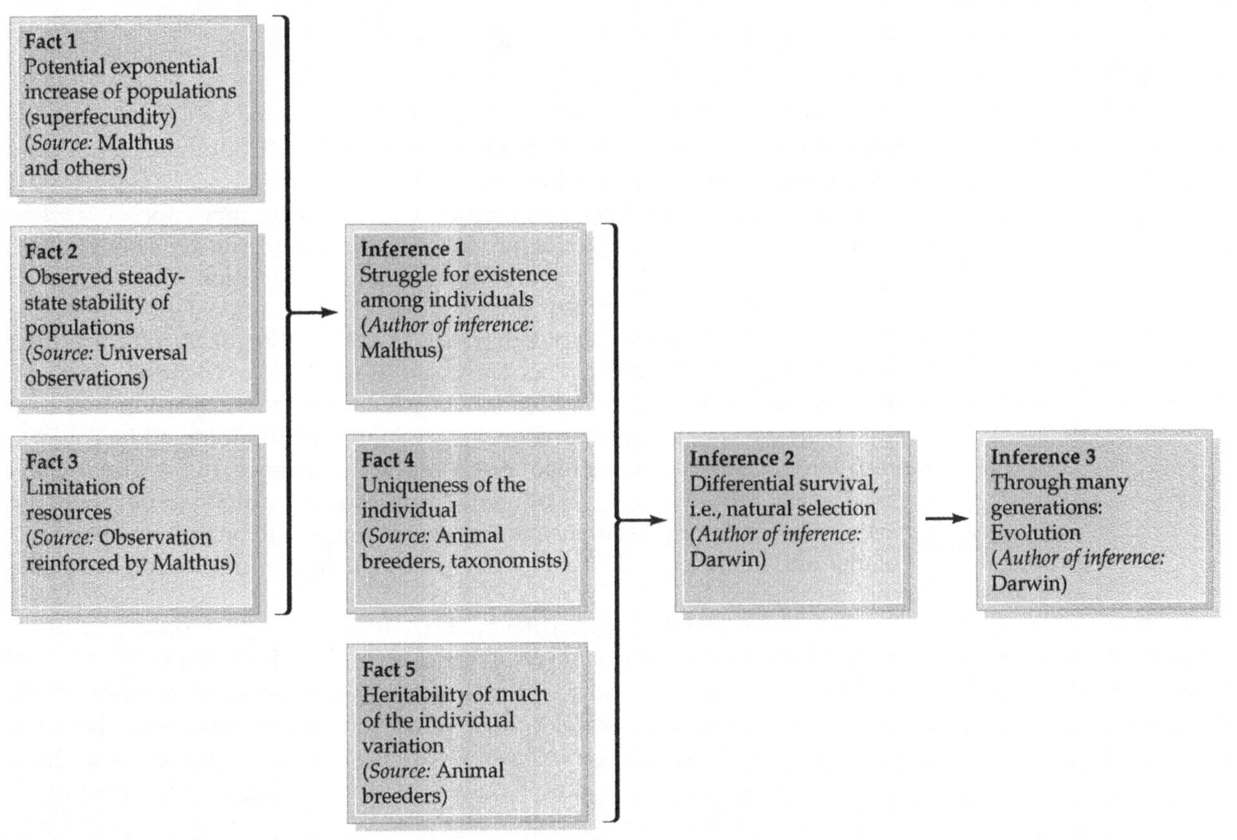

FIGURE 1.10
Zoologist Ernst Mayr reduced Darwin's explanatory model of evolution through natural selection to five facts and three inferences.

Thus, natural selection was presented as a process by which adaptive traits are preserved (through the survival and reproduction of their carriers) and maladaptive (or *less* adaptive) traits are winnowed out of species. This process occurs in both plants and animals, and true to Lyell's uniformitarian principles, Darwin described the evolutionary process as extremely slow and gradual. Such a process clearly could not have been responsible for species diversity on Bishop Ussher's 6,000-year-old earth, but by the mid-nineteenth century, Hutton, Cuvier, Lyell, and others had provided ample evidence for deep time.

The first presentation of the Darwin/Wallace evolutionary model was made at the Linnaean Society in London over a year prior to the *Origin's* publication. On July 1, 1858, a paper entitled "On the Tendency of Species to Form Varieties, and on the Perpetuation of Varieties and Species by Means of Selection" was read before the fellows of the society. This was the first publication to the world of Darwin's and Wallace's theory, and the world has not been the same since that day. Neither Darwin nor Wallace was present (Desmond and Moore, 1991).

It is impossible today to recreate the atmosphere of intellectual and moral shock that swept England when Darwin's book was published the following year. It was not that the evolution of plants or animals was so hard to swallow. After all, humans themselves had been responsible, through selective breeding, for the evolution of a number of domestic animals and a great variety of crops. Then there were those peculiar dinosaur bones that people had been digging up; they had to be explained, as did the growing evidence that the earth was not simply thousands of years old but hundreds of thousands, perhaps hundreds of millions. No, those things were not really the problem. What was so hard to accept was the implied suggestion that human beings were descended from a bunch of "repulsive, scratching, hairy apes and monkeys." Those awful monkeys! As one Victorian lady is reported to have said, "My dear, let us hope that it is not true, but if it is, let us pray that it will not become generally known."

The genius of Charles Darwin's evolutionary theory becomes apparent when one considers that he constructed it despite the lack of two critical pieces of information. Darwin knew neither the sources of spontaneous variation within each generation (the basis of Fact 4) nor the mechanisms of intergenerational inheritance (the basis of Fact 5). (As it happens, a contemporary researcher, Gregor Mendel, was hard at work on those very problems, but Darwin was unaware of Mendel's findings. See the next section for more on Mendel's work.) Furthermore, Darwin was very careful about the way he presented his theory to the world, doing all he could to minimize giving offense to his readers. Of prime importance, in *On the Origin of Species,* Darwin refrained from mentioning the question of human origins with the exception of a single timid sentence near the end: "Light will be thrown on the origin of man and his history" (Darwin, 1859/1964:488). But the implication was plain, and nobody missed it.

In 1863, Thomas H. Huxley, a friend of Darwin and an ardent propagandist for his theory, published *Evidence as to Man's Place in Nature.* This was the first book to address itself in an orderly and scientific way to the problem of human origins. By making many telling anatomical comparisons between humans and the apes, Huxley established that, of all animals on earth, the African great apes—the chimpanzee and gorilla—are most closely related to humans (Figure 1.11). He further stated that the evolutionary development of apes and humans had taken place in much the same way and according to the same laws. From this it followed that if prehuman fossils were ever found, older and older humanlike fossils would be found, leading eventually to types that would turn out to be ancestral to both apes and humans. And it was clear that Huxley thought these common ancestors would probably be found in Africa (Huxley, 1915).

Darwin, confronted by the same relationship of fossil species to living ones, saw that the latter were the modified descendants of the former. Carrying the case to its full conclusion in *The Descent of Man,* published in 1871 (1981), Darwin propounded the theory of an unbroken chain of organisms that began with the first forms of life and evolved to humans. Here was a true scientific theory, a theory of evolution sub-

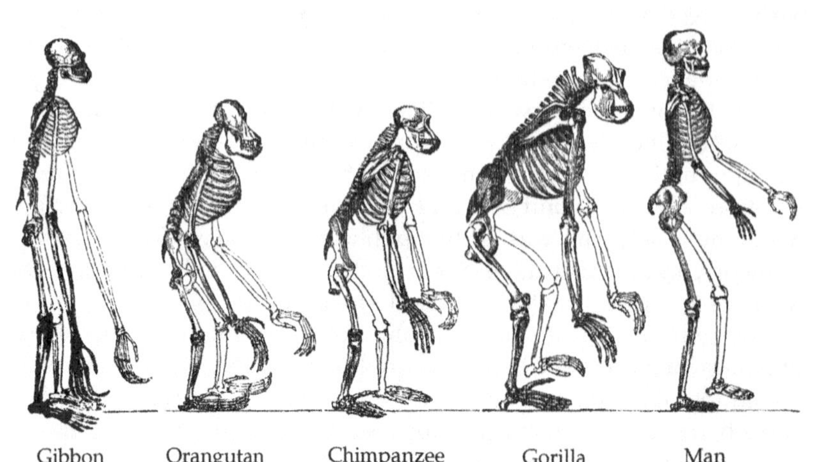

FIGURE 1.11
In 1863, Thomas H. Huxley published this drawing of the skeletons of four apes and a human to illustrate their extraordinary similarity. He wrote, "Whatever part of the animal fabric might be selected for comparison, the lower apes [monkeys] and the Gorilla would differ more than the Gorilla and the Man." All drawings are to the same scale except the gibbon, which is drawn to twice the scale.

ject to proof. But where was the proof? Where were the bones of this multitude of organisms? Surely, many of them should have survived in the earth, yet the fossils found up to Darwin's day supplied only the most fragmentary evidence. Where were the missing links? It was a painful time for the evolutionists. Despite all the logic in Huxley's and Darwin's views, they were difficult to support, because in Africa, or indeed anywhere else, there was an embarrassing lack of fossils resembling human beings.

At this turning point in the history of human knowledge, there had emerged two great and related ideas about the origin of nature and of humankind: (1) the earth is extremely ancient, long populated by many kinds of animals, some of which are no longer living, and (2) humans themselves, mutable creatures like the animals, have their ancestors far back in time. But how far back and who those ancestors were, nobody had even the slightest notion. Almost everything we know about our ancestry, we have learned in the past one hundred fifty years, much of it during the past half century (see Box 1.1).

BOX 1.1 CURRENT ISSUE

The Relevance of Paleoanthropology

Reviewers of earlier versions of this book indicated that students are interested in learning how its contents can have everyday relevance. To that end , we have created a series of Current Issue boxes that appear throughout the text. Other topics of present-day interest are discussed in the Postscript at the end of each chapter.

It may not be immediately obvious what possible relevance ancient bones and stones can have to our present occupations and problems. Almost any branch of science can immediately be seen to have a greater impact on the present world than the study of human evolution.

This is not, however, a realistic assessment of the value of our study. We all know now that we are the product of our genes and our environment and have been fashioned over millions of years to be as we are. Life has been evolving for more than two billion years, and we are one of its most remarkable products. It follows that we are the product of our past experience as a species. To a great extent, our bodies are adaptations to past environments and our minds are no different. The fact that we have evolved some degree of free will is the single factor that tends to free us a little from the stamp of history and prehistory. But our genes hold our personalities on a leash, and we cannot stray far from the anchor of our genetic blueprint.

Our study of bones and stones tells us how we were made: It is as simple as that. If you want to understand a complex mechanism, you find out how it is made and the principles that underlie its design. To understand ourselves, it is essential to understand how we were made and the principles that operated during our formation. That is, it is necessary to study and plot in detail the evolution of our bodies and behavior.

Why do we need to understand ourselves? For one thing, such knowledge may help us develop a world society capable of peacefully sharing and preserving the earth. The underlying essential unity of modern humans, as well as our physical and cultural diversity, is the result of our shared evolutionary history. Furthermore, examining our Darwinian development in the context of ancestral environments may help us understand the roots of such perplexing behaviors as human status seeking, harmful aggression, and shortsighted exploitation of the environment.

You may think that many of these issues fall within the purview of psychologists, not paleoanthropologists. Up to a point, that is true, but without the historic and prehistoric evidence, the psychologists can never fully understand their subject. All biological research must be done under the rubric of evolution. This is the essential and revealing key that alone can deliver the understanding we need.

The logic is inescapable. To understand ourselves, we must understand the past. That is why the study of human evolution, seemingly so far from everyday problems, is really the most basic and fundamental science of all. It lies at the root of all human studies, from psychology to political science and from medicine to management.

Gregor Mendel and the Problem of Heredity

Blending inheritance an outmoded theory stating that offspring receive a combination of all characteristics of each parent through the mixture of their bloods; superseded by Mendelian genetics.

True breeding (breeding true) the situation in which the members of a genetic strain resemble each other in all important characteristics and show little variability.

Dominant in genetics, describes a trait that is expressed in the *phenotype* even when the organism is carrying only one copy of the underlying hereditary material (one copy of the responsible *gene*).

Charles Darwin deduced the operation of natural selection even though he was missing two major pieces of the evolutionary puzzle: namely, the sources of variation and the mechanisms of heredity. From personal observations and reading, Darwin knew that all species contain a variety of individuals in every generation, and additionally, he shared the common knowledge that offspring often inherit parental traits (Mayr, 1991). Folk wisdom in Darwin's day held that blood was intimately involved in the passage of traits from parent to child, a belief that resulted in sayings such as "Blood will tell." Mother's and father's bloods (and therefore traits) were thought to be coalesced somehow in each of their children, but logical as it may have seemed, this notion of **blending inheritance** raised some formidable problems. After all, if each child is a blend of the parents' characteristics, the long-term effect should be an overall loss of variation within the population. That is, new individuals should be born increasingly alike in each succeeding generation as individual differences are diluted through blending. And yet the opposite is true: In sexually reproducing species, variability is maintained over time and often increases.

Unknown to Darwin, the problems that proved so intractable for him—variation and inheritance—were beginning to yield their secrets to an Augustinian monk named Gregor Johann Mendel (Figure 1.12). Born in a small village in what is now the Czech Republic, Mendel had "a special liking [for natural science]" (Orel, 1996:

FIGURE 1.12 Gregor Mendel's country childhood gave him a deep knowledge and sympathetic understanding of the plant world. As a monk with some leisure, he took up plant breeding in the monastery garden, with remarkable and brilliant results.

44). He learned much about plants and horticulture from his father, Anton, who was a small-scale farmer and fruit grower. Later, after entering the Augustinian monastery at Brunn and completing his university studies, Mendel combined his religious duties with a lengthy series of botanical experiments designed to elucidate the natural laws that control variation and inheritance.

The Experiments

Mendel's botanical studies began in about 1857 (Orel, 1996). By reviewing earlier studies of plant hybridization, he realized that most had been poorly designed and rather haphazardly carried out. He also realized that success depended not only on systematic work done on a large scale but, of equal importance, on selecting the right species for study. For his inheritance work, he needed **true-breeding** plants, plants that showed little spontaneous variation from generation to generation. He also needed a species whose pollination he could control easily, for otherwise systematic cross-fertilizations would be impossible. Mendel ended up choosing the common garden pea for most of his experimental work.

The garden pea was a good choice because it presented several traits that were easily observed and manipulated. Mendel chose seven characteristics for systematic investigation (illustrated in Figure 1.13), the most important of which, for our purposes here, were seed form and seed color—round or wrinkled, green or yellow. (The following discussion is based on Mayr, 1982, and Orel, 1996.) He was now ready to begin producing hybrids, and he started with a simple cross between wrinkled-pea and round-pea plants grown from seeds he had bought, taking great care to prevent accidental pollination from plants outside his study and removing the anthers or stigma of each flower (the male and female organs) to avoid self-fertilization. After the necessary time for fertilization, growth, and pea development, Mendel was able to observe the results of his experiment. Upon opening the pods, he found only round peas (Figure 1.14). The wrinkled trait, which had existed in half of the parent plants, seemed to have disappeared completely! (Similar disappearances of one variant or the other were found in Mendel's other first-generation hybrids—green pea color disappeared after a green-yellow cross, and short plant height disappeared after a short-tall cross.)

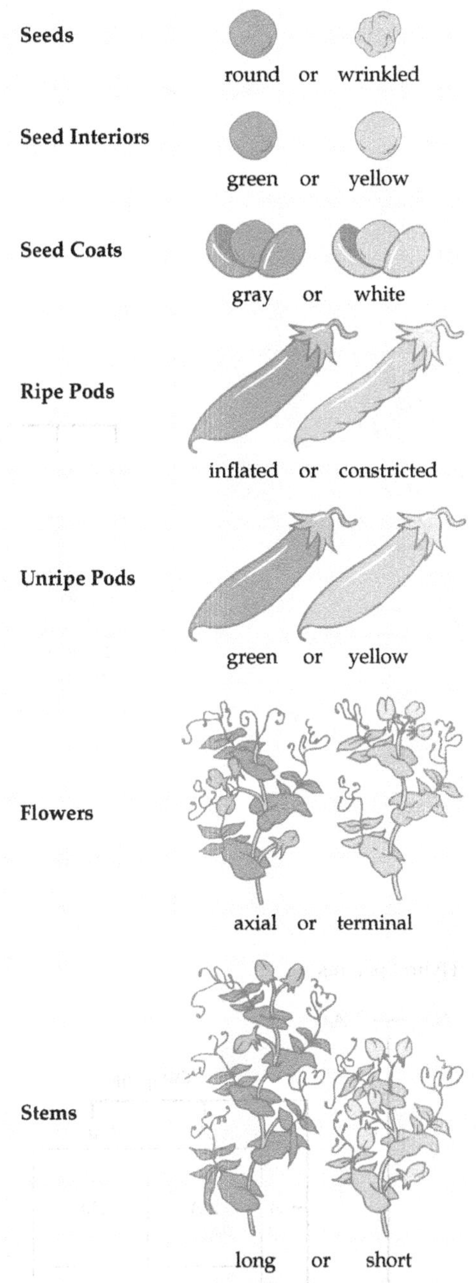

FIGURE 1.13 Mendel's pioneering observations of the pea plant were based on a comparison of these seven easily identifiable characteristics.

After due consideration, Mendel decided to call the characteristic that prevailed in the first hybrid generation **dominant** and the one that apparently disappeared **recessive.** But what, Mendel wondered, would happen to the dominant and recessive traits if the hybrids were allowed to self-fertilize as they would normally? He made the experiments and waited. When at last he could examine the traits of second-generation plants, Mendel found that the recessive characteristics had reappeared! In the round-wrinkled cross, for example, wrinkling was back in about one-third of the peas (Figure 1.14), and round and wrinkled peas could be found side by side in the same pod. In general, dominant traits outnumbered their recessive counterparts by a 3:1 ratio in the second generation.

And there were more surprises in store. When Mendel planted his second generation of peas and then allowed those plants to self-fertilize, he obtained mixed results. Recessive characteristics always bred true; for example, plants grown from wrinkled peas produced only wrinkled peas. Plants with dominant traits, however, came in two types: One-third were true-breeding, but two-thirds acted like hybrid

Recessive in genetics, describes a trait that is expressed only when the organism is carrying two copies of the underlying hereditary material (two copies of the responsible *gene*).

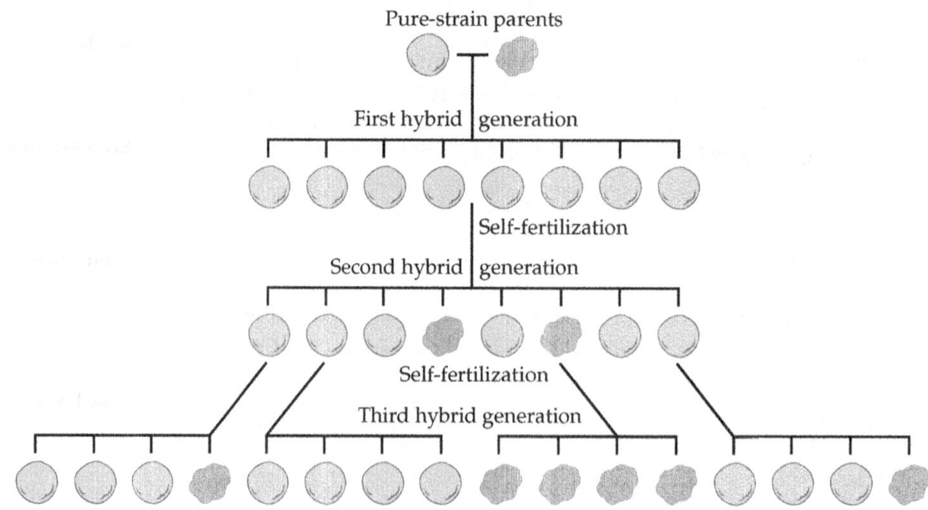

FIGURE 1.14
This figure shows the results obtained in successive generations when Mendel crossed pure-strain round and wrinkled peas. The first generation seeds were all round. The second hybrid generation contained both round and wrinkled peas, in a ratio of 3 to 1. In the third hybrid generation, Mendel found new combinations of characteristics. All of the wrinkled seeds had bred true (producing only wrinkled offspring); some of the round peas also bred true, while other round peas repeated the 3:1 ratio seen in the second generation.

Phenotype the observable characteristics of a plant or an animal; the expression of the *genotype*.

Genotype the genetic makeup of a plant or animal; the total information contained in all *genes* of the organism.

Genes primarily, functional segments of *chromosomes* in cell nuclei, which control the coding and inheritance of *phenotypic* traits; some genes also occur in *mitochondria*.

Homozygous having identical versions of a *gene* (*alleles*) for a particular trait.

Heterozygous having different versions of a *gene* (*alleles*) for a particular trait.

seeds of the first generation and produced both dominant and recessive offspring at a ratio of 3:1 (Figure 1.14). Pondering these results, Mendel drew several conclusions that took him a long way toward solving the riddle of heredity. First, he reasoned that an organism's visible characteristics (now called its **phenotype**) are not always an accurate representation of its set of hereditary qualities (now, its **genotype**). This discovery not only explained why some plants with dominant traits could produce mixed descendants but it also forced a second major conclusion: that hereditary qualities are nonreducible *particles*. These particles (now called **genes**) are not blended during sexual reproduction but rather retain their identities as they are passed from parents to offspring. And third, Mendel's mathematical results—his ratios of offsprings' traits—suggested that hereditary particles generally function as pairs, with a particle expressing its trait unless it is blocked (dominated) by its partner.

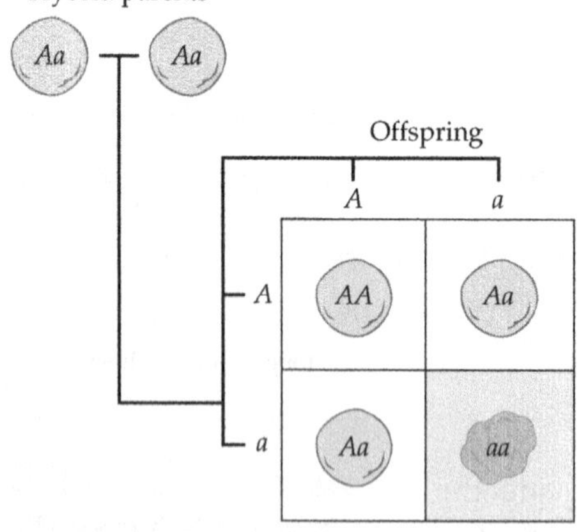

FIGURE 1.15
The results of self-fertilizing first-generation hybrid peas were explained by Mendel in this way: Using the letters *A* and *a* for the characters smooth and wrinkled, he accounted for the 3:1 proportion by proposing that *A* is always dominant to *a* in every hybrid.

A simple way to visualize the connection between hereditary pairs (genotype) and visible traits (phenotype) is shown in Figure 1.15. Here, dominant particles are labeled *A* and recessive ones *a*. With regard to the form of Mendel's peas, hybrids with *Aa* genotypes would be round (of course, so would all *AA* individuals). Crossing two such hybrids could potentially produce three different genotypes (*AA*, *Aa*, and *aa*) and both possible phenotypes (round and wrinkled). Today, individuals with similar genes for a trait (*AA* and *aa*) are said to be **homozygous,** while those with different genes (*Aa*) are described as **heterozygous.**

Mendel's Hereditary Principles

Mendel eventually looked at much more complex cases than just single contrasting characteristics. As shown in Figure 1.16, simultaneously studying two traits—pea form (round, wrinkled) and pea color (green, yellow)—produced a greatly enlarged set of possible genotypes reducible to four phenotypes with a 9:3:3:1 ratio. In addition, Mendel identified a few traits (for example, flower color in beans) that seemed to be controlled by two pairs of hereditary particles rather than one. In all, his work allowed Mendel to formulate several important biological principles (Mayr, 1982; Orel, 1996):

1. Heredity is transmitted by a large number of independent, nonreducible particles that occur as pairs in individual organisms. These hereditary particles retain their distinctive identities regardless of the nature of their pair-partners. This is the *principle of particulate heredity,* and it disproved the old notion of heredity as a matter of blending.
2. The traits of parental organisms will become segregated in predictable ratios in the progeny of hybrids. This *principle of segregation* is now understood to be based on the splitting of gene pairs during the production of sex cells (pollen and ovules, or sperm and eggs), with new pairs being formed in predictable ratios at fertilization (Singer and Berg, 1991).
3. Hereditary particles for different traits generally are inherited independently of one another. This is the *principle of independent assortment* (see Figure 1.16 for an illustration).

These principles, along with the detailed results of Mendel's long years of work, were read to the Brunn Society for the Study of Natural Science in 1865 and published in that society's proceedings in 1866. Unfortunately, Mendel's work found few interested readers, and virtually no one at the time recognized how far he had gone toward answering the basic questions about heredity. It would be the turn of the century before Mendel's work would be rediscovered, and after 1868, the man now widely viewed as the "father of genetics" devoted the rest of his life to leadership duties as abbot of his monastery (Orel, 1996).

Mendel considered himself to be an evolutionary researcher, and by 1863, he had read Darwin's book *On the Origin of Species.* It is interesting to speculate what might have taken place if the two men had ever met or corresponded. (Mayr [1982] is convinced that little, if any, creative exchange would have occurred.) As it turned out, they never made contact. Although Mendel traveled to England in 1862 to see the London International Exhibition, he did not make the sixteen-mile side trip to Down to meet Darwin. Perhaps he was too modest, or perhaps his inability to speak English held him back (Orel, 1996). In any event, it would be another seventy years before Darwinism and Mendelism were combined into modern evolutionary theories.

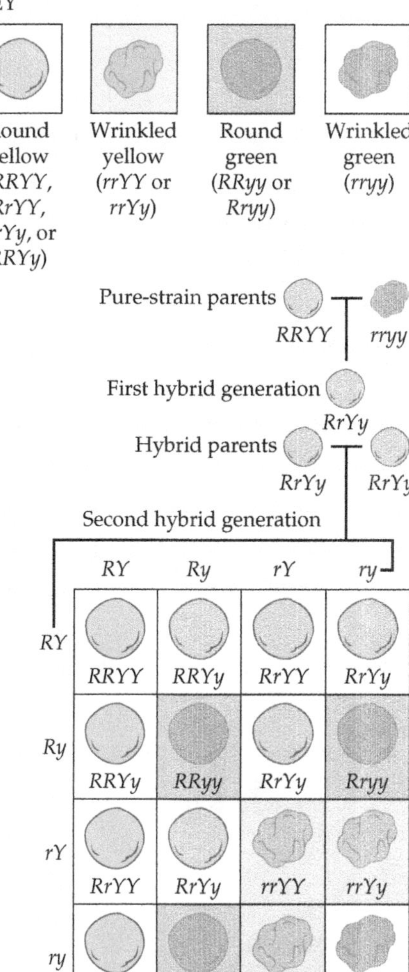

FIGURE 1.16 The Punnett square shows Mendel's law of independent assortment. A pea with two dominant characteristics (roundness and yellowness, *RR* and *YY*) is crossed with a pea having two recessive characteristics (wrinkledness and greenness, *rr* and *yy*). The hybrid combines all four genes of its parents (*RrYy*). If these hybrids are crossed, their genes have the potential to produce the combinations shown: four kinds of peas appearing in a ratio of 9:3:3:1.

Turn of the Century: Mendel Rediscovered, Natural Selection Out of Favor

Hugo De Vries and the Mutationists

The decades following Darwin's and Mendel's deaths in the 1880s found scientists in general agreement about the occurrence of evolutionary change but at odds concerning such basic questions as the sources of spontaneous phenotypic variation and the effectiveness of natural selection. The confusion among biologists was compounded by the fact that Mendel's detailed work on inheritance, having never gained much recognition when it was published, had been forgotten.

Among the workers caught in this muddle was Hugo De Vries, a botanist at the University of Amsterdam. De Vries accepted Darwin's thesis that descent with modification is the main law of change among organisms, but he wondered how large differences between species could ever be produced by natural selection, picking and choosing among small, individual variations. De Vries had a hunch that **mutations,** spontaneous (and sometimes substantial) changes in an organism's characteristics, were more important than natural selection in directing the path of evolution. Darwinians recognized the occasional sudden appearance of new traits—so-called *sports of nature*—but credited them only with secondary importance. For his studies of mutations, De Vries chose to work with the evening primrose, a plant capable of wide variations in each generation. His observations carried out for more than a decade reinforced De Vries's confidence in the power of mutations and also led him to several of the same conclusions that Mendel had formulated thirty-five years earlier, especially the conclusion that hereditary units are "distinct, separate, and independent" particles. Indeed, as De Vries conducted a literature search in 1900 prior to publishing his primrose data, he came across Mendel's long-lost paper and only then realized that much of his work had been anticipated by the Moravian monk. (By a remarkable coincidence, Mendel's paper was also rediscovered by two other researchers, one German and one Austrian, in that same year.) Behaving honorably, De Vries gave full credit to Mendel, whose discoveries were at last given the scientific acclaim they deserved (Mayr, 1982).

Mutation generally, a spontaneous change in the chemistry of a *gene* that can alter its *phenotypic* effect. The accumulation of such changes may contribute to the *evolution* of a new *species* of animal or plant.

Macromutation a large and genetically inherited change between parent and offspring.

And so, as the twentieth century got underway, Mendel's principles of inheritance had not only been rediscovered but also confirmed. The controversy between mutationists like De Vries and traditional Darwinians (believers in natural selection as the main evolutionary mechanism) continued to rage, however, with a new line of mutationist evidence being advanced: the evidence of mimicry in nature. Probably the most striking cases of mimicry involve cross-species matches in appearance, as demonstrated for butterflies in Figure 1.17. Often, mimics gain a degree of protection against predators, for example, by becoming the look-alikes of tough or bad-tasting prey species.

FIGURE 1.17
Mimicry occurs quite widely among animals (and even some plants). In this example, the monarch butterfly *Danais plexippus* (top) is mimicked by the viceroy butterfly *Limenitis archippus* (bottom). Both butterflies have an orange ground and black and white markings. Experiments have demonstrated the function and effectiveness of this mimicry: The monarch butterfly is protected from predators by its unpalatability; the viceroy is protected by mimicking it.

The mutationists claimed that such wonderful resemblances could have arisen only by mutation, since intermediate types—quarter-mimics or half-mimics that had abandoned their own original camouflage but had achieved only a portion of the model's protective coloration—would be maladaptive. How, except by mutation, could the elaborate markings and other bodily designs of mimics ever have come into being? Mimicry, the mutationists argued, is *the* outstanding proof of the power of mutations, a power that might even extend to the relatively instantaneous production of entirely new species through **macromutations.** (Such large-scale mutations—that may involve doubling or tripling the original genotype—are more common in plants than in animals, although not unknown among the latter.) For their part, the Darwinians vigorously disagreed with the idea of saltatorial (jumpy) evolution, and they backed up their arguments with a new weapon: mathematics (Mayr, 1982; Ridley, 1996).

The Emergence of the Modern Synthesis

That natural selection is, in fact, the primary mechanism of evolution was demonstrated in the early twentieth century by Ronald Aylmer Fisher, J. B. S. Haldane, Sewall Wright, and other mathematically inclined biologists. Fisher, in particular, zeroed in on the mutationists' pet phenomenon: mimicry. He proved conclusively that natural selection acting on small variations is the only force that could bring about the intricate matches of mimic to model. The coincidental occurrence of the same traits in mimics and models due to random mutations is so unlikely as to be mathematically impossible. Besides, said Fisher, the mutation theory explained neither why mimics and models are always found in the same regions and during the same season nor why mimicry is usually only "skin deep" (involves no more copying of traits than is necessary) (Dobzhansky, 1937). In the end, the mathematical arguments prevailed, and in accordance with Darwin's original position, natural selection reemerged as the main force driving evolutionary change. Mutation took on the role as the primary source of new genetic material. Thus, mutations contribute to phenotypic variations that are then either rejected or, more rarely, preserved and molded by the action of natural selection (Dobzhansky, 1937; Mayr, 1982; Ridley, 1996).

Progress in the newly formed science of Mendelian genetics continued during the first two decades of the twentieth century. It was not until the 1930s and 1940s, however, that Darwin's theory of natural selection was finally combined with Mendel's theory of heredity to produce a genetically based evolutionary model. Fisher, Haldane, and Wright were all part of this development, along with other scientists such as Julian Huxley (the grandson of T. H. Huxley), Theodosius Dobzhansky, and Ernst Mayr. The new model was dubbed the *synthetic theory of evolution* or, following the title of an important book by Julian Huxley, the *modern synthesis.* (It is also occasionally called *neo-Darwinism.*) The modern synthesis has proved remarkably resilient to subsequent testing and refinement, and today it prevails as the universally accepted evolutionary paradigm. The next chapter presents more detailed information about genetics and the ways that populations of organisms evolve (Mayr, 1982; Price, 1996; Ridley, 1996).

Summary

During the past four centuries, our understanding of the earth's origin—and our own—has changed dramatically. In the seventeenth century, the Christian creation myth of a divine origin was widely accepted in Europe, as was Bishop Ussher's calculation of the young age of the earth. The young earth theory fell victim to geological discoveries during the succeeding two hundred years, however, and in addition, in 1859, Charles Darwin published a convincing theory of evolution by natural selection that was quickly applied to the question of human origins. Darwin developed his theory without much knowledge about the source of phenotypic variations or the mechanisms of inheritance, but Mendel's work (which marked the beginning of the science of genetics) went a long way toward correcting that lack of knowledge. Building on Mendel's achievements, De Vries, Fisher, Haldane, Wright, Dobzhansky, and others produced a series of further discoveries in genetics. Finally, during the 1930s and 1940s, Darwin's theory of natural selection was united with Mendelian genetics to produce the synthetic theory of evolution, a theory that still guides the work of biologists (including physical anthropologists) today.

Postscript

Fundamental Judeo-Christian beliefs and biblical literalism are alive and well in the United States and several other parts of the world. A 1993 Gallup poll found that 49 percent of adult Americans believe that humans are the result of special creation by God within the last 10,000 years. While **creationism** is believed in by only a tiny minority of scientists, its acceptance by a substantial portion of the American populace has important implications. Creationists—or as many now prefer to be called,

Creationism the belief that humans and all life forms were specially created by God or some other divine force.

intelligent-design theorists (based on their belief in a divine Designer)—argue that their Bible-based explanation of human origins is as valid as the evolutionary explanation and thus deserves equal time in public school curricula. They insist that their studies are based on sound scientific principles and even refer to their work as *creation science* (Numbers, 1992).

Anthropologists, geologists, and other traditional scientists have responded to the fundamentalists' challenge by arguing that creation science is a sham and not science at all. The argument goes like this: Traditional scientists use a particular methodology as they try to establish the probabilistic validity of inferences about how the world works. This **scientific method** science works through the development of *theories* (broad sets of principles that explain bodies of facts) and *hypotheses.* Scientific theories are constantly tested by generating hypotheses (falsifiable research predictions), which are then tested by laboratory experimentation or field observations. If most of the predictions (hypotheses) generated by a theory prove to be correct, then the validity of the entire theory is supported. On the other hand, if one's hypotheses consistently prove to be wrong, the validity of one's theory will be destroyed. Based on the results of hypothesis testing, scientific theories are maintained unchanged, are modified, or are discarded (Mayr, 1982). The theory of evolution, for example, has been subjected to repeated tests ever since Darwin's day, and although extended and modified in places, it has survived essentially intact.

Scientific method the process of developing and testing hypotheses (by attempted falsification) that traditional scientists use to establish the probabilistic validity of their theories.

Scientists argue that the problem with creation science is that the fundamentalists' basic theory—that God created the world and its inhabitants recently and in a short time span—is not really open to falsification. Creationists may formulate hypotheses and gather data, but since their theory is truly an article of faith, there is no possibility of changing or discarding it, regardless of their results (Kehoe, 1985).

Creationists continue to press local school boards and textbook publishers to include their views. And traditional scientists continue to argue that while material on creationism may be included legitimately in Bible courses or studies of comparative religion, it does not belong in the science classroom. What do you think? Your stand on this question could well affect your children's future public education.

Review Questions

1. Describe the effects of Christian beliefs on the development of evolutionary theory and studies of human prehistory.
2. Discuss the development of deep time within European science. What were the implications of this development for evolutionary theory?
3. Georges Cuvier and Charles Lyell had very different ideas about the pattern and pace of geologic change. Compare Cuvier's catastrophism with Lyell's theory of uniformitarianism.
4. Describe how competition and natural selection are related in Charles Darwin's evolutionary model.
5. Explain how Gregor Mendel's work refuted the old concept of blending inheritance.
6. What is the synthetic theory of evolution? When was it developed and what are its constituent parts?

SUGGESTED FURTHER READING

Browne, Janet. *Charles Darwin: The Power of Place.* New York, Knopf, 2002.

Browne, Janet. *Charles Darwin: Voyaging.* New York, Knopf, 1995.

Darwin, Charles. *On the Origin of Species.* Cambridge (MA), Harvard University Press, 1964. (First published in 1859.)

Grayson, Donald. *The Establishment of Human Antiquity.* New York, Academic Press, 1983.

Larson, Edward. *Evolution.* New York, Modern Library, 2004.

Mayr, Ernst. *One Long Argument.* Cambridge (MA), Harvard University Press, 1991.

Mayr, Ernst. *The Growth of Biological Thought: Diversity, Evolution, and Inheritance.* Cambridge (MA), Harvard University Press, 1982.

Numbers, Ronald. *The Creationists.* New York, Knopf, 1992.

Price, Peter. *Biological Evolution.* Fort Worth, Saunders College Publishing, 1996.

INTERNET RESOURCES

UCMP EXHIBITION HALLS: EVOLUTION

www.ucmp.berkeley.edu/history/evolution.html

This web site provides biographical sketches of several scientists who contributed to "deep time" and/or evolutionary theories.

MENDELWEB

www.mendelweb.org

Information about the life and work of Gregor Mendel and the origins of classical genetics.

MENDEL MUSEUM

www.mendel-museum.org

Excellent site maintained by the Mendel Museum at the Abbey of St. Thomas, Brno. The site includes biographical information about Mendel, as well as animated descriptions of his botanical experiments.

NATIONAL CENTER FOR SCIENCE EDUCATION

www.natcenscied.org

Information about the continuing controversy over teaching evolution and "creation science" in the public schools.

VICTORIAN SCIENCE: AN OVERVIEW

www.victorianweb.org/science/sciov.html

Part of the Victorian Web, this site provides background information about Charles Darwin and other nineteenth-century scientists.

EVOLUTION CHANGE: DEEP TIME

www.pbs.org/wgbh/evolution/change/deeptime

This site includes an animated introduction to deep time and links to related geological and evolutionary topics.

USEFUL SEARCH TERMS:

Charles Darwin
creationism
Darwinism
deep time
evolution
Gregor Mendel

Chapter 2

Evolutionary Mechanisms

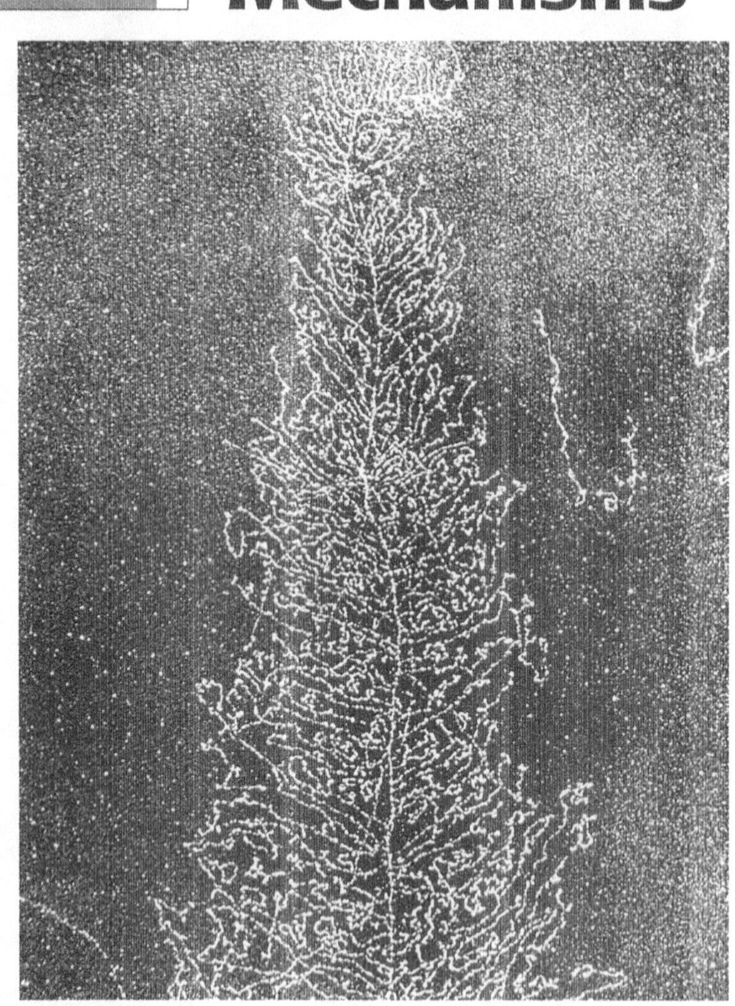

RNA strands (lateral branches) shown being synthesized on DNA (vertical line).

Evolution is always happening. What [geneticists mean by that is] the genes of this generation are not precisely what they were in the preceding generation. Nor will they be precisely the same in the next. And evolution is that change. And it is almost a certainty, a mathematical certainty, that the genes will never be the same.

Peter Grant, quoted in J. Weiner's *The Beak of the Finch* (1994: 126).

Overview

Chapter 2 provides a primer on the science of genetics and the mechanisms of evolutionary change. Taking its lead from the modern synthetic theory of evolution, the chapter focuses mainly on change at the level of the population but attempts throughout to show how the survival and reproduction of individuals contributes to the characteristics of the population. The chemistry (DNA, RNA) and functioning of genes are described, including the role genes play in protein synthesis. Next comes a discussion of the contributions of mutation and crossing-over to phenotypic variation at the level of the population, followed by material on the nature (and definition) of species. Gene flow, an important non-Darwinian mechanism, is examined as part of the biological species concept, and this is followed by descriptions of the evolutionary effects of natural selection, genetic drift, and the founder effect. The Hardy-Weinberg theorem, one of population geneticists' most useful tools, is then described. The chapter ends with discussions of speciation (particularly allopatric speciation), extinction, and the question of progress in evolution.

Levels of Selection and Change

The modern synthetic theory of evolution proposes that changes in species' traits are the results of altered frequencies of Mendel's hereditary particles—that is, altered gene frequencies. In strong contrast to the mutationists' theory, which focused on the spontaneous modifications of *individual* organisms as the basis of evolutionary change, the modern synthesis focuses on genetic changes produced by natural selection working within **populations** of plants and animals. (Typically, a population is a subunit of a *species.* Further information about the connection between populations and species is given on pages 36–37. For now, just think of a population as a geographically localized breeding group of conspecifics.)

Population usually, a local or breeding group; a group in which any two individuals have the potential of mating with each other.

Evolutionary biologist Ernst Mayr (1982) has described the emergence of the modern synthesis as a shift to "population thinking," and one of the main goals of this chapter is to get you used to thinking about biological change in this way. A second goal is to make sure that you understand how natural selection (aided by certain other processes) shapes groups of organisms over time. This primer on the mechanisms of evolutionary change is a necessary prerequisite for applying Darwinian theory to the specific case of human origins.

Of course, the mutationists were partially right in their belief that individual organisms contribute fundamentally to evolutionary change. But contributing to evolution is not the same as actually evolving personally. By definition, individuals cannot evolve; only populations can do that. That is, only populations can show the sort of intergenerational changes in genes and traits that qualify as evolution. Individuals make their contributions by surviving (or not), reproducing (or not), and getting their genes into the next generation (or not). And as certain individuals succeed and others fail, the population itself is modified over time.

Therefore, in order to understand evolution fully, you must learn to pay attention simultaneously to two levels of biological activity: individual organisms, each

TABLE 2.1 A Framework for Understanding Darwinian Evolution

Individual	Population
Genotype	Gene pool
Phenotype	Collective phenotype
Fitness	Degree of adaptation

Microevolution evolutionary change within *species*; *evolution* that affects *populations*.

Macroevolution evolutionary change that involves the origin or *extinction* of *species* or higher *taxonomic* groups.

Genes primarily, functional units of the *chromosomes* in cell nuclei, controlling the coding and inheritance of *phenotypic* traits; some genes also occur in *mitochondria*.

Chromosomes coiled, thread-like structures of *DNA*, bearing the *genes* and found in the nuclei of all plant and animal cells.

Mitochondria granular or rod-shaped bodies in the cytoplasm of cells that function in the metabolism of fat and proteins. Probably of bacterial origin.

trying to survive and reproduce, and populations, each reflecting the cumulative results of its members' efforts. At first, this sort of two-level awareness may seem difficult, but it gets easier with practice. As a framework to get you started, we can identify three types of linkage between individuals and their populations, as shown in Table 2.1.

It should be noted that technically, the discussion here addresses only the operation of **microevolution,** or evolution below the species level (that is, within populations). **Macroevolution,** which includes evolutionary events above the species level (that is, the origin or loss of species or higher groups) is briefly treated at the end of the chapter (Price, 1996; Ridley, 1996).

Microevolution: Genes, Genotypes, and Gene Pools

Every living creature is characterized by its genotype, its own entire set of **genes.** (Note: Some scientists prefer the term *genome* here, using genotype to refer only to subsets of genes linked to specific traits. We prefer the broader meaning of genotype.) The vast majority of genes are located in the nuclei of the individual's cells (Figure 2.1), where they are organized into structures called **chromosomes.** (This term, which means "colored bodies," refers to the fact that at certain stages of cell growth the chromosomes can be stained by researchers and viewed microscopically; see Figure 2.2). A few genes can also be found outside the nucleus within organelles called **mitochondria** (Figure 2.1), where they take the form of closed loops of hereditary material. Of the two types, nuclear and mitochondrial, nuclear genes are infinitely more important in the production of an organism's traits. (Mitochondrial genes seem to be related mainly to the or-

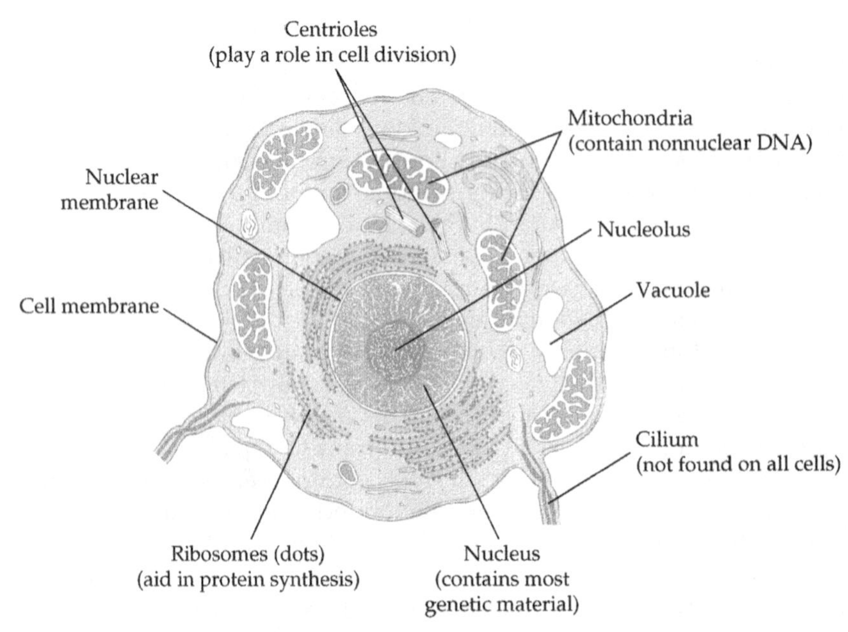

FIGURE 2.1
This simplified diagram of an animal cell shows the *nucleus* (containing the gene-bearing chromosomes) separated from the remainder of the cell's contents (the cytoplasm) by the nuclear membrane. Important structures to note within the cytoplasm include the *ribosomes,* which contribute to protein synthesis, and the *mitochondria,* which contain nonnuclear DNA.

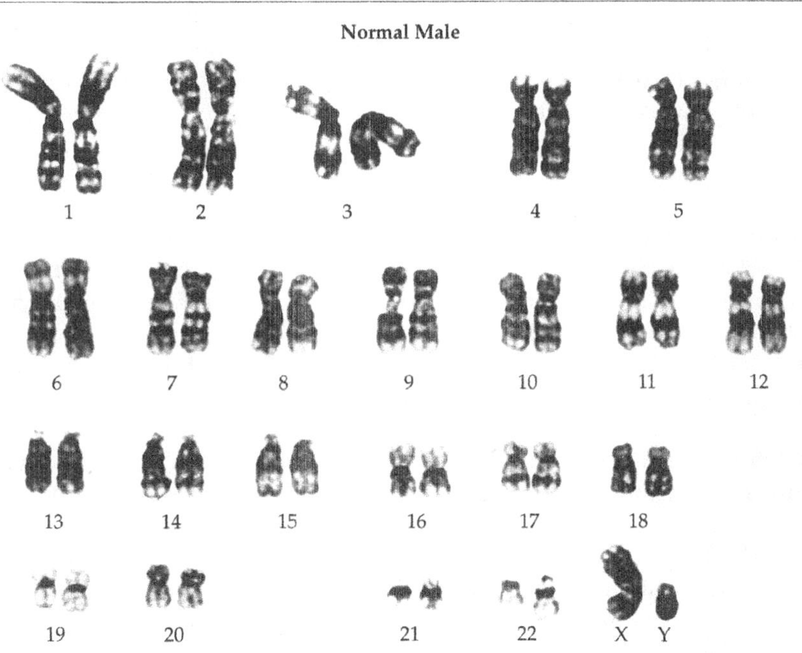

FIGURE 2.2 Humans have 46 chromosomes as 22 or 23 matching pairs. The sex chromosomes (labeled X and Y) are indicated in this photograph from a male human. Only males have the small Y chromosome, and so in this sex, the twenty-third pair cannot be matched. Females have two similar X chromosomes.

ganelles' own functioning and to general cell chemistry.) Nonetheless, mitochondrial genes may have the potential to help scientists analyze evolutionary events and relationships (more on this topic in Chapters 14 and 16; Molnar, 2002).

Genes provide, in effect, a blueprint for the construction, operation, and maintenance of individual organisms. So-called structural genes tend to produce, and thus end up being named for particular traits. For example, humans have eye color genes, skin color genes, genes that affect behavior, and even genes that determine susceptibility to certain diseases. Additionally, there is an important set of regulatory genes that control the developmental, metabolic, energetic, and biosynthetic activities of the body (Carroll, 2003; Singer and Berg, 1991). The genetic blueprint is rather flexible, however, and the details of the resulting phenotype—which specific traits make up an individual's phenotype—are always dependent on complex interactions among the organism's genes and between its genes and its environment. An obvious example of the latter interaction is body size. Genes for large body size may not be expressed fully when coupled with environmental factors such as poor nutrition and disease during development, and as a result, the adult individual will be smaller than its genetic potential for growth.

The gene-and-environment relationship is expressed in the following simple but important formula:

Genotype + Environment = Phenotype

Following Table 2.1, summing the genotypes of the members of a population yields information about the **gene pool.** A full inventory of a population's gene pool would list all of the various genes and their frequencies. This ideal situation has not yet been achieved for humans or any other species, although thanks to the recent completion of the Human Genome Project, most of the identities—but not the frequencies—of humans' genes are now known (Gibson and Muse, 2002; International Consortium, 2004; Venter et al., 2001).

Gene pool all of the *genes of a population* at a given time; summing genes within a species yields the species' gene pool.

Population geneticists can usually draw conclusions about the frequencies of only a few well-studied genes. A good example involves calculations of the M and N blood-type genes among the Quinault Indians, a Native American tribe from Washington State. Of the MN blood genes of the Quinaults, 63 percent are gene *M*, while the remaining 37 percent are gene *N*. If one could show a clear shift in these percentages over time, it would be strong proof of microevolution. Indeed, documenting change in the composition of a population's gene pool is the very best way to show that evolution has occurred.

Phenotypes and Collective Phenotypes

A second, although somewhat less satisfactory, way to show that population-level evolution has taken place is to document transgenerational phenotypic change. As described in Chapter 1, individual organisms possess not only genotypes, but also phenotypes. If we pool the trait data for all members of a population, we can draw conclusions about the population's **collective phenotype.** For continuous traits, such as body weight, statements about the collective phenotype take the form of a mean value plus a measure of variation around that mean (humans' average weight = 128 ± 2 lb [58 ± 1 kg]; the variation is best measured in standard deviations). For discontinuous traits, such as blood types, collective phenotype statements express the percentages shown by the various phenotypic states.

Collective phenotype the set of phenotypic averages and norms that characterize a *population* or *species*.

The Quinault blood-group data once again provide a good example. Among these Indians, almost exactly 50 percent of individuals show the MN blood *type* (note that blood types are different from blood genes), just over 38 percent show type M, and about 11 percent show type N. If these percentages were to change, scientists would be justified in concluding that evolution has probably occurred. Such a conclusion is warranted even though we may lack information about the population's genetic makeup—as is always the case for fossil populations. To summarize, microevolution can only be documented by demonstrating changes in either gene pools or collective phenotypes.

Genes, DNA, and RNA

But we're about to get ahead of ourselves. Clarifying how genotypes are related to gene pools and how phenotypes are related to collective phenotypes are important steps toward understanding the workings of evolution under the modern synthesis. The third linkage identified in Table 2.1 relates the *fitness* of individuals (usually defined by some measure of reproductive success) to the *adaptedness* of their populations (measured by phenotypic match to environmental conditions). These are key concepts and deserve full discussions, but first we need to backtrack and get a more thorough grounding in genetics. Of particular importance are the details of genes' location, composition, and functioning. (Most of this information is based on Singer and Berg [1991].)

As noted earlier, most genes occur as parts of chromosomes, those interesting threadlike structures found in cell nuclei. Each living species has a characteristic number of chromosomes, the so-called **diploid number** (symbolized $2n$). This is the full chromosomal count, and it occurs in all *somatic* cells (all cells except the **gametes,** eggs, and sperm). Gametes, or sex cells, in contrast, possess a **haploid number** of chromosomes, or half of the full count (symbolized n). Diploid numbers for humans and some of our close relatives include 42 in baboons, 48 in chimpanzees and gorillas, and 46 in people (Ankel-Simons, 1983).

Careful readers will have noticed that diploid numbers are always even. This is because somatic cells primarily contain pairs of **homologous chromosomes**—pairs that resemble each other in shape, size, and their sequence of genes (see Figure 2.2). The pair of **sex chromosomes,** however, is an exception to this rule. The X and Y chromosomes that determine femaleness or maleness are quite different in shape, size, and genetic contents (Figure 2.2). Among mammals, inheriting two Xs results in development as a female, while an XY combination results in development as a

Diploid number the full *chromosome* count in somatic cells (all cells except *gametes*)

Gametes reproductive *haploid* cells generated by *meiosis*, which fuse with *gametes* of the opposite sex in reproduction; in animals, eggs and sperm.

Haploid number the number of *chromosomes* carried by *gametes*; one-half of the full count carried by somatic cells.

Homologous chromosomes *chromosomes* that are similar in shape, size, and sequence of *genes*.

Sex chromosomes those *chromosomes* that carry *genes* that control gender (femaleness or maleness).

male. Obviously, in sexually reproducing species, babies' diploid numbers are produced by the union of haploid egg with haploid sperm at conception.

The possibility that the chromosomes might contain the cell's hereditary material was first suggested in 1902 by Walter Sutton in the United States and Theodor Boveri in Germany (Mayr, 1982). Numerous discoveries since then have amply confirmed this suggestion and collectively give us a detailed picture of the chemistry of chromosomes and genes. We now know that chromosomes consist of long, spiraling strands of **DNA** (*deoxyribonucleic acid*), a substance that was first discovered in 1869 by Friedrich Miescher and whose composition and structure were worked out by Francis Crick, Rosalind Franklin, James Watson, and Maurice Wilkins in 1953 (Figure 2.3; Maddox, 2003; Mayr, 1982).

DNA (deoxyribonucleic acid) a chemical substance found in *chromosomes* and *mitochondria* that reproduces itself and carries the *genetic code*.

Another way to understand genes, then, is to view them as basic functional subunits of DNA—segments of DNA that can be identified with particular phenotypic effects—that tend to occur at particular chromosomal locations or loci (singular, **locus**). But it's a little more complicated than that. A gene at a particular locus may show several different forms and these variants are called **alleles.** Alleles influence the same phenotypic trait, only differently. Gregor Mendel's work, described in Chapter 1, provided several examples of alleles and their pair-wise interactions. As shown in Figure 1.16, *R* and *r* represent alleles (variant types) of the gene for pea form. Depending on the combination of alleles that a new plant inherits during fertilization, it can be homozygous dominant (*RR*, producing round peas), heterozygous (*Rr*, also producing round peas), or homozygous recessive (*rr*, producing wrinkled peas). So far so good, but how do genes actually go about producing phenotypic traits? To answer that question, we must literally unravel the DNA molecule.

Locus the position of a nuclear *gene* on a *chromosome*; each locus can carry only one *allele* of a gene.

Alleles *genes* occupying equivalent positions on paired *chromosomes* yet producing different phenotypic effects when *homozygous*; alternative states of a gene, originally produced by *mutation*.

Nucleotides organic compounds, consisting of bases, sugars, and phosphates; found in cells either free or as part of polynucleotide chains.

The DNA of a chromosome consists of two long, interlocking polynucleotide chains arranged in a double helix (Figure 2.3). The backbone of each chain is a series of linked sugar and phosphate molecules (deoxyribose phosphates), and each sugar-phosphate unit is bonded to a single **nucleotide** base. These bases come in four varieties—(A) adenine, (T) thymine, (G) guanine, and (C) cytosine—and the two chains are held together in a helical structure by the bonds between complementary nucleotide bases (A with T, G with C). If the two chains are separated for individual analysis, each can be described by its sequence of nucleotide bases, for

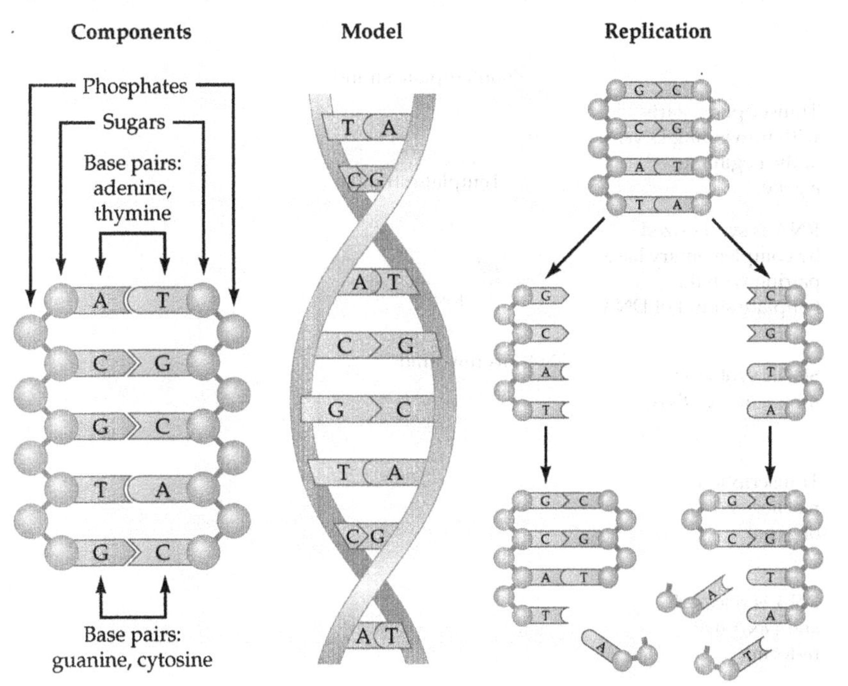

FIGURE 2.3
The DNA molecule is a double spiral (or helix) linked by four interlocking chemical subunits: the base pairs. Replication and protein synthesis take place by the splitting of the double helix: Each separate strand replicates by synthesizing its mirror image from the unit molecules floating in solution, as shown here.

Codon a *nucleotide* triplet that codes for the production of a particular *amino acid* during *protein* production.

Amino acids a group of organic compounds that act as building blocks for *proteins*.

RNA (ribonucleic acid) a compound found with *DNA* in cell nuclei and chemically close to DNA; transmits the *genetic code* from DNA to direct the production of *proteins*. May take two forms: messenger RNA (mRNA) or transfer RNA (tRNA).

Proteins molecules composed of chains of *amino acids*.

Exons segments of a *gene's DNA* that code for *protein* production.

Introns segments of a *gene's DNA* that do not code for *protein* production (so-called noncoding DNA).

Ribosomes cellular organelles that contribute to *protein* synthesis.

Satellite DNA tandem repetitions of *DNA* sequences that accumulate at certain locations on *chromosomes* and are usually noncoding.

example, ACGTTGCAA. The nucleotides work in groups of three adjacent bases (e.g., ACG; such a triplet is called a **codon**) to code for the production of particular **amino acids** as part of protein synthesis within the cell. (This is the first step in the production of phenotypic traits.) Each gene consists of a long sequence of codons (humans' genes range in size from a few hundred to tens of thousands of base pairs) that work together to produce a particular protein.

The DNA double helix actually becomes partially unraveled into two individual chains in two circumstances. First, this occurs as part of *chromosomal replication* (sometimes called *gene replication*) during both forms of cell division. During *mitosis*, the normal division process of somatic cells, all of the chromosomes form replicas (thus temporarily doubling the genes in the nucleus) and then the cell divides once. This results in identical twin copies of the original diploid cell. In contrast, during *meiosis*, the process of reduction division that results in gametes, a single act of chromosomal replication is followed by two episodes of cell division. This produces haploid sex cells (see Figure 2.7, page 35; meiosis is described in greater detail in a later section concerned with the sources of phenotypic variation). In any event, during both types of cell division, each polynucleotide chain serves as a template for the formation of its partner from newly synthesized sugar-phosphate-base units (Figure 2.3; see Alberts [2003] for more details on replication). The second circumstance of DNA unraveling is during the transcription of DNA information into **RNA** (*ribonucleic acid*) as a step toward protein synthesis (Figure 2.4). A brief look at protein synthesis reveals more details of the structure of genes and the process of phenotype production.

Proteins are complex molecules composed of long chains of amino acids. They take a variety of forms, and collectively, they coordinate and control our basic life processes, being involved in growth, development, reproduction, and bodily maintenance. Examples of proteins include hemoglobin (responsible for oxygen and carbon dioxide transport throughout the body), collagen and keratin (building blocks of connective tissues and hair), the antibodies active within our immune system, and the enzymes that catalyze our biochemical reactions. The cellular process that results in protein synthesis begins with partial unwinding of the DNA helix (Figure 2.4). Transcription of the DNA information then starts as a strand of *messenger RNA*

FIGURE 2.4
The basic sequence of events during DNA-to-RNA transcription.

Nontemplate strand
Transcription starts with unwinding DNA at the beginning of a gene.
Template strand
RNA is synthesized by complementary base pairing with the template strand of DNA.
RNA
Site of synthesis moves along DNA.
DNA has rewound
Transcription reaches end of gene.
RNA is released and DNA helix re-forms.

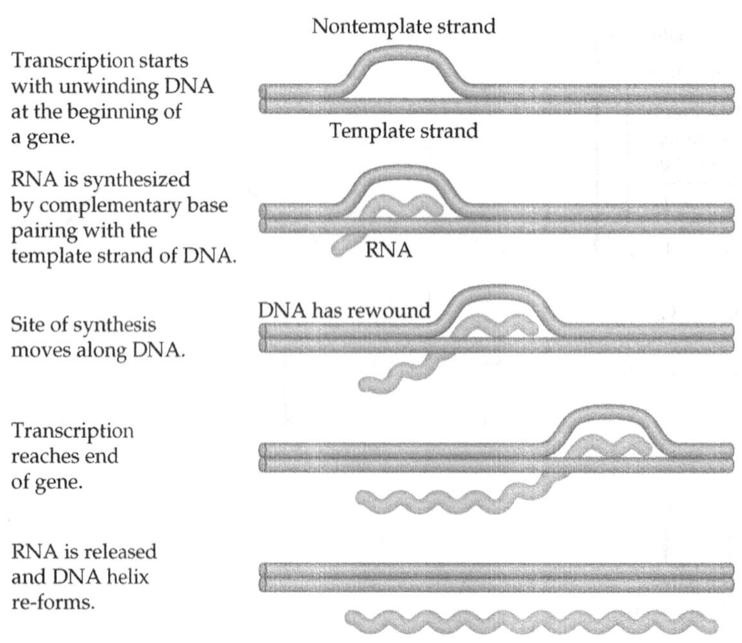

(mRNA) and is synthesized by complementary base pairing onto the DNA template. Interestingly, only certain portions of each gene's DNA, called **exon** segments, actually code for protein production. Long stretches of noncoding DNA, called **intron** segments, must therefore be removed from the mRNA template after transcription is completed. This is done through a process called *splicing* that leaves the mRNA with only exon information (Figure 2.5).

Once a gene has been completely transcribed, the mRNA strand is released, and the DNA helix re-forms. Messenger RNA is then engaged by particles called **ribosomes** that move along the mRNA chain and catalyze the translation of proteins, triplet codon by triplet codon (Figure 2.6). A key element in this process is the action of another form of RNA—*transfer RNA* (tRNA)—in engaging amino acids and then positioning them on the mRNA template. Bit by bit, amino acids are assembled into long protein chains, all of which will contribute to the formation or operation of the organism's phenotype.

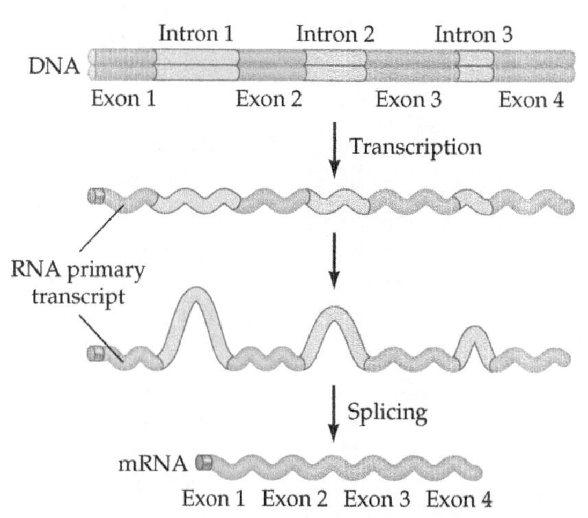

FIGURE 2.5
RNA splicing after transcription removes the noncoding introns and leaves only exon information.

Two final points need to be made before we end this section on the chemistry of genes. First, it bears repeating that by no means does all of a cell's nuclear DNA actually contribute to protein (and therefore phenotype) production. Introns are noncoding sequences, and surprisingly, they account for much more DNA than do exons. Furthermore, at certain points on chromosomes, tandem repetitions of DNA sequences (called **satellite DNA**) tend to accumulate, and these are also likely to

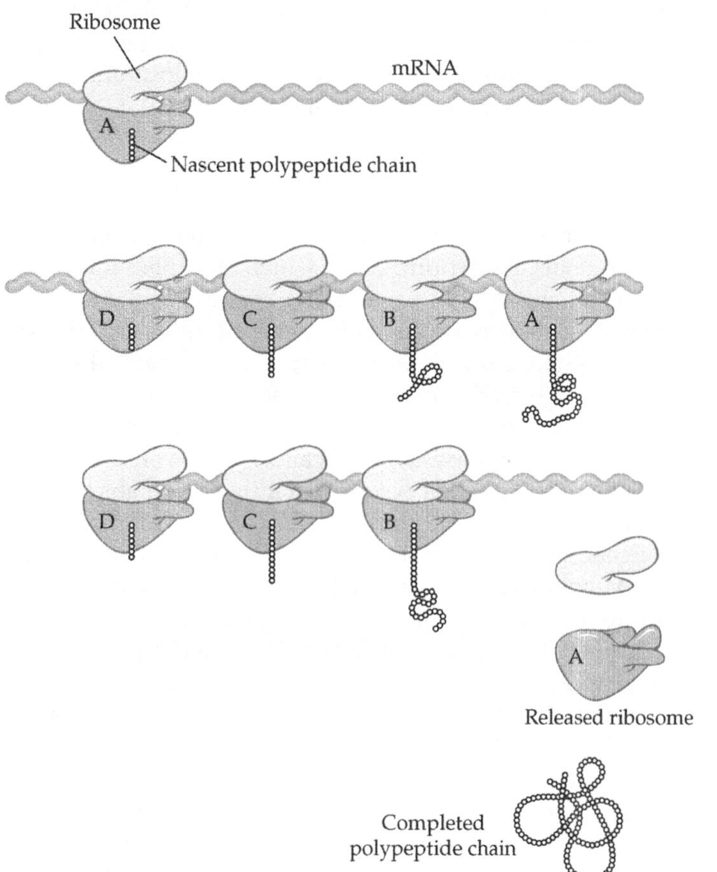

FIGURE 2.6
Multiple ribosomes sequentially engage mRNA after transcription and, aided by tRNA (not shown), catalyze the translation of the polypeptide chains that will form proteins. When a ribosome has completed its portion of polypeptide synthesis, it is released from the mRNA chain.

be noncoding. Current estimates of the total proportion of humans' DNA that is noncoding range from 75 to 90 percent (Ridley, 1996).

Just think how much sorting and splicing (Figure 2.5) is required to extract our (relatively few) exon sequences from all of the noncoding material surrounding them! Scientists have yet to learn precisely how and why the silent sequences of DNA accumulate, and what functions (if any) they serve. One idea is that the noncoding DNA may be organized into important *regulatory* regions that affect the expression of coding sequences. Other possibilities are that the noncoding DNA serves to keep genes correctly spaced within the three-dimensional DNA molecule and that it is an important reservoir for recombination (Makalowski, 2003). Some scientists, however, think it is just noncoding "junk" (Ridley, 1996).

The second point concerns the universal occurrence of the DNA genetic code (see Appendix 1). Scientists have found that in virtually all life forms, the same 61 DNA triplets encode the same 20 amino acids. Furthermore, one triplet (ATG) functions universally as a "start" codon, marking the beginning point for a protein coding sequence, while three triplets (TAA, TAG, TGA) function as "stop" markers (Ridley, 1996). This remarkable discovery argues as powerfully as the entire fossil record that all life has evolved from a single ancestral source. If Charles Darwin could come back to life and read these words, he might chuckle and say, "I told you so!"

Sources of Genetic and Phenotypic Variation

A resurrected Darwin would also be keenly interested in modern information about the sources of trait variation among conspecific organisms. Remember that Darwin formulated his evolutionary theory without the slightest notion as to why variation occurs in every new generation—he simply knew that you could count on it. Today, evolutionary biologists consider two distinctly different processes to be the main sources of phenotypic variation: gene mutations and chromosomal mixing and recombination during gamete production (meiosis and crossing-over; again, much of this discussion follows Singer and Berg [1991]).

Mutations

Modern humans are estimated to carry 20,000 to 25,000 genes per haploid gamete (International Consortium, 2004), which multiplies into 40,000 to 50,000 alleles per diploid somatic cell. As in all living creatures, spontaneous changes in humans' DNA sequences occur constantly and randomly. Such changes, called **point mutations,** can change the allelic identity of genes and influence an offspring's phenotype if they are carried on gametes and thus inherited. (Mutations in somatic cells also occur, but they cannot be inherited. Somatic mutations may contribute to the development of diseases such as cancer, however; see Box 2.1).

Point mutation usually, the substitution of one *nucleotide* in a single *codon* of a *gene* that affects *protein* synthesis and *genotype*; gene *mutation*.

Although mutations occur constantly, in humans they have a low average rate of about 1 mutation per 100,000 copies of a gene (rates vary for different genes, with some genes mutating at one-tenth this speed and others ten times as fast; Molnar, 1998). Mutations are possible in both coding DNA sequences, where they might alter protein synthesis, and in noncoding regions, where they might affect important regulatory functions (Carroll, 2003). The mutation rate of an organism's genes may be increased, however, through exposure to environmental stimuli such as radiation and certain chemicals. (The rate also increases with age.) H. J. Muller won the Nobel Prize in 1946 for his work on X-ray-induced mutations in fruit flies.

A point mutation may be as small as the substitution, addition, or loss of a single nucleotide base. Many point mutations are never expressed phenotypically because of DNA's ability for self-repair back to the original condition (Friedberg, 2003). (Specialized enzymes exist for DNA repair. Single-strand damage, such as missing or mismatched bases, is repaired using the undamaged strand as a template.

BOX 2.1 CURRENT ISSUE

The Upside and Downside of Genetics Research

Hardly a week goes by without a new breakthrough in biomedical science. Premature infants who would have died only a few decades ago are now saved. Immunizations protect us from many serious diseases. Organ transplants allow life-saving replacements for people with kidney and heart disease. In genetics, we've gained much understanding about inherited predispositions to diseases and pathologies, and this knowledge, along with new techniques for detecting "bad" genes, allows informed counseling of high-risk individuals (that is, people at personal risk of gene-related illness or would-be parents likely to pass detrimental genotypes to children). With the new knowledge, however, come new problems and difficult decisions. Consider an example.

Researchers have discovered that women with mutations in two genes—the so-called BRCA1 and BRCA2 genes—almost certainly run an elevated risk of breast and ovarian cancers. One recent study suggested that carriers of mutations at both loci—mainly Jewish women of Eastern or Central European ancestry—have a 56 percent chance of breast cancer and a 16 percent chance of ovarian cancer by age 70 (average risks for noncarriers are 8 percent and 2 percent for the two cancers, respectively; Kolata, 1997; see also King et al., 2003). Laboratory tests have been developed to identify people with mutated BRCA1 and BRCA2 genes, but the personal dilemma is how to respond to positive test results. Ideally, the genes themselves could be altered somehow and the risk of disease therefore reduced. Unfortunately, such genetic engineering is still only a possibility for the future, and the options presently available for cancer gene carriers are less than appealing. One can choose to do nothing and simply live with the risks, in the hope that further discoveries will allow the necessary gene therapy. Or one can opt for prophylactic removal of the breasts and ovaries, procedures that can dramatically reduce the risk of the cancers. (Some researchers are urging women with mutant genes to consider at least removal of the ovaries.)

But how is one to choose? Modern Americans grow up expecting to live to a ripe old age *and* to do so with normal, healthy bodies. We're not used to thinking of our bodies as our own worst enemies. We have no guidelines for deciding whether to coexist with an internal time bomb such as a cancer gene or to get rid of its likely target, despite the physical, emotional, and reproductive costs. Which path would you choose for yourself? Which would you choose for a loved one?

To take this example one step further, consider some of the possible ripple effects of increased biomedical knowledge. Imagine the case of a cancer gene carrier's medical history becoming known to a prospective employer or an insurance company. Do you think a woman ethically could be denied either a job or insurance coverage based solely on her *risk* of cancer? And if you don't think this sort of thing can happen, consider the following actual incident, reported by Joseph Levine and David Suzuki in their recent book, *The Secret of Life* (1993:203):

> One couple who knew that they were CF (cystic fibrosis) carriers asked their HMO (health maintenance organization) to pay for a genetic test on their unborn child during pregnancy. They were told that if the child tested positive, the HMO would cancel their health plan unless they agreed to an abortion. Only threatened legal action induced the HMO to withdraw that demand.

What's the take-home message? The Pandora's box of biomedical knowledge is wide open. Future discoveries will have both upside and downside effects, and the latter will test our wisdom and courage as individuals and our ethics as a society.

Double-strand damage can be repaired after chromosomal recombination during meiosis [see next section] provides unaltered DNA as a template.) Even when expressed, mutations do not necessarily produce completely new alleles or monstrous traits, such as legs growing out of a fly's head in place of antennae. Many mutations simply alter a gene from one known allele (and trait) to another, as in the case of humans' normal blood-clotting allele mutating into the allele that causes hemophilia, a pathological condition characterized by bleeding due to inadequate clotting. Sometimes, of course, entirely new genetic variants *are* produced, and therefore mutations must be ranked as the primary source of new alleles in a species' gene pool.

The question is, Are constantly occurring point mutations responsible generation after generation for the vast amount of individual phenotypic variation seen in all species? Probably not. First of all, the mutation rates are too low. And second, most new mutant alleles are quickly lost from the gene pool. In some cases, they are eliminated by natural selection, being selected against because they code for deleterious traits. Given the random nature of mutation, it is unusual for the process to produce immediately beneficial genetic changes. (Just as a random adjustment inside a computer is unlikely to improve its performance, a random addition to a species' gene pool is unlikely to be useful to anyone who inherits it.) Beneficial mutations, as well as those that are selectively neutral, also occur, of course, and both types are more likely to be maintained in the gene pool than those with negative results. In all cases, rarity is working against retention, however, and many mutant alleles disappear through chance loss alone (that is, by chance, they are not passed to offspring; Williams, 1997). Mutations do not serve, therefore, as the main source of phenotypic variation in each generation. A much better candidate exists for that important role: meiosis, the cell division process that produces eggs and sperm.

Meiosis and Crossing-Over

The reduction division process of meiosis is remarkable in many ways. Not only does it reduce the chromosome count of gametes to the haploid number, but it also provides the basis for extensive phenotypic variation in every generation by producing genetically unique sex cells. While mutation stands as the ultimate source of new alleles and allelic variation, meiosis must be viewed as the primary (and proximate) source of genotypic variety among individuals.

Meiosis involves one chromosomal replication and two cell divisions (Figure 2.7). Before the first cell division, each chromosome replicates itself to produce two **chromatids.** The duplicated chromosome with its two elements then pairs with its homologous partner, and this pairing yields clusters of four chromatids called *tetrads.* As the tetrads line up at the equator of the fibrous spindle that stretches between the **centrioles** (Metaphase I), the chromatids in each may overlap at points called **chiasmata. Crossing-over,** or the exchange of sections between homologous chromosomes, may then take place at these sites (Figure 2.8). During the next stage (Anaphase I), the homologous chromosomes (each still consisting of two chromatids) separate and move toward opposite poles of the spindle. (Technically, the two halves of the dividing cell are now haploid, since we count chromosomes, not chromatids.) At this point, any or all of the four chromatids formerly making up a tetrad may contain a different mixture of genetic material from their original condition.

Chromatid one of the two elements in a duplicated *chromosome.*

Centrioles minute granules present in many cells outside the nuclear membrane. The centriole divides in cell division, and the parts separate to form the poles of the spindle.

Chiasmata points where the *chromatids* of a tetrad overlap and segment exchange may occur; cross-over points (singular, *chiasma*).

Crossing-over the exchange of sections between *homologous chromosomes.*

Haplotype a sequence of linked *nucleotides* or loci that is exchanged as a block between *homologous chromosomes* during *meiosis.*

Note that because crossing-over tends to occur regularly at some spots on chromosomes and rarely at others, so-called **haplotype** blocks—sequences of linked nucleotides or loci that are exchanged as a unit—can usually be identified along a chromosome's length. Haplotype blocks show both internal variation (three to seven primary variants per block is typical) and geographic variation that can provide clues about a species's place of origin and subsequent migrations (Pääbo, 2003; Strickberger, 2000).

The first meiotic division is then completed, and the second begins. (In females of some species—such as our own—the first division in potential egg cells begins prenatally, is suspended between birth and puberty, and is then completed—along with the second division—by a few cells every month between puberty and menopause; R. Jones, 1991). The second meiotic division occurs without further replication of the genetic material and involves the separation of chromatids (Anaphase II). The potential result of meiosis is the production of four haploid "daughter" cells (this term is used for both sperm and egg cells), each genetically unique. This potential is realized in men (four sperm cells from each original parent cell), while in women, only one energy-rich egg is produced from every parent cell.

Evolutionary change via natural selection can proceed only if conspecifics vary phenotypically and trait differences are based, at least partially, on genetic differences.

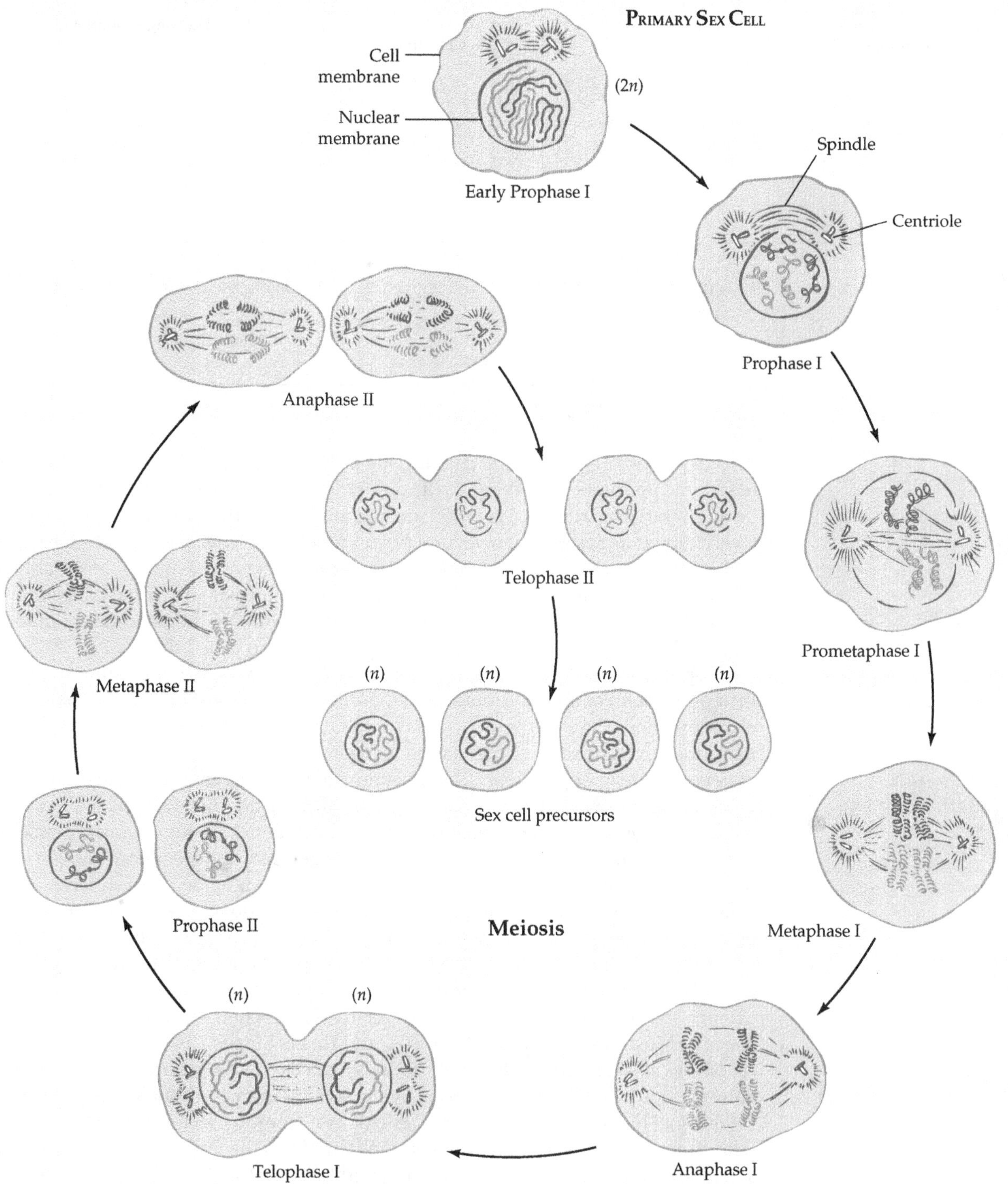

FIGURE 2.7
Meiosis. The single replication of genetic material occurs in Prophase I. Crossing-over within the tetrad takes place in Metaphase I, producing numerous reconstituted chromosomes. Two cell divisions then follow that (potentially) result in four haploid gamete precursors.

(Within a population, the proportion of phenotypic variance attributable to genetic variance is referred to as a trait's level of **heritability**.) Meiosis, with its genetic and chromosomal mixing, provides the basis for gene-based phenotypic variations. The stage is now set for evolution at the levels of the population and the species.

Heritability a property of *phenotypic* traits; the proportion of a trait's interindividual variance that is due to genetic variance.

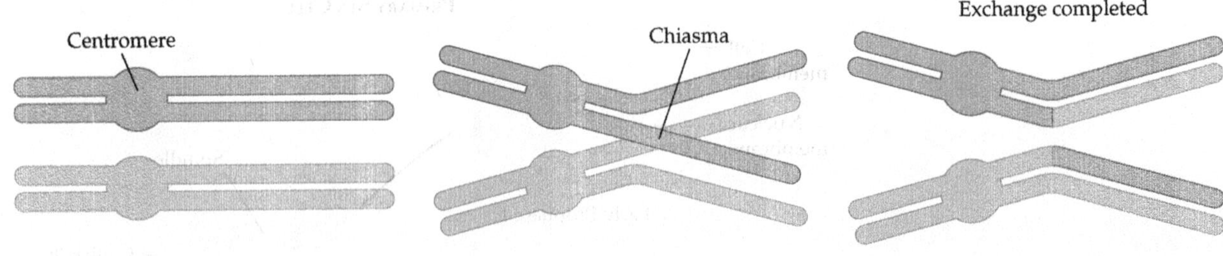

FIGURE 2.8
A simple example of crossing-over and segment exchange among the chromatids of a tetrad.

Populations and Species

Various Definitions of Species

As we discussed earlier in the chapter, the modern synthetic theory of evolution is based on "population thinking." Although individuals' contributions to evolution through the generation of variation are acknowledged, the focus is on population-level changes in gene frequencies and phenotypic traits. Now, populations have several interesting characteristics, the first being that they are usually identifiable in nature. That is, at any point in time, a population consists of a finite collection of conspecific individuals living in the same area and having the potential of mating with each other. (These breeding communities are also called **demes**.)

Deme the community of potentially interbreeding individuals at a locality.

Populations are anything but closed, however, and a second interesting feature is their permeable community boundaries that allow communication between neighboring populations through the (occasional or regular) exchange of members. In sexually reproducing creatures, these member exchanges almost always result in the movement of genes between populations. This phenomenon, called **gene flow,** usually has the result of decreasing differences (both genetic and phenotypic) *between* populations, while increasing variation of both sorts *within* each deme. In other words, thanks to gene flow, populations within a species are homogenized, both genetically and in their traits. (See, however, the study by Garant et al. [2005] for evidence of differentiating gene flow.) If a new and advantageous mutation crops up in one population, sooner or later it will be spread to all of the others. The occurrence of gene flow is what most evolutionary biologists would say binds a set of populations into a **species** (Figure 2.9).

Gene flow the transmission of *genes* between *populations*, which increases the variety of genes available to each and creates or maintains similarities in the genetic makeup of the populations.

Species following the biological species concept, a group of interbreeding natural *populations* that are reproductively isolated from other such groups.

If the presence of gene flow demonstrates permeable population boundaries *within* a species, does its absence reflect relatively impenetrable boundaries *between* species? Most biologists would say yes, and this is indeed the basis for the classical *biological species* concept, which defines a species as "a group of interbreeding natural populations that are reproductively isolated from other such groups" (Mayr, 1996:264). Here conspecifics are recognized not from the fact that they look alike (although this is almost always true as well) but from the fact that they mate exclusively (or almost exclusively, see below) with one another.

In virtually every biological species, one or more *isolating mechanisms* have evolved that have rendered organisms unable, or unwilling, to reproduce outside of their own species. Common isolating mechanisms that separate species include morphological differences (body shape, size, coloration, etc.), genetic and chromosomal differences (distinctive chromosome numbers and shapes), and perhaps most important of all, behavioral differences. Typical behavioral mechanisms include differences in breeding seasons and courtship patterns. Courtship, in particular, often involves complicated ritualistic behavior that is important in species recognition. (It should be noted that the word *natural* is very important to the biological species concept. The definition was never meant to apply to species that are naturally separated geographically but can interbreed in captivity. African lions [*Felis leo*] and Asian tigers [*Felis tigris*] may hybridize in zoos to produce "tiglons" and "ligers," but this does not mean that the two parent species are, in fact, one.)

The biological species definition is probably the best but by no means the only way to conceptualize and recognize species (Mayr, 1982, 1996; Strickberger, 2000). Morphological definitions (the so-called *typological species* concept, based on looking alike) were popular in Darwin's day, and they are still preferred by some scientists. The primary weakness of morphological definitions is the arbitrariness of trait selection for species classifications. Using different traits may result in researchers recognizing different numbers and patterns of species.

Other definitions, such as the *ecological species* concept, try to distinguish between species based on their different **ecological niches** (the set of resources and habitats exploited by each species). Like trait-based definitions, this approach also has problems, including the fact that in widespread species, there can be extensive niche diversification among demes (which would therefore have to be redefined as individual species). Overall, the biological species concept seems to be the best approach to species recognition, but even it has drawbacks.

Perhaps the greatest weakness of the biological species definition is that it makes the reproductive barriers between species sound too solid and universal. In fact, fertile hybridization (crossing) between widely recognized species is quite common among plants and occurs at least occasionally among animals. About 40 percent of duck and geese species have been known to hybridize, grey wolves (*Canis lupus*) produce fertile hybrids with coyotes (*Canis latrans*), and in Ethiopia, primatologists have documented anubis baboons (*Papio cynocephalus anubis*) cross-breeding with hamadryas baboons (*Papio hamadryas*; Kummer, 1995; Mayr, 1996; Weiner, 1994).

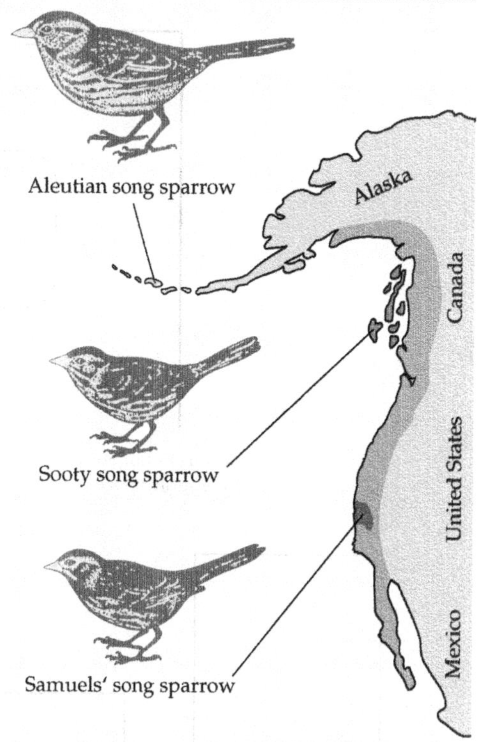

FIGURE 2.9 There are 34 subspecies of the song sparrow (*Passarella melodia*); 3 are shown here. Lines indicate the approximate breeding ranges of the illustrated subspecies, while those of 14 other distinct populations are shown by medium shading. Although birds at the northern and southern extremes of the geographic range do not interbreed directly, the unity of the species is maintained by extensive gene flow between neighboring populations all along the Pacific coast.

Even Ernst Mayr, one of the strongest supporters of the biological species concept, noted that "a leakage of genes occurs among many good 'reproductively isolated' species." By "gene leakage," he meant the transmission of genes from one species to another through hybridization followed by hybrids back-crossing with one of the original parent species. Mayr argued, however, that the biological species definition is by no means invalidated by this "messiness" in nature. In his view, despite the fact that reproductive "isolating mechanisms do not always prevent the *occasional* interbreeding of non-conspecific individuals . . . they nevertheless prevent the complete *fusion* of such species" (Mayr, 1996:265; emphasis added). And so it appears that despite occasional gene leakage from one species to another, most of the time, **assortative mating** (the tendency for creatures with similar phenotypes to mate with one another) and other behavioral and genetic mechanisms ensure species' integrity.

A second weakness of the biological species concept, and one that plagues evolutionary biologists, is that it is difficult to apply to fossil species, since we can never be sure about their reproductive behavior. Thus, when scientists try to identify and sort extinct species, they are forced to fall back on trait similarities and differences as the best indicators of reproductive isolation. The types and amounts of morphological distinctiveness needed for the identification of fossil species are usually based on studies of their closest living evolutionary relatives. For example, knowledge about morphological variation among modern humans, as well as that found among the living ape species, allows anthropologists to make informed decisions about the species of early human ancestors (see Chapter 7).

Ecological niche the set of resources and habitats exploited by a *species*.

Assortative mating the tendency of like to mate with like.

Darwinian Evolution: How Natural Selection Shapes Populations

Despite continuing disagreements among specialists over the precise definition(s) of species, it is clear that they do exist in nature and that they usually can be

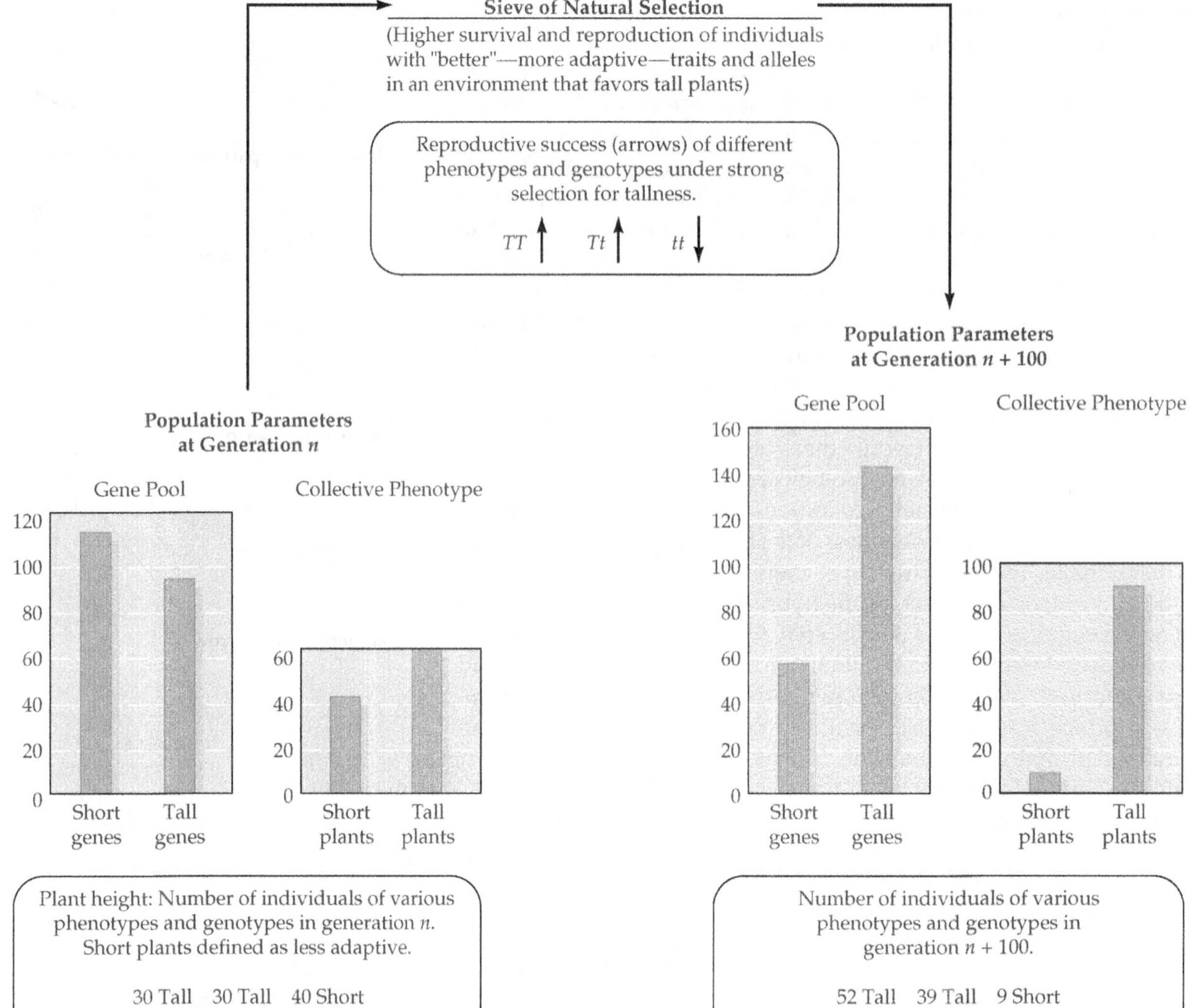
Sieve of Natural Selection
(Higher survival and reproduction of individuals with "better"—more adaptive—traits and alleles in an environment that favors tall plants)
Reproductive success (arrows) of different phenotypes and genotypes under strong selection for tallness.
TT Tt tt
Population Parameters at Generation n
Gene Pool
Collective Phenotype
Short genes
Tall genes
Short plants
Tall plants
Plant height: Number of individuals of various phenotypes and genotypes in generation n. Short plants defined as less adaptive.
30 Tall (TT) 30 Tall (Tt) 40 Short (tt)
Population Parameters at Generation n + 100
Gene Pool
Collective Phenotype
Short genes
Tall genes
Short plants
Tall plants
Number of individuals of various phenotypes and genotypes in generation n + 100.
52 Tall (TT) 39 Tall (Tt) 9 Short (tt)

FIGURE 2.10
A model of evolution by natural selection. In this example, pea plant height has two alleles: *T* (dominant) and *t* (recessive). The effects of selection for tallness from generations *n* to *n* + 100 are shown. Population size is held at 100 plants throughout the example.

subdivided into identifiable populations. (Very small species, with limited geographic ranges, may consist of only a single population. In this case, the species and the population are identical. Presumably, all new species that have resulted from the splitting or branching of an evolutionary lineage began as a single-population species. Species formation by branching is discussed at the end of this chapter.) Once in existence, a species may be stable or it may change with time. (Most species that last for a reasonable period probably experience both stability and change.) And of the handful of mechanisms that produce evolutionary change, the force that Charles Darwin dubbed *natural selection* is still widely regarded as the most important.

As noted in Chapter 1, natural selection is a straightforward and remarkably obvious concept, once you begin to think about it. (We have tried to diagram its operation in Figure 2.10.) In a nutshell, each population consists of individuals who vary in their genotypes and traits (remember the contributions that mutation and meiosis make to variation) and who are living under a distinct set of environmental

	(*a*) Selection coefficient = 0.05		(*b*) Selection Coefficient = 0.01	
	Gene Frequency		Gene Frequency	
Generation	***A***	*a*	***A***	*a*
0	0.01	0.99	0.01	0.99
100	0.44	0.56	0.026	0.974
200	0.81	0.19	0.067	0.933
300	0.89	0.11	0.15	0.85
400	0.93	0.07	0.28	0.72
500	0.95	0.05	0.43	0.57
600	0.96	0.04	0.55	0.45
700	0.96	0.04	0.65	0.35
800	0.97	0.03	0.72	0.28
900	0.97	0.03	0.77	0.23
1000	0.98	0.02	0.80	0.20

FIGURE 2.11
The results of a simulation of changes in the frequencies of alleles *A* and *a* during 1,000 generations of selection against the recessive allele. *(a)* Selection coefficient of 0.05 (*aa* individuals have a relative chance of survival of 95 percent, compared with 100 percent for *AA* and *Aa* individuals). *(b)* Selection coefficient of 0.01 (*aa* individuals have 99 percent chance of survival, compared to 100 percent for *AA* and *Aa*).

Source: Adapted from M. Ridley, 1996, *Evolution* (2nd edition). Reprinted by permission of Blackwell Science, Inc.

conditions (broadly defined to include physical conditions, food, water, and competing organisms). Individuals simply try to survive and reproduce, and other things being equal, those lucky few who possess traits that work in that environment succeed at both. Reproductively successful individuals pass their genes and traits on to the next generation, while nonreproducers obviously do not. Thus, with each passing generation, reproducers' alleles tend to increase in relative frequency (compared to the genes' alternate forms—alleles at the same loci—that were carried by nonreproducers) within the population gene pool and reproducers' phenotypic traits tend to become more common. The effects of natural selection can be measured as changes in the population's gene pool and/or shifts in the collective phenotype (Figures 2.10 and 2.11).

Charles Darwin envisioned natural selection as a process that operates slowly and that requires great stretches of time (and many generations) to perform its work. This may be true most of the time, and the results in Figure 2.11 show how small differences in the survival rates of different alleles (more correctly, the survival rates of the carriers of different alleles) can produce dramatic genetic shifts given enough time. Nonetheless, recent studies of fish, lizards, and even Darwin's Galápagos finches have demonstrated that under sufficiently strong environmental pressures, natural selection can move rapidly on occasion to transform a population or species (Losos et al., 1997; Weiner, 1994).

In response to environmental change, **directional natural selection** typically favors organisms that differ in particular ways from most of their conspecifics—for instance, by being a tall plant (Figure 2.10) or a small-bodied individual (Figure 2.12, part (*a*). Over time, such selection will increase average plant height and decrease average body size in the population. Natural selection does not always change things, however. At times (probably often), natural selection acts to preserve current gene frequencies and phenotypic distributions. Such **stabilizing natural selection**

Directional natural selection *natural selection* that operates in response to environmental change and produces shifts in the composition of a *population's gene pool* and *collective phenotype*.

Stabilizing natural selection *natural selection* that operates during periods when the environment is stable and maintains the genetic and phenotypic status quo within a *population*.

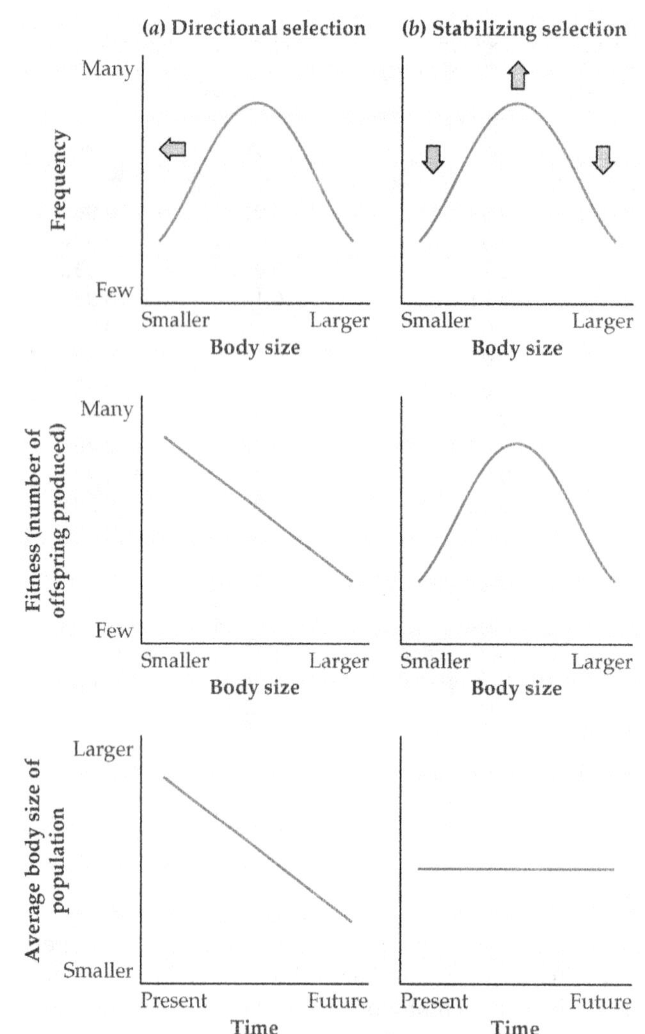

FIGURE 2.12
Diagrams of *(a)* directional natural selection and *(b)* stabilizing natural selection. The top row shows the frequency distribution of body size in a hypothetical population. Most individuals are of medium size, with some considerably smaller or larger. Arrows show the forces of selection. The middle row shows individuals' fitness, as measured by number of offspring. The bottom row shows the average body size in the population. Note that as directional selection favors smaller individuals, the average size drops over time. During stabilizing selection, however, medium-sized individuals have higher fitness than individuals at both size extremes, and mean size remains the same over time.

Source: Adapted from M. Ridley, 1996, *Evolution* (2nd edition). Reprinted by permission of Blackwell Science, Inc.

occurs when the environment is relatively constant (unchanging), and it operates by selecting against all individuals that deviate from the prevailing phenotypic norms (Figure 2.12*b*). Periods of **stasis** in the history of a species, when little or no evolutionary change occurs, are generally periods of stabilizing selection.

Stasis a period of evolutionary equilibrium or inactivity.

Natural selection is not the only evolutionary mechanism, but it ranks at the top of the list. In order to ensure your understanding of this important process, three clear examples of directional selection—including one from humans—are given in Box 2.2. In addition, a later section of this chapter explains the action of natural selection on humans' hemoglobin alleles, and Chapter 17 describes how the process has contributed to biological diversity among living people.

Sexual Selection

The preceding description of natural selection, as well as the examples in Box 2.2, illustrate organisms contending with elements of the physical environment (defined here as including food and predators). There is, however, another sort of Darwinian selection that involves creatures competing with other members of their own species for mates. Darwin mentioned this process of **sexual selection** in *On the Origin of Species,* which was published in 1859 (1964), and then described it more fully in 1871 in *The Descent of Man* (1981). He recognized two types of sexual selection.

Sexual selection a category including intrasexual competition for mates (usually aggressive and among males) and intersexual mate selection (usually of males by females).

BOX 2.2

Three Examples of Natural Selection at Work

1. Fur Color in Mice

In 1962, a mutant strain of house mice (*Mus musculus*) was discovered in a farm population in Missouri. Because of the effects of a single recessive allele, the mutant animals had pink eyes and pale yellow fur in contrast to the dark eyes and dark (agouti) fur of normal mice. The mutants interbred freely with the normal mice, and the two strains lived together in a granary used to store corn. The solid construction of the granary prevented the farm's numerous cats from entering.

In order to determine the relative proportions of mutants and normals, researchers periodically live-trapped the granary mice and released them (see table below). At the first trapping, the mutants accounted for about 28 percent of the population, and their representation increased steadily throughout 1962. In January 1963, because of an increase in the mouse population, the farmer made an opening in the granary wall to provide access for his cats. The cats immediately began to prey on the mice, and the pale yellow animals soon proved to be much more vulnerable to predation than their agouti conspecifics (probably because of greater visibility in the dimly lit corn crib). The percentage of mutants in the population fell to zero soon after the cats began their deadly work.

The allele responsible for the mutant coloration had not been completely removed from the population, however. In September 1963, at the urging of the researchers, the farmer sealed off the cats' entrance, and within three months the pale-colored mice had rebounded to about 5 percent of the population. In this example from nature, heritable differences in fur color were strongly affected by predator pressure (L. Brown, 1965).

2. Body Size and Bill Dimensions in Darwin's Finches

A species of Darwin's finch (*Geospiza fortis*) was studied on the Galápagos island of Daphne Major between 1975 and 1978. Birds were trapped and measured regularly, and data were collected on their feeding patterns. (They ate mostly seeds of various sorts and sizes.)

In 1977, Daphne Major experienced a severe drought that resulted in a sharp food shortage for the finches. Seeds of all sorts declined in abundance, but small seeds declined faster than large ones, and the result was a strong overall increase in the average size and hardness of the available seeds. (Averages for the "size-hardness index" for the seeds increased from a predrought figure of just over 4 to about 6 during the drought.)

In response to these environmental changes, the finches suffered an 85 percent drop in population size. Small birds suffered greater decimation than large ones, apparently because the smaller birds (with their smaller bills) had difficulty cracking and eating large, hard seeds. That is to say, smaller birds were strongly "selected against" because of the drought-related changes in food. Measurements taken after the drought (1978, see table on page 42) showed the effects of natural selection: Average body size in the population had increased, as had average bill size (Boag and Grant, 1981).

Date	Total Mice Trapped	Mutants as Percentage of Trapped Mice
Apr. 1962	32	28.1%
Aug. 1962	44	40.1%
Dec. 1962	58	46.6%
(Jan. 1963—cats allowed into granary)		
Apr. 1963	22	0.0%
Aug. 1963	29	0.0%
(Sept. 1963—cats excluded from granary)		
Dec. 1963	37	5.4%

(continued)

BOX 2.2 (continued)

Finch Traits	Predrought Mean	Postdrought Mean
Weight (g)	15.59	16.85
Bill length (mm)	10.68	11.07
Bill depth (mm)	9.42	9.96

3. Skin Color and Sunlight in Humans

Modern humans are much less hairy than their ancient ape relatives and appear to have been so throughout their entire history as a species (that is, for at least 195,000 years; McDougall et al., 2005). Most anthropologists conclude that the earliest populations of *Homo sapiens* lived in Africa, produced lots of melanin pigment in the epidermis of their skin, and were therefore dark in color. Such a condition would have provided many benefits to relatively hairless creatures living under the strong tropical sun. Among those benefits, it now appears, was the protection that heavy pigmentation provides for the body's stores of the B vitamin folate (folic acid). Studies of modern people have shown that folate deficiency is related to increased incidents of life-threatening birth defects, such as spina bifida (the failure of the spinal vertebrae arches to close around the spinal cord). Additionally, a deficiency of folate *may* be linked to low levels of spermatogenesis in men. Either way, insufficient folate can lead to reproductive failure in affected individuals.

The amount of epidermal pigmentation an individual produces also affects the ability of his or her skin to contribute to the formation of vitamin D, a substance that plays a key role in the production of babies with strong bones and the maintenance of healthy bones and immune systems in mothers. When ultraviolet B (UVB) radiation penetrates through the epidermis to the upper layers of the dermis, specialized cells produce *previtamin D*, which the kidneys later make into vitamin D.

In the sun-drenched regions where *Homo sapiens* first evolved, dark skin was an unmitigated blessing. It protected folate supplies while still allowing the absorption of enough UVB radiation to make vitamin D. However, in the human populations that began to migrate out of Africa and into more temperate and less sunny regions of the Old World, natural selection changed its pattern. Under conditions of reduced sunlight, lighter-skinned members of the migrating populations were favored. Lighter skin color allowed higher-latitude people to produce adequate vitamin D to stay healthy, despite the diminished UVB levels in their new habitats, while simultaneously, the reduction in sunlight eliminated it as a significant threat to folate.

Thus, throughout the course of *Homo sapiens'* evolutionary history, natural selection has favored dark skin color in some populations and light skin color in others. In all cases, the selection pressures were acting on physiological and/or morphological variables essential for survival and reproduction (see table below; Jablonski and Chaplin, 2002).

Natural Selection	Conditions			
Favored skin color	**Latitude**	**Annual UVB**	**Folate**	**Vitamin D**
Dark skin	Tropics	High dosage	Pigment provides protection	Despite dark skin, enough UVB gets through for vitamin D production
Light skin	Higher latitudes	Lower dosage	No need for folate protection	Despite lower UVB levels, light skin allows enough to penetrate for vitamin D production

The first kind was the result of competition among members of one sex (usually males) for the opposite sex. Good examples are found among the higher primates, such as some multimale baboon groups (Chapter 4), where the alpha male may have primary sexual access to most females in a troop as they near ovulation.

This reproductive pattern of behavior will select the genes for powerful and impressive males. Darwin's second kind of sexual selection involves differential choice by members of one sex for members of the opposite sex. This usually takes the form of the females' choice of some males in preference to others and is well known among both birds and primates (see Chapter 4). Both these phenomena are most commonly observed among polygamous species and play a much smaller part in a purely monogamous species in which every individual has a mate.

The role that sexual selection has played in human evolution is not yet understood, but it is clearly not a significant factor in a monogamous society with a 50:50 sex ratio. Insofar as human societies permit polygamy (and very many do) and insofar as the historical pattern was probably not monogamy (Chapter 9), it is possible that sexual selection has indeed brought about the evolution of some human traits. The kinds of characteristics in humans that may be a product of sexual selection are those which appear to advertise sexuality, such as hair patterns and types, body shape and breast development in women, and penis size in men. The second type of selection (differential choice of mate) has probably been more important in human evolution than intermale competition. The elucidation of this problem depends on knowledge of the mating patterns of early peoples—information that is probably unobtainable. Were matings a result of male-male competition, free choice, or were they arranged by parents or elders for political and economic reasons? The present arrangements may not tell us much about the past.

Other nonrandom mating systems found in animals and humans are **inbreeding** and **outbreeding.** Inbreeding occurs when sexual partners share a recent common ancestor (that is, when they are genetically related to some degree). In small, isolated animal and human populations, inbreeding may be the typical pattern, but it has its costs. It often results in the homozygous pairing of recessive genes and the expression of harmful traits in the phenotype.

Inbreeding mating among related individuals.

Outbreeding mating among unrelated individuals.

Mechanisms that promote outbreeding—such as one or both sexes leaving their natal group at adulthood—are widely found among nonhuman primates and other animals. Humans also practice outbreeding, which is promoted in most societies by extensive incest taboos and rules that insist on marriage with members of other clans for political and economic reasons. Outbreeding has the opposite genetic effect of inbreeding: Variation increases, and harmful recessives remain unexpressed and possibly accumulate, although the population may show improved health and lower mortality.

The mating system is therefore an important characteristic of a species and is linked not only to the species' social life as a whole but, as we will see, to many of its most striking anatomical adaptations.

Non-Darwinian Evolutionary Mechanisms

Although of primary importance, natural selection is not the only force in nature that shapes the genes and traits of populations and species. At least five other processes can be identified and assigned to a category called *non-Darwinian evolutionary mechanisms:* mutation, chromosomal recombination during meiosis (crossing-over), gene flow, the **founder effect,** and **genetic drift.** (The label *non-Darwinian* simply means that Charles Darwin was unaware of the biological processes in question. Their discoveries, mainly in the twentieth century, followed the development of the science of genetics.) The first three phenomena—mutation, crossing-over, and gene flow—have been described already and require little discussion here. All three of these processes usually produce random genetic and phenotypic variability within populations—variability that can then be shaped by natural selection. The last two phenomena—founder effects and genetic drift—also affect variability and thus feed natural selection, but they also may sometimes produce evolutionary change on their own.

Founder effect the genetic difference between a newly founded, separated *population* and its parent group. The founding population is usually different because its *gene pool* is only a segment of the parent group's.

Genetic drift the genetic changes in *populations* caused by random phenomena rather than by *natural selection*.

The founder effect and genetic drift are both special factors operating in very small populations. These small communities either may be the remnants of larger populations that have gone through size-reducing *bottlenecks* (for example, decimation by disease), or they may be *founder populations* started by a few individuals splintering off to establish a new breeding colony. Small, descendant populations often are not typical samples of the parent species. That is, just by chance alone, these populations may, from the very start, carry different gene frequencies and phenotypic norms than the parent species. In particular, the gene pool of such a small population may not contain the full assortment of rare alleles found among the parents, or on occasion, it may contain exceptionally high frequencies of previously rare alleles. The term *founder effect* can be used to describe the altered genetic and phenotypic qualities of small, descendant populations, evolutionary differences that may then be enhanced by natural selection (Ridley, 1996).

Small populations also become good candidates for yet another evolutionary mechanism: *genetic drift.* This mechanism involves chance intergenerational changes in the frequencies of alternate alleles (those at the same locus) with similar selection values. In such a population, rare alleles may be quickly lost or, alternatively, fixed (become widespread) in the gene pool because of several chance factors. For example, rare alleles may be lost when their few carriers die accidentally. (No natural selection is involved here, just pure chance.) Or perhaps the carriers survive but because of chance alone, fail to reproduce. Or finally, perhaps heterozygous individuals with rare alleles are lucky enough to survive and reproduce, but then just by chance, the alleles are absent from the particular sperm or egg cells involved in reproduction. In a similar way, these examples could be reworded to explain how rare alleles may become fixed by chance alone. Studies suggest that weak environmental selection pressures are critical in the operation of genetic drift. Thus, alleles with neutral or weak selection values should be good candidates for the effects of drift (Ridley, 1996).

Evidence for genetic drift has been obtained from experiments with small populations of the fruit fly *Drosophila,* but more interesting examples from natural populations can be found in the literature on human blood groups. (The nature and frequency of A, B, O, and other genetically determined blood groups are discussed in Chapter 17, but we will refer to them here briefly in this connection.)

Clear evidence of drift-generated variation in blood-group alleles has been reported for villages of varying sizes in the Parma River Valley in Italy. Blood samples were taken from the residents of large lowland villages, medium hill villages, and small mountain villages. When the amount of genetic variation in the ABO and Rh blood groups was plotted against village size, an inverse relationship was found. Thus, as predicted, when population (village) size went down, genetic variation due to genetic drift (chance) went up (Cavalli-Sforza and Cavalli-Sforza, 1995; Molnar, 2002). In a non-blood-group example, genetic drift is probably responsible for the relatively high rate of a particular eye defect on the Micronesian island of Pingelap. About 10 percent of the island's population shows the defect, which is almost nonexistent elsewhere in the world. Almost certainly, a mutation that occurred some time ago has become commonplace due to genetic drift (Cavalli-Sforza and Cavalli-Sforza, 1995). These data on the effects of drift are of particular interest because we believe that during much of human evolution, the species consisted of small bands of between 200 and 500 individuals.

In summary, it seems clear that founder effects and genetic drift—along with the other non-Darwinian mechanisms and, of course, natural selection—have made important contributions to the evolution of populations and species, including the human species. Mutation, crossing-over, and gene flow all produce increased variability within populations. (So does simple population growth, since an abundance of individuals means an abundance of new mutations.) Natural selection and founder effects have acted to decrease variation. Genetic drift, being a random process, can either enhance variability (when rare alleles become established or fixed in a gene pool) or reduce it (when rare alleles are lost).

The interplay of all these processes determines the evolutionary potential of an evolving lineage. Interestingly, however, even these various powerful forces acting in combination are usually unable to bring populations into perfect genetic and phenotypic harmony with their environments (that is, produce perfectly adapted populations). This is due to several factors, but high on the list is the extreme difficulty of eliminating detrimental recessive alleles completely, particularly if they are protected by the condition known as *balanced polymorphism.*

Polymorphism and Genetic Load

All populations of plants and animals (and hundreds of millions of people) carry some lethal or deleterious genes. These are termed the **genetic load.** Although these genes may be dominant, they are typically **co-dominant,** or recessive, and thus express their full effect only in homozygotes, when they may bring about a physical malformation or a fatal genetic disease.

An example of such a phenomenon is **sickle-cell anemia** (Molnar, 2002). Persons who are homozygous for the abnormal sickle-cell allele (Hb^S) are characterized by anemia due to red blood cells that become crescent-shaped when oxygen levels are low (Figure 2.13). Homozygotes for the normal allele (Hb^A) have round red blood cells, while heterozygotes produce both round and sickle cells, but more of the former. Sickle-cell disease is a life-threatening condition that is common in certain regions of West and Central Africa (Figure 2.14). In many Central African populations, from 20 to 40 percent of individuals are Hb^A Hb^S heterozygotes; 1 to 2 percent are Hb^S Hb^S homozygotes, who usually die soon after birth.

Because natural selection would ordinarily select out such an undesirable trait, we have to ask why such a high frequency of the Hb^S gene is maintained. In 1954, A. C. Allison, a British doctor, showed that the sickle-cell trait in its heterozygote condition affords protection against malarial infection and that the distribution of the Hb^S gene coincides with the distribution of the *Anopheles* mosquito, which carries malaria. The Hb^S gene was maintained by natural selection according to the balanced advantages and disadvantages that it offered: protection from disease for the Hb^A Hb^S carrier and death for the Hb^S Hb^S. This is an example of **balanced polymorphism.** *Polymorphism* usually refers to the expression of two or more alleles of a single gene in a population in more or less constant proportions. The human blood groups constitute further well-known examples.

Today in the United States, we live in an environment free of malaria, yet approximately 10 percent of Americans of African origin still carry the Hb^S gene (Molnar, 2002). Thus, it has become a complete liability and, in the rare homozygous state, is still a serious and often lethal condition. Clearly, a life-saving adaptation in one environment is part of humankind's genetic load in another.

We can see, then, that the survival values of genes are determined by the environment in which they are expressed. We can see, too, how natural selection acting on genetic variability can compromise between advantages and disadvantages, so that ordinarily lethal phenotypes are maintained in a population in balance with advantageous phenotypes. Of course, many rare recessive lethal genes are simply carried along in the gene pool because they are almost never expressed in a homozygote. Between balanced polymorphisms and rare recessives, it appears that most species will always bear the burden of a genetic load. But optimistically, our genetic load may represent a potential for variability that may in the future be necessary for survival, as it may have been in the past. Natural selection operates on phenotypes, that is, only on the expression of a proportion of the genotype. Hidden genetic variability is, to some extent, our insurance against environmental change.

A population's genetic load is obviously affected by the mutation rates of alleles that reduce fitness at some point in the life span (Strickberger, 2000). Additionally, individuals' chances of survival and reproduction can be sharply reduced by

Genetic load the *recessive genes* in a *population* that are harmful when expressed in the rare *homozygous* condition.

Co-dominant ther term for *alleles* that in *heterozygous* combination produce a *phenotype* distinct from either type of *homozygote*.

Sickle-cell anemia a genetically caused disease that can be fatal, in which the *red blood corpuscles* carry insufficient oxygen.

Balanced polymorphism the maintenance in a *population* of different *alleles* of a particular *gene* in proportion to the advantages offered by each (e.g., *sickle-cell* and normal *hemoglobin*).

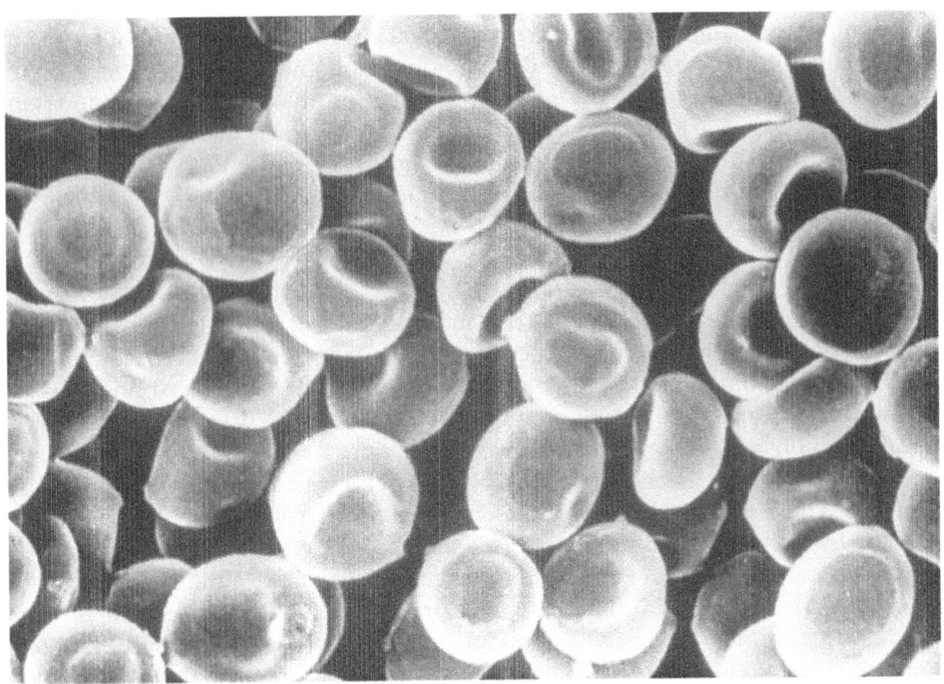

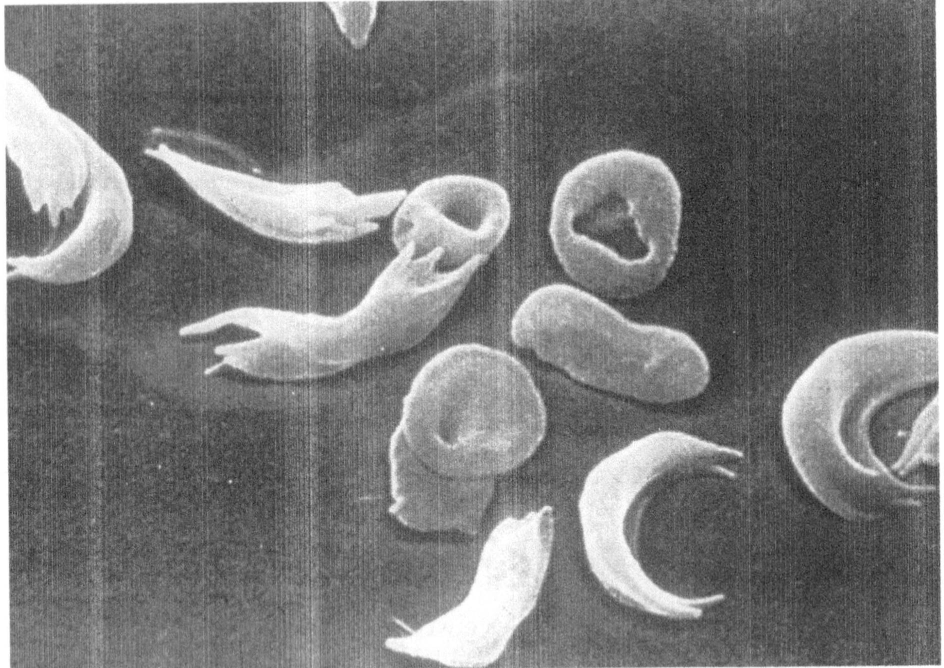

FIGURE 2.13
The sickle-cell trait is due to abnormal hemoglobin, which differs from normal hemoglobin in only 1 amino acid out of nearly 300 that constitute the protein. The red blood corpuscles in the top photograph appear normal; the bottom photograph shows the distortion that gives sickle-cell anemia its name.

several inherited chromosomal abnormalities. For example, in humans, *Down's syndrome* can affect both males and females who are born with an extra chromosome 21 (diploid count 46 + 1) and show some degree of mental retardation. *Turner's syndrome* involves girls born with only a single X chromosome (XO, 46 – 1) and results

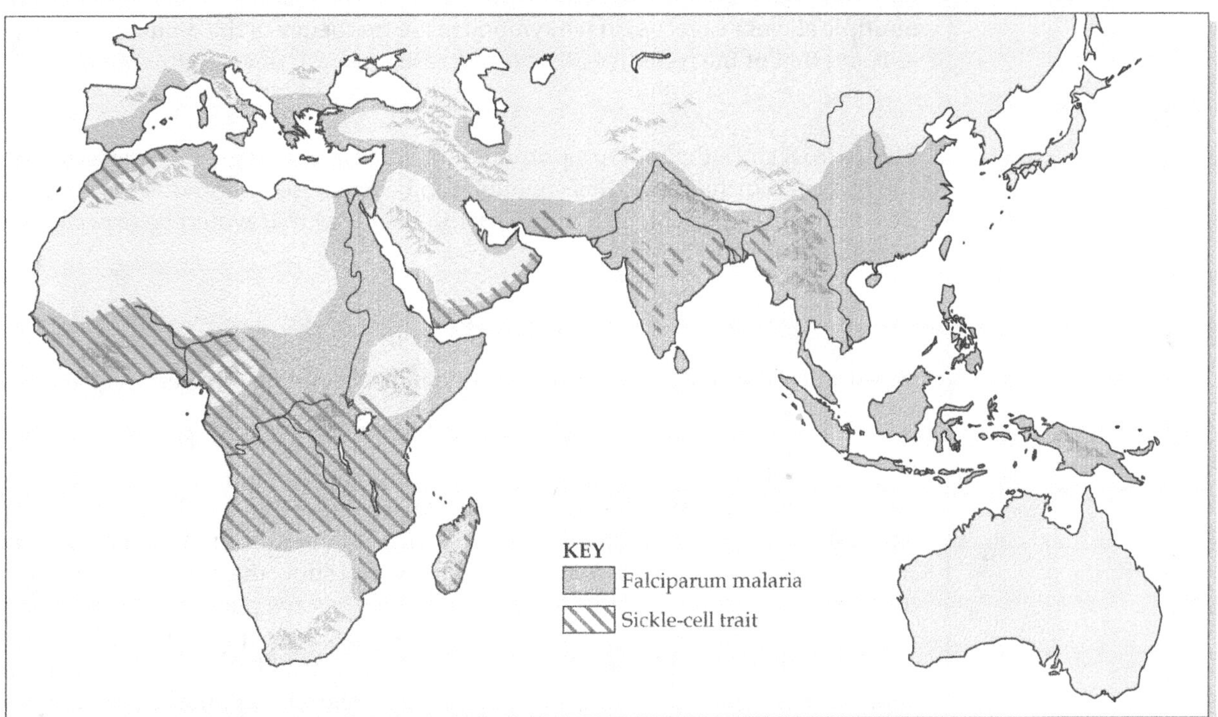

FIGURE 2.14
The coincidental occurence of the sickle-cell trait and malaria in parts of the Old World led us to understand why the abnormal hemoglobin Hb^S appears in these areas. Although disadvantageous elsewhere, in malarial areas, the sickling gene gives considerable protection against the dangerous malarial parasite. The two hemoglobin forms are in balance according to the advantages and disadvantages they offer. Therefore, this instance of the phenomenon of polymorphism is termed *balanced polymorphism*. Other genes give similar protection in other parts of the world where malaria occurs.

in short stature and poorly developed secondary sexual characteristics. And in *Klinefelter's syndrome* phenotypic males are born with an extra X chromosome (XXY, 46 + 1), a condition that renders them sterile (Delhanty, 1992; Molnar, 2002).

The Hardy-Weinberg Theorem

The preceding sections have established that evolution is a population-level phenomenon. Within their environments, living creatures strive to survive and reproduce, and their success or failure in getting their genes into succeeding generations determines the evolutionary trajectories of their populations. Populations can experience rapid evolutionary change, but in fact, most of the time they are probably in stasis, with little or no change occurring as long as the environment remains constant. It would obviously be very useful to be able to determine whether a population is evolving or in equilibrium (stable) for specific phenotypic traits. Geneticists have developed a procedure for this purpose, the *Hardy-Weinberg test*, which is a critical concept in population genetics (Molnar, 2002; Ridley, 1996).

In 1908, English mathematician G. H. Hardy and German physician W. Weinberg independently developed a formula for describing the proportions of a pair of alleles within a stable population. This formula allows researchers to calculate the expected frequencies of genotypes and phenotypes once they have obtained information about allele frequencies. Here's how it works. Imagine the simplest possible condition: a trait that is controlled by a single pair of alleles (*A*, *a*; note, however, that the Hardy-Weinberg formula can be expanded to handle cases with multiple alleles at a locus). If we symbolize the frequency of the dominant allele (A) as p and that of the recessive allele (a) as q, then we can develop this equation:

$$(1)\ p + q = 1$$

This is true, since the total proportion of the alleles at any given locus is equal to 100 percent. Furthermore, this equation can be expanded to produce the frequencies of the three possible genotypes (AA, Aa, and aa) that would be expected in a population at equilibrium:

$$(2)\ (p + q)^2 = 1$$
$$(3)\ p^2 + 2pq + q^2 = 1$$

Substituting the genotypes for their mathematical symbols, we get:

$$(4)\ AA + 2Aa + aa = 1$$

In other words, the frequencies of both homozygotes (AA and aa), plus the total frequency of the heterozygotes ($2Aa$), equal 100 percent of the population for the trait in question. Of course, with regard to their phenotypes, in this example both the AA homozygotes and the heterozygotes (Aa) would show the dominant form of the trait. Only the aa homozygotes would show the recessive phenotypic condition.

The genius of Hardy and Weinberg was to realize that under a certain set of conditions, the allele frequencies p and q will reach equilibrium in one generation and, assuming the conditions are maintained, remain in equilibrium indefinitely. The necessary conditions include large population size, random mating, no mutations, no selection, and no gene flow. Although these conditions may seem impossibly stringent at first glance, in fact, the Hardy-Weinberg theorem is rather robust and fits a number of natural populations rather well, despite their failure to meet one or more of the criteria.

For simple single recessive allele traits, the frequency of q can be easily determined from the occurrence of individuals showing the rare phenotype. And once q is known, p (and thus all genotypic frequencies) can be readily calculated. For example, a rare disorder caused by a single recessive allele in modern human populations is *Tay-Sachs disease.* Most common in Jews of Eastern European descent, people with Tay-Sachs experience nervous system degeneration, convulsions, and death at a young age. Although the frequency of Tay-Sachs disease varies strongly between populations, its incidence among Ashkenazic Jewish people in Eastern Europe and the United States is about 1 per 2,500 births, which makes q^2 equal to 0.0004 (Molnar, 2002). The value of q is therefore 0.02 in these groups, making the frequency of the recessive Tay-Sachs allele 2.0 percent in their widespread gene pool. From these figures, p can be calculated as 0.98 and p^2 (homozygous dominants) as 96.04 percent. Finally, the frequency of unafflicted carriers of the Tay-Sachs allele (the heterozygotes, $2pq$) can be calculated as 0.0392, or about 1 person in 25 among Ashkenazi Jews. (Comparable figures for non-Ashkenazi people in the same areas are 1 Tay-Sachs case per 500,000 births; $q^2 = 0.000002$; $q = 0.0014$; $p = 0.9986$, making p^2 [homozygous dominants] 99.72 percent of genotypes; $2pq$ [heterozygous individuals] = 0.0028 for a carrier rate of about 1 person in 358 [Molnar, 2002].)

The Tay-Sachs example illustrates one of the most important practical applications of the Hardy-Weinberg theorem: determining the equilibrium incidence of unexpressed recessive alleles that can produce serious human health problems. This is critically important because it indicates the level of need for programs that can prevent and cure these diseases. But what if the population is *not* in equilibrium for the trait in question? Then a second use of the theorem can be made by comparing the *expected* (that is, equilibrium) genotype frequencies (p^2, $2pq$, q^2) with *observed* frequencies that are determined by actually sampling the population. If the two sets of frequencies are significantly different, the population is not in equilibrium but rather evolving, probably due to natural selection or nonrandom mating. Such a finding could merit further research.

Measures of Fitness

We began this chapter with a table that identified three different types of linkage between individual organisms and their populations (Table 2.1). Two of those linkages—genotypes and gene pools, phenotypes and collective phenotypes—already have been discussed, and now is an appropriate time to describe the third: the relationship between individuals' **fitness** and their population's degree of *adaptation.*

Fitness an individual's relative degree of success in surviving and reproducing and thus in gaining genetic representation in succeeding generations.

Traditionally, fitness has been measured in terms of individual reproductive success, that is, how many offspring an organism produces and successfully rears. Since each offspring carries 50 percent of each parent's genes (in most organisms) and many parental traits, individual reproduction is a primary path to evolutionary fitness. (Obviously, survival to adulthood is necessary for individual reproductive success, but surviving without reproducing does not equal fitness as measured here. Equally obviously, simply possessing traits that are likely to lead to survival, such as strength, stamina, and general good health—the popular meaning of being fit—doesn't qualify as evolutionary fitness.)

Recently, the definition of evolutionary fitness has been extended in important ways. Thanks to the work of W. D. Hamilton (1964) and many others, we now realize that individual reproductive success is only one component of an organism's **inclusive fitness.** A second important component is the reproductive success of one's genetic kin. After all, in diploid organisms, parents and offspring and full siblings have 50 percent of their genes in common, half-sibs 25 percent, first cousins 12.5 percent, and so on. Assisting a relative to survive and reproduce is therefore a perfectly good way to get copies of one's own genes into future generations.

Inclusive fitness the sum total of an organism's individual reproductive success (number of offspring) plus portions of the reproductive success of genetic kin.

This realization also appears to explain several previously puzzling aspects of animals' (and perhaps humans') behavior. Animals often appear to behave altruistically, doing things that benefit others while inflicting a cost on the actor. (There are many examples, such as alarm calling, intervening in fights, and sharing food.) But if the recipients of such **bioaltruism** are the actor's kin, then acts that appear to be altruistic may in fact reap a genetic reward for the actor by helping relatives survive and reproduce. This insight is the basis for yet another evolutionary mechanism known as **kin selection.** Kin selection may well be the process by which behaviors that are apparently altruistic but in reality are likely to serve genetic self-interest may have evolved (Trivers, 1985; Wilson, 1975).

Bioaltruism behavior that appears to be altruistic but in fact is believed to benefit the animal indirectly by increasing its *inclusive fitness.*

Kin selection the selection of characteristics (and their *genes*) that increase the probability of the survival and reproduction of close relatives.

In any event, as individuals possessing advantageous traits (those that contribute to survival and successful reproduction within the prevailing environment) demonstrate their fitness by passing many copies of their genes into the next generation (in the form of offspring, grand-offspring, nieces, nephews, etc.), they drive up the frequencies of good-trait alleles relative to alleles that code for less advantageous traits. Thus, in the next generation, the population's collective phenotype will be shifted (slightly or strongly, depending on selection pressures) toward good traits. In other words, the population, viewed as a whole, will be *better adapted* to its environment than before. In this way, the actions of individuals as they face each day's challenges—feeding, survival, reproduction, parenting, aiding kin—contribute to the evolution of their population and species.

Macroevolution: Speciation

Speciation the production of new *species,* either through the gradual transformation or the splitting or branching of existing species.

Extinction the loss of a *species* due to the deaths of all its members.

Only three topics remain to be discussed in this chapter, but they are essential for an understanding of evolution. We need to look first at **speciation,** the processes by which new species come into existence; second at **extinction,** the processes by which species are lost; and finally at the notion of *progress* in evolution.

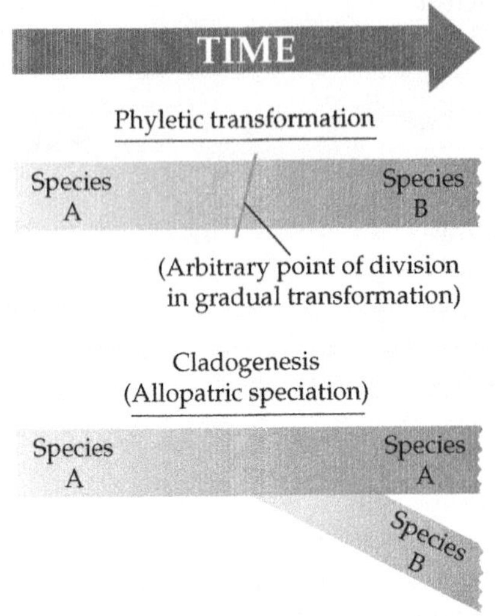

FIGURE 2.15 Phyletic transformation involves the gradual conversion (mainly through natural selection) of an entire species into a new species. While it occurs in nature, some scientists feel it is not a true form of speciation because it does not lead to an increase in species diversity. In contrast, allopatric speciation (a primary form of cladogenesis) involves branching of an existing species (usually due to the isolation of one or more populations) with the result that the total number of species is increased.

There appear to be two primary ways that new species are formed: **phyletic transformation** (also called *phyletic evolution, phyletic gradualism,* or *anagenesis*) and **cladogenesis** (Mayr, 1982, 1996). In its purest form, phyletic transformation involves the evolutionary conversion of an entire species into a species of phenotypically different descendants (Figure 2.15, top). Here, transformation within an evolving lineage results from the slow accumulation of adaptive changes wrought by natural selection. After sufficient trait change has built up, a new species name is deemed necessary by scientists studying the lineage, and so they coin one. In Figure 2.15, species A gradually converts into species B. Phyletic evolution thus involves losing one old species for each new one that is added. There is no increase in species diversity here, a fact that has led some researchers to balk at calling this process true speciation.

A further problem with phyletic transformation—at least for taxonomists trying to assign specimen names unambiguously—is that it complicates the identification of species in a lineage since their phenotypic boundaries are largely arbitrary (Figure 2.15). Sometimes, for ease of communication, researchers resolve the confusion by identifying **chronospecies,** lineage subdivisions that are as strongly time defined as they are trait defined. Criticisms aside, however, it is clear that phyletic transformations occur in nature and, furthermore, that anagenesis plays an important supporting role in cladogenetic speciation, increasing the divergence of populations that are splintering from their parent species.

The second speciation mode—cladogenesis—increases the diversity of life forms through the splitting or branching of existing species. Almost certainly, its most important form is **allopatric speciation.** (The name means "different localities" and refers to speciation among populations with different ranges; see Figure 2.15, bottom, and also Figure 2.16.) Allopatric speciation is thought to begin, typically, with the formation of a physical barrier between a peripheral population and the rest of its species. Such *geographic isolation*—perhaps produced by the formation of a new mountain range, volcanoes, geologic faults, a river changing its course, or some other topographic alteration—results in the interruption of gene flow between the separated population and the parent species. The maintenance of genetic and phenotypic continuity between the population and the parent species ends, and thereafter, mutations occurring on either side of the barrier will make the two units progressively different. Of course, thanks to the founder effect, the chances are good that the population and the parent species are substantially different genetically when geographic isolation becomes effective. The population's much smaller gene pool probably lacks a good number of the rare alleles found in the species' gene pool, as well as having different frequencies of even the common ones, and all of this will result in phenotypic differences in short order. Furthermore, if the isolated population is small (as seems generally to be the case in nature), genetic drift may add to its accumulating allelic differences from the parent species. And finally, natural selection will occur among the population's phenotypes (and associated genotypes) as it adapts the isolated community to its new environment, an environment that may differ significantly from that of the parent species (Price, 1996).

The combination of all of these evolutionary forces—no gene flow, accumulating mutations, founder effect, genetic drift, and natural selection working within a different environment—leads to increasing differences between the isolated population and the parent species. When the two have become sufficiently different so that they cannot or will not interbreed should they meet again (due to the disappearance of the barrier or to migration), they qualify as good species under the biological species concept: distinct breeding communities that are *reproductively isolated* from one another (Mayr, 1996). How long this might take—for a geographically isolated population to become reproductively isolated from its parent

Phyletic transformation the conversion (mainly through *natural selection*) of an entire *species* into a new species.

Cladogenesis branching evolution involving the splitting of a *species* or lineage.

Chronospecies the sort of *species* that are created when an unbroken evolutionary continuum is arbitrarily divided into time-defined units.

Allopatric speciation the production of new *species* through the splitting or branching of existing ones. The process begins with the geographic isolation of one or more *populations* from the bulk of the parent species.

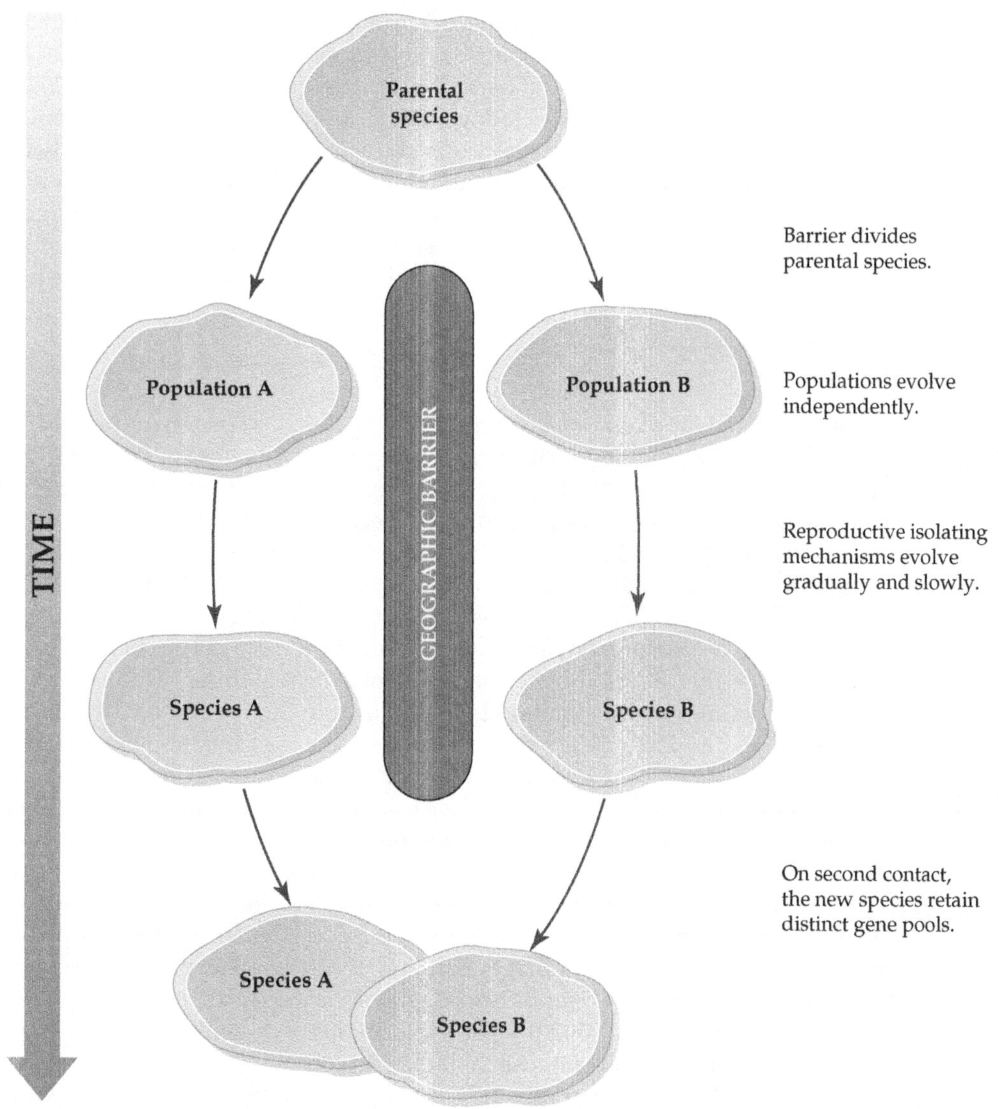

FIGURE 2.16
Geographic, or allopatric, speciation by division of populations resulting from a geographic barrier.

Source: Price, Peter. *Biological Evolution.* Fort Worth, Saunders College Publishing, 2001. p. 76.

species—undoubtedly differs from case to case. Some organisms mature and reproduce rapidly, while others are much slower. With all factors working at top speed, it seems likely that complete speciation might be achieved in several hundred to a few thousand generations.

There are other forms of cladogenesis, including **sympatric speciation** (the name means "same locality"), in which populations living in the same or overlapping ranges separate by adapting to different ecological niches, and **parapatric speciation** (which separates populations of sedentary organisms living in adjacent ranges). In some cases of cladogenetic separation of sympatric or parapatric populations, chromosomal rearrangements play a significant role. That is, differences in large structural rearrangements of chromosomes may reduce total gene flow between

Sympatric speciation *speciation* among *populations* with the same or overlapping geographic ranges.

Parapatric speciation *speciation* among *populations* of sedentary organisms with adjacent geographic ranges.

populations, *even though they are still interbreeding,* while simultaneously allowing new mutations and differences due to selection to accumulate within the rearranged segments. Such a process may have contributed to humans' separation from the line that led to chimpanzees (Navarro and Barton, 2003; Rieseberg and Livingstone, 2003).

Hybrid speciation *speciation* through hybridization between two good *species.*

And finally, there is even a noncladogenetic process call **hybrid speciation,** in which hybrids between two good species find themselves at an adaptive advantage in a particular ecological situation and therefore thrive. While all of these secondary speciation models are interesting and occur occasionally in nature, most scientists still think these processes have been much less important in the history of life than the allopatric production of new species. But enough about the birth of species. Let's turn our attention to how species die.

Macroevolution: Extinction

The term *extinction* is applied most commonly to the loss of a species due to the disappearance of all of its members. (It can also be applied to the loss of larger biological units such as genera or "families"—in zoology, collections of related genera.) We need to begin with a clarification, however, because there are at least two ways for a species to disappear. When a species becomes truly extinct, all of its members die—and their genes die with them. In contrast, when a species is phyletically transformed (Figure 2.15), its genes don't cease to exist but simply end up being housed in a different kind of creature. Phyletic transformation produces a type of pseudoextinction of species that should not be confused with the real thing. (Unfortunately, the two are sometimes devilishly hard to distinguish in the fossil record.)

In any event, disappearance, either by true extinction or the false extinction of phyletic transformation, is the inevitable fate of all species (humans included). While animal species typically last about 4 million years (among humans and our ancestors, the average is closer to 1 million years), it still remains true that the vast majority of all species that have ever lived are now extinct. But why do species become extinct? Is it, as D. M. Raup (1991) asked in a recent book, a matter of "bad genes or bad luck"?

Raup tends to side with bad luck, and there is a good deal of evidence supporting this point of view. It appears that, regardless of how well a species is adapted to its normal environment, sooner or later it will be exposed to such extraordinary biological or physical stresses that it will die. Examples of possible extinction-causing stressors include new and intense interspecific competition; extreme environmental changes due to fluctuations in sea level, global climate, and large-scale volcanism; and environmental and ecological disasters resulting from collisions of the earth with extraterrestrial objects (comets and asteroids). Raup favors the collision hypothesis as an explanation for many mass extinction events, particularly the event that killed off the dinosaurs 65 million years ago. (See Figure 5.5 for the dates of the five largest mass extinctions.)

The data on extinction—and especially the mass events—suggest that contrary to the teachings of Lyell and despite a day-to-day appearance of regularity and predictability, when one views the earth over geological time, it is clearly a dangerous and rather unpredictable place, periodically liable to large-scale, devastating environmental fluctuations. The extinctions that result from such fluctuations have played an important part in shaping the history of life on earth, and the existence of each living species is the result of a unique history of adaptation, speciation, and extinction. While natural selection has tended to improve species' adaptations to their normal environments and has combined with processes such as genetic drift to produce new species, extinction has operated to reduce species' diversity and to open up ecological niches. Happily for humans, vacating ecological niches tends to open the way for new evolutionary experimentation. Had the dinosaurs not become extinct, mammals might never have diversified and primates (including humans) might never have evolved.

Progress in Evolution

For most educated people, including the vast majority of scientists, the fact of evolution cannot be denied. Evolutionists often differ considerably, however, in their interpretations of pattern and meaning in the history of life. Among the commonly asked interpretative questions are these: Has evolution shown any broad trends? Has evolution been moving life toward some identifiable goal? Is evolution progressive, producing ever-better organisms over time?

Interestingly, Charles Darwin would probably have answered no to most, if not all, of these questions. In his books and personal correspondence, Darwin repeatedly expressed the view that natural selection works *locally*, producing a sequence of adaptive adjustments to changing local environments. Natural selection cannot see beyond the local level in order to produce broad trends, thought Darwin, and thus he resisted the notion of progress in life's history. For many people, however, progress and evolution have become synonymous, and they argue that there have been broad increases—progressive trends—in such variables as animals' size and overall organic complexity (including intelligence) throughout life's history.

Unfortunately for believers in evolutionary progress, a close examination of the evidence fails to provide strong support for their position. First, on the issue of size, recent tests of the so-called Cope's rule (named after its 1871 formulator, paleontologist Edward Drinker Cope), which states that body size tends to increase in an animal lineage during its evolution, have produced mixed results. While the inadequacy of Cope's rule has been demonstrated for marine organisms, fossil mammal species (particularly those whose members are already large) do show a tendency to increase about 9 percent in size over their immediate ancestors (Alroy, 1998). Second, with regard to organic complexity, recent studies suggest that the occasional evolution of creatures with increased complexity was predictable from random change alone, given the utter simplicity of the earliest living creatures, the bacteria. That there has been no overall trend toward increased organic complexity is shown by the fact that bacteria are still the predominant form of life on earth (Gould, 1996). And finally, concerning the evolution of intelligence, a widely accepted theory is that intelligence (and the correlated trait of brain enlargement) has evolved repeatedly among social animals as an adaptation for remembering and manipulating social relationships (see Chapters 9 and 13). Most mammals are social (that is, group-living) creatures, and this is particularly true for humans and our closest animal relatives, the primates (monkeys, apes, etc.). Therefore, humans' big brains—viewed against a background of big-brained mammalian and primate ancestors—become understandable as an extreme form of a common adaptation for life in a complex society (Dunbar, 1998). The fact that among modern people brain functioning includes self-consciousness may be simply a fluke, an accidental stroke of luck that was in no way preordained.

To most scientists, the persistence of the idea of progressive evolution seems to be mainly the result of humans' egocentric nearsightedness (see Box 2.3). Interestingly, however, there are some authoritative voices in the opposite corner. Paleontologist Simon Conway Morris (2003) has recently argued that once life was in existence on earth (or elsewhere, for that matter), progressive evolution was inevitable, including the ultimate production of intelligent humanoids. He even argues that homininlike creatures would have evolved on earth without the catastrophic demise of the dinosaurs (albeit with perhaps a 30 million year delay). Morris's interpretation of the history of life on earth makes fascinating reading, but at present, it expresses a minority opinion. For most paleoanthropologists and other evolutionary researchers, the evidence indicates that humans are the result of a series of (for us, happy) contingent events. And in the final analysis, despite our many marvelous qualities, we are the result of chance.

BOX 2.3

Some Thoughts on Evolution and Progress

For many modern people, reflection on the long journey that our ancestors have made from single-celled organisms to big-brained, self-aware creatures inevitably leads to the conclusion that evolution is progressive. As we argue in the text, however, this conclusion is more illusory than real, and here's why.

Both evolutionary theory and an obsession with progress are relatively recent developments, dating mainly from the nineteenth century. In medieval times, life seemed to continue more or less the same from generation to generation. There was no reason to expect scientific breakthroughs or significant philosophical developments. Alchemists still had not managed to make gold from lesser metals, try as they did. The created world was constant and stable. The concept of evolution brought the idea of progress into social consciousness, and to humans, who stood at the top of the chain of being, it seemed to confirm their natural superiority.

The reality is not quite so simple, however. Evolution is a process, operating in time, driven primarily by natural selection, which has produced a whole range of organisms from viruses to humans. The fact that some recently evolved creatures are large and complex is counterbalanced by the survival and diversification of older and simpler forms of life. The plant kingdom has achieved a dominant position on earth without the added sophistication of a nervous system or musculature. Our greatest competitors on earth today are minute and relatively simple viruses, bacteria, and protozoa. As disease organisms, they still play a major part in shaping human history.

It follows that evolution cannot be described as progressive; the process is characterized by change, the sole results of which are survival and reproduction. The success of a species could be measured in terms of its numbers, the gross weight of its biomass, its stability and longevity in time, its variety of adaptations, or its geographical range. We humans have a rapidly increasing population and biomass, yet these can hardly be called signs of progress, since this very increase puts the whole species in danger. Compared with the dinosaurs that ruled the world for more than 100 million years, we are merely upstarts and have no cause for self-congratulation on the basis of stability or longevity. We are a variable and widespread species, but that seems only to make the population explosion more dangerous, for there is now little wilderness remaining for the survival of many of those other species with which we share the planet and upon which we depend. No, none of these characteristics constitutes evolutionary success for humanity. The dinosaurs appear to have done better, although extinction was their ultimate fate.

So, in what way are we special? In what way could we be called the most successful and progressive species in the history of the planet? If we look at *Homo sapiens*, we see, for example, that the species is very complex (especially the nervous system) and is fully self-conscious (which is probably unique in the animal world). It has also intentionally altered its environment in a drastic manner. But we cannot be sure that it is necessarily progressive to be complex, or self-conscious, or to alter the environment; any of these characteristics could prove disastrous to its possessor and so to humankind. But human history does exemplify one evolutionary trend that appears to be truly progressive: *an increase in the range and variety of adjustments that the organism is capable of making in response to its environment*. This is the secret of our adaptation.

In order to respond to the environment, animals require a range of sense organs, a powerful brain to process the sensory inputs, and efficient and effective mechanical systems to bring about a whole range of responsive behavior. In *Homo sapiens*, we find a greater range of sensory input (we know more about our environment), more analytic processing of that input (a far more complex brain), and a greater range of motor outputs (i.e., of behavior and communication) than in any other species.

This much lies in our biology, but our culture has taken this trend much, much further. Microscopes, telescopes, a variety of sensors, and amplifiers of many kinds have vastly increased the range of environmental inputs. Books and computers aid memory, analysis, and prediction. Transportation and tools of every description help us amplify our behavior and satisfy our needs with increasing success. It is in this sense that we are more complex and in this sense that we are more adaptable than other species. If we are more adaptable, we are more likely to survive and maybe more likely to achieve long-term success.

The story of human evolution is a tale of increasing interaction with and control over our environment. Perhaps unfortunately, our adaptation has become so potent that we now run the risk of destroying the environment and ourselves with it. We must learn to control our unprecedented abilities for short-term manipulation and exploitation of the earth's resources. Clearly, we still have some way to travel on the evolutionary journey before we can call ourselves, without qualification, a successful and progressive species.

Summary

During the present century, the science of genetics has yielded numerous secrets that allow us to understand the workings of evolution. Phenotypic traits are encoded in genes—hereditary units, consisting of DNA, that occur on chromosomes within the nucleus of the cell. Offspring tend to look like their parents because of inherited genes, but because of genetic mixing during gamete production, offspring never look exactly like their parents or each other (with the single exception of identical siblings). This heritable variation in every generation allows natural selection to improve the degree of adaptation of populations.

Working along with other factors, such as geographic isolation, mutation, founder effect, and genetic drift, natural selection can lead to speciation. Species exist for varying amounts of time—some for many millions of years—but ultimately all species disappear. Some (several?) mass extinction events have probably been caused by comets or asteroids hitting the earth. Every species has a unique history of speciation, adaptation, and, in the end, extinction.

Finally, a variety of recent studies have confirmed that evolution is indeed a contingent process with few, if any, general trends encompassing large numbers of species. Despite the persistent human hope that we are the pinnacle of evolution and that evolution's flow has moved inexorably toward our morphology and self-conscious intelligence, all available evidence suggests that humans—like all other species—are the result mainly of chance and the action of natural selection.

Postscript

Every passing year brings an increase in humans' control over their own evolutionary future. Technological advances now enable many of the world's people to effectively short-circuit natural selection by using new means of controlling their environment, health, survival, and reproductive success. Is a geographic region too hot or cold or dry or humid for comfortable human living? No problem. We simply build artificial environments featuring cooling, heating, humidifying, or dehumidifying systems that allow easy living in any climate regardless of one's phenotype. Poor vision is corrected with eyeglasses, poor hearing with hearing aids, and lost teeth with dentures. Light-skinned people live and work safely in areas of high solar radiation thanks to clothing and sunscreen creams.

Today, medical advances allow the birth, survival, and reproduction of people with physical and mental impairments that would have been fatal in the past. At the same time, we are gaining genetic knowledge that, in combination with amniocentesis, may enable us at some future point to scan and even *tailor* genotypes prenatally, thus preventing unwanted traits—including impairments—from being expressed phenotypically. Indeed, for better or worse, we may soon be able to **clone** humans entirely! We are thus rapidly gaining control over both of the factors—genes and environment—that determine the fitness of individuals and the evolution of populations.

Clone a genetically identical organism asexually reproduced from an ancestral organism.

But increased control brings its own uncertainties. Consider the following questions:

- What are the implications of assisting increasing numbers of genetically and/or physically impaired people to be born and to reproduce? Will the genetic load of the species increase? Would the denial of medical assistance to *any* impaired individual (fetal or postnatal) be consistent with humane behavior?
- Should we attempt to eliminate undesirable human traits and develop desirable ones? If the answer is yes, who should decide which traits are which and

how should the decisions be made? Should genetic tailoring be allowed for strictly cosmetic reasons (e.g., to alter skin color or projected height)? How should species engineering be accomplished? (Humans have a very checkered history of such eugenics projects.) Might long-term disadvantages result from reducing genetic and phenotypic variability within our species?

Although the traditional set of evolutionary mechanisms (natural selection, mutation, gene flow, and genetic drift) continues to have some effect on modern humans (more on some populations than on others), it is clear that we are becoming something of a special case with regard to further evolution. Ever-increasing control over our evolutionary trajectory promises to bring a plethora of challenging questions for scientists, physicians, theologians, **bioethicists,** and laypersons alike.

Bioethicist a person who specializes in exploring the ethical dimensions of biological decisions.

Review Questions

1. What are genes, how do they determine phenotypic traits, and what happens when they mutate?
2. Describe the contributions made by point mutations and meiosis (crossing-over) to phenotypic variability in populations.
3. Describe the *biological species* concept. How must this concept be adjusted to account for the occasional case of "gene leakage" between species?
4. Explain how natural selection operates to shape the gene pools and collective phenotypes of populations. How does the fitness of individuals contribute to the degree of adaptation of the population?
5. How does allopatric speciation work? Why isn't phyletic transformation considered to be true speciation? Are there any other ways that new species can come into existence? If so, what are they?
6. Discuss the possibility of the extinction of our species. What circumstances could result in the extinction of humans?
7. Discuss the implications of humans being the result of chance, rather than the inevitable result of progressive evolution. Does this alter the way you look at yourself and your species?

SUGGESTED FURTHER READING

Gould, Stephen Jay. *Full House.* New York, Harmony Books, 1996.

Levine, Joseph, and David Suzuki. *The Secret of Life.* Boston, WGBH Educational Foundation, 1993.

Molnar, Stephen. *Human Variation,* 5th ed. Upper Saddle River (NJ), Prentice Hall, 2002.

Orel, Vítězslav. *Gregor Mendel: The First Geneticist.* Oxford, Oxford University Press, 1996.

Raup, David. *Extinction: Bad Genes or Bad Luck?* New York, W. W. Norton, 1991.

Weiner, Jonathan. *The Beak of the Finch.* New York, Vintage Books, 1994.

INTERNET RESOURCES

NATURAL SELECTION

http://en.wikipedia.org/wiki/Natural_selection

Produced by the Wikipedia encyclopedia, this site describes the process of natural selection, as well as providing links to several other evolutionary mechanisms.

The Origin of Species, Charles Darwin, Chapter 4 Natural Selection

www.literature.org/authors/darwin-charles/the-origin-of-species/chapter-04.html

Reprinted in its entirety is Darwin's chapter describing his primary evolutionary mechanism.

THE TALK.ORIGINS ARCHIVE

www.talkorigins.org

Good starting point for material on genetics, evolutionary processes, speciation models, and extinction. Search the archive for numerous topics related to evolution—particularly human evolution—and creationism.

SPECIATION

http://users.rcn.com/jkimball.ma.ultranet/BiologyPages/S/Speciation.html

This site describes the various speciation processes, illustrating allopatric speciation with Darwin's finches in the Galápagos.

EXTINCTION

www.peripatus.gen.nz/paleontology/extinction.html

Produced by Peripatus, this web site describes the processes that lead to extinction and identifies the several mass extinction events.

DNA FROM THE BEGINNING

www.dnaftb.org/dnaftb

Produced by the Cold Spring Harbor Laboratory, this site presents "an animated primer on the basics of DNA, genes, and heredity."

USEFUL SEARCH TERMS:

biological species concept
DNA
extinction
Human Genome Project
natural selection
sexual selection
speciation

Chapter 3

Humans among the Primates

A baby orangutan (*Pongo pygmaeus*) and friend.

What a piece of work is a man! How noble in reason! How infinite in faculties! In form and in moving, how express and admirable! In action how like an angel! In apprehension how like a god! The beauty of the world! The paragon of animals!

William Shakespeare, 1564–1616, Hamlet, II, ii.

Overview

The order Primates—that subgroup of mammals that includes lemurs, lorises, tarsiers, monkeys, apes, and humans—is quite ancient, and this chapter is devoted to its description. First appearing about 90 million years ago, the order is represented today by more than 200 widely diverse species. Originally shaped by life in the trees and an insectivorous diet, primates have evolved an array of distinctive adaptations, including freely moving limbs with grasping hands and feet, keen vision, and (at least among some primates) complex brains. Humans are in many ways typical primates, and our distinctive features can be best appreciated when considered against the primate background. Human specialities include habitual bipedal locomotion, extreme brain complexity, language and speech, and a cultural way of life. Thanks to cultural adaptations, humans have gained considerable control over their evolutionary future.

Names and Classifications

The first two chapters have shown how evolution works, but before we can start examining our past, we must first learn something about what we are like today. We cannot completely—or even partially—answer this question until we have answered simpler questions about our similarities to and differences from other animals. Humankind is biologically classified under the Latin name ***Homo sapiens***; *Homo* means "man," and *sapiens* "wise." The human has been called the thinking animal. The human has also been labeled a political animal, a tool-using animal, a social animal, a speaking animal, and the animal that is aware of itself. We are all these things and more.

Homo sapiens among living *primates*, the scientific name for modern humans; members of the *species* first appeared about 195,000 years ago.

The Latin name *Homo sapiens* was coined by the great Swedish biologist Carl von Linné as part of his classification of all plants and animals (Lewin, 1993). Although a practicing doctor for part of his life, Linnaeus (the Latinized form of his name, by which he is more commonly known) collected plants and animals in Europe and received specimens from collectors throughout the world. He began to develop a system for naming and classifying most of the then-known living organisms. He used a binomial (two-name) system to label each one, choosing Latin for the names because it was a convenient international language. He published his system of names in his famous book *Systema Naturae*, which ran to ten editions between 1735 and 1766 (Eiseley, 1958; Mayr, 1982).

It was already clear to biologists that some creatures were more similar to each other than to others; they seemed to be created on the same general plan. Linnaeus grouped the similar ones in classes and orders to form a hierarchic arrangement. (This is an example of **phenetic classification.**) In 1735, Linnaeus had put *Homo* in his first class of Quadrupeds in the order Anthropomorpha, with the apes (Simia) and the sloth. In the tenth edition (1758), he called humans *Homo sapiens* and placed them with monkeys and apes in the order called *Primates*. Although not based on a theory of evolution, this classification indicated anatomical similarities—similarities that disturbed Linnaeus, among others. In 1766, he wrote: "It is remarkable that the stupidest ape differs so little from the wisest man."

Phenetic classification a *taxonomy* based on physical similarities or differences between *species* or other *taxa*.

Taxonomy classification of plants or animals according to their relationships and the ordering of these groups into hierarchies. *Taxonomic* levels are ranks within these classifications, e.g., *species* or *genus*.

Phylogenetic classification a *taxonomy* that reflects evolutionary descent and is based on the pattern of primitive and *derived traits*; in traditional evolutionary classifications, traits may be given different weights.

Taxon a group of organisms at any level of a classification scheme (plural, taxa).

Cladistic classification on evolution-based *taxonomy* that gives equal weight to traits and requires *sister groups* to be similarly ranked.

Primitive trait a characteristic inherited from an early ancestor and widely shared among descendants.

Shared derived trait a characteristic inherited from a relatively recent ancestor and found among a few close *taxa*.

Unique derived trait a characteristic that is a unique evolutionary *adaptation* of a *species*.

Cladogram a branching tree diagram displaying evolutionary relationships among organisms.

Clade members of an evolutionary cluster (e.g., sister *species*) plus their common ancestor.

Much of Linnaeus's classification scheme is still used because his method has proved to be of immense value. An international system of nomenclature (the rules of naming) has become essential in the development of the biological sciences, and the Linnaean system has survived the development of evolutionary biology since Darwin. The theory of evolution changed the basis of the system, however, making it clear that the similarities seen by Linnaeus and others were in many cases a result of evolutionary or phylogenetic relationships. Groups based on anatomical likeness often proved to share a common ancestor. The form of the system of classification remained but its meaning altered. The hierarchy came to reflect relationship; the species became variable and adaptable. The species was no longer the expression of an ideal type created by God, which Linnaeus believed it to be, but the changing product of natural selection.

Today, we attempt in our classifications to reflect evolutionary relationships, and so the **taxonomies** we use are **phylogenetic classifications** (J. Klein and Takahata, 2002; Mayr, 1982). There are two sorts of phylogenetic naming systems, however, and they differ in the use of trait similarities and differences (character states) between species or higher **taxa.** Many modern evolutionary biologists—including an ever-increasing number of paleoanthropologists—favor arranging species in **cladistic classifications.** In such classifications, relationships between taxa are recognized strictly from the patterns of occurrence of **primitive traits, shared derived traits,** and **unique derived traits.**

Primitive traits are character states inherited from distant (early) ancestors. These traits are found in a broad array of the ancestors' descendants and thus provide little information about recent divisions among those same creatures. For example, in the **cladogram** shown in Figure 3.1, living Old World monkeys, apes, and humans all possess eight premolars in their adult dentition and also prehensile (grasping) hands. These primitive traits therefore identify the catarrhine **clade,** a grouping that is assumed to be **monophyletic** (descended from a single common ancestral species). The catarrhines can be split into two smaller clades: one with tails (the Cercopithecoidea) and one without tails (the Hominoidea). Note that the possession of the shared derived tail-less condition groups humans with living apes. Finally, recognizing humans' unique derived trait of nonprehensile feet allows further subdivision of the Hominoidea.

Cladistic classifications simply try to identify groups of species or higher taxa that possess traits that are similar by descent (so-called **homologous** traits). This methodology is generally quite successful in identifying evolutionary clusters, al-

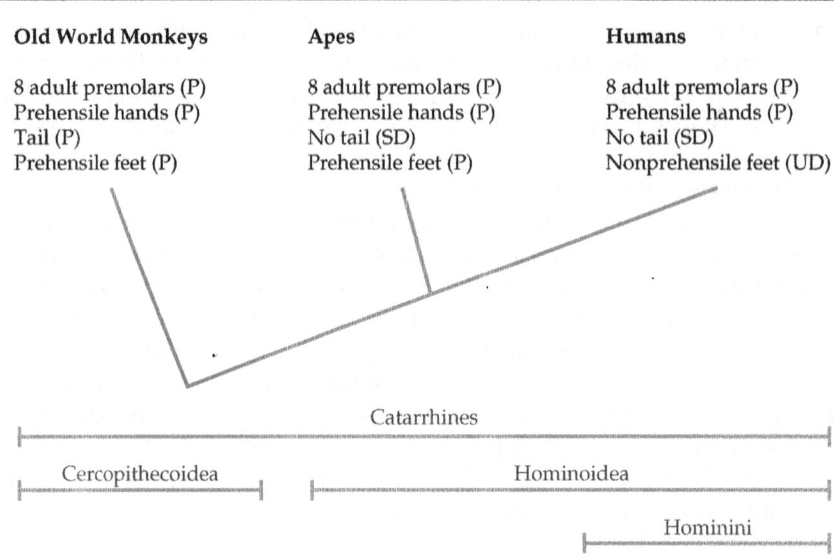

FIGURE 3.1 A cladogram comparing Old World monkeys, apes, and humans. Common names and traits are shown at the top. Traits are labeled as follows: P = primitive trait; SD = shared derived trait; UD = unique derived trait. Taxonomic labels are shown at the bottom.

though it can be confused by the occurrence of **homoplasies,** or trait similarities between unrelated species that are usually the result of independent adaptation to similar environments. Morphological traits still make up an important part of the data for cladistic analyses, but within the past few decades, molecular traits have also begun to be utilized (Klein and Takahata, 2002).

Cladistic classifications do have a few quirks worth noting. First, they do not include information about specific ancestor–descendant relationships. In Figure 3.1, for example, it is impossible to tell whether apes gave rise to humans through the evolution of nonprehensile feet or the reverse. (But the presence of grasping feet in the Cercopithecoidea, as well, suggests that that is the primitive condition, as shown in the figure.) Second, in cladistic analyses, **sister groups** are always given the same taxonomic rank; thus, the Old World monkeys and the ape–human group are both given superfamily status. And finally, cladistic analyses always treat individual traits equally. That is, particular traits—such as nonprehensile feet and increased brain size—are never viewed as providing information about different levels of organization or adaptation (i.e., evolutionary **grades;** Aiello and Dean, 1990; Conroy, 1997; Klein and Takahata, 2002).

The use of the evolutionary grade approach has characterized **traditional evolutionary classifications.** In these classifications, systematists routinely give different weights to traits and argue that sister groups most definitely *can* be assigned to different taxonomic levels. One problem with this approach is that it introduces an element of arbitrariness to classification, since systematists may differ on which traits they think deserve special emphasis. Should we view humans as having evolved to a higher evolutionary grade than apes because our brains are so much larger, or should differences in brain size be viewed as no more important than differences in arm and leg lengths? Furthermore, a second problem becomes obvious when both the living primates and their fossil forebears are classified together: Including extinct intermediate forms quickly shows the gaps between grades to be more apparent than real (i.e., only the absence of ancestral intermediates makes the gaps seem so meaningful). In order to avoid these problems and to make this book match as closely as possible the procedures of current researchers, we have chosen to depart from previous editions and use a cladistic classification of primates.

Whichever classification scheme is utilized, the close relationships of humans and the great apes with each other and with the lesser apes (the gibbons) have never been in question. The point was clearly made by T. H. Huxley in 1863 (Figure 1.11). Today, they are all placed in the superfamily Hominoidea. As noted, Linnaeus classified this group (or taxon) with the monkeys and some other animals under the name *Primates.* Linnaeus then grouped the primates with other furry, warm-blooded creatures that suckled their young in the class *Mammalia.* We mammals have backbones and share an even more general structure with such animals as fish and birds, with whom we constitute the subphylum Vertebrata. Humans' position in the grand hierarchy of the animal kingdom is summarized in Table 3.1.

Monophyletic a *clade* with a single common ancestor.

Homologous generally, traits that are shared by two or more *taxa* due to descent from a common ancestor.

Homoplasies trait resemblances between *taxa* due not to common ancestry but to other factors, such as independent adaptation to similar environments.

Sister groups in *cladistics*, the groups resulting from a dichotomous evolutionary branching event; initially ranked as sister *species*, these groups may change rank due to subsequent branching but must always maintain the same *taxonomic* level.

Grades arbitrarily defined levels of evolutionary development.

Traditional evolutionary classification a classification scheme that recognizes *grade*-level differences between sister groups.

The Primates

The list of animals included in the order Primates has been modified substantially since Linnaeus's time. He included the bats and *colugos* ("flying lemurs") as primates, but in 1873, these animals were removed by the English scientist St. George Mivart, who also provided a more detailed definition of the order. Mivart defined *primates* as placental mammals that possess the following traits: claws or nails; collarbones; eye sockets encircled by bone; **heterodont** dentition (specifically, having incisors, canines and molars); posterior lobe of the brain that includes a distinctive groove (the calcarine fissure); thumbs or big toes (or both) that are opposable; flat nail on big toe; caecum (pouchlike portion of the large intestine); pendulous penis; scrotal testes; and two nipples (Conroy, 1990).

Heterodont having several different types of teeth (incisors, *canines*, etc.), each with a different function.

TABLE 3.1 Classification of Humankind

Taxonomic Category	Group Including Humans	Primary Characteristics	Members
Kingdom	Animalia	Generally, moving freely and feeding by mouth	Vertebrates and others
Phylum	Chordata	Possession of a notochord at some stage of life	Vertebrates, sea squirts, amphioxus
Subphylum	Vertebrata	Bilaterally symmetrical animals with internal backbones and other bony skeletal structures	Mammals and others (e.g., fish, birds, reptiles)
Class	Mammalia	Vertebrates characterized by fur, warm bloodedness, suckling live-born young	Primates and others (e.g., dogs, bats, rodents)
Order	Primates	Mammals characterized by keen vision, grasping hands and feet, nails on digits, flexible limbs	Haplorhini and Strepsirhini (lemurs and lorises)
Suborder	Haplorhini	Primates characterized by bony eye sockets, hairy nose, lack of light-reflecting layer in retina, etc.	Anthropoidea and Tarsioidea
Hyporder	Anthropoidea	Primates with complex societies, diurnal activity rhythms, increased intelligence	Hominoidea and both Old World and New World monkeys
Superfamily	Hominoidea ("hominoids")*	Anthropoids with relatively erect posture, loss of tail, mobile limbs, five-cusped lower molars	Hominidae (great apes and humans) and Hylobatidae (gibbons)
Family	Hominidae ("hominids")*	Hominoids characterized by reduced arm length, increased elbow stability, increased body size, male/female size dimorphism	Homininae, Ponginae (orangutans), Gorillinae (gorillas)
Subfamily	Homininae ("hominines")*	African hominids marked by numerous shared derived genetic traits	Hominini and Panini (chimpanzees and bonobos)
Tribe	Hominini ("hominins")*	Hominines characterized by canine reduction and habitual bipedalism	Genera *Ardipithecus, Australopithecus, Kenyanthropus, Homo, Orrorin, Paranthropus, Sahelanthropus*
Subtribe	Hominina ("hominans")*	Hominins typically characterized by marked brain enlargement, skillful hands, evolving culture (including tool making)	*Homo sapiens* and all congeners
Genus and Species	*Homo Sapiens*	Hominans characterized by huge brain, vertical forehead, small face, chin, complex culture, language and speech.	Modern humans

Sources: Based on Delson, 2000; Klein and Takahata, 2002; Wood and Richmond, 2000.
*Common names in quotation marks.

During the twentieth century, this anatomical definition of the primates was to a great extent superseded by a definition based on the order's evolutionary trends. According to the English anatomist W. E. Le Gros Clark (as presented in his influential book *The Antecedents of Man* in 1959), primates are characterized by the retention of generalized limbs tipped with five grasping digits; the replacement of claws by nails; retention of a tail; expansion and elaboration of the brain; emphasis on vision; deemphasis on olfaction; loss of some teeth from the ancestral condition; retention of a simple molar cusp pattern; delayed maturation; and reduction of litter size to single infants (Table 3.2).

Today, more than 200 species of animals living in Africa, Asia, and the tropical Americas (Figure 3.2) are recognized as primates, and the diversity within the order is staggering. Primates range in size from the gorilla at an average weight of 258 pounds (117 kilograms) to the tiny Demidoff's dwarf bush baby at 2.3 ounces (65 grams). Some primates are exceedingly intelligent creatures, others seem to have

TABLE 3.2 Major Characteristics of Primates

A. Characteristics Relating to Motor Adaptations

1. Retention of ancestral mammalian limb structure, with five digits on hands and feet, and free mobility of limbs with unfused radius and fibula.
2. Evolution of mobile, grasping digits, with sensitive friction pads and nails replacing claws. Palmar surfaces with friction skin.
3. Retention of tail as an organ of balance (except in humans, apes, and a few monkeys) and as a grasping limb in some New World monkeys.
4. Evolution of erect posture in many groups, with extensive head rotation.
5. Evolution of nervous system to give precise and rapid control of musculature.

B. Characteristics Relating to Sensory Adaptations

1. Enlargement of the eyes, increasing amount of light and detail received.
2. Evolution of retina to increase sensitivity to low levels of illumination and to different frequencies (i.e., to color).
3. Eyes that look forward, with overlapping visual fields that give stereoscopic vision.
4. Enclosure of eyes in a bony ring in all living groups and a full bony socket in haplorhines.
5. Reduction in olfactory apparatus, especially the snout.
6. Internal ear structures enclosed within petrosal bone.

C. Dental Characteristics

1. Simple cusp patterns in molar teeth.
2. In most groups, 32 or 36 teeth.

D. General Characteristics

1. Lengthened period of maturation, of infant dependency, and of gestation, compared with most mammals. Relatively long life span.
2. Low reproductive rate, especially among Hominoidea.
3. Relatively large and complex brain, especially those parts involved in vision, tactile inputs, muscle coordination and control, and memory and learning.

run-of-the-mill mammalian intelligence. Most are very social creatures, but some live solitary lives; most are **diurnal,** but some are **nocturnal.** Dietary specialities range from insects to fruit to leaves (with humans adding a significant amount of animal flesh to the basic primate diet). In order to describe all of this diversity, a complex taxonomy is required (Table 3.3).

Diurnal active during the day, as *apes, monkeys,* and humans are.

Nocturnal active during the hours of darkness.

Semiorder a subdivision of an *order;* the order *Primates* (fossil and living) contains two semiorders: *Plesiadapiformes* and *Euprimates.*

Euprimates a *semiorder* of the *primates* that contains the living *strepsirhines* (lemurs and lorises) and *haplorhines* (*tarsiers, monkeys, apes,* and humans). Also called "primates of a modern aspect."

Plesiadapiformes a *semiorder* of the *primates* that is now extinct. Also called the "archaic primates."

Strepsirhini

When both fossil and extant primates are considered, two **semiorders** can be identified: the **Euprimates,** or true primates (primates of modern aspect), and the **Plesiadapiformes,** the Euprimates' extinct and archaic kin (Delson, 2000). Molecular data suggest that the primate order diverged from the other placental mammals some 90 million years ago (mya), but fossil euprimates were not known until about 35 million years (myr) later (R. D. Martin, 2003; Tavaré et al., 2002). An anatomical comparison of the two semiorders suggests that they may be sister groups rather than ancestor–descendant stocks (Conroy, 1990; R. D. Martin, 1990; Sargis, 2002). Details of plesiadapiform anatomy will be given in a later chapter, but as the common name *archaic primates* implies, they were more primitive than euprimates in many ways.

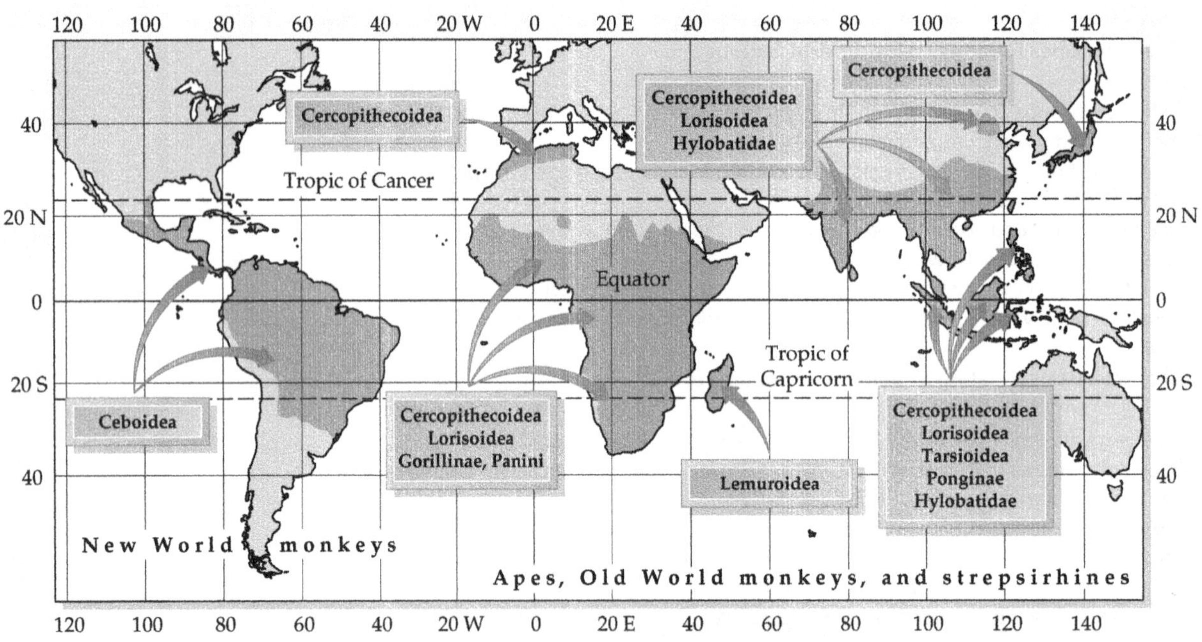

FIGURE 3.2
Worldwide distribution of nonhuman primates by superfamilies and families. Dark areas show the approximate ranges of nonhuman primates.

Source: Adapted from Napier and Napier, 1967.

Strepsirhines a suborder of the living *primates* that includes the Lemuroidea and Lorisoidea.

Haplorhines a suborder of the living *primates* that includes the Ceboidea, Cercopitheccoidea, and Hominoidea.

Prosimians a suborder used in traditional evolutionary classifications that contained the Lemuroidea, Lorisoidea, and Tarsioidea; not used in this book.

Anthropoid relating to humans, *apes*, and *monkeys*.

Focusing for now only on the living members of the primate order, two suborders can be discerned: the **Strepsirhines** and the **Haplorhines.** Both suborders were definitely in existence by about 55 mya, but one recent estimate suggests that they might have originated some 25 million years earlier (Conroy, 1990; R. D. Martin, 2003; Rasmussen, 2002). Living strepsirhines include the superfamilies Lemuroidea (which includes lemurs, aye-ayes, and other creatures; Figures 3.3 and 3.4) and Lorisoidea (lorises and bush babies; Figure 3.5). In traditional classifications utilizing an evolutionary grade approach, tarsiers (superfamily Tarsioidea; Figure 3.6) were combined with the lorisoids and lemuroids in a suborder called **Prosimii.** This was done because tarsiers clearly share numerous primitive characteristics with lorises and lemurs. Nonetheless, as will be shown shortly, tarsiers also share important derived traits with **anthropoids** (monkeys, apes, and humans), resemblances that many systematists think justify tarsiers' classification in the modern suborder Haplorhini (Table 3.3). In this book, the latter scheme will be followed, and the old grade name *prosimian* will not be used.

Toothcomb a dental specialization of *strepsirhines* in which the lower front teeth are closely spaced and forwardly inclined.

Quadrupedal moving on all four limbs.

Today, strepsirhines are found only in Africa, particularly on the island of Madagascar, and in Asia, and they are characterized by a suite of primitive traits (Table 3.4). In general, they are small- to medium-sized animals with a well developed olfactory apparatus, visual features that suggest a current or ancestral adaptation to nocturnal activity, claws on some digits, prehensile hands and feet (but poor opposability of the thumb), and a dental specialization called a **toothcomb** that is used for both foraging and grooming. Strepsirhines are arboreal animals that move about the forests of the Old World in a **quadrupedal** fashion or by clinging and leaping from one vertical support to another. On average, they are somewhat less social than haplorhines, often foraging solitarily or forming small social groups (often monogamous breeding units). They are also more committed to insect eating than the average haplorhine, although all eat fruit, as well.

TABLE 3.3 Partial Taxonomy of the Living Primates

Suborder	Hyporder	Infraorder	Superfamily	Family	Genus
Strepsirhini			Lemuroidea		13 genera
			Lorisoidea		9 genera
	Tarsiiformes				
Haplorhini			Tarsioidea		*Tarsius*
	Anthropoidea				
		Platyrrhini	Ceboidea		*Callithrix*
					Cebuella
					Saguinus
					Leontideus
					Callimico
					Pithecia
					Chiropotes
					Cacajao
					Aotus
					Callicebus
					Saimiri
					Cebus
					Alouatta
					Ateles
					Lagothrix
					Brachyteles
		Catarrhini	Cercopithecoidea		*Cercopithecus*
					Miopithecus
					Erythrocebus
					Allenopithecus
					Cercocebus
					Mandrillus
					Papio
					Theropithecus
					Macaca
					Cynopithecus
					Colobus
					Semnopithecus
					Presbytis
					Pygathrix
					Rhinopithecus
					Nasalis
					Simias
			Hominoidea	Hylobatidae	*Hylobates* (Gibbons)
				Hominidae	*Pongo* (Orangutans)
					Gorilla (Gorillas)
					Pan (Chimpanzees and Bonobos)
					Homo (Humans)

Note: Authors differ in details of primate classification. Family names are given only for the Hominoidea.
Sources: Based on Delson, 2000; Dolhinow and Fuentes, 1999; Falk, 2000; Wood and Richmond, 2000.

In several important ways, living strepsirhines bridge the anatomical gaps between haplorhines and both the archaic primates (Plesiadapiformes) and the order's primitive mammalian ancestors. For one thing, lemuroids and lorisoids lack the extensive eye protection found in haplorhines (Figure 3.7). While haplorhines show a complete bony eye socket (tarsiers' are nearly complete), all strepsirhines display

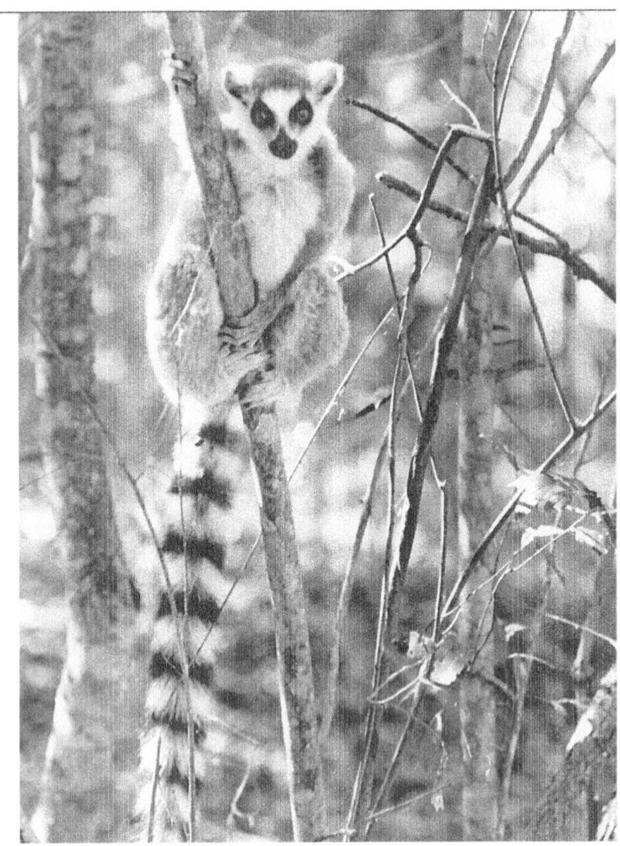

FIGURE 3.3
The ring-tailed lemur (*Lemur catta*) is typical of the Lemuroidea from Madagascar. The most striking features of lemurs are large, forward-looking eyes and long, separated fingers and toes. The ring-tail stands about 15 inches (38 centimeters) high.

FIGURE 3.4
The aye-aye is a solitary and nocturnal strepsirhine with the most unusual dentition of the entire order (see Figure 3.8). It has evolved enormous gnawing incisors, and the rest of its teeth have dwindled or disappeared.

FIGURE 3.5
The loris (*Loris tardigradus*) represents another group of strepsirhines (Lorisoidea) found in Africa and Asia. Lorises are smaller than lemurs but have very large eyes adapted for hunting insects and other small creatures at night. Lorises' bodies are about 8–14 inches (20–36 centimeters) long.

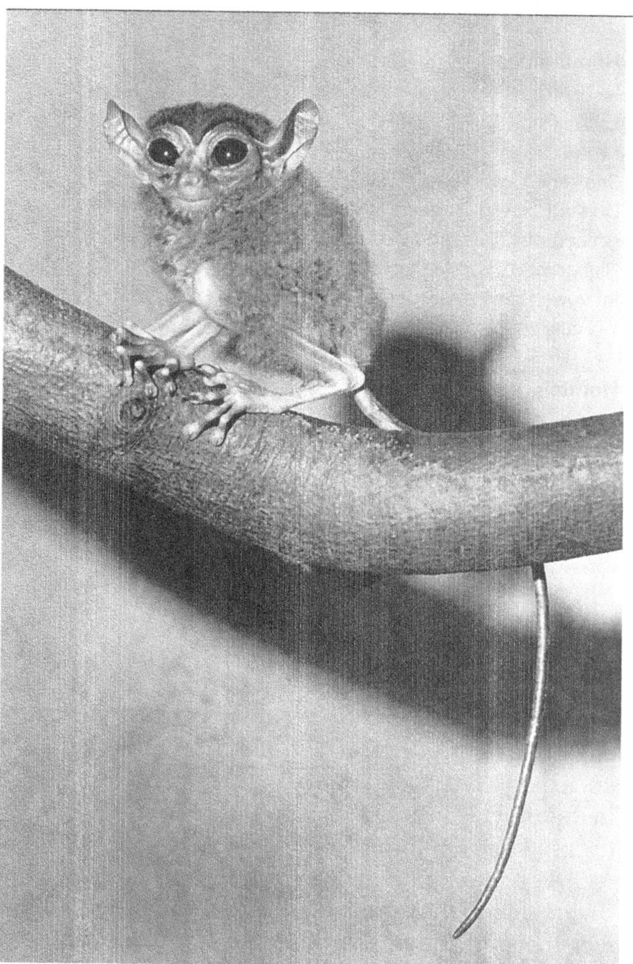

FIGURE 3.6
Three species of the primitive haplorhine the tarsier occur in Southeast Asia. With their enormous eyes, all are nocturnal, and most are forest living. Their diet consists mainly of insects. They weigh only just over 4 ounces (120 grams) but have long and powerful hind limbs adapted for leaping. They appear to have evolved little in 50 million years.

TABLE 3.4 Distinguishing Characteristics of Various Primate Taxa

Strepsirhines
Long muzzle tipped with a **rhinarium**
Tactile vibrissae (sensory whiskers)
Frenulum that anchors upper lip
Toilet claw on second toe
Postorbital bar only
Two-part frontal bone
Two-part mandible
Mandibular toothcomb in most species
Haplorhines
Reduced muzzle with a hairy nose (lack of rhinarium)
Lack of prominent whiskers
Reduced or absent frenulum (producing a mobile upper lip)
Nails (flat or modified) on all digits (tarsiers show two pedal claws)
Complete bony eye socket (tarsiers' sockets are nearly complete)
Fused frontal bone
Fused mandibular symphysis (not fused in tarsiers)
Lack of toothcomb
Retina that includes a **fovea**
Cerebral cortex that includes a central sulcus
Generally, opposable thumbs and big toes
Hominoidea
Lack of tail
Broad chest
Shortened lower back
Dorsally placed scapulae (shoulder blades)
Great mobility at shoulders, elbows, and wrists
Higher ratio of brain size to body size than in other primates
Increased complexity of folding of cerebral cortex
Y-5 cusp pattern of lower molars
Hominini
Reduced canine length
Nonprehensile big toes (especially in Hominina)
Pelvis and legs reflecting habitual bipedalism (short, wide iliac blades; enlarged iliac spines; close-knee stance)
Extreme brain enlargement and elaboration (especially in Hominina)

Rhinarium the moist, hairless nose characteristic of *strepsirhines* and of most nonprimate mammals.

Frenulum a flap of skin that tethers the upper lip to the jaw.

Fovea an area of the *haplorhine* retina that allows extremely detailed vision.

Opposable thumb the ability to hold thumb and index finger together in opposition, giving a *precision grip*.

Postorbital bar a bar of bone running around the outside margin of the orbits of *strepsirhines*.

Diastema a space in the toothrow that accommodates one or more teeth in the opposite jaw when the mouth is closed (plural, diastemata).

only a **postorbital bar** of bone extending from brow to cheekbone. Second, while both strepsirhines and haplorhines show a reduction in total tooth count from the ancestral dental formula (Figure 3.8), several strepsirhine species have retained the ancient three-cusped pattern in their upper molar teeth (tarsiers are also primitive in this trait). Third, strepsirhines still show the primitive clawed condition on some digits, while haplorhines show nails (usually flat, but sometimes compressed and recurved into pseudoclaws) on all digits. Fourth, while strepsirhines show greater divergence of the thumb than nonprimate mammals and have grasping hands and feet, they lack the extensive thumb opposability (and precision gripping) that characterizes most anthropoids (compare Figure 3.9 with Figures 3.17 and 3.18). Again, although classified as haplorhines, tarsiers are strepsirhine-like in the possession of a few clawed toes and nonopposable thumbs (Napier and Napier, 1967).

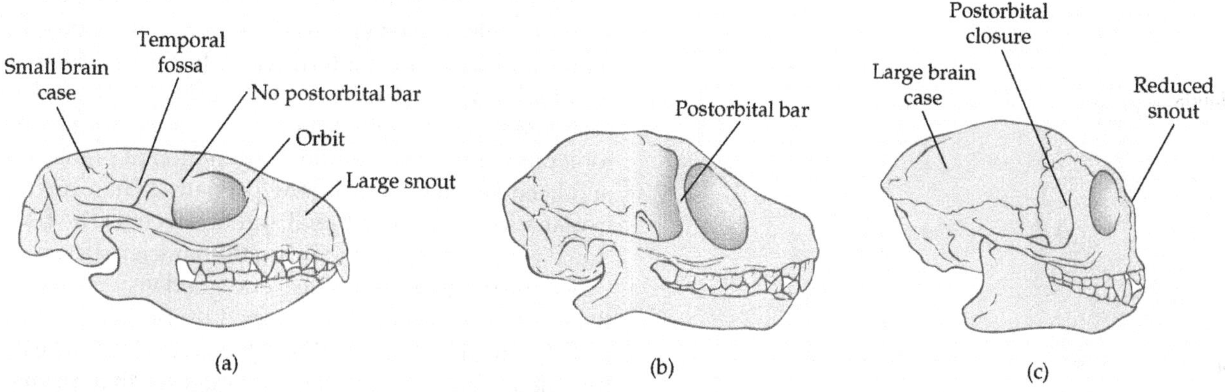

FIGURE 3.7
Comparative skull anatomy reveals several distinctive primate traits. Lateral views of (*a*) a non-primate mammal (hedgehog), (*b*) a lemuroid strepsirhine, and (*c*) an anthropoid (New World monkey). Skulls not drawn to scale.

Primate type	Dental formula
Primitive mammals	$\frac{3143}{3143}$
Strepsirhines	
Lemuroidea	$\frac{2133}{2133}$
Lorisoidea	$\frac{2133}{2133}$
Aye-aye	$\frac{1013}{1003}$
Haplorhines	
Tarsioidea	$\frac{2133}{1133}$
Ceboidea	$\frac{2133}{2133}$ or $\frac{2132}{2132}$
Cercopithecoidea	$\frac{2123}{2123}$
Hominoidea	$\frac{2123}{2123}$

Incisors | Premolars | Molars

Primitive mammals: I_1 C P_1 M_1

Strepsirhines (lemur): I_{1-2} C P_2 M_1

New World monkeys (spider monkey): I_1 C P_2 M_1

Old World monkeys (baboon): I_1 C P_3 M_1

Humans: I_1 C P_3 M_1

FIGURE 3.8
Dental formulae and lateral views of several primate varieties. Dental formulae represent half of the upper dentition over half of the lower and count (from left to right) numbers of permanent incisors, canines, premolars, and molars. In lemurs, I_{1-2} and the lower canines make up the toothcomb. Arrows mark the presence of a **diastema,** or gap in the toothrow.

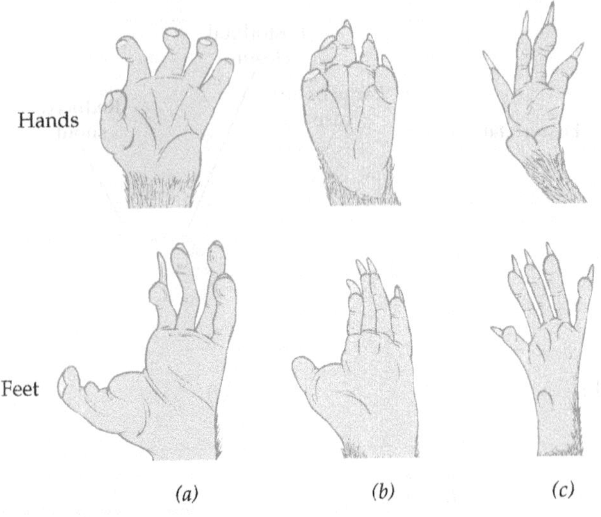

FIGURE 3.9
Comparisons of the hand and foot of (*a*) a bush baby (Lorisoidea) with two nonprimate mammals; an opossum (*b*) and a gray squirrel (*c*).

Stereoscopic vision vision produced by two eyes with overlapping fields, giving a sense of depth and distance; most highly evolved in hunting animals and *primates*.

Despite the retention of some primitive traits, however, strepsirhines show the distinctive euprimate combination of increased emphasis on vision plus grasping hands and feet. This pattern was inherited by the haplorhines, in whom further modifications of the sensory systems—such as a reduction of the olfactory sense—took place. But why did the combination of prehension and keen vision evolve among primates? There are two explanations, one traditional and one recent. The traditional explanation for the primate characteristics, especially grasping hands and feet and good vision, is called the *arboreal theory*. First developed by British scientists G. E. Smith (1927) and F. Wood Jones (1916) in the early twentieth century, this theory suggests that primate characteristics are essentially adaptations to life in the trees. Grasping extremities are viewed here as evolving for safe and lively movement through the irregular arboreal habitat. Similarly, keen vision is thought to have evolved to facilitate arboreal locomotion—particularly **stereoscopic vision**, with depth perception for judging distance before leaping—and for locating food and danger. The sense of smell was of limited use to arboreal animals, and its supporting structures (a long muzzle and large smell centers in the brain) dwindled.

The logic of the arboreal theory seemed entirely adequate for more than half a century. In the 1970s, however, American anthropologist Matt Cartmill began to probe that logic and the validity of the arboreal explanation. Cartmill (1974) observed that arboreal life does not necessarily select for primatelike characteristics. Many animals are perfectly at home in the trees without looking and acting like primates. Gray squirrels are a good example. Squirrels skitter through the branches, making leaps of many times their body length. Furthermore, they successfully locate food and detect danger in the trees. Squirrels manage all this even though their hands and feet are relatively nonprehensile and their eyes are much more wide set and laterally oriented than those of a primate, producing poorer depth perception. Moving the eyes closer together and forward produces increased overlap of the left and right visual fields, and increased overlap leads to better stereoscopic depth perception at close range (Figure 3.10).

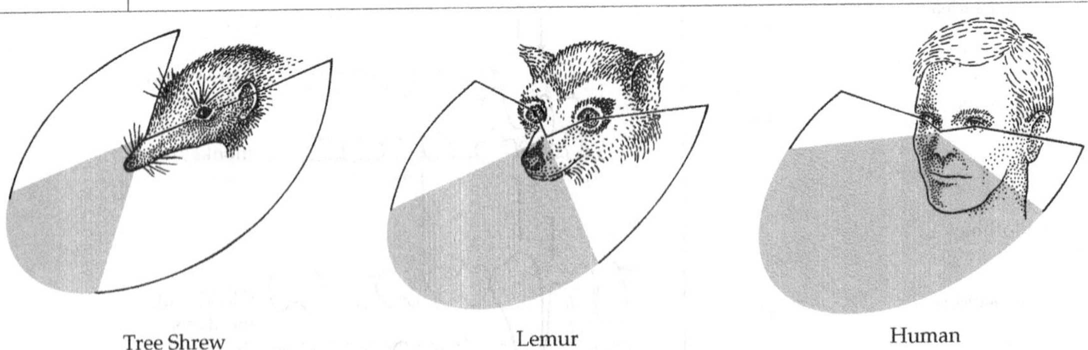

FIGURE 3.10
Stereoscopic vision is of great importance to primates, probably for both arboreal movement and foraging activities. The primitive tree shrew's eyes look sideways, and the visual fields have small overlap; in the lemur, the overlap is greater. In monkeys, apes, and humans, the extent of visual field overlap is great. Upright posture permits easy head rotation, which compensates for the loss of backward vision. As the eyes moved to the front of the face in primate evolution and vision became the primary sense, the sense of smell became less important, the snout was reduced, and the face flattened. Heads not drawn to scale.

Cartmill compared primates with other animals and found that close-set, forwardly directed eyes are characteristic of predators that rely on vision in hunting. Cats, owls, chameleons, and many other animals use their close-set eyes to locate prey and to judge the distance for a capturing leap or grab. For arboreal hunters, grasping feet stabilize the animal on its support, while grasping hands (one or both working together) make the capture.

Based on these discoveries, Cartmill (1974) fashioned the *visual predation theory* of primate evolution. This theory holds that among the primates, grasping extremities and keen vision originally evolved as adaptations for vision-directed predation on insects. (Such hunting is still common among some strepsirhines.) De-emphasis on the sense of smell—and reduction of the olfactory apparatus—is viewed here as the result of a migration of the eyes in an anterior direction. Approximation of the eyes could have constricted the olfactory connections between the muzzle and the brain and thus could have led to a reduced sense of smell.

In 1992, Cartmill modified his theory somewhat. By then, additional studies had identified several diurnal visual predators (e.g., mongooses and some tree shrews) that lack convergent eyes, suggesting that the first primates' nocturnal lifestyle also influenced their visual evolution. Because nocturnal creatures have wide-open irises, orbital convergence both enhances their stereoscopic, close-range depth perception *and* it improves the clarity of objects directly in front of the eyes. (In diurnal creatures, even those with widely spaced eyes, blurred objects are focused by constricting the pupils.) Thus, it was not just hunting but *nocturnal* hunting that shaped the primates' traits.

The visual predation theory is convincing in many ways, but recent findings suggest that primates' distinctive characteristics—especially grasping hands and feet and visual specializations—actually may have evolved in sequence, rather than as a single multifaceted package. In 2002, paleontologists Jonathan Bloch and Doug Boyer reported the recovery of a 55-myr-old plesiadapiform fossil (genus *Carpolestes*) that showed an opposable big toe tipped by a nail (not a claw) and capable of grasping small terminal branches. That same specimen also showed evidence of grasping specializations of the hand, but like all plesiadapiforms, its species lacked orbital convergence and a postorbital bar. Bloch and Boyer (2002) and others (Sargis, 2002) have concluded from this discovery that certain of the plesiadapiforms were actually the first to evolve the grasping adaptations that later became ubiquitous among the euprimates and that grasping abilities were refined in response to increased diversity of angiosperms (flowering plants; see also Sussman, 1991). Nocturnal, vision-directed predation on insects by the earliest euprimates may then have completed the grasping–vision adaptive package (Ravosa and Savakova, 2004).

Cartmill and his colleagues (Kirk et al., 2003) reject the above suggestion, countering that *Carpolestes* was not a plesiadapiform but rather belonged to a sister taxon to the archaic primates. The sequential development–single package question will be settled only by future fossil discoveries. If nothing else, however, the controversy (combined with the old arboreal theory) serves to underscore the presence of several factors that would have selected for grasping skills and keen vision among the evolving primates: the demands of arboreal locomotion, foraging on angiosperm plant parts, and the nocturnal hunting of insects.

Haplorhini

The suborder Haplorhini contains two so-called **hyporders:** Tarsiiformes and Anthropoidea (Table 3.3). The earliest fossil evidence of the tarsiiforms is dated just over 30 mya, while that of the anthropoids is 45 to 50 myr in age (Beard et al., 1994; Conroy, 1990; Ducrocq, 1998; Kay et al., 1997). Living representatives of the two hyporders include the tarsiers (Tarsiiformes) and the New World and Old World

Hyporder a *taxonomic* rank; a subdivision of a suborder.

monkeys, apes, and humans (Anthropoidea). As noted earlier, while tarsiers share several traits with strepsirhines, the list of tarsiiform–anthropoid shared derived traits is also extensive and supports their combination in the same suborder. Among the derived traits shared by tarsiiforms and anthropoids are the following features (Conroy, 1990; Falk, 2000; W. C. O. Hill, 1955):

1. hairy nose rather than a rhinarium
2. mobile upper lip
3. lack of a light-reflecting layer in the retina
4. similar arterial pattern supplying the middle ear
5. reduction in facial length
6. closely approximated orbits and complete (or nearly complete) bony sockets
7. reduced olfactory bulbs of the brain
8. tubular **ectotympanic bone**

Ectotympanic bone a middle ear bone that supports the eardrum.

Modern tarsiers (Figure 3.6) are found in the Philippines as well as on Borneo and certain other Southeast Asian islands. Small animals with enormous, bulging eyes, two pedal claws for self-grooming, and a primitive molar anatomy, tarsiers are nocturnal hunters *par excellence*, eating a variety of live prey, including insects, bats, birds, and snakes (Falk, 2000; Gursky, 2002). Socially, some species of tarsiers form male–female pairs that defend foraging territories, while in other species, mixed age and sex groups of up to six animals are seen together. Mating appears to be primarily monogamous (Bearder, 1987).

Besides the tarsiers, the living haplorhines include the New World and Old World monkeys (the Ceboidea and Cercopithecoidea, respectively; Figure 3.11), the apes (superfamily Hominoidea; Figure 3.12), and humans. As shown in Table 3.4, the anthropoids—indeed, all haplorhines—display numerous anatomical differences from the strepsirhines. Among anthropoids, the sense of smell has been reduced as the muzzle has been shortened and the rhinarium lost. The eyes of anthropoids are close together, forwardly directed, and protected by complete bony sockets. With the exception of the tiny marmosets and tamarins of the New World, anthropoids have flat nails on all of their digits. (The small callitrichid monkeys have "re-evolved" claws by compressing and curving their nails [Falk, 2000], and these pseudoclaws are used for moving about in squirrel fashion in the trees. Most anthropoids are large, heavy animals, however, that have only nails; claws cannot bear the weight of a big arboreal animal.) Anthropoids also have lower jaws that are fused at the midline, and their front teeth are vertically implanted (no toothcomb). And finally, as detailed in Chapter 13, anthropoids show increases in the relative size and complexity of the brain. Monkeys, apes, and humans have a larger and more complexly folded cerebral cortex than strepsirhines. To some extent, this is due to changes in the animals' sensory systems, but it is also related to increased intelligence (Ankel-Simons, 1983; Falk, 2000).

Platyrrhines an infraorder of the *anthropoids* that includes the *New World monkeys*.

Catarrhines an infraorder of the *anthropoids* that includes *Old World monkeys, apes*, and humans.

Prehensile adapted for grasping.

For the purpose of further anatomical comparisons, anthropoids may be divided into two infraorders: the **platyrrhines** and the **catarrhines** (Table 3.3). The first category includes the New World monkeys (superfamily Ceboidea), all of which are marked by round nostrils that are widely spaced and face laterally, and by a total of 12 premolars in the adult dentition. Catarrhines include the Old World monkeys, apes, and humans (superfamilies Cercopithecoidea and Hominoidea), and they are characterized by compressed, closely spaced, and downwardly directed nostrils and only eight permanent premolars (Figure 3.11). Comparing all monkeys with all hominoids generally, monkeys have long backs, narrow chests, laterally placed scapulae (shoulder blades) and a tail (Figure 3.13). Some ceboids have **prehensile** or grasping tails, but none of the cercopithecoids is so equipped. Monkeys also have a smaller range of motion at the shoulder than hominoids (Figure 3.14). These anatomical traits are correlated with habitual quadrupedal locomotion both in the trees and on the ground. Generally speaking, monkeys walk, run, and leap about on all fours. This is not to say that monkeys don't or can't do other things—

FIGURE 3.11
Old World monkeys (*top*): a long-tailed macaque (*left*) and a mandrill (*right*), both primarily adapted to terrestrial quadrupedalism. New World monkeys, such as the spider monkey (*bottom left and right*), are highly adapted to an arboreal life. Notice the long grasping tail in the New World monkey and its laterally opening nostrils. In contrast, the Old World monkeys' nostrils are downwardly directed.

some species show a good deal of hanging and swinging by their arms (or tail)—but the majority of species usually move about quadrupedally along the tops of branches.

The anatomy of hominoids (apes and humans; superfamily Hominoidea) differs significantly from that of monkeys. To start at the top, hominoids have larger brains than monkeys, and this larger brain size is correlated with new functional capabilities such as self-recognition (in some species) and learning by insight. Hominoids also have certain distinctive dental traits. Their lower molars show a characteristic arrangement of five cusps and grooves called the **Y-5 pattern.** Old World monkeys, in contrast, show a pattern of molar cusp morphology called **bilophodonty:** four cusps that are arranged in two pairs (front and rear), with the members of a pair connected by a transverse ridge of enamel (Figure 3.15).

Y-5 pattern an arrangement of the *cusps* and grooves of the lower *molars* that is characteristic of *hominoids*.

Bilophodonty the molar *cusp* pattern of *Old World monkeys*, featuring four *cusps* arranged in front and rear pairs.

FIGURE 3.12 Whereas the orangutan (*upper left*) and the gibbon (*upper right*) are still primarily arboreal, the gorilla (*lower left*) and the chimpanzee (*lower right*) have developed knuckle-walking as the form of locomotion most practical for their ground-based way of life. The fifth living ape, the bonobo, is shown in Figure 4.20.

Postcranial referring to any anatomical feature that is behind the head (in *quadrupeds*) or below the head (in *bipeds*).

With regard to **postcranial** anatomy, all hominoids show broad chests with dorsal scapulae; short, stiff backs; relatively long arms with mobile wrists, elbows, and shoulders; and no tail. These traits are probably adaptations for suspensory locomotion and posture (arm swinging or hanging), behaviors that are shown to some extent by all living apes, although not by humans. A closer look at the variety of hominoid locomotor patterns and their associated anatomical variations is instructive.

The most obvious distinction between apes and monkeys is that apes are built for a different mode of travel, having short, wide, shallow trunks and long, free-swinging arms that rotate at the shoulders. These adaptations allow apes to reach out in all directions in the trees, climbing arm over arm.

From their probable beginning as efficient climbers, the different families of apes have adapted in different ways. The gibbons (Hylobatidae) have evolved very long arms and hands and in this way are specialized for the horizontal arm-over-arm

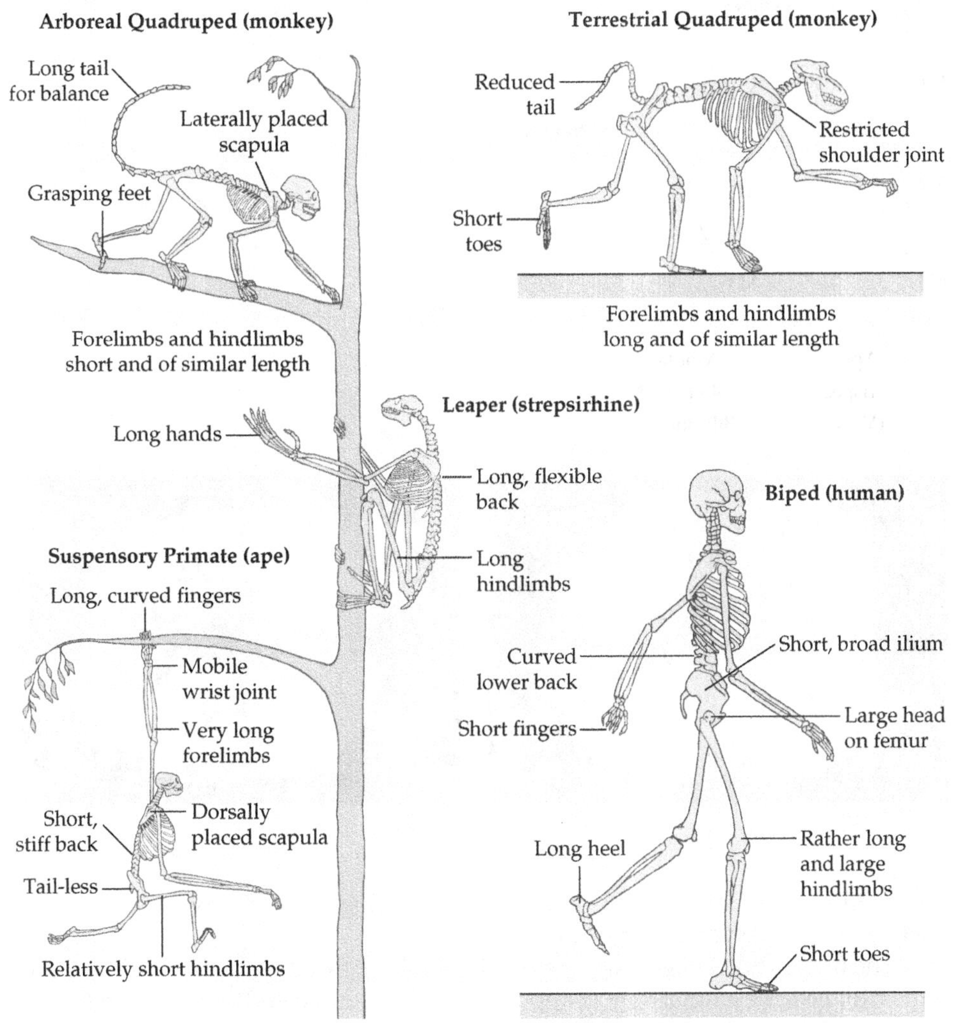

Arboreal Quadruped (monkey)
Long tail for balance
Laterally placed scapula
Grasping feet
Forelimbs and hindlimbs short and of similar length

Terrestrial Quadruped (monkey)
Reduced tail
Restricted shoulder joint
Short toes
Forelimbs and hindlimbs long and of similar length

Leaper (strepsirhine)
Long hands
Long, flexible back
Long hindlimbs

Suspensory Primate (ape)
Long, curved fingers
Mobile wrist joint
Very long forelimbs
Short, stiff back
Dorsally placed scapula
Tail-less
Relatively short hindlimbs

Biped (human)
Curved lower back
Short, broad ilium
Short fingers
Large head on femur
Long heel
Rather long and large hindlimbs
Short toes
Great toe aligned with other digits

FIGURE 3.13 Monkeys are generally arboreal or terrestrial quadrupeds, while hominoids engage in arboreal suspensory behavior, knuckle-walking, and bipedalism. This figure shows some of the anatomical features associated with each main type of primate locomotion.

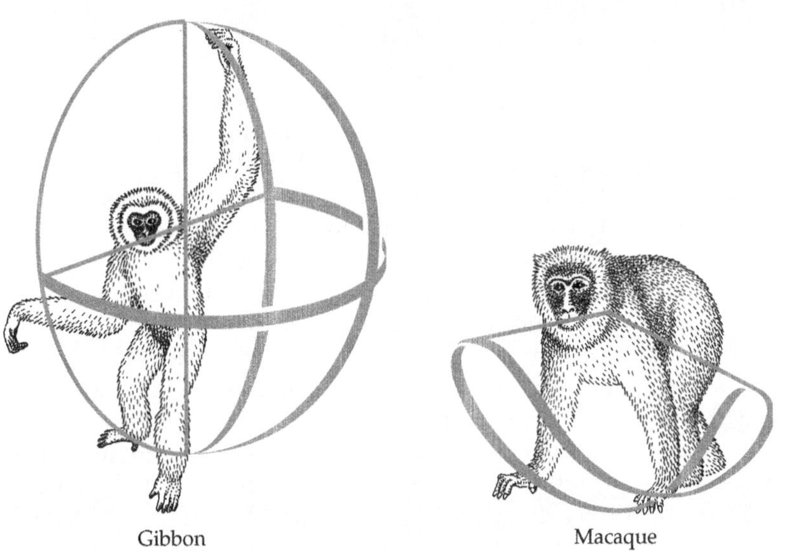

FIGURE 3.14 One of the basic differences between apes and monkeys lies in the greater freedom of movement that the former have in their forelimbs. Apes are climbers; many can also swing by their arms in trees and can move their arms freely in all directions (gibbon, *left*). Most monkeys (such as the Asian macaque, *right*), by contrast, are true quadrupeds. Since they travel on four limbs, they need move their front legs only backward and forward and a little to the side. They leap and jump in the trees and run across the ground.

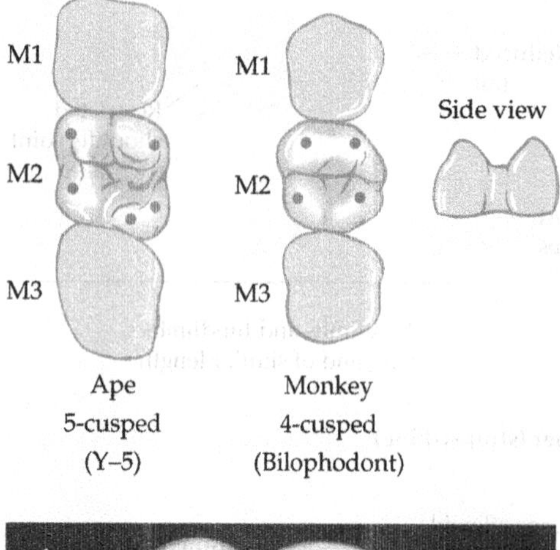

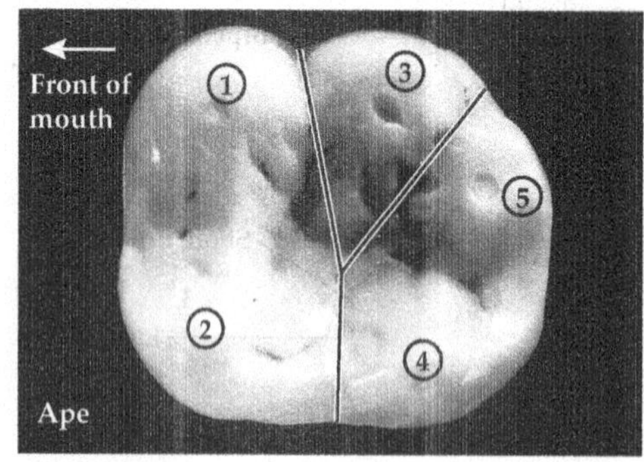

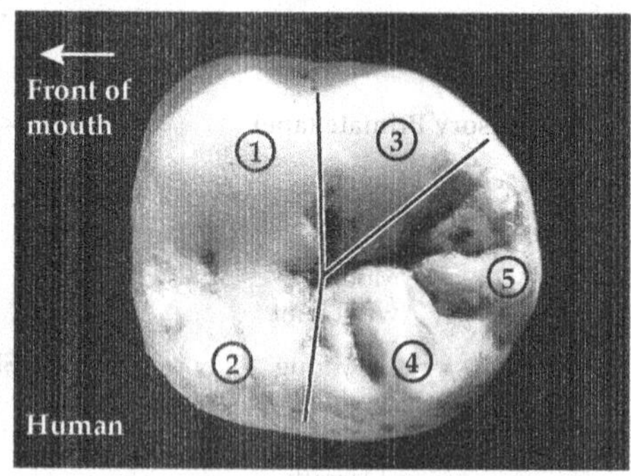

FIGURE 3.15 The cusp patterns of the lower molars enable us to distinguish apes and monkeys with ease. Old World monkeys show four paired cusps (the bilophodont pattern); front and rear cusps are clearly seen in a side view. In contrast, humans are relatively difficult to distinguish from apes on the basis of the molar teeth: both have five cusps following a Y-5 pattern. In some human lower molars, however, the fifth cusp has been lost, and it is commonly much reduced.

Brachiation an arboreal locomotor pattern featuring manual swinging from branch to branch.

locomotion called **brachiation** (Figure 3.12). Brachiating gibbons can travel with considerable speed and extraordinary grace.

The orangutan (*Pongo*) moves steadily, climbing through the trees with all four limbs: indeed, the animal almost appears to be four armed and four handed (Figure 3.12). On the ground, the orangutan moves quadrupedally with clenched fists and feet, although it occasionally walks on the palms of its hands. Both the gibbons and the orangutans are fully adapted to arboreal life, however, and show no specific terrestrial adaptations.

The African apes (part of the family Hominidae), however, do show such adaptations, and the larger varieties, especially the mountain gorilla, have almost deserted the trees for the ground, although they will still sleep in trees. Whereas the smaller chimpanzees and bonobos are good climbers, all African apes are adapted to terrestrial quadrupedalism, and they walk on the soles of their feet and the knuckles of their hands. The terrestrial skeletal adaptations are seen in the bones of their wrists and hands, which are modified to support the weight of the animals on their knuckles—on the second phalanx counting from the tip of the finger (Figure 3.12). Here, normal hairy skin is replaced by hairless friction skin, such as we find on the palms of our hands and the soles of our feet (Schultz, 1969).

Thus, the living apes, sharing a common ancestor which we believe was an arboreal climber that underwent a reduction in the tail, have each in their own way modified this original locomotor adaptation together with their skeleton and musculature. The tail was lost because a climber does not need an organ that balances and adjusts the aerodynamics of a leaping animal (Cartmill and Milton, 1977; Nakatsukasa et al., 2003). Human ancestors have taken a fourth route—to terrestrial bipedalism. Although we are still quite able as climbers, our lower limbs have undergone profound changes in adaptation to **bipedal** walking on the ground.

Bipedal moving erect on the hind limbs only.

Human Characteristics

Humans are very similar to the living apes in many ways, but the similarities are not equal across the various ape species and this fact is revealed in our taxonomy. As shown in Tables 3.1 and 3.3, humans are grouped with the large-bodied apes (the so-called great apes) in the family Hominidae, while the smaller but longer-armed gibbons are placed in their own family, Hylobatidae. Next, the orangutans—with their distinctive facial profile, small brows, and tall, ovoid orbits (Aiello and Dean, 1990)—can be separated into their own subfamily, Ponginae, leaving only the relations among the African apes and humans to be worked out. These relationships are, in fact, among the most difficult to determine, and researchers have struggled for years to sort the anatomical and molecular features of gorillas, chimpanzees (and bonobos), and humans into sensible shared–derived verses unique categories.

This problem of working out the evolutionary relations within the African hominid trichotomy has recently been solved to most workers' satisfaction by genetic comparisons. It now seems clear that humans and chimps (and by implication bonobos) have two to three times more genetic similarities with one another than either species has with gorillas (Klein and Takahata, 2002). Therefore, gorillas can be split off into their own subfamily, Gorillinae, leaving humans (genus *Homo*) and chimpanzees and bonobos (genus *Pan*) in the subfamily Homininae. The chimpanzee–bonobo clade is separated from humans at the tribal level: tribe Panini for the apes and Hominini for us. For convenience, the taxonomy of the living hominoids is given in Table 3.5.

These taxonomic niceties, however, do little to get at the essence of what distinguishes humans from apes, and indeed, the similarities are impressive. As shown in Table 3.6, compared to the other living hominoids, we are not exceptional for either adult body size or sexual dimorphism in body weight. Our average gestation length surpasses those of the largest apes by only a few days, and the weight of a human baby as a percentage of a woman's weight is well within the range of hominoid variation. True, humans do live longer than apes, but we also mature a bit more slowly, with the result that we are sexually immature for about the same percentage of our life span as our ape cousins.

So, what exactly is it that makes humans different from the apes and other primates? Four physical traits have overwhelming significance. The first three are a skeleton adapted for erect bipedalism (upright walking; Figure 3.13); eyes capable of sharp, three-dimensional vision in color; and hands that can both grip things powerfully and manipulate things nimbly. These features are found in some degree in many primates; it is their elaboration and special combination with one another that distinguishes humans. Controlling and making use of this equipment is humans' fourth significant trait: the brain. A physical organ itself, the human brain introduces the capacity for rational thought and, with the body, makes possible that other most human of all our abilities: speech.

TABLE 3.5 Taxonomy of the Living Hominoids

Superfamily Hominoidea
- Family Hylobatidae (genus *Hylobates*)
- Family Hominidae
  - Subfamily Ponginae (genus *Pongo*)
  - Subfamily Gorillinae (genus *Gorilla*)
  - Subfamily Homininae
    - Tribe Panini (genus *Pan*)
    - Tribe Hominini (genus *Homo*)

TABLE 3.6 Hominoid Life Histories: Body Size, Reproduction, Maturation, and Longevity

Trait	Humans (*Homo sapiens*)	Chimpanzees (*Pan troglodytes*)	Bonobos (*Pan paniscus*)	Gorillas (*Gorilla gorilla*)	Orangutans (*Pongo pygmaeus*)	Gibbons (*Hylobates* species)
Adult body weight: Female–Male range	100–200 lb. (40–70 kg)	73–132 lb. (33–60 kg)	73–99 lb. (33–45 kg)	159–386 lb. (72–175 kg)	82–179 lb. (37–81 kg)	11–24 lb. (5–11 kg)
Female body weight as % of Male body weight	81	78	73	51	46	94
Gestation (days)	267	228	230–240	256	260	210–231
Infant weight as % of Female body weight	5.5	4.0	?	2.6	4.0	6.0–7.5
Life span (yrs.)	75	> 50	> 50?	> 50	> 55	> 30?
Female sexual maturity (yrs.)	14.3	9.8	?	6.5	7	7–9
Female sexual immaturity as % of life span	19.1	20	?	13	13	23.3–30
Male sexual maturity (yrs.)	15	13	?	10	9.6	6.5
Male sexual immaturity as % of life span	20	26	?	20	17.5	21.7

Sources: Most data are averages taken from Dixson, 1998; Falk, 2000; Fleagle, 1988; Harvey et al., 1987; Molnar, 2002; Napier and Napier, 1985; Schultz, 1969; Tanner, 1992.

Bipedalism

The four distinguishing attributes uniquely combined in humans interact with one another. It is impossible to say that one led to the next or that one is necessarily more important than the others. Each reinforces the others and makes improvements in them possible. Nevertheless, one attribute stands out simply because it is so conspicuous: upright walking.

For all its apparent simplicity, walking is an adaptation that is extremely specialized. True, humans are not the only animals able to stand on their hind legs; birds, bears, and a number of our primate cousins occasionally do so. But with the exception of a few flightless birds, such as the ostrich, humans are the only animals that depend exclusively on two legs for everyday walking and running. Using two legs, a human has the endurance to outrun a deer and can carry heavier loads, pound for pound of body weight, than a donkey.

Like donkeys and horses, human beings have a variety of gaits; they amble, stride, jog, and sprint. The simple stride, though, is at once the most useful and the most peculiarly human way of getting from one place to another. Probably evolved to enable our African ancestors to cover many miles in a day's food gathering or scavenging, the long, free-swinging stride has taken us to every corner of the earth. Striding is no minor accomplishment. When compared with the way four-legged animals get about, human walking turns out to be a surprisingly complex feat. "Without split-second timing," said John Napier, a British authority on primates, "man would fall flat on his face; in fact with each step he takes, he teeters on the edge of catastrophe" (Napier, 1970:165). Human walking is actually a balancing act in which the muscles of the feet, legs, hips, and back are alternately contracted and relaxed according to synchronized orders from the brain and the spinal cord.

As Huxley showed in 1863, the human skeleton is closer in form to that of the African great apes than to that of any other animal. There are nevertheless striking

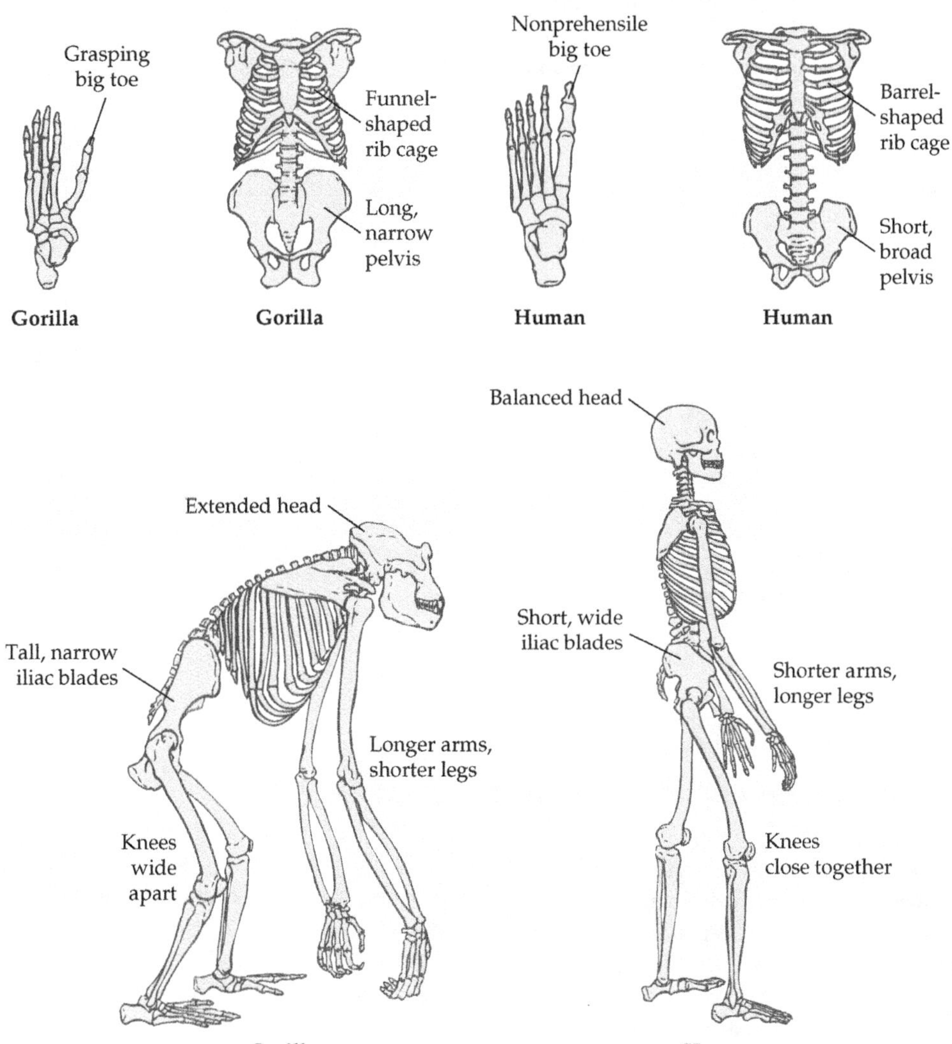

FIGURE 3.16 A comparison of key skeletal features of bipedal humans and quadrupedal apes.

differences between the human and the African ape skeletons—differences almost entirely due to the evolution among ancestral hominins (Table 3.1) of bipedal walking and among apes of quadrupedal knuckle-walking (Figure 3.16; see also Table 3.7). The human foot has lost the ability to grip with the big toe, and the toe itself has become long and robust, forming the ball of the foot—an essential pivot for the act of walking. Human arms are short and legs long, in relation to the length of the trunk, while the apes have relatively long arms and short legs, indicating that the arms are more important in locomotion. The human knee has been modified for the transmission of weight and can be locked when extended. Fundamental changes have occurred in the pelvis, as well. Compared to apes, our pelvis is shorter (a change that improved bipedal balance) and has a broader blade, or *ilium* (giving greater leverage to the muscles that hold the body erect). Additionally, our hip sockets have increased in relative size to match the greater weight they transmit compared to apes. Almost every bone in the body reflects the evolution of humans' and apes' distinctly different kinds of posture and locomotion.

Balanced bipedalism is uniquely human and beautiful in its efficiency and its superb adaptation of bone and muscle, brain and nerve to the tricky problem of moving about on two limbs. Our adaptations for bipedalism have not been perfected, however (Box 3.1). Back trouble, foot ailments, and difficulty in giving

TABLE 3.7 Hominoid Comparative Anatomy: Limbs and Hips

Trait	Humans	Chimpanzees	Bonobos	Gorillas	Orangutans	Gibbons
Arms as % of body weight[a]	8	16	16	?	18	20
Arm length × 100 divided by trunk length[a]	148	172	?	172	200	238
Legs as % of body weight[b]	30	18	24	?	18	18
Leg length × 100 divided by trunk length[b]	169	127	?	124	116	140
Ilium width × 100 divided by ilium length	126	66	56	92	74	49
Width of hip socket × 100 divided by ilium length	30	12	ca. 18	15	14	11

[a]Note that humans' arms are lighter and shorter than apes' arms.
[b]Humans' legs are heavier and longer than apes' legs.
Sources: Data from Aiello and Dean, 1990; Jungers and Susman, 1984; Schultz, 1968; Zihlman, 1984.

BOX 3.1 CURRENT ISSUE

Humans' Anatomical Imperfections

The human body is a marvelous and intricate piece of biological machinery. Indeed, that complexity is so impressive (at least to us) that it is often given as proof that we must be the result of divine design. Surely, the reasoning goes, only God could have made creatures with our intelligence, physical skills, and beauty. As Shakespeare said, "What a piece of work!" Well, lest you get carried away with that logic, let's run down a list of human imperfections related to the switch from quadrupedalism to bipedalism, problems that natural selection has not been able to correct (see also Price, 1996).

First, as an adaptation for a fully upright and balanced stance, humans evolved a strong curvature in the small of the back (see Figure 3.13; apes have a straight lower back). Unfortunately, the curved shape and increased pressure on the lower back due to carrying the full weight of the upper body have increased our vulnerability to painful conditions such as pulled muscles, slipped discs, lumbago (rheumatism), and scoliosis (lateral curvature of the spine).

Second, expanding brain size in our species has resulted in an increase in the size of a baby's head at birth. Women's average pelvic size has not been able to keep up, however (pelvic width is constrained by the biomechanical requirements of bipedalism), and the ensuing mismatch—newborn head lengths that are slightly bigger than mothers' pelvic widths—has resulted in more difficult deliveries than in other hominoids.

Third, humans' upright posture puts much more pressure on the muscles of our lower abdominal wall than is true for quadrupeds, and as a result, we commonly rupture those muscles (producing hernias) during heavy lifting or sometimes even as the result of vigorous coughing.

Fourth, because the human heart is so far above the ground, our blood can have a hard time overcoming the pull of gravity to make the return trip from the feet. A result: distended and swollen varicose veins, particularly in older people.

Fifth, humans' common complaint of hemorrhoids is related partly to our upright posture bringing extra pressure to bear on the blood vessels supplying the large intestine's lower end. As many sufferers can attest, these vessels can become swollen and quite painful.

And finally, bipedalism puts the full weight of the body on our feet alone (as opposed to quadrupeds' hands *and* feet). In the course of a human lifetime, this can result in painful calluses and fallen arches (flat feet), conditions that can be exacerbated by poorly designed or ill-fitting shoes.

And so, the human body *is* marvelous and also distinctly imperfect. Working with the material at hand, natural selection converted quadruped apes into bipedal humans. But, unfortunately for us, natural selection is concerned with survival, not perfection, and as a result, it has left us with several annoying and painful rough edges.

birth—common among humans—result partly from upright posture (Napier, 1970; Price, 1996). Indeed, natural selection does not necessarily generate perfection in any trait. Natural selection simply favors the trait variants that promote individuals' survival and reproduction in the current environment—nothing more. To our eyes, the results often seem to constitute a kind of perfection, but most traits are compromises.

Vision

Why is it so important to human evolution that we stand erect and walk on two legs? Part of the answer has to do with the human head. The head is where the eyes are, and the taller an animal stands, the more it sees. A quadrupedal baboon (genus *Papio*) with eyes that are 2 feet (0.6 meters) above the African **savanna** can detect low objects about 6 miles (almost 10 kilometers) away; eyes 5 feet (1.5 meters) above the ground can see 9 miles (14 kilometers) farther.

Savanna a tropical or subtropical grassland, often with scattered trees (woodland savanna).

The advantage of height is especially important because vision is the most important of our five major senses, and is the source of some 90 percent of the information stored in the brain. Human eyes are attuned precisely to human needs. In general, they are unsurpassed by any other eyes in the world. A hawk can see more sharply but cannot move its eyes easily and must move its head to follow its prey. A dragonfly can follow faster movement but cannot focus a sharp image. A horse can see almost completely behind its head but has difficulty seeing objects straight ahead at close range. Most important, human beings and their catarrhine primate relatives (the Old World monkeys and apes) have the special combination of full stereoscopic vision and **trichromatic** color vision—the latter trait perhaps originating as an adaptation for evaluating fruits and flowers in a shadowy environment (Figure 3.10; Deacon, 1992a; Jacobs, 1994/95). Catarrhine eyes, placed at the front of the head rather than at the sides, can focus together on an object so that it is perceived as a single three-dimensional image in the brain. And within this image, rich color vision allows catarrhines to pick out details by hue as well as by form, relationship, and brightness. Interestingly, those primates with trichromatic color vision are also the ones with the poorest sense of smell. Around 30 percent of the olfactory receptor genes of Old World monkeys and apes carry coding region disruptions that render them inoperative; the number of such pseudogenes rises to about 60 percent in humans. Thus, for reasons that are not well understood, it appears that there was "an exchange in the importance of these two senses [vision and smell] in primate evolution" (Gilad et al., 2004:123).

Trichromatic referring to the rich color vision produced by having three types of photopigments (molecules that absorb certain wavelengths of light) in the eye.

The special importance of vision among humans lies in its combination with two of our other features: terrestrial bipedalism, which locates our keen eyes well above the ground without having to climb a tree (giving hunters, for example, a wide and deep field of vision as they search for prey), and our mental and manual capacities for the skillful manipulation and modification of objects. Monkeys and apes may adopt a temporary bipedal stance or do some climbing to improve their view, but humans don't have to. And both monkeys and apes are somewhat limited when it comes to tool use and tool making—monkeys by their brain power and apes by their hands.

Hands

Humans stand up partly in order to see and stay up partly because they see so well. But the freedom that this posture gives to their arms and hands has proved even more decisive in distinguishing humans from monkeys and apes. Chimpanzees, although occasionally bipedal, are basically quadrupedal animals, and they lack free use of the arms. They can get around with a bunch of bananas in their arms, but they must always be ready to maintain their balance with the help of a knuckle on the ground. Humans have far less need for caution. Babies may crawl on all fours; old people may rely on canes; but most humans go about with never a thought of support by anything but their two legs. Their hands are free to grab, carry, and manipulate.

Not needing our hands for support, we have been able to use them for more complicated and more creative tasks. With 25 joints and 58 distinctly different motions, the human hand is one of the most advanced mechanisms produced by nature. Imagine a single tool that can meet the demands of tasks as varied as gripping a hammer, playing a violin, wringing out a towel, holding a pencil, and comforting a child with a touch.

Furthermore, while the hand itself may be a marvelous tool, it is used to full value only when it manipulates still other tools. This capacity is a second-stage benefit of upright walking. With our erect posture, our hands are free; with our hands free, we can use tools; with tools, we can get food more easily and exploit the environment in other ways to ensure our survival. Humans are not the only animals that use tools, but they are the only ones that have become *dependent* on tools. (Note, however, that the claim of tool dependency has recently been made for the nut-cracking chimpanzees of the Taï Forest in west Africa [Boesch and Boesch-Achermann, 2000]. This claim will be evaluated in the next chapter.)

Power grip a grip involving all fingers of the hand equally, as in grasping a baseball.

Precision grip a grip that involves opposing the tip of the thumb to the tips of the other fingers, allowing fine control of small objects.

There are two distinct ways of holding and using tools: the **power grip** and the **precision grip,** as John Napier (1970) termed them (Figure 3.17). Human infants and children begin with the power grip and progress to the precision grip. Think of how a child holds a spoon: first in the power grip, in its fist or between its fingers and palm, and later between the tips of the thumb and the first two fingers, in the precision grip. All primates have the power grip. It is the way they get firm hold of a tree branch. But only catarrhine primates have thumbs that are long enough or flexible enough to be completely opposable through rotation at the wrist, able to reach to the tips of all the other fingers and thus provide some degree of precision gripping. Apes and Old World monkeys differ in their grips, however, and unexpectedly, the monkeys are somewhat more like humans. As an adaptation for arboreal arm-swinging and arm-hanging, apes have evolved greatly elongated fingers, exclusive of the thumb. (See the hand length index in Table 3.8.) As a result, apes' thumbs are relatively quite short and, despite their potential full opposability, usually produce only an impaired precision grip (Figure 3.18). Humans' long, fully opposable thumbs and the independent control of our fingers make possible nearly all the movements necessary to handle tools, to make clothing, to write with a pencil, and to play a flute, for example.

TABLE 3.8 Hominoid Comparative Anatomy: Hands and Brains

Trait	Humans	Chimpanzees	Bonobos	Gorillas	Orangutans	Gibbons
Hand length × 100 divided by trunk length[a]	37	49	?	40	53	55
Thumb length × 100 divided by index finger length[a]	65	43	?	47	40	46
Brain size (sexes averaged)	1,330 cc	410 cc	349 cc	506 cc	413 cc	112 cc
Encephalization quotient (EQ)[b]	8.1	3.0	2.4	1.6	2.4	2.6

[a]Note that humans have relatively short hands but long thumbs.
[b]EQ expresses a species' actual brain size relative to the expected brain size calculated from body weight.
Sources: EQ calculations follow "Jerison column" in Aiello and Dean, 1990; Falk, 2000; Schultz, 1968, 1969; Napier, 1970.

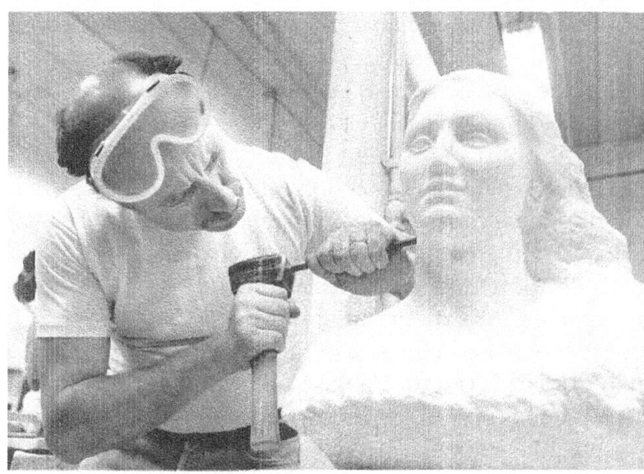

FIGURE 3.17
The power grip (*left*) and the precision grip (*right*) are illustrated in these photographs, together with the uniquely human independent control of the five fingers.

But the fine precision grip of humans would be a much less extraordinary adaptation without the complex brain that coordinates and directs its use. (This is demonstrated by the combination of clever hands and smallish brains, ranging from 60 to 200-plus cubic centimeters [Falk, 2000], in the Old World monkeys.) In the human lineage, manipulation, tool use, and the brain may have developed together. The hand carries out some of the most critical and complex orders of the brain, and as the hand grew more skillful, so did the brain.

The Brain

The human brain is not much to look at. On the dissecting table, it appears pinkish-gray and moist, and its surface is "marked by numerous irregular grooves . . . with intervening rounded eminences" (Goss, 1973:837). An ape's brain does not look very different. But there is a difference, and it is crucial. It lies in the extent of the gray

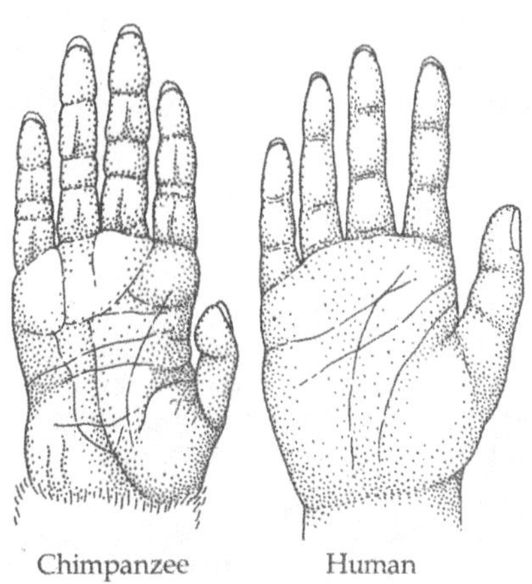

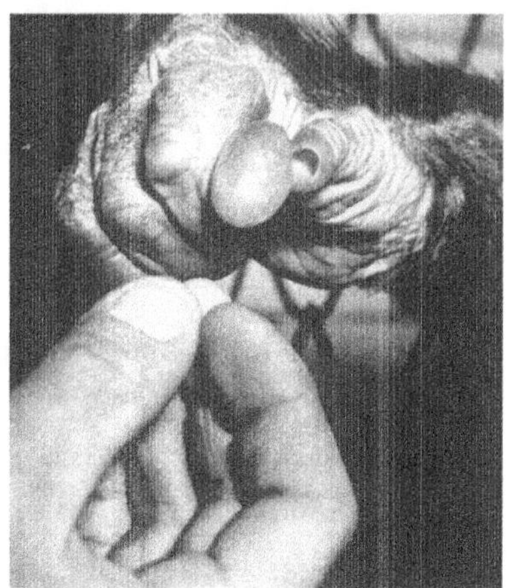

FIGURE 3.18
Although superficially like a human hand, the hand of a chimpanzee has a relatively short thumb and less independent control of the fingers. As the photograph shows, when the chimpanzee picks up an object between finger and thumb, it does not fully oppose the tip of the thumb to the tips of the fingers as do humans. Thus, compared to humans (and Old World monkeys), the ape's precision grip is somewhat impaired.

Neurons nerve cells; the basic units of the nervous system.

layer called the *cortex*, which constitutes the outer layer of the largest part of the brain, the *cerebrum*. The cortex, scientists now know, plays the major role in reasoned behavior, memory, and abstract thought—and also supervises the delicate and accurate muscular movements that control the precision grip (Deacon, 1992b; Washburn, 1960).

The cortex is quite thin, but it represents 80 percent of the volume of the human brain and contains most of the brain's estimated 10 billion nerve cells, or **neurons,** and the neurons' estimated 100 trillion connections (Pinker, 2002). If spread out flat, it would be about the size of a large newspaper page. It fits inside the head only by being compressed like a crumpled rag. This compression demonstrates that the cortex has all but outgrown its allotted space. Indeed, the human brain is more than eight times larger than expected for a mammal of our body size. (See the EQ values in Table 3.8.) Somehow, the increase in the size of the cortex has helped make our brain the uniquely human thing it is (Figure 3.19; see also Chapter 13). Recent work has shown that a gene known as *ASPM*, an important determinant of brain size, has been under intense selective pressure in the last several million years of human evolution (Wade, 2004; Zhang, 2003).

Although many mysteries about the brain remain to be solved, some of its secrets, particularly the importance of the huge cortex, are fairly well understood. The

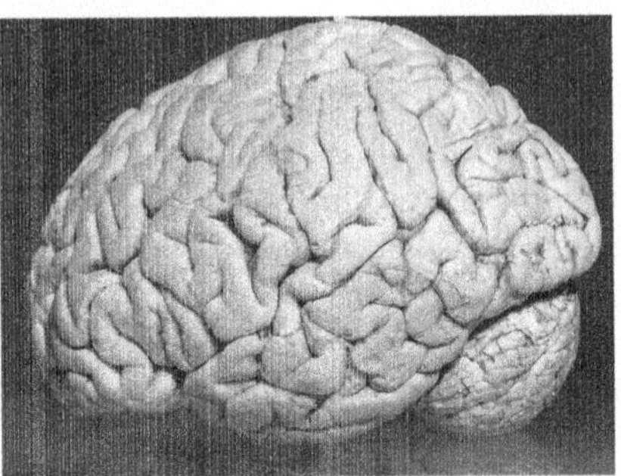

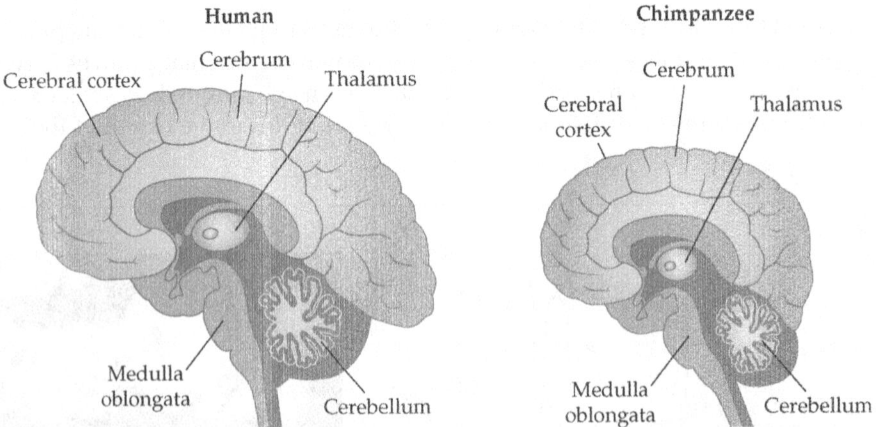

FIGURE 3.19

(top) Conscious mental activity takes place at the surface, or cortex, of the cerebral hemispheres, the two halves of the cerebrum. This cortex has evolved so much in primate evolution that in apes and humans, it is too large to be smooth, as it used to be, and is deeply folded. The bottom diagrams illustrate the importance of the cerebrum and its cortex in humans.

(bottom) Mid-brain view of a human (*left*) and chimpanzee (*right*).

Source: Drawings based on Swindler and Wood, 1973; not to scale. The photo shows a freshly dissected human brain.

cortex is not only the seat of intelligence but also, and perhaps more significantly, the part of the brain where sense impressions and memories are stored to be called forth and acted on as circumstances suggest. The working of the human cortex is affected by both genes and environment (i.e., learning and experience). Although we lack rigidly inborn programs for thinking and behaving, the human brain is equipped with mechanisms that influence what, when, and how easily we learn various things—for example, language and particular behavioral tendencies. As evolutionary biologist Steven Pinker has noted, it appears that the human brain comes "with a battery of emotions, drives, and faculties for reasoning and communicating, and that they have a common logic across cultures, are difficult to erase or redesign from scratch, were shaped by natural selection acting over the course of human evolution, and owe some of their basic design (and some of their variation) to information in the genome" (Pinker, 2002:73). The extent to which the human brain, with its obvious output of *reasoned behavior,* is fundamentally different from the brains of other animals—especially monkeys and apes—is an area of active research. Of particular importance is the question of the uniqueness of the human *mind.*

The most impressive mental ability of humans is not the ease with which we solve problems or reason through behavioral decisions. Rather, it is our ability to look inward and observe our own mental processes: Humans not only think but *know* they are thinking. We are conscious of what we know, believe, and feel, and we recognize knowledge, beliefs, and emotions in other people. (We are also quick to manipulate others' beliefs, emotions, and knowledge to our own advantage.)

In a word, humans have a *mind*—but is this also true of other primates? Primatologists Dorothy Cheney and Robert Seyfarth have summarized much of what is known about the problem of mind among nonhuman primates in their book *How Monkeys See the World* (1990). They find little evidence of mind among monkeys. Although monkeys know a lot about their physical and social environments, they differ from humans in their failure to use knowledge for personal gain—apparently because they "do not know what they know and cannot reflect upon their knowledge, their emotions, or their beliefs" (Cheney and Seyfarth, 1990:254). Monkeys apparently are unable to attribute mental states or impute motives to other individuals, and therefore these concepts do not affect how they behave. Furthermore, monkeys appear to have little if any self-awareness.

But, Cheney and Seyfarth continue, apes may be different. Research on apes (primarily chimpanzees) suggests that these animals may be far superior to monkeys in attributing mental states to each other: "There is strong suggestive evidence that chimpanzees, if not other apes, recognize that other individuals have beliefs and that their own behavior can affect those beliefs. Unlike monkeys, chimpanzees seem to understand each others' goals and motives. They deceive each other in more ways and in more contexts than monkeys, and they seem better than monkeys at recognizing both their own and other individuals' knowledge and limitations" (Cheney and Seyfarth, 1990:254). Very similar sentiments have been expressed recently by Christophe Boesch and Hedwige Boesch-Achermann (2000). Based on their observations of wild chimpanzees in the Taï Forest, they argue strongly that these apes possess a mind of sorts, although undoubtedly somewhat simpler than that of humans. If this proves to be true, an evolutionary continuum from mindless monkeys to mind-possessing humans—with apes in between—will have been demonstrated.

Language and Speech

The large and complex human brain has combined with certain critical bodily modifications to produce perhaps our most obvious unique traits: **language** and **speech.** Although virtually all animals communicate with their fellows, only humans think symbolically and transmit their thoughts by talking. Human speech—the oral expression of language—consists of a repertory of short, contrast-

Language the cognitive aspect of human communication, involving symbolic thinking structured by grammar.

Speech the oral expression of *language,* or spoken language; other expressions include signed and written language.

ing sounds that can be combined in an almost infinite number of ways. While animals communicate emotional state and, on occasion, limited information about their physical or social circumstances, humans routinely engage in complex linguistic exchanges of information or ideas.

Language and speech are so clearly dependent on brainpower that their dependence on the body is often overlooked. The role of the body is most clearly demonstrated by studies of chimpanzees. Chimpanzees have brains that appear to be adequate for some degree of abstract thought (Boesch and Boesch-Achermann, 2000). They can also produce a wide range of sounds. It seems that they should, then, be able to talk. Since the turn of the century, scientists have been trying to teach chimpanzees to speak. The best anyone has been able to do, after years of patient tutelage, is to get a chimpanzee to say "mama," "papa," and one or two other infant words (Jolly, 1985).

Only recently has the reason for this failure been traced. It involves not simply brain size but other aspects of the anatomy. Chimpanzees and gorillas are indeed able to use very simple sentences—but they cannot speak them. These apes lack the kind of pharynx, mouth, and tongue that enable humans to articulate vowels. With training, they can speak somewhat, not with auditory symbols, but with visual ones, such as the symbols of American Sign Language for the deaf or specially designed lexigrams (Jolly, 1985; Rumbaugh et al., 1994). The human remains the only creature that has developed both the physical structures and the powerful, specialized brain needed to produce speech.

Cultural Adaptation

Language was perhaps the last of our major biological characteristics to evolve. And with the gift of speech, we acquired an immensely powerful tool for the development and continuing evolution of the human way of life—a way of life based on cultural adaptation. Unlike the other primates, humans are no longer wholly at the mercy of their surroundings. Faced with environmental challenges, we invent cultural solutions, rather than evolve biological ones. (Apes also do this to a very limited extent, as described in Chapter 4.) Clothes, shelters, and heating and cooling systems help us deal with harsh climatic conditions. Tools, irrigation systems, and pesticides help us aggressively exploit the environment for food. Medical technology helps us deal with diseases and physical handicaps. Furthermore, thanks to language, human knowledge is cumulative: It increases steadily as each new generation's innovations are added to the summed knowledge passed down to it. Thus, **culture** evolves in a Lamarckian fashion, by the inheritance of acquired traits.

Culture humans' systems of learned behaviors, symbols, customs, beliefs, institutions, artifacts, and technology; characteristic of a group and transmitted by its members to their offspring.

The importance of humans' evolution of a wholly cultural way of life cannot be overemphasized. Our reliance on cultural adaptation has set us apart from the other primates. For better or worse, we are the only living primate species that exerts significant control over its own evolutionary future.

Summary

The first primates evolved about 90 million years ago. Today, the order is represented by more than 200 species and is characterized by extreme physical and behavioral diversity. The most basic primate traits—grasping hands and feet and stereoscopic vision with depth perception (plus the neural elaborations that go with these developments)—were most likely originally adaptations for feeding on plant parts and preying on insects in an arboreal habitat.

The living primates can be arranged in two suborders: Strepsirhini and Haplorhini. The strepsirhines were the first suborder to evolve, and today they are characterized by the retention of several primitive anatomical traits, including a keen sense of smell and relatively unprotected eyes. At present, these small (and often nocturnal) creatures are found only in Africa and Asia. The haplorhine suborder, today including tarsiers, monkeys, apes, and humans, first appeared about 45 to 50 million years ago. Compared to strepsirhines, living haplorhines show a reduced sense of smell, elaborated vision, and a more complex brain. Modern monkeys are found in Central and South America (superfamily Ceboidea) and in Africa and Asia (superfamily Cercopithecoidea). Most monkeys show some variety of quadrupedal locomotion in the trees.

The superfamily Hominoidea includes the apes and humans. While humans are found worldwide, apes are limited to Africa (chimpanzees, bonobos, and gorillas) and Asia (gibbons and orangutans). Apes tend to be large, tail-less, arboreal arm-swingers and arm-hangers (or their terrestrial descendants), while humans have evolved into terrestrial bipeds. Hominoids display the largest, most complex brain of all primates. Humans have shown unparalleled brain expansion and elaboration, and they are characterized by the unique possession of a fully developed mind. Other unique traits shown by humans include language and speech and cultural adaptation as a way of life. The latter has given humans considerable control over their evolutionary future.

Postscript

Along with many other species, nonhuman primates are currently in a state of global emergency. Of the 200-plus primate species, more than 50 percent are considered endangered or in some jeopardy, and one in five is likely to become extinct in just a few years if strict conservation measures are not begun immediately (Mittermeier and Cheney, 1987; Wolfheim, 1983). Among the species at greatest risk are several of Madagascar's strepsirhines (white-rumped black lemurs, golden and greater bamboo lemurs, and Tattersall's sifaka), the muriqui monkeys and lion tamarins of South America, the Tonkin snub-nosed monkeys, the Mentawai macaques, and Africa's red colobus monkeys. Most of the living apes are endangered to some degree, including Sumatran orangutans and mountain gorillas (IUCN).

Who is responsible for bringing so many of our evolutionary relatives to the brink of disaster? Unfortunately, we have no one to blame but ourselves. Through our use of primates for food, pets, and research subjects and our destruction of their natural habitats, we have become monkeys', apes' and strepsirhines' worst enemy. Let's consider the problem.

The global population of humans is now over 6 billion; this figure is predicted to rise to more than 10 billion by the middle of this century (Population Reference Bureau). Population growth is uneven from one country to the next, but the highest rates seem generally to be in underdeveloped tropical countries. All of these people need—and demand—food and living space, and in their efforts to meet these needs, they are causing massive habitat destruction. Habitat destruction impinges most directly on primates when it affects the tropical and subtropical forests since, as explained in this chapter, this is where most species naturally occur—and the forests of the world are being ravaged. Every year some 53,000 square miles (more than 137,000 square kilometers) of tropical and subtropical forest are destroyed worldwide—an area as big as the state of North Carolina (Earth Observatory). The forests are cut down to make space for agriculture and ranching, for fuel to be used locally, and for exportable wood. And as the forests go, so do their primate inhabitants. The primate-rich Amazonian forests are expected to be reduced by half in the next 25 years, while the Congo basin forests will decrease 25 percent in the same period (Mittermeier and Cheney, 1987).

In addition to habitat destruction, humans contribute to primate extinction by hunting the animals for food, killing them as pests, and capturing them to sell as pets or research subjects. Although capturing animals for sale has come under some control in the last few decades, it can still have a major impact on marginal species, and it is terribly inefficient: It has been estimated that traditional capture techniques result in five to ten animals killed for every one that is sold (Mittermeier and Cheney, 1987).

What, if anything, can (or should) we do about global habitat destruction and the plight of endangered primates? One response might be that we should do nothing; after all, extinction is a fact of life, and given enough time, the earth will surely adjust to humans' habitat and wildlife depredations. However, is this the wisest course? What do we stand to lose if the forests and their inhabitants are plundered completely? Perhaps we should move quickly to stop the destruction and save the endangered species, but how can we do it? After all, inhabitants of developed countries—comparatively well fed, well housed, and secure—are hardly in a strong moral position to tell people in poor, developing countries how to manage their forests and wildlife. Hard questions. And also questions that demand immediate answers and carry high stakes. What's *your* position on these issues?

Review Questions

1. Review the relative merits of the arboreal and visual predation theories as explanations of the common characteristics of primates. How do the recent discoveries concerning plesiadapiform prehension affect the validity of these theories?
2. Compare the anatomy of strepsirhines to that of haplorhine primates. Can haplorhines be said to have progressed beyond the strepsirhine condition?
3. Why are humans classified as hominoids rather than as monkeys? Describe how human anatomy resembles that of apes and differs from that of monkeys.
4. One can arrange the living primates so that it appears that evolution shaped the creatures to become increasingly humanlike. Discuss this notion of humans being the goal of primate evolution.
5. Do monkeys and apes have minds? Discuss the evidence, and consider the implications of how humans treat these animals.
6. What are the implications of humans now being largely in control of their own evolutionary future?

SUGGESTED FURTHER READING

Cartmill, Matt. "New Views on Primate Origins." *Evolutionary Anthropology,* 1:105–111, 1992.

Cartmill, Matt. "Rethinking Primate Origins." *Science,* 184:436–443, 1974.

Falk, Dean. *Primate Diversity.* New York, W. W. Norton, 2000.

Napier, John R. *The Roots of Mankind.* Washington, DC, Smithsonian Institution Press, 1970.

Napier, John R., and Prue H. Napier. *The Natural History of the Primates.* Cambridge (MA), MIT Press, 1985.

Sargis, Eric. "Primate Origins Nailed." *Science,* 298:1564–1565, 2002.

Schultz, Adolph. *The Life of Primates.* New York, Universe Books, 1969.

Sussman, Robert. "Primate Origins and the Evolution of Angiosperms." *American Journal of Primatology,* 23:209–223, 1991.

INTERNET RESOURCES

PRIMATE INFO NET: ABOUT THE PRIMATES
http://pin.primate.wisc.edu/aboutp

Maintained by the Wisconsin Regional Primate Research Center, this site provides extensive information about primates, as well as many links.

JOURNEY INTO PHYLOGENETIC SYSTEMATICS
www.ucmp.berkeley.edu/clad/clad4.html

Produced by the University of California Museum of Paleontology, this site describes the rationale, methods, and implications of cladistic analysis.

STATE OF THE WORLD'S FORESTS, 2003
www.fao.org/documents/show_cdr.asp?url_file=/DOCREP/005/Y7581E/y7581e00.htm

This extensive report was prepared by the UN Food and Agriculture Organization. See also the sites listed for Chapter 4.

USEFUL SEARCH TERMS:

bipedal locomotion
cladistics
haplorhines (tarsiers and anthropoids)
human anatomy
primates
strepsirhines (prosimians)

Chapter 4

The Behavior of Living Primates

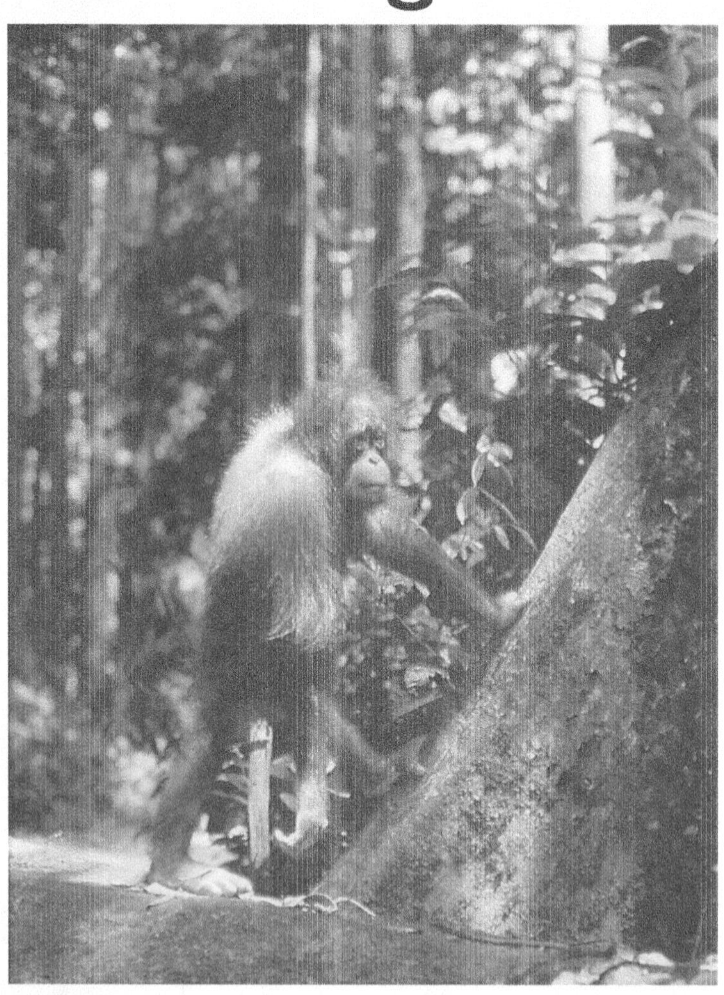

Studies of living apes such as this orangutan can yield important insights into the early stages of human evolution.

We love animals, we watch them with delight, we study their habits with ever-increasing curiosity; and we destroy them.

Kenneth Clark, 1903–1983. *Animals and Men*, Ch. 5.

Overview

The fossilized remains of our extinct ancestors provide important direct information about their anatomy but only limited (and indirect) information about their behavior. In order to make reasonable behavioral reconstructions, researchers often rely on analogies drawn from living human cultures (usually hunting-and-gathering peoples) and nonhuman primates. This chapter presents a broad summary of what scientists have learned about our nonhuman primate kin, including their diets, grouping patterns, social development, sexuality, dominance systems, and affiliative (friendly) relations. Particular emphasis is placed on the various living ape species—gibbons, orangutans, gorillas, chimpanzees, and bonobos—since the fossil record makes it clear that humans are descended from ape stock.

Studying Primates

Fossils can provide a very good indication of the course of evolution, but they are less good at indicating precisely how evolution came about. This limitation has been a source of frustration to anthropologists for many years—so much so that many are now looking for answers elsewhere than in the fossil record. One alternative field that is fruitful is the study of humankind's primate relatives, especially the monkeys and apes; closely related to us, they are even more closely related to our ancestors.

Recent developments in biochemistry have shown close similarities of DNA, cell proteins, and blood proteins including hemoglobin between humans and the other primates (Box 4.1). Now, thanks to an upsurge in studies of monkeys and apes in their natural environments, it is becoming clear that in their social behavior, too, they stand much closer to us than we had suspected. Many, like baboons, live in highly organized and cohesive groups. Others, like chimpanzees, live in more loosely organized communities. Whatever the size or structure of the social unit, some members are good friends, others dedicated enemies; some are collaborators, others rivals; some are popular, others shunned. Infant apes and monkeys, as they grow up, must learn a code of behavior, much as a human child must, and all the members of a group are linked by an elaborate system of communication that uses both sounds and gestures and shows considerable sophistication.

The comparison of ape and monkey behavior with human behavior, of course, must not be pushed too far. Yet in their daily routine and in many aspects of their relationships with their fellows, the nonhuman primates resemble humans in many surprising ways and throw much light on the roots of human behavior.

Early Work

Although new aspects of the connection between us and our primate kin are continually coming to light, the idea of studying primates is by no means a new one.

Casual and anecdotal comments on primates can be traced several centuries into the past but yield little reliable information. It was not until the early twentieth century that scientific studies of monkeys and apes began in earnest (Haraway, 1989; Loy and Peters, 1991; Ribnick, 1982). In the 1920s, psychobiologist Robert Yerkes

BOX 4.1

Biochemical Relations between Humans and Other Primates

Close relationships among humans, apes, and monkeys are demonstrated by our many anatomical similarities, as T. H. Huxley showed in 1863 (Figure 1.11). Within the last forty years, those close relationships have been verified by studies of anthropoids' biochemistry.

As shown in Table 4.1, measures of cross-species reactivity for the protein albumin reveal that humans have much closer links with the living apes than with monkeys or strepsirhines. Our close relations with the other hominoids is also shown by data on DNA hybridization, with the additional revelation that humans are more like the African apes than the gibbons from Asia. (DNA hybridization is a rather complex process that involves splitting a species' double-stranded DNA by heating it, and then comparing the nucleotide sequences on single DNA strands with strands from a second species.) Finally, the pooled results of amino acid sequencing studies of several different proteins go beyond the albumin evidence and suggest that humans are even closer to chimpanzees than to gorillas. (This has been confirmed recently by other genetic studies [Klein and Takahata, 2002].) Note that all of the numbers below can be read simply as measures of *relative evolutionary relationship.*

TABLE 4.1 Relationships between Humans and Other Primates Using Biochemical Markers

Biochemical Marker	Chimpanzee	Gorilla	Gibbon	Old World Monkey	New World Monkey	Strepsirhine	Source
Albumin reactivity	1.14	1.09	1.28	2.45	4.2	8.6	Sarich and Wilson (1967a, b)
DNA hybridization	2.3	2.4	6.4	9	—	—	Beneviste and Todaro (1976)
Amino acid sequencing	0.3	0.6	2.4	3.8	7.5	11.3	Goodman (1975)

Finally, although there is some disagreement among specialists, it seems reasonable to assume that molecular changes occur at approximately the same rate in different lineages of organisms. This means that measures of accumulated change can be used to estimate the date when lines leading to different living species diverged from their common ancestor. In other words, accumulated change can be used to construct **molecular clocks.** Table 4.2 lists humans' molecular divergence dates from the African ape lineage as well as from the lines of several other types of anthropoids. Note that these dates are estimates. Some paleontologists still feel that only fossils can give us conclusive evidence of divergence times.

TABLE 4.2 Estimated Times of Evolutionary Divergence among Higher Primates (in millions of years ago)

Species	Time of Divergence Based on Molecular Clock	Time of Divergence Based on Fossil Evidence
Humans and *Pan*[a]	6–7[b]	5–7
Humans and gorillas	8–10[b]	—
Humans and gibbons	~17[c]	12–21
Humans and Old World monkeys	22–27[c]	15–20
Humans and New World monkeys	~33[d]	~27

[a]Chimpanzees and bonobos.
[b]Dates from Sibley (1992).
[c]Dates from Friday (1992).
[d]Date from Sarich (1992).

observed captive chimpanzees in the United States and later sent two students, Henry Nissen and Harold Bingham, to Africa to study the chimpanzee and the gorilla, respectively. In 1930, Yerkes opened the Laboratories of Primate Biology at Orange Park, Florida, which later moved to Atlanta and were renamed the Yerkes Regional Primate Research Center. Behavioral studies, as well as studies of physiological matters, are carried out at the center.

Molecular clocks a variety of molecular measures for estimating the time of divergence of living *species* from the common ancestor.

The first systematic investigations of the behavior of apes and monkeys living under natural conditions were made by C. R. Carpenter. In the early 1930s, Carpenter journeyed to Barro Colorado Island in Panama to study howler monkeys (*Alouatta palliata*) and then traveled to Southeast Asia to observe gibbons. Later he set up a research colony of rhesus monkeys (*Macaca mulatta*) on Cayo Santiago, Puerto Rico. Carpenter published some revolutionary findings on monkey behavior. The results he obtained by viewing primates in the wild pointed up the limitations of studying primates in captivity, which had been the practice up to that time.

Around the same period, the South African zoologist Solly Zuckerman was studying baboons—first, hamadryas baboons (*Papio hamadryas*) in the London Zoo and then, chacma baboons (*Papio cynocephalus*) in South Africa. Zuckerman was especially interested in what these creatures' behavior might suggest about that of humans. He concluded that sexual behavior was the original force behind social organization among primates (Zuckerman, 1932), an idea that has since been alternately discredited and somewhat revived. But he was seriously misled by studying baboons in the zoo: Their behavior in captivity was quite different from the way they were later found to behave in the wild (Kummer, 1995).

Psychologists, too, took an interest in the behavior of nonhuman primates, particularly that of apes. The German scientist Wolfgang Köhler conducted experiments investigating chimpanzees' capacity to find solutions to problems, such as stacking boxes or using sticks to reach bundles of bananas (Köhler, 1927). In Russia, Nadie Kohts studied chimps' ability to discriminate between objects by size, color, and shape (Yerkes and Yerkes, 1929). And in the United States, Harry and Margaret Harlow studied the mother–infant bond in rhesus monkeys (Haraway, 1989; Jolly, 1985).

It is exceedingly difficult to do some kinds of experimental work in an animal's natural habitat—for example, hormone therapy and psychological testing. But however useful for gauging an individual animal's response to a specific stimulus or situation it is, observing apes or monkeys in artificial confinement provides only partial insight into normal primate behavior. The other handy spot for observation is the zoo, but there, too, the subjects' behavior can be distorted by the abnormal environment (Figure 4.1). For scientists interested in studying normal primate behavior, the best option is to observe monkeys and apes in their natural setting.

A major development in field research occurred after World War II, when primatologists in Japan established the Primate Research Group to study native Japanese macaques (*M. fuscata*) under natural conditions. At Takasakiyama, by setting up feeding stations that a macaque colony with 200-odd members visited regularly, scientists were able to observe one group of monkeys over an extended period (Altmann, 1965). On the island of Koshima, with an isolated macaque population, researchers not only recorded their subjects' customs but to some extent changed them, thereby gaining numerous insights into how the monkeys' behavior and social structure were determined (Kawai, 1965).

Recent Studies

The trend toward studying primates in their native habitats really caught hold in the late 1950s. Led by various anthropologists, a large number of young field workers, including both women and men, began pouring out all over the world from universities and museums in a dozen countries. In the late 1950s, they began by studying langurs and baboons. During the 1960s, they studied rhesus and langur

FIGURE 4.1
For many years, zoos housed primates in unnatural environments, which often resulted in distorted behavior. Here a gorilla has only dry leaves with which to build a nest. Happily, zoos are increasingly providing naturalistic enclosures for their primates (such as the Regenstein Center for African Apes at the Lincoln Park Zoo), although the best behavioral data still come from free-ranging animals.

monkeys in India and gorillas, chimpanzees, and many forest monkeys in Africa. During the 1960s and 1970s, they observed the gibbons and orangutans of southeast Asia. At various times, studies of New World monkeys have been conducted in Central and South America.

Today, roughly three-quarters of a century after the first scientific studies of monkeys and apes, hundreds of primatologists are at work around the world. Boasting their own professional associations and journals, these researchers are racing against the clock and global decay to understand our primate kin before many more species go extinct. As the following sections will show, primate studies have produced a wealth of detail about creatures that are fascinating for their own sake but doubly so for what they may reveal about human evolution.

Basis of Social Organization

Although, as shown in Chapter 3, monkeys and apes differ from each other in important ways, they also share many characteristics. Of these, certainly the most interesting is that they are all social species (except the orangutan) and that their societies are highly organized. We first need to ask ourselves several questions: What are the advantages of social life? Why are so many mammal and bird species social, and why have the Hominoidea developed this characteristic to such lengths? Four kinds of advantage are usually proposed by zoologists:

1. Several pairs of eyes are better than one in the detection of predators and in their avoidance. Defense by a group is also far more effective. Three or four male baboons constitute an impressive display and can frighten any predator, even a lion. A lone baboon is a dead baboon.

2. Competing for large food patches is more successful when done by groups rather than by individuals. We shall see that in some monkeys, social groups subdivide when food is sparse and widely scattered.
3. Reproductive advantages accrue from social groups because regular access to the opposite sex is ensured.
4. Social groups permit extensive socialization with peers and elders and the opportunity to learn from them. Among animals such as the higher primates, this is a factor of the greatest importance.

These factors are probably the most important in bringing about the selection of social life in animals such as primates. Although considerable variation may occur within a species, especially under different environmental conditions, only a few Old World primate species (including the gibbons and the siamang, a large gibbon) normally live in groups consisting of only an adult male, a female, and their young. The orang is unique in being more or less solitary. The remaining Old World monkeys and apes all live in social groups that number as many as 500 individuals but most commonly number between 10 and 50 (see Table 4.3 and Figure 4.2).

Mother + infant; lone males
(e.g., orangutans)

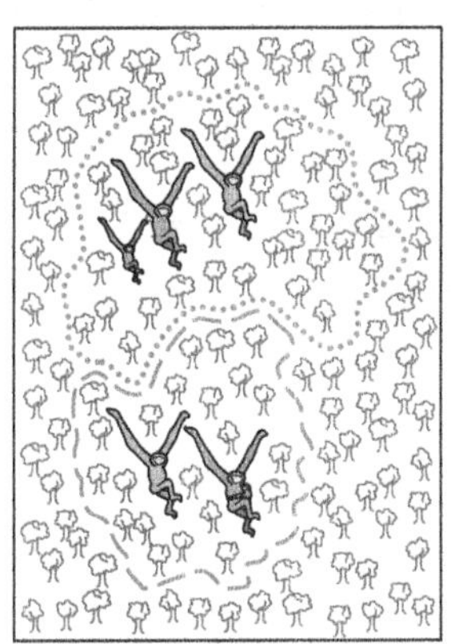

Monogamous family
(e.g., gibbons)

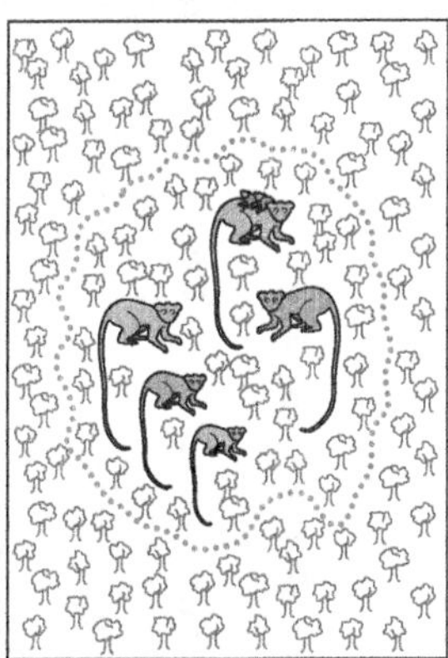

Multimale; unifemale
(e.g., some New World monkeys [*Saguinus*])

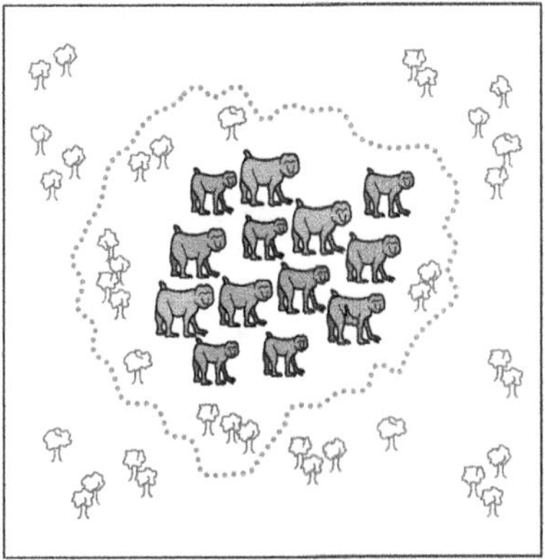

Multimale; multifemale
(e.g., macaques and baboons)

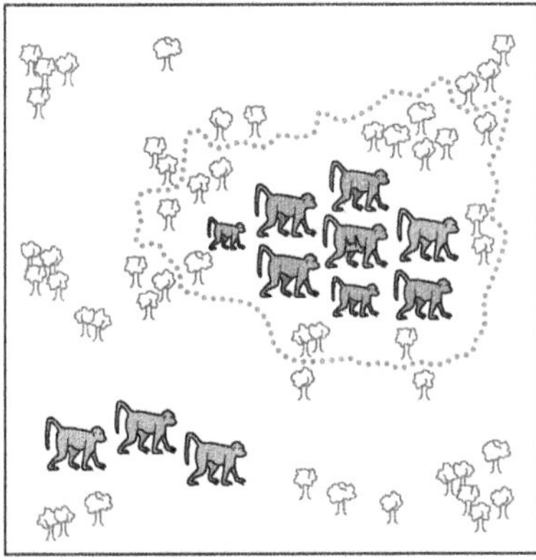

Unimale; multifemale
(e.g., patas monkeys [*Erythrocebus*] and gorillas)

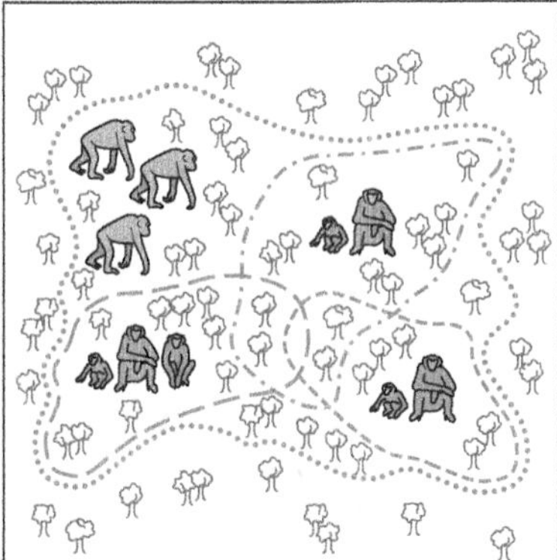

Multimale; multifemale; dispersed or "fusion–fission" community
(e.g., chimpanzees and bonobos)

FIGURE 4.2
Illustrations of the different types of primate society. Adult males are shown in color. Dotted and dashed lines indicate home ranges or territorial boundaries, depending on the species.

TABLE 4.3 Some Socioecological Characteristics of Old World Monkeys and Apes

	Japanese Macaques (*Macaca fuscata*)	Savanna Baboons (*Papio cynocephalus*)	Hanuman Langurs (*Presbytis entellus*)	White-Handed Gibbons (*Hylobates lar*)	Eastern Highland Gorillas (*Gorilla gorilla beringei*)	Orangutans (*Pongo pygmaeus*)	Chimpanzees (*Pan troglodytes*)	Bonobos (*Pan paniscus*)
Group size	35–55	10–185	10–65	Adult pair and 1 or 2 offspring	2–34	2 (mother and offspring)	20–105	50–120
Social structure	Multimale; multifemale	Multimale; multifemale	Multimale; unifemale, and possibly age-graded; multifemale	Monogamous families	Unimale or multimale with one dominant silverback male; also lone males; multifemale	Mother and infant; lone males	Multimale; multifemale; dispersed community	Multimale; multifemale; dispersed community
Habitat	Seasonal, deciduous and evergreen and montane and submontane areas	African acacia woodland, short grass savanna, forest	Deciduous to moist evergreen forests; sea level to high Himalayas	Forest	Lowland and mountain rain forests and bamboo forests	Indonesian jungles; herbivorous (mostly frugivorous) diet	Deciduous woodland; omnivorous (mostly frugivorous) diet	Lowland rain forest and swamp forest; omnivorous (mostly frugivorous) diet
Home range	0.1–10.4 mi^2 (0.27–27 km^2)	0.8–15.4 mi^2 (2.1–40 km^2)	0.04–3 mi^2 (0.1–7.8 km^2)	0.08–0.2 mi^2 (0.2–0.5 km^2)	1.5–4.2 mi^2 (4–11 km^2)	Females: 0.2–3.5 mi^2 (0.6–9 km^2) Males: 1.9–15.4 mi^2 (5–40 km^2)	2–215 mi^2 (5–560 km^2)	7.7–19.3 mi^2 (20–50 km^2)

Sources: Data from Cheney, 1987; Delgado and van Schaik, 2000; Doran and McNeilage, 1998, 2001; Melnick and Pearl, 1987; Nishida and Hiraiwa-Hasegawa, 1987; Rodman and Mitani, 1987; Stewart and Harcourt, 1987.

But how are these societies organized? Far from being structureless, primate societies are remarkably complex and stable. Order is maintained through a complex interrelationship of several factors. One is the animals' prolonged period of dependence: Infant apes and monkeys, like human infants, are far from self-sufficient and maintain prolonged relationships with their mothers. During this time, they learn roles and practice behaviors they will use as adults. Other factors are dominance and hierarchy. In many species, the adults of one or both sexes have quite a well-defined social rank within the group. Also important are the other relationships among adults, which to some extent are determined by kinship, friendship, sexual contacts and competition for resources.

Thinking about these factors, one quickly sees that they are among the most important regulators of human society, as well. Thus, for a very long time (we may assume) and for many species—for humans, for chimpanzees, and for baboons—the problem of life has been and still is largely the problem of getting along in a group.

Learning in Childhood

What is meant by a *prolonged* period of dependence? A kitten has become a cat by the time it is a year old. A comparably sized ring-tailed lemur takes over twice as long to reach adulthood. A male baboon takes seven to eight years to reach full social and biological maturity, a chimpanzee needs anywhere from ten to thirteen years, and a human even longer (Harvey et al., 1987). As a result, family ties—and especially those based on **matrilineal kinship**—among higher primates tend to be strong and lasting. This slow development among a group of supportive relatives is necessary for a higher primate to learn all the things it must to fit itself into a complex society, with many daily choices and varied personal interchange. During this period, the vulnerable young animal is protected by its kin and other members of the group.

Matrilineal kinship kinship traced through the maternal line.

Take chimpanzees, for example. For a young chimpanzee, life is full of learning opportunities: during play, during practice in nest building and tool use, and while watching adults forage, hunt, fight, reconcile, and have sex. Although adult apes are usually inadvertent models, they sometimes deliberately instruct youngsters, as has been observed for nut-cracking techniques among the Taï chimps (Boesch and Boesch-Achermann, 2000). Among humans, all sorts of purposeful teaching are routine. Since chimpanzee behavior, like that of virtually all primates, is based heavily on experience and learning, rather than being rigidly innate, young animals must absorb an enormous amount of social and ecological detail from their elders and peers in order to survive and reproduce. They accomplish this learning in the context of their family (usually, mother–infant and other matrilineal kin; occasionally, biparental units including siblings) and the larger social group. Collectively, the group's adults represent an important pool of knowledge from which youngsters can draw.

Studies of Hanuman langurs in India (Figure 4.3) have yielded a wealth of information on how the infants of one monkey species learn. These large monkeys live in groups containing several adult females and one or more adult males (Table 4.3). The adult females are organized in a dominance hierarchy that is shown by their respective abilities to displace one another from food and other resources. Mothers lavish attention on the distinctively dark new infants, but they also allow other females to hold, carry, and groom the baby—and many females, particularly nulliparous youngsters and pregnant adults, are anxious to engage in such "aunting," or **allomothering.** Mothers must be careful, however, as they sometimes have difficulty reclaiming their infants from high-ranking allomothers (Hrdy, 1977).

Allomothering typically, care or attention directed toward an infant by a female other than its mother (also called *aunting behavior*).

An older infant follows its mother about, copying her actions, learning to forage. It also spends much of its time in energetic activity, running, climbing, chasing, and wrestling—skills that will be invaluable as it reaches adulthood. As it interacts with its fellows, it learns its place in the group and develops socially and physically (Dolhinow, 1999).

Once young langurs are weaned, around the age of fifteen months, they become segregated by sex. Juvenile females mix more and more intimately with the

FIGURE 4.3
A juvenile female langur (*left*) holds a complaining infant while adult females groom each other. As the infants get older, they become more adventurous (*right*).

FIGURE 4.4
An adult male hamadryas baboon hugs an infant while yawning threateningly. Contacts such as these often mark the start of new one-male family units.

adult females and their infants. Now, the juveniles are the allomothers, holding infants and gaining experience for their own future role as mothers. The male juveniles, meanwhile, spend most of their free time playing. As they grow older, their play becomes ever more vigorous and adventurous (Hrdy, 1977). This is the young males' first step toward eventual emigration.

These female–male differences in play-mothering versus rough-and-tumble play are found in many primate species, including humans (Pinker, 2002). Some researchers view play as primarily practice for the behaviors needed for adult survival and reproduction (Hrdy, 1977; Symons, 1978). Others disagree, preferring to interpret play as a process and part "of the environment of development" of young primates (Dolhinow, 1999). Strong arguments can be made for both points of view, and all parties agree that play is a critical part of the transition from immaturity to adulthood (Walters, 1987).

Another factor that influences learning and development in primates is the species-specific pattern of adult involvement with youngsters. Mothers, of course, are involved with infant care and development in all species (Nicolson, 1991), although their styles may vary widely depending on such variables as temperament and dominance rank (Altmann, 1980). Males' involvement with infants is much less common than that of mothers. In monogamous species, males may make large paternal investments, carrying infants and even sharing food with them. In polygynous and promiscuous species—species with lower levels of paternity certainty—males' interactions with youngsters range from simple tolerance to strong attachment (Taub and Mehlman, 1991). At the attachment end of the spectrum, several cases of chimpanzee males "adopting" orphaned infants have been reported (Boesch and Boesch-Achermann, 2000). In an interesting twist of the use of male–infant attachment, hamadryas baboon males often start their one-male family units by first "mothering" infant females who will later become their mates

FIGURE 4.5
Confrontations among savanna baboons usually result in one individual's either presenting its rump in defeat or scampering off. For these two well-matched baboons, however, confrontation has resulted in fighting.

(Kummer, 1995; Figure 4.4). Humans, although displaying a wide variety of mating and marriage systems, are characterized by a very high level of male involvement with infants (Taub and Mehlman, 1991).

The Dominance Hierarchy

Part of growing up in most primate societies is establishing one's place in the group's social hierarchy. The concept of a status or **dominance hierarchy** among social animals is well recognized from chickens to gorillas. Sometimes called a "pecking order," the idea is a simple one. Dominance of one kind or another is a central factor in the social life of many higher primates, but its expression can be either simple or complex.

Dominance hierarchy the rank structuring of a *primate* group, usually based on winning and losing fights. For some purposes, the ranks within a subset of animals, such as the adult males, may be analyzed separately.

We can define *dominance* simply as the relative status or rank of an animal, as determined by its ability to compete successfully with other individuals for varying goals. Contested goals might include access to resources such as favorite foods or sleeping sites. Social resources, such as mates and grooming partners, are also contested. Dominant animals can also direct and control their own and others' aggression; in aggressive encounters, dominant animals consistently defeat less dominant animals (Figure 4.5).

In some species, dominance relationships are clear cut and static, and a social hierarchy can be recognized. Sometimes, such hierarchies are limited to one sex, but in other species, both males and females are integrated into a general hierarchy within which some animals may share a similar rank.

However, dominance hierarchies are always subject to influence by animals' personalities and by social variables, and a particular animal may be dominant or submissive under different circumstances. Successful aggression is not the only behavior that generates high status. An ingratiating personality can gain allies and lead to high status, while an ill-tempered, aggressive animal may get little social support. Alternatively, two or even three individuals may team up as a coalition to hold a top position that none alone could hold (Hall and DeVore, 1965). High-ranking animals move confidently through their troop, others deferring to them as a matter of course. Supportive relatives are particularly important in maintaining status, and macaque and baboon mothers will pass down their status from generation to generation through the female line (Hausfater, 1975; Sade, 1967). Also, among baboons, males of any age consistently dominate females of similar age (Hausfater, 1975). Adult males, however, have to establish their rank from scratch whenever they move from one troop to another (Walters and Seyfarth, 1987).

Dominance hierarchies are not usually stable for long. In one baboon troop studied over a long period, male ranks altered on average every thirteen to twenty-one days, while female ranks altered no more often than every fifty-seven days. Factors that brought about such changes included the movement of males in and out of the troop, births and deaths, and fighting within the troop (Hausfater, 1975).

Sex and Status

One of the most interesting questions for the evolutionary biologist is this: Do dominant individuals produce more young than subordinates? At first glance, this seems obviously to be the case for males, because in many species, such as savanna baboons, dominance can increase a male's sexual access to fertile females. In fact, the situation is anything but straightforward.

Several studies of baboons have reported positive correlations between male rank and reproduction. For example, primatologist Glenn Hausfater (1975) found that higher-ranked males clearly copulated more than lower-ranked males within his study group. To a large extent, this was due to the alpha male's being able to achieve unequaled access to females on the day of ovulation (determined retrospectively from the date of deflation of the females' **sex swellings**). But results such as these seem to be matched by an equal number of studies that find no correlation between male rank and reproduction. Furthermore, since males of many species change ranks frequently, measuring sexual success rates for ranks may not tell us much about the success of individual animals (or at best, we will obtain information on short-term reproductive success). That is, today's alpha male, with his high copulation rate, may well be tomorrow's subordinate male, stuck with a much lower reproductive performance. And males that live for many years may occupy several ranks and experience many fluctuations in their level of reproduction. Until longitudinal studies yield information on males' lifetime histories of rank and reproduction, firm correlations between these factors will remain elusive.

Sex swellings hormone-induced swellings on the hindquarters of certain *primate* females; generally correlated with ovulation.

It is also important to record that female choice does play a part in any male's sexual achievements, and many males court females for long periods of time in order to win their favors. Dominance is not a ticket to unlimited sexual access, although it certainly helps.

The behavior of chimpanzees is most instructive in this matter and shows how flexible the relations between sex and status can be. For some years, it has been known that wild chimpanzee males show at least three mating strategies (Goodall, 1986; Tutin, 1979). If a male is sufficiently high ranking (typically, the alpha male of the community), he may try to monopolize a sexually attractive female (a female with large sex swellings) by preventing the approach of other males. Such sexual possessiveness is often impossible for lower-ranking males, however, who usually opt for the strategy of frequent **opportunistic mating.** (This can involve several males' nonaggressively sharing sexual access to a particular female that copulates with them one after another.) Finally, a male of any rank may attempt—through skillful social manipulation and sometimes aggressive courting—to form a **consortship** with a female, which he then leads away to the periphery of the community range for several days of exclusive mating. Recently, a fourth strategy has been reported, in which two or three male allies cooperate to mate-guard sexually swollen females when there are several other males in the vicinity (Mitani et al., 2002).

Opportunistic mating mating done whenever and wherever the opportunity presents itself and with whatever partner is available.

Consortship generally, a period of exclusive sexual association and mating between a female and a male.

In general, then, wild chimpanzee males attempt to exert their dominance rank for reproductive gains whenever possible, but when this strategy is unworkable, they easily shift to other mating patterns, all of which include some likelihood of fathering infants. A recent overview of the connection between male rank and reproductive success concluded that there is a positive, albeit modest, correlation between these variables (Mitani et al., 2002; see also Boesch and Boesch-Achermann, 2000; Goodall, 1986). That is to say, males' efforts at achieving a high dominance rank probably result in some increased reproductive success, but mid- and low-ranking males may still sire some infants. Undoubtedly, female mate choice comes into play here. And to complicate the matter even further, there is evidence that the occasional chimp female is impregnated by a male from outside her community. This is almost certainly a rare event, however (Mitani et al., 2002), despite initial suggestions to the contrary (Gagneux et al., 1997).

Savanna baboons have been studied in great detail over many years by Shirley Strum at Gilgil in Kenya (Strum, 1987). It is now clear that adolescent males leave their home troops as a matter of course and move to neighboring troops. Here they attempt to become assimilated by making friends with high-ranking females. The approach to the female is made very slowly over a long period of time, and in due course, if the male is accepted, he begins to play with her infant for hours. Males generally make friends with infants as a means of winning female trust and of neutralizing the aggression of other males. If such a male becomes accepted by the female, he courts her and becomes her "friend," thereby becoming a full member of the troop. If he is sufficiently ingratiating and clever in developing his relationships, he may be able to copulate with this female or other females when they are sexually swollen. Among the Gilgil baboons, sexual conquest can be achieved more effectively by building friendships than by achieving dominance in the male hierarchy.

Males' ranks and reproductive strategies are only half of the story, of course: Females' dominance and mating patterns are equally fascinating. Longitudinal observations of baboons and better knowledge of kin relationships within the baboon troop have revealed that the long-term stability of the group depends not so much on the males as on the high-ranking females that constitute an ongoing aristocracy of their own, based on mother–daughter and sister–sister ties. Once established, this matrilineal aristocracy tends to perpetuate itself: The hierarchy of females is much more stable than that of males (Hausfater, 1975). The privileged—and usually related—females groom each other sociably, bringing up their infants in an atmosphere of comfort and security that is denied low-ranking females.

With regard to the question of female rank and reproductive success, recent studies have shown that the situation is just as complex as among males. Observations of the savanna baboons that inhabit Tanzania's Gombe National Park have shown that high-ranking females enjoy significant *short-term* advantages in reproduction compared to low-ranking females. Probably because of greater access to food, dominant females have shorter interbirth intervals, greater infant survival, and accelerated maturation of their daughters (Packer et al., 1995). These results seem to provide clear evidence why competition for rank would be beneficial for female baboons.

But short-term benefits can be deceptive, and among the Gombe baboons, no overall relationship exists between *lifetime* reproductive success and female dominance. This is because achieving and maintaining high rank takes a significant long-term reproductive toll on many females. Compared to low-ranking animals, dominant females experience a higher incidence of miscarriage and run a greater risk of being chronically infertile. Such stress-related reproductive failure represents the cost females pay for being at the top of the dominance hierarchy—a cost that is probably great enough to prevent female baboons from evolving into hyperaggressive status seekers (Dunbar, 1995; Packer et al., 1995).

In contrast to the baboon studies, however, analyses of thirty-five years of dominance and reproduction data from the female chimpanzees at Gombe *do* suggest lifetime benefits for high-ranking individuals. In a study that parallels many of the baboon findings, primatologists Anne Pusey, Jennifer Williams, and Jane Goodall (1997) recently reported that in comparison to lower-ranked individuals, dominant female chimps have significantly higher rates of infant survival, more rapid production of young, and daughters who mature (and thus begin their own reproductive careers) faster. It appears that high rank enables female chimpanzees to gain access to the best food sources, and being better nourished enhances maternal and infant health, as well as daughters' maturation rate. High-ranking female chimps probably escape negative stress effects (such as those identified for female baboons) because chimpanzee communities are dispersed and females typically forage alone (see Figure 4.2).

Overall, then, high rank has been shown to produce short-term reproductive benefits for both males and females in many primate species. Lifetime benefits, however, are harder to document, although they do seem to occur among female chimps. In any event, status hierarchies represent one means by which natural selection has brought order and organization to primate society. The tendency for an individual to attempt to increase its status is deep seated and is expressed among most higher primates and indeed, most social animals. Human societies are no exception: Status is just as pervasive and just as variable in its mode of expression as it is among other primates.

Sexual Physiology and Behavior

As we saw earlier, Solly Zuckerman's (1932) observations of hamadryas baboons in the London Zoo led him to conclude that the members of primate groups are bound to each other by the year-round urge to satisfy their sexual needs. This theory was bolstered by the effects of studying primates in zoos and laboratories, where seasonal reproductive cycles may be distorted and there may be an unusual use of sexual behavior to establish dominance and submission. Actually, as field studies have shown, many monkeys—for example, the rhesus and the Japanese macaques—breed only in a specific season, and their closely knit societies continue even when there is no primary sexual activity (Lindburg, 1971; Loy, 1971). Thus, the study of captive animals alone can prove misleading, and such data should be checked against field observations.

All Old World monkeys, apes, and humans share a basically similar sexual anatomy and physiology (Dixson, 1998). The ovarian–uterine cycle is about 28–35 days in length, with ovulation occurring near the middle and menstruation (shedding of the uterine lining) at the end. Counting the interval between periods of menstrual bleeding produces a measure of the **menstrual cycle.** Mapped on top of the menstrual cycle, however, is a pattern of behavioral fluctuation called the **estrus cycle.** In response to the changing levels of their sex hormones (mainly the estrogens and progesterone), primate females show monthly cycles in sexual **attractiveness** and **receptivity** and in their tendency to initiate mating. (This is called their degree of **proceptivity** [Beach, 1976].) A sexually active female—one that is simultaneously attractive, proceptive, and receptive—is commonly labeled as being in **estrus.** (In some species—baboons and chimpanzees, for example, as described earlier—females in estrus also display large, colorful sex swellings around the vulva, but it is behavior and not swelling or color that marks a female as estrous [Heape, 1900].)

Menstrual cycle the interval (generally, monthly) between periods of menstrual bleeding; especially characteristic of *catarrhine* females.

Estrus cycle the interval between periods of sexual *attractiveness* and activity of *primate* females; correlated with ovulation and the *menstrual cycle* but with great flexibility among *catarrhines*.

Attractiveness in *primate* studies, the aspect of female sexuality reflected by attention from males.

Receptivity the aspect of female sexuality reflected by cooperating in copulation.

Proceptivity the aspect of female sexuality reflected by inviting copulation.

Estrus the period, usually around ovulation, of sexual *attractiveness* and activity by *primate* and other mammalian females

Old World monkey and ape females show great flexibility in the occurrence of sexual behavior throughout the menstrual cycle. Copulations may occur early in the cycle, at ovulation, or near menstruation. (Pregnant females also continue to mate.) Indeed, females seem to have a moderate level of situation dependency in their sexual behavior that allows them to use sex to their advantage (perhaps to fool a potentially infanticidal male or to accommodate a sexually insistent one), regardless of their ovarian or hormonal condition. Nonetheless, among monkeys and apes, *most* sex takes place near ovulation during a period of estrus that lasts a week or so (Dixson, 1998; Hrdy and Whitten, 1987; Loy, 1987).

One of the primary differences between nonhuman primates and humans is the fact that women do not show strong estrus-type peaks in sexual behavior. Extending the sexual flexibility characteristic of monkeys and apes, human sexual behavior is marked by extreme situation dependency and mating throughout the menstrual cycle and during pregnancy. Although humans may retain some mild midcycle remnants of estrus (experts disagree on this point), it is clear that our sexual behavior is much more flexible and less controlled by hormones than that of our nonhuman relatives. But it is important not to overstate the contrast. While humans no longer show clear-cut estrus, monkeys and apes seem to anticipate human behavior with their moderate degree of situation dependency (Hrdy and Whitten, 1987; Loy, 1987). A pair of interesting questions is how and why hominins evolved such an extremely flexible system of sexual behavior (see Chapter 9).

The overt activities of nonhuman primate sexual behavior contrast with the covert nature of most human sexual behavior. For example, among nonhuman primates, sexual advances and mountings may occur at any time to reduce tension and appease anger. Male–male, male–female, female–male, and female–female mountings are commonly seen. Touching of genitals may occur as a greeting and is often seen in grooming sessions to solidify social relationships. Homosexual behavior, which is quite distinct from the social mountings mentioned above, has been described in several species. Sex is indeed a continuous and rich part of primate social life (de Waal, 2001; Dixson, 1998; Wolfe, 1991).

Sexual Selection among Primates

In 1871, Charles Darwin noted that competition for mates is unequal between the sexes of most species. The more vigorously competing sex tends to be bigger, and male–female differences in body form and color, decorative appendages, and behavioral displays may evolve, as well (Darwin, 1871/1981). In many primate species, males compete for females, since access to females sets an upper limit on males' reproductive success. (This is true of all mammals [Trivers, 1985].) This may be the reason that males tend to be larger than females—a form of **sexual dimorphism** that is not uncommon. Great apes, various baboon species, and a number of other monkeys have very considerable differences between the sexes in body size, weight, and size of canine teeth (see Table 3.6). Shoulder breadth and striking hair forms are often well developed in the males (Figure 4.6). Sex differences in size may vary from females being 50 percent the size of males among gorillas and baboons

Sexual dimorphism characteristic anatomical (and behavioral) differences between males and females of a *species*.

FIGURE 4.6 Hamadryas female with young and a male. The male is larger and heavier, and he carries a magnificent mane, which makes him look even larger. Males are also armed with huge canines, as shown in Figure 4.4.

to 78 percent among chimpanzees, 81 percent among humans, and 94 percent (near equality) among gibbons (Table 3.6).

It was once claimed that large, aggressive baboon males evolved as protectors of the troop against predators. If we look at higher primates as a whole, however, a much better explanation is the correlation between reproductive system and sexual dimorphism. **Monogynous** species, in which neither sex competes strongly for additional mates (for example, gibbons), show little sexual dimorphism. **Polygynous** species (such as savanna baboons), which live in multimale troops and offer greater sexual opportunities to large, powerful males, are quite dimorphic. It seems that in such a dimorphic species, both natural selection and sexual selection are generating large males. A comparison of dimorphism and the breeding system in a whole range of primates is considered by some primatologists to support this conclusion, although others are not sure whether intermale competition for mates is a fully adequate answer (Fedigan, 1982).

Monogyny in zoology, generally having only one mate.

Polygyny in zoology, the tendency for a male to have regular sexual access to two or more females.

Indeed, several other factors could be driving sexual dimorphism in body size among primates. It seems likely that larger males may be more successful at defending females and their infants against **infanticidal** attacks by other (usually, outsider) males. Such attacks have been documented in numerous species of monkeys, as well as among gorillas and chimpanzees (Enstam et al., 2002; Hrdy, 1977; Mitani et al., 2002; Struhsaker and Leland, 1987). In several of these cases, infant killing has been identified as an evolved strategy for male–male reproductive competition, since it not only eliminates rival males' progeny but also can function to shorten the time before the mother of the dead infant can conceive the infanticide's baby (Hrdy, 1977).

Infanticide the killing of infants.

Furthermore, several researchers have suggested that perhaps instead of focusing entirely on the benefits of an increase in males' size, we should examine "the adaptive advantages of females having become smaller" (Fedigan, 1982:59). Perhaps smallness in females has been selected for in order to reduce their nutritional needs in a poor environment, subject to the requirements of their reproductive physiology. There is some evidence to support this point of view, and it is becoming increasing clear that sexual dimorphism in size probably represents a grand evolutionary compromise of several factors acting on both males and females.

Finally, as Darwin pointed out, sexual selection has two faces, and same-sex competition (such as the male–male competition just discussed) is only one. The second kind of sexual selection involves members of one sex exercising a deliberate choice of certain traits in the opposite sex. If two males fight over a female and the victor then forces his attentions on her, the female cannot be said to have exercised much choice—or she had a "Hobson's choice," at best. (Mate with any male you choose, so long as you choose the winner of the fight.) But female primates do much more than make Hobson's choices. Like males, females have sexual strategies shaped by evolution to maximize reproductive success, and an important part of those strategies is playing an active role in mate selection.

Primatologist Meredith Small (1993) has recently reviewed the patterns of mate selection by primate females, and several of her conclusions are startling. She believes that females are more sexually assertive and less picky about their mates than has traditionally been held. Rather than waiting coyly for a male suitor, females are often sexually aggressive and actively solicit males. Further, females sometimes choose *not to be selective* and, as a result, mate rather promiscuously with the males of their group. Or they may make choices that seem to make little theoretical sense, as when they prefer outsiders of unknown fitness over male group mates characterized by proven fitness. Small concluded that primate females' main objective is to conserve time within their reproductive careers. "Get pregnant as soon as possible" seems to be the overriding guideline; the identity of the baby's father seems considerably less important. Small's views have aroused a good deal of controversy among primate researchers, but they are of extraordinary value in reminding us that it's not only males who do the sexual choosing.

FIGURE 4.7
Grooming has two main functions: to remove parasites and keep the fur clean and to establish and maintain social relationships. Here a relaxed female baboon encourages a dominant male to groom her, while a lower-ranking male watches from a proper distance.

Grooming and Social Interaction

Perhaps the most commonly observed form of social contact between higher primates is grooming. One monkey or ape grooms another by picking through its fur to clean out dirt, as well as parasites, which it then eats. Physically, grooming is an important cleaning mechanism, and it is highly effective. But to primates, grooming is far more than a form of hygiene. It is the most important means of social interaction among members of a group, and it serves a variety of purposes (Sade, 1965). For example, grooming seems to be an effective instrument for reducing tension of all kinds, as shown by baboons, macaques, and chimpanzees. At other times, it serves simply as an enjoyable pastime when the group is not in search of food. Much as humans gather in conversation groups, monkeys gather in grooming groups. The same function is served: the maintenance of friendly social relations. Being groomed is obviously enjoyable; the groomed animal sits or lies in an attitude of beatific contentment (Figure 4.7). Most grooming is done by females, and mothers regularly groom their young from birth. Subordinates groom their social superiors much more frequently than they are groomed in turn (Seyfarth, 1977). As one might expect, dominant males get much grooming and give little.

All of these observations suggest that grooming and sociality are complexly intertwined among primates—an arrangement that can have both health and reproductive benefits, as demonstrated among baboons. UCLA anthropologist Joan Silk and her colleagues recently reported that savanna baboon females that scored high on a "sociality index" (based on giving and receiving grooming and sitting near other adults) also had the highest one-year infant survival rates (Silk et al., 2003).

Nonetheless, while grooming appears simply to benefit all participants, when examined more closely, it also can be seen to carry costs in terms of the time involved—time that could have been directed toward other vital activities, such as foraging, mating, and resting. Since this is the case, it is not surprising that in many primate species, the vast majority of grooming episodes are between genetic kin (Gouzoules and Gouzoules, 1987; Kurland, 1977; Sade, 1965). This pattern, demonstrated elegantly for Japanese monkeys by Jeffrey Kurland, almost certainly evolved through the operation of kin selection, since grooming relatives should increase the inclusive fitness of all parties. Frequent grooming between pairs of nonrelatives, on the other hand, may well be due to evolved patterns of **reciprocal altruism,** in which both partners' overall fitness is improved by the regular exchange of altruistic favors (Trivers, 1985). Kurland's data also appear to document several cases of reciprocal grooming among nonkin pairs of macaques (Kurland, 1977, as cited by Gray, 1985).

Reciprocal altruism the trading of apparently altruistic acts by different individuals at different times; a variety of *bioaltruism.*

Kinship, reciprocity, sex, and dominance—these variables and others provide structure for the social groups of primates. Precisely how that structure is expressed, however, is strongly affected by the animals' physical environment, and it is to that topic that we now turn.

Territory and Ecology

The relationship between the social group and its environment is ultimately determined by the distribution and density of the natural resources essential to the animals' survival, by the density of competing animals (including humans), and by the pressure of predators. The social group becomes associated with a recognizable area of land or forest—called the **home range**—which contains sufficient space, food, water, and safe sleeping sites for all its members. Behavioral mechanisms bring about this spacing, which reduces the possibility of overexploiting the food resources and of having conflict over those resources. The home range of savanna baboons may be partly shared with other groups of the same species; it is always shared with other species, often with other primate species. Within this range, it is usually possible to define smaller areas—called **core areas**—containing resources absolutely essential for survival—in this case, sleeping trees (Figure 4.8). A core area becomes defended **territory** when it is actively defended against intruders from neighboring groups.

Home range the area a *primate* group uses for foraging, sleeping, and so on in a year.

Core area a portion of the *home range* that is used frequently.

Territory the area occupied and defended by individuals or groups of animals against *conspecifics.*

Different primate species use space in very different ways. In many species—such as savanna baboons (Figure 4.9), some vervet monkeys (*Cercopithecus aethiops*), orangutans, and gorillas—neighbors simply avoid each other by staying at a distance. At the other extreme, gibbons of both sexes display vigorously at the boundaries of their precisely defined territories to demonstrate their occupation of the area and their ferocity (Leighton, 1987), and male chimpanzees routinely patrol their territorial

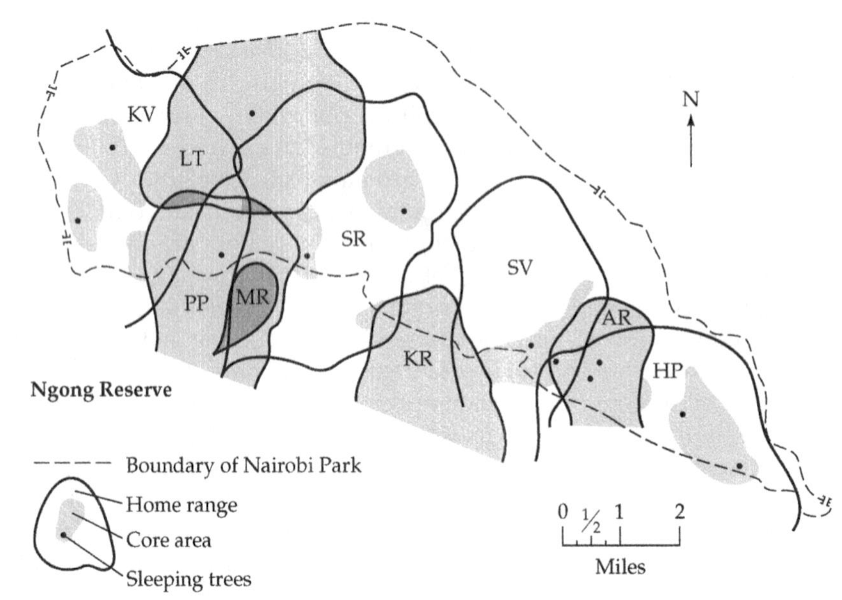

FIGURE 4.8
This plan shows the home ranges and core areas of the baboon troops in the Nairobi Park in 1960. The home ranges overlap considerably, but the core areas, which contain the baboons' sleeping trees, essential to each troop, are quite distinct. The letters refer to the different troops studied.

Source: Based on DeVore and Hall (1965).

FIGURE 4.9
Groves of sleeping trees, to which a savanna baboon troop returns each night, are an essential feature in the home range of every troop in open savanna country. In this photograph, the troop has left its grove of acacia trees at dawn and is preparing to move out into the open grasslands to feed.

boundaries watching for strangers (Boesch and Boesch-Achermann, 2000; Goodall, 1986). In some other primate species, groups may sometimes interact aggressively if they meet by chance, demonstrating a clear territorial sense (Cheney, 1987).

Why do some species defend a territory while others do not? The answer is uncertain, and a number of factors may be in operation. The resource base seems to be the key, and it appears that if food is patchy in space and unpredictable in time, an optimum feeding strategy is to form large groups and range over considerable areas of land (e.g., savanna baboons). Where food is concentrated in space and reliable in supply, the smaller groups may occupy a fixed and limited area (e.g., gibbons), and it is both possible and worthwhile to defend such an area. In the case of gibbons, the ultimate small group has evolved: a monogynous pair characterized by sexual equality of status and a sharing of social roles not found in other species.

In contrast, savanna baboons and some other monkeys that cover large home ranges are polygynous to **promiscuous,** having multimale groups. They do not defend their extensive home ranges and are not capable of doing so. The contrast in the use of space, the quality of the environment, and reproductive system is clear and significant.

Promiscuous both females and males having multiple sexual partners.

It must be added, however, that food distribution is not the whole story. Other essential resources—such as sleeping trees or cliffs (in treeless habitats) and water supply and forest density—may also contribute to how a primate species uses its environment and what form its reproductive system will take. The exact mechanisms operating and the factors involved are still poorly understood. The study of **socioecology** has produced important insights into primate behavior and social organization, as exemplified by the following thumbnail sketches of two types of baboons.

Socioecology the connection between *species'* ecological relations and their social behaviors; also the study of this connection.

Socioecology of East African Baboons

Baboons are extremely adaptable animals; they have not become as physically specialized as many other species, and they are thus able to suit themselves to a wide variety of living conditions. With no material culture to rely on, however, baboons must change their behavior and social organization in order to adapt to different environmental conditions.

Female-bonded groups social groups organized around a set of matrilineal families linked by bonds between the matriarchs.

Female philopatry when females live and reproduce in their natal group for life.

The savanna baboon generally lives close to trees to which it can flee and in which it can sleep and in a climate where there is a year-round supply of food, albeit sometimes patchily distributed. In this setting, baboons' **female-bonded** troops—consisting of several matrilineal families linked by bonds between the matriarchs, plus an assortment of immigrant adult males—are the key units in intergroup competition for food. Troops are built up through **female philopatry** and male transfers and occasionally exceed 150 animals in size (Table 4.3). As described earlier, within the troop, both female and male dominance hierarchies are discernable, ranks of mothers influence youngsters' ranks, and adult males dominate everyone. Intergroup competition for food patches and sleeping groves may take the form of threatening or fighting, or it may be a simple matter of smaller troops avoiding larger ones (Wrangham, 1987).

Harem polygyny in zoology, a group including one breeding male and multiple females; among humans, one husband and multiple wives and concubines.

Hamadryas baboon society is different. This baboon lives in dry and rocky sections of Ethiopia and the near desert of Somalia. In this environment, one-male groups characterized by **harem polygyny** are the rule the year round, although for safety, many groups come together at night on the sleeping cliffs. Hamadryas females transfer from their natal units, and therefore female–female relations within harems are not close (Kummer, 1995). The male–female relationship is more close knit. Each hamadryas male is continuously jealous of his harem, requiring his females to stay very close at all times. When he moves, they move—or get bitten. In hamadryas baboons' harsh and dry environment, where food is extremely widespread and dispersal is more important than direct confrontation with other foraging units, small one-male (polygynous) groups are an appropriate response.

Primate Feeding Strategies

Just as *reproductive strategy* refers to all those adaptations that maximize reproductive success, so a *feeding strategy* comprises the anatomical, physiological, and behavioral characteristics that permit animals to obtain energy efficiently by food acquisition. The strategy that should be favored by natural selection is the one that is most effective in metabolically converting food resources into energy and that is least expensive in terms of energy expenditure. A feeding strategy is optimal when, in addition to providing essential nutrients, its net energy yield per unit of time is at its highest.

Several kinds of feeding strategy can be identified among primates, and they are intimately connected with the animals' size, digestive capacity, and metabolic requirements. Small primates, like all small mammals, have high metabolic rates but relatively low total daily food requirements. This means that they need food items that deliver high energy levels per unit of body weight but not much food overall. Furthermore, being small, they have limited gut capacities that render them unable to retain food in the body and digest it slowly. Combined, these factors dictate that small primates will concentrate on high-energy, easily digested foods that may be very patchily distributed (rare) in the environment (Conroy, 1990; Richard, 1985).

Large primates, on the other hand, have rather the reverse set of requirements. They have relatively low metabolic rates but high total daily food requirements. Their bulky bodies need more food overall but a lower energy intake per unit of body weight. Additionally, thanks to their larger guts, big primates can digest hard-to-process foods in a leisurely fashion. Combined, these factors dictate that large primates will concentrate on low-energy and less-digestible food items that are readily available and can be consumed in bulk. Medium-sized primates should occupy a middle ground between the two metabolic and dietary extremes (Conroy, 1990; Richard, 1985).

When one categorizes primates' main food items in terms of abundance, energy content, and digestibility and then correlates the categories with body size, the results

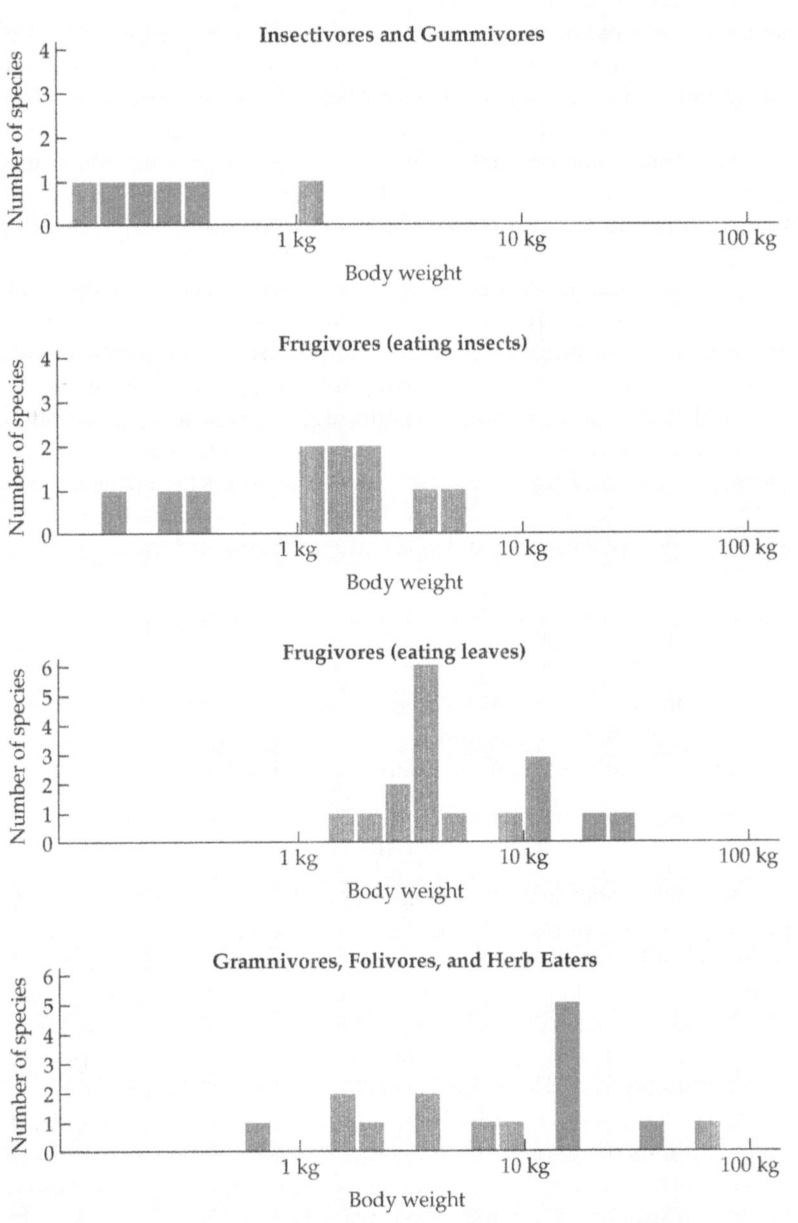

FIGURE 4.10
Grouping primate species by body weight and primary dietary component reveals correlations between these variables.

Source: Alison Richard, *Primates in Nature* (p. 185). New York, Freeman, 1985. Copyright W. H. Freeman and Company.

are instructive (Figure 4.10). The smallest primates (numerous strepsirhines and also tarsiers) subsist mainly on insects and/or gum—both easily digested foods—with insects being rare and high energy and gum being lower in energy but relatively abundant. Small- to medium-sized primates, such as South American capuchin monkeys (*Cebus*), eat mainly fruit (intermediate energy level, somewhat harder to digest, patchy but not rare) and some insects. Medium- to large-sized creatures, such as gibbons and spider monkeys, are fruit eaters who also ingest some leaves (low energy, hard to digest, abundant). And finally, the largest primates, including some of the bigger monkeys and apes, eat mainly the structural parts of plants—leaves, seeds, grass blades, and corms—all of which are abundant, medium to low in energy, and generally hard to digest. (Note, however, that while these are useful generalizations, there are also exceptions to the rule relating diet to body size [Richards, 1985].)

Dietary specialties are sometimes correlated with anatomical differences. For example, consider the large stomach of leaf-eating Colobine monkeys (*Colobus*), which consists of a forestomach (in which cellulose is digested) followed by a series of saclike chambers. Dietary specializations also tend to be correlated with dental differences among primate species. For example, animals such as tarsiers that commonly eat insects usually have enlarged and pointed incisors and canines for killing prey, and tall, sharp cusps on their molars and premolars for shearing insects into tiny, digestible fragments. Specialized leaf eaters likewise have high-crowned molars and premolars for slicing up foliage (this aids in the digestion of cellulose), but their incisors tend to be rather narrow. And finally, species that eat mainly fruits show yet another combination of traits: large, broad incisors with straight cutting edges (an adaptation for biting off chunks of tough-skinned fruits) and relatively small, low-crowned molars (which are adequate because the inner flesh of fruit is generally soft and needs little chewing) (Conroy, 1990). Information on the dental adaptations and the diet and body size generalizations of living primates can serve as a basis for inferring the food preferences of fossil species.

Finally, it should be noted that although primate species are often categorized by the principle components of their diets as **insectivores** (insect eaters), **gummivores** (gum eaters), **frugivores** (fruit eaters), **folivores** (leaf eaters), and **gramnivores** (grain or seed eaters), such labels are rather gross generalizations and may hide considerable dietary variation and cross-category consumption.

Insectivore as a dietary classification, a *species* that primarily eats insects.

Gummivore as a dietary classification, a *species* that primarily eats gum.

Frugivore as a dietary classification, a *species* that primarily eats fruit.

Folivore as a dietary classification, a *species* that primarily eats leaves and other foliage.

Gramnivore as a dietary classification, a *species* that primarily eats grain and other seeds.

The Apes

The environmental adaptations of the monkeys and their social organization make their study of interest to us, but it is, of course, not the monkeys but the apes that are our closest relatives among nonhuman primates.

Asiatic Apes: Gibbons and the Orangutan

Gibbons (six species including siamangs) and the orangutan are Asiatic apes. By a great number of external and internal measurements, including genetic ones, they are remarkably different from chimpanzees, bonobos, and gorillas. In fact, they are in some ways less like chimpanzees than are humans. These differences indicate separations far back in time, between 12 and 21 million years ago for gibbons and 13 to 16 million years ago for orangutans—long before the separation of human, gorilla, bonobo, and chimpanzee (see Table 4.2 and Sibley [1992]).

As we have seen, both gibbons and the orangutan are tree-dwelling animals today. Millions of years of climbing and reliance on the fruits and leaves of jungle trees has brought them to an extreme point of arboreal specialization. In the trees, they move superbly, each in its own way. The gibbon (Figure 4.11) is an airy flier that hangs from branches, swinging from one to another in a breathtaking arc, grabbing the next branch just long enough to launch itself in the direction of a third. For this brachiator, arms and hands are everything. Its fingers are extremely long, specialized to serve as powerful hooks to catch branches. Being the smallest ape, it has the smallest brain at 112 cubic centimeters (Table 3.8).

The orangutan is quite different (Figure 4.12). It is much larger: Adult males weigh more than 150 pounds (68 kilograms), compared to the gibbons' 11 to 24 pounds (5 to 11 kilograms) (Table 3.6). Obviously, an animal of this size cannot go careening through the branches. Orangutans have developed four prehensile hands that are well adapted to seizing or holding, and their limbs are so articulated that they can reach in any direction. There is almost nowhere in a tree that an orangutan cannot safely go, despite its great bulk, by careful gripping and climbing. The orangutan also has an absolutely larger brain than the gibbon (413 cubic centimeters on average), but when *relative* brain size is measured using the encephalization quotient (EQ), the two apes are seen to be very similar (Table 3.8).

The grouping patterns and mating systems of gibbons and orangutans are very different. Gibbons form monogynous families that are usually long lasting. Adult

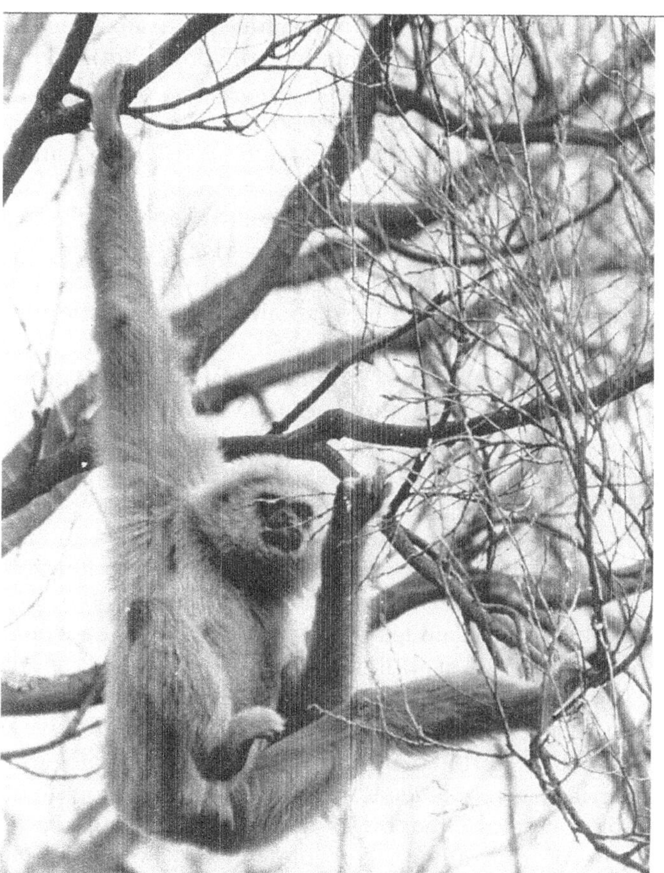

FIGURE 4.11
A gibbon hangs by an arm and steadies itself with a foot while feeding.

FIGURE 4.12
The orangutan of Indonesian Sumatra and Kalimantan (Borneo) is the most seriously threatened of the great apes. It has immensely long arms and relatively short legs with short thumbs and big toes. It is mainly arboreal but does cover considerable distances on the ground in emergencies. This is a juvenile.

Monomorphic both sexes showing the same trait (e.g., similar body size).

males and females are **monomorphic** in body size and canine tooth length and, as a result, are often codominant (equally dominant). Both sexes actively defend the family's arboreal territory (0.08 to 0.2 square miles; or 0.2 to 0.5 square kilometers) against encroachment by neighboring families. Subadults of both sexes disperse from their natal units (often after aggression by their same-sex parent) and start their own families (Leighton, 1987).

This traditional picture of stable and cooperative gibbon families is a bit too perfect, however, as shown by recent field studies. Independent observations by anthropologist Ulrich Reichard (1995) and psychologist Ryne Palombit (1994) have documented mate desertion by both male and female gibbons (this usually also involves forfeiture of territory), as well as extra-pair (in human terms, adulterous) copulations with neighbors. Within three wild gibbon groups in Thailand, Reichard found that extra-pair matings accounted for 12 percent of all copulations. These new data suggest that gibbons continually assess their mates and that both males and females are prepared to copulate adulterously and/or abandon their families in order to improve their personal reproductive prospects. This is a far cry from the old view of gibbons forming life-long nuclear families, and it strongly increases the behavioral similarities between gibbons and humankind.

In contrast to gibbons, adult orangutans of both sexes live solitary lives, and the only real social unit is that of a female and her dependent offspring. Adult males are twice the size of adult females, and males (even as subadults) generally dominate females. Each adult inhabits a large home range (0.2 to 3.5 square miles, or 0.6 to 9.0 square kilometers, for females), with an extensive overlap of males' and females' ranges. Adult males have several mating strategies. Some defend their ranges as territories from other adult males while pursuing sexual interactions with overlapping females. Other males, both full adults and subadults, do not defend a mating territory; rather, they move over large distances and seek matings opportunistically. Since both males and females have access to multiple sexual partners, the orangutan mating system is best described as promiscuous (Delgado and van Schaik, 2000; Rodman and Mitani, 1987).

Both gibbons and orangutans are basically frugivorous in their diets. Compared to other ape species, gibbons perform very little object manipulation and may be safely classed as non–tool users (although there was one observation of a leaf being used as a sponge for water dipping; McGrew, 1992). Wild orangutans, on the other hand, are much more accomplished tool users. The apes regularly drop twigs and topple snags as part of aggressive displays and also rub their faces with leaves (McGrew, 1992). Additionally, wild Sumatran orangs have been observed to fashion sticks into tools used to probe seeds from partly opened *Neesia* fruits and to extract insects, bits of insect nests, and honey from tree holes (van Schaik et al., 1996). Stick probes are usually held between the teeth, but occasionally they are handheld and applied with a power grip. (Precision gripping has not been observed, perhaps because of orangutans' relatively short thumbs; see Table 3.8.) And finally, rehabilitated female orangutans in east Malaysia have been seen to arrange several large leaves into "leaf-vessels," into which they spit partially masticated food. The food is then consumed gradually from the leaf-vessel (Rogers and Kaplan, 1994). In captivity, orangutans have shown quite extensive and complex tool use (McGrew, 1992).

But as noted earlier, gibbons and orangutans are humans' distant evolutionary kin. In contrast, it appears certain that humans share a common ancestor with some of the African apes as recently as 5 to 7 million years ago (Table 4.2). Therefore, we must examine our hominoid relatives from Africa in somewhat greater detail.

Gorillas: Behavior and Ecology

As discussed at the beginning of this chapter, molecular studies have shown that gorillas are somewhat more distant evolutionary relatives of humans than are chimpanzees and bonobos (Box 4.1). More precisely, the gorilla lineage diverged about 8 to

FIGURE 4.13
In Central Africa, Dian Fossey walks through the forest near her isolated field station with two young mountain gorillas. She studied this endangered primate in its native habitat from 1967 until her death in 1984.

Source: Bob Campbell, © National Geographic Society.

10 million years ago from the chimp–bonobo–human line. Therefore, chimpanzees and bonobos may tell us more about our last ape ancestor, but nonetheless gorillas are fascinating in their own right and provide additional insights into our primate heritage. Three types of gorillas are currently recognized: a western lowland subspecies (*Gorilla gorilla gorilla*), an eastern lowland subspecies (*G. g. gaueri*), and mountain gorillas (*G. g. beringei*). All three subspecies have been studied and are broadly similar, but of the three, the very best information comes from the mountain gorillas of East Africa.

Intensive scientific studies of mountain gorillas began with the work of George Schaller in 1959–1960. In 1967, Dian Fossey (Figure 4.13) arrived in the Virunga Volcano region with the goal of extending Schaller's findings. She established her camp—the beginning of the Karisoke Research Center—in the Rwandan sector of the volcanoes region and began work to habituate the local gorilla groups to her presence. Fossey lived and worked at Karisoke until 1984, and thanks to her observations—as well as those of a long list of students and colleagues who joined or followed her in the Virungas—we now have a remarkably detailed understanding of mountain gorilla life (Fossey, 1983). Unfortunately, Fossey's personal contribution to gorilla studies and conservation ended with her murder in December 1984. It is still unknown whether she died at the hands of poachers or other perpetrators (Stewart et al., 2001).

While the orangutan and gibbon have evolved into specialized tree dwellers, the gorilla's development has taken the direction of a great increase in size, along with a dietary switch from mainly arboreal foods to an abundant and bulky terrestrial diet of herbal leaves, stems, shoots, and pith. There are apparently subspecific differences in diet, however, and western lowland gorillas eat more fruit than do mountain gorillas and also regularly wade about in swamps foraging for aquatic herbs (Doran and McNeilage, 1998). The two specializations of great size and terrestrial diet go together: We may suppose size and strength have been selected

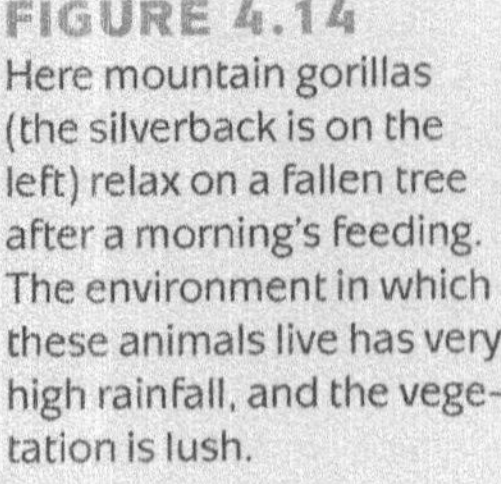

FIGURE 4.14
Here mountain gorillas (the silverback is on the left) relax on a fallen tree after a morning's feeding. The environment in which these animals live has very high rainfall, and the vegetation is lush.

because other animals will not attack the gorilla while it is on the ground eating. And because the gorilla is so large, it needs a great deal of just the kind of coarse vegetation that it finds in large quantities in the places it inhabits. This great ape retains the equipment for climbing and reaching: the long arms, the deft hands, and keen vision. Young gorillas are frisky and venturesome in the trees, but their elders are essentially ground animals. In fact, adult female mountain gorillas spend only 7 percent of their time in the trees and males only 2 percent (Doran and McNeilage, 1998).

With no predators to fear except humans and with plenty of food available, the gorillas Fossey encountered lived most of the time in a state of mild and amiable serenity (Figure 4.14). Most of them live in groups of two to thirty-four, each group led by a powerful silverback male, so called for the saddle of grizzled silver hair that the male grows when he reaches the age of ten. His dominance over the group is absolute but normally genial. Occasionally, a young gorilla will get too frolicsome and will be silenced by a glare or a threatening slap on the ground by an adult. Sometimes, a couple of females will begin to scream at each other until the leader glares at them, when they promptly quiet down. Except for particularly irascible silverbacks, the leaders are usually quite approachable. Females nestle against them, and infants crawl over their huge bodies. When a band of gorillas is at rest, the young play, the mothers tend their infants, and the other adults lie at peace and soak up the sun (Fossey, 1983).

Gorilla groups are not territorial; rather, they move about within nondefended home ranges in search of food and other resources (Doran and McNeilage, 1998). They do not use tools to obtain food or for any other purpose, although they may be frequent tool users in captivity (Boysen et al., 1999). The gorilla mating system approximates harem polygyny, and a silverback male typically has several sexual partners, while females have only one. It is important to note, however, that about one-quarter of mountain gorilla groups contain more than one silverback male. In these groups, the dominant silverback does most of the mating, but subordinate males are not completely excluded and therefore females may have multiple mates. Female gorillas routinely emigrate from their natal group and males may do so, as well, although the percentage of transferring males seems to be lower in mountain gorillas than in some lowland populations (Doran and McNeilage, 1998; Yamagiwa and Kahekwa, 2001). Within a group, the strongest social bonds are between females and their silverback leader. Bonds between unrelated females are quite weak (Watts, 2001).

Even though gorillas usually present a mild demeanor to the outside world, protected as they are by their immense strength, they can be aggressive in rivalry between males over females and in other aspects of reproductive behavior. Maturing and/or subordinate silverbacks can improve their mating opportunities only by kidnapping females from other groups, by usurping the position of the dominant silverback male (often their father) in their own group, or by awaiting his death. Sometimes, the females support an up-and-coming male against an older one. The group leaders, in turn, must defend their own females against kidnapping and the subsequent likelihood of infanticide by extra-group males (Fossey, 1983). As in some other primates, killing infants in order to bring newly acquired females quickly back to sexual cycling seems to be an evolved reproductive strategy among mountain gorillas, although perhaps not among the lowland subspecies (Doran and McNeilage, 1998; Yamagiwa and Kahekwa, 2001).

Studies of all of the gorilla subspecies are continuing today, some with more urgency than others. In Dian Fossey's beloved Virunga Volcanoes, political instability and poaching still threaten the mountain gorillas (Steklis and Gerald-Steklis, 2001), which may yet disappear before they are fully understood.

FIGURE 4.15
Jane Goodall has been a pioneer in the study of wild animals. By undertaking a long behavioral study of wild chimpanzees since 1960, she has contributed greatly to our understanding both of chimpanzees and by implication of ourselves.

Goodall and the Gombe Chimpanzees

As with the gorilla, long and devoted field observations have helped us understand something of chimpanzee behavior. Paleoanthropologist Louis Leakey knew of a community of chimpanzees that lived in a hilly wooded tract near the Gombe Stream, a river running into Lake Tanganyika in western Tanzania. He was interested in anything that had to do with primates; furthermore, he thought that the present-day stream, with its woodland and grassland environment, closely resembled the environment inhabited by early hominins. He persuaded Jane Goodall to undertake a study of the Gombe chimps (Goodall, 1986).

In 1960, when Goodall arrived in what is now the Gombe National Park, she set up camp near the lakeshore and began looking for chimpanzees in an area of about 15 square miles (39 square kilometers). Her plan was to watch the animals discreetly, not getting too close, just accustoming them to her presence, as a preliminary to closer acquaintance. Many months later, she was still watching from a distance, still treated with suspicion by the shy chimpanzees. Ultimately, after a period of rejection that would have discouraged a less dedicated person, she was accepted, not by all the chimpanzees but by many of them (Figure 4.15). Goodall's studies revealed the chimpanzee to be an animal whose biology, behavior, and social organization provoke all kinds of speculations about the emergence of humankind (see Box 4.2).

BOX 4.2 **CURRENT ISSUE**

Genetic Relations between Humans and Chimpanzees

One often reads the claim that humans and chimpanzees are about 99 percent genetically identical. This startling statistic, which reflects humans' recent evolutionary separation from the chimp–bonobo lineage, excites our interest in several ways. Some people experience increased empathy with chimpanzees and devote themselves to ape conservation efforts. Others ponder the science fiction possibilities of chimp–human hybridization!

But what sense can we actually make of the 99 percent claim? After all, humans and chimps *seem* very different. We are taller, smaller toothed, less hairy, bigger brained, and have different limb proportions than chimpanzees. Furthermore, we mature more slowly, live longer, and reproduce more often. And finally, thanks to our large and complex brains, humans have minds, language, and culture—three attributes that chimpanzees may possess partially, but imperfectly (see later sections of this chapter and also Chapter 13). So what's with the claim of genetic near identity?

As it turns out, there are actually several ways to measure human–chimp genetic relatedness, and the various measures don't necessarily give the same results (Price, 1996). For starters, the 99 percent figure is based on comparisons of the amino acid sequences of functionally similar proteins (for example, comparing our hemoglobin *a* protein with that of a chimp). Many such polypeptide chains are absolutely the same in chimps and humans, while others differ by only a single amino acid. In contrast, while functionally similar proteins may be the same across the species, the polypeptide products of alleles at similar chromosomal loci often are not. Electrophoretic comparisons (which involve placing proteins in an electric field and measuring their migration patterns across a starch gel) suggest that humans and chimps are only 52 percent identical in their alleles at an average locus. Finally, humans and chimpanzees show several chromosomal differences. As noted in Chapter 2, the species differ in their diploid numbers: forty-six for us and forty-eight for chimps. Our chromosome two is the result of fusing the ancestral ape chromosomes twelve and thirteen, both of which still exist separately in chimpanzees, while other human–chimp chromosomal differences can be traced to inversions (in which stretches of genetic material are reversed on a chromosome) or the addition or loss of chunks of DNA.

The situation, therefore, is considerably more complicated than simply labeling humans and chimps as 99 percent the same. Nonetheless, all of the evidence agrees that *organismal* (anatomical and behavioral) differences between the species have evolved at a much faster rate than *molecular* (chromosomal, allelic, protein) differences. One way this could have happened is if many (most?) of the detectable genetic differences have involved regulatory genes—genes that affect the body's growth, development, and maintenance—rather than structural genes that code for building blocks such as flesh and bones (Price, 1996). In other words, humans and chimpanzees may differ not so much in *what* they're made of as in *how* they're made.

So, the next time you hear the 99 percent measure being bandied about, you might want to point out that while humans and chimps consist of the same bodily bricks and mortar, we differ mightily from chimps when measured by the finished product: the evolved architecture of our bodies, brains, and behaviors. These evolved differences clearly preclude gene leakage between the species in nature and would almost certainly foil the efforts of any scientist mad enough to try creating an ape–human Chimpenstein in the laboratory.

Chimpanzees occur in a broad band across West and Central Africa, from Senegal and the Ivory Coast in the west to Uganda and Tanzania in the east (Figure 4.16). Of all the great apes, the chimpanzee is the least specialized. In size, it is a neat compromise: small enough to get about in trees and big enough to take care of itself on the ground against predators, particularly since it usually travels in bands, which are sections of a larger community. As a result, it is at home in both worlds. Although still a fruit eater whose favorite staple is ripe figs, it is a generalist–opportunist and will eat a wide variety of other fruit and vegetation, together with some meat: birds' eggs or fledglings, insects, lizards or small snakes, and occasionally a young baboon, colobus monkey, or bush pig (Boesch and Boesch-Achermann, 2000; Goodall, 1986; Stanford, 1999).

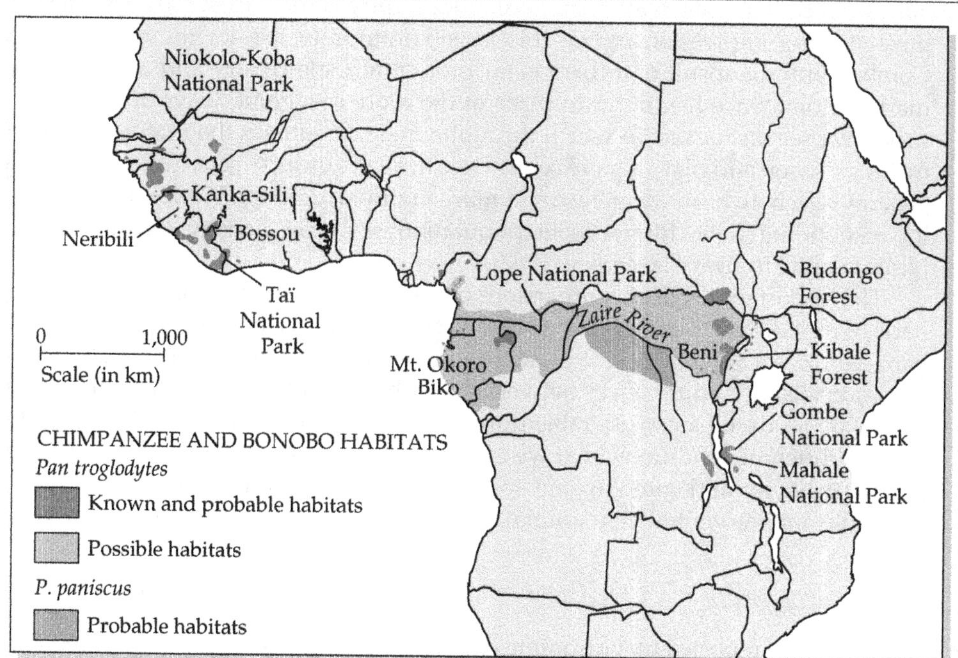

FIGURE 4.16
Chimpanzee and bonobo distribution follows the band of tropical rain forest across Central Africa. A number of study areas are identified.

Source: Based on Goodall, 1986.

Chimpanzee society is not typical of the higher primates. The Gombe animals live in dispersed communities of from forty to sixty individuals, and the bonding between them is loose. The term **fusion–fission** has been applied to chimpanzee society. Individuals of either sex have almost complete freedom to come and go as they wish. The membership of temporary subgroups is constantly changing. Adults and adolescents can and do forage, travel, and sleep alone, sometimes for days at a time. An individual rarely sees all the members of the community on the same day and probably never sees them two days in succession. An animal may travel one day with a large, noisy, and excitable gathering and the next day completely alone. Females may spend many days alone or with their young; males tend to be more gregarious. This flexibility of chimpanzee society is one of its most remarkable characteristics.

Fusion–fission community a society that includes several individuals of both sexes and all ages and is characterized by the formation and dissolution of temporary subgroups.

In addition to their fusion–fission characteristic, chimpanzee communities can be classed as multimale–multifemale, since they contain several adult individuals of each sex. Young females habitually emigrate from their natal community to live and breed elsewhere as adults, while males routinely remain in the community of their birth. Although there is considerable variation among chimpanzee populations, this emigration pattern typically results in relatively weak social bonds between females but strong bonds (often based on kinship) between males. Heterosexual social bonds also appear to be intermediate in strength, and grooming between the sexes is less common and of shorter duration than grooming between males (Boesch and Boesch-Ackermann, 2000; Goodall, 1986).

As noted earlier, male chimpanzees strive to achieve high dominance rank, and within each community, one male can be recognized as the alpha animal. Males form strong alliances with one another, and support from allies (often kin) may be crucial to achieving and maintaining high rank. Dominance relations exist among females, but they are not as clear cut as the male hierarchy, although older females generally dominate younger ones (Goodall, 1986).

Nishida and the Mahale Mountain Chimpanzees

In 1966, Toshisada Nishida and Junichiro Itani, with a small team from Kyoto University in Japan, set out to study another group of chimpanzees not far south of Gombe, in the Mahale Mountains of Tanzania. Since that time, they have maintained almost continuous observation of a large community of more than 100 apes. The first most striking impression is that this large community has far more males than Gombe, with the result that there is far more intermale rivalry and a much more marked dominance hierarchy. In place of the more easygoing ways of the Gombe males, we see a situation in which the alpha male dominates the matings of all females in season and plays a more central role in all the group's activities. Interactions generally seem to be more intense and more highly structured. We see social behavior responding to a difference in population size and density (Nishida, 1990; Nishida and Hiraiwa-Hasegawa, 1987).

The important result of comparisons of this sort (and we now have studies from parts of west Africa to compare with those of east Africa) is the realization that chimpanzees have a very flexible and adaptable behavior repertoire. There are subtle (and not so subtle) differences between the behaviors of every community, and it is only by studying a considerable number of different populations, living under slightly different conditions, that we can begin to learn the full repertoire of chimpanzee behavior and come to gain some insight into the total potential of this remarkable and very intelligent animal.

The Chimpanzee as Hunter

Goodall (1986) reported that a hunting chimpanzee is unmistakable. Compared with other chimpanzee behaviors, there is something out of the ordinary about hunting behavior, observed much more often among males than among females. There is in it something purposeful, tense, and inward that other chimpanzees recognize and respond to. Sometimes, they just watch the hunter intently. Sometimes, other chimpanzees move to adjacent trees to cut off the escape of the quarry, a young baboon or a small arboreal monkey. On several occasions observed by Goodall, the quarry was a young baboon whose screams brought adult baboons rushing to its defense. In the ensuing hullabaloo, the youngster more often than not escaped. But Goodall saw chimpanzees killing and eating small- to medium-sized animals (monkeys, pigs, small antelopes) often enough to realize that meat is an important part of the apes' diet.

Since Goodall's pioneering work, observations by Nishida (1990) at Mahale, Christophe Boesch and Hedwige Boesch-Achermann (2000) in the Taï National Park (Ivory Coast), and Craig Stanford (1996, 1999) at Gombe have added much new information about hunting and meat eating by chimpanzees. First, we now know that chimps' main prey species is the red colobus monkey (*Colobus badius*). Chimpanzees hunt red colobus at all three major study sites, and at Gombe, where up to 150 monkeys may be killed during a peak hunting year, the apes have a strong negative effect on colobus population size. Second, we now realize that meat can be a substantial part of the diet for particular populations of chimpanzees. At Gombe, Stanford has estimated that during a good hunting year, the chimps may consume more than 270 pounds (600 kilograms) of meat. This would bring the meat consumption of adult males (who hunt much more frequently than females and thus eat more meat) to a point near the low end of the range for human hunters and gatherers (i.e., between 5 to 10 percent of the diet). And finally, scientists have now observed much more complex hunts than those recorded at Gombe in the dense rain forest at Taï in west Africa.

Observations on the Taï chimps have been made for more than twenty years by the husband-and-wife team of Christophe Boesch and Hedwige Boesch-Achermann, primatologists operating out of the Swiss Center for Scientific Research. They have found that red colobus hunts at Taï more often involve groups of chimp males using more complicated strategies than at Gombe. For example, the Taï chimps often take on different roles during colobus hunts: Some males function as drivers, others encircle the fleeing monkeys to keep them from dispersing, and yet others race ahead to block the monkeys' arboreal pathway. The chances of a kill are greatly enhanced by larger hunting parties, and after a successful hunt, cooperating males may share meat generously. Such regular sharing of the kill presumably encourages future co-

FIGURE 4.17
The upper chimpanzee is holding the rib cage of a small monkey; the two lower chimpanzees are begging. Frequently, the hunter will share the remains of the kill.

operation (Boesch and Boesch-Achermann, 2000). Of course, simpler hunts—arboreal pursuits of monkeys by single chimps or pouncing on piglets and fawns when they are discovered hiding in the grass—also occur at all chimpanzee study sites.

Clearly, chimpanzees all across Africa are excited by meat and very fond of it. As described earlier, adult males do most of the hunting, but at some sites, females may make regular kills as well (Goodall, 1986). Rarely do chimpanzees scavenge meat from the kills of other predators or from natural deaths (Boesch and Boesch-Achermann, 2000). Meat is chewed long and reflectively, usually with a mouthful of leaves added. Sometimes, the carcass is shared in an orderly fashion by the successful hunter(s), with bits of meat being torn off and handed out to begging group mates (Figure 4.17). Males tend to share with other males (most often with kin, allies, and co-hunters) and also with estrous females. Indeed, the regularity of chimpanzee males apparently swapping meat for sex has led Craig Stanford to suggest that males "decide to hunt with an awareness that procuring colobus meat may enhance their access to [sexually] swollen females" (1996:104).

The revelation that chimpanzees hunt and eat meat—and share it, as well—has enormous implications in explaining the development of hunting and sharing among hominins. It now becomes possible to speculate that these traits were brought to the savanna from the forest. We no longer have to puzzle over how a propensity for meat eating began in a creature with a fruit-eating ancestry; it was already there, as we now know it is in most primates. All this propensity needed was encouragement in a new environment.

The First Herbalists?

To this section on chimpanzee diet, we can now add a most remarkable postscript. Recent studies in East Africa have revealed that on certain occasions, chimpanzees will chew the pith or eat a few leaves of particular plants that have been shown to have medicinal properties (Huffman and Wrangham, 1994; Wrangham and Goodall, 1989). The chimps seem to sense when they need these plants, and they evidently have the knowledge to select particular species. How do we know they are medicinal? In the first place, they are certainly not part of the chimp's regular diet and are eaten only quite uncommonly and when other more popular food plants are available. The leaves are not particularly palatable, for the chimps do not chew them but swallow them like a pill. Second, the local people use some of these same plants, in particular, species of *Aspilia,* in the same way. Finally, the plants turn out on analysis to contain an antibiotic (thiarubrine-A) that is potent against bacteria, viruses, fungi, and even parasitic worms!

Although it has not been proved, it does appear that chimpanzees—and occasionally, gorillas and bonobos, as well—are deliberately dosing themselves when they feel unwell with one or more of a number of species of plants that have very definite medicinal qualities (Huffman and Wrangham, 1994). Research is now proceeding to look into any value these plants may have in western medicine.

Tools and Weapons

One of the most stunning discoveries of the chimpanzee studies is the fact that these apes make and use a wide variety of simple tools (see Table 4.4). Despite their relatively short thumbs and impaired precision grip (see Figure 3.18 and Table 3.8), chimpanzees fish for termites with sticks and stems (Figure 4.18), make sponges of wadded leaves, hammer open nuts with stones, and occasionally use natural objects as weapons. The exact value of these activities to chimpanzees' survival is hard to measure, but it seems clear that they allow the apes to adapt to a variety of habitats and facilitate the extraction of otherwise inaccessible food items. Each new generation learns tool-using patterns from the previous one. The youngsters have many opportunities to learn: They watch their elders intently, often copying what they do, and occasionally they are deliberately taught by adults (Boesch and Boesch-Achermann, 2000).

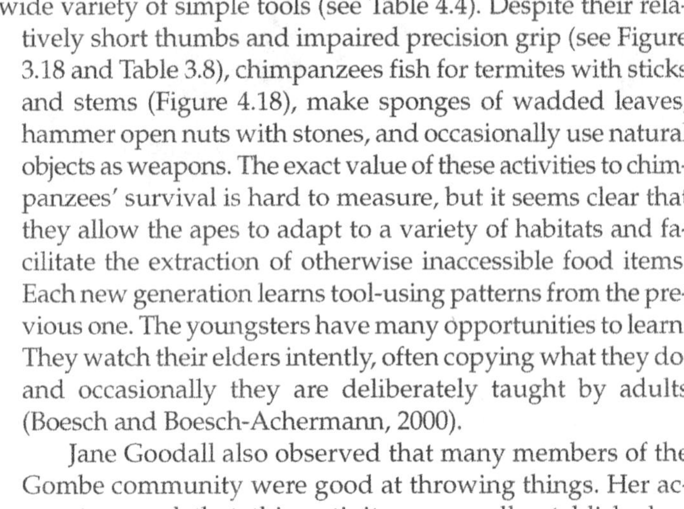

FIGURE 4.18
Jane Goodall observed chimpanzees fishing with short twigs for termites in mounds. The chimpanzees prepared the twigs by stripping off the leaves and breaking the twigs to a certain length. In fact, they made a tool.

Jane Goodall also observed that many members of the Gombe community were good at throwing things. Her accounts reveal that this activity was well established at Gombe; a number of males tried it and in a variety of circumstances. Even often woefully inaccurate throwing seems useful to a chimpanzee. In chimpanzee life, there is a great deal of bluffing and aggressive display. During such activity, an animal will jump up and down, wave its arms, hoot, shriek, and charge forward. This behavior looks especially disconcerting if it is accompanied by a shower of sticks, waste, or stones. The fact that throwing is useful as an aggressive display explains why it is now established as part of the species' behavior. In their throwing behavior, chimpanzees have clearly hit on a most effective way of dealing with predators and other opponents—a technique that surely would have been equally valuable to early hominins.

Studies from all over Africa suggest that in different regions of their range, chimpanzees show cultural differences in behavior generally and in tool use. (See the Postscript to this chapter.) Different kinds of probes are used in fishing for termites, from light wands to stout sticks used for heavy digging (McGrew, 1992). The hominin use of digging sticks is foreshadowed by these primates.

In the Taï Forest, chimpanzees have been observed using sticks and stones to break open nuts. At Bossou, in Guinea, west Africa, chimpanzees use two stones to smash open palm nuts. They place the nut in the cavity of one flat stone (platform stone) and smash it with a hammer stone (Figure 4.19; Boesch and Boesch-Achermann, 2000; McGrew, 1992). The apes are even capable of leaving behind an

TABLE 4.4 A Partial List of Tool-Use Patterns Shown by Wild Apes

Tool or Behavior Pattern	Chimpanzees	Bonobos	Gorillas	Orangutans
Sticks as probes for termite (or other insect) fishing or for honey extraction	X			X
Wadded leaf sponges	X			
Leaf-vessels to hold food				X
Leaves as rain hats		X		X
Leaves wiped, rubbed on body	X	X		X
Branches dragged, torn, dropped in display	X	X	X	X
Branches, rocks as hammers for nut cracking	X			
Roots, rocks as anvils for nut cracking	X			
Leaf petiole of oil palms for pestle-pounding in palm crown	X			
Rocks, branches waved, thrown at opponents	X			

Sources: Goodall, 1986; Ingmanson, 1996; McGrew, 1992; Rogers and Kaplan, 1994; van Schaik and Fox, 1996; Yamakoshi and Sugiyama, 1995.

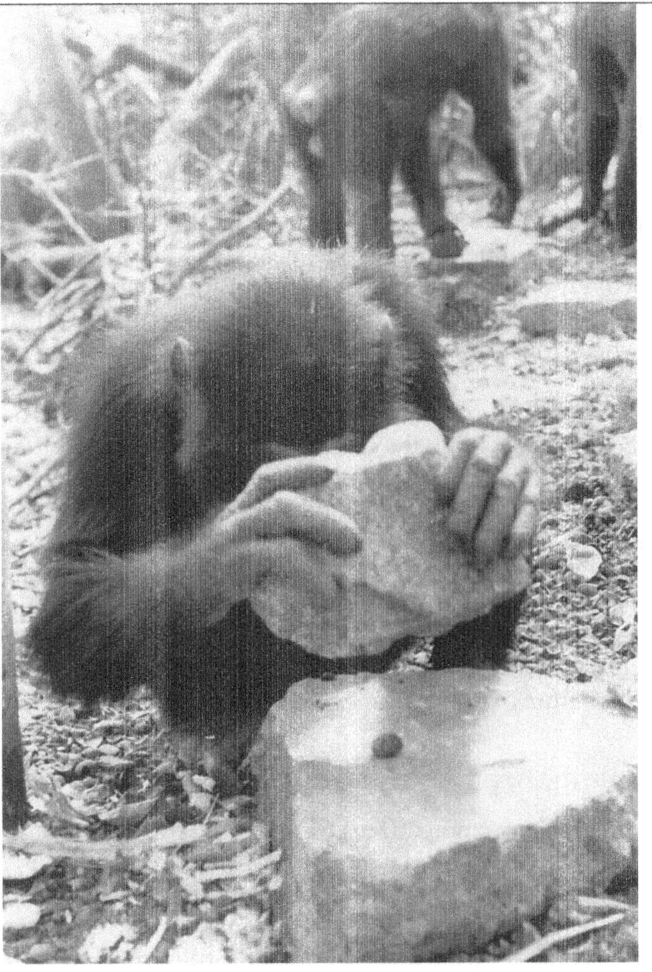

FIGURE 4.19 Chimpanzee using a hammer stone and an anvil to crack open oil palm nuts.

archaeological record of their tool-using behavior. Recently, scientists working at Taï excavated a chimpanzee nut-cracking site and recovered identifiable hammer stones, detached flakes, and bits of shattered rock. Although modified by use, rather than intentionally beforehand, these implements showed a strong resemblance to the stone tools attributed to early hominins (Bower, 2002).

Thus, among chimpanzees, we have evidence of the use of tools as weapons, digging sticks, and nut crackers and as implements for the collection of social insects such as termites and ants. Even the use of stone tools—so important in hominin evolution—is seen in chimpanzees' hammer-stone-and-anvil nut processing. But two additional interesting and suggestive observations must be made. First, female chimpanzees appear to use tools more often and more efficiently than do males. As noted by McGrew (1992), most chimpanzee tool use occurs during sessions of insect gathering (termite fishing and ant dipping), and females show much higher levels of insectivory than males. With regard to nut-cracking behavior, at Taï, where Boesch and Boesch-Achermann (2000) described the apes as dependent on tool use during the nut season, chimp females were considerably more active than males at opening nuts. Second, tool use rarely occurs in the context of hunting and eating mammalian prey—which, as noted earlier, are primarily male activities—although occasionally sticks are used to pick marrow from broken bones or leaf wads are used to clean out an opened braincase.

Can these findings on sex differences in chimpanzee tool use be applied to early hominins? In McGrew's words, "If the parallels between observed ape and hypothesized proto-[hominin] data are genuine, then the evolutionary origins of tool-use are more likely to have come from solitary, female gathering and not from social, male hunting" (1992: 118). Further data bearing on this point are eagerly awaited.

Murder and War

Data from several study sites have revealed that encounters between chimpanzee communities may in fact be sought and may become very aggressive. The best data come from Jane Goodall's (1986) observations at Gombe. There, it was observed that parties of up to ten adult males, sometimes accompanied by females and young, might patrol peripheral areas near the boundary of the community territory and actively search for signs of neighboring groups. Contact might result in displays until one or both groups gave up or fled and returned to the core area of their range. When single chimpanzees or very small parties were encountered, they might be chased and even attacked, often brutally. Males were observed setting out as a small group with the clear intention of stalking a neighbor. They silently moved through the forest, avoiding the crackle of branches or leaves underfoot.

Such behavior is known to have resulted in what can only be called brutal murder, clearly cold blooded and calculated. Goodall has described one four-year period at Gombe as essentially a war, during which an entire community was annihilated, so that the victorious males and their females were able to move into the unoccupied territory. This behavior looks all too familiar, and the whole question of intercommunity relations and aggression among chimpanzees is now a subject of active research. Understanding it is important to those studying the evolution and nature of human violence (Wrangham and Peterson, 1996).

Chimpanzee Politics

Research on chimpanzees in the wild (Boesch and Boesch-Achermann, 2000; Goodall, 1986; Nishida, 1990) and in captivity (de Waal, 1982) has shown time and again that these apes are masters of political manipulation. In their never-ending competition for food, sex, and dominance rank, chimpanzees use short-term coalitions, long-term alliances, divide-and-rule strategies, intimidating aggression, and

reconciliation. They favor kin, punish cheaters, and attempt to deceive one another. All in all, chimps possess an impressive array of tactics for primates that lack speech.

Reconciliation the act of restoring friendly relations.

In this size-dimorphic species, males do most of the posturing, threatening, and maneuvering, but females can be important coalition partners and allies, as well as the limited reproductive resource for which males struggle the hardest. Frans de Waal (1982) reported that within a captive colony at the Burgers' Zoo in Arnhem, Holland, senior females occasionally defused male–male competition by confiscating rocks from the hands of angry combatants! Kinship and personality traits influence the animals' patterns of political infighting, and in addition, there seem to be population differences in behavior. At Taï, for example, coalitions during fighting tended to disrupt the existing dominance hierarchy among the males, while at Mahale, they tended to support the existing ranks (Boesch and Boesch-Achermann, 2000).

The importance of reconciliation and peace making has been stressed by de Waal in a more recent book (1989), where he has extended his studies to macaque monkeys and bonobos. It is clear that peace making and other stabilizing social mechanisms of reconciliation are vital for a stable, adaptive, and successful society. Almost all these behaviors have been observed in wild chimp populations and serve to counteract the constant competition.

Bonobos: The Best Evolutionary Model for Early Hominins?

One ape species remains to be described: *Pan paniscus,* the bonobo (pygmy chimpanzee). Although recognized for more than half a century, this species has been essentially unstudied until the last three decades. As data on bonobos have been forthcoming, however, they have been particularly tantalizing for anthropologists, since in some ways these are the apes that most closely resemble humans in their behavior. Some scientists believe, therefore, that bonobos are an especially good model for studies of early hominin evolution.

Bonobos are found in Central Africa in the lowland rain forests and swamp forests south of the Zaire River (Figure 4.16). They are about the size of the smallest subspecies of chimpanzees (*Pan troglodytes*), although bonobos are somewhat more slender, with narrower shoulders and longer legs. In addition, bonobos have smaller brow ridges and ears and lighter-colored lips than chimpanzees, and the hair on their heads is parted down the center. As in the other African apes, sexual dimorphism in body size is significant among bonobos, and females' body weight is about three-quarters that of males (see Table 3.6).

Bonobos live in multimale–multifemale communities that are characterized by the fusion–fission subgrouping already described for chimpanzees: Females appear to emigrate from their natal communities, but males rarely do so. Interestingly, the tendency of bonobo males to remain in their natal communities is not correlated with strong male–male relationships, as it is among chimpanzees. The strongest social bonds among adult bonobos are either between females or between males and females. Adult males tend not to develop close relations with one another, but rather they remain strongly bonded to their mothers, associating with them frequently. Newly immigrated females use affiliative and sexual interactions (genito–genital rubbing, see following) to establish friendly relationships with unrelated resident females, and coalitions of bonded females dominate males and limit males' access to preferred feeding sites. Bonobo females develop distinct dominance relationships, and the support of a high-ranking mother can enhance an adult son's rank among the males. In general, bonobo females have much more influence within their communities—and bonobo males have less—than is true for their chimpanzee counterparts (de Waal and Lanting, 1997; Hohmann and Fruth, 2002; Parish, 1994, 1996; Stanford, 1998; F. White, 1992b, 1996).

A community of bonobos includes between 50 and 120 animals and inhabits a range of about 8 to 19 square miles (20 to 50 square kilometers; Table 4.2). The apes spend most of their time in the trees foraging for fruits, a diet supplemented with

FIGURE 4.20
Bonobos stand and move bipedally much more frequently than chimpanzees.

Source: Frans de Waal and Frans Lanting, *Bonobo: The Forgotten Ape* (p. 53). Berkeley, University of California Press, 1997. Copyright by Frans Lanting, Santa Cruz, CA.

other plant parts, insects, and some meat. Food is regularly shared. Unlike chimpanzees, bonobos apparently do not use tools to obtain or process either plant or animal foods. Among the few tool-use patterns recorded for bonobos are making rain hats from leafy boughs, wiping feces from their bodies with leaves, and dragging branches in display.

In another contrast to chimpanzees, bonobo communities show extensively overlapping home ranges and often fail to defend their ranges as true territories. Thus, there is little if any chimpanzee-style territorial patrolling. When subgroups from different bonobo communities meet in the forest, they initially display hostility but may soon begin to interact in a friendly and sexual fashion. First, females from the two communities engage in genital rubbing and then grooming. Youngsters from the different groups begin to play. Finally, adult males may participate in scrotal rubbing with their counterparts from the other group. Amazingly, even copulations between males and females from different communities can take place during these relatively relaxed encounters—something no self-respecting chimpanzee male would ever allow (de Waal and Lanting, 1997; Fruth and Hohmann, 2002; Ingmanson, 1996; F. White, 1992a, 1996).

Among the similarities claimed for bonobos and humans, most are sexual but one is postural. Studies of captive animals have suggested that bonobos stand and walk bipedally more often (and with greater ease) than chimpanzees or gorillas (Figure 4.20). While this may be true, no one is claiming that bonobos are habitual bipeds. In fact, a recent field study showed that bipedalism represented less than 2 percent of the total locomotion of its wild bonobo subjects (F. White, 1992a).

The similarities in sexual behavior, however, are more striking and possibly more important. Compared to chimpanzees, bonobo females resume sexual activity fairly quickly following parturition (after only 12 versus about 51 months), and they have a much higher proportion of sexually swollen days prior to the next delivery (27 percent versus about 5 percent). To some extent, this is offset by chimpanzee females having a higher copulation rate when they are in estrus, but the overall effect is for bonobo females to be attractive, proceptive, and receptive more often than their chimp counterparts (Furuichi and Hashimoto, 2002). Humans, of course, resemble bonobos in being sexually active most of the time, rather than rarely but intensely.

But the sexual similarities take two more interesting twists. First, while virtually all chimpanzee copulations are ventrodorsal (the male mounts the female from the rear), some 25 to 30 percent of bonobo matings are ventroventral (Nishida and Hiraiwa-Hasegawa, 1987). Of the two sexes, female bonobos seem to be particularly fond of face-to-face sex; several instances have been recorded of females interrupting ventrodorsal copulations in order to change their position and embrace the male ventrally. And second, bonobos are without a doubt the most inventive of all the apes in their sexual variations. Bonobos show all of the possible combinations of sexual partners: opposite sex, same sex, and old and young. Pairs of females frequently embrace ventrally and rub their genitals together, while males mount one another and occasionally "fence" (mutually rub) with their erect penises. Sex is used by bonobos to reduce tension and resolve conflicts. As Frans de Waal has remarked about this make-love-not-war species, "The chimpanzee resolves sexual issues with power; the bonobo resolves power issues with sex" (de Waal and Lanting, 1997:32). Indeed, some researchers believe that frequent female–female and male–female sexual contacts explain why these relationships are stronger among bonobos than among chimpanzees.

Finally, similar to chimpanzees, bonobo males compete with one another for dominance rank within their communities. Interestingly, the support of his mother is often critically important for a bonobo male to successfully rise in rank, an achievement that can have important reproductive payoffs (and inclusive fitness payoffs for his mother). Recently, males' dominance ranks have been shown to be positively correlated with both copulation rate (Kano, 1996) and number of offspring sired (Gerloff et al., 1999). Studies of bonobos are in their infancy. Assuming that humans allow (and assist) bonobos to avoid extinction, this species promises to yield critical information for interpreting human evolution.

Speculations about Ape–Human Common Ancestors

Studies of chromosomes and DNA are beginning to allow fine-grained distinctions about humans' evolutionary relationships with the African apes (see Box 4.1). Most molecular research suggests that humans, bonobos, and chimpanzees are a clade with a common ancestor that lived about 5 to 7 million years ago (the gorilla lineage having diverged a couple of million years before). These studies further suggest that the chimp and bonobo lines may have separated only within the last 2.5 to 3 million years, so that they are extremely close sister species. Thus, based on data from living humans, chimpanzees, and bonobos, we can speculate cautiously about the probable characteristics of their last common ancestor (an ape-grade creature whose exact identity has yet to be established).

As summarized in Table 4.5, it seems likely that humans' last ape ancestor formed multimale–multifemale communities that were characterized by fusion–fission subgrouping. Female emigration from the natal community was probably the prevalent pattern, but it is unclear whether territorial defense by males occurred. Sexual behavior was probably variable and situation dependent. (That is, hormonal control of sex was moderate to low, but whether mating occurred constantly or mainly during estrus-related peaks is not certain.) Males almost certainly had

TABLE 4.5 Characteristics of Chimpanzees, Bonobos, Humans, and Their Common Ancestor

Trait	Chimpanzees	Bonobos	Humans	Common Ancestor
Social group[a]	MM–MF community; fusion–fission	MM–MF community; fusion–fission	MM–MF community; fusion–fission	MM–MF community; fusion–fission
Females or males change groups	Females	Females	Females more often	Females
Male–male bonds	Strong	Weak	Strong	?
Female–female bonds	Weak	Strong	Weak to moderate	?
Male–female bonds	Weak	Strong	Strong	?
Territorial defense	Common, by males	Little, if any	Common, by males	?
Mating system	Promiscuity	Promiscuity	Mild polygyny to promiscuity	Multiple mates for males (for females too?)
Sexual swelling	Yes	Yes	No	?
Sexual activity[b]	5%	27%	Near 100%?	?
Hormonal control of female sexuality	Moderate	Moderate to low	Low	Moderate to low
Copulation pattern	Ventrodorsal	Ventrodorsal > ventroventral	Variable	?
Paternal investment by males	Slight	Slight	Moderate to strong	?
Tool use	Frequent, with many patterns	Rare, with few patterns	Very frequent, with many patterns	Probably present (varied patterns?)
Meat eating	Yes, common	Yes, occasional	Yes, variable	Yes
Food sharing	Routine	Routine	Frequent	Yes
Bipedal stance	Rare	More common than in chimps	Habitual	At least occasional

[a]MM, multimale; MF, multifemale.
[b]Percentage of interbirth interval with swelling and/or copulations.

access to multiple mates, and the same may have been true of females. The common ancestor probably engaged in some tool use (the extent is uncertain), included meat in its diet, and at least occasionally shared food. And finally, bipedal standing and walking almost certainly occurred on occasion, although not habitually.

Beyond this admittedly sketchy characterization, speculations become very tenuous, but even this incomplete picture of our last ape ancestors is useful in generating evolutionary hypotheses for further testing. Humans appear to be the descendants of social, female-emigrating, polygynous-to-promiscuous, tool-using apes that relished a bit of meat in the diet and at least occasionally stood and moved upright. But what was involved in the evolutionary transformation of such a creature into a hominin? To begin to answer that question, we need to focus not on shared traits but on behavioral and anatomical differences between apes and humans. We will examine such differences in the next chapter as we take a look at some fossil candidates for the office of Common Ancestor.

Summary

Knowledge of the behavior of living primates is an important component in the study of human origins and human nature. Since primate studies began in the early part of this century, they have produced much useful information about our evolutionary relatives, the monkeys and apes. As shown in this chapter, primates are extremely social creatures whose complex behavioral repertoires are based mainly on learning. Their societies are structured by several types of relationships, especially dominance relations, kinship, and affiliative relations (the last based commonly on grooming). Patterns of sexual behavior vary from species to species, but the levels of reproductive success and the identities of sexual partners are commonly influenced by dominance and female choice. Among the apes, chimpanzees and bonobos are clearly the closest evolutionary relatives of humans; gorillas rank third. Comparisons among chimpanzees, bonobos, and humans have revealed much about the likely traits of our common ancestor and enable us to formulate numerous evolutionary hypotheses for testing.

Postscript

Do chimpanzees have culture? A deceptively simple question perhaps. A knee-jerk answer might be "No, of course not—they're animals!" But how does one classify an animal that makes and uses tools and that shows regional variation in both tool use and social behavior? (Boesch, 2003; Boesch and Boesch-Achermann, 2000). When anthropology originated in the nineteenth century (long before the primatological studies that would muddy the interspecific waters), culture was recognized as uniquely human and dependent on complex thought and language (see Stocking, 1987). Early cultural anthropologists (who produced nearly as many definitions as they themselves numbered) were certain about culture's unique state as a human attribute and did not consider the question of its development from prehistoric times.

The nascent science of archaeology forced the issue of cultural origins in the nineteenth century. Early collectors of stone tools and other artifacts were properly cautious, however, and talked of the beginning of human *material culture*. This qualified term reflected the view that simple tools are not always accurate indicators of a total cultural system. This view follows from the fact that tool-making skills can be learned by observation alone, without language-based instruction. The implication was and still is that material culture might well have preceded the full range of cultural manifestations in the course of human evolution.

Modern anthropology has made progress in understanding culture and its definitive features, but there is still room for debate. A modern definition describes *culture* as the totality of behavior of a social group that is passed down the generations by learning and symbolic means. This broad definition covers all modern cultural manifestations—rituals, beliefs, material objects, social institutions, and so on—and grounds them in the three key elements of learning, symbolic transmission, and behavior as the property of society.

But to return to the original question: How well do chimpanzees and other nonhuman primates match our current understanding of culture? Following the revised definition, we can recognize some apparently cultural behavior among monkeys as well as among tool-making chimpanzees. But for many workers, the critical addition of symbolic transmission to the definition seems clearly to distinguish human culture from the nonsymbolic protoculture of nonhuman primates. The transition from protoculture to culture came, then, with the evolution of symbolic language.

Not everyone agrees with this point of view, however, and among the dissenters are primatologists W. C. McGrew, Christophe Boesch, and Hedwige Boesch-Achermann. In his book *Chimpanzee Material Culture* (1992), McGrew sets out eight criteria for identifying cultural acts among nonlinguistic creatures such as chimps: innovation, dissemination, standardization, durability, diffusion, tradition, nonsubsistence, and naturalness. He concludes that no single chimpanzee population satisfies all eight conditions but that all conditions (except perhaps diffusion) are met by the behavior of some chimps in some cases. He also describes differences in grooming patterns between chimp populations that would automatically be

Heuristic devices devices that facilitate or stimulate further investigation and thought.

described as cultural differences if shown by humans but that are denied that label when they are shown by apes. McGrew's argument strongly implies that while definitions of culture are important **heuristic devices** for social scientists, they usually also have the unspoken function of separating humans from all nonhumans.

Boesch and Boesch-Achermann (2000) go even further than McGrew. They argue that chimpanzees show not only complex tool-making and tool-using patterns but also some symbolic behavior, the capacity for deliberate teaching of youngsters, and a type of theory of mind. Boesch (2003:89) summarizes the position in favor of recognizing chimpanzees as truly cultural primates in these words:

> What we observe in different chimpanzee groups nicely matches our definition of culture as a set of behaviors learned from group members and not genetically transmitted, mainly independent from ecological conditions, and shared between members of some specific groups. In addition, the flexibility of the chimpanzees' culture allows them to shape their environment to gain access to important new food sources, develop arbitrary signs that have shared meaning, and develop subcultures that distinguish individual groups from their neighbors.

And there the argument sits, with the apes showing more and more evidence of at least culturelike behavior but never quite satisfying the (increasingly torturous?) criteria of some traditionalists. Are the defenders of human uniqueness being unreasonably anthropocentric and/or practicing poor science in their construction and application of cultural definitions? Is it more reasonable to view both chimpanzees and humans as culture-bearing creatures, although differing enormously in the complexity of their respective systems? What is the right approach, and what implications do the different views have for how we regard and treat our ape relatives?

Review Questions

1. Studies of primate behavior are commonly conducted both in the field and in captivity. Discuss the strengths and weaknesses of research in these two settings.
2. Why do most primates live in groups? What are the advantages and disadvantages of social living? What mechanisms have the animals evolved to cope with the disadvantages of group life?
3. How does the sexual behavior of primate males and females differ? How is sexual behavior affected by rank, age, kinship, and hormonal condition? What is *situation-dependent sex?*
4. How do primates relate to their habitat? Define and compare the following three concepts: home range, core area, territory.
5. Describe tool use among chimpanzees, and explore the implications of the chimp data for the evolution of tool use among hominins.
6. Why do some anthropologists think that bonobos make a better model for hominin evolution than chimpanzees? Develop some questions about hominin evolution to which one could apply a bonobo model.
7. Describe the (speculative) characteristics of the chimpanzee–bonobo–human common ancestor.

SUGGESTED FURTHER READING

Boesch, Christophe, and Hedwige Boesch-Achermann. *The Chimpanzees of the Taï Forest.* Oxford, Oxford University Press, 2000.

de Waal, Frans, and Frans Lanting. *Bonobo: The Forgotten Ape.* Berkeley, University of California Press, 1997.

Fossey, Dian. *Gorillas in the Mist.* Boston, Houghton Mifflin, 1983.

Galdikas, Biruté. *Reflections of Eden: My Years With the Orangutans of Borneo.* Boston, Little, Brown, 1995.

Goodall, Jane. *The Chimpanzees of Gombe.* Cambridge (MA), Harvard University Press, 1986.

Kummer, Hans. *In Quest of the Sacred Baboon.* Princeton, Princeton University Press, 1995.

Nishida, Toshisada. *The Chimpanzees of the Mahale Mountains.* Tokyo, University of Tokyo Press, 1990.

INTERNET RESOURCES

LIVING LINKS

www.emory.edu/LIVING_LINKS/index.html

Focused on the research of primatologist Frans de Waal, this web site describes some of the work being done at Emory University and the Yerkes Primate Research Center. A particularly good site for students interested in ape studies.

AFRICAN APE STUDY SITES

http://weber.ucsd.edu/~jmoore/apesites/index.html

This useful site lists over 20 sites where African apes (chimpanzees, bonobos, gorillas) are now or have been studied. For each site, information is provided on ecology, ape demography, research contacts, and important publications.

GREAT APES SURVIVAL PROJECT—GRASP

www.unep.org/grasp

Sponsored by the United Nations Environment Programme, this site provides information about the threat of extinction faced by the four great ape species.

BABOON FACT FILES

www.outtoafrica.nl/animals/engbaboon.html?zenden=2&subsoort_id=1&bestemming_id=1

This site includes lots of information about baboons and links to other similar sites.

THE JANE GOODALL INSTITUTE: CHIMPANZEE CENTRAL

www.janegoodall.org/chimp_central/chimpanzees/gombe/tool.asp

Produced with the aid of veteran field researcher Jane Goodall, this site describes chimp behavior and conservation status.

ASP AMERICAN SOCIETY OF PRIMATOLOGISTS

www.asp.org

Produced by the main American organization devoted to the study and conservation of primates, this site contains useful research information and links.

USEFUL SEARCH TERMS:

apes
bonobos
chimpanzees
gibbons
gorillas
monkeys
orangutans

Chapter 5

Apes and Other Ancestors: Prehominin Evolution

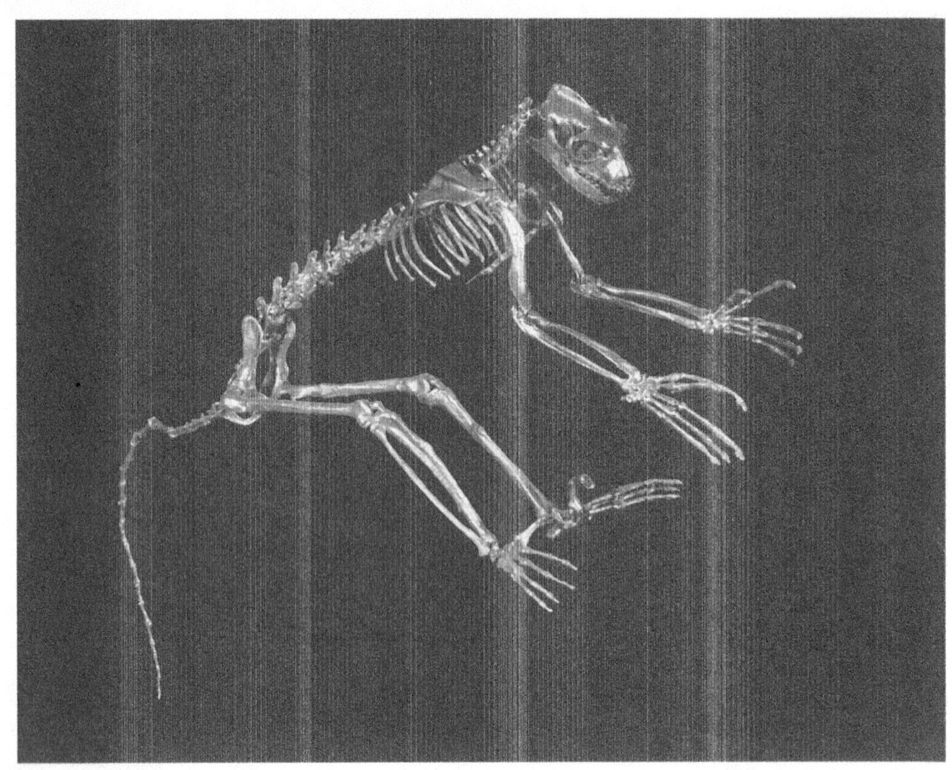

The Eocene strepsirhine *Notharctus* (family Adapidae) may have been an early ancestor of modern lemurs. Its skeleton features a long spine, grasping hands and feet, and a postorbital bar.

It is an axiom of mine that when you have excluded the impossible, whatever remains, however improbable, must be the truth.

Arthur Conan Doyle, 1859–1930. *The Adventures of Sherlock Holmes:* The Beryl Coronet.

Overview

This chapter describes the evolutionary beginnings of the primates, a mammalian order that originated at least 65 and perhaps as many as 90 million years ago (mya). The more primitive of the two primate semiorders—the Plesiadapiformes, or archaic primates—first appeared in the Cretaceous period and seems to have evolved in the northern latitudes. Primates of a modern aspect, classified in the semiorder Euprimates, first appeared during the early Eocene epoch in the northern hemisphere and possibly originated in Asia. These first euprimates were roughly comparable in their anatomy to modern lemurs and lorises, although both the strepsirhine and haplorhine suborders were represented. Anthropoid primates—with their improved vision, reduced sense of smell, and more complex brains—evolved around 45 mya, with the superfamily Hominoidea making its debut around 20 mya.

The early hominoids fell into two categories: dental apes, which resembled modern apes only in their dental and cranial traits (postcranially, they were more like monkeys); and suspensory apes, which also showed adaptations for forelimb-dominated locomotion (arm-swinging and arm-hanging). After a period of considerable success, when evolutionary radiations increased their diversity and geographic expansion carried them into Europe and Asia, the apes began to decline in number and variety during a period of late Miocene climatic cooling. It was at this time—some 5 to 7 million years ago—that modern humans' last ape ancestors are thought to have lived, although their precise identity is still unknown.

We do know, however, what it took to convert those apes into hominins: primarily, the remodeling of quadrupedal creatures into bipeds. And because understanding this conversion is an essential prerequisite to studying the hominin fossil record, the last sections of the chapter are devoted to a description of the anatomy of bipedalism.

Mini-TIMELINE

Date (Years Ago or Geologic Period or Epoch)	Evolutionary Events	Important Taxa
5–7 million	First hominins	*Ardipithecus, Orrorin, Sahelanthropus*
Late Miocene	Apes decline strongly	*Khoratpithecus, Oreopithecus*
Mid Miocene	Apes spread and diversify	*Dryopithecus, Equatorius-Kenyapithecus, Sivapithecus*
Early Miocene	First apes; first Old World monkeys	*Proconsul, Morotopithecus,* monkey subfamily Victoriapithecinae
Late Oligocene	First New World monkeys	*Branisella*
Early Oligocene	Anthropoids diversify	*Aegyptopithecus*
Mid Eocene	First anthropoids; strepsirhines diversify	*Algeripithecus, Eosimias*
Early Eocene	First euprimates	Superfamilies Adapoidea and Omomyoidea
Late Cretaceous	First fossil plesiadapiforms	*Purgatorius*

Studying Fossils

The study of prehistoric humans is linked inextricably with the study of all other primate fossils. Humans' characteristics evolved out of those of earlier, nonhuman species, and so in order to understand ourselves, we must analyze the remains of ancient archaic primates and euprimates. Luckily, fragments of these creatures are being discovered in ever-increasing numbers, and anthropologists can reconstruct (cautiously) their anatomical and behavioral (including socioecological) traits through comparisons with living primates. Additionally, interpretations of fossils are based on estimates of their age, and thanks to advances in **geology, paleontology,** and especially atomic physics, scientists usually can determine age with considerable accuracy. Once we have all of the information before us—anatomy, behavior, and age—we can begin to group our primate ancestors into species, genera, and larger lineages and to work out those lineages' evolutionary connections.

Geology the study of the earth's physical formation, its nature, and its continuing development.

Paleontology the study of the fossil remains and biology of organisms that lived in the past.

At least, that's how it works in theory. The tasks of fossil interpretation and the reconstruction of phylogenies are complicated immensely by the simple fact that all primates converge in their various traits as one goes back in time. In other words, telling modern strepsirhines, monkeys, apes, and humans apart is easy because all have evolved in a somewhat different manner, with different sets of primitive and derived traits, and so they simply don't look or act alike. But since all living primates are descended from a common ancestor, the farther back we go, the more similar their fossil remains become. Indeed, as later sections of this chapter will show, even the application of such general labels as "monkeys" and "apes" becomes difficult as we move back in time.

Looking far back into the past is absolutely necessary, however, because relatively recent developments that led to humankind were made possible only by earlier developments. Much of who and what we are was determined by the evolutionary histories of our prehominin ancestors, and so it is to those creatures that this chapter is devoted.

Dating Procedures

Before we begin analyzing traits and reconstructing evolutionary lineages, it is important to say a bit more about what fossils are and how scientists go about dating them. Regarding the first point, fossils are traces of deceased organisms that (typically) are preserved in rock. Most often the hard parts—shells, bones, and especially teeth—are preserved as their original molecules are replaced by minerals. Under certain rare circumstances, traces of the soft parts of ancient organisms (gills, guts, feathers) also may be preserved. Most fossilization takes place as dead organisms are covered by muddy sediments at the bottom of a sea or lake or at the bend of a river. Fossils can also accumulate in caves and sinkholes as dead creatures are covered by rock falls and washed-in or blown-in soil (or, as during the late stages of hominin prehistory, covered by the living debris of subsequent human cave dwellers). Of course, deliberate burial can also lead to fossilization, but this practice is a very recent one and limited to the human lineage.

In the two centuries that have passed since the work of Cuvier and others began to reveal the importance of the fossil record, many different procedures have been developed to provide dates for ancient remains. Detailed descriptions of several important dating methods are given in Appendix 2 at the end of the book, but a brief overview of dating is useful here.

Stratigraphy the sequence of geologic strata, or rock layers, formed by materials deposited by water or wind; also the study of this sequence.

First of all, within the science of geology the subdiscipline known as **stratigraphy** attempts to interpret the production of rock layers—whether they occurred by the underwater deposition of sediments, by glacial or volcanic action, or by the accumulation of windblown soil—and their subsequent rearrangement, if any, as the result of earth movements and weathering (Figure 5.1). Stratigraphic information allows the **relative dating** of any fossils contained in the various rock layers; in undisturbed strata, the oldest layers are the deepest, and both strata and fossils get younger as one nears the surface. Although stratigraphy alone doesn't tell us a fossil's actual age, simply knowing that one specimen is older or younger than another can be critically important for working out evolutionary sequences.

Relative dating estimating the ages of *geologic* deposits (and the *fossils* in them) by determining their *stratigraphic* level in relation to other deposits whose relative or absolute age is known.

Furthermore, because every species has a finite lifetime between its origin and extinction, well-studied fossil lineages—with known sequences of species dated relative to one another—can be used to date other material by **faunal correlation.** For example, a newly discovered hominin specimen found in the same rock layer as a variety of pig known to be ancient within the pig lineage can properly be assumed to be quite old, as well. Better yet, if the actual age of the fossil pig species has been determined (see the methodologies that follow), that same age can be attributed to the hominin material (Lewin, 1987).

Faunal correlation dating a site by the similarity of its animal *fossils* to those of another site that may carry a reliable *absolute date*.

Finally, the claim that fossils from a particular site come from the same rock layer and therefore are the same relative age can be tested by analyzing their levels of certain chemicals, usually nitrogen (which is lost during fossilization) and uranium and fluorine (both of which commonly accumulate in bones from groundwater). Noncontemporaneous specimens will show different chemical levels.

Methods for **absolute dating,** which provide actual ages for strata and/or fossils, are a much more recent scientific development than stratigraphy (F. H. Brown, 1992). Many of these procedures are based on atomic physics and the natural tendency of one element (or isotope, a variety of a particular element) to decay into some other element (or isotope). For example, both carbon 14 (an unstable isotope) and carbon 12 (stable) are present in the atmosphere; C^{14} is produced naturally from nitrogen (Figure 5.2). Organisms incorporate both types of carbon when they are alive. After death, C^{14} decays at a known rate and by measuring the ratio between the two carbon isotopes, one can determine how long ago death (usually coincident with fossilization) occurred. Somewhat similarly, potassium 40 breaks down into the gaseous element argon in volcanic rocks and measuring the potassium–argon (symbolized K/Ar) ratio provides dates for these strata and any fossils they contain. (This procedure is especially important in East Africa, where volcanic activity was widespread in the past.) A newly developed test, the Ar^{40}/Ar^{39} procedure, is derived from K/Ar dating.

Absolute dating determining the age in years of *geologic* deposits (and the *fossils* in them). This may be done by examining the chemical composition of rock fragments containing radioactive substances, which decay at known rates.

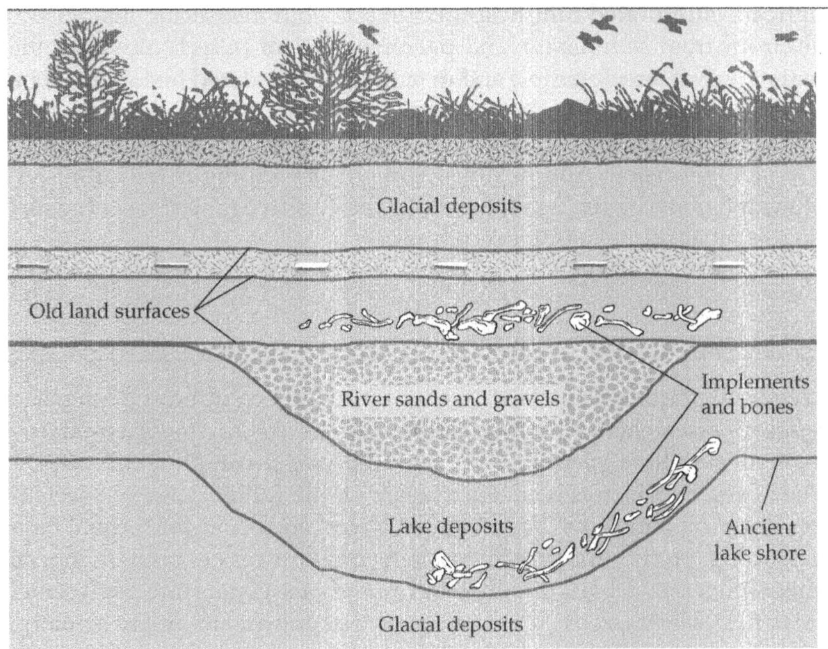

FIGURE 5.1 Fossils are found in deposits formed by the action of glaciers and rivers or laid down in ancient riverbeds, lakes, estuaries, and seas. Some deposits are windblown and may contain volcanic ash. Fossils are laid down in more or less horizontal beds, or *strata*, as shown here. *Stratigraphy* is the science that attempts to understand stratigraphic deposition—its form, its sequence, and its age.

FIGURE 5.2
Radiocarbon dating is used for organic materials. Carbon 14, or C^{14}, is an unstable form of carbon (the stable form is carbon 12). A certain proportion of C^{14} exists in the atmosphere and as carbon dioxide (CO_2) is absorbed and incorporated by plants in the form of carbohydrates. Animals absorb C^{14} by eating the plants. Thereafter, the C^{14} disintegrates at a known rate (the half-life). The extent of this disintegration can be measured and related to the amount of C^{14} remaining, and so too the age of the organic material.

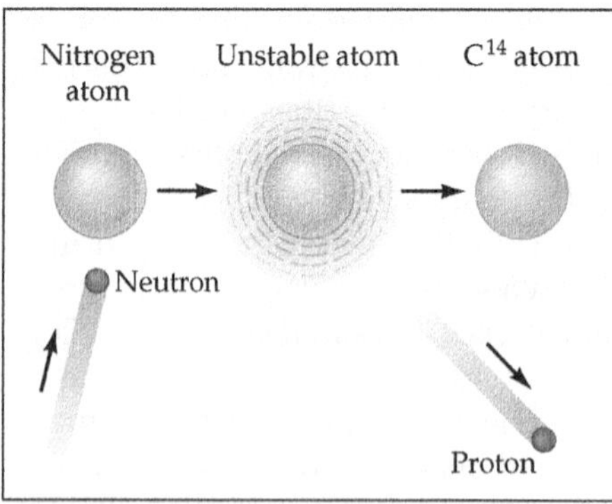

1. Nitrogen atom becomes C^{14} atom in the atmosphere.

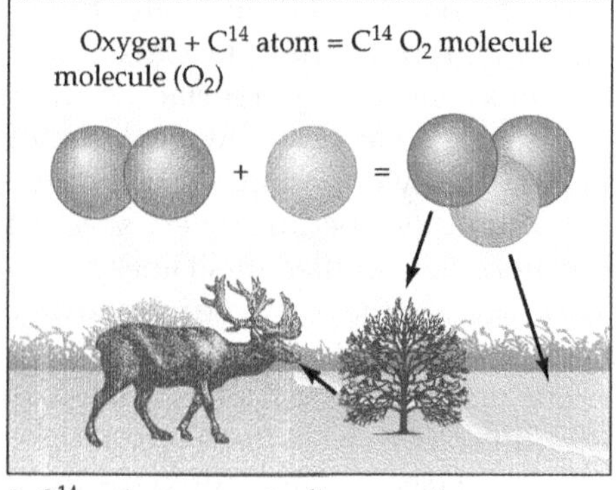

2. C^{14} and oxygen enter live organisms.

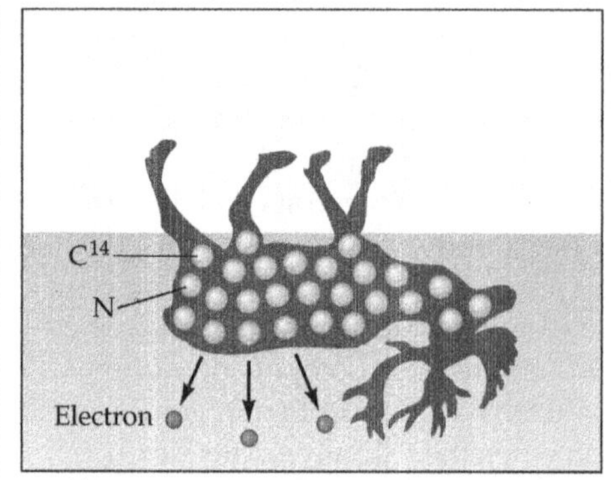

3. C^{14} atoms disintegrate.

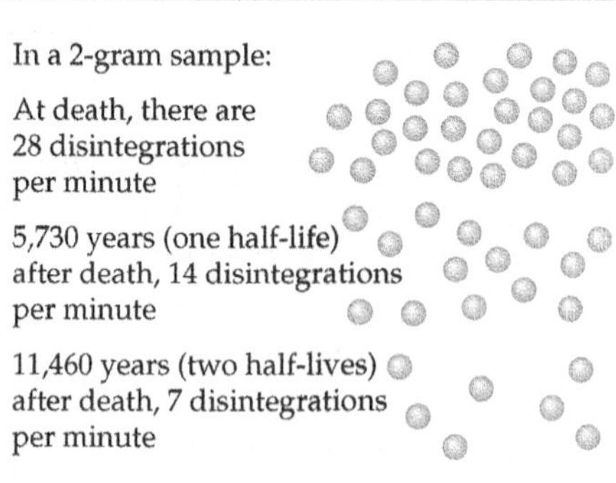

4. C^{14} continues to disintegrate at an orderly, predictable rate, allowing calculation of the age.

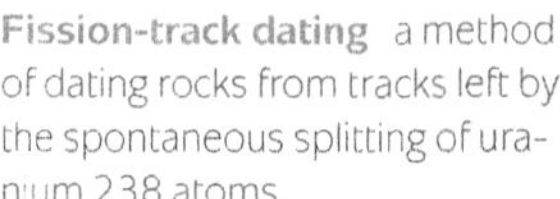

Fission-track dating a method of dating rocks from tracks left by the spontaneous splitting of uranium 238 atoms.

Thermoluminescence a method of dating pottery and stone tools by heating them to release trapped electrons; the electrons produce measurable light.

Optically stimulated luminescence a method of dating sediments by stimulating them with intense light; such stimulation causes the sediments to release trapped electrons and produce measurable light.

Paleomagnetism magnetism preserved in rock originally generated by the earth's magnetic field. Past fluctuations in the intensity and direction of this field allow correlation between strata; a form of *relative dating* that can be used for *absolute dating* because the historic pattern of magnetic fluctuations and reversals is known and dated.

Eocene the *geologic* epoch extending from 56 to 34 million years BP.

Several additional dating procedures, many based in one way or another on radioactive decay, have been developed and are described in Appendix 2. These include **fission-track dating** (based on tracks made in mineral crystals by spontaneously splitting uranium 238 atoms), **thermoluminescence** (TL, based on the release of trapped electrons from pottery and rocks heated in fires by early humans), **optically stimulated luminescence** (like TL, but measuring the release of trapped electrons from sediments), and **paleomagnetism** (which measures the fossilized magnetism in a rock sample and matches it with a dated history of global magnetic reversals; see Figure 5.3). Altogether, the various relative and absolute dating techniques enable scientists to pinpoint the ages of most (but not all) fossils with considerable precision. And as noted earlier, such dating is critical for evolutionary interpretations. Figure 5.4 summarizes the effective time spans of some of the most important absolute dating procedures.

The Earliest Primates

Trying to unravel the earliest stages of primate evolution is a long-standing challenge for researchers. The oldest known fossils of primates of a modern aspect date back to 55 million years ago, the early **Eocene** epoch (Ni et al., 2004; Figure 5.5). These first euprimates were creatures with the full package of specialties, including grasping hands and feet, orbital convergence, and postorbital bars. From the beginning of the euprimate fossil record, however, both living suborders—strepsirhines and haplorhines—and numerous genera are represented (Conroy, 1990; R. D. Martin, 2004), a fact implying that euprimates might actually have come into existence and started to diversify long before their known fossils began to accumulate. Indeed, one recent study has estimated that euprimates first evolved

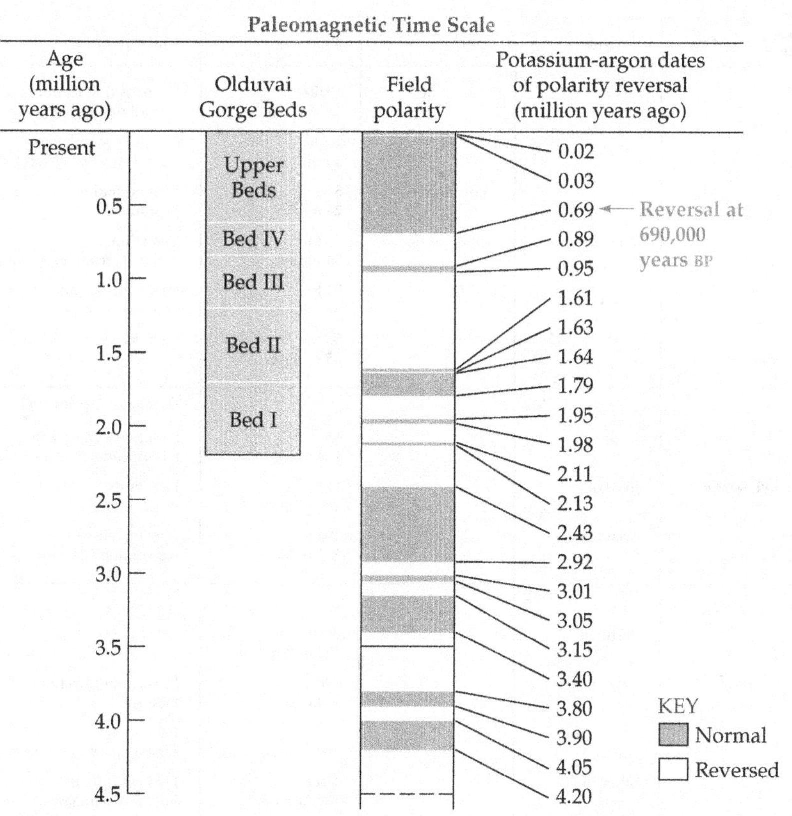

FIGURE 5.3 The left-hand column shows the sequence of beds from the important fossil locality of Olduvai Gorge, while the right-hand column shows known reversals in world magnetic polarity during the past 4.5 million years. The evidence is obtained by measuring the polarity of volcanic lavas, which can also be potassium-argon dated. Deposits that are only roughly dated by relative methods can often be more accurately dated by the measurement of their magnetic polarity and referral to this chart.

Source: Based partly on F. H. Brown, 1992.

about 82 mya (Tavaré et al., 2002)—well before the extinction of the dinosaurs and the beginning of the so-called age of mammals with the **Paleocene** epoch.

But does the 82 myr date truly mark the start of the order Primates? Some researchers think not. They refer to molecular data that trace our order's separation from other mammals back some 90 myr to the mid **Cretaceous** period; the separation of strepsirhines and haplorhines then followed some 8 million years later (Tavaré et al., 2002). If this scenario is correct, however, who might the hypothesized premodern primates have been and what might they have been like?

For many years, the arboreal and mainly insectivorous tree shrews (Figure 5.8) were considered to be primitive primates and probably to resemble the first members of our order (Le Gros Clark, 1959). Although they were reclassified in the 1970s and placed in their own order (Scandentia), tree shrews may still provide useful clues concerning the features of primates' last mammalian ancestor (Rasmussen, 2002; Sargis, 2004). And in fact, the fossil group that many scientists now consider to be the oldest known primates—the **plesiadapiforms**—do resemble tree shrews

Paleocene the *geologic* epoch extending from 65 to 56 million years BP.

Cretaceous a period of the Mesozoic era, dating 65 to 144 million years ago.

Plesiadapiforms the common name for *extinct primates* belonging to the *semiorder Plesiadapiformes*.

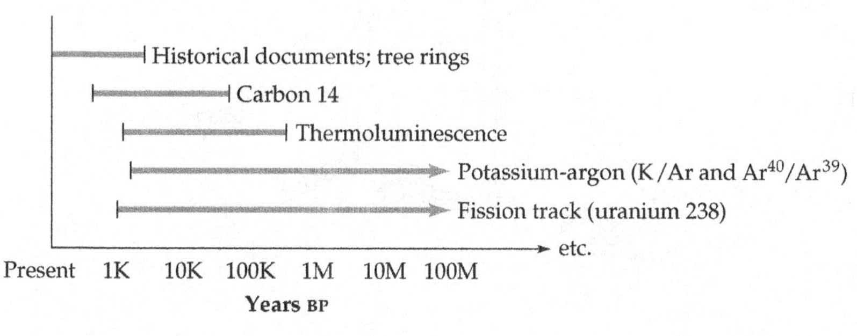

FIGURE 5.4 Approximate ranges of time in which dates can be established by the methods discussed in this chapter. The time scale is logarithmic: K = thousand years; M = million years.

Sources: F. H. Brown, 1992; Deino et al., 1998; Feathers, 1996; Wagner, 1996.

FIGURE 5.5
The vast span of the geologic time scale is divided into eras, periods, and epochs, as shown in this chart. It is hard to comprehend fully the great period of time during which nature and humankind have evolved. If the almost 500 million years of vertebrate evolution are symbolized by one hour of time, then euprimate evolution took seven minutes and human evolution occurred in the last twelve seconds of that hour. ME = mass extinction event.

Sources: Dates primarily based on R. A. Martin (2004) and Mundil et al. (2004).

Years BP / Eras	Period	Epoch	Years BP	Main Events
CENOZOIC	Quaternary	Pleistocene	10,000 to 1.8 million	Humans first learn to use and control fire in temperate zones
		Pliocene	1.8 to 5 million	Genus *Homo* appears Age of *Australopithecus, Paranthropus*
		Miocene	5 to 24 million	First hominins First apes
	Tertiary	Oligocene	24 to 34 million	Catarrhines and platyrrhines separate
		Eocene	34 to 56 million	First anthropoids First euprimates
65 million		Paleocene	56 to 65 million	*Purgatorius*
MESOZOIC	ME			First archaic primates?
	Cretaceous		65 to 144 million	First flowering plants Disappearance of large dinosaurs
	Jurassic		144 to 206 million	First birds
	ME			
253 million	Triassic		206 to 253 million	First mammals Age of Reptiles begins
PALEOZOIC	ME			
	Permian		253 to 290 million	
	Carboniferous		290 to 354 million	First coniferous trees First reptiles
	ME			
	Devonian		354 to 409 million	First forests First amphibians, insects, and bony fish
	Silurian		409 to 439 million	First land plants First fish with jaws
	ME			
	Ordovician		439 to 495 million	First vertebrates: armored fish without jaws
543 million	Cambrian		495 to 543 million	First shell-bearing animals
PRECAMBRIAN			600 million	First multicellular animals
			3.5 billion	First living things: algae, bacteria
			4 billion	Formation of primordial seas
			4.5 billion	Formation of earth

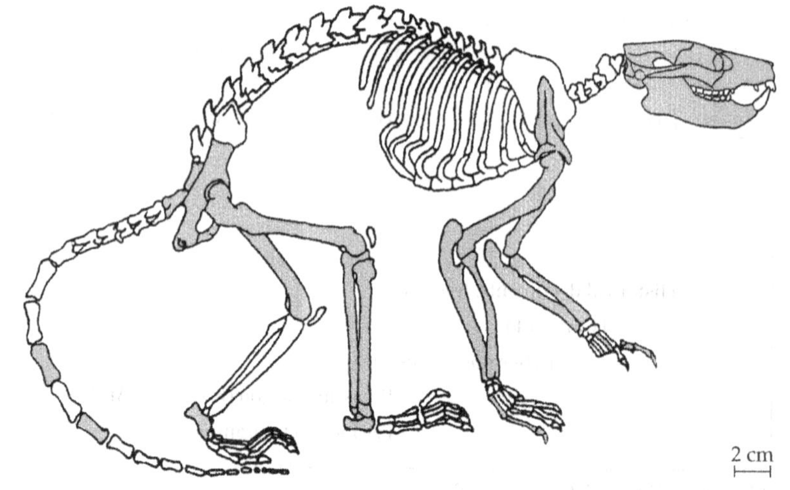

FIGURE 5.6
Reconstructed skeleton of *Plesiadapis tricuspidens.* Elements that are unshaded are conjectured; other elements are known from fossil material. Note the rodentlike dentition and missing postorbital bars.

Source: Robert D. Martin (1990).

in several primitive features, including low skulls and small brains (Rasmussen, 2002; Sargis, 2004; Figure 5.6).

The plesiadapiforms were chipmunk- to cat-sized creatures that moved about on the ground and in the trees. Their remains come mainly from North American and European deposits of the Paleocene epoch, and the oldest known genus is called ***Purgatorius*** (65-plus million years old from Montana; Van Valen and Sloan, 1965). Plesiadapiforms enjoyed warm-temperate to subtropical climates even in the higher northern latitudes, and their diets were varied, with some species being mainly insectivorous and others gramnivorous, folivorous, or frugivorous. Virtually all plesiadapiforms had enlarged, rodentlike incisors, which in some species were modified for cropping vegetation (Conroy, 1990; Figure 5.6). Their main claim to primate status has long been the details of their molar anatomy, but in many ways (e.g., the lack of postorbital bars and orbital convergence; typically, claws on semiprehensile digits; specialized front teeth), the plesiadapiforms seem very different from euprimates (Rasmussen, 2002).

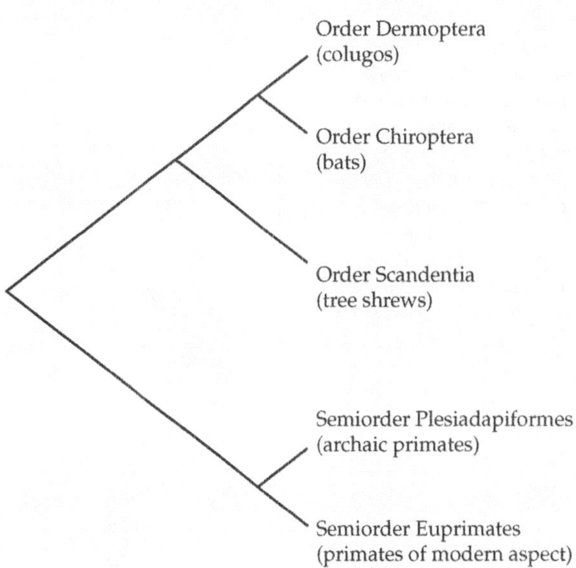

FIGURE 5.7
Cladogram showing the relationships between primates and their closest evolutionary relatives.
Source: Sargis, (2002).

Considering the full set of plesiadapiform characteristics, however, it seems reasonable to include them as archaic members of the order Primates and to place them in their own semiorder, Plesiadapiformes (Table 5.1). Six families belong to this semiorder, among them **Plesiadapidae, Paromomyidae,** and **Carpolestidae** (Conroy, 1990; R. D. Martin, 1990). The semiorder arrangement reflects a combination of similarities and significant differences between Plesiadapiformes and Euprimates. (Interestingly, two new derived traits shared by euprimates and certain plesiadapiforms have recently been reported. At least one paromomyid species showed a pattern of middle ear nerve canal placement previously thought to be unique to euprimates [Silcox, 2003], and a new study of the foot of a carpolestid variety revealed a big toe that was capable of grasping small terminal branches and probably bore a nail, not a claw [Bloch and Boyer, 2002].)

But were the plesiadapiforms ancestral to the modern primates? Probably not. In the opinion of most experts, they were too specialized to fill that role. Rather, they should be viewed as an archaic sister group to euprimates (Figure 5.7). Nonetheless, a knowledge of plesiadapid anatomy provides important clues about the possible path of euprimate evolution. For example, the discovery that at least one form of Paleocene carpolestid simultaneously lacked orbital convergence and possessed opposable big toes has suggested to some researchers that, as proposed by the

Purgatorius an *extinct genus* of *plesiadapiform*, dating to about 65 mya.

Plesiadapidae a family of *extinct* archaic *primates*; a family of the *semiorder Plesiadapiformes*.

Paromomyidae a family of *extinct* archaic *primates*; a family of the *semiorder Plesiadapiformes*.

Carpolestidae a family of *extinct* archaic *primates*; a family of the *semiorder Plesiadapiformes*.

TABLE 5.1 Partial Taxonomy of the Fossil and Living Primates

Semiorder	Suborder	Family (Plesiadapiformes only)
Plesiadapiformes		
		Carpolestidae
		Microsyopidae
		Paromomyidae
		Picrodontidae
		Plesiadapidae
		Saxonellidae
Euprimates		
	Strepsirhini	
	Haplorhini	

FIGURE 5.8
Tree shrews are found in Southeast Asia. They are primitive mammals and may be similar to the first primates. Their appearance is somewhat similar to that of the squirrel, but they are quite distinct from any rodent. Their bodies are about 5 inches (13 centimeters) long.

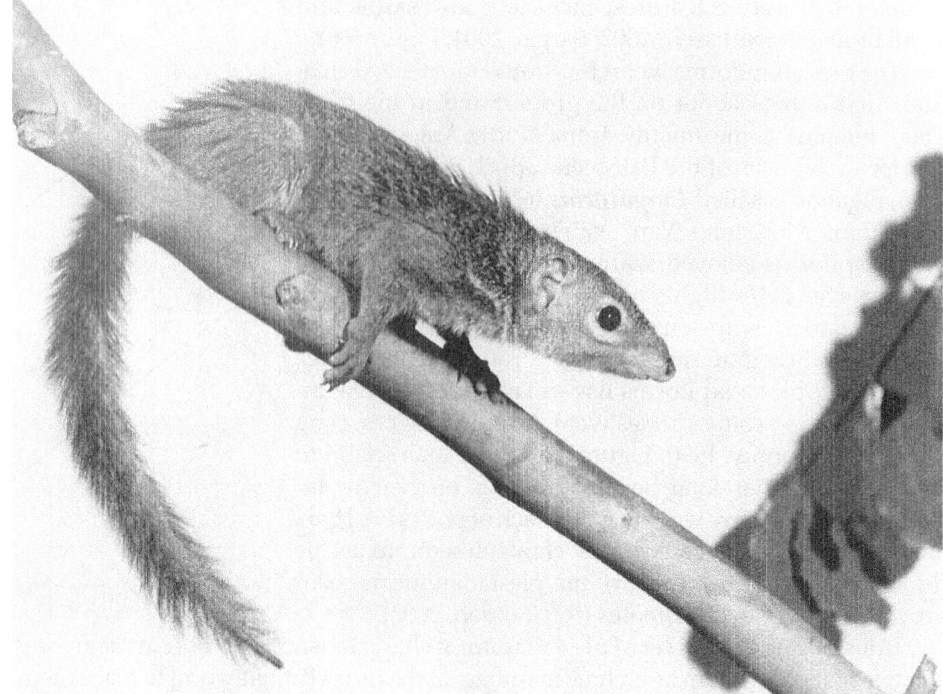

arboreal theory, euprimates' grasping extremities first evolved for treetop locomotion and plant food foraging, not for predation on insects (Bloch and Boyer, 2002; Sargis, 2002). (Not surprisingly, the visual predation hypothesis supporters reject this notion [Kirk et al., 2003].)

Colugos nonprimate *mammals* from Asia known for arboreal gliding; misnamed "flying lemurs."

And so, we are left without a clear idea of the ancestors of our now double-pronged Primate order. Besides tree shrews, primates are most similar to **colugos** (misnamed "flying lemurs," order Dermoptera) and bats (order Chiroptera) (Figure 5.7). Perhaps continued comparisons with these creatures and additional fossil discoveries will eventually lead to the identification of our missing forebears. One thing is clear, however, and that is that none of the plesiadapiforms survived beyond the Eocene. By the succeeding Oligocene epoch, the euprimates had the order to themselves (R. D. Martin, 1990).

Undoubted Primate Fossils

The semiorder Euprimates literally burst upon the paleontological scene at the beginning of the Eocene epoch (55 mya). Dozens of euprimate genera have been discovered from Eocene deposits in the northern hemisphere, including sites in North America, Europe, and Asia. Given this, many experts think the evidence is convincing for a northern origin for the semiorder (Tavaré et al., 2002), and some suggest Asia as the most likely spot (Beard, 1998, as cited by Hooker et al., 1999). An earlier suggestion of an African origin for euprimates was based on a fossil named ***Altiatlasius*** from the late Paleocene of Morocco (Rasmussen, 2002). Recently, however, new discoveries have forced a reanalysis of *Altiatlasius*, which now seems most likely to have been a plesiadapiform migrant that dispersed southward from North America via Europe (Hooker et al., 1999). Paralleling uncertainties about the ancestry of the entire Primate order, the immediate forebears of the euprimates are unknown at present.

Altiatlasius once thought to be the oldest known *euprimate fossil*; a *plesiadapiform* from the late *Paleocene* of North Africa.

The first euprimates were marked with the full array of modern traits: grasping hands and feet, close-set eyes bounded by postorbital bars, and teeth that allowed them to feed on a mixed diet of insects and/or plant products (Covert, 2002; Rasmussen, 2002). Experts continue to argue whether these were primarily adap-

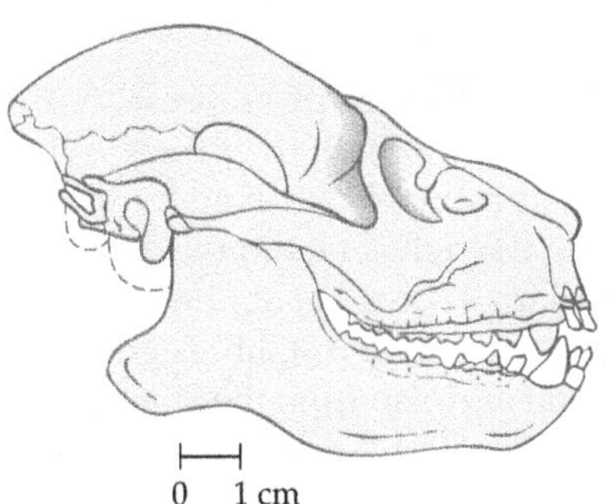

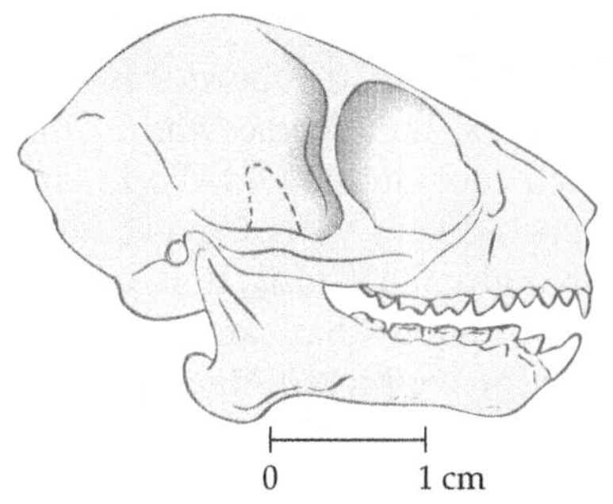

FIGURE 5.9
Representative skulls of early euprimates. Adapid (*Leptadapis magnus*) shown at left and omomyid (*Necrolemur antiquus*) to the right. Both are from European mid Eocene deposits.

tations for visual predation on insects or harvesting the terminal-branch products of the diversifying angiosperms (flowering plants; see Ni et al., 2004). Both of the modern euprimate suborders were represented from the outset: strepsirhines by the Eocene superfamily **Adapoidea** (commonly, the adapids) and haplorhines by the superfamily **Omomyoidea** (commonly, the omomyids; Figure 5.9). Some authorities describe the members of these two superfamilies as lemurlike and tarsierlike, respectively (Delson and Tattersall, 2000), and while others disagree, this does seem to reflect their evolutionary relationships: Adapids were probably ancestral to modern lemurs and lorises and omomyids to modern tarsiers and anthropoids (Covert, 2002). Additional specimens are needed to solidify the early euprimates' evolutionary connections, and time is of the essence, since many of the important fossil deposits are threatened by commercial excavation (Box 5.1).

Adapoidea and Omomyoidea superfamilies of *Eocene euprimates;* now extinct.

BOX 5.1 CURRENT ISSUE

Old Bones for Sale

People everywhere are fascinated by evidence of ancient life, be it artifacts from prehistoric cultures or the fossil remains of our human forebears or earlier creatures. Over the centuries, that fascination has taken a rather heavy toll on prehistoric cultural sites, with looters doing considerable destruction in search of marketable artifacts, including bits and pieces of ancient monuments. Recently, strong pressure has been brought to bear (mainly by indigenous people claiming descent from specific prehistoric groups) that has helped to slow the archaeological pilfering and bring the human antiquities trade under control.

But what about the nonhuman fossil trade? For better or worse, sales of fossils appear to be growing rapidly. The remains of ancient mollusks, arthropods, fishes, and plants are commonly seen in rock shops and nature stores, and they are also for sale on the World Wide Web, through catalogs, and at auctions. Even the remains of ancient primates sometimes show up in the listings and go to the highest bidder.

The obvious problem here is that fossils that are sold into private collections are usually unavailable for scientific study. (Even if they end up in public museums, many commercial fossils are of little scientific value since they lack information on geologic context.) In the United States, many important fossil deposits are located on federal public lands, and collection at those sites historically has been allowed only by permission and for educational and scientific purposes—the rationale being that fossils on federal lands belong to the public at large and thus should not be exploited for private gain. (Some 80 to 90 percent of Americans agree with this position.)

Within the last few years, however, commercial fossil hunters and their supporters have been trying to open up federal public lands for nonscientific collection and sales. It has become a classic public versus private interest controversy. What's your opinion on this question: Restriction of fossil collecting to specialists working for the (educational and scientific) public good or unrestricted collection and free enterprise? Americans hate to have their activities restricted by government regulations, but should they be free to sell fossil prosimians from public lands? Does every basement collection need an omomyid?

Tarsiiformes and Anthropoids Evolve

The Euprimate suborder of the Haplorhini is currently represented by two hyporders: Tarsiiformes and Anthropoidea (Table 3.3). Both of these hyporders have their roots in the Old World, and both had probably evolved by the early Eocene epoch (Beard, 2002; Covert, 2002). Among the oldest tarsiid remains are those from Shanghuang, China, that date to about 45 mya (Beard et al., 1994). Anthropoid fossils of about that same age have been reported from Glib Zegdou in the North African country of Algeria (***Algeripithecus***) and also from the Shanghuang deposits in China (***Eosimias;*** Beard, 2002; Beard et al., 1994). Additional anthropoid remains dating to the late middle Eocene–early **Oligocene** have been discovered in Egypt's Fayum Depression (e.g., ***Catopithecus*** and other members of the extinct group called the **oligopithecines;** Rasmussen and Simons, 1992; Simons and Rasmussen, 1996), Algeria (***Biretia;*** Beard, 2002), Thailand (***Siamopithecus;*** Chaimanee et al., 1997), and Myanmar (formerly Burma; genera include ***Myanmarpithecus;*** Ciochon and Gunnell, 2002). (Two other genera long thought to be Burmese anthropoids, *Pondaungia* and *Amphipithecus,* have been claimed recently to be adapid strepsirhines [Ciochon and Gunnell, 2002].) Given the similarity in age of the African and Asian anthropoid remains and their wide distribution on both continents, it is currently impossible to pinpoint the place of origin of this hyporder (compare Beard, 2002, with Dagosto, 2002).

Algeripithecus an *anthropoid primate* from the early-middle *Eocene* epoch of North Africa.

Eosimias an *anthropoid* from the mid *Eocene* epoch of China.

Oligocene the *geologic* epoch extending from 34 to 24 million years BP.

Catopithecus a particularly well-known *oligopithecine* from the Fayum in Africa.

Oligopithecines a late *Eocene anthropoid;* many have been collected from Egypt's Fayum Depression.

Biretia an early *anthropoid* from Algeria.

Siamopithecus a late *Eocene anthropoid* from Thailand.

Myanmarpithecus an early *anthropoid* from Myanmar (formerly Burma).

A closer look at the oligopithecines from northern Africa will provide a better idea of what the early anthropoids looked like and how they behaved. Around 36 mya, the Fayum Depression was a tropical and swampy region lying along the southern shore of the Mediterranean. Heavily wooded in parts and laced with rivers, it provided a prime habitat for the diversifying anthropoids. Among the oligopithecine genera were *Oligopithecus, Proteopithecus,* and *Catopithecus.* All were small-bodied (about 2.2 pounds, or 1 kilogram) forest dwellers that probably ate a mixed diet of fruit and insects. Among the fossils of *Catopithecus* is a well-preserved skull that demonstrates such diagnostic anthropoid traits as bony eye sockets and fused frontal bones.

But the oligopithecines were not typically anthropoid in all of their features. Demonstrating that anthropoid traits evolved in mosaic fashion, rather than all at once, the oligopithecines still showed a low ratio of brain size to body size as well as some strepsirhinelike features in their jaws and teeth. *Catopithecus,* for example, had an unfused mandibular symphysis. Interestingly, the oligopithecines varied somewhat in their dental formulae: While *Catopithecus* had a total of eight premolars, *Proteopithecus* had twelve. Although too generalized to be classified as either monkeys or apes, the oligopithecines give us a good view of the anatomy, diet, and habitat of early anthropoids (Rasmussen and Simons, 1992; Simons and Rasmussen, 1996).

Oligocene Anthropoids

By the early Oligocene epoch, anthropoids were enjoying much success in Africa. Several genera had evolved, including *Parapithecus, Propliopithecus, Apidium* (Figure 5.10), and ***Aegyptopithecus*** (Figures 5.10 and 5.11). Although these creatures showed some advances over their Eocene ancestors, analyses of their total morphological patterns show that they were still very primitive. *Parapithecus* and *Apidium* are best classified as basal anthropoids that preceded the evolutionary separation of platyrrhines and catarrhines (Fleagle, 1988). *Propliopithecus* and *Aegyptopithecus,* on the other hand, can be identified as catarrhines, although both were too primitive to be classified further as either monkeys or apes.

Aegyptopithecus a basal *catarrhine* from the Fayum in Africa; dated to the *Oligocene* epoch.

A detailed analysis of the total morphology of *Aegyptopithecus* shows how such a conclusion is reached (Conroy, 1990; Fleagle, 1988). Although certain dental features suggest that *Aegyptopithecus* had evolved into an ape-grade creature—

Branisella boliviana an *Oligocene platyrrhine monkey* from Bolivia.

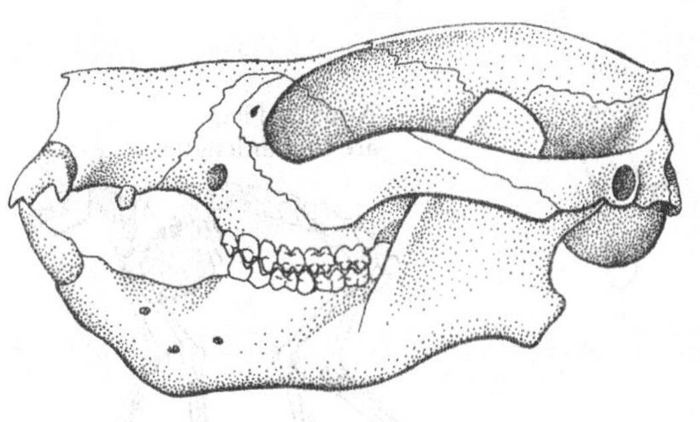

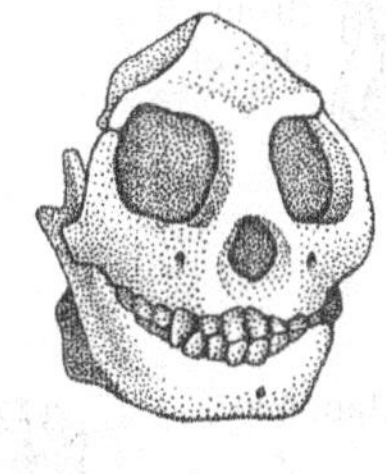

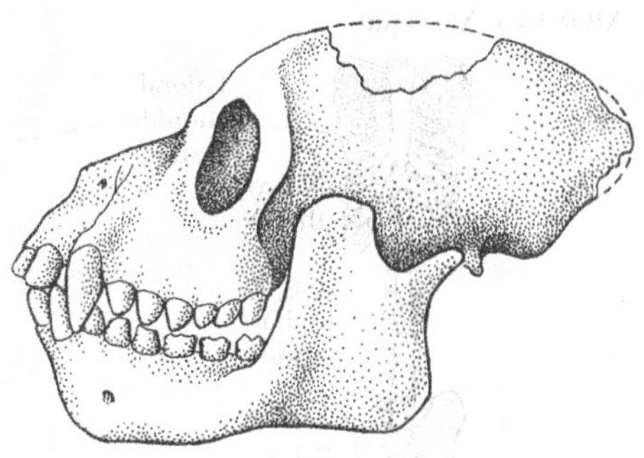

FIGURE 5.10
The orbits of living primates are surrounded by a ring of bone that constitutes a lateral extension of the frontal bone joining the cheekbone. This structure protects the large, forward-pointing eyes. Fossil anthropoids such as *Apidium* had these laterally bounded orbits and also a full bony socket, as did the more advanced *Aegyptopithecus*. In more primitive archaic primates, such as *Plesiadapis*, the orbit was open at the back and side. The scale is 60 percent actual size.

2123/2123 dental formula, five-cusped (but not yet Y-5) molars, rectangular dental arcade (Figure 5.11)—other features are distinctly monkey-like. *Aegyptopithecus* was an arboreal quadruped, rather than an arm-hanger or arm-swinger, sported a tail, and had a monkey-shaped skull. (See Figure 5.12 for anatomical comparisons of modern monkeys and apes.) Thus, given their mosaic anatomy, *Propliopithecus* and *Aegyptopithecus* are best regarded as generalized catarrhines that may have been on or near the ancestral line for all later anthropoids of the Old World (Benefit, 1999; Conroy, 1990; but see R. D. Martin, 1990). The stage was set for the evolution of the modern superfamilies of monkeys and apes.

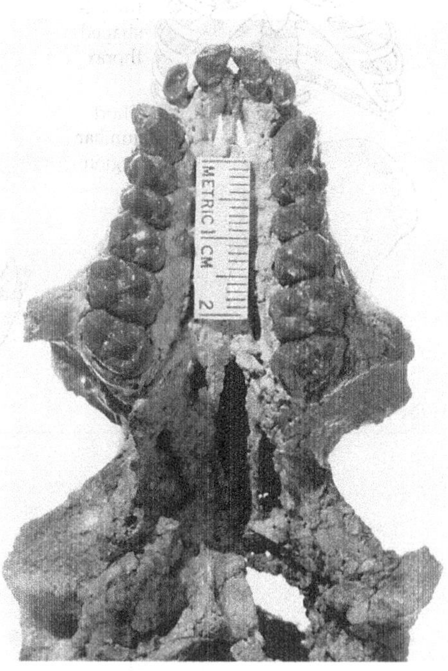

FIGURE 5.11
The palate of *Aegyptopithecus* shows a somewhat apelike dentition and almost rectangular dental arcade. The creature, however, was very small, as indicated by the scale. This specimen was discovered by Elwyn Simons in the Fayum region of Egypt. It is dated about 32 million years BP.

Evolution of the New World Monkeys

Humans are catarrhine primates whose evolutionary origins reside in the Old World. That being the case, the history of the New World monkeys is of rather secondary importance to the story being told here. Nonetheless, the evolutionary appearance of these "second cousins" of ours deserves at least a brief description before we move on to fossil apes.

The oldest fossils of platyrrhine monkeys come from late Oligocene deposits in Bolivia. ***Branisella boliviana,*** a smallish (2.2 pounds, 1 kilogram) New World monkey variety, lived some 25 to 26 mya (Fleagle and Tejedor, 2002). Other genera—such as the Patagonian monkeys *Dolichocebus, Homunculus,* and *Tremacebus*—are probably a few million years younger (R. D. Martin, 1990). These finds reveal a 20-million-year gap between the first appearance of anthropoids in Africa and Asia and their (apparent) arrival in the New World. But where did the first platyrrhines come from and how did they reach the Americas?

The best explanation at present is that they came from Africa and crossed the South Atlantic by a combination of island hopping and rafting aboard floating mats of vegetation. Geophysical studies have shown that during the Oligocene epoch, the continents of Africa, North America, and South America were in about the same relative positions to one another as they are today. The primary difference in geophysical relations was the absence of a land connection between North and South

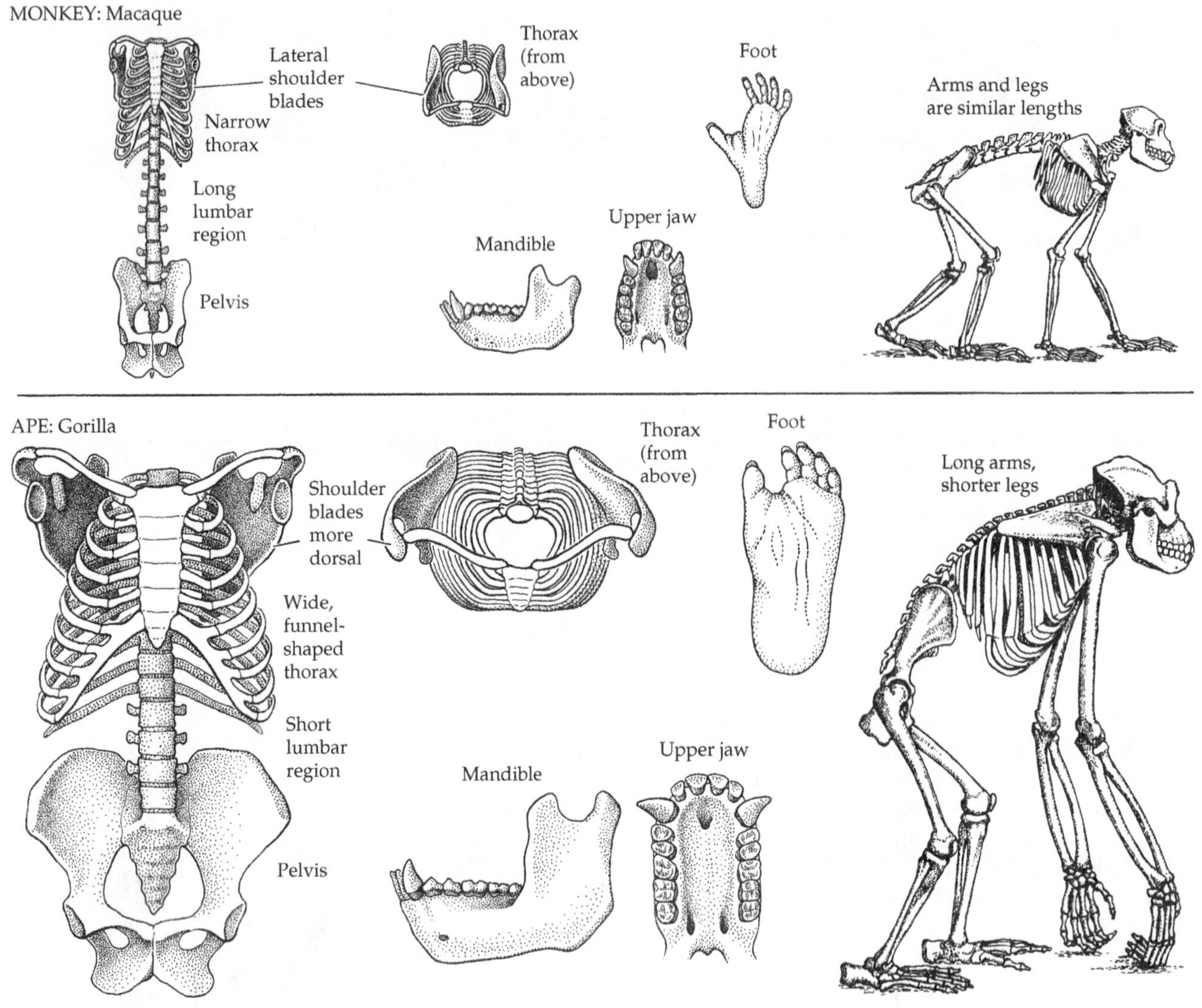

FIGURE 5.12
Ape and monkey skeletons have much in common. Nonetheless, apes are more like humans than like monkeys in skeletal structure. Note the different proportions of the limbs; the form of the rib cage and shoulder blade; and the use of hands in locomotion. Scale is approximately one-twentieth actual size. Note that the macaque shown has a relatively short tail.

America; the two continents were separated by the Caribbean Sea. A reconstruction of Oligocene ocean currents suggests that primates would have been carried from Africa to South America much more readily than from North America. Additionally, there may well have been mid-Atlantic islands in existence during the Oligocene that would have aided the east–west migration of platyrrhine ancestors (Conroy, 1990; Fleagle, 1988; Fleagle and Tejedor, 2002).

Once in South and Central America, the platyrrhines diversified strongly to produce the great variety of New World monkeys alive today. They made no contribution, however, to the evolution of humankind.

The Miocene: Apes at Last

Miocene the *geologic* epoch extending from 24 to 5 million years BP.

The earliest known members of the superfamily Hominoidea—that is, the first apes—appear in the fossil record from the early **Miocene** epoch and date to about

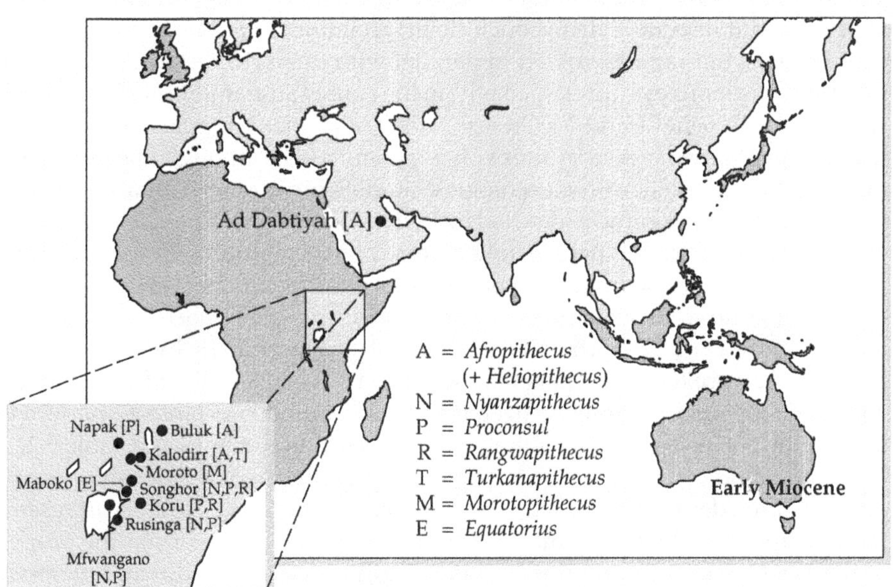

FIGURE 5.13 Map of the Old World showing the sites that have produced ape remains dating to the early Miocene. Note that these earliest apes were concentrated in Africa.

Source: Based on Kelley, 1992.

20 million years of age (Conroy, 1990; Gebo et al., 1997). The absolutely oldest genera, ***Morotopithecus*** and ***Proconsul***, are from African sites, as are most of the other early Miocene forms (Figure 5.13 and Table 5.2), making an African origin for hominoids a safe conclusion. Cercopithecoid monkeys apparently evolved at roughly the same time (by at least 15 to 18 mya; Benefit, 1999; R. D. Martin, 1990). Details of the

Morotopithecus a *genus* of *apes* that inhabited East Africa during the early *Miocene*.

Proconsul an *ape genus* from East Africa that lived during the early *Miocene* epoch.

TABLE 5.2 Fossil Ape Genera

Age	Genus	Location
Early Miocene	*Proconsul*	Africa
	Morotopithecus	Africa
	Micropithecus	Africa
	Limnopithecus	Africa
	Dendropithecus	Africa
	Rangwapithecus	Africa
	Turkanapithecus	Africa
?	*Dionysopithecus*[c]	Asia
Early to Mid Miocene	*Afropithecus*	Africa, Saudi Arabia
	Nyanzapithecus	Africa
Mid Miocene	*Nacholapithecus*	Africa
	Equatorius	Africa
	Kenyapithecus	Africa
	Otavipithecus	Africa
Mid to Late Miocene	*Dryopithecus*[a]	Europe
	Pliopithecus	Europe
	Sivapithecus[a, b]	Africa, Asia, Europe
Late Miocene	*Khoratpithecus*	Asia
	Laccopithecus	Asia
	Lufengpithecus	Asia
	Oreopithecus	Europe
Late Miocene to Pleistocene	*Gigantopithecus*	Asia

[a]*Rudapithecus* is lumped with *Dryopithecus* by some authors and with *Sivapithecus* by others.
[b]Includes *Ouranopithecus* and the Pasalar fossils from Figure 5.16, and also *Ramapithecus* and *Ankarapithecus*.
[c]The early Miocene date of this taxon is questionable.
Sources: Conroy, 1990; Conroy et al., 1993; Gebo et al., 1997; Nakatsukasa et al., 2003; Ward et al., 1999.

evolutionary differentiation of the two living catarrhine superfamilies are unclear at present, but it seems safe to conclude that hominoids did not descend from cercopithecoids, but rather evolved in parallel with them (Kingdon, 2003). The earliest catarrhine monkeys are classed within the extinct subfamily **Victoriapithecinae,** (Benefit, 1999; Benefit and McCrossin, 1997), and many species used more open habitats than those favored by the evolving hominoids. Although interesting in their own right (and excellent socioecological models for certain habitats, as shown in Chapter 4), the Cercopithecoidea had little, if any, effect on hominin evolution. (Even so, competition from an increasingly diverse and numerous collection of monkeys may have affected ape migration patterns, as described later [Kingdon, 2003].)

Victoriapithecinae *an extinct subfamily of the earliest catarrhine monkeys.*

The apes do concern us, however, and during the early Miocene, they were busy adapting to a warm East African environment covered mostly by forest and woodlands. Most were forest animals who subsisted on a mixed diet of fruit and leaves, and they ranged from monkey-sized creatures to animals as large as modern gorillas (Begun, 2003). As shown by the genus names in Figure 5.13 and Table 5.2, these early hominoids were a diverse lot, and their evolutionary relationships are not at all clear. Indeed, they were so diverse that many genera (e.g., *Proconsul*) resembled modern apes only in their dental and cranial traits (a fact that brings the proper use of the label "ape" into question; see Box 5.2). From the neck down, *Proconsul* and

BOX 5.2

Naming Problems and Fossil Hominoids

What makes an ape an ape? Or in slightly more stylish form, what is the essence of apeness?

Answering this question is easy if we think only of living apes: Apes are big primates with distinctive Y-5 molar teeth (Figure 3.15), relatively large brains, and no tail. Furthermore, their locomotor patterns are distinctly forelimb dominated; in the trees, they often hang or swing about by their arms, and as adaptations for this sort of movement they have short, stiff backs, long arms, and shoulder and elbow joints that allow a wide range of movement. So far, so good. But as this chapter shows, the suite of features that characterizes modern apes was not present in all early hominoids—and this creates a terminology problem.

The very earliest catarrhines, such as the Oligocene primate *Aegyptopithecus*, showed a mixture of primitive traits that were sorted out differently in the evolutionary lineages leading to today's monkeys and apes. These early catarrhines are described as *generalized* because they combined certain apelike dental features with a monkeylike, tail-equipped body that was adapted for arboreal quadrupedalism rather than forelimb suspension. By about 18 mya, the Old World monkeys had emerged as a distinct evolutionary family that retained the old pattern of arboreal quadrupedalism and combined it with new dental specializations such as four-cusped, bilophodont molars (Figure 3.15). The emergence of the dentally distinct Old World monkeys left a group of catarrhine "remainders," all of which were characterized by old-style five-cusped (now Y-5) molars but which were wonderfully diverse in their postcranial anatomies.

All of these Y-5 species are classified within the superfamily Hominoidea and a few—including *Morotopithecus, Dryopithecus,* and *Oreopithecus,* which possessed bodies adapted for suspensory locomotion—are clearly apes in the modern sense of the word. (As indicated in the text, these genera—particularly *Morotopithecus*—were separated in space and time, suggesting that forelimb-dominated locomotion may have evolved independently more than once among the hominoids. But that's another story.)

But what about the others? What evolutionary sense can we make of—and specifically, what should we call—creatures such as *Proconsul* whose dental and cranial traits earned them a place among the hominoids, but whose bodies looked like that of a monkey?

Taking those questions in order, since all living apes show forelimb-dominated locomotion and human anatomy indicates descent from a swinging-and-hanging ancestor, it is clear that at some point the monkeylike hominoids disappeared entirely, leaving the superfamily to be represented exclusively by suspensory creatures. When and why this happened are both unknown at present and researchers anxiously are seeking new fossils to settle these issues. As to what we should call the Y-5 "nonswingers," at present there is no good term. Harvard's David Pilbeam (1996) prefers the accurate but awkward label "hominoids of archaic aspect," while the authors of this book have opted for "dental apes." What would you call these monkeylike hominoids? If you have an opinion, e-mail us at the addresses given in the Preface to this book.

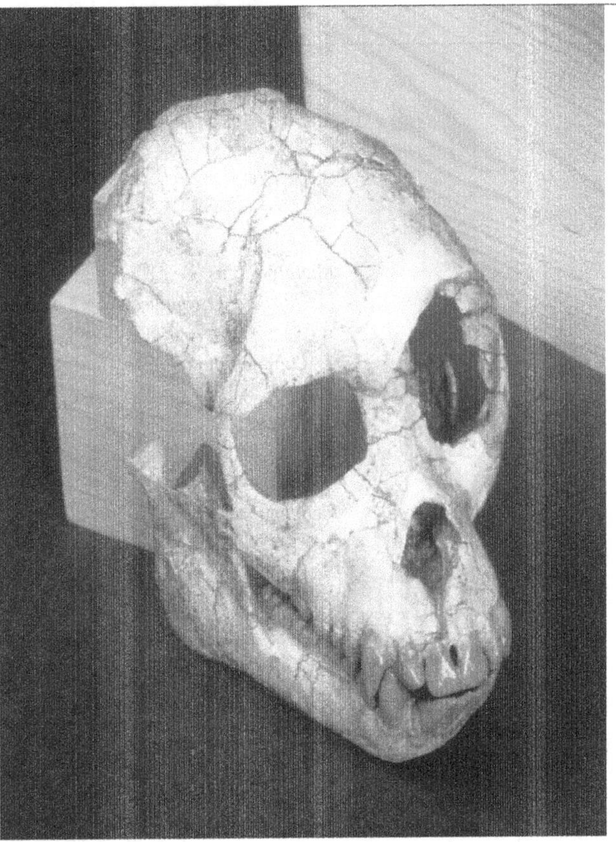

FIGURE 5.14
The skull of *Proconsul* is a typical ape skull. It combines a low cranial vault, projecting muzzle, and large anterior teeth.

several others had more anatomical similarities to monkeys than to today's chimpanzees, orangutans, and gorillas (Figure 5.14 and 5.15). A few Miocene genera, however—particularly *Morotopithecus*, ***Oreopithecus***, and ***Dryopithecus***—had evolved adaptations for suspensory postures and locomotion and thus looked like modern apes both above and below the neck (that is, cranially, dentally, *and* postcranially). David Pilbeam of Harvard University refers to the first category of creatures (e.g., *Proconsul*) as "hominoids of archaic aspect" and the second as "hominoids of modern aspect" (Pilbeam, 1996). We prefer the shorter terms "dental apes" and "suspensory apes" (see Box 5.2).

Oreopithecus **and** ***Dryopithecus*** ape genera from the mid to late *Miocene* of Europe.

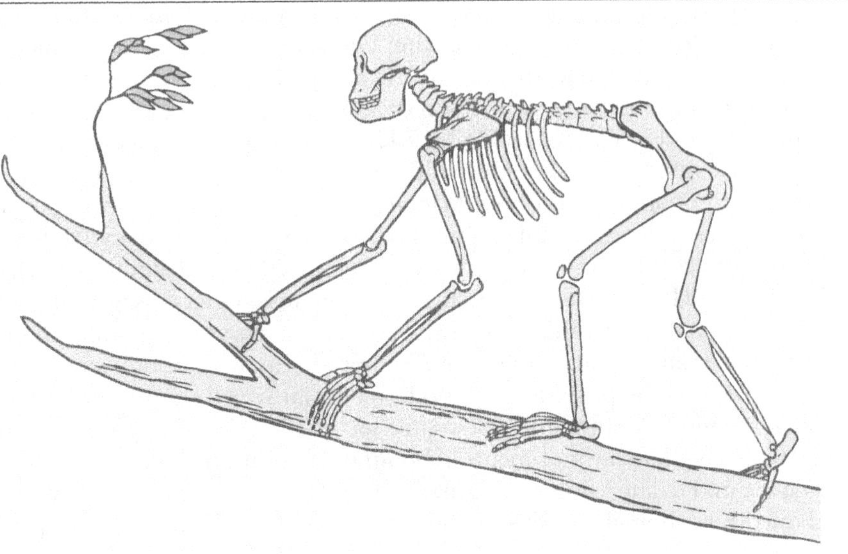

FIGURE 5.15
Reconstructed skeleton of *Proconsul*. Note the slender torso, the monkeylike limb proportions, and (possibly) the lack of a tail. (As discussed in the text, authorities disagree on this point.)

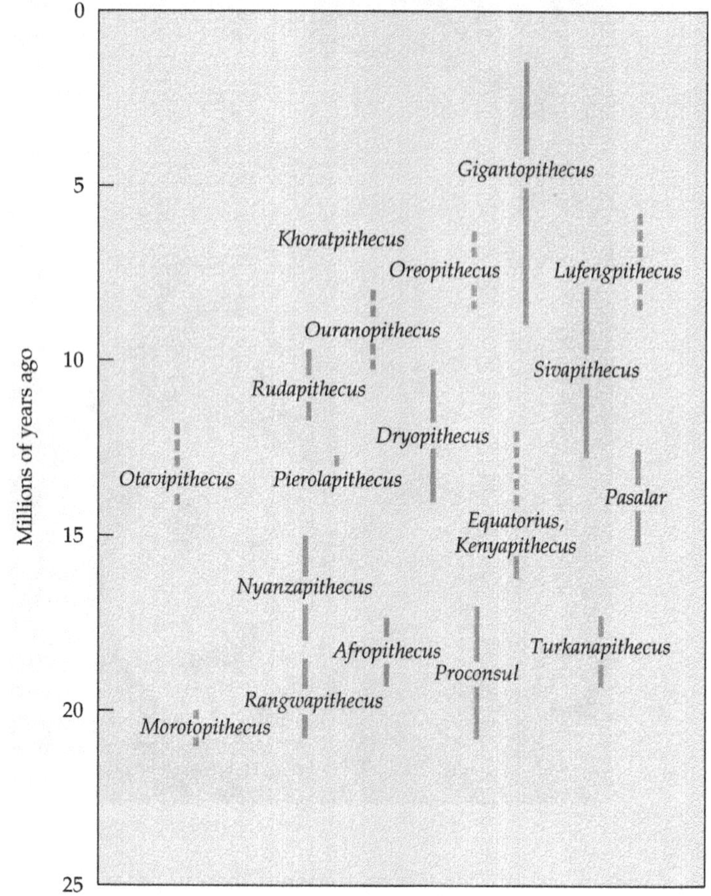

FIGURE 5.16 Selected fossil ape genera are shown here along with their time ranges. (Solid lines denote well-known ranges; dashed lines indicate probable ranges.)

Sources: Data primarily from Kelley, 1992; Conroy et al., 1993; Gebo et al., 1997; and Ward et al., 1999.

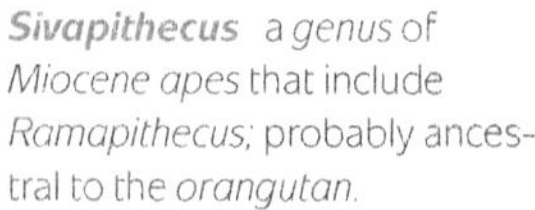
Sivapithecus a *genus* of *Miocene apes* that include *Ramapithecus*; probably ancestral to the *orangutan*.

Dental apes, in the form of *Proconsul*, show up right at the very beginning of hominoid history, some 17 to 20 million years ago (Figure 5.16). As represented by ***Sivapithecus***, *Lufengpithecus*, and others, the dental apes continued until the late stages of the Miocene (Figure 5.16) and they are known from Africa, Asia, and Europe. The well-known African genus *Proconsul* (Figures 5.14 and 5.15) serves as a good example of these archaic hominoids. As expected from a catarrhine, *Proconsul*'s protruding muzzle showed a dental formula of 2123/2123. In addition, it had projecting and pointed canine teeth, upper canines that sheared against the lower anterior premolars, and postcanine toothrows that were generally parallel. Other features worth mentioning are *Proconsul*'s strongly receding forehead and low-vaulted braincase.

Despite its apelike teeth and skull, however, *Proconsul* showed few similarities to modern apes from the neck down (Begun, 2003; Simons, 1992). As summarized in Table 3.4 and illustrated in Figure 5.12, modern apes have a broad chest, a short lower back, no tail, and shoulders and arms modified for forelimb-dominated locomotion (arm-hanging and arm-swinging). In contrast to modern apes, however, *Proconsul* had a long, flexible spine; a narrow torso; and monkeylike limb proportions (Figure 5.15). Many authorities (e.g., Begun [2003] and Simons [1992]) conclude that *Proconsul* lacked a tail, although some other researchers disagree (Benefit, 1999). Judging from its postcranial remains, *Proconsul* was a rather generalized quadruped, certainly not an animal adapted for forelimb-dominated arboreal movement.

As regards the postcranially modern apes, it was thought until quite recently that adaptations for forelimb-dominated locomotion (arm-hanging and arm-swinging) were very late developments in hominoid evolution. For example, *Sivapithecus*, from the mid to late Miocene (Figures 5.16 and 5.17), shows elbow joints apparently adapted for arboreal suspension, but the rest of its skeleton suggests quadrupedal

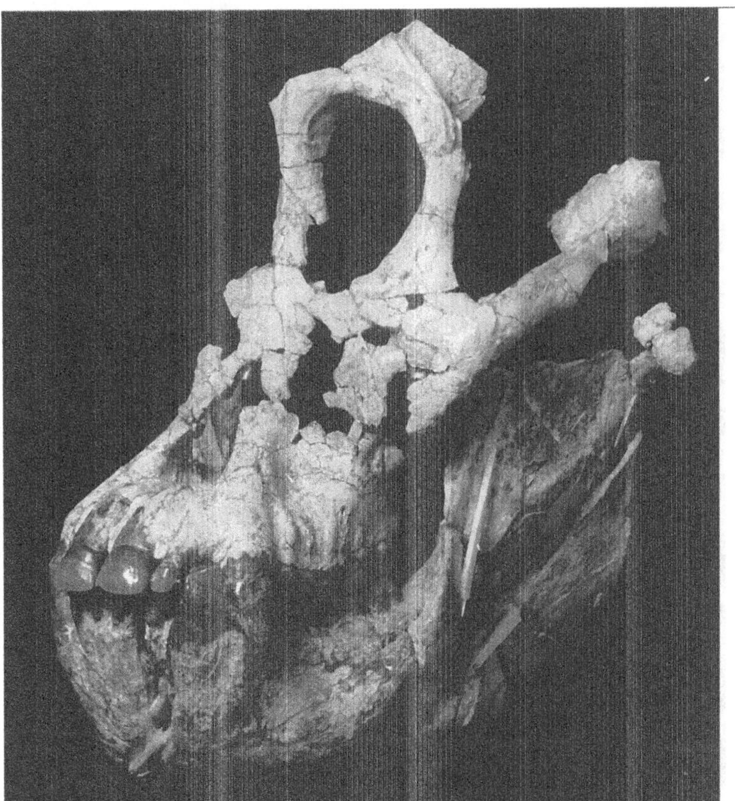

FIGURE 5.17
This *Sivapithecus indicus* skull was found in northeast Pakistan by David Pilbeam and his research team from Harvard. The shape of the orbits and profile of the face of *Sivapithecus* suggest a connection to modern orangutans.

walking (Begun, 2003; Kelley, 1992). The oldest known full-fledged hanger-and-swinger was thought to be *Oreopithecus bambolii*, which inhabited Europe around 8 million years ago. This unique hominoid had a short trunk and a broad thorax, long arms and short legs, and elbow joints like those of living apes (Fleagle, 1988). Unfortunately, the evolutionary relationships of *Oreopithecus* are extremely obscure.

The recent discoveries of new suspensory apes have pushed the advent of forelimb-dominated locomotion far back in hominoid history. First, in 1996, Spanish paleontologists Salvador Moyà-Solà and Meike Köhler published evidence that the European species *Dryopithecus laietanus* was an upright climber and swinger 9.5 million years ago. Fossils from the Spanish site of Can Llobateres revealed that like modern apes, *D. laietanus* showed a short back, broad thorax, dorsally positioned shoulder blades, long arms and short legs, and large hands with long, powerful fingers (Figure 5.18). Clearly indicative of suspensory locomotion, these traits have convinced Moyà-Solà and Köhler (1996) that *Dryopithecus* is closely related to modern apes (Figure 5.19).

A second new find, however, is much older than Can Llobateres and thus even more exciting. In 1997, a team of researchers headed by Daniel Gebo of Northern Illinois University announced evidence of an upright climber and brachiator dating to 20.6 million years of age. Named *Morotopithecus bishopi* and recovered from a site in northeastern Uganda (Figure 5.13), this ancient hominoid showed a short, stiff back, broadening of the thorax, and modifications of the shoulder that allowed "climbing, a slow to moderate speed of brachiation, . . . quadrupedalism, and . . . an arm-hanging posture" (Gebo et al., 1997: 402). Its discoverers suspect that *Morotopithecus*, which was quite large at about 100 pounds (45 kilograms), is not directly ancestral to modern hominoids but rather represents a sister taxon that split off early from the lineage of living apes (Figure 5.19). Nonetheless, evidence from *Morotopithecus* may provide important clues to the evolutionary pathway that led from small-bodied, primitive catarrhines to large-bodied, suspensory apes (MacLatchy, 2004).

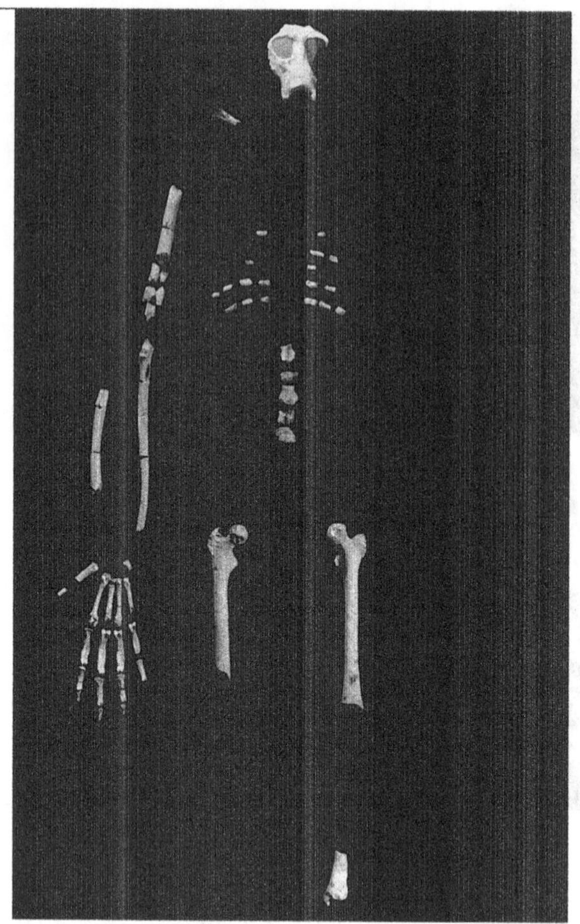

FIGURE 5.18 The skeleton of *Dryopithecus laietanus* from Can Llobateres (Spain). Note the long arm, large hand, and long, powerful fingers. All of these traits suggest forelimb-dominated, suspensory locomotion.

Finally, in 2004, a new ape species from Spain, *Pierolapithecus catalaunicus*, was described that possessed monkeylike hands (suggesting quadrupedalism) but also evidence of habitually upright trunk (suggesting vertical climbing; Moyà-Solà et al., 2004). This surprising combination of traits in the 13-million-year-old *P. catalaunicus* (Figure 5.16) shows that all upright hominoids were not necessarily arm hangers and swingers. Vertical climbing and suspensory locomotion may well have evolved independently, at least on occasion.

In sum, the evidence from *Oreopithecus*, *Dryopithecus*, *Morotopithecus*, and *Pierolapithecus*, in combination with that from the dental apes, indicates that hominoids have experimented with a variety of locomotor adaptations throughout the

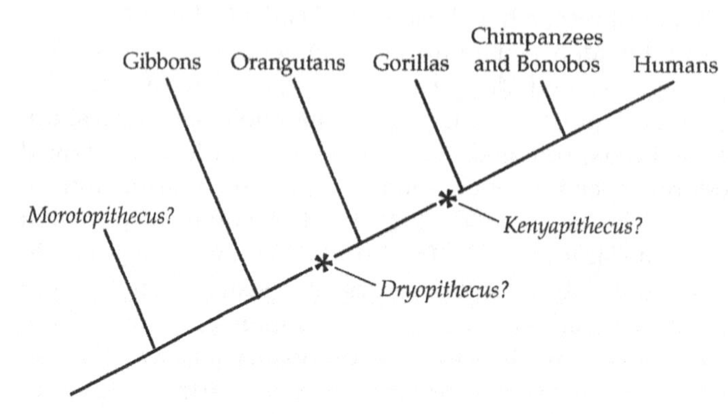

FIGURE 5.19 This branching diagram shows the possible placement of *Morotopithecus*, *Dryopithecus*, and *Kenyapithecus* on the evolutionary tree of hominoids. The diagram has no time scale.

superfamily's long history. Most fossil species opted for *pronograde* locomotion (monkeylike quadrupedalism with the spine horizontal), but a few showed *orthograde* (spine upright) vertical climbing and/or suspensory patterns similar to today's apes. Practitioners of both pronograde and orthograde patterns tended to move through the trees slowly and cautiously, especially the larger species (Nakatsukasa et al., 2003). Slow arboreal movement, in turn, allowed the reduction or complete loss of the tail. Having a tail helps arboreal runners and leapers to maintain their balance, but for slow climbers and swingers, a tail simply represents an unnecessary physiological expense (Kingdon, 2003). Although, as mentioned earlier, there is some controversy over the question of tail loss for particular genera (e.g., *Proconsul*), it has been proved for others (*Nacholapithecus:* Nakatsukasa et al., 2003) and ultimately came to be a general feature of the hominoid superfamily. At some point in hominoid evolution, the pronograde genera all went extinct, leaving only orthograde locomotors among the living apes. The reasons for this are unknown.

After their evolutionary origin in Africa around 20 mya, the early apes experienced an interesting and complex history of intercontinental migration (Figure 5.20; Begun, 2003; Kingdon, 2003; Kordos and Begun, 2002). Studies of **continental drift** have shown that while Africa was in about its modern position relative to Eurasia by the early Miocene, high sea levels prevented extensive movement of species between the two land masses. Sea levels dropped around 16.5 to 17 mya, however, and it seems that one or more species of African apes took advantage of the newly emerged land bridge to migrate from northeast Africa into western Eurasia. These migrants (or their descendants) eventually spread into western Europe and Far

Continental drift a theory that describes the movements of continental land masses throughout the earth's history.

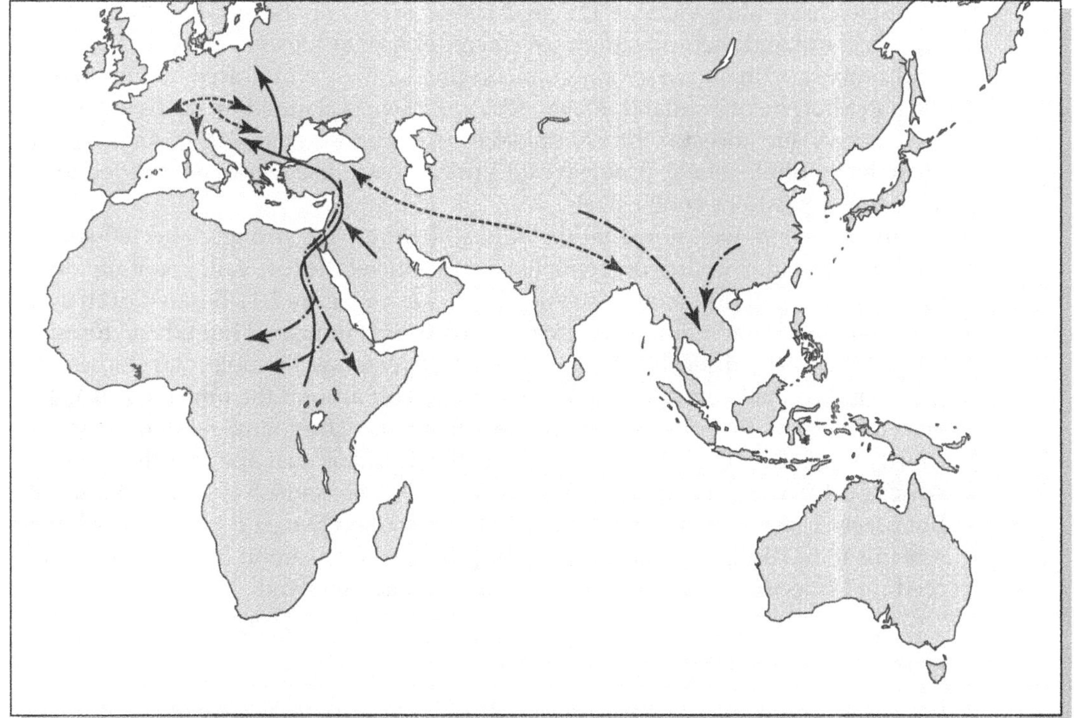

FIGURE 5.20
Migrations of early apes. The solid lines represent original northward movements from Africa and Arabia, ca. 16.5 to 17 mya. The dashed lines represent spread within Europe and into south Asia, ca. 8 to 16.5 mya. Dashed-and-dotted lines represent movement of the Dryopithecine lineage back to Africa and the Sivapithecine lineage into southeast Asia, ca. 6 to 9 mya.

Source: Based on Begun, 2003.

Eastern Asia and gave rise to an ape radiation that included such mid to late Miocene genera as *Dryopithecus, Oranopithecus, Lufengpithecus,* and *Sivapithecus* (see Figure 5.16).

After enjoying several million years of life in subtropical Eurasia, however, the now-diversified apes experienced strong climatic challenges in the late Miocene. The development of Old World mountain ranges, changes in ocean currents, and several other geophysical factors combined to cool off the Eurasian climate. Changes in temperature and rainfall patterns resulted in the replacement of forests with woodlands and grasslands in much of midlatitude Eurasia and also in east Africa. Far Eastern apes migrated south into the southeast Asian tropics to escape the increasing cold and in that location gave rise to the orangutan lineage (modern subfamily Ponginae; Table 3.1). European and western Asian apes, however—including the ancestors of humans, chimps, bonobos, and gorillas (subfamilies Homininae and Gorillinae; Table 3.1)—tended to return to Africa and its remaining tropical forest. These southern migrations are thought to have occurred some 6 to 9 million years ago (Begun, 2003).

This scenario of multiple migrations between and within Africa and Eurasia therefore accounts for the evolution of the Asian great ape, the orangutan, from *Sivapithecus* stock and the African great apes (and ultimately, humans) from either *Dryopithecus* or *Ouranopithecus* stock (Begun, 2003; Kordos and Begun, 2002). There are other scenarios, however. For example, throughout the Miocene, there were still resident apes in Africa—*Otavipithecus* in the south and the *Equatorius-Kenyapithecus* lineage in the east (Conroy et al., 1993; C. Ward et al., 1999)—and some researchers prefer an indigenous ancestor for modern African hominids. Monte McCrossin of Southern Illinois University believes that the *Equatorius-Kenyapithecus* line contains 14-million-year-old evidence for an African origin of the gorilla–chimpanzee–human clade and the appearance of a semiterrestrial lifestyle (McCrossin, 1997). Additionally, with regard to orangutan origins, a newly announced hominoid from the late Miocene of Thailand, *Khoratpithecus piriyai,* is claimed by its discoverers to be a more likely ancestor than *Sivapithecus* (Chaimanee et al., 2004). As is true for virtually all phylogenetic problems, additional fossil discoveries are needed to answer these questions conclusively.

In any event, we know that the African habitat was strongly affected some 8 million years ago by earth movements that produced the Rift Valley running down the eastern side of the continent (Coppens, 1994; see Figure 7.1). Because of changes in air circulation and rainfall, the area west of the Rift remained humid and forested, while to the east, a drier climate produced open savannas. Biomolecular studies suggest that the gorilla lineage may have branched off around the time the Rift Valley was formed, with hominins separating from the chimpanzee–bonobo lineage shortly thereafter (Figure 5.21). It appears that humans' last ape ancestors lived in Africa (as Darwin predicted) during the late Miocene, some 5 to 7 mya (Table 4.2). But precisely what those apes were, what they looked like, and how they behaved remains to be discovered. Regardless, big changes were afoot: By early in the succeeding **Pliocene** epoch, unequivocal hominins had evolved.

Pliocene the *geologic* epoch extending from 5 to 1.8 million years BP.

Apes to Hominins: The Anatomical Criteria

We are now poised to review the fossil record of the human lineage, the tribe *Hominini.* Indeed, most of the remainder of this book is devoted to that purpose. Before surveying the hominin remains, however, it is important to set out very clearly the minimum criteria for including a fossil species in that category.

As reviewed in Chapter 3, living hominins (modern humans) are distinguished by several traits, including short, incisorlike canine teeth (Figure 5.22); skulls with flat faces and huge brains (Figure 5.23); fully opposable thumbs that give us a fine

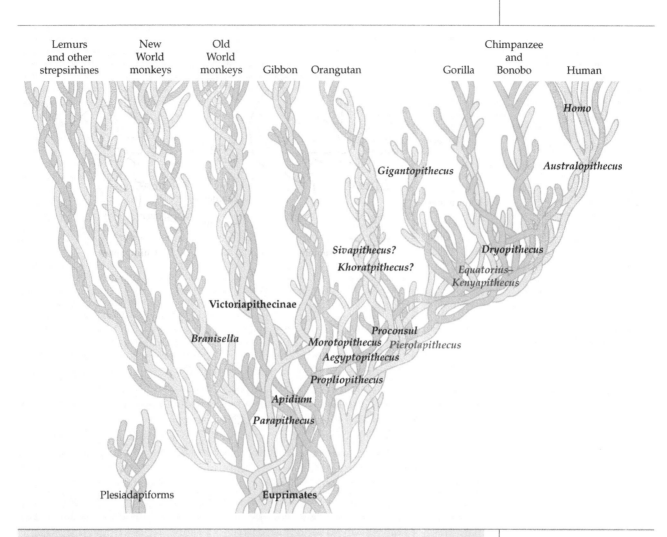

Lemurs and other strepsirhines
New World monkeys
Old World monkeys
Gibbon
Orangutan
Gorilla
Chimpanzee and Bonobo
Human
Homo
Australopithecus
Gigantopithecus
Sivapithecus?
Khoratpithecus?
Dryopithecus
Equatorius–Kenyapithecus
Victoriapithecinae
Branisella
Proconsul
Morotopithecus
Pierolapithecus
Aegyptopithecus
Propliopithecus
Apidium
Parapithecus
Plesiadapiforms
Euprimates

FIGURE 5.21
Evolutionary trees, or dendrograms, are always greatly oversimplified and in certain ways inaccurate, but they nevertheless give a good indication of the relative ages and phylogenetic relationships of the species shown. The multiplicity of lines indicates that any evolving lineage contains an unknown number of divergent populations that may or may not be different species. Many such populations become extinct. The chart is highly speculative.

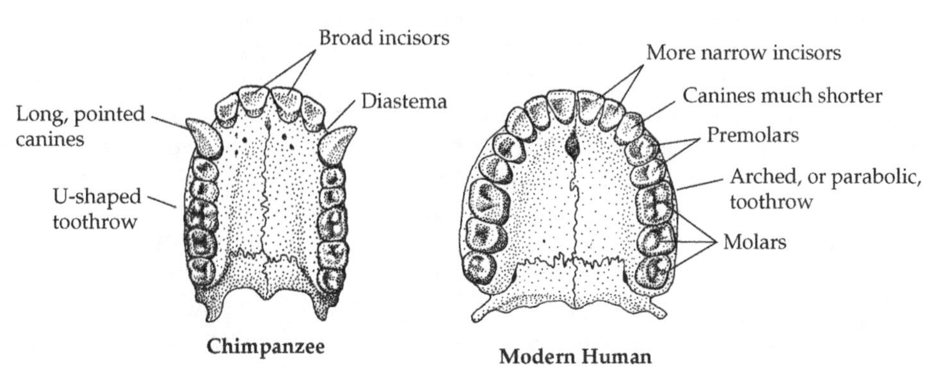

FIGURE 5.22
The dentition of the upper jaw of an ape (a chimpanzee) and that of a human are compared. Notice the distinct shape of the toothrow, as well as the ape's large canines and diastemata.

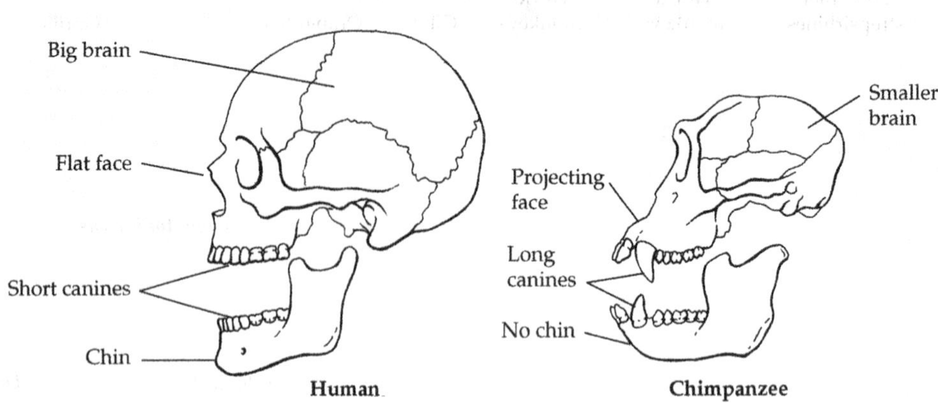

FIGURE 5.23 The ape and human skulls are quite distinct. The chimpanzee has a large jaw with large canines, especially in the male skull shown here. In humans, the teeth are smaller, and the canines generally project no farther than the other teeth. Humans also show a distinct chin, whereas apes do not. The enlarged braincase of humans brings about a more vertical alignment of the face and jaws. The scale is approximately one-fifth actual size.

precision grip; and numerous adaptations of the back, hips, legs, and feet that facilitate bipedal locomotion. Of these traits, only two—the first to evolve—are useful markers of the earliest hominins: reduced canine length and adaptations for bipedalism. But even these two are not equally useful. Some of the late Miocene apes (*Ouranopithecus*, for example) had relatively short canines, while those of some early hominins were relatively long in comparison to those of later members of the human tribe. Therefore, in the final analysis, only evidence of habitual bipedalism unmistakably marks a fossil species as hominin.

Modern apes are long-armed and short-legged arborealists. They climb, swing, or hang about in the trees using forelimb-dominated movements, and when they come to the ground, they walk quadrupedally. As adaptations for these locomotor patterns, apes have evolved (or retained) a distinct suite of postcranial traits (Aiello and Dean, 1990; Alexander, 1992; Lovejoy, 1988). They have short, stiff, straight backs; tall, narrow pelvic bones similar to those of monkeys; widely spaced knees and feet (a **wide-knee stance;** Figure 5.24); and divergent big toes capable of grasping branches during climbing.

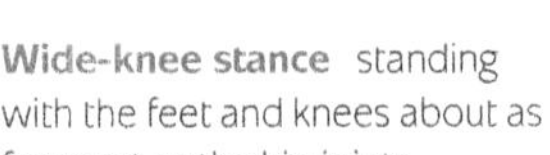

Wide-knee stance standing with the feet and knees about as far apart as the hip joints.

Iliac blade the broad portion of the *ilium*, one of the bones of the *pelvis*.

Anterior inferior iliac spine a projection from the *ilium* that serves as an attachment point for certain thigh muscles and also the *iliofemoral ligament*.

Ischium one of the bones of the *pelvis*.

Sacrum the part of the vertebral column that articulates with the *pelvis* and forms the dorsal portion of the pelvic girdle.

Hamstrings muscles of the hips and the back of the thigh; thigh extensors.

Specifically with regard to the pelvis, the following distinctive anatomical traits can be identified in apes (Figure 5.25): (1) the **iliac blade** is tall and narrow and shows no sign of forward curvature into a *pelvic bowl;* (2) the **anterior inferior iliac spine** is very small and undeveloped; (3) the shaft of the **ischium** lies essentially in a straight line with the main portion of the ilium; and (4) the **sacrum** (the wedge of fused vertebrae that articulates with the pelvic bones) is relatively narrow. Additionally, with regard to the femur, or thighbone, the ape's wide-knee stance results in the lack of an angled shaft at the knee (Figure 5.24).

Equipped with this set of anatomical features, apes are capable only of energetically expensive and (somewhat) unstable bipedalism. A bipedal ape stands in a bent-hip, bent-knee posture with its center of gravity high above and anterior to the hip joints (Figure 5.26). This semi-upright posture is needed to produce an angle between the ischium and the femur—an angle that allows the **hamstring** muscles to extend (retract) the thigh—but it is maintained only with considerable muscular effort. When an ape walks, it takes short steps (the knee never passes behind the hip joints) and it balances by swaying its trunk to one side as the opposite leg is swinging forward (Figure 5.27). This "waddle-and-teeter" bipedalism is the best an ape can do, given its anatomy, but it is a most imperfect means of locomotion (Aiello and Dean, 1990; Pilbeam, 1972).

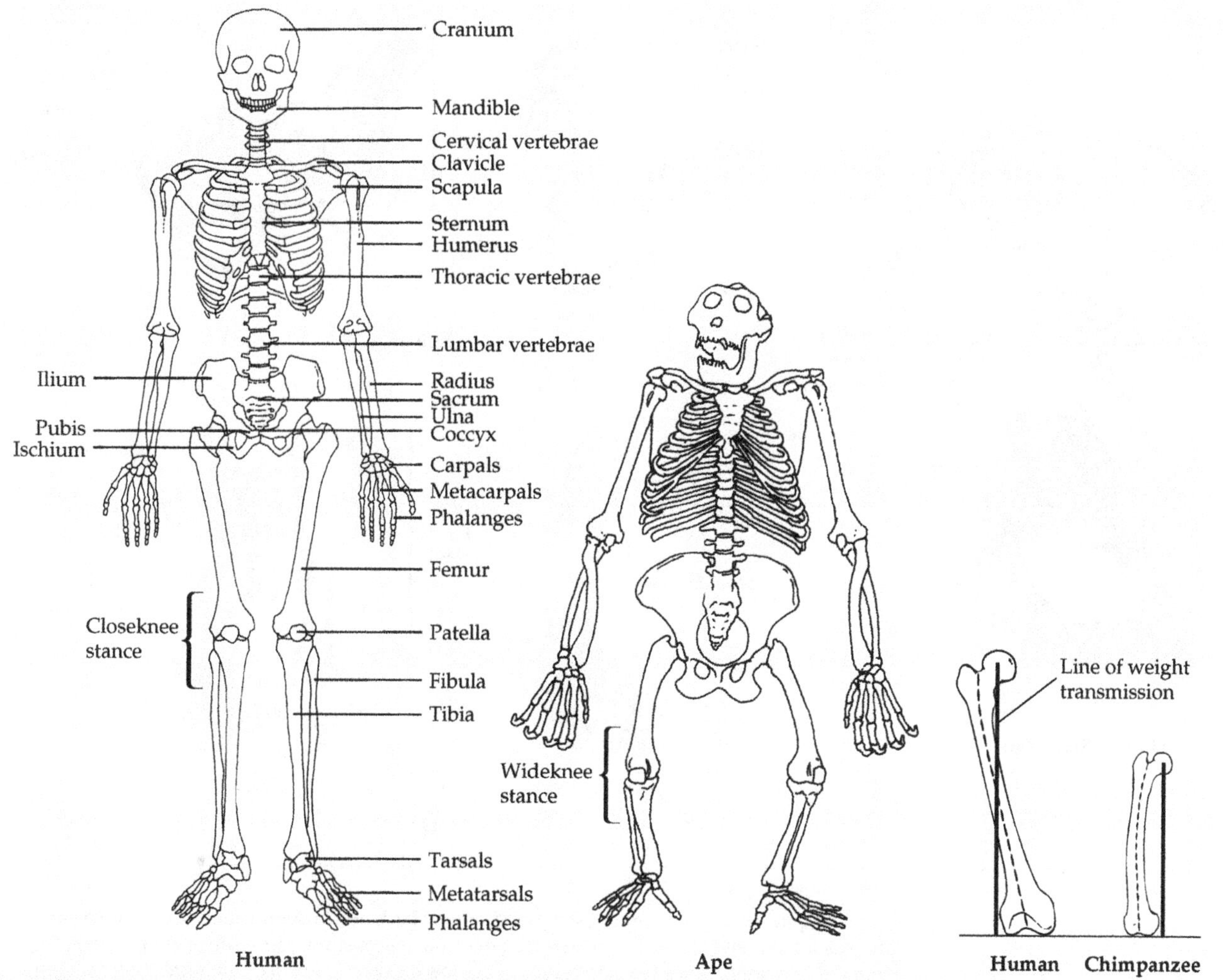

FIGURE 5.24
Humans *(left)* have evolved a close-knee stance, while bipedal apes *(center)* show a wide-knee posture. Postural and locomotor differences are reflected in the ape's lack of an angled femoral shaft in contrast to humans, who have one *(right)*.

In contrast to apes, the human pelvis (Figure 5.25) features (1) a short iliac blade that has been widened and bent posteriorly (as shown by the deep **sciatic notch**); (2) anterior curvature and lateral flaring of the iliac blades to produce a bowl-shaped pelvic girdle; (3) strong enlargement of the anterior inferior iliac spine; (4) realignment of the ischium relative to the ilium; and (5) a wide sacrum (Aiello and Dean, 1990; Alexander, 1992; Lovejoy, 1988; Pilbeam, 1972). These evolutionary modifications went a long way toward perfecting bipedal walking.

Sciatic notch a deep indentation of the *dorsal* edge of the *hominin ilium*.

In conjunction with the development of a **lumbar curve** in the back, posterior expansion and bending of the iliac blades brought the human trunk over the hip joints and allowed straightening of the legs, while lowering the center of gravity to a point within the pelvic bowl (Figure 5.26). This greatly increased the energy efficiency of bipedalism and reduced its instability. The evolution of a pelvic bowl with broad, flaring walls allowed the lesser gluteal muscles (**gluteus medius** and **gluteus minimus**) to function as powerful lateral stabilizers of the trunk during walking (no more teetering to balance the body and free the swing leg; Figure 5.28). Expansion of the anterior inferior iliac spine facilitated pulling the thigh forward

Lumbar curve the forward curvature of the vertebral column in the lower back that helps bring the *hominin* trunk over the hip joints.

Gluteus medius and gluteus minimus muscles of the hip; lateral stabilizers of the *pelvis* in modern humans.

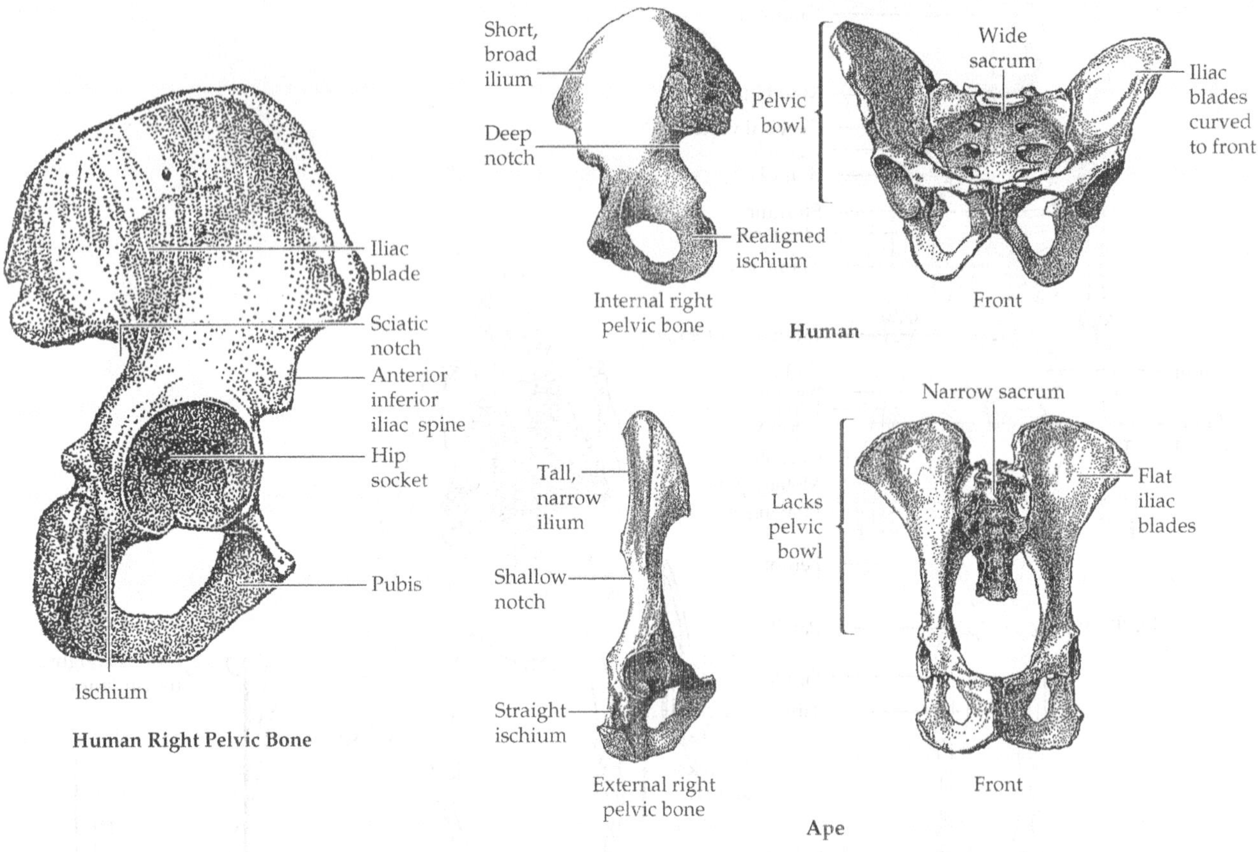

FIGURE 5.25
The right pelvic bone of a human *(left)* has a broad iliac blade, a deep sciatic notch, and a large anterior inferior iliac spine. The two pelvic bones plus the sacrum form a distinct pelvic bowl in humans *(top right)*, while the iliac blades of an ape show no bowl-like curvature *(bottom right)*. Drawings on right are not to scale. See also Figure 7.10 for photographs of ape and human pelvic bowls.

FIGURE 5.26
A bipedal ape *(left)* stands with its feet wide apart and with a bent-hip, bent-knee posture. The ape's center of gravity *(see dot)* is located high above and anterior to the hip joints. In contrast, a bipedal human *(right)* has its feet close together, and the center of gravity is located within the pelvic girdle.

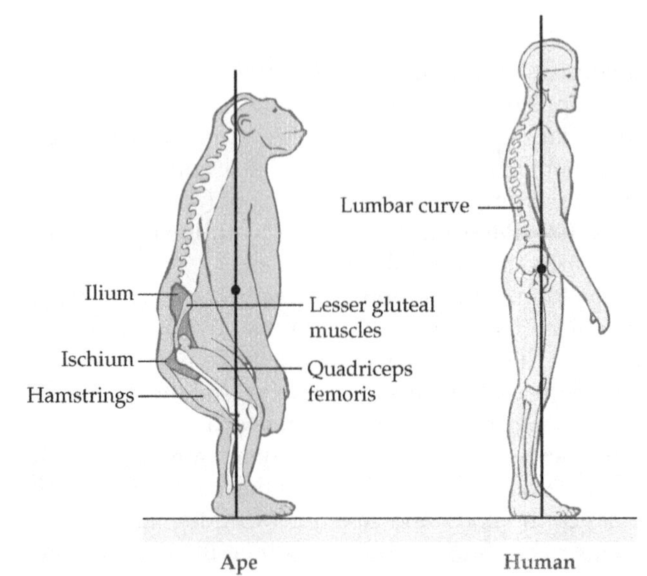

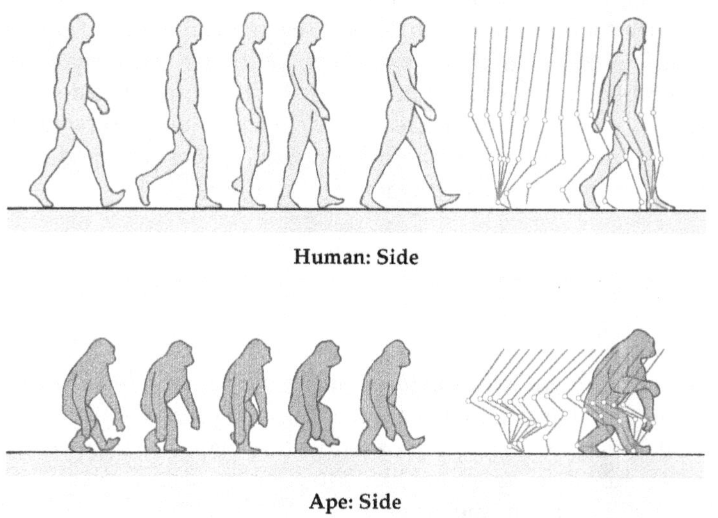

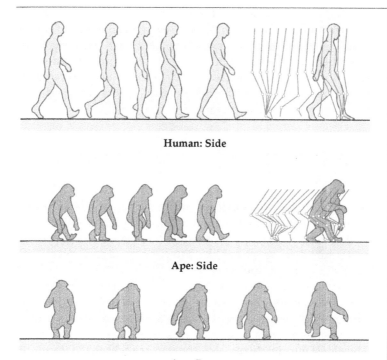

FIGURE 5.27
Side views of bipedalism in humans and apes reveal that the human knee extends backward past the hips with each step, producing a long stride. In contrast, the ape waddles forward with short steps. A rear view shows how a bipedal ape teeters from side to side in order to balance its weight over the fixed leg.

(flexion) and also provided space for humans' large **iliofemoral ligament,** an anatomical feature that stabilizes the trunk against backward movement at the hips (Figure 5.28). And finally, the realignment of the ischium relative to the ilium resulted in an angle between the ischium and the femur that allows the thigh-extending hamstrings to work well with the body fully upright. This last change, in turn, allowed humans to take nice long strides on knees that swing back past the hips (no more waddling; Figure 5.27).

Iliofemoral ligament the ligament that prevents backward movement of the trunk at the human hip.

Two other changes in humans' postcranial anatomy deserve to be mentioned. We evolved a **close-knee stance** that pulled our feet nearer the body's midline, making lateral balancing of the trunk much easier than in wide-kneed apes and producing an angled femoral shaft (Figure 5.24). Additionally, we evolved nondivergent and nonprehensile big toes that function to propel our bodies forward during bipedal movement.

Close-knee stance standing with the feet and knees closer together than the hip joints.

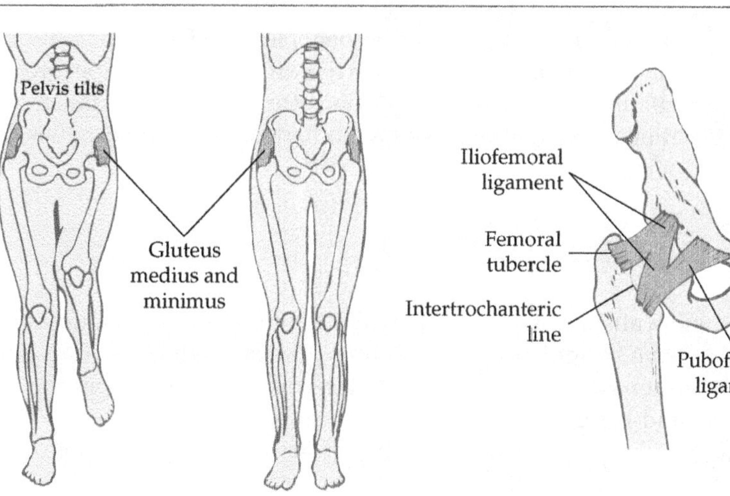

FIGURE 5.28
(Left) The lesser gluteal muscles of humans (gluteus medius and gluteus minimus) provide lateral stabilization of the pelvis over the fixed leg during bipedalism. *(Right)* A front view of the pelvis and the femur also shows the position of humans' iliofemoral ligament.

The pelvic anatomies of living apes and humans reveal two ends of an evolutionary continuum. We can expect the pelvic remains of early hominins to be intermediate between these extremes, with the very first members of our tribe resembling apes more than people. But the primary criterion for classifying a fossil species as hominin is clear: evidence of habitual bipedal movement. This criterion should be kept firmly in mind as we review the evidence of the beginnings of the hominin lineage in the next few chapters.

Summary

As currently known, the fossil and molecular evidence indicates that the primate order probably originated about 90 million years ago during the late Cretaceous period. This date is an approximation, however, based on very incomplete evidence, and future discoveries are likely to push the actual point of origin millions of years in one direction or the other.

Based on recent studies, archaic arboreal creatures such as *Purgatorius* should be included in the order Primates as the semiorder Plesiadapiformes. Preceding but probably not ancestral to primates of a modern aspect—the semiorder Euprimates—the plesiadapiforms possessed rodentlike front teeth and lacked postorbital bars. The oldest euprimate remains come from rocks that date about 55 myr of age. These creatures—including from the outset representatives of the two modern suborders, Strepsirhini and Haplorhini—seem to have originated in the Northern hemisphere, but whether that means North America, Europe, or Asia is unclear at present. By the Oligocene epoch, the plesiadapiforms were extinct and the euprimates had the order to themselves.

Anthropoid primates had evolved by about 45 mya, although the continent of origin (Africa or Asia?) is hotly debated, and catarrhines were in existence by early Oligocene times in Africa. New World (platyrrhine) monkey fossils first appear in Bolivian deposits dating 25 to 26 myr of age. These creatures were probably the descendants of African anthropoids that traveled to South America by island hopping and/or rafting. Old World monkeys and hominoids (early apes) had differentiated by about 20 mya, and an African homeland for the hominoids now seems conclusive. Represented initially by both *dental apes* with monkeylike lower bodies and *suspensory apes* with postcranial adaptations for arm-hanging and arm-swinging, the early hominoids showed a complex pattern of migration between Africa and Eurasia during the mid to late Miocene.

The stock that gave rise to modern African apes (gorillas, chimpanzees, and bonobos) and ultimately to humans may have evolved in Eurasia and then returned to Africa. Humans' last ape ancestor probably lived in East Africa around 5 to 7 mya. Two key anatomical changes distinguish hominins from their ape forebears: reduced canine length and lower-body adaptations for habitual bipedalism. The latter set of modifications is complex and involved changes in the spine, pelvis, legs, and feet.

Postscript

To knuckle-walk or not to knuckle-walk? That is (sort of) the question that anthropologists have struggled with for years. More accurately, the question is whether or not hominins descended from knuckle-walking apes as opposed to orthograde swingers-and-hangers.

Supporters of a knuckle-walking ancestry for hominins point out that all three living African apes (gorillas, chimpanzees, and bonobos) show this type of locomotion, with only the fourth member of the African hominoid clade—humans—lacking it. Therefore, the argument goes, it seems clear that knuckle-walking must have evolved just once, sometime before the divergence of the gorilla lineage about 8 to 10 million years ago (see Table 4.2) and that only humans have departed from the ancestral way of getting around. This is certainly the most parsimonious (least complicated) hypothesis, since it involves the lowest number of locomotor innovations: Knuckle-walking evolves once and bipedalism evolves once.

Scientists who support a knuckle-walking ancestry for humans base their argument on anatomical similarities between hominins and modern African apes. Two recent studies, for example, found several minute features of the wrists of modern humans and two premodern hominin species (*Australopithecus anamensis* and *Australopithecus afarensis,* both 3 to 4 myr old; see Chapter 7) that are interpreted as the remnants of ancestral adaptations for knuckle-walking (Richmond and Strait, 2000; Richmond et al., 2001). These paleoanthropologists argue that the evidence is convincing that hominin bipedalism was preceded by a knuckle-walking phase.

Other researchers are not so sure, however. They argue that hominins' putative knuckle-walking indicators may have other and better biological and mechanical explanations (Dainton, 2001; Lovejoy et al., 2001). Thus, the anatomists—the very specialists who should be able to solve this puzzle—are deeply divided. Presumably, a close analysis of the very earliest members of the human lineage should settle the issue, but here the fossil record lets us down. There are currently three genera dating to 5.5 to 7 mya from Africa that can make a reasonable claim to be the first hominin: *Sahelanthropus, Orrorin,* and *Ardipithecus.* Unfortunately, all three genera are represented by such scanty fossil remains that their locomotor anatomy cannot be determined with certainty (see Chapter 7). So, are we descended from knuckle-walkers? The jury is still out on that question. Stay tuned for further anatomical studies and fossil discoveries.

Review Questions

1. The plesiadapiforms are considered in this book to have been an archaic (and now extinct) semiorder of the Primates. How did the anatomy of these archaic creatures differ from that of the Euprimates (primates of modern aspect)?
2. When and where did the semiorder of the Euprimates arise? What evolutionary connections (if any) link the first euprimates with the living suborders Strepsirhini and Haplorhini?
3. Describe the differences and similarities between the *dental* and *suspensory* apes of the Miocene epoch. Which sort of ape gave rise to hominins?
4. What do we know about the age, location, identity, and behavior of hominins' last ape ancestor?
5. What anatomical traits differentiate the tribe Hominini from the chimpanzee–bonobo lineage?
6. Describe hominins' anatomical adaptations for habitual bipedalism, and provide functional explanations.

SUGGESTED FURTHER READING

Aiello, Leslie, and Christopher Dean. *An Introduction to Human Evolutionary Anatomy.* London, Academic Press, 1990.

Begun, David. "Planet of the Apes." *Scientific American,* 289(2):74–83, 2003.

Benefit, Brenda. "*Victoriapithecus:* The Key to Old World Monkey and Catarrhine Origins." *Evolutionary Anthropology,* 7:155–174, 1999.

Conroy, Glenn. *Primate Evolution.* New York, W. W. Norton, 1990.

Hartwig, Walter C. (ed.). *The Primate Fossil Record.* Cambridge, Cambridge University Press, 2002.

Martin, Robert D. *Primate Origins and Evolution.* Princeton, Princeton University Press, 1990.

INTERNET RESOURCES

PRIMATE-LIKE MAMMALS: A STUNNING DIVERSITY IN THE TREE TOPS
www.paleocene-mammals.de/primates.htm
This site introduces the controversial plesiadapiforms and discusses their classification as primates.

Aegyptopithecus zeuxis
http://members.tripod.com/cacajao/aegyptopithecus_zeuxis.html
Information on this important early catarrhine.

PLANET OF THE APES
www.primates.com/history
Recent *Scientific American* article describing the major features of ape evolution.

BLACKWELL SYNERGY: ACQUISITION OF BIPEDALISM
www.blackwell-synergy.com/links/doi/10.1111/j.0021-8782.2004.00290.x/full
Recent article from the *Journal of Anatomy* discussing the fossil evidence for the advent of hominin bipedalism.

USEFUL SEARCH TERMS:

anatomy of bipedalism
ape evolution
bipedal locomotion
fossil apes (monkeys, primates)
human pelvis (feet, legs)

Chapter 5 Timeline

Cro-Magnon, Neandertal, and *Homo erectus*

CENOZOIC

Early strepsirhines

65 million

First plesiadapiforms, ca. 90 mya?

MESOZOIC

First mammals

253 million

PALEOZOIC

First vertebrates

543 million

PRECAMBRIAN

YEARS BP	FOSSIL RECORD	PRIMATES
Pleistocene		*Homo*
2 million	Early *Homo*	
Pliocene	*Australopithecus* and *Paranthropus*	
5 million		
	Earliest hominins? *Ardipithecus, Sahelanthropus, Orrorin*	Australopiths
	Sivapithecus in Asia and Europe	
Miocene	*Equatorins–Kenyapithecus* in Africa	
	Morotopithecus and *Proconsul* in Africa	Apes
25 million	*Branisella*	Platyrrhines appear
Oligocene		
	Aegyptopithecus at Fayum	Basal catarrhines
35 million	Oligopithecines in Africa	
Eocene		Early anthropoids
	Eosimias in China and *Algeripithecus* in Algeria	
	Adapoidea, Omomyoidea	First euprimates
58 million		
Paleocene		
65 million		
Late Cretaceous period	*Purgatorius*	First fossil plesiadapiforms

BACK BEYOND THE APES

The time scale of primate evolution is immense and may extend back some 90 million years. The first part of primate history was the age of the plesiadapiforms and first euprimates. By 20 million years ago, the apes were established in Africa, and for this reason, we too find our origin on this continent. By about 15 million years ago, the apes had spread into Eurasia.

Chapter 6

The South African Hominins

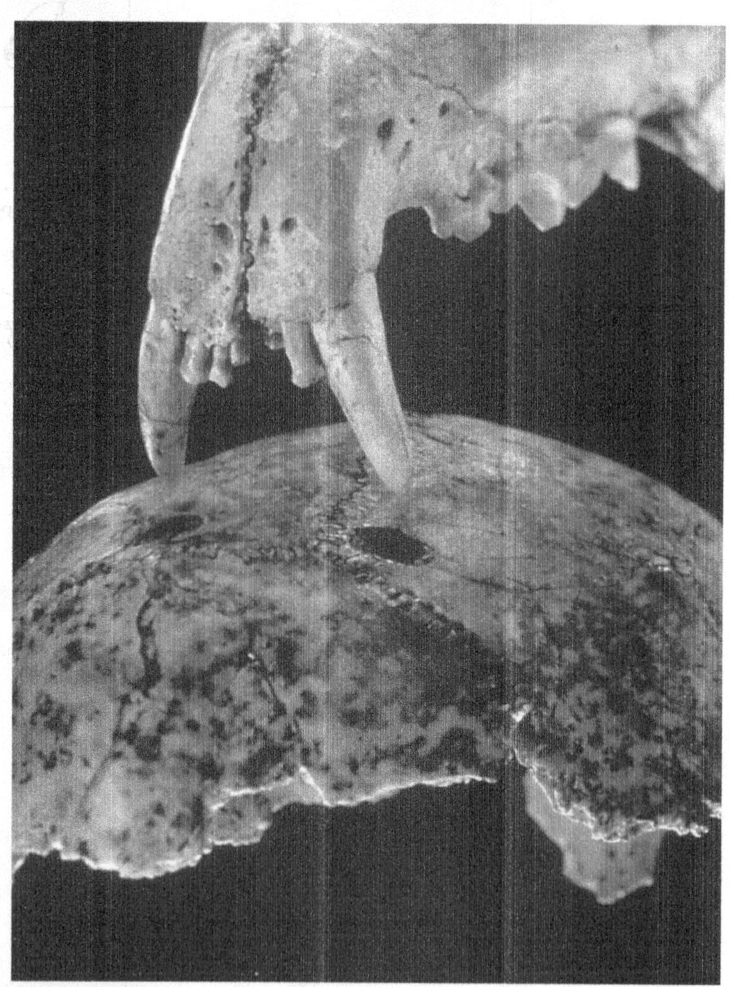

Early hominins probably served as prey for leopards and other large cats, as shown by this *Paranthropus robustus* skull fragment from the Swartkrans site. Indentations on the skull neatly match the lower canines of a leopard jaw from the same deposit.

In each great region of the world the living mammals are closely related to the extinct species of the same region. It is, therefore, probable that Africa was formerly inhabited by extinct apes closely allied to the gorilla and chimpanzee; and as these two species are now man's nearest allies, it is somewhat more probable that our early progenitors lived on the African continent than elsewhere.

Charles Darwin, 1809–1882. *The Descent of Man.*

Overview

The human tribe—the tribe, Hominini—branched off from ape stock some 5 to 7 million years ago. All members of that tribe, living and fossil, are referred to as *hominins* and can be placed in one of two subtribes: Australopithecina (containing the genera *Ardipithecus, Australopithecus, Kenyaothropus, Paranthropus, Orrorin,* and *Sahelanthropus*) and Hominina (containing the genus *Homo*).

The australopith subtribe was the earliest to evolve, and the first fossil evidence of these ancient bipeds was discovered in South Africa by Raymond Dart in 1924. Dart named his discovery *Australopithecus africanus* and claimed that it was intermediate between modern apes and humans. Dart's claims were largely dismissed by the scientific community until additional and more complete australopith materials were discovered by Robert Broom in the 1930s. Included in the new finds were the fossils of a species of australopith equipped with massive grinding teeth. Broom named this new creature *Paranthropus robustus.* Today, the hominin status of the australopiths is firmly established, and it is known that they roamed South Africa from 3 million years BP (and possibly earlier) to just a million years ago. Furthermore, there is evidence that certain of the South African australopiths used bone digging implements and possibly even manufactured stone tools.

The Science of Paleoanthropology

We are now ready to address the main topics of this book: paleoanthropology and the evidence for human evolution. The first five chapters have laid the groundwork for this inquiry by providing basic knowledge about evolutionary processes, genetics, primate socioecology and behavior, and the prehominin fossil record.

Mini-TIMELINE

Date or Age	Fossil Discoveries or Evolutionary Events
(A) Date (years AD)	
1995	"Little Foot" described from Sterkfontein
1965–1966	Brain, Tobias work at Swartkrans, Sterkfontein
1950	Le Gros Clark classifies australopiths as hominins
1938	Broom discovers first *Paranthropus*
1924	Dart discovers first *Australopithecus*
(B) Age (million years BP)	
2.0–1.0	*Paranthropus robustus* inhabits South Africa
3.5 (4?)–1.7	*Australopithecus africanus* inhabits South Africa

BOX 6.1

Special Skills to Study Fossil Sites

Paleoanthropological work can involve many different specialists, some of whom are listed below. These scientists work both in field and lab settings, and some people working on a single project may fill more than one role. For example, a paleoanthropologist may also be an archaeologist or a physical anthropologist.

Paleoanthropologists	In charge of investigations from start to finish, they must pick the site, get permission to excavate, obtain financial support, hire the labor, and organize, plan, and supervise the work in progress. Finally, they must integrate the data collected by each of the specialists and publish their conclusions.
Geologists	Often assist in selecting the site. Their knowledge of the geologic history of the region is indispensable in determining the relative ages of fossils. Their study of the strata at the site determines the natural processes—deposition, volcanic action—that laid the strata down and the conditions under which fossilization took place.
Archaeologists	Study humankind's past material culture: tools of stone, bone, and wood; living sites, settlement patterns, and food remains; art and ritual.
Physical anthropologists	Specialists in the comparative anatomy of apes and humans, they evaluate remains found at the site and the evolutionary status of fossil hominins who lived there.
Draftspeople/Illustrators	Record the exact position of all fossils, tools, and other artifacts as excavated, marking their relationships to each other in both the horizontal and vertical planes; prepare illustrations of specimens.
Geochemists	With geophysicists, conduct chemical and physical tests in the laboratory to determine the absolute ages of materials found at the site. They may also study the chemical composition of bones and artifacts.
Paleontologists/Faunal analysts	Study the fossil animal remains found at the site. From the finds, they can learn much about the ecology and the eating habits of early humans, as well as the paleoenvironment and age of the site.
Palynologists	Specialize in the study and identification of fossil plant pollen, which may shed light on early humankind's environment and diet and the climate at the time.
Pedologists	Experts on soil and its chemical composition, their findings round out the picture of the environment as it once was.
Petrologists	Identify and classify the rocks and minerals found around the site. They can determine the nature of rocks from which tools were made and identify stones that do not occur naturally in the area, which would indicate that the stones were imported by early humans.
Photographers	Document fossil remains and artifacts and their associations as they are uncovered, record work in progress and the use of special equipment, and provide overall views of the site as well as of personnel at work.
Preparators	At the site, preserve and protect fossils and artifacts with various hardening agents and make plaster casts for particularly fragile bones and other organic remains. In the laboratory, they clean and restore the specimens, making them ready for study by various specialists.
Surveyors	Map the general region of the site and the site itself, plotting it in relation to natural landmarks and making a detailed record of its contours before they are obliterated by digging.
Taphonomists	Study the condition and arrangement of the fossils in relation to the deposits which carry them to determine the origin and formation of the fossil assemblage.

Paleoanthropology had its start in the mid-nineteenth century with the first discoveries in Europe of the fossils of premodern humans—the Neandertals (see Chapter 14)—and with a landmark initial publication by T. H. Huxley, *Evidence as to Man's Place in Nature* (1863/1915). As detailed in later chapters, around the turn of the twentieth century, new fossils from the Far East took evidence of the hominin tribe not just tens of thousands but a million years into the past and back to a much more primitive anatomy. The twentieth century itself began with a blind lead from Britain—the fraudulent Piltdown remains (discussed later). Then researchers hit pay dirt with the discovery of the first **australopiths** from South Africa, creatures who seemed to be very near the evolutionary origin of bipedal walking. This was the beginning of a long line of discoveries from Africa that continues to this day.

Australopith a member of the *hominin* subtribe Australopithecina; any representative of the *genera Ardipithecus, Australopithecus, Kenyanthropus, Paranthropus, Orrorin*, and *Sahelanthropus*.

This chapter describes those first australopith finds and the rough-and-ready field techniques then in use by paleoanthropologists. Fast-forwarding to the twenty-first century, we find that paleoanthropology is now a very complicated field of inquiry compared to its humble beginnings. Today, the location, excavation, dating, analysis, and interpretation of hominin fossils requires the combined skills of a team of specialists (see Box 6.1). Sites are excavated with extreme care (Figure 6.1), and all fossils, artifacts, and other significant features are plotted on maps for further study. Geologists, paleontologists, and other scientists help to reconstruct the ancient landscape and ecosystem in detail. Laboratory analyses of fossils and the publication of results may take several years after the original discoveries. The old days of publishing hasty descriptions and speculations about new fossils are (thankfully) just about gone. But early discoveries, such as that made by Raymond Dart in South Africa in 1924, took place under very different circumstances. Large teams of specialists, such as those listed in Box 6.1 were unknown, as was the instantaneous, worldwide communication that takes place today via e-mail. It is to Dart's story that we now turn.

FIGURE 6.1 Controlled excavations at the australopith site of Swartkrans, South Africa. The grid system is used for plotting artifacts and fossils.

TABLE 6.1 Hominin Taxonomy I: Australopiths

Taxon	Age (mya)	First Described
Tribe Hominini ("hominins")		
Subtribe Australopithecina ("australopiths")		
Genus *Sahelanthropus*	~7–6	2002
Genus *Orrorin*	~6	2001
Genus *Ardipithecus*	5.8–4.4	1994–1995
Species *Ar. kadabba*	5.8–5.2	2001–2004
Species *Ar. ramidus*	4.4	1994–1995
Genus *Kenyanthropus*	3.5–3.2	2001
Genus *Australopithecus*	4.2–1.7	1925
Species *A. anamensis*	4.2–3.9	1995
Species *A. afarensis*	4.2–2.5	1978
Species *A. bahrelghazali*	~3.5–3.0	1996
Species *A. africanus*	3.5 (4?)–1.7	1925
Species *A. garhi*	2.5	1999
Genus *Paranthropus*	2.6–1.0	1938
Species *P. aethiopicus*	2.6–2.3	1968, 1985
Species *P. boisei*	2.4–1.3	1959, 1960
Species *P. robustus*	2–1	1938
Subtribe Hominina ("hominans")*		
Genus *Homo*		

*Names, ages, and dates of the hominan species are given in Table 8.1.

As Dart's tale is told, however, it is important to note that for the moment, our narrative is structured around paleoanthropological history—that is, a description of the South African australopiths following the order in which they were discovered—rather than the chronological ages of the various genera and species. To aid in understanding the fossils along both dimensions, the australopiths from South Africa and elsewhere are listed in Table 6.1, along with their ages and the dates of their initial descriptions.

Dart's Discovery of the Taung Skull

The importance of bipedalism cannot be overestimated. Bipedalism is much more than a mere rearing up and running about. As we have seen, it involves structural changes of the hips, legs, and feet that are found in hominins but not in apes. Somehow and for reasons that remain hazy, in the late Miocene epoch of Africa, the adaptations of bipedalism made their appearance in at least one kind of hominoid.

The first tangible evidence that a two-legged primate existed in the distant past came from an unexpected place: the Transvaal region of South Africa (Dart, 1925; Dart and Craig, 1967). Raymond Dart, professor of anatomy at the University of the Witwatersrand in Johannesburg, South Africa, encouraged his students to send him rock fragments that contained fossils. In 1924, a student brought him a fossil baboon skull that had come from a limestone quarry at a place named Taung, 200 miles (320 kilometers) from Johannesburg (see Figure 6.2). Hoping to obtain more fossils, particularly another baboon skull, Dart persuaded the quarry owner to save bone-bearing rocks, and in due course, he was sent two boxes of fragmented materials.

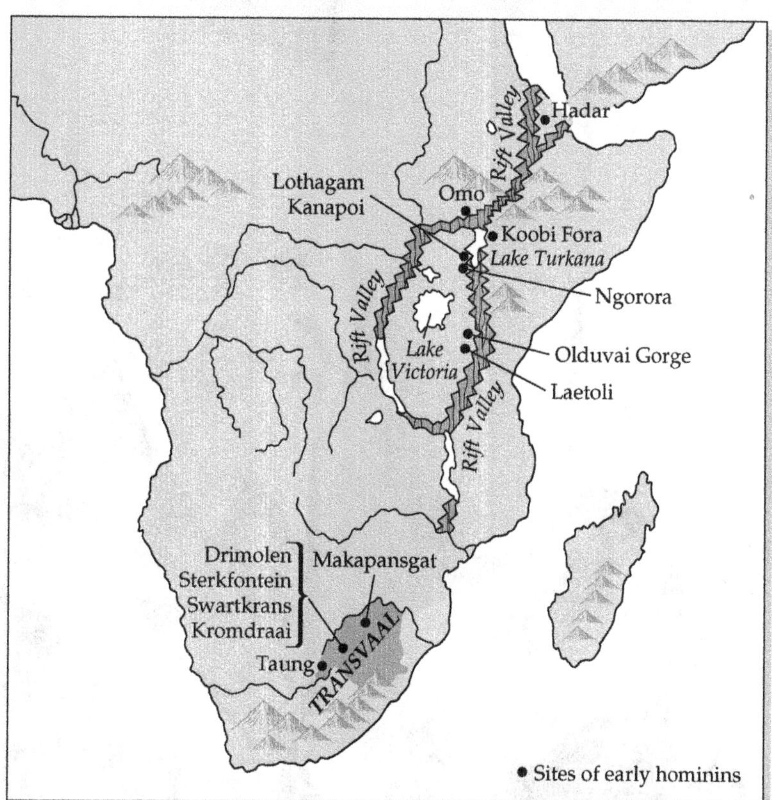

FIGURE 6.2
The earliest knowledge of australopiths came from the Transvaal region in South Africa. At a number of sites in this area, fossils were preserved in caves and hollows in the dolomite bedrock. Although their absolute age is not accurately known, they are broadly dated between 3.5 and 1 million years BP.

Dart found nothing of great interest in the first box, but his eye hit on something very strange in the second. On the top of the heap lay not a skull but the next best thing to it: an oddly shaped rounded piece of rock that appeared to be the mold of the inside of a skull. Searching the rest of the box, Dart found another piece of rock with a curved depression into which this mold fitted: part of the skull itself. In this second rock, Dart could dimly perceive the outline of a broken piece of skull and the back of a lower jaw. He was looking from the rear at the inside of something's or somebody's head.

An **endocast** (a fossilized cast of the interior of a skull) of any species of primate would have been a notable discovery, but one look at this antique fragment sent Dart's mind racing. The animal's brain capacity appeared to be three times larger than an ancient baboon's and perhaps even larger than a modern adult chimpanzee's. The exciting thought struck Dart that he might be holding in his hands the "missing link" between ape and human.

Endocast a *fossilized* cast of the interior of a skull; may reveal much about brain size and shape.

Dart's first problem was to free the rest of the strange skull from the surrounding stone. Working with a hammer, chisels, and a sharpened knitting needle, he slowly uncovered a face that was remarkably apelike, not baboonlike at all. Yet it was not overhung by the low brow of an ape but surmounted by a forehead. But what sort of ape, Dart wondered, might have lived long ago on that grassy plateau?

Apes lived in tropical forests, but according to the prevailing wisdom, there had been no such forests in South Africa for more than 100 million years. Rather, South Africa was believed to have always remained a dry, relatively undisturbed veld, much as it is today. Throughout prehistory, the nearest natural habitat of apes was more than 2,000 miles (3,200 kilometers) north of Taung. Could some different kind of ape have found a way to adapt itself to life in an arid, open land?

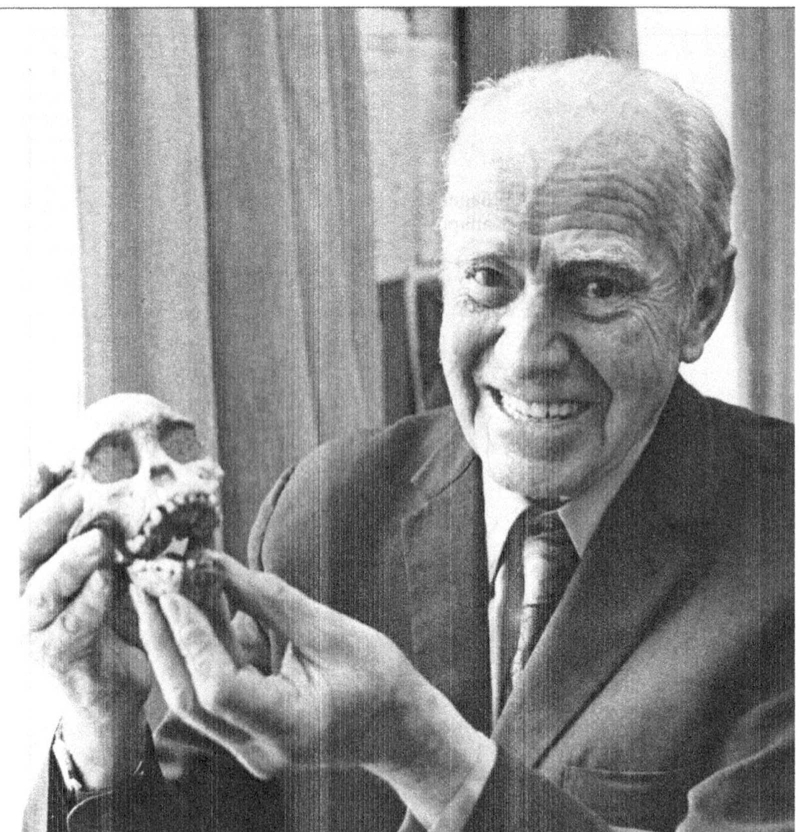

FIGURE 6.3
In 1924, Raymond Dart startled the anthropological world with his discovery of a small fossil skull from a quarry at Taung in South Africa. (The height of the skull and jaw is about 5 inches or 13 centimeters.) The following year, he named the Taung specimen *Australopithecus africanus* and boldly declared it to be a human ancestor.

The Evidence and Dart's Interpretation

Dart continued his exacting labor, and on the seventy-third day, the stone parted and he saw the face and most of the skull of a child now thought to have died at three to four years of age (Figure 6.3). It had a full set of milk teeth; the permanent molars were just beginning to erupt; and the canines, like those of humans, were quite small. After Dart studied his find carefully, he realized that the set of the skull suggested that the child had walked upright. One bit of evidence was the position of the **foramen magnum,** the large hole through which the spinal cord passes into the skull on its way to the brain. In apes, the foramen magnum is near the back of the skull, reflecting the sloping position of the spinal column in quadrupedal posture. But in the Taung skull, it faced almost directly downward (Figure 6.4): The Taung child had carried its head balanced atop its spine. Dart was certain that the creature had stood erect.

Foramen magnum the large opening in the cranial base, through which the spinal cord passes to the brain.

In the 1920s, all known premodern hominins—the Neandertals, Java man, and even the fraudulent Piltdown fossil (all discussed later)—seemed to be recognizably human creatures that were apelike in one or more traits. The Taung fossil, however, appeared to be just the reverse: an ape with some humanlike features. The question before Dart was how to classify a creature that combined an ape-sized brain with an upright stance and humanlike teeth. In his report to the British scientific journal *Nature,* Dart took the bit between his teeth and declared that he had discovered an extinct link between humans and their ape ancestors. He christened his find ***Australopithecus africanus,*** or "southern ape of Africa" (Dart, 1925). Newspaper headlines around the world proclaimed that the "missing link" had been found.

Australopithecus a *genus* of the tribe Hominini, subtribe Australopithecina; contains five *species*: *A. afarensis*, *A. africanus*, *A. anamensis*, *A. bahrelghazali*, and *A. garhi*.

Australopithecus africanus an *australopith species* that inhabited South Africa 3.5 (4?) to 1.7 million years ago.

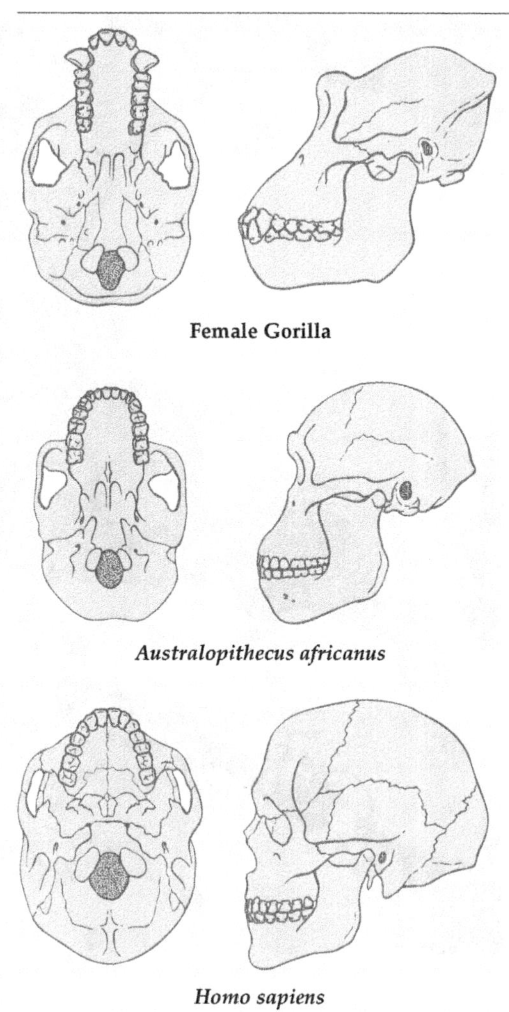

FIGURE 6.4
Improvement in the balance of the head during human evolution has involved movement of the **occipital condyles** and the associated foramen magnum (shown stippled) forward. (The occipital condyles are the bearing surfaces of the skull on the uppermost vertebra—the atlas; the foramen magnum is the hole in the base of the skull through which the spinal cord passes.) In this important characteristic of the skull base, *Australopithecus* is intermediate between apes (here, a gorilla *[top]* is illustrated) and modern humans *(bottom)*. Scale is approximately one-fifth actual size.

Dart's Claims Dismissed

Dart's report was intensely interesting to a number of scientists in Europe, not so much for the human attributes he claimed for the Taung creature as for the inexplicable presence of an ape so far south. The general conclusion was that this was a young specimen of an ancient chimpanzeelike or gorillalike species, but how it had wandered where no ape had ever before been known to go was extremely puzzling. As for Dart's claim that the Taung child represented an early human ancestor and a true missing link? That notion was met with a good deal of skepticism. Some of Dart's most powerful scientific colleagues thought he had simply found an odd ape and that humans were more likely descended from creatures like **Piltdown man** (P. Bowler, 1986; Keith, 1950; see Box 6.2 on p. 169).

Given this skepticism, Dart was encouraged by a warm congratulatory letter from Robert Broom, a Scottish physician who had hunted fossils, particularly fossils of mammal-like reptiles, in many parts of South Africa (Figure 6.5). Two weeks after the letter arrived, Broom himself appeared at Dart's laboratory. He spent a weekend studying the Taung child intensively and became convinced that it was truly a connecting link between the apes and humans. He said so firmly in an article in *Nature* (Broom, 1925). After the first flare-up of attention, however, Dart's child was either forgotten or dismissed by most scientists. Nonetheless, Dart continued to study the skull.

Occipital condyles pads of bone on the base of the skull that articulate with the uppermost vertebra.

Piltdown man a doctored modern human skull and ape jaw that was "discovered" in 1911 and supposed to represent a very primitive human, *Eoanthropus dawsoni*, but later exposed as a hoax in 1953.

FIGURE 6.5
Robert Broom was a passionate fossil hunter and distinguished paleontologist. He kept working until his death at age 85.

Dentition of Taung

Dart worked away at the Taung skull almost daily for more than four years. In 1929, he succeeded in separating the upper and lower jaws, and for the first time, he could examine the entire pattern of the teeth and get a good look at their grinding surfaces (Dart and Craig, 1967).

What he found strengthened his case that the fossil was neither an ape nor a baboon. In apes, as we have seen (Chapter 5), the front teeth are large because they are used for fighting and for tearing up the tough vegetable matter that forms much of an ape's diet. Ape canines, in particular, are so large that there must be spaces (diastemata) between the teeth of the upper jaw to accommodate the lower canines when the jaw is closed (Figure 6.6, p. 170). At the same time, apes' jaws are relatively longer than humans' jaws and heavier, too; thus, and the muscles needed to move them are more massive. The Taung child, although a young individual and therefore lacking typical adult characters, could be judged to be distinctly more humanlike than apelike in all these characteristics. Its nicely curved jaw was shorter than a young ape's and more lightly made. Its canines and incisors were relatively small and set closely together. In fact, though the molars were larger than is now normal, most of the teeth could have belonged to a child of today (Figure 6.7, p. 171).

In the minds of Dart and Broom, any lingering doubts about the hominin nature of the creature vanished, but skeptics, they suspected, would take more convincing. What was needed was an adult skull, and also some legs or pelvic bones, to support the claim of erect posture that the position of the foramen magnum suggested. Broom was determined to find this evidence.

BOX 6.2

The Piltdown Fraud

In December 1922, Raymond Dart left England, bound for Johannesburg, South Africa, and a new job at the University of Witwatersrand. He had recently finished a stint as senior demonstrator at University College, London, under the supervision of the renowned anthropologist and neuroanatomist Grafton Elliot Smith (Dart and Craig, 1967).

At the time, Elliot Smith was one of England's most senior scientists. Along with Arthur Keith and Arthur Smith Woodward (both later "Sir Arthurs") and W. L. H. Duckworth, Elliot Smith exerted enormous influence on British anthropology and paleontology in the first half of the twentieth century. These men trained students, wrote important books, developed influential theories, and of the greatest significance for Dart, made approving or dismissive public comments about new fossil finds. Elliot Smith, in particular, had a special theoretical hobbyhorse: his notion that in human evolution, "the brain had led the way." That is, Smith believed that the expansion and elaboration of the human brain had preceded all other major evolutionary events—including dental changes and bipedalism—and indeed had made them possible (Landau, 1991; Smith, 1927).

At the time of Dart's announcement of *Australopithecus africanus,* Elliot Smith and his colleagues were preoccupied with other fossils more obviously related to humans: the small-brained Java man (discovered in 1891; see Chapter 10) and, delightfully, from England itself, the large-brained Piltdown man. Piltdown seemed to fit the "brain led the way" theory perfectly.

The Piltdown fossils (Figure 6.8, p. 171) were brought to public attention by amateur archaeologist Charles Dawson and paleontologist Arthur Smith Woodward. Dawson had made the original discovery of apparently ancient skull fragments in a gravel pit near Piltdown Common, Sussex, in 1911. With Smith Woodward's help, additional remains were recovered in 1912, and in 1913, Jesuit paleontologist Teilhard de Chardin retrieved a lower canine tooth from the Piltdown gravels. When the pieces were reconstructed, they produced a very large (almost 1,500 cubic centimeters) and high-vaulted braincase with an apelike jaw and somewhat projecting lower canines. Elliot Smith's theories seemed to be verified: Piltdown man combined a modern-sized brain with a primitive dentition. Furthermore, it was thought that *Eoanthropus dawsoni* ("Dawson's dawn man"), as the Piltdown specimen had been officially dubbed, was quite old—probably Pliocene in age (Spencer, 1990).

Dart's announcement of the Taung fossil elicited cool reactions from British anthropologists who were enamored with other possible ancestors. Elliot Smith admitted that its brain was unusually large for an ape but disagreed with Dart's conclusion that it had walked bipedally (Smith, 1925, 1927). Smith's continuing preoccupation with Piltdown is shown by the fact that in his 1927 book, he devoted about three times as many pages to the English fossil as to Dart's Taung child. (Piltdown man was also included in Smith's human evolutionary tree [1927:2], while *Australopithecus* was omitted entirely.) Keith's dismissive reaction was that *Australopithecus* belonged in "the same group or subfamily as the chimpanzee and gorilla" (1925:234) and that it was "much too late in the scale of time to have any place in man's ancestry" (Dart and Craig, 1967:42). Smith Woodward—significantly, a co-discoverer of Piltdown—opined that the Taung fossil would have little bearing on deciding the place of origin of humans (Woodward, 1925).

For forty years, Piltdown man influenced researchers' interpretations of human evolution. Unfortunately, with each new find, Piltdown became more and more of an oddity. The accumulating collection of australopith fossils and new remains from China and elsewhere all seemed to proclaim that the legs and the teeth, not the brain, had led the way in human evolution. Finally, in the early 1950s, scientists at Oxford University and the British Natural History Museum initiated a series of new analyses to test the unspeakable possibility that the Piltdown fossil was a fraud. To their dismay, the tests proved beyond a doubt that a hoax had been perpetrated. Bones had been stained and broken, and teeth had been filed flat in order to make it appear that the skull and the jaw belonged to the same ancient creature. In reality, an ape's jaw had been combined with a human skull, and the best scientific minds in the world had been hoodwinked (Weiner, 1995).

Over the years, several people were held up as suspects by amateur sleuths bent on solving the Piltdown hoax. Many thought that Dawson, the original discoverer, was the joker; others believed Arthur Keith, Teilhard de Chardin, or even Elliot Smith himself to be the culprit (Spencer, 1990). Only in May 1996 was the mystery finally solved. Based on materials found in an old trunk stored in a loft at the British Natural History Museum, it appeared certain that the hoaxer was one Martin Hinton, museum curator of zoology at the time of the fraud.

(continued)

BOX 6.2 *(continued)*

Hinton had the materials and the experience to pull off the hoax, and he apparently had the motive: It seems he was angry at his boss, Arthur Smith Woodward, over money (specifically, how Hinton was to be paid for a cataloging project taken on during his vacation; Gee, 1996).

Ironically, over the years, Piltdown has changed from an embarrassment to anthropology to a useful reminder not to become overly invested in a particular theory or to put unqualified trust in new discoveries that fit one's expectations. *Eoanthropus* now serves to remind us that science makes progress only through a mix of hard work, insight, skepticism, data sharing, and careful verification or falsification of results. Such a mix of further data collection and analysis led to the recognition of the Taung child as a hominin by the 1950s.

Discoveries of Robert Broom

It was 1936 before Broom discovered additional fossils that supported the Taung child's claim of hominin status. Working then as the curator of vertebrate paleontology at the Transvaal Museum in Pretoria, Broom found the key remains in a quarry at Sterkfontein, a village not far from Pretoria (Figure 6.2; Broom, 1950; Reader, 1988).

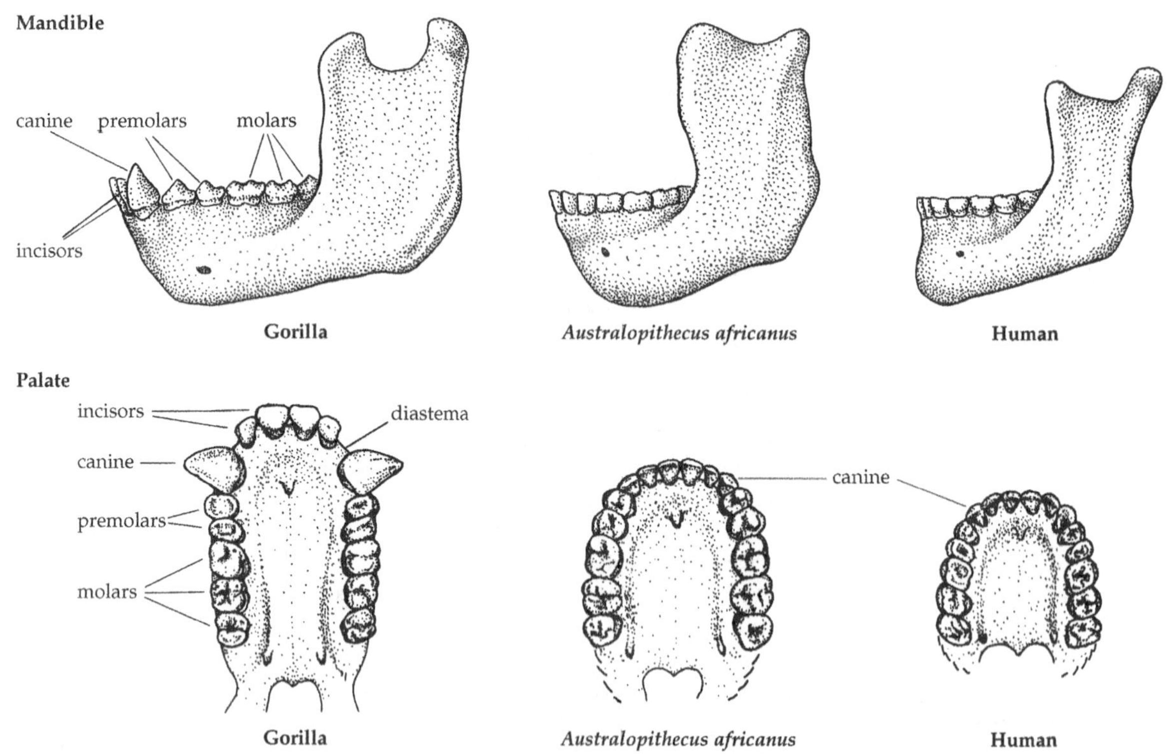

FIGURE 6.6
These drawings show a lateral view of the mandibles (lower jaws) and a full view of the palates (upper jaws) of a gorilla, an adult *Australopithecus africanus*, and a modern human. The striking difference in the size and form of the canine teeth is clear, and in the gorilla palate, we can see the gaps or diastemata, into which the lower canines fit on each side. The difference in the shape of the dental arcade in ape and hominid is also striking. The lateral view also shows distinct tooth wear: The ape teeth are used to crush and tear; the hominin teeth are used to crush and grind, which causes the typical flat wear of the hominin dentition. The drawings are not to scale.

A Skull from Sterkfontein

Ever since the first mining camps were opened during the South African gold rush of 1886, the people of the Sterkfontein area had been picking up fossilized remains of baboons, and perhaps, unknowingly, hominins. The limeworks at Sterkfontein had even issued a little guidebook: "Come to Sterkfontein and Find the Missing Link." When Broom first visited the quarry, the manager, who had worked at Taung and knew about the *Australopithecus* child's skull, promised Broom that he would keep a sharp lookout for anything similar. That similar something appeared in August 1936 and consisted of two-thirds of a superb brain cast, both sides of an upper jaw, and fragments of a braincase. When the fragments were pieced together, Broom had parts of the skull of an adult *Australopithecus.*

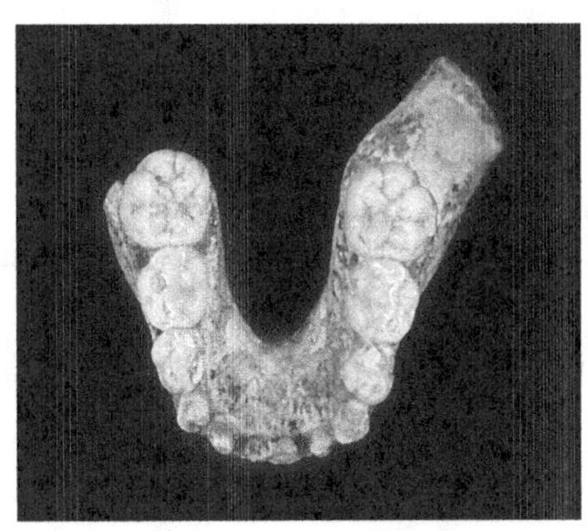

FIGURE 6.7 Lower dentition of the Taung child (*Australopithecus africanus*). The largest teeth are the first permanent molars.

Paranthropus robustus at Kromdraai

For two years, Broom, now in his seventies, continued to visit his fossil gold mine. One June day in 1938, the quarry manager met Broom and handed him an upper jaw with one molar in place. He had obtained it from a schoolboy who lived on a farm at Kromdraai, less than a mile (1.6 kilometers) away. Broom found the boy and was rewarded when the lad pulled out of his pocket "four of the most wonderful teeth ever seen in the world's history"(Broom, 1950:50).

After school, the boy led Broom to the site of the jaw's discovery, where several additional pieces of the same specimen were eventually found. When the fragments were put together, Broom had most of another australopith skull. It was characterized by a short, flat face; a cranial capacity of about 600 cubic centimeters; small, humanlike canines and incisors; and huge premolars and molars. The new fossil was sufficiently different from the Taung and Sterkfontein specimens (not to mention modern humans), particularly in its grinding tooth **megadontia,** that Broom felt justified in creating a new genus and species to hold it: ***Paranthropus robustus,*** or "robust near-man" (Box 6.3). Comparing the total fossil assemblage at Kromdraai with that from Sterkfontein, Broom estimated that *Paranthropus* was probably older than the *Australopithecus* specimens from the

Megadontia the condition of having enlarged teeth relative to body size.

Paranthropus robustus australopith *species* that lived in South Africa 2.0–1.0 mya; called *Australopithecus robustus* by some authors.

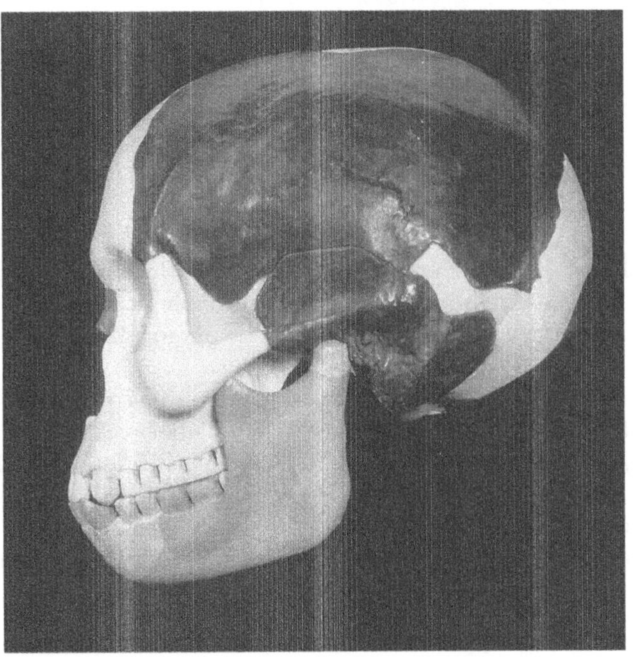

FIGURE 6.8 The fraudulent Piltdown skull, here reconstructed, led scientists astray for forty years in their understanding of human evolution. The black shaded area of the skull distinguishes the original fragments. The remainder is reconstruction.

BOX 6.3

Characteristics of the South African Australopiths[a]

Trait	*Australopithecus africanus*	*Paranthropus robustus*
Height	F: 3.8 ft (115 cm) M: 4.5 ft (138 cm) (F is 83% of M)	F: 3.6 ft (110 cm) M: 4.3 ft (132 cm) (F is 83% of M)
Weight	F: 55–66 lb (25–30 kg) M: 90–132 lb (41–60 kg) (F about 54% of M)	F: 71–88 lb (32–40 kg) M: 88–176 lb (40–80 kg) (F about 60% of M)
Brain size (sexes combined)	454 cc mean (405–515 cc range)[b]	503 cc? (Mean reflects measures of 476 and 530 cc for one specimen)
Cranium	**Prognathic** face; lacks sagittal crest; low, flat forehead; low-vaulted braincase; lacks flexure (arching) of cranial base[c]	Face is wide, flattish, and "dished"; sagittal crest; low, flat forehead; low-vaulted braincase; some flexure (arching) of cranial base[c]
Dentition	Parabolic toothrow; short, incisor-like canines; no diastemata; lower P3s have two cusps; smaller grinding teeth than *P. robustus*	Parabolic toothrow; short, incisor-like canines; small anterior teeth; no diastemata; lower P3s have two or more cusps; very large grinding teeth
Diet	Mostly fruits and leaves; also, possibly grasses, sedges, some meat	Harder, tougher items than *A. africanus* (more nuts? gritty tubers?); some meat? Termites?
Limbs	Longer and larger arms and shorter legs than modern humans; apelike tibia; grasping big toes	Longer arms and shorter legs than modern humans; humanlike (nongrasping) big toes
Pelvis	Short, broad ilia; pelvic bowl nearly complete; short ischial shafts realigned in modern manner; pelvis wide between hip joints	Short, broad ilia; weak iliofemoral ligaments (?); shortening of ischial shaft (?); pelvis wide between hip joints
Locomotion	Bipedalism and arboreal climbing	Bipedalism
Known dates (million years BP)	3.5 (4?)–1.7[d]	2.0–1.0

[a]Mean values for height, weight, and brain size are sometimes based on small samples and may change with additional fossil discoveries. For additional technical details and diagnostic traits, see Appendix 3. See text for data sources, in addition to Aiello and Dean (1990), Conroy (1990), and Grine (1993).
[b]The brain size of Sterkfontein fossil 505 is controversial. It is taken here as 515 cubic centimeters.
[c]A fully flexed (arched) cranial base suggests the presence of the throat anatomy that allows modern speech (see Chapter 13).
[d]An age of approximately 4 myr has been claimed for some Sterkfontein specimens (Partridge et al., 2003), but this is disputed (Berger et al., 2002; Gibbons, 2003).

Prognathic having the lower face and jaws projecting in front of the upper parts of the face.

Paranthropus a *genus* of the tribe Hominini, subtribe Australopithecina; contains three *species*: *P. robustus*, *P. boisei*, and *P. aethiopicus*.

Sagittal crest a ridge of bone running front to rear along the midline of the skull; serves to attach certain jaw muscles.

latter site: mid versus late Pleistocene (Broom, 1938). In fact, subsequent studies have shown that Broom had the chronological order reversed: *Australopithecus* inhabited South Africa a million years or more before the advent of *Paranthropus* (see Table 6.1).

Broom continued to search, and in due course, he had more megadont fossils to work with, having struck a rich find in a cave at Swartkrans (Figures 6.9 and 6.10), just across the valley from Sterkfontein (Reader, 1988). The new material he found confirmed that the *Paranthropus* grinding teeth were huge in proportion to the size of the front teeth and that on its skull, *P. robustus* had a bony ridge or crest, called a **sagittal crest,** to anchor large jaw muscles (Figure 6.10). These characteristics suggested that the creature was a vegetarian and chewed up large quantities of tough vegetable food, as a gorilla does today.

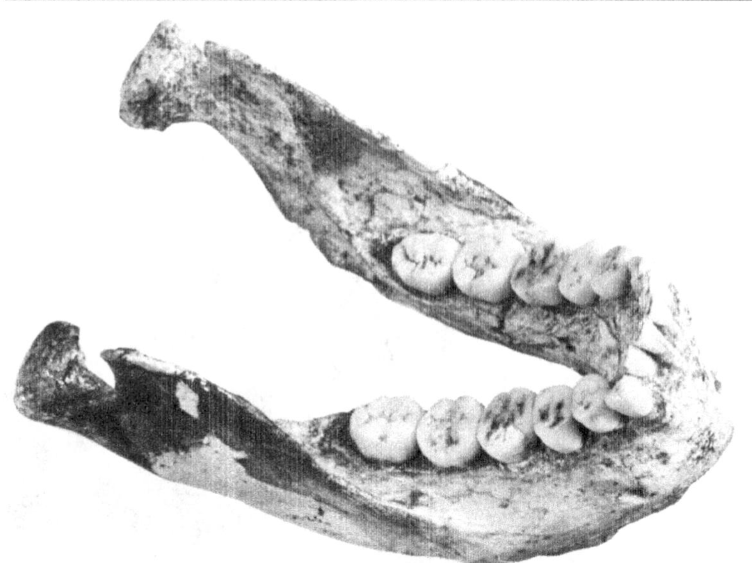

FIGURE 6.9
The almost perfectly preserved jaw of *Paranthropus robustus* found at Swartkrans. Note the huge molars and premolars and the diminutive front teeth that characterize the megadont genus. This photograph is approximately three-quarters actual size.

Further Discoveries at Sterkfontein

The 1930s gave way to the 1940s, World War II came and went, and still the statuses of *Australopithecus* and *Paranthropus* were unclear. Were they apes or hominins? Were they directly ancestral to humans or evolutionary deadends? More fossils were needed, and it was the indefatigable Broom who supplied them.

In 1947, Broom resumed working at Sterkfontein. One day, a blast in some unpromising cave debris revealed the first of a series of important discoveries. When the smoke cleared, the upper half of an adult female australopith skull (Figure 6.11) sparkled in the sunlight. The lower half lay embedded in a block of stone nearby. The specimen's jaw protruded and her forehead was low, but still, there was an

Zygomatic arch the bony arch running from the cheekbone back to the auditory meatus.

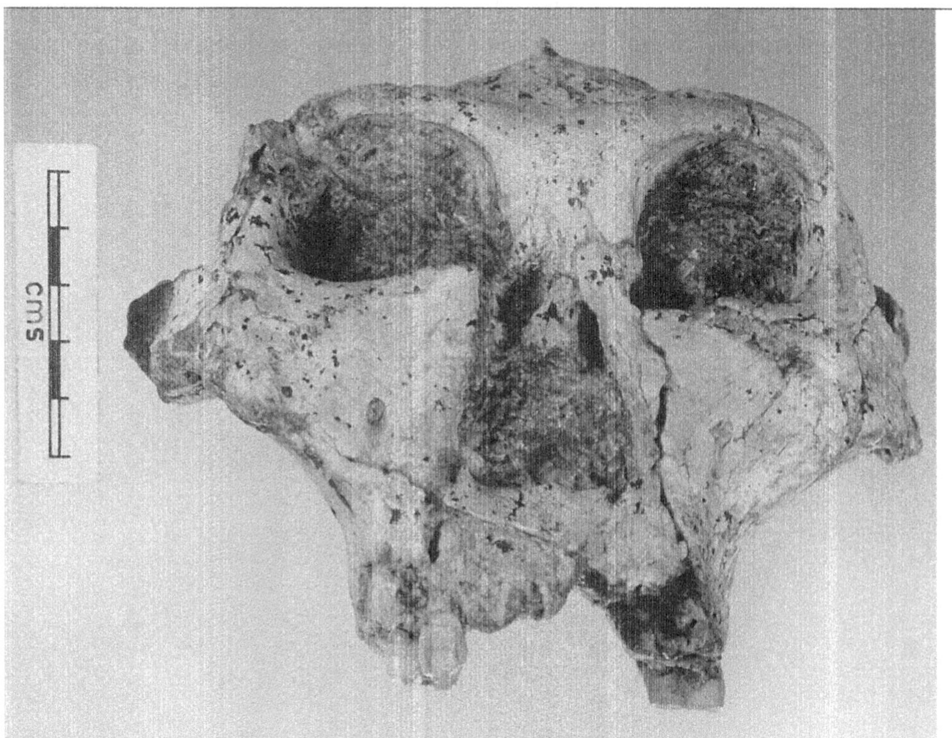

FIGURE 6.10
A skull of *Paranthropus robustus* from Swartkrans (museum catalog number SK48). Note the broad face, the large **zygomatic arches**, and the sagittal crest atop the skull.

FIGURE 6.11
This magnificent skull of *Australopithecus africanus* was found at Sterkfontein by Robert Broom in 1947. Although the teeth and jawbone are missing, the skull is otherwise complete and undistorted—a rare find. The photograph is approximately one-half actual size.

unmistakable quality of humanness about her. Her cranial capacity was 485 cubic centimeters.

This discovery was followed by other important finds (Figures 6.12 and 6.13): first, a male jaw with an intact canine tooth worn level with the other teeth, as human canines are, and later, a nearly perfect female pelvis. This was, after the skull, the most important discovery. There was no doubt that it had belonged to a creature that had walked and run upright, much as we do (Dart and Craig, 1967; Box 6.3).

When Broom's Sterkfontein pelvis was reconstructed (Figure 6.14), it suggested a near-modern type of terrestrial bipedalism. Its short, broad iliac blades testified to a low center of gravity and formed a nearly complete pelvic bowl. Furthermore,

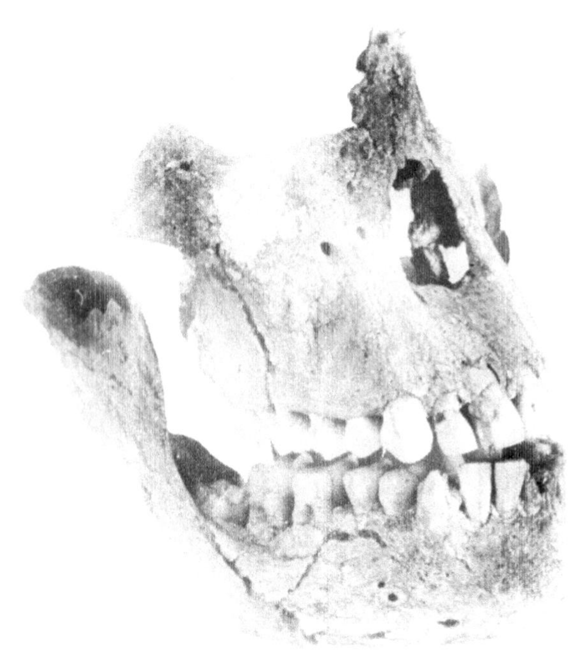

FIGURE 6.12
These beautifully preserved jaws were found at Sterkfontein by John Robinson, Broom's successor as curator at the Transvaal museum. This specimen has unusually large canine teeth for *Australopithecus africanus*.

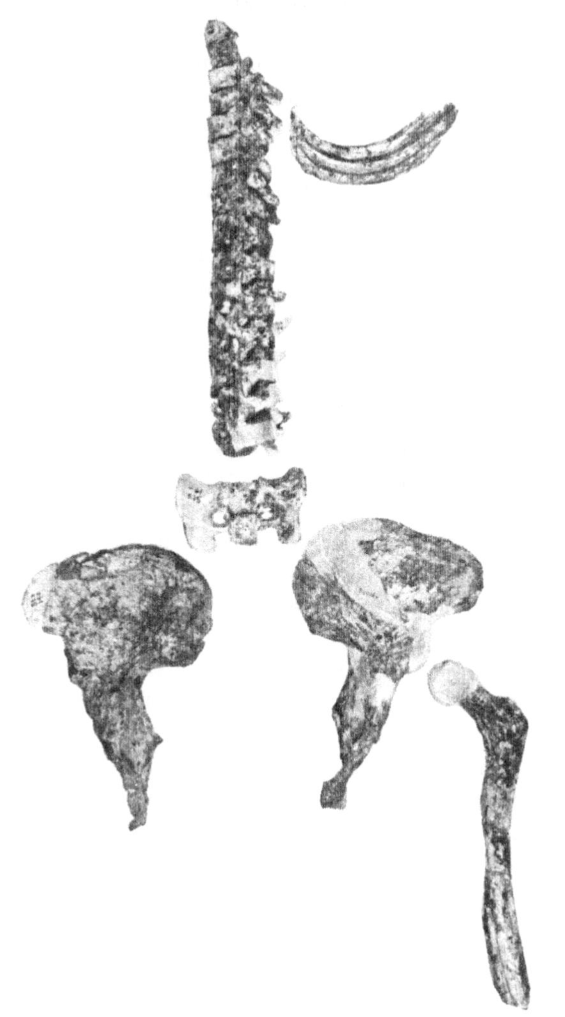

FIGURE 6.13
The skeletal remains of *Australopithecus africanus* found by Robert Broom at Sterkfontein. These bones are believed to have belonged to a female that was no more than 4 feet 3 inches (1.3 meters) tall. The pelvic bones were of exceptional importance in proving that *Australopithecus* was bipedal, as Dart had claimed in 1925. The photograph is approximately one-quarter actual size.

the ischial shafts were relatively short and realigned with the ilia in a modern manner, while the anterior inferior iliac spines were enlarged (LeGros Clark, 1967; Robinson, 1972). In all, the pelvis seemed to provide perfect confirmation of Dart's original claim: that *Australopithecus africanus* was an upright inhabitant of the South African savanna.

This interpretation of *A. africanus,* as an exclusively bipedal and terrestrial and rather humanlike species, may not be entirely accurate, however. In 1995,

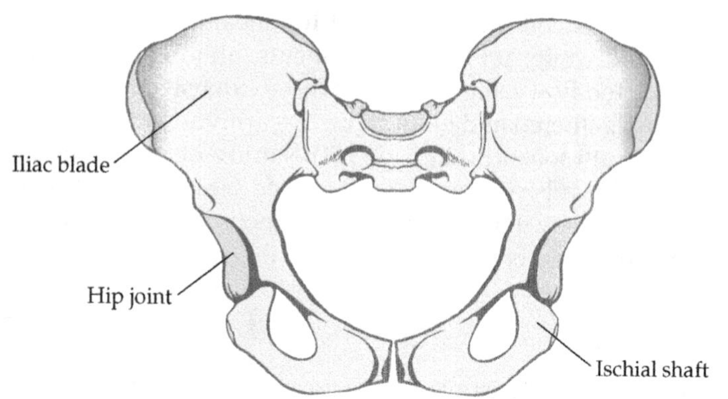

FIGURE 6.14
The restored pelvic girdle of *Australopithecus africanus* from Sterkfontein. The wide pelvis has short, broad iliac blades; forwardly curved ilia producing a nearly complete pelvic bowl; and short ischial shafts that have been realigned in the modern manner. It is clearly the pelvis of a biped.

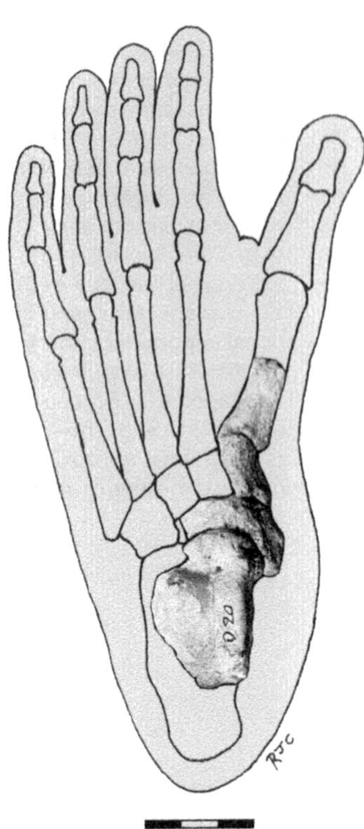

FIGURE 6.15
This drawing shows the reconstructed foot of *Australopithecus africanus* found at Sterkfontein. "Little Foot," as the fossil is called by its discoverers, displays adaptations for bipedalism at the rear of the foot and adaptations for climbing—primarily the grasping big toe—at the front. The fossil may be as much as 3.5 million years old. This figure is approximately one-half actual size.

researchers announced the discovery of four articulating (connecting to one another) foot bones from Sterkfontein that may be 3.5 million years old (Figure 6.15). Dubbed "Little Foot" and attributed to *Australopithecus africanus,* these bones show adaptations for bipedalism at the rear of the foot, as well as the clear presence of an apelike, grasping big toe at the front (Clarke and Tobias, 1995). The"Little Foot" report was followed in 1996 by a 2.7-million-year-old *A. africanus* tibia (shin bone) that shows evidence of apelike mobility at the knee joint (Berger and Tobias, 1996). Finally, in 1998, evidence was presented that suggests *A. africanus* may have had much larger forelimbs relative to the size of their hindlimbs than in modern humans—that is, distinctly apelike body proportions (McHenry and Berger, 1998).

Together, the new data suggest that *A. africanus,* while bipedal, was also equipped for arboreal, climbing activities. Interestingly, the 1996 paper also cited new evidence that in the distant past, Sterkfontein may have been somewhat wooded, rather than strictly open grassland—an adjustment to the reconstructed habitat that agrees nicely with the new picture of *A. africanus* locomotion.

Interestingly, the few postcranial remains known from *Paranthropus robustus* have also revealed adaptations for habitual bipedalism, although perhaps not for climbing. Unlike *A. africanus, P. robustus* had nongrasping big toes, although they still had somewhat apelike limb proportions (Aiello and Dean, 1990; Box 6.3).

By the late 1940s, a total of five South African sites had produced australopith remains. (Others have been discovered since then; see Figure 6.2.) These creatures were finally recognized as hominins in 1950 after detailed study of the accumulated fossils by British anatomist W. E. Le Gros Clark (Le Gros Clark, 1955, 1967). Controversies continued, however (and remain in force today) about the South African australopiths' possible evolutionary relationships to each other and to modern humans and over the question of whether they made and used tools. It is to that topic that we now turn.

Fossils and Artifacts

Which, if either, of the two South African fossil types had led to humans still remained an unanswered question. Researchers knew that if stone tools or other implements could be associated with either type, some light might be shed on the matter.

Evidence of *Australopithecus* Tool Making at Makapansgat?

Osteodontokeratic culture the culture of bone, tooth, and horn tools hypothesized by Raymond Dart for *A. africanus*; now largely dismissed.

Taphonomy the scientific study of the conditions under which objects are preserved as *fossils.*

In 1947, after eighteen years of concentrating on his work in anatomy at the University of Witwatersrand, Dart returned to the search for "dawn man." He analyzed thousands of fossilized animal bones associated with further remains of *Australopithecus africans* that had been found in cave deposits 200 miles (320 kilometers) to the north of Sterkfontein, at Makapansgat (Figure 6.16). He called the collection an **osteodontokeratic culture** (meaning a culture of bone, tooth, and horn); (Dart and Craig, 1967). His arguments, although ingenious, were not widely accepted. Today, it seems clear that these extensive collections represent the remains of bones gathered and gnawed on by carnivores and porcupines, rather than being australopith tools (Brain, 1981). The study of the origin and formation of assemblages of fossils such as these is termed **taphonomy.** It is, as we will see, a branch of paleontology that has proved of immense value in understanding prehistoric environments and early hominin behavior (see Box 6.1).

Definite Tools Found at Sterkfontein and Swartkrans

The evidence of australopith material culture at Makapansgat thus turned out to be a false lead. But beginning in the 1950s and continuing right up to the present,

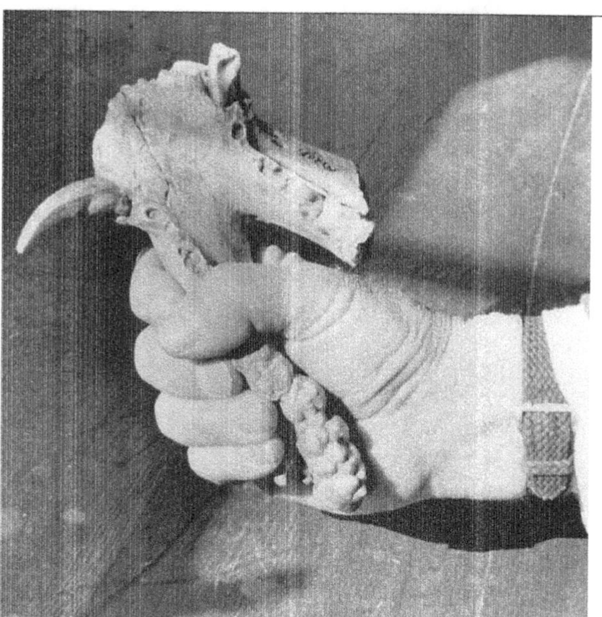

FIGURE 6.16 Raymond Dart firmly believed that *Australopithecus africanus* used animal bones as a wide variety of tools. Here, he demonstrates a pick.

clear and definite evidence of tool making and tool use has been forthcoming from both Sterkfontein and Swartkrans. Unfortunately, much of the new evidence is difficult to interpret, for two reasons.

First, there is the problem of the complex geology of these sites. Both consist of limestone caverns and sinkholes filled with **breccia**—a hard jumble of bones, stones, and sand dropped or washed in from the surface and then calcified by lime-bearing solutions. The caverns, sinkholes, and breccia form a complicated pattern of layers and pockets (so-called breccia *infills*) that are very hard to date either absolutely or relative to one another. Additionally, the contents of a particular infill may have accumulated so slowly that it samples several past environments, and therefore individual items in the infill's contents—including tools and hominin fossils—may not be at all contemporaneous (Conroy, 1990; Kuman and Clarke, 2000). Second, it appears that as many as three different hominin species, including two australopiths and an early form of *Homo*, may have been recovered from these sites. Combining this diversity of hominin types with the complex geology, and throwing in a dash of disagreement among researchers about the species classification of particular fossils, has made the identification of the South African tool makers a difficult task.

Breccia a lime-cemented jumble of sand, stones, and bones; a common cave fill in South Africa.

In any event, here are the data. Simple pebble tools and flakes were discovered at Sterkfontein in 1957 (Figure 6.17; Howell, 1973). These artifacts come from a layer called Member 5 (estimated to be about 2.0 to 1.7 myr old), which also contains hominin remains considered to be from *Paranthropus robustus* (Figure 6.18). Just slightly older than Member 5 is the so-called StW 53 infill, which contains no stone tools but does contain hominin fossils traditionally classed as ***Homo habilis*** (discussed in Chapter 8) but more recently referred to *Australopithecus* sp. (i.e., species indeterminate; Kuman and Clarke, 2000). Fossils traditionally classed as *Australopithecus africanus* have been found in Members 4 and 2 (Little Foot is from layer 2), both of which lack tools (Conroy, 1990).

Homo habilis one of the two *species* of "early *Homo*"; inhabited South and East Africa 2.3 to 1.6 million years ago.

At Swartkrans, a half-century of additional work since the days of Robert Broom has produced many more fossils and a lot of stone and bone tools (Conroy, 1990). *Paranthropus robustus* fossils come from the three lowest layers, which collectively date from about 1.8 to 1.0 mya. In addition, hominin remains referred to ***Homo erectus*** have been recovered from deposits that date back 1.8 to 1.5 myr. Pebble tools and flakes are found throughout the Swartkrans geological sequence and date as far back as 1.8 million years. Finally, several dozen bone tools from Swartkrans (and one from Sterkfontein Member 5) have been shown recently to have probably been used for digging into local termite mounds (Backwell and d'Errico, 2001).

Homo erectus a *hominin species* that inhabited much of the Old World between 1.9(?) million and at least 300,000 years BP; successor to "early *Homo*."

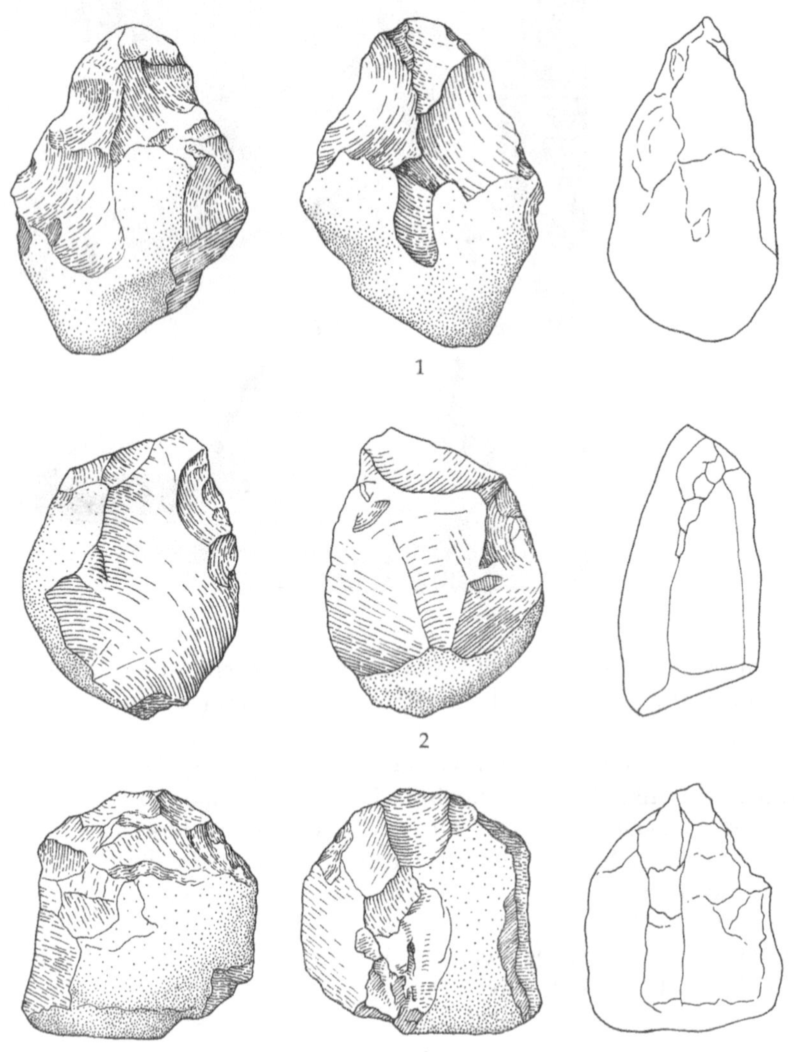

FIGURE 6.17
These primitive stone choppers from Sterkfontein were the first to be discovered in association with hominin remains in South Africa. Recent research has shown that they were not associated with *Australopithecus africanus* but are from a higher level of the cave deposits. The drawings are approximately 40 percent natural size.

So, to summarize the evidence from South Africa: *Paranthropus robustus* is regularly found associated with stone and bone tools and seems likely to have produced material culture; *Australopithecus africanus* is nowhere found associated with tools and may have lacked nonbiodegradable implements; *Homo erectus* (who would later become an accomplished stone tool maker throughout the Old World) is found with stone tools at Swartkrans and may have produced some of them; and as for *Homo habilis* (who *may* be present at Sterkfontein), the question of tool making is irresolvable at present. A fascinating addendum to these findings is Randall Susman's analysis of the hand bones of *P. robustus*, which reveals that this hominin had a fully opposable thumb and was capable of a precision grip (Susman, 1994). Thus, there seems to be no anatomical bar to viewing *Paranthropus robustus* as an australopith tool maker.

Comments on Australopith Phylogeny

Thus far, we have said nothing about the possible evolutionary relationships between the South African australopiths. There are some anatomical indications, especially in facial traits, that *Australopithecus africanus* was ancestral to *Paranthropus robustus* (Conroy, 1990; Rak, 1985), and such an arrangement agrees with the relative ages of the two species. Other bits of evidence, however, suggest that *A. africanus* was on the

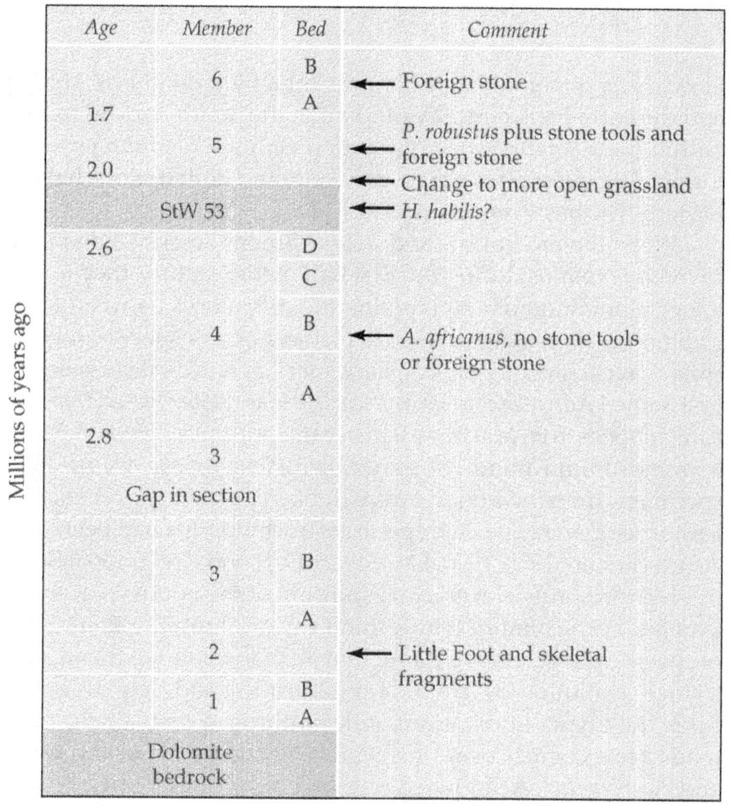

Millions of years ago

Age	*Member*	*Bed*	*Comment*
	6	B	← Foreign stone
		A	
1.7	5		← *P. robustus* plus stone tools and foreign stone
2.0			← Change to more open grassland
	StW 53		← *H. habilis?*
2.6		D	
		C	
	4	B	← *A. africanus*, no stone tools or foreign stone
		A	
2.8	3		
	Gap in section		
	3	B	
		A	
	2		← Little Foot and skeletal fragments
	1	B	
		A	
	Dolomite bedrock		

FIGURE 6.18 This diagram shows the various strata (identified as "Members") at the Sterkfontein site. Note the extreme age of Member 2, which contained Little Foot. Most *Australopithecus africanus* fossils come from Member 4, while stone and bone tools, fossils of *Homo habilis*, and possibly the remains of *Paranthropus* have been found in Member 5.

evolutionary line that led to the genus *Homo* and was not ancestral to *Paranthropus* (Tattersell, 1995a). For its part, *Paranthropus robustus*—along with its entire genus—seems to have gone extinct about a million years ago without leaving any descendants. Further evidence on this point, as well as additional details about the overall pattern of hominin evolution, will be presented in later chapters (see especially Chapter 8).

Summary

In 1924, Raymond Dart named a new primate genus and species, *Australopithecus africanus*, based on his study of a child's skull from Taung. Dart's claims—that the new species was bipedal and that it stood halfway between apes and humans—were dismissed by most of his colleagues. He did make one important convert, however, and that was Robert Broom, who immediately began to search the dolomite caves of the Transvaal and soon found more australopith remains, including those of a different species with massive teeth—*Paranthropus robustus*. In 1949, Wilfrid Le Gros Clark of Oxford University assessed the australopith finds, which by then included pelvic bones and other postcranial remains, and pronounced them hominin and bipedal.

In the three-quarters of a century since the australopiths were first identified, extensive excavations in South Africa have established several facts (see Box 6.3). *Australopithecus africanus* was present in the region from about 3.5 to 1.7 million years BP. This species was definitely bipedal when on the ground but probably continued to engage in arboreal climbing, as well. There are few, if any, indications that *A. africanus* was a tool maker. The second type of South African australopith, *Paranthropus robustus*, has emerged as more habitually terrestrial than *A. africanus* and as a possible tool user and tool maker. *P. robustus* apparently lived in the region from 2.0 to 1.0 mya. While *A. africanus* may have been ancestral to later, more modern hominins, it now seems certain that *Paranthropus robustus* was destined to become extinct without descendants.

Postscript

How many genera of australopiths inhabited Southern Africa in the late Pliocene and the early Pleistocene? Could all of the South African fossils be accommodated within *Australopithecus*, or is a second genus—*Paranthropus*—needed for the robust forms? The question is not an easy one, and both options have loyal and vocal supporters. The basic issues are as follow.

When Raymond Dart and Robert Broom described and named their newly discovered hominins during the first half of this century, they followed a grand paleontological tradition of emphasizing the differences between fossils, rather than their commonalities, and they created a plethora of new species and genus labels. The Taung child was christened *Australopithecus africanus.* Gracile fossils from Sterkfontein were first named *Australopithecus transvaalensis* and later *Plesianthropus transvaalensis,* while similar bones from Makapansgat became *Australopithecus prometheus.* The big-toothed hominids from Kromdraai were called *Paranthropus robustus,* but equally megadont specimens from Swartkrans were dubbed *Paranthropus crassidens.* By mid century, at least three genera and five species of australopiths had been suggested for Southern Africa (Broom, 1938, 1950; Dart, 1925; Dart and Craig, 1967; Reader, 1988).

More recently, the original splitting of the South African fossils into numerous taxa has been countered by a trend toward lumping them into a minimal number of species and genera. Arguing that all of the South African australopiths represent a single evolutionary grade of organization and emphasizing the anatomical features they have in common, paleoanthropologists of the last few decades have tended to recognize only one genus (*Australopithecus*) and two species (*A. africanus* and *A. robustus*). Acknowledging diversity within unity, however, the two species were often described as representing a "gracile lineage" and a "robust lineage" (Note in Box 6.3 that *P. robustus* was slightly heavier than *A. africanus,* although the two species were about equally short.)

Within just the past few years, the argument for splitting the lineages into separate genera has been renewed with vigor. Much of this argument is based on the results of modern cladistic analyses that show, in the words of paleoanthropologist F. E. Grine, "that the 'robust' australopithecines [from both South and East Africa] form a monophyletic clade [indicating] the validity (and the necessity) of the generic name *Paranthropus*" (1993:201). (In this case, a monophyletic clade is a group of species marked by shared derived traits and containing only species more closely related to each other than to any species outside the clade.) Harvard professor emeritus of anthropology William Howells agrees with the revival of *Paranthropus,* noting that the anatomical differences between gracile and robust australopiths at least equal those between living chimpanzees and gorillas, which are classified in separate genera (*Pan* and *Gorilla;* Howells, 1993). Numerous other authors are also using the two-genus scheme.

We find the arguments convincing that the South and East African robusts form a monophyletic clade and that anatomically they are significantly different from the gracile forms, particularly in their facial features and enlarged postcanine teeth (see Appendix 3). Therefore, in this book we have adopted the two-genus classification for the South African australopiths. But do we consider the matter settled? Not by a long shot. Many paleoanthropologists—particularly in the United States—still prefer the more conservative one-genus classification (e.g., Kappelman, 1996). One can only hope that additional fossil finds and new analyses will settle the issue definitively.

Review Questions

1. In 1925, Raymond Dart claimed that *Australopithecus africanus* was an evolutionary link between apes and people. Why was his claim rejected by most of his anthropological and anatomical colleagues?

2. Describe the anatomical and behavioral differences between the two South African australopith genera and between each one and modern humans.
3. Should the South African australopiths be placed in a single genus or two genera? What are the arguments on each side of the question?
4. Traditionally, many anthropologists have concluded that none of the South African australopiths made or used tools. Review the current evidence, and evaluate the strength of that conclusion.

SUGGESTED FURTHER READING

Aiello, Leslie, and Christopher Dean. *An Introduction to Human Evolutionary Anatomy.* London, Academic Press, 1990.

Broom, Robert. *Finding the Missing Link.* London, Watts, 1950.

Conroy, Glenn. C. *Reconstructing Human Origins.* New York, W. W. Norton, 1997.

Dart, Raymond, and Dennis Craig. *Adventures with the Missing Link.* Philadelphia, Institute Press, 1967.

Grine, F. E. "Australopithecine Taxonomy and Phylogeny: Historical Background and Recent Interpretation," in R. L. Ciochon and J. G. Fleagle, eds., *The Human Evolution Source Book.* Englewood Cliffs (NJ), Prentice Hall, 1993.

Le Gros Clark, W. E. *Man-Apes or Ape-Man?* New York, Holt, Rinehart & Winston, 1967.

Tattersall, Ian. *The Fossil Trail.* New York, Oxford University Press, 1995.

Tattersall, Ian, and Jeffrey Schwartz. *Extinct Humans.* New York, Westview Press, 2000.

INTERNET RESOURCES

Australopithecus africanus

www.mnh.si.edu/anthro/humanorigins/ha/afri.html

Maintained by the Smithsonian Institution, this site contains useful information and photographs of *A. africanus* specimens.

MAJOR FOSSIL FIND AT STERKFONTEIN CAVES

http://virtual.yosemite.cc.ca.us/anthro/NEWS/major_fossil_find_at_sterkfontei.htm

This site focuses on the 1998 discovery of an australopith skeleton at Sterkfontein, but it includes links to other South African sites such as Taung.

THE TALK.ORIGINS ARCHIVE: FOSSIL HOMINIDS

www.talkorigins.org/faqs/homs

Discussions of australopith and other hominin fossils, particularly from an evolutionary versus creationism perspective.

Paranthropus Robustus

www.mnh.si.edu/anthro/humanorigins/ha/rob.htm

This is a sister site from the Smithsonian Institution, matching that for *A. africanus* mentioned above.

BIOGRAPHIES: RAYMOND DART

www.talkorigins.org/faqs/homs/rdart.html

This site provides a profile of the man who made the original australopith discovery.

BIOGRAPHIES: ROBERT BROOM

www.talkorigins.org/faqs/homs/rbroom.html

A second profile of an early paleoanthropologist from the Talk.Origins site.

USEFUL SEARCH TERMS:

australopiths
Australopithecus africanus
osteodontokeratic culture
Paranthropus robustus
Sterkfontein
Taung
South African fossil hominins

Chapter 6 Timeline

HOLOCENE

10,000

CENOZOIC

Proconsul

Apidium, Aegyptopithecus,* and *Propliopithecus

Eosimias

Early strepsirhines

65 million

MESOZOIC

First mammals

253 million

PALEOZOIC

YEARS AD	DISCOVERIES
1998	*Australopithecus* skeleton found at Sterkfontein
1995	Little Foot discovered at Sterkfontein
1966	Tobias starts work at Sterkfontein
1965	Brain starts work at Swartkrans
1957	Discovery of stone tools at Sterkfontein
1950	Definitive assessments by Le Gros Clark published
1948	*Paranthropus* found at Swartkrans
1947	*Australopithecus africanus* skull and pelvis found at Sterkfontein; Dart discovers *Australopithecus* at Makapansgat
1938	*Paranthropus robustus* discovered by Broom at Kromdraai
1936	Broom's first adult *Australopithecus* found at Sterkfontein
1925	Dart's publication on *Australopithecus africanus*
1924	Dart discovers *Australopithecus africanus* from Taung

YEARS BP	FOSSIL RECORD	
		Later *Homo* species
		Homo erectus/ergaster
2 million	*Paranthropus robustus* at Kromdraai and Swartkrans with *Homo*	*Homo* and *Paranthropus robustus*
	Australopithecus africanus at Sterkfontein and Makapansgat	*Australopithecus africanus*
5 million		
	Origin of bipedalism	Ancient apes
	Sivapithecus in Europe and in Asia	
10 million		
15 million	*Equatorius–Kenyapithecus* in Africa	

THE TRANSVAAL HOMINIDS

The history of discoveries in South Africa is a fascinating story still unfolding *(top right)*. The age of the fossils *(bottom right)* is still a matter of some uncertainty, although luminescence dating and other procedures have clarified the situation a good deal.

Chapter 7

East Africa and the Sahel: A Multitude of Australopiths

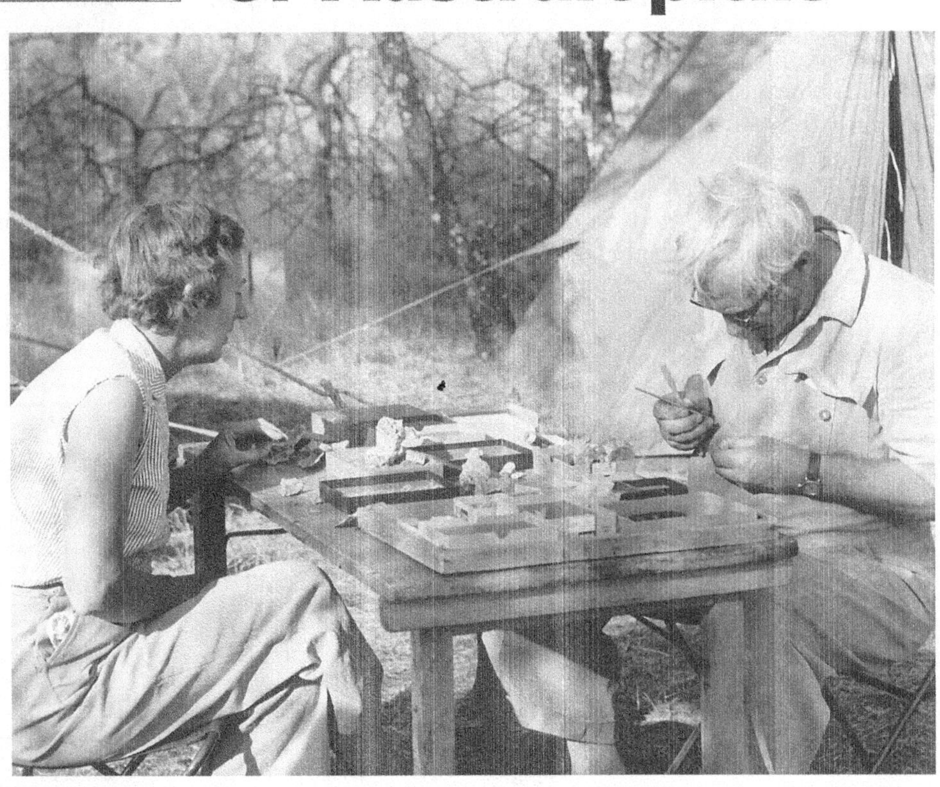

Mary and Louis Leakey were a productive paleoanthropological team for many decades in East Africa.

Ex Africa semper aliquid novi. ("Africa always has something new.")
Pliny the Elder, 23–79. *Natural History,* Book VIII.

Overview

Early hominin fossils belonging to the subtribe Australopithecina have been discovered not only in South Africa but at numerous locations in east and north central Africa, as well. Since the first australopith remains were recovered from Tanzania in 1959, new species and genera have been forthcoming at an amazing rate. The oldest fossils are from Chad in the African Sahel (*Sahelanthropus,* 7 to 6 myr old) and from Kenya (*Orrorin,* ca. 6 myr of age). Next in age is *Ardipithecus kadabba* from Ethiopia, a newly named species from late Miocene deposits dating 5.8 myr of age. Three additional genera—*Australopithecus, Kenyanthropus,* and *Paranthropus*—and a second *Ardipithecus* species (*Ar. ramidus*) are represented by fossils from several sites centered on East Africa's Rift Valley (plus one site in Chad) and are of **Plio-Pleistocene** age.

Plio-Pleistocene a combination of the last two epochs of the Cenozoic era; the *Pliocene* lasted from 5 to 1.8 million years BP, and the *Pleistocene* from 1.8 million to 10,000 years BP.

The six East African/Sahel genera contain a total of eleven species (see the Mini-Timeline below) that varied significantly in body build, dental measurements, and brain size. All walked upright when on the ground, and some may have made tools. Given their ape-sized brains, however, they almost certainly lacked speech and language. Experts disagree about the phylogenetic relations of most of these species, as well as those of the South African australopiths. A discussion of australopith phylogeny will follow descriptions of the oldest representatives of *Homo* in Chapter 8.

A Half-Century of Australopiths from East Africa and the Sahel

Thanks to a multitude of discoveries during the last 50 years, East Africa—broadly defined to include all the countries bordering on the Rift Valley network that crisscrosses the region—plus Chad in the Sub-Saharan Sahel (Figure 7.1) now boasts six

Mini-TIMELINE

Australopith Species	Location	Geological Age (mya)	Discoverer (Team Leader)	Date of Discovery
Sahelanthropus tchadensis	Chad	7–6	M. Brunet	2002
Orrorin tugenensis	Kenya	~6	M. Pickford and B. Senut	2001
Ardipithecus kadabba	Ethiopia	5.8–5.2	Y. Haile-Selassie	2001–2004
Ardipithecus ramidus	Ethiopia	4.4	T. White	1994–1995
Kenyanthropus platyops	Kenya	3.5–3.2	Meave Leakey	2001
Australopithecus anamensis	Kenya	4.2–3.9	Meave Leakey	1995
Australopithecus afarensis	Ethiopia, Kenya, Tanzania	4.2–2.5	D. Johanson	1978
Australopithecus bahrelghazali	Chad	3.5–3.0	M. Brunet	1996
Paranthropus aethiopicus	Ethiopia, Kenya	2.6–2.3	C. Arambourg	1968
Australopithecus garhi	Ethiopia	2.5	B. Asfaw	1999
Paranthropus boisei	Ethiopia, Kenya, Tanzania, Malawi	2.4–1.3	L. Leakey	1959

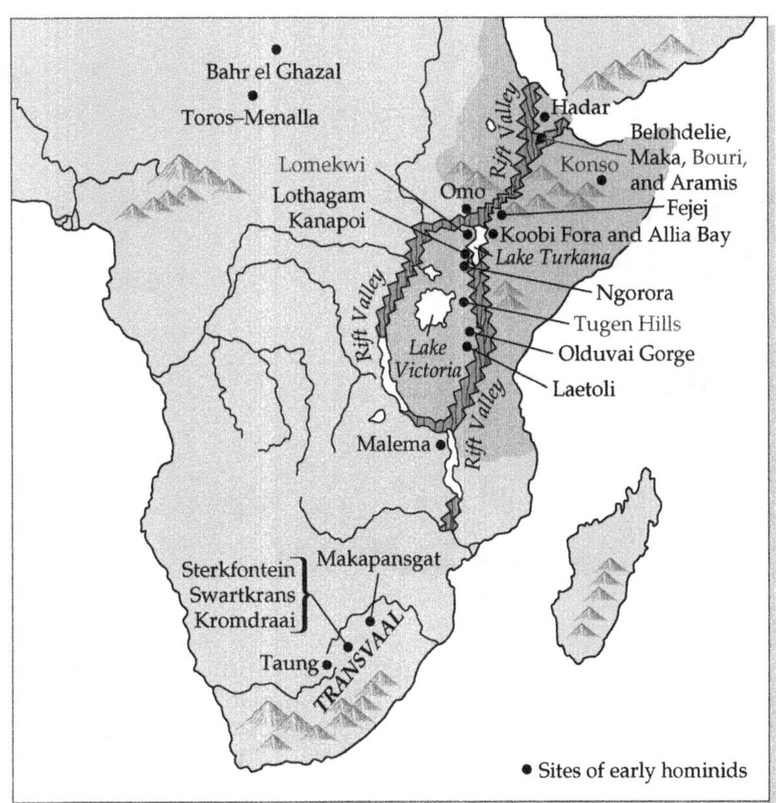

FIGURE 7.1 Southern, eastern, and north central Africa, showing some of the many sites in which australopith fossils have been discovered.

genera and eleven species of australopiths. Two of these taxa are relatively well known. Represented by several specimens, *Australopithecus afarensis* and *Paranthropus boisei* can be described with anatomical thoroughness. The rest of the East African/Sahel species (see the Mini-Timeline), however, are poorly known from a handful of specimens and sites. For these species, a few distinguishing traits can be listed, but full descriptions require additional fossils.

In this chapter, we begin by telling the story of a remarkable fossil-hunting family—the Leakeys—and the first australopith discovery in East Africa. Originally named ***Zinjanthropus boisei*** but later incorporated into the genus *Paranthropus*, this species will be described in detail. Next, the wide-ranging and well-represented species *Australopithecus afarensis* will be treated in terms of its discovery story and its anatomy. These two detailed descriptions will then be followed by shorter discussions of the lesser-known australopiths—discussions that work their way back in time to the very oldest known hominins, *Ardipithecus kadabba*, *Orrorin*, and *Sahelanthropus*. A summary section on australopith lifestyles and behavior will close the chapter.

Zinjanthropus boisei the original name for the *australopith species* now called *Paranthropus boisei*.

And now, we begin our East African odyssey in Tanzania's remarkable Olduvai Gorge (Figure 7.2).

Discoveries at Olduvai

The questions that archaeologists were trying to answer in South Africa's Transvaal—namely, who were the first hominins and did they use tools of any sort?—brought the attention of anthropologists to another part of the continent. During the 1950s, distinguished archaeologists Louis Leakey and Mary Leakey were finding the remains of an extensive pebble-tool industry 2,000 miles (3,200 kilometers) north of the South African grasslands in a dry river canyon in northern Tanzania called Olduvai Gorge (Figures 7.1 and 7.2).

FIGURE 7.2
Olduvai Gorge is a remarkable landform as well as a fossil gold mine. In this photograph, the layers of sedimentary rock are obvious.

Olduvai Gorge is an abrupt rent in the earth, some 25 miles (40 kilometers) long and 300 feet (90 meters) deep. Like a miniature Grand Canyon, its sides display different strata laid bare by the cutting of an ancient river (Figure 7.2). A German entomologist named Wilhelm Kattwinkel found the gorge in 1911 when he almost fell into its depths as he broke through some bush on the edge. A hasty exploration showed the place to be a rich source of animal fossils. Some of the fossils that Kattwinkel took back to Berlin were so unusual that an expedition, headed by Hans Reck, was sent out in 1913 to explore further. Its investigations were ended by World War I, and after the war, Reck was unable to raise funds to resume operations. Eventually, he wrote to Louis Leakey, then the curator of the Coryndon Memorial Museum at Nairobi, urging him to take over, but Leakey had to wait until 1931 before he could raise the money for an expedition to Olduvai (Reader, 1988).

One season spent exploring the gorge was enough to convince Leakey that Olduvai was "a veritable paradise for the prehistorian as well as for the palaeontologist" (L. S. B. Leakey, 1966:295). He found pebble tools in his first year there, but no fossil evidence as to who had made them. For years, as money and transport permitted, Leakey returned to the gorge, along with his wife, Mary, and their sons. From each of the four principal beds that overlie one another from the canyon bottom to the surface of the plain some 300 feet (90 meters) above, the Leakeys eventually recovered an enormous number of animal fossils, many from species previously unknown to science. But except for a couple of scraps of skull found in 1935, evidence of ancient hominins continued to elude them (Reader, 1988).

Discovery of *Paranthropus boisei*

Oldowan tool industry the earliest known stone-tool *culture*, dating 2.5 million years into the past. The products were very crude stone *choppers* and *flakes*.

Sagittal suture the line of union joining the two main side bones of the braincase.

For twenty-eight years, the Leakeys (Figures 7.3 and 7.4) were engaged in one of the most persistent and unrewarding efforts in the history of anthropology. Olduvai was several days of rough driving from Nairobi, and the Leakeys could seldom afford more than a few weeks a year at the gorge. Olduvai was also stiflingly hot, and water had to be hauled from a spring miles away. By the summer of 1959, about all Louis and Mary had to show for their efforts (besides animal fossils) was a small collection of what they believed to be the oldest stone implements ever seen, collectively called the **Oldowan tool industry.**

On July 17, 1959, Louis awakened with a fever and a headache. His wife insisted that he remain in camp. But the work season was drawing to an end and the day could not be lost, so Mary drove to the point where the party was working. As she walked slowly along the hillside of Bed I, the lowest layer of the gorge, a piece of skull bone exposed by recent erosion caught her eye. Searching higher along the slope, she found two big hominin teeth. She marked the spot with a small piece of stone and sped back to camp (Reader, 1988).

Louis heard the car racing up the road and sprang up in alarm, thinking that his wife had been bitten by a snake. But as the car stopped, he heard Mary shout, "I've got him!" The "him," she felt sure, was a hominin fossil—the early human they had been seeking for so many years. Louis's fever and headache forgotten, he jumped in the car, and the couple drove back as fast as they could.

The Leakeys went to work with camel's hair brushes and dental picks. At the end of nineteen days, they had about 400 fragments of the skull and teeth of a young australopith.

While undertaking the delicate task of assembling the bits and pieces, the Leakeys continued to excavate the site. Not only had they discovered the oldest hominin skull found to that time in eastern Africa, but they had also unearthed what appeared to be a campsite of this ancient creature. Scattered on what had been the margins of an ancient lake were many tools made of flaked stone and pebbles, along with waste chips. Lying about, too, were the fossil bones of animals: complete remains of rats, mice, frogs, lizards, birds, snakes, tortoises as well as some young pigs and parts of small antelopes. But there were no remains of large animals. Nearly all these bones were broken, and it seemed to the Leakeys that their hominin had killed and eaten the other animals.

FIGURE 7.3
Distinguished archaeologist Mary Leakey worked at numerous African sites, including Olduvai and Laetoli, until her retirement in 1984.

The skull that took shape from the fragments uncovered at the campsite (Figure 7.5) had several interesting features. For instance, the wisdom teeth were unworn and the suture joining the two halves of the skull, the **sagittal suture,** had not yet closed, indicating that it was a young adult. The likelihood that it was a male followed from the presence of a sagittal crest. In brain size and in general appearance,

FIGURE 7.4
Louis Leakey was somewhat eccentric but a passionate, brilliant man. In this photo from the 1960s, he is examining some of his important and numerous discoveries with his son, Richard.

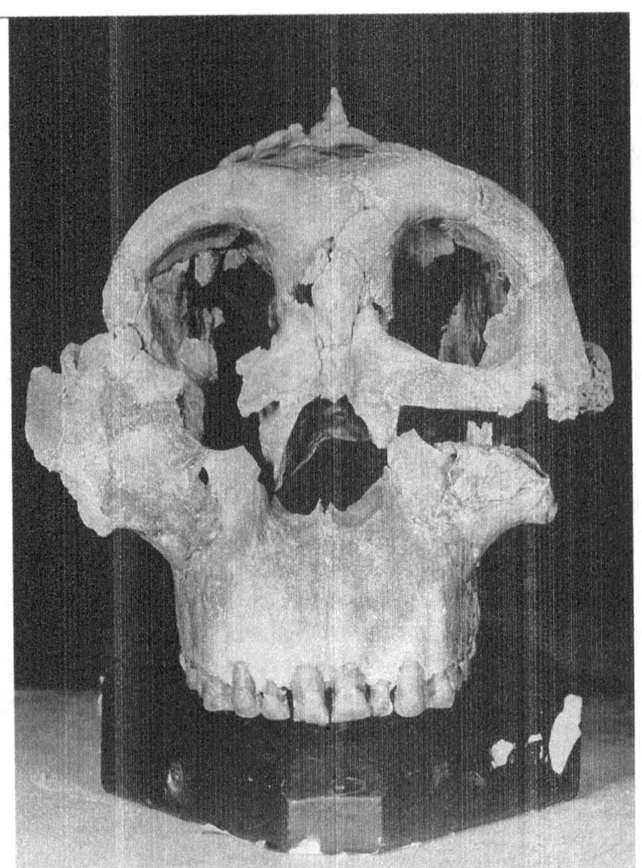

FIGURE 7.5
Zinjanthropus, the immense skull found by Mary Leakey at Olduvai in 1959. It is now classified as *Paranthropus boisei*. This photograph is approximately 45 percent actual size.

the skull broadly resembled *Paranthropus robustus* of the south. The face attached to the low cranium was more massive than in *P. robustus*, however, and the back teeth were larger (Grine, 1993; see Appendix 3).

These and other differences eventually led Louis to create a new genus and species for the Olduvai hominin: *Zinjanthropus boisei* (L. S. B. Leakey, 1959). (*Zinj* means "eastern Africa" in Arabic; *boisei* was selected in honor of Charles Boise, one of the Leakeys' financial backers.) Subsequent analyses, however, have emphasized the similarities, rather than the differences, between the Olduvai fossil and *P. robustus*, and today, the skull is classified as ***Paranthropus boisei.***

Paranthropus boisei a megadont *australopith species* that lived in East Africa 2.4 to 1.3 million years ago; also known as *Australopithecus boisei*.

Fortunately, the age of the Leakeys' fossil could be determined using the then-new method of potassium-argon dating (Appendix 2). These tests revealed the startling age of about 1.75 million years, an age repeatedly confirmed by retests. This was an extraordinary date, and it supported the claim of great antiquity for all the australopiths, including those from South Africa.

But several important questions remained unanswered, despite firm information about the antiquity of the *P. boisei* fossils from Olduvai. Chief among those questions was whether *Paranthropus* was responsible for the Bed I flake and chopper tools. Initially, the Leakeys thought that was probably the case, but they later changed their minds following the recovery of more modern hominin remains ("early *Homo*"; see Chapter 8) from the same rock layer. Today, the problem is still unresolved. Many paleoanthropologists prefer to attribute the Bed I tools to early *Homo* (e.g., Schick and Toth, 1993), while some agree with Randall Susman (1994; see Chapter 6) that the smaller-brained *Paranthropus* could (also?) have made the stone implements. It is hoped that further research will clarify the situation.

Fossils from Kenya and Ethiopia Reveal Details of *P. boisei* Anatomy

In the late 1960s, paleoanthropologists turned their attention to new sites in the Horn of Africa. In extreme southwestern Ethiopia, fossil-hunting teams headed by French scientists Camille Arambourg and Yves Coppens and American F. Clark Howell began work at separate sites in the Omo River Valley (Figure 7.1). Although desolate and scorching hot, this region holds a treasure of old and accessible fossils, including those of early hominins. At Omo, geological deposits from Plio-Pleistocene times (most strata dating between 4 and 1.4 myr of age) have been conveniently heaved to the surface by ancient convulsions of the earth, and numerous volcanoes have left datable ash layers. Compared to Olduvai Gorge, where the fossil deposits only go back about 1.9 million years, the evolutionary record at Omo is about half again as deep (Conroy, 1997; Howell, 1976; Reader, 1988).

The Omo Valley began immediately to produce numerous animal fossils: invertebrates, fish, reptiles, antelopes, pigs, "false sabertooth" cats, hippos, and extinct varieties of monkeys. Hominin remains—primarily teeth—were also found, including several specimens attributable to *Paranthropus boisei* (Howell, 1976). The *P. boisei* materials were beginning to accumulate into a tidy sample.

Meanwhile, in 1969, Richard Leakey, Louis and Mary's 25-year-old son, was leading his own research team into the fossil-rich sandstone deposits east of Lake Turkana in northern Kenya. At two sites, Ileret and Ķoobi Fora, this team discovered three superb skulls, more than two dozen mandibles or parts of mandibles, some arm and leg bone fragments, and isolated teeth, amounting to more than 100 specimens in all. Much of this material from *P. boisei* and dates from about 2 to 1.3 million years ago (Figure 7.6). When these East Turkana fossils are combined with the Omo and Olduvai finds and with a fragmentary upper jaw recently found in Malawi (Kullmer et al., 1999), there are enough materials in the way of young and old individuals, both males and females, and enough variation in dentition for the outlines of a variable population of the megadont *Paranthropus boisei* to begin to reveal itself.

Having a population to study, instead of an individual fossil, is extremely important. No two people today are exactly alike; no two australopiths were, either. For that reason, drawing conclusions from a single fossil is risky. Measurements can be taken of a single fossil and theories can be built up as a result of those measurements, but this information may be misleading because the fossil may not be typical. Only when a large number of specimens is available can variations be taken into account (Box 7.1). If visitors from outer space were to describe and name *Homo sapiens* by examining one skeleton—for example, that of a short, heavy-boned Inuit (Eskimo)—they certainly might be excused if they thought they had another species when they discovered a second skeleton of a 6.5 feet (2 meters), slender-boned Watusi tribesman from Central Africa.

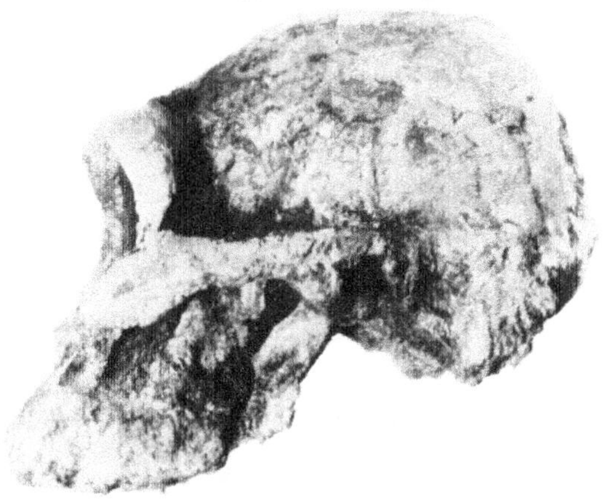

FIGURE 7.6
This skull (museum number KNM-ER 406) of *Paranthropus boisei*, found at Koobi Fora, is similar in many ways to that found at Olduvai (Figure 7.5). This photograph is approximately 30 percent actual size.

That is why the *P. boisei* population that is emerging is so valuable. It begins to indicate some of the limits of variability beyond which no members of the species went. Any creature that does exceed those limits significantly can be presumed to be from a different species.

A population analysis of *P. boisei* shows this species to have been quite similar to the South African megadont hominin, *P. robustus*. Like *P. robustus* (Figure 6.10), *P. boisei* had a bony crest along the top of its skull, but its crest is more pronounced for the anchoring of even bigger muscles to work a more massive jaw containing larger molars. This complex of features indicates a life adapted to eating large

BOX 7.1

Determining the Characteristics of a Previously Unknown Fossil Species

Drawing conclusions about extinct species from their fossil remains is a tricky business. Individual specimens are sure to vary and it is rare indeed for a single fossil to display the full suite of traits typical of its species. Furthermore, each species' set of defining parameters is actually a mix of discrete characteristics (e.g., its dental formula or the presence of a toothcomb) and characteristics that are continuous in their distribution (e.g., body weight, brain size, enamel thickness). While a species' set of discrete diagnostic traits may be made clear by only a few fossil specimens, establishing mean values and ranges for continuous traits obviously requires the recovery of a sample population.

The following example uses the continuous trait of cranial capacity in an imaginary species of apes to show how calculated parameters change as a population of fossil specimens grows. Note the fluctuations in mean brain size and range of cranial volume as additional skulls are added to the set of known fossils.

A. The Fossils

From left to right, skulls are shown in the order of their discovery and with their brain sizes in cubic centimeters.

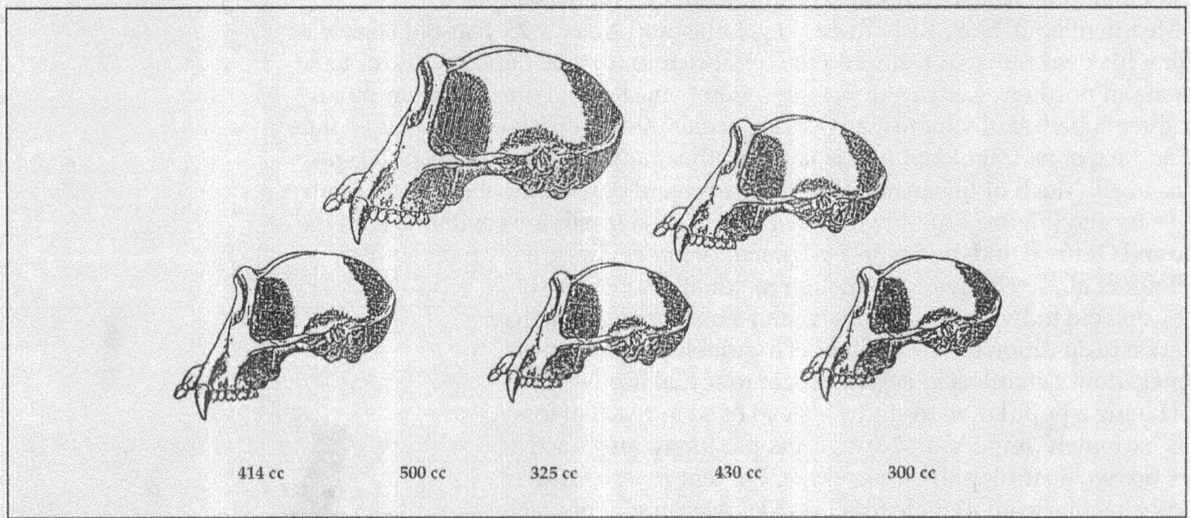

Source: Drawings based on Le Gros Clark, 1959.

B. Sample Populations and Calculations of Brain Size

Specimens in Sample	Mean Cranial Capacity	Change vs. Previous Mean
Skull 1	414 cc (range incalculable)	–
Skulls 1 & 2	457 cc (range 414–500 cc)	+ 10.4%
Skulls 1–3	413 cc (range 325–500 cc)	– 9.6%
Skulls 1–4	417 cc (range 325–500 cc)	+ 1.0%
Skulls 1–5	394 cc (range 300–500 cc)	– 5.5%

Note: Lest this made-up example seem unrealistic in the small size of its specimen population, compare the numbers of adult skulls with measurable cranial capacities known in 1996 from the South African australopiths: *Australopithecus africanus*, 11; *Paranthropus robustus*, 8 (data from Wolpoff, 1996). Small sample size remains a problem for virtually all extinct hominin species and each new discovery has the potential to alter previous lists of defining characteristics.

BOX 7.2

Characteristics of *Paranthropus boisei*[a]

Trait	*Paranthropus boisei*
Height	F: 4.1 ft (124 cm) M: 4.5 ft (137 cm) (F is 90% of M)
Weight	F: 75–88 lb (34–40 kg) M: 108–176 lb (49–80 kg) (F is 57% of M)
Brain size (sexes combined)	465 cc mean (390–500 cc range)
Cranium	Tall, broad, "dished" face; sagittal crest; low forehead; low-vaulted braincase; some flexure of cranial base; anterior location of foramen magnum
Dentition	Parabolic toothrow; small incisors and canines; huge grinding teeth; lower P3s often have 3+ cusps
Diet	Hard, tough, fibrous vegetable foods; some meat
Limbs	Unknown
Pelvis	Unknown
Locomotion	Bipedalism (based on foramen magnum placement)
Known dates (million years B.P.)	2.4–1.3

[a]Mean values, or range of values, for anatomical measurements may change with additional fossil discoveries. For additional technical details and diagnostic traits, see Appendix 3.
Sources: Falk et al., 2000; Grine, 1993; Suwa et al., 1997; and Wood and Richmond, 2000.

amounts of coarse, tough vegetable matter. It is the same adaptation as *P. robustus* but larger and more elaborately evolved (Box 7.2). Other details of the face and skull separate these two megadont species (see Appendix 3), and details of their habitat preferences may do so, as well (this is discussed in a later section). Both *P. boisei* and *P. robustus* have been found in association—but not necessarily *exclusive* association—with chopper and flake tools. Interpreting the evidence for material culture and technology by *Paranthropus* continues to be a controversial subject among paleoanthropologists.

With this brief description of *Paranthropus boisei,* we now turn our attention to the other well-known australopith from East Africa: *Australopithecus afarensis.*

Australopithecus afarensis: A Second Australopith from Ethiopia

The Ethiopian site of Hadar is located about 130 miles (210 kilometers) northeast of Addis Ababa along the Awash River (Figures 7.1 and 7.7). This part of the African Rift system consists of a maze of arid and scorching badlands that present a formidable challenge to fossil hunters. Searching the Hadar badlands is worth the effort, however, because a multitude of fossils—including those of australopiths—are there to be found, as shown by a series of important discoveries that began in 1973. That year, an international expedition led by Maurice Taieb and Yves Coppens from

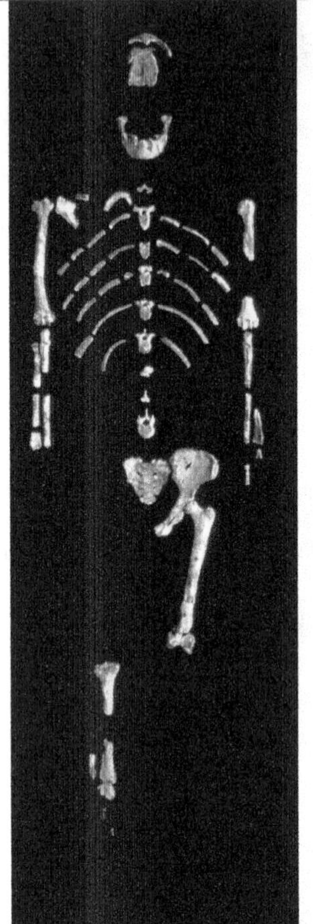

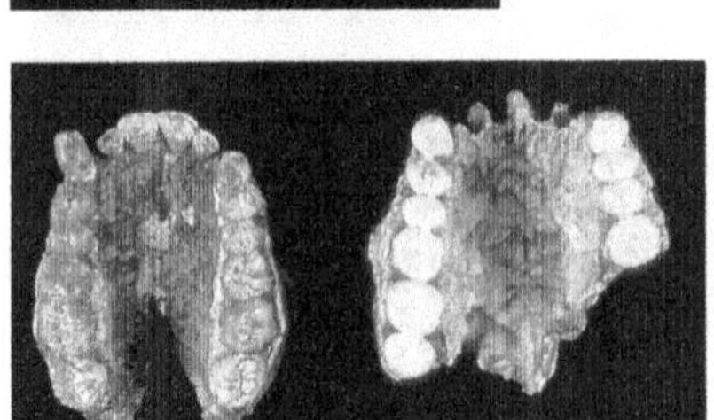

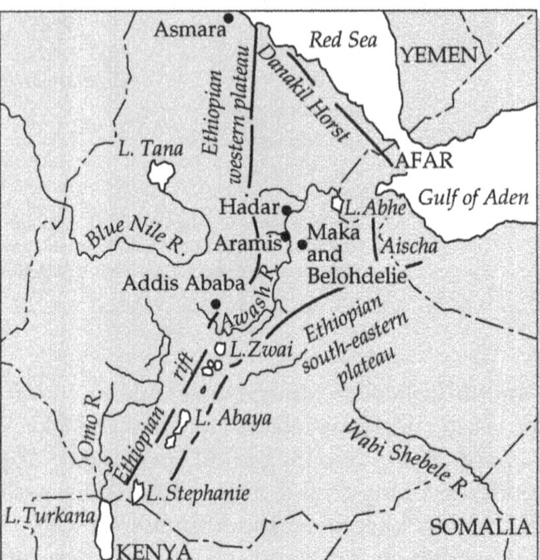

FIGURE 7.7 Important hominin remains have been recovered from the extensive stratified deposits at Hadar *(top and bottom, right)* in the Afar region of Ethiopia. At this site, Donald C. Johanson and his team discovered the bones of a skeleton in 1974. (*top left*). "Lucy," as the skeleton is called, lived by a lake about 3 million years ago; she was only 3.5 to 4 feet (about 1.1 meters) tall and died when she was in her early twenties. Based on this and other discoveries, Johanson and his colleagues named a new species, *Australopithecus afarensis*. Also found in this region was a complete palate, dated at around 3.8 million years. In the *bottom left* photograph, it is compared with a cast of a *Homo erectus* palate *(right)* that is less than 1 million years old. Their similarities suggest that the Afar palate may have been ancestral to *Homo*.

France and Don Johanson from the United States made several extremely important fossil finds (Johnson and Edey, 1981). During the first season at Hadar, Johanson found a hominin knee joint that dated to about 3 mya. Furthermore, an examination of its anatomy proved conclusively that the creature to whom the knee belonged had a close-knee stance and walked erect (Figure 7.8). Here was evidence of habitual bipedalism far older than anything known before. Hadar suddenly became the most intriguing prehistoric site on earth.

Johanson and his group returned to Hadar in the fall of 1974 and proceeded to make additional spectacular finds. On one particularly lucky December day, the team found the partial skeleton of a 3-million-year-old australopith that has become one of the world's most famous fossils (Johanson and Edey, 1981; Reader, 1988). Given the name Lucy, the skeleton (from locality 288), which was 40 percent complete, represented a very small *Australopithecus* (Figure 7.7). Although the knee joint and the pelvis again carry the marks of habitual bipedalism, the skull is primitive, as are other features of the skeleton (Johanson and White, 1979).

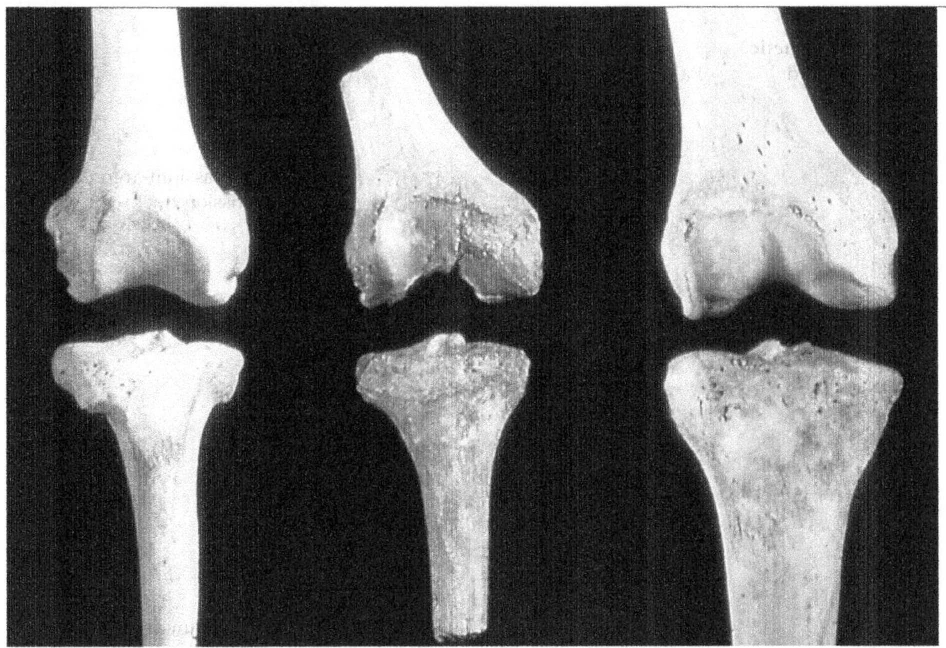

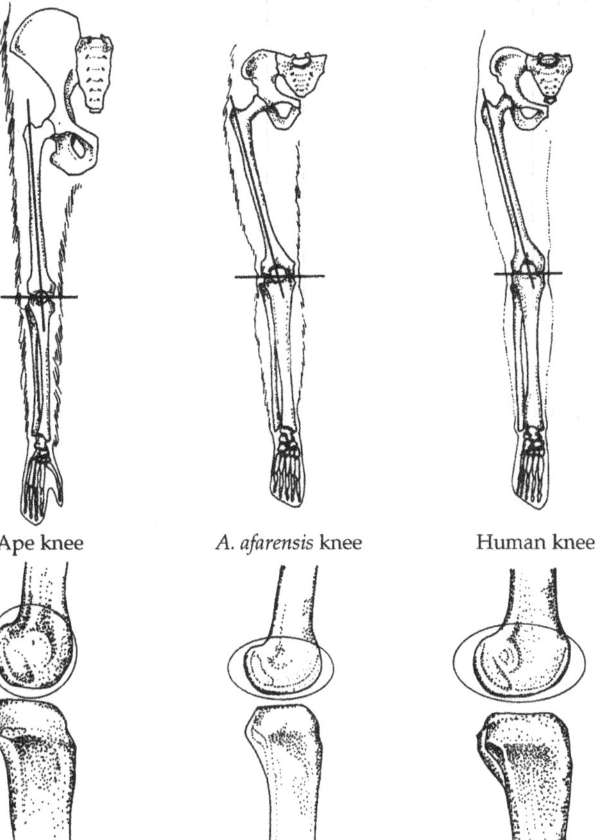

FIGURE 7.8
The interpretation of the *Australopithecus afarensis* knee bones can be understood from this figure. The critical character is the plane of the condyles of the knee joint (*circled below*) in relation to the shaft of the femur. The frontal photograph of right knees shows that in the ape (*left*) the alignment is such that the leg is straight when the knee is extended. In humans (*right*) and in *A. afarensis* (*middle*), the alignment is such that the leg is angled at the knee. This is partially a product of the broadening of the pelvis (*top drawings*). The lower drawings show that the bearing surfaces of the knee condyles are broadened in bipedal species as an adaptation to the greater weight transmitted through the knee.

The 1975 season brought further remarkable discoveries. At a single site (locality 333), Johanson's team found a mixed collection of some 200 teeth and bone fragments, representing at least thirteen australopiths, including males, females, and at least four children. The strange thing about this precious haul was that the hominin bones were all associated and from a single level, not mixed with animal bones, as such fossils usually are. They have been called the "first family."

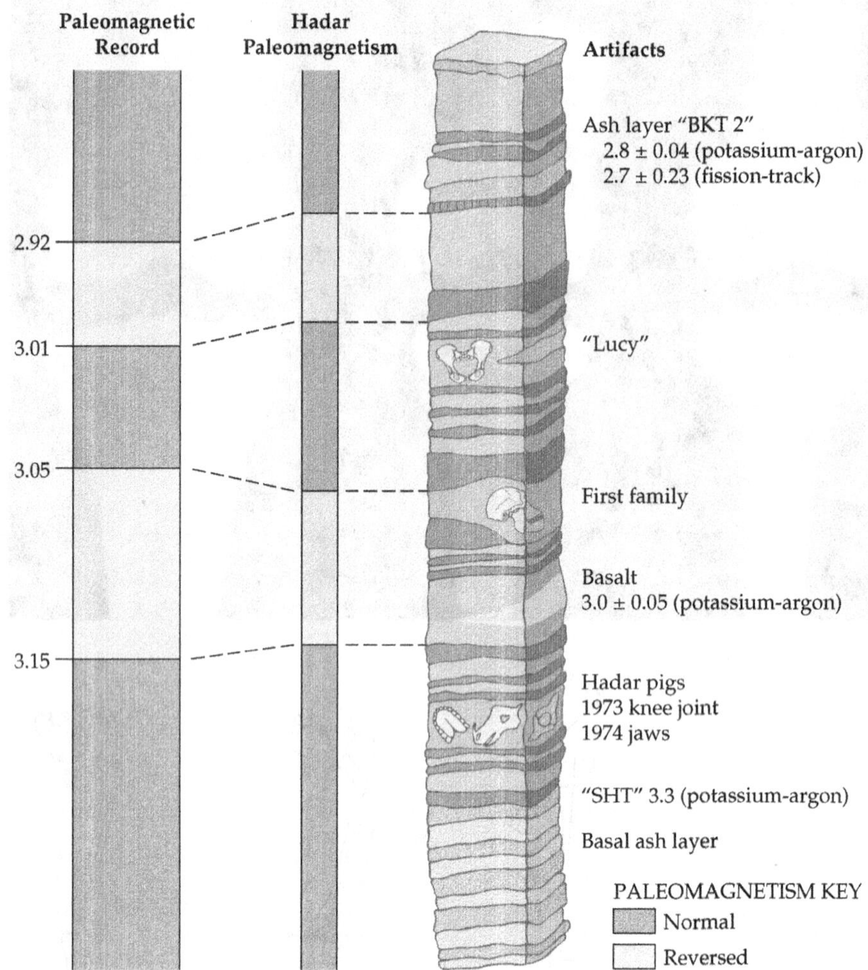

FIGURE 7.9 Stratigraphic column at Hadar showing chronometric dates in million years BP and probable paleomagnetic match.

The final field season of 1976 was concerned mainly with stratigraphy and dating. Researchers now believe that the Hadar australopiths fall into the time range 2.8 to 3.3 mya (Figure 7.9). The potassium-argon dates in this section agree with fission-track dates and have been cross-checked by the chemical signatures of the tuffs, while the fauna (in particular, the pig fossils) from the section also support the dates. Figure 7.9 also shows how the paleomagnetism of the section conforms to the paleomagnetic record. In summary, the site is quite well dated, although further dates from below the fossil-bearing strata would help sandwich the lower collection of fossils (Johanson and Edey, 1981).

Australopithecus afarensis an *australopith species* that inhabited East Africa from 4.2 to 2.5 million years ago.

The fossils from Hadar were described by Johanson and his associates (1978) and assigned to a new and very primitive species of *Australopithecus*: ***A. afarensis.*** The characteristics of this species are described below and summarized in Box 7.3.

The body size of *Australopithecus afarensis* apparently varied considerably both within a sex and between sexes (sexual dimorphism). Some females, like Lucy, may have been just over 3 feet (about 1 meter) tall, while large males may have been as much as 5 feet (1.5 meters) tall. Weight probably varied from 66 to as much as 154 pounds (30 to 70 kilograms). (It should be noted that the extent of sexual dimorphism in this species has been challenged, most recently by Reno et al. [2003].) All individuals, although small by modern standards, were powerfully built: The bones were thick for their size and carried markings suggesting that they had been well muscled.

As we have seen, the evidence of the knee joint makes it clear that, like all other hominins, *A. afarensis* was habitually bipedal. Indeed, the likelihood that *A. afarensis* was more committed to a terrestrial way of life than South Africa's *A. africanus* is suggested by the fact that Lucy and her kin possessed humanlike, nonopposable

BOX 7.3

Characteristics of *Australopithecus afarensis*[a]

Trait	*Australopithecus afarensis*
Height	F: 3.3–3.4 ft (100–105 cm) M: 5.0 ft (151 cm) (F is 68% of M)
Weight	F: 66 lb (30 kg) M: 99–154 lb (45–70 kg) (F is 52% of M)
Brain size (sexes combined)	470 cc mean (375–540 cc range)
Cranium	Prognathic face; low, flat forehead; low-vaulted braincase; large brows; unflexed cranial base
Dentition	U-shaped toothrow; relatively large anterior teeth (incisors and canines); moderately large molars; canines that project somewhat; upper jaw diastemata; lower P3s at least semisectorial
Diet	Fruit and other plant foods; some meat(?)
Limbs	Long arms relative to legs; curved finger and toe bones (adaptations for arboreal movement?); close-knee stance
Pelvis	Short, broad iliac blades; incomplete pelvic bowl; weak iliofemoral ligament; ischial shaft relatively shorter than in apes but not yet realigned in modern fashion; pelvis wide between hip joints
Locomotion	Bipedalism and possibly arboreal climbing
Known dates (million years BP)	4.2–2.5

[a]Mean values, and ranges of values, for anatomical measurements may change with additional fossil discoveries. For additional technical details and diagnostic traits, see Appendix 3. Primary sources include Conroy (1997), Johanson and White (1979), and Wood and Richmond (2000).

(nongrasping) big toes (Wood and Richmond, 2000). As described in Chapter 6, the big toes of *A. africanus* were divergent digits probably used for climbing, at least if "Little Foot" is properly assigned to that taxon. In the upper body, however, even *A. afarensis* may show signs of continuing arboreality, including relatively longer arms and shorter legs than those of modern humans, rather apelike wrist bones, and curved fingers (another apelike trait). In rebuttal, researchers who believe that *Australopithecus afarensis* was essentially fully terrestrial note that these creatures had short fingers (those of apes are long) and that the retention of some apelike traits is predictable in early hominins such as Lucy that recently evolved from ape ancestors. (See Stern [2000] and C. Ward [2002] for thorough discussions of this question.)

The pelvis of *A. afarensis* shows unmistakable adaptations for habitual bipedalism (Figure 7.10). First, the iliac blades are short and broad, and deep sciatic notches indicate the extent of backward expansion and bending. Thus, the center of gravity of *A. afarensis* was considerably lower than that of an ape, and as a consequence, bipedal balancing was much more stable and energy efficient. Second, the iliac blades of *A. afarensis* are curved toward the front of the body, producing a partial pelvic bowl. Third, the anterior inferior iliac spines are well developed and mark the upper attachment of powerful **rectus femoris** muscles that flexed the *A. afarensis* thigh and extended the lower leg during bipedal walking. And finally, the ischial shaft is relatively short compared to the shaft of an ape.

Rectus femoris one of the muscles that flexes the hominin thigh.

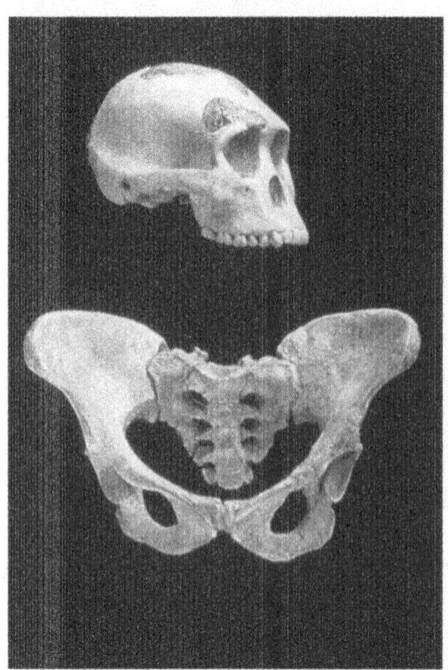

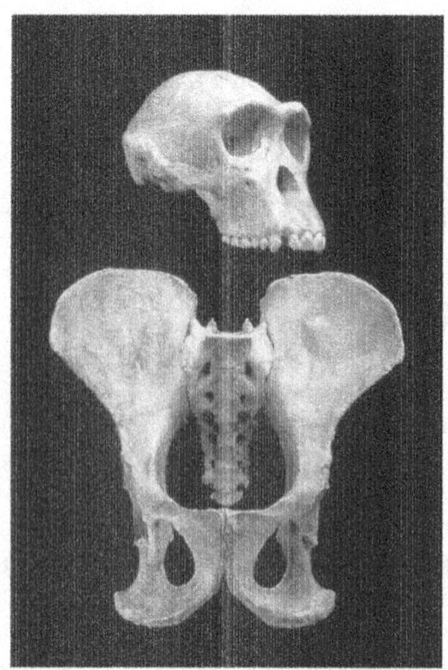

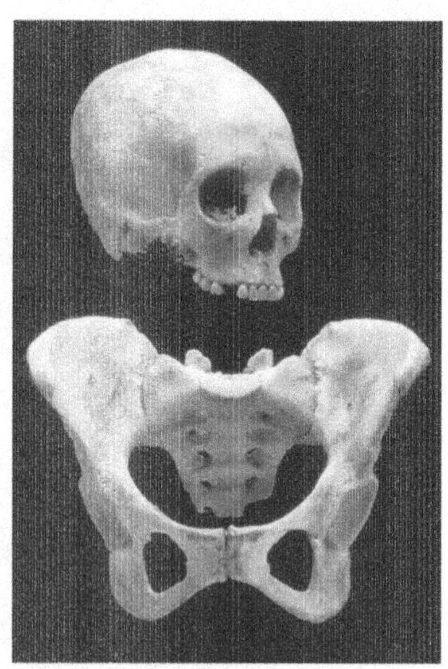

FIGURE 7.10
The restored pelvic girdle of *A. afarensis* (*left*) compared with that of a modern human (*right*) and a chimpanzee (*center*). Note the shorter, broader ilia and more bowl-like pelvis of *A. afarensis* compared to that of the ape. Also visible are the deep sciatic notches and extreme pelvic width (hip joint to hip joint) of *A. afarensis*. A typical skull for each species is shown with the corresponding pelvis.

In combination with these humanlike features, however, there are clear pelvic indications that the evolutionary transformation was not complete and that *A. afarensis* may not have shown modern bipedal locomotion. These indications include the incomplete pelvic bowl, the lack of modern realignment of the ischial shafts, the extreme width (hip joint to hip joint) of the pelvic girdle, and evidence that the iliofemoral ligaments may have been small and weak. This combination of derived and primitive traits has convinced some anthropologists and anatomists that *Australopithecus afarensis* showed a distinctively different kind of bipedalism than modern humans, perhaps one with apelike balancing mechanisms and more twisting of the trunk (Stern, 2000; C. Ward, 2002).

The skull bones of *Australopithecus afarensis* reveal a rather primitive mixture of traits (Figure 7.11). The face was prognathic, the forehead receded strongly from

FIGURE 7.11
Composite reconstruction based on *A. afarensis* fossil skull fragments found at Hadar. Reconstruction by Tim White and William Kimbel. The photographs are approximately 25 percent actual size.

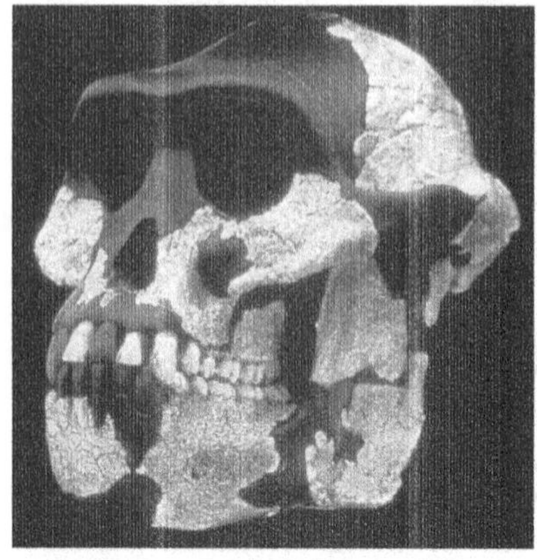

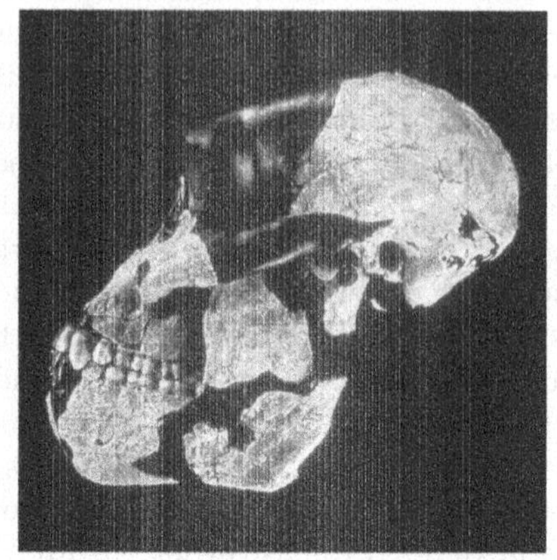

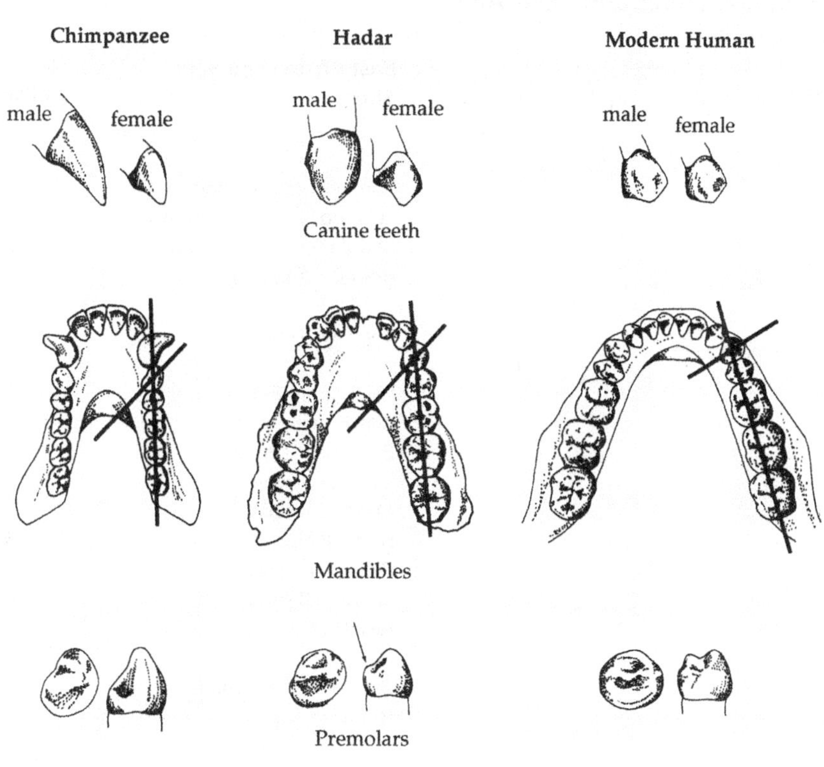

FIGURE 7.12 Comparison of Hadar (*A. afarensis*) with chimpanzee and modern human dentitions. At the *top*, a comparison of the male and female upper canines of each species. Notice the pointed ape canines and the blunt human teeth, together with the considerable sexual dimorphism in the ape and Hadar teeth. *Below* this, the three mandibles are illustrated. Notice the intermediate traits of the Hadar mandible. The lines show the alignment of the first lower premolar in relation to the molar series as a whole. At the *bottom*, a typical first lower premolar is illustrated. The ape premolar is one-cusped; the human premolar two-cusped. The Hadar premolar illustrated has a small lingual cusp (*arrow*) and is intermediate in form.

behind large brows, and the braincase was low-vaulted—a distinctly apelike cranium indeed. Furthermore, *A. afarensis*'s average cranial capacity of 470 cubic centimeters (range 375 to 540 cc) was only slightly larger than that of a chimpanzee (410 cubic centimeters mean).

Finally, the *A. afarensis* dentition is of great importance: It is apelike in many respects. In particular, the upper canine is somewhat pointed, with a large root, and is reminiscent of that of an ape; it also shows noticeable sexual dimorphism (Figure 7.12). The lower canines are associated with small diastemata in the upper jaw. At the same time, the first lower premolar (P3) is also remarkable in lacking or having only a small internal (lingual) secondary cusp; yet the tooth is not truly apelike, for the apes have no second cusp, but only one single large one. It is, as Johanson says, "a tooth in transition" (Johanson and Edey, 1981:270). The molar teeth show the kind of wear we associate with modern humans, with an indication of the grinding of grit-laden foods. In some specimens, the canines show beginning wear from the apex. Finally, the shape of the toothrow is more apelike than human, as is the profile of the face (Figures 7.11 and 7.12).

Altogether, the *A. afarensis* fossils show a remarkable set of traits that place them squarely in the tribe Hominini yet reveal many similarities to apes. Two and a half decades' work has made *A. afarensis* one of the best known of all fossil hominin species.

The species *A. afarensis* includes more than the Hadar fossils (see Table 7.1). In addition, there are 4-million-year-old Kenyan remains from Allia Bay, east of Lake Turkana; nearly equally ancient Ethiopian fossils from Middle Awash sites, such as Maka and Belohdelie; and 4.2-million-year-old specimens from Fejej in the Omo River basin (Coffing et al., 1994; Conroy, 1997; Kappelman et al., 1996). Although the extremely old (5.6 myr) mandibular fragment from Lothagam, Kenya, has been assigned to *A. afarensis* by some workers (Hill et al., 1992), others are more cautious, noting that its morphology also matches that of other australopiths, especially *Ardipithecus* (described in a later section; White et al., 1994). Opting for caution ourselves, we favor putting the Lothagam fossil in suspension *pro tem.* Finally, among the most important

TABLE 7.1 Important Australopith Sites and Their Ages

Species	South African Sites	Age (Million Years)[a]	East African and Sahel Sites	Age (Million Years)[b]
Sahelanthropus tchadensis			Toros–Menalla (Chad)	~7–6
Orrorin tugenensis			Lukeino Formation (Kenya)	~6
Ardipithecus kadabba			Middle Awash (Ethiopia)	5.8–5.2
Ardipithecus ramidus			Aramis (Ethiopia)	4.4
Kenyanthropus platyops			Lomekwi (Kenya)	3.5–3.2
Australopithecus afarensis			Fejej (Ethiopia)	4.2–4.0
			Allia Bay (Kenya)	4
			Belohdelie (Ethiopia)	3.8
			Laetoli (Tanzania)	3.8–3.6
			Maka (Ethiopia)	3.4
			Hadar (Ethiopia)	3.4–3.0
			Omo (Ethiopia)	3.0–2.5
Australopithecus anamensis			Kanapoi (Kenya)	4.2–3.9
			Allia Bay (Kenya)	3.9
Australopithecus bahrelghazali			Bahr el Ghazal (Chad)	~3.5–3.0
Australopithecus garhi			Bouri (Ethiopia)	2.5
Australopithecus africanus	Sterkfontein (SA)	3.5 (4?)–2.5		
	Makapansgat (SA)	3.0–2.5		
	Taung (SA)	2.8–2.6		
	Gladysvale (SA)	2.5–1.7		
Paranthropus aethiopicus			Omo (Ethiopia)	2.6–2.3
			West Turkana (Kenya)	2.5
Paranthropus boisei			Malema (Malawi)	2.4
			Omo (Ethiopia)	2.3–1.5
			Koobi Fora (Kenya)	2.0–1.3
			Olduvai (Tanzania)	1.8
			Peninj (Tanzania)	1.5
			Konso (Ethiopia)	1.4
Paranthropus robustus	Sterkfontein (SA)	2.0–1.7		
	Drimolen (SA)	2.0–1.5		
	Kromdraai (SA)	~2–1		
	Swartkrans (SA)	1.8–1.0		

[a]Dates attributed to South African sites often are based not on chronometric procedures but on comparative analyses of fauna. Nonetheless, these dates probably do bracket the times of existence of the various hominin species.
[b]Most of the dates for sites from East Africa and the Sahel are based on chronometric procedures and are therefore quite accurate.
Sources: Conroy (1997) and Wood and Richmond (2000), in addition to the numerous references cited in the text for particular hominin species.

A. afarensis fossils are the remains from a remarkable site in northern Kenya called Laetoli.

Beginning with an early Leakey expedition in 1935, a rich collection of hominin fossils has been recovered at Laetoli, a site south of Olduvai Gorge and over 1,000 miles (1,600 kilometers) from Hadar (Figure 7.1). Many of these fossils were found by Mary Leakey's research team in the 1970s, and they include numerous jaws and dental remains. Although there has been some disagreement over the inclusion of the Laetoli fossils in *Australopithecus afarensis* (Hartwig-Scherer, 1993; Johanson and Edey,

1981; Reader, 1988), discoveries elsewhere and additional analyses have convinced most workers that this classification is correct (White et al., 1993). In particular, the problem of combining fossils from sites 1,000 miles apart in a single species was eased by the discovery of *A. afarensis* remains from Allia Bay and Fejej, both about halfway between the two extremes (Figure 7.1). It now seems clear that *Australopithecus afarensis* was simply an anatomically variable and very widespread variety of hominin.

In any event, in addition to its fossils, the Laetoli site has produced another sort of evidence regarding the hominin status and behavior of *A. afarensis:* a remarkable set of preserved footprints that date to 3.6 million years ago (Conroy, 1997). In 1978, Paul Abell, a geochemist from the University of Rhode Island who was working at Laetoli, made another discovery that was, if possible, more remarkable than the fossil finds. Sandwiched in layers of volcanic ash were the preserved footprints of a whole range of animals, including elephants, rhinoceroses, many types of antelope, three kinds of giraffe, a saber-toothed cat, and many other species, all now extinct. One of these other species was a hominin: Clearly impressed in the ash layer, hominin tracks cover a distance of more than 150 feet (45 meters; Reader, 1988). Portions of the tracks are slightly eroded, but several intact prints are preserved (Figure 7.13). The pattern and form of the footprints are like those made in soft sand by modern humans and suggest (like the other evidence) an evolved bipedalism. The smaller and larger footprints (on the basis of modern people's foot size) suggest a stature ranging from about 4 to 5 feet (1.2 to 1.5 meters; Conroy, 1997). This discovery is a most remarkable one, and it is unique in paleontology for the number of mammalian species represented: A large proportion of the Laetoli Pliocene fauna have left their imprint. Above all, it is quite clear that *Australopithecus afarensis* was walking very nearly like a human just after 4 million years ago—and perhaps earlier.

Finally, before leaving *A. afarensis* and turning to the numerous lesser-known australopiths from East Africa and the Sahel, it should be noted that there is no evidence for stone tool manufacture by Lucy and her kind (Table 7.2). Given the first

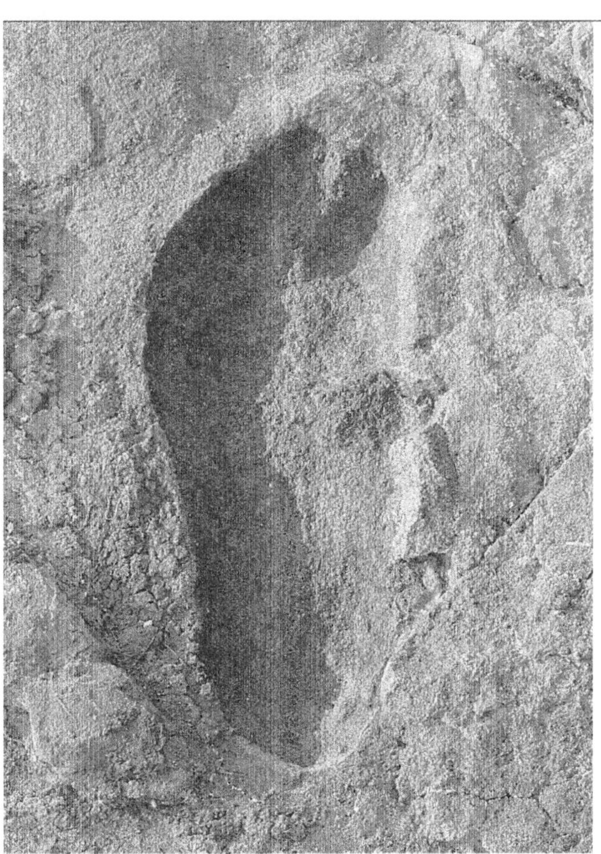

FIGURE 7.13
The Laetoli site has produced a unique record of the footprints of animals dated from about 3.6 million years BP. The footprints of a large proportion of the fossil species are present, including those of *Australopithecus afarensis*, as shown in this picture.

appearance of Oldowan tools in East Africa around 2.5 to 2.6 mya (Panger et al., 2002), it appears that *Australopithecus afarensis* predated the development of stone technology (R. Klein, 2000). As argued earlier for other australopith species, however, chimpanzeelike tool use and biodegradable tool manufacture cannot be ruled out.

Lesser-Known Australopith Species

Australopithecus anamensis

Australopithecus anamensis a *species* of *australopith* that inhabited East Africa from 4.2 to 3.9 million years ago.

The Leakey family has been blessed with three generations of talented fossil hunters. First, of course, there were Louis and Mary, whose pioneering work at Olduvai Gorge was described early in this chapter. Their rich paleontological legacy was carried on by sons Jonathan and Richard; by Richard's wife, Meave; and most recently by granddaughter Louise Leaky. In 1995, Meave Leakey and her team made headlines with the announcement of a very ancient australopith from the Kenyan sites of Kanapoi and Allia Bay (M. Leakey et al., 1995). The new hominin type, named ***Australopithecus anamensis,*** clearly is one of if not *the* oldest species of *Australopithecus* yet discovered. This claim is supported by Ar^{40}/AR^{39} dates of 4.2 to 3.9 mya—a range of dates that places *A. anamensis* father back in time than all but the most ancient fossils of *A. afarensis* (Table 7.1).

The remains of *A. anamensis* have been gathered from river deposits at Allia Bay and lakeside deposits at Kanapoi. (The two sites lie some 90 miles [145 kilometers] apart and on opposite sides of Lake Turkana; see Figure 7.1.) The Allia Bay fossils occur as a "bone bed," and each fragment was rolled and weathered as it was swept into position by a precursor of the modern Omo River. Among the Allia Bay fossils, one finds aquatic animals (fish, crocodiles, and hippopotamuses), as well as the bones of leaf-eating monkeys and woodland antelopes—remains that collectively suggest a gallery forest habitat along the river. In contrast, the Kanapoi site probably combined "dry, possibly open, wooded or bushland conditions [with] a wide gallery forest" (M. Leakey et al., 1995: 571). The remains of kudus, impalas, hyaenas, and a semi-terrestrial monkey called *Parapapio* (an early ancestor of today's baboons) confirm the somewhat more open conditions at Kanapoi. Meave Leakey and her team believe that the early hominins who lived at the two sites utilized a wide range of habitats.

So, what sort of hominin was *Australopithecus anamensis*? As one might expect this far back in time, it was a bipedal species that still showed a goodly number of apelike traits throughout its body (Box 7.4). The list of fossils recovered thus far includes numerous teeth, upper and lower jaw fragments (Figure 7.14), part of an elbow, a piece of temporal bone from the skull that includes a distinctively narrow and elliptical external acoustic meatus (ear opening), and the top and bottom portions of a right tibia (shin bone; Figure 7.15). The tibia fragments clearly show that *A. anamensis* was habitually bipedal. Unlike the shin bone of an ape, the tibia of *A. anamensis* showed a distinctively hominin knee joint, extra spongy bone just below the knee to absorb the shock of upright walking, and a bony buttress at the ankle to facilitate weight bearing. Furthermore, according to Leakey and Walker (1997), the elbow joint seems to indicate that *A. anamensis* was not a knuckle-walker, although whether it showed any other apelike locomotor patterns—such as arboreal climbing—remains an open question.

In contrast to its hominin-type lower body, several features of the face and jaws of *Australopithecus anamensis* were strongly apelike, some even more so than the same traits of *A. afarensis* (C. Ward et al., 1999). For example, *A. anamensis* showed a primitive U-shaped toothrow, a mandibular symphysis that sloped strongly backward and upper canines with enormous roots. (Those same canines wore flat at the tip, however, rather than remaining pointed as in modern apes; see Figure 7.14.) More modern dental traits included thick tooth enamel, a feature that suggests some adaptation to a diet including hard food items.

BOX 7.4

Characteristics of *Australopithecus anamensis*[a]

Trait	*Australopithecus anamensis*
Height	Unknown
Weight[b]	104–121 lb (47–55 kg)
Brain size	Unknown
Cranium	Mandibular symphysis slopes strongly down and back, suggesting facial prognathism; external acoustic meatus (ear canal) is small and apelike in outline
Dentition	U-shaped toothrows; all canines have long, robust roots; lower canines show strong size sexual dimorphism; lower P3 is very asymmetrical, with a centrally positioned and blunt main cusp (semisectorial?); thick molar enamel
Diet	Fruit and foliage; thick enamel suggests a diet including some hard items
Limbs	Elbow anatomy seems to rule out knuckle-walking; condyles of tibia differ from those of apes in both size and shape; top of tibia shows extra spongy bone for shock absorption; bottom of tibia shows extra bony buttressing at ankle
Pelvis	Unknown
Locomotion	Bipedalism (unknown whether accompanied by arboreal climbing)
Known dates (million years BP)	4.2–3.9

[a]Values for anatomical measurements may change with additional fossil discoveries. For additional technical details and diagnostic traits, see Appendix 3.
[b]Weight estimated for one (presumably male) individual.
Sources: M. Leakey et al., 1995, 1998.

In summary, *Australopithecus anamensis* lived between 4.2 and 3.9 mya and showed a slightly more apelike anatomy than its near contemporary *A. afarensis*. It moved bipedally through the habitats of East Africa, apparently using both open bushland and forested terrain. To date, *A. anamensis* remains have not been found in association with tools of any sort.

Australopithecus bahrelghazali

The dust had barely settled from the Leakey group's naming of *A. anamensis* before another new hominin hit the press. In November 1995, a team led by Michel Brunet of the University of Poitiers announced the discovery of an australopith mandible from the Sahel site of Bahr el Ghazal in Chad (Figure 7.1). The find excited tremendous interest among paleoanthropologists because it extended the known range of the australopiths to some 1,500 miles (2,500 kilometers) west of the Rift Valley. Brunet and his colleagues gave the fossil from Chad the species name ***Australopithecus bahrelghazali*** (Brunet et al., 1995, 1996).

Australopithecus bahrel-ghazali a species of *australopith* known from Chad and dating 3.5 to 3.0 million years ago.

The Bahr el Ghazal mandible, which has been dated by faunal correlation with Hadar deposits at 3.5 to 3.0 mya, preserves only the front portion of the jaw (from the symphysis back to the last premolar). Included in the jaw are all of the canines and premolars and one lateral incisor. As indicated in Box 7.5 (and also in Appendix 3), very little can be concluded about the anatomy and adaptations of this hominin because of the limited sample of fossils. *Australopithecus bahrel-ghazali* had short but

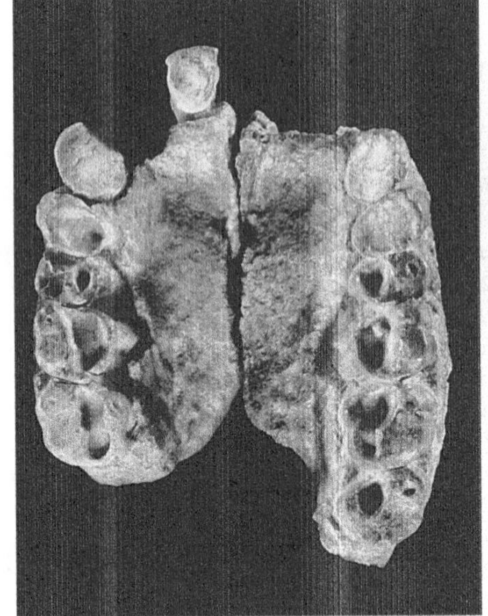

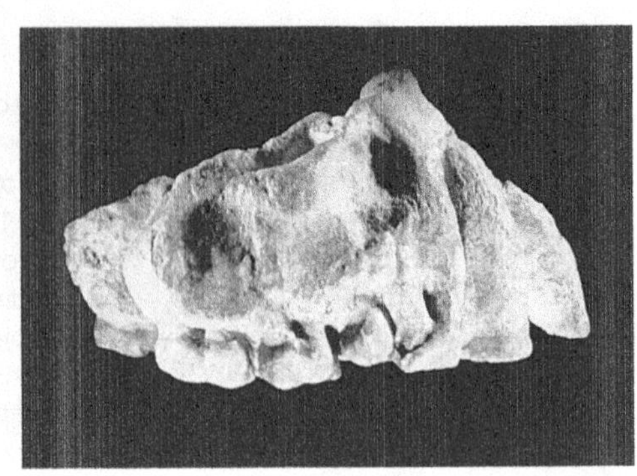

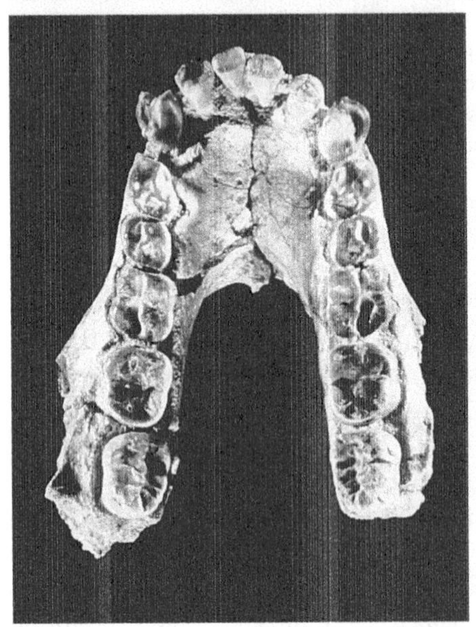

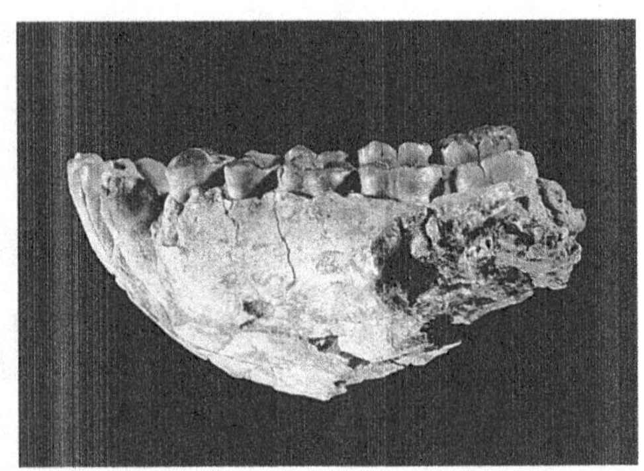

FIGURE 7.14
The upper dentition of *Australopithecus anamensis* (*top row*) shows a U-shaped toothrow and massive canine roots. The same toothrow configuration is present in the mandible (*bottom row*), which also shows a strongly sloping symphysis.

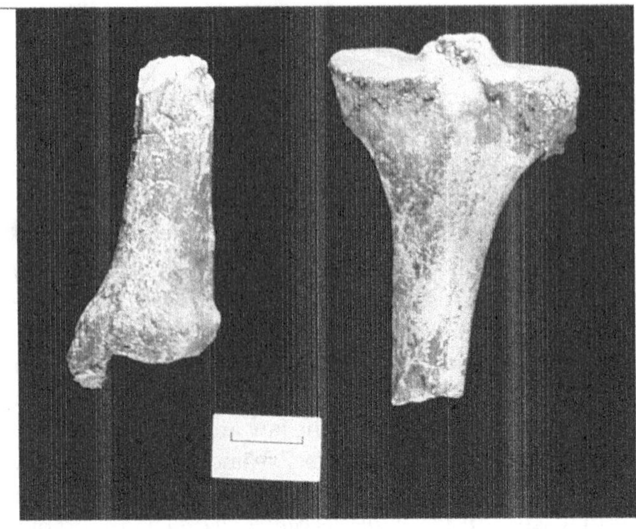

FIGURE 7.15
The top of the *A. anamensis* tibia from Kanapoi (*right*) shows extra spongy bone just below the knee. This would have helped to absorb the shock of bipedal walking. The lower end of the tibia (*left*) has extra bony buttressing at the ankle—again, for shock absorption and stability.

BOX 7.5

Characteristics of *Australopithecus bahrelghazali*[a]

Trait	*Australopithecus bahrelghazali*
Height, weight, and brain size	Unknown
Cranium	Mandibular symphysis shows a unique outline, particularly on the lingual (internal) surface
Dentition	Short, pointed lower canines; bicuspid (nonsectorial) lower P3s (this implies short upper canines); three-rooted lower premolars; premolar enamel thicker than in *Ardipithecus* but thin compared to other australopiths
Diet	Few hard items in the diet? Mostly fruit and foliage?
Limbs and pelvis	Unknown
Locomotion	Bipedalism (assumed)
Known dates (million years BP)	3.5–3.0

[a]For additional technical details and diagnostic traits, see Appendix 3.
Source: Brunet et al., 1996.

pointed canines, bicuspid (nonsectorial) lower P3s, and a unique outline of the mandibular symphysis. Furthermore, it differed from other *Australopithecus* and *Paranthropus* species in its three-rooted lower premolars (theirs were two-rooted) and its thinner premolar enamel. Collectively, these traits support at least the provisional listing of *A. bahrelghazali* as a new australopith species (Table 7.1).

A. bahrelghazali apparently inhabited a lakeside environment that included both gallery forest and wooded savanna with open grassy patches. Furthermore, judging from its thin enamel, this early species apparently subsisted rather exclusively on soft foods—undoubtedly mostly fruits, foliage, and vegetables. No tools have been found associated with this species.

Australopithecus garhi

Between 1996 and 1998, a multinational team of paleoanthropologists, archaeologists, and geologists from thirteen countries recovered the remains of yet another ancient hominin from Ethiopia—this one, from the west Awash site of Bouri (Asfaw et al., 1999; Figure 7.1). Of primary diagnostic value among the Bouri fossils was a partial cranium—complete with the upper dentition and much of the face—that dates back 2.5 myr (de Heinzelin et al., 1999). This fossil now serves as the **type specimen** for a new australopith species, ***Australopithecus garhi,*** and its features are summarized in Box 7.6.

Type specimen the *fossil* specimen that serves as the basis for identifying all other individuals in a *species;* usually the original specimen to be found.

Australopithecus garhi a *species* of *australopith* from Ethiopia and dating 2.5 million years ago.

Bouri had more tricks up its sleeve than a single skull, however. At a spot just over 300 yards (precisely, 278 meters) from the cranium, that same 2.5-million-year-old stratum yielded a partial skeleton—postcranial remains that included arm and leg fragments and one toe bone. The discoverers have been cautious about concluding that the skull and skeleton are from the same species, but their analysis implies that they suspect that was the case (see also Wood and Richmond, 2000). Here, we *do* make that assumption and therefore include several postcranial traits in Box 7.6.

Based on the sparse remains currently known, *Australopithecus garhi* seems rather apelike in many features (Asfaw et al., 1999). The type specimen (thought to be a male) has a prognathic lower face, U-shaped maxillary toothrow, smallish

BOX 7.6

Characteristics of *Australopithecus garhi*[a]

Trait	*Australopithecus garhi*
Height and weight	Unknown
Brain size[b]	450 cc
Cranium	Prognathic lower face; lack of facial "dishing"; well-developed brows; marked postorbital constriction; sagittal cresting (in male)
Dentition	Postcanine megadontia in maxilla; broad upper canines and medial incisors; short (nonprojecting) upper canines; procumbent upper incisors; moderately thick enamel
Diet	Megadontia suggests a diet that included some hard items; presence of butchered animal remains suggests that meat and marrow were consumed
Limbs	Relatively long arms (especially forearms); lengthening of the femur suggests a refinement related to habitual bipedalism
Pelvis	Unknown
Locomotion	Bipedalism (inferred from femoral lengthening)
Known dates (million years BP)	2.5

[a]Values for anatomical measurements will change with additional fossil discoveries. For additional technical details and diagnostic traits, see Appendix 3.
[b]Based on one (presumably male) specimen.
Sources: Asfaw et al., 1999; de Heinzelin et al., 1999.

sagittal crest, and marked postorbital constriction in front of its 450 cubic centimeter braincase. Its dentition reveals the curious combination of postcanine megadontia paired with broad canines and central incisors. (In the *Paranthropus* species, postcanine megadontia is paired with *reduced* size of the anterior teeth.) Intriguingly, the partial skeleton—here, viewed as *A. garhi*—shows some distinctly modern traits that contrast strongly with the primitive skull. Of special interest, the femur shows clear lengthening compared to other australopiths and apes and thus constitutes the earliest known step in the evolution of modern humans' long legs. The fact that the arms, and especially the forearms, of *A. garhi* continued to be relatively long reflects mosaic development in hominins' limb proportions.

But the final Bouri trick may be the most spectacular of all. At the same location that produced the partial skeleton, researchers found animal bones that had been smashed for marrow extraction and also cut with (presumably, Oldowan) stone tools (de Heinzelin et al., 1999). These cut marks from 2.5 mya are the oldest known evidence of hominin butchery, but whether they were made by stone-tool-wielding *A. garhi* (as seems logical, since that is the only species presently recognized from Bouri) or some other hominin remains to be established.

Paranthropus aethiopicus

During the fossil expeditions of the late 1960s, a French team under the direction of Camille Arambourg and Yves Coppens made several discoveries of australopith remains in their assigned section of the Omo River Valley. Among those remains was a distinctive megadont jaw originally classed as *Paraustralopithecus aethiopicus* but now included in ***Paranthropus aethiopicus*** (Wood and Richmond, 2000).

Paranthropus aethiopicus a *megadont australopith species* that inhabited East Africa 2.6 to 2.3 million years ago.

This taxon was significantly expanded in 1985 with the discovery of an ancient and blackened skull from the west side of Lake Turkana (Walker et al., 1986). From

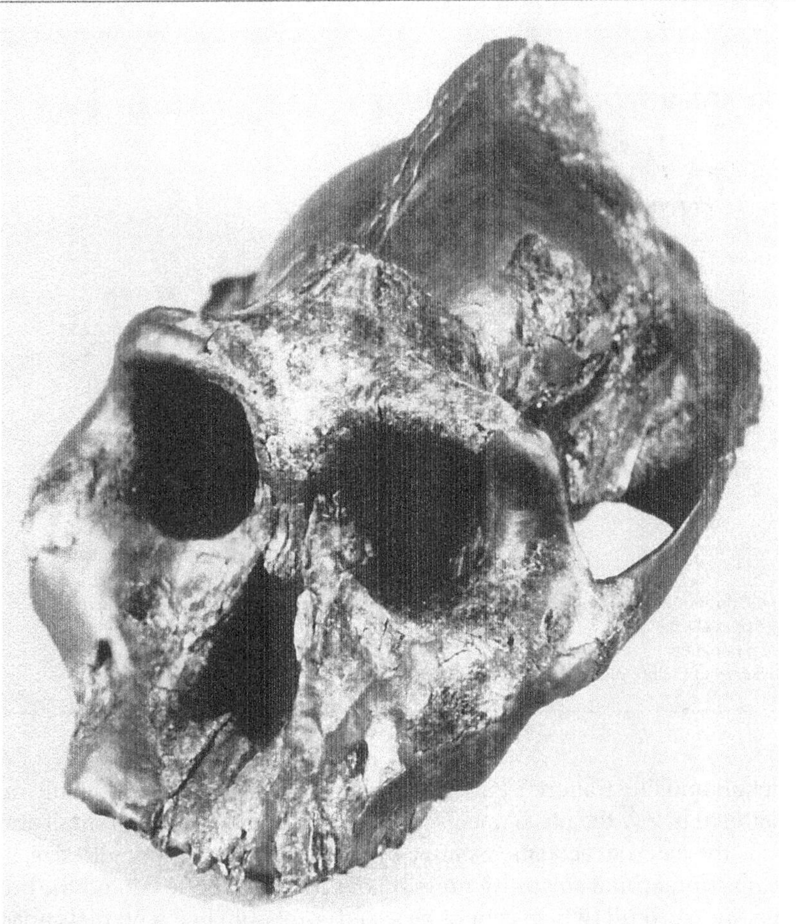

FIGURE 7.16 The Black Skull (museum number KNM-WT 17000) is classed as *Paranthropus aethiopicus*. Although a member of the megadont clade, it resembles *Australopithecus afarensis* in several traits. This photograph is about 60 percent actual size.

deposits dating about 2.5 million years of age, an excavating team headed by Alan Walker and Richard Leakey recovered a nearly toothless cranium (museum catalog number KNM-WT 17000, dubbed the "Black Skull" because of its coloration) and a partial mandible. Although much larger, the mandible is otherwise similar to the jaw found years earlier by French scientists at Omo. The west Turkana cranium is massively built and quite prognathic (Figure 7.16). It features a low forehead and a small braincase (410 cubic centimeters) and is topped by a sagittal crest that would have anchored large jaw muscles. The zygomatic arches flare widely to the side, and the face is somewhat "dished" (concave) in appearance. The few measurable teeth and tooth roots indicate that the grinding teeth were as large as those of *Paranthropus boisei.*

Although *P. aethiopicus* is known from only a few fossils and is still somewhat conroversial, it is considered a valid australopith taxon here. Particulars of its anatomy are given in Box 7.7 and Appendix 3.

Kenyanthropus platyops

Six years after her announcement of *Australopithecus anamensis,* Meave Leakey and her team followed that success with another and perhaps even more spectacular find: an entirely new genus of East African hominins named ***Kenyanthropus platyops.*** The new taxon was announced in 2001 and was based on 3.5 to 3.2-million-year-old fossils from the West Turkana site of Lomekwi (Figure 7.1). Among the key discoveries was a distorted cranium that showed such "a unique combination of derived facial and primitive neurocranial features" (M. Leakey et al., 2001: 433) that the team felt the creation of a new genus was appropriate.

Kenyanthropus platyops an *australopith genus* and *species* from East Africa that dates back to 3.5 to 3.2 million years of age.

Kenyanthropus platyops is characterized by a face that is tall in the malar (cheekbone) region and has anteriorly positioned zygomatic processes (see Appendix 3 for

BOX 7.7

Characteristics of *Paranthropus aethiopicus*[a]

Trait	*Paranthropus aethiopicus*
Height and weight	Unknown
Brain size	410 cc[b]
Cranium	"Dished" face; large sagittal crest; low forehead; low-vaulted braincase (compared to *P. boisei:* unflexed cranial base; shallow jaw joint; extreme facial prognathism; parietal bones flared strongly at the mastoid)
Dentition	Grinding tooth megadontia equals that of *P. boisei*
Diet, limbs, and pelvis	Unknown
Locomotion	Bipedalism (assumed)
Known dates (million years BP)	2.6–2.3

[a]Values for anatomical measurements will change as additional specimens are found. For further technical details and diagnostic traits, see Appendix 3.
[b]Based on a single (male?) specimen.
Sources: Grine, 1993; Walker et al., 1986; Wood and Richmond, 2000.

details and illustrations). Furthermore, the face is quite flat, with only moderate prognathism below the nasal opening. The nasal opening itself is small and narrow, and so is the external acoustic meatus. Brow ridges are of moderate size, and thus there is no supraorbital sulcus (depression of the frontal bone behind the brows). The single known skull (which cannot be sexed) probably had a cranial capacity in the 400 to 500 cubic centimeter range. The flat face of *K. platyops* was equipped with small molars capped with thick enamel (M. Leakey et al., 2001; Box 7.8). Interestingly, of all

BOX 7.8

Characteristics of *Kenyanthropus platyops*[a]

Trait	*Kenyanthropus platyops*
Height and weight	Unknown
Brain size	400–500 cc[b]
Cranium	Tall malar region; anteriorly positioned zygomatic processes; flat transverse facial contour below nasal opening; moderate subnasal prognathism; entrance to nasal cavity is stepped; small and narrow nasal opening and external acoustic meatus; no supraorbital sulcus
Dentition	Small upper molars; thick molar enamel
Diet, limbs and pelvis	Unknown
Locomotion	Bipedalism (assumed)
Known dates (million years BP)	3.5–3.2

[a]Values for anatomical measurements will change as additional specimens are found. For further technical details and diagnostic traits, see Appendix 3.
[b]Based on one distorted specimen.
Source: M. Leakey et al., 2001.

the various early hominin types, *K. platyops* is most similar to *Homo rudolfensis*, although whether the species' similarities reflect a close phylogenetic relationship or mere convergent evolution is unclear (McHenry, 2002; more on this in a later section).

Kenyanthropus platyops lived near a shallow lake in a well-watered and predominantly woodland habitat, although with some open grasslands. The diet of this species is unknown at present, but its discoverers think that *K. platyops*'s unique features indicate the use of "a distinct dietary adaptive zone" (M. Leakey et al., 2001: 439). To date, there is no evidence of tool use by this mid Pliocene hominin type.

Ardipithecus ramidus

One last species of Plio-Pleistocene australopiths remains to be described: ***Ardipithecus ramidus*** from Ethiopia. Fossils assigned to this species were recovered between 1992 and 1994 by an American–Japanese–Ethiopian research team working in early Pliocene deposits at the Middle Awash site of Aramis (Figure 7.1). The remains of *Ar. ramidus* are relatively extensive but, unfortunately, not completely analyzed. From the 1992–1993 field season, there are several teeth, a partial mandible, some skull fragments, and four arm bones—three of which are from the left arm of a single individual (White et al., 1994, 1995). Back in the field in 1994, the researchers made additional important finds, including a partial skeleton that preserved key portions of the locomotor anatomy (vertebral column, pelvis, legs; Conroy, 1997). All of these remains have been dated to about 4.4 myr of age (WoldeGabriel et al., 1994).

Ardipithecus ramidus an *australopith species* from Ethiopia that dates back to 4.4 million years of age.

Reflecting the fact that it is often easier to collect fossils than to prepare and analyze them, the 1994 skeleton has still not been fully described. Despite this lack of important information, certain conclusions can be drawn regarding the anatomy and behavior of this previously unknown genus and species (Box 7.9). *Ardipithecus*

BOX 7.9

Characteristics of *Ardipithecus ramidus*[a]

Trait	*Ardipithecus ramidus*
Height	At least 3.3 ft (100 cm; upper height limit and sexual dimorphism unknown)
Weight	At least 66 lb (30 kg; upper weight limit and sexual dimorphism unknown)
Brain size	Unknown
Cranium	Forwardly positioned foramen magnum; small occipital condyles; very flat surface of jaw joint
Dentition	Canines lower, blunter, and more incisiform than those of apes but less incisiform and larger (relative to the postcanine teeth) than those of *A. afarensis*; lower anterior premolars (P3s) show evidence of reduced sectorial functioning; thin enamel on canines and molars; apelike anatomy of lower first deciduous molar
Diet	Unknown (thin molar enamel may rule out "hard object feeder")
Limbs	Arm bones showing a mosaic of hominin and ape traits; elliptical shape of the head of the humerus and the anatomy of the elbow joint resemble those of later hominins; pelvic and lower limb anatomy unknown
Locomotion	Bipedalism (knuckle-walking can be ruled out)
Known dates (million years BP)	4.4

[a]For additional technical details and diagnostic traits, see Appendix 3.
Source: T. White et al., 1994.

ramidus showed canines that were shorter and more incisiform than those of apes but less incisiform and larger (relative to the postcanine teeth) than those of *A. afarensis*; lower anterior premolars (P3s) that show some honing function, but less than in apes; enamel on canines and molars that is thin compared to that of *A. afarensis* but approximates the condition in chimpanzees; similar to other australopiths but in contrast to apes, a forwardly placed foramen magnum; and finally, a shape of the head of the humerus (upper arm bone) and the anatomy of the elbow joint resembling that of later hominins, not of apes. One additional characteristic that strongly differentiates *Ar. ramidus* from *A. afarensis* is the extremely apelike anatomy of the lower first deciduous molar found at Aramis.

White et al. (1994) believe that the Aramis fossils show enough derived features to be safely included in the hominin tribe. They point particularly to homininlike modifications in the canine and lower P3 complex, the positioning of the foramen magnum, and the elbow anatomy. To its discoverers, *Ar. ramidus* fulfills virtually all the theoretical expectations of a species just this side of the ape–hominin split.

Doubters, however, argue that only undeniable proof of habitual bipedalism will validate *Ar. ramidus* as a hominin. The primary evidence at the moment is the species' forwardly positioned foramen magnum (Box 7.9) and therein lies the importance of the 1994 skeleton and its postcranial remains. Evidence from those fossils could nail down *Ar. ramidus*'s claim to be a member of the human tribe and, furthermore, a biped that inhabited not an open savanna but rather a wooded habitat (WoldeGabriel et al., 1994). In the meantime, very recent discoveries of an even older species of *Ardipithecus, Ar. kadabba,* have taken the genus back into the Miocene epoch (Haile-Selassie et al., 2004). And it is to this ancient time period that we must look for the absolute beginnings of our lineage.

Back in Time: Australopiths from the Miocene

Ardipithecus kadabba

The twenty-first century has gotten off to a remarkable start as regards the search for the oldest hominins. Thanks to the efforts of a record number of fossil-hunting teams and the fact that expanded geological information now allows researchers to locate and intensively survey sites of great age, paleoanthropologists have recently taken the history of the hominin tribe back into the late Miocene epoch.

In 1997, scientists working in the Middle Awash Valley of Ethiopia's Afar Rift discovered eleven dental and postcranial fragments that were initially assigned to a subspecies of *Ardipithecus ramidus, Ar. ramidus kadabba* (Haile-Selassie, 2001). Further field work in 2002, however, produced an additional six teeth whose anatomy convinced researchers that they were working not with a subspecies of a known type but with an entirely new species: ***Ardipithecus kadabba.*** The fact that the remains, now totaling some 19 bits in all, could be dated to a period 5.8 to 5.2 mya—tantalizingly close to the calculated divergence of hominins from their last ape ancestors (Table 4.2)—greatly increased their anthropological interest (Haile-Selassie, 2001; Haile-Selasssie et al., 2004; WoldeGabriel et al., 2001).

Ardipithecus kadabba an *australopith species* from Ethiopia that dates back to 5.8 to 5.2 million years of age.

Recovered from deposits that represent a predominantly wet and wooded habitat (with some wooded grassland thrown into the mix; WoldeGabriel et al., 2001), the fossils of *Ar. kadabba* show the following anatomical features (see also Box 7.10): a toe bone that is consistent with bipedalism similar to that of *Australopithecus afarensis;* lower lateral incisors that are comparable in shape to those of later hominins and distinct from those of chimpanzees; upper M3s (third molars) that are apelike in their cusp count ($n = 4$) and overall shape; projecting, interlocking upper and lower canines that (at least in the upper jaw) equal those of female chimpanzees in length; lower P3s that show a

BOX 7.10

Characteristics of *Ardipithecus kadabba*[a]

Trait	*Ardipithecus kadabba*
Height and weight	Unknown
Brain size	Unknown
Cranium	Unknown
Dentition	Lower lateral incisor is similar to later hominins and narrower than in *Pan troglodytes;* morphology of lower canine and wear of upper canine suggest less than fully functional C/P3 honing complex; upper canines as long as those of female *P. troglodytes;* upper M3s are apelike in cusp count and overall shape; enamel thickness comparable to *Ardipithecus ramidus*(?)
Diet	Unknown
Limbs	Curved finger bone similar to that of *Australopithecus afarensis;* olecranon fossa of humerus is less elliptical and deeper than in later hominins; ulnar shaft more curved than in later hominins; toe bone similar to those of *A. afarensis*
Pelvis	Unknown
Locomotion	Bipedalism (assumed for genus)
Known dates (million years BP)	5.8–5.2

[a]See Appendix 3 for additional details and diagnostic features.
Sources: Haile-Selassie, 2001; Haile-Selassie et al., 2004.

small mesiobuccal (Appendix 3, Figure A.5) wear facet caused by contact with the upper canine but also limited wear on the distal–lingual crown face of the upper canines, which suggests honing was reduced compared to apes (Haile-Selassie, 2001; Haile-Selassie et al., 2004). Overall, *Ardipithecus kadabba* shows a strong mix of apelike and clearly hominin traits. Especially with regard to the degree of canine–premolar honing, *Ar. kadabba* seems to be just our side of the ape–hominin divide.

Little more can be said about this ancient taxon, except that in many dental traits, *Ardipithecus kadabba* is broadly similar to the two remaining Miocene genera, *Orrorin* and *Sahelanthropus.* Haile-Selassie et al. (2004) caution that distinguishing these three taxa is difficult, if not impossible, at this stage of our knowledge.

Orrorin tugenensis

Yet another apparent ancestor claimed by its discoverers to be just our side of the ape–hominin divide was announced in 2001 by a joint French–Kenyan team headed by Brigitte Senut and Martin Pickford (Senut et al., 2001). From sites in the Tugen Hills of western Kenya (Figure 7.1), the team recovered just over a dozen fossils from deposits of the Lukeino Formation that are 6 million years old or thereabouts (Deino et al., 2002). The remains were placed in a new genus and species, ***Orrorin tugenensis,*** and informally called "Millennium Man," since they were found in the year 2000 (Gibbons, 2002). Most importantly, among the remains were such diagnostic fragments as partial femurs, a distal humerus that includes a portion of the elbow joint, and an upper canine (Senut et al., 2001).

Orrorin tugenensis *an australopith genus* and *species* from western Kenya that dates back to 6 million years of age.

The best evidence for bipedalism by *Orrorin*—and by extrapolation, for its hominin status—comes from the femoral fragments. The head of the femur—the part of the bone that most directly bears the weight of the upper body during bipedal standing and walking—is relatively larger than in the "Lucy" specimen of *Australopithecus afarensis.* Furthermore, the posterior surface of the top of the femur may show a distinctive groove (the obturator externus groove [see Aiello and Dean, 1990]) that Senut et al. (2001) claim is indicative of frequent bipedalism. Both of these bits of evidence have been questioned by other experts, however—femoral head size because it is affected by body weight as well as locomotor pattern (Aiello and Dean, 1990) and the obturator externus groove because it may reflect reduced ischial length but not necessarily bipedalism (Stern and Susman, 1983). Equally controversial are claims that the distribution of cortical bone at *Orrorin*'s femoral neck-shaft junction proves bipedalism (Galik et al., 2004; Gibbons, 2004). As one cautious skeptic has pointed out, the details of the *lower* femur "would be more likely to make the bipedalism case by revealing the structure of the knee" (Balter, 2001: 1461). But unfortunately, a knee of *Orrorin* has yet to be found. Interestingly, the fragmentary humerus of *Orrorin* may show some adaptations for climbing, and the same is true for a single curved finger bone (Senut et al., 2001). Overall, the postcranial evidence from this new genus is suggestive of bipedalism but not conclusive.

In the *Orrorin* dentition, evidence of hominin status is perhaps even more elusive. While it is true that the molars resemble those of most later australopiths in their thick layer of enamel, the single upper canine recovered so far for the genus is about the same size and shape as those of female chimpanzees and displays an apelike groove down its front surface (Senut et al., 2001).

No tools were found in association with the *Orrorin tugenensis* remains, and as yet, no measurable skulls have been discovered. The primary anatomical traits of this species are listed in Box 7.11. Only further fossil discoveries will prove beyond doubt whether this ancient creature belonged to the hominin tribe.

BOX 7.11

Characteristics of *Orrorin tugenensis*[a]

Trait	*Orrorin tugenensis*
Height	"Equivalent to a female chimpanzee" (2.5 ft; 77.5 cm)
Weight	"Equivalent to a female chimpanzee" (66 lb; 30 kg)
Brain size and cranium	Unknown
Dentition	Large upper central incisor; upper canine pointed, "almost sectorial," and grooved on mesial surface (similar to female chimpanzees' upper canines); thick enamel on molars; lower molars are "small *Homo*-like rectangular" teeth; body of mandible relatively deep below M3
Diet	Unknown
Limbs	Large, spherical femoral head; femoral neck is elongated; obturator groove present; muscle insertions on humerus indicate some climbing; curved finger bones
Pelvis	Unknown
Locomotion	Bipedalism(?) and possibly some climbing
Known dates (million years BP)	6

[a]See Appendix 3 for additional details and diagnostic features.
Source: Senut et al., 2001.

Sahelanthropus tchadensis

The long list of East African and Sahel australopiths is nearing its end. Only one more genus and species remains to be described before we try to reach some general conclusions about these early hominins as well as those from South Africa. But this last australopith is certainly worthy of close consideration. It is from a rather unusual place—Chad, in the Sahel—and at 6 to 7 million years of age it is the oldest known member of the tribe Hominini. Its name is ***Sahelanthropus tchadensis.***

Sahelanthropus tchadensis an *australopith genus* and *species* from Chad that dates back to 6 to 7 million years of age.

Sahelanthropus was discovered by a joint French–Chadian research team in 2001 at the site of Toros–Menalla (TM) 266 in the middle of the Djurab Desert (Figure 7.1). On July 19, 2001, student researcher Ahounta Djimdoumalbaye was fossil hunting amidst the windblown sands when he discovered fragments of what turned out to be a remarkably complete cranium (Figure 7.17). The skull (probably from a male) was small brained and big browed, and it showed a small sagittal crest near the back of the braincase. Clearly hominoid but with a unique set of traits, the find was judged to represent a new genus and species of hominin, and the formal name *Sahelanthropus tchadensis* ("Sahel man from Chad") was chosen (Brunet et al., 2002). Informally, the fossil is called "Toumaï, which means "hope of life" in the local language ("Toumaï" web site). Additional searching by the team produced a few lower jaw fragments and some teeth but no postcranial remains (Lemonick and Dorfman, 2002). Along with the hominin remains, the TM 266 site has produced numerous fossils of fish, crocodiles, and amphibious mammals, as well as primates, elephants, and grazing animals. The reconstructed habitat is a lakeside gallery forest and some grasslands, and the calculated age (derived by faunal correlation with radiometrically dated sites) is late Miocene, about 6 to 7 myr of age (Vignaud et al., 2002).

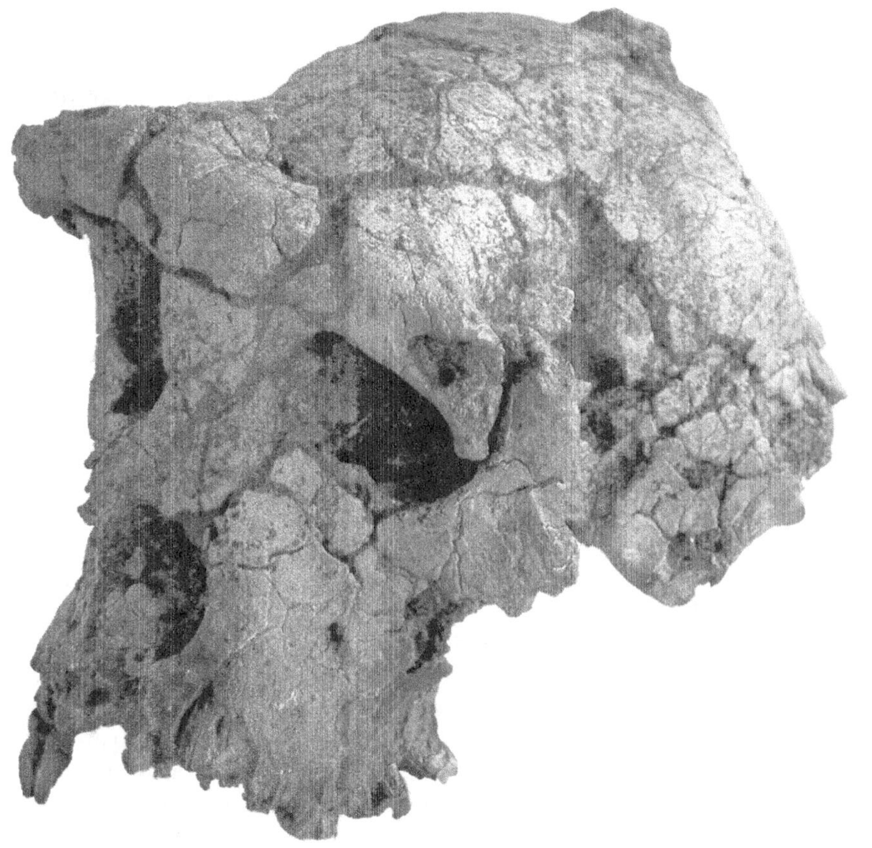

FIGURE 7.17 The skull of *Sahelanthropus tchadensis* shows a tall but not particularly prognathic face that is capped by huge brows. A posteriorly located sagittal crest is also visible.

BOX 7.12

Characteristics of *Sahelanthropus tchadensis*[a]

Trait	*Sahelanthropus tchadensis*
Height and weight	Unknown
Brain size[b]	320–380 cc
Cranium	Relatively flat face with little lower face prognathism; face wide at top and narrow at bottom; long, narrow cranial base; large, continuous supraorbital torus; no supratoral sulcus; marked postorbital constriction; small sagittal crest at rear of skull; large nuchal crest; foramen magnum relatively far forward
Dentition	Relatively small incisors; small (presumably male) upper canines; upper and lower canines worn at the tip; apparently no upper canine–lower P3 honing complex; molars with low and rounded cusps; moderately thick enamel on cheek teeth (>*Pan* but <*Australopithecus*)
Diet	Unknown
Limbs and pelvis	Unknown
Locomotion	Bipedalism (judging from foramen magnum placement)
Known dates (million years BP)	7–6

[a]See Appendix 3 for additional details and diagnostic traits.
[b]Based on single specimen, presumably a male.
Source: Brunet et al., 2002.

A thorough anatomical analysis of *Sahelanthropus* has revealed that this species showed a combination of apelike and hominin traits (Brunet et al., 2002; Box 7.12). Skull characteristics include a rather flat face that is wide at the top and narrow at the bottom; a small and low-vaulted braincase (estimated volume of 320 to 380 cubic centimeters); huge supraorbital torus (brows); marked postorbital constriction; and a small, posteriorly located sagittal crest. The huge brows deserve special mention because they are relatively larger than those of a male gorilla. Unlike a gorilla, however, *Sahelanthropus* lacked a prognathic lower face and large canines. Perhaps the best cranial indicator that *Sahelanthropus* was bipedal is the relatively anterior position of the foramen magnum (as far forward as in *Ardipithecus ramidus;* also see Figure 6.4). Postcranial remains are needed to verify this locomotor classification, however.

The *Sahelanthropus* dentition was apelike in its U-shaped dental arch but similar to later hominins in reduced canine size, apical canine wear, and (apparently) the lack of an upper canine–lower P3 honing complex. (The lower P3 has not been found but is assumed to have been nonsectorial.) Enamel thickness of the grinding teeth was intermediate between that of chimpanzees and *Australopithecus* species (Brunet et al., 2002).

All told, *Sahelanthropus* is a wonderful mosaic of ape and hominin traits. As Bernard Wood has commented, "From the back it looks like a chimpanzee, whereas from the front it could pass for a 1.75-million-year-old advanced australopith" (B. Wood, 2002:134). Given the new species' mix of traits (some of which are undoubtedly useful phylogenetic indicators and others deceptive anatomical convergences), Wood concludes that it might be a stem hominin but that this may be impossible to prove. Other skeptics are more blunt. Milford Wolpoff of the

University of Michigan, writing with Brigitte Senut, Martin Pickford (the latter two being the discoverers of *Orrorin*, one will remember) and John Hawks, argue that *Sahelanthropus* was actually an ape and (attacking the evidence of foramen magnum placement) certainly not an obligate biped. They suggest that *Sahelpithecus* might be a more appropriate name (Wolpoff et al., 2002). Further complicating the issue is the fact that dentally, there is very little difference among the three claimants as Miocene hominins: *Sahelanthropus, Orrorin*, and *Ardipithecus kadabba*. Some researchers suspect that further discoveries will show these remains actually represent only one genus and perhaps only a single species within that genus (Haile-Selassie et al., 2004; Lemonick and Dorfman, 2002).

Lifestyles of the Australopiths

So much for the nuts and bolts of the australopith fossil record. Along with Chapter 6, this chapter so far has been concerned with presenting the details about the discoveries, locations, ages, and anatomies of the thirteen species of australopiths (see Table 6.1 for a taxonomic refresher). They come from a variety of sites in South, East, and north central Africa and cover a combined time range of 7 to 1 mya (Table 7.1).

But now it's time to put some flesh on those dry bones and to make a few educated speculations about how the various early hominins lived. The anatomical and archaeological evidence provides a good basis for such speculations, of course, but in addition, paleoanthropologists routinely apply models developed from the socioecology and behavior of nonhuman primates (especially the apes) and from modern humans who still live by hunting and gathering. It is important to keep in mind, however, that all reconstructions of australopith life ways are *hypotheses*, and as such, they require further scrutiny and scientific testing. Some will eventually be accepted as proved facts; others will be rejected in favor of alternative interpretations.

Perhaps the best way to begin this synthesis is to divide the thirteen proposed australopiths into two chronological groups—Miocene species versus those from the Plio-Pleistocene—and to ask whether they meet the basic criteria for inclusion as hominins: canine reduction and habitual bipedalism.

The first category includes three genera and species: *Sahelanthropus tchadensis, Orrorin tugenensis*, and *Ardipithecus kadabba*. A look at Table 7.2, which summarizes certain key traits for all the australopith types, shows that none of the Miocene species is on particularly firm ground with regard to its hominin status. Both *Orrorin* and *Ardipithecus kadabba* show projecting and pointed upper canines—very apelike (specifically, female chimplike) teeth for both species, although the *Ar. kadabba* discoverers point to details of the canine base that they say link their fossil but not *Orrorin* to later hominins (Haile-Selassie, 2001; Haile-Selassie et al., 2004). In the very oldest species, *Sahelanthropus*, the upper canines (of a presumably male specimen) do appear to be shorter than those of male apes and to indicate a lack of canine–lower P3 honing, but these interpretations have been challenged. Turning to evidence for bipedalism among the Miocene species, *Sahelanthropus* depends on the placement of its foramen magnum (challenged), *Orrorin* on the details of the upper femur (challenged), and *Ar. kadabba* on a single toe bone (challenged). In short, any or all of these creatures *could* be hominins—indeed, they could all be the *same species* of hominin (Haile-Selassie et al., 2004)—but each of their claims requires substantiation.

It should also be kept in mind that among these Miocene types, researchers may possibly have found the remains of the last ape–human common ancestor. In that connection, it is interesting that Jonathan Kingdon (2003) has speculated recently that the last common ancestor was a "ground ape" that lived in the coastal forests of East Africa sometime between 7.8 and 6.2 mya. It was this ground ape, in Kingdon's view, that originally evolved shortening and widening of the pelvis, changes in the trunk, and forward movement of the foramen magnum as adaptations for "squat feeding." Only later did these modifications serve as precursors for habitual bipedalism in the common ancestor's descendants (Kingdon, 2003). This is an intriguing hypothesis that, if true (and it has yet to be tested), will require researchers to think about the meaning of hominins' diagnostic traits in an entirely new way.

Assuming for now, however, that one or more of the Miocene species is actually an early hominin and that, contrary to Kingdon (2003), their adaptations *do* reflect the beginnings of habitual bipedalism, what conclusions can we draw about the context of that critical development? The answer seems to be that bipedalism probably evolved within a primarily forested or wooded habitat, not on the African savanna, as traditionally thought (Dart, 1925; Napier, 1970). *Sahelanthropus, Orrorin,* and *Ar. kadabba* all apparently utilized mainly wooded terrain, often near lakes or streams (Wong, 2003). As we will see in the next chapter, this discovery has important implications for hypotheses about the beginnings of bipedal locomotion.

Dietary preferences are unknown for the three Miocene species, and so are their capacities for tool use and tool making. At present, no tools (stone or otherwise) have been found in association with these early hominins, but it is important to remember that the current absence of evidence is not necessarily strong evidence of the absence of tool use and tool making. After all, these creatures are estimated to have been just about as brainy as modern chimpanzees, and chimps are talented and varied tool users and makers.

When we turn to the australopiths from the Plio-Pleistocene, our synthesis becomes both more detailed and less speculative. The hominin status of these ten species is generally conceded, although some—*Kenyanthropus platyops, Paranthropus boisei,* and *Australopithecus bahrelghazali*—lack postcranial evidence. (These species are so similar in other ways to well established hominins that their bipedalism is assumed, pending the discovery of supporting or refuting fossils.) A progressive reduction in canine length can be discerned beginning about 4 million years ago, and by about 2.5 to 3 mya, hominins' canines had become quite incisiform. Unequivocal proof of habitual bipedalism is provided by both *A. afarensis* and *A. anamensis* by about 4 mya, but whether this locomotion was the same as modern humans' is a matter of active debate. Australopith bipedalism may well have been less energy efficient than our way of getting around, perhaps especially for long-range walking (Wood and Richmond, 2000). Nonetheless, it must have been a relatively stable adaptation of most (if not all) australopith species, given their longevity in the fossil record. (*A. afarensis* lasted for 1.7 million years, and both *A. africanus* and *P. robustus* lasted for 1 million; Table 7.1.) Theories addressing the evolution and use of bipedalism by the earliest hominins are explored in the next chapter.

Interestingly, adopting bipedalism apparently did not require completely forsaking the trees—at least not initially (Hunt, 1998). *A. africanus, A. afarensis,* and perhaps even the *Paranthropus* species show anatomical evidence of both the derived trait of terrestrial bipedalism and the likely continuation of some arboreal climbing. (Note that separating working adaptations from primitive retentions is a complex matter; see Stern [2000] and C. Ward [2002].) Furthermore, the australopiths' anatomical adaptations to bipedalism may have evolved in a mosaic fashion. One study reported that CT (computed tomography) images of *A. africanus* and *P. robustus* skulls show **semicircular canal** morphologies like those of apes, not of modern humans, and suggested that these australopiths may have been *facultative* (optional, dependent on conditions) rather than *obligate* bipeds (Spoor et al., 1994). However, because other researchers (Graf and Vidal, 1996) have challenged the notion of a functional connection between locomotor pattern and semicircular canal morphology, we are without closure on this point.

Semicircular canals the fluid-filled canals of the inner ear that control balance and coordination.

As shown in Table 7.2, the strong likelihood that hominin bipedalism evolved in forested or wooded circumstances is reinforced by data from the Plio-Pleistocene

TABLE 7.2 Australopith Anatomy and Habits

Species	Brain Size (cc)	Canine Length	$C\text{-}P_3$ Honing	Proof of Bipedalism	Habitat	Diet	Tool Use or Tool Making
Sahelanthropus tchadensis	320–380	Somewhat shortened?[a]	Probably absent	Foramen magnum placement[a]	Forest and grassland	Unknown	Unknown
Orrorin tugenensis	Unknown	Projecting and pointed[b,c]	Unknown	Femoral head and muscle attachments[d]	Forest?	Unknown	Unknown
Ardipithecus kadabba	Unknown	Projecting and pointed[c]	Not fully functional	Toe bone similar to those of *A. afarensis*[e]	Woodland and grassland	Unknown	Unknown
Ardipithecus ramidus	Unknown	Lower, blunter than in apes	Less than apes (absent?)	Foramen magnum placement	Primarily woodland	Not hard object feeders	Unknown
Kenyanthropus platyops	400–500	Unknown	Unknown	Postcranial remains lacking	Woodland and grassland	Unknown	Unknown
Australopithecus anamensis	Unknown	Large but with apical wear	Semi-sectorial?	Anatomy of tibia	Woodland and grassland?	Fruit, foliage, hard items?	Unknown
Australopithecus afarensis	375–540	Somewhat projecting	Semi-sectorial	Anatomy of pelvis and knees	Woodland and grassland	Small, hard-husked fruit	Unknown
Australopithecus bahrelghazali	Unknown	Short but pointed	Absent	Postcranial remains lacking	Forest and grassland	Not hard object feeders	Unknown
Australopithecus africanus	405–515	Short and incisiform	Absent	Anatomy of pelvis	Grassland with some woods	Fruit, foliage, some meat?	Apparently neither
Australopithecus garhi	450	Short and incisiform	Absent	Assumed from femoral lengthening	Lakeside grasslands	Some hard items; meat?[f]	Butchering with stone tools?[g]
Paranthropus aethiopicus	410	Unknown	Unknown	Postcranial remains lacking	Wooded?	Unknown	Unknown
Paranthropus boisei	390–500	Short and incisiform	Absent	Foramen magnum placement	Open woods and grassland	Fibrous fruits and foliage?	No exclusive association with tools[h]
Paranthropus robustus	476–530	Short and incisiform	Absent	Anatomy of pelvis and foot	Bush/wooded grasslands	Grass, tubers, termites, and meat	Bone digging tools; stone tools possible

[a]Challenged by Wolpoff et al. (2002).
[b]Challenged by Haile-Selasssie (2001).
[c]Comparable to the canines of a female chimpanzee.
[d]Challenged by Aiello and Collard (2001) and in Gibbons (2002).
[e]Challenged in Wong (2003).
[f]Assuming the Bouri cut marks were made by this species.
[g]These tools were not found in direct association with the remains of *A. garhi*.
[h]*Homo habilis* is thought by many researchers to have made the Oldowan tools at Olduvai Bed I.

Sources: Wood and Richmond, 2000; T. White, 2002. Also see the various species descriptions in the text.

FIGURE 7.18 Reconstruction of a group of australopiths (*Paranthropus robustus*) foraging on the South African grasslands.

australopiths. All of these species utilized a mixture of habitat types—forest, woodland, bush, and grasslands—usually in close proximity to a water source, such as a lake or river. Some species, such as *P. robustus*, may have been particularly drawn to open and grassy habitats, but all used a mosaic of environments (Figure 7.18; Wood and Richmond, 2000).

Within their mixed habitats, the australopiths ate an equally mixed diet. Although the exact proportions undoubtedly varied from species to species and region to region, the australopith diet consisted mainly of fibrous fruits, supplemented with leaves, tubers, nuts, insects, and most likely, meat (Grine, 1993; Hunt, 1998; Wood and Richmond, 2000). This interpretation is based mainly on the anatomy of australopith teeth (including size, enamel thickness, and microwear) and skulls, but other findings have contributed, as well. Termite foraging has recently been suggested for *P. robustus* based on the discovery of bone digging tools at Swartkrans (Backwell and d'Errico, 2001). Additionally, the possibility of meat eating by the australopiths has been suggested first from low strontium-to-calcium ratios in *P. robustus* fossils (which matches the chemical profile of modern carnivores, not herbivores; I. Stewart, 1992) and second from analyses of the stable carbon (C^{13}) content of *A. africanus* teeth from Makapansgat (Sponheimer and Lee-Thorp, 1999). The *A. africanus* teeth provide evidence of a C^{13}-enriched diet such as grasses, sedges, and/or the animals that ate those plants. Of course, there is nothing particularly startling in these descriptions of the reconstructed australopith diet: Bonobos and especially chimpanzees engage in insectivory and some meat eating, and these practices are likely to have been in place for the last ape–hominin common ancestor (Table 4.5).

Tool use and tool making by the Plio-Pleistocene australopiths are hotly debated topics at present. The evidence continues to accumulate, however, that both practices *may* have been present. Bone slivers used for digging into termite mounds have been attributed to *P. robustus,* as previously described. Furthermore, the hand anatomy of both *P. robustus* and *A. africanus* was such that precision gripping and tool making should have been possible (Wood and Richmond, 2000), and as noted in the previous chapter, some researchers already attribute the Swartkrans pebble tools to the australopiths there. Similarly, it is possible but has not yet been proved that the cut-marked animal bones at Bouri were the work of implement-wielding *A. garhi.* It should be clearly noted, however, that many (most?) paleoanthropologists and archaeologists continue to reserve the beginnings of stone tool manufacture for the first representatives of the genus *Homo* and that there is still much to be learned about the history of hominin technology (Panger et al., 2002).

With regard to possible grouping patterns, the reconstruction of the last ape–hominin common ancestor (Table 4.5) implies that the australopiths lived in fusion–fission communities that contained multiple males and females. This may never be demonstrable, however, and almost equally elusive is information on australopith mating systems. To some workers, the moderate to extreme sexual dimorphism in body size shown by the best-known australopiths suggests polygynous mating systems complete with lots of male–male breeding competition; other specialists are not so sure and favor the early evolution of hominin monogamy (Lovejoy, 1993; Reno et al., 2003).

Finally, as regards the communication skills of the australopiths, the safest bet seems to be that they could not talk, and this is based on three sorts of evidence. First, while it is granted that some species (*P. boisei* and *P. robustus*) show a degree of cranial base flexure that anticipates the anatomy of modern humans (see Chapter 13), most australopiths do not, suggesting a lack of the throat proportions needed for speech. Second, the conclusion that speech was absent is reinforced by data on the size of the australopith hypoglossal canal, the opening that carries the nerves responsible for varying the shape of the human tongue during speech. In contrast to the large hypoglossal canal of modern humans but similar to the condition in chimpanzees, *A. africanus* (the only australopith studied so far) shows a small canal, implying a lack of fine control of the tongue (Kay et al., 1998). Third, a lack of speech is supported by the observation that the australopiths had a level of encephalization that was only a bit advanced beyond that of chimpanzees (McHenry, 2002). In other words, they probably lacked the mental equipment for speech. Like modern apes, the australopiths probably used a combination of nonlinguistic calls, gestures, postures, and facial expressions to communicate with one another.

And that concludes our brief sketch of australopith life ways and brings us to the end of this chapter. A discussion of the australopiths' evolutionary relations is provided in next chapter, following descriptions of the earliest **hominans** (members of the subtribe **Hominina** and the genus *Homo*). As we will see, the boundary between the australopiths and early *Homo* is currently under discussion (and possibly revision).

Hominan a member of the subtribe *Hominina*; a member of any *species* belonging to the *genus Homo*.

Hominina a subtribe of the tribe Hominini that contains the *genus Homo* and all of its living and *fossil species*.

Summary

Since the discovery of *Zinjanthropus* (now *Paranthropus boisei*) at Olduvai Gorge in 1959, East Africa and the Sahel have produced the remains of a variety of Miocene and Plio-Pleistocene hominins that collectively have established that continent as the birthplace of the human tribe. At present, six genera and eleven species of australopiths (hominin subtribe Australopithecina) are known from the East Africa–Sahel regions, and two additional species are known from South Africa. The East African–Sahel materials include the very oldest australopiths: *Sahelanthropus, Orrorin,* and *Ardipithecus kadabba,* all from deposits between 5.2 and 7.0 million years of age.

The australopiths (considering now all known species) were or were becoming habitual bipeds and also were experiencing key dental modifications that took them away from apelike traits and toward those of modern humans. They were small-bodied (roughly, chimpanzee-sized) and small-brained hominins who utilized both wooded and grassy habitats and who ate a varied diet, including fibrous fruits, leaves, nuts, insects, and probably some meat. Their cranial and vocal tract anatomies and brain size suggest a lack of speech. There is evidence, however, that some australopith species *may* have made and used tools, including simple Oldowan choppers and flakes.

Why these first hominins started down the evolutionary path toward modern bipedalism is a topic for the next chapter. Nonetheless, an accumulating body of evidence suggests that this development occurred in forested or wooded habitats, not in response to life on the African savanna. Judging from the fossils presently known, the subtribe Australopithecina had disappeared from East Africa and the Sahel by about 1.3 million years ago and from South Africa by 1 million years ago.

Postscript

As shown in Tables 6.1 and 7.1, the subtribe of the australopiths is now believed to have contained quite a variety of hominin types. Splitters and lumpers (see the Postscript to Chapter 6) will always disagree about taxonomic designations, but for this book, we have presented a six-genus and thirteen-species division of the australopiths.

Do we expect that this taxonomy will stand the test of time? Not on your life. Thanks to the continuing discoveries of new forms and the reanalysis of old ones, australopith taxonomy (indeed, the taxonomy of all hominins) will always be in a state of flux. A particular set of species and genus names is useful only so long as it provides a reasonable picture of the diversity and relationships of fossil populations, and as our information base and fossil collections increase, adding new names and changing old ones is inevitable. Robert Broom's *Paranthropus crassidens* from Swartkrans is now called *P. robustus*; the Leakeys' *Zinjanthropus boisei* is now *Paranthropus boisei*; the genus name *Ardipithecus* was coined in 1995 to accommodate the Aramis fossils. Just recently, in fact, the increase in new taxon names has been dramatic. Thanks to growing numbers of paleoanthropologists, improved search techniques, and long, hot hours fossil hunting, three new australopith genera—*Sahelanthropus, Orrorin,* and *Kenyanthropus*—have been added since the turn of the twenty-first century!

Why do we bother to point this out? Mainly because we hope to recruit some of the best and brightest readers of this book into the exciting and dynamic field of paleoanthropology. The constant flow of new discoveries, new laboratory procedures, new theories and controversies (e.g., forest versus savanna development of bipedalism), and the like bears witness to the fact that there is still much work to do and much to learn before we will truly understand the origin of humankind. Without a doubt, the next several decades are going to be exciting ones for paleoanthropologists. And so, although we can't promise a life quite as romantic and adventuresome as Indiana Jones's, if you have a flair for science, a willingness to work hard in the fossil fields and/or the laboratory, and an interest in foreign travel, you just might want to consider a career spent solving the greatest whodunit of all time: the mystery of human origins.

Review Questions

1. What are the grounds for classifying the species *aethiopicus, boisei,* and *robustus* within the single genus *Paranthropus*? What do these species have in common? How do they differ from one another and, in particular, from their contemporaries in the genus *Australopithecus*?
2. Summarize and compare the evidence for bipedalism in the Miocene australopiths (*Sahelanthropus, Orrorin,* and *Ardipithecus kadabba*) and the Plio-Pleistocene species *Australopithecus anamensis* and *Australopithecus afarensis.*

3. Summarize and compare the evidence for dental modernization (especially reduction in canine size and the loss of canine–lower P3 honing) in the Miocene australopiths and the Plio-Pleistocene species *A. anamensis* and *A. afarensis*.
4. Describe the lifestyles of the australopith genera *Australopithecus* and *Paranthropus*. Be sure to include information about habitat, locomotion (i.e., the variety, if any, of locomotor patterns), diet, material culture, and evidence regarding speech.

SUGGESTED FURTHER READING

Aiello, Leslie, and Christopher Dean. *An Introduction to Human Evolutionary Anatomy.* London, Academic Press, 1990.

Conroy, Glenn. *Reconstructing Human Origins.* New York, W. W. Norton, 1997.

Johanson, Donald, and Blake Edgar. *From Lucy to Language.* New York, Simon & Schuster, 1996.

Kingdon, Jonathan. *Lowly Origin.* Princeton, Princeton University Press, 2003.

Tattersall, Ian, and Jeffrey Schwartz. *Extinct Humans.* New York, Westview Press, 2000.

Wood, Bernard, and Brian Richmond. "Human Evolution: Taxonomy and Paleobiology." *Journal of Anatomy,* 196:19–60, 2000.

INTERNET RESOURCES

"TOUMAÏ THE HUMAN ANCESTOR"

www.cnrs.fr/cw/fr/pres/compress/Toumai/Tounaigb/resumegb.html

Produced by the discoverers of the *Sahelanthropus* fossil, this site provides details of that ancient hominin from Chad.

EVOLUTION: HUMANS: ORIGINS OF HUMANKIND

www.pbs.org/wgbh/evolution/humans/humankind/a.html

Maintained by PBS, this site includes thumbnail sketches of several hominin species, including such early australopiths as *Orrorin* and *Ardipithecus.*

Orrorin tugenensis

www.modernhumanorigins.com/tugenensis.html

An anatomically detailed description of the 6-million-year-old fossils from Kenya.

BECOMING HUMAN

www.becominghuman.org

Produced by the Institute of Human Origins, this site includes a nice video presentation about the discovery of *Australopithecus afarensis* and human evolution in general.

Kenyanthropus platyops

www.modernhumanorigins.com/platyops.html

Detailed anatomical information on this new australopith from East Africa.

THE LEAKEY FOUNDATION

www.leakeyfoundation.org

This site includes bibliographical sketches of the fossil-hunting Leakey family, and describes modern research supported by the Foundation.

USEFUL SEARCH TERMS:

Ardipithecus
Australopithecus afarensis
Australopithecus anamensis
Kenyanthropus
Leakey (Louis, Mary, Richard, Meave)
Paranthropus boisei
Olduvai Gorge
Orrorin
Sahelanthropus

Chapter 7 Timeline

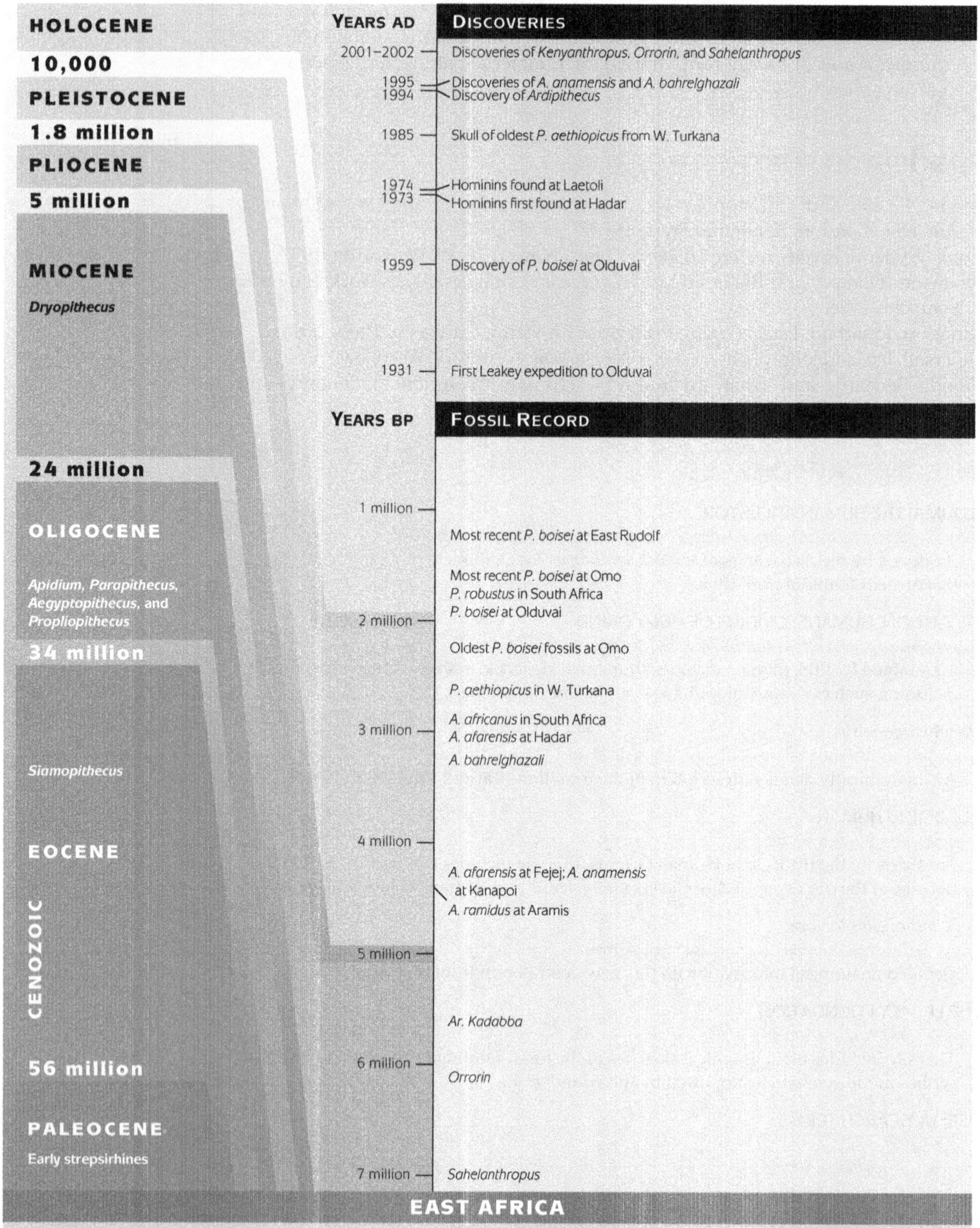

HOLOCENE
10,000
PLEISTOCENE
1.8 million
PLIOCENE
5 million
MIOCENE
Dryopithecus
24 million
OLIGOCENE
Apidium, Parapithecus, Aegyptopithecus, and *Propliopithecus*
34 million
Siamopithecus
EOCENE
CENOZOIC
56 million
PALEOCENE
Early strepsirhines

YEARS AD	DISCOVERIES
2001–2002	Discoveries of *Kenyanthropus, Orrorin,* and *Sahelanthropus*
1995	Discoveries of *A. anamensis* and *A. bahrelghazali*
1994	Discovery of *Ardipithecus*
1985	Skull of oldest *P. aethiopicus* from W. Turkana
1974	Hominins found at Laetoli
1973	Hominins first found at Hadar
1959	Discovery of *P. boisei* at Olduvai
1931	First Leakey expedition to Olduvai

YEARS BP	FOSSIL RECORD
1 million	
	Most recent *P. boisei* at East Rudolf
	Most recent *P. boisei* at Omo
	P. robustus in South Africa
	P. boisei at Olduvai
2 million	
	Oldest *P. boisei* fossils at Omo
	P. aethiopicus in W. Turkana
	A. africanus in South Africa
3 million	
	A. afarensis at Hadar
	A. bahrelghazali
4 million	
	A. afarensis at Fejej; *A. anamensis* at Kanapoi
	A. ramidus at Aramis
5 million	
	Ar. Kadabba
6 million	
	Orrorin
7 million	*Sahelanthropus*

EAST AFRICA

The story of discoveries in East Africa and the Sahel is as exciting as that of South Africa, and new discoveries are reported every year. Dating of fossil deposits is far more secure in these areas than in South Africa because there has been much volcanic activity since the early Miocene and chronometric dating is therefore possible. Many of the deposits, moreover, are very thick and span a considerable time range.

Chapter 8

East Africa: The Advent of *Homo*

An artist's conception of how early *Homo* might have looked while chipping an Oldowan tool some 2 million years ago.

Intelligence . . . is the faculty of making artificial objects . . .

Henri Bergson, 1859–1941. *L'Evolution Creatrice.*

More brain, O Lord, more brain!

George Meredith, 1828–1909. *Modern Love.*

Overview

Based on molecular evidence and the current fossil record, the tribe Hominini originated in Africa around 7 to 6 mya, during the late Miocene epoch. Despite showing a good deal of variation, the first hominins can be grouped within a single subtribe (*Australopithecina;* informally, *australopiths*). Miocene australopiths included *Sahelanthropus, Orrorin,* and *Ardipithecus kadabba.* During the early to mid Pliocene, the genera *Australopithecus* and *Kenyanthropus* were added, and the older australopith types apparently went extinct. Around 2.5 mya, for reasons that are not well understood, hominins experienced considerable extinction and speciation. The large and varied genus *Australopithecus* was lost in East Africa and the Sahel (although it survived for another 0.8 myr in South Africa), and two new genera—*Paranthropus* and *Homo*—appeared. Thus, at 2.5 mya or shortly thereafter, a new hominin subtribe, *Hominina* (informally, *hominans*) came into existence and has continued until the present day (now in a single remaining species, *Homo sapiens*). Although the evolutionary relationships between the australopiths and hominans are controversial, it does appear that some variety of *Australopithecus* was ancestral to the genus *Homo.*

Two species of the earliest hominans can be identified: *Homo habilis* (2.3 to 1.6 million years BP) and *Homo rudolfensis* (2.4 to 1.6 million years BP). Both were terrestrial bipeds (although not necessarily walking exactly like modern humans), and both had significantly larger brains than their australopith forebears. Furthermore, it appears that one or both of these "early *Homo*" species routinely made Oldowan stone tools—a development that paleoanthropologists believe signals increased meat in the diet. Early *Homo* spread from northeast to South Africa and survived until 1.6 mya. By 1.8 mya, at the latest, early *Homo* (most likely, *Homo habilis*) had given rise to *Homo erectus.*

Mini-TIMELINE

Date or Age	Fossil Discoveries or Evolutionary Events
(A) Date (years AD)	
1997	2.5-million-year-old Oldowan tools found at Gona
1994	*Homo habilis* (?) found associated with Oldowan tools at Kada Hadar
1960	Discovery of first *Homo habilis* fossils at Olduvai Gorge
(B) Age (million years BP)	
1.0–1.3	*Paranthropus* goes extinct
1.8	Oldest definite *Homo erectus* fossils
2.3 (?)–1.6	*Homo habilis* inhabits first East, then South Africa
2.4–1.6	*Homo rudolfensis* inhabits East Africa

First Evidence of the Hominans

As described in Chapters 6 and 7, the beginning of the hominin story is concerned exclusively with tales of the australopiths. Represented by six genera and thirteen species (Table 6.1), the subtribe Australopithecina enjoyed about 4.5 million years of existence in Africa without competition from more advanced hominin types (roughly 7 to 2.5 million years BP). Then, about 2.5 million years ago, a critical (for us) evolutionary development took place: One of the australopith species gave rise by cladogenesis to different sorts of creatures, ones that were bigger brained than their ancestors and definitely produced a lithic culture—that is, a culture based on the use of stone tools. Paleoanthropologists classify these new creatures as *Homo*, the first representatives of the subtribe Hominina (Table 8.1), and this chapter is devoted to their story.

The Discovery of *Homo habilis*

Recall from Chapter 7 that in 1959, Mary and Louis Leakey hit paleontological pay dirt in Bed I of Olduvai Gorge. That was the year they discovered the skull of *Zinjanthropus* (now *Paranthropus*) *boisei*, a creature that they suspected was responsible for the numerous Oldowan stone choppers and flakes also found at the site. That conclusion was short lived, however, because just the next year, a better candidate for the office of stone tool maker showed up: a hominin with a much bigger brain than *Zinjanthropus.*

Early in 1960, the Leakeys' son, Jonathan, uncovered some teeth and bone fragments of a second Bed I hominin. Although found at broadly the same stratigraphic level as *Paranthropus* (*Zinjanthropus*) *boisei* and not far away, Louis Leakey realized the bones represented a creature far closer to modern humans than *P. boisei,* with its huge molars and sagittal crest. The new fossil showed much smaller grinding

TABLE 8.1 Hominin Taxonomy II: Hominans

Taxon	Age (million years or thousand years)	First Described
Tribe Hominini (hominins)		
Subtribe Australopithecina (australopiths)*		
Genera		
Sahelanthropus		
Orrorin		
Ardipithecus		
Australopithecus		
Kenyanthropus		
Paranthropus		
Subtribe Hominina (hominans)		
Genus		
Homo		
Species *H. rudolfensis*	2.4–1.6 myr	1986, 1992
Species *H. habilis*	2.3–1.6 myr	1964
Species *H. erectus*	1.9 myr–27 (?) kyr	1892, 1944
Species *H. heidelbergensis*	850–100 kyr	1908
Species *H. neanderthalensis*	~350–27 kyr	1864
Species *H. floresiensis*	>38–18 kyr	2004
Species *H. sapiens*	195 kyr–present	1758

*See Table 6.1 and Chapters 6 and 7 for more details.

TABLE 8.2 A Partial Record of Early *Homo* Fossil Sites

Species	South African Sites	Age (million years)[a]	East African Sites	Age (million years)
Homo habilis	Sterkfontein[b]	<2.6 & >2.0	Hadar	2.3
	Swartkrans	1.8–1.5	Omo & Koobi Fora	2.0–1.8
			Olduvai Gorge	1.9–1.6
Homo rudolfensis			Uraha (Malawi)	2.4
			Omo & Koobi Fora	2.0–1.6

[a]As noted in Table 7.1, the East African sites are dated more accurately than those from South Africa.
[b]This skull is considered to be *Australopithecus* sp. by Kuman and Clarke (2000).
Sources: See sources listed in the text.

Homo rudolfensis one of the two *species* of "early *Homo*"; inhabited East Africa 2.4 to 1.6 million years ago.

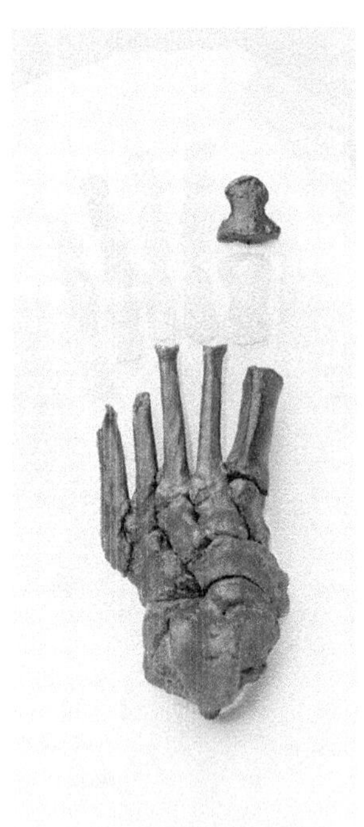

FIGURE 8.1
The *Homo habilis* foot from Olduvai Gorge (OH 8). Almost all of the toe bones (phalanges) are missing, as is part of the heel. This photograph is about one-third actual size.

teeth and relatively larger front teeth than *Zinjanthropus,* as well as a larger braincase. By 1964, a thorough analysis of the large-brained specimen, plus the discovery of additional and confirming fossils, convinced Leakey and his co-workers that the Bed I tool maker was not *P. boisei* but a previously unknown species that they named *Homo habilis* ("handy man"; L. S. B. Leakey et al., 1964; Reader, 1988).

Homo habilis remains that span a period from 2.0 to 1.6 mya have now been recovered from Olduvai Gorge, from Omo in extreme southwest Ethiopia, and from Koobi Fora in Kenya (Table 8.2 and Figure 7.1; Wood, 1992; Wood and Richmond, 2000). In addition, a 2.3-million-year-old maxilla (upper jaw) from Hadar has been assigned to this species (Kimbel et al., 1996), as have cranial remains from Sterkfontein that date somewhere between 2.0 and 2.6 mya (Hughes and Tobias, 1997; Kuman and Clarke, 2000; note that Kuman and Clarke consider this material to be *Australopithecus* sp.). Finally, a partial cranium dating 1.8 to 1.5 mya from Swartkrans may also belong to this taxon (Grine et al., 1993). A reasonable overall time range for *H. habilis* is about 2.3 to 1.6 mya (Table 8.1).

Among the most important specimens discovered thus far is a partial foot from Olduvai (OH 8; the toe bones and part of the heel are missing; see Figure 8.1), a very fragmented skull from the same locality, and a much more complete skull from Koobi Fora that dates 1.9 million years of age (KNM-ER 1813; Figure 8.2, *right*). Finally, in the mid 1980s, Donald Johanson and Tim White worked at Olduvai Gorge for four seasons and recovered a fragmentary skeleton that has been attributed to *Homo habilis* (OH 62). This find is particularly important because it provides critical information about body size, limb proportions, and other aspects of the postcranial anatomy of this species (Johanson and Shreeve, 1989).

The taxonomic validity of *Homo habilis* is now widely accepted, although this was not the case initially, as described below. Indeed, over the years, so much variable fossil material was attributed to *Homo habilis* that many scientists started to believe that it had come to contain specimens from more than one species. Splitting the *H. habilis* bone collection led to the naming of a second early hominan, ***Homo rudolfensis*** (Wood, 1992). Together, the two species are commonly referred to as "early *Homo.*"

In any event, the main characteristics of *Homo habilis* (as adjusted after the removal of the *H. rudolfensis* material) are summarized in Box 8.1. Comparisons with Boxes 6.3 and 7.3 show that *Homo habilis* may have had much in common with South Africa's *Australopithecus africanus* and East Africa's *A. afarensis.* Traditionally, researchers have concluded that body size was very similar in the three species, that all showed rather apelike limb proportions (relatively long arms and short legs), and that all showed some indication of continuing arboreal activity (the OH 8 foot may have had a partially divergent, grasping big toe; Kidd et al., 1996). (As discussed in a later section, however, certain of these conclusions have recently been challenged.) The dentition of *Homo habilis* was much more modern than that of *A. afarensis* but only marginally more so than that of *A. africanus.*

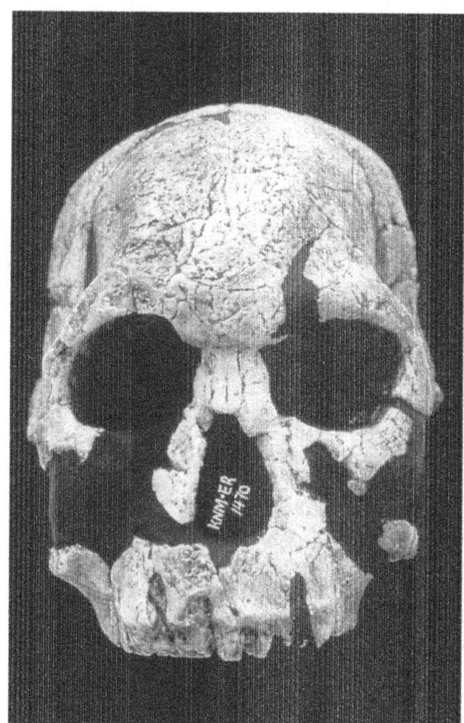

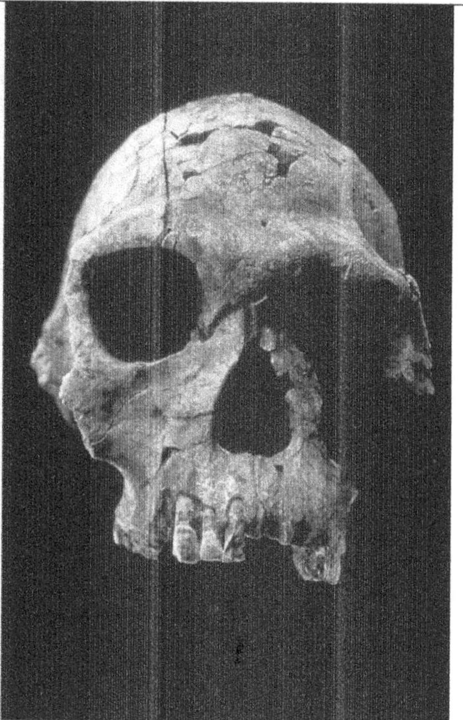

FIGURE 8.2
Homo rudolfensis (KNM-ER 1470; *left*) compared with *Homo habilis* (KNM-ER 1813; *right*). Note the differences in size of braincase between the two early *Homo* species. Both photos are about 45 percent actual size.

BOX 8.1

Characteristics of *Homo habilis*[a]

Trait	*Homo habilis*
Height[b]	F: 3.3 ft (100 cm) M: ?
Weight[b]	F: 71 lb (32 kg) M: 82 lb (37 kg) (F about 86% of M)
Brain size	612 cc mean (509–674 cc range)
Cranium	Somewhat prognathic face; incipient brow ridge; fore-shortened palate; no sagittal crest; rounded mandibular base
Dentition	Narrower lower grinding teeth than in *Homo rudolfensis*; mostly single-rooted lower premolars
Limbs[c]	Possibly, longer arms and shorter legs than modern humans; feet retaining adaptations for climbing
Locomotion	Bipedalism (probably relatively modern)
Known dates (million years BP)	2.3–1.6

[a]Mean values for anatomical measurements may change with additional fossil discoveries. For additional technical details and diagnostic traits, see Appendix 3.
[b]Estimates of height and weight will need to be recalculated if limb lengths are changed following Haeusler and McHenry (2004).
[c]Haeusler and McHenry (2004) conclude that *Homo habilis* probably had humanlike long legs but apelike long forearms.
Sources: Aiello and Dean, 1990; Wood, 1992.

TABLE 8.3 Cranial Capacities for Apes and Certain Hominin Species

Species	Range of Cranial Capacity (cc)	Average Cranial Capacity (cc)
Chimpanzees	282–500	410
Gorillas	340–752	506
Sahelanthropus tchadensis	320–380	Unknown
Australopithecus afarensis	375–540	470
Australopithecus africanus	405–515	454
Australopithecus garhi	Unknown	450
Kenyanthropus platyops	400–500	Unknown
Paranthropus robustus	476–530	Unknown
Paranthropus boisei	390–500	465
Paranthropus aethiopicus	Unknown	410
Homo habilis	509–674	612
Homo rudolfensis	752–810	781
Homo erectus	600–1,251	962
Modern humans	1,000–2,000	1,330

Note: Measurements of cranial capacity are always given in cubic centimeters (cc; a cubic centimeter equals about 0.06 in^3); the size of the brain itself is usually somewhat smaller because the cranial cavity also contains other structures. The above figures are approximate: For the two African apes, they are based on rather small samples, and in the case of the fossil groups, the samples are extremely small and may prove to be misleading. Furthermore, a recent study by Conroy et. al. (1998) suggests that cranial capacities measured using traditional techniques may well be inflated compared to those done with modern CT scans and computer imaging. For modern humans, rare extremes exceeding even the approximate range given above have been found; the average figure is based on a limited number of samples. Slight variations in these figures will be found in other authors' works.

As a general rule and within an order, species of animals with larger brains are more intelligent than those with smaller brains, but this does not hold among species of different body sizes. The significance of brain size is considered in Chapter 13. Within a species, variations in brain size are not believed to be related to intelligence among normal individuals. Fossils are attributed to *Homo habilis* and *Homo rudolfensis* following Wood (1992). West Turkana fossil KNM-WT 17000 is classified as *P. aethiopicus*.

Sources: Data from Walker et al. (1986), Tobias (1985), Aiello and Dean (1990), Brown et al. (1993), Falk et al. (2000), and other sources cited in the text.

It is immediately clear that among the primary factors differentiating *Homo habilis* from the australopiths was brain size. With an average of 612 cubic centimeters, *Homo habilis* had a bigger brain than apes and the various australopiths, but a much smaller brain than modern people or the well-established hominan ***Homo erectus*** (Table 8.3). But what do these differences say about taxonomy? Specifically, do the brain size data help us decide whether *habilis* is a hominan or an australopith?

Homo erectus *a hominin species* that inhabited much of the Old World between 1.9(?) million and at least 300,000 years BP; successor to "early *Homo*."

Classifying *Homo habilis*

Homo habilis earned neither its name nor its credentials easily. A few anthropologists preferred to identify it as an advanced type of *A. africanus* and not deserving *Homo* status at all (Le Gros Clark, 1967; J. Robinson, 1972). Some still identify it in this way (Wood and Collard, 1999a, b). Its qualifications as a distinct species have been in question from the day it was named.

Should it be called *Homo habilis* or *Australopithecus habilis?* Compared to the certified human beings of the genus *Homo* that came after, it seems scarcely human; compared to the more primitive types that preceded, its human credentials improve. This disconcerting shift of perspective always occurs when the eye runs down a series of fossils that are closely related to one another. The differences among them are often differences in degree—not in kind—and obviously become more pronounced as one takes one's examples from more widely separated time zones. The more obvious characteristics of *Homo* are comparative: an increasingly large brain, a higher forehead, a "more delicate" jaw, and longer legs. But in an evolving lineage, where do we draw the line?

The Question of Brain Size

The question of brain size continues to arise. In the 1940s, British anatomist Arthur Keith chose to draw the line marking the appearance of humanity where the brain capacity touched 750 cubic centimeters (Keith, 1949). Anything below that, according to Keith, was not human; anything above it was. (Most modern people have brains in the 1,200 to 1,600 cubic centimeter range, although smaller and larger brains regularly occur; see Table 8.3). More recently, Wilfrid Le Gros Clark put the minimum at 700 cubic centimeters (Le Gros Clark, 1955, 1959). Le Gros Clark's choice, unlike Keith's, was not arbitrary; it reflected the state of the fossil record at the time it was made: No accepted "human" skulls were known to exist with cranial capacities of less than 700 cubic centimeters. Implicit in this situation, of course, was the possibility that an apparently human specimen with a slightly smaller brain might be discovered any day.

Homo habilis laid this problem right at the scientists' doorstep. The great difficulty in deciding whether it was human lay in the fact that the type specimen from Olduvai had a brain capacity estimated to be about 657 cubic centimeters—just under Le Gros Clark's limit. Since then, five other *H. habilis* skulls have been measured by two experts: Phillip Tobias and Ralph Holloway. They came up with surprisingly uniform figures for these skulls. They range in capacity from 509 to 674 cubic centimeters and average about 612 cubic centimeters (Aiello and Dean, 1990). Too small brained for a "human"? Perhaps, but probably too large brained for a typical australopith, whose mean cranial capacity was only about 450 cubic centimeters (Table 8.3).

What is the meaning of brain size? How significant is the steady increase in cranial capacity that we find in human evolution? Large brains are found in large animals generally, and the brains of elephants and whales are very much larger than those of humans. As a general rule, among mammals, brain size can best be interpreted when it is related to body size, and a doubling of body size during the evolution of a lineage usually results in a considerable increase in brain size (see Chapter 13).

When we look at the figures in Table 8.3, therefore, we should consider the size of the animal itself. For example, the stature of *A. afarensis* varied from 3.3 to 5 feet (1 to 1.5 meters) tall, while that of modern humans varies from approximately 4.5 to over 6 feet (1.4 to 1.8 meters). The difference in relative brain size is therefore not quite as great as the table might suggest. It should not be forgotten, however, that many human populations—of pygmies, for example—fall into the range of stature for *A. afarensis* yet have brains in the region of 1,200 to over 1,400 cubic centimeters—three times as large (Coon, 1963). A consideration of stature is therefore not going to alter very seriously the significance of the figures for the hominins listed in Table 8.3. (But see the challenging questions raised by the newly discovered dwarfed species *Homo floresiensis* in the Postscript to Chapter 15.)

As it turned out, Leakey and his colleagues didn't confront any of the hard questions about the meaning of brain size when they named *Homo habilis* in 1964. In the end, in order to get their Olduvai find into *Homo,* they simply redefined our genus by lowering its "cerebral Rubicon." Down from Arthur Keith's 750 cubic centimeters and Le Gros Clark's 700 cubic centimeters, Leakey and his team proposed a lower limit of 600 cubic centimeters for the absolute brain size of any specimen to be included in *Homo* (L. S. B. Leakey et al., 1964). With the bar reset within its reach, *habilis* vaulted promptly into the genus *Homo,* and it has been there for forty years.

The old question of "Australopith or hominan?" has not gone away, however; indeed, that discussion is back in full force. But before continuing with the complexities of *habilis*'s classification, let's take a look at its contemporary, *Homo rudolfensis,* whose taxonomy is also under scrutiny.

Evidence of *Homo* at Koobi Fora

Early in the work at Koobi Fora (early 1970s), it became clear that the Lake Turkana region contained fossils of hominins other than *Paranthropus.* Over time, a number of specimens were recovered of larger-brained creatures that did not fit well into either *Australopithecus* or *Paranthropus*. One of the finest fossils carries the museum number KNM-ER 1470, and it is an almost complete cranium and face but with the skull base and jaw missing (Figure 8.2). ER 1470 combines a large face with strongly built zygomatic arches and relatively large molar teeth (much smaller than in *Paranthropus*, however; Wood, 1992). The skull is relatively lightly built, and the braincase is considerably larger than any australopith's at 752 cubic centimeters (Aiello and Dean, 1990).

As the search for fossils continued at Koobi Fora, several other specimens of relatively large-brained hominins were discovered, including the splendid skull labeled ER-1813 (Figure 8.2). But what to call the nonaustralopiths from Koobi Fora? Initially, they were lumped in with similar specimens from Olduvai Gorge and classified as *Homo habilis*. This is still the position taken by some researchers. Others argue, however, that there is too much variation in the combined Olduvai and Koobi Fora assemblage to be contained in a single species—even a species with marked sexual dimorphism in body size.

It now seems increasingly likely that *Homo habilis*, as traditionally defined, probably contained at least two species. In 1992, Bernard Wood proposed the following solution to the problem (a solution that we have adopted for this textbook): Retain the name *Homo habilis* for the Olduvai material and some of the fossils from Omo and Koobi Fora (including ER-1813), and classify ER-1470 and certain other Omo, Uraha, and Koobi Fora specimens as belonging to a new species, *Homo rudolfensis* (Wood, 1992).

If the early *Homo* fossils from Olduvai and Koobi Fora are sorted in this way, interesting differences appear between the two resulting species (compare Boxes 8.1 and 8.2). *Homo habilis* (as now narrowly defined) has the more primitive-looking skull, with some prognathism, an incipient brow ridge, and a much smaller

BOX 8.2

Characteristics of *Homo rudolfensis*[a]

Trait	*Homo rudolfensis*
Height[b] (sexes combined)	4.9 ft (150 cm) (?)
Weight[b]	F: 112 lb (51 kg) M: 132 lb (60 kg) (F about 85% of M)
Brain size (sexes combined)	781 cc mean (752–810 cc range)
Cranium	Flat face; no brow ridge; large palate; no sagittal crest; everted mandibular base
Dentition	Broader lower grinding teeth than *Homo habilis*; multirooted lower premolars
Limbs[b]	Limb proportions unknown; feet possibly more like those of later humans than was true for *H. habilis*
Locomotion	Bipedalism (probably relatively modern)
Known dates (million years BP)	2.4–1.6

[a]Mean values for anatomical measurements may change with additional fossil discoveries. For additional technical details and diagnostic traits, see Appendix 3.
[b]Estimates of height and weight will need to be recalculated if long legs were present (see Haeusler and McHenry, 2004).
Sources: Aiello and Dean, 1990; Wood, 1992.

brain (although brain size is increased by about one-third over the australopith average). Additionally, the postcranial anatomy of the newly defined *Homo habilis* includes small body size, australopithlike limb proportions (but see the discussion that follows), and adaptations of the feet for climbing—features that suggest the continuation of arboreal activities in addition to terrestrial bipedalism. On the progressive side, however, the teeth of *Homo habilis* seem more like those of later hominans than do the teeth of *Homo rudolfensis*. For its part, *Homo rudolfensis* has a larger body, a flatter face, and a larger brain than *H. habilis* (showing about a two-thirds increase in brain size over the australopith average), but these are combined with broad grinding teeth that remind one of *Paranthropus*. And while the limb proportions of *Homo rudolfensis* are currently unknown, certain features of the foot and the thigh are quite similar to those of later *Homo* species. The few pelvic remains of early *Homo* suggest that these hominans showed an almost modern form of bipedalism.

As just noted, the proper classification of *H. habilis* and *H. rudolfensis* has recently become a matter of vigorous discussion among paleoanthropologists due to a combination of new analyses and new fossil finds. In 1999, Bernard Wood—who has a long history of trying to figure out what is and is not *Homo*—and his colleague Mark Collard published detailed comparisons of *habilis* and *rudolfensis* versus the then-known australopiths and several widely accepted hominans. Based on functional analyses of six global traits (body size, body shape, locomotion, jaws and teeth, development, and brain size), these investigators concluded that *habilis* was australopithlike, rather than humanlike or intermediate, for all six measures! Regarding *rudolfensis,* the first three traits could not be compared because of a paucity of fossils, but jaws and teeth, development, and brain size were all judged to be australopithlike (Wood and Collard, 1999a, b). Wood and Collard (1999b:70) recommended that "both *H. habilis* and *H. rudolfensis* should be transferred to the genus *Australopithecus*" in order to make *Homo* once again a monophyletic genus.

In the best scientific tradition, Wood and Collard's suggestion concerning taxonomic revision for early *Homo* has set off a series of follow-up studies. A recent analysis of dental growth patterns by Christopher Dean et al. (2001) supported the proposed name changes. In contrast, a new study of absolute and relative limb lengths done by Martin Haeusler and Henry McHenry (2004) opposed the revision. Haeusler and McHenry concluded that *Homo habilis* (and probably *Homo rudolfensis,* as well) had humanlike long legs, rather than the short legs characteristic of australopiths, and may well have engaged in long-distance terrestrial travel. (Interestingly, *Homo habilis*'s upper limbs were found to have some rather apelike traits, such as quite long forearms.) As noted in Boxes 8.1 and 8.2, accepting the notion that early *Homo* experienced lengthening of the legs will force the recalculation of average heights and weights, and to date, this has not been done to our knowledge.

To further complicate matters, as part of its announcement in 2001 of the flat-faced genus *Kenyanthropus,* Meave Leakey's team suggested that based on strong resemblances, *H. rudolfensis* might best be transferred to that new taxon (M. Leakey et al., 2001). Some paleoanthropologists, including Ian Tattersall (2003), have already acted on that suggestion and now include *Kenyanthropus rudolfensis* in their hominin phylogenies. (Note that within the hominin taxonomy used in this book, both Wood and Collard's and Leakey et al.'s suggestions amount to redefining *habilis* and *rudolfensis* as australopiths, rather than hominans.)

Finally, a 1.8-million-year-old maxilla that was found recently in the little-explored western portion of Olduvai Gorge seems to bridge the morphological gap between *habilis* and *rudolfensis.* This suggests that the two never were distinct species in the first place (Blumenschine et al., 2003).

In summary, the classifications of *habilis* and *rudolfensis* as hominans are being seriously questioned by an increasing number of paleoanthropologists. In effect, this means that the boundary between the two hominin subtribes—Australopithecina and

Hominina—may change in the near future in terms of the diagnostic criteria and fossils included and excluded. It is our sense, however, that revisionists in favor of treating *habilis* and *rudolfensis* as australopiths are still in the minority, and so in this book, we have followed the tradition of regarding them as early representatives of *Homo*.

The two species of early *Homo* overlapped temporally for 700,000 years or more (Table 8.2), and at least at Koobi Fora, they overlapped geographically, as well. *Homo rudolfensis* was apparently the first to evolve and may have been strictly an East African form. Recent discoveries at the Uraha site west of Lake Malawi have set the earliest date for *Homo rudolfensis* at about 2.4 mya. *Homo habilis* ranged from Koobi Fora, Omo, and Hadar in the north to Sterkfontein and Swartkrans in the south. But what do we know about the daily lives of early *Homo?* And furthermore, what conclusions can we draw about the evolutionary relationships linking *H. habilis* and *H. rudolfensis* to the various australopiths, to each other, and to later (undoubted) hominans? It is to these two questions that we now turn our attention.

Early Hominan Lifestyles

In light of the fact that both species of early *Homo* are thought to be immediate descendants of some form or forms of australopith, it should come as no surprise that paleoanthropologists think they lived a rather australopithlike lifestyle, albeit with one or two significant differences. Like the australopiths, early *Homo* utilized a mixed bag of habitats, including lake floodplains, gallery forests, woodlands, and savanna (Blumenschine et al., 2003; Kimbel et al., 1996; Kuman and Clarke, 2000). Their primary locomotor adaptation to that mosaic environment was clearly terrestrial bipedalism, although certain apelike anatomical features suggest a somewhat nonmodern way of walking and the continuation of some amount of arboreal climbing. In particular, primitive features of the feet of *Homo habilis* (for example, a somewhat divergent big toe) have convinced some researchers that these hominans had a distinctly nonmodern gait; others are not so sure. Furthermore, while the very meager postcranial remains attributed to *H. rudolfensis* look a bit more like those of modern humans (especially a talus from Koobi Fora), the species classification for this material has been questioned (Aiello and Dean, 1990; Wood, 1992; Wood and Richmond, 2000). In all, considerably more material is needed before we can say for sure how early *Homo* moved and precisely what sorts of habitats these hominans favored.

Unfortunately, we must be satisfied with equally fuzzy conclusions about the social groups, mating patterns, and communication skills of early *Homo.* Judging from traditional body weight estimates, *H. habilis* and *H. rudolfensis* were less sexually dimorphic in size than the australopiths. This suggests that they also were less likely to have had polygynous mating systems, but more precise conclusions are impossible at present. Whether early *Homo* moved about the African landscape in family groups or troops is equally unclear, although it does seem safe to rule out orangutanlike solitary ranging, given the predator pressure the first hominans must have faced. Finally, larger brains no doubt meant more complex communication skills than those of the australopiths, but speech and language still seem to have been beyond the capabilities of early *Homo* (Wood and Collard, 1999a). This conclusion is supported by evidence that they probably retained apelike proportions of the vocal tract (including an unflexed cranial base; see Chapter 13) and also by the simple nature of the Oldowan stone tools that they are assumed to have made.

The Oldowan stone tools bring us to the evidence that, for over thirty years, most researchers have believed has provided a relatively clear behavioral dividing line between the first hominans and the australopiths: Early *Homo* (one or both forms) is thought to have made and used stone tools on a regular basis, while the australopiths were at best casual makers and users of stone tools (Schick and Toth, 1993). The oldest known stone tools have been recovered from the site of Gona, in the Hadar region of Ethiopia, and they are dated at 2.6 to 2.5 million years of age (Semaw et al., 1997).

Consisting of simple cores, whole flakes, and flaking debris (see Chapter 9), the Gona assemblage is a clear example of the Oldowan tool industry. At Gona, sharp flakes were struck off cores and then used as cutting implements, while the cores themselves apparently were used as hammerstones and multipurpose pounders. (This can be detected from the way the cores are pitted and battered.) Other ancient Oldowan assemblages have come from Omo (2.4 to 2.3 mya), the Semliki River Valley in the western Rift (2.3 mya), and, of course, Olduvai Gorge (1.9 to 1.7 mya; Panger et al., 2002).

Admittedly, absolutely conclusive proof that the various Oldowan assemblages were made by early *Homo* is still lacking, but one recent discovery was very nearly the "smoking gun" that archaeologists have been seeking. At the Kada Hadar site in Ethiopia, an upper jaw of early *Homo* (most likely *H. habilis*) was found "closely associated" with 2.3-million-year-old Oldowan tools (Kimbel et al; 1996:550). Pending the discovery of a skeleton with tool in hand, we find this sort of sole association of early *Homo* with Oldowan tools to be convincing, and so for the remainder of this book, we treat the first hominans as stone tool makers without further qualifying remarks.

Early *Homo* may not have been alone in their stone-knapping habits, however. New discoveries have added to a growing body of evidence that one or more species of australopiths may also have made and used Oldowan tools. Besides the anatomical and archaeological evidence suggesting a link between *Paranthropus* and stone industries at Sterkfontein and Swartkrans (see Chapter 6), Ethiopia's Bouri region has yielded 2.5-million-year-old mammal bones that show both percussion marks and stone tool cut marks that were *possibly* made by *Australopithecus garhi* (de Heinzelin et al., 1999). The old idea that stone technology serves as a clear behavioral boundary between the australopiths and hominans may well be on the way out.

It appears that all of the early stone-knapping hominins, whether australopiths or hominans, probably used Oldowan tools primarily to process meat (Kimbel et al., 1996). Furthermore, the *regular* production of Oldowan choppers and flakes by early *Homo* is thought to signal a significant increase in the amount of meat in their diet (Schick and Toth, 1993). Whether meat was obtained primarily through active hunting or scavenging from carnivore kills and other carcasses is unclear, but the latter seems most likely (Potts, 1996). Oldowan choppers were used to batter open bones so the marrow could be consumed, and sharp-edged flakes were used for dismembering carcasses and cutting flesh away from bone. As noted in the next chapter, this dietary shift toward carnivory could have had important effects on encephalization in early *Homo*.

Beyond these remarks, only one other comment concerning the diet of early *Homo* is possible. Namely, the relatively larger, multirooted grinding teeth of *Homo rudolfensis* suggest that members of that species ate more tough and hard food items (nuts, roots, seeds, etc.) than did *Homo habilis*.

Early Hominin Phylogenies

Adding the two early *Homo* species to all of the australopiths described in Chapters 6 and 7, we now have a grand total of fifteen hominin varieties to consider. As such, it is high time to try to make some phylogenetic sense of them. This is easier said than done, however, and in reality, researchers are all over the board with regard to their reconstructions of hominin evolution. This is due, in part, to the variety in traits that experts emphasize as they try to identify ancestor–descendant relationships. Moreover, while the hominin fossil record is impressive and continues to grow by leaps and bounds, it is still actually quite incomplete, and thus, the intermediate forms between many fossil species and genera are still "missing links." Given this state of affairs, we have chosen to present three phylogenies from recent publications and then to see what consensus, if any, can be drawn from them.

Figure 8.3 presents phylogenetic schemes by anthropologists Ian Tattersall (American Museum of Natural History) and Jonathan Kingdon (Oxford University).

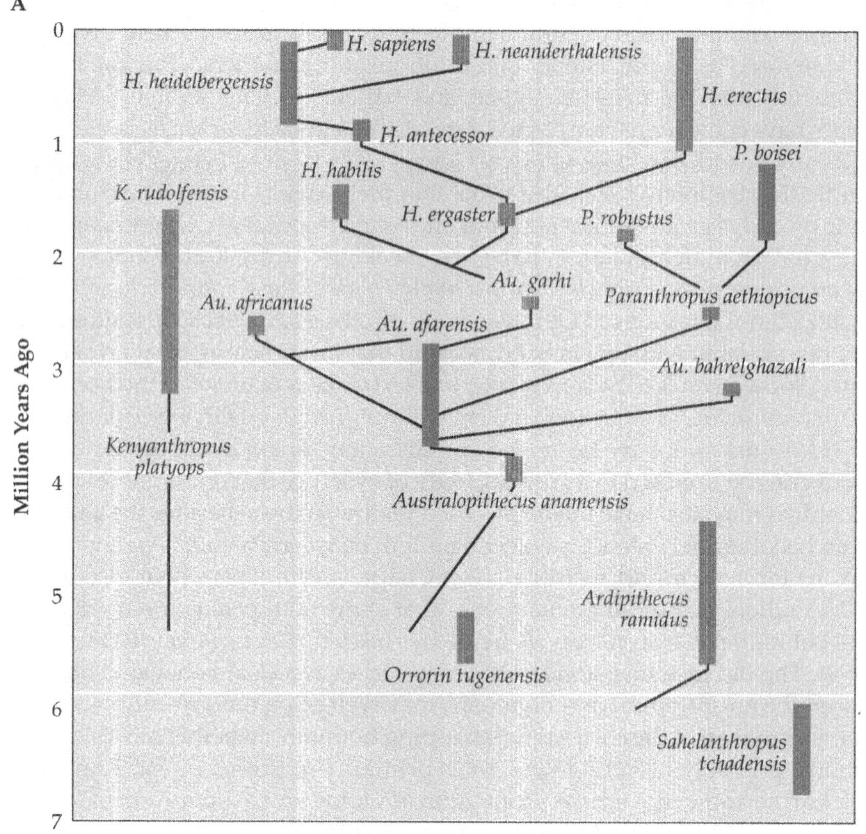

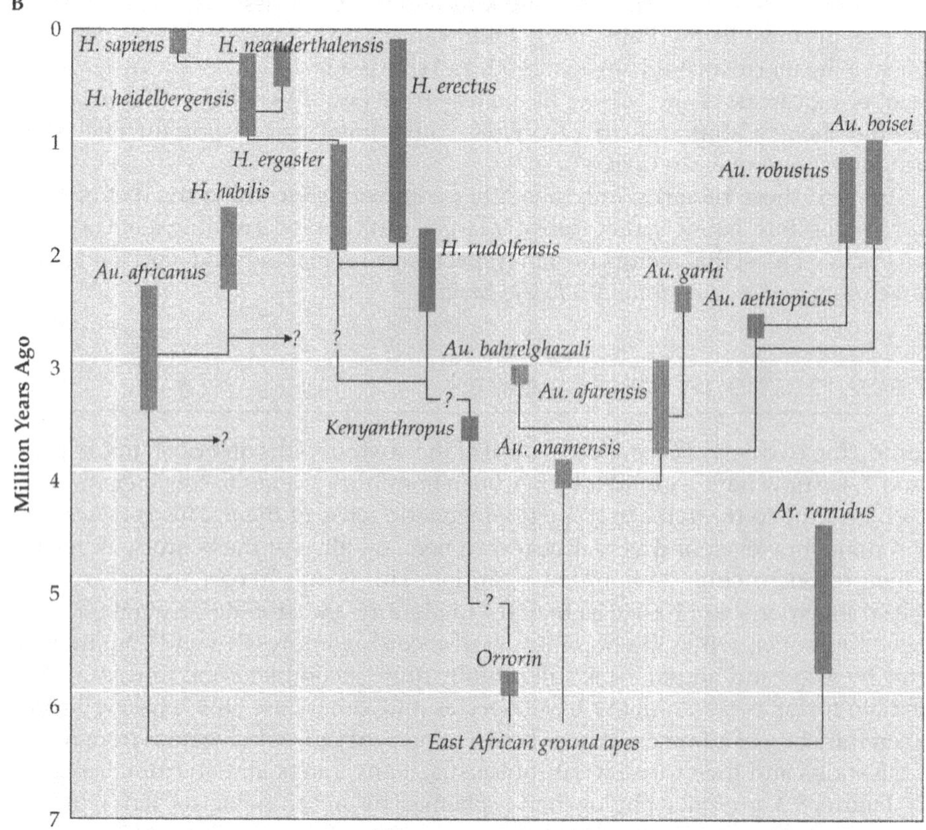

FIGURE 8.3
Two recent phylogenies of the hominins. Scheme A is taken from Tattersall (2003), and scheme B is from Kingdon (2003). Tattersall's abbreviations include *Au.* = *Australopithecus; P.* = *Paranthropus; K.* = *Kenyanthropus; H.* = *Homo.* Kingdon's phylogeny includes a mix of genus names without species and species names without genera, but based on the text of this and previous chapters, these can easily be deciphered. "Lucy," in Kingdon's scheme, represents *Australopithecus afarensis.* Note that both of these evolutionary trees were published before the announcement of *Ardipithecus kadabba* as a species. For our purposes, the lower (oldest) end of the *Ardipithecus* line in both trees can be taken as representing *Ar. kadabba.*

Sources: (a) Based on Ian Tattersall (p. 26), "Once We Were Not Alone." *Scientific American* (Special Edition), 13(2):20–27, 2003. Copyright by Ian Tattersall, American Museum of Natural History. (b) Based on Jonathan Kingdon (p. 232), *Lowly Origin.* Princeton, Princeton University Press, 2003. Copyright Princeton U. Press.

Both phylogenies were published before the 2004 naming of *Ardipithecus kadabba* as a species, and therefore, neither includes that taxon. Likewise, neither scheme includes the brand-new hominan species *Homo floresiensis* (see Chapter 15, Postscript). Both schemes do include the *Ardipithecus* lineage, however, and *Ar. kadabba* can be envisioned as the oldest member of that evolutionary line. Otherwise, both Tattersall and Kingdon have plotted virtually all known hominin taxa in hypothesized ancestor–descendant relationships. (Note that Kingdon considers *Sahelanthropus* to have been an ape, and therefore, that taxon is missing from his evolutionary tree.)

Reviewing Tattersall's (2003) phylogeny, we find the following interpretations of the hominin fossil record, as it is currently known:

- None of the Miocene species is clearly ancestral to later australopiths.
- *Australopithecus afarensis* is identified as the immediate ancestor of the *Paranthropus* subclade *and* as a species on the direct line to *Homo* (via other australopiths).
- The last australopith ancestor of hominans was probably *Australopithecus garhi.*
- Although *Homo habilis* qualifies as a hominan, *rudolfensis* is identified as an australopith (?) and part of the *Kenyanthropus* subclade, viewed here as a deadend.
- *Paranthropus* went extinct without descendants.
- *Homo* experienced diversification after its appearance but today is represented only by *H. sapiens.*

Turning to Kingdon's (2003) phylogeny—which, as described in Chapter 7, is derived from a hypothetical ancestral "East African ground ape"—the following interpretations are found:

- Hominans and most of the australopiths probably descended from different Miocene ancestors. (*Orrorin* was ancestral to the ultimately hominan clade, while a different and unknown ancestor gave rise to many of the *Australopithecus* and all of the *Paranthropus* species.)
- *Australopithecus anamensis, A. afarensis, A. bahrelghazali, A. garhi,* and the three *Paranthropus* species (here transferred to the genus *Australopithecus*) are all identified as members of a deadend australopith subclade and thus disconnected from the hominan line.
- *Australopithecus africanus* is identified as the ancestor of *Homo habilis,* but the latter species is viewed as a deadend.
- *Kenyanthropus* may have been on the direct line to both *Homo rudolfensis* and all undoubted hominans.
- After its origin, *Homo* experienced diversification but today is represented only by *H. sapiens.*

And finally, the hominin phylogeny published in 2003 by philosopher Camilo Cela-Conde (Universitat de las Islas Baleares, Spain) and geneticist Francisco Ayala (University of California, Irvine) shows yet another arrangement and some different names (Cela-Conde and Ayala, 2003; Figure 8.4):

- *Sahelanthropus* is identified as a basal hominin, but its relationship to later members of the tribe is unknown.
- A lineage identified as *Praeanthropus,* which includes several species called *Australopithecus* by other workers, is envisioned as occupying a central position in hominin evolution. (It is grounded in the Miocene species *Praeanthropus tugenensis* [called *Orrorin tugenensis* by others] and identified as ancestral, at various times, to a deadend *Ardipithecus* subclade, a deadend *Australopithecus* subclade [which includes species classified by others as *Paranthropus*], and a *Homo* subclade.)
- The *Homo* subclade begins with *H. platyops* (classified by other workers as *Kenyanthropus*), ends with *H. sapiens,* and includes (among other species) both *H. habilis* and *H. rudolfensis.*

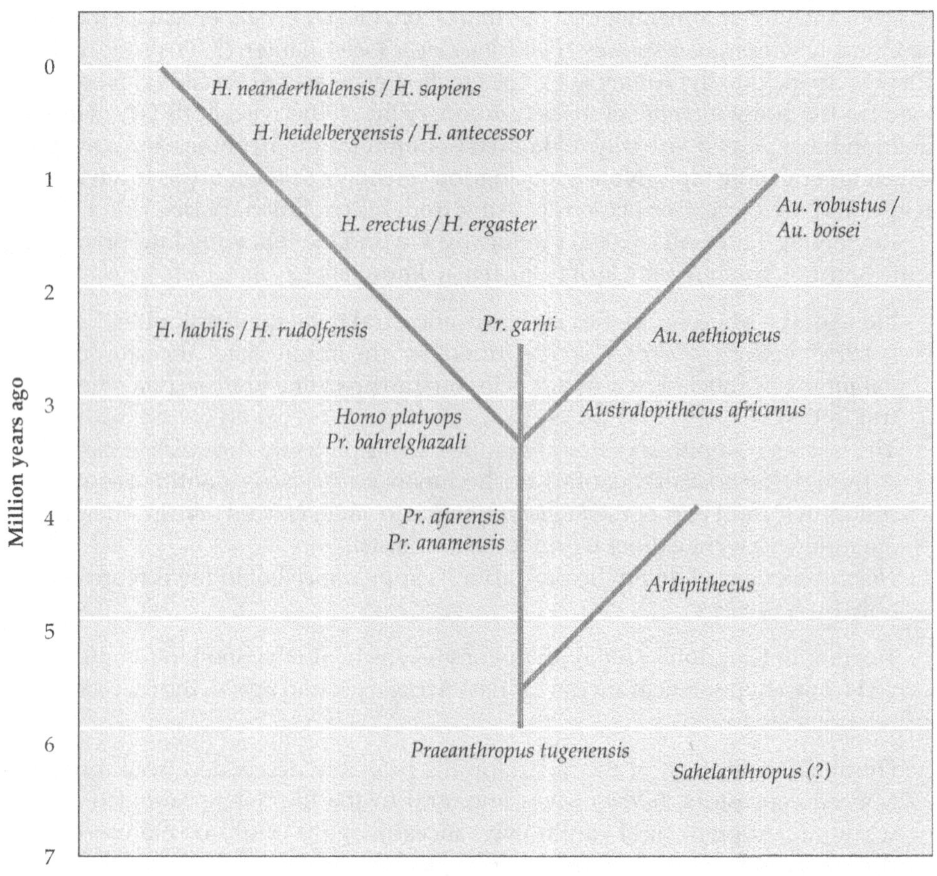

FIGURE 8.4

Hominim phylogeny redrawn from Cela-Conde and Ayala (2003). In this scheme, only four genus names are used, and several species are transferred from their traditional genera. A new genus called *Praeanthropus* is shown, containing four species called *Australopithecus* elsewhere plus the Kenyan genus called *Orrorin* elsewhere. The three species called *Paranthropus* elsewhere are here renamed *Australopithecus*. The genus called *Kenyanthropus* elsewhere is here included in *Homo*. Finally, as in the schemes shown in Figure 8.3, the base of Cela-Conde and Ayala's *Ardipithecus* branch can be regarded as *Ar. kadabba* and the top as *Ar. ramidus*.

Source: Based on Camilo Cela-Conde and Francisco Ayala (p. 7687), "Genea of the Human Lineage." *Proceedings of the National Academy of Sciences*, 100:7684–7689, 2003. Copyright by Francisco Ayala, Dept. of Ecology and Evolutionary Biology, University of California, Irvine.

In their use of the taxon *Praeanthropus* (a name that has been around for a half century but is rarely used), Cela-Conde and Ayala (2003) are in agreement with Senut et al. (2001), the discoverers of *Orrorin*. Senut and her colleagues prefer to keep *Orrorin* in its own genus, however, while viewing it as definitely ancestral to *Praeanthropus*.

Remember that these three phylogenies were picked for discussion solely because they were recently published and therefore include all known hominin species (with the exceptions of *Ardipithecus kadabba* and *Homo floresiensis*) and because they demonstrate the wide range of plausible interpretations. Given that caveat, what common threads can we find running through these evolutionary schemes? In two of the three, *Orrorin* (or *Praeanthropus*) *tugenensis* is identified as the Miocene ancestor of the line that ultimately gave rise to *Homo*. Similarly, two phylogenies identify *Australopithecus afarensis* as the immediate ancestor of the megadont subclade that included *robustus, boisei,* and *aethiopicus*—a subclade that all three schemes interpret as going extinct without descendants. And finally, *Australopithecus* (or *Praeanthropus*) *garhi* is seen as occupying or being close to occupying an ancestral position to *Homo* in two phylogenies, but it is on a definite side branch in the third.

For what it is worth, the authors of this book favor Tattersall's (2003) phylogeny, or something like it, over the other two. Regardless, all three have interesting and heuristically valuable features, and all will change as new fossils are discovered and old ones are reanalyzed. Reassuringly, despite their differences in names and particular ancestor–descendant arrangements, all modern phylogenies (the three discussed here plus others) can be distilled into the same limited set of major conclusions:

- Hominins originated in Africa during the late Miocene epoch.
- One or more of the Miocene species gave rise to the Plio-Pleistocene australopiths, who diversified strongly.
- The australopiths went extinct by about 1 mya, but not before some form (of *Australopithecus,* most workers would say) had given rise to *Homo.*

For the moment, this is the best we can do to unravel the first 5 million years or so of hominin evolution. Each year brings new breakthroughs, however, and bit by bit, our ancestors' true phylogenetic relations undoubtedly will emerge.

Summary

Around 2.5 million years ago, for reasons that are not well understood (but see the Postscript to Chapter 9), the tribe Hominini experienced a significant evolutionary shake-up: The last East African representatives of the once diverse genus *Australopithecus* died out and two new genera appeared, *Paranthropus* and *Homo.* The latter marked the origin of the subtribe Hominina. Shortly after its evolutionary appearance, *Homo* was present in at least two forms, *H. habilis* and *H. rudolfensis,* both showing relatively modern bipedalism and one or both making Oldowan stone tools. With significantly larger brains than the australopiths, the two early *Homo* species were undoubtedly somewhat smarter than their predecessors and probably had more complex communication systems, although it seems unlikely that they had speech and language. Stone tool manufacture and use probably points to more meat in the early hominans' diet, but anthropologists are undecided about how additional meat was obtained (scavenging or active hunting?).

In any event, along with the *Paranthropus* forms (with which early *Homo* had a long temporal overlap and even spatial overlap, at some sites), the first hominans haunted the gallery forests, woodlands, and savannas of both East and South Africa for very nearly a million years. And although the early *Homo* species were not quite at the point where most anthropologists are comfortable calling them "human" (admittedly, this is a matter of taste; there are no established criteria for the use of that term), one of them (probably *H. habilis*) gave rise to a species that clearly deserves that label: *Homo erectus.*

Postscript

In the woodlands and savannas of Africa, the australopiths rode the crest of hominin evolution for about 4.5 million years. Various genera came and went; *Sahelanthropus* and *Orrorin* were probably extinct by the end of the Miocene, and *Ardipithecus* likely disappeared soon thereafter. *Kenyanthropus* is thought by some anthropologists to have left descendants (see preceding discussion), but the megadont subclade of the

Paranthropus species clearly did not. Most researchers conclude that it was the genus *Australopithecus* that happened to give rise near the end of the Pliocene to more humanlike creatures (hominans) of the genus *Homo.* Many of the genes we carry about today were inherited from those *Australopithecus* forebears.

But how do scientists decide that early *Homo*—*H. habilis* and *H. rudolfensis*—were members of our genus and not simply advanced australopiths? What derived traits do these species share with later varieties of *Homo* that mark the genus boundary? As it turns out, this is not an easy question, and the answer has become more complex as the fossil record around the Plio-Pleistocene dividing line has become better known. One trait stands out above all others, of course, and that is *Homo's* increased brain size. A convenient (but arbitrary) dividing line appears to be about 600 cubic centimeters: *Homo* is above that figure and the australopiths below. In addition, thanks to modern cladistic analyses, we can expand the defining criteria for *Homo* using the following list (traits 2 to 9 are taken from Wood, 1992). Compared to the australopiths, *Homo* shows the following:

1. larger brain (roughly 600 cubic centimeters and up)
2. thicker bones of the braincase
3. reduced postorbital constriction (narrowing of the skull at the temples)
4. occipital bone that makes an increased contribution to the cranial sagittal arc length
5. higher cranial vault
6. foramen magnum farther forward
7. flatter lower face
8. narrowed tooth crowns (especially the lower premolars)
9. shorter molar toothrow

Using only this list of traits—all cranial and dental—*habilis* and *rudolfensis* seem clearly to be hominans (Wood, 1992). (It should be noted, however, that while the average brain size for *H. habilis* is 612 cubic centimeters, some individual crania fall below 600 cubic centimeters [Aiello and Dean, 1990].) Recently, however, another very important criterion has been emphasized for including a variety of species within the same genus: shared adaptive strategy. Rethinking his 1992 conclusions, Bernard Wood (working with Mark Collard) has recently decided that the developmental schedule, overall anatomical adaptations, and reconstructed habitat use and diet of *habilis* and *rudolfensis* indicate an australopithlike adaptive strategy: relatively rapid maturation and a combination of terrestrial bipedalism and arboreal climbing in search of a mechanically demanding diet (Wood and Collard, 1999b). Consequently, Wood now favors transferring *habilis* and *rudolfensis* to the genus *Australopithecus.*

Interestingly, a second pair of researchers, Cela-Conde and Ayala (2003), recently reached exactly the opposite taxonomic conclusion based on their analysis of shared adaptive strategy. Concluding that *habilis* and *rudolfensis* were "early forms of the lineage that adapted to the savanna by means of a nonspecialized diet, eventually developing lithic tools for scavenging and hunting purposes" (2003: 7687), Cela-Conde and Ayala left both species in the genus *Homo.*

As noted in the text, the authors of this book favor the second position. The last word on the australopith–hominan boundary has not been written, however.

Review Questions

1. Describe the anatomical traits of *Homo habilis* and *Homo rudolfensis.* How do these species of early *Homo* differ physically from their *Australopithecus* ancestors?
2. Describe the behavioral traits (group type, mating system, diet, lithic culture) of early *Homo.* Compare these traits with similar information for *Australopithecus* and *Paranthropus.*

3. Describe the possible evolutionary relations of the early *Homo* species. Which australopith type(s) do you think gave rise to them, and which early hominan variety do you think gave rise to *Homo erectus?*
4. Discuss whether or not the earliest hominans (or even the australopiths) should be called "humans." What criteria would you establish for the use of this term?

SUGGESTED FURTHER READING

Cela-Conde, Camilo, and Francisco Ayala. "Genera of the Human Lineage." *Proceedings of the National Academy of Sciences,* 100:7684–7689, 2003.

Johanson, Donald, and Blake Edgar. *From Lucy to Language.* New York, Simon & Schuster, 1996.

Tattersall, Ian. "Once We Were Not Alone." *Scientific American* (Special Edition), 13(2):20–27, 2003.

Wood, Bernard. "Origin and Evolution of the Genus *Homo.*" *Nature,* 355:783–790, 1992.

Wood, Bernard, and Mark Collard. "The Human Genus." *Science,* 284:65–71, 1999.

INTERNET RESOURCES

Homo habilis
www.mnh.si.edu/anthro/humanorigins/ha/hab.html
Useful descriptions and excellent illustrations of several key specimens.

ARCHAEOLOGY.INFO: *Homo habilis*
www.archaeologyinfo.com/homohabilis.htm
This site provides a detailed anatomical description of this early *Homo* species.

ARCHAEOLOGY.INFO: *Homo rudolfensis*
www.archaeologyinfo.com/homorudolfensis.htm
Matching the site for *H. habilis,* this web site gives details about the anatomy and classification of *Homo rudolfensis.*

ORIGINSNET: OLDOWAN ERA
www.originsnet.org/eraold.html
This site provides a listing of archaeological locales that have produced Oldowan tools. Also included are descriptions and photographs of various Oldowan styles.

HUMAN ANCESTORS HALL: EARLY HUMAN PHYLOGENY
www.mnh.si.edu/anthro/humanorigins/ha/a_tree.html
There are numerous evolutionary trees for hominins available on the web. This scheme is from the Smithsonian Institution.

USEFUL SEARCH TERMS:

"early Homo"
fossil hominans
genus Homo
Homo habilis
Homo rudolfensis
Lower Paleolithic
Oldowan tools

Chapter 8 Timeline

	Years AD	Discoveries
HOLOCENE	1997	2.5-million-year-old Oldowan tools discovered at Gona
10,000	1995	2.4-million-year-old *Homo rudolfensis* jaw discovered at Uraha
PLEISTOCENE	1994	*Homo habilis* found associated with Oldowan tools at Kada Hadar
1.8 million	1969	First Koobi Fora expedition
PLIOCENE	1967	First Omo expedition
5 million	1960	Discovery of first *Homo habilis* fossils at Olduvai Gorge
MIOCENE *Dryopithecus*	1931	First Leakey expedition to Olduvai Gorge

	Years BP	Fossil Record
24 million		
OLIGOCENE *Apidium, Parapithecus, Aegyptopithecus, and Propliopithecus*	1 million – 1.3 million	Most recent *Paranthropus* fossils at Swartkrans and Koobi Fora
34 million	1.6 million	Most recent *Homo habilis* fossils at Olduvai Gorge; most recent *H. rudolfensis* fossils from East Africa
Siamopithecus	2 million	*Homo habilis* at Sterkfontein
EOCENE	2.3 million	*Homo habilis* fossil at Hadar
CENOZOIC	2.4 million	Oldest *Homo rudolfensis* remains at Uraha
56 million	3 million	
PALEOCENE Early strepsirhines	4 million	
	5 million	
	6 million	

THE ADVENT OF *HOMO*

The earliest hominans, members of the genus *Homo*, have been recovered from sites in Northeast and East Africa. At least one variety of early *Homo*, *H. habilis*, also inhabited South Africa around 2 million years ago.

Chapter 9

The Evolution of Hominin Behavior

Footprints from Laetoli, Tanzania, dated at 3.6 million years old, attest to the bipedalism of *Australopithecus afarensis.*

As unto the bow the cord is,
So unto the man is woman;
Though she bends him, she obeys him,
Though she draws him, yet she follows;
Useless each without the other!

Henry Wadsworth Longfellow, 1807–1882, *The Song of Hiawatha*, x.

Overview

Working with fossils and artifacts and with information about the behavior of modern humans and nonhuman primates, anthropologists attempt to reconstruct the evolution of hominins' lifestyles. This chapter describes the current state of such reconstructions and focuses on three primary topics: the selection pressures that favored the evolution of bipedalism; the nature and use of early stone tools; and the likely socioecology of early hominins. With regard to the first topic, several hypotheses are reviewed, including those linking bipedalism with tool and weapon use, energy efficiency, body temperature regulation, life in variable habitats, reproductive success, wading-foraging, and descent from squat-feeding apes. Furthermore, the secondary links between bipedalism and childbirth patterns and bipedalism and canine tooth morphology are described. The bipedalism sections are followed by a discussion of the nature and probable use of Oldowan choppers and flakes and a look at early hominins' probable ranging and subsistence patterns.

Hominin Characteristics

In the last three chapters, we have introduced a multitude of Miocene and Plio-Pleistocene australopiths, as well as the two earliest species of hominans: *Homo habilis* and *Homo rudolfensis.* The various descriptions have tended to focus on the hard facts of each species' anatomical credentials for classification as hominins—primarily, evidence of habitual bipedalism and canine reduction—with little space given to explaining why and under what circumstances those anatomical features evolved. Now, it is time to go back and fill in the theoretical background for the first stages of hominin evolution. As will become apparent, providing clear answers to *how* and *why* questions about humans' evolutionary past is often quite a challenge.

As we have seen, hominins are characterized by a rather distinctive set of evolving traits, including habitual bipedalism, canine reduction (shortening and blunting), brain enlargement, speech and language, and technology (i.e., the development of material culture, especially tools). While the fossil record makes it clear that these traits evolved individually and in a mosaic fashion, rather than as a monolithic unit—bipedalism and canine reduction appearing early; brain enlargement, speech and language, and complex tools later—it is nonetheless true that they were intricately interrelated and variously set limits on or facilitated the development of one another.

Since the mid nineteenth century, scientists have theorized about the course of hominin evolution, developing sometimes elaborate hypotheses about the environmental conditions that selected for our package of traits and the sequence of trait development. Here, we will focus primarily on relatively recent hypotheses about the advent of bipedalism, canine reduction, and stone tool technology. Discussions of the evolution of human society and our enlarged brains will be provided later.

Before we begin, however, a cautionary note is in order: It is important to remember that all evolutionary speculations are in fact *hypotheses*, useful for stimulating thought and research but requiring further scrutiny. Simply sounding plausible does not make an evolutionary explanation true. Only extensive testing will enable paleoanthropologists to reject some of the following ideas and to give increased credence to others.

Bipedal Locomotion

In the Beginning

The fossil and molecular data agree that hominins diverged from apes sometime between 5 and 7 million years ago (Table 4.2). Although the exact identity of our ape forebears remains to be discovered, our own postcranial anatomy—and more especially, that of the australopiths and early hominans—provides clear evidence that those ancestral apes were arboreal creatures that engaged in arm-swinging and arm-hanging, as well as quadrupedal climbing. If modern chimpanzees and bonobos are accurate models, our ape ancestors were rather generalized in locomotion, food tastes, and habitat use and lived in or near the mosaic environment of the forest–woodland-savanna **ecotone.**

Ecotone an area where two or more ecological zones meet.

As ecotone dwellers, our ape ancestors were faced with an ever-changing (and ever-challenging) mix of resources and opportunities. Food sources—both arboreal and terrestrial—changed seasonally, annually, and across the millennia. Predator pressures waxed and waned, as did the opportunities and need for tool use. During the Miocene and Pliocene epochs, African forests shrank in size and grasslands showed significant expansion (Potts, 1996), and we can imagine our ape ancestors, particularly those living near the forest edge, coming to the ground on a regular basis to forage and travel, just as chimpanzees do today. At some point, more or less continuous ground living and bipedalism made survival and reproductive sense, and individuals with large or small adaptations for terrestrial living–feeding–moving were favored.

Undoubtedly, the transitions from tree living to ground living and from quadrupedalism to bipedalism were gradual rather than abrupt. Old adaptations for arboreality were slow to disappear, as shown by australopith anatomy. Nonetheless, for reasons that are only beginning to become clear, natural selection acting on individuals' variations and population differences ultimately produced recognizable hominins. One or more of the following scenarios may help us understand how and why that transformation took place.

Tool Use and Bipedalism

In his 1871 book *The Descent of Man,* Charles Darwin speculated that bipedalism must have evolved rather quickly among protohominins after they began to live on the ground. The change from quadrupedalism to an upright posture, which involved our ancestors' feet being "rendered flat, and the great toe [losing] the power of prehension," then had the important ripple effect of making object manipulation and tool use possible. After all, Darwin noted, "The hands and arms could hardly have become perfect enough to have manufactured weapons, or to have hurled stones and spears with a true aim, as long as they were habitually used for locomotion" (Darwin, 1871/1981: 141). Darwin further envisioned a positive feedback loop ultimately developing between bipedalism and tool use, with increased sophistication in one leading to progress in the other. Thus, considering the entire intertwined history of posture and manual dexterity, "The free use of the arms and hands [was] partly the cause and partly the result of man's erect posture" (Darwin, 1871/1981:144).

In the 1960s and 1970s, American anthropologist Sherwood Washburn reached the same conclusion as Darwin concerning a posture-and-tool use feedback loop during the earliest stages of hominin evolution. However, informed by a decade of data on wild chimpanzee material culture, Washburn put more emphasis on ape tool use as the antecedent behavior (Washburn, 1960; Washburn and Moore, 1974). In his view, "[In] many populations of apes over some millions of years minimal tool-use was present. In some of these populations the carrying of tools and the products of tool-use became so important that selection favored those groups of apes in which bipedal locomotion was most efficient" (Washburn and Moore, 1974: 122). For Washburn, the argument had become primarily one of tools first and bipedalism second.

But today, over a century after Darwin's book and four decades after Washburn's paper, it is still hard to know what to make of the tools–bipedalism connection. As we have seen from the fossils of *Australopithecus anamensis*, habitual bipedalism can be demonstrated clearly from about 4.2 mya, and the evidence of earlier bipedalism by *Sahelanthropus*, *Orrorin*, and *Ardipithecus* is strongly suggestive. With their ape-sized brains and hands at least as dexterous as those of modern apes, it seems possible that there was some degree of tool use by the various australopiths. Modern chimps, however, show us not only that apes can be tool users, but also that it's possible to be an occasional tool user and remain a quadruped. Therefore, chimp-type tool use might or might not have been sufficient to select for habitual bipedalism in the protohominins. A follow-up question then becomes, What about stone tool manufacture and use? Here the answer seems easier: Because the clear appearance of bipedalism predates the oldest stone tools by at least 1.7 million years, stone tool technology can be confidently ruled out as the stimulus for bipedalism.

In summary, the tools-and-bipedalism question remains something of a riddle. However, because the earliest hominins do not appear to have exceeded a chimpanzee level of technology, Washburn's (1960) argument that tool use was the trigger for locomotor change remains unconvincing.

Energy Efficiency and Bipedalism

A second theory about the origin of hominin bipedalism is the notion that it was favored by selection because it was more energy efficient than the terrestrial quadrupedalism of our last ape ancestor. The energy efficiency of different locomotor patterns is usually measured by standardized oxygen consumption. Modern humans show the greatest energy efficiency when they are walking at a moderate pace; indeed, our walking bipedalism is slightly more efficient than an average mammal's ambling along quadrupedally at the same speed. (We are not very efficient runners, however, using about twice as much energy as a running quadrupedal mammal of the same body size. This fact suggests that if energy efficiency played a role, bipedalism probably evolved to allow us to walk, not run [Steudel, 1996].)

But, of course, hominins descended not from an "average quadrupedal mammal" but from a quadrupedal ape, and so comparisons with living apes should provide even more specific clues to the evolution of our bipedalism. Energy studies of chimpanzees have shown that these apes consume oxygen at the same rate whether they are moving bipedally or quadrupedally. Regardless of how they are moving, however, chimps' energy efficiency compares poorly with that of other (equivalently sized) quadrupeds. Therefore, since bipedal humans have a slight energy edge on the average nonprimate quadruped, there is no doubt that human walking is *significantly* more efficient than chimpanzee quadrupedalism (Steudel, 1996).

Results such as these have convinced several researchers that selection for energy-efficient walking was probably an important factor in the evolution of hominin bipedalism (e.g., Rodman and McHenry, 1980), the main idea being that our ancestors were moving long distances each day as they traveled between widely separated food sources scattered throughout the forest–woodland–savanna ecotone. Primatologist Lynne Isbell and her colleague Truman Young have argued that faced with Miocene–Pliocene forest shrinkage and patchy food distribution, the earliest hominins had to evolve either energy-efficient locomotor abilities or smaller group sizes. Smaller groups (with fewer mouths to feed and thus a reduced need for travel to find the necessary food) would have been at a disadvantage in intergroup competition, however, and our ancestors opted for energy-efficient movement. Bipedalism allowed them to maintain large group size, move rapidly and with minimal energy expenditure between distant food patches, and then drive away rival foragers once they got there (Isbell and Young, 1996).

Not everyone is convinced, however. Karen Steudel of the University of Wisconsin argues that the *earliest* hominin bipeds—with their apelike bodies and perhaps an inability to fully extend the leg past the hip—would not have been particularly energy efficient. She can see natural selection improving efficiency once the transition to routine bipedalism had been made, but she rejects the notion that efficiency triggered that transition (Steudel, 1996).

And so, anthropologists are presently split on the question of energy efficiency as a selection pressure for the evolution of hominin bipedalism (see also Leonard and Robertson, 2001; Steudel-Numbers, 2001). Even if proponents of the efficiency model prove to be right, however, it is possible that other factors may also have been at work selecting for upright walking, including the need for body temperature regulation.

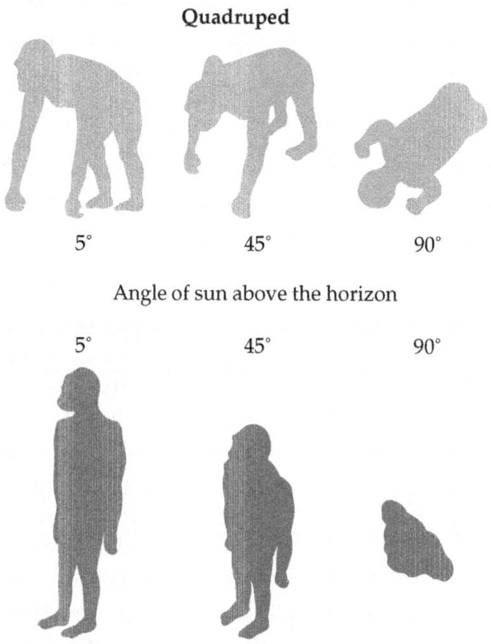

FIGURE 9.1 Models of hypothetical early hominins show how much body surface is exposed to direct solar radiation by quadrupeds (*top*) versus bipeds (*bottom*). From left to right, the sun is low on the horizon, 45 degrees above the horizon, and directly overhead. Note the small amount of body surface exposed by a biped at midday.

Body Temperature and Bipedalism

Certain hypotheses explaining the evolution of hominin bipedalism are more dependent than others on the traditional view that it occurred on the sun-drenched African savanna. One interesting savanna-based scenario is the product of British physiologist Peter Wheeler, who has delved into the connection between body temperature and bipedalism (Wheeler, 1991a, 1991b, 1993). As anyone who has walked across the African plains knows, one of the most formidable problems facing a diurnal primate living on the savanna is regulating its body temperature. Overexposure to the rays of the equatorial sun can build up a dangerous heat load, and thus we might expect that savanna-dwelling early hominins evolved mechanisms to prevent excessive heat buildup and/or to rapidly dissipate body heat once it had accumulated. Wheeler has looked into this problem, and he is convinced that the solution may provide clues to the evolution of bipedalism.

Two key variables affect the accumulation of heat from direct solar radiation: the amount of body surface a creature has exposed to the sun's rays and the intensity (or heat) of those rays. Using scale models of australopiths in various postures (Figure 9.1), Wheeler found that when the sun is near the horizon or about 45 degrees above it (thus emitting cool to moderately warm rays), quadrupeds and bipeds have similar amounts of body surface exposed and accumulate equivalent heat loads. However, at noon, when the sun is directly overhead and its rays are the most intense, the heat load buildup of a biped is 60 percent less than that of a quadruped because of the biped's minimal surface exposure.

Wheeler has also calculated that bipedalism would aid in the dissipation of any body heat that did manage to accumulate. Bipeds are farther from the hot ground surface than are quadrupeds, and thus a biped's skin contacts cooler and faster-moving air currents; this contact aids in heat loss through convection. Such convectional cooling would, of course, be enhanced by the loss of thick body hair; the loss would allow an essentially naked surface to be held aloft in the cool breezes. Thus, the temperature regulation model may help to explain the reduction of human body hair. Wheeler believes that early hominins might have increased their convectional heat loss by as much as one-third by adopting bipedalism.

The combination of lower heat buildup and easy heat dissipation could have reduced the early hominins' dependence on shade and allowed them to remain active throughout much of the equatorial day and at relatively high temperatures. Furthermore, if heat loss could be accomplished mainly through convectional cooling, rather than by evaporative cooling through sweating, hominins' dependence on water would have been lowered. Wheeler has suggested that early bipeds may have required some 40 percent less water each day than a quadrupedal ape living under the same conditions. If true, this would have freed the early hominins to range widely across the savanna as they foraged.

Now clearly, Wheeler's beautiful theory must somehow deal with the ugly fact that many of the australopith sites seem to have been extensively wooded (Table 7.2). Nonetheless, Wheeler's faith in his hypothesis has yet to be shaken. He argues that some of the sites that have produced the oldest *conclusive* evidence for bipedalism were open enough for his model to have worked. He says, "If you look at the oldest evidence for bipedalism—Laetoli, and now the [*Australopithecus*] *anamensis* sites—these are actually [relatively] open habitats" (Shreeve, 1996:122). Other researchers disagree with that environmental assessment, however (Shreeve, 1996), and with the recent spate of discoveries of shade-dwelling australopiths—*Sahelanthropus, Orrorin,* and *Ardipithecus kadabba*—a good deal of the steam has gone out of Wheeler's argument.

Habitat Variability/Instability and Bipedalism

In a book entitled *Humanity's Descent*, Rick Potts of the Smithsonian Institution has proposed yet another habitat-related scenario for the evolution of bipedalism. In Potts's (1996) view, late Miocene–early Pliocene times in Africa were marked not only by habitat diversity (i.e., mixed habitats or ecotones) but also by dramatic habitat instability. According to Potts, environmental cycles (hotter/colder, wetter/dryer) and their accompanying habitat shifts (more/less forest, woodland, savanna) occurred much more often than traditionally portrayed, and the resulting long-term instability selected for behavioral and anatomical flexibility and generality among the early hominins. He says, "The benefits of walking erect are found in mobility itself. The distinctive two-leggedness of the early australopiths . . . afforded a certain flexibility of movement. Its success resided in the opportunities it gave to adjust locomotor style to changing landscapes" (Potts, 1996:98). Noting that the australopiths' terrestrial walking can only be understood in the context of their concurrent arboreal adaptations, Potts argues that these early hominins evolved a mixed locomotor package that gave them access to the best of both worlds. The australopiths were thus "liberated from [the] trees" and "unindentured to the ground" (Potts, 1996:91). It remained for later hominin species, especially *Homo erectus* (see Chapter 10), to make a full commitment to terrestrial life and leave the trees for good.

Foraging Postures and Bipedalism

Two new hypotheses relate the beginning of hominin bipedalism to particular foraging patterns and postural adaptations. The first hypothesis, by Belgian anthropologist Marc Verhaegen and his colleagues (Verhaegen et al., 2002), proposes that hominin bipedalism began as an adaptation for wetland wading and climbing, as our earliest ancestors foraged for plants in shallow water and alongside streams. These researchers attempt to support their argument with data on certain aspects of the australopiths' anatomy and reconstructed habitats and new observations of wading–foraging by wild gorillas (Doran and McNeilage, 1998). The hypothesis further suggests that early hominans (genus *Homo*) continued and elaborated on the australopiths' semiaquatic lifestyle and eventually "evolved diving abilities and dispersed along [Africa's] Indian Ocean" coast, where they depended heavily on marine foods such as shellfish (Verhaegen et al., 2002:216). Our understanding of the fossil and other evidence leads us to conclude that this hypothesis is unlikely to stand close scrutiny and testing.

A second new hypothesis (which seems to us somewhat more plausible) has hominin bipedalism originating from a set of anatomical *preadaptations* that evolved back in the Miocene among certain "squat-feeding ground apes" (Kingdon, 2003). In his new book *Lowly Origin,* Jonathan Kingdon speculates that hominins originated in the East African forests as the descendants of "ground apes" that practiced a pattern he calls *squat feeding.* He envisions creatures that spent most of their foraging time on the ground, utilized significantly less fruit than arboreal apes, and showed strong dietary increases in leaf litter fauna, small mammals, ground-dwelling birds, and herbaceous plants. Furthermore, Kingdon thinks the squat-feeding habit would have selected for important anatomical changes, including the evolution of a stable flexed-leg and broad-pelvis base; a flexible waist, complete with a lumbar curve; a more vertical spine and better head balance; and mobile shoulders. Among the pelvic changes that are hypothesized to have accompanied squat feeding are shortening and broadening of both the iliac blades and the sacrum.

Kingdon (2003) believes that in the context of small and rich feeding territories requiring only short bouts of actual travel, these modifications would have served squat feeders very well. In his view, these same modifications would have functioned later as preadaptations for energy-efficient bipedal standing in an altered environment that presented forest-edge opportunities for upright food gathering. Bipedal *walking* would have become energy efficient at an even later stage, after some additional changes in the pelvis and legs, and might then have been important for inland migration by creatures such as *Orrorin* and/or *Ardipithecus* (Kingdon, 2003). The entire hypothesis—that bipedal hominins evolved from squat-feeding apes with already altered trunks, hips, and legs—is intriguing but will require considerable verification.

Reproduction and Bipedalism

Tool use, energy efficiency, temperature regulation, habitat variability, and foraging postures—these are only a few of the many explanations that have been offered for bipedalism. Other hypotheses include the possibilities that bipedalism evolved to allow long-distance surveillance for predators (Shreeve, 1996) or that bipedal displays fostered social control in early hominin groups (Jablonski and Chaplin, 1992). One thing is clear: Regardless of what selection pressure(s) led to habitual bipedalism, evolution worked through the enhanced reproductive success of those individuals that were best suited for upright movement. American anthropologist Owen Lovejoy has emphasized the direct effects of bipedalism on hominins' reproductive efficiency (Lovejoy, 1981). His hypothesis links bipedalism with the evolution of several unique features of human reproduction (Figure 9.2).

Two major reproductive changes distinguish humans from the apes: the loss of estrus and strong paternal investment in children. Humans have continued the trend, first seen clearly among the apes, of relaxed hormonal control of sexual behavior. In our species, the ancient estrus cycle of sexual behavior has nearly, if not completely, disappeared, and ovulation is now hidden from both women and men. These changes, and particularly the concealment of ovulation, make it difficult for both sexes to determine the paternity of offspring. Only within exclusive sexual relationships can one be sure that the male mate is the father of the female's children. This

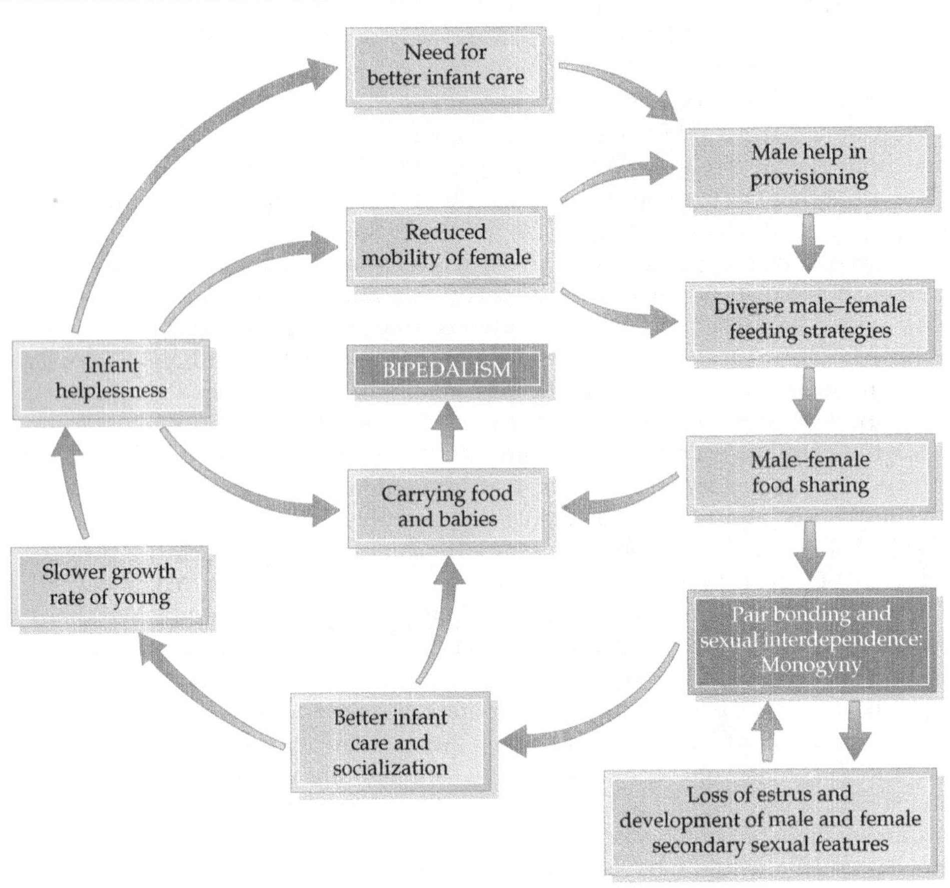

FIGURE 9.2 Behavioral adaptations of early hominins according to Lovejoy (1981), drawn as a feedback system.

is critically important, since kin-selection theory predicts that males will invest time, energy, and resources only in youngsters carrying their genes (Trivers, 1985).

Lovejoy (1981), who flatly rejects the energy-efficiency and body temperature models of bipedalism, focuses his attention on behavior that has direct, positive effects on the production and rearing of offspring. Arguing that a primary difference between humans and apes is our greater birthrate (i.e., a shorter interbirth interval), he suggests that among the earliest hominins, some males began to provide for females and young regularly. Such provisioning—locating, collecting, and furnishing food—would have reduced both the amount of parental investment required from females (they would not have been solely responsible for finding food for themselves and their babies) and the mortality risks of females and young (they would not have been ranging as far for food, and thus their risk of injury would be lower). The energy saved by provisioned females would then have been turned into increased reproduction, and infant mortality would have dropped.

But where does bipedalism come in? Lovejoy (1981) argues that effective provisioning would have required bipedal locomotion so that males' hands were free to carry food. Bipedal, provisioning males would have been favored by natural selection over nonprovisioning, quadrupedal males, but only if males were actually investing in their own young. Thus Lovejoy speculates that provisioning males must have had a high degree of paternity certainty. He envisions such certainty as being the result of the evolution of monogamous "pair-bonded" nuclear families. Males provisioned only their female mates and their young, and because of the adults' **pair bond** (reinforced by the frequent copulation required for conception, now that ovulation was hidden), females remained sexually faithful to their mates during the males' foraging trips.

Pair bond a psychological relationship between mates; thought to be marked by sexual faithfulness.

Lovejoy's scenario, although ingeniously tying together locomotion, reproduction, and family structure, has come under intense criticism. For one thing, it can be argued that the apparent sexual dimorphism in the australopiths supports the notion of some form of polygynous mating system, not monogamy (or more properly, monogyny). Lovejoy recognized this problem in 1981 but argued that *canine* monomorphism was a better indicator of hominins' mating patterns than body size dimorphism (see also Lovejoy, 1993). That argument may now be moot, however, since new analyses of australopith postcranial remains have reopened the entire question of body size dimorphism (Reno et al., 2003).

The dimorphism issue clearly is unsettled, but a further counterargument against the idea of monogamy being characteristic of early hominins is that it isn't even characteristic of living humans, who have been described—taking all modern societies into consideration—as "mildly polygynous" (Symons, 1979). Furthermore, there seems to be very little evidence that an evolved pair bond characterizes modern humans. Humans form social and sexual relationships of varying duration, but there is little evidence that we have been shaped by evolution to form long-lasting, exclusive pair bonds (Symons, 1979). And if modern people lack long-lasting or permanent pair bonds, there is no basis for attributing them to early hominins.

And so at present, a number of evolutionary scenarios attempt to account for the appearance of habitual bipedalism. It is worth repeating that these explanations are working hypotheses, none of which has been falsified unequivocally, and that they all have interesting and attractive features. Indeed, because each hypothesis may hold a grain of truth, it seems reasonable and probable that some *combination* of selection pressures, rather than a single evolutionary factor, led to erect walking. Additional speculative research and new fossil finds may someday help us to solve the riddle of bipedalism.

The Relationship of Bipedalism to Other Hominin Traits: Birth Pattern

While habitual bipedalism is *the* most distinctive hominin trait, others are almost as diagnostic. Some are anatomical traits, such as short, incisorlike canine teeth and (among *Homo*) big brains. Others are social attributes, such as an evolutionary tendency toward increasingly complex interpersonal relationships and societies. How is bipedalism linked to these important secondary traits?

Dealing with the social category, American anthropologist Wenda Trevathan (1987, 1988) and others have speculated on the possible effects of bipedalism on childbirth and, by extension, on hominin sociality. As shown in the preceding chapters, the evolution of bipedalism involved a good deal of remodeling of the hominin pelvis. In particular, the shape of the **birth canal** changed from the ape's long oval, becoming quite wide transversely (from side to side) but shallow sagittally (from front to back) in *Australopithecus* (Figure 9.3). Later, in *Homo*, the canal regained a relatively long sagittal dimension—particularly at the exit, or outlet—producing a more rounded shape (Figure 9.3).

Birth canal the passage through the mother's pelvis by means of which an infant is born.

In nonhuman primates, babies are sagittally oriented throughout birth. There is no fetal rotation, and newborns exit the canal face to face with their mothers. In this way, mother monkeys and apes routinely assist in delivery by reaching down and pulling emerging infants up and toward their chests in a curve that matches the normal flexion of the babies' bodies. Interestingly, the human delivery pattern is very different (Figure 9.3, *right*). A modern human baby, with its large skull, negotiates the birth canal by entering with the head oriented transversely. It then rotates 90 degrees into a sagittal position before exiting the canal facing the sacrum—that is, with its back toward the mother's face. A human mother is therefore in a bad position to assist in delivery, since her infant is exiting "down and back." Pulling an emerging human infant up toward the mother's breast would bend it dangerously against the normal flexion of its body.

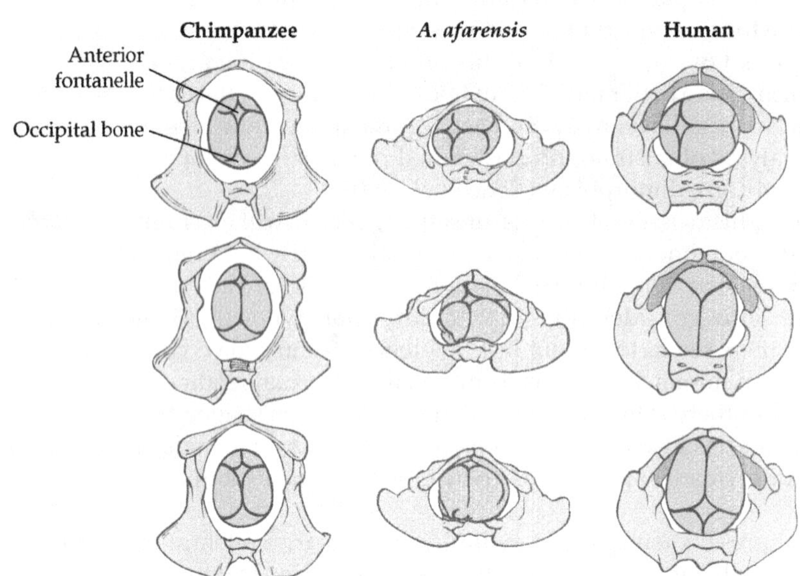

FIGURE 9.3
Three views of the fit between the fetal head and the birth canal in chimpanzees (*left*), *Australopithecus afarensis* (*center*), and modern humans (*right*). The top view shows the orientation of the fetal head at the entrance (inlet) to the birth canal; the middle view is at midcanal; the bottom view is at the exit (outlet). Fetal head size in *Australopithecus* is speculative and controversial.

Trevathan (1987, 1988) has speculated that at some point in human evolution, with the introduction of fetal rotation and down-and-back delivery, hominin mothers would have benefited significantly from the assistance of birth attendants. Seeking and giving assistance at births is viewed as contributing to the development of empathy, communication, and cooperation among the evolving hominins. Although speculative, this is an intriguing notion. However, there is a major problem in determining when the human birth pattern originated. Trevathan thinks this might have occurred among the australopiths, but others think that australopith births were as fast and trouble free as those of apes and that down-and-back human deliveries are probably the result of strong brain expansion within the genus *Homo*. If the latter view is correct, the human birth pattern is probably not much more than 2 million years old.

Bipedalism and Canine Reduction

Moving to the connection between bipedalism and canine shortening, in 1960, Sherwood Washburn, champion of the theory that tool use preceded and possibly stimulated bipedalism, called attention to the fact that the australopiths had relatively small canine teeth that would have been of little value in aggression or defense. In contrast, in all other large, ground-dwelling primates—chimpanzees, gorillas, and particularly baboons—the male's canines are enormous teeth, true fangs. Among their uses are self-defense against large and dangerous terrestrial predators. As part of his scenario for early hominin evolution, Washburn argued that the loss of large canines must have been balanced by some other means of self-defense—namely, the use of various objects as weapons.

As noted at the beginning of this chapter, the hypothesis that tool use triggered bipedalism remains to be falsified completely, but the supporting evidence is unconvincing. In that case, are there other explanations of canine reduction? If it was not related to tool use, what caused it? Clifford Jolly (1970) of New York University suggested an answer to that question. Jolly proposed that the evolution of hominins was marked by a shift from ape-type frugivory to a diet that included a significantly higher proportion of small, hard objects, such as seeds, nuts, and tubers—items that would have been plentiful in the forest–woodland–savanna ecotone. The evolutionary scenario proposed by Jolly became known as the *seed-eating hypothesis* (Jolly, 1970).

Jolly's hypothesis—which included speculations not only about canine reduction in hominins but also about postcranial preadaptations for bipedalism—was based on comparative data taken from savanna baboons (genus *Papio*) and **gelada** monkeys (genus *Theropithecus;* highly terrestrial, grass-and-rhizome feeders from Ethiopia). Compared to the more frugivorous savanna baboons, Jolly found that the grass-mincing geladas showed somewhat smaller canines and incisors, skull and jaw proportions that maximized crushing force between the opposing molars, and more constant truncal erectness while sitting and foraging. The last element, truncal erectness, was suggested as a probable preadaptation for hominins' eventual bipedalism. (Jonathan Kingdon [2003] acknowledges Jolly's early contribution to Kingdon's new squat-feeding ape theory of bipedalism.) Canine reduction was explained by Jolly as either an adaptation to reduce "locking" between the opposing toothrows—a change that would have resulted in "increased efficiency in rotary chewing" of small, hard objects (Jolly, 1970:15)—or, alternatively, as a side effect of **pleiotropic genes** acting mainly to reduce incisor size. Jolly downplayed a connection between tool use and canine reduction, since he thought the dental change could be linked convincingly to dietary factors.

Gelada a *species* of terrestrial *monkey* related to baboons found in the mountains of Ethopia; *Theropithecus gelada*.

Pleiotropic genes *genes* that influence more than one *phenotypic* trait.

Jolly's (1970) hypothesis has been received with a mixture of skepticism and support. To some, the model seems to fit well with the dental specializations of the *Paranthropus* megadonts but not so well with the teeth of other Plio-Pleistocene australopiths (e.g., *A. afarensis;* Conroy, 1997). Just recently, however, it received a boost from the discoveries of *Sahelanthropus* and *Orrorin,* both of which show significantly thicker molar enamel than in apes (Brunet et al., 2002; Senut et al., 2001). Thickened molar enamel would seem to go well with a diet that required prolonged and vigorous chewing, and if either or both of these Miocene species correctly reflects the dental adaptations of the first hominins, Jolly's notion gains strength. Interestingly, the third claimant for Miocene hominin status—*Ardipithecus*—shows chimplike enamel thickness that is hard to reconcile with a diet of small, hard objects (White et al., 1994).

One of Jolly's most vigorous critics is American anthropologist Leonard Greenfield, who believes that flawed assumptions about dental mechanics underlie the seed-eating model. Greenfield (1992) has suggested as a substitute his *dual-selection hypothesis.* This model proposes that two forms of selection shaped canine tooth anatomy: selection for use as a weapon and selection for incisorlike functions. These selective forces tended to move canine anatomy in mutually exclusive directions and therefore can be viewed as competing with one another. If the weapon-use function prevailed, the canines would be long, fanglike teeth, but if incisorlike selection was stronger, the canines would be short and have broader cutting edges. Finally, and of major importance, the dual-selection hypothesis assumes that if selection for weapon-use functions diminished, canines would *automatically* shift toward an incisorlike anatomy.

Greenfield's model is interesting and may have some merit, but even if it proves to be correct and applicable to hominins, it leaves critical questions unanswered: For example, did the canines of early hominins get shorter and broader because they were no longer needed as weapons or because they were *strongly* needed as additional incisorlike teeth? In fact, little has changed since 1995, when J. M. Plavcan and Jay Kelley summed up the situation with regard to hominins' dental changes as follows: "At this point . . . we are aware of no hypothesis that satisfactorily explains canine reduction" (Plavcan and Kelley, 1996:387). We can only hope that future discoveries and ideas will bring clarity to this problem of dental hominization.

This brief review has touched on some past and present explanations for the main hominin adaptations. Clearly, definitive answers to many important *how* and *why* questions are still lacking. There seems little doubt, however, that once hominins had some of the major behavioral and anatomical cards on the table, particularly bipedalism and simple technology, a complex **positive feedback** system could have developed.

Positive feedback the process in which a positive change in one component of a system brings about changes in other components, which in turn brings about further positive changes in the first component.

One such feedback system is shown in Figure 9.4. Although certain loops in this system are questionable, others—such as those connecting the triangle of technology (tool making), subsistence, and intelligence (brain size)—were almost certainly of great importance, at least once *Homo* had evolved. While studying Figure 9.4,

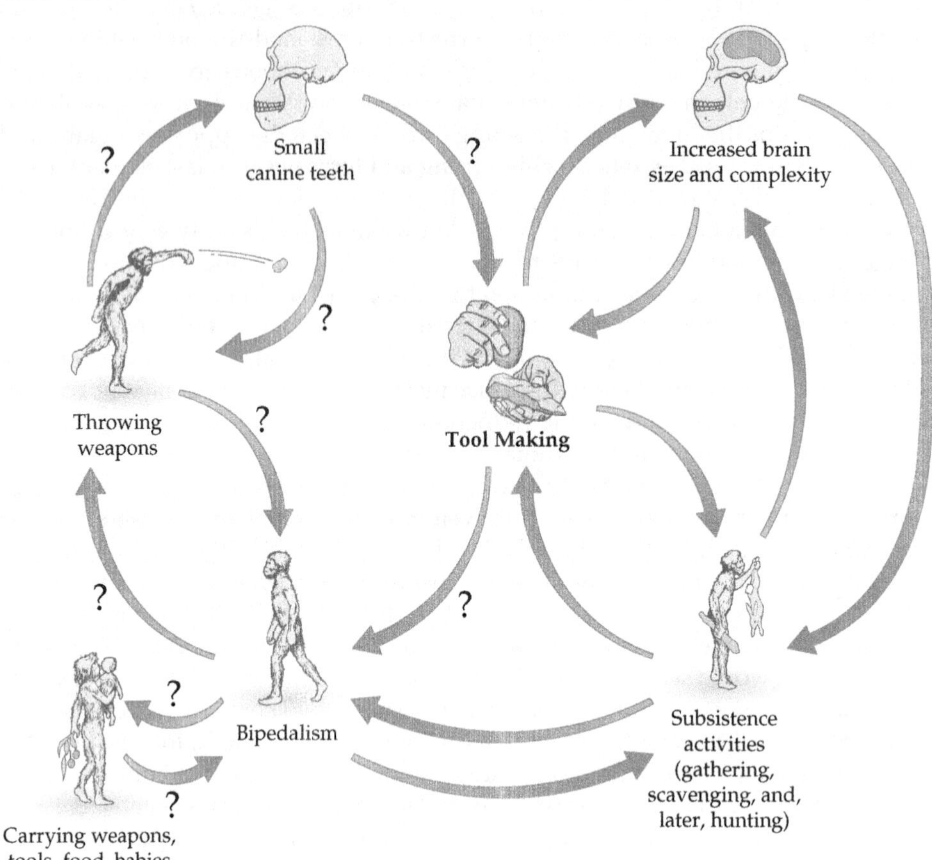

FIGURE 9.4 Numerous feedback systems occur in nature and are often interlocking. Negative feedback maintains stability, and positive feedback brings about major adaptive changes that constitute evolution. Shown here in simplified form is a positive feedback system that may have been important in hominin evolution.

however, we must keep in mind that this and all speculation-based feedback models are primarily heuristic devices. The danger inherent in model building is that we may begin to have too much trust in the model as a representation of the real world. Most of the feedback loops shown in the figure await rigorous testing (see Box 9.1).

Early Technology

As suggested in an earlier chapter, we suspect that early hominins inherited an aptitude for tool use from their last ape ancestor. How and why tool use—and at some point, tool making—became increasingly complex are questions that are difficult to answer. When, for example, did our ancestors begin to recognize that certain implements were useful enough either to be carried with them or for their locations to be remembered? (In this connection, it is interesting to note that wild chimpanzees at Taï apparently possess mental maps, including the locations of good hammer stones and how far they were, when last seen, from nut trees [Boesch and Boesch-Achermann, 2000].) Or again, how did the uniquely hominin practice of making tools from stones begin? Was it from discovering that flakes that were accidentally knocked off hammer stones made useful cutting tools? In any event, once stone tools were in use, the presence and activities of our ancestors became much easier to trace and decipher. And it is to the beginnings of stone technology that we devote most of the rest of this chapter.

Earliest Stone Industry: The Oldowan

The magnet that drew Louis and Mary Leakey back to Olduvai Gorge year after year was the large number of extremely primitive stone implements. Mary Leakey

BOX 9.1 CURRENT ISSUE

Still Lots to Do

This chapter's discussions about how and why hominins became bipeds and acquired short canines, reveals both the variety of our evolutionary scenarios and the depths of our residual ignorance. Paleoanthropologists have many hypotheses that explain the events of human evolution, but virtually all of these hypotheses require further refinement and testing before they can be considered proved in a scientific sense. For example, Washburn's (1960) weapons use hypothesis, Jolly's (1970) seed-eating hypothesis, and Greenfield's (1992) dual-selection hypothesis all address the problem of canine reduction among hominins. Each explanation has something to recommend it, but each also has weaknesses or is somehow incomplete.

We draw attention to this cloud of anthropological ignorance in order to point out its silver lining of future opportunities. As noted in an earlier Current Issue item, there are still lots of hominin fossils out there to be found and the pace of discovery is picking up. But in addition to work in the fossil fields, there are many theoretical breakthroughs still to be made, increasingly sophisticated analyses to be done, and new approaches devised for solving old problems.

For example, not long ago, the anthropological world was set agog with the news that DNA taken from ancient Neandertal bones revealed that these people were genetically distinct and so can be considered a separate species from *Homo sapiens*. This sort of application of advanced genetics techniques to problems in the fossil record is unprecedented and promises further surprises as it becomes widely used. Additionally, new information and procedures in physiology, anatomy, and growth; chronometric dating; archaeology (especially lithic analysis); and primatology, to name just a few fields, are all successfully being brought to bear on problems of human evolution.

The point is this: Students often ask about the opportunities for careers in anthropology. While we have no crystal ball to tell us about tomorrow's job market, we can say with certainty that there is much exciting work is left to be done in paleoanthropology. If that field seems to be the right choice for you, talk to your professor or academic advisor for more information or contact the American Association of Physical Anthropologists. (The AAPA Internet site is www.physanth.org.)

made the study of these objects her special province. Her monograph on the stone culture at Olduvai covers material taken from the gorge's lowest strata, known as Beds I and II, and a time period that extends from 1.2 to 2.2 million years ago (M. Leakey, 1971; Table 9.1).

TABLE 9.1 Stratified Beds and Fossils at Olduvai Gorge

Approximate Age (Years)	Bed	Fossils and Industry
620,000–100,000	Upper beds	*Homo sapiens*
840,000–620,000	Bed IV	Fossils of *Homo erectus* Late Acheulean hand axes and cleavers
1.2 million–840,000	Bed III	No fossils Few artifacts
1.7–1.2 million	Bed II	*Homo erectus* and early Acheulean tools *Homo habilis* and Oldowan tools
2.2–1.7 million	Bed I	*Paranthropus boisei* and *Homo habilis* Oldowan choppers
2.2 million	Volcanic lava	

Note: The ages of the upper beds are still rather uncertain. Bed I fossil sites date 1.9–1.7 mya.

FIGURE 9.5
An Oldowan chopper was usually made by striking some flakes from a rounded cobble to give a cutting edge. It is one of the simplest stone implements. The scale here is approximately twice actual size.

Acheulean industry a stone tool tradition that first appeared about 1.7 million years ago in Africa.

Choppers small, generally ovoid stones with a few *flakes* removed to produce a partial cutting edge.

Flakes sharp-edged fragments struck from a larger stone; may then be used as a cutting tool.

Mary Leakey found that there were two stone-working traditions at Olduvai. One, the **Acheulean industry**, appears first in Bed II and will be discussed in Chapter 11. The other, the Oldowan, is the older and more primitive and occurs throughout Bed I, as well as at other early African sites (see Chapters 6, 7, and 8). Its signature implements are what anthropologists for a long time called *pebble tools* but what Mary Leakey preferred to call **choppers**. Many of the chopping tools at Olduvai are of hen's egg size or larger, some of them 3 or 4 inches (8 to 10 centimeters) across. In addition to the choppers, Oldowan sites typically contain numerous stone flakes.

An Oldowan chopper (Figure 9.5) is about the most basic stone implement one can possibly imagine could be recognized by archaeologists. The chopper was typically made from a *cobble*, a stone that had been worn smooth by sand and water action. The stone selected was often that of a close-grained, hard, smooth-textured material, such as quartz, flint, chert, or, at Olduvai, hardened lava.

To turn a cobble into a sharp-edged tool, an early tool maker had only to smash one end down hard on a nearby boulder or to balance it on the boulder and give it a good whack with another rock. If the cobble were hit at the right angle with enough force, a large chip would fly off. Another whack would knock off a second chip next to the first, leaving a jagged edge or perhaps a point on one end of the stone. There were large choppers and small ones. The tool was presumably held as one would hold a rock while banging downward, with a direct hammering or chopping motion. The small chips knocked off during the manufacture of choppers are known as **flakes**. Sharper than choppers, they often may have been more useful than the core.

But how were the Oldowan choppers and flakes used? What do they tell us about the lifestyle of their makers? Archaeologists Kathy Schick and Nicholas Toth have made an in-depth study of these questions, and their discoveries are revealing. In or-

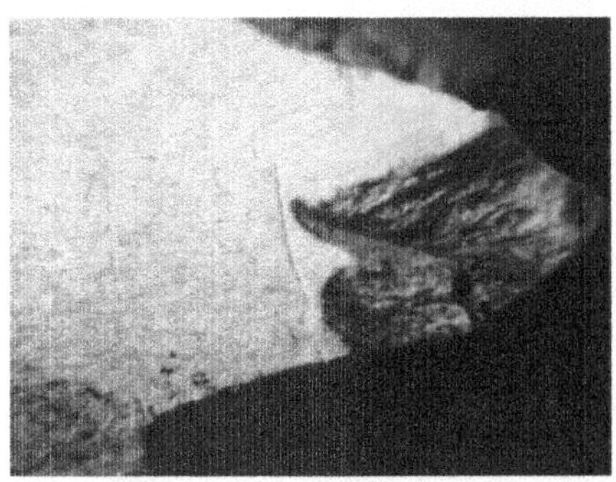

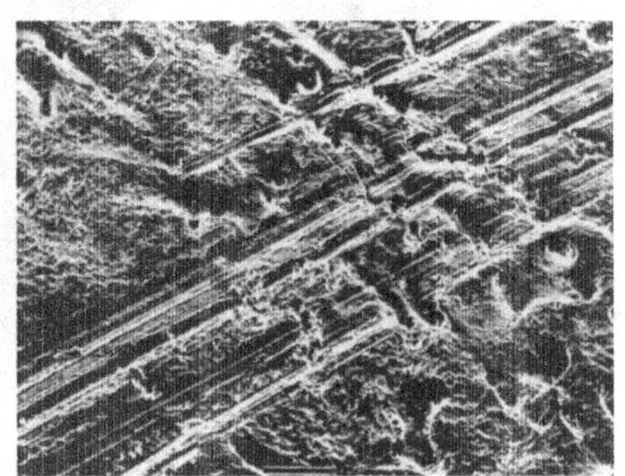

FIGURE 9.6
Marks on the surfaces of fossil bones, such as those from Olduvai Gorge (*left*), can be produced in several ways, including by stone tools or the teeth of carnivores. Under a scanning electron microscope, cuts made by stone tools (*right*) typically contain parallel striations in the bottom of the groove. These cuts can be clearly distinguished from the marks made by the teeth of carnivores.

der to extract the maximum information from the ancient stone implements, Schick and Toth (1993) have used a combination of traditional and innovative techniques. They have studied the occurrence and distribution of Oldowan tools at the various African sites and also the fossil bone assemblages associated with the tools. In addition, they have conducted numerous field experiments using newly made flakes and choppers to butcher animals that have died naturally and to smash animal long bones for marrow. Finally, they have utilized data from electron microscope studies of cut marks on fossil bones (Figure 9.6) and **microwear** on tool surfaces. (The microwear pattern of chips, pits, and polish can provide excellent clues as to how a tool was used.)

Microwear the microscopic pattern of scratches, pits, and polish produced during the use of a stone tool.

Based on all of their various analyses, Schick and Toth (1993) have concluded that the principal reason for the emergence of stone tool technology among hominins was for quick and efficient butchering of animal carcasses before eating them on the spot or carrying them elsewhere for later consumption. Flakes were found to be excellent implements for skinning, defleshing, and dismembering animal carcasses (Figure 9.7)—even better than choppers, so often thought of as the premier Oldowan tools. (Indeed, many choppers may be nothing more than **débitage**, or waste cores left after flake manufacture.) Using simple flake tools, Schick and Toth were able to skin even an elephant with its inch-thick hide! Choppers were useful for dismembering carcasses and, along with unmodified cobbles, for bone breaking (Figure 9.8).

Débitage the debris produced during stone tool manufacture.

We should not conclude that Oldowan tools were used only for meat processing, however. Microwear analyses have identified tools used for cutting soft plants and others used to work wood (Schick and Toth, 1993). Hammer stones were no doubt used to crush nuts, and the use, if any, of **manuports** (unmodified stones brought from elsewhere to the site by hominins) is unknown. Nonetheless, based on their work, Schick and Toth believe that the primary message of the oldest stone tools is a significant increase in meat eating by early hominins.

Manuports unmodified stones that could not have occurred naturally in an archaeological site and must have been carried there; how manuports were used is unknown.

Because progress in the early Stone Age was slow, the beginnings of the Oldowan tool industry were probably far older than would be indicated even by the Gona site, which dates the earliest known stone tools to 2.6 to 2.5 million years BP (Chapter 8). But how much older, no one yet has the slightest idea. After 2.5 million BP, tool making and hominin evolution went hand in hand, but the earliest steps are unknown (Panger et al., 2002).

Identifying both ancient tools and ancient tool makers can be tricky. Archaeologists can usually distinguish between primitive stone tools and naturally

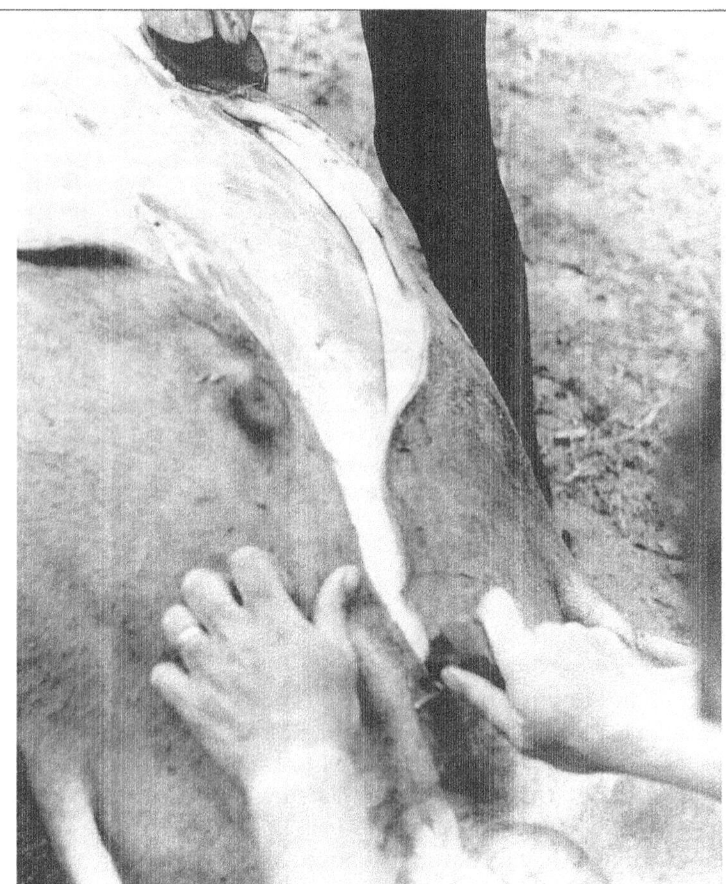

FIGURE 9.7
Archaeologists experimentally skinning a wildebeest (that died of natural causes) with a lava flake. Simple, sharp flakes are excellent tools for skinning, defleshing, and dismembering animal carcasses.

occurring rocks because the artifacts satisfy one or more of the following criteria: an organized chipping pattern; evidence of being transported to the site from some other locality; association with bones showing cut marks; and association with other undoubted artifacts or structures. Identifying the Oldowan tool makers is currently a very controversial topic, as discussed in earlier chapters. Virtually all paleoanthro-

FIGURE 9.8
The use of a stone chopper and an anvil to crack a limb bone in order to expose the marrow.

pologists attribute stone tool–making abilities to early *Homo,* and indeed, the Leakeys ended up assigning the Bed I stone tools at Olduvai Gorge to *Homo habilis,* rather than its contemporary, *Paranthropus* (*Zinjanthropus*) *boisei* (L.S.B. Leakey et al., 1964). Forty years of additional discoveries and analyses, however, have opened the very real possibility that some of the australopiths may have been stone tool makers, too. We can hope that further work will clear up this important question, but for now, let's turn our attention to what the Olduvai stone tools and bone assemblages may tell us about evolving hominin behavior, regardless of which ancient species—hominan, australopith, or both—produced them.

Interpreting Early Hominin Sites

During their decades of work at Olduvai Gorge, Mary and Louis Leakey and their sons and co-workers laid bare numerous ancient hominin sites (Leakey, 1971; Table 9.1). Marked by the occurrence of hominin bones and/or Oldowan tools, often in association with animal bones, many of these sites were originally called **occupation levels,** suggesting that the hominins found there actually camped on the spot. We are now wary of jumping to that conclusion, however. Only after a team of experts—archaeologists, geologists, paleontologists, paleoanthropologists, and taphonomists—has thoroughly studied a site can its true nature be understood.

Occupation level the land surface occupied by prehistoric *hominins.*

The oldest sites at Olduvai come from Bed I and date between 1.9 and 1.7 million years old (Table 9.1). Sites at this level have produced Oldowan stone tools in abundance and also (sometimes at the same location) fossils of both the megadont australopith *Paranthropus boisei* and *Homo habilis.*

The first difficulty in interpreting a particular site is to determine which hominin species (one? more?) produced it. For some decades, researchers were confident that the presence of stone tools indicated the activities of *Homo habilis,* but as noted earlier, we can no longer make that easy assumption.

Next, comes the issue of trying to imagine how hominins might have lived nearly 2 million years ago. What living analogues should we use? Should we assume that although much smaller brained, the Bed I hominins behaved more or less like modern humans? Or should we envision them as advanced apes? If we adopt the ape analogy, we risk underinterpreting the Olduvai sites, perhaps especially those produced by *H. habilis.* On the other hand, if we view either *P. boisei* or *Homo habilis* as primitive, long-armed little humans, we risk overinterpretation. It is the latter error that some workers think we have been making for years.

During the 1970s and early 1980s, many workers, including Mary Leakey (1971) and archaeologist Glynn Isaac, used an analogy from modern hunter-and-gatherer cultures to interpret the Bed I sites. They concluded that many of the sites were probably **home bases,** where group members gathered to share food, to socialize, to make tools, and to sleep (Isaac, 1983). Concentrations of stone artifacts, along with animal bones bearing cut marks and percussion scars from stone hammers, provided clear evidence of regular meat consumption at many sites. Following the hunter–gatherer analogy, it was assumed that the Oldowan tool makers practiced a sexual division of labor, with males bringing in most of the meat and females gathering plant foods. At least one site (Olduvai DK-I) produced a circular concentration of stones that Mary Leakey interpreted as the remains of a hut or windbreak (Isaac, 1983; Schick and Toth, 1993). In all, a very humanlike lifestyle was envisioned.

Home base a place where *hominin* groups gathered for socializing, food sharing, and sleeping.

Views on the lifestyle of the Oldowan tool makers began to change in the 1970s and 1980s, as many workers became convinced that these hominins had been overly humanized. Early hominin sites can be complicated to interpret. In some cases, artifacts may be concentrated in a particular area due to the activities of flowing water. In other cases, artifacts and animal bones may be associated because both were dropped around a water source that attracted both humans and animals.

The study of *taphonomy* is concerned with understanding these types of complex relationships. Taphonomic studies by Pat Shipman (1983) and others began to show that hominins shared the Olduvai sites with a variety of large carnivores, thus weakening the idea that these were the safe, social home bases originally envisioned. Furthermore, studies of the bone accumulations suggested that Bed I hominins were mainly scavengers—stealing from carnivore kills or using the carcasses of animals that had died naturally—and not full-fledged hunters (Shipman, 1983). Archaeologist Lewis Binford suggested that the Bed I sites were no more than "scavenging stations," where hominins brought portions of large animal carcasses for consumption. Certain sites were regularly used because they allowed easy monitoring of the surrounding area for predators. Sleeping was done elsewhere, away from the remains of the day's meals, which would have attracted hyenas and other dangerous animals (Schick and Toth, 1993).

Rick Potts (1984, 1993, 1996) has suggested alternatively that the Olduvai Bed I sites mainly represent places where raw and worked stone was cached for the handy processing of animal foods obtained nearby. Potts has proposed a resource transport hypothesis that involves Oldowan tool makers bringing raw stone from sources several kilometers away and caching it at a number of locations within the group's territory or range. (The original selection of a cache site may have been purely accidental and was very likely related to finding an available carcass on the spot.) Stone tools could have been made at the cache sites for use elsewhere, but more frequently, portions of carcasses were transported to the tool-making site for processing. This idea is very similar to Binford's scavenging-station model, with the key addition of cached stone resources. Again, camping and sleeping at the food-processing sites is deemed unlikely by Potts because such locations would have attracted carnivores interested in leftover meat and bones. In this connection, Potts interprets the DK-I "windbreak" as merely a concentration of lava rocks broken up by the roots of an ancient tree and not as the remains of a shelter at all (Reader, 1988). Also important is the fact that neither Binford's nor Potts's models necessarily include a sexual division of labor or food sharing (but neither do they preclude such behavior).

Most current interpretations of the subsistence, ranging, and tool-using patterns of late Pliocene–early Pleistocene hominins are therefore much more conservative than they were thirty years ago. Nonetheless, in a minor reversal of this conservative trend, Washington University anthropologists Lisa Rose and Fiona Marshall have suggested that Plio-Pleistocene hominins at Olduvai and Koobi Fora probably *did* use certain spots as home bases. Rose and Marshall (1996) reason that foraging for meat (whether by scavenging or hunting) would have brought early hominins into contact with dangerous carnivores. However, rather than avoiding or fleeing from predators, they speculate that the hominins might have cooperated to drive them away from kills, and then, after the carcass had been transported to a home base (a regularly used site that also offered water, accommodations for safe sleeping, etc.), they would have cooperated once again to defend it against any carnivorous visitors. Thus, in the Rose and Marshall scenario, meat eating would have fostered increased sociality and home bases would "have become foci for a range of social, foraging, toolmaking, and carcass-processing activities [albeit with no implications for] a monogamous social organization or a well-defined sexual division of labor" (1996: 319). Other studies have supported Rose and Marshall's suggestion that Plio-Pleistocene hominins were gaining regular access to meaty carcasses, either by hunting or by "power scavenging"—aggressively driving away predators or other scavengers (Bunn, 1996; Domínguez-Rodrigo and Pickering, 2003).

And so anthropologists continue to search for the best ways to interpret early hominins' behavior. Lacking clear analogues for either the australopiths or early *Homo*, some researchers prefer to view them as apelike, while others think of them as more humanlike. Almost certainly, the truth lies in between. Few anthropologists are tempted to apply the term *human* to any of these ancient creatures.

What Triggered Brain Expansion in Early *Homo*?

Group Size, Subsistence, and Brain Metabolism

Before we end this chapter, it seems reasonable to ask whether any of the lifestyle interpretations just described for early *Homo* provide any insights into their brain expansion compared to the australopiths. Certainly, once bigger brains were in existence, they would have allowed various other advances—increasingly sophisticated material culture and communication patterns, for example (see Figure 9.4). But what might have triggered the evolution of bigger brains in the first place?

Although fully aware that evolutionary speculations are risky endeavors, let's try our hand at one. We think the key elements in hominan brain expansion might have been group size, complex subsistence patterns, and the high nutritional value of meat. Robin Dunbar (1998) has produced evidence that among the living primates, there is a strong positive relationship between brain size and the size of a species' social groups. The implication is that the original function of big brains was to keep track of a complex network of social information: group-mates' identities, dominance relationships, alliances and friendships, grudges and debts. Remembering and manipulating social relationships and socially important information has clear effects on survival and reproduction, and there is every reason to believe that this was true among the early hominans.

Using an equation that related brain size to group size for primates, Aiello and Dunbar (1993) plugged in early *Homo*'s brain size and came up with an estimated group size of eighty-two individuals. (Note that these are "cognitive groups," including individuals about whom one has social knowledge, but not necessarily with whom one lives on a daily basis.) So, if the analysis is right, early *Homo* lived in a complex social environment within which a big brain would have been a great help in dealing with everyday life. That's evolutionary variable number one.

Variable number two involves subsistence and ranging patterns. Various studies have shown that among primates, large brains also are correlated with diet. For example, omnivores are thought to have large brains partly because their lifestyle requires complex strategies for extracting high-quality foodstuffs. Similarly, primates with large home ranges (e.g., frugivores compared to folivores) seem to have bigger brains so they can handle a sophisticated "mental map" of their feeding area (Dunbar, 1998; Fleagle, 1988). The archaeological record supports both points for early *Homo*: The first hominans ate a complex, omnivorous diet, including plant and animal products, and they apparently ranged over wide areas in the process of locating food and also raw stone for tool making.

So far, so good. But can we connect the dots between group size and subsistence for early *Homo*? We think so, by linking Dunbar's line of reasoning with that of Rose and Marshall. If early *Homo* not only lived in groups but also actively scavenged for meat in groups, the hominans could have increased their odds for success by cooperatively driving predators away from kills and cooperatively defending kills against other hominins.

That brings us to evolutionary variable number three. Big brains are metabolically expensive organs. (It has been calculated that the modern human brain has a mass-specific metabolic rate nine times greater than the average mass-specific rate of the body as a whole; see Chapter 11.) Moreover, meat is an energy-rich food. If the early hominans successfully increased their meat intake (and this is suggested by studies of Oldowan tools), this would have allowed brain expansion because the enhanced diet could nourish a larger brain.

And so the links are as follows: Big brains were selected for by pressures favoring increased social intelligence (group living) and subsistence intelligence (omnivory and wide ranging). Group living facilitated cooperative scavenging (and possibly also small-scale hunting) and thus increased meat consumption. And more meat in the diet allowed the expansion of metabolically expensive brains.

Masticatory Genes

An alternative and intriguing explanation for brain expansion in early *Homo* has just been published (Currie, 2004; Stedman et al., 2004), and it involves an ancient mutation in a gene affecting jaw muscle mass. Monkeys and apes with large jaw muscles are characterized by active *MYH16* genes that produce so-called myosin heavy chain proteins. These proteins accumulate in jaw muscle cells and result in large, powerful temporalis and masseter muscles—muscles large enough to exert contractile forces capable of affecting craniofacial shape, including limiting the size of the braincase.

Stedman et al. estimate that about 2.4 mya, hominins experienced a mutation that rendered the *MYH16* gene inactive. This resulted in shorter and weaker muscle fibers in the jaws and possibly "removed an evolutionary constraint on encephalization" (2004: 418). The resulting increase in brain size (the adaptive significance of which is not addressed by Stedman et al.) would have resulted in the beginning of the hominan subtribe and the creatures we recognize as early *Homo.*

All of these explanations for brain expansion in early *Homo*—group size, diet, and metabolism versus jaw muscle mutations—are interesting and plausible but require further testing. And, of course, these are not the only scenarios about the cause or causes of hominan encephalization. About all we can say for sure is that something happened around 2.5 million years ago that propelled the early hominans beyond their australopith ancestors in both intelligence and material culture. But early *Homo* was also due to be outstripped by a descendant—*Homo erectus*, just after 2 million years BP.

Summary

The primary hallmark of hominins is bipedalism, yet as this chapter has demonstrated, we have only an imperfect understanding of the selection pressures that produced our characteristic form of locomotion. Increased energy efficiency (compared to ape quadrupedalism), body temperature control, and adapting to variable and unstable habitats appear to be among the best explanations for the evolution of bipedalism, although there are several other suggestions that cannot be discounted entirely, such as freeing the hands for tool use and carrying things. Two new hypotheses link the origin of bipedalism to an ancestry of wading and climbing, on the one hand, and to postcranial modifications accumulated during a period of terrestrial squat feeding, on the other. Furthermore, the connections between bipedalism and both modern birth patterns and canine tooth reduction remain unclear. Undoubtedly, several variables—both anatomical and behavioral—were involved in a complex feedback system throughout hominin evolution.

As described in this chapter, our interpretations of late Pliocene and early Pleistocene hominins are in a state of rapid change, and our understanding of the beginnings of a modern human way of life is incomplete. Anthropologists of the 1970s and 1980s viewed these creatures, and especially early *Homo,* as food-sharing, shelter-building hunter–gatherers, who established base camps on the African plains and who might even have formed pair-bonded monogynous families.

Recent analyses challenge several of these ideas. Although *Homo habilis* was clearly more of a meat eater than the australopiths, we can have no confidence that these hominans hunted game any larger than that taken by chimpanzees. Indeed, most indications are that early *Homo* obtained most of its meat by scavenging on animals that had died of natural causes or from carnivore kills. (Note, however, that some researchers think this involved aggressive power scavenging, rather than simply skulking about until the predators went away.)

Likewise, we are speculating on thin evidence if we attribute the beginnings of a sexual division of labor to early *Homo*. Certainly, at some point in hominin evolution, subsistence activities were partitioned sexually, so that women mainly gathered plants and men hunted for animal foods. And it seems logical that the sexual division of labor was linked to the beginnings of significant food sharing. But we are outrunning our data if we confidently attribute these modern behaviors to early *Homo*, whose subsistence patterns may have been entirely unlike those of any living hominoid.

In summary, for now, we must be content with an uncertain picture of the evolution of hominins' diagnostic anatomical traits, just as we are uncertain about the lifestyles—and in some cases, the identities—of the Oldowan tool makers. Even the first members of the hominan subtribe—*Homo habilis* and *Homo rudolfensis*—apparently lived just outside the cultural circle that defines *humanity*. In strong contrast, however, we can confidently describe the evolutionary descendants of early *Homo* as living a human lifestyle (i.e., a lifestyle broadly similar to that of modern people). And it is to these ancestors, *Homo erectus*, that we now turn our attention.

Postscript

In his classic work *On the Origin of Species*, Charles Darwin (1859/1964) presented a model of continuous and gradual evolutionary change. In his descriptions of adaptation and speciation, Darwin put particular emphasis on the effects of intra- and interspecific competition (while also noting that organisms struggle with the physical environment) and repeatedly stated his belief that "Natura non facit saltum" ("Nature does not make jumps"; Darwin, 1859/1964:206 and elsewhere). In Darwin's world—following the teachings of the geologist Charles Lyell—organic change was slow and stately.

In contrast to Darwinian slowness and uniformity, some researchers are beginning to present evidence for periods of accelerated tempo in evolution, including the evolution of hominins. A current supporter of this view is paleontologist Elisabeth Vrba of Yale University, who argues that life's history has been shaped by a process she calls "turnover pulse." According to Vrba (1985, 1993), in response to dramatic (and, in the context of geological time, relatively rapid) change in the physical environment, entire communities of organisms may experience spurts (pulses) of speciation. And while these pulses do not involve any new or mysterious evolutionary processes, they are triggered primarily by environmental fluctuations that break up ecosystems long in equilibrium.

Vrba's work has identified at least one turnover pulse episode with implications for hominin evolution: during the late Pliocene about 2.5 mya. This turnover pulse event was apparently triggered by a 10 to 20 degree Fahrenheit drop in global temperatures and increased aridity on the continents—changes that, in turn, were due to continental drifting and altered global air and water circulation. In eastern and southern Africa, the cooling and drying trends resulted in the spread of grasslands and a reduction in bush and tree cover; in northern Africa, the Sahara desert developed.

The late Pliocene event witnessed the extinction of numerous older antelope species and the appearance of many modern genera, including several—like *Oryx*—that are strongly adapted to arid environments. Furthermore, many varieties of African animals, including early elephants, pigs, horses, bovids, and rhinos, showed dental changes that indicate an adaptation to diets with more tough and abrasive foodstuffs. And finally, as part of the 2.5-million-year BP turnover pulse, hominins experienced an adaptive radiation that resulted in the appearance of *Paranthropus* (with its huge grinding teeth) and early *Homo* (*H. habilis* and *H. rudolfensis*).

Vrba's (1985, 1993) turnover pulse hypothesis has drawn both proponents and critics. Among the critics are Anna Behrensmeyer and several colleagues at the Smithsonian Institution. Their analysis of mammalian taxa in the Lake Turkana region searched unsuccessfully for a "marked pulse" in species turnover between 2.8 and 2.5 mya (Behrensmeyer et al., 1997:1591).

Only time will tell whether Vrba's hypothesis will be accepted as a real evolutionary phenomenon, but in the meantime, it is worth noting that it has much in common with the cladogenetic speciation model called **punctuated equilibrium**, which hypothesizes that most species experience lengthy periods of stasis (equilibrium) that are occasionally interrupted (punctuated) by rapid evolution and speciation by branching (Eldredge and Gould, 1972).

Punctuated equilibrium the hypothesis that most *species* have long periods of *stasis*, interrupted by episodes of rapid evolutionary change and *speciation* by *branching*.

Together, the punctuated equilibrium and turnover pulse hypotheses (assuming both are verified) could provide an important extension to evolutionary theories. Slow, steady Darwinian gradualism occurs under some ecological conditions, but when the physical environment shifts dramatically, individual species and entire communities of organisms may be thrown into pulses of accelerated speciation, extinction, and dispersion, as long-established ecosystems are disrupted. Presumably, hominins were not immune to such drastic changes.

Review Questions

1. Review the evidence supporting the idea that tool use stimulated the beginnings of habitual bipedalism. If this hypothesis is true, what type and frequency of tool use do you think were involved?
2. Compare the various hypotheses about the origin of hominin bipedalism. Arrange the hypotheses in order from the most to the least likely, and then present evidence to support your ordering system.
3. Owen Lovejoy and others have argued that hominins evolved a pair bond and a tendency toward monogyny. Discuss the evidence for and against these propositions.
4. In the nineteenth century, it was argued that "the brain led the way" in hominin evolution—that is, that brain expansion and elaboration evolved early and other human traits (bipedalism, tool use, language, etc.) followed. Discuss the brain-first theory, based on your knowledge of the sequence of appearance of distinctive hominin traits.
5. Describe the forms and functions of Oldowan tools. What do these tools suggest about the subsistence patterns of their makers?
6. Which behavioral analogue do you prefer for interpreting the behavior of early *Homo*—chimpanzees or modern humans? Or should some combination of analogues be used? Explain your position.
7. What sort of group structure and mating pattern do you think characterized the australopiths? What about early *Homo*? Present evidence to support your conclusions.

SUGGESTED FURTHER READING

Jolly, Clifford. "The Seed-Eaters: A New Model of Hominid Differentiation Based on a Baboon Analogy." *Man*, 5(1):5–26, 1970.

Kingdon, Jonathan. *Lowly Origin*. Princeton, Princeton University Press, 2003.

Lovejoy, C. Owen. "Evolution of Human Walking." *Scientific American*, 259:118–125, 1988.

Schick, Kathy, and Nicholas Toth. *Making Silent Stones Speak*. New York, Simon & Schuster, 1993.

Shreeve, James. "Sunset on the Savanna." *Discover,* 17(7):116–125, 1996.

Trevathan, Wenda. *Human Birth: An Evolutionary Perspective.* New York, Aldine de Gruyter, 1987.

Wheeler, Peter. "Human Ancestors Walked Tall, Stayed Cool." *Natural History,* 102(8):65–67, 1993.

INTERNET RESOURCES

THE ORIGIN OF HOMINID BIPEDALISM

www.riverapes.com/AHAH/ComparativeBiology/Bipedalism/Bipedalism.htm

A useful summary table of the various hypotheses for hominin bipedalism. Links from the table lead to explanations and key publications.

PHILO.SOPHISTRY: COMPARATIVE BIPEDALISM

www.philosophistry.com/static/bipedalism.html

Another web site devoted to the problems of how and why bipedal standing and moving evolves among animals. This one considers several nonprimate species.

THE EVOLUTION OF HUMAN ORIGINS

http://rcp.missouri.edu/carolward/pdfs/Ward-AAA.pdf

In this 2003 paper, paleoanthropologist Carol Ward takes a look at theories and recent developments in the study of hominin origins. Also available in html format.

THE SOCIAL BRAIN HYPOTHESIS

http://psych.colorado.edu/~tito/sp03/7536/Dunbar_1998.pdf

This article by Robin Dunbar outlines his theory that primate (including hominin) brains are correlated with social complexity. Also available in html format.

SPECIES, SPECIATION, AND THE ENVIRONMENT

www.actionbioscience.org/evolution/eldredge.html

Biologist Niles Eldredge discusses several hypotheses about the production of new species, including Elizabeth Vrba's "turnover pulse" model.

USEFUL SEARCH TERMS:

evolution of bipedalism
experimental archaeology
hominin canine reduction
origin of Homo
Seed-eating hypothesis
Social brain hypothesis
stone knapping

Chapter 10

Discovering *Homo erectus*

Begun in the 1920s, excavations at the Chinese site of Zhoukoudian have produced the remains of some forty *Homo erectus* individuals as well as thousands of stone tools.

Then felt I like some watcher of the skies
When a new planet swims into his ken;
Or like stout Cortez, when with eagle eyes
He stared at the Pacific—and all his men
Looked at each other with a wild surmise—
Silent, upon a peak in Darien.

John Keats, 1795–1821. "On First Looking into Chapman's Homer."

Overview

In 1887, a young Dutchman named Eugene Dubois (Figure 10.1) quit his job as a university professor and sailed to the East Indies in search of the "missing link." Incredibly, within four years, he had accomplished his objective with the discovery of *Pithecanthropus erectus* in Java. Although Dubois's claim that ***Pithecanthropus*** was a "venerable ape-man" was greeted skeptically by the scientific community, it wasn't too many years before confirming fossils were unearthed in China and given the name ***Sinanthropus pekinensis.*** Today, *Pithecanthropus* and *Sinanthropus*, along with fossils from Africa and Europe, are classified as *Homo erectus*, an early to mid Pleistocene species thought to be on the direct ancestral line to modern humans.

Pithecanthropus the original *genus* name given by Eugene Dubois to *fossil* material from Java; now classified as *H. erectus*.

Sinanthropus pekinensis the original name given by Davidson Black to ancient *fossils* from Zhoukoudian; now classified as *Homo erectus*.

This chapter describes the various *Homo erectus* discoveries as well as the species' subsequent migrations across the Old World. The anatomy of *Homo erectus* is described in some detail, and the evidence for language and speech in this species is reviewed. The chapter ends with a brief description of the probable evolutionary relationships of *Homo erectus*.

FIGURE 10.1
An 1883 photograph shows Eugene Dubois (1858–1940) as a teacher in Amsterdam.

Homo heidelbergensis successor to *Homo erectus*, first appearing about 800,000 to 600,000 years BP; ancestral to both *Homo sapiens* and the *Neandertals*.

One final introductory comment is in order before beginning the chapter: In several of the following sections, we have found it necessary to discuss later evolutionary events and to refer to ***Homo heidelbergensis***, a species that many believe originated from *Homo erectus* stock some 800,000 to 600,000 years ago and later gave rise to modern humans (*Homo sapiens*). References made here to *H. heidelbergensis* result mainly from the half-million-year period of overlap between that species and late populations of *Homo erectus* and paleoanthropologists' uncertainty over the classification of particular fossils and/or the species assignment of new behavior patterns.

Mini-TIMELINE

Date or Age	Fossil Discoveries or Evolutionary Events
(A) Date (years AD)	
1996	Fossils from Ngandong and Sambungmacan are re-dated
1994	*Homo erectus* fossils from Sangiran and Modjokerto are re-dated
1984	Nariokotome *H. erectus* skeleton found
1929	First skull of *Sinanthropus* discovered
1891	Eugene Dubois discovers first *Pithecanthropus* fossils
(B) Age (million years BP)	
1.8–1.6	*Homo erectus* at Dmanisi, Republic of Georgia
1.8–1.7	Oldest (?) Asian *H. erectus* fossils at Sangiran and Modjokerto
1.8	Oldest African *H. erectus* fossils at Koobi Fora
1.9	Hominins inhabit Longgupo Cave, China

Eugene Dubois and the Quest for the Missing Link

By the late nineteenth century, books such as Charles Darwin's (1871/1981) *The Descent of Man* and Thomas Huxley's (1863/1915) *Man's Place in Nature* in England and Ernst Haeckel's (1868) *Natürliche Schöpfungsgeschichte* in Germany had brought the possibility of human evolution to the public's attention. Still, the claim that humankind was merely an offshoot of an ape was rejected by most laypersons and by many eminent scientists, as well. No one had yet found any fossils proving a link between apes and humans. Most of those who doubted our primate origins did so not merely through acceptance of the biblical account of creation but also because for a long time, there was no really convincing fossil evidence to support human evolution. Some scientists took the lack of any fossils of intermediate humanlike apes as proof that no such creatures had ever existed. At the other extreme, some of Darwin's early supporters rushed forward with fanciful pedigrees for humankind, making up in enthusiasm what they lacked in evidence (Haeckel, 1868).

Eugene Dubois was born in Holland in 1858 and grew up in this atmosphere of often bitter debate over human origins. Although the Dubois family was conventional and religious, the home atmosphere was not one of narrow-minded provincial piety, and the boy's interest in science was encouraged. Dubois went to medical school but, choosing academic life over medical practice, became an instructor in anatomy at Amsterdam University. He was fascinated by the many different evolutionary trees that were being published in both learned and popular journals and was much influenced by the work of Haeckel. For a few years, Dubois delivered his lectures and did his anatomy research, but an idea was taking hold in him: to establish the human place in evolution and set the record straight, once and for all, by finding a fossil of a primitive creature that was the clear forerunner of humans (Shipman, 2001; Theunissen, 1989).

Dubois Begins Work in the East Indies

Dubois set about deciding where to look for humans' evolutionary ancestors. Taking his cue from Darwin, Haeckel, and others, he settled on the tropics. Darwin (1871/1981:206) had suggested that our tree-dwelling progenitors lived in "some warm, forest-clad land"; Alfred Russel Wallace (1885) had also recommended that our forebears be sought in a tropical zone.

Wallace had lived in Malaysia and noted that the islands of Sumatra and Borneo (Figure 10.2) are the home of both the gibbon and the orangutan, one of the most advanced species of ape. He wrote, "With what interest must every naturalist look forward to the time when the caves and tertiary deposits of the tropics may be thoroughly examined, and the past history and earliest appearance of the great man-like apes be at length made known" (Wallace, 1885:72). Wallace's curiosity about these islands and their caves proved contagious, and Dubois began to think seriously of going to the Dutch East Indies to explore the caves himself. The more he read about the geology and natural history of the region, the more convinced he became that the missing link would be discovered there.

At age twenty-nine, Eugene Dubois gave up his professional position and set out to find the fossil of a creature that would prove the relationship between humans and apes. Dubois's planning focused on Sumatra, then under Dutch rule and therefore a practical place for a Dutch citizen to launch a paleontological expedition. To finance such an expedition, Dubois enlisted for a term of eight years as a surgeon in the Royal Dutch East Indies Army. Once in the Indies, he hoped to persuade his commanding officer to give him release time for his research. In

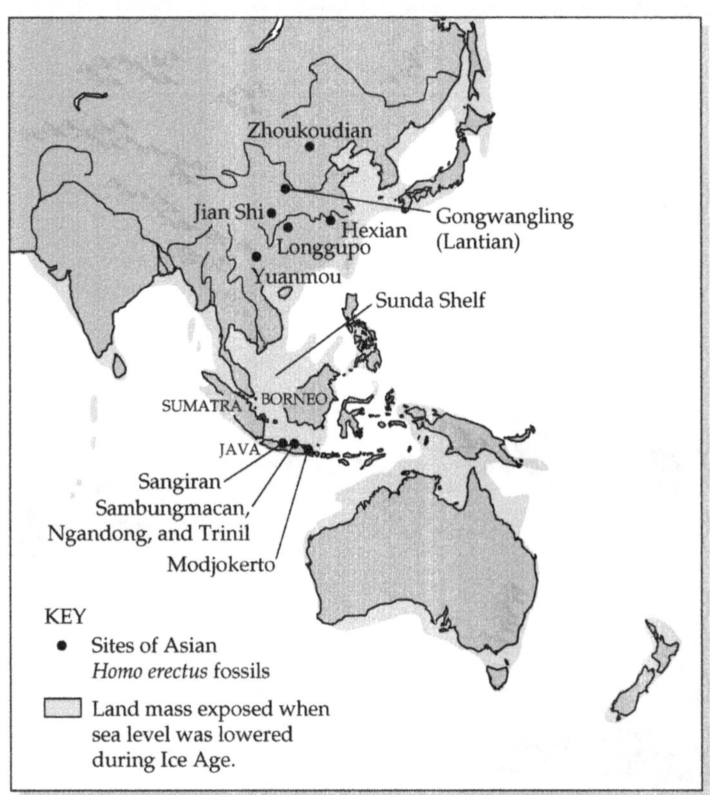

FIGURE 10.2 Important Asian *Homo erectus* sites. During glacial periods, when far more water was locked up in the polar and continental ice sheets than today, the world sea level fell. During the coldest periods, the maximum lowering of the sea appears to have been more than 330 feet (100 meters), which would have enlarged considerably the land masses available for occupation by plant and animal life. Throughout the Pleistocene, the sea level fluctuated extensively.

October 1887, Dubois sailed with his wife and infant daughter for Sumatra (Shipman, 2001).

For the first two years in Sumatra, Dubois's investigations of a great many limestone caves and deposits produced fossils of apes and other species but no "missing links." Dubois was sufficiently successful, however, that the colonial government decided to help with the search by giving him a crew of convicts and forced laborers (farmers working off their taxes, rather than paying with a portion of their crops), as well as two enlisted men to oversee them. Most importantly, Dubois was relieved of his medical duties in order to devote full attention to the explorations. In 1890, Dubois, with his family in tow, moved his operation to the island of Java, lured by the recent discovery of human fossils at the site of Wadjak. He immediately began to investigate caves, rock shelters, and other fossil deposits (Shipman, 2001).

Discovery of *Pithecanthropus*

To Dubois, the most promising site on the island seemed to be an exposed and stratified embankment along the Solo River, near the small village of Trinil in the center of Java (Figures 10.2 and 10.3). There, in the months when the river was low, Dubois could survey a bank 45 feet (14 meters) high of ancient river deposits with clearly defined layers of fine volcanic debris and sandstone (Dubois, 1896/1971).

Excavations at Trinil were begun in the summer of 1891 and immediately produced animal fossils, including extinct species of buffalo and elephants (*Stegodon*). The first primate fossil—an upper third molar (M3) from an apelike creature—was discovered in September from a rock layer about 5 feet (1.5 meters) below the low water level. Dubois initially interpreted this tooth as belonging to an Asian variety of chimpanzee but later changed his mind and attributed it to his ape-man. It was only one month later, in October 1891, that Dubois's crew hit real pay dirt. Still digging near the spot that had produced the molar, they found a faceless skullcap only 3 feet (0.9 meters) away (Figure 10.4). Dubois's wildest dream had come true! After coming halfway around the world, he had indeed found a "missing link" between humans and apes (Dubois, 1896/1971; Shipman, 2001; Theunissen, 1989).

FIGURE 10.3 At this bend in the Solo River at Trinil, Java, Dubois excavated the terraced bank where the Java fossils were found, at a depth of 48 feet (14.6 meters).

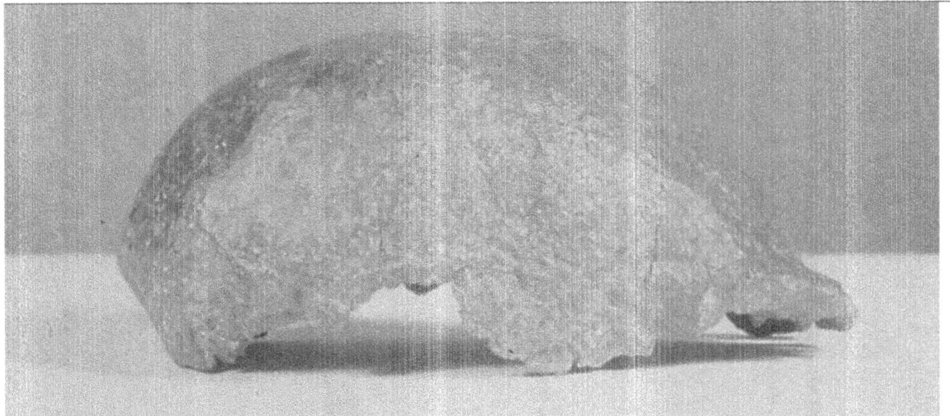

FIGURE 10.4
The skullcap of *Pithecanthropus erectus* was Dubois's greatest find. It was to be nearly forty years before another skull of this kind was found. This photograph is approximately 60 percent actual size.

Shortly after these finds were made, the rains came, the river rose, and digging had to be suspended until the following year. When digging resumed in 1892, Dubois cut a new excavation in the same deposit from which the strange cranium had been recovered. About 49 feet (15 meters) upstream from where the skull was found, he discovered another even more surprising primate fossil. This one was unmistakable. It was the left femur, or thighbone, of a primate that had walked erect! It resembled a human thighbone in almost every respect, except that it was heavier (Figure 10.5). Could the curious tooth, the problematic skull, and the unexpected thighbone all have belonged to the same individual? The implications were staggering (Theunissen, 1989).

Dubois measured and studied the apelike skull and the humanlike femur from Trinil and, in 1892, announced that the skull and femur had belonged to the same creature, which he believed to have been an upright species of chimpanzee that he called *Anthropopithecus erectus.* In 1893, however, he changed his mind and the species' name. After further study of the femur and after calculating that the fossil skullcap would have held a brain 2.4 times larger than that of an adult chimp, Dubois borrowed the name of Haeckel's hypothetical human ancestor and christened his fossil *Pithecanthropus erectus* (from the Greek *pithekos,* "ape," and *anthropos,* "man"). By appropriating this name for his Java find, Dubois boldly filed his claim to have found, as he cabled his friends in Europe, the "Missing Link of Darwin." He attributed it to a late Pliocene age (Theunissen, 1989).

The bones of *Pithecanthropus erectus* were one of the greatest fossil finds ever made, and even though he had only those few incomplete specimens, Dubois fully realized their importance. We now believe that *Pithecanthropus erectus* was actually an early human, a vital link in the chain of human evolution, not the half-ape Dubois had supposed it to be. We also now believe the Trinil skull to date from the middle Pleistocene—perhaps 800,000 to just over a million years BP (see Table 10.1).

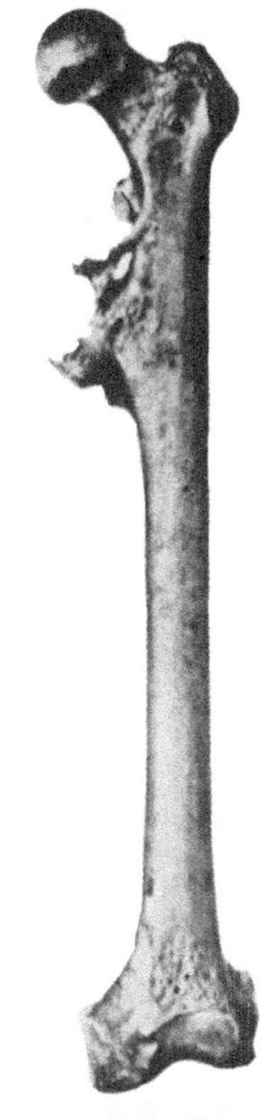

FIGURE 10.5
The first femur that Dubois found appeared very modern and indicated an upright posture. The growth of bone on its inner surface near the top is an unusual pathological condition (probably myositis ossificans, an inflammatory disease of muscles that produce extra bony deposits) that is also found occasionally in modern humans but has no evolutionary significance. This photograph is just under 25 percent actual size.

Java Controversy

Even before Dubois could show his discoveries to colleagues in Europe, his precious fossils became the focus of a raging scientific controversy that embroiled him throughout the rest of his life (Shipman, 2001; Theunissen, 1989). His reports were met with skepticism. Some critics insisted that the fossil bones did not belong together at all and suggested that Dubois had simply made the mistake of mixing the skull and teeth of an ape with the thighbone of a human who had died nearby. Dubois was denounced from pulpit and from podium, for clergy and scientists were almost equally angry and skeptical about his finds. The combination of apelike head and upright posture ran directly contrary to the belief that the development of a larger, better brain had come first in the separation of the human stock from earlier anthropoids. Scientists expected a being with a human head and an apelike body, not the reverse (Smith, 1927).

TABLE 10.1 A Partial Record of *Homo erectus* Fossils

Continent	Site	Age (Years BP)
Africa	Salé	300,000–200,000
	Sidi Abderrahman	300,000–200,000
	Thomas Quarries	350,000–240,000
	Lainyamok	600,000
	Ternifine	650,000
	Melka Kunture	900,000
	Olorgesailie	970,000–900,000
	Daka	1.0 million
	Olduvai Gorge	1.2 million–600,000
	Omo	1.4 million
	Nariokotome	1.5 million
	Swartkrans[a]	1.8–1.5 million
	Koobi Fora	1.8–1.6 million
Asia	Ngandong [Solo]	46,000–27,000
	Sambungmacan	53,000–27,000
	Jian Shi	300,000–200,000
	Zhoukoudian	670,000–410,000
	Hexian	700,000–250,000
	Gongwangling [Lantian]	700,000
	Yuanmou	900,000–500,000
	Trinil	1.0–0.8 million
	Sangiran	1.7 million–500,000
	Modjokerto	1.8 million
	Longgupo[b]	1.9–1.7 million
Europe	Dmanisi	1.7 million

[a]Some workers argue that the *Homo* fossils from Swartkrans do not fit easily into *H. erectus* and require their own species designation. We have opted to retain the traditional *H. erectus* classification, pending further information.
[b]Although its discoverers claim the Longgupo Cave fossils may represent *H. habilis*, a more conservative view is that they are best assigned to early *Homo erectus*.
Sources: Sources for most dates are given in the text. Also see Boaz and Ciochon, 2004; Conroy, 1997; Klein, 1999; and Potts et al., 2004.

The arrival of the fossils themselves for close inspection did not settle the arguments. In 1895, Dubois presented *Pithecanthropus* to the Third International Congress of Zoology at Leiden, announcing at this time the discovery from his collection of a second molar from Trinil. Almost at once, a quarrel broke out over the species' interpretation: Some scientists believed that *Pithecanthropus* was an ape that had humanlike characteristics, while others thought it was a human that had apelike attributes. Only a few scientists were inclined to agree with Dubois that the fossils represented a transitional form, or "missing link," between apes and humans.

For a while, Dubois patiently defended his claim for *Pithecanthropus.* He gave his colleagues as much detailed knowledge of the fossils as he could. He exhibited the bones at scientific meetings throughout Europe, showed them to any scientists who wanted to examine them, and published detailed descriptions. In spite of all Dubois's efforts, however, the attacks on *Pithecanthropus* continued and he took them personally. Deeply hurt by the refusal of other scientists to accept his interpretation of the bones, he withdrew the remains of *Pithecanthropus* from the public realm and refused to allow even scientific colleagues to examine them. He then turned his attention to research on brain evolution.

In 1922, an international effort was begun to persuade Dubois to once again make his fossils available for study. Soon afterward, Dubois opened his strongboxes for Alés Hrdlička of the Smithsonian Institution and thereafter again exhibited *Pithecanthropus* at scientific meetings. Between 1932 and 1935, continued examinations of the vast fossil collections that Dubois had brought back from the East Indies led to the discovery of five more fragmentary femora. These displayed the same characteristics as the original Trinil femur, thus proving beyond a doubt that *Pithecanthropus* was indeed a biped. At the same time, however, these discoveries undermined Dubois's argument that the original femur, molars, and skullcap were from the same individual.

Although fraught with controversy and not a little personal unhappiness, Eugene Dubois's accomplishment remains quite remarkable. He set out to find evidence of ape-to-human evolution and succeeded in his quest. As always happens in these cases, however, Dubois's time in the spotlight was relatively brief. In 1927, the attention of the scientific world was drawn to China and the discovery of a new species dubbed "Peking Man."

Twentieth-Century Discoveries

Search for Human Fossils in China

The years following Dubois's discovery saw several important additions to the hominin fossil record: the Mauer mandible (now thought to be *Homo heidelbergensis*) was discovered near Heidelberg, Germany, in 1907; the fraudulent Piltdown remains were announced in England between 1912 and 1913; and Dart's baby *Australopithecus africanus* from Taung was described in 1925. None of these finds, however, shed much light on Dubois's *Pithecanthropus erectus* fossils. That light came in 1927 with the discovery of more Asian "missing links" at the Chinese site of Zhoukoudian near Beijing (Peking).

The discovery of "Peking man" in 1927, resulted from the efforts—some direct and some indirect—of an interesting set of scientists. Henry Fairfield Osborn, head of the American Museum of Natural History, had raised interest in the topic of human evolution on the Asian mainland in the early 1920s. Osborne's belief that the high plateaus of Asia would yield fossil humans led him to send a series of expeditions to Mongolia between 1922 and 1925. Led by explorer and hunter Roy Chapman Andrews, these expeditions produced several fabulous discoveries, such as the first dinosaur eggs, but no evidence of human evolution (Andrews, 1926). In the meantime, Canadian physician Davidson Black was combining his duties as anatomy professor at Peking Union Medical College with a bit of fossil hunting. Aware that the so-called **dragon bones** (fossil bones and teeth) for sale in Chinese drugstores as medicinal ingredients occasionally included specimens of either ancient apes or ancient humans, Black had come to China in 1919 hoping to combine his anatomical vocation and anthropological avocation (Boaz and Ciochon, 2004).

Dragon bones the ancient Chinese term for *fossils* of various sorts that were collected and ground into medicines.

Black's plans of finding time for fossil hunting when he reached China were discouraged by the president of the Peking Union Medical College. Nonetheless, Black struck up a paleontological collaboration with a Swedish geologist named J. Gunnar Andersson, who had worked in China for years. Along with a young colleague, Otto Zdansky, Andersson had conducted excavations between 1921 and 1923 at a site called Dragon Bone Hill—now usually called Zhoukoudian, after a nearby village. In the course of those excavations, Zdansky discovered two hominin teeth, but in an apparent attempt to publish about them himself, he did not tell Andersson, who only learned about the hominin presence at Zhoukoudian in 1926. Andersson then shared this new information with Black, and together, they made the public announcement of the fossils that immediately became known as "Peking Man" (Black, 1926). In collaboration with the Geological Survey of China, plans were made for further excavations at Zhoukoudian under Black's general supervision (Boaz and Ciochon, 2004; Jia and Huang, 1990).

Sinanthropus Discovered

Work started up again at Dragon Bone Hill in 1927. The limestone of the hill was honeycombed with collapsed caves and fossil-filled fissures. Digging in this hard, compacted fill material proved difficult; blasting was often necessary.

In October 1927, just before the first season's work was to end, another hominin tooth was found. Black studied the tooth exhaustively. Struck by its size and cusp pattern, he became convinced that it was a very ancient human molar. Without waiting for any further proof, Black announced the discovery of a new genus and species of prehistoric human: *Sinanthropus pekinensis,* "Chinese man of Peking." Scientists were startled at the naming, given the paucity of fossil evidence for *Sinanthropus,* but the gamble paid off for Black, and he was able to obtain funding for continued excavations.

Black's belief in the humanness of *Sinanthropus* was vindicated quickly. In 1928, fossil jaws and more teeth were found, and the next year, Pei Wenzhong, a Chinese archaeologist and the new field supervisor at Zhoukoudian, turned up the first skull of *Sinanthropus.* It was a cold December afternoon and along with four other men, Pei was working by candle light in a deep crevice that already had produced several fossils. Observers at the surface heard the hammering of the excavators suddenly go dead and then heard Pei shout out, "What's that? A human skull!" (Jia and Huang, 1990:64). One of several skullcaps eventually recovered from Zhoukoudian (Figure 10.6), the precious fossil was carefully preserved in plaster, wrapped in burlap and cotton padding, and hand delivered by Pei to Davidson Black four days later. To describe Black as "elated" is putting it mildly.

Black spent the next four months freeing the skullcap from the surrounding stone. When it was entirely clean, he separated all the bones, made a cast of each one, and then reassembled the pieces. The cranial capacity of the skull, now known as Zhoukoudian III, came to about 915 cubic centimeters, marking its owner as definitely humanlike in this respect (Aiello and Dean, 1990).

Intensive Work at Zhoukoudian

The news made headlines around the world. Excavations at Zhoukoudian were reorganized on a broader basis and went on for almost ten more years, finally taking on the proportions of a grand engineering project.

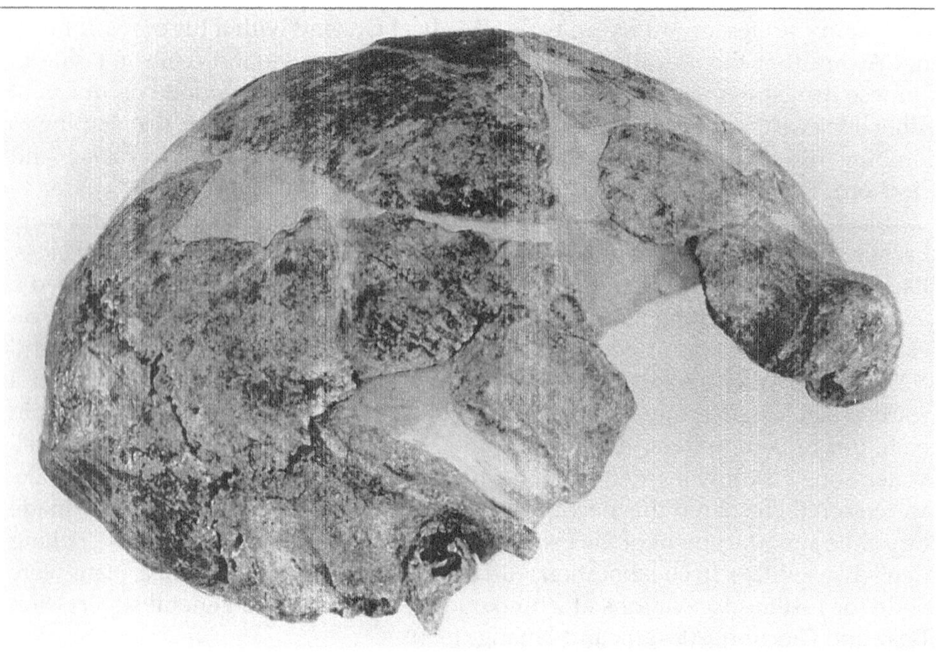

FIGURE 10.6 Although not the first to be discovered, this is one of several skullcaps of "Peking man" (*Homo erectus*) recovered from Zhoukoudian.

FIGURE 10.7 Franz Weidenreich (*left*, shown here with an unidentified colleague) succeeded Davidson Black at Peking Union Medical College in 1935 and pursued the excavations at Zhoukoudian with equal fervor.

As work advanced, a whole hillside was sliced off, revealing deposits 160 feet (almost 50 meters) deep (see photo on p. 262). The excavations cut through a compact mixture of limestone, clay, and animal and human debris. Large carnivores had occupied the Dragon Bone Hill cave for long periods of time, as shown by the bones of extinct creatures such as cave bears and giant hyenas. "Peking Man" also had used the cave between about 670,000 and 410,000 years ago (Table 10.1), probably staying mainly near its well-lit entrance, rather than challenging the hyenas residing in the depths (Boaz and Ciochon, 2004). The fossilized remains of these early humans continued to turn up regularly throughout the excavations of the 1930s, and by 1937, parts of more than forty individuals had been found. Included in the inventory of hominan fossils were six **calvariae** (skulls without faces or mandibles); several skull, face, and jaw fragments; numerous teeth; and assorted postcranial remains (Conroy, 1997).

Calvaria a braincase; that is, a skull minus the facial skeleton and lower jaw (plural, *calvariae*).

Black organized the work, kept detailed records of all the finds, classified them, and made casts, drawings, and photographs of the heavy volume of material pouring into Beijing. Tragically, he did not live to savor the full bounty of Zhoukoudian. He died of a heart attack in 1934, but he had seen enough to realize the site's extraordinary significance. The Rockefeller Foundation sought carefully for a successor and chose Franz Weidenreich, then a visiting professor of anatomy at the University of Chicago (Figure 10.7). Before Nazis' policies drove him from his native Germany, Weidenreich had completed important studies of several European fossil hominans (Boaz and Ciochon, 2004).

Assessment of *Sinanthropus*

After Weidenreich's arrival at Zhoukoudian in 1935, only two more seasons of undisturbed digging could be carried out. The Sino–Japanese War broke out in the summer of 1937, and the archaeologists had to take refuge. And with the approach of World War II, Weidenreich concentrated on making accurate drawings and casts of the skulls and published detailed photographs and descriptions of every important

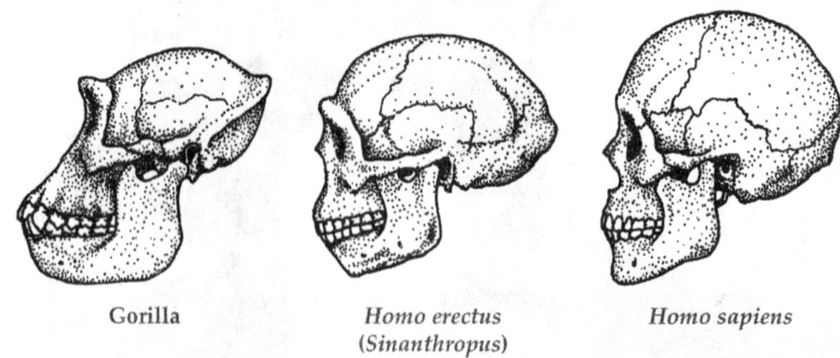

FIGURE 10.8
Skulls of a female gorilla, *Sinanthropus*, and a modern Chinese person (all equally reduced). Note the size and form of the braincase in relation to the jaws.

fossil. He began a classic series of studies of the fossils, all showing that *Sinanthropus* was not a link between apes and humans but an actual human, although a very primitive one.

Sinanthropus clearly walked upright like modern humans and also shared our trait of small, incisiform canine teeth. Furthermore, with an average cranial capacity of just over 1,000 cubic centimeters (Weidenreich, 1943), *Sinanthropus* was considerably nearer the mean for modern humans (1,330 cubic centimeters) than that of the largest-brained ape, the gorilla (about 500 cubic centimeters; Figure 10.8). But what of that preeminently human trait: culture? Was there evidence at Zhoukoudian that *Sinanthropus* had lived a cultural lifestyle, as do modern people?

Culture at Zhoukoudian

Insofar as the manufacture and use of stone tools is proof of a cultural lifestyle, the answer to the question just posed is yes. The Zhoukoudian excavations produced tens of thousands of stone artifacts, mostly made from quartz and mostly of the rather simple flake-and-chopper variety. Animal bones were found, as well, that showed stone tool cut marks, indicating that *Sinanthropus* defleshed carcasses at least occasionally (although whether they had killed the beasts themselves or scavenged from predator kills is another matter). Evidence for the use of antler and bone implements also has been reported but is currently controversial (Boaz and Ciochon, 2004).

Equally controversial is the suggestion that *Sinanthropus* regularly used fire for cooking and/or driving away predators at Dragon Bone Hill. Bits of burned bone have been found, but whether the fires in question were accidental or under hominan control is still uncertain. Meat was undoubtedly an important dietary component, however, and, it has been suggested, so were hackberry seeds. (Skeptics disagree on the last point.) The archaeological evidence from Zhoukoudian will be discussed further in the next chapter, but even a cursory analysis suggests at least a simple cultural existence (Boaz and Ciochon, 2004).

Relationship of *Pithecanthropus* and *Sinanthropus*

But how did the Chinese species compare with Dubois's *Pithecanthropus* from Java? Davidson Black suspected that they were very similar, but at the time of his death in 1934, comparisons between the Chinese and Javanese species were hampered by limited fossil collections from both regions. The situation improved when more fossils attributed to *Pithecanthropus* were discovered in the mid 1930s. Of particular importance, German paleontologist G. H. R. von Koenigswald found a child's skull at the Javanese site of Mojokerto in 1936 and an adult's skull at Sangiran in 1937 (Figure 10.2; Boaz and Ciochon, 2004; Swisher et al., 2000). The Sangiran skull was a particularly close match to Dubois's Trinil calvaria; indeed, the resemblance was "as [close] as one egg [to] another" (von Koenigswald and Weidenreich, 1939:927).

In 1939, a historic meeting of *Sinanthropus* and *Pithecanthropus* took place in Weidenreich's laboratory, when von Koenigswald paid a visit and brought his Java fossils along to compare them with the Zhoukoudian finds. The two scientists concluded that *Pithecanthropus* and *Sinanthropus* were indeed close relations and they said so in a joint paper published in *Nature:* "Considered from the general point of view of human evolution, [*Pithecanthropus*] and [*Sinanthropus*] . . . are related to each other in the same way as two different races of present mankind" (von Koenigswald and Weidenreich, 1939:928).

The aging Eugene Dubois bitterly opposed this conclusion, continuing to insist that his own find was quite distinct from all others (Shipman, 2001). But von Koenigswald and Weidenreich were little disturbed by his protests. More upsetting was the rumble of war.

Fate of the Java and Beijing Fossils

In Java, von Koenigswald knew that it was only a matter of time until the island would be seized. He quietly gave some of his most valuable fossils for safekeeping to a Swiss geologist and a Swedish journalist, neutrals in the conflict between the Allies and Axis powers. (The journalist put the teeth in milk bottles and buried them one night in his garden.) When the Japanese occupied Java in 1942, they demanded that von Koenigswald give up his fossils. He surrendered a few but substituted plaster casts for some of the originals. At the end of the war, von Koenigswald tracked down and reassembled all the fossils. The single skull that had been taken to Japan (as a birthday present for the Emperor) was returned in the late 1940s. *Pithecanthropus* had survived the disaster of World War II (von Koenigswald, 1956).

The Peking Man fossils were not so fortunate as those from Java. The start of the Sino–Japanese war in 1937 resulted in the end of excavation at Zhoukoudian and the occupation of Beijing by the Japanese. Initially, it was believed that the occupying forces posed no threat to the *Sinanthropus* fossils, and so they remained at the Peking Union Medical College. By early 1941, however, Weidenreich, along with officials of the Geological Survey of China, had become sufficiently concerned to request the removal of the specimens to safety in the United States. Despite their warnings, the president of the Medical College remained convinced that the fossils were in no danger. He therefore denied the request to ship them abroad and instead fired Weidenreich (who went to New York). The situation in China had deteriorated enough by November 1941, however, that the *Sinanthropus* fossils were finally crated up for transport to the United States (Boaz and Ciochon, 2004).

At this point, the story becomes absolutely muddled. The Peking Man fossils never made it to the United States, but it is unknown whether they were lost (or hidden?) at the Medical College, the U.S. Legation in Beijing, the U.S. Marine barracks next door to the Legation, or the port city of Qinhuangdao. The rumor has been disproved that they were loaded onto an American steamship that was subsequently sunk, but to this day, the original *Sinanthropus* specimens have not turned up, despite diligent searching by many people. Luckily, Weidenreich had overseen the preparation of a superb series of fossil casts, and those did survive. The casts, along with Weidenreich's excellent descriptions and photographs, preserve much information about the original Zhoukoudian fossils (Boaz and Ciochon, 2004).

During the 1940s, it became increasingly clear that *Pithecanthropus* showed strong anatomical resemblances to modern humans, *Homo sapiens.* As a result, in 1951, as part of a general taxonomic house cleaning, *Pithecanthropus,* in all of its Asian forms, was formally sunk into the single species *Homo erectus* (Figure 10.9; Howells, 1980). And no sooner had the new species been established than it proved to have some surprises up its sleeve. Discoveries over the following half century have shown that *Homo erectus* is much older than initial estimates and was much more widely spread across the Old World.

FIGURE 10.9
The reconstruction of the skull and jaw of *Homo erectus* is based on numerous fossil finds. The general form of the face can also be reconstructed with reasonable accuracy, but we have little information on such important features as nostrils, lips, and hair.

Homo erectus Fossils from Africa

Since the 1950s, the African continent has yielded numerous fossils of *Homo erectus* from a variety of locations (Figure 10.10 and Table 10.1). In 1954, *Homo erectus* mandibles dating 650,000 years BP were discovered at the northwest African site of Ternifine, Algeria. The next year, another jaw was recovered from slightly younger deposits at the coastal Moroccan site of Sidi Abderrahman, and in 1971, cranial fragments of late *Homo erectus* also were reported from Salé, Morocco (Conroy, 1997; Klein, 1989).

Fossils from South and East Africa have pushed the species farther and farther into the past. The Swartkrans site has produced remains dating between 1.8 and 1.5 million years of age that *may* represent *Homo erectus* (see Chapter 6). In 1960, Louis Leakey recovered undoubted *Homo erectus* remains (museum number OH 9) dating 1.2 million years BP from Tanzania's Olduvai Gorge. (Since then, younger *H. erectus* fossils, circa 600,000 to 700,000 years of age, have also been found at Olduvai.) Just north of Olduvai, the Kenyan site of Lainyamok has yielded *Homo erectus* teeth and limb bones dating around 600,000 years BP, while the central Ethiopian site of Melka Kunturé has produced a cranial fragment that may go back 900,000 years. In 2003, Ethiopia contributed another *H. erectus* skull and some postcranial remains from a 1.0-million-year-old site called Daka in the Middle Awash region (Asfaw et al., 2002).

The distinction of producing the most ancient remains of East African *Homo erectus,* however, belongs to the Omo region of extreme southwestern Ethiopia and the east and west shores of Lake Turkana in Kenya. Relevant Omo fossils date to 1.4 million years ago, while discoveries in east Turkana's Koobi Fora region carry *Homo erectus* all the way back to 1.8 million years BP Among the Koobi Fora fossils is a superb skull, designated KNM ER-3733, whose owner boasted a cranial capacity of 850 cubic centimeters some 1.7 mya (Figure 10.11; Klein, 1989).

But of all the African specimens, the *Homo erectus* boy from the west Turkana site of Nariokotome is perhaps the most exciting (Walker and Leakey, 1993). Initially

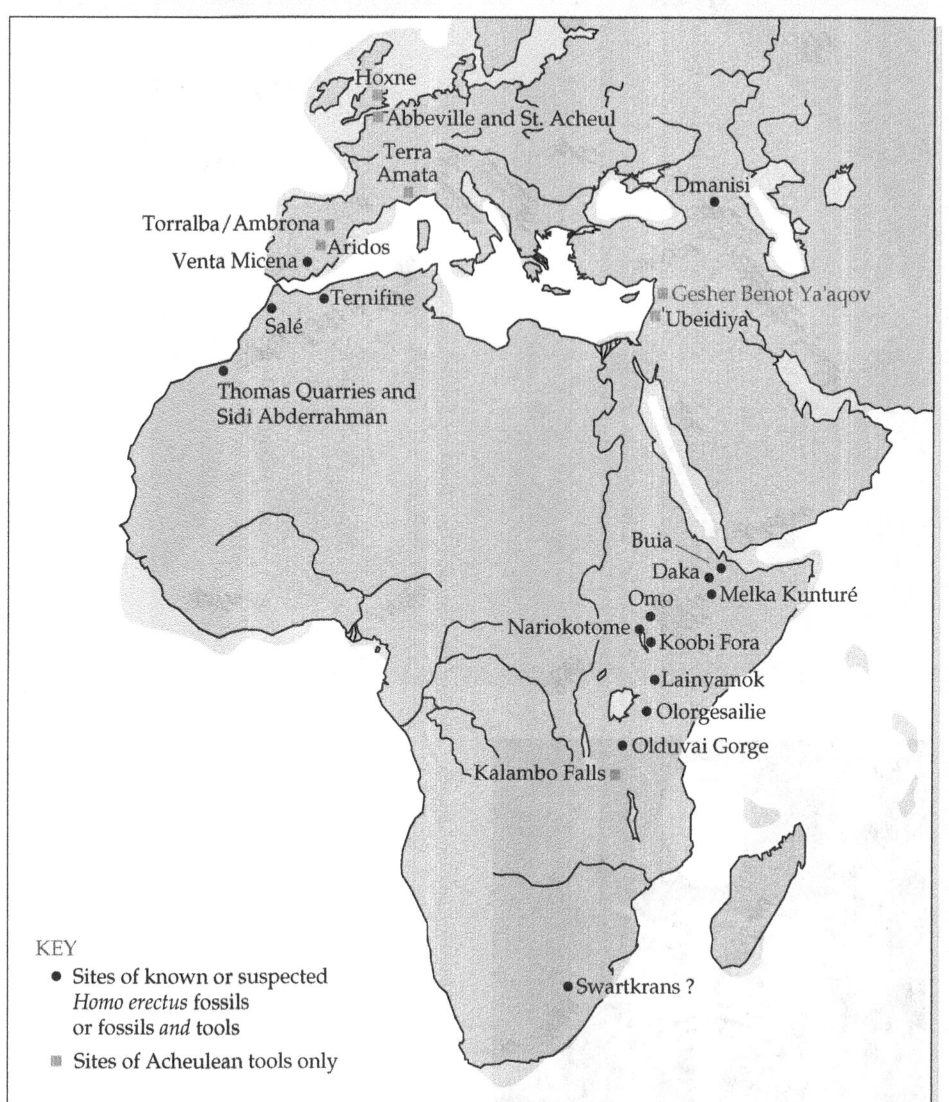

FIGURE 10.10
Since the earliest discoveries in East Asia, a number of sites in Europe and Africa have yielded fossil remains of *Homo erectus* and/or Acheulean tools. On this map, the coastline is shown as it might have been during a period of glaciation when the sea level fell.

discovered in 1984 by the veteran fossil hunter Kamoya Kimeu, the specimen consists of a nearly complete skeleton (Figure 10.12) that lacks only the left humerus (upper arm bone), both radii (lower arm bones), and most of the bones of the hands and feet. Dated to 1.5 million years BP, the Nariokotome boy was about twelve years old when he died (perhaps from the septicemia of a gum infection after the loss of a lower milk molar) and came to lie in a shallow swamp that was probably replenished seasonally by the floodwaters of the Omo River. After death, the body lay relatively undisturbed in the quiet water as it gradually decomposed. Small portions of the body were very likely eaten by scavenging catfish, and the skeleton was dispersed and damaged somewhat as large wading animals trampled and kicked the bones. Most of the skeleton, however, settled quietly into the mud and began the long wait until its discovery 1.5 million years later.

The nearly complete nature of the Nariokotome skeleton has allowed detailed studies of *Homo erectus* anatomy never before possible. The boy was about 5.3 feet (160 centimeters) tall at death and would very likely have grown to be a big man of about 6.1 feet (185 centimeters) and 150 pounds (68 kilograms). His boyhood cranial capacity of 880 cubic centimeters would probably have expanded to about 909

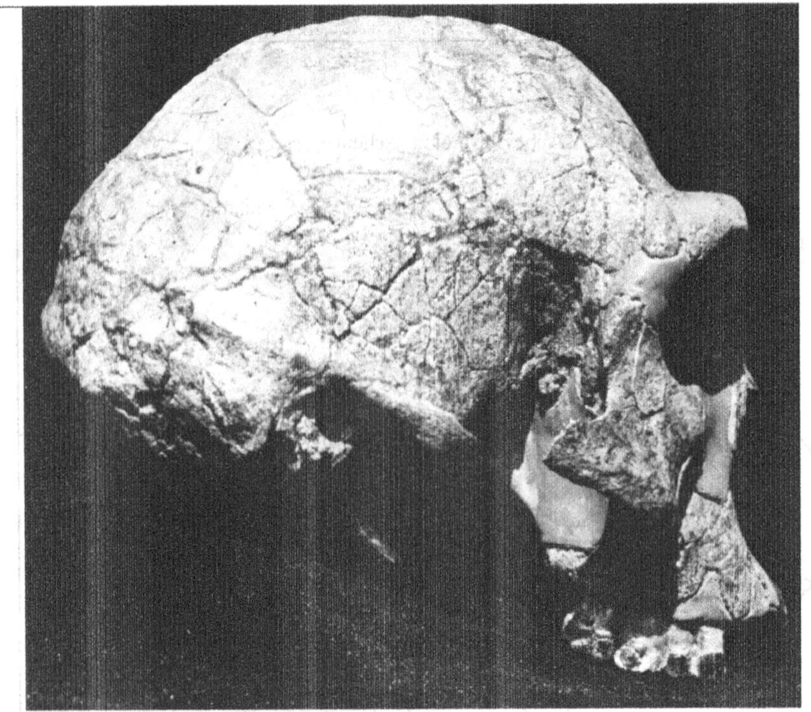

FIGURE 10.11 This skull from Koobi Fora in Kenya is one of the best-preserved skulls that belongs to the species *Homo erectus*. The present evidence suggests it may be 1.7 million years old. This photograph is approximately one-third actual size.

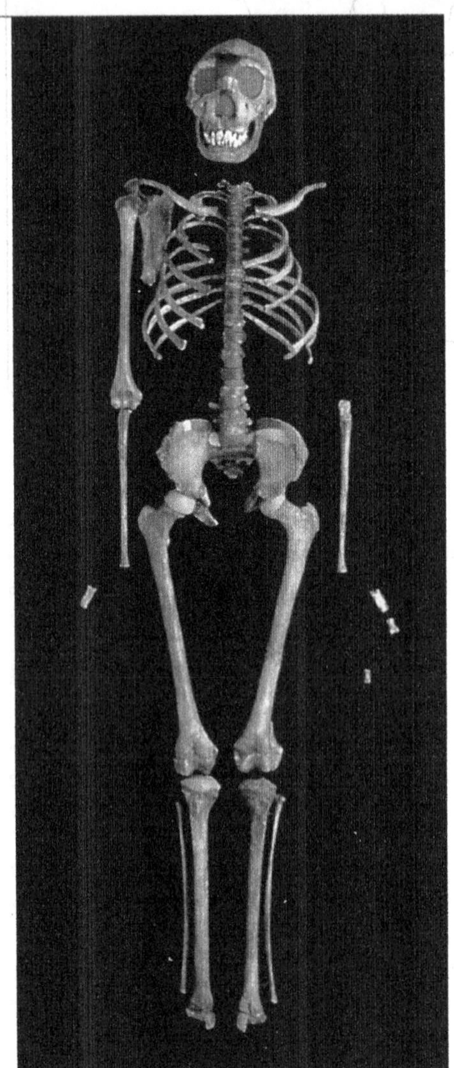

FIGURE 10.12 The most complete early hominan skeleton ever found was discovered at Nariokotome, west of Lake Turkana, Kenya, in 1984 and was excavated from sediments that are dated close to 1.5 million years ago. The skeleton, known as KNM-WT 15000, belongs to a twelve-year-old *Homo erectus* boy who would have grown into an adult more than 6 feet (1.8 meters) in height.

cubic centimeters when he became an adult (68 percent of the modern human average). He had long arms and legs and a slender torso—bodily proportions identical to those of modern people who are adapted to hot, dry climates. His estimated adult pelvic dimensions, if characteristic of the species, suggest that *Homo erectus* newborns had a relatively small brain (perhaps about 200 cubic centimeters) and that, as in modern humans, rapid brain growth then continued for the first part of an infant's life. And finally, details of his thoracic (rib cage) vertebrae suggest that *Homo erectus* may have lacked the fine muscular control over breathing that is required for speech (more on this in a later section; Walker, 1993b; see also the chapters in Walker and Leakey, 1993).

Evidence of *Homo erectus* in Europe: Many Artifacts, Few Fossils

As detailed in the next chapter, after about 1.5 mya, *Homo erectus* people in Africa, parts of Europe, and western Asia produced a new and distinctive type of stone tool industry called the Acheulean. In addition, *H. erectus* populations everywhere continued to make and use Oldowan flakes and choppers, and in Eastern Asia these were their only stone implements (Boaz and Ciochon, 2004; Schick and Toth, 1993). Both Acheulean and Oldowan sites attributed to *Homo erectus* have been excavated in Europe, but only a handful of *H. erectus* fossils have come from that continent. Perhaps the most tantalizing specimens—three skulls, two mandibles, and several postcranial fragments—come from the Caucasus site of Dmanisi in extreme southeastern Europe (Figure 10.10; Antón, 2003; Gabunia et al., 2001; Vekua et al., 2002). Dated to 1.7 million years of age and associated with Oldowan-type chopper and flakes, the Dmanisi fossils are considered to be very primitive representatives of *Homo erectus*, although some specimens also show strong similarities to *Homo habilis* (Vekua et al., 2002).

Although these are the only definite fossils of *Homo erectus* to come from Europe, we would be remiss not to mention the controversial material from Venta Micena near Orce in southern Spain (see Figure 10.10). Dated by paleomagnetism and faunal studies to about 1.6 million years ago, Venta Micena has produced Oldowan tools, the remains of several immigrant animal species from nearby Africa (including hippos, ancestral zebras, and ancestral hyenas), and a skull fragment that some workers have attributed to *Homo* (species indeterminate, but probably *erectus;* Borja et al., 1997). The hominin nature of the Orce remains has not gone unchallenged, however (Moyà-Solà and Köhler, 1997; Palmqvist, 1997), and the latest analysis seems to prove that the skull fragment is actually from a large ruminant (i.e., a cow or deer; Martínez-Navarro, 2002).

Nonetheless, the site itself is tremendously exciting because of its extreme age and undoubted stone tools. At 1.6 million years of age, Venta Micena is clearly the oldest hominin site in Western Europe, nearly matching Dmanisi in its antiquity. Furthermore, the Spanish material shows that the human exodus from Africa occurred at both ends of the Mediterranean, rather than simply through the Middle East.

More Fossils and Some Surprising Dates from Asia

World War II caused a temporary break in paleoanthropological activities in Asia, but during the second half of the twentieth century, exploration resumed and more *Homo erectus* specimens were discovered. In China, intermittent work was resumed at Zhoukoudian, and new dental, cranial, and postcranial material, was recovered (Boaz and Ciochon, 2004). Additionally, Chinese workers found *Homo erectus* remains at several new sites, including Gongwangling (where the finds included a partial skull with an estimated cranial capacity of about 780 cubic centimeters),

Yuanmou, and Hexian (Figure 10.2). The Hexian material, which is no older than 700,000 and perhaps as young as 250,000 years BP (Table 10.1), represents at least three *H. erectus* individuals and was discovered in 1980–1981. Finally, and most intriguing of all, excavations carried out between 1985 and 1988 at the Longgupo Cave site in Sichuan Province (Figure 10.2) may have produced the very oldest evidence of hominins in Asia. The Longgupo fossils include a partial mandible with the left P4 and M1 and an upper incisor. Found in association with two apparent Oldowan tools, the teeth show similarities to both *Homo erectus* and *Homo habilis* and carry a paleomagnetic date of 1.9 to 1.7 million years ago. For simplification and because of their early date and lack of diagnostic traits, we have chosen to treat the Longgupo fossils in this text as early *Homo erectus*. Nonetheless, some researchers (including the fossils' discoverers) think the teeth, and thus the first Asians, are best classified as a pre-*erectus* hominin type (Boaz and Ciochon 2004; Conroy, 1997).

Java, too, has continued to produce *Homo erectus* fossils (some of them questionable, see following) since Indonesia's independence in 1945. Included in the new discoveries are calvariae and postcranial fossils from Ngandong (found between 1976 and 1980), more skulls from Sambungmacan (1973 and 2003), and an exceptionally complete cranium from Sangiran (found in 1993 and estimated to have a cranial capacity of 856 cubic centimeters; Baba et al., 2003; Conroy, 1997).

The most exciting news from Java, however, is not about newly discovered fossils but about the new and startling dates that have been determined for some long-known remains. First, as background, until recently, the consensus was that *H. erectus* had originated in Africa about 1.8 million years ago from early *Homo* stock (either *H. habilis* or *H. rudolfensis*), and then, about 1 mya, as a result of increased intelligence and cultural complexity, the species was able to expand its geographic range out of Africa and into Europe and Asia, reaching Java no later than 900,000 to 800,000 years BP. It was a tidy scenario and one that seemed adequate for many years but is no more, thanks to new information.

Recently, a joint American–Indonesian research team has re-dated two of the classic Javanese *H. erectus* sites. Using an Ar^{40}/Ar^{39} dating technique, the team—headed by geochronologists Carl Swisher and Garniss Curtis—determined in 1994 that *Homo erectus* inhabited the Sangiran region more than 1.66 million years ago and the Modjokerto region as early as 1.81 million years BP (Swisher et al., 1994). Thus, it appears that *Homo erectus* may have inhabited extreme Southeast Asia fully a million years earlier than traditionally believed and could be equally old in Asia, Africa, and Europe. This new evidence alone could mean that the species' place of origin and subsequent migrations may have to be revised.

But there's one more bit of evidence to be considered, and it, too, may weigh against the traditional migration scenario. If the discoverers of the Longgupo Cave hominin are correct in identifying their find as belonging to a pre-*erectus* species (Huang et al., 1995), it would go far toward proving that early *Homo* was the first hominin type to spread out of African, not *H. erectus*. On the other hand, if a slightly older African *Homo erectus* specimen turns up in the future, enormous amounts of time probably are not needed for the traditional Africa-to-Asia expansion. For example, an African origin for *H. erectus* at 2.0 million years ago, followed by a leisurely spread of 1 mile (1.6 kilometers) every ten years would have put hominins at Longgupo Cave and in Java 100,000 years later. In any event, only time and further discoveries will help to answer these questions. As things stand presently, none of the possible points of origin—Africa, Asia, or somewhere in between—can be definitely ruled out for *Homo erectus*.

Regardless of when and where they originated, however, *Homo erectus* apparently stayed around for a very long time based on new dates for the Javanese sites of Ngandong and Sambungmacan (Table 10.1 and Figure 10.2). Based on chronometric dates taken from fossil water buffalo teeth collected at the two sites, geochronologists have estimated the age of Ngandong at 46,000 to 27,000 years BP and that of Sambungmacan at 53,000 to 27,000 BP (Swisher et al., 1996). Thus, late *Homo erectus* may have overlapped in time with *Homo sapiens* in southeast Asia, with the implication that local *H. erectus* populations probably were not ancestral to modern Asians. (Recent excavations do suggest, however, that Asian *Homo erectus* people gave rise to a dwarfed hominan type that is now extinct: *Homo floresiensis* [see Chapter 15, Postscript].)

Finally, it must be noted that not all paleoanthropologists concur in classifying Ngandong and Sambungmacan as *H. erectus* but rather argue from enlarged brain size and other modernish features that they are best placed in *Homo sapiens* (Wolpoff, 1996). In this book, however, we have adopted what we judge to be the majority opinion and included Ngandong and Sambungmacan as bona fide *Homo erectus* populations (see Antón, 2002, 2003; Rightmire, 1990).

The Anatomy of *Homo erectus*

Fossils attributed to *Homo erectus* therefore cover an enormous time span (1.9 million to possibly about 27,000 years BP; Box 10.1) and an equally impressive geographical range (from South Africa to southeast Asia). As a consequence of its longevity and geographic spread, *Homo erectus* shows a good deal of anatomical variability—too much, in fact, for some researchers (e.g., Wood and Richmond, 2000), who argue that certain early African specimens should be put in a separate species from classic Asian *H. erectus.* These workers argue that the material traditionally included in *Homo erectus* should be divided, retaining the name *Homo erectus* for the Asian fossils from Java and China and classifying at least the early African remains from Lake Turkana (KNM ER-3733 and 3883, and the Nariokotome boy, KNM WT-15000) as a separate species called ***Homo ergaster.*** (Interestingly, certain later African fossils, such as Louis Leakey's 1.2-million-year-old skull from Olduvai Gorge, would be left in *H. erectus.*) Supporters of this scheme view *H. ergaster* as more closely related (and more likely to be ancestral) to modern humans than was Asian *Homo erectus* (Tattersall, 2003).

Homo ergaster the *species* name given by some *paleoanthropologists* to certain African *fossils* regarded by most workers as early *Homo erectus*.

Other scientists disagree with the proposed taxonomic split, however, and chief among the dissenters is G. Philip Rightmire (1990, 1992). Rightmire and like-minded paleoanthropologists conclude that there is insufficient anatomical difference to justify the recognition of two separate species, arguing that *Homo erectus*'s anatomical variability simply matched its geographic spread. (Note that some researchers, such as Boaz and Ciochon [2004], do recognize subspecific distinctions.) The single-species group points out that many of the traits claimed to be distinctive, derived features of Asian *Homo erectus* can also be identified on some of the early African specimens. For example, **sagittal keeling** of the frontal and/or parietal bones is common among the Asian fossils, but it is also present on KNM ER-3733 and 3883 from East Africa (Figure 10.13). The single-species position has gained further support from the recent discoveries in Africa of two 1-million-year-old skulls that bridge the claimed anatomical gap between Asian *H. erectus* and the "*H. ergaster*" specimens: Buia (from Eritrea; Abbate et al., 1998) and Daka (from Ethiopia; Asfaw et al., 2002).

Sagittal keel a slightly raised ridge running down the center of a skull; smaller than a *sagittal crest*.

For the moment, the authors of this book find the single-species position to be the most convincing and thus retain the traditional classification scheme and treat *Homo erectus* as one variable and widespread species. We hasten to add, however, that this taxonomy does not imply that the evolutionary descendants of *H. erectus* (i.e., *Homo heidelbergensis,* see following) were equally related to the African and Asian populations of the ancestral species. As shown in Figure 10.14, part b, a speciation event located in Africa could have produced descendants who carried more African than Asian traits. With these taxonomic issues out of the way, we can proceed to the anatomy.

In many important ways, *Homo erectus* had reached anatomical modernity. On average, these people were as tall and as heavy as modern humans (compare Boxes

FIGURE 10.13
Homo erectus skulls from Africa (*left*) and Asia (*center*) are compared. Shared traits include the long, low-vaulted, and wide braincase; large brows; an angled occipital region; and an occipital ridge. Also, both African and Asian *Homo erectus* skulls may show some sagittal keeling. A superior view of the skull of *H. erectus* (*right*) reveals a marked postorbital constriction (specimen from Zhoukoudian).

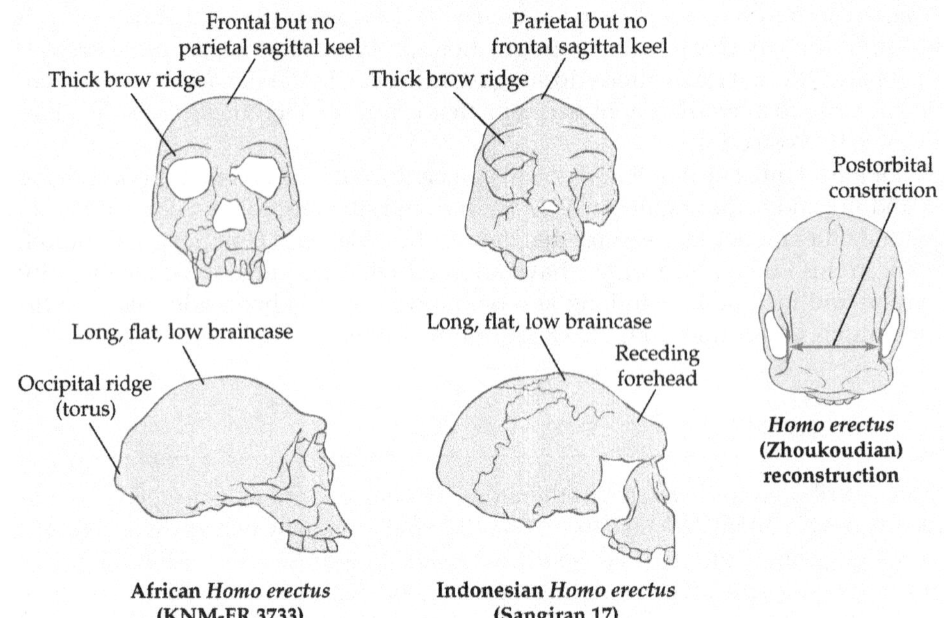

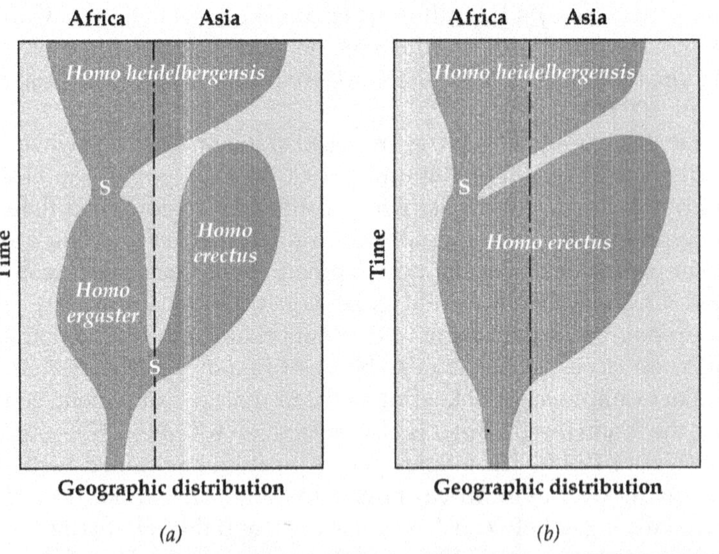

FIGURE 10.14
In phylogenetic scheme *(a)*, the African species *Homo ergaster* gives rise first to the Asian species *Homo erectus* and later to the worldwide species *Homo heidelbergensis*. This view is favored by Bernard Wood, Ian Tattersall, and others, and it would successfully explain why modern humans show few of the anatomical specializations of Asian *H. erectus*. Scheme *(a)* does require, however, splitting mid Pleistocene hominins into two species. Phylogenetic scheme *(b)*, on the other hand, retains all mid Pleistocene hominins in the single, widespread species *Homo erectus*. Stronger African than Asian resemblances for *Homo heidelbergensis* are then explained by that taxon's speciation event occurring in Africa. The authors of this text prefer scheme *(b)*, given the available evidence. The letter S marks a speciation event.

Source: Based on Harrison, 1993.

BOX 10.1

Characteristics of *Homo erectus*[a]

Trait	*Homo erectus*
Height (sexes combined)	4.9–6.1 ft (148–185 cm)
Weight (sexes combined)	101–150 lb (46-68 kg)
Brain size (sexes combined)	962 cc mean (600–1,251 cc range)
Cranium	Long, low-vaulted (platycephalic) braincase, widest at the base; large brow ridges; some sagittal keeling common; thick skull bones; variable flexion of cranial base; **occipital torus**
Dentition	Both anterior and posterior teeth smaller than those of early *Homo*
Limbs	Relative arm and leg lengths within modern human range of variation
Locomotion	Bipedalism (fully modern)
Distribution	Africa, Asia, Europe
Known dates (years BP)	1.9 million to possibly 27,000

[a]For additional technical details and diagnostic traits, see Appendix 3.
Sources: Aiello and Dean, 1990, Antón, 2002, 2003; Rightmire, 1990, 1992.

10.1 and 15.1; Antón, 2003). They seem to have had a modern body build, with a distinct waist instead of the potbelly that probably characterized earlier hominins (Aiello and Wheeler, 1995; this finding has implications for the diet of *Homo erectus,* as discussed in Chapter 11). Furthermore, the limb proportions of *H. erectus* were similar to those of modern humans (note that new data suggest that this may have been true for *Homo habilis,* as well; Haeusler and McHenry, 2004). There can be no doubt that *Homo erectus* stood and moved in a fully modern, upright fashion.

Occipital torus a ridge running side to side across the occipital bone.

Despite their modern postcranial skeletons, however, *Homo erectus* individuals differed greatly from modern people in their brain size and cranial anatomy. Overall, the average brain size for *Homo erectus* was 962 cubic centimeters (range 600 to 1,251 cubic centimeters; Antón, 2003; see Box 10.1). This cranial capacity was 1.2 to 1.6 times larger than in early *Homo* but still only 72 percent of the modern average (Table 8.3). Furthermore, because brain expansion in *Homo erectus* was matched, to some extent, by increased body size, the species' relative brain size (brain size controlling for body weight) was not dramatically greater than that of early *Homo* (see Chapter 13). Additionally, the enlarged *H. erectus* brain was still encased in a primitive-looking container (Figures 10.11 and 10.13). The skull of *Homo erectus* was constructed of thick cranial bones, and it was long, low vaulted, and widest at the base, a combination of traits labeled **platycephalic** (Rightmire, 1990, 1992).

Platycephalic a term describing a skull that is long, low vaulted, and wide.

The front of the cranium was topped with huge brow ridges, and behind those brows, the skull showed a distinct postorbital constriction at the temples. Often, particularly in the Asian specimens, the top of the skull showed a distinct sagittal keel. (The function of this feature, like many others, is unknown.) And finally, at the back, the skull of *Homo erectus* was ridged and angled sharply toward the cranial base (Figure 10.13), and the cranial base itself tended to be rather flat and unflexed, lacking the arched configuration characteristic of modern humans (Aiello and Dean, 1990; Rightmire, 1990; note that this trait is variable, however, as described by Baba et al., 2003, and Ross and Henneberg, 1995).

Several researchers have attempted to determine whether *Homo erectus* showed any significant evolutionary changes in anatomy during its long period of existence. In a recent statement on the subject, G. P. Rightmire (2004) concluded that *Homo erectus* did, in fact, show a steady (anagenetic) increase in brain size of some 165 cubic centimeters every million years. This pattern was broken only by the cladogenetic origin of *H. erectus*'s bigger-brained descendant, *Homo heidelbergensis*, around 800,000 years ago (Rightmire, 2004). Whether or not *H. erectus*'s steadily increasing brain size had any behavioral implications will be examined in the next chapter.

Anatomical Evidence of Speech and Language

A crucial question that so far has defied our attempts at an answer concerns the beginnings of those uniquely human traits, speech and language (see Chapter 3 for definitions). The australopiths all seemed too small brained and behaviorally primitive to have had language and speech. Early representatives of *Homo* showed a strong increase in brain size and definite stone tool technology, but most workers hesitate to regard them as linguistic creatures. But what about *Homo erectus*? Surely, with all we know about the anatomy of this species, we can draw some clear conclusions about its linguistic capacities.

Unfortunately, it seems that when it comes to elucidating speech and language evolution, additional anatomical knowledge has exacerbated rather than reduced the problem. Certainly, *Homo erectus* had an absolutely larger brain than its evolutionary predecessors, but this only increases the likelihood rather than proving conclusively that they produced spoken language. An examination of the brain's so-called language areas (see Chapter 13) is also inconclusive.

Broca's area a part of the human *cerebral cortex* involved with the hierarchical organization of grammar and the manual combination of objects.

Wernicke's area a part of the human *cerebral cortex* essential in comprehending and producing meaningful *speech*.

Hemispherical asymmetry the condition in which the two cerebral hemispheres differ in one or more dimensions. In most modern humans, the left hemisphere is somewhat larger than the right.

Although **Broca's area** in the inferior frontal lobe is well developed in *Homo erectus* (Begun and Walker, 1993), recent research on modern humans has shown that this cortical region supports both the hierarchical organization of grammar and the manual combination of objects, including tool use (Greenfield, 1991). Whether the manual coordination involved in tool manufacture and use or the production of hierarchically organized speech or both were associated with Broca's area development in *Homo erectus* is unknown. Furthermore, **Wernicke's area** in the temporal lobe appears to be extremely difficult to assess for most ancient skulls—including those of *Homo erectus*—because of distortion during fossilization (Walker, 1993a). And finally, **hemispherical asymmetry** in the cerebrum—demonstrable in the Nariokotome boy and very likely associated in that specimen with right-handedness—cannot be trusted as a guide to language abilities since asymmetry (including left-hemisphere dominance for vocalizations) has been documented for monkeys and apes (Falk, 1992).

Two negative bits of anatomical evidence argue against fully modern language in *Homo erectus*. First, although there is some variation among specimens, the cranial base is generally flatter (less strongly flexed) than in modern humans. As detailed in Chapter 13, this suggests a short pharynx and an inability to produce the full range of modern vowel sounds. Second, analyses of the vertebral canals of the Nariokotome boy have revealed dimensions similar to those of monkeys and apes in the thoracic (rib cage) region (MacLarnon, 1993; Figure 10.15). In contrast, modern humans have enlarged canals in their thoracic vertebrae, possibly to accommodate increased nerve connections with the rib cage muscles that control this part of the breathing apparatus. The small thoracic canals found in *Homo erectus* suggest that this species lacked the fine control of breathing that is essential for modern speech (MacLarnon and Hewitt, 2004; Walker, 1993a, 1993b).

So, could *Homo erectus* talk? The best answer from anatomy is a rather unsatisfying "maybe." It is entirely possible that archaeology may be a better guide to these capacities than is anatomy. This is an important point to keep in mind when we examine the archaeological evidence gathered from *Homo erectus* sites (Chapter 11).

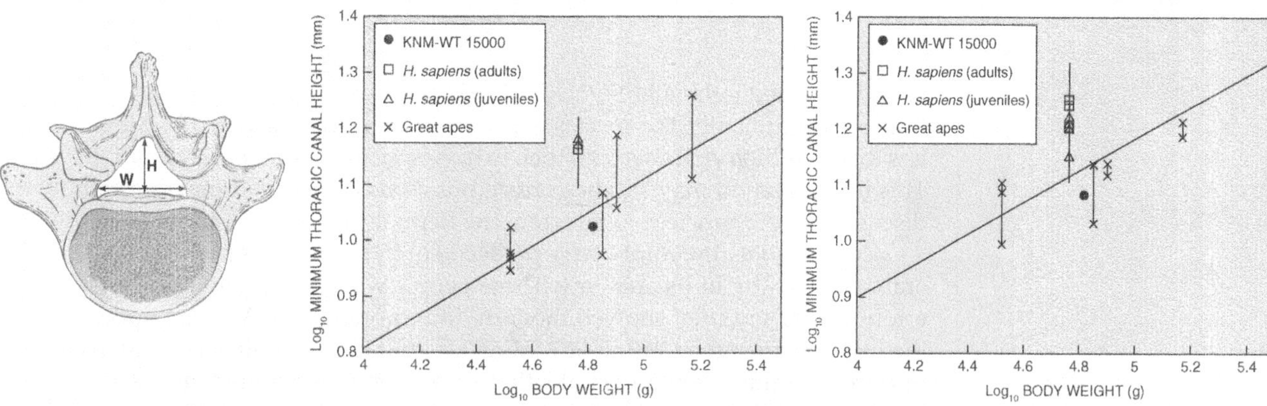

FIGURE 10.15
A representative human vertebra (*left*) showing the vertebral canal and how it can be measured. The Nariokotome boy (KNM-WT 15000) had smaller thoracic canal measurements than both adult and juvenile modern humans (*center* and *right*). The KNM-WT 15000 dimensions are roughly comparable to those of some apes.

Evolutionary Relationships of *Homo erectus*

Our interpretation of the fossil evidence is that *Homo erectus* evolved from some form of early *Homo* around 1.9 million years BP. As explained earlier, it is impossible at present to pinpoint the place of origin of *H. erectus,* although an East African homeland still seems most likely. Following its advent, *Homo erectus* spread across the face of the Old World—eventually occupying portions of Africa, Asia, and Europe—and may have survived until about 53,000 to 27,000 years ago in a few Old World culs-de-sac.

At some point in the mid Pleistocene—roughly, sometime around 800,000 to 600,000 BP, judging by fossils discovered in Southern Europe and Africa—*Homo erectus* gave rise to a new and bigger-brained descendant that many paleoanthropologists call *Homo heidelbergensis.* (Note that some workers still interpret *Homo erectus* as evolving into "archaic *Homo sapiens*"; Chapter 12). As shown in schematic form in Figure 10.14, this speciation event probably occurred in Africa or Western Eurasia (Rightmire, 1996). Undoubtedly more intelligent than their ancestors and with a more complex culture, *Homo heidelbergensis* lived on eventually to give rise to both modern humans and the Neandertals.

Finally, in addition to producing *H. heidelbergensis,* a very recent discovery on the Indonesian island of Flores suggests that *Homo erectus* gave rise there (or somewhere nearby) to a dwarfed descendant: *Homo floresiensis* (Brown et al., 2004; Morwood et al., 2004). This miniaturized species arose sometime prior to 38,000 years ago and lived until at least 18,000 years BP before going extinct (see Figure 12.9 and Chapter 15, Postscript).

Those are the bare bones of the *Homo erectus* story. They appeared, they survived, they begat descendants, and they became extinct. But many questions remain unanswered. What adaptations—cultural as well as biological—enabled them to survive for the better part of two million years? In order to understand *Homo erectus* more completely, we must now turn to the archaeological record.

Summary

First discovered in Java in 1891, *Homo erectus* is now known from Asia, Africa, and Europe. Traditionally, the species was thought to have originated in Africa slightly less than 2 million years ago and then to have spread to other parts of the Old World. This interpretation may still be correct, but it has been called into question by the discovery of very ancient fossils from the Republic of Georgia, China, and Java.

Compared to its evolutionary predecessors, *Homo erectus* had achieved considerable modernity in its anatomy. These people were as tall and as heavy as modern humans, and they showed modern limb proportions. Average brain size had increased to more than 960 cubic centimeters, but the big brains were still contained in rather primitive-looking skulls that were long, low vaulted, and widest at the base. Despite their large brains, however, there is only weak anatomical evidence that *Homo erectus* had language. In particular, details of the thoracic vertebral canals may indicate that they lacked the breathing control needed for modern speech. *Homo erectus* survived for almost 2 million years, and while most populations seem to have gone extinct about 300,000 to 200,000 years ago, relict populations such as Ngandong and Sambungmacan may have lived as recently as 53,000 to 27,000 years BP.

Some researchers believe that the anatomical variability of *Homo erectus* justifies splitting the taxon into two species: The name *Homo erectus* would be retained for specimens from Olduvai Gorge and Asia, while the name *Homo ergaster* would be introduced for early African specimens from the Lake Turkana region. We do not believe that such a step is warranted at present and thus have treated *Homo erectus* as a single, anatomically variable, widely spread species.

Postscript

The hominan fossils from Longuppo Cave in Sichuan Province, China, are ancient, fragmentary, and potentially very important (Ciochon, 1995; Huang et al., 1995; Larick and Ciochon, 1996). Recovered in 1995 from 1.78- to 1.96-million-year-old deposits, the fossil specimens include an upper incisor and a mandibular fragment containing the last premolar (P4) and first molar (M1). They were found in association with two very crude artifacts—a battered cobble and a chipped flake—that resemble the Oldowan tools from numerous African sites. The Longuppo jaw fragment, in particular, shows some traits that seem unusually primitive for Asian *Homo erectus*, including certain aspects of cusp arrangement on both teeth and the fact that the P4 has a bifid root (most *H. erectus* P4s have single roots; Wood and Turner, 1995). Indeed, the discoverers of the Chinese specimens were strongly reminded of *Homo habilis* and/or very early African *H. erectus* (i.e., *ergaster*) by the results of their anatomical analyses.

As noted earlier in this chapter, a primary question raised by the Longuppo fossils is whether they disprove the claim that *Homo erectus* was the first hominin species to expand its range out of Africa. Rather, do they show that *Homo habilis* was the first true globetrotter, making the 6,000-mile journey from East Africa to East Asia equipped only with Oldowan technology? Unfortunately, the Longuppo fossils by themselves are too scrappy and worn to answer this question conclusively, but other fossils may help to come up with an answer.

About one-third of the way from East Africa to China is the Georgian site of Dmanisi. The main path from Africa to Georgia lies through the Levantine Corridor, where recent excavations have documented the presence of hominins between 1.7 and 2.0 myr ago (Ron and Levi, 2001). The Dmanisi site itself, dated to about 1.75

mya, has produced three hominin crania and other fossil remains, as well as numerous Oldowan stone tools. The latest skull to be found at Dmanisi is a very small-brained individual (600 cubic centimeters) who shows a strong combination of *habilis*-like and *erectus*-like traits. The skull's discoverers have provisionally assigned it (and the rest of the Dmanisi collection) to *H. erectus* (i.e., *ergaster*), but note that "it can be argued that this population is closely related to *Homo habilis* (*sensu stricto*) as known from Olduvai Gorge [and] Koobi Fora" (Vekua et al, 2002:88).

The third piece of evidence supporting the possibility of an Africa-to-Asia migration by *H. habilis* is the recent reanalysis of body proportions in that species. As noted in an earlier chapter, Martin Haeusler and Henry McHenry (2004) have determined that *Homo habilis* may actually have had long legs, rather than the short, apish lower limbs traditionally attributed to this species. Although further proof is needed, if this turns out to be the case, long-distance (including transcontinental) travel by *H. habilis* will not seem so physically impossible after all.

But scientists are typically conservative, the Longuppo fossils are scrappy and worn, and those from Dmanisi are maddeningly ambiguous in their diagnostic traits. As a result of this combination of factors, both the Longuppo and Dmanisi remains have been classified (and thus treated in this book) as early *Homo erectus* (broadly defined) pending more information. So, while it seems, to quote G. P. Rightmire, as if "the first people out of Africa came out with a little pea brain" (Gore, 2002), the species designation of those first travelers has yet to be nailed down. As is so often the case in science, we must stay tuned.

Review Questions

1. Summarize the anatomical differences between *Homo erectus* and early *Homo.* How did *Homo erectus* differ anatomically from modern humans?
2. Discuss the reasoning that led Eugene Dubois to search for the "missing link" in Java. How do modern paleoanthropologists decide where to search for fossils?
3. There are few indications from anatomy—other than gross brain size—that *Homo erectus* had language. Discuss how a hominid species might have lived for nearly 2 million years and inhabited both tropical and temperate habitats *without* modern language.
4. Discuss the implications of Longgupo Cave, Dmanisi, and the re-dated Javanese fossils from Sangiran and Modjokerto for our interpretations of the origin and spread of *Homo erectus.*
5. Discuss the implications of the possible young ages (53,000 to 27,000 BP) recently calculated for the fossils from Ngandong and Sambungmacan. What do these dates suggest about the link between *H. erectus* and modern Asians?

SUGGESTED FURTHER READING

Boaz, Noel, and Russell Ciochon. *Dragon Bone Hill.* Oxford, Oxford University Press, 2004.

Jia, Lanpo, and Weiwen Huang. *The Story of Peking Man.* Oxford, Oxford University Press, 1990.

Rightmire, G. P. *The Evolution of Homo erectus.* Cambridge, Cambridge University Press, 1990.

Swisher, III, Carl, Garniss Curtis, and Roger Lewin. *Java Man.* New York, Scribners, 2000.

Theunissen, Bert. *Eugene Dubois and the Ape-Man from Java.* Dordrecht, Kluwer, 1989.

Walker, Alan, and Richard Leakey, eds. *The Nariokotome Homo erectus Skeleton.* Cambridge (MA), Harvard University Press, 1993.

INTERNET RESOURCES

HOMO ERECTUS

www.mnh.si.edu/anthro/humanorigins/ha/erec.html

Produced by the Smithsonian Institution as part of its Human Ancestors Hall, this site includes photographs of several important *H. erectus* specimens and a description of the species.

ARCHAEOLOGY.INFO: *HOMO ERECTUS*

www.archaeologyinfo.com/homoerectus.htm

This site presents another good description of this early hominan species, this time with lots of anatomical details.

BIOGRAPHIES: EUGENE DUBOIS

www.talkorigins.org/faqs/homs/edubois.html

A nice biography of the original discoverer of *Pithecanthropus,* including a discussion of his last views on its human like or ape like nature.

HOMO ERGASTER

www.mnh.si.edu/anthro/humanorigins/ha/erg.html

Although this text does not recognize *Homo ergaster* as a separate species, many pale-oanthropologists do so and therefore this Smithsonian website may be of interest.

USEFUL SEARCH TERMS:

Eugene Dubois
Homo erectus
Homo ergaster
Longgupo Cave
Nariokotome boy
Pithecanthropus
Sinanthropus
Zhoukoudian

Chapter 10 Timeline

HOLOCENE
10,000
PLEISTOCENE
1.8 million
Earliest Oldowan tools at Omo and Hadar
PLIOCENE
5 million
Earliest australopiths
10 million
15 million
MIOCENE
Proconsul
20 million
24 million
OLIGOCENE
Apidium, Parapithecus, and *Aegyptopithecus*
CENOZOIC

YEARS AD	DISCOVERIES
1991–2002	*H. erectus* at Dmanisi
1984	*H. erectus* skeleton found at Nariokotome, West Turkana
1975	*H. erectus* at Koobi Fora
1960	*H. erectus* at Olduvai
1955	*H. erectus* at Ternifine
1936	New finds in Java
1929	First skull of *Sinanthropus*
1921	Excavation begins at Zhoukoudian
1894	Dubois's treatise on *Pithecanthropus*
1891	Dubois discovers *Pithecanthropus* skull in Java

YEARS BP	FOSSIL RECORD
(?) 53,000–27,000	Ngandong and Sambungmacan
600,000	*H. erectus* at Zhoukoudian (Beijing fossils) and at Ternifine
	H. erectus at Trinil (Java)
1 million	
	Olduvai *H. erectus*
1.4 million	*H. erectus* at Koobi Fora and Modjokerto (Java); *P. robustus* in South Africa; *H. habilis* and *P. boisei* at Olduvai; early *Homo* and *P. boisei* at Koobi Fora
1.8 million	
1.9 million	Hominins at Longgupo Cave
2.2 million	
	A. africanus in South Africa
2.6 million	
3 million	*A. afarensis* at Hadar
3.7 million	*A. afarensis* at Laetoli
4.2 million	*A. anamensis* in Kenya
4.4 million	*A. ramidus* at Aramis

SELECT HOMININS

Homo heidelbergensis
Homo erectus
Early *Homo*
Australopithecus africanus
Australopithecus afarensis
Australopithecus anamensis
Ardipithecus ramidus

DISCOVERING *HOMO ERECTUS*

Discoveries of *Homo erectus* have been made throughout the Old World since the first Java finds in 1891. *Homo erectus*'s predecessors, early *Homo*, were intermediates between the ancestral australopiths and themselves.

Chapter 11

Environment, Technology, and Society of *Homo erectus*

These early Acheulean hand axes from Peninj, Tanzania, are made from large lava flakes.

Man is a tool-making animal.

Benjamin Franklin, 1706–1790.

Overview

As currently known, the fossil record indicates that prior to the appearance of *Homo erectus,* hominins' geographic range was limited to Africa. (The Longgupo Cave fossils are treated as early *Homo erectus* here.) All that changed with the evolution of *H. erectus,* however, and by 1.8 million years BP, these hominans were spread from Africa to extreme southeast Asia and were beginning a period of existence that would last over 1.75 million years. But what allowed such phenomenal geographic spread and species longevity?

This chapter examines several cultural innovations and behavioral changes that might have contributed to the success of *H. erectus:* stone-knapping advances that resulted in Acheulean bifacial tools; the beginnings of shelter construction and the control and use of fire; and increased dependence on meat eating.

Homo erectus: New Questions about an Old Species

For more than a quarter of a century, the story of *Homo erectus*—including time and place of origin, geographic spread, and role in human evolution—seemed straightforward. Anthropologists seemed to have many more answers about the species than questions. Now, all of that has changed. With the evidence of *Homo erectus* fossils from Asia that are fully as old as the first African representatives of the species, we face more questions than answers.

Although the issue is debatable, *Homo erectus* can still claim the distinction of being the first hominin species to exist outside Africa, and in our view, it still seems reasonable to assume an African origin for the species since all convincing pre–*H. erectus* hominin fossils are from that continent. Furthermore, *Homo erectus* enjoyed impressive longevity as a species and great geographic spread. Nonetheless, many traditional scenarios about connections between cultural (particularly technological) developments, socioecology, and geographic spread must be reexamined. It is time to stop and take stock of what we know and don't know about these early hominans and their lifeways, and it is to that end that this chapter is dedicated.

Mini-TIMELINE

Age (Years BP)	Fossil Discoveries or Evolutionary Events
400,000–300,000	Regular use of fire confirmed; oldest shelter construction
790,000	Hearths in Israel document beginning use of fire
1.5 million	Nariokotome *Homo erectus* skeleton
1.7 million	First Acheulean tools (Africa)
1.8 million	*Homo erectus* present in Africa, Java, and the Caucasus
1.9 million	Oldest known *Homo erectus*(?) from Longgupo Cave, China
2.6–2.5 million	Oldest Oldowan choppers and flakes

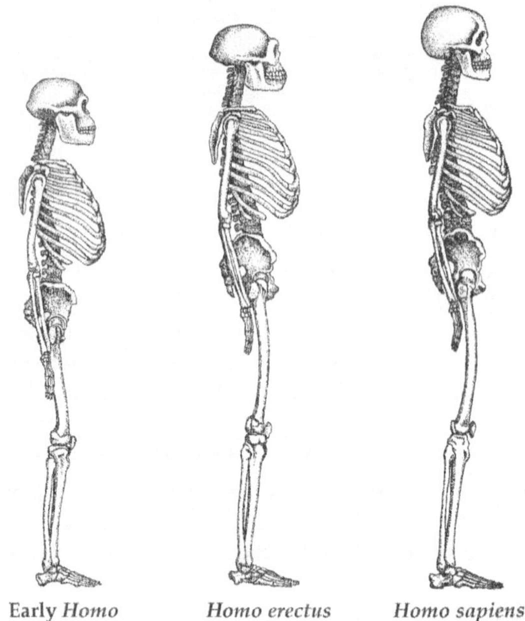

FIGURE 11.1
The anatomy of *Homo erectus* was becoming very modern in most features and distinct from early *Homo*; the differences in the skull are the most striking. In addition, *Homo erectus* probably had longer legs and shorter arms than their ancestors. Stature is a very variable characteristic, and some living populations of *Homo sapiens* are smaller than the average *Homo erectus* and no bigger than the skeleton of early *Homo* shown here. The thorax of early *Homo* was probably more apelike (funnel shaped) than that of *Homo erectus*, although it does not show clearly in this side view. The bones known from the right side of the body are colored.

To start with an anatomical recap, *Homo erectus* seems quite modern physically in many ways (Jellema et al., 1993; Ruff and Walker, 1993). These hominans were about as tall and at least as heavy as people today, and they had modern limb proportions. Additionally, *Homo erectus* had a barrel-shaped thorax above a distinct waist. This body build, which also characterizes modern humans, contrasts strongly with the funnel-shaped rib cage of apes. The strong implication is that, like modern people, *Homo erectus* had a linear and relatively slender body shape, distinctly different from the potbellied bodies of apes and earlier hominins (the reconstructed thorax of *Australopithecus afarensis* is strongly funnel shaped; Aiello and Wheeler, 1995).

Despite the similarities, however, there are also clear differences between *H. erectus* and modern people. First, *Homo erectus* possessed a brain that was only about two-thirds modern size, and as we have seen, that brain was packaged in a rather primitive-looking skull. The thick-boned cranium of *Homo erectus* was long, low vaulted, and wide at the base. Additionally, the face was more prognathic than that of modern humans, sticking out in front of the braincase rather than being tucked underneath the frontal portion of the cranium (Figure 11.1). Studies of the surface anatomy of the *Homo erectus* brain, combined with other aspects of anatomy, fail to provide compelling evidence for complex modern language.

Habitat

Given their Old World–wide geographic spread, it no surprise that *Homo erectus* utilized a variety of habitats. At Nariokotome in East Africa, the tropical environment 1.5

myr ago included an intermittently inundated flood basin of the Omo River, which would have been covered in reeds and lush grasses after the rainy season. Additionally, there was a border of riparian forest and some amount of thornbush on the higher ground away from the river (Feibel and Brown, 1993). Animal fossils from Nariokotome reflect the mixed nature of the habitat and include freshwater fish and snails, a monitor lizard, hippopotamuses, and extinct warthogs (Harris and Leakey, 1993).

In contrast, the 1.75-million-year-old Dmanisi site in the Republic of Georgia, situated at 44 degrees North latitude, was distinctly nontropical. *Homo erectus* people living there would have enjoyed a moderately dry and temperate Mediterranean climate and a location that featured forest–steppe vegetation as well as nearby fresh water. Animals present at Dmanisi included voles, marmots, bears, extinct equids, and deer (Dmanisi).

Finally, at the mid Pleistocene (ca. 500,000 BP) Zhoukoudian cave site in China, located near the fortieth parallel, *Homo erectus* lived under temperate-to-cold conditions during interglacial times. The area was probably generally forested and supported an animal community that included deer and elk, a horse species, rhinos, elephants, and pigs. It is entirely possible that this site had to be abandoned when the interglacial period ended and very cold weather returned to the region (Boaz and Ciochon, 2004).

Thus, environmental flexibility was a primary characteristic of *Homo erectus*. These hominans managed to make a living in a wide variety of climates, habitat types, and animal communities. Extreme cold seems to have been one of the few ecological circumstances that kept them from inhabiting an area. But what enabled them to achieve this level of ecological adaptability? Undoubtedly, it had much to do with their unprecedented (for hominins) level of intelligence and the cultural advances that big brains made possible. It is time to take a closer look at *Homo erectus*'s culture, beginning with their stone technology.

Stone Tools

As described in Chapter 9, stone tool technology got its start with either the australopiths or early *Homo*, and by the time *Homo erectus* appeared, Oldowan choppers and flake tools had been in use for at least half a million years. For another 100,000 to 400,000 years, Oldowan tools continued to be the top-of-the-line implements for early *Homo erectus* in Africa. The same may have been true in Asia, although the association of early Asian (i.e., Javanese) *Homo erectus* with stone tools of *any sort* remains questionable (Schick and Toth, 1993).

In any event, around 1.7 million years BP, Africa witnessed a significant advance in stone tool technology: the development of the Acheulean industry of bifacially flaked tools and its premier implement, the **hand ax.** Named after a much later French site at St. Acheul, where hand axes were found in abundance, the Acheulean tool kit included not only bifacial hand axes, picks, and cleavers (Figure 11.2) but

Hand ax a bifacially flaked stone implement that characterized the *Acheulean industry*.

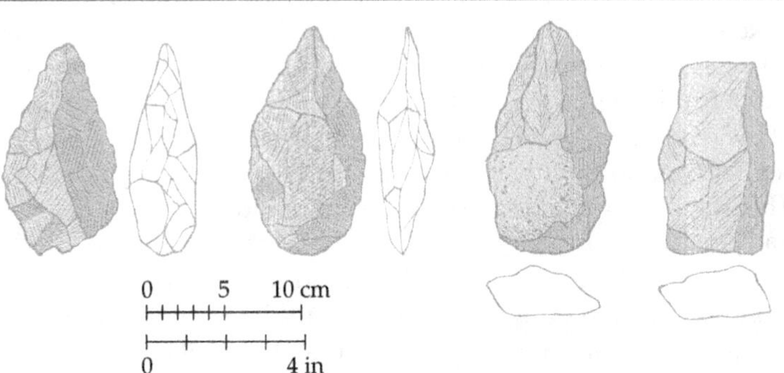

FIGURE 11.2 These early Acheulean artifacts are from Olduvai Gorge and date to approximately 1.5 million years BP. From *left* to *right*, three hand axes (the right one is quite crude in its chipping) and a cleaver are shown. Note the cleaver's straight bit.

also an assortment of Oldowan-type choppers and flakes, suggesting that the more primitive implements continued to serve important functions (Schick and Toth, 1993).

Lithic technology stone tool technology.

In order to understand the nature of this advance in **lithic technology,** we need to take a closer look at how stone tools are made. First of all, not all stones are suitable for use in tool production. Rocks of a coarse, granular composition, such as granite, are almost useless for making chipped tools; they do not fracture along smooth, clean edges but tend to crumble. The ideal stone from the point of view of the tool maker is hard, tough, and of a smooth, fine-grained consistency. Stone of this type fractures into sharp flakes, rather than crumbling. Flint was the most common of the desirable tool stones in Western Europe, and the typical Acheulean implement there was a flint hand ax. In Africa, Acheulean tools were often fashioned from large lava flakes.

Combining various kinds of stone with various ways of working them produces a surprising variety of results. The finer grained the stone, the flatter and more leaflike the flakes that can be chipped loose from it. The size and shape of these flakes can be further controlled by how they are separated from the original stone. They may be knocked loose by a hammer or pried loose by a pointed stick or bone. The angle at which the hammer blow is struck can be changed to produce either a small, thick flake or a large, thin one. Also, different kinds of hammers produce different kinds of flakes. Relatively soft hammers of wood or bone produce one kind, hard stone hammers produce another. Even the way a tool is held while it is being made will affect the kind of flake that can be struck from it: When it is held in the hand, the results are not the same as when it is balanced on a rock anvil (Schick and Toth, 1993).

Core and Flake Tools

Core tool an implement shaped from the core of a rock nodule.

Flake tool an implement made from a *flake* struck from a larger stone.

Despite all the variations in techniques and materials, however, there are still only two basic categories of tools: **core tools** and **flake tools.** To make a core tool, one takes a lump of stone and knocks chips from it until it has the desired size and shape; the core of stone that remains is the tool (Figure 11.3). A flake tool, as its name implies, typically is a chip struck from a core. It may be large or small, and it may be used as it is or further flaked or chipped, somewhat in the manner of a core tool. In any event, the flake itself, and not the core from which it was struck, is the tool.

In the earliest days of tool making, flake tools were very simple. Whatever happened to fly off a core could be put to use if it had a sharp edge. In general, flakes were effective cutting tools because their edges were sharper than the edges that could be produced on core choppers, which were more useful for heavy hacking. As time went on, more and more skills were developed in the manufacture of flakes, and eventually, it became a much more sophisticated method of tool making than the simple core technique.

The Acheulean industry is noted for its use of a prepared core in the production of its characteristic implement, the *biface,* a tool whose cutting edge has been flaked more carefully on both sides to make it straighter and sharper than the primitive Oldowan chopper. This may seem like an awfully small improvement, but it was a fundamental one and made possible much more efficient tools. The purpose of the two-sided, or bifacial, technique was to change the shape of the core from essentially round to flattish, for only with a flat stone can one get a decent cutting edge. The first step in making an Acheulean hand ax was to rough out the core until it had somewhat the shape of a turtle shell, thickest in the middle and thinning to a coarse edge all around. This edge could then be trimmed with more delicate little scallops of flaking (Figure 11.4). The cutting surfaces thus produced were longer, straighter, and considerably keener than those of any Oldowan chopper.

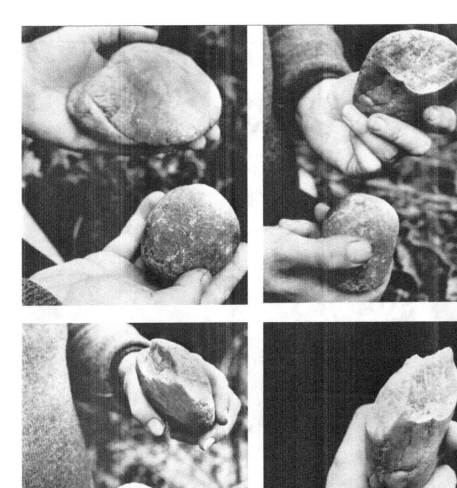

FIGURE 11.3
Stone tool making is not simple; it requires skill and much practice. Most people, however, can learn how to make simple tools. These photographs show Francois Bordes making a chopping tool (*bottom right*).

One technological improvement that permitted the more controlled working required to shape an Acheulean hand ax was the use of different kinds of hammers. In earlier times, it appears, the tool maker knocked flakes from the stone core with another piece of stone. The hard shock of rock on rock tended to leave deep, irregular scars and wavy cutting edges. But a wood or bone hammer, being softer, gave its user much greater control over flaking. Such implements left shallower, cleaner scars on the core and produced sharper and straighter cutting edges. In time, the use of stone was pretty much restricted to the preliminary rough shaping of a hand ax, and all the fine work around the edges was done with wood, antler, and bone. The finished hand ax was usually pear shaped or pointed (Schick and Toth, 1993).

Another type of implement that appears for the first time in the Acheulean industry is the **cleaver.** A cleaver had a straight cutting edge at one end and actually looked much more like a modern ax head than the pointed hand axes did. It was probably used for heavy chopping or for hacking through the joints of large animals (Figure 11.2).

Cleaver an *Acheulean* stone implement with a straight cutting edge at one end; probably used for butchering animal carcasses.

As noted earlier, Acheulean tools originated in Africa around 1.7 million years ago. They were then produced continuously (along with a few Oldowan choppers

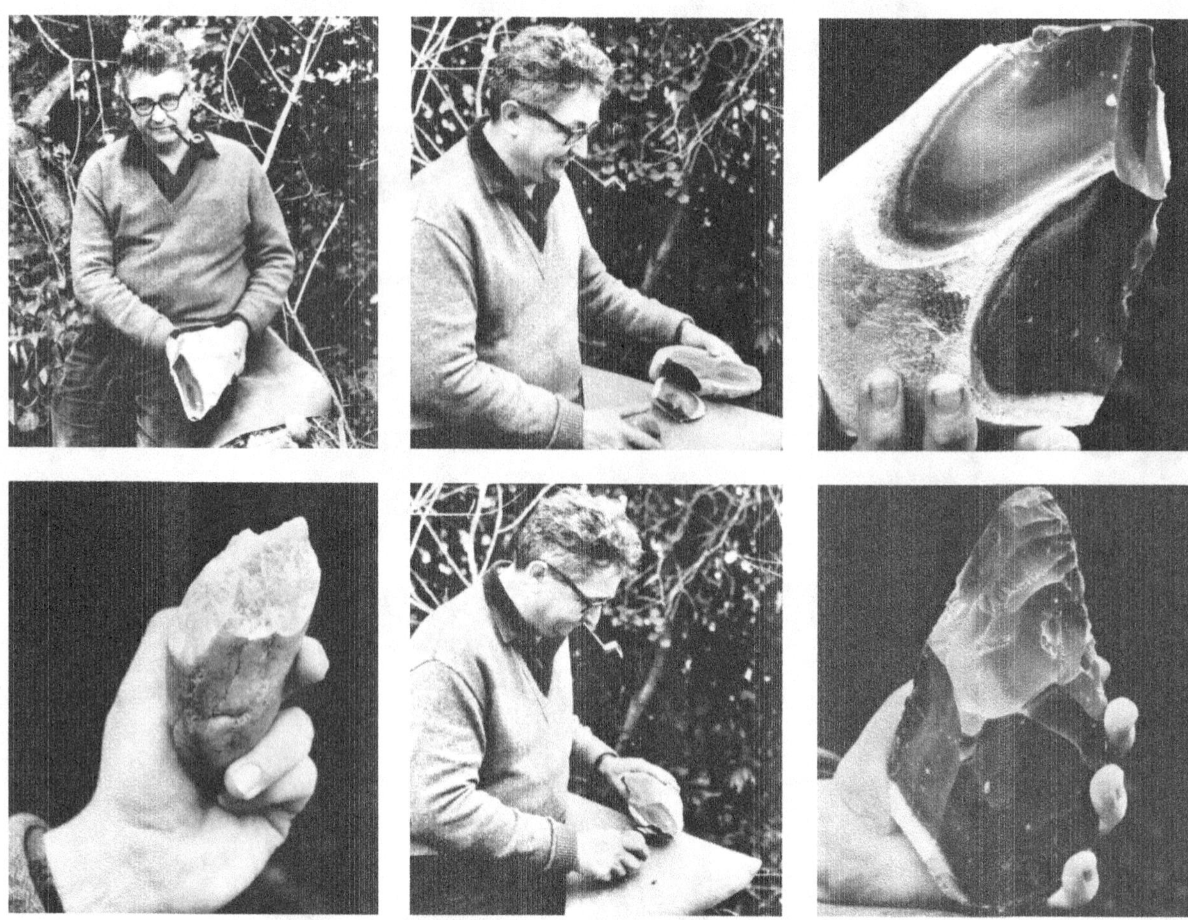

FIGURE 11.4
Making a hand ax is more difficult than making a chopping tool, as shown by these photographs of Francois Bordes. Having knocked the end off a large flint nodule, Bordes has prepared a striking platform (*upper left*). Using a hammer stone, he proceeds to strike off several large flakes, roughing out the general shape (*upper center, upper right, and lower left*). He then switches to an antler hammer, working both sides of the tool to thin out and retouch the edge (*lower center*). The final product, with long, straight, sharp edges (*lower right*), is one of the types of tools used for thousands of years by *Homo erectus* and *Homo heidelbergensis*.

and flakes) throughout *Homo erectus*'s long African residency and beyond, finally disappearing about 250,000 years BP (Klein, 2000). Acheulean tools were being made in the Middle East by 1 mya, as shown at the site of 'Ubeidiya in Israel, and they were present in Europe as early as 500,000 to 600,000 years BP (Pitts and Roberts, 1998; Klein, 2000) and in northeastern Pakistan by 400,000 to 730,000 years BP. Several later sites in Africa and Europe show that the Acheulean tradition survived *Homo erectus* in some areas and was continued for a time by their descendants. Generally, Acheulean tools from sites clearly older than 400,000 to 500,000 years BP are attributed to *Homo erectus,* even in the absence of confirming fossils. At several important Acheulean sites, however, the tool makers' species identity remains ambiguous because the sites lack hominin fossils and they date to a period when *Homo erectus* and *Homo heidelbergensis* overlapped in time. Examples of Acheulean assemblages that could have been produced by either late *H. erectus* or *Homo heidelbergensis* include Africa's Kalambo Falls; Torralba and Ambrona in Spain; Abbeville, St. Acheul, and Terra Amata in France; and Hoxne in England (Figure 10.10; Klein, 1989).

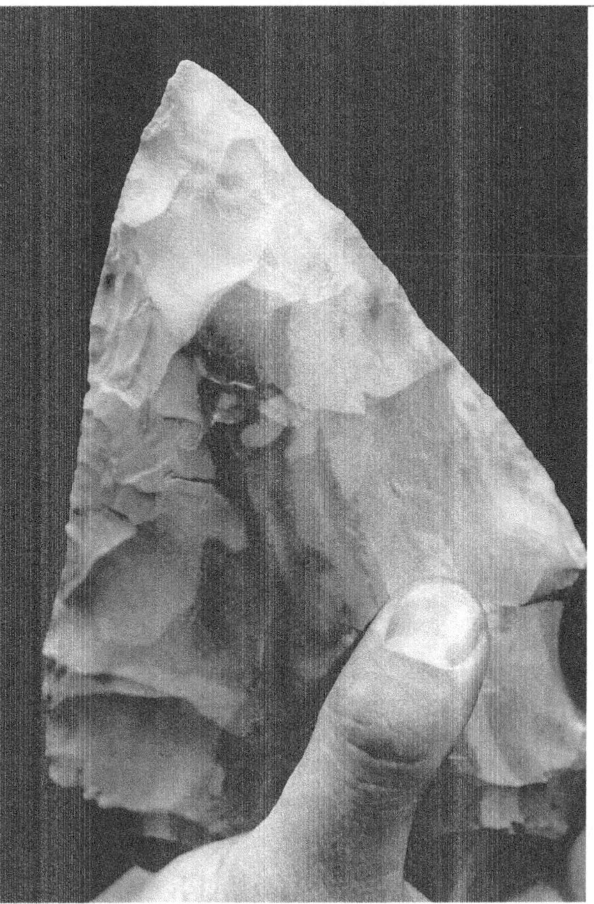

FIGURE 11.5
Held in the palm of the hand, an Acheulean hand ax would have been an excellent tool for dismembering and butchering animal carcasses.

Wherever they are found, Acheulean hand axes and cleavers are generally interpreted as being implements for processing animal carcasses (Figure 11.5). True, the cleavers could have been used to chop and shape wood, but according to archaeologists Kathy Schick and Nicholas Toth (1993), the wear pattern on cleaver bits is more suggestive of use on soft material, such as hides and meat. Schick and Toth believe that Acheulean tools represent an adaptation for "habitual and systematic butchery, [and] especially the dismembering of large animal carcasses," as *Homo erectus* experienced a strong dietary shift toward more meat consumption (1993:260). Schick and Toth leave unanswered the question of whether meat was obtained primarily by scavenging or by hunting.

Interestingly, no sites in China or Southeast Asia are included in the inventory of Acheulean locales. In fact, there is strong evidence that Acheulean tools were never produced in much of the Far East. As first pointed out in 1948 by Hallam Movius (then of Harvard University), Acheulean sites are common in Africa, the Middle East, Europe, and much of western Asia, but they are strangely absent in far eastern and southeastern Asia. The line dividing the Old World into Acheulean and non-Acheulean regions became known as the **Movius line** (Figure 11.6). Hand-ax cultures flourished to the west and south of the line, but in the east, only choppers and flake tools were found (Gowlett, 1992; Klein, 2000). (Today, we know the actual situation wasn't quite as clear as first described. There are a few examples of crude hand axes from sites in South Korea and China but nothing that is clearly Acheulean. Also, there are some African and European sites contemporaneous with the Acheulean that produced only chopper and flake assemblages. Nonetheless, the Movius line remains a useful heuristic device for archaeologists [Schick and Toth, 1993].)

Movius line The geographic dividing line between the *Acheulean* tradition in the West and non-Acheulean *lithic* traditions in eastern and southeastern Asia.

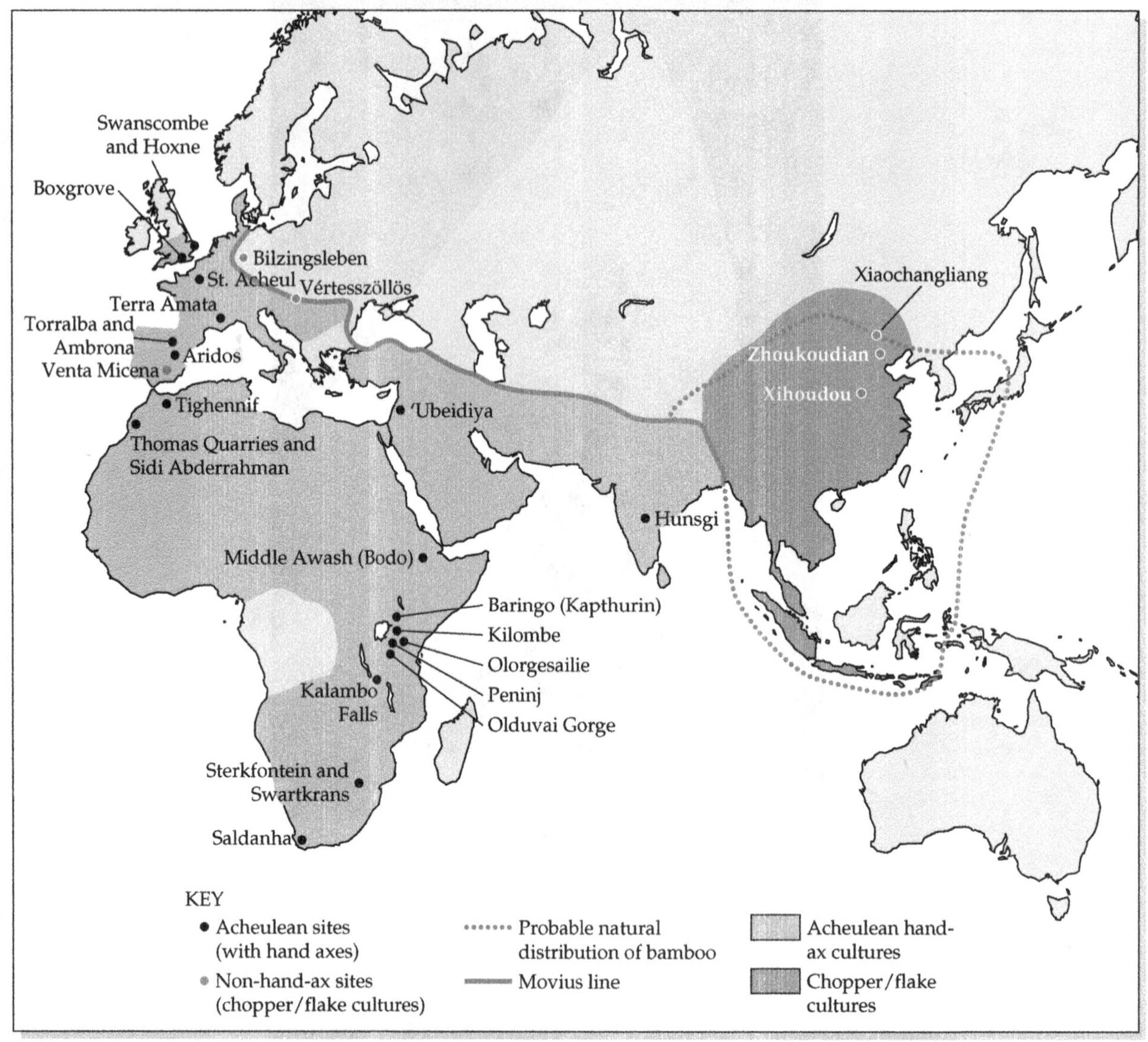

FIGURE 11.6
The Movius line divides the world of *Homo erectus* and its immediate descendants into Acheulean hand-ax cultures to the west and chopper-flake cultures to the east. Note that in the east and in southeast Asia, the absence of hand-ax cultures coincides closely with the presence of bamboo.

But why were there no Acheulean hand-ax cultures in the eastern extremes of Asia? Traditionally, this has been a hard question to answer, since researchers believed until quite recently that *Homo erectus*'s departure from Africa postdated the invention of Acheulean tools by over half a million years. If *Homo erectus* left Africa with Acheulean technology, why didn't the tradition arrive in eastern Asia? Was it discarded or forgotten along the way? The new dates from Java help solve this riddle somewhat, since they place *Homo erectus* in southeast Asia at least 100,000 years *before* the advent of the Acheulean in Africa. It thus appears that even if, as traditionally thought, *Homo erectus* turns out to be a native African species that spread to Asia, its initial migration predated the development of Acheulean tools. Thus, a chronological barrier might have prevented the introduction of Acheulean technology to eastern Asia.

Schick and Toth (1993) have listed several other explanations for the absence of the Acheulean tradition from eastern Asia. Perhaps it was due to a paucity of suitable raw stone; coarse quartz is common in the East, but fine-grained flints, cherts, and lavas are rare. This distribution of raw materials would lend itself to the production of Oldowan choppers but not to bifacial hand axes requiring extensive chipping. Alternatively, the absence of the Acheulean tools may be related to different functional requirements in Asia compared to the West. If the Acheulean developed as an adaptation for meat processing by African hominans operating in open country, it may have been distinctly less useful in the closed and forested habitats of Asia, where large prey animals were probably less common and vegetable foods easier to harvest.

Certainly, the most intriguing of the explanations for the "missing Acheulean" is the suggestion by anthropologist Geoffrey Pope (1989, 1993) and others that, in far eastern and southeastern Asia, bamboo tools were used in place of stone implements to perform a variety of tasks. To quote Pope, "There are few useful tools that cannot be constructed from bamboo. Cooking and storage containers, knives, spears, heavy and light projectile points, elaborate traps, rope, fasteners [and] clothing . . . can be manufactured from bamboo" (1989:53). When a bamboo stalk is split, it produces razor-sharp "stick knives" that can be used to butcher animals or perform other hacking and scraping jobs. Such bamboo utensils are still used in some parts of the world today (Figure 11.7), and as Pope has pointed out, the natural distribution of bamboo coincides closely with those Asian areas that lack Acheulean tools (Figure 11.6). Pope's conclusions remind us that *Homo erectus* (like its ancestors) almost certainly used a variety of biodegradable tools (whether bamboo or some other material), which do not survive archaeologically. Such tools would always have been of great importance and their development could have been of as great value to the evolving hominins as was their stone industry.

We can conclude, therefore, that while the Acheulean tradition, with its hand axes and cleavers, was an important lithic advance by *Homo erectus* over older technologies, it constituted only one of several adaptive patterns used by the species. Clever and behaviorally flexible, *Homo erectus* was capable of adjusting its material culture to the local resources and functional requirements. Nonetheless, the Acheulean tradition clearly reflected significant cognitive progress by *Homo erectus* over its evolutionary predecessors. As American anthropologist A. J. Jelinek

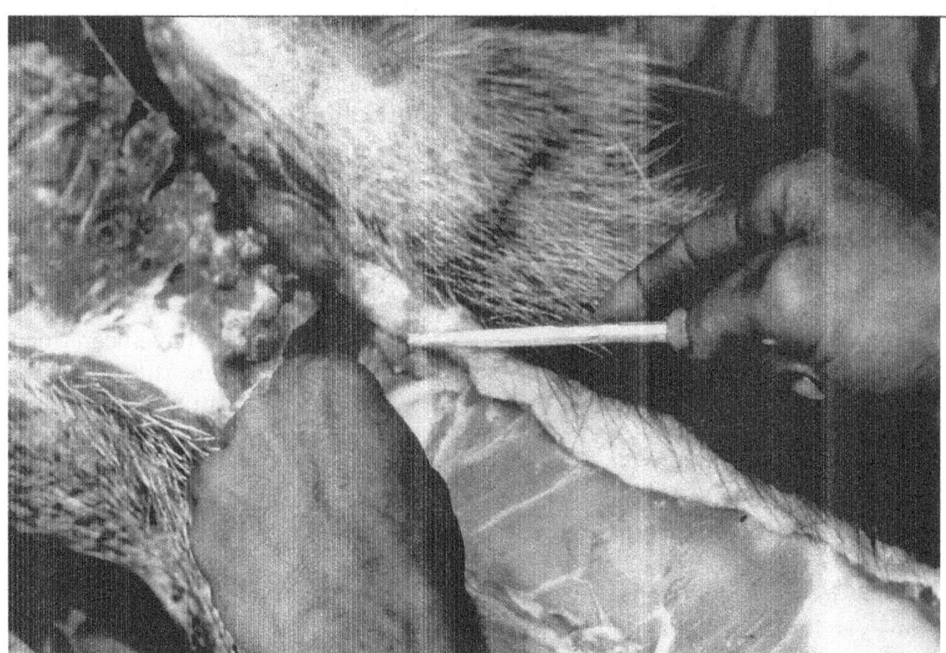

FIGURE 11.7
Split bamboo has razor-sharp edges and can be used as a stick knife. Here, a bamboo knife is used to butcher a pig in New Guinea.

remarked, Acheulean tools were the first "fully conceived implements whose final form is regularly patterned and in no way suggested by the shape or exterior texture of the stone from which they were made. This is certainly a significant step in conceptualization" (1977:29).

Interestingly, once in existence, the Acheulean tradition showed very little overall change during perhaps 1.5 million years. Harvard's William Howells (1993:118) has referred to this lack of change as a "general stagnation" in material culture, and he has attributed it to a long period of little advance in intelligence and communication skills—a stasis that apparently was interrupted only by the evolution of *Homo heidelbergensis.*

Shelter and Fire

As noted earlier, *Homo erectus* populations adapted successfully to a variety of climates and habitats throughout the Old World. This adaptation was primarily a cultural phenomenon, however, and wherever they were found, *H. erectus* populations seem to have retained basically a tropical body build (relatively tall and linear, although with some regional variation in height; Antón, 2003). Undoubtedly, such hominans would have found winters at Dmanisi, Zhoukoudian, and other high-latitude sites quite trying, so what cultural advances (in addition to their tools of stone and other materials) made it possible for them to survive?

Certainly, *Homo erectus* would have gained some relief from the elements by seeking refuge in caves and rock shelters (Boaz and Ciochon, 2004). But would this behavior have been enough? For years, scientists have searched for—and argued about—evidence that *Homo erectus* had gained additional protection against its environment through the construction of shelters and the control and use of fire. The evidence is sparse and difficult to interpret, but a review of it should prove instructive.

To begin with the evidence for "domestic architectural features" (shelters and huts), at the site of Soleihac in southeastern France, *Homo erectus* apparently left a collection of choppers and flakes (no hand axes) a little more than 900,000 years ago. Also from Soleihac comes a rather mysterious line of basalt blocks 66 feet (20 meters) long. It is difficult to know what to make of the line of stones. Are they all that's left of a shelter, or are they a natural feature of the site? Some researchers, such as paleoanthropologist Richard Klein, are clearly skeptical. According to Klein "[The basalt line] may represent the oldest structural remnant in Europe, *if it is truly of human origin*" (1989:213; italics added).

For the next, and considerably more impressive, evidence of shelter construction, we must jump forward a half million years to the 400,000- to 300,000-year-old French site of Terra Amata (located under the modern city of Nice). Excavated in the 1960s by Henry de Lumley (1969), the site is claimed to have revealed evidence in the form of ancient postholes and concentrated artifacts of several huts measuring 26 to 49 feet (8 to 15 meters) long by 13 to 20 feet (4 to 6 meters) wide. De Lumley concluded that the hut roofs had been supported by two or more large posts and that the walls were made of saplings and branches (Figure 11.8). Shelters very similar in size and construction to those envisioned by de Lumley have been documented among some modern hunter-and-gatherer groups (Figure 11.8).

In addition to the apparent remains of ancient shelters, Terra Amata also produced evidence of the control and use of fire. In the center of each reconstructed hut was a hearth, a fairly compact area of baked and discolored sand, and some hearths were ringed by a windscreen of stones, suggesting that the shelters were rather drafty (Figure 11.8). Whether the fires were used for cooking or warmth (or both) is hard to determine.

The most problematic aspect of Terra Amata is not the archaeological evidence, however; rather, it is our inability to determine accurately the hominin species re-

FIGURE 11.8
The drawing at *right* reconstructs the kind of huts that Henry De Lumley excavated at Terra Amata in France. The hut has been cut away to show the method of construction. The exact form of the roof is uncertain, but this type of construction is common in some human groups today, as can be seen in the photograph of a San hut in the northern Kalahari (*left*). The drawing shows some worked stones in the center. The oval of rocks and the central postholes were the main clues to the size and form of construction at Terra Amata.

sponsible for the site. Terra Amata has produced no fossil remains of its inhabitants that would allow their identification. Couple that fact with the young age of the site—perhaps 300,000 years BP—and it becomes clear that either late *Homo erectus* or *Homo heidelbergensis* might have been the builders and fire makers of Terra Amata. This complication rather cuts the legs out from under any convincing argument for *Homo erectus* as a builder, at any rate. (For more information on fire, see below.) If these hominans *ever* started constructing shelters, it was very late—indeed, just before the bulk of the species went extinct. Certainly, there is no evidence that making shelters contributed to *Homo erectus*'s geographic expansion.

Documenting the use of fire by *Homo erectus* is a bit easier than proving that they built shelters, but not much. Evidence suggesting that hominins used fire as early as 1.6 to 1.5 myr ago has been reported from several sites, including Koobi Fora and Chesowanja in Kenya and Swartkrans in South Africa (Bellomo, 1994; Schick and Toth, 1993). All of these reports have been challenged, however, and all may be the result of natural fires, not hominin activities (Klein, 1999).

What is needed is convincing evidence of the existence of hearths, and precisely that sort of proof has recently been reported for a 790,000-year-old Israeli site called Gesher Benot Ya'aqov (GBY; Goren-Inbar et al., 2004). At GBY, burned flint artifacts belonging to the Acheulean industry were found in association with bits of burnt wood, and of critical importance, the stone tools were spatially clustered, strongly suggesting the presence of hearths. Unfortunately, no hominin remains have been recovered from GBY, and its date of 790,000 BP falls into the overlap zone between *Homo erectus* (1.9 myr to 27 kyr) and *Homo heidelbergensis* (850 to 100 kyr; see Chapter 12)—a state of affairs that led the excavators of GBY to refrain from assigning the site to a particular hominin type. Nonetheless, it seems to us that the odds favor GBY as being a *Homo erectus* site, and so we tentatively accept it as evidence of the use of fire by that species.

Finally, at the 670,000 to 410,000-year-old Chinese site of Zhoukoudian, evidence has been found for both natural and hominin-associated fires and for a couple of cases of roasting horses' heads (Binford and Stone, 1986). Although researchers

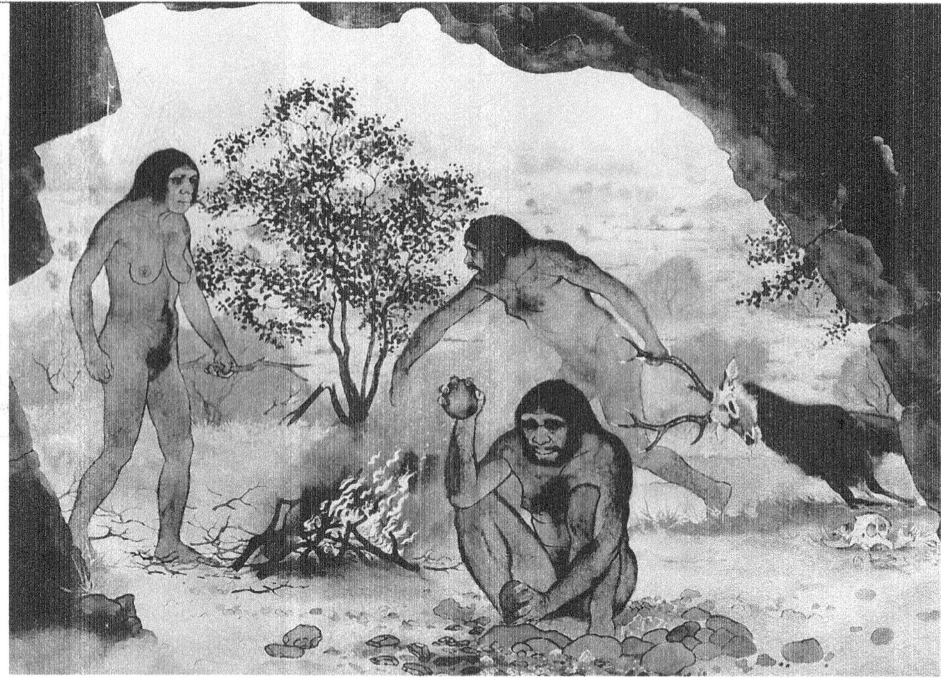

FIGURE 11.9
This painting by English artist Maurice Wilson dates from 1950 and shows a typical home-hearth-and hunting interpretation of *Homo erectus.*

disagree on the extent of *Homo erectus*'s use of fire at Zhoukoudian (compare Binford and Ho [1985] with Boaz and Ciochon [2004]), it now appears that this site does document at least occasional controlled use of fire during late *H. erectus* times. One recent suggestion is that *Homo erectus* at Zhoukoudian used fire primarily to drive away the cave's resident hyenas so they could scavenge the carnivores' kills (Boaz and Ciochon, 2004), but there also appears to be some evidence for hearths (Klein, 1999). Still, it seems premature to conclude that domestic scenes such as that painted in 1950 and shown in Figure 11.9—a blazing hearth fed by a female wood gatherer, a male (hunter?) dragging home a deer carcass, and a male tool maker working away near the fire—were regular events at Zhoukoudian. What we can safely conclude about the *Homo erectus* lifestyle will be discussed more fully in a later section.

In summary then, regarding fire, *Homo erectus* probably was in control of this important tool by about three-quarters of a million years ago—much too late for fire to have been a key element in the species' geographic spread. Once under control, fire provided protection from predators, warmth, a tool for scavenging, and the means to (occasionally) cook one's food. That brings us to what we know about the diet of *Homo erectus* and how it was obtained.

Subsistence Patterns and Diet

Early discoveries of *Homo erectus* fossils in association with stone tools and animal bones readily lent themselves to the interpretation of a hunting-and-gathering way of life—an interpretation that anthropologists eagerly embraced. The *Homo erectus* inhabitants of Zhoukoudian in China were described as deer hunters who consumed cooked meals that combined venison with local plant products such as hackberries (Wu and Lin, 1983). Similarly, in Africa, the Olorgesailie site (ca. 600,000 years old) was interpreted as showing that *Homo erectus* hunters occasionally preyed on fellow primates, including giant gelada baboons (Isaac, 1968). These and other bits of data were then combined into an elaborate picture of the society and lifestyle of *Homo erectus* that generally tended to portray these Plio-Pleistocene hominins as an early version of modern human hunters-and-gatherers.

In recent years, several of the original studies describing *Homo erectus* as a hunter-and-gatherer have come under intense criticism. For example, Binford and Stone (1986) reexamined the material from the late *H. erectus* site of Zhoukoudian and concluded that there is very little *conclusive* evidence of systematic hunting. Comparisons of the Zhoukoudian animal bones with faunal remains from both carnivore (especially hyena) dens and undoubted hunting sites (such as the 105,000-year-old European site of Combe Grenal) convinced these researchers that the Chinese assemblage was primarily the result of animal activity rather than hunting and gathering. A few of the deer and horse bones at Zhoukoudian showed cut marks from stone tools that overlay gnaw marks by carnivores, suggesting hominin scavenging. While acknowledging that *Homo erectus* certainly used the Zhoukoudian cave site, Binford and Stone concluded that at Zhoukoudian, "all the positive evidence is consistent with what is believed to be evidence for [hominin] scavenging [and] there are *no positive indicators* of hunting in the available data" (1986:468, italics in the original).

A very recent analysis by Boaz and Ciochon (2004) agrees with Binford and Stone's conclusion that at Zhoukoudian, *Homo erectus* obtained meat primarily by scavenging, not hunting. (Thus, the hunter in Figure 11.9, who appears to be dragging home a relatively intact deer carcass, seems to have been more imaginary than real.) The same subsistence classification—primarily scavengers, not hunters—now appears to be applicable to *Homo erectus* populations wherever they are found (Klein, 2000).

Nonetheless, even if *Homo erectus* remained scavengers-and-gathers, rather than hunters, they still must have been very good at their meat procurement techniques. This conclusion seems inescapable from the considerable indirect evidence for strongly increased meat consumption compared to all earlier hominins. First, there is the matter of their advance in stone tool technology. As noted earlier, archaeologists Kathy Schick and Nicholas Toth (1993), among others, have concluded that Acheulean hand axes and cleavers were used primarily for dismembering and butchering large animal carcasses. This conclusion is based on studies of the artifacts' design and wear patterns, as well as on experimental studies of how they could have been used most effectively. It appears, therefore, that the development of the Acheulean tradition is a clear indicator of a distinct shift toward greater reliance on meat by *Homo erectus*. The absence of Acheulean tools in Eastern and Southeastern Asia may well be related to the presence of fewer game animals in tropical forests than in open grasslands, although as discussed above, other explanations may apply, as well.

The second sort of evidence in favor of more meat eating by *Homo erectus* involves anatomy—specifically, the size and shape of these early hominans. With regard to body size, Alan Walker (1993a) has concluded that *Homo erectus* was a species of big individuals, comparable to the top 17 percent of modern human populations in height and within the modern range with regard to weight (possibly with a slightly higher average weight). Furthermore, Walker argues that early African *Homo erectus* differed little in body size from late Asian members of the species, implying a long period of anatomical stasis once an adaptive body build had evolved. Compared to early *Homo* (*H. habilis* and *H. rudolfensis*), *Homo erectus* showed an increase in body size of one-quarter to one-third (compare Boxes 8.1, 8.2, and 10.1). It seems difficult to explain an increase in body size of this magnitude without postulating increased meat consumption.

As for *Homo erectus*'s body shape, two aspects concern us: the enormous enlargement of the brain and the coincidental reduction of the gastrointestinal tract. As noted in Chapter 10, *Homo erectus* showed a 20 to 60 percent increase in brain size compared to the two species of early *Homo*. Furthermore, as shown by analyses of the Nariokotome skeleton, *Homo erectus* was probably the first hominin type to show a barrel-shaped thorax and a distinct waist, similar to modern human

TABLE 11.1 Mass-Specific Organ Metabolic Rates in Humans[a]

Organ	Metabolic Rate in W. Kg^{-1} (watts per kilogram)
Brain	11.2
Liver and gastrointestinal tract	12.2
Skeletal muscle	0.5
Lung	6.7
Skin	0.3
Whole-body average	1.3

[a]Mass-specific organ metabolic rates are those for a 65 kilogram human male with a bodily basal metabolism rate (BMR) of 90.6 watts. The average mass-specific metabolic rate of the human body as a whole is 1.3 W. Kg^{-1}.
Source: Data from Aschoff et al. (1971), as reported by Aiello and Wheeler (1995); reprinted by permission of the University of Chicago Press.

anatomy. Earlier species apparently possessed funnel-shaped rib cages and potbellies like living apes. This modification in the shape of the *H. erectus* thorax suggests significant reduction in the size of the gastrointestinal tract (Aiello and Wheeler, 1995). Both brains and intestines are metabolically expensive organs with a mass-specific (i.e., organ- or part-specific) metabolic rate much higher than the average mass-specific rate for the body as a whole (Table 11.1).

Researchers Leslie Aiello and Peter Wheeler (1995) believe there were only two ways to accommodate the increased energy demands of the big brain of *Homo erectus:* Either raise the overall basal metabolism rate of the body, or compensate for brain growth by reducing the size of some other metabolically expensive organs. All indications are that our forebears evolved down the second path. Modern humans show a standard basal metabolism rate for mammals our size, but we have much bigger brains and smaller gastrointestinal tracts than expected (Figure 11.10). Furthermore, the energetic savings realized by reducing the digestive system are approximately the same as the added costs of a larger brain. Beginning with *Homo erectus*, hominans experienced an evolutionary trade-off of intestines for brains.

Reducing the digestive system has dietary implications, of course, which brings us back to the question of *Homo erectus*'s subsistence patterns. Animals that depend

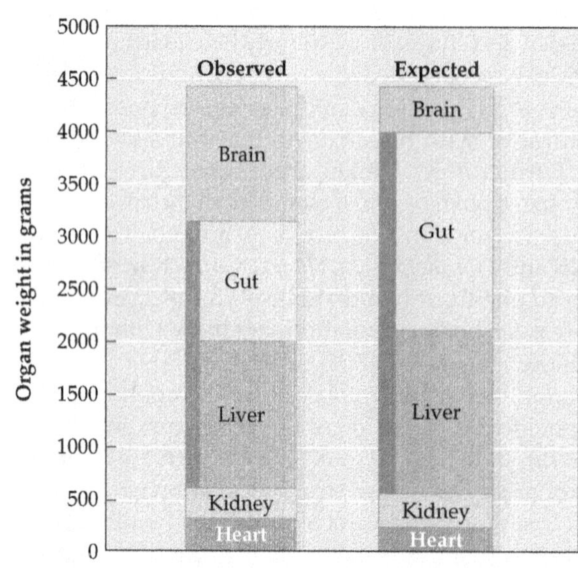

FIGURE 11.10 The *right-hand* column shows the organ weights predicted (expected) for a 143 pound (65 kilogram) human with typical primate organ sizes. The *left-hand* column shows the actual (observed) organ weights found in 65-kilogram modern people. The modern human brain is almost three times larger than expected, while the gut is 40 percent smaller.

Source: From Aiello and Wheeler, 1995; reprinted by permission of the University of Chicago Press.

on poor-quality (low energy) and hard-to-digest diets (folivores and, to a lesser extent, frugivores) consume large quantities of food and then process it slowly in their large stomachs and intestines. More carnivorous animals, on the other hand, eating higher-quality (higher-energy) and more digestible diets, need both less food and smaller digestive organs for its processing. We agree with Aiello and Wheeler (1995) that the anatomical evidence places *Homo erectus* in the latter group. Apparently, by becoming super-scavengers (on top of continuing the sort of small-scale hunting we have attributed to the australopiths and early *Homo*), *Homo erectus* populations were able to strongly increase the energy-rich meat component of their diet. This meat-intensive diet required less digestive effort than was true for earlier hominins—thus allowing gastrointestinal reduction—and simultaneously provided plenty of energy for their expanding brains.

As discussed in Chapter 9, several factors have been suggested as triggers for brain expansion among hominins, with the pressures for increased social intelligence and subsistence intelligence being high on the list. The evolution of a super-scavenging-and-gathering lifestyle by *Homo erectus* would have simultaneously relaxed the metabolic constraints on brain growth and intensified the selective pressure for further expansion. A nice feedback loop would have been established: Eating more meat contributed to bigger brains, bigger brains equaled greater intelligence, and greater intelligence allowed the invention of more clever ways to obtain meat and other high-energy foods.

Society

As we have noted before, trying to reconstruct the social groupings and behaviors of extinct hominin species is a very risky business. Behavioral patterns and relationships do not fossilize. Nonetheless, anatomy and/or archaeology sometimes can provide useful hints about social phenomena, and so we will take the evidence available and see what can be said about *Homo erectus* in this regard.

Group Size and Structure

First of all, based on the species' average brain size, it has been estimated that a typical *Homo erectus* group might have contained just over one hundred individuals (Aiello and Dunbar, 1993). But how was such a group organized? Was it stratified or egalitarian? Were there families, as we know them today?

Unfortunately, virtually all of these questions are currently unanswerable, although some useful hints can be provided. Regarding stratification, it can be said that no *Homo erectus* site has produced evidence of differential wealth or status (no signs of personal adornment have been discovered, for example). Whether this indicates egalitarian societies is uncertain, however. With regard to family types, we cannot say whether these hominans were organized into pair-bonded monogynous units, polygynous harems, or otherwise, but a significant reduction (compared to earlier hominins) in body size dimorphism has suggested to some researchers that polygyny was on the wane and pair-bonding on the rise (Deacon, 1997). Other analysts are not so sure about a decrease in male–male sexual competition, however, since the size dimorphism shift was primarily the result of *H. erectus* females getting larger, not males moving toward females in body size (Key and Aiello, 1999).

One thing, however, is quite clear: Due to increases in the size of their own bodies and in the size of their babies' brains, *Homo erectus* females were at a strong disadvantage (compared to males) in relative energetic load (Key and Aiello, 1999). This energy imbalance was related in complex ways to females' energy costs of reproduction and infant care and, in turn, to their social relations. Let's examine this problem more closely.

Increased Reproduction Costs for Females

Altricial the state of being born helpless and requiring parental care.

Secondary altriciality the phenomenon of an infant's motor skills requiring a lengthy period of postnatal development, as opposed to its sensory systems, which are functional at birth or soon after; characteristic of *H. erectus* and later *hominins*.

An analysis of the energy costs of reproduction for *Homo erectus* females must start with the species' pattern of fetal and infantile brain growth. Among modern humans, because of constraints on women's pelvic dimensions related to efficient bipedal locomotion, babies are born with brains that are only about 25 percent of adult size. (In comparison, ape infants have accomplished 35 to 61 percent of total brain growth at birth [Schultz, 1968; see Box 11.1].) As we all know, modern human babies are **altricial,** or helpless at birth and completely dependent on adult care. Ours is a particular kind of helplessness, however, that is called **secondary altriciality** because it affects mainly the motor skills and not the senses. Although their sensory systems quickly become functional, modern babies' motor skills take a long time to develop. But our babies are accomplishing something vital during their period of motor helplessness: They are undergoing very rapid postnatal brain growth (significantly faster than in apes; Key and Aiello, 1999) that will carry them to about 70 percent of adult brain size by one year of age (Hrdy, 1999). Thus, modern babies play catch-up in brain growth during their first year of life but only at the cost of requiring full-time care. And of course, since humans are mammals, the responsibility for the care and feeding of dependent infants falls primarily on their mothers, producing an immediate distinction between women and men in relative energy load.

The pelvis of the *Homo erectus* boy from Nariokotome has been studied by Alan Walker and Christopher Ruff (1993). From the adolescent's pelvis, Walker and Ruff have calculated the probable pelvic dimensions of *Homo erectus* adults and concluded that this species resembled modern humans in producing secondarily altricial infants. Among *Homo erectus* people, infants' brains were probably about 22 percent of adult size at birth but grew rapidly (perhaps more rapidly than in modern humans [Coqueugniot et al., 2004]) during the immediate postnatal period, when the infants were almost certainly totally dependent on adult care. The strong implication of this finding is that, as among modern humans, *Homo erectus* women were cast in the role of primary caretakers for extremely helpless infants with high energy demands during childhood, and this raised women's relative energy load enormously.

Family in human society, generally a unit marked by interdependent subsistence, sexual relationships among adults, and parent–offspring relationships.

There are several ways that *Homo erectus* women might have gotten help to manage the energetic costs of maintaining their own larger than ever bodies *and* gestating and nurturing big-brained, secondarily altricial infants (Key and Aiello, 1999). One possibility is an increase in paternal investment in mates and offspring. This could have led to the evolution of that human institution, the **family.** Alternately, there could have been an increase in female–female cooperation in child care and other support. Some researchers think the phenomenon of menopause and women's postreproductive contributions to their daughters' health and reproduction might have evolved as *Homo erectus*'s solution to out-of-control female energy loads. (The fitness benefits of such behaviors have recently been demonstrated in modern humans [Lahdenperä et al., 2004].) Increased investment by fathers or by grandmothers? At this point, it is impossible to determine which pattern (both? neither?) was characteristic of *Homo erectus*.

Aggression

All animal species display some aggression, of course, and undoubtedly, *Homo erectus* was no exception. As evidence, a few crania from Zhoukoudian show depressed fractures that may have been inflicted by group mates. Recently, paleoanthropologists Noel Boaz and Russell Ciochon (2004) made the interesting suggestion that intraspecific aggression might have been responsible for the evolution of unusually thick skull bones in *H. erectus*. Boaz and Ciochon hypothesize that as part of

BOX 11.1 **CURRENT ISSUE**

Brains, Babies, and Bipedalism

Human babies are born with heads much too large for their bodies. Far from being concerned about this anatomical mismatch, however, most people think it makes the top-heavy little rascals all the more attractive. Well, newborns with big heads may be cute, but they spell trouble for a significant number of human births and thus provide a good example of an evolutionary compromise between competing selection pressures. The following table (from Rosenberg, 1992) contains data for apes and humans on the relative size of newborns' heads compared to the smallest dimension of mothers' birth canals. (For apes, cranial breadth is given as a percentage of the width of the birth canal inlet [top of the canal]; for humans, cranial length, not breadth, is given as a percentage of inlet width, since that is the dimension that squeezes through the inlet's transverse diameter.)

The numbers show that baby apes' heads are considerably smaller than their mothers' birth canals. As a consequence, ape births tend to be quick (usually two hours or less) and difficult deliveries are unusual. In comparison, human babies have heads that are slightly longer than their mothers' birth canals are wide. Thus, human deliveries routinely take three to four times as long as those of apes and run a much higher risk of complications.

One measure of the degree of difficulty of human births is the maternal mortality rate. According to Laurel Cobb (personal communication), an international consultant on maternal and child health, worldwide, about 320 women die giving birth for every 100,000 new babies. (Forty percent of these deaths are due to obstructed labor or hemorrhage.) In less developed countries, where medical care is often inadequate, as many as 900 maternal deaths per 100,000 live births can occur. Of the two figures, the second undoubtedly comes closer to measuring maternal mortality among *Homo sapiens* prior to the advent of effective medical care.

Species	Infant Head as Percentage of Pelvic Inlet Width
Orangutans	73.1
Chimpanzees	72.4
Gorillas	64.4
Modern humans	101.8

The evolutionary conflict noted above pitted the biomechanical requirements of bipedalism against the need for larger birth canals as brain size rose in the genus *Homo*. Compared to the australopiths, modern humans show both bigger brains (two to three times larger among adults) and more narrow pelvises. (This made lateral balancing easier and bipedalism more energy efficient.) Among the apes and perhaps the australopiths, as well, nearly half of total brain growth occurs before birth, but for this pattern to have been continued among large-brained *Homo*, the birth canal needed to be enlarged. Lateral expansion (widening) of the pelvis was not mechanically feasible, however, because it would have required either increasing the mass of the lesser gluteal muscles or lengthening the neck of the femur (see Chapter 5 and Figure 5.28).

Given these anatomical constraints and the continuing strong pressure for brain enlargement, natural selection fashioned the modern human compromise: Match the newborn head to the maternal birth canal as closely as possible, and reduce the prenatal percentage of total brain growth to about 25 percent. As described in this chapter, the latter change led to the phenomenon of secondary altriciality.

Pain and difficulty in childbirth are part of the human condition. Biblical literalists believe this was part of God's curse on Eve for her disobedience in the Garden of Eden. Evolutionary biologists, on the other hand, understand it as the result of natural selection generating a tightly balanced compromise between bipedal locomotion and prenatal brain development.

their mating competition, young *Homo erectus* males regularly head bashed one another and that the species evolved extremely thick (pachyostotic) skull bones as a defensive adaptation. This is not the only explanation offered by Boaz and Ciochon for **pachyostosis,** but it is the one they favor. Further investigation is justified, particularly to see if evidence for head trauma is found in more populations than just the one at Zhoukoudian. If not, head bashing can be written off as a local cultural phenomenon, rather than a species-typical trait.

Pachyostosis literally, "thick-boned"; used here to describe the skull bones of *Homo erectus*.

Continuing with the theme of aggression, over a half century ago, Franz Weidenreich suggested that the faceless and baseless crania from Zhoukoudian were proof of hominin cannibalism at the site (Jia and Huang, 1990). Since then, much of the bone breakage and other damage at Zhoukoudian—including the removal of the face and cranial base from several specimens—has been convincingly explained as hyena activity (Binford and Ho, 1985), thus (temporarily) exculpating *Homo erectus* from cannibalism. Just recently, however, Boaz and Ciochon (2004) have renewed the claim, pointing to stone tool cut marks on Skull V from the Chinese cave. But the evidence of a single skull from a single locality, although suggestive, is hard to stretch into a specieswide trait. Further data are needed before the question of *Homo erectus*'s cannibalism can be finally decided.

Beyond these two points—the possibilities of intraspecific head bashing and occasional cannibalism—the data on aggression become too thin to allow even speculation. Did *Homo erectus* aggressively defend territories? Did they wage war on other groups? Answers to these questions must be deferred to future investigators.

Communication

Finally, before leaving *Homo erectus,* we need to revisit briefly the question of speech and language. In Chapter 10, it was concluded from evidence of small thoracic canals and somewhat flatter cranial bases than modern humans (a variable trait, however) that *Homo erectus* probably lacked modern speech. What exactly does this mean?

At least one linguist has suggested that *Homo erectus* produced a *proto-language*—a "concatenation of vocabulary items according to pragmatic pressures (e.g., put the 'word' for the most salient idea first), with no level of grammatical organization involving phrases or inflections or grammatical words such as determiners, auxiliaries, or case-markers" (Hurford, 1999:188). If this is true, *Homo erectus* might have been capable of only a sort of "Tarzan talk" ("Me Tarzan, You Jane"), despite its 962 cubic centimeter brain.

Other linguists are more generous. Terrence Deacon (1997) thinks *Homo erectus* thought and communicated symbolically but still talked in a way characterized by more mouth-produced than throat-produced sounds, few vowels and rapid changes of tone, lots of consonants and oral clicks, and only short phrases. Ann MacLarnon and Gwen Hewitt (2004) agree that *Homo erectus*'s sound sequences (phrases) would have been short, given their inefficient breathing control.

Finally, going even farther than Deacon, Brown University's Philip Lieberman—who has been investigating language evolution for almost forty years—believes that "*Homo erectus* most likely talked, had large vocabularies, and commanded fairly complex syntax" (2002:58).

And so, expert opinions range from using proto-language to being competent speakers. These interpretations will be improved by future discoveries and studies, but one thing is certain now: Nonmodern as they may have been, *Homo erectus*'s speech and language capacities were adequate for the task. As such, they enabled this species of early hominans to spread across the Old World and to enjoy a tenure of almost 2 million years.

Summary

Homo erectus evolved around 1.9 million years ago, and within 100,000 years, it had spread from Africa to extreme southeastern Asia. What enabled this phenomenal geographic spread? Was it increased intelligence? Certainly, this must have played a part, as *Homo erectus* showed a significant jump in overall brain size compared to

TABLE 11.2 A Distribution of the Technological and Subsistence Innovations of *Homo erectus* to Early, Middle, and Late Stages of the Species' Span[a]

Stage	Bracketing Dates (Million Years BP)	Technological or Subsistence Innovation
Early *Homo erectus*	1.9–1.2	Acheulean industry (Oldowan continues as well). Super-scavenging-and-gathering lifestyle (more meat).
Middle *Homo erectus*	1.2–0.6	Control and use of fire (possibly). Acheulean continues west of Movius line, Oldowan to the east.
Late *Homo erectus*	0.6–0.03	Shelters (possibly).

[a]Stages were arbitrarily defined as approximately 600,000-year periods.

early *Homo*. But precisely how increased intelligence aided the species' spread and longevity is unclear. Was it spoken language? Maybe, but the indicators are mixed. *Homo erectus* probably had a large enough brain for language, but it may not have had the fine control of breathing that modern speech requires. If these hominans produced spoken language, it probably was not as rich in sounds or as rapid and complex as that of modern humans.

But what of culture? Surely, there were key cultural advances that set *Homo erectus* apart from early *Homo* and enabled its success. Again, the only possible answer is "maybe." Admittedly, this is not very satisfying, but for a couple of reasons, it is the best we can do at present. First, we are limited primarily to statements about the *material culture* of *H. erectus*—that is, their tools and other artifacts. Social and behavioral traits—such as group composition, level of social organization, territoriality, and cooperation in (and/or division of) subsistence activities—do not fossilize and can only be inferred. And inferred cultural advances must be considered only as hypotheses for investigation, not as reliable explanations of other phenomena. Thus, we can draw solid conclusions only about a greatly impoverished version of culture—but that's the nature of the archaeological data currently available.

Second, although the innovations in material culture are there, in most cases, the timing is wrong—at least wrong in order for them to work as explanations of *Homo erectus*'s initial geographic spread. As summarized in Table 11.2, only one technological advance can be attributed undeniably to early *Homo erectus:* the development of the Acheulean lithic tradition, with its bifacial tools, particularly hand axes and cleavers. As discussed earlier, this innovation in stone tool technology probably signaled a shift into a super-scavenging-and-gathering mode and enabled the exploitation of energy- and nutrient-rich animal products with an entirely new intensity. Other cultural innovations frequently attributed to *Homo erectus,* such as the control and use of fire and shelter construction, probably came only in the middle or late stages of the species' tenure, if at all.

Unfortunately—at least for our understanding of the Old World wide spread of *Homo erectus*—even the appearance of Acheulean tools postdates the exodus from Africa. The very earliest dates given for Acheulean technology are 1.7 million years ago, and many archaeologists prefer 1.5 to 1.4 mya. Since *Homo erectus* people (or their ancestors?) *had* to have left Africa before 1.8 million years BP, the conclusion seems inescapable that they did so with tools no more complex than Oldowan choppers and flakes. Their successful colonization of Eurasia is all the more impressive.

As noted by several researchers, *Homo erectus* was a very stable species once its basic adaptive niche had taken shape. After inventing Acheulean tools and becoming super-scavengers, *Homo erectus* showed little if any cultural change that can be seen in the archaeological record for well over a million years! The next big change in hominan evolution—the hunting way of life—had to await the appearance of *H. erectus*'s descendants, *Homo heidelbergensis.*

Postscript

As detailed in this chapter, the combination of factors that enabled *Homo erectus* to spread from Africa to southern Europe and even as far as modern-day Indonesia remains unclear. Lithic innovations may have played a role, but the evidence is equivocal. Shelter construction and the regular use of fire probably came too late to have made a difference. A recent archaeological report, however, has suggested another technological breakthrough that might have fostered *H. erectus*'s geographic spread: boat building.

Archaeologist Mike Morwood of the University of New England (New South Wales, Australia) and his co-workers announced in 1998 the discovery of ancient chopper and flake tools from the east Indonesian island of Flores. Dated by the zircon fission-track technique to between 900,000 and 800,000 years BP, the Flores tools seem almost certainly to have been the work of *Homo erectus*, since they greatly predate the evolution of modern humans and since *Homo heidelbergensis* fossils have not been found in this part of the world (see Chapters 12 for details).

The most interesting aspect of the Flores tools, however, is related to the island's location. Because it is surrounded by deep-water straits, Flores seems unlikely to have been connected by a land bridge to the rest of Southeast Asia during the Pleistocene—not even at the peak of the various glaciations, when sea levels would have been dramatically lower than today. This means that whoever made the Flores stone tools had to cross about 12 miles (19 kilometers) of open water to colonize the island. Morwood and his colleagues thus conclude that mid-Pleistocene *Homo erectus* people in Indonesia were able to construct some sort of watercraft that were sufficiently reliable to take out on the open sea.

Homo erectus as boat builder? The possibility has important implications for our interpretations of *Homo erectus*'s intelligence and communication (that is, linguistic) skills, and it could help to explain how the species moved so rapidly across certain portions of the Old World. Further evidence such as that from Flores is eagerly awaited.

Review Questions

1. Describe the innovations in material culture attributed to *Homo erectus*. Which ones are we sure of, and which are we not? Where do these innovations fall within the species' time span?
2. Speculate about why *Homo erectus* was apparently very stable over time with regard to material culture. What anatomical or environmental factors might have contributed to this stasis?
3. There seems to be evidence that *Homo erectus* could not produce modern speech. If this is true, how do you think the species communicated? How might a lack of modern language have affected the species' potential for cultural change?
4. Why have so few Acheulean hand axes been found in eastern and southeastern Asia? Give as many explanations as you can for their absence.
5. Describe the hypothesized relationships among brain size, digestive system size, and diet of *Homo erectus*. Discuss the various ways brain enlargement could be both the result of evolutionary pressures and the trigger for further evolution.

SUGGESTED FURTHER READING

Aiello, Leslie, and Peter Wheeler. "The Expensive-Tissue Hypothesis." *Current Anthropology*, 36:199–221, 1995.

Boaz, Noel, and Russell Ciochon. *Dragon Bone Hill.* Oxford, Oxford University Press, 2004.

de Lumley, Henry. "A Paleolithic Camp at Nice." *Scientific American,* 220(5):42–50, 1969.

Klein, Richard. *The Human Career,* 2nd ed. Chicago, University of Chicago Press, 1999.

Pope, Geoffrey. "Bamboo and Human Evolution." *Natural History,* 98(10):48–57, 1989.

Schick, Kathy, and Nicholas Toth. *Making Silent Stones Speak.* New York, Simon & Schuster, 1993.

INTERNET RESOURCES

DMANISI

www.dmanisi.org.ge

A description of this important Eurasian site, its hominin remains, stone tools, and paleoenvironment.

ACHEULEAN HANDAXES

http://home.wanadoo.nl/marco.langbroek/acheul.html

This site gives a general description of and chronology for the Acheulean tradition, as well as a few illustrations of hand axes.

SCIENCE NEWS ONLINE: ANCIENT ASIAN TOOLS CROSSED THE LINE

www.sciencenews.org/articles/20000304/fob1.asp

A report of recent findings that challenge the notion that Acheulean tools never moved east of the Movius line.

STONE AGE HABITATS

www.personal.psu.edu/users/w/x/wxk116/habitat

This site presents an interesting survey of evidence for early shelter construction. Note that on this web site the stone circle from Olduvai Gorge is not accepted as clear evidence of shelter construction.

BRAZILIAN JOURNAL OF GENETICS: BRAINS AND GUTS IN HUMAN EVOLUTION

www.scielo.br/scielo.php?pid=S0100-84551997000100023&script=sci_arttext&tlng=en

A 1997 article by Leslie Aiello explaining the expensive tissue hypothesis in detail.

HEADSTRONG HOMINIDS

www.naturalhistorymag.com/0204/0204_feature.html

This recent article by Noel Boaz and Russell Ciochon presents a sexual-selection explanation for the thick skull bones of *Homo erectus.*

USEFUL SEARCH TERMS:

Acheulean tools
Dmanisi
Expensive tissue hypothesis
hand axes
Homo erectus *culture*
Movius line

Chapter 11 Timeline

Epoch	Years BP	Fossils and Behaviors	Lithic Ages
HOLOCENE			
10,000			
PLEISTOCENE	53,000–27,000	Ngandong and Sambungmacan fossils	Upper Paleolithic (40,000 BP)
	100,000		Middle Paleolithic (250,000 BP)
1.8 million	200,000		
	300,000	Regular use of fire; oldest shelters	
PLIOCENE	400,000		Lower Paleolithic
5 million	500,000	*H. erectus* at Zhoukoudian, China	
	600,000		
	700,000	*H. erectus* at Gongwangling (Lantian), China	
	800,000	Hearths at Gesher Benot Ya'aqov, Israel	
	900,000	*H. erectus* at Trinil, Java	
	1 million		
	1.25 million		
	1.4 million		
	1.5 million	Nariokotome boy	
	1.6 million		
MIOCENE	1.7 million	Beginnings of Acheulean tradition	
	1.8 million	*H. erectus* in Africa, the Caucasus, and Java	
	1.9 million	Hominins at Longgupo Cave, China	
	2 million	Hominins spread out of Africa (?)	
	2.6–2.5 million	Oldest Oldowan tools at Gona, Ethiopia	

Developing the Acheulean stone tool tradition seems to have been the primary technological innovation of *Homo erectus*. Researchers disagree whether and/or when these hominans used fire and built shelters.

Chapter 12

Homo heidelbergensis and the Advent of the Hunting Way of Life

Homo heidelbergensis hunters using wooden spears attack their prey.

[Hunting] is a way of life, and the success of this adaptation (in its total social, technical, and psychological dimensions) has dominated the course of human evolution for hundreds of thousands of years. In a very real sense our intellect, interests, emotions, and basic social life—all are evolutionary products of the success of the hunting adaptation.

Sherwood Washburn and C. S. Lancaster, From *Man the Hunter* (1968)

Overview

As described in earlier chapters of this book, from the very beginning, hominins have probably practiced various forms of small-scale hunting. Several lines of evidence suggest that the australopiths consumed meat as part of their regular diet, and the assumption was made that on occasion, they caught and killed small prey in the same ways as do modern chimpanzees. Meat eating gained in importance with the evolution of hominans, however, as demonstrated by the Oldowan tools and larger brains of early *Homo* and by further brain growth and the development of sophisticated Acheulean butchering tools by *Homo erectus*. Nonetheless, archaeology indicates that most of the meat consumed by these hominans came not from hunting but rather from scavenging from carnivore kills.

The first true hunting species, as shown by preserved spears and other evidence, was the immediate descendant of *H. erectus*—namely, *Homo heidelbergensis*. First appearing approximately 850,000 years ago, *Homo heidelbergensis* showed even further expansion of the brain, modernizing trends of the face and teeth, and improved communication abilities compared to *H. erectus*. This species may also have shown certain of the social adaptations found in modern hunting-and-gathering people. Finally, like its immediate ancestor, *Homo heidelbergensis* spread across the Old World, becoming the dominant hominin species at the time. This chapter is devoted to an examination of the *H. heidelbergensis* fossil record, anatomy, and lifeways.

Mini-TIMELINE

Date or Age	Fossil Discoveries or Evolutionary Events
(A) Date (years AD)	
1995	TD6 *H. heidelbergensis* fossils (Spain) announced
1994	Ceprano skull found in Italy
1978	Dali skull discovered in northern China
1976	Bodo fossil found in Ethiopia
1921	Kabwe skull found in Zambia
1907	Mauer jaw (*H. heidelbergensis* type specimen) found in Germany
(B) Age (years BP)	
100,000	Approximate extinction date of *Homo heidelbergensis*
~200,000	Dali skull
500,000	Boxgrove and Mauer fossils
600,000	Bodo skull
800,000	Gran Dolina (TD6) fossils
~850,000	Ceprano skull (oldest known *H. heidelbergensis*?)

The Descendants of *Homo erectus*

Perhaps 900,000 to 800,000 years ago, a new species of humans split off from *Homo erectus*. This speciation event—which many investigators conclude occurred in Africa or Western Eurasia (Rightmire, 1998)—produced a larger-brained and smaller-jawed type of human classified here as *Homo heidelbergensis*. Subsequent migrations carried these still-premodern people throughout Africa, into Europe, and east as far as modern China. Within the confines of Europe, *H. heidelbergensis* gave rise to the even larger-brained Neandertals around 300,000 years ago. And some 150,000 years later and back in Africa, a different *Homo heidelbergensis* population apparently evolved into anatomically modern people (*Homo sapiens*).

When expressed this way, the outlines of mid to late Pleistocene human evolution seem simple. In reality, however, they are anything but clear. As described in this chapter, the three-part division of the successors of *Homo erectus*—into *Homo heidelbergensis, Homo neanderthalensis,* and *Homo sapiens*—is accepted by many but not all paleoanthropologists. The species names given to particular fossils are often controversial, origins and extinctions of individual species are generally hard to identify, and the possibility exists that additional species from this time period will be named in the future. Nonetheless, despite the remaining uncertainty, the evolutionary relationships described above serve well as a provisional framework for analyzing mid to late Pleistocene human remains. Problems with the framework will be pointed out as we go along. In this chapter, we first turn our attention to *H. heidelbergensis*.

Speciation in the Middle Pleistocene: *Homo heidelbergensis*

African Fossils

In 1921, laborers mining lead and zinc ore in Zambia (previously Northern Rhodesia), thousands of miles from Europe, uncovered an ancient skull and other human bones. The fossil fragments came from a cave in a knoll called Broken Hill, which rose above plateau country just north of the Zambesi River, at a place called Kabwe (see Figure 12.1 and Table 12.1). The presence of stone tools and extinct animal bones indicated considerable age, and indeed, the skull is currently dated about 400,000 years BP (Klein, 1999).

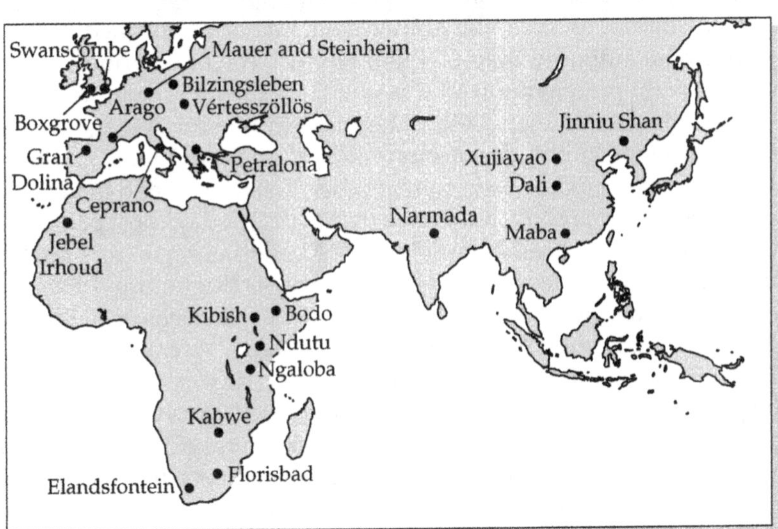

FIGURE 12.1 Fossils of *Homo heidelbergensis* have been found in Africa, Asia, and Europe. This map shows only a sample of all known sites.

TABLE 12.1 A Partial Record of *Homo heidelbergensis* Sites

Geographic Area	Site	Age (Years BP)
Africa	Ngaloba (LH18)	150,000–90,000
	Singa (Sudan)	170,000–150,000
	Jebel Irhoud	190,000–90,000
	Omo Kibish 2	195,000
	Florisbad	~260,000
	Kabwe	~400,000
	Elandsfontein	~400,000
	Ndutu	~400,000
	Bodo	600,000
Asia	Xujiayao	125,000–100,000
	Maba	140,000–119,000
	Dali	230,000–180,000
	Jinniushan	280,000–200,000
	Yunxian	~580,000
	Narmada	600,000–400,000
Europe	Bilzingsleben	~300,000
	Petralona	400,000–250,000
	Swanscombe	400,000–250,000
	Steinheim	400,000–300,000
	Vértessöllös	~400,000
	Arago	~450,000
	Boxgrove	500,000
	Mauer	500,000
	Atapuerca (Gran Dolina, TD6)	~800,000
	Ceprano	~850,000

Source: Klein, 1999, Manzi, 2004, and Rightmire, 2004.

The Kabwe skull showed a mixture of primitive and advanced features (Figure 12.2). Among the primitive traits were its wide cranial base, receding and slightly keeled forehead, and large-sized brows (Conroy, 1997). On the advanced side, however, the skull showed distinct right and left brows that were thick medially but tapered at the side (in contrast to the more continuous browridge of *Homo erectus*) and a very large brain size of 1,280 cubic centimeters (Klein, 1999; Wood and Richmond, 2000). Initially called "Rhodesian Man," the specimen reminded scholars at the time of the Neandertal fossils from Europe (see Chapter 14).

Nonetheless, by 1927, the Kabwe skull had been assigned to the genus *Homo* by no less an authority than G. Elliot Smith. "The most primitive member of the genus *Homo* at present known" was what he called this creature, whose brain was only 50 cubic centimeters below the modern human average (Smith, 1927:116). (Remember that Smith's declaration was made before Dubois's *Pithecanthropus* and Black's *Sinanthropus* had been combined as *Homo erectus* and many years before the discoveries of *Homo habilis* and *Homo rudolfensis*.) Today, most paleoanthropologists (but not all, as described below) assign "Rhodesian Man" to a rather progressive mid Pleistocene species named *H. heidelbergensis* (Rightmire, 1998).

Since the discovery at Kabwe, several other specimens of *H. heidelbergensis* have been recovered from African sites (Table 12.1). A cranium found in 1953 at Elandsfontein, South Africa (near Saldanha Bay), is very similar to the Kabwe fossil and probably about the same age. Also around 400,000 years old is the crushed skull from the Tanzanian site of Ndutu that was found in 1973. And finally, a jawless cranium discovered in 1976 at Bodo, Ethiopia, carried the African fossil record of *Homo heidelbergensis* all the way back to 600,000 years BP (Conroy, 1997; Conroy et al., 1978).

The Bodo skull (Figure 12.3)—with its massive face, large brows, and thick cranial bones—is reminiscent of *Homo erectus* in many respects. Nonetheless, it also has a suite of more *sapiens*-like features, including distinct right and left brows (as in Kabwe); changed proportions of the frontal bone; vertical nasal margin, rather than forward sloping; widening of the braincase further up the sides of the skull than in earlier hominans; a shallow jaw joint; and last but not least, a 1,250 cubic centimeter brain (Conroy et al., 2000; Johanson and Edgar, 1996; Rightmire, 1996, 1998, 2004).

Found in association with Acheulean hand axes and cleavers (Conroy, 1997), the Bodo skull also shows some intriguing stone tool damage of its own. Diagnostic stone tool cut marks occur around the skull's eye sockets, forehead, cheekbones, and elsewhere (Johanson and Edgar, 1996). These cut marks clearly demonstrate that "around 600,000 years ago, this individual was intentionally defleshed, in the earliest such incident known. But whether the butcher ate any of this flesh cannot be answered" (Johanson and Edgar, 1996:93).

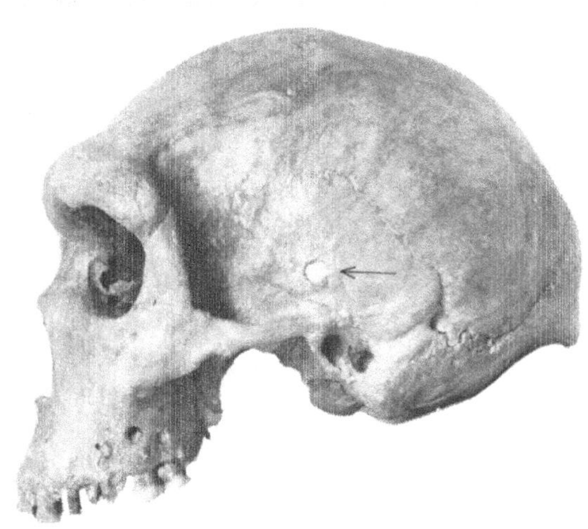

FIGURE 12.2 *Homo heidelbergensis* people flourished during the mid Pleistocene in Africa. This skull from Kabwe, in Zambia, is exceptionally powerfully built. The hole in the temporal bone (*arrow*) was probably caused during life by a small tumor. This photograph is approximately 40 percent actual size.

Asian Fossils

Asia, too, has contributed its share of apparent *Homo heidelbergensis* remains, some quite ancient (Table 12.1). Examples include the fossil from the Narmada Valley in north-central India. In 1982, reseachers unearthed a heavy skullcap now dated at 600,000 to 400,000 years BP. The skull is heavily built and reminiscent of *Homo erectus* fossils; it also has about a 1,200 cubic centimeter brain, however, and a relatively vertical forehead (Klein, 1999). Overall, the Narmada skull seems best classified as *Homo heidelbergensis*. It is associated with hand axes and cleavers, and its considerable importance lies in the way it links Europe and China both geographically and anatomically.

China also has produced several fossils that can be classified (at least provisionally) as *Homo heidelbergensis*, including some with impressively early dates (see Table 12.1 and Figure 12.1). From the site of Dali in north China, a nearly complete skull

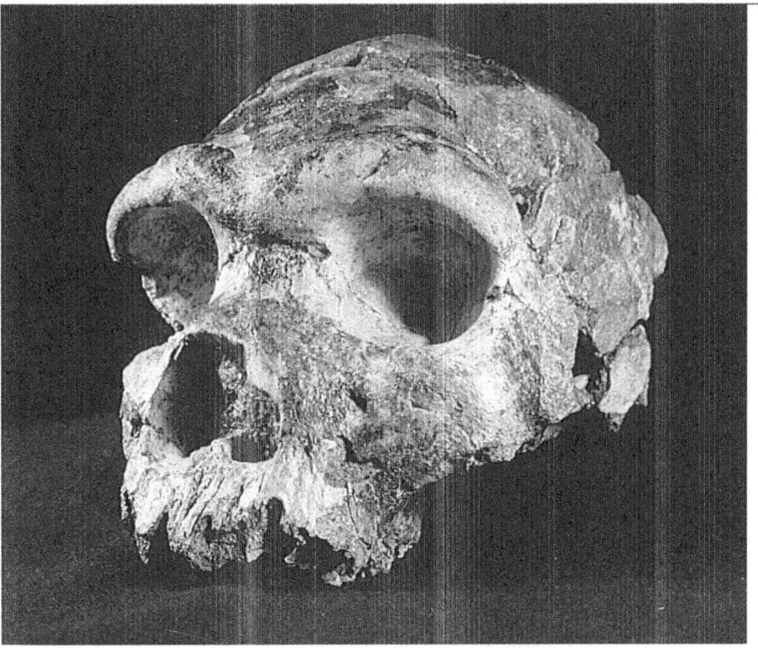

FIGURE 12.3 The Bodo cranium is the oldest African *Homo heidelbergensis*, dating to 600,000 years BP. This skull is about 70 percent actual size.

dating 230,000 to 180,000 years BP was discovered. The Dali fossil resembles *Homo erectus* in its long, low, thick-walled cranium and large brow ridges, but it seems more modern in the higher placement of maximum cranial width and reduced postorbital constriction (Klein, 1999). With a cranial capacity of 1,120 cubic centimeters (Rightmire, 2004), Dali seems best classified as Chinese *Homo heidelbergensis,* at least tentatively. Similar classification appears appropriate for fossil remains from the sites of Xujiayao (125,000 to 100,000 years BP), Maba (140,000 to 119,000 years BP), Jinniushan and possibly Yunxian. The Jinniushan site has yielded a probable *Homo heidelbergensis* skull with an impressive cranial capacity of 1,300 cubic centimeters that dates from about 280,000 to 200,000 years ago. Yunxian has produced two crania that are even older—probably about 580,000 years of age—but whose mixture of *erectus*-like and more modern traits makes them hard to classify (Li and Etler, 1992; Yunxian). The Yunxian skulls are tentatively included in *Homo heidelbergensis* pending further information.

European Fossils

Several European sites have produced fossils assigned to *Homo heidelbergensis,* including the oldest known remains of that taxon. To begin with a discovery made in 1907, quarry workers found a chinless mandible at the site of Mauer near Heidelberg, Germany (Figure 12.1). This fossil was the first to carry the name *H. heidelbergensis* (given to it by the paleontologist Otto Schoetensack), and it has become the type specimen for the species. The Mauer jaw is around 500,000 years old and shows similarities both to its *Homo erectus* ancestors (in its lack of a chin and overall robustness) and to *Homo sapiens* (in its molar size); (Conroy, 1997; Johanson and Edgar, 1996).

Other interesting fossils were discovered in the mid 1930s in Thames River gravel deposits near the English village of Swanscombe (Figure 12.4). At that site a human skull was unearthed that has been dated to about 400,000 to 250,000 years BP. The partial skull consists only of three bones—both parietals and the occipital—which makes it difficult to classify with certainty (Conroy, 1997).

A very similar skull—this time with a face—was discovered at Steinheim, Germany, in 1933. Approximately the same age as Swanscombe (Table 12.1), the Steinheim fossil has a braincase that is more or less similar to the English specimen and that held a 1,100 cubic centimeter brain. The Steinheim skull also shows rather heavy brows and a low forehead (Figure 12.4; Conroy, 1997). Unfortunately, like Swanscombe, the Steinheim fossil is hard to classify, despite its more complete nature. Both fossils are anatomically intermediate between *Homo erectus* and modern humans, and neither is clearly a Neandertal (Johanson and Edgar, 1996). As a temporary measure, Steinheim and Swanscombe are treated here as *Homo heidelbergensis,* although it is possible that they were actually early members of the Neandertal lineage (see Chapter 14).

The oldest hominin fossil known from England was excavated in 1993 at the site of Boxgrove in West Sussex (Figure 12.1). The fossil is a fragment of a massive left tibia,

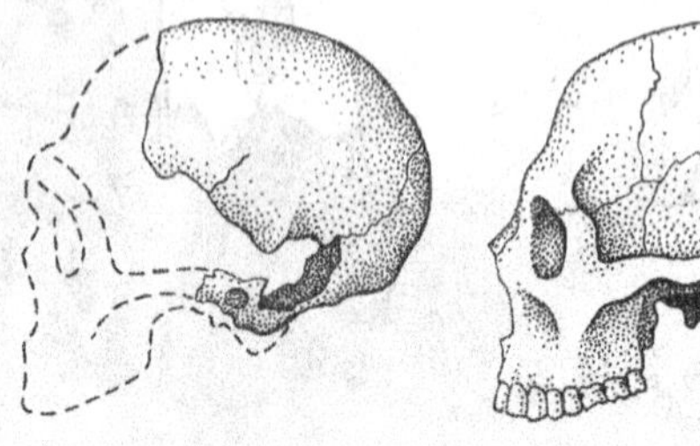
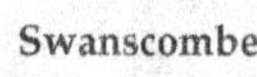

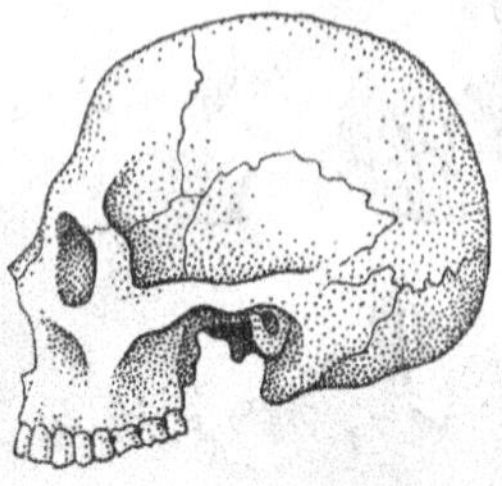

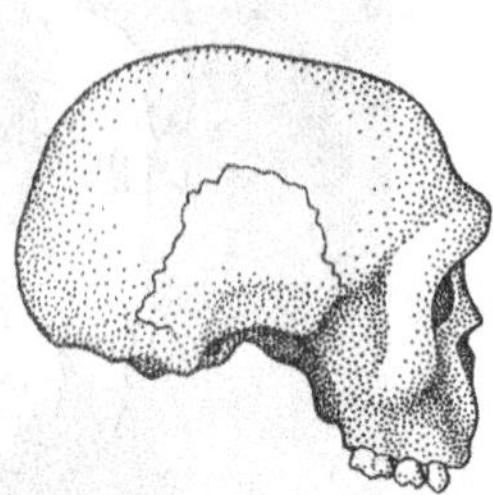

FIGURE 12.4
The Swanscombe and Steinheim skulls compared with the skull of a modern human being. The form of the back of the skull is quite comparable; the differences lie in the face. This drawing is just under 25 percent actual size.

or shinbone, and is roughly the same age as Mauer (Table 12.1). Analyses of the bone suggest assignment to *Homo heidelbergensis* (Roberts et al., 1994). Besides being the earliest evidence of hominin occupancy of the British Isles, the Boxgrove tibia is exciting because it is accompanied by Acheulean stone tools (Pitts and Roberts, 1998). As noted in Chapter 11, a critical absence of hominin fossils leaves the identity of the tool makers uncertain at several Acheulean sites in Europe—particularly sites that fall within the period of *Homo erectus–Homo heidelbergensis* overlap. At Boxgrove, however, it seems clear that a half million years ago, the latter people made and used Acheulean tools, and this discovery will no doubt have implications for interpreting other sites.

In 1960, the Greek site of Petralona (Figure 12.1) produced a large-brained (1,230 cubic centimeters) *Homo heidelbergensis* skull (Rightmire, 2004). Dating approximately to 400,000 to 250,000 years BP, the Petralona skull shares some features with *Homo erectus* and others with the more modern specimen from Kabwe in Africa. Certain features of the Petralona face and braincase suggest links to the later Neandertals (Johanson and Edgar, 1996). Also resembling *Homo erectus* to some extent, but with a projected brain size that seems too large and cranial bones that seem too thin, are some scrappy remains from Vértesszöllös in Hungary (Figure 12.1; Conroy, 1997).

In 1971, fossil humans from approximately 450,000 years BP were discovered at Arago near Tautavel in the Pyrenees (Figure 12.1). Among the remains were a ruggedly built skull (probably that of a young man), a partial hip bone, two mandibles, and assorted other fossils (Conroy, 1997). The skull (Figure 12.5) showed a forward-jutting face, heavy brow ridges, a slanting forehead, and a 1,166 cubic centimeter braincase (Rightmire, 2004). The two jaws were both chinless, and along with the other Arago remains, they are classified here as *Homo heidelbergensis.*

The sites mentioned thus far document the existence of *Homo heidelbergensis* in Europe between about 500,000 and 250,000 years BP (Table 12.1). Two additional sites

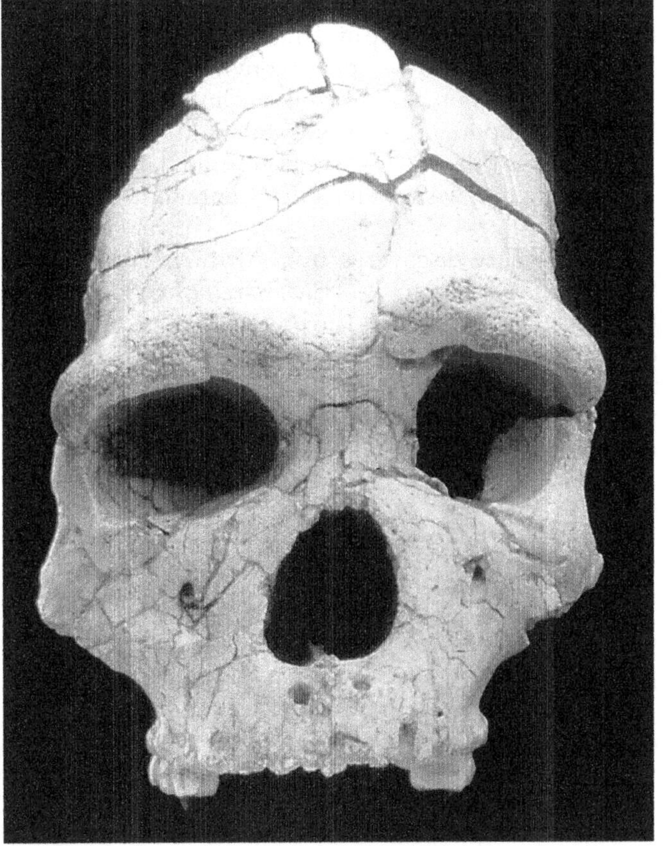

FIGURE 12.5
The skull from Arago is much more robust than those from Swanscombe and Steinheim. This photograph is approximately 60 percent actual size.

take the European tenure of the species back to just under 1 million years ago. These two sites—Gran Dolina in the Atapuerca hills of northern Spain and Ceprano in central Italy (Figure 12.1)—also represent the very oldest remains of *Homo heidelbergensis* from the entire Old World. As such, they provide our best approximation of the origin of this species.

Located some 125 miles (200 kilometers) north of Madrid, the Gran Dolina site in the Sierra de Atapuerca contains a treasure trove of mid Pleistocene hominan fossils. From a deep level called the Aurora stratum, or TD6, researchers at Gran Dolina have recovered early human fossils dated by paleomagnetism to about 800,000 BP (Arsuaga, 2000; Bermúdez de Castro et al., 1999; Carbonell et al., 1995). Found in association with a pre-Acheulean chopper-and-flake tool assemblage, the TD6 fossils (which represent at least six individuals) show smaller jaws and teeth than *Homo erectus*, a cranial capacity of more than 1,000 cubic centimeters, separated brow ridges, and in at least one specimen—a juvenile designated ATD6–69—modern-looking midfacial features (Bermúdez de Castro et al., 1997). Indeed, although the Gran Dolina hominans were initially assigned to *Homo heidelbergensis* (Carbonell et al., 1995), the facial features of ATD6–69, along with certain other cranial and dental traits, have convinced the Spanish team excavating the site that the TD6 materials constitute a new species of premodern humans: ***Homo antecessor*** (Bermúdez de Castro et al., 1997). Initial reactions to the new species designation were mixed, however (Gibbons, 1997), and many anthropologists prefer to keep the TD6 fossils in *Homo heidelbergensis*, at least for the time being. In this book, we take a conservative approach and lump the TD6 fossils into *Homo heidelbergensis*. (For more information on the controversial question of mid Pleistocene hominan taxonomy, see the Postscript to this chapter.)

Homo antecessor the proposed new *species* name for certain *fossils* from the site of Gran Dolina, Spain; a taxon not recognized as valid in this book.

And finally, in 1994, the Italian site of Ceprano produced a partial cranium with big brows and a brain just over 1,000 cubic centimeters in size (Ascenzi et al., 1996). Dated by a combination of K/Ar and stratigraphic procedures to 900,000 to 800,000 BP (Manzi, 2004; date taken here as approximately 850,000 years ago; Table 12.1), the Ceprano fossil was initially assigned to *Homo erectus* by its discoverers and others (Clarke, 2000). Despite undeniable *Homo erectus*–like features, however, a recent reanalysis of the skull has argued convincingly that its modern traits (e.g., weak postorbital constriction, lack of vault keeling, and double-arched brow) carry greater taxonomic importance and that it should be put in the same taxon as the Gran Dolina fossils (Manzi, 2004; see also Antón [2003] on the removal of Ceprano from *H. erectus*). Thus, we have included Ceprano as the oldest known example of *Homo heidelbergensis*.

In summary, discoveries from Africa, Asia, and Europe indicate that by about 850,000 to 600,000 years ago, *Homo erectus* had given rise to a more modern human type, *Homo heidelbergensis*. The precise location of that transition is unclear at present, but Africa or Western Eurasia seems most likely (Rightmire, 1998). After spreading widely across the Old World, *H. heidelbergensis* lasted until perhaps 100,000 years BP, and maybe even later (Table 12.1). Following a description of the anatomy of *Homo heidelbergensis*, we will take a look at the behavior and probable evolutionary relationships of this species.

The Anatomy of *Homo heidelbergensis*

Compared to their *Homo erectus* ancestors, *Homo heidelbergensis* people had made progress toward modernity in several points of anatomy (see Box 12.1 and Figure 12.6; unless otherwise indicated, anatomical details come from Conroy [1997] and Rightmire [1996, 1998, 2004]). Perhaps the most significant advance was in their brain size, which now averaged 1,212 cubic centimeters—a 25 percent increase over the *Homo erectus* average (compare Box 10.1). Increased brain size was accompanied by a rise in the height of the cranial vault (the bones of which were still generally quite thick), while brow size, facial prognathism, and tooth sizes all showed declines.

BOX 12.1

Characteristics of *Homo heidelbergensis*[a]

Trait	*Homo heidelbergensis*
Height (sexes combined)	Essentially modern? >4.9 ft (>150 cm)
Weight (sexes combined)	Essentially modern? 77–185 lb (35–84 kg)
Brain size (sexes combined)	1,212 cc mean (1,100–1,305 cc range)
Cranium	Compared to *Homo erectus:* smaller and separated brows; higher cranial vault; less prognathic face; incipient chin on some specimens; variability in degree of cranial base flexure
Dentition	Similar to *Homo erectus,* but with smaller teeth overall
Limbs	Modern arm and leg proportions; massive construction suggests a powerful body
Locomotion	Bipedalism
Distribution	Africa, Asia, Europe
Known dates	~850,000–100,000(?) years BP

[a]Mean values for anatomical measurements may change with the addition of new fossil discoveries. For additional technical details and diagnostic traits, see Appendix 3.
Sources: Conroy, 1997; Kappelman, 1996; Rightmire, 1996, 1998, 2004.

Brows also showed a change in shape from the straight, shelf-like structures of *Homo erectus* to curved prominences above the separate eye sockets. Most *Homo heidelbergensis* individuals (e.g., Mauer and Arago) continued to lack a distinct chin, but some specimens do show incipient development of this feature. Equally variable is the degree of flexure of the cranial base (an important indicator of how the vocal apparatus was configured), with some specimens (e.g., Kabwe) approaching the modern condition (Ross and Henneberg, 1995). Finally, *Homo heidelbergensis* faces were sometimes quite broad and had rather large noses (e.g., Bodo and Kabwe).

Few conclusions can be drawn about the postcranial skeleton of *Homo heidelbergensis* because of a paucity of relevant fossils. It seems likely that these people were essentially modern in their overall height and weight (Aiello and Dean, 1990; Mietto et al., 2003; Molnar, 2002). However, there are some tantalizing hints that they

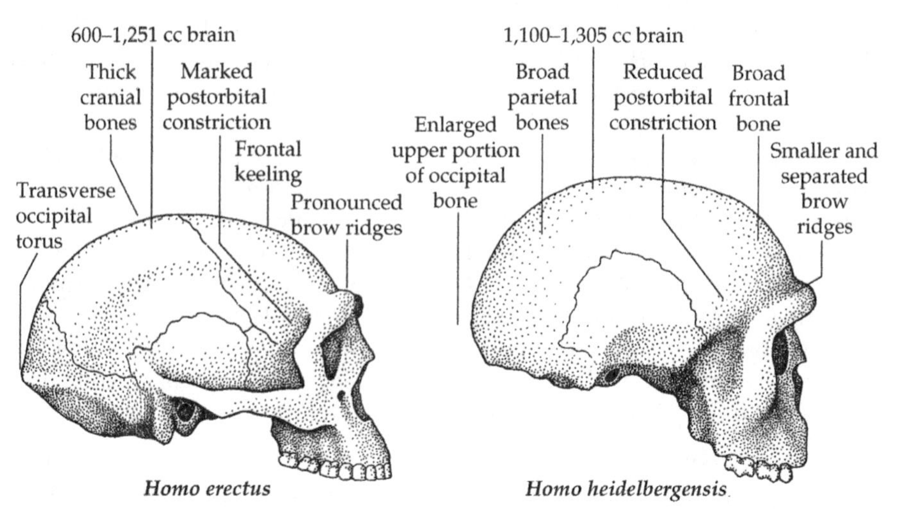

FIGURE 12.6 Compared to *Homo erectus, Homo heidelbergensis*—represented here by the Steinheim fossil—showed much larger brains and more modern cranial anatomies. Nonetheless, that species also retained such primitive traits as relatively large brows. Several distinctive traits are listed for both species, and others are given in Appendix 3. The drawings are about one-quarter actual size.

might have been much more powerfully built than modern humans. For example, the fragmentary tibia from Boxgrove, England, has very large midshaft dimensions and thick walls. Robust femoral and tibial fragments were also found at Kabwe (Roberts et al., 1994). Modern humans have apparently experienced a significant reduction in bodily robustness compared to their *H. heidelbergensis* forebears (Kappelman, 1996; Ruff et al., 1997).

Not surprisingly, given the species' wide range and the likelihood of interpopulation differences in adaptations, *Homo heidelbergensis* shows not only temporal but geographic variability. Nonetheless, there appears to be enough internal consistency to consider it a valid taxon, at least until further discoveries that might prove the case to be otherwise.

The Advent of the Hunting Lifestyle: Technological and Social Developments

In contrast to *Homo erectus,* whom we described as a super-scavenging-and-gathering species, *Homo heidelbergensis* people seem clearly to have achieved a subsistence level that deserves the label *hunting-and-gathering*. This lifestyle would have involved the active pursuit of game of various sizes—in addition to plant food gathering and, undoubtedly, some continuing scavenging for meat—and would have moved hominans into the role of top-level carnivores (Roebroeks, 2001). Some anthropologists have argued that the hunting lifestyle was a strong determinant of hominans' further evolution in the areas of society, psychology, communication, and technology (Washburn and Lancaster, 1968), but others are not so sure (Cartmill, 1993). In this section, we will see what the archaeological and fossil data reveal about the life ways of *Homo heidelbergensis* and perhaps venture a speculation or two about what their societies might have been like.

Evidence for Hunting

Before reviewing the evidence for hunting by *Homo heidelbergensis* people, a caveat is in order: As described earlier, this species first appeared around 850,000 to 800,000 years BP and lasted for perhaps 750,000 million years. Furthermore, we believe it was spread from Europe to Africa and on to Eastern Asia and thus undoubtedly utilized a wide variety of habitats. Given this amount of chronologic, geographic, and environmental spread, it is almost a certainty that *H. heidelbergensis* populations varied, perhaps widely, in their subsistence patterns. With particular regard to hunting, they probably put more emphasis on this behavior in some regions (and habitats) than in others and perhaps also at different times in the species' overall tenure. Therefore, any broad statement about *Homo heidelbergensis*'s hunting behaviors runs the risk of being overly simplistic and too generalized. Nonetheless, we think it is a risk worth taking, and so here is the evidence for hunting by these mid Pleistocene people, beginning with the oldest sites.

Disappointingly, the approximately 850,000-year-old Ceprano site in Italy tells us very little about its inhabitants' subsistence behaviors. The skull from Ceprano was probably associated with a chopper-and-flake (Oldowan) lithic industry (Manzi, 2004), but few, if any, faunal remains seem to have been recovered.

The Gran Dolina (Atapuerca TD6) cave site, in contrast, is very informative and strongly suggests hunting 800,000 years ago by this *Homo heidelbergensis* population. Although they produced only an Oldowan chopper-and-flake tool industry, the Gran Dolina people butchered and ate both small and large animals. In the words of the Gran Dolina excavators,

> Data for survivorship and density suggest that . . . complete small-sized [prey animals] were brought into the cave [as well as] partial carcasses of large ungulates. . . . Percussion

> marks, cut-marks and fractures provide evidence of human activity on the fossil bone remains and provide evidence for the consumption of animal food. The role of . . . carnivores at [TD6] was probably unimportant. All of the remains with superimposed carnivore tooth marks and [hominan] cut marks indicate that the [hominans] had priority access." (Bermúdez de Castro et al., 1999:696)

These data come close to presenting a convincing case for hunting, although even the TD6 researchers admit that a bit of competitive scavenging might have occurred.

Now we must fast-forward 300,000 years to the Boxgrove site in England. There, excavators found *Homo heidelbergensis* remains, many hand axes and other tools belonging to the Acheulean industry, and clear evidence (including diagnostic microwear) that the stone tools were used to butcher the carcasses of rhinos, horses, and red deer (Pitts and Roberts, 1998). Additionally, some of the long bones had been smashed with stone hammers in order to get at the nutritious marrow inside. But the question remains, Were the animal remains at Boxgrove obtained by hominan hunting or scavenging? A strong suggestion that they were the result of hunting comes from the 1995 discovery of a horse scapula with a (partial) circular hole through it. That hole, the Boxgrove scientists concluded, almost certainly was made by a wooden spear (Pitts and Roberts, 1998).

And exactly what the Boxgrove spear might have been like was revealed by a discovery in 1995 at the German site of Schöningen (Thieme, 1997). From 400,000-year-old organic mud deposits, archaeologists recovered three wooden spears ranging in length from 6 to 7.5 feet (1.8 to 2.3 meters). Made from spruce, the Schöningen spears were sharpened at one end, resembled modern javelins, and almost certainly "were made as projectile weapons rather than thrusting spears or lances" (Thieme, 1997:809). Also found at the site were numerous flint tools and more than 10,000 animal bones (mostly horse remains), many of which bore stone tool cut marks. The excavator of Schöningen, German archaeologist Hartmut Thieme, concluded that his

> discovery of spears designed for throwing means that theories of the development of hunting capacities and subsistence strategies of Middle Pleistocene [hominans] must be revised, as well-balanced, sophisticated hunting weapons were common from an early period of the Middle Pleistocene onwards. Accordingly, meat from hunting may have provided a larger dietary contribution than has previously been acknowledged." (1997:810)

In our view, these three sites—Atapuerca TD6, Boxgrove, and Schöningen—provide convincing evidence that some *Homo heidelbergensis* populations lived a hunting-and-gathering lifestyle, and we shall classify the species accordingly. We must hasten to note, however, that the case for *H. heidelbergensis* as hunters-and-gatherers is not airtight. There are sites such as Elandsfontein (Table 12.1) where hunting versus scavenging cannot be decided (Klein, 1999). Furthermore, since no hominin remains were discovered at Schöningen, our attribution of that site (and its remarkable spears) to *Homo heidelbergensis* is based solely on its age (squarely in the middle of the *H. heidelbergensis* time span, late in the *H. erectus* time span, and before the definite appearance of the Neandertals; see Chapter 14).

As noted earlier, some room must be left in our characterization of *Homo heidelbergensis* for variation in subsistence patterns, and it may well be significant that the best evidence for hunting by this species comes from northern temperate zone sites (Roebroeks, 2001). In any event, we have said about all there is to say in support of the mid Pleistocene appearance of the hunting life. Given that, we now turn our attention to a more detailed look at the stone tool technology of *H. heidelbergensis*.

Lithic Technology

The stone tool industries of *Homo heidelbergensis* bridge the gap between the Lower Paleolithic (characterized by Oldowan choppers and flakes and Acheulean hand axes) and the next lithic stage, the **Middle Paleolithic.** Recognized mainly by declining numbers of hand axes and the invention of the **Levallois technique** for the production of

Middle Paleolithic: a period of stone tool manufacture in the Old World (mainly Europe, Africa, and Western Asia) that lasted from about 250,000 to 40,000 years BP.

Levallois technique a stone-knapping method in which a core is shaped to allow a *flake* of predetermined size and shape to be detached; originated at least 250,000 years BP.

BOX 12.2

Invention of the Levallois Technique

A significant advance in stone tool technology occurred at the start of the Middle Paleolithic and may be attributable to *Homo heidelbergensis.* Prior to that time, early *Homo* and *H. erectus* tool makers had produced flake tools by simply hitting a large core with a hammer stone. The resulting flakes were unpredictable in their sizes and shapes, but they served well enough as butchering implements.

Some 300,000 to 250,000 years ago, however, some particularly ingenious stone-knappers developed a sophisticated new technique for making flake tools. Called the *Levallois technique* after the Parisian suburb where such tools were first discovered by archaeologists, the procedure involves carefully preparing a stone core and then producing a finished implement with a single blow (Stringer and Gamble, 1993; Figure 12.7). First, a nodule of flint or other stone is chipped around the sides and on the top. This produces a prepared core that looks something like a tortoise and removes all (or most) of the nodule's original surface. Then the prepared core is given a well-aimed blow at a point on one end. This detaches a flake of predetermined size and shape, with long, sharp cutting edges.

Much less wasteful of raw material than earlier flaking methods, the Levallois technique also represents a remarkable insight into the potential of stone, for no tool is visible until the very end of the process. (In contrast, in the making of a hand axe, the tool gradually and reassuringly takes shape as the stone-knapper works.) The invention of the technique is thought to have taken place in Africa by at least 250,000 years BP, and possibly as early as 300,000 years ago.

prepared flakes (see Box 12.2), the Middle Paleolithic is reckoned by many archaeologists to have begun around 250,000 years ago and lasted until about 40,000 years BP (Klein, 1999; Schick and Toth, 1993; Stringer and Gamble, 1993). As expected, given the postulated descent of *Homo heidelbergensis* from *H. erectus,* the oldest tool kits known for the younger species tend to continue the Acheulean hand axe tradition or the production of simple chopper-and-flake tools (Table 12.2). For example, the Bodo skull from Ethiopia—which dates to 600,000 years BP—was found in association with Acheulean hand axes and cleavers. The same is true for other early African fossils such

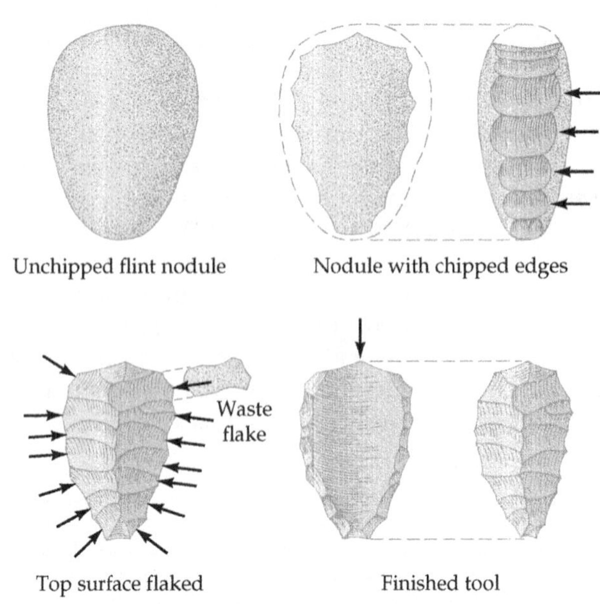

FIGURE 12.7 The Levallois flake has a distinctive predetermined shape. The tool maker first prepared a nodule by trimming its sides (*top right*). This core was then further refined by the flaking of small chips from the front and back surfaces. This is known as a *tortoise core* because of its appearance. A final brisk blow at one end removed the finished flake (*bottom right*), already sharp and in need of no further retouching. These drawings are approximately one-fourth actual size.

TABLE 12.2 A Partial Record of *Homo heidelbergensis* Lithic Cultures

Geographic Area	Site/Fossil	Age (Years BP)	Tool Kit
Africa	Jebel Irhoud	190,000–90,000	Mousterian, Levallois-flaked tools
	Kabwe	~400,000	Sangoan tools
	Elandsfontein	~400,000	Acheulean tools (probable)
	Ndutu	~400,000	Acheulean tools
	Bodo	600,000	Acheulean tools
Asia	Xujiayao (China)	125,000–100,000	Flake tools (no hand axes)
	Dali (China)	230,000–180,000	Flake tools (no hand axes)
	Narmada (India)	600,000–400,000	Acheulean tools
Europe	Vértessöllös	~400,000	Flake tools, choppers (no hand axes)
	Swanscombe	400,000–250,000	Flakes, choppers and Acheulean tools
	Bilzingsleben	~300,000	Flake tools (no hand axes)
	Arago	450,000	Late Acheulean, including small flake tools
	Boxgrove	500,000	Early Acheulean hand axes
	Gran Dolina	~800,000	Flake tools, choppers (no hand axes)

Sources: See Table 12.1. Also see Conroy, 1997; Schick and Toth, 1993.

as Ndutu and Elandsfontein, as well as remains from the 500,000- to 450,000-year-old European sites of Boxgrove (England) and Arago (France). The easternmost Acheulean assemblage that can be attributed to *Homo heidelbergensis* comes from Narmada in India and dates to 600,000 to 400,000 years BP. Interestingly, the 800,000-year-old bones from Gran Dolina in the Atapuerca mountains are not accompanied by Acheulean tools but rather by a flake-and-chopper assemblage that lacks hand axes.

A second feature of the lithic industries produced by *Homo heidelbergensis* is their diversity. This is not unexpected, of course, given the wide geographic spread of *H. heidelbergensis* and the fact that *Homo erectus*'s tool kits also showed regional distinctions (see Chapter 11). As shown in Table 12.2, *Homo heidelbergensis* people in Eastern Asia continued the local tradition of producing nondescript flake tools and pebble choppers (implements that may have been used in combination with bamboo tools; see Chapter 11). The Levallois technique apparently never spread to that part of the Old World. In contrast, African and Western Asian assemblages included Levallois flake tools and a variety of implements including scrapers, choppers, and **denticulates.** In East and Central Africa, *Homo heidelbergensis* people made stone tools attributed to the **Sangoan industry.** The Kabwe fossil, dated to about 400,000 years BP, was found in association with several such implements. Although the Sangoan included some hand axes and scrapers, its most distinctive tools were long, narrow, and heavy stone picks that may have been used for woodworking by archaic populations adapted to forested environments (Schick and Toth, 1993). But perhaps the most intriguing African lithic assemblage of all is that from Jebel Irhoud in Morocco. Here, *Homo heidelbergensis* people produced a stone tool industry that has been classified as *Mousterian* (see Chapter 14). Complete with Levallois-flaked implements, the Jebel Irhoud tool assemblage is unusual because Mousterian tools are almost always associated with Neandertals, but the human remains from this site show no Neandertal affinities (Stringer and Gamble, 1993). No good explanation for this archaeological puzzle is known at present.

Denticulates stone implements made with toothed or notched edges

Sangoan the *Middle Paleolithic* tool industry from East and Central Africa; associated with *Homo heidelbergensis.*

Nonlithic Artifacts

Evidence of nonlithic adaptations of *H. heidelbergensis* people is sparse. As noted in Chapter 11, they may have been responsible for the shelters and hearths found at Terra Amata, and other evidence that *H. heidelbergensis* people controlled and used fire includes the reports of possible hearths at Schöningen (Thieme, 1997) and the 300,000-year-old Bilzingseben site in Germany (Schick and Toth, 1993). With regard to clothing, it seems most unlikely that humans would have been able to inhabit the cold middle regions of Europe 500,000 to 250,000 years ago without at least the rudiments of bodily coverings, but conclusive evidence has yet to be discovered. Finally, at present, we simply have no information about any belief systems, burial practices, or artistic products of *Homo heidelbergensis.*

Homo heidelbergensis Society

In 1968, Sherwood Washburn and C. S. Lancaster published a paper entitled "The Evolution of Hunting" that has become something of an anthropological classic. In that paper (which is quoted at the head of this chapter), Washburn and Lancaster argued that beginning with *Homo erectus,* hominans lived a hunting lifestyle for over one-half million years (up to the development of agriculture just a few thousand years ago). Furthermore, "the success of this particularly human way of life . . . dominated human evolution and determined the relation of biology and culture for thousands of years" (1968:296). Among other things, it was claimed that the hunting adaptation strongly affected the subsequent evolution of humans' mentality (intelligence and other aspects of our psychology, including aggressiveness), society (inter- and intrasexual relations and the family), communication skills, technology, and our attitudes toward the natural world. Then, based on anthropologists' knowledge of extant hunting societies, Washburn and Lancaster listed a package of traits that defined the lifestyle:

- emphasis on intermale cooperation, particularly as related to planning and carrying out hunts and butchering prey
- sexual division of labor, especially as regards subsistence activities and child care
- food sharing
- emphasis on knowledge of other species and large geographical areas
- emphasis on technical skill
- emphasis on male aggressiveness (as shown by men's pleasure in hunting and killing prey and their enjoyment of war)
- emphasis on the interdependence of men, women, and children (including food sharing), with the result of the evolution of the family
- pair-bonding, incest taboos, and exogamy as aspects of family relations

Since its appearance, Washburn and Lancaster's analysis has proved to be both controversial and heuristically important. Critics have argued with various aspects of what quickly became known as the "hunting hypothesis" (see Cartmill [1993] for an overview of the controversy), and proponents of the model have wrestled with the problem of how it might be applied, in whole or in part, to premodern hominins (see this chapter's Postscript). As argued in this and the previous chapter, it seems best to mark the beginning of a hunting lifestyle with *Homo heidelbergensis,* not *H. erectus.* But having made that taxonomic shift, what conclusions, if any, can we draw about the applicability of the Washburn–Lancaster model to *Homo heidelbergensis?* What do we know (from either biology or archaeology) about the personal relations, societal structure, and intergroup relations of this species?

The short answer is "very little for certain." A typical *Homo heidelbergensis cognitive group* (the set of individuals known personally) has been calculated at about 131 people (Aiello and Dunbar, 1993). Presumably, intelligence and language skills would have been at a premium within such groups to handle social knowledge (ranks, relationships, alliances, grievances, debts owed and paid, etc.) and increasingly complex communication. With regard to intelligence, the significant jump in brain size compared to *Homo erectus* suggests that *H. heidelbergensis* people were indeed considerably smarter than their immediate forebears (but whether for social, ecological, or technical reasons is unclear). Additionally, increased intelligence is indicated by archaeological evidence that *Homo heidelbergensis* produced a more sophisticated tool kit than that of *Homo erectus* (Rightmire, 2004). With regard to communication, a recent analysis by MacLarnon and Hewitt (1999) concluded that *Homo heidelbergensis* probably had the basic package of breath control, tongue innervation, and throat (pharyngeal) proportions to allow complex (modern?) speech. But were these early humans smarter and more talkative *because of hunting*? As noted by Leiden University's Wil Roebroeks, improved communication skills would have facilitated the "exchange of information about resources and coordination of foraging activities" (2001:452). Clearly, however, this would have benefited both hunters *and* gatherers, leaving unanswered the question of whether hunting was the primary causal factor.

Within a *Homo heidelbergensis* group, women would still have been struggling with relatively high energy loads (as documented for *Homo erectus;* see Chapter 11) and faced with the care of secondarily altricial infants. Therefore, like their immediate forebears, they would have needed some support from their group mates. Whether that support came from a mate–husband, from other women, or elsewhere is unknown. Was the institution of the family present at this time? We think the answer is "probably," but it is impossible to prove. Certainly, the finer aspects of modern mating and familial relations—exogamy, incest taboos, and marriage—remain far beyond our abilities of detection.

For those populations of *Homo heidelbergensis* for which hunting seems certain—Gran Dolina, Boxgrove, Schöningen—two aspects of the Washburn–Lancaster model seem definitely to apply: a sexual division of labor and the concomitant practice of food sharing. Given the restrictions on energy, long-distance ranging, and quiet stalking placed on women by their child care obligations, men must have fallen naturally into the role of hunters and women into that of gatherers. The two sexes probably shared the fruits (literally, for women) of their subsistence labors at the end of the day at "meeting places" (Roebroeks, 2001). Interestingly, a sexual division of labor means that in many places, female gatherers undoubtedly provided the bulk of the food for *Homo heidelbergensis* groups. Among modern hunting-and-gathering cultures, meat typically constitutes 20 to 40 percent of the diet, with the rest consisting of vegetable foods gathered mainly by women (Figure 12.8; Foley, 1992).

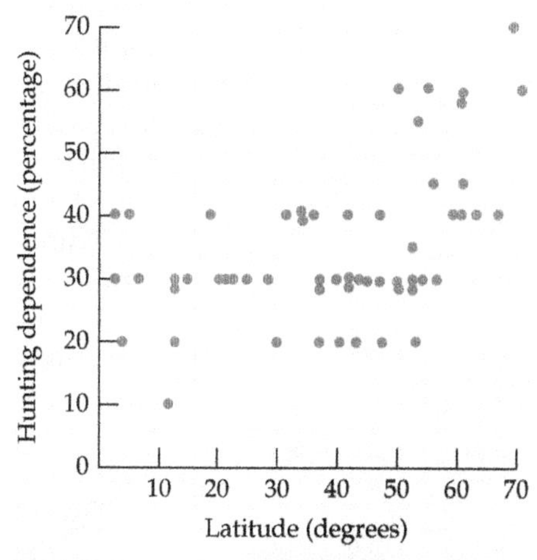

FIGURE 12.8 Among living hunters-and-gatherers, the percentage of food obtained through hunting varies strongly with latitude. In tropical and subtropical areas, hunting generally contributes 10 to 40 percent of the total food, while in higher latitudes (as among certain Eskimo groups), the bulk of the diet may come from meat.

Source: Data from Foley, 1992.

With regard to the question of aggressiveness—at least, intraspecific aggressiveness—the sites of Gran Dolina and Bodo have produced some fascinating data. As mentioned earlier, the Bodo skull showed stone tool cut marks, indicating that it had been defleshed. Whether that defleshing was part of a ritual act and/or a cannibalistic meal cannot be determined. At Gran Dolina, however, the evidence for *routine* (as opposed to *survival*) cannibalism is clearer. In the words of the excavators, at TD6 "[Human] and animal fossil bones show clear evidence of butchering, bone marrow extraction and peeling fracture. Human and faunal remains appear completely mixed. . . . [This suggests] gastronomic cannibalism" (Bermúdez de Castro et al., 1999:697). Of particular importance here is the observation that the location and distribution of butchering marks on human and animal bones were the same (Arsuaga, 2000). At TD6, people were food, but whether cannibalism was limited to foreigners or included group mates is uncertain.

And that is really about all that can be concluded about *Homo heidelbergensis* culture. Hunters-and-gatherers in some regions, although probably still super-scavengers-and-gatherers in others, these people were the most intelligent and most communicative hominins yet to evolve. Their societies undoubtedly had a complex structure, but beyond the family, exactly what form that structure took is hard to say. Were they territorial? Did groups interact in a friendly or aggressive fashion? Did they bury their dead (even occasionally) or practice rituals or sing around the campfire?

Only additional discoveries and analyses will help answer these questions. As we will see in later chapters, however, we can do much better at describing the lives of *Homo heidelbergensis*'s descendants—namely, the Neandertals and the first modern humans.

The Descendants of *Homo heidelbergensis*

In this chapter, we have lumped all of the immediate descendants of *H. erectus* into a single mid to late Pleistocene species, *Homo heidelbergensis,* which existed from about 850,000 to 100,000 years BP. We agree with Rightmire (1996, 1998) that the *erectus*-to-*heidelbergensis* speciation event probably occurred in Africa (see Figure 10.14). Two recent discoveries in the eastern part of that continent lend support to this conclusion. Both the 1-million-year-old cranium from Buia, Eritrea (Abbate et al., 1998) and the 970,000- to 900,000-year-old fossils from Olorgesailie, Kenya (Potts et al., 2004), show a mixture of primitive (*erectus*-like) and progressive (*H. sapiens*–like) traits. The Olorgesailie skull, in particular, resembles the Bodo, Kabwe, and Ceprano fossils in its double-arched brows. Together, Buia and Olorgesailie provide anatomical and temporal links between *Homo erectus* and *Homo heidelbergensis.*

In our opinion, most anthropologists agree with this lumping of mid Pleistocene, non-Neandertal hominans into *Homo heidelbergensis,* but by no means is everyone comfortable with this arrangement. As just a few examples of dissenters, Conroy (1997) groups all such specimens under the label "archaic *Homo sapiens*"; the Atapuerca researchers now classify the Gran Dolina fossils as *Homo antecessor* (Bermúdez de Castro et al., 1997); Manzi (2004) places the Ceprano skull in *Homo antecessor* while Clarke (2000) regards it as *Homo erectus;* and Mallegni et al. (2003) elevate the Ceprano specimen to *Homo cepranensis.* In East Asia, Klein (1999) is more comfortable classifying the fossils from Dali, Jinniushan, and Maba as late *Homo erectus* than as *H. heidelbergensis.* Only time, more fossils, and more studies will sort out this confusion and disagreement. Nonetheless, as a working arrangement, we think a unitary *H. heidelbergensis* serves quite well.

The fossil evidence shows that after its origin, *H. heidelbergensis* spread both north and east, becoming the second hominan species to migrate out of Africa. Its initial movement into Europe apparently got as far as the southern part of the continent and no further. Movement by *H. heidelbergensis* people north of the Pyrenees and Alps did not occur until around 500,000 years ago (Roebroeks, 2001). Moving east, the species was in present-day India by 600,000 to 400,000 BP and reached the Far East soon after (Table 12.1). Exactly how these *Homo heidelbergensis* migrants might have interacted with *H. erectus* populations already in place throughout the Old World is completely unknown.

As detailed in later chapters and diagramed in Figure 12.9, *Homo heidelbergensis* is thought to have given rise (at different times and in different places) to modern humans (*Homo sapiens*) and to the Neandertals (*Homo neanderthalensis*). The *heidelbergensis*-to-*sapiens* speciation event is dated to no later than 195,000 years ago (McDougall et al., 2005) and the advent of the Neandertals to around 300,000 BP. The enigmatic Neandertals will be dealt with in Chapter 14, but first, we must take a break from fossils in order to examine more closely the evolution of language.

Summary

Around 850,000 years ago, *Homo erectus* gave rise to a more advanced species of hominan called here *Homo heidelbergensis.* After their origin in Africa, these people spread into Europe and as far to the east as present-day China. Compared to *H. erectus, Homo heidelbergensis* showed a significantly larger brain, more modern features of the skull and face, and more anatomical evidence of the ability to speak. In con-

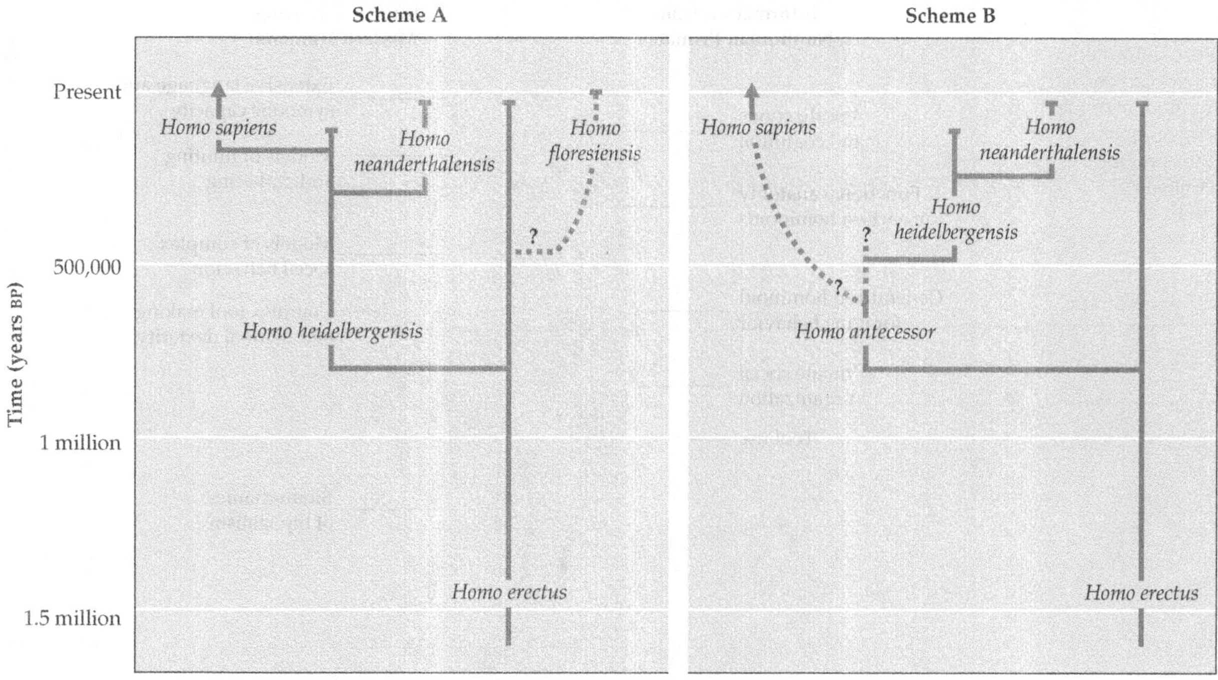

FIGURE 12.9
Two alternative schemes for mid to late Pleistocene human evolution are shown. (A) Here, *Homo erectus* gives rise to *H. heidelbergensis*, which is the common ancestor of modern humans and the Neandertals. (B) Alternately, *Homo erectus* gives rise to *Homo antecessor*, who is the common ancestor of modern humans and *H. heidelbergensis*, with the latter being ancestral to the Neandertals. The recently discovered dwarfed species *Homo floresiensis* (discussed at the end of Chapter 15) is shown in scheme (A), which is the phylogeny favored by the authors of this text.

trast to its anatomical progress, however, the species' lithic culture remained at the level of choppers and flakes or Acheulean hand axes. Clear evidence of a hunting-and-gathering lifestyle has come from a handful of sites, but some *H. heidelbergensis* populations may have remained super-scavengers-and-gatherers. The development of the hunting way of life may have had important behavioral and social implications for some *Homo heidelbergensis* groups. *H. heidelbergensis* is thought to have given rise to the Neandertals around 300,000 years ago. Some 105,000 years later, a different *H. heidelbergensis* population apparently was ancestral to modern humans (*Homo sapiens*).

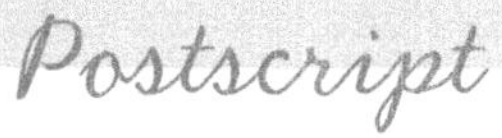

Postscript

For paleoanthropologists and archaeologists, interpreting the fossils and artifacts that they discover is both the bane of their existence and the best part of their job. How can we ever know what prehistoric tools were used for or how the tool makers organized and lived their lives?

These are difficult questions precisely because there are few established principles regarding how interpretations of ancient bones and stones should be carried out. Although modern researchers are much less prone to make hasty speculations than their predecessors were, preferring to force recovered bones and artifacts to *prove* the existence of particular behavioral patterns, guidelines for interpretations are still fuzzy,

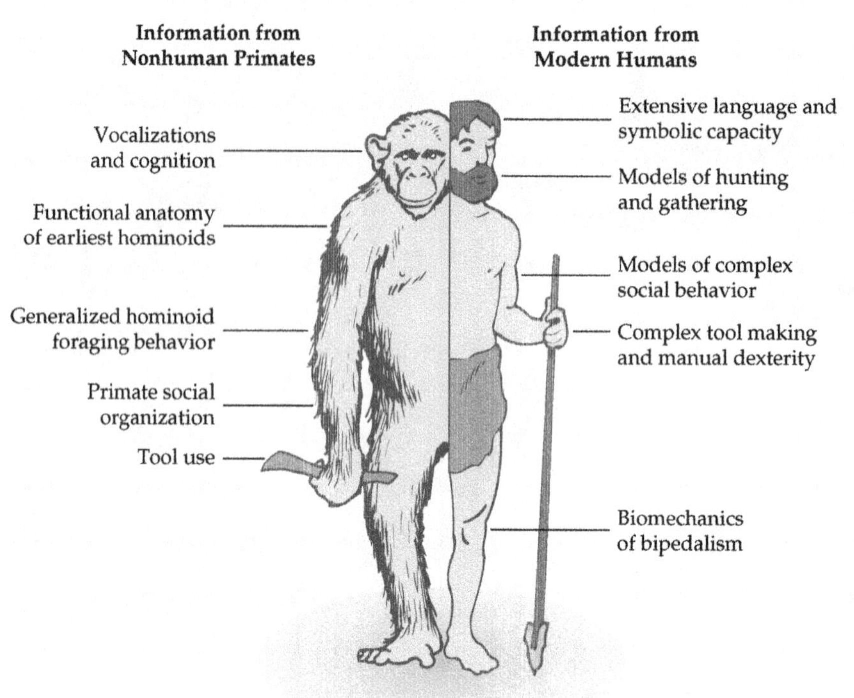

FIGURE 12.10 This figure shows some of the sorts of information researchers can derive from nonhuman primates and living humans that aid in the interpretation of extinct hominins.

and therefore disagreements among specialists are legion. Consider the problem of analogue models (Foley, 1992).

Two sources of information are commonly used to interpret the behavior of prehistoric hominins: data from modern people still practicing hunting-and-gathering and data from nonhuman primates (usually apes; Figure 12.10). Conclusions about extinct hominin types are then reached by a process of triangulation; that is, nonmodern hominins are described as behaviorally intermediate between modern hunters-and-gatherers and apes, with humanlike traits predominating in relatively recent species and apelike traits predominating in very ancient hominin types. Thus, *Homo heidelbergensis* has been described in this chapter as a sort of primitive human, while the australopiths were interpreted earlier as more like apes.

In principle, there is nothing wrong with this sort of triangulation. Problems arise, however, in determining which analogue model—modern hunters-and-gatherers or apes—is most appropriate in each case and (perhaps more importantly) because reliance on these two established models sometimes seems to limit our imagination and prevent us from considering the possibility of adaptive systems unlike those known in any living primate. Leaving some room for imaginative interpretations (always tentative and constructed as testable hypotheses) is quite important, since comparative information from apes is limited by the small number of living species and since comparative data from modern hunters-and-gatherers, almost all of whom live in marginal habitats, may not be representative of the past, when hunting-and-gathering people had access to richer environments. And finally, it must be remembered that arguing from living systems to systems that are extinct is a multistep process that involves data gathering at several levels, rather than a simple transference from the present to the past.

Review Questions

1. Compare the anatomy of *Homo heidelbergensis* with that of *Homo erectus*. In what ways was *H. heidelbergensis* more modern than its immediate forebear?

2. Compare the culture of *Homo heidelbergensis* with that of *Homo erectus*. Can you detect any progressive changes in lithic technology, evidence for control of fire, shelter construction, or the like?
3. We have described some *Homo heidelbergensis* populations as living a hunting-and-gathering lifestyle. What archaeological evidence is there for this conclusion?
4. Assuming that some *H. heidelbergensis* people were hunters-and-gatherers, what implications (if any) does this have for their behavior and social structure?
5. Do you think *Homo heidelbergensis* was any more human than *Homo erectus*? If so, how was it expressed? In your view, what are the diagnostic features of humanness?

SUGGESTED FURTHER READING

Bermúdez de Castro, J., et al. "The TD6 (Aurora Stratum) Hominid Site: Final Remarks and New Questions." *Journal of Human Evolution*, 37:695–700, 1999.

Klein, Richard. "Archaeology and the Evolution of Human Behavior." *Evolutionary Anthropology*, 9:17–36, 2000.

Johanson, Donald, and Blake Edgar. *From Lucy to Language*. New York, Simon & Schuster, 1996.

Pitts, Michael, and Mark Roberts. *Fairweather Eden*. New York, Fromm International, 1998.

Rightmire, G. P. "Human Evolution in the Middle Pleistocene: The Role of *Homo heidelbergensis*." *Evolutionary Anthropology*, 6:218–227, 1998.

Tattersall, Ian, and Jeffrey Schwartz. *Extinct Humans*. New York, Westview Press, 2000.

INTERNET RESOURCES

Homo heidelbergensis
www.mnh.si.edu/anthro/humanorigins/ha/heid.htm
This Smithsonian site presents a brief description of these descendants of *H. erectus*.

ARCHAEOLOGY.INFO: *Homo heidelbergensis*
www.archaeologyinfo.com/homoheidelbergensis.htm
More information, including anatomical details, about this species.

BOXGROVE PROJECTS: BOXGROVE EXCAVATIONS
http://freespace.virgin.net/mi.pope/site/sitehome.htm
This site provides interesting information on a *Homo heidelbergensis* site in England.

ATAPUERCA: THE HUMANS OF GRAN DOLINA
www.amnh.org/exhibitions/atapuerca/granhumans/index.php
Produced by the American Museum of Natural History, this web site describes the fossils from the Gran Dolina site in Spain. These materials are classified as *Homo heidelbergensis* in this textbook.

PREHISTORY SECTION: U. R. V. ATAPUERCA RESEARCH TEAM
http://romani.iua.urv.es/welcome.html
This site contains full information on the various excavations in the Sierra de Atapuerca and the hominins that have been discovered there.

PNAS: A CRANIUM FOR THE EARLIEST EUROPEANS
www.pubmedcentral.nih.gov/articlerender.fcgi?artid=55569
A detailed morphological analysis of the ~850,000-year-old skull from Ceprano, Italy.

USEFUL SEARCH TERMS:

Atapuerca
Bodo fossil
Boxgrove
evolution of hunting
Homo antecessor
Homo heidelbergensis
hunting and gathering

Chapter 12 Timeline

HOLOCENE		YEARS AD	HOMO HEIDELBERGENSIS DISCOVERIES
10,000			
		1997	Wooden Spears at Schöningen
		1996	At Ceprano
100,000	Approximate extinction of *H. heidelbergensis*	1995	At Atapuerca TD6
		1994	At Boxgrove
200,000			
250,000	Dali		
300,000	Bilzingsleben		
350,000	Swanscombe, Steinheim		
400,000	Petralona, Kabwe, Elandsfontein		
500,000	Mauer and Boxgrove Narmada		
		1978	At Dali
600,000	Bodo	1976	At Bodo
PLEISTOCENE			
		1971	At Arago
800,000	Gran Dolina TD6 Ceprano		
900,000			
1 million	Last australopiths extinct		
	H. habilis at Olduvai		
		1935	At Swanscombe
1.8 million	*H. erectus* in Africa, the Caucasus, and Java	1933	At Steinheim
2 million			
		1921	At Kabwe (Broken Hill)
PLIOCENE			
	H. rudolfensis		
2.5 million	Earliest Oldowan tools	1907	Mauer jaw found (type specimen)

DISCOVERY OF *HOMO HEIDELBERGENSIS*

Chapter 13

The Evolution of Language and the Brain

These naturally occurring endocasts from South Africa give a good idea of the topography of the australopith brain.

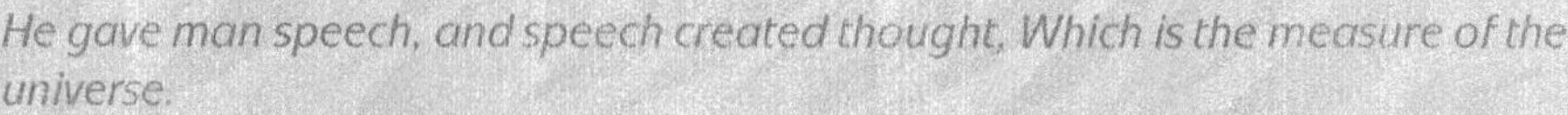

He gave man speech, and speech created thought, Which is the measure of the universe.

Percy Bysshe Shelley, 1792–1822. *Prometheus Unbound*, II, IV, 72–73.

Speech was given to man to disguise his thoughts.

Attributed to Charles Maurice de Talleyrand, 1754–1838.

Overview

Of all of the various traits of living humans, spoken language appears to be unique. At first glance, language and speech seem to separate us rather cleanly from all other living organisms, and virtually all theories of human origins include spoken language as a key evolutionary milestone in our history. But how wide is the "language gap" between humans and other animals, when did it first appear, and how closely is it related to differences in brain anatomy?

This chapter addresses these and other questions as it describes the anatomical specializations (brain size and organization and throat and mouth anatomy) that enable humans to talk. The chapter also compares human language to the communication patterns of wild monkeys and apes, discusses apes' abilities to learn gestural and computer-based language systems in the laboratory, and reviews the hominin fossil record for evidence of the beginnings of spoken language. The chapter ends with a discussion of the archaeological evidence for the appearance of human mind.

Ways of Communicating

As the social life of humans grew more complex, the ability to communicate must also have developed. Spoken language, we can now see, was humankind's passport to a totally new level of social relationship, organization, and thought. Although undoubtedly rooted in the vocal and gestural communication patterns of our primate and australopith ancestors, spoken language moved humans far beyond our forebears' nonlinguistic world into a realm all our own. But how, when, and why did it evolve?

Theories on the Origins of Speech

When did humans begin to speak? How did they start? What did their first words sound like? For centuries, philosophers, historians, and others have struggled with these questions, trying (among other things) to determine whether speech and language were God-instilled or human-achieved attributes. Not surprisingly,

Mini-TIMELINE

Date (Years BP)	Species and Reconstructed Communication
160,000–present	*Homo sapiens:* modern speech and language; modern mind
850,000–100,000(?)	*Homo heidelbergensis:* modern speech and language as well as mind approaching modernity (?)
1.9 million–27,000	*Homo erectus:* rudimentary speech and language (at best); primitive mind (?)
2.4–1.6 million	Early *Homo:* probably lacked speech and language; primitive mind (?)
7.0–1.0 million	Australopiths: almost certainly lacked speech and language; apelike mind (?)

Charles Darwin preferred a naturalistic explanation, and in *The Descent of Man,* he suggested "that language owes its origin to the imitation and modification, aided by signs and gestures, of various natural sounds, the voices of other animals, and man's own instinctive cries" (1871/1981:I, 56). Since the nineteenth century, Darwin's evolutionary theory has provided a useful framework for studies of the gradual acquisition of speech and language.

A half century after Darwin, Grafton Elliot Smith (1927) linked the origin of speech to increased muscular control in a way that anticipated certain modern theories. Smith wrote that the

> perfection of cerebral control over muscular actions made it possible for the Ape-Man to learn to imitate the sounds around him, for the art of learning is a training not only of the motor centres and the muscles concerned, but also of all muscles, because posture involves the whole body and it is more or less concerned in every act. The benefits that accrued from educating the hands added to the power of controlling other muscles, such as those concerned with articulate speech. (1927:69)

Smith further theorized that in addition to imitating sounds that they heard, our ancestors began to *name objects and events* and to *use imperative verbs.* Combining the two practices (naming and commanding), "it became possible for men to communicate [in simple sentences]" (1927:173).

Today, theories about the origins of speech and language have multiplied, but we are still a long way from any consensus on the issue (Holden, 2004). Arguing along the same lines as Elliot Smith did years earlier, Philip Lieberman (2002) thinks there was probably a connection between the evolution of hominin bipedalism and speech and language. The increased motor control needed for upright standing and walking—control that was mediated by the development of new neural connections between the brain's cortex and its deep structures—would have been a preadaptation for language development. According to Lieberman, these connections provide the "'sequencing engine' that makes [both verbal and movement] combinations possible" (Holden, 2004:1317).

Other researchers focus not so much on the neural underpinnings (both modern and evolutionary) of speech and language as on the usefulness of comparative animal studies to reveal the origin of our communication system. Scientists like David McNeill of the University of Chicago and Michael Corballis of the University of Auckland emphasize the probable importance of gestures as an early stage in language evolution (Holden, 2004). Marc Hauser of Harvard, on the other hand, prefers to focus on the calls of monkeys and apes as likely evolutionary precursors of speech (Holden, 2004), as does Charles Snowdon (2001) of the University of Wisconsin. Hauser et al. (2002) have argued that most of the elements of language (broadly defined) are present in a wide variety of species and that only **recursion**—the production of messages containing imbedded elements that can be understood only in relation to other elements and certain operating rules—sets humans apart from all other creatures. Let's take a closer look at some of the animal (especially primate) studies, postponing a closer look at brain anatomy to a later section of this chapter.

Recursion the production of messages containing imbedded elements that can be understood only in relation to other elements and certain operating rules.

Communication among Animals

Nonhuman vertebrates and insects have some intriguing ways of communicating. Honeybees perform a kind of dance on the honeycomb; the dance accurately transmits information about the direction, distance, and nature of a food source. Dogs and wolves use scents to communicate in addition to barks, howls, and growls; they also use a system of visual signals that includes not only facial expression and body movement but also the position of the tail.

Communications get more complex as the social organizations of animals do, and next to ourselves, the nonhuman primates have some of the most intricate

FIGURE 13.1
Facial expression is one of the most important modes of nonverbal communication in both chimpanzees and people. The functions of such expressions in the two species are quite closely related.

systems of all. Far from depending only on vocalizations, nonhuman primates seem to rely heavily on combinations of gestures, facial expressions, and postures as well as scents and sounds (Figure 13.1). They apparently are able to lend many shades of meaning to this body language vocabulary. Often, they use sounds as a means of calling attention to their other signals. For some occasions, however, only sounds will do. On sensing danger, for instance, a rhesus monkey will give a shriek that causes its companions to seek shelter frantically.

This wordless communication system serves the nonhuman primates extremely well. As social animals living in troops, they use it to keep in touch with one another at all times. More important, it allows individuals to display their feelings and to recognize the intentions and moods of others, enabling them to react appropriately. Many of the signals express the established hierarchy of dominance and submission within the group (Figure 13.2). Different signals—vocal and visual—help individuals stay in contact when moving through the community territory. Still other signals promote mating behavior or foster good mother–infant relations.

Yet for all its complexity and however well suited it may be to the needs of monkeys and apes, such a communication system falls far short of humans' spoken lan-

FIGURE 13.2
A young male chimpanzee presents his rump to a dominant male in a gesture of appeasement. Reassured by the touch of the dominant male, the youngster turns to face his superior.

guage. As far as is known, nonhuman primates in the wild are limited in the ways they can refer to specific things in their environment and cannot communicate thought through the complex phonetic codes called *words* that are used by humans. Nor do they seem able to refer easily to the past or future with the aid of their signals. For them, what is out of sight is usually out of mind. The signal system narrowly circumscribes what can be communicated, and vocalizations and facial expressions are under much less voluntary control than in our species.

This is not to say that the nonhuman primates' vocal signals are entirely unspecific. Consider, for example, the danger-call system of the African vervet monkeys, which have three alarm calls for three kinds of predator and a fourth for baboons (Cheney and Seyfarth, 1990). The vervets use a chitter for snakes (Figure 13.3), a chirp for ground-dwelling carnivores, and a "r-raup" sound to warn of birds of prey. When tape recordings of their alarm calls are played back to them, a chirp is enough to send the vervets scrambling to the tips of branches, well out of reach of ground animals, whereas a "r-raup" launches them from the trees into the thickets below, where predatory birds cannot get at them. As the young mature, they are able to make finer distinctions between the different alarm calls. A cry of "Watch out—eagle!" is beyond their capabilities, but it is also beyond their needs. They do not have to know whether it is an eagle or a hawk diving on them; what matters is that they get the message that the danger is from above, so that they can flee in the right direction.

Young vervets sometimes make mistakes in giving alarm calls, and as they grow up, they improve their performance. The calls can also be adapted and modified for different circumstances. This evidence suggests that the alarm calls are learned or are reinforced by learning rather than being simply innate (Cheney and Seyfarth, 1990).

In addition to vervets' predator-specific alarm calls, some other species of nonhuman primates are also capable of conveying specific environmental information by using vocalizations. For example, rhesus macaques have five acoustically different scream vocalizations that they can give when threatened or attacked. These screams are essentially recruitment devices (cries for help), and primatologists Harold Gouzoules, Sarah Gonzoules, and Peter Marler (1986) have found that the particular scream an animal gives depends on the identity of its opponent (kin or nonkin, dominant or subordinate) and the severity of the fight. Group mates are clearly able to screen the various calls for help, and their responses match the caller's level of danger.

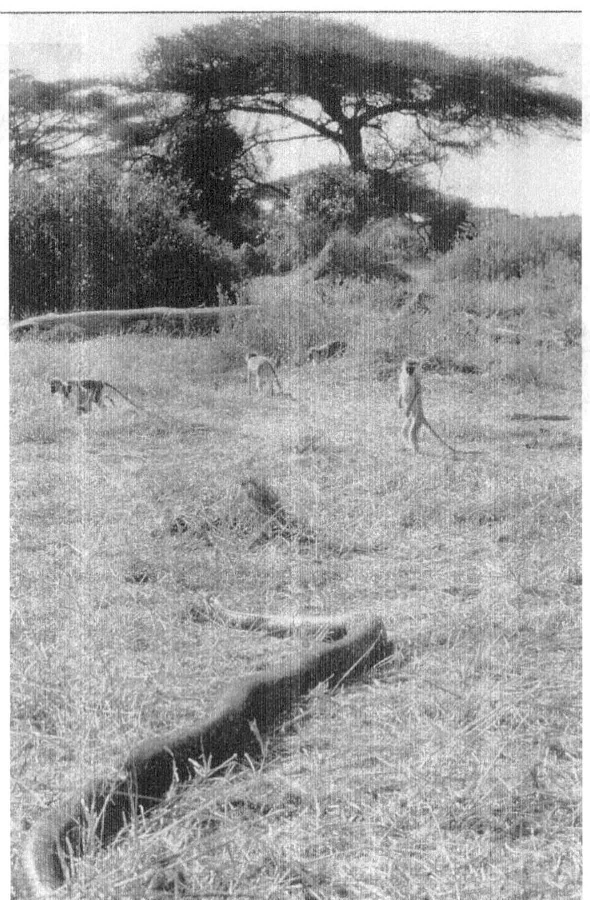

FIGURE 13.3
These vervets (*Cercopithecus aethiops*) are responding to the presence of a python. The appropriate snake alarm call caused the monkeys to run to the nearby acacia trees.

Distinct alarm calls like those of vervet monkeys or foe-specific screams like those of rhesus monkeys may be more widespread than we know. However, based on current knowledge, the vocalizations that are most typical of the higher primates, such as grunts and barks, and that have been well studied in a number of species, especially chimpanzees, are quite distinct and do not indicate a particular feature of the environment so much as an inner state of excitement.

Limbic and Nonlimbic Communication

In their function as well as in their causation, the vocal and visual signals used by nonhuman primates can be divided into two kinds. The majority of these signals—probably most of the vocal signals, as we have seen—express inner emotional and physiological states and are under only limited voluntary control. They allow all members of the troop to monitor the emotional status of all other members. All signals of this sort are generated mainly by a group of structures in the brain known collectively as the **limbic system** (the "emotional brain"). These signals come from below the level of conscious awareness, just as the human scream is generated (T. Deacon, 1997).

Limbic system the emotional brain; a group of structures in the brain that are important in regulating such behavior as eating, drinking, aggression, sexual activity, and expressions of emotion. Proportionately smaller in humans than in other *primates*, it operates below the level of consciousness.

In contrast to these signals, some gestures appear to communicate conscious will or intent. A chimpanzee holds out its hand as a gesture of submissive greeting or raises it in threat. A subordinate chimp anxiously presents to a superior male, backing rump first toward him (Figure 13.2). These conscious gestures, which are normal, voluntary movements, have taken on a role in communication. Because of the intentions and wishes they symbolize, they fall into a category different from the expressions of raw emotion we considered earlier. They are probably generated primarily by higher (cortical) centers of the brain, whose control functions have been superimposed over autonomous limbic control (T. Deacon, 1997).

Both emotional and volitional communication are seen in our own behavior. We, too, have a repertory of wordless signals that universally express emotions: A person has only to smile to demonstrate friendly intentions; clenched fists and jaws, scowls, and frowns are unmistakable signs of anger or disappointment; and the laugh, the cry, and the scream are direct expressions of inner psychological and physiological states. Humans even have acquired an involuntary signal other primates do not have: the blush, over which most people have little or no control, but which sends a clear message about what is going on inside the brain. And when humans are most excited, they often show it by speechlessness. Such basic signals are in a different category from the many other body motions humans use, such as shaking and nodding the head, shrugging the shoulders, and clapping the hands; these are really abbreviated substitutes for spoken language and vary in meaning from one place to another. Nonverbal communication is still an essential component in modern human relationships (Figure 13.1).

In this context, the observations made of vervet monkeys by Dorothy Cheney and Robert Seyfarth (1990) are of particular interest. Alarm calls, which appear to benefit kin (i.e., kin selection) as well as the alarmist itself (as a result of reciprocal altruism), are made by many social species of birds and mammals. Among primates, vervets' alarm calls have received the most detailed study. It is clear that these calls, described earlier, refer to objects in the vervets' environment and are not merely expressions of emotion. Furthermore, the sounds are arbitrary and do not resemble in any way the objects to which they refer. However, it must be added that there is certainly an affective component of emphasis, such as volume, length, or rate of delivery, just as there is in human language.

To students of language evolution, the vervets are fascinating. The monkeys' alarm calls may well be based on more than simple limbic control, and they show many similarities to human words. As noted by Hauser et al., however, "Additional evidence is required before such signals can be considered as precursors for, or homologs of, human words" (2002:1576). Alarm calls probably refer to things in the world in a different way than words do (T. Deacon, 1997), and there is currently no convincing evidence that they demonstrate symbolic thinking by either the caller or the listener. Furthermore, alarm calls show little plasticity in final form or context of application and no evidence of recombination into more complex messages. Human language, on the other hand, is all about flexibility, openness, and symbolism (T. Deacon, 1997; Snowdon, 2001).

Nature of Language

Spoken language provides a magnificently efficient and versatile means of communication (T. Deacon, 1997; Snowden, 2001). It is a complex system of chains of symbols to which meanings have been assigned by cultural convention. The number of meanings that can be so assigned is, in practice, infinite. Its coded series of sounds conveys conscious thought many times faster than any other method of signaling can—faster than hand signs, moving pictures, and even other kinds of vocalizations. Through language, humans can step outside themselves and give things and people names, reflect about others and themselves, and refer to the past and the future. Most important of all, language gives people the capacity to share their thoughts. With this ability, discussion, complex bargaining, and democratic processes all became possible.

Whenever and however spoken language evolved—and as noted in earlier chapters, its full development probably postdated *Homo erectus*, despite that species' worldwide spread—it was the new and extraordinarily efficient means by which humans acquired and passed on from one generation to the next the flexible network of learned, rather than genetically inherited, behavior patterns and the knowledge that allowed them to alter their environment and adapt to new ones. Once language had evolved, culture had a symbolic form that changed its whole nature. From this point in human evolution, culture and its medium—language—were necessary for survival.

Ability to Speak

Although it has long been clear that this watershed in evolution occurred largely because of the ability to use words to communicate symbolic meaning, it was not at all clear until recently why humans alone, and not their intelligent close relatives the apes, are capable of speech. After all, apes have much of the vocal apparatus—lips, a tongue, and a larynx or voice box with vocal cords—that humans have.

Talking Apes?

In 1871, Charles Darwin remarked that apes possess vocal organs "which with long-continued practice might have been used for speech" but are not. He blamed this state of affairs on apes' limited intelligence. "The fact of the higher apes not using their vocal organs for speech, no doubt depends on their intelligence not having been sufficiently advanced," he noted (1871/1981:I, 59). Nonetheless, 80 years later, Darwin's insight did not stop Keith Hayes and Cathy Hayes from attempting to teach Viki, a home-reared chimpanzee, to speak (Desmond, 1979). Although the Hayeses devoted 6 years of painstaking effort to the project, in the end, all that a frustrated Viki could manage were heavily accented attempts at "Mama," "Papa," "cup," and "up." Interestingly, "she *understood* spoken English commands, and often acted on them, even if she could not speak back" (Desmond, 1979:28; italics in the original).

A more recent experiment made by Robert Gardner and Beatrice Gardner (1969) produced better results. A chimpanzee named Washoe learned by age five to understand several hundred hand signals of the standard American Sign Language (ASL) of the deaf and to use about 130 of them in her productive vocabulary (Wallman, 1992; Figure 13.4). With these, she learned to name things and express her wants and needs by using those names. Another chimpanzee, Sarah, learned to communicate with her keepers by selecting from a number of plastic chips that carried particular meanings, which she placed on a magnetic board. A third chim-

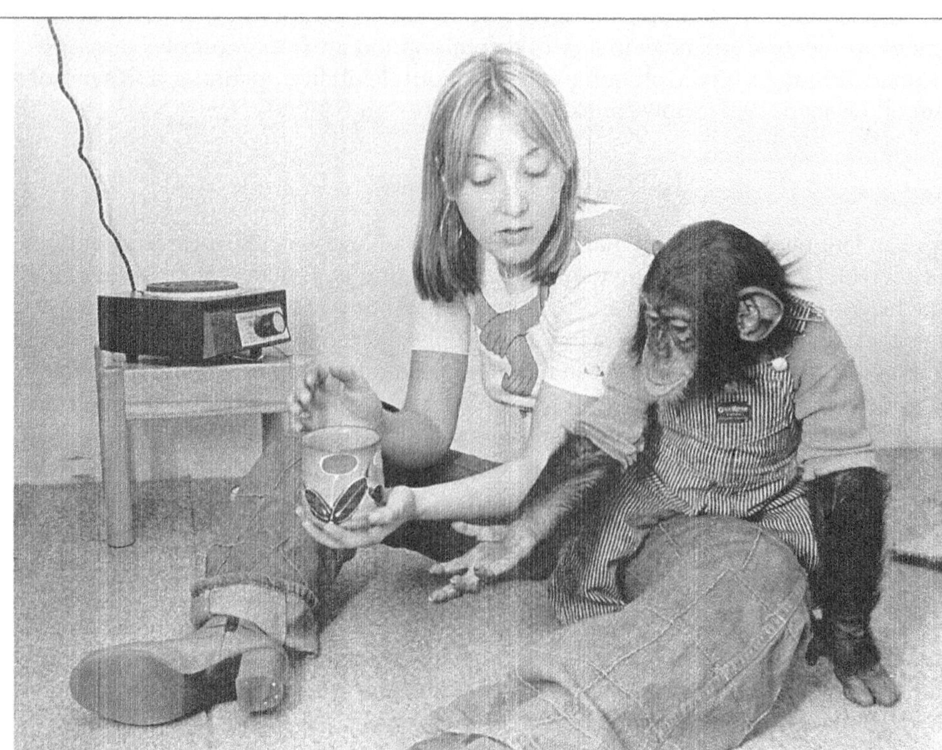

FIGURE 13.4
One of the projects for teaching a chimpanzee sign language was run by Columbia University psychologist Herbert Terrace. In this photograph, his subject, Nim Chimpsky, is signing "give" to his teacher and companion, Laura Petitto.

panzee, Lana, learned to communicate by pressing buttons on a computer keyboard. A gorilla, Koko, trained in ASL by Penny Patterson of Stanford, has learned a vocabulary of more than 250 hand signals and understands many more. Other researchers are teaching the orangutan.

Constant training by humans enables these apes to associate visual symbols not only with concrete objects but also with such abstracts as adjectives, verbs, and even prepositions. With these symbols, it is claimed that apes can construct simple sentences, which they use to express their desires. It is said that they can also lie, abuse their trainers, and invent new expressions. Examples of the latter include "water bird" for swan (Washoe), "white tiger" for zebra, and "bottle match" for cigarette lighter (Koko) (Wallman, 1992).

But of all the ape subjects used thus far in language studies, perhaps the most accomplished is Kanzi, a male bonobo under observation at Georgia State University (Savage-Rumbaugh and Lewin, 1994). Psychobiologist Sue Savage-Rumbaugh has worked with Kanzi since his infancy. Kanzi showed early an outstanding and spontaneous ability to master the meaning of lexigrams (word symbols or icons) on a computer keyboard, and after learning a number of lexigrams, he began to combine them to produce the occasional multiword message (such as "Matata group room tickle," in which he requested that his mother, Matata, be allowed to join in a tickling session in the group room). But even more impressive, as a youngster, Kanzi began to comprehend a certain amount of spoken English, and by age five, he was able to respond correctly to Savage-Rumbaugh's spoken requests and directives. (Kanzi has even shown the ability to respond appropriately to some novel sentences the first time he heard them.) Furthermore, it appears that as part of his spontaneous development of speech comprehension—which reminds one of the Hayeses' experience with Viki—Kanzi may have picked up a bit of English **syntax.** Additionally, according to Savage-Rumbaugh, Kanzi's lexigram-encoded messages to his human companions often include examples of ape-invented syntactic rules (Savage-Rumbaugh and Lewin, 1994).

Syntax the rules of structure in *language*.

It is difficult to know precisely what to make of the linguistic feats of Kanzi and the other ape language subjects. (For a skeptical view of apes' language abilities, see the conclusions of the Nim Chimpsky researchers [Wallman, 1992]; Nim is shown in Figure 13.4.) Clearly, these apes have a certain capacity for symbol comprehension and use, but their best efforts still do not exceed those of a two- to three-year-old human child. These studies show that with exposure to humans (and usually after considerable instruction), apes can learn symbols and use a symbolic means of communication, sometimes with a bit of simple syntax. In all cases, however, they produce messages only by gesture or icon manipulation, not by means of their vocal apparatus. A basic problem remains, as well, in "that we have little idea what [its acquired] signs mean to an ape" (Jolly, 1985:435).

Nonetheless, Kanzi, Koko, Lana, Washoe, and the others have certainly narrowed the "language gap" between apes and humans. As Kathleen Gibson (1994) of the University of Texas and other researchers have argued, these results strongly suggest that a *quantitative,* rather than *qualitative,* gap in communication capacities separates humans from their ape relations. It remains true, however, that ape language certainly does not amount to human language in the complete sense, and most importantly, it is never expressed as speech.

The Pharynx

A clear boundary between apes and humans becomes obvious when one considers means of language transmission. Spoken language requires equipment, both physical and mental, that apes and monkeys simply do not have (see Figure 13.5). The adult human tongue, for example, is thicker than that of monkeys and apes, and unlike theirs, it bends in a sharp angle into the throat. In addition, the human

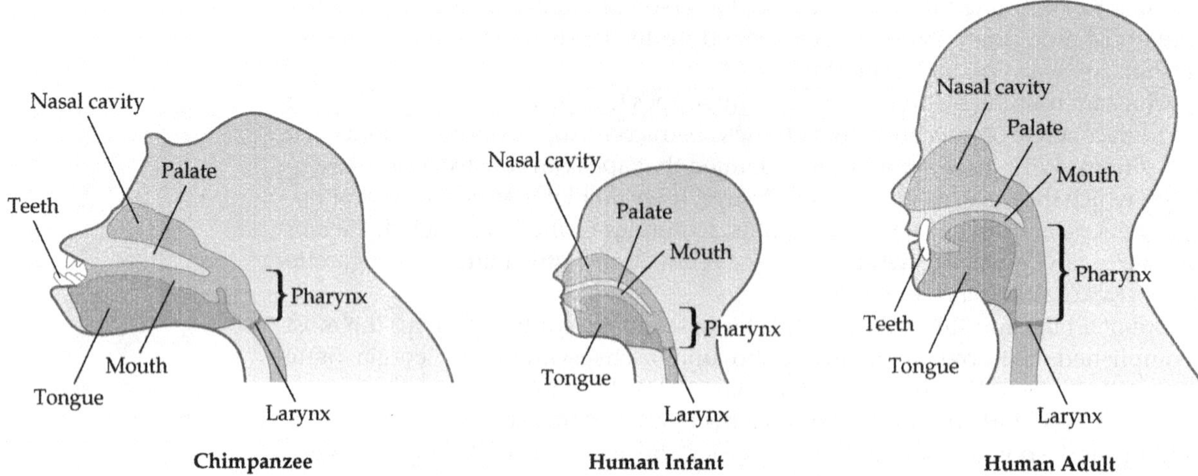

FIGURE 13.5
Insights into the speaking ability of early hominins have come from comparisons of the vocal apparatus of modern human adults and babies with that of a chimpanzee. To form words, sounds must be modulated by the pharynx, which lies above the larynx. The human newborn resembles the chimpanzee, with its high larynx and short pharynx. By the age of five, the child's larynx has descended from the level of the fourth cervical vertebra to that of the seventh, and the long human pharynx is complete.

Larynx the voice box; the organ in the throat containing the vocal cords; important in human *speech* production.

Pharynx the throat above the *larynx*.

larynx, with its vocal cords, is farther down the throat than the ape larynx. The part of the throat above the larynx, the **pharynx,** is proportionately much longer in humans than in any other primates (Aiello and Dean, 1990; P. Lieberman, 1992, 2002).

The pharynx serves as a combined opening for the windpipe (trachea), which goes to the lungs and the gullet (esophagus), which leads to the stomach. As the anchor for the base of the tongue, it also plays a fundamental part in producing speech, and this is where the longer human pharynx becomes important. It is the pharynx that modifies the sounds made by the vocal cords and gives them the varying tones that language requires. To provide this control, the muscles of the pharynx walls and the base of the tongue move continuously during speech, constantly and precisely varying the dimensions of the pharynx. These dimensional changes produce much the same effect on sounds that an organ achieves with its dozens of pipes of different lengths and diameters, each making a particular tone. Clearly, the pharynx is extremely important to speech.

Monkeys and apes, lacking the human vocal equipment, vary the shape of only their mouths when they vocalize; there is practically no variation of the pharynx. The oral cavity of the mouth is large, and the tongue is incapable of forming a number of important speech sounds. In particular, apes cannot produce the vowels [i] (as in the word *see*), [u] (as in the word *do*), and [a] (as in the word *ma*). Of special importance is the fact that apes lack the so-called supervowel [i], which is among the most easily understood of all speech sounds and helps human listeners rapidly decode complex bundles of consonants and vowels (P. Lieberman, 2002).

The same limitation restricts the vocalization of human babies, who at birth are unable to make the three vowel sounds just described. For at least six weeks, a baby's tongue remains immobile during its cries. It rests almost entirely within the mouth, as in nonhuman primates, and the larynx sits high in the throat. This arrangement permits babies as well as all other primates to swallow and breathe at the same time without danger of choking. By the time babies reach the babbling stage, at around three months, the base of the tongue and the larynx have begun to descend into the throat, enlarging the pharyngeal region. Not until this development is complete, which occurs by about the age of five, are humans physically equipped to make all of the speech sounds that distinguish them from their simian relatives (P. Lieberman, 1992, 2002).

Speech and Language Centers in the Human Brain

Other equally important reasons that humans can talk and nonhuman primates cannot have to do with the brain. Thirty years ago, scientists believed that speech and language were abilities controlled by a few interconnected areas in our **cerebral cortex,** the convoluted outer layer of the brain (Figure 13.6). These sites included Broca's area in the inferior frontal lobe, Wernicke's area in the temporal lobe, and the **angular gyrus** in the inferior parietal lobe. Respectively, these areas were thought to control articulation, language comprehension, and the cross-modal association of sensory information. Furthermore, Broca's and Wernicke's areas were understood to be connected by a tract of nerve fibers called the *arcuate fasciculus,* an arrangement that facilitated the coordination of language production and comprehension. And finally, these cortical areas were described as occurring exclusively in the dominant left cerebral hemisphere in most people (95 percent of right-handers and 70 percent of left-handers), and since they are somewhat enlarged compared to the other side, they produced measurable brain asymmetry (Aiello and Dean, 1990; Campbell, 1976; Corballis, 1991; Wallman, 1992).

Cerebral cortex the gray, wrinkled, outer layer of the brain; largely responsible for memory and, in humans, reasoned behavior and abstract thought; also referred to as the *neocortex.*

Angular gyrus the part of the human *cerebral cortex* that allows the information received from different senses to be associated.

The functioning of these few speech–language areas was seen as relatively straightforward. Broca's area is located close to the motor cortex that controls the muscles of the face, jaw, tongue, pharynx, and larynx (Figure 13.6). Impulses transmitted from Broca's area were thought to mainly affect speech *production,* as shown by the slow and labored articulation of people with classic Broca's *aphasia* (a loss or impairment of speech) due to damage in this region. Damage to Wernicke's area, on the other hand, produced a different sort of aphasia: speech that was fluent (well articulated) but meaningless. Thus, Wernicke's area was interpreted as the seat of language *comprehension.* Apes were thought to possess neither a Broca's area nor a Wernicke's area and thus (in addition to their vocal tract drawbacks) to lack the neurological equipment necessary for speech and language (Campbell, 1976; T. Deacon, 1992b; P. Lieberman, 2002).

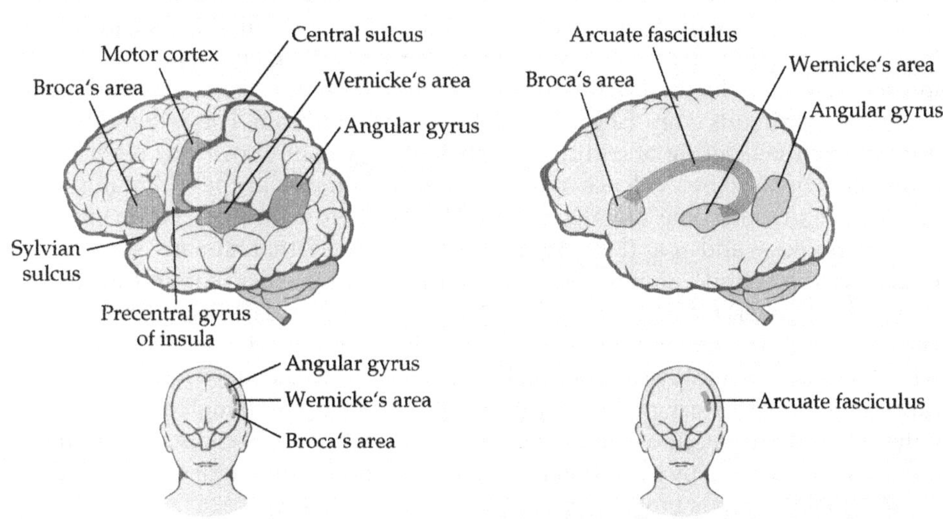

FIGURE 13.6 The areas of the brain cortex (surface layer) involved in speech production are shown in the *left* drawing. The drawing at the *right* shows the arcuate fasciculus, which links Wernicke's area to Broca's area deep within the brain. Wernicke's area and the angular gyrus are also involved in the decoding of speech.

Basal ganglia subcortical structures located deep within the brain; often connected to the *cerebral cortex* via neural circuits.

In the past three decades, researchers have discovered that while much of the old understanding of speech–language functioning is true, the situation is much more complex than originally thought. Using a variety of new techniques, researchers have found new speech–language areas and circuits and expanded the known functions of old areas. Regarding new areas, it is now known that a portion of the precentral gyrus of the *insula* (cortical tissue under the frontal and temporal lobes; Figure 13.6) helps to coordinate articulation (Dronkers, 1996). Additionally, evidence has been reported for neural circuits between Broca's area and subcortical structures collectively called the **basal ganglia** (P. Lieberman, 2002). These so-called cortical–striatal–cortical circuits also make a contribution to speech and language. In fact, it now appears that full-blown Broca's aphasia does not occur without some subcortical or insular damage. Interestingly, at least some of the cortical–striatal–cortical circuits represent connections with the limbic system of the human brain, reflecting the fact that our volitional language system is piggy-backed atop the old primate emotional call system (Robinson, 1976). Finally, it is now known that there are neural connections between Broca's area in the frontal lobe and portions of the cerebellum on the opposite side of the brain. Cerebellar regions seem to become activated during such language tasks as repeating and associating words (T. Deacon, 1997).

With regard to expanded functions for well-known cortical sites, Broca's area is now thought to contribute not only to speech production but also to the *comprehension* of both syntax and sentences, partly through its involvement in the brain's "'verbal working memory,' a short-term neural memory buffer" (P. Lieberman, 2002:48). This finding came from studies using PET technology (positron emission tomography), a technique allowing scientists to observe cranial blood flow in conscious humans performing various speech–language and/or manual tasks. Not surprisingly, Wernicke's area and other brain regions also contribute to verbal working memory, as do "right hemisphere homologies of Wernicke's and Broca's areas" (P. Lieberman, 2002:51). Finally, PET studies have shown that Broca's area affects not only speech and language but also the "hierarchical organization of [manual] object-combination activity" (P. Greenfield, 1991: 536). As noted at the start of this chapter, some researchers think it is not accidental that the human frontal lobe is involved in both the control of bodily movements *and* speech and language. Philip Lieberman (2002) has suggested that the elaboration of cortical–striatal–cortical circuits as part of the evolution of hominin bipedalism served as a preadaptation for the later appearance of language.

And so, moving far beyond the simplistic picture of thirty years ago, we now know that when humans are speaking and listening, their brains are in a flurry of activity involving a number of different interconnected regions. Rather than having speech–language activities localized in a few regions, humans' numerous communication circuits link many different areas of the brain and pull together such functions as articulation, comprehension, and memory as well as emotional and sensory information input. Incredibly, this maze of interconnected and functionally dependent areas and circuits is an elaboration of the old primate brain. This is demonstrated not only by the layering of cortical speech–language control over the older limbic call system but also by evidence of Broca's area asymmetry in apes (Cantalupo and Hopkins, 2001) and some lateralization (left hemisphere control) of certain vocalizations in monkeys and apes (Falk, 1992). Further evidence that humans' speech–language system is build atop an older set of primate capacities is found in the fact (mentioned earlier) that the bonobo Kanzi and the chimpanzee Viki understood spoken commands from their trainers. Sue Savage-Rumbaugh and others thus insist that while apes demonstrably cannot speak, "the conclusion that apes have [an innate] capacity for *language* can no longer be evaded" (Savage-Rumbaugh et al., 1998:206; italics added). Although we don't know exactly how the ape's communication system was transformed by evolution into that of symbolic humans, it seems worth repeating that the gap is probably quantitative, not qualitative.

But leaving comparative brain studies for a moment, is there anything to be learned from the hominin fossil record regarding the means or timing of the acquisition of speech? Let's take a look at some changes in the skull that contributed to our ability to talk.

Evolution of Speech

It is currently impossible to pinpoint when hominins began to use language: the development of speech and other human characteristics was probably infinitely gradual. But for the process to start, the vocal apparatus had to be modified and the brain had to evolve. This development must have taken hundreds of thousands of years. Some small mutations may have enabled *Australopithecus* to make a few voluntary sounds, providing an edge in the competition for survival. The ability to signal one another through a more extensive repertory of **phonemes** would have been a definite advantage to the australopiths' descendants. And then, as the number of phonemes grew, brain development could have permitted more precise differentiation between them and new combinations of them, so that primitive words may have taken shape.

Phonemes the smallest sound components of *language*.

All the while, the brain and the vocal apparatus would have been involved in a feedback relationship with each other, changes in one fostering development of the other: The success of the cortex in forming a rudimentary sound code would have affected the vocal apparatus, and this, in turn, would have helped enlarge the speech centers of the brain, and so on, until the rudiments of speech appeared. Then hominins were ready to begin combining a few separate sounds, or words—representing specific elements of terrain, the hunt, the family, and seasonal changes—into simple combinations that conveyed a great deal of information.

Phonation: Flexing the Cranial Base

What this first speech sounded like depended on how far the dual development of vocal apparatus and brain equipment had progressed. Linguist Philip Lieberman's (1992, 2002) analysis of the character of modern speech emphasizes the importance of the human vocal equipment. He has pointed out that the pharynx is essential for producing the vowel sounds [i], [u], and [a], which are crucial to all modern languages, from English to Kirghiz. Virtually all meaningful segments of human speech contain one or more of these sounds. Combining these vowel sounds with a wide assortment of consonants, the human vocal apparatus can produce an infinite number of variations but also, and more important, can connect them with great rapidity in the coded series of sounds that is spoken language.

This involves the putting together of separate phonetic segments into a sound that can be understood as one word. A person saying *bat*, for instance, does not articulate the fragments of sound represented by the letters *b*, *a*, and *t* but combines these elements into one syllable. This ability to combine sounds gives the voice the ability to put together and transmit more than 25 phonetic segments a second (P. Lieberman, 1992).

The key to human phonation lies in the position of the larynx. As we have seen, during modern human growth, the pharynx lengthens and the larynx descends in the neck, so that by about the age of five, the low larynx separates humans from all other primates. Early on, researchers realized that if they could identify skeletal features that documented the low larynx–long pharynx condition in fossil hominins, they would have gone a long way toward reconstructing the phonetic abilities of our ancestors. Initially, it appeared that the amount of flexion shown by the cranial base provided a clear indication of vocal tract dimensions, and the first comparative studies of such flexion were done in the 1970s and 1980s. Based on measurements of the *exterior* of the skull, Laitman et al. (1979) and Laitman and Heimbuch (1982) concluded that the australopiths were very apelike in their vocal tracts and the Neandertals were relatively apelike, but mid-Pleistocene specimens such as Kabwe and Steinheim (now classified as *Homo heidelbergensis*) were relatively modern (Figure 13.7).

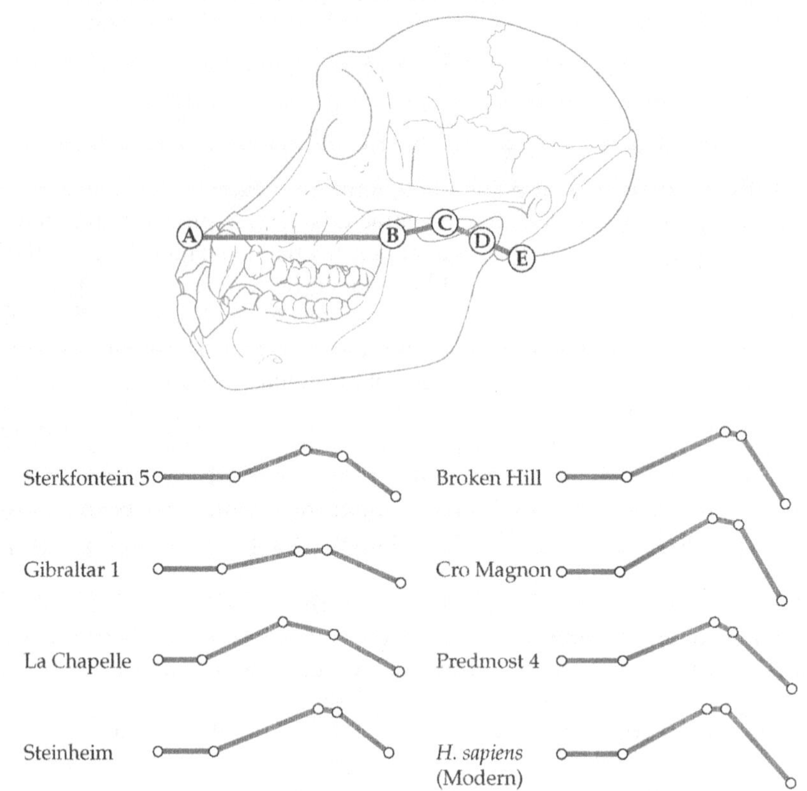

FIGURE 13.7

The cranial base profiles of fossil hominins and modern humans suggest the recent development of full basicranial flexion and modern throat proportions. As shown here on the skull of a female chimpanzee (*top*), profiles are measured by connecting five midline points: *A*, prosthion (most anterior point on the alveolar process—toothbearing ridge—of the upper jaw); *B*, staphylion (near the posterior edge of the hard palate); *C*, hormion (near the posterior edge of the vomer, one of the internal bones of the face); *D*, sphenobasion (a point on the sphenoid/occipital articulation); and *E*, basion (midpoint of the anterior margin of the foramen magnum). At the bottom of the figure, cranial base profiles are shown for an australopith (Sterkfontein 5), two Neandertals (Gibraltar and La Chapelle), two *Homo heidelbergensis* specimens (Steinheim and Broken Hill [=Kabwe]), two fossil *Homo sapiens* (Cro-Magnon and Predmost 4), and modern humans.

Source: Figure modified from J. Laitman, R. Heimbuch, and E. Crelin, "The Basicranium of Fossil Hominids as an Indicator of Their Upper Respiratory Systems." *American Journal of Physical Anthropology*, 51, 1979. Copyright © 1979, John Wiley and Sons, Inc. Reprinted by permission of Wiley-Liss, Inc., a subsidiary of John Wiley and Sons, Inc.)

The early studies of basicranial flexion were challenged in the 1990s. Using CT (computed tomography) measurements of the *interior* of the skull, Ross and Henneberg (1995) concluded that the degree of basicranial flexion was about the same in *Australopithecus africanus, Homo erectus, Homo heidelbergensis* (Kabwe), and modern humans. The clear implication of this finding was that these fossil hominins probably differed little in their phonetic capacities. Importantly, these researchers also noted that external and internal measurements of flexion "bear little if any relationship to each other" (1995:587).

Finally, in 1999, Daniel Lieberman and Robert McCarthy conducted a comparison of internal versus external cranial base angles with regard to their usefulness in predicting vocal tract dimensions in apes and hominins. In their results, Lieberman and McCarthy strongly questioned the validity of all such measures and concluded that, quite simply, "measurements of cranial base angulation cannot be used to make inferences about the dimensions of the human vocal tract" (1999:512).

With these varying research results, what sense can we make of basicranial flexion and the evolution of speech? Taking a position similar to that of Lewin and Foley (2004), we are not quite ready to give up the connection altogether. As Philip Lieberman (2002:56) argued, "The only apparent selective advantage that the human [low larynx–long pharynx vocal tract] yields is to enhance the robustness of speech reception. . . . There would have been no selective advantage for the retention of variations that yielded the modern human [vocal tract dimensions] in the absence of speech." Accepting this argument, we will continue to apply basicranial flexion data, along with other sorts of evidence, to the problem of vocal tract reconstruction. As described in earlier chapters, the vocal tract, brain size, and archaeological evidence seem to converge on the conclusion that the full range of modern speech sounds probably did not appear until at least 750,000 years ago.

Articulation: Oral Cavity Dimensions and Tongue Innervation

During human speech, the pharyngeal cavity and the larynx together generate the vowel sounds, but it is the tongue and lips that produce articulation of these sounds by interspersing the vowels with consonants. Research by Linda Duchin (1990) of the University of Washington, Seattle, has shown how very different the tongue musculature and oral cavity of the chimpanzee are from those of humans.

In chimpanzees, the palate and the mandible create a much longer oral cavity than in humans, and the muscles that support and move the tongue (its extrinsic muscles) lie in slightly different places and are set at different angles than those of humans. The **hyoid** bone, to which some of these muscles are attached, lies in a different position in apes: higher and farther back than in humans. Altogether, these differences mean that control of the tongue in apes is less efficient than in humans. Furthermore, because of the larger oral cavity in apes, the tongue cannot reach all the necessary contact points needed to create consonants during phonation. In humans, the position of the anchorage of the tongue muscles and the smaller oral cavity mean that the tongue can move very rapidly from point to point in the mouth to create the fast-changing consonants of speech (Duchin, 1990).

Hyoid a bone of the throat positioned just above the *larynx* and just below the *mandible*; provides attachment for one of the muscles of the tongue and for certain muscles of the front of the neck.

Measurements of the oral cavities of *Homo erectus* and Neandertal fossil skulls fall close to or into the human range and distinguish them clearly from the chimpanzee (Duchin, 1990). This would appear to imply that these fossil hominins may have had some potential for articulate speech. Interestingly, certain of these suggestive findings have been reinforced recently by the research of Richard Kay, Matt Cartmill, and Michelle Balow (1998) on the anatomy of the **hypoglossal canal** in hominoids. This canal carries the nerve to the muscles of the tongue, and Kay et al. think canal size was probably correlated closely with tongue coordination and the capacity for speech. Their comparisons of canal cross-sectional areas in modern African apes, living humans, and several fossil hominins produced some fascinating results. Specimens of *Australopithecus africanus* and possibly *Homo habilis* were found to be similar to apes with regard to hypoglossal canal size, and both early hominin types had significantly smaller canals than modern humans. In contrast, the hypoglossal canals of Neandertal and *Homo heidelbergensis* people had reached modern size, reinforcing the basicranial flexion and other evidence that modern vocal capacities may have begun in the middle Pleistocene, well before the appearance of *Homo sapiens*.

Hypoglossal canal an opening in the *occipital bone* just anterior to the *occipital condyle*; allows passage of the hypoglossal nerve to the tongue musculature.

The Brain

Humans among Mammals

Our analyses up to this point have shown that the simple observation that humans talk and apes do not is related to several anatomical differences between people and all other living hominids. Humans have unique adaptations of the vocal tract (probably related to our basicranial flexion) and of the oral cavity that allow speech, as well as numerous and elaborated brain regions that facilitate language production and comprehension. And of course, widening our perspective on ape–human brain differences shows that we also enjoy an enormous increase in overall size (see Table 3.8).

As shown by the fossil hominin species already reviewed, overall brain size in our tribe has effectively tripled in the past 7 million years, and many researchers still rely heavily on overall brain size as they speculate about such things as the appearance of language and modern culture. Overall, brain size is a very gross measure, however, and ape–human differences—as well as changes during the course of hominin evolution—need to be examined in much finer terms. Thus, we now turn to a closer look at the human brain in mammalian (and especially primate) context.

In order to really understand the evolutionary increase in brain size that hominins have experienced—and that modern humans now exemplify—we need to relate it to body size, for a simple increase in body size itself (accompanied by an appropriate increase in brain size) can occur rapidly in evolution and is not an unusual occurrence. To relate brain size to body size, we need to calculate how large a brain a typical anthropoid would have if it were to have a body the same size as ours. The answer reveals that the present human brain is between three and four times larger than we would expect in a primate of our build (Rilling and Insel, 1999). It appears, then, that our brain's tripling in size occurred despite only a moderate increase in our body size. This is perhaps the most significant anatomical fact about the species *Homo sapiens*.

Encephalization quotient (EQ) in mammals, a number expressing observed brain size in a particular species relative to expected brain size calculated from body weight.

This characteristic is perhaps even more striking when we remember that monkeys and apes have large brains in relation to body weight compared to other land animals. California psychiatrist Harry Jerison (1973) has introduced the **encephalization quotient (EQ)** to compare relative brain sizes. The EQ is calculated by relating the brain size of each species to the size expected for an average mammal of the same body weight. By definition, an average mammal has an EQ of 1.0. If the relative brain size is smaller than average, then the EQ has a value of less than 1.0; if the relative brain size is larger than average, then the EQ ranges above 1.0. Figure 13.8 very briefly summarizes Jerison's results. Insectivores and rodents are in one group, with EQs generally below 1.0. Ungulates (hoofed mammals), carnivores, and strepsirhines make

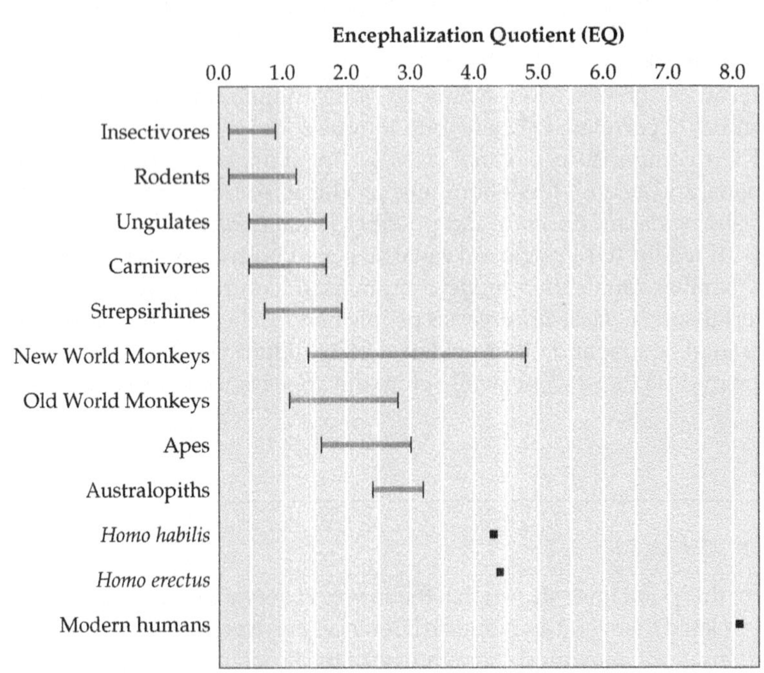

FIGURE 13.8
The encephalization quotient (EQ) is shown here for several groups of mammals, including a number of hominins. For most groups, a range of EQ values is shown by a horizontal line; for two hominin species, small sample sizes allow only EQ means (shown by dots).

Sources: Data for non-anthropoids: Jerison, 1973; for monkeys and hominins, Aiello and Dean, 1990 (following Jerison's procedures).

TABLE 13.1 Brain Weight as Percentage of Body Weight for Selected Mammals

Species	Brain Weight as % of Body Weight
Squirrel monkeys (NW monkeys)	3.70
Tarsiers (*T. syrichta*, Philippines)	3.20
Modern humans	**2.44**
Saddleback tamarins (NW monkeys)	2.38
Rhesus macaques (OW monkeys)	2.08
Chimpanzees	1.13
Australopithecus afarensis	1.06
Dolphins	1.06
Domestic cats	0.91
Orangutans	0.78
Squirrels	0.67
Gorillas	0.40
Elephants	0.18
Sperm whales	0.02

Sources: Harvey et al., 1987; Serendip; WonderQuest.

a second group, with EQs hovering around 1.0. Monkeys and apes do better, with EQs ranging between 1.1 and 4.8. Modern humans have an average EQ of about 8.1.

A slightly less sophisticated way to compare brain sizes across species is simply to look at overall brain weight as a percentage of body weight (Table 13.1). The modern human brain accounts for about 2.44 percent of our body weight, a figure that is very similar to the results for certain tamarin monkeys from South America. Humans clearly surpass the living apes on this measure but are, in turn, surpassed by Philippine tarsiers and squirrel monkeys from the New World. Both tarsiers and squirrel monkeys are small-bodied, insectivorous species (Bearder, 1987; Robinson and Janson, 1987) that undoubtedly have high metabolism rates—a trait thought to be linked to the evolution of large brains (Harvey et al., 1987). As expected, humans' brain weight percentage also clearly exceeds the percentages of nonprimate species, such as dolphins, cats, and squirrels, and even of such absolutely large-brained creatures as elephants (4.5 kg [9.9 lb] brain; Serendip) and sperm whales (7.8 kg [17.2 lb] brain; WonderQuest). In the latter species, body size has increased so much more than brain size that their brain weight percentages have fallen to 0.18 and 0.02, respectively.

And so, in general, the brains of humans and the other haplorhines are relatively larger than those of nonprimate mammals, and within the Primate order, human brain enlargement is unequalled. But narrowing our focus, can we detect any *patterns* in primate brain enlargement? Have some parts of the brain increased while others have lagged behind? Studies conducted some years ago by Heinz Stephan of the Max-Planck Institute began to provide answers to these questions. Stephan (1972) found that many phylogenetically old portions of the primate brain, including aspects of the limbic system (the old "emotional brain"), have shown very little progression in size, while the neocortex (cerebral cortex) has expanded dramatically compared to the situation in other mammals. More recent work has supported and extended Stephan's findings. For example, magnetic resonance imaging (MRI) studies of a variety of monkeys and apes have shown that humans have a significantly larger neocortex than expected for an anthropoid of our body size—a claim that no other anthropoid species can make (Figure 13.9; Rilling and Insel, 1999). Furthermore, both components of the human neocortex—the gray matter, composed mainly of nerve cell bodies, and the underlying cerebral white matter, consisting largely of

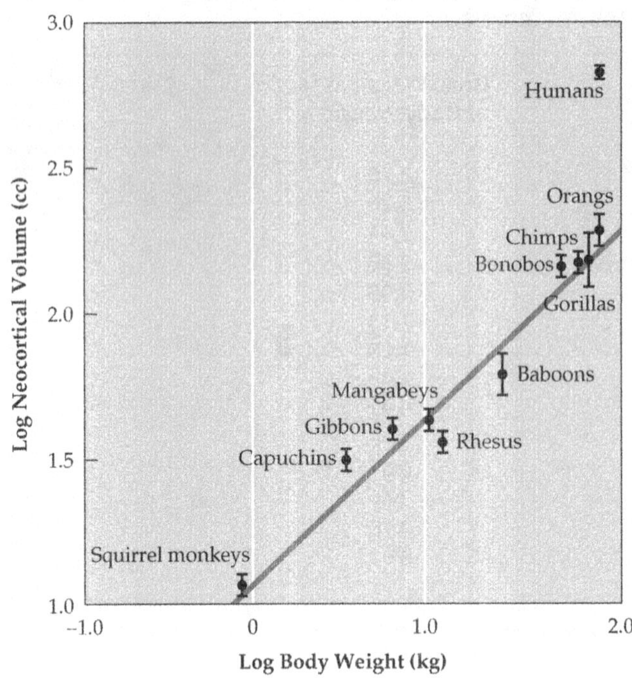

FIGURE 13.9 Relative neocortical size in anthropoid primates. Logarithmic plots of neocortical gray matter volume *versus* body weight.

Source: Rilling and Insel, 1999.

Axon processes extending from nerve cell bodies that carry information to other cells.

axons (processes extending from the cell body that carry information to other cells)—are significantly larger than predicted by body size. In effect, this means that compared to monkeys and apes, humans have experienced a unique increase in both the number and the connections of cortical cells. Our brains are not only the biggest, absolutely *and* relatively, among the primates, but they also show the highest degree of interneuron connectivity (Rilling and Insel, 1999).

Interestingly, the MRI studies disagree slightly on the question of whether the expansion of the human neocortex has been relatively uniform across the surface of the brain. Katerina Semendeferi and Hanna Damasio (2000) outlined and measured total size for three neocortical regions in the living hominoids: frontal lobe, temporal lobe, and the combined parieto-occipital region. They found that in humans, all three regions are *about* the same relative sizes as those in the great apes (Table 13.2 and Figure 13.10).

On the face of it, this finding seems to directly challenge the widespread notion that humans have uniquely enlarged frontal lobes. But when other investigators looked

TABLE 13.2 Comparison of Major Brain Regions and Gyrification in Hominoids

Species	Frontal Lobe[a]	Temporal Lobe[a]	Parieto–Occipital Region[a]	Gyrification Index[b]
Modern humans	36.8	18.1	36.4	2.57
Bonobos	34.9	16.6	37.6	2.17
Chimpanzees	34.8	17.2	37.0	2.19
Gorillas	35.1	14.0	39.9	2.07
Orangutans	36.3	16.8	35.5	2.29
Gibbons	28.4	18.9	39.2	1.90

[a]Percentage of hemispheres.
[b]A measure of the amount of cortical folding.
Sources: Regional percentages: Semendeferi and Damasio, 2000; Gyrification index: Rilling and Insel, 1999.

beyond simple lobe size and focused on lobe *folding*, the traditional idea was supported. James Rilling and Thomas Insel (1999) found that not only is the entire human neocortex more complexly folded than in the other hominoids (see the **gyrification index** in Table 13.2), but also that unique amounts of folding are found in the prefrontal region (where Broca's area is located) *and* in the vicinity of Wernicke's area. Rilling and Insel think their gyrification data demonstrate "unique evolutionary modification in the [frontal and temporal regions] involved in . . . symbolic thinking, knowledge of appropriate social behavior, decision-making, planning to achieve goals, and working memory [as well as] comprehension and production of language" (1999:219).

In sum, the various studies have shown that compared to other primates, humans are characterized by the following set of quantitative and qualitative features: a larger whole brain (whether measured absolutely or by EQ); a larger neocortex; more gray matter (neuronal cells); more white matter (axons); more total gyrification of the neocortex; and unique gyrification in the prefrontal and temporal lobes. Not only are our brains three to four times larger than those of apes, but we also show greater interneuron connectivity and special development in those areas involved in symbolic thinking, memory, and communication. Truly a remarkable organ, the human brain. But what evolutionary factors might have led to its extreme development and especially to the phenomenon we call "the mind"? Let us now turn to those questions.

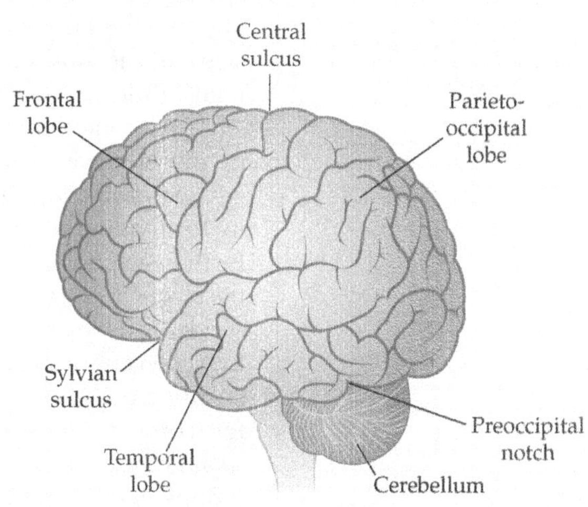

FIGURE 13.10 The neocortical regions compared by Semendeferi and Damasio, 2000 (frontal lobe, temporal lobe, parieto-occipital lobes). See Table 13.2 for data.

Source: Semendeferi and Damasio, 2000.

Group Size, Brain Size, Language, and Radiators

An interesting theory that links encephalization and language to increasing group size has been presented by Leslie Aiello and Robin Dunbar (1993). As noted earlier, Dunbar (1998) and others have shown that among the primates brain size is correlated positively with group size, suggesting selection for social intelligence (Figure 13.11). Larger social groups mean more relationships to coordinate, a task that

Gyrification index a quantitative measure of cortical folding.

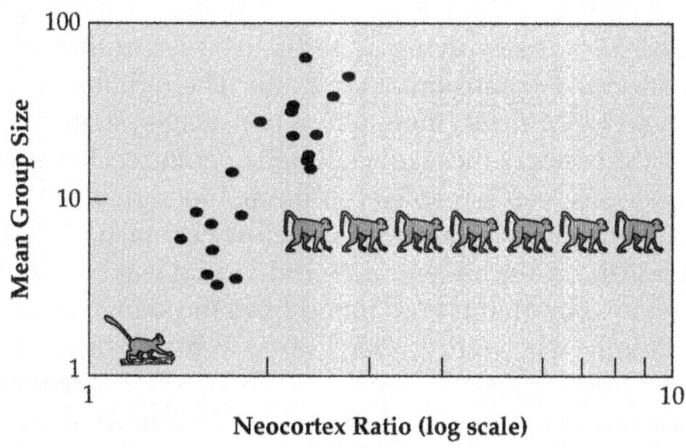

FIGURE 13.11 When relative neocortex size (the neocortex ratio) is plotted against mean group size for nonhuman primates, a strong positive correlation is revealed. As shown by the icons, the strepsirhines' values are clustered in the *lower left* portion of the chart. All of the highest values are from monkey and ape species.

Source: Figure modified from R. I. M. Dunbar, "The Social Brain Hypothesis." *Evolutionary Anthropology*, 66:178–190, 1998. Copyright © 1998, John Wiley and Sons, Inc. Reprinted by permission of Wiley-Liss, Inc., a subsidiary of John Wiley and Sons, Inc.

monkeys and apes usually accomplish by grooming one another. Total daily grooming time therefore also shows positive correlations with both brain size and group size and can amount to 20 percent of the day before it begins to compromise the animals' time budgets for other activities such as feeding, resting, and travel.

Aiello and Dunbar (1993) hypothesize that hominin evolution was characterized by pressure for ever-larger groups because bigger groups would have meant increased protection against predators and other dangers, as well as an improved ability to compete successfully against other hominin groups for food and space. They further suspect that as hominin groups continued to grow, they eventually reached the size where grooming was no longer viable as the main way of coordinating and servicing the expanding number of social relationships. At about the point where 25 to 30 percent of the day would have been needed for enough physical grooming to ensure group cohesion, time budget constraints should have selected for some other form of social lubrication. Aiello and Dunbar conclude that language evolved as that social lubricant: a form of vocal grooming that facilitated the maintenance of large groups. Based on their calculations of the relationship between relative neocortex size and group size, Aiello and Dunbar suggest that the critical language-inducing group size was reached by the middle Pleistocene (about 250,000 years BP). Thus, language with significant social information content had its first effects among *Homo heidelbergensis* (albeit after a gradual evolutionary development). This conclusion is in agreement with the data presented in earlier chapters.

Brain growth and language obviously carried enormous survival and reproductive benefits for our hominin ancestors, and Aiello and Dunbar (1993) may be correct in concluding that pressure for larger groups was the driving factor behind these related developments. Nonetheless, it may have been a simple and early change in the brain's cooling system that made them possible. Paleoneurologist Dean Falk (1992) has developed what she calls the "radiator" theory of brain evolution. According to Falk, in response to their evolving bipedalism, the australopiths developed new means of draining blood from their (elevated) braincases. *Paranthropus* (and, in Falk's opinion, *Australopithecus afarensis*, as well) evolved a system in which an enlarged occipital-marginal (O/M) sinus delivered blood to the vertebral plexus at the base of the skull (Figure 13.12). This system worked well enough as long as the brain was not overheated and remained relatively small, and thus Falk concludes that the robust australopiths probably lived mainly in forests, rather than on the savanna, and that their potential for brain growth was limited.

In contrast to *Paranthropus* and *A. afarensis*, however, Falk describes *Australopithecus africanus* and *Homo* as evolving a "radiator" system that allowed both savanna living *and* continued expansion of the brain. The radiators worked like this: Instead of an enlarged O/M sinus, there was a two-way system of emissary veins that passed through the bones of the skull via small openings called foramina (Figure 13.12). The emissary veins were capable of draining blood *from* the braincase to the vertebral plexus when the individual was at or below normal body temperature and of pumping blood *into* the braincase when the individual was overheated. This two-way system allowed evaporation-cooled blood from the skin to be shunted to overheated brains in hominins who were working up a sweat during their gathering and scavenging (and later hunting) on the tropical savanna. And the radiator system was wonderfully modifiable. Over time, the *A. africanus–Homo* lineage evolved more and more emissary veins that allowed better and better temperature regulation. To quote Falk, "[The cranial radiator system] released thermal constraints that had previously kept brain size in check" (1992:163). Apparently, hominins' cranial radiators allowed them to combine diurnal exploitation of the tropical savanna with continued brain expansion. (It is worth noting, however, that this interesting theory has not gone unchallenged. In particular, Braga and Boesch [1997] have questioned Falk's conclusions. Further research by both supporters and opponents will be necessary before the ultimate fate of the radiator theory is known.)

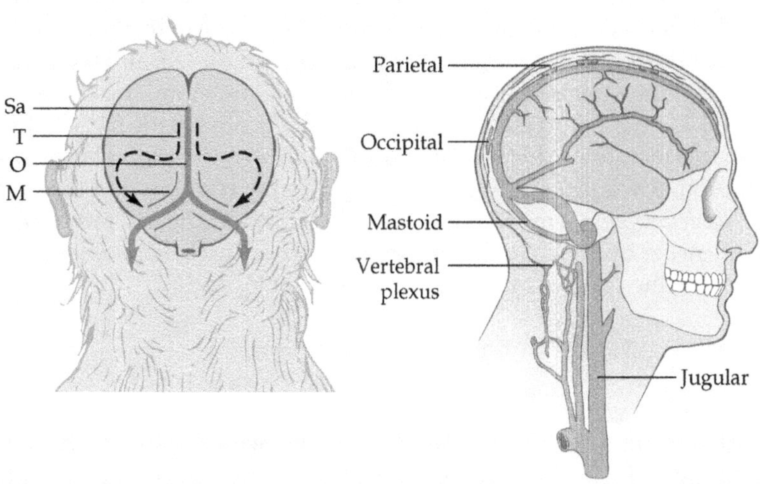

FIGURE 13.12
Blood flow from the cranium of a *Paranthropus* australopith is shown at *left* (rear view of skull). In addition to exiting the skull via the superior sagittal sinus (Sa), blood drained out through the enlarged occipital sinus (O) and marginal sinus (M). The transverse sinus (T) was of relatively little importance in these hominins. In contrast, in the *A. africanus/Homo* lineage, a radiator network of emissary veins evolved for cranial drainage and brain cooling. The side view of a modern human skull at *right* shows the parietal, occipital, and mastoid emissary veins and their drainage target, the vertebral plexus.

Further work is needed on the problem of what was driving and/or releasing increased encephalization among the evolving hominins, but in the meantime, it is becoming ever easier to document the stepwise nature of that process. In 1996, John Kappelman, of the University of Texas, devised a method for calculating body mass in extinct hominins from the size of their orbital apertures (eye sockets). Kappelman combined his body mass estimates with data on brain size to produce EQ values for several of the australopith and hominin species known at the time. The results of these calculations are presented in Table 13.3, but because he used a different formula from Jerison (1973; Figure 13.8), Kappelman's EQ values for premodern hominins have been converted to percentages of his score for modern humans. As an example, *Homo heidelbergensis* showed about two-thirds of the modern level of encephalization. When the broad sweep of these relative EQ scores is considered, a roughly 10-point increase is seen between the australopiths and early *Homo*, 5- to 6-point increases are seen from early *Homo* to *H. erectus* and also from *H. erectus* to *H. heidelbergensis*, and a 32-point jump is seen from *H. heidelbergensis* to modern people.

TABLE 13.3 Relative EQ Values for Selected Fossil Hominin Types

Species	EQ Value as % of Modern Humans' EQ
Homo sapiens	100.00
Homo neanderthalensis	77.04
Homo heidelbergensis	67.74
Homo erectus	62.05
Early *Homo* (*H. habilis* & *H. rudolfensis*)	55.60
Australopithecus africanus	55.98
Paranthropus boisei	40.61
Paranthropus aethiopicus	39.28
Australopith mean	45.29

Source: Kappelman, 1996.

Although these are interesting results, they should be taken only as a rough approximation of increasing encephalization and intelligence in the hominin lineage. Remember that EQ is affected both by body size and brain size, and these variables did not evolve at the same rate. Thus, the apparently large jump in scores between *H. heidelbergensis* and modern people is undoubtedly related to the facts that we generally weigh less than they did (Ruff et al. 1997) *and* have 10 percent larger brains—a combination that would have inflated our EQ value compared to theirs. In any event, if *H. heidelbergensis* was the first species to produce nearly modern speech, as suggested earlier by Aiello and Dunbar (1993), those archaic people did so with about two-thirds the relative brain power that we enjoy today.

The Evolution of Mind

To close this chapter, we should discuss briefly what many people would say is the most important result of humans' brain growth: the evolution of a theory of mind. According to psychologists, having a theory of mind involves being able to attribute beliefs, knowledge, and emotions to oneself and to others (Cheney and Seyfarth, 1990). In species that possess a theory of mind, individuals benefit by using these attributed mental states to manipulate others—for example, by sharing or denying information and through deception. Although more evidence is needed, it appears that by the time apes reach adolescence, they *may* possess something like a theory of mind, judging from examples of deception and from the fact that they seem to have some self-awareness. Monkeys, on the other hand, apparently lack such a theory completely (see Chapter 3). Precisely when during hominin evolution a theory of mind developed is unclear.

Recently, Steven Mithen (1996) of the University of Reading used the archaeological record to reconstruct the evolution of the human mind. His results, although speculative, are interesting. Mithen assumed that hominins descended from ape ancestors with modular brains—that is, brains that were partitioned into separate functional domains. The three domains attributed to the ape–hominin common ancestor are *general intelligence* (the center of trial-and-error and associative learning, foraging decisions, tool use, etc.), *social intelligence* (responsible for information about relationships with group mates), and *natural history intelligence* (responsible for information about the environment and resources). The three domains were viewed as complementary to one another but with few interconnections—a condition that prevented the flow of information and insights from one area to another. Mithen described this as a "Swiss Army Knife" type of brain, with intelligence domains that functioned just as individually as the various blades, screwdrivers, scissors, and other tools in a modern Swiss Army Knife.

From the strictly modular brain of our last ape ancestor, Mithen (1996) envisioned a series of increasingly interconnected brains evolving. In general, the various functional domains are interpreted as increasing in size and complexity during hominin evolution but continuing to operate in a stand-alone fashion (that is, to have few, if any, interconnections). At the level of early *Homo*, Mithen envisioned the evolution of a new domain of *technical intelligence*. (His evidence is the first stone tools.) This particular domain is hypothesized to have grown rapidly in size, reaching a level of considerable importance among *Homo erectus* super-scavengers-and-gatherers (Figure 13.13[a]). Also at the *Homo erectus* level, Mithen concluded that an incipient language domain evolved as an offshoot of social intelligence.

Despite these new functional areas, however, the evolving hominin brain, according to Mithen (1996), was still essentially a Swiss Army Knife affair as recently as 200,000 years ago. Indeed, it is not until the appearance of *Homo sapiens* that Mithen finally saw evidence of extensive interdomain connections. Modern humans were interpreted as having brains with full cognitive fluidity—as characterized by the free flow of information and ideas among the various intelligence domains—and, by implication, a complete theory of mind (Figure 13.13[b]).

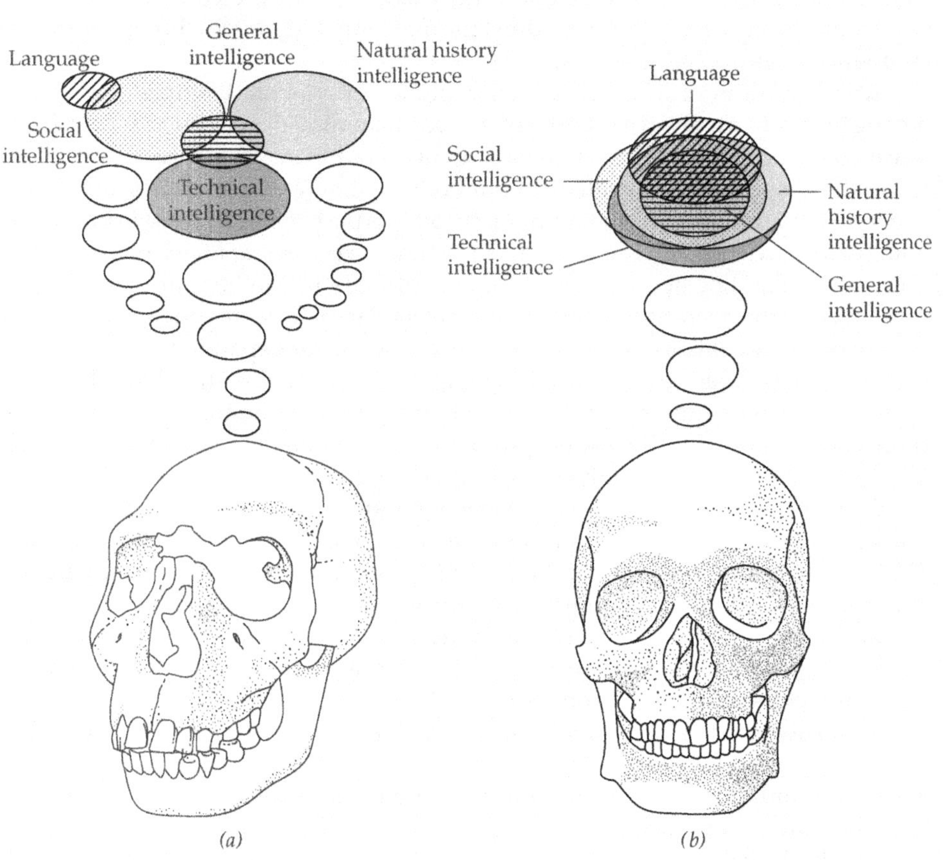

FIGURE 13.13
(*a*) By the time of *Homo erectus*, according to Steven Mithen (1996), technical intelligence had evolved as well as a small language domain, and natural history intelligence had increased in size and complexity. Few interdomain connections are envisioned, however.
(*b*) Only among *Homo sapiens* does Mithen recognize a modern mind with full cognitive fluidity—that is, numerous interdomain connections, as shown by overlapping symbols. The skulls are not drawn to scale.

Mithen's analysis is interesting but requires extensive testing. Tracing the evolution of the human mind—one of the few features that sets our species apart from all other animals and a key element in our global domination—remains a formidable challenge.

Summary

Language is perhaps the most remarkable and distinctive characteristic of humans. In its spoken form, it combines a variety of features: the arbitrary form of speech units (sounds, words) with regard to their referents, the combination of units following elaborate rules of syntax, the ability to refer to things not physically present and to the past and future, and the openness of the system to the invention of new units. *In their entirety,* these features differentiate us quite cleanly from the rest of the animal world, even though apes have been shown to possess rudimentary language capacities. Combined with culture, spoken language must have provided a strong stimulus to human evolution and contributed significantly to our modern way of life.

It is this central importance of language that makes our inability to pinpoint its evolutionary beginnings so frustrating. Clearly, human language must have evolved from the gesture-and-call system of hominins' last ape ancestors, but experts vigorously disagree on exactly how the transition proceeded. Some scholars focus on primate calls as the likely precursors of speech. Others argue that gestures and/or other behaviors involving bodily motor control were of prime importance (the latter mainly as a preadaptation). And cross-cutting this debate is the finding from work with signing and lexigram-using apes that these creatures' brains possess some basic capacity for understanding language, even though they are anatomically incapable of speech.

A few things are clear, however. The evolution of symbolic language and speech among hominins involved a number of related anatomical developments. First, brain size increased dramatically, such that today, humans have a brain three to four times larger than expected for a primate of our body weight (and eight times larger than expected for a similarly sized mammal). Second, as part of that increase in brain size, hominins experienced an increase in neocortical nerve cells *and* nerve connectivity. Third, the expanding neocortex assumed the primary role in hominin communication, layering the operation of several speech and language areas on top of the older system of limbic control of primate calls. As the neocortex expanded, extensive connections (the cortical–striatal–cortical circuits) were formed with older, subcortical areas, as well as circuits that linked the emerging speech–language regions. These connections eventually allowed the production of symbolic and volitional language, in contrast to primates' (mainly) emotional communication. Fourth and finally, the vocal apparatus of hominins changed in ways that allowed humans to produce the full set of vowel sounds and a rapid-fire stream of combined vowels and consonants. These changes included modifications of the proportions of the throat (apparently in connection with flexion of the basicranium) and the oral cavity.

Returning to brain size, its strong increase over the course of hominin evolution is obvious from the fossil record, but scholars are still undecided exactly what factor or factors selected for brain growth. A need for increased social intelligence has been suggested as one important selective force. Equally fuzzy is our understanding of precisely how the human *mind* evolved. Some researchers think this was a matter of individual mental modules becoming elaborated and interconnected, but others are unconvinced.

Finally, despite a spate of recent work on the subject, reconstructing the speech and language abilities of extinct hominins is still a matter of considerable guesswork. It seems reasonable to deny speech and language to the australopiths and early *Homo. Homo erectus* probably possessed some sort of speech and language, but the anatomy of these early Pleistocene hominins suggests that their speech (at least) was not fully modern. The earliest species thought to have had fully developed speech and language is *Homo heidelbergensis.* If this determination is accurate, modern communication extends back a half million years or more into the past.

Postscript

When we use the term *spoken language,* most readers will naturally think of the languages they are familiar with—for example, English and Spanish. But some very fascinating languages, commonly known as the *click languages,* are very different indeed. Click languages are spoken primarily in Africa, and daily conversations in these languages may consist largely of clicking sounds that are made by movement of the tongue and inward air movements. (Movie buffs who have seen *The Gods Must Be Crazy* will remember the click language spoken in that film, which is technically known as Ju | 'hoansi.)

Recent linguistic research has highlighted the potential importance of click communication in the early development of language (Pennisi, 2004). Linguist Bonny Sands (personal communication, 2004), of Northern Arizona University, is engaged in a project to document click languages, which are rapidly disappearing. Sands and other researchers have found that although click languages are only spoken by about 30 African groups today, they are still amazingly diverse. Sands is particularly interested in Hadzane, a language spoken by about 1,000 people in northern Tanzania called the Hadzabe. Hadzane does not appear to be closely related to any other known click language and two explanations may account for this: Hadzane may have had a separate origin from the other click languages, or Hadzane and the other click languages may derive from an ancient protoclick language.

Some current genetic work supports the idea that all click languages are extremely old (Pennisi, 2004). Alec Knight and Joanna Mountain from Stanford University are studying the DNA of the Hadzabe, who are geographically isolated from most other current click speakers, who live 1,250 miles (2,000 kilometers) away in Southern Africa. Knight and Mountain were particularly interested in comparing Hadzabe DNA to that of the San people of Southern Africa, who also speak a click language. Knight and Mountain hypothesized that if the Hadzabe had moved into Tanzania from the south, then their genetic data would show that they were related to the San. In fact, the genetic sequences of these two groups were very different, suggesting that the groups have long and separate histories (Pennisi, 2004).

One of the most intriguing aspects of the click languages is their use in hunting. Living Hadzabe people have told Alec Knight that they use clicks when they hunt, since those sounds are similar to those that occur in the natural environment. Thus, some scientists theorize that the first human language may have been a click language. Other researchers, such as Sands (personal communication, 2004), are not convinced of such a close relationship between human genetic data and language evolution. As Sands points out, "The Hadzabe use clicks when they hunt simply because they speak when they hunt." Moreover, Sands also notes that in many cultures, domesticated animals clearly understand that some clicks are human-created noises. For example, a lateral click is used as "giddy up" for horses, and people often make bilabial clicks at their pets to get their attention. In addition, just making clicks is different than using them as consonants in syllables as part of a language. Sands argues that there is little reason to consider clicks "the oldest sounds" in the human language tool kit.

Given that speech itself does not fossilize, we must make inferences about its origins from the types of indirect evidence discussed in this chapter, including the form of the vocal tract and the skull, ape communication, brain configuration, and genetic studies (Holden, 2004). It seems likely that the origin of human speech will remain a fascinating yet controversial subject for years to come.

Review Questions

1. Compare the communication systems of modern humans and animals. How are animals limited in their communication compared to people? What similarities, if any, do animals' communication systems show to humans' language and speech?
2. Discuss the connections between the evolution of language and the human theory of mind.
3. How do the following cortical areas affect speech and language among modern humans: Broca's area, Wernicke's area, the angular gyrus, cortical–striatal–cortical circuits, and the limbic system?
4. Compare the brains of apes and modern humans with regard to absolute size, EQ, and the development of the speech–language areas.
5. Describe the evolutionary changes in the vocal tract and oral cavity that have made human speech possible.
6. Describe the Aiello and Dunbar (1993) theory that language development was triggered by the increasing size of human groups. What evidence do they have for group sizes among extinct hominins?
7. Discuss the evidence (anatomical and archaeological) for and against the presence of language and speech in the various fossil hominin species. When do *you* think linguistic communication evolved and under what circumstances?

SUGGESTED FURTHER READING

Cheney, Dorothy, and Robert Seyfarth. *How Monkeys See the World.* Chicago, University of Chicago Press, 1990.

Dunbar, Robin. *Grooming, Gossip, and the Evolution of Language.* Cambridge (MA), Harvard University Press, 1996.

Falk, Dean. *Braindance.* New York, Henry Holt, 1992.

Lieberman, Philip. "On the Nature and Evolution of the Neural Bases of Human Language." *Yearbook of Physical Anthropology,* 45:36–62, 2002.

Savage-Rumbaugh, Sue, Stuart Shanker, and Talbot Taylor. *Apes, Language, and the Human Mind.* New York, Oxford University Press, 1998.

Wallman, Joel. *Aping Language.* Cambridge, Cambridge University Press, 1992.

INTERNET RESOURCES

CHIMPANZEE COMMUNICATIONS AND THE EVOLUTION OF HUMAN LANGUAGE

www.gps.caltech.edu/~rkopp/collegepapers/chimps.html

A thoughtful article about the usefulness of ape language studies for understanding the evolution of human language.

VERVET MONKEY VOCALIZATIONS

www.wjh.harvard.edu/~mnkylab/media/vervetcalls.html

Want to hear what vervet alarm calls sound like? This web site produced by Harvard's Marc Hauser lets you do so.

DESIGN FEATURES OF LANGUAGE

http://bowland-files.lancs.ac.uk/chimp/langac/LECTURE4/4design.htm

A useful list of the design features of human language. Be sure to also click on the "chimp studies" button of this web site.

READING, WRITING, AND SPEAKING: WHERE DOES LANGUAGE LIVE?

http://williamcalvin.com/Bk1/bk1ch3.htm

This site provides access to several chapters written by William Calvin and George Ojemann about human brain functions.

ON THE NATURE AND EVOLUTION OF THE NEURAL BASES OF HUMAN LANGUAGE

http://lts3.algonquincollege.com/Everest2004/mainsite/neural_language.pdf

Philip Lieberman's latest statement about the numerous brain areas responsible for speech and language.

BRAINDANCE

www.albany.edu/braindance

Focusing mainly on the work of veteran paleoneurologist Dean Falk, this site also has useful links to other sources of information on the evolution of the human brain.

USEFUL SEARCH TERMS:

ape language studies
evolution of language
human brain evolution
Kanzi
speech-language areas of the brain
Washoe

Chapter 14

The Neandertal Enigma

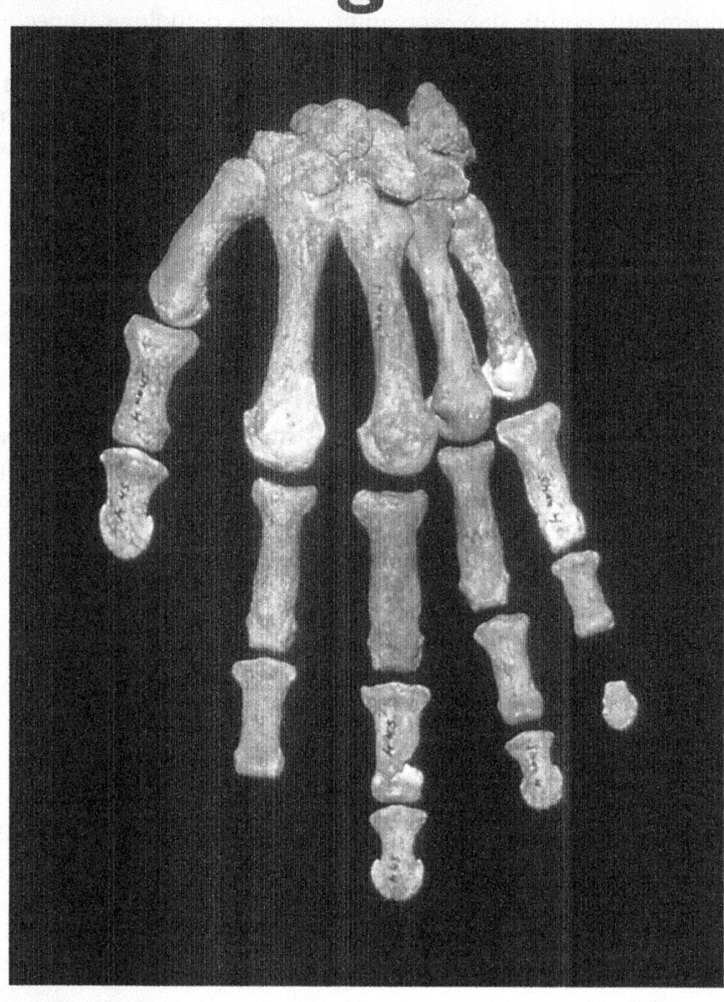

These Neandertal hand bones provide evidence of great strength and a powerful grip.

The savage . . . breathes only peace and liberty; he desires only to live and be free from labour.

Jean-Jacques Rousseau, 1712–1778. *A Discourse on the Origin of Inequality.*

The brutish appearance of [Neandertal Man's] energetic and clumsy body [along with] the heavy-jawed skull . . . declares the predominance of functions of a purely vegetative or bestial kind over the functions of mind.

Marcellin Boule, 1861–1942. *Fossil Men: Elements of Human Palaeontology.*

Overview

Of all the fossil hominin species, the Neandertals surely take the prize for being the best known and least understood. When Neandertal remains were first discovered during the nineteenth century, they were interpreted as pathological specimens of modern people. Early in the twentieth century, Neandertals were interpreted as a divergent and very apelike variety of humankind. Today, we know that after descending from *H. heidelbergensis* forebears about 350,000 years ago, ***Homo neanderthalensis*** people inhabited portions of Europe and the Middle East for over 300 millennia.

Homo neanderthalensis a *species* of humans that inhabited Europe and the Middle East from about 350,000 to 27,000 BP; descended from *Homo heidelbergensis*, the species' common name is usually spelled *Neandertal*.

The distinctive anatomy of the classic Neandertal included a stocky body build, a low-vaulted and big-browed skull, a larger brain than in modern humans, and a prognathic face with a large nose and swept-back cheekbones. Accomplished but small-scale hunters, the Neandertals produced a lithic culture called the Mousterian that shows links to the older Acheulean industry. Beyond their stone tools, however, the Neandertals' culture seems rather impoverished, with only hints of nonsubsistence artifacts.

Around 27,000 years ago, the Neandertals finally disappeared, apparently driven to extinction by competition from modern peoples who began moving into Europe about 40,000 BP. Recent mitochondrial DNA studies suggest that the Neandertals contributed few, if any, genes to the modern European gene pool, but

Mini-TIMELINE

Date or Age	Fossil Discoveries or Evolutionary Events
(A) Date (years AD)	
1997	Genetic evidence suggests Neandertals were a distinct species
1992	Early Neandertals found at Sima de los Huesos (Atapuerca, Spain)
1953	Neandertal burials discovered at Shanidar Cave, Iraq
1929	First Neandertal remains from the Levant discovered (Tabun)
1913	Boule's monograph on the La Chapelle skeleton
1848–1856	Neandertal discoveries in Gibraltar and Germany
(B) Age (years BP)	
~27,000	Approximate date of Neandertals' extinction
34,000	Carved bone and ivory ornaments among late Neandertals
82,000–43,000	Bone flutes possibly carved by Neandertals
90,000–30,000	Period of the classic Neandertals
250,000	Approximate beginning of the Middle Paleolithic
~350,000	Oldest known Neandertals inhabited Atapuerca Hills, Spain

some scholars disagree. In any event, by just after 27,000 years ago, the Neandertals had vanished and *Homo sapiens* had Europe to itself.

First View of Neandertals

Of all the kinds of prehistoric peoples, certainly those who project the clearest image are the Neandertals. For many, they are *the* Stone Age humans, shambling, beetle-browed louts who prowled the earth during the time of the glaciers. The Neandertals got such a poor reputation among the general public because early on, they were grievously misjudged by the experts. For many years, paleoanthropologists regarded Neandertals as a brutish breed that at best represented an insignificant side branch of the human family tree. Only recently has this misjudgment been remedied, and it now seems clear that they were members of a distinct and accomplished species. From perhaps as early as 350,000 years ago to about 27,000 years ago, they expanded the regions occupied by humans into arctic climates, devised ingenious stone tools to exploit nature, developed a relatively complex society, and possibly opened the door to the world of the supernatural. Clearly, they were people of considerable talents.

Why did the experts misjudge the Neandertals? Many reasons can be given: the scarcity of fossils, errors in reconstructing bone fragments, and other technical difficulties. But perhaps more important, these problems were compounded by an accident of timing. To tell the story of the Neandertals, we have to return again to the nineteenth century—to a time even before the publication of Darwin's *On the Origin of Species* (1859/1964), when almost no one believed that humankind had ever had a primitive ancestor.

The first fossil skull ever to be positively identified as belonging to an ancient human was that of a Neandertal. No one was prepared for the sight of a primitive-looking skeleton in the human closet, and when such a skeleton was found in 1856, it caught everyone off guard. Having nothing with which to compare the first Neandertal skull except the skull of a modern human, scientists of the time were struck more by the differences between the two than the similarities. Today, the reverse is true. Compared to their predecessors, *Homo erectus,* Neandertals showed considerable evolutionary advancement. They may have been a little shorter than the average modern European and considerably heavier featured, squatter, and more muscular than most, but with regard to brain size and some other features, they compare well to modern people.

First Discovery

The first Neandertal to be recognized as a primitive human was discovered in 1856, not far from the city of Düsseldorf, Germany, where a tributary stream of the Rhine flows through a steep-sided gorge known as the Neander Valley—*Neanderthal* in nineteenth-century German (Stringer and Gamble, 1993; Trinkaus and Shipman, 1993; see Figure 14.5). In 1856, the flanks of the gorge were being quarried for limestone. During the summer, workers blasted open a small cave, and as they dug their pickaxes into the floor of the cave, they uncovered a number of ancient bones. But the quarriers were intent on limestone; they did not pay much attention to the bones, and most of what was probably a complete skeleton of a Neandertal was lost. Only the skullcap (Figure 14.1), ribs, part of the pelvis, and some limb bones were saved.

The owner of the quarry thought these fragments belonged to a bear, and he presented them to a local science teacher, J. K. Fuhlrott, who was known to be interested in such things. Fuhlrott had enough knowledge of anatomy to realize that the skeletal remains came not from a bear but from a most extraordinary human with thick limb bones and a heavy, slanted brow. The appearance of the bones

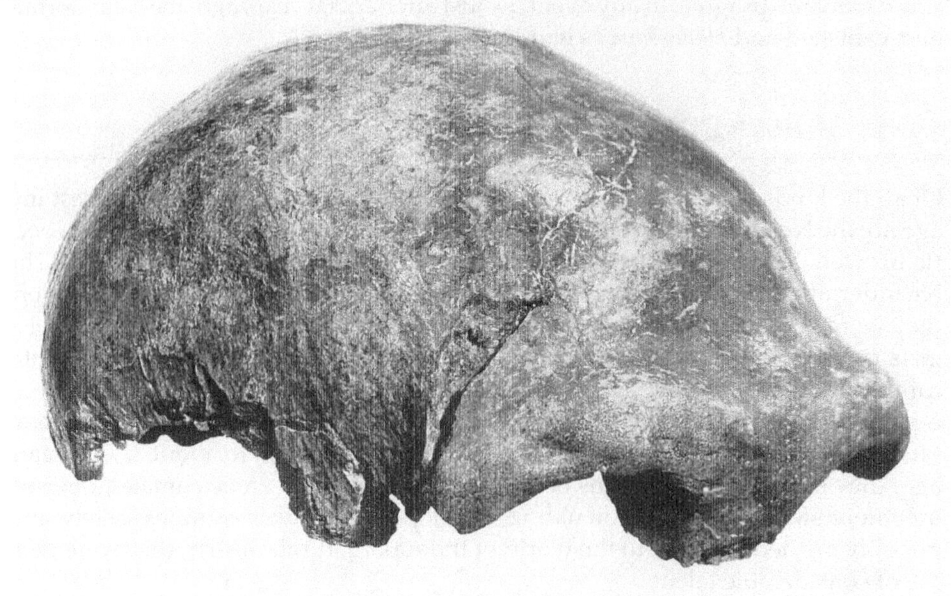

FIGURE 14.1
The skullcap from the Neander Valley is possibly the most famous fossil discovery ever made. Following its discovery in 1856, it was thought by many to be the skull of some pathological idiot. Today, we know that it belonged to an early but by no means excessively primitive variety of humans. This photograph is just over one-half actual size.

suggested to Fuhlrott that they were fossilized and thus very ancient. Furthermore, their primitive characteristics hinted at an entirely unknown variety of ancient humans.

Knowing that this judgment was bound to be disputed, Fuhlrott called in Hermann Schaaffhausen, professor of anatomy at the University of Bonn. Schaaffhausen agreed that the bones represented an ancient race of humans. He had in mind, however, an age of no more than a few thousand years. The fossil fragments could have come, he suggested, from some barbarian who had lived in Northern Europe before the Celtic and Germanic tribes arrived (Trinkaus and Shipman, 1993).

Schaaffhausen can hardly be criticized for missing the truth about the bones from the Neander Valley: The scientific community of 1856 did not realize that humankind had been on earth for a substantial length of time, and no respectable scientist believed that people had ever existed in any form other than that of the modern human. Such a notion would have been directly contrary to a belief in Genesis.

Indeed, as noted in Chapter 1, creationist beliefs were still in the ascendancy in the early 1850s, although the old notion of a very young earth was beginning to be passé, particularly among scholars. A few odd, humanlike bones had been discovered in Europe in the eighteenth century and the first half of the nineteenth century, but it took the publication of Darwin's *On the Origin of Species* in 1859 (1964) to open the way to recognize the bones as fossilized relics of human evolution.

Homo neanderthalensis?

In 1856, experts familiar with human skeletons and skull structure could see some very peculiar things about the Neander Valley skull (see Figure 14.1). It was clearly humanlike, yet it had strongly developed eyebrow ridges and a retreating forehead, and it was much flatter on top and more bulging in the back than is typical of the skull of a modern human. Was the skull normal or pathological? Schaaffhausen came down on the side of normality, but some of his scientific colleagues were not so sure.

Darwin heard about these remarkable bones but never investigated them. However, his friend and supporter Thomas H. Huxley undertook a thorough study of the unprecedented skull. Schaaffhausen had determined that the cranium could hold 63 cubic inches (1,030 cubic centimeters) of water; complete, it would have contained 75 cubic inches (1,230 cubic centimeters), which is not far from the average cranial volume of many modern people. Such a modern-sized brain impressed Huxley, and then, too, the limb bones, although on the bulky side, were "quite those of an European of middle stature" (Huxley, 1863/1915:206).

"Under whatever aspect we view this cranium," wrote Huxley in 1863, "we meet with ape-like characteristics, stamping it as the most pithecoid [apelike] of human crania yet discovered." In view of the large cranial capacity, however, Huxley did not see Neandertal as an ancestral form. He wrote, "In no sense can the Neanderthal bones be regarded as the remains of a human being intermediate between Men and Apes." Noting that the fossils were more nearly allied to the apes than these creatures are to monkeys and strepsirhines, he concluded that they were human. "In still older strata," Huxley wondered evolutionarily, "do the fossilized bones of an ape more anthropoid, or a Man more pithecoid, than any yet known await the researches of some unborn palaeontologist?" (Huxley, 1863/1915:205, 206, 209).

William King, professor of geology at Queen's College in Galway, Ireland, accepted the German fossil as an extinct form of humanity. In 1863, King suggested at a scientific meeting that the specimen be placed in a separate species, *Homo neanderthalensis.* In giving the fossil the genus name *Homo,* King was acknowledging a general similarity to humankind, but he believed that he could not add the species name for modern humans, *sapiens,* because, as he wrote, "The Neanderthal skull is so eminently [simian] . . . I feel myself constrained to believe that the thoughts and desires which once dwelt within it never soared beyond those of the brute" (Trinkaus and Shipman, 1993:88).

Rickets a pathological condition involving curvature of the bones; caused by insufficient vitamin D.

King's taxonomic assessment was closer to being correct than anyone else's, but unfortunately, more authoritative (albeit erroneous) opinions carried the day. Along with some others, distinguished German pathologist Rudolf Virchow endorsed the notion that the Neander Valley specimen was modern, probably imbecilic, and pathological, having suffered from **rickets** at some time in its life. A colleague of Virchow's went so far as to suggest that the large brows of the Neandertal were caused by a lifetime of frowning! Not surprisingly, Virchow's attitude toward the Neander Valley remains fit perfectly with his distain for evolutionary theories (Boule, 1923; Trinkaus and Shipman, 1993). Furthermore, the acceptance of Virchow's conservative and antievolutionary position by other scholars was made easier by the fact that there was no clear evidence, either faunal or stratigraphic, that the Neander Valley specimen was really ancient (Reader, 1988). Evidence for the applicability of Darwin's theory to human history would ultimately be forthcoming, but the first Neandertal specimen provided little support.

The Neandertal Discoveries Accumulate

Very soon after the announcement of the Neander Valley find, other similar specimens came to light (Boule, 1923; R. Klein, 1999). In 1864, a Neandertal skull was brought forward that had been found on Gibraltar almost 20 years earlier. In 1866, a robust lower jaw lacking a chin (i.e., with a receding mandibular symphysis) was unearthed at La Naulette in Belgium. This time, the evidence for antiquity was good: The jaw was found in association with the bones of mammoths and other extinct creatures. Nonetheless, Virchow dismissed the Belgian fossil as a pathological modern—an interpretation he also applied to a second mandible recovered from the Moravian site of Šipka. And finally, in 1886, another Belgian site called Spy produced two Neandertal skulls and other bones. As at La Naulette, the evidence for great age was convincing. The Spy bones were found with the remains of mammoths and woolly rhinoceroses and with chipped stone tools.

The additional specimens all showed strong points of resemblance to the Neander Valley remains, and collectively, they began to turn the tide against the "pathology" theory (Trinkhaus and Shipman, 1993). But how did the big-browed

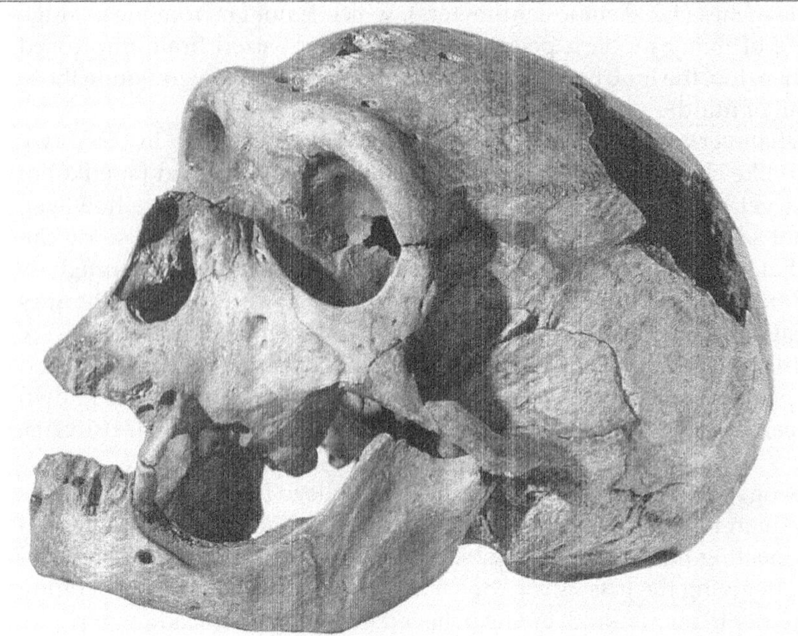

FIGURE 14.2
The skull of the old man of La Chapelle-aux-Saints shows that he lost many teeth during life. He was less than 5 feet (1.5 meters) tall and bent by arthritis, but he had a large cranial capacity of about 1,625 cubic centimeters. The average modern human capacity is 1,330 cubic centimeters. The photograph is approximately 45 percent actual size.

and robustly built Neandertals link up with modern humans? Were they our forebears or merely wayward "first cousins"? Opinions were varied as the nineteenth century drew to a close.

La Chapelle-aux-Saints and Other Finds

In the first decade of the twentieth century, archaeologists were at work in the Dordogne region of southwestern France (see Figure 14.5). From the 1860s on, countless stone tools had been found in this region, proof that the Dordogne had been a population center in ancient times. Beginning in 1908, a magnificent series of Neandertal fossils was also discovered. One of the first fossils to turn up was the skeleton of an old man in a cave near the village of La Chapelle-aux-Saints (Figure 14.2). A nearby cave at Le Moustier yielded the skeleton of a Neandertal youth. A rock shelter at La Ferrassie produced adult male and female Neandertals and later the remains of several children (see Figure 14.3). Another rock shelter at La Quina held parts of several Neandertal skeletons (Boule, 1923).

The great value of these materials was their completeness. The bones from Spy had given a rough portrait of the Neandertal people, but as long as the fossil record remained essentially fragmentary, venturesome scholars could leap to extremes and see them as either *Homo sapiens* or very apelike. The wealth of skeletal materials from southwestern France seemed to promise enough data to set the most vivid imagination to rest. With it, scientists would be able to reconstruct what a Neandertal looked like and study the physical resemblances—or lack of them—between Neandertals and modern humans.

Boule's Reconstruction

As it happened, the specimen from La Chapelle-aux-Saints was selected for a comprehensive analysis and reconstruction of the Neandertal skeleton. The task of rebuilding the skeleton fell to a French paleontologist named Marcellin Boule, of the French National Museum of Natural History (Boule, 1923). On this project, Boule had an unusually fine set of bones to work with. The materials were well preserved, and although some of the bones were broken, everything of importance was available except some teeth and vertebrae.

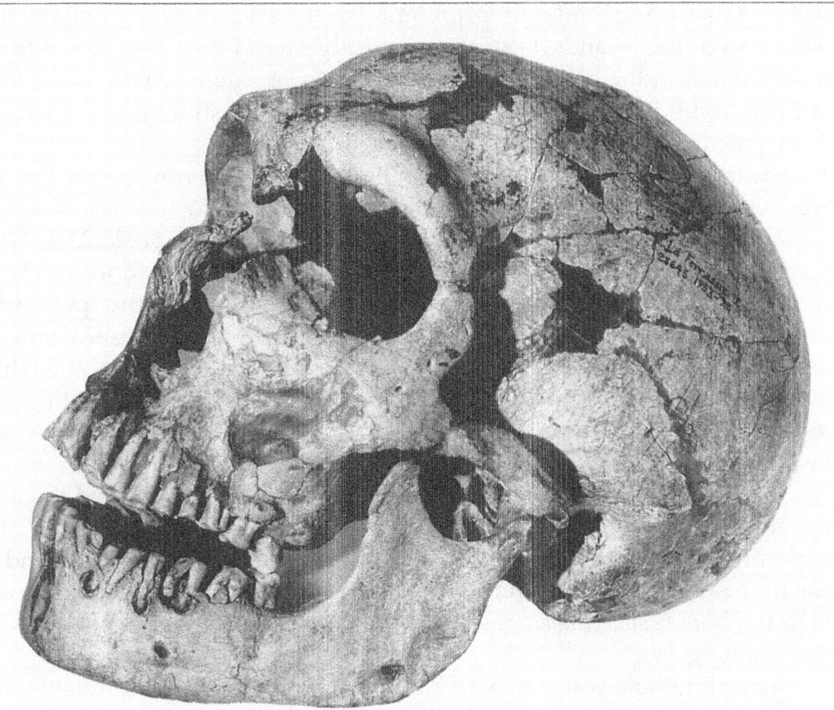

FIGURE 14.3
The male skeleton from La Ferrassie, buried with five others, had an even larger cranial capacity than the La Chappelle man: 1,689 cubic centimeters. His front teeth show a rare type of extreme wear that is found today among some Inuit tribes and other hunting people. It may have been caused by chewing animal skins to soften them for clothing. This photograph is just over 40 percent actual size.

Despite the completeness and good condition of the bones, Boule proceeded to commit an astonishing series of errors—and they were not corrected for decades. Boule's mistakes—due in equal parts to his theoretical leanings, his habit of ignoring important work by others when it suited him, and the fact that human paleontology was in its infancy—combined to make the reconstructed skeleton appear quite apelike from head to toe (Trinkaus and Shipman, 1993; Figure 14.4). He mistakenly arranged the foot bones so that the big toe diverged from the other toes like an opposable thumb, which implied that Neandertals walked on the outer part of

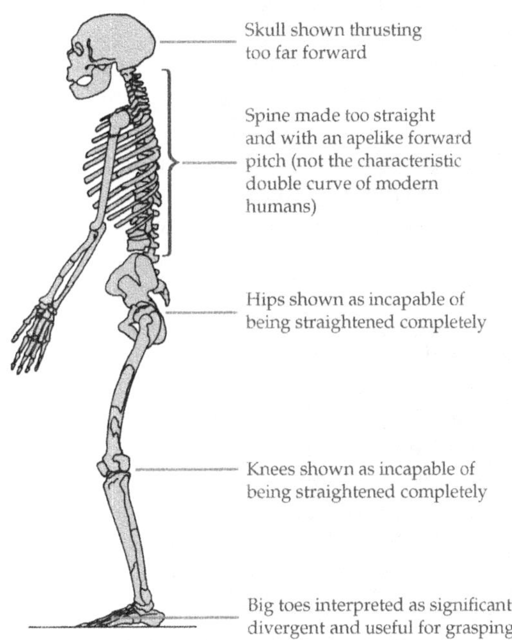

FIGURE 14.4
Marcellin Boule made a series of errors when he reconstructed the skeleton from La Chapelle-aux-Saints and so implied that all Neandertal people walked with a stooping gait and bent knees.

their feet, like apes. Boule's interpretation of the knee joint was equally incorrect: He declared that Neandertals could not fully extend their legs, a fact that would have resulted in the bent-knee gait that observers could readily see the skeleton would adopt if it could walk. In every respect, the posture of Boule's reconstruction seemed nonhuman (Tattersall, 1995a, b).

The most devastating conclusion of Boule's study was on the intelligence of the man from La Chapelle-aux-Saints. Boule dismissed the fossil's large cranial capacity, saying, "Large heads are not always the best heads" (1923:231). He looked mainly at the long, low skull—and perceived severe mental inferiority. He cited the interior of the skull as support for this judgment; measuring the space behind the retreating forehead, the paleontologist determined to his satisfaction that the Neandertal brain had possessed a smallish frontal lobe, which was then thought to be the center of higher intelligence. And so Boule ranked the fossil man's brainpower somewhere between that of apes and modern humans—but closer to that of the apes (Boule, 1923).

Cro-Magnon an anatomically modern human living in Europe between 40,000 and 10,000 years ago.

Boule wrote disparagingly of the apelike Neandertal body and the likelihood that these archaic humans "possessed only a rudimentary psychic nature . . . markedly inferior to that of any modern race whatever" (1923:236). And when it was time to classify the Neander Valley man and his conspecifics, Boule relegated them to *Homo neanderthalensis*—in his view, a separate, aberrant species that had died out long ago.

Marcellin Boule was a man of excellent reputation and formidable diligence, virtues that made his errors all the more serious. Between 1911 and 1913, he published his conclusions in three exhaustive volumes. Packed with detail and ringing with confidence, these monographs had tremendous influence on scientists and the public alike. Although a few prehistorians stuck to their view that the Neandertals were respectable ancestors of modern humans, practically everyone now believed that such a lineage had been proved impossible.

The sheer force of Boule's work was not the only reason for its acceptance. Some circumstantial evidence pointed toward an evolutionary gap between the Neandertals and the later **Cro-Magnons,** who by this time were acknowledged to be the immediate ancestors of present-day Europeans. (The Cro-Magnons are discussed in Chapters 15 and 16.) Even if the Neandertals were not quite as debased as Boule supposed, they definitely looked different from the anatomically modern Cro-Magnons, and no one had come across a fossil that indicated an evolutionary transition between the two. Without an intermediate fossil, it was only prudent to assume that the Cro-Magnons derived from stock that had been occupying Europe or some other part of the world during or possibly before the era of the Neandertals, thus granting the Neandertals no significance in human evolution.

Furthermore, archaeologists believed that there was no cultural connection between the Neandertal and the Cro-Magnon peoples (Boule, 1923). The stone tools of the Cro-Magnons seemed markedly more sophisticated than Neandertal implements. And when archaeologists dug down through successive layers in caves, they sometimes found sterile layers between the Neandertal deposits and the deposits left by Cro-Magnons, indicating that no one had occupied the cave for a time. It appeared that the Neandertals and their characteristic Mousterian culture had experienced an "apparently sudden disappearance . . . [and then been replaced] by men of the same type as now occupy Europe" (Keith, 1920:135–136).

For the better part of the twentieth century, the classification of the Neandertals and their place in hominin evolution was in dispute. Some paleoanthropologists preferred to follow William King's lead of 1864 and give them a separate species designation, *Homo neanderthalensis.* Others opted to include the Neandertals within *Homo sapiens* but as a distinct subspecies: *H. sapiens neanderthalensis.* As a result of this uncertainty, there has been continuing controversy about whether the Neandertals made a genetic contribution to modern people.

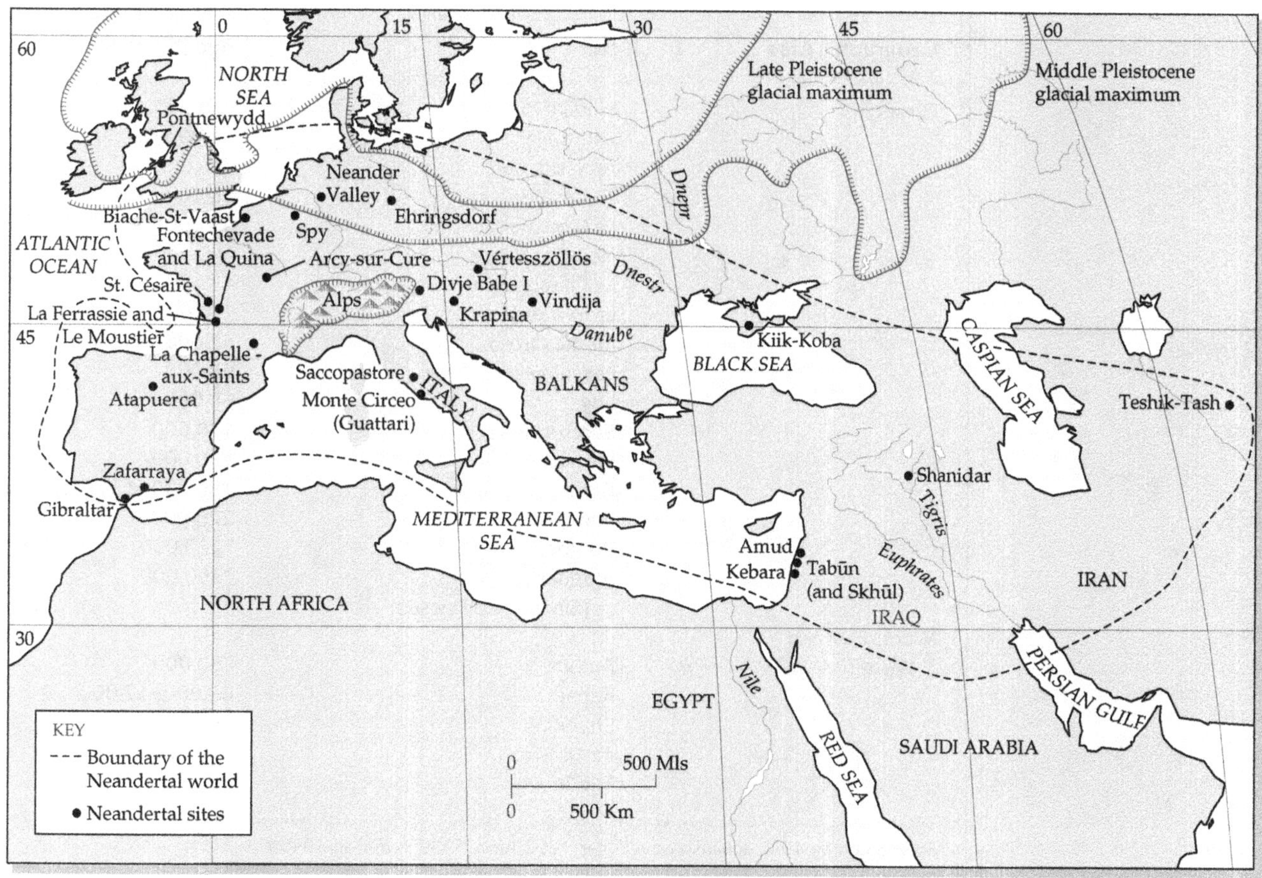

FIGURE 14.5
The Neandertals' world extended over Europe, the Middle East, and portions of Western Asia. Only a few of the known Neandertal sites are shown.

Source: After Annick Peterson from *In Search of the Neanderthals* by Christopher Stringer and Clive Gamble. © 1993 Christopher Stringer and Clive Gamble. Reprinted by permission of the publishers, Thames and Hudson.

As detailed in a later section, many of these problems recently have been clarified by the extraction and analysis of Neandertal DNA. This genetic research suggests that the Neandertals did belong to a different species from modern people, and thus it is unlikely that we carry many (if any) of their genes. Furthermore, there is evidence that the Neandertal species is much older than anyone ever expected, having split off from the line leading to modern humans at least 350,000 years ago. But *Homo sapiens* or not, archaeological studies and fossil discoveries made since Boule's day have shown that the Neandertals were a very capable and successful species that spread widely across Europe and Western Asia. It is to those later discoveries and studies that we now turn our attention.

Neandertals in Europe and Beyond

Marcellin Boule had depicted the Neandertals as creatures that might have had a hard time surviving, much less thriving, in the world. But if geographic range is any measure of success, these archaic people seem to have done quite well. As shown in Figure 14.5, Neandertal remains and artifacts have been recovered from

TABLE 14.1 A Partial Record of Neandertal Sites

Geographic Area	Site	Age (Years BP)
Europe	Vindija	~28,000
	Zafarraya	33,000–27,000
	Arcy-sur-Cure	~34,000
	St. Césaire	36,000–32,000
	Le Moustier	41,000
	Neander Valley	~45,000
	La Chapelle-aux-Saints	47,000
	La Ferrassie	~50,000
	Monte Circeo	52,000
	La Quina	64,000
	Spy	68,000
	Saccopastore	120,000
	Krapina	130,000
	Biache-St.-Vaast	180,000–130,000
	Ehringsdorf	225,000
	Pontnewydd	~225,000
	Atapuerca (Sima de los Huesos)	~350,000
Middle East and Western Asia	Amud	~50,000
	Kebara	65,000–47,000
	Shanidar	70,000–50,000
	Teshik-Tash	~70,000
	Tabūn	150,000 (?)–75,000

Source: Conroy, 1997; Johanson and Edgar, 1996; Klein, 1999; Tattersall, 1995b.

the western extremes of Europe (from Gibraltar and possibly Pontnewydd in Wales), throughout the bulk of that continent, and to the east as far as Israel, Iraq, and Uzbekistan. (Teshik-Tash is one of the easternmost sites.) In fact, the world of the Neandertals was quite extensive, covering an area some 4,000 miles (6,400 kilometers) east to west and 1,500 miles (2,400 kilometers) north to south (Stringer and Gamble, 1993). The fossil record shows that they inhabited that world for over 300,000 years, and biomolecular estimates may increase that figure to as much as 500,000 years (discussed in a later section). Furthermore, the archaeological record shows that the Neandertals' culture was rich and included a number of modern traits, at least in incipient form. They were very much like us in many ways but quite different in others. Table 14.1 lists several of the more important Neandertal sites, along with their ages.

Discoveries from Israel

During the early 1930s, a joint Anglo–American fossil expedition had extraordinary good luck in two caves on the slopes of Mount Carmel (see Figure 14.5). The first find, at Mugharet et-Tabūn (Cave of the Oven), was a female skeleton, definitely Neandertal but possessing a skull slightly higher domed than usual and with a more vertical forehead. A second Mount Carmel site, Mugharet es-Skhūl (Cave of the Kids), yielded remains of ten individuals. Some resembled Neandertals in a few features, others looked more advanced, and one approached the appearance of modern humans (Figure 14.6). This last individual displayed only a trace of the Neandertal brow ridge, but the forehead was steeper, the jaw more delicate, the chin more pronounced, and the shape of the cranium distinctly modern. Today, we have further important

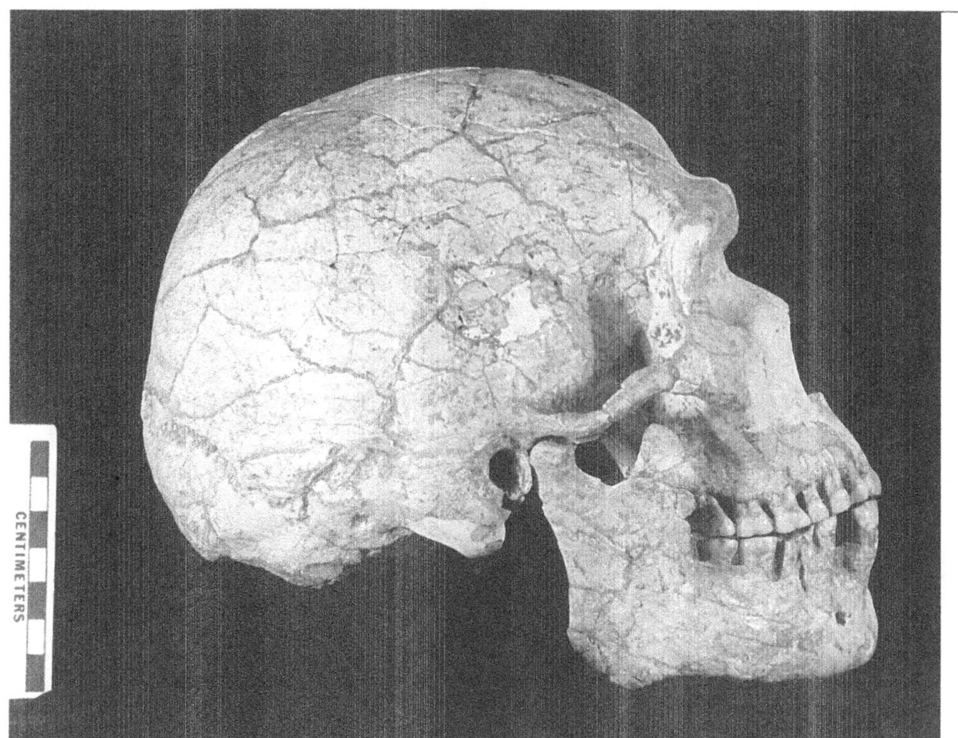

FIGURE 14.6 The skull of an early *Homo sapiens* fossil from the cave of Skhūl on the slopes of Mount Carmel. This skull shows several modern features, including a chin and a relatively steep forehead. The photograph is about 45 percent actual size.

discoveries from Israel: undoubted Neandertal skeletons from Amud and Kebara, and several more of the modern-looking skeletons from Qafzeh (south of Nazareth). The variation exhibited is striking (Stringer and Gamble, 1993). The sites from this region appear to span a period from about 150,000 to 47,000 years BP.

The initial impression left by the Skhūl and Qafzeh people was that they occupied an evolutionary middle ground between the Neandertals and modern humans. They were certainly extremely variable in form. Today, both the Skhūl and Qafzeh specimens are classified as early representatives of *Homo sapiens,* albeit with a good deal of anatomical diversity.

Until fairly recently, it was believed by many anthropologists that the Levant (eastern Mediterranean area) provided solid evidence for the evolutionary transition of Neandertals into modern humans. This conclusion was based on early indications that the more modern Skhūl and Qafzeh people *postdated* the Israeli Neandertals. Recent advances in dating techniques, however, have effectively reversed the situation. The Skhūl and Qafzeh fossils are now dated to between 130,000 and 80,000 years BP, while the Levantine Neandertals appear to have inhabited the area some 75,000 to 50,000 BP years ago (Shea, 2003). (Note that the Tabūn 1 specimen is somewhat problematic here, due to an uncertain provenance. This Neandertal woman may be as much as 150,000 years old, but then again, she could be half that age [Klein, 1999].) On balance, it seems reasonable to conclude that more modern people were in the Levant *before* the Neandertals and, furthermore, that the moderns may have been driven out (or driven extinct locally) by competition from the late-arriving archaics (Shea, 2003).

Other Middle Eastern/Western Asian sites are worth mentioning before we return to Europe for the alpha and omega of the Neandertal specimens. First, the site of Shanidar in the Zagros Mountains of Iraq (Figure 14.5) yielded several Neandertal skeletons during excavations carried out between 1951 and 1960 (Solecki, 1971). Dated about 50,000 years BP or a little earlier, the Shanidar skeletons show fully developed and typical Neandertal traits and also a very high incident of antemortem (predeath) trauma, including broken ribs, scalp wounds, apparent stab wounds, and degenerative joint disease. As paleoanthropologist Glenn Conroy of Washington University remarked, "The Neandertals clearly had a tough time of it" as they hunted and gathered and perhaps also fought with one another (1997:446). Second, the easternmost Neandertal remains showed up in 1938 during work at the cave site of Teshik-Tash located in the Bajsun-Tau Mountains of Uzbekistan, about 78 miles (125 kilometers) south of Samarkand (Figure 14.5). At this rugged, high-altitude site, a young Neandertal boy was found buried, and it appeared that some care had been given to the interment (Stringer and Gamble, 1993).

The Oldest and Youngest Neandertals

For the most exciting recent fossil finds of Neandertals, however, we must return to Europe. In the hills of northern Spain, researchers have uncovered evidence of the very oldest members of the Neandertal lineage. The materials come from the site of the Sima de los Huesos (Pit of Bones) in the Sierra de Atapuerca, some 150 miles (250 kilometers) due north of Madrid (Figure 14.5). In the Sima de los Huesos, the remains of at least 28 early humans have been found deep in a cave, scattered about a small chamber at the bottom of a narrow shaft 40 feet (13 meters) deep. Intermingled with the bones of bears and other animals, the human remains in the Pit of Bones apparently accumulated as people living near the cave's mouth disposed of their dead by dumping them down the shaft (Arsuaga, 2000; Arsuaga et al., 1993).

Carrying a minimum age of 350,000 BP but possibly as old as 400,000 to 500,000 years BP (Bischoff et al., 2003), the Sima de los Huesos fossils share many traits with *Homo erectus* and other features with modern *Homo sapiens*. The majority of their anatomical characteristics, however—including the shape of the brows, projection of the face, and the shape of the back of the braincase (see Figure 14.7)—are shared

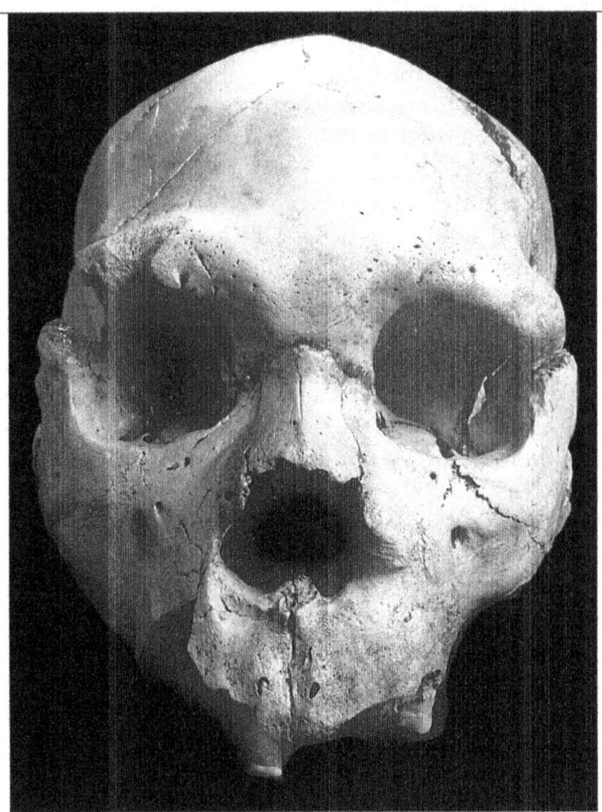

FIGURE 14.7 This skull from the Spanish site of Sima de los Huesos in the Sierra de Atapuerca displays several evolving Neandertal traits, including large brows and midfacial prognathism. Its cranial capacity was 1,125 cubic centimeters. This photograph is about 55 percent actual size.

with undoubted Neandertals, and thus they are classified here as the oldest known members of that lineage.

Southern Europe has also produced the *youngest* Neandertal remains—fossils that may mark the end of the species both on the continent and entirely. At the Croatian site of Vindija (Figure 14.5), paleoanthropologist Fred Smith and his colleagues have recovered Neandertal fossils dated to about 28,000 years ago. Interestingly, the Vindija people were somewhat less robust than most Neandertals and resembled modern humans in certain features (Stringer and Gamble, 1993; Smith, 2002). (This finding will be discussed in more detail in Chapter 15 in connection with the evolution of anatomically modern people.) And finally, the southern Spanish cave site of Zafarraya (Figure 14.5) has produced typical Neandertal stone tools dating to 27,000 years BP and Neandertal fossils from somewhat older deposits (33,000 years BP; Klein, 1999; Tattersall, 1995b). Together, these sites suggest that just under 30,000 years ago, the Neandertals came to their end in the lands bordering the Adriatic and Mediterranean Seas.

So much for our selective review of Neandertal discoveries. Let us now turn to the anatomy of these archaic humans.

Neandertal Anatomy

As noted earlier, Marcellin Boule's misanalysis of the La Chapelle-aux-Saints Neandertal skeleton misled anthropologists for quite some time. We now have a much more accurate picture of Neandertal anatomy, thanks to the discovery and study of many additional fossils.

Several of the more important anatomical features of the Neandertals are summarized in Box 14.1. As shown there, they were well within the range of modern body size (height and weight), although on average, they were shorter and considerably more stocky than most living people. The Neandertals were built to

BOX 14.1

Characteristics of the Neandertals[a]

Trait	*Homo neanderthalensis*
Height (sexes combined)	4.9–5.6 ft (150–170 cm)
Weight (sexes combined)	110–143 lb (50–65 kg)
Brain size (sexes combined)	~1,450 cc mean (1,125–1,750 cc range)
Cranium	Occipital depression (*suprainiac fossa*); occipital torus; large nose; midfacial prognathism; variability in degree of cranial base flexure; modern hyoid bone
Dentition	Large incisors: gap behind lower M3
Limbs	Robust, stocky physique as adaptation to cold; short legs; powerful hands
Locomotion	Bipedalism
Distribution	Middle East, Europe, Western Asia
Known dates	~350,000–27,000 years BP

[a]Mean values for anatomical measurements may change with the addition of new fossil discoveries. For additional technical details and diagnostic traits, see Appendix 3.
Sources: Conroy, 1997; Klein, 1999; Stringer and Gamble, 1993; Tattersall, 1995b.

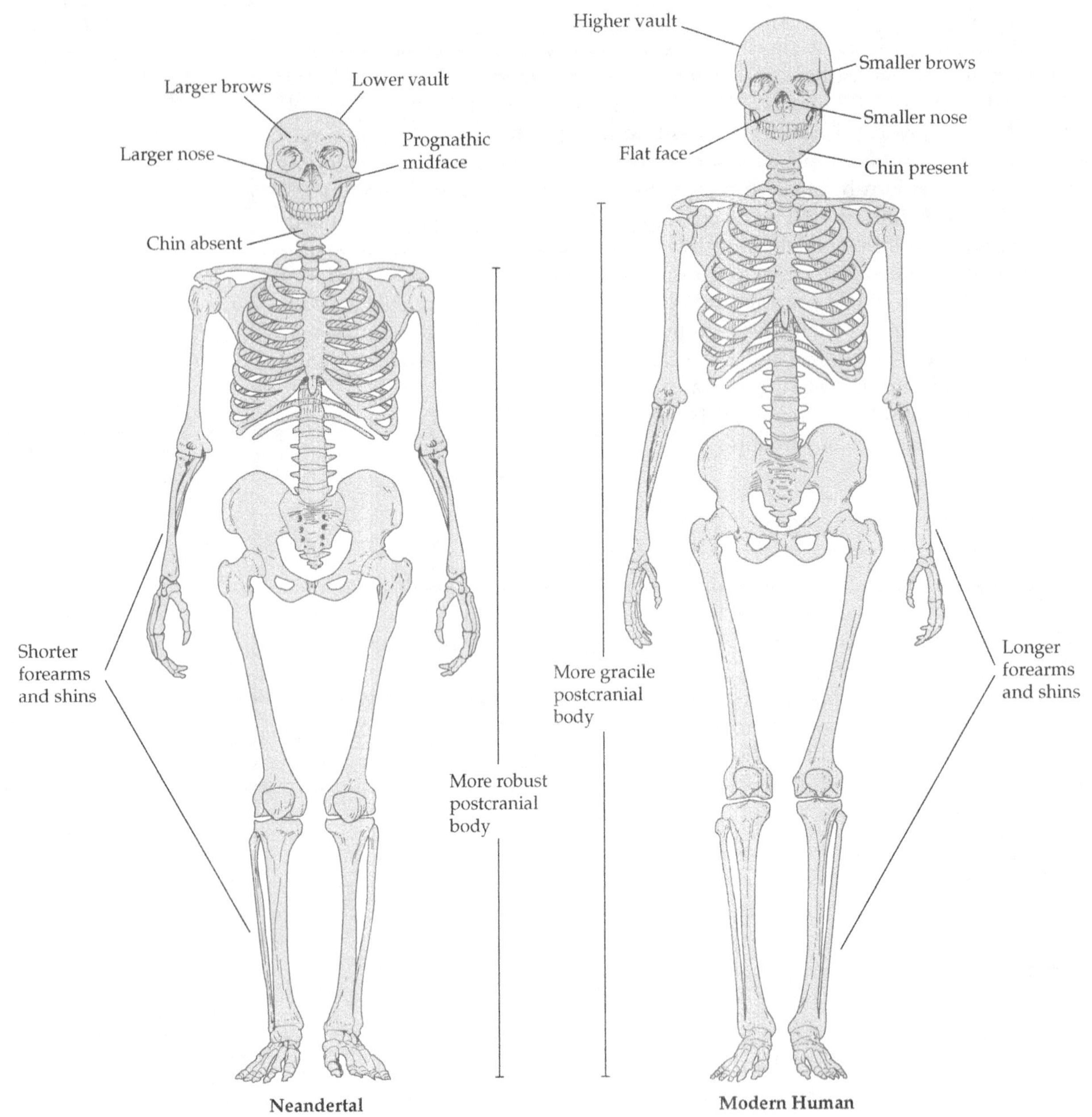

FIGURE 14.8
A comparision of Neandertal (*left*) and modern human (*right*) skeletons. The Neandertals possessed a shorter, more robust body, with a broad chest and powerful arms and hands. Note also the interspecific differences in brow size and height of the cranial vault.
Source: From *The Last Neanderthal* by Ian Tattersall. New York, Macmillan, 1995.

withstand the extreme cold of the European ice ages (Holliday, 1997; Weaver, 2003). Their broad bodies and relatively short limbs helped to conserve heat in accordance with Bergmann's and Allen's rules (discussed in Chapter 17; see Figure 14.8). They were also built for strength, with thick limb bones, broad shoulder blades that anchored powerful arm muscles, and massive hands (see the chapter-opener illustration).

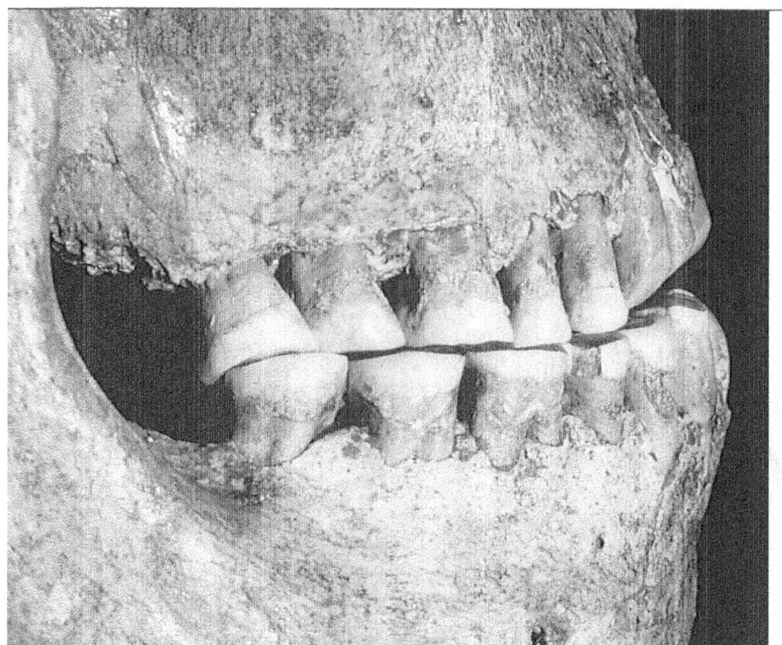

FIGURE 14.9
A lateral view of the dentition of a Neandertal from Shanidar, Iraq. The retromolar gap is obvious at the *left,* and strong wear can be seen on the upper-front teeth (*right*).

Atop their ruggedly built bodies, the Neandertals carried large and distinctive heads. Their skulls showed a long and rather low-vaulted braincase; midfacial prognathism; cheekbones that were swept back rather than laterally flaring; a large nose; large brow ridges; and variability in the degree of cranial base flexure (see Figures 14.2, 14.3, 14.4, and 14.8). Additionally, the Neandertal occipital bone at the back of the skull tended to protrude somewhat and featured a characteristic depression or pit for the attachment of neck muscles, the **suprainiac fossa.** And within their big skulls, the Neandertals possessed equally large brains. Average brain size calculated over their entire 350,000 to 27,000 BP time period is about 1,450 cubic centimeters—some 9 percent more than modern humans' average size (1,330 cubic centimeters) and almost 20 percent more than that of the Neandertals' immediate ancestors, *Homo heidelbergensis.*

Suprainiac fossa a characteristic depression of the occipital bone of *Neandertals.*

The Neandertals' jaws and teeth also had certain distinctive features (see Figures 14.2 and 14.3). The mandible usually lacked a chin, although some individuals showed incipient development of this trait. Midfacial prognathism resulted in the lower toothrow being moved forward, producing a characteristic space between the last molar and the **ramus** of the mandible (the **retromolar gap**). Finally, many Neandertal fossils show extreme wear of the front teeth (Figure 14.9), a feature thought to reflect the use of the teeth as tools (Figure 14.10).

Ramus the vertical portion of the *mandible;* as opposed to the mandibular body, which bears the teeth.

Retromolar gap the space between the M3 and the mandibular *ramus;* characteristic of *Neandertals.*

In summary, the Neandertals were smallish but powerful and rugged people who thrived for over 300,000 years in Europe and certain adjacent areas. Although the latest studies show that they probably were not us—that is, not *Homo sapiens*—but rather a distinct species, *Homo neanderthalensis,* they were a remarkable offshoot of hominin evolution and produced a complex culture, to which we will now turn.

Surviving in an Ice Age World

The ice age world of the Neandertals was a very inhospitable place at times. When glacial ice sheets advanced into Europe from the North Pole and from mountain ranges such as the Alps (Figure 14.5), sea levels dropped, ambient temperatures plummeted, forests gave way to expanding grassy plains as annual rainfall declined, and significant changes occurred in the animal community. Mean annual temper-

FIGURE 14.10 The American Museum of Natural History's reconstruction of a classic Neandertal group. Note how the woman in the center is anchoring an animal skin with her teeth as she scrapes it with a stone tool. Such use of the teeth would have caused the wear seen in Figure 14.9.

atures in midlatitude Europe fell as much as 16 degrees centigrade during glacial periods compared to the milder interglacials (Klein, 1999). (To illustrate the impact of a decline of this magnitude, consider how such cooling would affect modern-day Paris. A typical July day with a high of 76 degrees Fahrenheit [25 degrees centigrade] would drop to a rather brisk 48 degrees Fahrenheit [9 degrees centigrade]. While not picnic weather, it was bearable. But in January, the average daily high of 43 degrees Fahrenheit [6 degrees centigrade] would plummet to a rather icy 14 degrees Fahrenheit [–10 degrees centigrade].) As the ice age temperatures dropped and the vegetation changed, temperate animals would have moved toward the equator and cold-loving species would have moved in to replace them. Cold temperatures and open grasslands would have favored grazing animals, such as red deer, reindeer, horses, and woolly mammoths (Klein, 1999; Stringer and Gamble, 1993; Tattersall, 1995b).

Matching the dates of Neandertal sites with reconstructions of the Pleistocene ice sheets suggests that these people first inhabited Europe during a cold phase that was in progress 350,000 years ago (Figure 14.11). Thereafter, temperatures waxed and waned in approximately 100,000-year cycles, with strong cold peaks at about 130,000 and 30,000 years BP and a smaller cold peak at around 70,000 BP Most of the European Neandertal sites date from the long cold period of 70,000 to 30,000 BP (Table 14.1).

The Neandertals had both biological and cultural adaptations that enabled them to survive the ice age conditions, deal with predators, obtain adequate food, and reproduce successfully for over 300,000 years. A review of those adaptations will be instructive (Table 14.2).

Biological Adaptations

Certain aspects of the distinctive Neandertal anatomy can be interpreted as cold climate adaptations. First, of primary importance, their short-limbed and bulky bodies clearly were molded by the need to retain body heat. Such a body build, similar to that found among modern Inuits living in the far northern latitudes (Holliday,

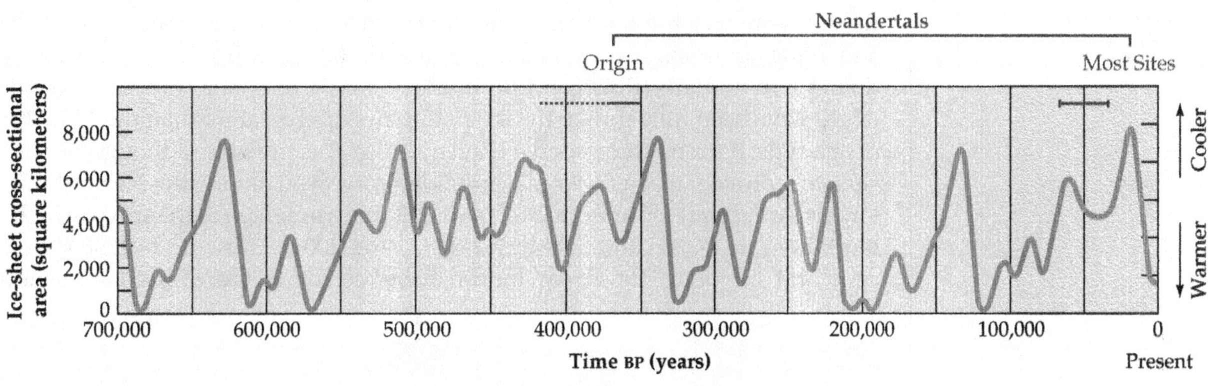

FIGURE 14.11
The Pleistocene ice ages most probably were caused by periodic variations in the geometry of the earth's orbit. Some of the key evidence for these variations comes from oxygen isotope analysis of cores drilled from the deep sea. From these data, it has proved possible to calculate the cross-sectional area of ice sheets at any time during the past 700,000 years. As we see in this chart, the main peaks of cold weather occurred approximately every 100,000 years, but many other cold oscillations came between these peaks.

Source: Covey, 1984.

1997; Molnar, 2002; see also Chapter 17), minimizes the ratio of surface area to weight and thus reduces heat loss. Second, the large Neandertal nose *may* have been an adaptation for warming and moisturizing cold, dry air before it reached the lungs (Coon, 1963). (Alternately, big noses might not have been selected for at all but instead represent a side effect of midfacial prognathism and/or selection for large maxillary incisors [Klein, 1999; Molnar, 2002].) Third, it is possible that the Neandertals had such a large brain because it, too, may have aided in body heat conservation (Stringer and Gamble, 1993). Note, however, that this suggestion is negated to some extent by the fact that the Neandertal skull was much longer than it was wide (i.e., **cephalic index** of 70 to 76 [Hooton, 1946]), a morphology that should have caused heat *loss* (Molnar, 2002).

Cephalic index a skull measurement sometimes used by *anthropologists*; defined as skull breadth/length × 100.

TABLE 14.2 Neandertals' Adaptations to the Ice Age

A. Biological Trait	Function
Robust and stocky physique	Retained body heat, following Bergmann's Rule
Short forearms and shins	Retained body heat, following Allen's Rule
Large nose	Warmed and moisturized cold, dry air?
Large brain	Aided in conserving body heat?
Early maturation	Allowed early reproduction in order to balance a short life span in a hazardous environment.

B. Cultural or Social Trait	Function
Spears tipped with stone points	Increased success in hunting
Use of animal skins as clothing and possibly shelters	Provided protection from cold and wind
Support and care of old and infirm	Yielded inclusive fitness benefits?

Sources: See references cited in the text.

One additional and intriguing biological adaptation has recently been suggested for the Neandertals. Based on a study of enamel development rates in several fossil and living hominins, it appears that the Neandertals grew up significantly faster than do modern humans (Rozzi and Bermúdez de Castro, 2004). Thus, the Neandertals might have been fully grown by about 15 years of age, rather than the 18 to 20 years of age typical for modern people (Kelley, 2004). It is possible, although not yet conclusively proved, that a faster maturation rate evolved among the Neandertals to allow an earlier start for reproduction and that this was linked to the species' high adult mortality rate (Rozzi and Bermúdez de Castro, 2004). Grow up fast, start breeding early, and die young. Those may, indeed, have been the facts of life for the Neandertals.

Cultural Adaptations: Lithic Technology

The Neandertals' ability to survive and spread throughout the northern latitudes must have been due, at least in part, to cultural advances, and chief among these were new stone-knapping techniques and a variety of new tools. Early in the final glacial cycle, they invented a new stone-working method that brought about the permanent ascendancy of the versatile tools made from flakes over those made by shaping a heavy core. Fine flake tools had now been made for a long time by the Levallois technique, but the new method was more productive (Stringer and Gamble, 1993). Stone tool remains indicate that at this period, people began to trim a nodule of stone around the edges to make a disk-shaped core; then, aiming hammer blows toward the center of the disk, they repeatedly rapped at its edges, knocking off flake after flake until the core was almost entirely used up. Finally, the unfinished flakes were further trimmed so that they had edges for work on wood, carcasses, or hides (Figure 14.12).

The virtue of the new **disk-core technique** was twofold. It permitted the production of large numbers of usable flakes with little effort, and because flakes could be retouched easily so that they had a shape or an edge, the new technique ushered in an era of specialization in tools. Neandertal tool kits were far more versatile than those of earlier peoples. Francois Bordes, a French archaeologist who was at one time the world's foremost expert on Neandertal stone crafting, listed more than 60 distinct types of cutting, scraping, piercing, and gouging tools (Stringer and Gamble, 1993).

Disk-core technique a *Neandertal* stone-knapping method in which a core is trimmed to disk shape and numerous *flakes* are then chipped off; the flakes are then generally retouched.

New weapons may also have been made at this time. Spears were improved when pointed flakes were attached to long pieces of wood by being wedged into the wood or tied with thongs. (The best evidence for this is from the Levant [Shea, 2003].) With such an arsenal of tools, the Neandertals could tap natural resources as never before. Confirming this point, recent archaeological and taphonomic studies conducted in the Middle East by American researchers Curtis Marean and Soo Yeun Kim (1998) and John Shea (1998, 2003) confirm that the Neandertals were active and vigorous hunters (as opposed to mainly scavengers of meat) and that in that area they regularly preyed on herd-dwelling species such as dromedaries, wild horses, and ibexes (see also Marean and Assefa, 1999).

The notion that hunting was among the most important—and in some areas, *the* most important—of the Neandertals' subsistence activities has been strengthened recently by chemical studies done on the fossils from Vindija Cave in Croatia (Richards et al., 2000). Analysis of the stable isotopes of carbon and nitrogen in the collagen of the Vindija people "overwhelmingly points to the Neanderthals behaving as top-level carnivores, obtaining almost all of their dietary protein from animal sources" (Richards et al, 2000:7663). Significantly, much of this meat was apparently obtained at close range, judging from the large numbers of stone spear points at some sites. Dangerous, close-range ambush-style hunting seems to have been a favorite practice of some Neandertal populations (Shea, 2003).

Everywhere north of the Sahara and eastward as far as Teshik-Tash, retouched flakes became the preeminent tools during the late Pleistocene. The tools made within this broad area are collectively placed in the **Mousterian industry** (see Figure 14.12), after the French site of Le Moustier, where such tools were first found in the 1860s. The makers of this wide-ranging culture were usually Neandertals, but in the Middle East, Mousterian tools have also been found in association with early anatomically modern people, and at Jebel Irhoud in Morocco, they were made by *Homo heidelbergensis* (Stringer and Gamble, 1993).

Mousterian industry a *Middle Paleolithic* tool industry from Europe and the Middle East; primarily associated with the *Neandertals*.

The abundance and variety of scrapers in the Neandertals' tool kits confirms our suspicions that these people must have spent enormous amounts of time preparing animal hides for use as loose-fitting clothing and possibly in the construction of shelters. Despite the toll that hide scraping took on their teeth (see Figures 14.9 and 14.10), making clothes of some sort was probably a necessity, at least for the mid-latitude Neandertal populations. A lack of bone needles suggests that skins were not sewn together, however (Tattersall, 1995b). Indeed, in strong contrast to Upper Paleolithic

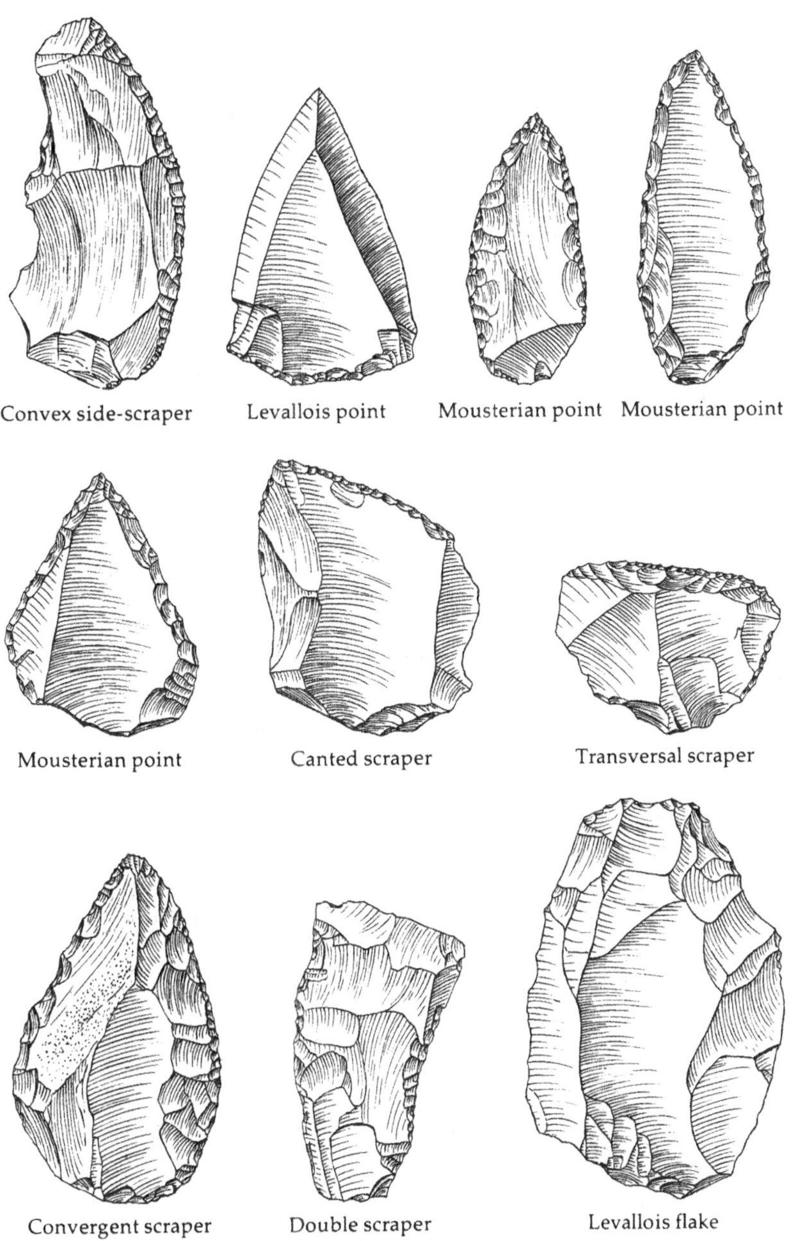

FIGURE 14.12 Flint tools of the typical Mousterian. The points are carefully worked and retouching is expertly done, usually on two sides. These drawings are approximately one-half actual size.

people, the Neandertals made little use of either bone or antler as raw materials for tools. By this time, of course, fire was well under control and no doubt essential for the Neandertals' survival in the very coldest parts of their range.

So much for technology. What other inferences can we draw about Neandertal culture? As it turns out, there are quite a few.

Rituals and Bear Cults

Red ocher a powdered mineral and earth mixture used as a red pigment.

Thirty years ago, it was widely accepted that the Neandertals practiced various forms of rituals to influence their luck and safety in the hunt or to gain power over dangerous predators (Campbell, 1976). Among these supposed rites were magical target practice, which comprised flinging clay pellets at animal-shaped formations deep inside caves, and the ritual butchering of an occasional prey animal, after which it was decorated with **red ocher.** Furthermore, there seemed to be good evidence that the Neandertals treated the skulls and other bones of cave bears in a ritual fashion. At 9 feet (2.7 meters) tall, the cave bear, *Ursus spelaeus,* was a nasty piece of work, and it competed with the Neandertals for cave space. Early twentieth century excavations at the Swiss site of Drachenloch ("Dragons Cave") suggested that Neandertals had ritually arranged bear bones within the cave, including caching them in stone cists dug into the floor. "Thus began the notion of Neandertal `bear cults,' with bears the subject of worship or other ritual activities that maybe included deliberate sacrifice, and that must surely have involved some type of feeling for the spiritual" (Tattersall, 1995b:95). Note that in all of these cases, Neandertal nature was thought to have been basically modern—an assumption that led to the general conclusion that they, like us, tried to manipulate supernatural forces to their advantage.

Unfortunately for the neatness of this picture, an additional three decades of research have shown that virtually *none* of it stands up to close examination and new data. The target practice and ritual butchering interpretations probably were simply the products of excavators' overly active imaginations. And the distribution of bear bones inside the caves turned out to be entirely naturalistic—the result of the bears' own shuffling about, such that skulls were sometimes kicked against the cave walls or under fallen slabs. Particularly telling is the fact that none of the supposed bear cult caves has produced either stone tools or cut-marked bones attesting to human activity (Klein, 1999; Tattersall, 1995b). To borrow a quote from T. H. Huxley (Anonymous, 1955:266), the case for Neandertal hunting/bear rituals was "a beautiful hypothesis [slain] by an ugly fact" (i.e., inadequate proof). Nonetheless, the Neandertals *do* show some evidence of ritual and perhaps even an appreciation of the spiritual, but for that we must turn to their burial practices.

Death and Burials

Of all the various indications of the Neandertals' humanness, their practice of burying their dead, at least on occasion, is perhaps the best documented and easiest to interpret. Death is life's bitterest fact, the inescapable defeat at the end of the long struggle to survive and prosper. Modern humans are universally saddened by death, and the evidence from numerous Neandertal sites strongly indicates that these archaic people felt the same.

The original Neandertal—the fossil from the Neander Valley—had probably been buried, but the excavation was such an accidental and amateurish job that all signs of deliberate interment were destroyed. The remains of Marcellin Boule's La Chapelle man were removed more carefully, and the presence of a burial pit was obvious to the excavator. Demonstrable or probable burials were also found at La Ferrassie, Kebara, Shanidar, Kiik-Koba, Tabūn, Amud, Teshik-Tash, and elsewhere. In all, about 20 well-documented (and several more probable) Mousterian burials are known (Klein, 1999).

Occasionally, a Neandertal site will yield multiple burials, with the most spectacular example being La Ferrassie in France, excavated between 1912 and 1934

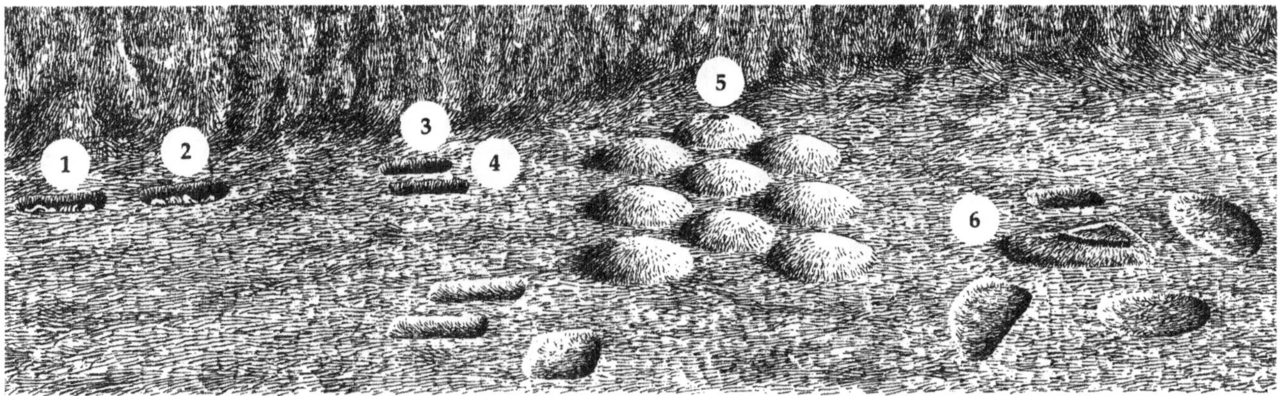

FIGURE 14.13
The care that Neandertals sometimes lavished on their dead seems clear at La Ferrassie, in France. There, archaeologists discovered what may be a 70,000-year-old family cemetery, containing the skeletons of two adults and several children. The drawing here shows a site about 85 feet (26 meters) long. The presumed parents were buried head to head (at locations *1* and *2* in the drawing); two skeletons (*3* and *4*), possibly of their children, each about five years old, were neatly interred near their father's feet. The significance of the nine small mounds is not clear, but one contained the bones of a newborn infant and three flint tools (*5*). The triangular stone (*6*) covered the grave of another child.

(Figure 14.13). At La Ferrassie, seven burials were discovered, including a man, a woman, and five children ranging in age from infancy to about six. One of the children "was headless; the skull was buried a short distance away, covered with a large stone marked with a series of artificial, cuplike depressions" (Trinkaus and Shipman, 1993:255). In addition, flint tools may have been placed in some of the graves. These findings raised numerous questions in the early 1900s, and they still do. Were these people related, thus making this site a family cemetery? Were they the victims of an epidemic or some other calamity? And why was one child's body buried separately from its head? Even today, we still can only speculate about the meaning of the La Ferrassie death assemblage.

The Neandertal burials are, in fact, the oldest known hominin interments, but what, if anything do they tell us about the spiritual beliefs of these people? In answering this intriguing question, researchers have tended to separate into conservative and liberal camps (Klein, 1999; Stringer and Gamble, 1993). The liberals argue that the Neandertals often buried *grave goods* (stone tools and/or meaty animal parts) with their corpses, believing that these items would be useful in some sort of afterlife. Conservatives counter that artifacts and animal bones are common items in the soil surrounding Neandertal graves, and so their occasional presence *in* graves was probably accidental. Liberals point to the occasional lump of red ocher in Middle Eastern graves as an indication that Neandertal corpses were sometimes decorated. (This pigment was definitely so used by early modern humans.) Conservatives respond by pointing to the complete absence of ocher in the graves of European Neandertals. To liberals, the fact that many Neandertal corpses were buried folded into the fetal position suggests a belief in rebirth into an otherworldly afterlife. Conservatives, on the other hand, point out that a flexed corpse needs a smaller grave than an extended one. The bottom line for conservatives is that the Neandertals were probably practicing nonsymbolic and nonreligious corpse disposal (Stringer and Gamble, 1993). The bottom line for liberals is a much more *sapiens*-like interpretation of the Neandertals' behavior and spiritual beliefs.

Perhaps the one burial site that brings the two interpretative camps into strongest opposition is Shanidar Cave in Iraq, excavated by Ralph Solecki between 1951 and

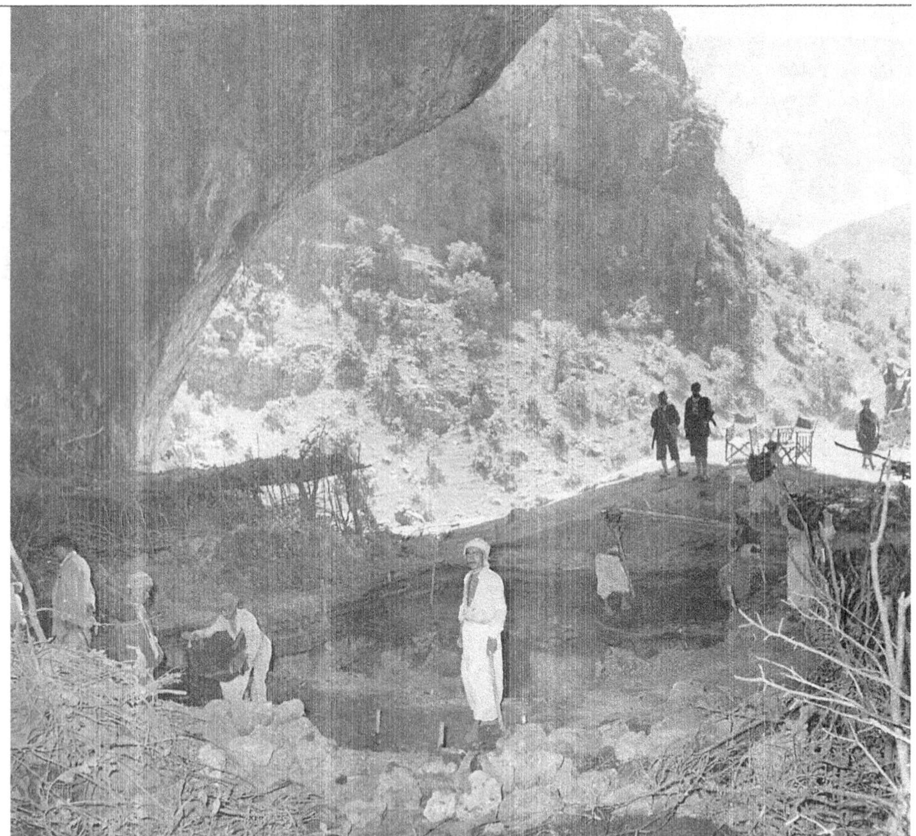

FIGURE 14.14 Just fifty years ago, Kurdish shepherds, shown here helping with the excavations at Shanidar, still used the cave to shelter themselves and their animals during the cold winters, much as their predecessors did thousands of years ago.

1960 (Solecki, 1971; Figure 14.14). At Shanidar, Solecki dug down through compressed deposits to uncover a total of nine burials. At the back of the cave, in a layer estimated to be 50,000 years old, he found the grave of a hunter with a badly crushed skull. As a routine procedure, Solecki collected samples of the soil in and around the grave (shown in Figure 14.15) and sent them to a laboratory at the Musée de l'Homme in France. There, his colleague Arlette Leroi-Gourhan checked the pollen count, hoping it would provide useful information on the prevailing climate and vegetation.

What she found was completely unexpected. Pollen was present in the grave in unprecedented abundance. Even more astonishing, some of it appeared in clusters, and a few clusters had been preserved along with the parts of the flowers that had supported them. Leroi-Gourhan concluded that no birds or animals or wind could possibly have deposited the material in such a way in the recess of the cave. Masses of flowers may have been placed in the grave by the companions of the dead man. Furthermore, the hunter apparently had been laid to rest on a woven bedding of pine boughs and flowers; more blossoms may very well have been strewn over his body.

Microscopic examination of the pollen indicated that it came from numerous species of bright-colored flowers, related to grape hyacinth, bachelor's button, hollyhock, and groundsel. Some of these plants are used in poultices and herbal remedies by contemporary peoples in Iraq. Perhaps the Neandertal mourners, too, believed that the blossoms possessed medicinal properties and added them to the grave in an effort to heal the fallen hunter in the afterlife. On the other hand, the flowers may have been put there in the same spirit that moves people today to place flowers on graves and gravestones.

These are powerful images, suggesting modern reactions to death. But not all researchers agree with Solecki's and Leroi-Gourhan's interpretation. Some prefer instead a completely naturalistic explanation for the pollen distribution patterns,

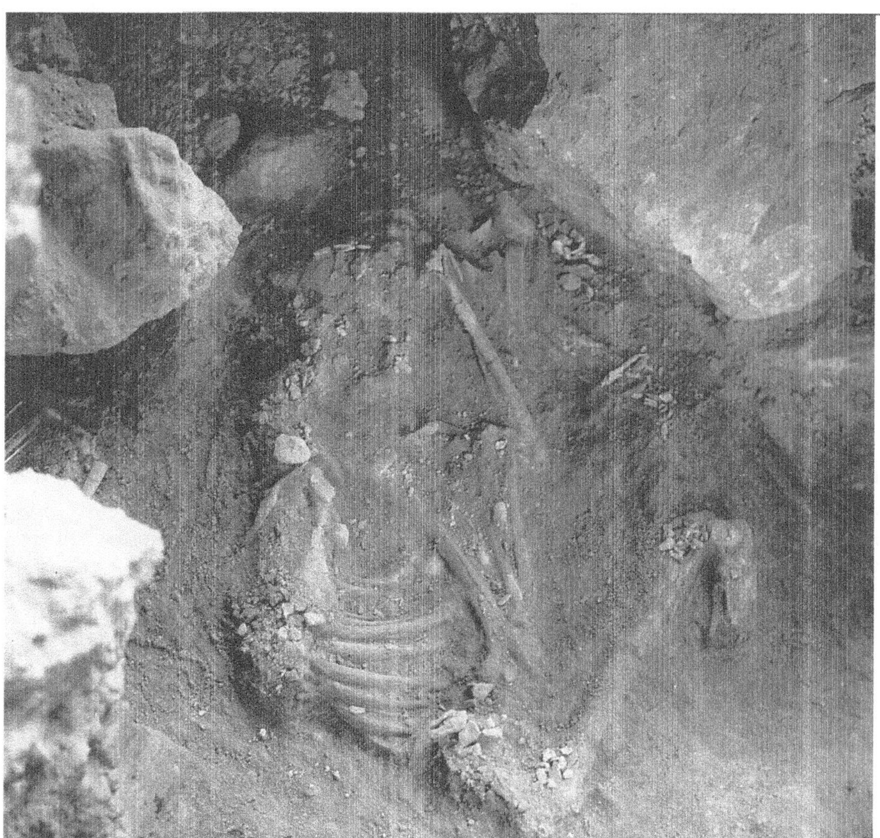

FIGURE 14.15 The skeleton known as Shanidar 4, which pollen tests suggest was buried with bunches of wild flowers related to hyacinths, daisies, and hollyhocks. The age is about 50,000 years.

such as the action of burrowing animals (Stringer and Gamble, 1993). The case of the Shanidar flower burial remains problematic.

To sum up, while there is no doubt that the Neandertals performed some deliberate burials, we have no idea what percentage of corpses were interred. Furthermore, it is unclear whether other older forms of funerary rites were practiced. For example, many (most?) scientists interpret the evidence from the approximately 350,000-year-old site of Sima de los Huesos in Spain as showing corpse disposal of the simplest sort—pitching dead individuals down a deep shaft at the back of a cave. Even there, however, some researchers find room to read funeral rituals into the archaeological evidence (Arsuaga, 2000). In short, the Neandertals' attitudes toward death, the details of their treatment of corpses, and their spiritual nature all remain elusive, despite 150 years of unearthing their remains.

The Old and the Disabled

The burial evidence shows that the Neandertals had sufficient concern for their group mates to occasionally give them ritual treatment at death, but what about during life? Were they, like modern humans, solicitous about one another's health? Or turning to the dark side of human nature, is there evidence that the Neandertals could have been brutally indifferent, perhaps even violent, toward one another?

For many researchers, a clear indication of the Neandertals' humanness was their treatment of old and disabled individuals. The man of La Chapelle-aux-Saints, for instance, was long past his prime when he died. His skeleton reveals that he had been bent over by arthritis and could not possibly have taken part in a hunt (Trinkaus and Shipman, 1993). Even the act of eating must have been difficult for him because he had lost all but two teeth. Had he lived at some earlier time, he might well have been abandoned to starve after his economic usefulness to the group was over. But the Neandertals evidently were not ruled by such stern logic. This man's companions unselfishly provided food, and they probably even softened it for him by partially chewing it.

Another possible instance of caring Neandertals comes from the Bau de l'Aubesier rock shelter in southern France. There, excavators recovered a jawbone that was toothless and diseased, suggesting that the individual would have needed help to acquire and ingest food (Lebel and Trinkaus, 2002). Other scholars have argued, however, that since the occasional nonhuman primate can survive in the wild without teeth, mandibles such as that from l'Aubesier do not provide convincing evidence for the Neandertals' care of the disabled (DeGusta, 2003).

Concern for the disabled is suggested also by remains at Shanidar. Some of the bones found there belonged to a 40-year-old man who was probably killed by a rockfall. Study of his skeleton revealed that before his accidental death, he had had the use of only one arm; his right arm and shoulder were poorly developed, probably because of an accident in childhood or a birth defect. Despite the major disability, he lived to a ripe age. His front teeth were unusually worn, suggesting that he spent much of his time chewing animal hides to soften them for use as clothes or perhaps that he used his teeth in lieu of his arm to hold objects (Solecki, 1971).

Evidence of Violence

The fact that the Neandertals and other early humans could find a place in their society for aged and disabled individuals does not necessarily mean that they were always full of love for one another. Indeed, at many sites, there is evidence of the violent side of Neandertal nature. For example, at Shanidar, one of the ribs of the fossil of a hunter was deeply grooved by the point of a weapon, probably a wooden spear. The top had penetrated the man's chest and perhaps punctured a lung, but this hunter had somehow survived the wound, for the bone showed signs of healing (Solecki, 1971). The original Neandertal man from Germany had also survived a grievous injury, although his recovery was incomplete: His left elbow bones were so misshapen that he could not have raised his hand to his mouth (Day, 1965). Whether the damage was done by human or beast or accident will never be known.

Evidence of Cannibalism?

That archaic people sometimes killed one another should surprise no one, and the suggestion has already been made for *Homo heidelbergensis* that they also occasionally ate one another. *Occasionally* seems to be the operative word here, however, because despite several Neandertal sites having been claimed to reveal evidence of cannibalism, few such claims have withstood close scrutiny (Klein, 1999).

Perhaps the best evidence for cannibalistic practices comes from the Croatian site of Krapina and the French site of Moula-Guercy. At Krapina, the Neandertal remains were scattered, disarticulated, and smashed. Long bones had been splintered in a way that allowed access to the edible marrow, and some bones showed signs of having been cut with stone tools or burned (Trinkaus and Shipman, 1993). The original excavator of Krapina, Karl Dragutin Gorjanovic-Kramberger, speculated that the local Neandertals "ate their fellow tribesmen, and what's more, they cracked open the hollow bones and sucked out the marrow" (Trinkaus and Shipman, 1993:170). On the face of it, this evidence seems to present a good case for cannibalism. Nonetheless, skeptics have counterargued that the Krapina bones may simply reflect crushing by rock falls and the defleshing of skeletons as part of a funerary ritual (Klein, 1999). Since neither argument can be proved conclusively, the Krapina case remains equivocal.

More convincing evidence of Neandertal cannibalism has come from Moula-Guercy in the Ardèche region of France (Defleur et al., 1999). Careful excavation and analysis has shown that 100,000 years ago, Neandertals there butchered their own kind using exactly the same methods they applied to deer carcasses. To be specific, they hacked off other Neandertals' arms and feet, removed their jaw muscles from their skull vaults, cut out their tongues, and defleshed their thighs. Unlike the suggestion for Krapina, the researchers found "no evidence that modifications to the [hominin] . . . bones from Moula-Guercy represent any form of mortuary ritual" (Defleur et al., 1999:131). Whether this demonstrable cannibalism at the French site was the result of limited food resources or other factors could not be determined.

In sum, as we might have predicted, given their similarity and close relationship to modern humans, the Neandertals were apparently capable of both humane acts and acts of utter brutality. These findings may give us some insights into the Neandertal mind, but first, we need to look at one or two more aspects of material culture.

Beginnings of Art and Music?

As will be explained in Chapter 16, one of the hallmarks of the Upper Paleolithic was a dramatic flowering of art—engravings, statuary, and magnificent cave paintings. A few tantalizing artifacts suggest that the Neandertals may have dabbled in art just before and coincidental to the arrival of modern humans, but they managed only a generally low level of accomplishment (Gibbons, 2001; Tattersall, 1995).

As noted earlier, the Neandertals occasionally made use of such natural pigments as red and yellow ocher and black manganese. These occur at Neandertal sites in powder form and sometimes in pencil-shaped pieces that show signs of being rubbed on a soft surface, such as human skin or animal hides (Klein, 1999).

There is no sign of a representational engraving or statuary from this era, but there are a few indications that the Neandertals were beginning to sense the visual possibilities of the materials around them. Several Neandertal sites have produced objects claimed to be simple works of art, including perforated and grooved animal bones and teeth and incised pebbles and bones (Klein, 1999). Almost all of these objects are vulnerable to naturalistic explanations of production, however, and so by themselves do not confirm an artistic streak in Neandertal nature.

Without a doubt, the best evidence for Neandertal art comes from the Chatelperronian industry (discussed in Chapter 15), a regional tool culture from southwest France and Spain that dates to about 40,000 to 27,000 BP. At the site of Arcy-sur-Cure in the Paris basin, 34,000-year-old Neandertal remains have been found in association with "a rich bone industry as well as personal ornaments" (Hublin et al., 1996:224). Among the Arcy-sur-Cure artifacts is a fairly elaborately carved bone ornament (Figure 14.16), as well as dozens of other "animal teeth and pieces of ivory, bone, or shell that are pierced or grooved, presumably for hanging as beads or pendants" (Klein, 2000:31). Interestingly, the Chatelperronian culture also produced certain stone tools (blade tools, including burins) that are usually associated with the Upper Paleolithic and anatomically modern people, as well as evidence for shelter construction (Klein, 2000).

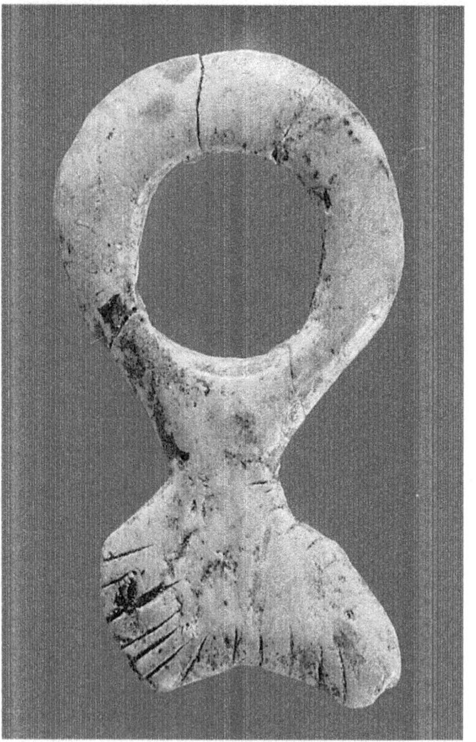

FIGURE 14.16
This carved bone pendant comes from the site of Arcy-sur-Cure (France). Dating to 34,000 years BP, it is thought by some archaeologists to be the work of Neandertals who had been exposed to the culture of Upper Paleolithic *Homo sapiens*. This photograph is not to scale.

The intriguing and unanswered question about the Chatelperronian culture is whether it represents artistic and technological innovation among the late Neandertals or a case of archaic humans borrowing Upper Paleolithic cultural traits from anatomically modern people who, by that time, were also residing in Southwestern Europe. By itself, the eleventh-hour show of artistic activity by the Chatelperronian people does not substantiate the broader claim of the Neandertals as artists.

But if examples of material art are scanty, evidence of the performing arts—music, song, dance—was nonexistent for the Neandertals until just recently. In 1995, the Neandertal cave site of Divje Babe I in northwestern Slovenia (Figure 14.5) yielded a fragmentary cave bear bone that was perforated with four round holes, all nicely aligned and on one side. After making comparisons with similar Upper Paleolithic objects, the bone's discoverer, paleontologist Ivan Turk of the Slovenian Academy of Sciences, concluded that it is probably all that is left of a Neandertal flute (Wilford, 1996). If Turk is correct, the Divje Babe I artifact, dated to 82,000 to 43,000 years BP, is not simply the oldest but also the only evidence for music making by the Neandertals. Marcel Otte (2000), of the Université of Liège, also believes the bone fragment is a Mousterian musical instrument. Commenting on the find, University of Washington paleoanthropologist Erik Trinkaus noted that the flute "reinforces the basic humanness of the Neandertals" (Wilford, 1996).

The notion of Neandertal-as-musician has not gone unchallenged, however. Three years after the Divje Babe I flute was discovered, a detailed taphonomic analysis of the bone was done by French researcher Francesco d'Errico and his colleagues (d'Errico et al., 1998). This study made a strong case for the flute being nothing more than a bear bone that had been gnawed and punctured by other carnivores (probably other bears). If d'Errico et al. are right, the beginnings of music cannot be detected until the Upper Paleolithic, and a claimed *sapiens*-like trait of the Neandertals is refuted.

Society, Language, and Mind

Average cognitive group size among the Neandertals has been estimated at about 144 individuals (Aiello and Dunbar, 1993). This is very similar to the cognitive groups of modern people, but whether it reflects the actual size of a Neandertal band or has any relation to regional population size is difficult to say. One thing that can be concluded, however, is that Neandertal bands probably lacked internal differentiation. The scarcity of markers of social stratification (e.g., personal ornamentation, elaborate burials, etc.) suggests that these people lived in egalitarian bands. Furthermore, with regard to population size, the frequency and distribution of Neandertal sites suggests that these people were less numerous overall than their anatomically modern successors, perhaps because they were less efficient at exploiting the available food resources (Klein, 1999). The Neandertals were mobile hunting-and-gathering people who lived off the land season by season. They appear to have lacked the strategies and/or the technology to store food stocks (meat, marrow, grease) against lean-season shortages (Marean and Assefa,1999; Stringer and Gamble, 1993).

There is also evidence that the Neandertals lived out their lives much more locally than their anatomically modern successors. Archaeologists have determined that raw materials, such as flint for tools, were moved much shorter distances during Neandertal times than during the Upper Paleolithic (Stringer and Gamble, 1993). (Note, however, that the Neandertals' hunting ranges may have been bigger than those of their Upper Paleolithic successors [Marean and Assefa, 1999].) We are left with the impression that the Neandertals lived a local, small-group, low-population-density existence and that they made the implements and other items that they needed to survive but little else.

The relatively simple Neandertal lifestyle—simple, that is, compared to that of Upper Paleolithic *Homo sapiens* (see Chapters 15 and 16)—*may* have been related to simplicity in communication. It has been suggested that the Neandertals had a primitive configuration of the vocal tract and therefore could not produce the full range of modern vowel sounds (Lieberman, 2002; Tattersall, 1995b). Furthermore, as discussed in a later section, it may also have been the case that the Neandertal mind was limited in its speech information storage capacity compared to modern people (Wynn and Coolidge, 2004). The question of speech–language modernity has not been conclusively answered, however, and evidence from the size of the Neandertal hypoglossal canal (Kay et al., 1998) suggests relatively sophisticated communication skills, as does the size of the cognitive group (Aiello and Dunbar, 1993).

The question of the Neandertal mind is particularly interesting, and in a recent paper, anthropologist Thomas Wynn and psychologist Frederick Coolidge (2004) joined forces to probe its nature and to compare it to the mind of living humans. Using theories and techniques from cognitive neuropsychology, cognitive anthropology, and cognitive archaeology, Wynn and Coolidge produced a fascinating and informative picture of Neandertal mentality.

Wynn and Coolidge's primary question was whether Neandertals differed from modern humans in the quantity and quality of their *working memory.* In this study, working memory was conceived as a three-part cognitive system combining *central executive functioning* (controlling attention to task and decision making) with two so-called "slave" systems: a *phonological loop* (articulatory storage that functions to hold and use speech-based information) and a *visuospatial loop* (storage providing "an interface for visual and spatial information" [2004:469]). Furthermore, two sorts of working memory were recognized: *long-term working memory* (L-TWM), which is concerned with expert cognition (the storage of knowledge about technical skills, such as stone knapping), and *enhanced working memory* (EWM), which allows complex communication, cultural creativity, and conscious experimentation.

Based on their analysis of Mousterian lithic technology, Wynn and Coolidge concluded that the Neandertals had achieved the same level of expert technical cognition (based on L-TWM) as modern humans. But while "[such] expert cognition was very effective and flexible, and able to deal with all of the problems of Neandertal life, . . . [it did not produce] regular innovation and experimentation" (2004:478). The Neandertals' material culture varied and changed "on a scale and at a rate that would appear to rule out conscious experimentation and creativity. These are . . . the stuff of enhanced working memory" (2004:476).

Wynn and Coolidge hypothesized that the modern human EWM first appeared some 100,000 to 50,000 years ago as the result of a relatively minor genetic mutation among early *Homo sapiens* people. This mutation is thought to have affected mainly the phonological loop of the cognitive system and therefore to have had its most significant impact on language. "Increased phonological storage may have allowed modern humans greater [long-term] articulatory . . . storage, greater self-reflection, . . . the beginnings of introspection, . . . increases in syntactical complexity, . . . [and] greater morphemological richness" (2004:481). Compared to the Neandertals, early modern people's declarative sentences probably contained more information, their commands were probably more complex, and their questions probably asked for more specific information. Wynn and Coolidge concluded that "the language of Neandertals may have been pragmatically restricted to declarative, imperative, and exclamatory modes of speech. Interrogative speech was probably more limited, and . . . subjunctive speech ["what if" statements] may have been non-existent or severely limited, as was the use of the future tense" (2004:482).

This study thus provides neuropsychological support for the anatomical evidence (discussed earlier) that Neandertals did not have fully modern language. Furthermore, it links limited language capacities with relative cultural stagnation among the Neandertals. The idea that a language-enhancing mutation might have jump-started the cultural explosion that occurred after the appearance of *Homo sapiens* will be discussed in more detail in the next chapter.

Finally, based on their analysis of the Neandertals' culture and mind, Wynn and Coolidge inferred the following personality traits for these archaic humans: "bravery, low levels of harm avoidance, . . . perhaps greater difficulties in making cost-benefit analyses, . . . stoicism, . . . [and perhaps] cruelty" (2004:479). These traits served the Neandertals well in their dangerous and violent hunting-and-gathering lifestyle, and to some extent, they are all found among modern people. As a suite of traits, however—a personality profile, if you will—they do seem to separate the Neandertals from their modern cousins.

The Neandertals' Evolutionary Fate

As outlined in Chapter 12, we believe that the Neandertals were one of two species of hominans to descend (at different times and probably in different places) from *Homo heidelbergensis* (see Figure 12.9). The other species, of course, was *Homo sapiens*, and exactly how modern people are related to the Neandertals—as evolutionary sister species, perhaps, or as their partial descendants—will be discussed in detail in the next chapter. In any event, two important conclusions can be reached at this point.

First, the Neandertals were a separate species from anatomically modern humans: *Homo neanderthalensis* versus *Homo sapiens*. In the last few years, researchers have been able to extract mitochondrial DNA (**mtDNA**) from the bones of three different Neandertal specimens, as well as two early modern humans dated approximately 24,000 years BP (Caramelli et al., 2003; Krings et al., 1997; Ovchinnikov et al., 2000). Cross-species comparisons revealed that the Neandertals were similar to one another in their mtDNA profiles but significantly different from both modern humans and anatomically modern near-contemporaries (Cro-Magnons; see Chapter 15). These results strongly suggest that the Neandertals were a separate species of hominans from *Homo sapiens* (but see Relethford, 2001), a conclusion that is reinforced by the distinct anatomical differences between these two human types. This taxonomic arrangement has widely replaced an older classification of the Neandertals as an archaic subspecies of *Homo sapiens*: *H. sapiens neanderthalensis*. Reference to the Neandertals as "archaic *Homo sapiens*" can still be found in some texts, however (e.g., Stanford et al., 2006).

mtDNA genetic material found in the *mitochondria* of cells.

Second, it is clear that the Neandertals went extinct just after 30,000 years ago. The circumstances of their disappearance and replacement by modern people are hazy, however, and in Chapter 15, we will discuss the possibility that, distinct species or not, some "gene leakage" might have occurred between Neandertals and Cro-Magnons around 30,000 years ago.

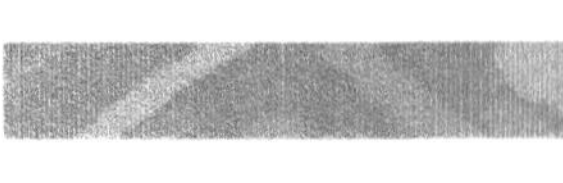

Summary

The Neandertals descended from *Homo heidelbergensis* stock 350,000 years ago or just a bit earlier. The exact point of origin is not known, but the oldest Neandertal specimens are from the Sima de los Huesos site in Spain. Between their origin and their disappearance around 27,000 years BP, the Neandertals spread all across Europe, Western Asia, and the Middle East. An anatomically distinctive hominan species, the Neandertals showed numerous biological adaptations for cold weather living. Their bodies were stocky and short limbed to enhance heat retention, and their noses were large and protruding, possibly for warming and moisturizing cold air. The Neandertals possessed a remarkably large brain, but their cranial anatomy was different than that of *Homo sapiens* (long, low skulls with large brows) and their language and mental processing (mind) may well have been limited compared to modern people.

Making their living by hunting and gathering, the Neandertals produced a distinctive lithic culture called the Mousterian. Other than their stone tools, however, their material culture was quite limited. Only near the end of their tenure as a species did the Neandertals produce any evidence of art, and then, it was possibly in imitation of contemporary modern people. The Neandertals did practice deliberate burial, however, at least on occasion, although precisely what this tells us about their spiritual nature (if any) is unclear. They also occasionally engaged in cannibalism, but again, the circumstances and meaning of this practice are unclear. Mitochondrial DNA analyses have shown that the Neandertals were a separate species, *Homo ne-*

anderthalensis, from modern people. It seems unlikely that they made a substantial genetic contribution to modern Europeans, but the possibility of some limited interbreeding with the Cro-Magnons cannot be conclusively disproved.

Upon the demise of the Neandertals some 27,000 years ago, anatomically modern humans—*Homo sapiens*—became the undisputed dominant hominin species on earth. But given the recent announcement of the dwarfed form *Homo floresiensis,* they were apparently not the only human type alive. It is to the appearance of *Homo sapiens* that we now turn.

Postscript

Humans are simultaneously fascinated and horrified by the thought of cannibalism. It's one of those "Ugh, that's awful . . . but please tell me more!" kinds of topics. We wince and grimace, but we read every gory detail about survival cannibalism following a plane crash or the possibility of ritual cannibalism in cultures other than our own. We can't imagine being cannibals ourselves, but for some reason, we are fascinated that others might be now or might have been in the past. That fascination has led to numerous allegations of cannibalism but to little universally accepted evidence for the practice either historically or prehistorically. That situation may be changing, however.

Some scholars, such as American anthropologist William Arens, believe that cannibalism has rarely been practiced by humankind. In his 1979 book *The Man-Eating Myth,* Arens concluded that "the available evidence does not permit the facile assumption that [cannibalism] was or has ever been a prevalent cultural feature. It is more reasonable to conclude that the idea of the cannibalistic nature of others is a myth" (Arens, 1979:182). These sentiments were echoed by British researcher Paul Bahn of Hull University: "There are no reliable first-hand witnesses of [cannibalism], and almost all [historical and ethnographic] reports are based on hearsay" (Bahn, 1992:330).

Contrary to the position taken by Arens and Bahn, however, many anthropologists, are beginning to get comfortable with the notion that throughout history, hominins may occasionally have eaten one another. There is the evidence that the Bodo *Homo heidelbergensis* specimen was scalped and that the Neandertals at Krapina and Moula-Guercy ate human flesh. Some have argued that there is evidence for cannibalism from the American Southwest, as well.

Working with prehistoric remains from the Four Corners area (where New Mexico, Arizona, Utah, and Colorado join), Christy Turner of Arizona State University and the late Jacqueline Turner developed a *minimal taphonomic signature* for determining whether cannibalism had occurred at a prehistoric site. As described in their 1999 book *Man Corn,* before cannibalism can be accepted as probable, six features of perimortem (near-death) bone damage have to be present: (1) extensive breakage, (2) cut marks, (3) anvil abrasions (marks made when bones scoot across an anvil as they are smashed), (4) burning, (5) pot polish (a characteristic polish that develops on the tips of bone fragments as they are cooked in a pottery vessel), and (6) many missing vertebrae (which have a tendency to be smashed to bits as the bones are being prepared for cooking). Using this yardstick, the Turners claim to have documented cannibalism in several dozen sites dating between 800 and 1,100 years ago. The Turners do not believe that this cannibalism was a response to starvation conditions but rather that it was a combination of religious rituals and social control that was brought into the Southwest by immigrants from Mesoamerica. (It should be noted that the Turners' claims are not without controversy among archaelogists.)

On balance, therefore, the evidence suggests that cannibalism has occurred occasionally among recent people and among our evolutionary forebears. (This includes chimpanzees, who occasionally eat one another.) The circumstances of eating human flesh may include dire emergencies, rituals, prolonged shortages of other food sources, and the desire to terrorize and control enemy groups. It appears that cannibalism is an unpleasant but sometimes real component of human behavior.

Review Questions

1. Describe the culture of the Neandertals, including both its material and behavioral aspects. Argue for or against the notion that the Neandertals were behaviorally human in the modern sense.
2. Describe how the Neandertals treated their dead. Were they actually practicing burial rites or simply corpse disposal? (Be sure to include the Sima de los Huesos Neandertals in your analysis.) Do you think the Neandertals' treatment of the dead reveals a developing spirituality? Why or why not?
3. From 1911 to 1913, Marcellin Boule described the Neandertals as "bestial" creatures who represented "an inferior type [of hominid] closer to the Apes than to any other human group." Based on your knowledge of Neandertal anatomy and culture, how would you respond to Boule?
4. Describe the distinctive anatomical features of the Neandertals. Which ones seem clearly to be adaptations to cold weather living? How did the Neandertals differ physically from their *Homo heidelbergensis* ancestors?
5. What conclusions have researchers reached about the functioning of the Neandertal mind? What evidence (if any) is there that these archaic humans differed mentally from modern people?
6. Could the Neandertals talk? And if so, how well? Compare the speech and language skills of the Neandertals with those of modern humans.

SUGGESTED FURTHER READING

Solecki, Ralph. *Shanidar: The First Flower People.* New York, Knopf, 1971.

Stringer, Christopher, and Clive Gamble. *In Search of the Neandertals.* New York, Thames & Hudson, 1993.

Tattersall, Ian. *The Last Neanderthal.* New York, Macmillan, 1995.

Trinkaus, Erik, and Pat Shipman. *The Neandertals.* New York, Knopf, 1993.

Turner, II, Christy, and Jacqueline Turner. *Man Corn.* Salt Lake City, University of Utah Press, 1999.

White, Tim. *Prehistoric Cannibalism at Mancos 5MTUMR-2346.* Princeton, Princeton University Press, 1992.

INTERNET RESOURCES

Homo neanderthalensis

www.mnh.si.edu/anthro/humanorigins/ha/neand.htm

This is another Smithsonian Institution hominin site, with information and photos of Neandertal fossils.

ARCHAEOLOGY.INFO: *Homo neanderthalensis*

www.archaeologyinfo.com/homoneaderthalensis.htm

This description by C. D. Kreger provides anatomical details for this interesting hominan species.

THE EXPERT NEANDERTAL MIND

http://web.uccs.edu/twynn/Expert.htm

This 2004 article provides an interesting and important analysis of Neandertal cognition.

ATAPUERCA: SIMA DE LOS HUESOS: THE PIT OF BONES
www.amnh.org/exhibitions/atapuerca/sima/index.php
This page is sponsored by the American Museum of Natural History and describes one of the oldest Neandertal sites in Europe.

CAVE BEARS
www.personal.psu.edu/users/w/x/wxk116/cavebears
An interesting description of these creatures, whose remains are often found in Neandertal and Cro-Magnon sites.

CAVE FINDS REVIVE NEANDERTAL CANNIBALISM
www.sciencenews.org/pages/sn_arc99/10_2_99/fob4.htm
Did the Neandertals occasionally eat one another? This article explores the question.

ART: EVOLUTION OR REVOLUTION?
http://cas.bellarmine.edu/tietjen/images/art(evolution_or_revolution).htm
This web site explores the topic of the beginning of art and whether the Neandertals made a contribution.

USEFUL SEARCH TERMS:
Homo neanderthalensis
La Chapelle-aux-Saints
Marcellin Boule
Mousterian culture
Neandertals
Sima de los Huesos (Atapuerca)

Chapter 14 Timeline

Period / Years	Years BP	Industry	Fossils and Artifacts
HOLOCENE			
10,000			
UPPER PALEOLITHIC			
40,000			
MIDDLE PALEOLITHIC	28,000	Chatelperronian culture	Vindija (possible cannibalism)
	30,000		Arcy-sur-Cure art
			St. Césaire
	40,000		Le Moustier
			La Chapelle
250,000	50,000	Mousterian Industry in Middle East and Europe	Shanidar flower burial
			La Ferrassie
			Shanidar fossils
			Charred skulls at Hortus
			Tabūn
Homo erectus at Zhoukoudian			La Quina, Spy fossils
500,000			Teshik-Tash goat horn burial
			Disk-core technique of tool making originated
			Kiik-Koba burials
			Skhūl, Qafzeh burials
	100,000		
	150,000		Moula-Guercy cannibalism
	200,000		
	250,000		Levallois technique originated
1 million *Paranthropus* extinct	300,000		
LOWER PALEOLITHIC	350,000	Acheulean Industry	Sima de los Huesos fossils and corpse disposal
	400,000		
	450,000		
1.5 million			
Acheulean industry originated *H. erectus* in Africa, the Caucasus, and Java			
1.8 million			

NEANDERTAL DISCOVERIES AND CULTURE

Chapter 15

The Final Transformation: The Evolution of Modern Humans

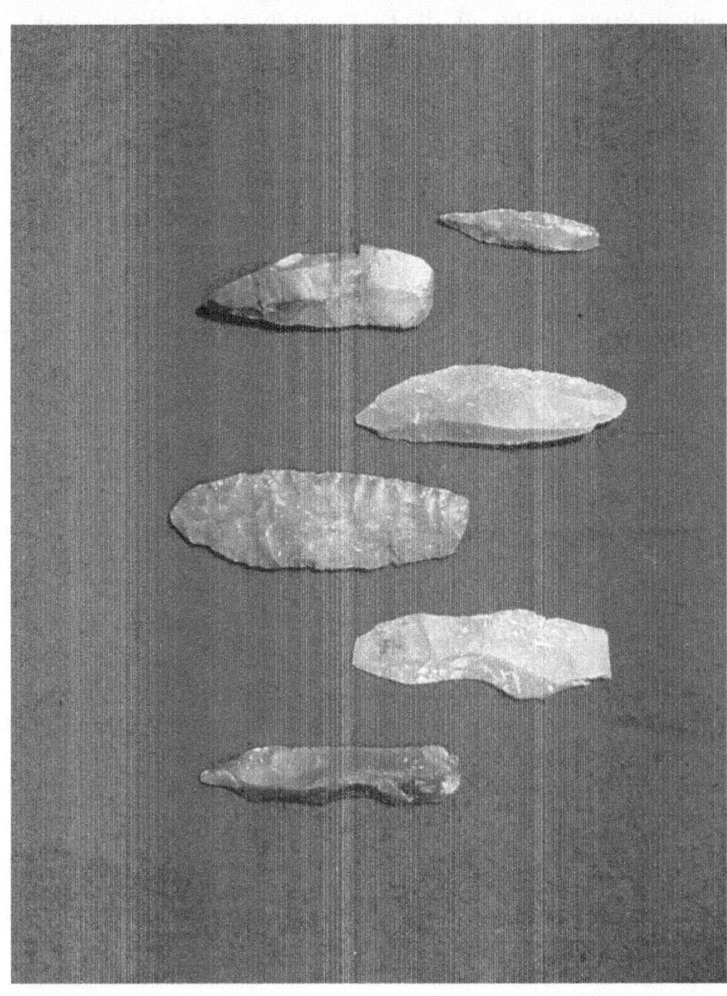

Blade tools from the Upper Paleolithic in France.

The troubles of our proud and angry dust are from eternity, and shall not fail.
Bear them, we can, and if we can we must.

A. E. Housman, 1859–1936. *Last Poems*, ix.

Overview

It appears that fully modern people (*Homo sapiens*) evolved from *Homo heidelbergensis* stock around 195,000 years ago, but the details—biological, cultural, and geographic—of that transformation are matters of considerable controversy. Two major evolutionary scenarios are currently being debated. The multiregional model holds that modern humans evolved more or less independently in several geographic regions, the species' unity being maintained by gene flow. In contrast, the so-called Out of Africa model holds that anatomically modern people evolved only once, most likely in Africa or the Middle East, and then spread quickly across the Old World, replacing all nonmodern hominins. The amount of interbreeding, if any, between resident nonmoderns (archaics) and invading moderns is a matter of great controversy.

This chapter discusses the evidence—cultural, anatomical, molecular, and fossil—supporting these competing evolutionary models. In addition, the spread of modern humans to the Americas and to Australia is described.

Early Discoveries of Anatomically Modern People

In recent years, prehistorians have begun to seek the origins of modern humankind in diverse parts of the globe: Africa, Asia, and Australia. But the story of the discovery of early modern remains begins in the Dordogne region of France (Figure 15.1), where archaeologists have excavated and analyzed and argued since 1868, when the first site was laid bare. This important discovery takes us back again to the nineteenth century, 12 years after the first Neandertal find but still long before anyone really understood its implications or the full meaning of human evolution.

Discovery in the Dordogne

The first discovery of modern human fossils was made by railway workers cutting into a hillside just outside the village of Les Eyzies, France. From an overhanging rock shelter in one of the region's many limestone cliffs came bones and what looked like stone tools. Scientists summoned to the site soon uncovered the remains of at

Mini-TIMELINE

Date (Years BP)	Evolutionary Events or Cultural Developments
12,500	Native Americans at Monte Verde (Chile)
38,000–18,000	*Homo floresiensis* present on Flores
40,000–10,000	Upper Paleolithic in Europe
40,000–20,000	Possible time of first human migration into the Americas
55,000	Humans present in Northern Australia
195,000	Oldest fossils of anatomically modern humans
200,000	Possible start of *Homo heidelbergensis–Homo sapiens* speciation event

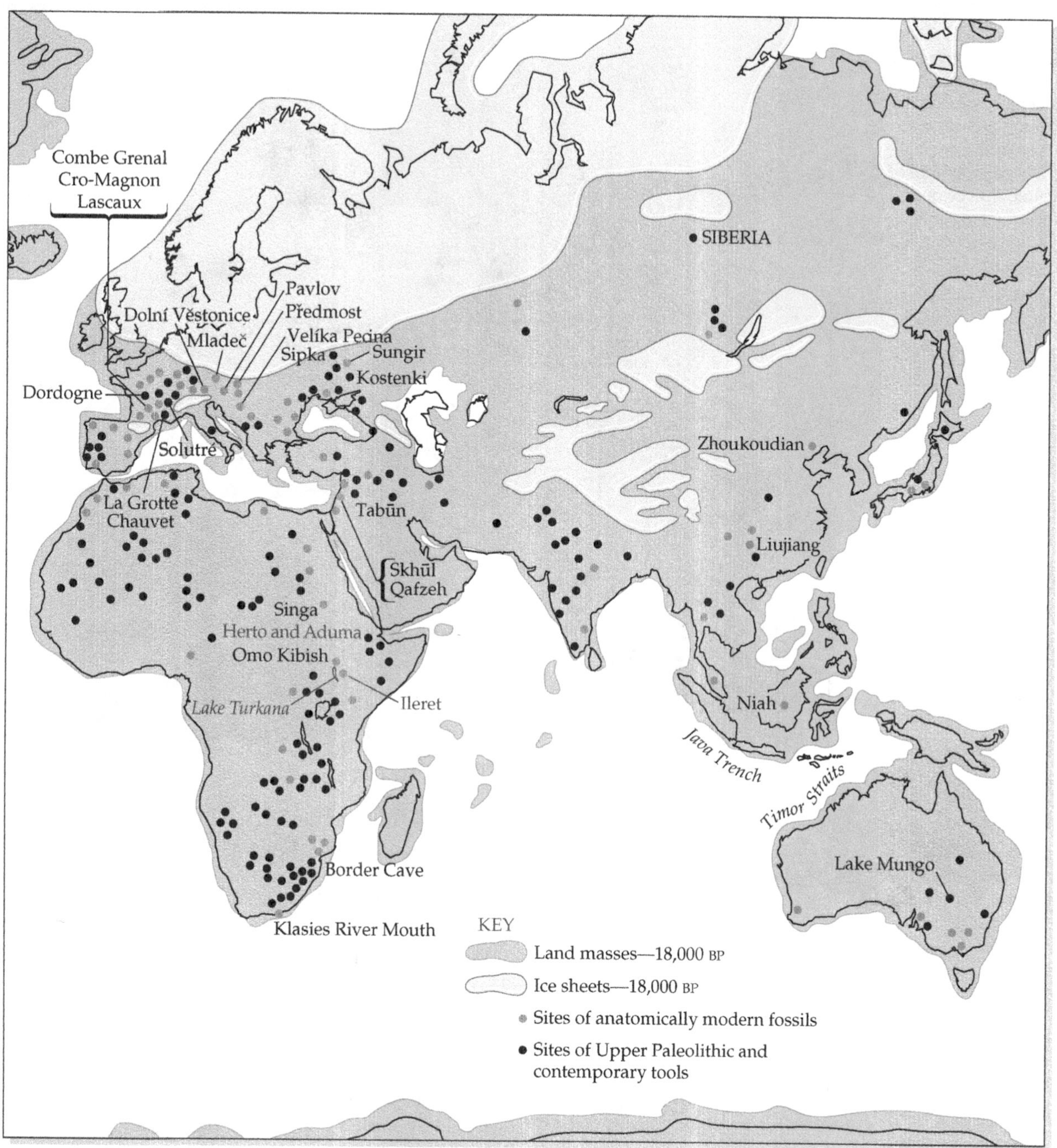

FIGURE 15.1
Anatomically modern fossils and related archaeological sites are today being discovered in many regions of the Old World. Humans of modern aspect lived in many places and varied environments, and their population and technology rapidly developed.

least five human skeletons: a middle-aged man, two younger men, a young woman, and a young child (Klein, 1999). The skeletons were similar to those of modern humans and were buried with flint tools and weapons, seashells pierced with holes, and animal teeth similarly perforated to make ornaments (Day, 1965).

The name of the rock shelter was Cro-Magnon, and that label was affixed to these newfound humans. In the succeeding years, the name was broadened to

FIGURE 15.2
Excavation of a rock shelter in the Dordogne called Abri Pataud. A steel grid has been constructed to enable the excavator to plot the depth and position of every fragment of archaeological evidence. The overhanging limestone cliffs extend upward and outward.

include all anatomically modern people inhabiting Europe between about 40,000 and 10,000 years ago, during a period technically known as the **Upper Paleolithic.**

Upper Paleolithic a period of stone tool manufacture in the Old World that lasted from about 40,000 to 10,000 BP; associated primarily with anatomically modern humans.

The limestone cliffs and caves in the Dordogne region seem particularly adaptable to human habitation (see Figure 15.2). Some of the caves and rock shelters are high on cliff faces and therefore effectively commanded the approach of animals, friends, and enemies. Additionally, the entire Dordogne must have been exceptionally rich in natural resources. The mountains to the east of Les Eyzies would have provided good summer hunting of reindeer, horses, and bison. To the west, the coastal plain stretching toward the Atlantic would also have been good grazing (and thus good hunting) ground. And finally, streams such as the Vézère River would have provided abundant aquatic resources for humans clever enough to harvest them.

And it is clear that the Cro-Magnon people *were* clever. They were, after all, us—*Homo sapiens*, anatomically modern humans. Their bodies were different from those of their forebearers, and their culture was considerably more complex. Indeed, the culture of the Cro-Magnons, as well as that of early moderns from Africa and elsewhere, showed such a spurt of elaboration that an entire chapter will be devoted to its description (Chapter 16). Leading up to that, the present chapter will concentrate on a survey of early *Homo sapiens* fossils, the various models put forth to explain how archaic people evolved into modern ones, and the anatomical changes that the transition involved.

Before we begin, however, it is important to point out that the Cro-Magnon remains *do not* represent the absolute oldest *Homo sapiens* specimens, only the first ones to be discovered. The inhabitants of the Cro-Magnon cave lived about 30,000 years ago (Klein, 1999), and as shown by the brief list of discoveries in Table 15.1, anatomically modern humans had existed for well over 160 millennia before that.

TABLE 15.1 A Partial Record of Fossil *Homo sapiens* Sites

Site	Age (Years BP)
Africa	
Omo Kibish, Ethiopia	195,000
Herto, Ethiopia	160,000–154,000
Klasies River Mouth, South Africa	115,000–60,000
Border Cave, South Africa	90,000–50,000
Middle East	
Skhūl and Qafzeh, Israel	120,000–80,000
Europe	
Bacho Kiro, Bulgaria	39,000–29,000
Asia	
Liujiang, China	30,000–10,000
Zhoukoudian, China (Upper Cave)	29,000–11,000
Australia and Indonesia	
Niah Cave, Borneo	~40,000
Lake Mungo, Australia	40,000

Sources: Bowler et al., 2003; Center for the Study of Chinese Prehistory; Churchill and Smith, 2000; Conroy, 1997; Klein, 1999; McDougall et al., 2005; White et al., 2003.

The Anatomy of *Homo sapiens*

What do all of these hominans—from the 195,000-year-old Omo Kibish people to modern humans beings around the world—have in common? What anatomical traits, in other words, are diagnostic for our species? Interestingly, this is actually a fairly difficult question to answer because of the extensive variability seen in *Homo sapiens'* anatomy—chronologically, geographically, and between people from the same population (Wood and Richmond, 2000). Nonetheless, even a fuzzy set of diagnostic traits is better than none, and therefore our inventory of such traits is shown in the following list (see also Figure 15.3, Box 15.1, and Appendix 3; primary sources for traits include Lieberman et al. [2002], Wood and Richmond [2000], and Wynn and Coolidge [2004]).

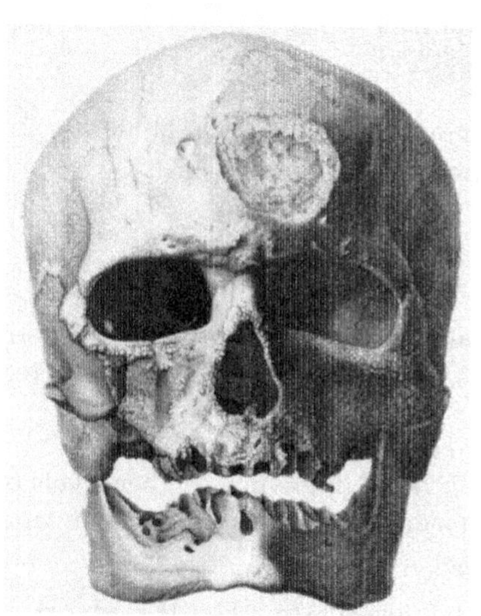

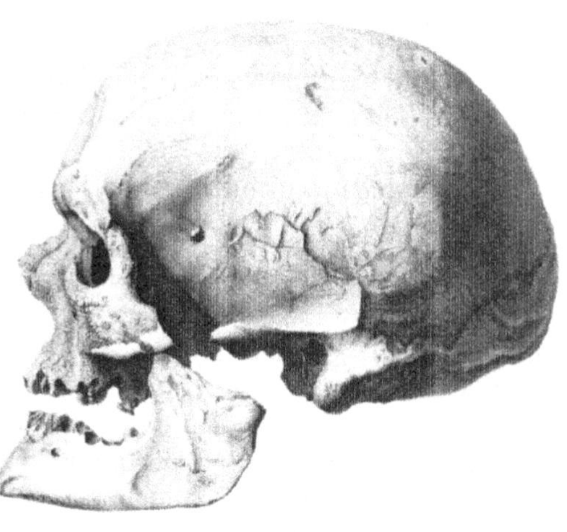

FIGURE 15.3 Nineteenth-century drawings of the fossilized skull from Cro-Magnon, France, the first of the very early specimens of modern *Homo sapiens* to be found. Notice the well-developed chin and the high forehead. These drawings are approximately one-third actual size.

BOX 15.1

Characteristics of Anatomically Modern People (*Homo sapiens*)[a]

Trait	*Homo sapiens*
Height (sexes combined)	ca. 5 to 6 ft (140–185 cm)—extremely variable (F is 90%–95% of M)
Weight (sexes combined)	ca. 100 to 200 lb (40–70 kg)—extremely variable (F is 90%–95% of M)
Brain size (sexes combined)	1,330 cc mean (1,000–2,000 cc range)
Cranium	High-vaulted, globular skull with widest point high on the sides; small brows; high forehead; little facial prognathism; flexed cranial base; canine fossa
Dentition	On average, smaller front and rear teeth and a more lightly built jaw than the archaics; definite chin
Limbs	Relatively long legs and short arms overall; body build that varies strongly with climatic conditions but generally linear
Distribution	Africa, Asia, Europe, Australia, Americas
Known dates	ca. 195,000 years BP to present

[a]For additional technical details and diagnostic traits, see Appendix 3.

Cranium

- relatively small face (both height and length are reduced compared to archaic humans—i.e., *H. heidelbergensis* and the Neandertals)
- neurocranial globularity
- flexed cranial base (see Postcranial traits following)
- vertical forehead
- small brows
- canine fossa (a shallow depression on the upper jaw lateral to the bulge that marks the canine root)
- distinct chin

Dentition

- premolars and molars that are small both absolutely and relative to body mass
- smaller and weaker jaws than in archaic humans

Postcranial Body

- vocal tract with low larynx and long pharynx (see Cranial traits above)
- reduced body mass compared to that of the archaic humans
- linear physique
- short pubic ramus but large pelvic inlet

Brain and Mind

- mean brain size of 1330 cubic centimeters (almost a 10 percent increase over our direct ancestors *H. heidelbergensis* but 8 percent smaller than our collateral relatives, the Neandertals)
- Jerison encephalization quotient (EQ) score of 8.1 (see Chapter 13)
- enhanced working memory (EWM) now in place (allowing "higher levels of innovation, thought experiment, and narrative complexity" [Wynn and Coolidge, 2004:484] than in archaic humans)

As demonstrated by this list, the main changes that marked the advent of anatomical modernity involved the shape of the skull and the *quality* of the brain.

Our skull became more rounded and lightly built and our face less prognathic than those of our *Homo heidelbergensis* ancestors. And as a result of altered cranial shape and vocal tract dimensions, plus the attainment of EWM, modern speech and language appeared. Modern cognition and communication, in turn, facilitated an explosion of cultural innovation. And not long after this package of modern traits evolved, *Homo sapiens* was the sole large-brained hominin species left on earth. Precisely how this came about is a matter of considerable controversy among anthropologists, as the next several sections will show.

Selection for Modern Human Anatomy

As just described, the main adaptive changes that converted archaic humans into anatomically modern people involved modifications of the skull—primarily braincase globularization, basicranial flexion, facial reduction, and the development of the chin. But what selection pressures were driving this suite of changes? Many researchers are now convinced that humankind's anatomical modernization was a multifaceted adaptation that occurred primarily for enhanced speech and language.

Rutgers University anthropologist Daniel Lieberman (1998) recently used CT scans and radiographs to compare the cranial anatomy of living people with that of several fossil hominans. He determined that a single evolutionary change—namely, shortening the sphenoid bone in the cranial base—probably triggered the final steps in the modernization of the human skull. (To better understand the concept of sphenoid shortening, refer to Figure A.2 in Appendix 3 and also to Figure 13.7. In the latter figure, sphenoid shortening would reduce the horizontal distance between points B and D.)

Lieberman's (1998) data show that a modern human's sphenoid is significantly shorter than that of a Neandertal (our collateral relative) and *Homo heidelbergensis* (our actual ancestors). A shorter sphenoid led to reduced facial prognathism, and that, in turn, led to smaller brows, a more vertical forehead, and a rounded skull shape. Of primary importance, however, is the fact that shortening the sphenoid bone would have "contribute[d] to the unique proportions of the human vocal tract, in which the horizontal component is roughly equal in length to its vertical component. . . . This configuration improves the ability to produce acoustically distinct speech sounds" (D. Lieberman, 1998:161). The linguistic Lieberman—Philip of Brown University—agrees with Daniel Lieberman's bottom line that increasingly complex speech provided the "selective advantage for the anatomical development of the face, skull, and vocal tract that marks anatomically modern human beings" (P. Lieberman, 2002:56).

Additionally, that distinctive human feature, the chin (Schwartz and Tattersall, 2000), may also have been influenced by selection for modern speech. The chin provides external reinforcement at our **mandibular symphysis** against the stresses of lateral grinding by the molars. Other primates, including other hominins, typically show *internal* reinforcement at the symphysis in the form of either a so-called simian shelf or a mandibular torus (Figure 15.4). Some scientists suggest that among modern humans, internal reinforcement would have been selected against because as our faces got shorter, extra bone on the inside of the lower jaw would have been dangerously close to the blood vessels, windpipe, and larynx in our necks (Campbell, 1985; DuBrul and Sicher, 1954). Given these anatomical constraints, natural selection found a compromise: The lower margin of our lightly buttressed symphysis was everted slightly (turned outward), producing a chin.

Mandibular symphysis the midline connecting the right and left halves of the lower jaw.

Thus, evidence of several sorts suggests that selection for complex speech and language was a major force during the last phases of human evolution and that it affected cranial, vocal tract, and brain modifications. An important question is how the various archaic humans, the Neandertals and others, contributed to that process, if at all. During the late Pleistocene, *Homo sapiens* appeared and, with the notable exception of the newly discovered dwarfed species *Homo floresiensis* (see the

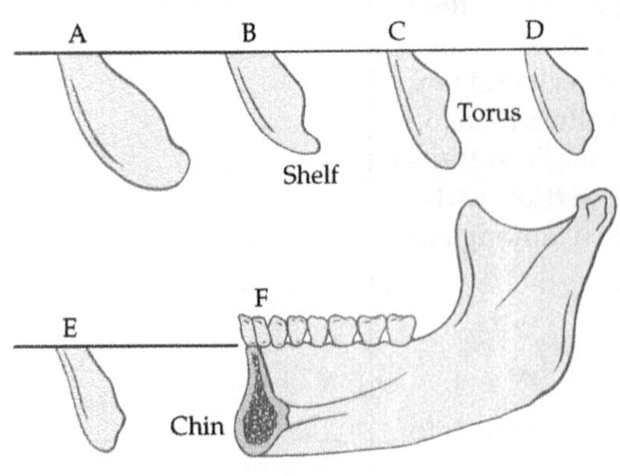

FIGURE 15.4
Cross-sections of the symphyseal region of several nonhuman primates and hominids: *(A)* gorilla, *(B)* chimpanzee, *(C) A. africanus*, *(D* and *E)* archaic *Homo*, and *(F)* modern human. For all drawings, the front of the jaw is to the left and the internal surface to the right. Note that internal buttressing can occur as a simian shelf of bone at the lower margin of the jaw and/or a mandibular torus higher on the symphysis.

Postscript to this chapter), all nonmodern human types disappeared. But what was the connection between those events?

Fate of the Archaic Humans

What became of the Neandertals and other archaics who struggled to sustain their developing humanity? Some paleoanthropologists advocate a multiregional model of anagenetic transformation and believe that many if not all—including the European Neandertals—evolved into modern humans. Other researchers, however, believe that most archaic populations became extinct and were replaced by modern people who originated in Africa and then spread across the world. These are the extreme positions—multiregional versus "Out of Africa"—and there are numerous intermediate scenarios that combine elements of both views (Smith, 2002). In the next several sections, we will look at the archaeological and fossil evidence for the various models of modern human origins.

Sequence of Tools

With regard to the Neandertals, in particular, paleoanthropologists and archaeologists have long hoped that the tools they left behind would yield a clear picture of their passing. And for a while, the separation of Neandertals from *Homo sapiens* appeared to be clean, as described by Richard Klein: "At most sites that contain both Neanderthal/Middle Paleolithic and modern human/Upper Paleolithic occupations, the Upper Paleolithic layers overlie the Middle Paleolithic ones with no evidence for either contact or for a substantial gap in time. The implication [was] for a very rapid replacement with little or no interaction" (1999:30). Further studies on the innovations involved in the Middle to Upper Paleolithic shift and the archaeology of Europe have shown, however, that the situation is more complex than originally thought.

Flakes and Blades

As explained in previous chapters, the Lower Paleolithic period included such early stone tool styles as the Oldowan and the Acheulean—tools that were produced by a variety of hominins ranging (probably) from some australopiths to *Homo heidelbergensis*. The term *Middle Paleolithic,* on the other hand, refers essentially to Mousterian tools produced by the Neandertals and/or certain modern or near-modern contemporaries in Europe, the Middle East, and North Africa (Schick and Toth, 1993). (Sub-Saharan African tool industries contemporaneous with the Middle Paleolithic to the north are usually referred to as *Middle Stone Age [MSA]* cultures.) Following the Middle Paleolithic/MSA, lithic cultures worldwide moved into a period labeled the *Upper Paleolithic* (or *Later Stone Age [LSA]* in sub-Saharan Africa) and are attributable almost without exception to anatomically modern people.

Blade tools slender, sharp *flake* tools that are at least twice as long as they are wide.

Most Middle Paleolithic/MSA tools consist of flat flakes shaped and retouched to provide the desired working edge. Upper Paleolithic tool makers produced flakes, too, but they specialized in a kind known as **blades,** which are essentially parallel sided and at least twice as long as they are wide (Schnick and Toth, 1993). This shift in the fundamental unit of the tool kit is marked enough so that many collections of Middle and Upper Paleolithic tools can be distinguished at a glance.

Blades are more economical to make than flakes because they yield more cutting edge per pound of stone. Progress is also apparent in craftsmanship. Tools of the Upper Paleolithic/LSA are more finely made, requiring extremely precise chipping to produce the desired point, notch, or cutting edge. And there are many more kinds of special-purpose tools. Upper Paleolithic/LSA kits often include a high percentage of **burins**—chisel-like tools that were useful, as we will see, for cutting bone, antler, and ivory.

Burin a chisel-like tool used to shape other materials, such as bone, antler, and wood; a tool for making other tools.

Indeed, the use of nonlithic materials that could be shaped, such as bone, antler and ivory, is an important marker distinguishing Upper Paleolithic/LSA assemblages from those of earlier cultures (Klein and Edgar, 2002). In addition, as detailed in Chapter 16, the Upper Paleolithic/LSA saw the true beginnings of art, the full development of elaborate burial rituals, the refinement of shelter construction and use of fire, and the development of extensive trade networks.

The details of the technological shift from the Middle Paleolithic/MSA to the Upper Paleolithic/LSA are hazy, despite many years of diligent archaeological work. In Asia, Upper Paleolithic industries began to appear in some areas around 40,000 to 25,000 years BP (Klein, 1999). Among the most interesting of these early locations is the 27,000-year-old site of Yana RHS in the Siberian Arctic (Pitulko et al., 2004). Yana RHS is potentially classifiable as early Upper Paleolithic because even though it lacks blade tools, the site has produced a spear foreshaft made of woolly rhinoceros horn, as well as two foreshafts made from mammoth ivory. As noted earlier, manufacturing tools from a variety of organic materials was a diagnostic feature of the emerging Upper Paleolithic.

In contrast to Asia, prehistoric Australians never produced Upper Paleolithic stone tools (continuing instead with a core-and-flake tradition), although they did show other "modern behavioral markers [such] as formal bone artifacts, art, [and] complex burials" (Klein, 1999:569). (Among these artworks are 25,000-year-old rock paintings.) And it has become clear recently that in Europe, Western Asia (including the Middle East), and Africa, the transition was not as clean as once thought (Klein, 1999; Stringer and Gamble, 1993). For example, the Mousterian industry included some blade tools, although they "tend to be much more casually made than their true Upper Paleolithic counterparts" (Klein, 1999:429).

Furthermore, in both the Middle East (at Tabūn) and South Africa (at Klasies River Mouth), cultural sequences have been discovered that show blade assemblages alternating with Mousterian or other Middle Paleolithic/MSA industries. Some archaeologists now speak of the early and tentative appearance of "pre–Upper Paleolithic" stone technology between 70,000 and 50,000 years ago, 10,000 years or more before the traditional date for the start of the Upper Paleolithic.

One example of modern behavior that occurred before the start of the Upper Paleolithic/LSA is worth further description. At the 77,000-year-old site of Blombos Cave, South Africa, archaeologists have found MSA-type stone tools in association with well-made bone tools, including awls and projectile points, perforated shells that were almost certainly worn as beads, and engraved pieces of red ocher that come close to being obvious works of art (Henshilwood et al., 2001, 2002, 2004). Whether archaic or anatomically modern humans made the Blombos Cave artifacts is unclear, but in any event, they document a clear flash of modern behavior well before the beginning of the Upper Paleolithic in Europe.

Finally, several other sites provide evidence against rigid associations of the Middle Paleolithic/MSA with archaic people only and the Upper Paleolithic/LSA solely with *Homo sapiens*. At Skhūl and Qafzeh in the Middle East, early anatomically modern (or near-modern) fossils were accompanied by Mousterian implements, while at the French sites of Arcy-sur-Cure and St. Césaire, undoubted Neandertal fossils (dating to 34,000 years BP at Arcy-sur-Cure) were found in association with an Upper Paleolithic industry called the **Chatelperronian** (Klein, 2000; Stringer and Gamble, 1993).

Chatelperronian an *Upper Paleolithic* tool culture of Western Europe; largely contemporaneous with the *Aurignacian* culture (37,000 to 29,000 years BP).

Aurignacian and Chatelperronian Industries

Known primarily from northern Spain and France, the **Aurignacian** and Chatelperronian industries marked the appearance of the Upper Paleolithic in Europe. Broadly contemporaneous, these cultural traditions shared an emphasis on

Aurignacian an *Upper Paleolithic*, mainly European tool culture that existed from about 37,000 to 29,000 years ago.

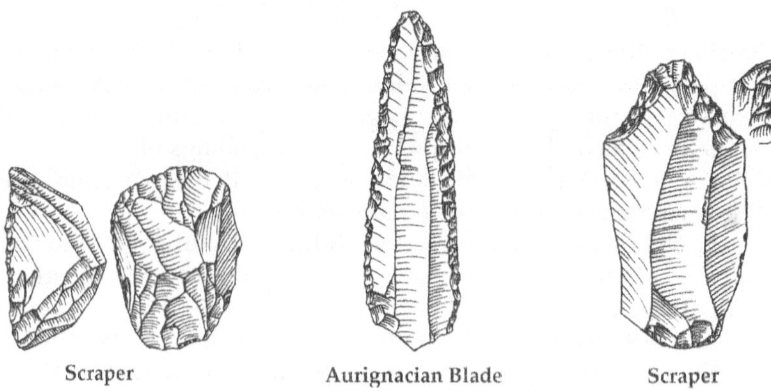

FIGURE 15.5 Aurignacian tools of the Upper Paleolithic were made by Cro-Magnon people. The most typical Aurignacian tool was the blade, much longer and narrower than any scraper. The Aurignacian retouching was very fine. The tools were made from a specially prepared core. These drawings are approximately one-half actual size.

blade technology, plus the appearance of well-made bone implements and objects of personal adornment such as beads and pendants. Despite their similarities, however, the Aurignacian and Chatelperronian industries appear to tell very different stories about the early phases of the European Upper Paleolithic.

The Aurignacian industry (Figure 15.5), with its finely retouched blade tools, was so completely unlike any typical Middle Paleolithic style that it almost certainly was imported into Western Europe, apparently by modern humans arriving from the east. At most European sites, the Aurignacian replaced the preceding Mousterian culture more or less abruptly, a fact suggesting to many anthropologists the rapid replacement of the Neandertals by fully modern humans (Klein, 1999; Klein and Edgar, 2002).

In contrast, the Chatelperronian industry (Figure 15.6) seems to have been an indigenous development that originated in Spain and France from a variant of the Mousterian (the Mousterian of Acheulean tradition). In addition to sidescrapers, denticulates, and Mousterian points, the Chatelperronian included blades, burins, endscrapers, and numerous bone artifacts (Klein, 2000). As noted earlier, the Chatelperronian is associated with Neandertal remains at St. Césaire and Arcy-sur-Cure. The question is, Do these sites really reflect Neandertal involvement in the development of the European Upper Paleolithic? More important, do they provide evidence that the Neandertals evolved physically into modern Europeans?

Although there are sharp differences of opinion on the subject, many paleoanthropologists agree with Richard Klein (2000; Klein and Edgar, 2002) that the Chatelperronian is best explained as being the result of traits diffusing from the Aurignacian into an otherwise Mousterian cultural context. In other words, the Chatelperronian may well reflect cultural diffusion from modern Europeans to Neandertals and need not imply any ancestor–descendant relationship between the two.

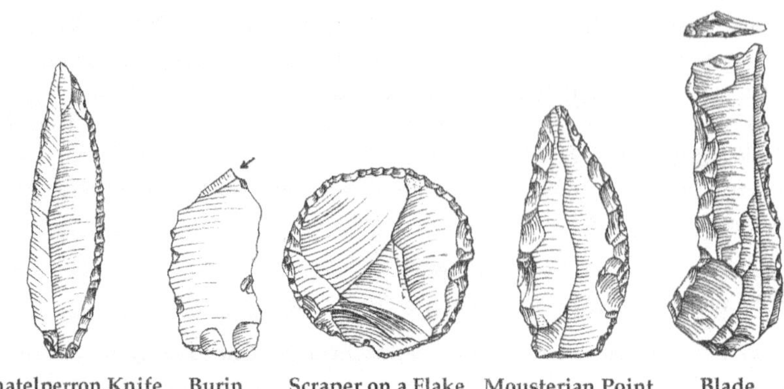

FIGURE 15.6 Typical Chatelperronian tools of the Upper Paleolithic. This tradition began with strongly marked Mousterian features and included Mousterian points, flakes, and other tools. Later tool kits contained a high proportion of burins and points. These drawings are approximately one-half actual size.

In summary, the archaeological record provides a general but by no means fine-grained picture of the disappearance of the Middle Paleolithic/MSA and its replacement (in whole or in part, depending on the region) by more elaborate Upper Paleolithic/LSA cultures. This changeover began about 50,000 years ago (perhaps a bit earlier in Africa and a bit later in Asia and Europe) and seems broadly to reflect the replacement of archaic humans (Neandertals in Europe and the Middle East; primarily *Homo heidelbergensis* elsewhere?) by anatomically modern people. Richard Klein and others think the cultural transformation was the result of the achievement of full modernity of the human brain (Klein and Edgar, 2002). Cognitive evolution researchers Wynn and Coolidge (2004) describe the same event as the achievement of "enhanced working memory." The details of the *biological* transformation of archaics into moderns remain fuzzy, however, and for more information on that point, we now turn to the fossil record.

The Fossil Record

Theoretically, a relatively complete fossil record from about 200,000 to 30,000 years ago should yield a pretty clear picture of the rise of *Homo sapiens* and the demise of the archaic humans. Unfortunately, the record is far from complete (although it is better in some regions than in others). Moreover, it is proving devilishly difficult to interpret everywhere.

One straightforward and instructive way to start a review of the fossils is to list the oldest specimens of anatomically modern people from all regions of the Old World. (The Americas can be ignored, since it is clear that *Homo sapiens* did not originate there.) As shown in Table 15.1, the most ancient evidence of modern people has been discovered in northeastern Africa and South Africa.

In 1967, hominan remains were discovered at the site of Omo Kibish in Southern Ethiopia (Figure 15.1; Day, 1969). Among the remains were two crania, Omo Kibish 1 and 2, the first-numbered of which was readily identified as belonging to *Homo sapiens*. (The second-numbered skull, although contemporaneous with Omo 1 and undoubtedly from a conspecific, was considerably more archaic in its anatomy [Table 15.2].) Until just recently, the Omo Kibish fossils were thought to be at most 130,000 years old, but new dates from the site have pushed their age back to 195,000

TABLE 15.2 Selected Human Fossils from Africa, Dated between 400,000 and 50,000 Years BP

Site	Anatomical Type	Approximate Age	Date of Discovery
Ndutu, Tanzania	Archaic[a]	~400,000	1973
Elandsfontein, RSA[b]	Archaic	~400,000	1953
Ileret, Kenya	Intermediate?	300,000–270,000	1992
Florisbad, RSA	Intermediate	~260,000	1932
Kabwe, Zambia	Archaic	~400,000	1921
Singa, Sudan	Intermediate	170,000–150,000	1924
Omo Kibish 1, Ethiopia	Modern	195,000	1967
Omo Kibish 2, Ethiopia	Modern?	195,000	1967
Ngaloba, Laetoli, Tanzania	Intermediate	150,000–90,000	1978
Klasies River Mouth, RSA	Modern	115,000–60,000	1972
Border Cave, RSA	Modern	90,000–50,000	1941
Die Kelders Cave, RSA	Modern	71,000–45,000	1976
Equus Cave, RSA	Modern	71,000–27,000(?)	1985
Dar-es-Soltan, Cave 2, Morocco	Modern	127,000–40,000(?)	1975

[a]Most of the archaic and intermediate fossils listed here are tentatively classified as *Homo heidelbergensis* (see Table 14.2).
[b]Republic of South Africa.
Source: Bräuer et al., 1997; McDougall et al., 2005.

years BP (McDougall et al., 2005). At present, therefore, these fossils can claim the distinction of being the oldest evidence of modern humans.

Not far behind the Omo Kibish crania come hominan remains from Herto, Ethiopia, that may date back to 160,000 years BP. They are sufficiently modern to be placed in our species but sufficiently different to warrant a subspecies designation: *Homo sapiens idaltu.* Furthermore, the Herto fossils show evidence of descent from African *H. heidelbergensis* people, as represented by Bodo and Kabwe (T. White et al., 2003). Next in line after Herto are specimens from the South African sites of Klasies River Mouth (100,000 years BP; Klein, 1999) and Border Cave (90,000 to 50,000 years BP). And finally, shifting our focus just slightly to the Middle East, the Israeli sites of Skhūl and Qafzeh have produced anatomically modern (some might say near-modern) remains that date to about 100,000 years BP (Klein, 1999).

Modern specimens from Europe, Asia, and Australia are notably younger than those from Africa, clearly suggesting that continent as our species' birthplace. European sites such as Bacho Kiro in Bulgaria *may* take the fossils of modern people back to about 39,000 years ago (Churchill and Smith, 2000).

In Asia, the oldest anatomically modern fossils come from Liujiang and the Upper Cave at Zhoukoudian, both in China. The Liujiang remains may be as much as 30,000 years of age, and those from Zhoukoudian may date back to 29,000 years BP (Center for the Study of Chinese Prehistory; Conroy, 1997). Interestingly, Indonesia and Australia have produced even older modern fossils than mainland Asia. Remains dating to about 40,000 years BP have come from Niah Cave in Borneo (Conroy, 1997) and from Lake Mungo in Australia (Bowler et al., 2003).

Read literally, this list of oldest specimens suggests that modern humans originated in Africa 195,000 or more years ago and then, beginning perhaps 70,000 years BP (Foley and Lahr, 2004), began to show major dispersals across the Old World, replacing their predecessors. And this may have been *exactly* how it happened. Some researchers, however, think the fossil record contains not just archaics and moderns but transitional near-moderns, as well, and that these transitional specimens may show evidence of European, Asian, and Indonesian contributions to the emergence of *Homo sapiens.* Let's take a closer look at is this multiregional model of modern origins.

The Multiregional Model

All specialists agree that the transition of archaic humans into *Homo sapiens* involved elevation and rounding of the cranial vault (which produced a fairly steep forehead); full flexion of the cranial base; reduction of the brows; development of a distinct chin; and some decrease in the size of the face and teeth (see Box 15.1 and Figure 15.7). Average brain size may have gone up or down a bit, depending on whether one believes we evolved only from *Homo heidelbergensis* or from all archaics generally (see following). Additionally, there were almost certainly advances in mental abilities and communication with the evolution of *Homo sapiens.* Despite general agreement on the biological modifications of modernity, however, paleoanthropologists have recently disagreed sharply on the specifics of *Homo sapiens*'s evolution. As noted earlier, two primary models (as well as several intermediate schemes) have been proposed.

The first model hypothesizes that modern humans evolved more or less simultaneously across the entire Old World from several ancestral populations (Wolpoff, 1996). Dubbed the *multiregional model* and illustrated in Figure 15.8 (*top*), this scheme envisions a broad-scale transformation of *Homo erectus* into modern humans via several geographically varying archaic populations. In other words, all or most archaic humans from around the Old World—including the Neandertals and the people we are calling *Homo heidelbergensis*—are hypothesized as having contributed to the modern gene pool.

In order for this sort of transformation to work, its supporters propose that there was extensive gene flow among the various populations of *Homo erectus* and later populations of archaic people. (Gene flow is shown as dashed lines in Figure 15.8.) Africa is viewed as exchanging genes with Eurasia, which in turn shared alleles with

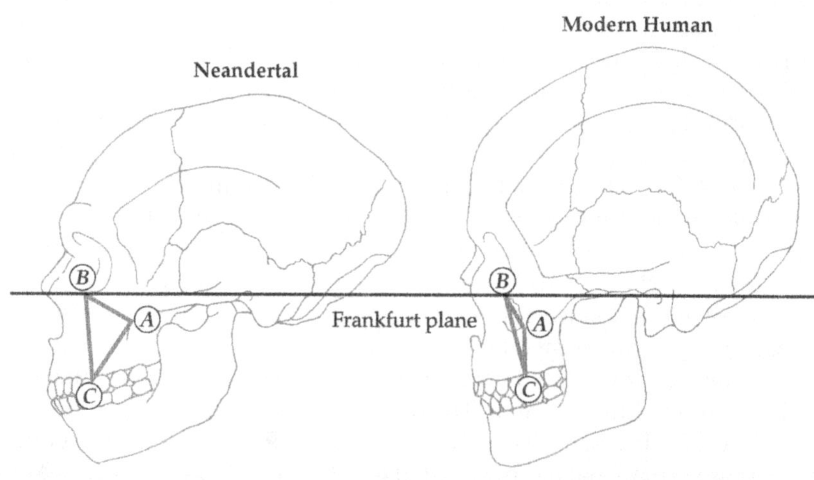

FIGURE 15.7
This comparison of a representative archaic (the classic Neandertal from La Chapelle) and a modern human provides an extreme example of the cranial differences between archaic people and *Homo sapiens*. The anatomical distance between modern humans and our actual ancestors, the *Homo heidelbergensis* people, was probably not quite so great. The horizontal line called the *Frankfurt plane*, which passes through the lower margin of the orbit and the auditory meatus (ear hole), enables the skulls to be drawn in comparable orientation. Differences in the A-B-C triangles reflect the midfacial prognathism of the Neandertal compared to the nonprognathic modern face.

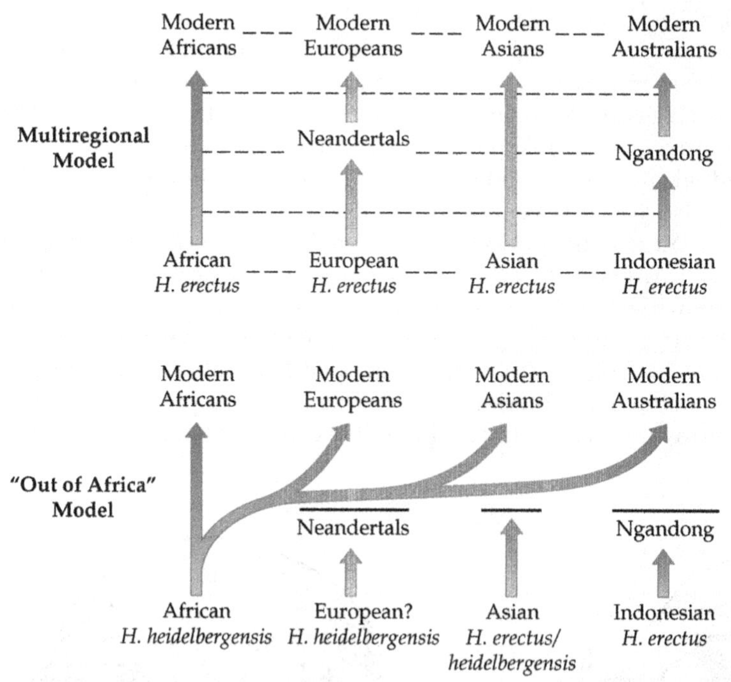

FIGURE 15.8
The multiregional model proposes that *Homo erectus* people on each continent evolved through various archaic types into modern humans. In this model, intercontinental gene flow is shown by horizontal dashed lines. In contrast, the "Out of Africa" model envisions modern *Homo sapiens* evolving once—in Africa from *Homo heidelbergensis* ancestors—and then migrating throughout the Old World replacing their archaic predecessors. Note that details about the evolutionary connections among *Homo erectus, Homo heidelbergensis,* and the Neandertals are not shown in the bottom model but can be found in Figure 12.9.

Source: Based on Stringer and Gamble, 1993.

East and Southeast Asia and Australia. Because of gene flow, multiregional supporters argue, new traits evolving in one region would have been carried inevitably to all other regions, and thus all of humanity would have evolved together from the level of *H. erectus* to full modernity. (Note that in the most recent versions of the multiregional model, all humans from about 2 million years BP to the present are viewed as constituting a single species: *Homo sapiens.* Thus, specimens treated in this book as *Homo erectus, H. heidelbergensis,* Neandertals, and anatomically modern humans are lumped into one anagenetically evolving lineage [D'Agnese, 2002; Wolpoff, 1996]. This arrangement has the advantage of removing the barriers to gene flow that accompany classifying the various hominans into different biological species.)

A review of the evidence for multiregionalism can profitably begin in the Middle East, where an ancestral relationship between archaic and undeniably modern people seems possible, with the fossils from Zuttiyeh, Skhūl, and Qafzeh somewhat bridging the evolutionary gap. The oldest of these three sites is Zuttiyeh cave in Israel. In the mid 1920s, a distinctly archaic partial face plus frontal bone was found there (Figure 15.9) that has been dated to 350,000 to 250,000 years BP (Wolpoff, 1996). Unfortunately, the fragmentary nature of the Zuttiyeh fossil and its mosaic of traits allow numerous comparisons but very little certainty with regard to its phylogenetic connections. With its large brows (centrally thickened and thinning laterally), receding frontal, and gracile zygomatic bones, the Zuttiyeh face shows some similarities to the archaic skull from Steinheim, Germany (Table 12.1). Looking eastward, it has also been noted that Zuttiyeh's flat upper face and frontal contours resemble the *Homo erectus* population from Zhoukoudian, China. Finally, considering only possible Middle East connections, some workers think Zuttiyeh was ancestral to the Skhūl and Qafzeh people, while others regard it as a member of the Neandertal lineage. For their parts, the Skhūl (100,000 to 80,000 years BP) and Qafzeh (120,000 to 90,000 years BP) fossils look somewhat transitional, since each includes some primitive features, although on balance, both probably fit best within the modern category (Table 15.1; Stringer and Gamble, 1993). For example, Skhūl 5 shows moderate brow ridge development (Figure 14.6), while Qafzeh 9 shows rather significant facial prognathism. Taken together, Zuttiyeh, Qafzeh, and Skhūl *may* document a gradual archaic-to-modern transition in the Middle East, but other interpretations also are possible (F. Smith, 2002).

In Europe, some genetic connection between the Neandertals and modern people seems possible from the fact that the most recent archaic specimens anticipate modern features while the oldest true moderns appear rather primitive. In the first category are the late Neandertals (more than 32,000 to 28,000 years BP) from Hortus in France, Vindija in Croatia, and Kūlna in the Czech Republic. These people have been described as showing "anterior dental reduction, an incipient mental eminence [chin], . . . a narrow nasal aperture and possible canine fossa, . . . and reduced fa-

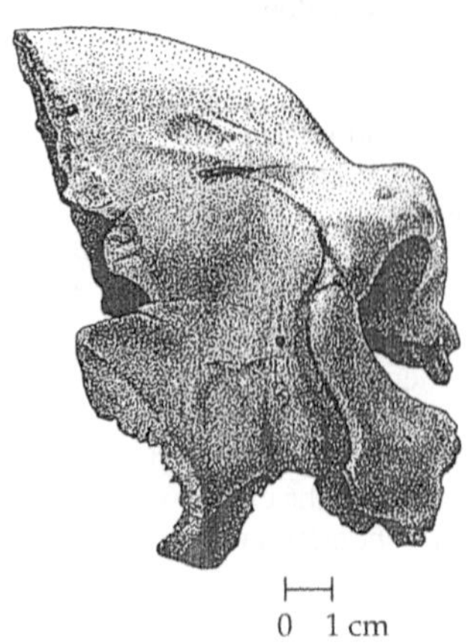

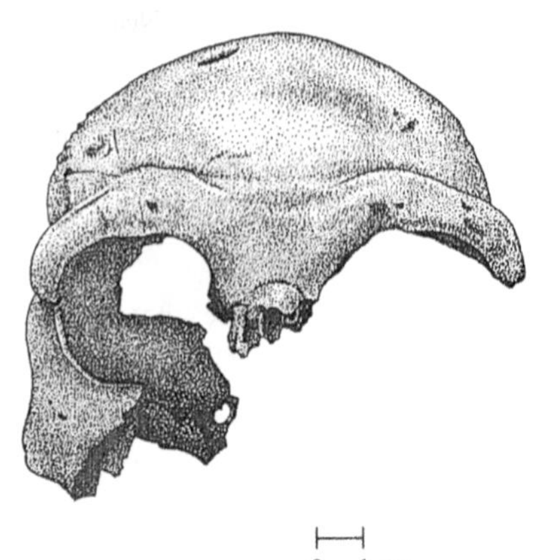

FIGURE 15.9 Side and front views of the fragmentary face from Zuttiyeh, Israel. Dated at 350,000 to 250,000 years BP, this specimen is drawn slightly less than one-half actual size. The scale below each view represents 1 centimeter.

cial proportions" (F. Smith, 2002:446). In the second category are the specimens from Mladeč (the Czech Republic) and Velíka Pečina (Croatia). Both are probably more than 30,000 years old and therefore among the oldest European *Homo sapiens* fossils, and both show a mosaic of traits, including some Neandertal-like features (e.g., thick cranial bones and large brow ridges among the Mladeč people; Churchill and Smith, 2000; Wolpoff, 1996).

By far the most intriguing recent contribution to the question of Neandertals' links to modern humans is the 1998 discovery of the Abrigo do Lagar Velho skeleton in Portugal (Duarte et al., 1999). This approximately 25,000-year-old fossil consists of the remains of a young child who was buried with pierced shells and red ocher and who shows a strong mixture of Neandertal-like and *sapiens*-like traits. The discoverers of Lagar Velho concluded that the specimen is a hybrid that documents generations of extensive interbreeding between Neandertals and anatomically modern people (Duarte et al., 1999; Kunzig, 1999). Skeptics have counterargued that the skeleton is simply a "chunky [modern] child" (Tattersall and Schwartz, 1999), but at present, neither side can prove its position conclusively.

An interesting side issue is whether demonstrating the hybrid status of Lagar Velho would prove that the Neandertals and Cro-Magnons were actually conspecifics, as suggested by the biological species concept (see Chapter 2). Clifford Jolly, for one, thinks that such a conclusion would not be obligatory. Using analogical data on hybridization among Old World monkeys, Jolly (2001) has argued that given the recentness of their last common ancestor, fertile interbreeding between Neandertals and Cro-Magnons should have been possible, even though they were morphologically distinct enough to warrant giving them separate species names.

The possibility that the Neandertals were strongly ancestral to modern Europeans has long been promoted by at least a few anthropologists, including, in particular, Ales Hrdlicka in the 1920s (Trinkaus and Shipman, 1993) and C. Loring Brace (1995) and Milford Wolpoff (1996) more recently. And as described above, there is some fossil evidence to support this view. In Wolpoff's current version of the multiregional model, this was simply part of an Old World–wide process of anagenetic change, not a true speciation event.

Arguments for regional continuity in China are based on claims that certain dental and cranial traits show long histories of evolutionary occurrence in that area. In particular, evidence for a broad and flat face is claimed to link fossil and modern inhabitants of the Far East. The proposed continuity sequence in China views the archaic fossils from Dali, Jinniushan, Maba, and Xujiayao (all dated to 280,000 to 100,000 years BP) as evolutionary descendants of the Zhoukoudian *Homo erectus* people and as the probable ancestors of modern populations such as that from Liujiang (Table 15.1; Wolpoff, 1996).

In the Indonesian/Australian region, a medley of cranial features has been used to argue that modern Australian Aborigines are descended from Javanese *Homo erectus* via intermediate populations such as Ngandong, Java, and (later) Willandra Lakes, Australia (same location as Lake Mungo in Figure 15.1; Thorne and Wolpoff, 2003). Among the traits claimed to show evolutionary continuity in this part of the Old World are details of facial anatomy and degree of facial prognathism (Wolpoff, 1996). Nonetheless, evidence that the Ngandong fossils are quite young—perhaps as young as 27,000 years BP (Table 10.1)—may bar them from a role as the Aborigines' ancestors, since modern people have lived in Australia for at least 40,000 years.

Furthermore, anatomical links between the late Pleistocene specimen from Willandra Lakes (WLH 50) with Ngandong, on the one hand, and modern Aborigines, on the other, have been challenged. Stringer (1998) found WLH 50 to be no closer metrically to the Ngandong population than to a sample of African archaics (e.g., Jebel Irhoud, Ngaloba, and Singa) and the primitive-looking modern Omo Kibish 2. Additionally, Stringer's study suggested that with regard to its modern traits, WLH 50 is somewhat closer to the Middle Eastern specimens from Skhūl and Qafzeh than it is to modern Australian Aborigines.

Finally, certain fossils in Africa from the period between 400,000 and 27,000 years BP *may* constitute an evolutionary series of humans from fully archaic to intermediate to anatomically modern (see Table 15.2). Very robust archaic skulls include the Kabwe fossil from Zambia and the Elandsfontein skull fragments from South Africa. These two skulls date to about 400,000 years BP. Moving into the intermediate category, the Ileret cranium from Kenya, recently dated at 300,000 to 270,000 years BP, has been described as archaic but showing some anatomical traits that approach modernity (Braüer et al., 1997). Additionally, Omo Kibish 2 is a primitive-looking modern from Ethiopia that dates to 195,000 BP, and the Ngaloba fossil is a lightly built archaic from Tanzania that dates between 150,000 and 90,000 years BP. Lastly, the fossil remains of fully modern humans go back 195,000 years at the Omo Kibish site (Omo 1 specimen), with the South African sites of Klasies River Mouth (115,000 to 60,000 years BP) and Border Cave (90,000 to 50,000 years BP) being just slightly younger (Table 15.2).

This overview of the fossil evidence for the multiregional model has been brief and selective, but it gives a general sense of the database used by those researchers who have argued for a broad-scale anagenetic transformation of *Homo erectus* into modern humans via various archaic populations. In fact, an extreme version of multiregionalism is rare among present-day paleoanthropologists, with a softer version involving varying degrees of assimilation of archaic genes within the invading moderns' gene pool becoming increasingly popular (F. Smith, 2002).

Several reasons can be given to explain this softening of the extreme multiregional stance. First, as shown in Table 15.1, the fossil record continues to point consistently toward Africa as the place of modern humans' first appearance. Not only do the accumulating fossils consistently indicate an African origin followed by outward migration, but they also keep pushing that origin further and further into the past—at least 195,000 years in the past, according to the redated Omo Kibish remains. Second, the African origin and migration suggested by the fossil record is strongly supported by genetic and morphological data, as described in the next section. And third, the occurrence of anatomically intermediate individuals and populations may not reflect *in situ* and parallel anagenetic change as much as pulses of interbreeding, as invading moderns moved out of Africa and contacted resident archaics across the Old World. In the following sections, we will take a close look at the "Out of Africa" model.

The "Out of Africa" Model

Without a doubt, one of the strongest pieces of evidence for this cladogenetic model is the clear occurrence of anatomically modern humans in the adjacent regions of Africa and the Middle East long before they showed up in Europe, Asia, and Australia—a pattern that strongly implies a single, branching origin. As shown in Table 15.1, modern humans were apparently living in Northeast Africa as early as 195,000 years ago. By 120,000 to 80,000 years ago, modern people were inhabiting such Middle Eastern sites as Skhūl and Qafzeh.

In comparison, the appearance of anatomically modern humans outside Africa and the Middle East was much later. Fossil evidence for the presence of *Homo sapiens* first appears in Europe, Asia, Indonesia, and Australia between 40,000 and 30,000 years ago (Table 15.1). Interestingly, there is *archaeological* evidence of human occupation, presumably by modern people, in northern Australia as early as 60,000 years BP (Klein and Edgar, 2002; O'Connell and Allen, 1998). Taken together, these "first appearance" dates provide strong, although not conclusive, proof for the Out of Africa theory.

In addition, detailed comparative analyses of the known fossils also seem primarily to support the Out of Africa model. For example, Cambridge University anthropologist Marta Mirazon Lahr (1994) took a close look at the cranial traits claimed to reflect morphological continuity from *Homo erectus* to modern people in East Asia and Australia. She concluded that the features in question "are not exclusive to these regions, either spatially or temporally, and some occur at a higher incidence in other populations" (1994:49). Based on her studies, Lahr favors the hypothesis of a single African origin for modern humans.

In a similar vein, American scientist Diane Waddle (1994) has conducted a matrix correlation test of the multiregional and Out of Africa models. Using more than 150 different cranial traits and measurements, Waddle calculated and compared overall "morphological distances" between groups of fossils arranged by region (West Europe, East Europe, Southwest Asia, Africa) and age (600,000 to 125,000, 125,000 to 32,000, and 32,000 to 8,000; all in years BP). Waddle ran her comparisons several times, varying the hypothetical place of initial appearance of modern humans and the amount and pattern of gene flow between regions. In the end, she concluded that the study "support[ed] a single African and/or [Middle Eastern] origin for modern humans" (1994:452).

Other analyses comparing fossil crania with one another and with modern humans also have supported an African origin followed by Old World–wide migration. This was the primary conclusion of Neves et al. (1999), who also found a particularly strong anatomical difference between the Ngandong fossils (treated in this book as late *Homo erectus*) and modern humans, including Native Australians. Significantly, Ngandong has long been claimed to represent a transitional link between the earliest Indonesian hominans and modern Australian Aborigines (e.g., Coon, 1963; Weidenreich, 1946; Wolpoff, 1996; see also Figure 15.8). Additionally, as mentioned earlier, Stringer (1998) has challenged claims (F. Smith, 2002; Wolpoff, 1996) that WLH 50, a late Pleistocene fossil from Australia, has close connections either with Ngandong or modern Aborigines.

Finally, there are now several genetic and molecular studies that bear on the multiregional versus African origin question. For example, a team of researchers led by A. M. Bowcock (1994) of the University of Texas has analyzed diversity in humans' polymorphic microsatellite alleles, reasoning that the oldest populations should show the greatest amount of genetic variation. (As a reminder, satellites are usually noncoding DNA sequences that accumulate at certain points on chromosomes; see Chapter 2.) Using genetic information from 148 people representing 14 indigenous populations and five continents, Bowcock et al. found that the "diversity of microsatellites is highest in Africa, which . . . supports the hypothesis of an African origin for [modern] humans" (1994:455). Similar results have been published just recently from another study of microsatellite diversity (Ayub et al, 2003), which included the fascinating finding that the San people of South Africa may be the descendants of one of the very first modern human populations to evolve.

Additional support for the African origin model comes from studies of genetic variation in certain regions of the Y chromosome—variation that is inherited only through the male line (Hammer, 1995; Hammer and Zegura, 1996). When diversity in the YAP (Y Alu polymorphism) region of that chromosome was examined, African populations were found to contain more variation than non-African groups, a finding that supports the idea that humans have been living in Africa longer than elsewhere. In fact, researchers estimate that the first man to show the pattern of Y chromosome mutations since inherited by all men worldwide—an individual dubbed our "African Adam"—lived around 170,000 to 190,000 years ago. Interestingly, however, the Y chromosome data also showed evidence of some Asian patterns occurring among modern Africans, rather than strictly the reverse. It appears likely, therefore, that initial movements of early modern humans from Africa to Asia were probably followed at some later time(s) by back-migrations in the opposite direction.

The conclusion that the first anatomically modern Asians were migrants from Africa—rather than the results of an independent evolutionary origin *in situ*—has gained strong support from a study of the genetic profiles of 28 present-day Chinese populations. Chinese geneticist J. Y. Chu and colleagues (1998) used genetic information to work out the most likely ancestral migration routes into and throughout Asia. They noted that, "it is now probably safe to conclude that modern humans originating in Africa constitute the majority of the current gene pool in East Asia" (Chu et al., 1998:11766). And three years after the work of Chu et al. was published, a follow-up study involving several of the same researchers (plus others) reached an even stronger conclusion: "[Our] result indicates that modern humans of African origin *completely* replaced earlier populations in East Asia" (Ke et al., 2001:1151; italics added).

Without a doubt, however, the best-known genetic studies probing the place and date of modern humans' origin are those focused on mitochondrial DNA (mtDNA). This work has attracted tremendous media attention, but it has also been something of a "two steps forward, one step backward" affair because of the initial publication of somewhat flawed results. Although some anthropologists have come to distrust the mtDNA studies, most believe the studies provide important information about recent human evolution. A closer look at this research follows.

Analyses of mtDNA (Figure 12.1) were pioneered by the late Allan Wilson of the University of California, Berkeley, and his research team in the late 1980s. Because mtDNA is found only in the cytoplasm of the cell and because sperm provides almost no cytoplasm to the fertilized egg, no mtDNA is inherited from the father. (That is, fertilization involves the combination of only the *nuclear* DNA of egg and sperm.) Thus, the genetic codes carried by a cell's mtDNA come from the mother alone, and each of us carries the mtDNA that we inherited from our mother, her mother, our maternal great-grandmother, and so on along a single genealogical line. This is quite a different mode of inheritance from that of nuclear DNA, which comes from an expanding network of grandparents of both sexes. Our ancestral mtDNA lineage converges with that of others with whom we share female grandparents to produce an expanding inverted tree of relationships (Figure 15.10).

Note that the exclusively matrilineal inheritance of mtDNA means that variant sequences (i.e., mutant forms of the mtDNA molecule) can easily be lost from a population—especially a small one—by chance alone. All it takes is for the woman or women carrying the variation either not to reproduce at all or to have only sons

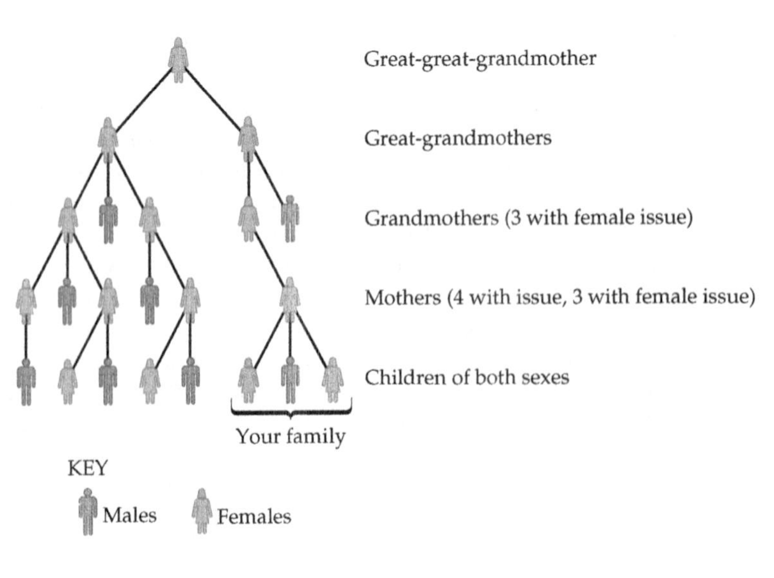

FIGURE 15.10 Mitochondrial DNA (mtDNA) is passed from one generation to another only through females in the cytoplasm of their egg cells. None is carried in the spermatozoa. If you trace your ancestry through your mother and your maternal female grandparents, you will eventually find that you share a single great-great-grandmother with the entire human race. The latest research suggests that this ancestor was an African who lived about 200,000 years ago. In this chart, such an ancestry is set out for five generations.

(who would inherit their mother's mtDNA but then be unable to pass it on to their own offspring).

Wilson and his colleagues, Rebecca Cann and Mark Stoneking, analyzed data from 147 people from five different parts of the world and then compared the geographic regions in terms of mtDNA diversity (Cann et al., 1987). Diversity in the mtDNA sequence was predicted to have increased over time within all of the populations due to mutations. Furthermore, assuming a single point of origin followed by dispersal, migrant populations everywhere were predicted to have lower levels of mtDNA diversity because of the so-called founder effect. That is, because dispersing populations were believed to be small, there should have been significant genetic bottlenecking, resulting in reduced mtDNA (as well as nuclear DNA) diversity in the new populations.

When Wilson's team reviewed their results, they concluded that Africa had the greatest level of mtDNA diversity and therefore was probably the home of the first modern humans (Cann et al., 1987). When the press got wind of this finding, it hailed the discovery of humankind's "African Eve."

Unfortunately, there were flaws in the initial mtDNA study, and they were quickly discovered by skeptics (Stoneking, 1993). Yet even after these problems were corrected in subsequent re-studies, the bottom line never seemed to change: "[All] mtDNA types in contemporary populations trace[d] back to a single ancestor [and] this ancestor probably lived in Africa" (Stoneking, 1993:62). The best estimate of the age of that last common mtDNA ancestor for humankind was about 200,000 years ago.

The latest round of mtDNA research seems to have eliminated most of the bugs from the system and to have extended the genetic database of the work, solidifying its conclusions in the process. Whereas early mtDNA work was done on only a portion of the mitochondrial molecule (the so-called control region, constituting 7 percent or less of the mtDNA genome), the new studies have succeeded in analyzing variations in the entire 16,500-base-pair-long sequence (Ingman et al., 2000). The improvements have not led to any major revision of the mtDNA story, however. Diversity across the entire molecular sequence still points to a single origin of modern humans in Africa sometime between 220,000 and 120,000 years BP.

A fascinating and important extension of the mtDNA studies during the past decade has been the successful extraction and analysis of genetic material from fossilized hominan remains. In 1997, a joint German and American research team succeeded in extracting mtDNA from the original Neandertal (Neander Valley) specimen (Krings et al., 1997). When it was compared to similar material from modern humans, the Neander Valley hominan's mtDNA was found to be significantly different (i.e., about 27 base-pair differences versus an average of about 8 differences between living humans from different populations). This suggested to the researchers that the Neandertals and modern people belonged to different species—*H. neanderthalensis* versus *H. sapiens*—and that the Neandertals became extinct without contributing mtDNA to living humans. Two follow-up studies on other Neandertal specimens confirmed the Neander Valley results and showed that the Neandertals were similar among themselves in mtDNA sequences (Krings et al., 2000; Ovchinnikov et al., 2000).

Even more recently, researchers have compared Neandertal mtDNA with genetic material extracted from two 25,000- to 23,000-year-old Cro-Magnon specimens (Caramelli et al., 2003) and that from an approximately 60,000-year-old Native Australian (Adcock et al., 2001). The two Cro-Magnons were found to be very similar to living humans (i.e., 2 to 3 base-pair differences on average) but significantly different from the Neandertals (23 to 28 base-pair differences; Caramelli et al., 2003). Similarly, the Australian specimen LM3 from Lake Mungo—ancient but clearly anatomically modern—was found to resemble other *Homo sapiens* much more than it did the Neandertals (see also Caramelli et al., 2003). (The fact that the LM3 sequence is unusually different from that of other moderns is interesting, but it may well "represent only a type that became extinct after modern humans spread from

Africa" [Klein and Edgar, 2002:247]. In any event, it does not challenge the data on relative amounts of total mtDNA diversity found in modern populations that sparked the "African Eve" notion in the first place.)

All of these studies are consistent in suggesting that the Neandertals made no mtDNA contribution to the modern human (especially European) gene pool. While that may be true, it is important to note that the mtDNA studies do not prove that Neandertals made no *nuclear* DNA contribution to modern Europeans and their descendants (Relethford, 2001). Remember that mtDNA and nuclear DNA have very different modes of inheritance (matrilineal versus biparental) and that mtDNA variants are much more easily lost by chance alone than are nuclear gene variants. "Just because all Neanderthal mtDNAs were lost does not mean that Neanderthal alleles at other loci were also lost" (Nordborg, 2004:264).

It remains possible that Cro-Magnons and Neandertals interbred somewhat—although probably not "as members of the same randomly mating population" (Jobling et al., 2004:261)—and that modern Europeans have some Neandertal nuclear DNA in their makeup. Proving a complete genetic break between *Homo sapiens* and the Neandertals requires information on nuclear DNA and mtDNA, and multiregional advocates argue that "there is morphological evidence for the survival of Neandertal [nuclear] genes in Europe after the arrival of [Cro-Magnon] people" (Adcock et al., 2001). Moreoever, it bears repeating that if we cannot prove conclusively a lack of interbreeding between archaic humans and *Homo sapiens* in Europe, where we have the best genetic and morphological evidence, we certainly cannot do so in other parts of the Old World.

So, to summarize this discussion of modern human origins, the following points seem to be warranted by the data at hand:

- The geographic distribution of the oldest anatomically modern fossils favors an African origin at least 195,000 years BP.
- Comparative anatomical studies also favor an African origin followed by dispersals to other continents.
- Studies of living humans' polymorphic microsatellite alleles and Y chromosomes add further support for the "Out of Africa" model, as do studies of mitochondrial DNA diversity.
- Comparisons of mtDNA sequences generally suggest genetic differences and little interbreeding between modern and archaic humans (especially the Neandertals), although they fail to prove conclusively that *no* interbreeding occurred.
- Persistent claims of morphological continuity and/or actual hybrids between archaic humans and modern people in Europe and Indonesia/Australia suggest the possibility of some interbreeding.
- Comparative primate studies suggest that fertile interbreeding should have been possible among "all human lineages stemming from [*Homo erectus*]" (Jolly, 2001:196). This applies whether we sort the various morphs into different species or regard them as conspecifics.

It appears, then, that the preponderance of evidence favors the "Out of Africa" model over multiregionalism. Nonetheless, given the nagging evidence of some morphological continuity and the inability of genetics to entirely disprove interbreeding, we favor a "limited admixture" scenario over either of the extreme models. This intermediate model acknowledges the likelihood of some fertile interbreeding between archaic people and *Homo sapiens* but agrees with Pearson (2004) that archaic humans probably contributed less than 10 percent of the modern gene pool (but see Templeton, 2002). The limited admixture model firmly maintains that the main features of modern human anatomy and the modern gene pool are African in origin. In essence, the biological core of every living person is overwhelmingly African.

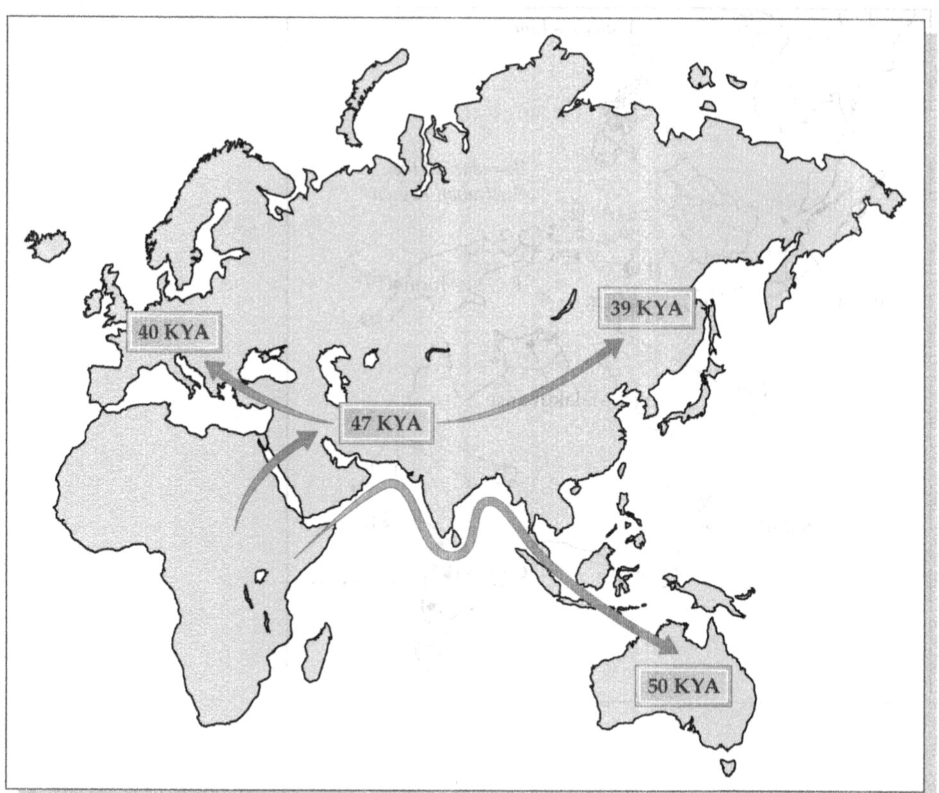

FIGURE 15.11 This map shows the minimum dates for modern humans' entry into the Middle East, Western Europe, Siberia, and Australia. The dispersal toward Indonesia and Australia probably began about 70,000 years BP, and that toward Eurasia about 50,000 years ago.

Source: Jobling et al., 2004.

Dispersals from the African Homeland

The fossil record indicates that modern humans were present in Northeast Africa by 195,000 years ago (Table 15.1). By 120,000 to 80,000 years BP, they had trickled into the Middle East and were living in present-day Israel. The first major dispersal out of Africa, however, probably occurred around 70,000 years ago and followed a southern route all the way to the Far East and Australia (Figure 15.11). A second major dispersal, about 50,000 to 40,000 years ago, carried *Homo sapiens* north into Eurasia and then west into Europe proper and east toward Siberia (Foley and Lahr, 2004; Jobling et al., 2004). Human occupation of the Americas followed shortly after colonization of the Siberian north. Evidence for early human settlements in Europe is discussed in some detail in Chapter 16, but to end the present chapter, let's take a brief look at humans' entry into Australia and the Americas.

Australia

Although the vast ice caps of the last glaciation locked up enough of the world's water to drop sea levels hundreds of feet, adding great expanses of dry land to the continents, such extensions never joined Australia to the mainland of Southeast Asia. The subsidence of waters from the comparatively shallow Sunda Shelf (Figure 15.12) united Borneo, Java, and Sumatra to Asia proper and probably exposed numerous small islands stretching to the east. But between Australia and Sunda still remained the waters of the Timor Trough, which was 10,000 feet (3,050 meters) deep and over 50 miles (80 kilometers) wide—a formidable challenge to early human migrants.

It was long assumed that *Homo sapiens* did not reach Australia until the ancestors of the modern Aborigines arrived within the last 10,000 years (R. Klein, 1999). Then, in 1968, archaeologists digging near Lake Mungo in New South Wales

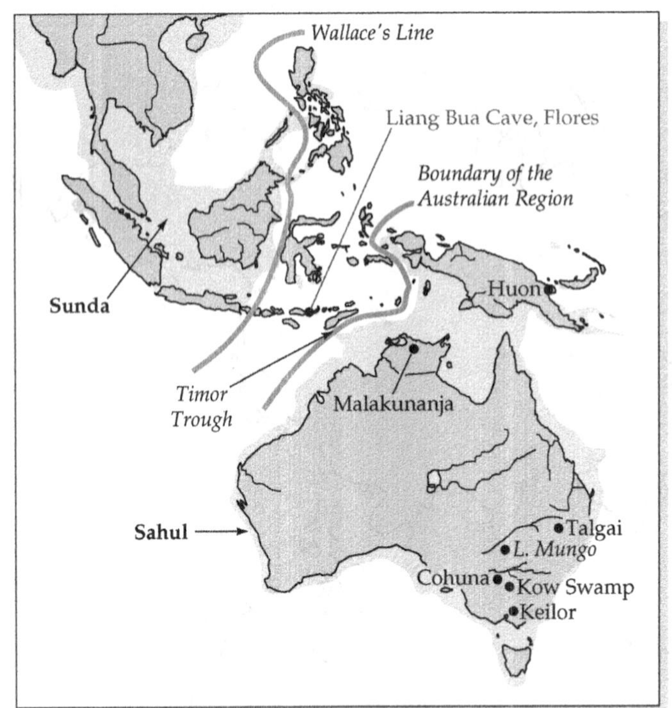

FIGURE 15.12 This map of Southeast Asia and Indonesia/Australia shows the two ancient land masses Sunda and Sahul, which were separated by the Timor Trough. The shaded area indicates the coastline that would be exposed by a drop in the sea level of 490 feet (150 meters). Wallace's Line represents the edge of the Sunda region. A few important archaeological sites are shown, as well.

Source: Adapted from J. P. White and J. F. O'Connell, 1979.

discovered a 40,000-year-old skeleton that was unmistakably modern in its anatomy. The same site also yielded archaeological evidence dating back as far as 50,000 years BP (Figure 15.12; Bowler et al., 2003). In a stroke, the history of human occupation in Australia had gained respectable time depth.

Dates from other Australian archaeological sites, such as Malakunanja in the Northern Territory (Figure 15.12), have been claimed to go back as far as 60,000 years BP (Klein and Edgar, 2002; Roberts et al., 2001), but these very early dates have been challenged (O'Connell and Allen, 1998). On balance, it appears that humans had probably reached Australia by around 50,000 years ago and were certainly in residence by 40,000 years BP (Jobling et al., 2004). Significantly, the Australian megafauna (including animals weighing 100 pounds [45 kilograms] or more) experienced widespread extinction not long after modern humans reached the continent; whether this was from overhunting or human-triggered ecological disruption is unclear, however (Roberts et al., 2001).

The most likely route of entry for the first modern Australians was from the Sunda region to the northwest (Figure 15.12). Despite the fact that sea levels were some 230 feet (70 meters) lower 50,000 years ago than at present (Jobling et al., 2004), these early migrants still had to cross huge gaps of open water. Their success in doing so suggests "purposeful voyaging by groups possessed of surprisingly sophisticated boat-building and navigation skills . . . [and] adds an important new dimension to [our] picture of early modern human behavioral and technological capabilities" (O'Connell and Allen, 1998:143).

The Americas

Fossil evidence for the entry of modern humans into the Americas goes back about 13,500 years (Jobling et al., 2004). The absolutely oldest specimen found thus far is "Luzia," a skeleton from Brazil that has been dated to 13,500 years BP. Not far behind are the specimens from Buhl, Idaho (approximately 12,900 years BP); Prince of Wales Island, Alaska (approximately 11,000 years BP); Spirit Cave, Nevada (10,600 years BP); and Kennewick, Washington (9,400 years BP). The last specimen,

Kennewick Man, has been the subject of a prolonged legal struggle between local Native Americans, who are anxious to rebury the remains, and a group of scientists, who wish to study the skeleton and compare it to living humans (Thomas, 2000).

Archaeological evidence *may* take human occupation in the Americas back even further than the fossil record. The Paleoindian culture called Clovis, best known for its distinctive stone spear points and accomplished big-game hunting, probably dates back to about 13,500 years BP (Jobling et al., 2004; but for a later date for Clovis see Meltzer, 1993, 1997). The foreshafts that Clovis people attached to their spears were very similar to those found at the 27,000-year-old Siberian site of Yana RHS, suggesting a cultural (and ancestral?) connection between these two populations. (This connection is controversial, however.) Additionally, there is a reliably dated (non-Clovis) site from Chile, the Monte Verde site, that documents human occupation in the southern portions of South America by about 12,500 years BP (Meltzer, 1997; Wilford, 1999).

There is some possibility, however, that the Americas were penetrated long before the Clovis and Monte Verde people. A handful of archaeological sites suggest a very early occupation: Cactus Hill, Virginia (circa 18,000 BP); Caverna da Pedra Pintada, Brazil (between 16,000 and 9,500 BP); and Meadowcroft, Pennsylvania (circa 23,000 years BP; Jobling et al., 2004; R. Klein, 1999; Roosevelt et al., 1996). The problem is that the dates for all of these sites have been challenged, and so even collectively, they do not provide conclusive proof of the existence of pre-Clovis/Monte Verde people.

There is somewhat more agreement among scientists about *how* the first Americans arrived than about *when*. Despite some disputes, most experts agree that humans entered the Americas via Beringia (Figure 15.13). Going overland, they

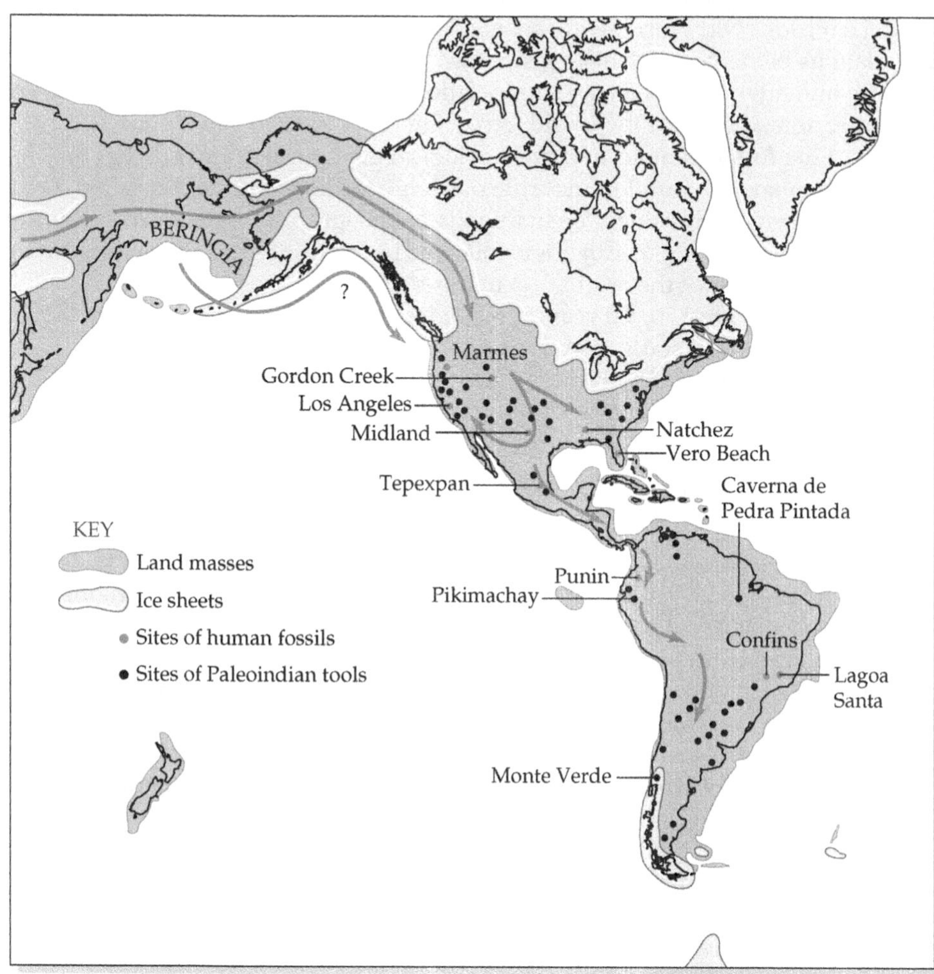

FIGURE 15.13 Much is still to be learned about the arrival of humankind in the New World. This map gives an idea of the migrants' most probable routes and of the extent of the land mass during the last glaciation.

would have gotten no further than present-day Alaska, however, until about 13,500 years ago. This is because glaciers blocked the path from about 36,000 to 13,500 years BP. Around 13,500 years ago, an ice-free corridor opened up that allowed north–south traffic (Jobling et al., 2004). Alternately, it has been suggested that the first Americans traveled south along the Pacific coast in boats of some sort (Hall et al., 2004; Jobling et al., 2004; Wilford, 1999). However they came, it now seems likely that there were several waves of immigration, possibly by "different founding populations [originating] from different places" (Dillehay, 2003). The peopling of the Americas remains very much under investigation, and new discoveries continue to inform our thinking.

With their entry into the Americas, *Homo sapiens* essentially completed the modern occupation of the globe. (For details on eleventh-hour migrations, see Diamond [1997].) In the next chapter, we will examine in some detail the kinds of culture early modern people brought with them wherever they wandered.

Summary

Anatomically modern people—*Homo sapiens*—originated at least 195,000 years ago, and their oldest remains have been found in Africa. The final anatomical transformation involved neurocranial globularization, facial reduction, and the development of modern proportions of the vocal tract. Most, if not all, of these adaptations seem to have been driven by selection for complex speech.

Two main scenarios have been proposed to explain the origin of modern humans: the multiregional model and the "Out of Africa" model. The multiregional model envisions Old World–wide anagenetic evolution, with different geographic populations being connected by gene flow. The Out of Africa model argues that modern humans originated via a single cladogenetic speciation event in Africa and thereafter spread around the world, replacing all of their archaic predecessors. A review of the fossil, genetic, and archaeological evidence strongly favors the Out of Africa explanation but does not rule out some fertile interbreeding between invading moderns and resident archaics in some geographical areas. Therefore, an assimilation model (i.e., African origin followed by some interbreeding) seems more accurate than either of the original, extreme scenarios.

Beginning around 70,000 years ago, modern humans started to disperse out of Africa—first east and south to Asia and Indonesia/Australia and later north into Eurasia. Modern humans had reached Australia by about 50,000 years ago, Western Europe by about 40,000 years ago, and the Americas by about 13,500 years ago.

Expanded Postscript

In an earlier chapter, we remarked that paleoanthropology is an ever-changing field of study and that countless fossils remain to be found, each with the potential to radically alter our understanding of human evolution. In a dramatic demonstration of that fact, a new species of the genus *Homo* was announced just as the writing of this book was being completed (P. Brown et al., 2004; Morwood et al., 2004). The new hominan—named ***Homo floresiensis*** in honor of its homeland on the Indonesian island of Flores—adds a new and very recent branch to humans' evolutionary tree and gives us our first dwarfed relative.

Homo floresiensis a *hominan species* that inhabited the Indonesian island of Flores from before 38,000 to 18,000 years BP.

In September 2003, the nonfossilized remains of *Homo floresiensis* were found by an international team of researchers in Liang Bua Cave near the provincial capital of Ruteng. The bones came mainly from a single skeleton (LB1) and included the skull, mandible, and much of the lower body (parts of the backbone, pelvis, legs, feet, and hands). An isolated lower premolar and an isolated radius (part of the forearm) were also found. The premolar could be confidently assigned to *H. floresiensis,* but the radius could only be assigned provisionally. The skeleton was situated next to the cave wall and showed no signs of deliberate burial.

Without a doubt, the two most unexpected aspects of the new species are its young age and its miniaturized condition. Radiocarbon, luminescence, and other dating procedures all point toward an age of 38,000 to 18,000 years BP for *Homo floresiensis.* Since there is evidence that *Homo sapiens* had reached Flores at least 35,000 years ago (if not earlier), anatomically modern people coexisted with *H. floresiensis* for over 15 millennia. This strongly suggests the two species exploited different ecological niches.

In their anatomy, *H. floresiensis* people combined primitive *Homo erectus*–like traits with derived dwarfed features. The former category included long, low-vaulted, and thick-boned skulls; moderately large brows; and a chinless mandible. With regard to their uniquely miniaturized anatomy, judging from the LB1 skeleton (thought to be an adult female), *Homo floresiensis* people were probably only about 3.5 feet (106 centimeters) tall and weighed around 57 pounds (26 kg). Brain size was also strongly miniaturized, measuring only 380 cubic centimeters in the LB1 skeleton (see Box 15.2 and Appendix 3 for more anatomical details).

The best explanation for the small size of the *Homo floresiensis* people is that they were the result of *island dwarfing.* Presumably, they were the descendants of modern-size *Homo erectus* ancestors but then experienced miniaturization thanks to natural selection "for small size in a low calorific environment, either after isolation on Flores,

BOX 15.2

Characteristics of *Homo floresiensis*[a]

Trait	*Homo floresiensis*
Height[b]	3.5 ft (106 cm)
Weight[b]	35–79 lb (16–36 kg) (midrange estimate: 57 lb, 26 kg)
Brain size[b]	380 cc
Cranium	Less facial prognathism than in *Australopithecus;* moderate supraorbital torus, accompanied by supraorbital sulcus; skull long, low vaulted, and widest near the base; flexed cranial base; thick cranial vault bones
Dentition	Parabolic toothrow; short canines but possibly a small maxillary diastema; grinding teeth somewhat megadont compared to *H. sapiens* but much less than in the australopiths
Diet	Archaeological evidence suggests hunting of juvenile dwarfed elephants (*Stegodon*)
Limbs	Femur broadly similar to *H. sapiens,* although much smaller; arm anatomy virtually unknown
Pelvis	Iliac blade is short and wide; greater lateral flare of the iliac blades than in *H. sapiens*
Locomotion	Bipedalism
Known dates	> 38,000 to 18,000 BP

[a]Values for anatomical measurements will change with additional fossil discoveries. For additional technical details and diagnostic traits, see Appendix 3.
[b]Based on one (presumably female) specimen.
Sources: Brown et al., 2004; Morwood et al., 2004.

or another insular environment in southeastern Asia" (Brown et al., 2004:1060; Diamond, 2004). This phenomenon of island dwarfism is known for other mammals and, indeed, also affected the indigenous elephants (*Stegodon*) on Flores (Lahr and Foley, 2004). Interestingly, the dwarfing process was more pronounced in the brain of *H. floresiensis* than in the body, rendering these people much less encephalized generally than modern human pygmies (Lahr and Foley, 2004). Small or not, however, the brain of *Homo floresiensis* was quite advanced in its details. Paleoneurologist Dean Falk and her colleagues have studied a computer-generated model of the brain of LB1 and found, among other modern features, that the frontal lobes were enlarged and highly folded (Balter, 2005). Brain anatomy like this implies aspects of higher cognition such as "undertaking initiatives and planning future actions" (Balter, 2005: 1386), and supports the notions that *Homo floresiensis* controlled fire and made stone tools. Tools found in Liang Bua Cave included burins and large and small blades, the latter possibly used by *H. floresiensis* to hunt dwarf elephants (Morwood et al., 2004; Wong, 2005).

Homo floresiensis presents us with a cautionary example as well as several puzzles. First, it is important to remember that only a single skeleton (plus a tooth and an arm bone) has been described. Other specimens are needed to confirm the unique anatomical mix of this creature and thus to verify its designation as a bona fide species. Without additional specimens, researchers cannot compare *H. floresiensis* with other hominins for such important parameters such as sexual dimorphism. Nor, for that matter, can we be absolutely sure that LB1 is not an abnormal specimen. Skeptics have already claimed that it is nothing more than a microcephalic modern human (Wong, 2005), but the new details on brain anatomy appear to refute that argument (Balter, 2005).

With regard to puzzles, besides making it necessary for all paleoanthropologists to become more familiar with the process and occurrence of island dwarfing, *Homo floresiensis* presents us with a challenging naming problem. As outlined in earlier chapters, a brain size of at least 600 cubic centimeters has long been a prerequisite for a species' inclusion in the genus *Homo.* But on Flores, we seem to have a very small-brained descendant of undoubtedly large-brained ancestors. Does the fact of *floresiensis*'s almost certain descent from *Homo erectus* entitle it to a place in that genus, or does its absolutely small cranial capacity (380 cubic centimeters in LB1) prevent it from being called *Homo?* (Calculating the EQ for the dwarfed Flores specimen is no help here because its body mass estimate is so uncertain. The *H. floresiensis* EQ could either be comparable to that of *H. erectus* or *H. habilis* or considerably lower [Brown et al, 2004].) It will be interesting in the coming months to follow the professional discussion about the proper name for the Flores specimen.

A second puzzle, of course, is how *H. floresiensis* and *H. sapiens* interacted once the latter species arrived in Flores. Did they compete for resources and space? Did they make contact, either friendly or aggressive? Did modern humans help to hasten the extinction of their dwarfed relatives? Only further study and (with luck) additional specimens will answer these questions and solve the taxonomic difficulties.

Those studies and discoveries lie in the future, however. For now, it is enough to enjoy the excitement of finding a new and remarkably different branch of the hominin tribe. It now seems likely that *Homo erectus* gave rise to more than one descendant: *H. heidelbergensis* in Africa or Southern Europe and, halfway around the world, *Homo floresiensis.* Who knows what surprises the next fossil discovery will bring?

Review Questions

1. Summarize the evidence supporting the "Out of Africa" model of the appearance of anatomically modern people. What weaknesses do you see in the model?
2. Summarize the evidence supporting the multiregional model of the appearance of anatomically modern people. What weaknesses do you see in the model? How would widescale anagenetic transformation take place?

3. Compare the anatomy of *Homo sapiens* to that of archaic humans and provide explanations for the changes. What anatomical features, if any, are unique to our species?
4. Describe the peopling of the Americas and Australia. When and how were these regions first entered and by whom?

SUGGESTED FURTHER READING

Diamond, Jared. *Guns, Germs, and Steel.* New York, W. W. Norton, 1997.

Jobling, Mark, Matthew Hurles, and Chris Tyler-Smith. *Human Evolutionary Genetics: Origins, Peoples and Disease.* New York, Garland, 2004.

Klein, Richard, and Blake Edgar. *The Dawn of Human Culture.* New York, Wiley, 2002.

Stringer, Christopher, and Robin McKie. *African Exodus.* New York, Henry Holt, 1996.

Sykes, Bryan. *The Seven Daughters of Eve.* New York, W. W. Norton, 2001.

INTERNET RESOURCES

THE ORIGIN OF MODERN HUMANS: MULTIREGIONAL AND REPLACEMENT THEORIES
http://calvin.linfield.edu/~mrobert/origins.html

Produced by biologist Michael Roberts, this site provides an examination of the two primary models for the evolution of modern people. Last updated in July 2002.

MITOCHONDRIAL DNA CLARIFIES HUMAN EVOLUTION
www.actionbioscience.org/evolution/ingman.html

Australian geneticist Max Ingman discusses the impact of mtDNA research on the question of modern origins.

NEWS AND VIEWS: OUT OF ETHIOPIA
www.nhm.ac.uk/palaeontology/v&a/cbs/Nature423CBS.pdf

Chris Stringer's commentary on the 2003 discovery of 160,000-year-old anatomically modern fossils in Ethiopia.

PNAS: THE EARLY UPPER PALEOLITHIC HUMAN SKELETON FROM THE ABRIGO DO LAGAR VELHO
www.pnas.org/cgi/content/full/96/13/7604

This site contains the 1999 report of the skeleton from Portugal claimed by some to be a Neandertal-*Homo sapiens* hybrid.

THE MTDNA DEBATE
www.geocities.com/CapeCanaveral/Launchpad/3917/mtdna.html

Links to lots of web sites about mtDNA, including several discussing how these studies bear on the question of Neandertal ancestry for modern Europeans.

FLORES MAN SPECIAL
www.nature.com/news/specials/flores/index.html

This news special from the journal *Nature* contains details of the recent discovery of a dwarfed species of late Pleistocene humans from Indonesia.

USEFUL SEARCH TERMS:

Herto fossils
Homo floresiensis
Homo sapiens
modern human origins
mtDNA studies
Multiregional hypothesis
Out of Africa hypothesis

Chapter 15 Timeline

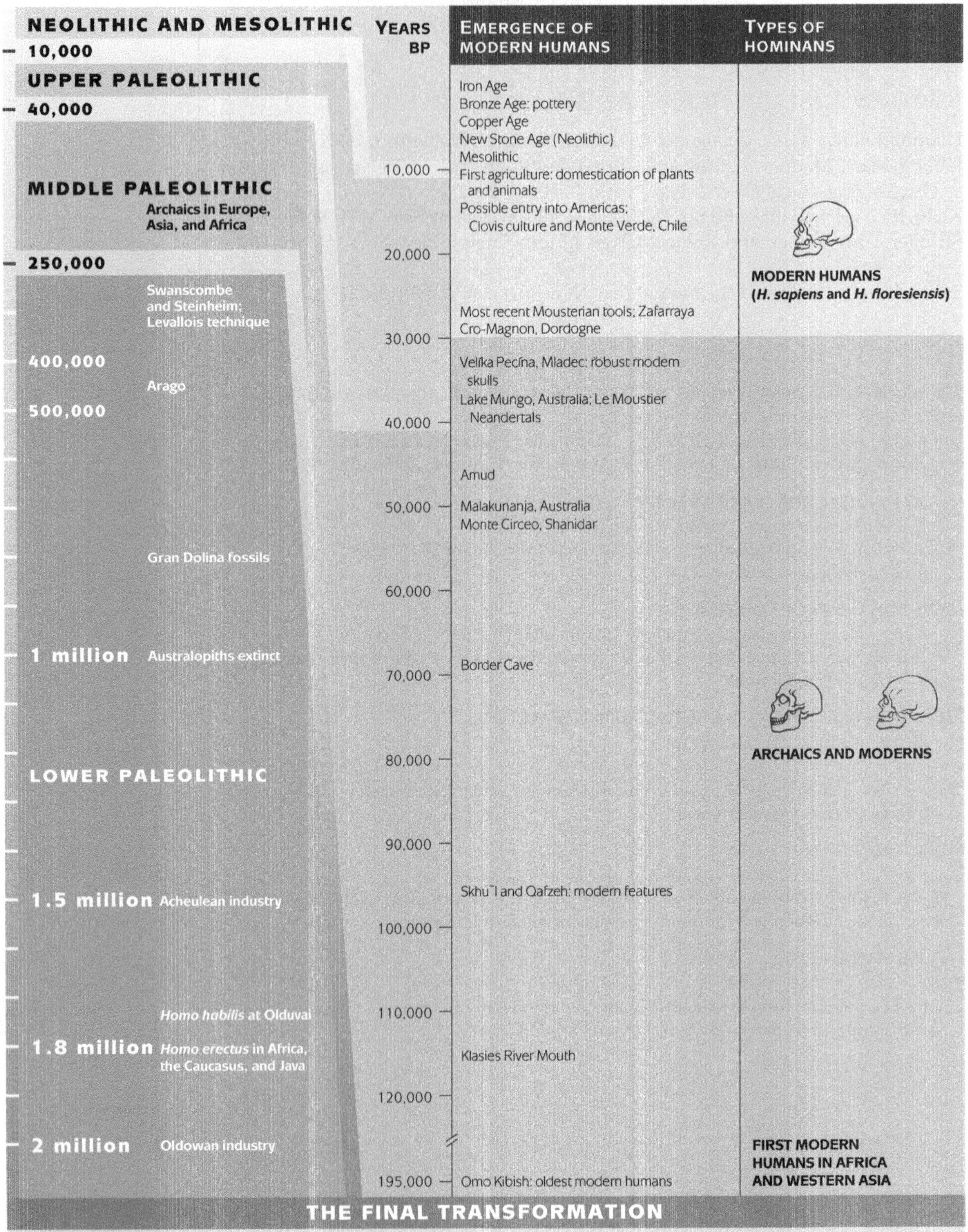

NEOLITHIC AND MESOLITHIC
10,000
UPPER PALEOLITHIC
40,000
MIDDLE PALEOLITHIC
Archaics in Europe, Asia, and Africa
250,000
Swanscombe and Steinheim; Levallois technique
400,000
Arago
500,000
Gran Dolina fossils
1 million Australopiths extinct
LOWER PALEOLITHIC
1.5 million Acheulean industry
Homo habilis at Olduvai
1.8 million *Homo erectus* in Africa, the Caucasus, and Java
2 million Oldowan industry

YEARS BP	EMERGENCE OF MODERN HUMANS	TYPES OF HOMINANS
	Iron Age Bronze Age: pottery Copper Age New Stone Age (Neolithic) Mesolithic	
10,000	First agriculture: domestication of plants and animals Possible entry into Americas; Clovis culture and Monte Verde, Chile	
20,000		MODERN HUMANS (*H. sapiens* and *H. floresiensis*)
	Most recent Mousterian tools; Zafarraya Cro-Magnon, Dordogne	
30,000	Velika Pecina, Mladec: robust modern skulls Lake Mungo, Australia; Le Moustier Neandertals	
40,000	Amud	
50,000	Malakunanja, Australia Monte Circeo, Shanidar	
60,000		
	Border Cave	
70,000		ARCHAICS AND MODERNS
80,000		
90,000	Skhu¯l and Qafzeh: modern features	
100,000		
110,000	Klasies River Mouth	
120,000		
195,000	Omo Kibish: oldest modern humans	FIRST MODERN HUMANS IN AFRICA AND WESTERN ASIA

THE FINAL TRANSFORMATION

This chart shows the approximate chronology of the Middle to Upper Paleolithic sequence. Many dates are approximate.

Chapter 16

The Advent of Modern Culture

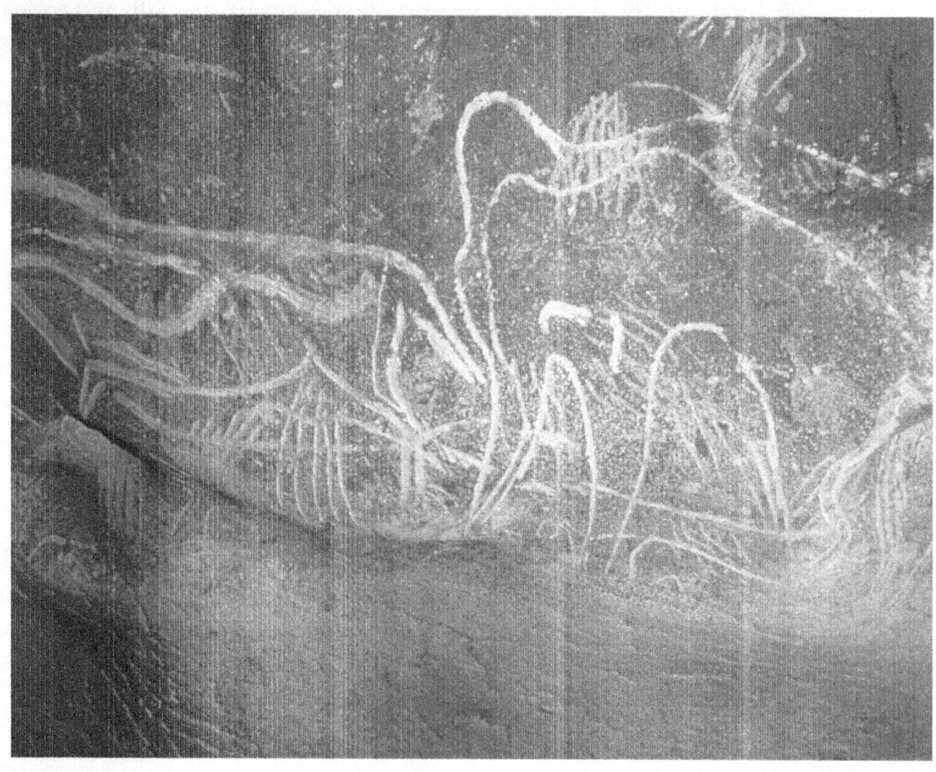

Mammoths and other animals move across the walls of the Chauvet Cave, discovered in France in 1994.

Human life is everywhere a state in which much is to be endured and little to be enjoyed.

Samuel Johnson, 1709–1784. *Rasselas*, Ch. 7.

Overview

The evolution of anatomically modern humans—*Homo sapiens*—was followed by a significant upswing in cultural complexity, and this chapter is concerned with describing that cultural surge. Increased control was gained over the production and use of fire; improved gathering, fishing, and hunting techniques ensured a dependable food supply and allowed a degree of sedentary living; and technology was broadened by the invention of new tool types and the increased use of bone, antler, and ivory as raw materials.

Furthermore, there was a strong improvement in artistic skills and endeavors—resulting in beautiful rock-shelter and cave art, carved ivory and bone implements, and clay sculptures—and also the elaboration of funeral rites, very likely reflecting the development of religion. And finally, elements of material culture indicate that societies were becoming more complex and probably stratified during this time. Humankind was now modern not only anatomically but intellectually, as well.

The Later Stone Age–Upper Paleolithic Surge in Cultural Complexity

By about 40,000 years ago, anatomically modern humans (*Homo sapiens*) were spread across Africa, Eurasia, and Indonesia/Australia. They inhabited a wide variety of environments, including tropical and temperate forests, woodland savannas, grassy steppes, and rocky seacoasts. In some areas, they struggled annually with cold and snow and with seasons of scarcity. In other areas, where the climate was more benign, life was a little easier. Everywhere, *Homo sapiens* exploited their environment with greater efficiency than had their forebears. Some populations continued to move seasonally, following the annual rhythms of animal and plant availability; others managed to live a somewhat more sedentary life by focusing on continuously available foods.

Mini-TIMELINE

Date (Years BP)	Evolutionary Events or Cultural Developments
10,000	End of Upper Paleolithic
16,500–11,000	Magdalenian culture (blade tools and harpoons)
20,000	Probable first use of bow and arrow
21,000–16,500	Solutrean culture (laurel-leaf blades)
27,000–21,000	Perigordian culture (female figurines)
33,000–30,000	Oldest cave art (La Grotte Chauvet)
40,000–27,000	Aurignacian culture
~45,000–40,000	Start of Upper Paleolithic
~50,000–45,000	Start of Later Stone Age
195,000	Oldest fossils of *Homo sapiens* (Omo Kibish)

Humankind achieved anatomical modernity 195,000 years ago or thereabouts, apparently as part of a speciation event in Africa. We have seen that this modernization involved facial reduction, globularization of the skull, and the attainment of modern proportions of the vocal tract—changes that many researchers think were due to selection for increasingly complex speech (D. Lieberman, 1998; P. Lieberman, 2002). That may be true, but confusingly, there seems to have been a lag of about 100,000 to 50,000 years between the attainment of modern cranial–facial anatomy and the spurt in cultural complexity that marks the presence of modern behavior. As Richard Klein and Blake Edgar have noted, "The people who lived in Africa between 130,000 and 50,000 years ago may have been modern or near-modern in form, but they were behaviorally similar to [archaic humans such as] the Neanderthals" (2002:230). Were their cognitive and/or communication skills not as sophisticated as their cranial and vocal tract anatomies imply?

No one knows for sure, but it is beginning to appear that that may have been the case and that something special happened to early *Homo sapiens* around 100,000 to 50,000 years BP. Richard Klein, Thomas Wynn, Frederick Coolidge and others conclude that the "special something" was a mutation that finally produced our fully modern brain and speech (Klein and Edgar, 2002; Wynn and Coolidge, 2004). Wynn and Coolidge describe such a mutation as producing *EWM* (*enhanced working memory*), complete with "higher levels of innovation, thought experiment, and narrative complexity [than in archaic humans]" (2004:484).

The creative spurt or explosion that marked behavioral modernity—sometimes referred to as the "big bang" of human culture (Klein and Edgar, 2002)—resulted in the Later Stone Age (LSA) in Africa and the Upper Paleolithic (UP) in Eurasia. The LSA's beginning can be dated around 50,000 to 45,000 years ago, and the UP appeared some 5,000 years later. Compared to the Middle Stone Age/Middle Paleolithic, the LSA and the UP shared the following set of cultural advances: an increased number of stone tool types; the production of many sorts of bone artifacts; the production of works of art and items for personal decoration; an increase in burial elaboration that suggests ritual interment; and increased subsistence efficiency and population densities (Klein and Edgar, 2002). Collectively, these innovations may explain why moderns dispersing from Africa were able to replace or "swamp" (genetically and culturally) resident archaics between 70,000 and 27,000 years ago.

Work is continuing on the question of what triggered the LSA/UP "big bang." (There are other explanations besides the neural mutation hypothesis [Klein and Edgar, 2002].) Here, we will focus on certain aspects of *Homo sapiens*'s cultural bloom as it was manifested across the Old World.

Mastery of Fire

LSA/UP people added new dimensions to the use of fire. As shown by the occasional discovery of firestones made of **iron pyrite,** they had the ability to strike a fire quickly whenever they needed one. Additionally, they had learned how to construct hearths so that their fires would burn hotter (R. Klein, 1999). The evidence of this comes from sites in Central and Eastern Europe, where some hearths include shallow grooves in the bottom and a channel curving away like a tail. This configuration fed more air to the fire, which then burned hotter.

Iron pyrite a mineral substance (iron disulfide) that, when struck with flint, makes sparks that will start a fire.

The people who built these special hearths needed them because of the type of fuel they used. In an area where wood was scarce, they had to turn for fuel to a material that normally does not burn well: bone (Burenhult, 1993). Although bone is hard to ignite and burns inefficiently, being only about 25 percent combustible material, it gives off adequate heat. That these people did burn it is proved by the lack of charred wood and the considerable quantities of bone ash found in their specially vented hearths.

The hearth was home, and the LSA/Upper Paleolithic people, who changed so much else, also changed the concept of home. Even though some lived in the same caves and rock shelters that had protected their predecessors, in other areas, they produced sturdily built shelters in open country (Burenhult, 1993a; R. Klein, 1999).

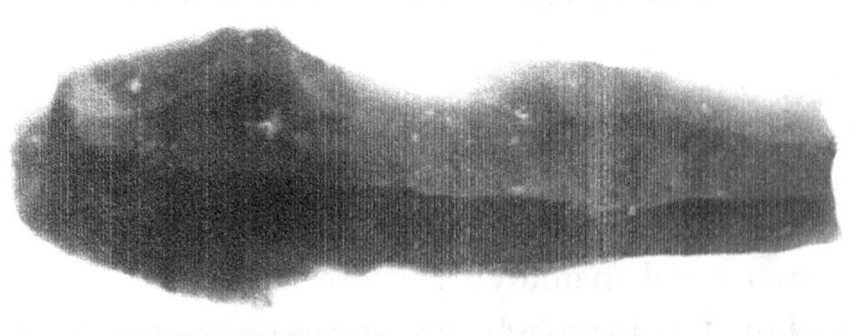

FIGURE 16.1
This Upper Paleolithic burin is an early chisel, which was a new and important technological development. Its main use was perhaps to make other tools of wood or bone. This photograph is approximately one-half actual size.

Tool Specialization

Compared to their archaic forebears, LSA/UP people produced a greater variety of tools from a greater variety of materials. In both the LSA and the UP, we also see a lot of change through time in artifact industries. This is in strong contrast to the Middle Paleolithic, which was relatively uniform in both time and space. Among the LSA/UP lithic implements were knives and scrapers (in LSA cultures, these were often "backed" or dulled along one edge), drills and saws, burins for shaping softer materials, ceremonial blades, and spear and arrow points. In Upper Paleolithic cultures, blade tools were commonplace. Long, narrow, and razor-sharp, blades were used unmodified as knives and as the raw material for other tool types, such as endscrapers and burins. Furthermore, small bladelets were apparently mounted in handles of some sort to produce composite tools. Interestingly, the LSA differed from the UP in the relative scarcity of both blades and burins, another indication of geographic variability in this time period. The classic European UP sequence (see the Mini-Timeline at the beginning of this chapter)—with the named industries of Aurignacian, Perigordian, Solutrean, and Magdalenian—also exemplifies this variability (R. Klein, 1999; Klein and Edgar, 2002).

Clearly, one of the most important UP tools was the cutter called a *burin* (see Figure 16.1). It is tempting to say that Upper Paleolithic people invented the burin, but it had existed in a few Neandertal tool kits, and a few burinlike tools are sometimes found in the tool assemblages of *Homo erectus*. In the hands of early anatomically modern people, however, the burin was gradually improved and became more important and much more prevalent.

A burin was a kind of chisel. It was a tool with a strong, sharply beveled edge or point used to cut, incise, and shape other materials, such as bone, antler, and wood. That is to say, the burin's chief function was the manufacture of other tools and implements. With a tool that made other tools, technology could expand many times faster than ever before.

Bone, antler, and ivory were the wonder materials of those times, much as plastics are today. Less brittle and therefore more workable than flint and much stronger and more durable than wood, they could be cut, grooved, chiseled, scraped, sharpened, and shaped. They could be finely worked into tiny implements like needles, or they could be used for heavy work. A deer antler made an excellent pick. A mammoth's leg bone cracked lengthwise needed only minor modifications and a handle to become an efficient shovel. Ivory could be steamed and bent, processes adding yet another dimension to tool making.

Best of all, the very animals hunted and depended on for food provided these materials in abundance. All animals have bone, of course, and many large animals—red deer, reindeer, mammoth—had antlers or tusks, as well. Antlers seemed almost to be nature's gift to humans because they did not even have to kill an animal to obtain them: Every year, deer shed their old ones, which lie on the ground for the picking up. Because reindeer and red deer were at one time or another perhaps the most abundant game animals in Western Europe, antler was used there more than bone or ivory. In parts of Eastern Europe and Siberia, where wood was relatively scarce, the skeletons and tusks of mammoths that had died natural deaths or had been trapped by hunters were a source of tools (Semenov, 1964). In Tasmania, stout bone points were made from the lower legs of wallabies (Cosgrove, 1993).

With its strong chisel point, a burin could easily scratch or dig into ivory or bone without breaking. To cut up a bone, the tool maker could incise a deep groove around the bone and then, with a sharp blow, break it cleanly at the cut. To get slivers for

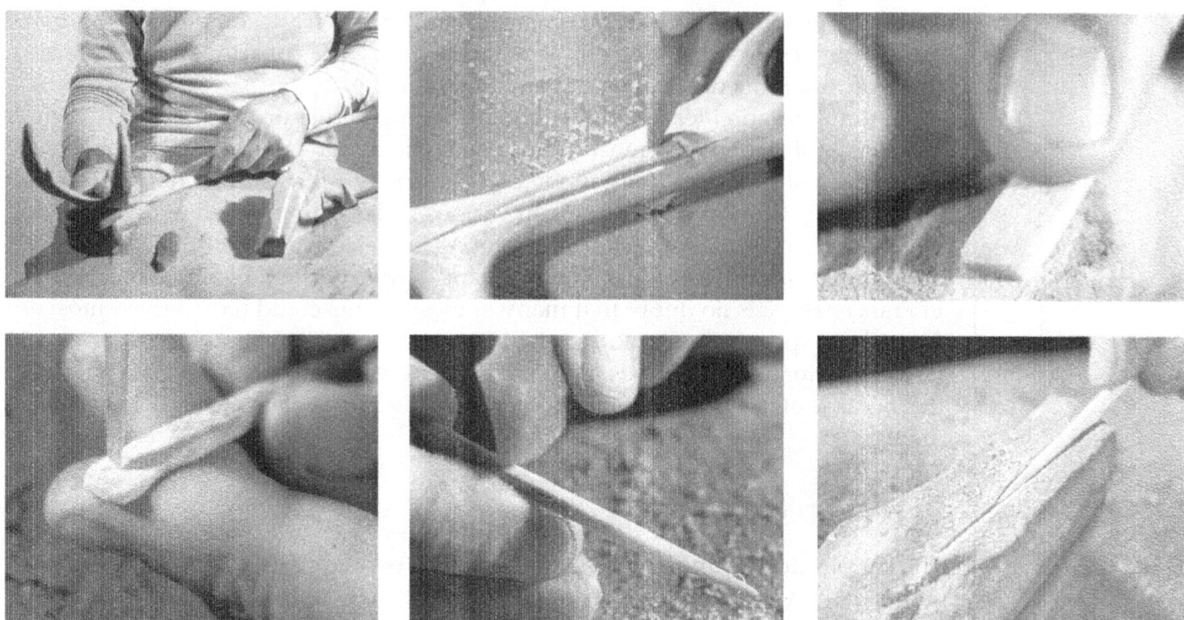

FIGURE 16.2
The slow process of making a needle out of an antler can be broken down into six steps.

needles, points, and awls, it was necessary only to draw a burin repeatedly lengthwise down a bone to score two parallel grooves deep enough to hit the soft center. Then the piece of hard material between the grooves was pried out and ground to shape (Figure 16.2). Other pieces of bone could be turned into spatulas, scrapers, beads, bracelets, digging tools, spear points, lances, and barbed harpoon tips.

Solutrean Laurel-leaf Blades

Improvement in stone tools was crucial to the developing Upper Paleolithic technical mastery. It is ironic that, despite all efforts to decipher them, no one really knows what purpose was served by the most beautiful examples of this new skill. Anyone who has ever held and examined a tool such as the magnificent laurel-leaf blade (Figure 16.3) must eventually wonder how this implement could have been used. Too delicate for a knife, too big and fragile for a spearhead, so beautifully

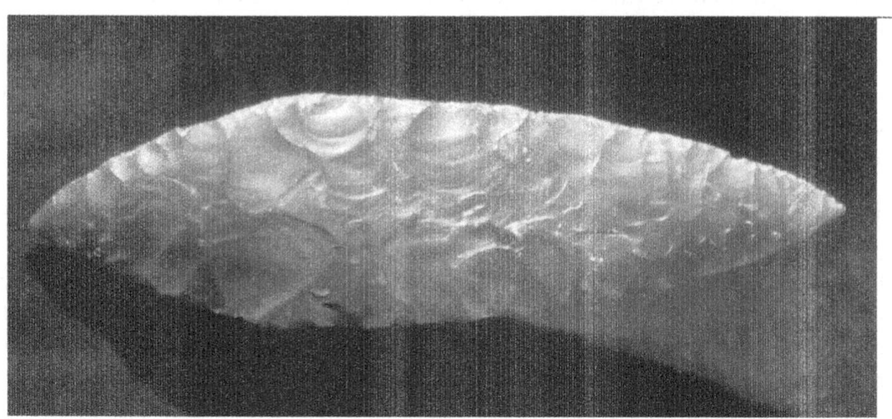

FIGURE 16.3
A laurel-leaf blade is so delicate that it could have served no practical purpose. This blade—11 inches (28 centimeters) long but only 0.4 inches (1 centimeter) thick—may have been a ceremonial object. These finely chipped blades are part of the Solutrean tool industry.

crafted a piece of flint seems to be a showpiece. Clearly, to produce an object of such daring proportions required craftsmanship bordering on art, and perhaps this masterpiece and others like it may have been just that: works of art that served an aesthetic or ritual function, rather than a utilitarian one.

If the large laurel-leaf blades were made for no useful purpose, they were clearly an instance of technology transcending itself. The smaller, everyday implements on which such showpieces were modeled had strictly practical functions. They are known in the thousands and come in various styles from sites all over the world. Stone points in various sizes have been found in Western and Central European excavations at cultural levels called **Solutrean**—a style typified by finds from Solutré in France. There is no doubt that many of these points could have served most effectively as spear points or knives with razor-sharp edges. Flint knives are equal, if not superior, to steel knives in their cutting power. The only drawback of flint is that because of its brittleness, it breaks more easily than metal and has to be replaced more often.

Solutrean an *Upper Paleolithic* culture existing in Western Europe between 21,000 and 16,500 years BP; best known for its laurel-leaf blades.

Hunters Par Excellence

The various deadly implements of the LSA/UP people—first spears and harpoons and later, bows and arrows—as well as the abundant animal remains in their living sites bear mute testimony to the hunting skills of these early humans. Reindeer, mammoths, bison, and horses were common game animals across Eurasia (R. Klein, 1999). At Solutré, in France (Figure 15.1), the fossilized remains of tens of thousands of horses have been found, and it is thought that Upper Paleolithic hunters either drove the animals over a nearby precipice or used the cliff edge "as a barrier to hedge the animals in, allowing them to be separated and slaughtered" (Burenhult, 1993a:92). It is likely that late Pleistocene people all across the world understood as much about hunting large herd animals as any humans in history. They undoubtedly knew just which plants the animals preferred to eat, when seasonal migrations began and how fast the animals traveled, and what panicked them and what soothed them. They knew how to ambush animals, how to encircle them, and how to kill them at close range and, using spear throwers and bows and arrows, at a safe distance.

These people's profound understanding of their prey, combined with significant technical advances in their hunting equipment, paid off in increased food supplies. Hunters had long had wooden spears with fire-hardened tips or sharp stone heads to thrust or throw at their prey, but the effectiveness of a hand-thrown spear must have been limited. Upper Paleolithic hunters made the spear a much more effective weapon by inventing the spear thrower (commonly referred to today by its Aztec name, the **atlatl**).

Atlatl an Aztec name for the spear thrower, a rodlike device used as an extension of the arm that greatly increases both the distance and impact of a throw.

The oldest evidence of this rodlike device dates from about 17,000 years BP, and comes from Europe (Hutchings and Brüchert, 1997). More than 70 reindeer–antler spear throwers have turned up in southwestern France and near Lake Constance along the northeastern border of Switzerland. There is a curious dearth of them elsewhere in the Old World, perhaps because they may have been made of wood and rotted away. By about 10,000 years ago, the wooden spear thrower was being used by the Indians of North and South America. The Inuit used it until recently, and some Australian Aborigines still use it today, calling it a *womera* (Figure 16.4).

The spear thrower is, in the simplest explanation, an extension of the arm. It is 1 to 2 feet (30 to 60 centimeters) long, with a handle at one end and a point or hook at the other that engages the butt end of the spear. Hunters hold the thrower behind their shoulder, hook up, and lay the spear along the thrower so that the spear points forward and slightly upward. During the throw, they keep hold of the thrower, which may have a thong tied to its end to go around their wrist. When throwing, they swing their arms forward and snap their wrist, launching the spear

FIGURE 16.4
The method of throwing a spear has not changed since spear throwers were introduced in Upper Paleolithic times about 17,000 years ago. Here, an Australian is shown poised to throw his stone-tipped spear. The womera, or spear thrower, can be clearly seen.

with great velocity from the end of the thrower at the top of its arc, in this way taking advantage of the centrifugal force generated. The spear travels faster than if hand thrown because the extension of the throwing arm provides more leverage; the spear thrower's end moves faster than the hand holding it.

Ethnographic observations and experiments have demonstrated the great advantages a spear thrower gives. A light spear can be thrown no more than 115 to 130 feet (35 to 40 meters) when launched directly from a hunter's hand, but it can be projected over 260 feet (80 meters) with a spear thrower (Semenov, 1964). Increased distance of throw may not have been the primary benefit, however. Experimental archaeologists W. K. Hutchings and L. W. Brüchert (1997) suggest that most hunting with the atlatl was done at distances of 50 to 65 feet (15 to 20 meters) from the prey, with experienced hunters hitting their target almost half of the time. Of particular importance, hits were often fatal or disabling, since atlatl-thrown spears generate enormous kinetic energy and highly lethal killing impact. (Surprisingly, the atlatl produces more kinetic energy than arrows shot from either traditional or modern bows.) The combination of greater range (compared to hand-thrown spears) and greater impact undoubtedly worked to the Upper Paleolithic hunters' advantage.

The first spear throwers were undoubtedly of wood, as the Australian womeras are today, but soon they were also being made from antler. People of the Upper Paleolithic **Magdalenian** culture embellished many of their throwers with carved figures and designs, including exquisite renderings of horses, deer, ibex, bison, birds, and fish (Leroi-Gourhan, 1965). These carvings on weaponry represent a combination of aesthetics and utility that is echoed in many aspects of Magdalenian life.

Magdalenian an *Upper Paleolithic* culture existing in Western Europe from about 16,500 to 11,000 years BP; produced many *blade* tools and prototype harpoons.

Other functional advances were in the spear itself. By this time, hunters had realized that a barbed point does more damage than a smooth one. Harpoon-style points, fashioned from bone or antler, often had several barbs on one or both sides (Figure 16.5). Another development stemmed from the difficulty of killing an animal outright by one spear wound alone; hunters would have to follow their wounded prey for a while until loss of blood made it weak enough for them to kill. To speed this process, some hunters carved bone spearheads with grooves along each side—runnels apparently designed to increase the flow of blood from the wound (R. Klein, 1999).

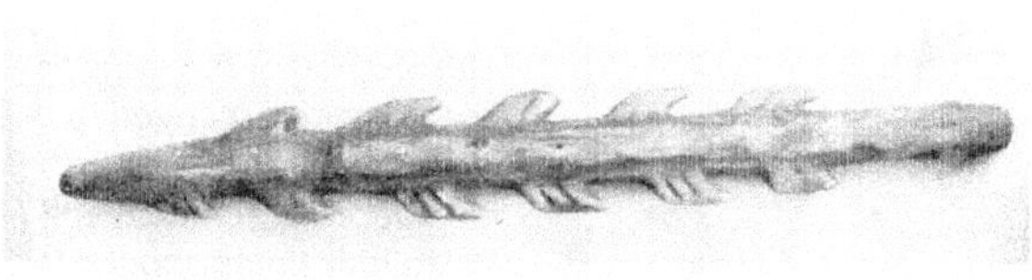

FIGURE 16.5 This beautifully made Magdalenian harpoon was part of a highly developed collection of fishing tackle. This photograph is about 90 percent actual size.

The Bow and Arrow

An interesting puzzle is the use of the bow and arrow. There is no clear-cut archaeological evidence that people used such a weapon until around 20,000 years ago (Schick and Toth, 1993; Klein and Edgar, 2002). But because bows are normally made of wood and sinew or gut, it would be a lucky accident indeed if any had survived the last ice age, and so the lack of evidence cannot be taken as conclusive. Among the best early evidence of the bow and arrow are microliths and bone foreshafts produced by LSA people in Africa. These artifacts closely resemble historic arrow points and foreshafts from the region.

Certainly, the bow would have given hunters the advantage of increased stealth. The spear thrower, no matter how valuable an aid, required hunters to break cover and stand out in the open, where they could be spotted by their prey. Moreover, an unsuccessful launch would scare off the target. But with the bow, hunters could remain hidden. If they missed with the first arrow, they could likely shoot again. Moreover, the arrow was swifter than the spear and it could be shot at a variety of animals—big and small, standing, running, or on the wing—with a good chance of hitting them.

Fishing Gear

Perhaps as important as the invention of the spear thrower or the bow in helping LSA/UP people expand their food supply and make a living in varied environments was the development of fishing gear. Human groups had earlier availed themselves of the bounty offered by streams, rivers, and the sea, but for some, fishing now became almost a way of life.

The oldest known bone fishhooks come from European sites about 14,000 years old. LSA coastal sites, such as Blombos Cave and Klasies River Mouth, have yielded toothpick-size fish *gorges,* small slivers of bone that were probably used with a leather or sinew line tied around the middle. When the baited gorge was swallowed by a fish, it cocked sideways in its throat in such a way as not to come out easily, and the catch was made (R. Klein, 1999; Klein and Edgar, 2002). Furthermore, small, grooved cylindrical stones found at those same LSA sites may have been weights on nets made of thongs or plant fibers. With a net, two or three people could catch a whole shoal of fish on one sweep.

The subsistence system of Later Stone Age and Upper Paleolithic people thus involved the exploitation of a wide variety of resources: herbivores, fish, shellfish, and fowl (Gore, 2000; Klein and Edgar, 2002). That dietary package would have been rounded out, of course, by the addition of gathered wild plant foods, and recent discoveries in the Levant have shown just how important the latter resources were to some populations.

Ohalo II in Israel is a 23,000-year-old Upper Paleolithic site on the shores of the Sea of Galilee. Archaeologists digging at Ohalo II between 1989 and 2001 discovered the remains of several huts and hearths, chipped and ground stone tools, and numerous animal bones (Weiss et al., 2004). Most important, however, due to the unusual preservation conditions at the site, the researchers also recovered an enormous collection of plant remains. Chief among the Ohalo II plant foods were grass seeds, including those of the wild cereals emmer wheat and barley, as well as several small-grained grasses, such as brome, foxtail, and alkali grass. Testifying to their dietary importance, grains of several types were found "concentrated around a grinding stone, which was discovered *in situ*" in one of the hut sites (2004:9552). Thus, grass seeds were gathered in quantity, ground up, and then (undoubtedly) cooked in some manner before being eaten by the Ohalo II people. These activities clearly set the stage for the domestication of cereals in the Levant some 13,000 years after Ohalo II.

Bone Needles and Sewn Clothing

Upper Paleolithic people inhabiting the higher latitudes of Eurasia would have benefited from any cultural improvement in their protection against the cold of the ice age. Carefully sewn, fitted clothing was part of the equipment that enabled them to conquer the far north and eventually to penetrate North America.

The hide clothing of these people was probably much like that of today's Inuit. A tunic or pullover with tightly sewn seams to keep heat from escaping, pants easily tucked into boots, and some sort of sock, perhaps of fur, would have been warm enough in all but the coldest weather. For frigid days, outer clothing consisting of a hooded parka, mittens, and high boots would have kept a person from freezing.

What is our evidence that the people had clothing of this sort? Bone needles were in existence 19,000 to 18,000 years ago in Europe (R. Klein, 1999; see Figure 16.2), strongly suggesting that these people wore sewn clothing. And in addition, we have the evidence of the 5,000-year-old Iceman discovered in 1991 in the Italian Alps (Discovery Channel; Sykes, 2001). Although he lived thousands of years after the Upper Paleolithic, it seems reasonable to assume that the Iceman's attire—stitched leather clothes (including leggings), a bear fur hat, and a braided grass cloak over it all—probably resembled the garments of his UP forebears.

Art and Ritual

Cave Art

Until now, our discussion of LSA and UP people has centered on their improvements in working stone and particularly bone and on the cultural developments furthered by these technological improvements. Notable as these changes were, it is the intellectual and spiritual achievements of these people that make them so impressive to us today. Particularly striking is their astounding artistic ability, a talent that may have been due to the evolution of a completely modern mind.

There are dozens of examples of cave art in France alone. These date from more than 30,000 to 10,000 years BP and are attributed primarily to the Solutrean and Magdalenian peoples (Leroi-Gourhan, 1965). Equally ancient rock art sites have been found in Tanzania and in the southern African nation of Namibia. At the Namibian site of Apollo Cave, rock slabs painted with the outlines of animals have been recovered that date to between 28,000 and 19,000 years BP (J. Deacon, 1999; Lewis-Williams, 1983). Similarly aged paintings have come from Australia. Red paint from the Sandy Creek site in Queensland is reported to date back 25,000 years, and petroglyphs from other Australian sites may be over 40,000 years old (Bahn, 1995/96). By the latest Pleistocene, rock art had also appeared in India and the Americas. All of these sites show that Upper Paleolithic peoples and their contemporaries outside Europe were close observers of the animals they hunted as well as magnificent artists. More than that, the record they left behind shows that they had a sufficiently sophisticated way of life to be able to appreciate and encourage their own talents and to work them into their rituals.

Traditionally, the paintings and carvings of these people have been interpreted as closely associated with their spiritual life. One strong indication is seen in the places they chose to put wall paintings. The caves in the Dordogne region of France are basically of two kinds. The rock overhangs, more or less open and facing out over the valleys, are full of the signs of many generations of occupancy; tools lie in all strata in their floors, together with buried skeletons and hearths. Some fragments of wall decoration have been found in the open shelters; perhaps originally, there were more that have since been destroyed by exposure to the elements.

The most spectacular wall art is confined to true caves: deep underground fissures with long galleries and passages (Leroi-Gourhan, 1965). They are dark, mysterious, and very cold; they could be entered only by people holding stone lamps or torches. Certainly, these caverns were inappropriate as dwelling places, and their inner chambers show little or no evidence of having been lived in. By nature removed from day-to-day life, these caves may well have been used as shrines and for the performance of certain rites.

Painting and Hunting Magic

Important early observations about the location of cave art were made by the late Abbé Henri Breuil, a French priest who devoted his life to the study of prehistory. Breuil and subsequent students of cave art have all noted that the paintings or engravings were often made in the least convenient places for viewing: in narrow niches, behind protrusions of rock, sometimes in areas that must have been not only difficult but actually dangerous for the artist to work in. For some reason, the art needed to be veiled in secrecy.

Sympathetic hunting magic the use of rituals and associated artifacts that practitioners believed would ensure success and safety in the hunt.

What was its purpose, then? The traditional explanation is that cave art was a vehicle for magic—more specifically, a vehicle for a form known as **sympathetic hunting magic** (Conkey, 1993; Dickson, 1990). LSA/UP people were strong and intelligent, and they were well equipped with all kinds of weapons, from spears and knives to harpoons and nets. They could ambush animals and stampede them. And as we have seen, they left behind them impressive records of their prowess. Nevertheless, despite their formidable powers, they walked always in the shadow of unpredictable and incomprehensible events, which they may have seen as malign forces. Doubtless, they felt it necessary to try to forestall misfortune and injury—and perhaps death, for some of the animals they came up against were extremely dangerous. Perhaps they believed, like so many people living today, that magic could help them not only dodge misfortune but also gain control over the animals they wanted to kill. By painting the animals' pictures, they became, in effect, the animals' masters and strengthened their chances of dealing the prey a mortal wound during the hunt.

This interpretation of the paintings as hunting magic has a variety of evidence to support it. First and most direct is the large number of game animals depicted (Figure 16.6) and the fact that several were painted with feathery darts of some sort in or near them. Good examples of the latter category include the apparently pregnant horse and the "Chinese" horse, both from the cave of Lascaux, France (Figure

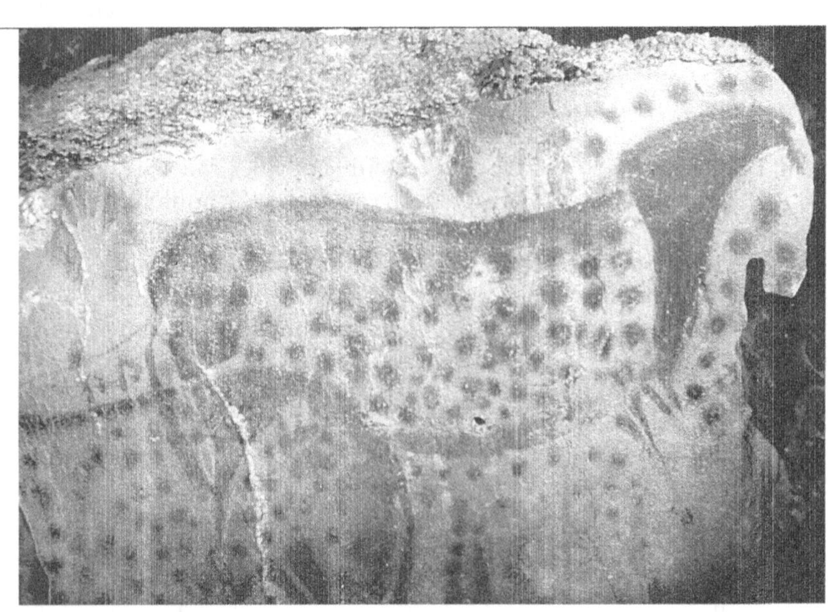

FIGURE 16.6 Covered with dots and surrounded by handprints, a painting of two horses in the Pech-Merle cave (Dordogne) may represent hunting magic. Alternately, the horses could have been produced over time as part of cult ceremonies of some sort, as suggested by Burenhult (1993b).

FIGURE 16.7
An apparently pregnant horse gallops across the limestone ceiling of Lascaux. The slash marks above its shoulders may indicate spears. Lascaux, among the finest of all the painted caves of southwestern France, is a Magdalenian masterpiece, dated about 17,000 years BP.

16.7). Also at Lascaux is a bison shown with a spear through its belly and its entrails spilling out. Interestingly, a prostrate humanlike figure (the hunter?) lies helplessly in front of the bison's lowered horns (Leroi-Gourhan, 1965), perhaps reflecting the dangers inherent in pursuing big game.

Second, there is a hint of hunting magic in the practice of superimposing one picture over another (Dickson, 1990). This phenomenon has been observed over and over again in the caves. In one spot at Lascaux, the paintings are four layers deep, even though there is plenty of empty wall space nearby. If the painters had meant simply to express themselves or give pleasure to others, they probably would have started with a clean wall surface for each animal depicted. The concentration of paintings in one spot, one atop another, suggests that the placement of the painting was somehow important and that the overpainting was done for a purpose. Certain areas of the cave were favored for some reason, and it would be logical to suppose that paintings that had previously brought hunters good luck came, in themselves, to be regarded as good hunting magic. Because ritual depends on duplicating as closely as possible a procedure that has proved successful in the past, certain spots in the cave would come to be regarded as lucky.

Hunting magic may also explain the occasional human–beast figures found in caves, strange-looking creatures with human bodies and animal or bird heads called *therianthropes.* Many anthropologists believe that these creatures represented shamans or sorcerers, who must have played an important part in the lives of the artists (Dickson, 1990). The humanlike figure from Lascaux, mentioned earlier, that was painted sprawled before a wounded bison is a therianthrope, complete with a bird's head and beak (Leroi-Gourhan, 1965). Does this figure depict a shaman, or was it produced by a shaman as part of a hunting-related ceremony? No one knows for sure.

Despite the logic and the long-term popularity of the hunting magic hypothesis, however, some researchers believe that it is not the only—and perhaps not even the best—interpretation of cave imagery. For example, Margaret Conkey (1993), of the University of California at Berkeley, and others have pointed out that the cave paintings and sculptures are generally of animal species *other* than those that figured heavily in Upper Paleolithic diets. While roughly 65 percent of the European cave images depict either horses or bison, two other species—red deer and reindeer—actually dominate the food refuse. Thus, if the images were intended to ensure success in the hunt, they didn't work very well—at least as reflected by the remains of ancient meals.

Furthermore, the idea that many of the cave sites were shrines whose images accumulated over long periods and repeated visits has been called into question. Recent analyses of pollen in cave sediments and of paint composition ("pigment recipes") suggest that in some cases, complex images, including depictions of groups and/or superimposed animals, were painted quickly and on one occasion. Results such as these tend to weaken (but not completely refute) the traditional notion that the caves were used over thousands of years by many generations of hopeful hunters.

Art and Fertility

Thus, although hunting magic may explain a great deal of cave art, that interpretation is not airtight. Some authorities believe that these animals and cryptic geometrical signs are sexual in nature and that the paintings were fertility magic. Horses, does, and cows were painted with swollen bellies (as in Figure 16.7), which have been interpreted as a sign of advanced pregnancy. In other paintings, udders were enlarged, as if to emphasize the rich supply of milk that the mother would be capable of giving to any offspring that might be born.

The fertility of prey animals was a natural concern of the hunters. Scarcity of food must have been a periodic problem in many regions, and the need to feed increasing numbers of people may well have led the Cro-Magnons to encourage the natural productiveness of their game with fertility magic.

Other authorities think that cave art, although sexual in content, was far less utilitarian in its purpose. Instead of fertility magic, they see it as an attempt to express in visual symbols the dual forces in human nature: male and female. The most notable spokesperson for this post-Freudian point of view is French anthropologist André Leroi-Gourhan, who has made an extensive study of cave art (1965). Leroi-Gourhan charted the frequency of occurrence of the various kinds of animals and signs, along with their locations in the caves and their positions in relation to each other. He thinks that most of the paintings and drawings have specific sexual connotations—that deer and bear are masculine, as are such signs as spears and clubs, whereas cattle and bison, as well as the enclosed figures that other authorities identify as traps in support of the theory of hunting magic, are feminine.

Taking an entirely new approach, Alexander Marshack (1991) has examined the smaller portable items of Upper Paleolithic art under a low-powered microscope. He has made many surprising observations and has drawn some startling, if controversial, conclusions. A beautiful horse 2.5 inches (6 centimeters) long, carved in mammoth ivory and from the site of Vogelherd in Germany, is one of the earliest known examples of animal sculpture, dating from about 30,000 years BP. The carefully carved ear, nose, mouth, and mane have been worn down by persistent handling. At some time during this use, a fresh angle or dart was engraved in its flank, apparently symbolizing an act of actual or ritualized killing. The object was touched and used often and seems to have served some important purpose.

A second example described by Marshack is the image of a horse engraved on a horse's pelvis from the site of Paglicci in Italy. Microscopic examination of the image indicated that the horse had been symbolically killed 27 times. Twenty-seven feathered darts or spears were engraved on and around the horse, each made by a different engraving point and in a different style, possibly over a considerable period of time.

But Marshack (1991) has noticed other details. On some portable items, he has found small marks, often in series, made at different times by different tools, which

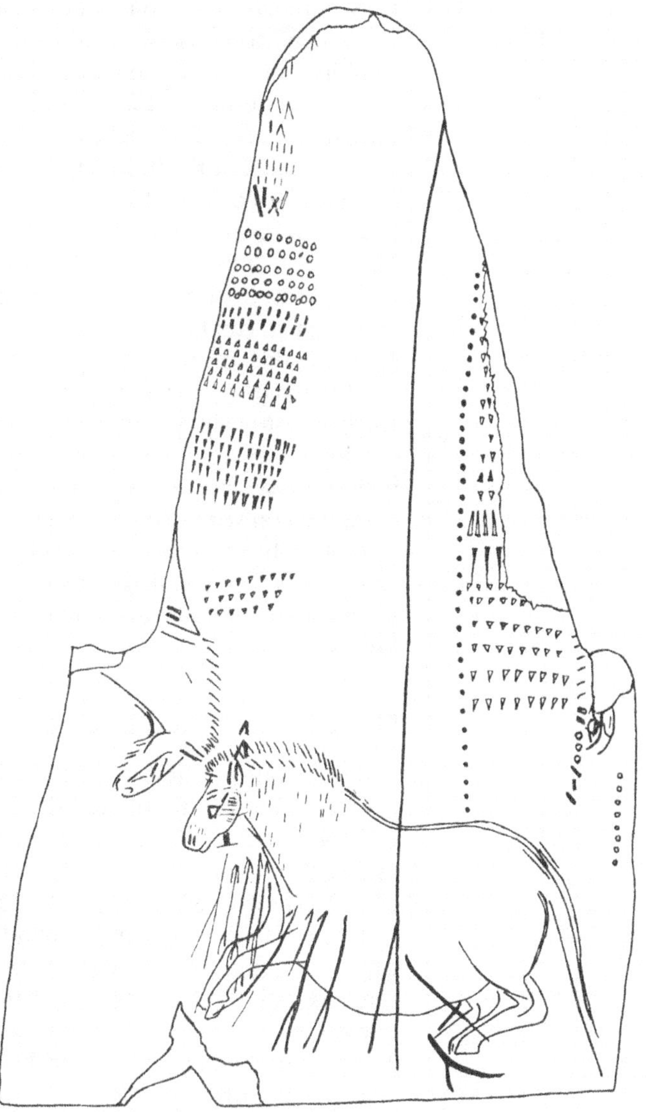

FIGURE 16.8
At *left*, a fragment of an antler tool from La Marche, France. This is the earliest known artifact containing two types of notations: cumulative markings and naturalistic sketches. The markings may be related to the gestation period of a horse. The line drawing (*right*) shows the entire surface of the antler fragment.

seem to indicate some sort of notation or numerical record. One particularly interesting antler fragment, from La Marche in the Dordogne, shows both a pregnant horse and a lengthy notation consisting of small notches in rows made from the tip downward, in lines of 11 (Figure 16.8). Marshack points out that 11 is the number of months in the gestation of a horse. Other notations on other fragments suggest that the phases of the moon were being logged.

Marshack's work has opened our eyes to the fact that these people were probably much more sophisticated than anyone had supposed. They were not only great artists but also possibly on the brink of developing arithmetic and even perhaps the beginning of very primitive writing. We do not yet understand the meanings of all the materials that they have left us, but we do know that they are ancestors for whom we should have the greatest respect.

When the work of Leroi-Gourhan, Marshack, Lewis-Williams, and others is combined with traditional interpretations, it becomes clear that Later Stone Age and Upper Paleolithic art may have had multiple functions—as hunting magic or fertility magic, as part of initiation rites, perhaps for communication between groups (see the Postscript to this chapter), and possibly even as a part of complex religious ceremonies (Dickson, 1990). But how can we tease apart these various functions for a more complete understanding? The first and most important step, according to Margaret Conkey (1993), is to stop viewing LSA/UP imagery as a functionally monolithic phenomenon and to begin disentangling it into its various imagery systems, which can be linked to specific social and historical contexts. Future analyses using this approach promise to produce fascinating results.

But whatever the images' meanings, the skill of the artists and the beauty of their work are astonishing. They painted in various tones of black, red, yellow, and brown obtained from natural clays and mineral oxides. Sometimes, they mixed their colors with charcoal and animal fat to make a thick pigment, which they used like a crayon or daubed on with primitive paintbrushes. At other times, they seem to have blown dry colors directly onto the wall in powder form, possibly through a hollow bird bone. Once applied to a wall, the colors were slowly absorbed by the limestone. Thanks to the constant humidity and temperature of the caves, much of Paleolithic art in Western Europe has retained its original brilliance for 20,000 years, some of it for even longer.

New Cave Discoveries Extend the Age of Paleolithic Art

Although one might assume that all of the painted caves of Europe had long since been found, three discoveries during the past decade have proven otherwise. First, in 1994, a spectacular painted cave was found in the Ardèche region of southern France (Chauvet et al., 1996). Named for Jean-Marie Chauvet, the leader of the discovery team, Chauvet Cave (see Figure 15.1) contains paintings that challenge Lascaux in their splendor, as detailed below. And then in the year 2000, two other caves were found: Cussac Cave, not far from Lascaux (Cussac Cave) and Fumane Cave in Italy (Balter, 2000). Cussac Cave probably dates to about 28,000 years BP, while the drawings from Fumane Cave (which were produced by applying red ocher to stone) may be the world's oldest known cave paintings at 36,500 to 32,000 years of age (BBC News).

Of these three new caves, only Chauvet has been thoroughly described (Chauvet et al., 1996). Dating about 32,000 to 31,000 years BP and attributed to the Aurignacian culture, the Chauvet Cave contains hundreds of vivid paintings of mammoths, horses, bears, woolly rhinos, lions, and hyenas. It has also produced the oldest images of owls and a panther. Long lines of well-proportioned and beautifully done animal images stretch along the cave walls. Usually, the paintings are faithful to nature, but in one whimsical departure, a young mammoth was depicted with spheres for feet. The floor of the cave yielded a few small patches of charcoal—possibly the remains of fires for lighting purposes—a handful of flint tools, and many cave bear bones. (Clearly, bears and humans both used the cave at times.) Intriguingly, in one of the cave's chambers, a cave bear skull was found perched all alone atop a huge stone block. To some, this discovery brings back old ideas about cave bear cults among prehistoric Europeans (see Chapter 14), but archaeologist Jean Clottes (1996) argues against a too hasty return to those notions.

Sculpture and Ceramics

In addition to painting, Upper Paleolithic people showed considerable proficiency as sculptors and engravers. In early examples of their skill, they incised the outlines of animals on cave walls. Later artists went on to develop the more advanced technique of carving subjects in high relief, often using the contours of the walls.

These artists also made complete statues in the round. In doing so, they left us a means of gaining further insights into Stone Age life and thought. In 2003, excavations in the Hohle Fels Cave in southwestern Germany produced three ancient carvings done from mammoth ivory. "The finds include the oldest known representation of a bird, a therianthropic sculpture [combining felid and human characteristics] and an animal that most closely resembles a horse" (Conard, 2003:830). These works of figurative art have been dated to more than 30,000 years BP.

By about 27,000 years ago, statues were also being made from a mixture of clay and ground bone that had been hardened by firing (R. Klein, 1999). The first evidence of firing comes from Dolní Věstonice in the Czech Republic (Figure 15.1). At that site, researchers found a kiln where the bone and clay mixture was fired into a new, rock-hard material. This is the first example in technological history of a process that was to become ubiquitous and would eventually be used in producing glass, bronze, steel, nylon, and most of the other materials of everyday life: the combination and treatment of two or more dissimilar substances to make a useful product unlike either starting substance. Ceramic remains from Dolní Věstonice include hundreds of fragments of animal and human figurines.

Perigordian an *Upper Paleolithic* culture of Western Europe dating 27,000 to 21,000 years BP.

Female Figurines

Without a doubt, of all the works of Upper Paleolithic representational art, the female figurines—the so-called Venus figures—are the most intriguing. Such figurines have a very wide distribution at Upper Paleolithic sites over much of Europe and eastward as far as western Siberia and Ukraine (R. Klein, 1999). Although they vary a good deal in appearance, they have some significant things in common, the most obvious being that the sculptors' interest was focused on the torso. The arms and/or legs are often made unnaturally small in proportion to the trunk, and in some cases, they are merely suggested (see Figures 16.9 and 16.10). The heads are also small and typically show little attempt to portray facial features, although the famous Venus of Willendorf, a 4 inch (10 centimeter) figurine made of limestone, does have a wavy hairdo executed with considerable care (Figure 16.10). All the emphasis is on the bodies, with their female characteristics—breasts, belly, and buttocks—greatly exaggerated in size. They look like tiny earth goddesses or fertility figures, and a good deal of informed speculation suggests that this is what they were. Many of them show the polish of long use and some the remains of red ocher, which indicates that they were symbolically painted (Leroi-Gourhan, 1965).

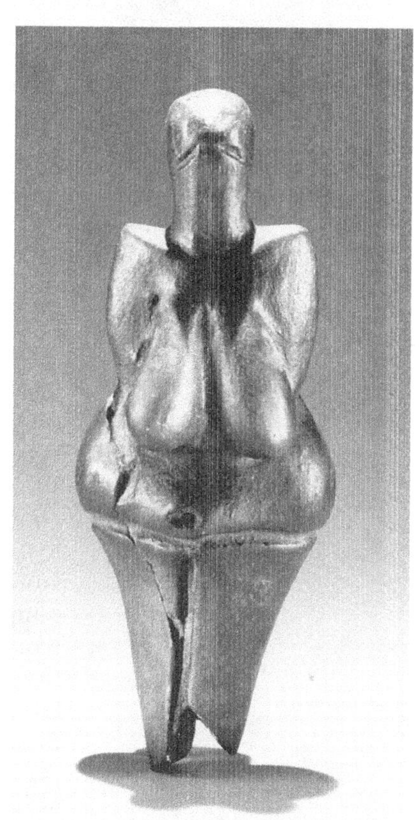

FIGURE 16.9 This Czech clay figure from Dolní Věstonice shows the Venus's typical traits: huge breasts and belly and shapeless arms. This figure's legs are now broken, but they probably had no feet. The photograph is approximately 80 percent actual size.

Some evidence supporting the idea that they were fertility figures is based on where the statuettes were found and when they are believed to have been made (Burenhult, 1993a, 1993c; Dickson, 1990). The majority of them come from the period of the Upper **Perigordian** (or Gravettian), a Paleolithic culture of Western Europe that existed between 27,000 and 21,000 years ago. During this period, the weather ranged from cool to very cold. In the cold periods, it was bitter in the extreme, especially on the Eastern European plains; nevertheless, many people continued to live there. Some made their homes in shallow pits that they dug in the ground and then roofed over with hides or other material. The vague outlines of the walls of many of these sunken huts can still be seen. The interesting thing is that these sites contain abundant examples of these female figurines, and they are often found lying right next to the walls or buried near hearths. The figurines themselves often taper to a point at the bottom, as if they had been designed to be stuck into the earth or into a base of some sort.

FIGURE 16.10
Small female figures, such as the Venus of Willendorf in Austria, were widespread in Europe 20,000 years ago. Note the intricate hairdo.

Life would have been hard during the years preceding the last glacial peak, and ensuring the survival of the group would have been of paramount importance. It thus seems quite possible that the Venus figurines were indeed fertility images or mother goddesses. There are other interpretations of the statuettes, however. Some scientists argue that because the Venus figures are not limited to fecund females, "young girls, nonpregnant 'middle-age' females, . . . and old women past child-bearing age" are all depicted—they may reflect an increase in the general (or specifically spiritual?) importance of women among European Upper Paleolithic people (Dickson, 1990; quote from p. 213). Another possibility is that the figurines functioned to identify and reinforce social alliances. The Venuses showed a common style over vast stretches of Europe and Western Asia and therefore might have "aid[ed] social communication and cooperation [as] distant relatives and strangers, individuals and groups identif[ied] with each other through sharing a common, recognizable symbolism" (Stringer and Gamble, 1993:211). Were the little figures worshipped as goddesses or venerated as symbols of ethnic solidarity or women's cultural importance? No one knows for sure.

Burial Customs and Rites

Upper Paleolithic people were concerned about death as well as life, and their treatment of the dead was careful and thoughtful. The bodies were often placed in graves dug in the ashes of previously occupied living sites, and in many places, it was a common practice to sprinkle the deceased with red ocher, perhaps in an effort to bring back the flush of life to pallid skin. The practice of including grave offerings was now commonplace (Figure 16.11). An extravagant example is the grave of two children (shown in Figure 16.12) that was excavated during the 1960s in a Paleolithic settlement about 130 miles (210 kilometers) northeast of Moscow, at Sungir (Figure 15.1). The grave suggests that the children were from a very important and/or affluent family and that Sungir society was significantly stratified. The two children—a boy 12 to 13 years old and a girl about three years younger—were laid out in a line, skull to skull. Both had been dressed from head to toe in clothing decorated with ivory beads carved from mammoth tusks, and they wore pendants and pins of the same material. Under the boy's left shoulder was a sculpted ivory mammoth, and both children were equipped with an assortment of ivory weapons, such as lances, spears, and daggers. The lances had been formed from a split mammoth bone that had been warmed over a fire in order to be straightened, a technique that requires considerable sophistication (Formicola and Buzhilova, 2004; R. Klein, 1999).

As noted, the elaborate nature of the double burial suggests social stratification at Sungir, but there is another intriguing aspect to it: The young girl's skeleton shows pathological shortening and bowing of the femora (Formicola and Buzhilova, 2004). Although the precise etiology of her abnormality is unclear, there is some evidence that her condition may have been related to the richness of the grave. Burials from at least two other European Upper Paleolithic sites combine physical abnormalities with spectacular grave goods, suggesting to some scholars that " 'abnormality' was part of a complex belief system reflected by sophisticated ritual activity and highly developed symbolism" (Formicola and Buzhilova, 2004:196).

Synthesizing Art, Ritual, and Religion in the Upper Paleolithic

American archaeologist D. Bruce Dickson (1990) has synthesized the evidence on European Upper Paleolithic burial practices and art and reached a set of interesting—

FIGURE 16.11
The skeleton of a man lies just as the body was buried 23,000 years ago in an ocher-sprinkled grave at Sungir, northeast of Moscow. The man was ceremoniously laid to rest, laden with beads, a headband of carved mammoth ivory, and the teeth of arctic foxes, in what appears to have been a burial ground. This suggests that the hunter–gatherers of Sungir lived part of the year in a settled community, where they developed complex customs.

and heuristically valuable—conclusions. Dickson believes that the elaborate burials of the Upper Paleolithic indicate a more complex and socially differentiated society than that of the Middle Paleolithic. Furthermore, since complex societies are supported by complex institutions, religious institutions in the Upper Paleolithic probably exceeded the simple shamanistic cult with its part-time religious specialist.

Dickson believes that religious rituals, conducted fundamentally in "an attempt to control nature and society by supernatural means" (1990:203), involved shamanistic direction of a community of participants. Community rituals, according to Dickson, were likely to be performed seasonally, when, following the rhythms of

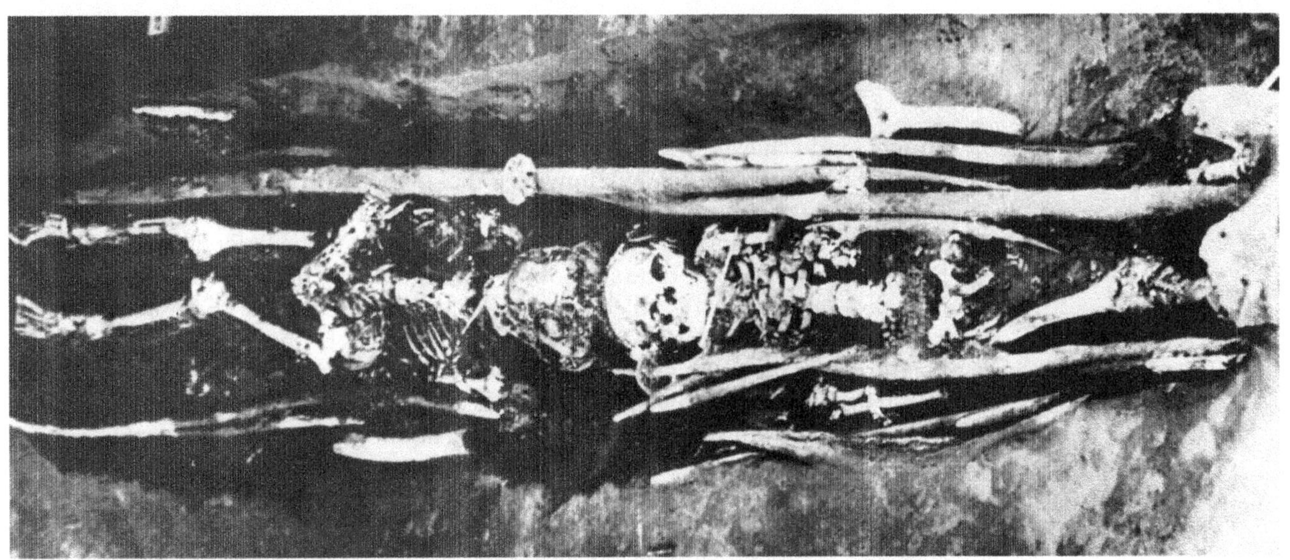

FIGURE 16.12
The skeletons of two children who died 23,000 years ago lie head to head in a grave at Sungir in Russia. The elaborateness of their grave suggests that the children were laid to rest amid solemn ritual.

their subsistence activities, Upper Paleolithic groups aggregated at the painted caves that served as their ceremonial centers. Annual visits to such ceremonial centers may account for the evidence that they were used and their art added to repeatedly. Seasonal aggregations and societywide rituals would have fostered group integrity and continuity, and shared religious beliefs may even have promoted friendly interactions and information sharing among widely separated cultures. Finally, Dickson believes that woven into the ritual practices of Upper Paleolithic people were concepts about the passage of time and about human sexuality, "especially the periodicity and fecundity of women" (1990:215). Thus, the Venus figurines and also artifacts suggesting notation systems are seen as facets of a larger and quite elaborate belief system.

The more we learn about these early modern people from the evidence of their living sites, the narrower the gap becomes between them and us. But it will never be entirely closed. The intimate details of social life, the games children played, the gestures and courtesies that give a society flavor—all these have necessarily vanished. We have no knowledge of how one person addressed another or what words they used. And we will never know.

Some details have enlightened us, however, and some generalizations can be made. As the first modern people stretched their powers, they came to separate themselves from nature's control in ways that their ancestors could not have dreamed of. Spread as they soon were throughout the Old and New Worlds, they were adapting to a vast range of environments and developing a host of different cultures and languages. What we have described is based mainly on archaeological research in Europe—a very small part indeed of the whole world. Everywhere, culture moved ahead and blossomed in an endless variety of forms, and society developed in a thousand complex ways. The ability to exploit such a variety of environments led to great growth in the numbers of people, and populations increased as much as tenfold in some parts of the world. By the end of the Later Stone Age/Upper Paleolithic, some 10,000 years ago, the stage was set for the last steps in the emergence of modern culture: agriculture, domestication of animals, metal working, complex forms of social and political life, writing, and perhaps even war.

Summary

Humankind achieved anatomical modernity at least 195,000 years ago. It was not until around 50,000 years ago, however, that evidence of behavioral modernity—modern human culture—began to appear. The "big bang" of human culture is first seen in the archaeological record of Africa in the form of the Later Stone Age (LSA). Perhaps 5,000 years after the start of the LSA, an elaboration of culture can be seen in Eurasia, and there, it is called the Upper Paleolithic (UP). The LSA and UP shared many cultural advances: increased types of stone tools; the production of formal bone artifacts; the production of works of art and personal adornment; increasingly elaborate burials; and increased subsistence efficiency. In some areas, the intensive use of gathered wild grains anticipated the later development of plant domestication. All of these advances may well have been the result of the evolution of a fully modern mind and modern speech.

Of all of the LSA/UP cultural advances, the art—including rock art, cave paintings, and sculpture—of these early modern humans is probably the most impressive. Cave and rock art dates back to 30,000 years BP in Africa, Europe, and Australia. In the caves of Upper Paleolithic Europe, these extraordinary paintings have been linked to hunting magic and other ceremonial activities, but no one knows for sure why they were produced or how they were used. The same is true for the Venus figurines, although for these artworks, the connection with fertility rites seems fairly strong.

By the end of the LSA/UP, some 10,000 years ago, *Homo sapiens* had migrated all across the Old World and reached Australia and the Americas. The modern human mind—with its enormous capacity for symbolic thinking, complex communication, and cultural innovation—was in existence. The stage was set for the domestication of plants and animals and the change from a migratory hunting-and-gathering way of life to a much more sedentary existence.

Postscript

Many students of Upper Paleolithic art believe that the cave paintings and sculptures preserve a kind of text and that if we can break the code of the various symbols, we will be able to reconstruct a good deal of what Upper Paleolithic people thought and how they interacted. Shared symbolism may have facilitated trading or cooperative hunting between widely scattered human groups. Additionally, some artistic symbols may have conveyed complex messages either within or between groups. Consider the case of the handprints.

In several, but by no means all, of the painted caves, images of animals and other objects are accompanied by impressions of human hands (see Figure 16.6). European sites known for their handprints include Gargas, Abri Labatut, Tibiran, and Les Combarelles in France and El Castillo and El Pindal in Spain. These handprints have several binary features: They are either traced (negative representation) or painted (positive representation); left- or right-handed; red or black in color; whole or mutilated (apparently missing digits). As discussed by D. Bruce Dickson (1990), the various attributes combine to produce sixteen distinct types of handprints (e.g., traced-left-red-whole versus painted-right-black-mutilated). Furthermore, as Dickson points out, if one counts fingers, the number of possible combinations rises to 40. One can imagine handprints being used simply as signatures after the completion of particularly elaborate pieces of cave art ("So-and-so painted this") or as complex, coded messages between groups that routinely visited the same cave sites ("So-and-so was here recently and wishes the reader of this message ill").

Alternately, of course, the handprints may carry no meaning whatsoever, in which case they would fall into the same category as modern doodles. Messages or doodles? Only time and further research will tell. One thing is clear, however: The full meaning of Upper Paleolithic art remains to be revealed, and many surprises lie ahead.

Review Questions

1. The so-called "big bang" of human cultural innovation occurred during the Later Stone Age in Africa and the Upper Paleolithic in Eurasia. What sort of cultural advances did this big bang include? How did the LSA and UP differ in terms of new traits and/or the timing of cultural elaboration?
2. Describe the expanded use of bone, antler, and ivory as raw materials during the LSA/UP. How did the blade-based tool called a *burin* contribute to this development?
3. It has been said that the LSA/UP people were more efficient hunters and gatherers than archaic humans. What evidence is there for increased food sources and/or new subsistence technology?
4. Describe the cave art of the Upper Paleolithic. Speculate on how cave paintings and sculptures may have been incorporated into rituals of various sorts. Compare your speculations with the use of icons in modern religions.
5. Speculate about the relative status of women and men within Upper Paleolithic societies. Which sex do you think made the greater contribution to subsistence

activities? To tool making? To art? To religion? In each case, explain the basis of your speculations. In particular, do you think the female figurines indicate that European Upper Paleolithic people traced their descent matrilineally or that they worshiped female deities?

SUGGESTED FURTHER READING

Burenhult, Göran (ed.). *The First Humans: Human Origins and History to 10,000 BC.* New York, HarperSanFrancisco, 1993.

Chauvet, Jean-Marie, Eliette Deschamps, and Christian Hillaire. *Dawn of Art: The Chauvet Cave.* New York, Abrams, 1996.

Dickson, D. Bruce. *The Dawn of Belief.* Tucson, University of Arizona Press, 1990.

Klein, Richard, and Blake Edgar. *The Dawn of Human Culture.* New York, John Wiley & Sons, 2002.

Leroi-Gourhan, André. *Treasures of Prehistoric Art.* New York, Abrams, 1965.

Lewis-Williams, J. David. *The Rock Art of Southern Africa.* Cambridge, Cambridge University Press, 1983.

Marshack, Alexander. *The Roots of Civilization.* Mount Kisco (NY), Moyer Bell Limited, 1991.

INTERNET RESOURCES

UPPER PALEOLITHIC FRANCE

www.beloit.edu/~museum/logan/paleoexhibit/upperpaleo.htm

Produced by the Logan Museum of Anthropology in Beloit, Wisconsin, this site contains useful information and illustrations about Upper Paleolithic cultures in France between about 40,000 and 9,000 years ago.

BEHAVIORAL AND BIOLOGICAL ORIGINS OF MODERN HUMANS

www.accessexcellence.org/BF/bf02/klein

Produced by the National Health Museum, this site presents Prof. Richard Klein's views on the late stages of humans' cultural and biological evolution.

EARLY MODERN HUMAN CULTURE

http://anthro.palomar.edu/homo2/sapiens_culture.htm

This web site gives an interesting overview of the evolution of modern culture and includes information on subsistence patterns, tools, and art.

OHALO II

http://ohalo.haifa.ac.il

The 23,000-year-old Israeli UP site of Ohalo II, with its evidence for early and intensive plant exploitation, is described here.

THE CAVE OF CHAUVET—PONT-D'ARC

www.culture.gouv.fr/culture/arcnat/chauvet/en

Produced by the French Ministry of Culture, this excellent site allows a self-guided tour through the painted cave.

SOUTHERN AFRICAN ROCK ART

www.museums.org.za/sam/resource/arch/rockart.htm

Rock art is not limited to Europe, of course, and this site provides an introduction to examples from South Africa.

USEFUL SEARCH TERMS:

cave art (paintings)
Cro-Magnon humans
Late Stone Age
modern human culture
Upper Paleolithic
Venus figurines

Chapter 16 Timeline

NEOLITHIC AND MESOLITHIC
- 10,000

UPPER PALEOLITHIC
- 40,000

MIDDLE PALEOLITHIC
- 250,000

LOWER PALEOLITHIC

Years BP	Event
	Swanscombe and Steinheim; Levallois technique
400,000	
	Arago
500,000	
	Gran Dolina fossils
1 million	Australopiths extinct
1.5 million	Acheulean industry
	Homo habilis at Olduvai
1.8 million	*Homo erectus* in Africa, the Caucasus, and Java
2 million	Oldowan industry

YEARS BP	FOSSILS AND ARCHAEOLOGICAL RECORD	MAJOR CULTURAL PHASES OF WESTERN EUROPE AND AFRICA
		Europe / *Africa*
		NEOLITHIC AND MESOLITHIC CULTURES
10,000	First farmers; Possible entry into Americas	UPPER PALEOLITHIC (Europe) / LATER STONE AGE (Africa): MAGDALENIAN
	Sungir burials; bow and arrow in Africa; Cave art and figurines	SOLUTREAN; PERIGORDIAN (=GRAVETTIAN)
	Zafarraya Neandertals; Cro-Magnon; Chauvet cave art; St. Césaire Neandertals; Modern skull at Niah; Lake Mungo, Australia, fossils	AURIGNACIAN/CHATELPERRONIAN
	Amud Neandertals; La Chapelle Neandertals	
50,000	Shanidar fossils and flower burial; Disk-core technique used	MIDDLE PALEOLITHIC (Europe) / MIDDLE STONE AGE (Africa): MOUSTERIAN
	Skhūl and Qafzeh fossils	
100,000	Klasies River Mouth fossils	
130,000		
195,000	Omo Kibish: oldest modern humans	

Many of the dates given to finds are based on indirect evidence and are estimates; the dates given to cultural phases are approximations.

Chapter 17

The Human Condition

A street scene in any modern city reveals humans' biological diversity at a glance.

But man, proud man,
Drest in a little brief authority,
Most ignorant of what he's most assured,
His glassy essence, like an angry ape,
Plays such fantastic tricks before high heaven
As make the angels weep.

William Shakespeare, 1564–1616. *Measure for Measure,* **II, ii.**

Overview

Hominin evolution has been under way for an estimated 7 million years. The earliest phase involved the australopiths, whose lifeways and anatomies served them in good stead for millions of years. About 2.4 million years ago, however, a new and significantly brainier type of hominin evolved: the first representatives of the genus *Homo.*

The hominans changed rather dramatically after their first appearance. They became bigger and smarter and better communicators; radically broadened their subsistence systems, first by becoming hunters-and-gatherers and later by domesticating plants and animals; and evolved a tremendously complex cultural lifestyle. Although several extinct hominan species are known, today, the subtribe (and indeed the entire tribe Hominini) is represented by only one species: modern humans, *Homo sapiens.*

This final chapter deals primarily with the extreme physical variability of living humans and with our traditional way of understanding that variability: through the construction of racial classifications. It shows how most anatomical variations can be understood as adaptations to different environments, mere surface features rather than deep lines of division across humanity. It argues that among humans, race has little or no validity as a biological concept (although it is quite important sociologically) and that therefore biology cannot be used as a justification for racist attitudes and behavior. The chapter concludes with a discussion of some of the challenges that await humans in the future, including limiting global population size and wisely using our growing control over our own evolution.

The Story of Humankind

It is hard to realize that the story we have recounted in these chapters took millions of years to enact. The development of lithic technology alone has taken more than 2 million years since the invention of the first stone tools. During this incredibly long period of emergence, the animal that became *Homo sapiens* has been shaped by environment and social experience—both body and culture changing in adaptation (Figure 17.1).

Evolutionary biology, of which paleoanthropology is a division, makes this much clear to us: Each species is a product of its genes and its environment. Genetic diversity and allele frequencies within all species are affected by the same set of processes: mutation and gene flow (both of which increase diversity); genetic drift, bottlenecks, and founder effects (all of which tend to reduce diversity); and natural selection (which, acting in response to specific environmental parameters, reduces overall diversity while increasing the frequency of fit traits and their alleles). In general, because of their long evolutionary history, most living species seem well adapted to their current environments.

It is important to remember, however, that natural selection—indeed, evolution in general—has not been directed toward any goal in terms of trait development

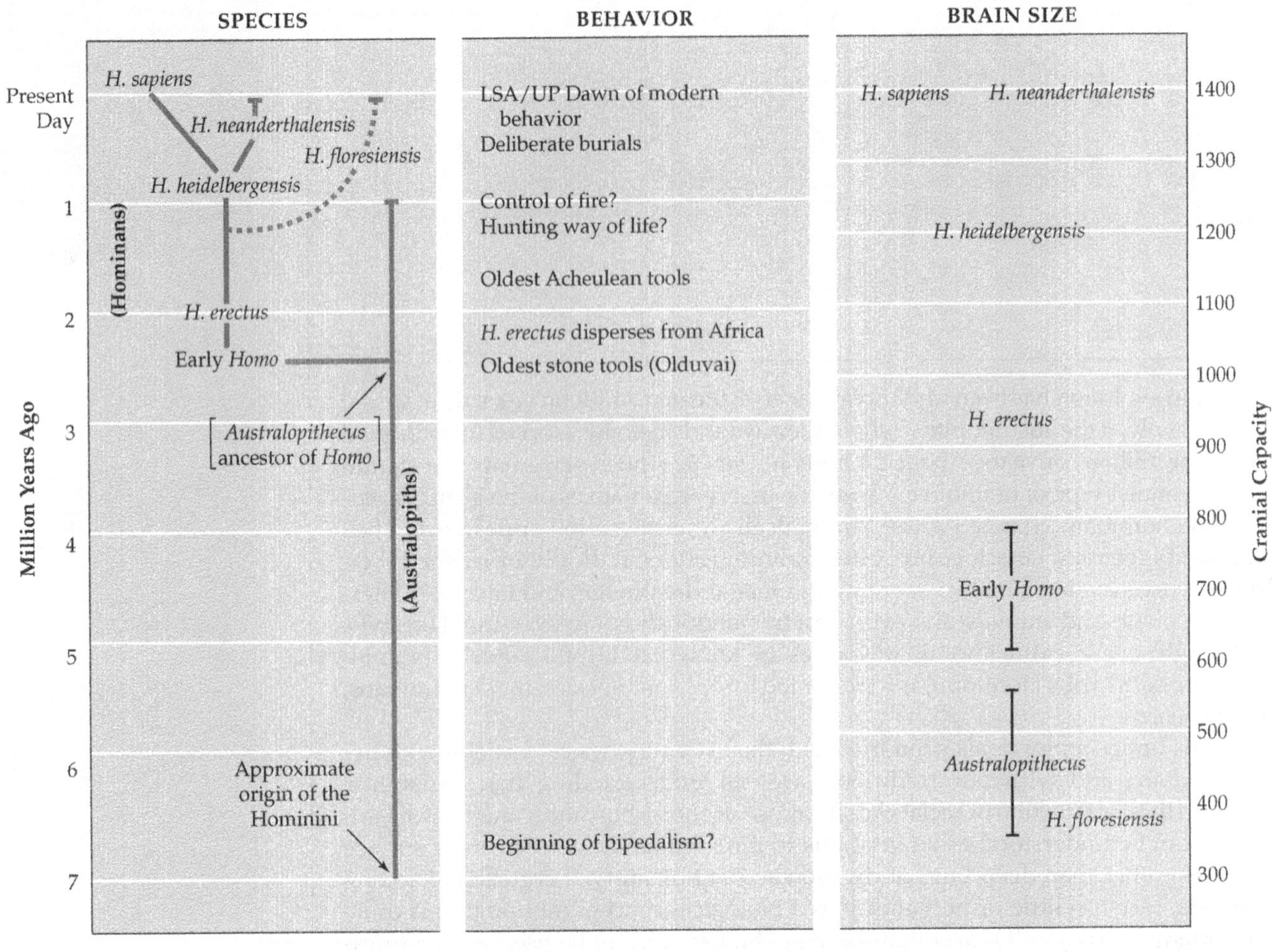

FIGURE 17.1
This summary chart shows an abbreviated account of hominin phylogeny (*left*), behavioral evolution (*center*), and increasing brain size (*right*). Mean brain sizes are shown for *H. sapiens* and the Neandertals (combined), *H. heidelbergensis*, and *H. erectus*. Range of brain sizes is shown for "early" *Homo* and the combined australopiths, with the names located near the mean values.

or species production. We *Homo sapiens* with our big brains are the result of a blind dance among genes, traits, and environment, and that dance had one underlying theme: Genes and traits that maximized survival and reproduction were favored and spread. Still, we can never understand either the genesis or the function of a characteristic without considering the environment in which it evolved.

Environmental History and Adaptation

The story of the human environment is relatively clear and forms the first part of the story of human evolution. The African forests and woodlands formed the womb that held our ape ancestors and from which the earliest hominins emerged into the world. As our ancestors evolved, they spread to open woodlands and tropical savannas throughout the Old World. As they expanded north into the temperate zones, they came to occupy an increasing number of different *biomes*, or ecological zones. To temperate grassland and woodland alike they adapted and eventually also to the cool **taiga** (subarctic coniferous forests) and icy tundra. Some populations

Taiga the northern coniferous forest bordering the *tundra*.

moved in and out of the northern taiga and followed game to alpine pastures. Other populations began to exploit the regions bordering deserts or reentered the tropical rain forests. Everywhere, humans evolved the flexibility to live in a variety of biomes—and they were the first primate type to do so.

Humankind owed this flexibility to the evolution of a remarkable and extraordinarily adaptable body and of an astounding brain. We have seen how the australopiths emerged as the first hominins, evolving (often in a mosaic fashion) humanlike teeth and postcranial adaptations for habitual bipedalism. Clever creatures that they were, the australopiths may well have begun the practice of stone tool manufacture, yet in many ways, their existence seems to have resembled that of modern chimpanzees.

Just after 2.5 million years ago, some form of *Australopithecus* gave rise to bigger brained, (definitely) stone tool-making creatures that we now classify as hominans: early *Homo*, including *H. rudolfensis* and *H. habilis*. Next in line came *Homo erectus*, perhaps the first species modern enough to be called *human* and probably the first hominin type to spread out of Africa. *H. erectus*, in turn, gave rise to *Homo heidelbergensis* around 850,000 years BP and that archaic species—along with its own descendants, the Neandertals (*H. neanderthalensis*)—occupied a variety of habitats and temperature zones, thanks to increasingly technological cultures.

Finally, modern people (*Homo sapiens*) evolved around 195,000 years ago—most probably in Africa from a *H. heidelbergensis* population—and ultimately spread throughout the Old World and into the Americas and Australia. With the exception of some remote islands, the entire worldwide expansion was probably completed before the end of the Paleolithic, bringing us almost to the later stone ages, the **Mesolithic** and Neolithic (Diamond, 1997).

Mesolithic a *Stone Age* period recognizable at some European sites and characterized by the use of small stone tools called microliths; lasting at most 2,000 years, the Mesolithic followed the *Paleolithic* and preceded the *Neolithic*.

The human organism, miraculous though it may seem in its complexity, was and is a product of natural selection: The human brain was no more than what was needed for survival and successful reproduction in a variety of different physical and social environments. From an average of perhaps 400 cubic centimeters some 7 million years ago, human cranial capacity has risen to vary between 1,000 and 2,000 cubic centimeters. This increase in size has been exceedingly rapid by evolutionary measure and has produced a brain of unprecedented complexity.

Altruism and Bioaltruism among Humans

The question inevitably arises of whether we are more than a superior kind of animal, and if so, in what way. Have we, in some sense, escaped from the constraints of our animal ancestry? Are we really different in kind from the animals that share our world?

For centuries, philosophers have been trying to define the unique qualities that set us apart from the animal kingdom. We have language, technology, complex society, and even civilization. Some writers have proposed ethics as the most profound characteristic that clearly divides human from beast. Do humans alone show the virtue of unselfishness or altruism? If they do, does this not finally separate them at a profound level from the selfish and competitive law of natural selection?

As mentioned in Chapters 2 and 4, nonhuman primates have been observed engaging in many types of kin-selected altruism, as well as reciprocal altruism between nonkin. Humans also show these sorts of altruistic behaviors, and it now seems clear that many of our most highly esteemed characteristics—including generosity and selflessness—are at least partially the result of selection for genetic maximization (Alexander, 1979; Betzig, 1997; Gray, 1985; Symons, 1979). Evolutionary models have been proposed that explain human altruism in terms of **group selection**—that is, the preservation of traits (and their underlying genes) that benefit the social group rather than benefiting individual actors (Wynne-Edwards, 1962). However, these models have not found widespread popularity (but see Sober and Wilson, 1998).

Group selection a theoretical model in which *natural selection* is presumed to operate not on the individual animal but on a social group as a unit.

Do humans show any kind of altruism that is not based in some biological advantage and is not seen in other species? Edward O. Wilson, who discussed this question at some length in his book *On Human Nature* (1978), has concluded that since we, too (with our brains), are a product of natural selection, it is not likely that we should have developed behavior that operates against natural selection. If biological fitness demands altruism, then it will appear in human societies. But if altruism operated to lower individuals' inclusive fitness, then it surely would never become established as a common behavior pattern. Wilson writes:

> Genes hold culture on a leash. The leash is very long, but inevitably values will be constrained in accordance with their effect on the human gene pool. . . . Human behavior—like the deepest capacities for emotional response which drive and guide it—is the circuitous technique by which human genetic material has been and will be kept intact. Morality has no other demonstrable ultimate function. (1978:167)

A review of instances of human altruism produces few examples in which there is not a well-recognized reward for a risk taken, even if the reward is promised in the next life. Human society has developed reciprocal altruism to the point where it is all pervasive, and society has developed sanctions against failure to act altruistically—that is, against selfishness. Experienced swimmers are expected to save a drowning person even if that person is completely unknown to them, and they frequently do so.

Much human behavior appears nonadaptive or maladaptive: We can choose not to bear children; we can commit suicide. As Wilson (1978) says, the genetic leash is long. Reason has given us freedom from the lower brain centers, the limbic system, which makes animals do what they have to do. We can determine our actions without reference to our limbic needs, and we can even go against our nature—as *individuals.* But for the *species,* such behavior would spell suicide. In this sense, we are still held by our genes on that unbreakable leash.

The ultimate human mystery lies perhaps in locating the origin of the aspirations that seem so far removed from our biological needs: dreams of dazzling creativity; dreams of a better world founded in equality; dreams of achievements and experience in poetry, music, art, and science. The mystery lies in understanding these new goals that our dreams have set us—goals that arise far from our biological heritage and yet give meaning to the lives of so many people. Human adaptability and reason give us, as individuals, freedom to follow these goals at whatever cost. It is in this sense that we have left the kingdom of animals and gained considerable freedom from our genes.

Cultural History

Adaptability and reason have also led to the third part of our story, the human specialty that was also a response to the environment: culture. Traditionally, culture has been viewed as consisting of those behaviors and ideas that are the property of the society and maintained by mutual learning and teaching by its members. In human evolution, language became a new means of transmitting and recording cultural data. Language was a unique and revolutionary organic adaptation, certainly one of the most important developments in human evolution. It opened up new possibilities of existence and allowed a surge in human technology.

The first developments of technology came at an unimaginably slow rate (Figure 17.1). Any idea of progress would have been entirely foreign to early hominins. But, roughly coincidental with increasing encephalization, technological progress did occur, however slowly. From chimplike tool use and biodegradable implements, hominins progressed to sharp stone flakes and simple choppers. Slowly, over millions of years, they improved the cutting edge and varied the form of their tools for different purposes. The large hand ax and the knifelike blade appeared; manual skill became essential to the development of technology. Fire began to be kept alive in the hearth. The rate of change quickened, and cultural developments came more rapidly (Figure 17.2). Some developments—such as the control of fire, shelter construction, and clothing—were probably crucial for hominins' worldwide spread, especially for their penetration into harsh environments and survival during periods of ice age cooling. Of critical importance, each cultural advance allowed more efficient and extensive exploitation of environmental resources than ever before—a positive feedback loop such as that shown in Figure 17.2.

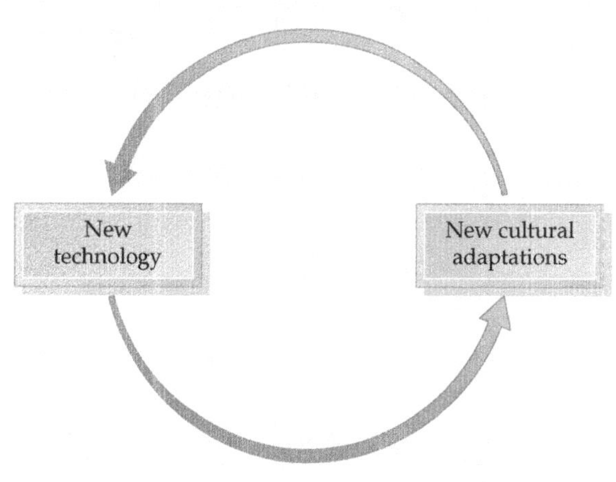

FIGURE 17.2 Positive feedback loops can be either constructive and creative or destructive. In either case, they tend to accelerate change in their components. This loop brings about accelerating cultural and technological changes.

Domestication of Plants and Animals

Eventually, humans learned to exploit their environment in a more fundamental way. They became increasingly skilled and effective hunters-and-gatherers. They learned to select and breed animals. After generations of gathering wild grains, they planted seeds and harvested cereals, becoming farmers.

Identification of the first evidence of the domestication of animals presents problems: The process of turning wild animals into tame ones will generate few identifiable archaeological remains, although after a considerable period of selective breeding, new breeds can be recognized by changes in skeletal structure. Dogs were probably the first animal type to be domesticated, and new mitochondrial DNA evidence suggests that occurred in East Asia around 15,000 years ago (Savolainen et al., 2002). Dogs seem to have been widely spread across Eurasia and North America by about 10,000 years BP (Diamond, 1997; Leonard et al., 2002). Sheep and goats were being bred selectively in the Middle East 10,000 years ago (Figure 17.3), as were pigs, both there and in the Far East (Diamond, 1997). Cattle joined the list of domesticated species a thousand years or so later and may

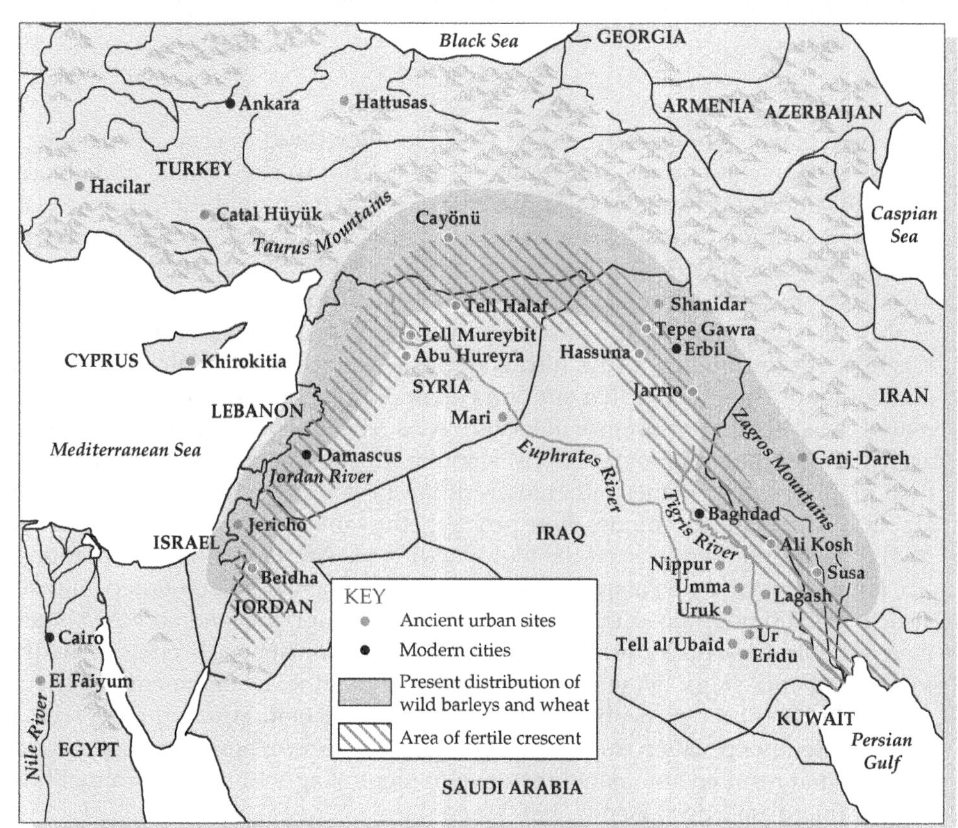

FIGURE 17.3 This map of the Middle East shows the Fertile Crescent, where the domestication of certain plants began about 10,000 years ago. The earliest villages and towns also developed in this region of agricultural wealth.

TABLE 17.1 Selected Wild Vegetables and Animals Domesticated in the Three Primary Zones of Agricultural Development

Zone	Plants	Animals
Middle East	Almonds	Cattle
	Apricots	Dogs
	Barley	Goats
	Dates	Horses
	Figs	Pigs
	Grapes	Sheep
	Lentils	
	Olives	
	Peas	
	Rye	
	Wheat	
China and Southeast Asia	Bananas	Banteng[a]
	Coconuts	Dogs
	Millet	Pigs
	Rice	Yak
	Soybeans	
	Sugarcane	
South and Central America	Avocados	Alpaca
	Beans	Guinea pig
	Chili	Llama
	Cocoa	
	Corn	
	Gourds	
	Peanuts	
	Potatoes	
	Squashes	

[a] Javanese wild cow.

have been tamed in more than one Old World location (Bradley et al., 1998). Horses, water buffaloes, and camels were domesticated in Eurasia and llamas and alpacas in South America between 6,000 and 4,500 years ago (Diamond, 1997).

The beginning of agriculture is still a mystery, and its details may always remain so (Diamond, 1997; Bar-Yosef, 1998). The first evidence of agriculture—of sowing, harvesting, and selecting various grains—dates from about 10,000 years BP and again comes from the Middle East (Figure 17.3). Agriculture also appeared about this time or soon after in north China and Mexico and somewhat later in Peru. The cultivation of rice—a crop that supports an enormous percentage of modern humans—was an early occurrence in Eastern Asia. The independent development of agriculture in these different regions is one of the most remarkable events in human prehistory. The plants and animals domesticated in each area were different (Table 17.1), but the techniques were probably the same: The farmers collected and sowed seeds and then selected the high-yielding varieties for continued planting.

Hunting persisted in many areas, and in some, where humans herded animals, agriculture did not follow until much later, even though the land and the climate were suitable. Clearly, the development of agriculture must have been slow, involving a number of steps. Some researchers believe that the development of agricultural techniques brought with it a rapid increase in population; others contend that the increase in population came first (following sedentism) and that the pressures for food that resulted stimulated the development of agriculture and animal husbandry (Bar-Yosef, 1998; Wenke, 1997).

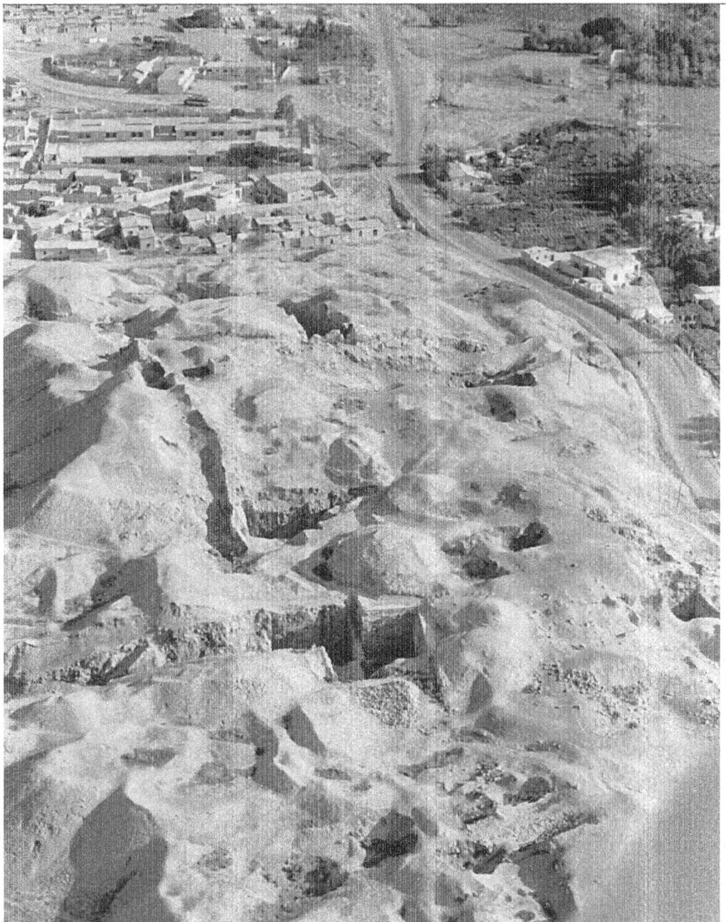

FIGURE 17.4
An aerial view of Jericho, taken some years ago, shows the modern city and the dirt mound 50 feet (15 meters) high, under which lie buried the many cities and walls of ancient Jericho. One excavation trench can be seen cutting from the left at the bottom of the photograph.

Whatever the order of events, it seems clear that the two factors would soon have come to interact in the manner of positive feedback, which would have resulted in a period of relatively rapid change in both population and culture. Certainly, the increase in population that we believe accompanied sedentism would have triggered the need for an even greater and more reliable food supply. And resource domestication occurred only where the appropriate plants and animals existed and the climate was right. The accidental distributions of domesticable species and favorable climates have shaped much of recent human history (Diamond, 1997).

Complex Societies

The agricultural revolution has had enormous effects on the earth and on humans. Agriculture has made possible a vast increase in the world's population (discussed later), and it set the stage for a further cultural development of equal significance: the development of cities and metal technology, the coming of complex societies often referred to as "civilization".

Civilization—marked by urbanized, state-level societies—first appeared in Mesopotamia (the area centered on the Tigris and Euphrates Rivers; Figure 17.3) and Egypt around 5,000 years ago (Fagan, 1999). Before that, however, these areas and the Levant had seen the growth of substantial settlements, including some large enough to be called early cities. Of particular importance were the sites of Abu Hureyra on the banks of the Euphrates and Jericho on the Jordan River (Fagan, 1999; Moore et al., 2000; Figures 17.3 and 17.4). Both of these settlements started out as small villages (Abu Hureyra at about 11,500 years BP and Jericho at about 10,500 BP) and then grew significantly after the advent of farming. Jericho was large and prosperous enough to build "massive stone walls complete with towers and a [deep] rock-cut ditch" around the city, although whether for defense or flood control is unclear (Fagan, 1999:139).

Agriculture brought with it the production of surplus food (that is, more than the farmers themselves needed), and this development, in turn, allowed certain of the early city dwellers to specialize in arts and crafts of an ever-widening variety. Trade flourished: At Jericho, turquoise, obsidian, and seashells passed through the city, together with much else of which we have no trace (Fagan, 1999). The north–south trade route on which the city lay was an important stimulus to its development. But civilization probably would not have grown from these early roots without improvements in agriculture. The greatest cities grew in areas of rich agricultural land, where the productivity was greatest; they reflected the agricultural foundation on which they necessarily were based.

The earliest achievements of civilization—including organized religion and government, weaving, writing, and metal technology—are too numerous to list, let alone discuss, but they reflect an accelerating process of development from prehistory into history. Above all, it was developing technology that brought about the astonishing growth and complexity of human culture.

Environment, human biology, culture—these three are all important threads of the human story we have told. During humankind's emergence, each acted on the others in mutual feedback; any change in one selected for adjustment in the others. This relationship was something new in evolution, for learning to change the environment was something no animal had ever done before, beyond building a nest or preparing a small arena for courtship.

The changes in environment brought about by the early farmers sometimes brought only short-term benefits. Gary Rollefson and Ilse Köhler-Rollefson (1992) of San Diego State University have uncovered strong evidence that deforestation caused a collapse of early civilization in parts of the Levant around 6,500 years BP. The area was rapidly depopulated at this time, and evidence suggests clearly that this depopulation was due not so much to a change in rainfall as to the extensive felling of woodland. Trees were used as fuel for, among other things, the production of lime plaster. As time passed, the final destruction of the woodland habitat was completed by the herds of goats that ranged over the one-time forest lands and consumed the tender saplings. Then the steep hills eroded rapidly, the soils were lost, and the flourishing communities, which had developed throughout the area, disappeared.

This is just one very significant example of how humans have changed and, in doing so, destroyed their own productive environments. Such changes have occurred in many parts of the world since the coming of animal husbandry and agriculture brought our ancestors to the doors of civilization (Diamond, 2005). The pattern has been repeated the world over but was especially devastating around the Mediterranean basin and in the Middle East, where the goat had been so widely domesticated. Humans may change their environment drastically—and as we can now see, such changes can turn out to be to their ultimate disadvantage.

Human Variability

Within this dynamic system unique to humankind, in which the human body and its environment are related through culture, all three components show considerable variability. In our physical variability, humankind is not alone in the animal or plant worlds. Variability in behavior and appearance is characteristic of all living organisms as their environment varies, and it is probably no greater in humans than in many other species. Every individual (except identical twins) carries different genetic material; differences due to age and sex also exist. Beyond this, we find variability that has evolved in response to local (and equally variable) environmental conditions. Humans' physical variations may be found both within and between populations, and in the past, such physical differences were often used by anthropologists to construct racial classifications that subdivided humanity.

We will argue in a later section that all such classifications have little meaning and that race is not a useful biological concept when applied to humans. Nonetheless, there are many good reasons for studying human variation apart from race construction, including learning how trait variations correlate with differing environments and susceptibility to certain diseases. Therefore, before addressing the race issue, we will review some of the major physical variations of modern humans. We will be concerned with traits of three main kinds: (1) anatomical features, such as skin color, hair form, and body shape; (2) physiological traits, such as metabolic rate and hormone activity, growth rate, color blindness, and genetic diseases; and (3) characteristics of the blood (biochemical traits).

Anatomical Traits

Perhaps the most easily noticed physical characteristic of humans is skin color. Depending on the amount of melanin in the epidermis, human skin varies from very light ("white") to very dark (dark brown or black). As shown in Figure 17.5, skin color is found to be very closely correlated with latitude when analyzed globally (Robins, 1991). People with dark skin colors are found nearest to the equator, and lighter populations inhabit higher northern and southern latitudes. As explained to some extent earlier in the book, this distribution of skin tones seems to reflect a complex pattern of adaptation by our ancestral populations. In equatorial and subequatorial regions, people are subjected to intense ultraviolet (UV) radiation, and bombardment by UV rays can be extremely harmful.

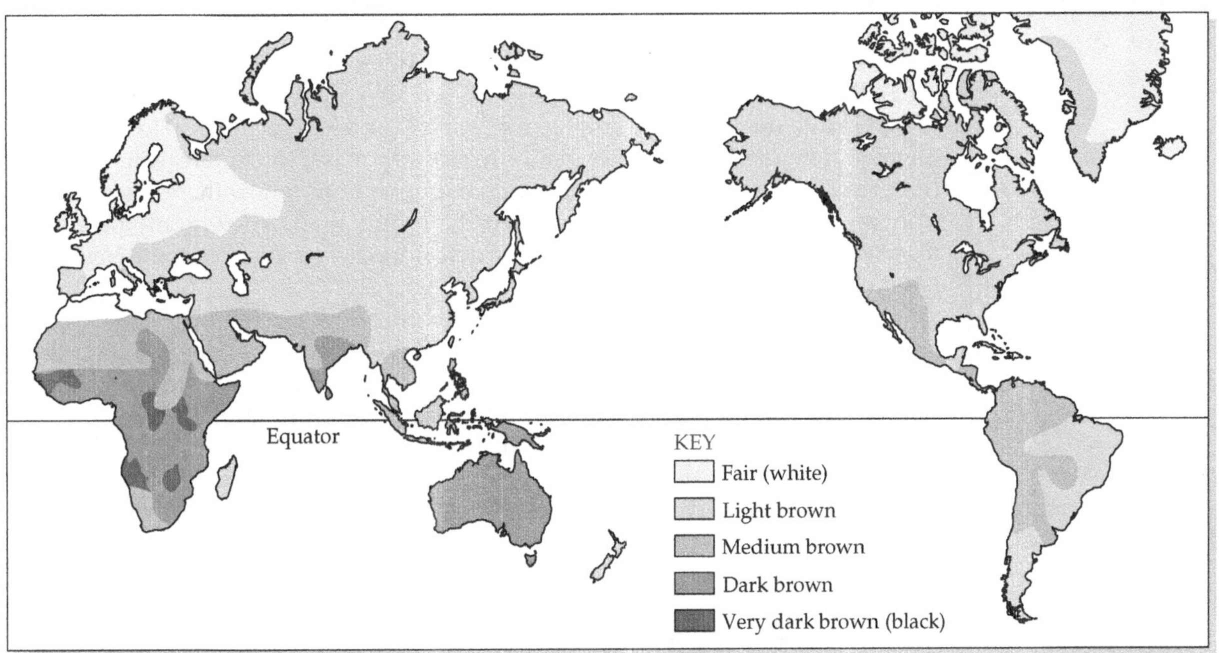

FIGURE 17.5
This global map shows the distribution of skin colors in indigenous populations. Note the clear correlation between skin color and latitude.

One relatively short-term hazard is sunburn, which may result in an inability to sweat efficiently and thus to reduce body heat. Sunburn-induced impairment of sweating may even lead to hyperthermia and death during heavy exercise by light-skinned individuals with a heavy solar heat load (Molnar, 2002). A second potentially harmful effect is sunlight-induced breakdown of the B vitamin folate (folic acid), a hazard that is prevented by having dark skin color (Jablonski and Chaplin, 2002; see Box 2.2). Since folate is essential for DNA synthesis and the production of healthy babies, such melanistic protection would be strongly favored in high sunlight regions. And a third hazard, of course, is that prolonged exposure to UV radiation may lead to skin cancer and its sometimes deadly consequences. Heavy epidermal concentrations of melanin help to protect tropical people against the ravages of UV radiation. Among equatorial and subequatorial populations, skin cancer rates are relatively low, and sweat glands are protected from UV-induced blockage (Molnar, 2002). Thus, there has been strong selection for dark skin colors in regions of intense and prolonged sunlight.

The sun-and-skin problem took on a different dimension in those human populations that migrated north and south away from the sunny regions. In the higher latitudes, sunburn damage, folate breakdown, and skin cancer became less significant threats, while an inability to produce enough vitamin D gained in importance. (see Box 2.2). Human populations that migrated to higher latitudes must have experienced selection for lighter skin color (reduced pigmentation) in order to enhance vitamin D production. Skin color thus turns out to be a very clear example of evolutionary adaptation among modern people. It is a striking trait but very superficial, both literally and figuratively.

Another trait with clear adaptive consequences is body build (Molnar, 2002). In the nineteenth century, Carl Bergmann, a German physiologist interested in the relationships among body mass, surface area, and heat production in warm-blooded animals, observed that populations occupying the coldest parts of a species' range tended to be bulkier—that is, more compact—than those living in the warmer parts (*Bergmann's rule*). Not long after Bergmann offered this insight, American J. A. Allen added that the protruding parts of the body, such as limbs, fingers, ears, and tails, tend to be relatively shorter in the cooler parts of the species' range than in its warmer regions (*Allen's rule*). In cool regions, these adaptations in body build decrease surface area in relation to mass, reducing heat loss. In warm regions, they increase surface area in relation to mass, thus increasing heat loss (Figure 17.6; Molnar, 2002). Modern human populations follow these rules derived from animal studies, and it seems clear that populations known only from their fossilized remains did the same. (See the description of the Nariokotome *Homo erectus* skeleton in Chapter 10.)

Living humans also show variations in hair form, from tight curls to waves to straight hair. Although the adaptive significance, if any, of the various hair patterns has yet to be fully worked out, living populations around the world clearly differ in their typical hair form while also showing much intrapopulational variation. Similarly, no clear adaptive function has yet been proved for the fold of skin that occurs in the upper eyelid of some living people, the **epicanthic fold** (Figure 17.7). Epicanthic folds are common among Asian people, some Native Americans, and the Khoisan (Bushmen and Hottentot) people of Southern Africa. Research is continuing on the significance of these and other variable human traits. No doubt, in some cases, differences in selection and adaptation will be the correct explanation; for other traits, variation may be the result of more random processes, such as genetic drift.

Epicanthic fold a fold of skin above the inner border of the eye; characteristic of Asiatic, some Native American, and Khoisan people.

One of the neatest demonstrations of environmental adaptation is that relating nose shape (expressed as the nasal index: breadth/length × 100) to the humidity of the air (expressed as vapor pressure). Moistening the air is a prime function of the nasal epithelium; the moisture content of the air must be brought up to 100 percent

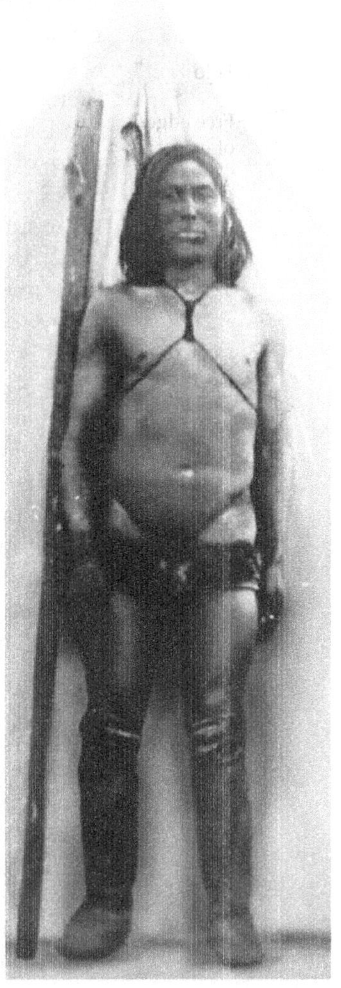

FIGURE 17.6 These individuals represent populations that demonstrate Bergmann's and Allen's rules. The African, on the *left*, tall and slim, has long extremities and a high ratio of surface area to mass. The Inuit, on the *right* has short extremities and a low ratio of surface area to mass, which reduces heat loss. The photographs are at the same scale.

relative humidity at body temperature before the air enters the lungs; otherwise, they will be damaged. It seems clear that people adapted to areas of dry air (deserts and high mountains) will tend to have narrow noses, while those adapted to moist air will usually have broad noses. The correlation can be demonstrated (Hooton, 1946; Molnar, 2002), and the explanation appears valid (see Figure 17.8).

The important thing to remember is that the differences in human anatomy mentioned here are relatively slight. Moreover, anatomical traits vary continuously: Noses vary from narrow to broad, hair varies by infinitesimal gradations from straight to tightly curled, and skin color varies from very light to black. These features are determined by numerous genes and are not discretely segregated into just a few phenotypes.

Physiological Traits

Physiological traits that vary within and between human populations are probably less well known than the more obvious anatomical differences, but they are also significant and reflect adaptation. The basal metabolic rate, which is related to the level of body heat production, varies, as might be predicted, according to the mean annual temperature (Harrison et al., 1977). Bone growth rate and maturation age also seem to vary, even though both are also greatly influenced by nutrition. The age at which teeth appear and their order of eruption vary, as well (Eveleth and

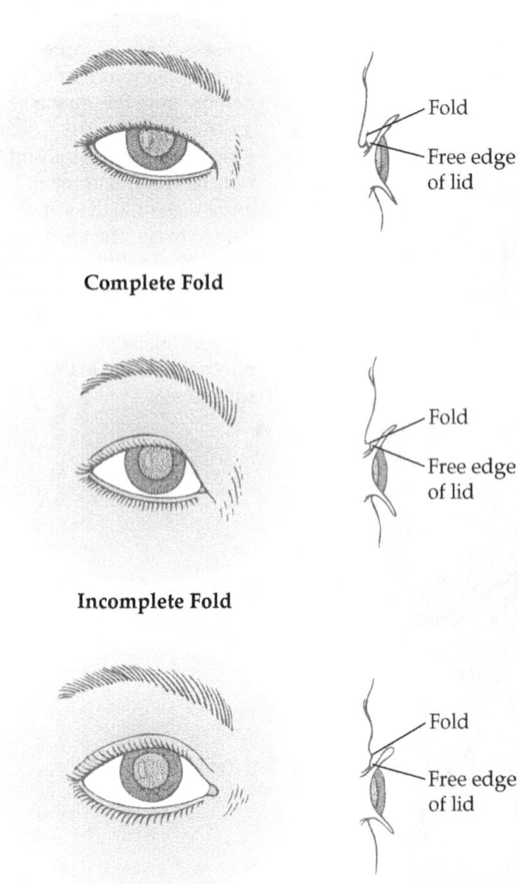

FIGURE 17.7
Asiatic peoples are distinguished by an extra fold of skin in the upper eyelid, which covers all or part of its edge. This fold is also found among some Native Americans and among some of the Khoisan peoples of South Africa.

Tanner, 1990). Protein structure, keenness of taste, drug sensitivity, balance of urinary substances, ear wax type, and lactose intolerence (due to a deficiency of the lactose enzyme) also show measurable differences (Molnar, 2002). And as we have seen, DNA carries recognizable differences. The better we become able to measure these sometimes trivial differences, the more of them we are likely to find.

Probably the most important physiological differences are those subtle genetic variations that give rise to disease (Molnar, 2002). Because they are based on only one or two genes, these traits are discrete; that is, they are either present or absent. We discussed one of them, sickle-cell anemia, in Chapter 2. Some other genetic diseases are just as dangerous but are limited to small populations. In the Mediterranean region, there is *favism*, which is a genetically determined allergy to the broad bean and results in severe anemia. Other hereditary disorders are much more widespread and occur more commonly in one population than another. One such disorder is *phenylketonuria (PKU)*, an inability to develop an essential enzyme, which usually results in brain damage and mental retardation. PKU is most common in some areas of Europe. It is rare among persons of African or Asian descent.

A disease like sickle-cell anemia that appears mostly in the Mediterranean region and in parts of Asia, rather than in Africa is *thalassemia* (Molnar, 2002). In afflicted individuals, the resulting anemia is so serious that they rarely reach reproductive age. But homozygous individuals who completely lack the thalassemia allele may die early of serious malaria. It is in the heterozygous state that the trait is present but not serious and provides some protection from malaria. Thus, the advantages and disadvantages of the gene in the population have remained in balance while malaria itself continues to thrive. Although most genetic diseases may simply be part of humans' genetic load, it is likely that some, like sickle-cell anemia and thalassemia, are part of such an adaptive equilibrium, termed balanced polymorphism (see Chapter 2).

Blood Groups

The third group of variable traits, the blood groups, have great medical significance (Jobling, et al., 2004; Molnar, 2002). When the possibility of blood transfusions was first investigated during the nineteenth century, it quickly became clear that introducing one individual's blood into another's bloodstream could be fatal.

Blood consists of a liquid component, the **blood plasma,** and three main types of cells: the **red blood cells,** which contain the red pigment hemoglobin and carry oxygen to all the parts of the body; the much larger **white blood cells,** or **leukocytes,** which defend against infection; and the smallest cells, the **platelets,** which maintain the circulatory system as a whole. (The liquid remaining after a clot has formed is called the **serum.**) The red cells have a protein coat whose molecules function as **antigens;** when introduced into another individual, antigens trigger the production of specific **antibodies,** other proteins that help protect the body against foreign substances. Microscopic examination of the blood of two people mixed together has shown that difficulties with transfusions come from the reactions between antigens and antibodies.

Safe transfusions now rest on biologist Karl Landsteiner's brilliant discovery in 1900 of the existence of different **blood groups** (Molnar, 2002). Transfusions of

Blood plasma a clear liquid component of blood that carries the *red blood cells, white blood cells*, and *platelets*.

Red blood cells (corpuscles) vertebrate blood cells lacking nuclei and containing *hemoglobin*.

White blood cells (leukocytes) vertebrate blood cells lacking *hemoglobin*.

Platelets minute blood cells associated with clotting.

Serum the liquid remaining after blood has clotted.

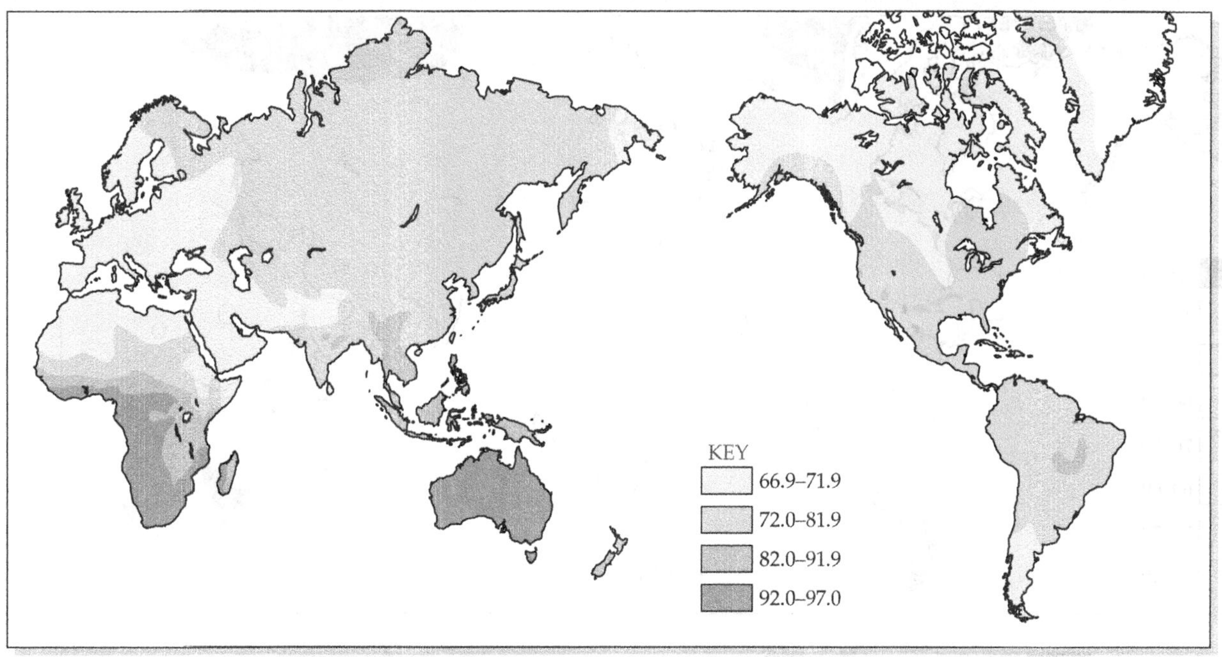

FIGURE 17.8
Nose form varies both within and between human populations. This map shows the distribution of typical nasal index values around the globe; a higher index number indicates a broader nose.

the wrong kind of blood can cause the recipient's red blood cells to *agglutinate*, or clump together, and sometimes to burst. The **agglutination** can result in clots that block the blood's flow. Landsteiner discovered that the blood (actually, the antigens) of one individual may trigger the production and agglutination of another individual's antibodies, causing clots. Landsteiner labeled with the letter O the blood of individuals that never agglutinated the blood of other persons but that would in turn be agglutinated by some foreign blood cells. (Modern labels are given here for Landsteiner's groups.) Blood of yet other individuals that was agglutinated he labeled A. The blood that agglutinated A blood and could itself be agglutinated by A blood was labeled type B.

Thus, there were three types: A, B, and O. Blood group A carries antigen A and develops anti-B antibodies. Blood group B contains antigen B and develops anti-A antibodies. Group O contains no antigens but develops both antibodies. Group AB (discovered later) carries antigens A and B but produces neither antibody. Type AB people can receive A, B, or O blood, but types A and B can receive only their own groups and type O, and type O people can receive only type O blood. Type O people, then, are universal donors, while type AB people are universal recipients. (The distribution of types A and O throughout the world is shown in Figure 17.9.)

Discovery of the ABO blood groups was followed by the discovery of many others (some of which are listed in Figure 17.10), the most important of which is the rhesus (Rh) system, identified in 1940. The rhesus system is responsible for an important disease that can kill newborn babies by destroying their blood cells. The cause of the disease is incompatibility between mother and child for the rhesus antigen D. If the mother is Rh-negative (lacks the D antigen) and the child is Rh-positive (possesses the D antigen), then the mother may form anti-D antibodies at the time of the child's birth, when some of the child's blood may enter the mother's bloodstream. In a second pregnancy, this antibody may pass through the placental barrier, coating and

Antigens any organic substances recognized by the body as foreign that stimulate the production of *antibodies*.

Antibody a protein produced as a defense mechanism to attack a foreign substance invading the body.

Blood groups groups of individuals whose blood can be mixed without *agglutination* (e.g., Groups A, B, O, and AB).

Agglutination the clumping of *red blood cells* as a result of the reaction of *antibodies* to an *antigen*.

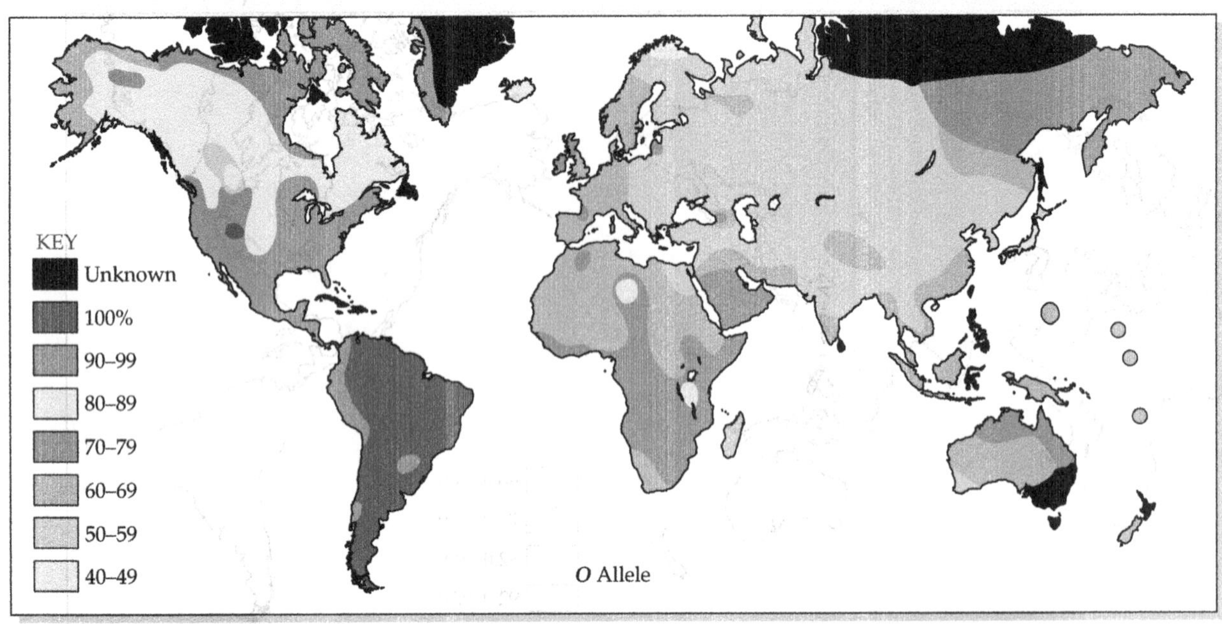

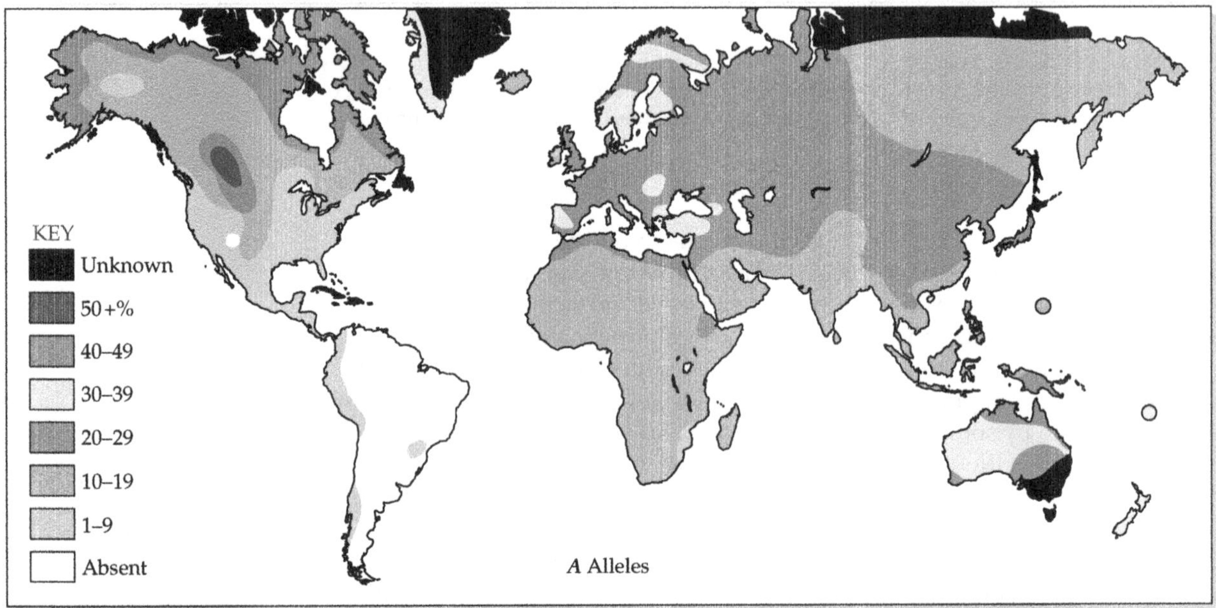

FIGURE 17.9

These maps give some idea of the distribution and frequency of the commonest ABO blood group alleles, *O* and the two *A* alleles (A_1 and A_2 combined for the lower map). This is an example of the kind of genetic data now available for human populations. The *upper* map charts the distribution of the predominant group O allele, which is common in the New World and especially in South America. The *lower* map plots the group A alleles, which are reasonably common in the Old World but rare in many parts of the New World and virtually absent from South America.

destroying the red blood cells of the fetus if it has Rh-positive blood. This destruction of the fetal red cells, which is called *erythroblastosis fetalis,* can be fatal to a developing child. The risk of erythroblastosis disease increases with each Rh-incompatible pregnancy, but the disease can now be prevented by giving the mother an injection of powerful anti-D antibody after the birth of the first Rh-positive child. The injec-

Blood group system	Allele	World range	Europeans	Africans: Non-Khoisan	Africans: Khoisan	Asians	Native Americans	Australians and Oceanics
ABO	A_1	0–45	5–40	8–30	0–15	0–45	0–20	8–38
	A_2	0–37	1–37	1–8	0–5	0–5	0	0
	B	0–33	4–18	10–20	2	16–25	0–4	0–13
	O	39–100	46–75	52–70	75–78	39–68	68–100	51–79
Rhesus	*cde–*	0–46	25–46	4–29	0	0–5	0	0
	cDe+	0–95	1–5	34–82	84–89	0–4	0–7	1–9
	CDe+	0–95	39–55	0–21	9–14	60–76	32–68	68–95
	cDE+	0–61	6–17	0–19	2	19–31	23–61	2–20
MNS	*N*	8–78	33–51	39–53	41	37–45	9–35	73–97
	NS	5–74	25–65	22–59	41	38	5–22	69–74
P	*P*	4–84	41–64	50–84	?	17	15–79	12–67
Lewis	*Lewis*	0–67	34–50	41	?	39	0–34	0–67
Duffy	*Duffy*	0-100	37–82	0–6	8	90–100	22–99	100
Diego	*Diego*	0–34	0	0	0	0–5	0–34	0
Gamma globulin	*Gm*	23–100	23–37	100	100	100	100	100
Haptoglobin	Hp^1	9–87	9–44	40–87	29	23–28	32–73	46–63

FIGURE 17.10
The frequencies of some blood group alleles present in different populations show the extent of variation in these genetic characters. Three different alleles for the rhesus-positive condition are listed (*cDe, CDe, cDE*). Alleles of the blood serum components gamma globulin and haptoglobin are also listed.

tion destroys any Rh-positive red cells from the infant remaining in the mother's bloodstream and so inhibits future anti-D antibody production (Molnar, 2002).

The alleles that determine blood types vary widely both within and between populations. Some data on the occurrence of these alleles are given in Figure 17.10. Note how many of the alleles show extensive intrapopulational variation and also overlap between populations.

Genes and Disease

The study of blood groups, an important medical advance, led to an understanding of their role as adaptations against certain diseases (Molnar, 2002). For example, type A persons show relatively high susceptibility to stomach cancer, pernicious anemia, smallpox, bronchial pneumonia, and rheumatic heart disease, while the other ABO types enjoy some degree of protection from these diseases. Type O individuals run a relatively high risk for duodenal and gastric ulcers, cholera, and plague. Type B individuals are highly susceptible to certain *E. coli* infections and the associated diarrhea. Some of the other blood systems (see Figure 17.10) also show disease-related adaptations. For example, one of the Duffy types provides resistance to vivax malaria, and certain Rh types may give some protection against rheumatic fever. The evidence seems clear that diseases have been important selection factors in the evolution and geographic distribution of humans' blood group systems.

Research into the relationship of disease and human genetics is progressing rapidly. One particular medical and genetic problem is presented by people who carry a genetic condition such as sickle-cell anemia in places where malaria is no longer present. Without the malaria to maintain the balance of the polymorphism, the sickle-cell gene should be reduced in the gene pool as a result of natural selection against both homozygotes and heterozygotes. Some of this sort of selection does occur, but mercifully, for sickle-cell sufferers and carriers, it is not nearly as severe as one might think, thanks to modern medicine and modern lifestyles. Persons who are homozygous for sickle-cell anemia (about 1 in 400 to 500 African American births) can be treated with blood transfusions, pain medications, and a new drug called hydroxyurea (American Sickle Cell Anemia Association). Nonetheless, their life expectancy of about 45 years (Jobling et al., 2004) is significantly shorter than that of nonafflicted people. Sickle-cell carriers (heterozygotes) also run an increased chance of exercise-related death compared to people with normal red cells (Sickle Cell Disease), but this and other health risks can be minimized through attention to lifestyle and activity.

A second medical and genetic problem concerns the possibility of a connection between resistance to HIV (the virus that causes AIDS) in some modern human populations and their ancestors' exposure to the bubonic plague or Black Death back in the fourteenth century (Kolata, 1998; Stephens et al., 1998). Roughly 10 percent of people of European descent, and particularly those people from the more northerly parts of the continent, carry a gene called *CCR5Δ32* that protects them against the AIDS virus. Although common in Europe, the HIV resistant gene becomes scarce around the Mediterranean, and it is low to absent in modern Africans, Asians, and Native Americans—a distribution that matches the geographic occurrence of the bubonic plague. Researchers are busy testing the hypothesis that a mutant gene appeared in Europe a few hundred years ago, became a stable part of the regional gene pool because it provided carriers with protection against the bubonic plague, and by a stroke of luck also provides their modern descendants with protection against HIV (Jobling et al., 2004). If future experiments verify the connection between bubonic plague survival and HIV resistance, it will provide yet another example of how epidemic diseases can affect the course of human evolution.

The Question of Race

Biological Races

The preceding sections have documented what is widely known: Humans, both within their local populations and around the world, vary anatomically and physiologically. In this variation, humans resemble most animal species occupying diverse geographical areas with diverse climates. Such species typically show variation in size and appearance—that is, in superficial (surface) characteristics that respond rapidly to environmental differences. These variations are often described by zoologists as demarcating **races** if they are of a minor nature or *subspecies* if they are more striking.

Races divisions of a *species*, usually based on physical or behavioral differences and less well marked than subspecies. Many anthropologists reject the concept of biological races of living humans.

In the course of human evolution, populations of our species have adapted to just about every ecological zone on the surface of the earth, excluding Antarctica, and have evolved morphological and physiological adaptations to the temperature, solar radiation, humidity, vegetation, and such of each zone. Furthermore, some genetic and phenotypic differences among human groups can be attributed to varying degrees of geographic isolation (which can reduce gene flow), social factors (such as mate-selection patterns), and genetic drift. Singly or in combination, these factors have produced genetic variation and often striking external differences between humans from different populations (Molnar, 2002; see Figure 17.6).

The crucial question, of course, is what sense can we make of all this variation? Are there identifiable subdivisions of *Homo sapiens* that we can all agree are biological races? And if so, who are they, how do they differ, and how far back in time can they be traced? Alternately, should the notion of biological races be discarded in favor of some other understanding of humans' obvious diversity? Let's take a closer look at the race concept as it has been applied to our species.

For more than 200 years, patterns of physical variation have been used by anthropologists (and also by nonspecialists, in the form of *folk concepts*) to classify people into races. Typically, races have been viewed as divisions of *Homo sapiens* with the following two main attributes:

1. *Distinctive sets of physical traits.* Although virtually all racial classifications rest mainly on differences in skin color, other characteristics—nose, lip, and eye shapes, hair color and texture, facial shapes, and so on—are typically presented as closely correlated with skin color variations.

2. *Distinctive geographic distributions.* Varying from relatively small areas to entire continents, racial distributions are generally described as they were at initial European contact—that is, about 1,500 AD.

To these physical and spatial attributes, a temporal dimension can be added. Scientists and laypersons, as well, have often assumed that the human races are the result of:

3. *Separate and possibly lengthy histories of existence.* There are many ways to look at this issue. Some pre-Darwinian theorists believed that "distinct boundaries between races [were] established at the creation" (Molnar, 2002:7). Going even further, Darwin's contemporary, Louis Agassiz (among others), concluded that the various categories of humankind were actually different divinely created species (Gould, 1981). And finally, twentieth-century anthropologist Carleton Coon (1963) argued that the geographic races of humans had long and reasonably separate evolutionary histories.

This traditional view of human races—separate histories, separate locations, homogeneous clusters of diagnostic traits—has begun to break down recently as new information on diversity (particularly genetic diversity) has accumulated. Over the past few decades, many anthropologists have grown disenchanted with racial classifications and become convinced that race is neither a useful nor valid biological concept for understanding human diversity (Littlefield et al., 1982; Shanklin, 1994). This position is widely accepted among *cultural* anthropologists, but *physical* anthropologists are divided on the issue. While most physical anthropology textbooks (and most practitioners?) now argue against the validity of biological races, some specialists, especially some **forensic anthropologists,** continue to advocate the concept. As articulated by George Gill (2000) of the University of Wyoming, these workers find racial divisions quite useful as they attempt to identify crime victims using skeletal evidence.

Forensic anthropologists physical *anthropologists* who apply their expertise to matters of law, such as the identification of human remains.

The basic problem with designating biological races of humans is that they are seemingly obvious and not obvious at the same time. Although some scientists argue that race is demonstrable from anatomical traits, races tend to become fuzzy (arbitrarily defined) when genetic data are applied. This confusing situation allows room for disagreement among anthropologists, depending on their theoretical and applied interests. For forensic anthropologists, designating biological races provides a useful set of pigeonholes for their skeletal identifications. For anthropologists using genetic data, however, the race concept becomes unworkable because interracial variation pales in comparison to shared genes and because internal variation is found in every population.

And so, as with many scientific controversies, the question of biological races of humans hinges on definitions, criteria of identification, and levels of measurement. Comparing the two primary approaches to racial classification—anatomical traits versus genetics—provides some interesting insights into the issue. First, classifications based on surface features alone—such as skin color, hair texture, nose shape, eye folds, and the like—are by far the oldest and have played a major role in shaping our folk concept of race. These classifications have tended to lump people into a few categories based mainly on skin color and geography. For example, in 1735, Linnaeus came up with a list of four races: American (Reddish), European (White), Asiatic (Yellow), and Negro (Black). Comte de Buffon, J. F. Blumenbach, and Georges Cuvier produced similar short lists during the eighteenth century (Molnar, 2002).

The problem with these classifications is that they are based on characteristics that are not discrete but rather grade imperceptibly from one geographic group to the next. Blumenbach recognized these gradations as early as 1775, when he noted, "One variety of mankind does so sensibly pass into the other, that you cannot mark out the limits between them" (quoted in Montagu, 1945:12). Nowadays, scientists describe graded features as having *clinal* distributions (that is, they show geographical gradations). Two well studied human examples are skin color (Figure 17.5) and nose form (Figure 17.8). The clinal distribution of anatomical traits is a problem for racial typologists for several reasons. First, as Blumenbach noted, one race blends smoothly into the next, and therefore, defining racial boundaries is quite arbitrary. Second, no geographic race is particularly homogeneous with regard to clinal characteristics. (Note in Figure 17.5 that Africans are not all uniformly dark nor are Europeans all uniformly white.) And third, the clinal distributions of several different traits—each supposedly diagnostic for a racial group—usually do not match very well. A comparison of Figures 17.5 and 17.8 shows that skin color and nose form differ significantly in their distribution patterns. What sense can we make of the fact that people from Somalia share dark brown skin with other Sub-Saharan Africans but usually have noses shaped like those of Europeans? As Stephen Molnar (2002) has remarked, to group Africans into a single "Negroid" race is to incorrectly treat them as if they were homogeneous when they are not. The same could be said, of course, about any of the other traditional "skin color" geographical races.

Identifying human biological races from clinally distributed anatomical features, therefore, is problematic at best, and given this, many anthropologists have abandoned the attempt as arbitrary and pointless. But having said that, it is important to note that because hominan evolution has included some reproductive separation of geographic populations and a limited amount of region-specific trait development, there seems to be enough anatomical distinctiveness between the major populations that forensic anthropologists such as George Gill can usually put crime remains into the correct slot from among a few "racial" pigeonholes. For these workers, the long tradition of anatomically based racial classifications (Hooton, 1946) is still useful.

In the mid twentieth century, genetic data began to be used in creating racial classifications of humans. This did little to clear up the issues of racial identity and validity, however, for several reasons: namely, genes, too, are usually clinally distributed (see Figure 17.9), and, furthermore, scientists have never agreed among themselves about the appropriate level for genetic analysis. Genetic differences have been found at the level of local breeding populations, as well as between continental clusters of populations (Dobzhansky, 1937; Garn, 1965; Molnar, 2002). But if the term *race* is equated with "a breeding population [sharing] a common history, and a common locale" (Garn, 1965:6), then *dozens* of modern human races exist today and more undoubtedly existed in the past. Thus, using the "breeding population" definition, Garn (1965) identified 9 geographical, or "primary," races (see Figure 17.11) and 32 modern "local" races! The lack of agreement between anatomic and genetic racial classifications, plus the seemingly endless numbers of genetically distinct breeding populations, has convinced many anthropologists that using a racial typology is the wrong way to understand humans' biological diversity.

The demonstration from genetics that there could be as few as six (Boyd, 1950) or as many as several dozen human races strongly suggested that creating a typology was a biologically meaningless exercise. Interestingly, although the intent was to illuminate our racial divisions, a main effect of these genetics studies was to provide unequivocal proof of a high level of human unity. In 1972, Harvard biologist R. C. Lewontin published the results of a study of genetic diversity within and between several traditionally defined geographic races (i.e., Africans, Native Americans, Mongoloids, Caucasians, South Asian Aborigines, Australian Aborigines, and Oceanians). Lewontin's results, shown in Figure 17.12, revealed that just over 85 percent of human genetic diversity, based on genes for physiological character traits, occurs between individuals belonging to the same population (generally, the same nation or tribe). An additional 8.3 percent of genetic variation is accounted for by differences between populations within the same traditional race (for example, between West Africans and Bantus). This leaves only 6.3 percent of genetic diversity accounted for by interracial differences! Thus, even if one is in-

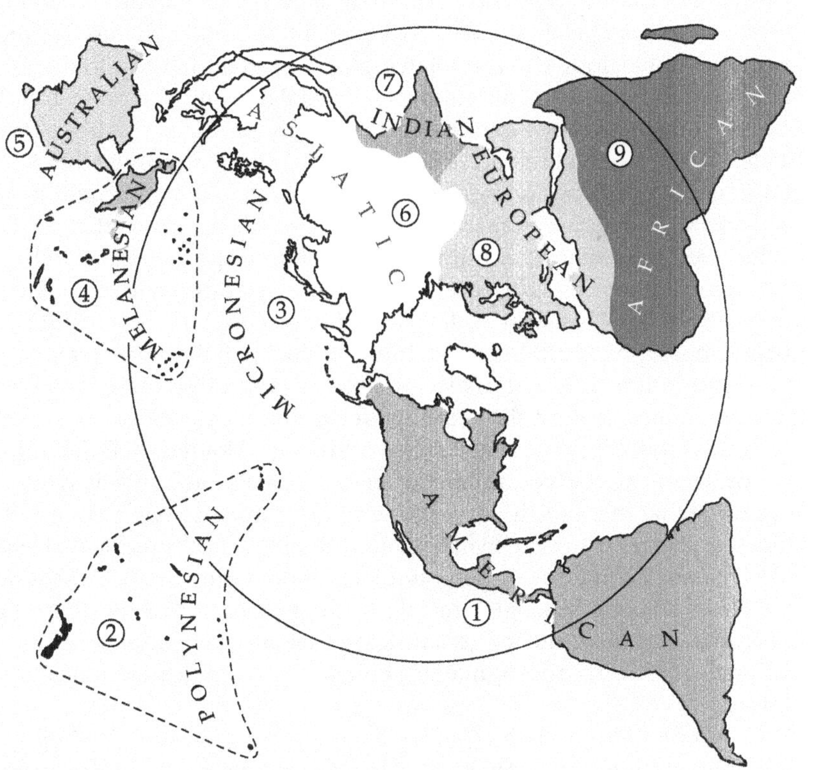

FIGURE 17.11 A polar-projection map showing the nine geographic races of humans envisioned by anthropologist Stanley Garn in 1965.

Source: From S. M. Garn, *Human Races*, 2nd edition, 1965. Courtesy of Charles C Thomas, Publisher, Ltd., Springfield, Illinois.

clined to believe in the existence of biological races among humans, these data argue strongly that such entities make only a small overall contribution to genetic variation among humans. Subsequent studies have verified Lewontin's general results time and again, suggesting to many anthropologists that it "no longer makes sense to adhere to arbitrary racial categories" (Brown and Armelagos, 2001:34).

	PERCENTAGE OF TOTAL DIVERSITY FOR GENE(S)		
Gene	Within Populations in %	Within Races between Populations in %	Between Races
Hp	89.3	5.1	5.6
Ag	83.4	—	—
Lp	93.9	—	—
Xm	99.7	—	—
Ap	92.7	6.2	1.1
6PGD	87.5	5.8	6.7
PGM	94.2	3.3	2.5
Ak	84.8	2.1	13.1
Kidd	74.1	21.1	4.8
Duffy	63.6	10.5	25.9
Lewis	96.6	3.2	0.2
Kell	90.1	7.3	2.6
Lutheran	69.4	21.4	9.2
P	94.9	2.9	2.2
MNS	91.1	4.1	4.8
Rh	67.4	7.3	25.3
ABO	90.7	6.3	3.0
Mean	85.4	8.3	6.3

FIGURE 17.12 Analyses such as this one indicate that the vast majority of genetic diversity in humans exists *within* so-called races, not *between* them.

Source: Lewontin, 1972.

It is important to note, however, that the relatively small number of so-called between-race genetic differences (6.3 percent of total diversity, as measured by Lewontin) can include disease-related alleles of great interest to the medical community. For that reason, some support for racial labeling as a proxy for place of evolutionary origin has been expressed recently by physicians. Although doctors are divided on the issue (Holden, 2003; Schwartz, 2001), many argue that knowing a patient's continent of ancestral origin can provide valuable information about his or her chances of carrying certain disease-related genes. It appears that, as with anatomical features, the vagaries of human evolution have produced small but important geographic differences in disease-related genes. In addition to the sickle-cell anemia and *CCRΔ532* (HIV resistance) alleles mentioned earlier in this chapter, there are significant geographical differences in the frequencies of the genes for such ailments as cystic fibrosis and Huntington disease (Jobling et al., 2004). Additionally, it is known that populations around the world differ in the incidence of the *CYP2D6* alleles, which affect the ability to metabolize certain drugs (Holden, 2003; Jobling et al., 2004).

Physicians who advocate categorizing their patients as black, white, Asian, and such argue that this simply serves to remind them that people from different parts of the world carry different health-related genotypes. They argue that "self-reported ancestry can facilitate assessments of epidemiological risks" (Rosenberg et al., 2002:2381). Opponents of such racial profiling respond that race-based generalizations can never substitute for genetic tests done on each patient and also worry that profiling could "unfairly stigmatize some patients and lead to inferior health care" (Holden, 2003:594).

In summary, two distinct views have emerged on the question of biological races of living humans. Some physical anthropologists (especially forensic specialists) and some physicians find geographic race typologies practically useful and therefore valid. Most other researchers disagree, however, concluding instead that biological races of humans are arbitrarily defined, indeterminate in number, and of little heuristic value. Virtually all cultural anthropologists and a good many (most?) physical anthropologists belong to the latter category. Racial skeptics argue that the investigation of individual traits and genes, including their distribution and evolutionary histories, is a better way to understand human evolution than the construction of race classifications. As discussed in the next section, skeptics are also worried about race typologies resulting in racist behaviors.

One aspect of the race question has become clear in the last half century, however: Thanks to the genetic studies, all parties now agree that underneath our external diversity, humans manifest enormous genetic unity. In the words of geneticist Luca Cavalli-Sforza, "It is because they are external that [so-called] racial differences strike us so forcibly, and we automatically assume that differences of similar magnitude exist below the surface, in the rest of our genetic makeup. This is simply not so: the remainder of our genetic makeup hardly differs at all" (Cavalli-Sforza and Cavalli-Sforza, 1995:124).

Ethnic and Other Social Groups

It would be a wonderful world indeed if anthropologists' repudiation of biological races could put an end to divisions between human populations and bring on an age of global unity. Such a world remains a utopian dream, however, because regardless of whether race has any biological reality, *as a social construct*, it is alive and well in most modern cultures. This is undoubtedly linked to humans' tendency to focus on all sorts of differences between people and to divide the world into "we–they" groups.

Ethnic group a group of people perceived as sharing a common and distinctive *culture*.

Grouping schemes based on real or imagined differences in behavior, customs, or genealogy (descent) result in the identification of **ethnic groups.** This term, which is much less emotionally charged than *race*, is now commonly applied both to huge collections of people (for example, Asian Americans) as well as small populations. Breaking free of our old fixation on physical differences is difficult, however, and people commonly take phenotype into consideration as they (consciously or unconsciously) make ethnic group distinctions.

Ethnic divisions can serve good and valid purposes. They may foster unity and pride within minority communities, serve as the focal point for political solidarity, or facilitate the preservation of a population's cultural heritage. On the other hand, when either the biological race concept or ethnic divisions are combined with another human tendency, our inclination to **xenophobia** (see Box 17.1), the result all too often is discrimination or **racism,** defined here as the belief that human groups can be ranked as superior or inferior to one another and their members treated accordingly. Racism is responsible for a multitude of evils, ranging from job discrimination to genocide.

Xenophobia a fear or hatred of foreigners.

Racism the assumption of inherent superiority of certain *races* and the consequent discrimination against others.

Perhaps the most strongly held folk belief—and certainly one of the most divisive—is the notion that ethnic groups (or racial groups, to typologists) differ significantly and unalterably in intelligence and the genes that code for it. Simply put, there is no good evidence for this belief. The question of intelligence was carefully examined in the mid 1990s by a task force appointed by the American Psychological Association. The report of that task force included the following findings (Neisser et al., 1996):

- There are multiple forms of intelligence (e.g., analytic, creative, and practical) and no single instrument (i.e., **IQ test**) comes close to measuring them all.
- To date, IQ tests have focused mainly on analytical skills and had little success measuring such important things as creativity, practical knowledge, social skills, and wisdom.

IQ tests tests that supposedly measure an individual's intelligence quotient. Many consider such tests flawed and of little value, particularly for cross-cultural comparisons.

BOX 17.1 CURRENT ISSUE

Xenophobia, an Outmoded Adaptation

Why, in the face of overwhelming evidence of humans' biological unity, do we still find superficial physical differences (for example, in skin, hair, and facial features) so striking? And furthermore, why do we so easily develop attitudes of distrust and dislike toward people we classify—based on those same superficial traits—as different from ourselves?

Partial answers to these questions can be derived from knowledge of humans' sensory systems and certain of our evolved but now outmoded behavioral tendencies. First of all, we are overwhelmingly visual animals. Following in the ancient anthropoid pattern, hominins have always relied for survival mainly on the evidence of their eyes, and consequently, modern humans are masters at noticing visual details. Among the most important visual details, of course, were the physical features of conspecifics. From those features, our ancestors obtained important information about group mates' probable kin relations, age, health, and reproductive condition that helped them make decisions about altruistic investments, mate selection, and alliances.

Of course, visual clues would also have allowed the identification of strangers (members of other groups or tribes, territorial invaders), a distinction that—judging from observations of monkeys and apes—often would have triggered a hostile reaction. In humans' prehistoric past, when strangers may have spelled trouble more often than they do today, such xenophobia could have been an adaptive first emotion. In our modern cultures, however, where we are constantly encountering physically and ethnically diverse people, xenophobia has become outmoded and undesirable. No longer the correct first emotion for survival, it has become maladaptive.

Thus, the explanation of our modern condition, but how can we change it? (We assume everyone agrees that reducing xenophobia and racism is a worthwhile goal.) Although distrust and dislike of strangers may be an evolved human tendency, that does not make it wise, morally right, or inevitable. Happily, because our behaviors are much more strongly shaped by learning than by genes, it should be possible to remove the basis of xenophobia through determined education by parents, peers, and society. With a strong effort, we should be able to move out of the xenophobic dark ages and into a modern world that accepts and values diversity.

- Intelligence, while heritable to some extent, is also strongly affected by environmental factors, such as an individual's educational history, family environment, socioeconomic level, and general health.
- An individual's intelligence is not stable throughout the life course. Rather, it changes with age, education, and experience.
- Inter-ethnic differences in mean IQ scores have been reported, but they are hard to interpret and their validity has been challenged. Cultural factors may well affect group scores, but the available evidence fails to support a genetic explanation for differences. The connections, if any, between ethnicity (race) and intelligence have yet to be clarified.

What sense, then, can we make of the ethnic divisions that criss-cross humankind? Unlike biological races, which many scientists would argue are products of our imagination, ethnic groups are demonstrably real factors in today's world. Sometimes, ethnic divisions are forces for good, but they can also be abused and turned to evil purposes. Differential treatment of ethnic (racial) groups based on perceived inferiority amounts to racist behavior and can never be justified. Any attempt to turn anthropological or psychological data to the support of racism is an utter perversion of the goals of those sciences.

Challenges for the Future

Population and Evolutionary Success

The hominin story began 7 million years ago in Africa. From rather humble beginnings, our species has evolved to become the dominant force on the planet. Physically and culturally diverse, humans are spread throughout all regions of the globe. Yes, we are a grand evolutionary success, yet ironically, our very success may contribute to our undoing.

Consider the issue of human population size. Edward S. Deevey (1960) has estimated that the hominin population of the earth 1 million years ago was little more than 100,000 individuals. By 300,000 years ago, at or near the end of *Homo erectus*'s tenancy, the human population had climbed to 1 million, and by 25,000 years ago, during the Upper Paleolithic, it had jumped to perhaps more than 3 million. (Note that there may have been significant bottlenecks within the broad trend of population growth. Modern humans—*Homo sapiens*—may have numbered between 5,000 and 10,000 shortly after their evolutionary origin.) The world population has risen at an increasingly steep pace since the Upper Paleolithic (Figure 17.13).

The population, according to Deevey (1960), has probably not risen in a steady curve. Rather, the increase in the world's population has had a series of surges, reflecting the great cultural innovations associated with hominin evolution. The first cultural innovation, of course, was the development of stone tools. This advance allowed hominins to exploit their environments more intensively. The population density of Africa in the days of the crude Oldowan industry, has been estimated at about 1 individual per 100 square miles (260 square kilometers). By the end of the Paleolithic, humans had spread around the world, and their density had probably risen tenfold.

The second innovation was the double discovery of how to grow crops and how to domesticate animals. This event came about 10,000 years ago. This second innovation facilated the creation of large, permanent settlements. Even nomads herding animals could exist in far greater concentrations on a given area of land than could hunters. The effect on world population was extraordinary. In 4,000 years, it jumped from an estimated 5 million to 86 million.

The third innovation was the Industrial Age. It had its beginnings about 300 years ago, when the human population of the world was in the neighborhood of 550 million. World population has been ballooning ever since and today is 6 billion. If it continues at its present rate of increase, it will double within 50 years.

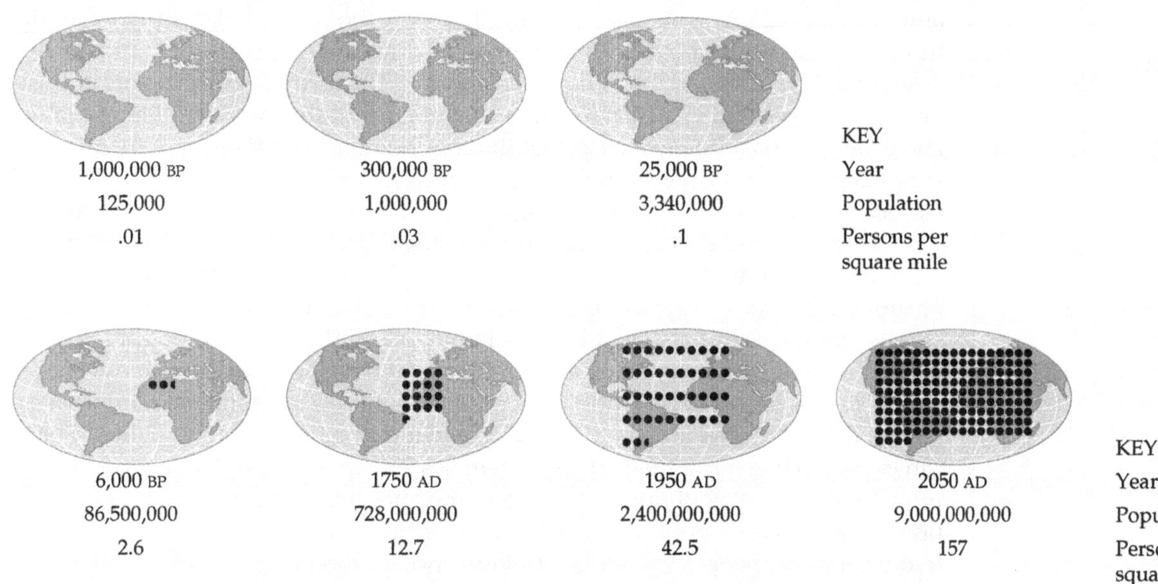

FIGURE 17.13
Until about 25,000 years BP, humankind was a stable part of the equilibrium existing among animals and plants. With better hunting technology, animal domestication, and agriculture, humans began to increase dramatically and to destroy the wilderness of which they had been a part. The figures given for the populations of the past are, of course, estimates. That for 2050 AD is a projection by the U.S. Census Bureau (U.S. Census Bureau).

Note: Dots indicate persons per square mile.

Although these figures are impressive, even more impressive is the *acceleration* in population growth. It took over 1 million years to get through the first phase; the second took only 10,000 years; and the third has been going on for only a few hundred. How long it will continue or what the human population of the earth will ultimately be is anybody's guess. But we can be sure that because the surface of the earth is finite, as are its resources, present rates of increase will bring us to the limit very soon.

Limits to Growth

It seems clear that the increase in our population is due primarily to making greater and greater use of the available resources. When a forest is cleared and crops are grown in its place, all the sunlight in that area is contributing to synthesis of food for humans. When wild animals grazing in meadows and savanna grasslands are killed and replaced by cattle, sheep, and goats, conversion of plant energy into animal protein is turned fully to human benefit.

In these cases, we can see that the ultimate limitation is the amount of energy that can be delivered by the sun to the earth's surface and turned into carbohydrates by photosynthesis in green plants. Other limiting factors are the other requirements of plants: water, minerals, and appropriate soil. Lack of water in particular has long been a problem for farmers, although they have occasionally overcome it with irrigation. But even with advanced technology, we cannot obtain food from all the earth; the ultimate limits are firm both on the land and in the oceans. Eventually, as Thomas Malthus predicted in 1798, these limits will indeed halt human population growth, if we do not bring about stabilization voluntarily.

But the continuing expansion of agriculture and animal husbandry cannot be taken to the ultimate limits set by the area of the earth's land masses without destroying all the natural wilderness and the miraculous array of wild plants and animals that occupy it. As discussed in Chapter 3, the continued destruction of the tropical forests poses a serious and immediate threat of extinction for many nonhuman primate species and the indigenous humans. The further expansion of agribusiness or even peasant agriculture will be destructive to the quality of life we value, and ecologists have made it clear that the continuing loss of forest in particular has very dangerous and irreversible results. We now know that much of the earth's land surface is, in fact, not well suited to agriculture but is best left in its natural state.

In some parts of the world, famine is already becoming a normal condition, and malnutrition is found on many continents. People are dying of hunger by the tens of thousands, partly because the increase in population is due not merely to increased resources but also to advances in medicine. These have brought about an increased **life expectancy.** An australopith might have been lucky to live 20 years, and *Homo erectus* probably added a decade to that life expectancy. Neolithic *Homo sapiens* lived between 30 and 40 years, while today, a citizen of the United States can expect to live more than 70 years (females 79.8 and males 74.4 years; U.S. Gov Info Resources). A doubling of life expectancy has brought a doubling of population without a corresponding increase in our efficiency in using resources. Thus, in many countries people live longer, but not enough food is grown to feed them all.

Life expectancy the average age at death of individuals born into a particular population.

Large segments of human society have certainly come a long way: in life span, in efficiency in extracting resources, in population density, in technological complexity, and in increased physical comfort. Whether we are really better off as a species, and whether our progress will continue, remains to be seen. For a species like ours, whose survival depends on culture (which is based on knowledge), it is essential to use all available knowledge and understanding to achieve better adaptation to a changing environment. This is perhaps our most difficult problem: Each new cultural adaptation we make alters the environment to which we are adapting. New adaptations increase population; greater population densities require further adaptations; new adaptations deplete world resources; resource depletion requires further adaptation; and so it goes on. We find ourselves in a vicious circle of ever-increasing instability (Figure 17.14). Essential now is an all-out attempt to break that accelerating positive feedback loop and bring about new stability in global population size, in technological investment, and in resource consumption (Figure 17.15). (See Smail, 2002, 2003a, and 2003b for a thoughtful discussion of the human population problem.)

Population size is certainly a measure of evolutionary success, but another measure that may be more significant is evolutionary longevity. *Homo sapiens*'s 195,000 years is nothing in universal and geologic time, and millions of species have evolved and become extinct in earth history. Compared with most mammals, we are infants of evolution. From this point of view, our apparent present success can

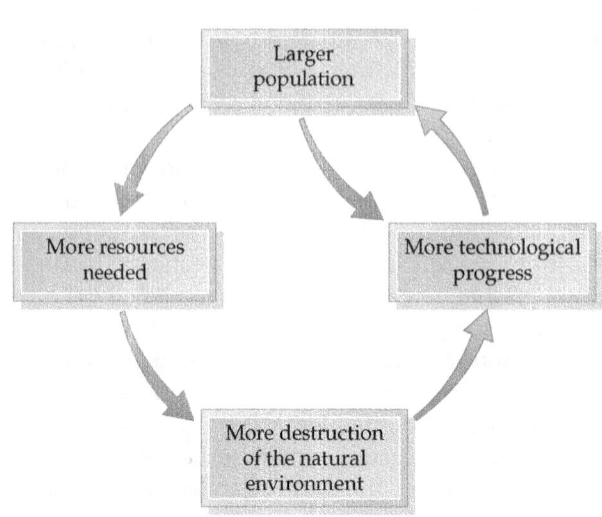

FIGURE 17.14
This positive feedback loop is the most dangerous to us, since it is accelerating very rapidly and involves environmental destruction. With the resource base of our livelihood seriously depleted, the survival of even our present number is threatened.

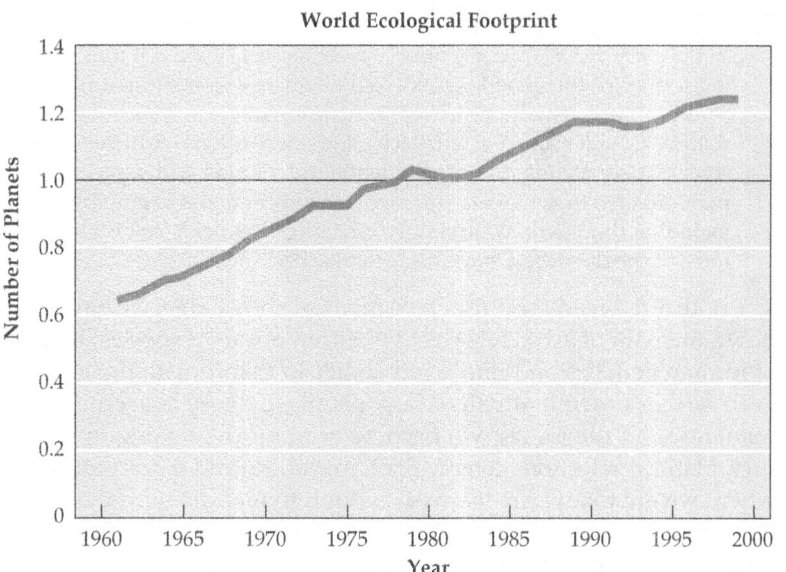

FIGURE 17.15
The ecological footprint is a measure of humanity's use of renewable natural resources. It grew by 80 percent between 1961 and 1999, to a level 20 percent above the earth's biological capacity. It is expressed as number of planets, where one planet equals the total biologically productive capacity of the earth in any one year. Natural resource consumption can exceed the planet's productive capacity by depleting the earth's natural capital, but this this cannot by sustained indefinately.

Source: World Wildlife Fund.

continue only if we can achieve some sort of stability in our relationship with the earth's resources. Otherwise, we run the risk of perishing as a species.

Gaining Control over Our Evolution

The scale of global overpopulation is so great and the solutions so seemingly elusive that most of us have a hard time even imagining, much less dealing with, the problem. Other challenges of the twenty-first century will be much more immediate and personal. For example, with each passing year, humans gain more and more control over their health, reproduction, and evolutionary future. With more control, however, will come increasingly difficult choices.

The evolutionary processes described by Charles Darwin and later biologists will, of course, continue to operate in the future. Mutations and new gene combinations will continue to provide the raw material for natural selection. According to British geneticist Steve Jones (1992), the mutation rate due to external agents will probably remain stable in the near future. Mutations due to delayed reproduction, however, may be expected to rise. This rise will be related to the fact that modern people are having children later than has been true during most of human evolution. Jones estimates that today's mean age at first reproduction is about five years later than it was 10,000 years ago (before the agricultural revolution). Because cells (including those that produce sperm and eggs) become increasingly mutation prone as they age, we can expect an increased number of newborns carrying mutant alleles (Jones, 1992).

This predicted rise in the mutation rate will coincide with the medical and scientific communities' increased ability to deal with genetic problems. As discussed in Chapter 2 and elsewhere, by using procedures such as amniocentesis, we can already learn not only the sex but also a great deal about the genotype of a developing fetus—information that parents may use to terminate a pregnancy for one reason or another. In the future, prospective parents will be able to learn even more about their unborn children, including genetic predispositions for numerous diseases and the presence or absence of genes for desired phenotypic traits. How will this information be used? Will we limit ourselves to curing (through such procedures as gene therapy) or preventing diseases? Or will our desire for perfect children result in increased abortions and genetic engineering for cosmetic effects? And looking beyond parents and offspring, how will society use additional genetic information?

Science writer Joseph Levine and geneticist David Suzuki (1993) have written about how such information might be abused. Here is a chilling real-life case:

> In the early 1970s . . . compulsory screening for sickle-cell trait [i.e., for persons carrying a copy of the gene for sickle-cell anemia] was instituted in at least twelve states. Screening was usually restricted to African-Americans (although 7 percent of subjects with sickle-cell trait were not black), and it was often conducted without informed consent. Inadequate regard for confidentiality, coupled with a preexisting history of racial prejudice, led to denial of insurance coverage and loss of employment for black people, including those who were simply carriers of the sickle-cell trait and showed no symptoms of the disease. (Levine and Suzuki, 1993; 202–203)

With our already sophisticated medical knowledge, we have taken several steps down the path of artificial selection within our own species. Increased knowledge of human genetics and improved ability to manipulate the genotype will take us even farther down that path. Many people are very concerned about these developments, and the issues will become even more pressing in the twenty-first century. Natural selection, genetic drift, mutation, and other natural processes got us where we are today. Are we wise enough to meddle with the selection systems of the future? Jeremy Rifkin of the Foundation for Economic Trends and other opponents of genetic engineering believe that the answer is no. According to Rifkin, "Perhaps none of us is wise enough, has the clairvoyance, the wisdom, to dictate basic changes in millions of years of genetic evolution. I don't think any of us should have that power. I think it's an unwarranted power and should not be exercised" (quoted in Levine and Suzuki, 1993; 218–219).

We are in the midst of a revolution in biological information and medical sophistication that has far-reaching implications for the future of humans. That future will also be affected by our burgeoning global population and by our stressed and deteriorating global environment. Our intelligence and cultural ingenuity—both products of our evolutionary history—brought us this far. We have no choice but to trust them to give us the vision and the tools to cope with our own success.

Summary

Cultural developments have proceeded at an ever-accelerating pace since the evolutionary appearance of anatomically modern humans. Plant and animal domestication was under way by 10,000 years BP, and the establishment of modern civilization soon followed. These developments facilitated or accompanied a strong surge in human population growth around the world. Human evolution did not stop with the attainment of modernity, however, and differential adaptation (very likely combined with a bit of genetic drift) led to physical diversity within and between human populations.

The question of whether modern humans can be divided into racial units is a contentious one. Some anthropologists and some physicians find the notion of identifying geographical races of humans both useful and valid. Most anthropologists, however, feel that biological races of humans are arbitrary by definition and indeterminate in number, which makes the concept useless as applied to our species. Certainly, with regard to genetics, it is clear that most human variation occurs *within* traditionally defined races and that only a small percentage occurs *between* them. Nonetheless, in line with humans' strong tendency to dichotomize the world into "we–they" units, distinct ethnic groups most definitely exist and may serve good and valid purposes within society. Ethnic divisions, like racial classifications, however, may also lead to racist and discriminatory attitudes and behaviors, and we must be constantly on guard against these evils.

The primary challenges for humankind in the twenty-first century include gaining control over global population growth, restricting our runaway use of the earth's finite resources, and dealing with the technological, genetic, and medical advances that allow us an ever-increasing measure of control over our evolutionary future.

Postscript

This brings to an end our history of human evolution. We hope you have enjoyed it and that this is only one of many anthropology books you will read during your college years and beyond. The story of humankind, whether read from the viewpoint of physical or cultural anthropology, is endlessly fascinating, and new discoveries are constantly being made. It is fascinating partly because it tells of a mammalian family that began with only one outstanding attribute—bipedalism—and that evolved the intelligence and the behavioral complexity to hold the fate of the world in its prehensile hands. But primarily, of course, it is fascinating because it is *our* story and ends with modern humans representing the sole surviving twig of the hominin evolutionary bush.

But the hominin story goes beyond being merely fascinating. It is also *important* because it gives us a clear picture of modern human equality and thus allows us to look to the future with a degree of optimism. Optimism is sometimes a rare commodity. As we prepare the ninth edition of this textbook, wars and insurgencies going on all over the globe, terror attacks are common, and so-called ethnic cleansing seems to be occurring once again in Africa. How, one might ask, in the light of these events, can we speak of optimism?

We are optimistic because of our deep belief in the unity of humankind. The fossil record shows that all modern people are the descendants of African ancestors who lived a short 195,000 years ago. Although in the intervening years, people have spread all over the globe, adapted to a variety of environments, and developed substantial genetic and physical diversity, that diversity is swamped by our overwhelming similarities. As noted in this chapter, only 6.3 percent of genetic diversity occurs between traditionally defined human races. Recent common ancestry and overwhelming genetic similarities—from these two facts flows the inescapable inference of *human unity.*

We are certainly not the first to make this inference, nor will we be the last. Human unity is a principle worth discovering and describing over and over, in the hope that humanity will finally get the message and move from genocide and international confrontation to peaceful coexistence and cooperation. The challenges facing humankind in the twenty-first century will put a premium on human unity and cooperation as never before. In order to make any significant headway against population growth, resource depletion, and human misery, we must act as a global community. But the development of such a community clearly hinges on our acceptance of one another as absolute equals. It will take massive teamwork, and we call on every reader of this book to contribute to that effort.

Review Questions

1. Discuss the connection between genes and culture. Specifically, discuss how humans' moral systems may have evolved.
2. Humans' global population is currently burgeoning. Describe the various developments over the course of human evolution that have allowed massive population growth.
3. Argue for or against the proposition that humans can be subdivided into biological races. Be sure to provide supporting evidence for your argument.
4. What is the difference between race and racism? Can races exist without racist attitudes and behavior?
5. Argue for or against the proposition that future human evolution will be controlled mainly by self-directed artificial selection, not by natural selection.
6. What, if anything, can we learn from the study of human evolution that will help guide our individual and societal decisions in the future?

SUGGESTED FURTHER READING

Campbell, Bernard. *Human Ecology: The Story of Our Place in Nature from Prehistory to the Present*, 2nd ed. New York, Aldine de Gruyter, 1995.

Cavalli-Sforza, Luigi Luca, Paolo Menozzi, and Alberto Piazza. *The History and Geography of Human Genes*. Princeton, Princeton University Press, 1994.

Diamond, Jared. *Guns, Germs, and Steel*. New York, W. W. Norton, 1997.

Gould, Stephen Jay. *The Mismeasure of Man*. New York, W. W. Norton, 1981.

Molnar, Stephen. *Human Variation: Races, Types, and Ethnic Groups*, 5th ed. Upper Saddle River (NJ), Prentice Hall, 2002.

Shanklin, Eugenia. *Anthropology and Race*. Belmont (CA), Wadsworth, 1994.

Shipman, Pat. *The Evolution of Racism*. New York, Simon & Schuster, 1994.

INTERNET RESOURCES

REINTRODUCING GROUP SELECTION TO THE HUMAN BEHAVIORAL SCIENCES
www.bbsonline.org/documents/a/00/00/04/60

Biologist David Sloan Wilson sees group selection as an important factor in human behavioral evolution. This article introduces you to some of his thinking.

EARLY PLANT DOMESTICATION IN MESOAMERICA
www.athenapub.com/nwdom1.htm

Excerpted from an *Athena Review* article, this paper describes the evidence for plant domestication in the New World.

MINORITIES, RACE, AND GENOMICS
www.ornl.gov/sci/techresources/Human_Genome/elsi/minorities.shtml

Part of the Human Genome Project Information effort, this site includes lots of useful links to papers discussing the complex issue of human biological races.

THE EVOLUTION OF HUMAN SKIN COLORATION
www.calacademy.org/research/anthropology/Jablonski/printable_files/skin.pdf

Nina Joblonski and George Chaplin's theory of the evolution of human skin colors is presented in this web site.

ABO BLOOD TYPES
http://anthro.palomar.edu/blood/ABO_system.htm

As the name indicates, this site explains the frequencies and inheritance of the ABO blood types.

FORENSIC ANTHROPOLOGY AND HUMAN OSTEOLOGY RESOURCES
www.forensicanthro.com

For readers interested in learning more about forensic anthropology, this web site has the important links.

WORLD POPULATION INFORMATION
www.census.gov/ipc/www/world.html

Produced by the U.S. Census Bureau, this site contains links to information on the current world population and predictions for the future.

USEFUL SEARCH TERMS:

biological races of humans
human biological diversity
Human Genome Project
plant (animal) domestication
race
skin colors
world population growth

Appendix 1

The Genetic Code

DNA Codon	Amino Acid	DNA Codon	Amino Acid
GCA	alanine	AGA	arginine
GCG	alanine	AGG	arginine
GCT	alanine	CGA	arginine
GCC	alanine	CGG	arginine
		CGT	arginine
GAT	aspartic acid	CGC	arginine
GAC	aspartic acid		
		AAT	asparagine
TGT	cysteine	AAC	asparagine
TGC	cysteine		
		GAA	glutamic acid
CAA	glutamine	GAG	glutamic acid
CAG	glutamine		
		GGA	glycine
CAT	histidine	GGG	glycine
CAC	histidine	GGT	glycine
		GGC	glycine
ATA	isoleucine		
ATT	isoleucine	TTA	leucine
ATC	isoleucine	TTG	leucine
		CTA	leucine
AAA	lysine	CTG	leucine
AAG	lysine	CTT	leucine
		CTC	leucine
ATG	methionine/**start**		
		TTT	phenylalanine
CCA	proline	TTC	phenylalanine
CCG	proline		
CCT	proline	AGT	serine
CCC	proline	AGC	serine
		TCA	serine
ACA	threonine	TCG	serine
ACG	threonine	TCT	serine
ACT	threonine	TCC	serine
ACC	threonine		
		TGG	tryptophan
TAT	tyrosine		
TAC	tyrosine	GTA	valine
		GTG	valine
TAA	**stop**	GTT	valine
TAG	**stop**	GTC	valine
TGA	**stop**		

Appendix 2

Dating Procedures for Fossil Remains

The problem of determining the age of fossils is handled in several ways. The first is through *geology*, the study of the earth itself. This branch of science is concerned with the location, size, and nature of the various layers of clay, silt, sand, lava, limestone, and other kinds of rock that constitute the earth's surface and with their relationship to one another. It examines certain processes, such as continental drift, erosion, the accumulation of layers of silt at the bottom of the sea, and their compaction into rock again by heat and pressure.

Analysis of these layers, or *strata*—a scientific discipline known as *stratigraphy*—permits the working out of a rough picture of past earth history (Figures 5.1, 5.5). From this information, the fossils found in different rock structures can be arranged in order of age. The deepest strata are the oldest, and the more recent levels are laid down above them. Thus, fossils in the upper strata are relatively younger than those in the lower strata. These data, however, do not give us the absolute age of the fossils in years. Moreover, the dates for the fossils are considered to be **indirect dates,** since the fossils themselves are not dated, but rather the layers in which they are found.

Indirect date a date on material that is associated with the object in question; for example, a human skull may be associated with a particular sedimentary layer that is dated by the K/Ar method to 2 million years BP, thus indirectly dating the skull to 2 million years BP, also.

The second way to determine relative age is by studying the fossils themselves. Fossil types are usually not the same in different layers. Animals evolved through time, and since all species have finite lifetimes (i.e., ultimately go extinct), their fossils provide clues of their own, particularly if the time sequence can be worked out. The evolution of the horse, for example, is very well known through fossils (Cowen, 1990; Strickberger, 2000). Over a period of about 60 million years, the creature developed from an animal the size of a dog with four toes on the front feet and three on the back to the modern large animal with one toe per foot; the numerous intermediate fossil stages located in various geological strata tell this story with great clarity. Fossils of ancestral horses become tools for dating, because any other animal or plant fossil that occurs in the same layer as one of the ancestral horses can be considered of the same age. Once relative ages are established, one fossil can help date another. This method is called *dating by faunal correlation* (Pilbeam, 1992).

One problem paleontologists have had to face is establishing contemporaneity when fossils from the same site are said to be associated but their association is questioned. This problem is now less serious than in earlier days, for two reasons. First, today we can check claims of contemporaneity and association by chemically analyzing the bone: Bones of roughly the same age should have roughly the same chemical analyses (Conroy, 1997). The chemicals usually assayed are nitrogen (which occurs in bone in the form of the protein collagen and is lost slowly during fossilization) and uranium and fluorine (both of which frequently enter bone from the surrounding groundwater and increase in concentration over a long period). Such analyses can be very valuable in establishing contemporaneity at a site: They are especially valuable if it is suspected that a skeleton has been buried within a deposit that is substantially older than the skeleton itself.

The second reason that contemporaneity can be more clearly established today is that more careful records of excavations are now being kept. Early investigators usually failed to realize the importance of carefully analyzing fossil sites and the position of fossils. Too often, they dug with reckless abandon, recovering only the largest bones and major pieces of worked stone. They did not appreciate the information they could get from the position of things relative to one another—and from the surrounding earth itself.

Through the constant cross-checking and fitting together of enormous amounts of both rock and fossil evidence, geologists have been able to fit together quite a detailed succession of rock formations and fossils from the present back to the distant Cambrian period (Figure 5.5). But this succession provides only the relative dating of fossils; the absolute, or chronometric dating, of the fossils is still lacking.

Fortunately, atomic physics provides us with some very valuable techniques for obtaining chronometric dates of geological formations (and in some cases, bones), which have revolutionized our study of human evolution. We know that certain radioactive elements discharge energy at a constant rate, known as the decay rate. Radium, for example, turns slowly but steadily into lead. Once this steady decay rate is known, it is only a matter of using laboratory technique to determine how old a piece of radium is by measuring how much of it is still radium and how much is lead.

One long-lasting radioactive substance used for chronometric dating is potassium 40 (F. H. Brown, 1992). This material breaks down into the gas argon at the relatively slow rate of one-half of the original potassium every 1,250 million years. (This is known as potassium 40's **half-life.**) Because potassium 40 is found in volcanic ash and lava, **potassium-argon** (abbreviated K/Ar) **dating** can be used to date fossils located in volcanic rock or ash or sandwiched between two layers of volcanic matter. The clock starts as the lava or ash cools (argon produced previously escaped while the lava was heated in the volcano), and it continues to run steadily with the breakdown of potassium 40. The age of the rock can therefore be calculated with remarkable precision by determining the ratio of argon gas to potassium 40. Problems arise when the rock sample containing the potassium also contains air (which itself contains small quantities of argon) or if the rock has been reheated by later volcanic eruptions, which may have driven off the argon already produced by radioactive decay. The other more general difficulty is that the method can be used to date fossils only from areas where volcanic eruptions occurred at about the same time as the fossils were deposited. Fortunately, many of the most important fossil sites in East Africa are in areas where volcanic activity was widespread, but in much of Asia, the Americas, and Europe, this method cannot be used.

Half-life the time it takes for half of any quantity of a radioactive element to decay to its fission products.

Potassium-argon dating *chronometric dating* in which age is determined by measurement of the decay of radioactive potassium 40.

An important development that supports this technique involves recognizing ash layers that have been deposited over wide areas. It has been shown that each ash layer (or **tuff,** as such a layer is often called) can be recognized by a unique analysis of its mineral components; that is, each tuff has its own chemical signature. Because of this characteristic, dated tuffs can be recognized over very great distances; their spread may be thousands of miles in extent (Feibel, 1999). Thus, it is possible to correlate tuffs from sites as far apart as Kenya, Ethiopia, and the Indian Ocean, where they can be recognized in deep-sea cores. In this way, dated tuffs may be widely mapped, and their K/Ar dates in one area checked against their K/Ar dating in another.

Tuff a rocklike substance formed from volcanic ash.

A derivation from K/Ar dating is the Ar^{40}/Ar^{39} procedure (Deino et al., 1998). In this test, previously irradiated crystals are melted with a laser beam in order to release argon. The procedure has the advantage of being extremely precise, even when very small mineral samples are tested. Together, the K/Ar and Ar^{40}/Ar^{39} procedures can date rocks over a wide span of time, from only a few tens of thousands to many millions of years ago.

Another useful radioactive element is carbon 14, which reverts to atmospheric nitrogen (Figure 5.2; F. H. Brown, 1992; Conroy, 1997). Physicist Willard Libby showed that carbon 14 is present in the atmosphere as carbon dioxide (CO_2) and is incorporated into all plant material. In the plant, the proportion of carbon 14 to the stable atom carbon 12 is the same as the proportion of the two in the atmosphere.

The clock starts when the CO_2 is taken into the plant (which animals may feed on) and is buried as either fiber or wood, or as the collagen in bone, or as charcoal left by a fire. After an organism's death, the carbon 14 it contains breaks down, and the proportion of carbon 12 increases. The laboratory technique measures the ratio of carbon 14 to carbon 12 in these prehistoric samples. Carbon 14 has a half-life of only 5,730 years, and therefore, measurements of the age of carbon compounds cover a relatively short period. The method is most useful for organic remains between 500 and 40,000 years old, although its range can be extended somewhat farther into the past. When an object such as a piece of charcoal or a fossil bone is dated by the radiocarbon method, this is considered to be a **direct date,** since the object itself is dated.

Direct date a date on an object itself; for example, a piece of bone may be directly dated by the radiocarbon method.

Errors in the radiocarbon method arise from a number of factors. It was originally supposed that the carbon 14 level in the atmosphere was constant, but we now know that it is not. Volcanoes produce CO_2 without carbon 14, which causes local reductions in the level of carbon 14 in the atmosphere. A more serious variation is in the atmospheric level itself, which alters according to variations in the chemical reactions in the upper atmosphere that create the carbon 14 in the first place. Comparing carbon 14 dates with the dates from tree rings (**dendrochronology**), annually deposited sediment layers, and stalagmites suggests that as one goes back in time, the radiocarbon procedure tends to underestimate the true age of a dated object. Therefore, it is now routine for researchers to convert raw carbon 14 dates into *calibrated years* before publication (Beck et al., 2001; CALIB Radiocarbon Calibration; Jobling et al., 2004).

Dendrochronology a dating procedure that involves counting the annual growth of rings of trees.

Another dating method that depends in a different way on radioactive decay is the *fission-track method* (Wagner, 1996). The rare radioactive element uranium 238 splits spontaneously to create a minute region of crystal disruption in a mineral. The disruption is called a *track.* In the laboratory, microscopic examination can determine track densities in mineral crystals containing uranium 238 in proportion to total uranium content. Since the rate of spontaneous fission is known, the age of the crystal can be calculated. The clock is started with the eruption of volcanoes, and so this method has the same geographic limitations as the potassium-argon method.

The main value of the fission-track method at present is as a cross-check on the potassium-argon method. The same volcanic samples can often be used, and the comparison aids in the detection of errors. The fission-track method itself has other problems. With low uranium content and rather recently formed minerals, the track density will be low. Heating eliminates tracks. (As we have seen, heating also causes problems in potassium-argon dating.) Fission-track dating, however, has proved of great value in dating samples from the beginning of the earth to about 300,000 years ago. It is now being used quite widely in dating early periods of human evolution in volcanically active regions.

Two additional methods of dating that depend on radioactivity are *thermoluminescence (TL)* and *optically stimulated luminescence (OSL)* (Feathers, 1996). Both procedures measure the emission of light from crystalline materials that have been stimulated in some way: In TL, the stimulation is by heat, whereas in OSL, it is by exposing the sample to intense light of narrow wavelength. Both types of stimulation release electrons trapped in the sample, and this produces measurable light.

To further understand luminescence dating, here is how TL works: Over a period of time, electrons become trapped in the crystal structure of buried substances (including pottery and stone tools) as they are irradiated by naturally occurring uranium, thorium, and potassium 40. (For accurate dating, the traps must have been emptied prior to electron accumulation by a zeroing event, such as heating by fire.) When the irradiated substances are reheated in the laboratory, the electrons are released with a quantity of light proportional to the number of electrons trapped. If the rate of electron accumulation can be established, the amount of light emitted can be used to measure the time elapsed since the test substance was originally heated. TL works best with pottery, but it can also be used on burnt flints and hearth stones. (OSL is used to date sediments, and it works best with wind-blown deposits, since the OSL zeroing event is exposure to light.)

Both types of luminescence dating have remaining problems—such as estimating the rate of electron entrapment and controlling for *fading*, the natural and gradual loss of trapped electrons—but they have great potential and have recently been used to establish some important dates. Of particular importance is the fact that the range of usefulness of luminescence dating overlaps those of carbon 14 and potassium-argon (see Figure 5.4).

Finally, the value of radioactive dating has been greatly increased by its use to date periodic changes in the global magnetic field (Kappleman, 1993; Ludwig and Renne, 2000). It appears that the north–south magnetic field of our planet has reversed its direction many times during the earth's history. (During periods of reversal, a compass needle would point south instead of north.) The direction of an ancient magnetic field can be detected by laboratory measurements of the fossilized magnetism in rocks, combined with information on how those rocks were oriented (north–south) at the site of their collection. Such paleomagnetism dates from around the world have enabled geophysicists to construct detailed time charts of normal and reversed periods (see Figure 5.3). These data help scientists determine the age of sites that lack independent chronometric dates but whose paleomagnetism profiles are known.

Appendix 3

Diagnostic Traits of the Hominins

This appendix lists selected general and species-specific diagnostic traits for the various hominin species. These lists (which vary in length, depending on available knowledge of the different species) are intended to supplement the general descriptions provided in boxes throughout the text with selected anatomical details. For further elucidation of these traits, interested readers are directed to the publications cited at the head of each species' list. To assist students in using the following technical material, a set of illustrative diagrams are provided at the end of the appendix. Throughout the appendix, we follow the standard procedures of labeling the permanent teeth with capital letters and the deciduous teeth with lowercase letters and of using superscript/subscript numbers to designate specific upper and lower teeth, respectively.

Diagnostic traits of *Sahelanthropus tchadensis* (Brunet et al., 2002)

A. General diagnostic traits (see also Box 7.12):
- large canine fossa
- large mastoid process
- small occipital condyles
- maxillary toothrow U-shaped and narrow
- broad interorbital pillar producing wide-set eyes
- broad glenoid cavity and large postglenoid process
- large mental foramen located below P_4/M_1
- upper canines thicker mesiodistally than buccolingually
- premolars with two roots

B. Traits distinguishing this species from living and fossil apes:
- (from all living apes) smaller canines with wear at the tip
- (from *Pongo*) nonconcave lateral facial profile, wider interorbital pillar, larger supraorbital torus
- (from *Gorilla*) less lower-face prognathism, no supratoral sulcus, smaller canines
- (from *Pan*) shorter face, larger brows, longer braincase, more narrow basicranium, thicker enamel on grinding teeth
- (from *Dryopithecus*) less lower-face prognathism, wider interorbital pillar, larger supraorbital torus, thicker enamel on grinding teeth

C. Traits distinguishing this species from other hominins:
- (from *Homo*) smaller cranial capacity, very large supraorbital torus, large I^1, nonincisiform canines
- (from *Orrorin*) I^1 with multiple tubercles on lingual surface, apical wear of upper canines
- (from *Ardipithecus*) I^1 with distinctive lingual crests, upper canines less incisiform, P_4 with two roots

- (from *Australopithecus*) less lower-face prognathism, more continuous brow ridge, more elongated braincase, nonincisiform canines, thinner enamel on grinding teeth
- (from *Kenyanthropus*) narrower and more convex face, greater postorbital constriction, larger nuchal crest
- (from *Paranthropus*) face narrower across the malar region, zygomatic process of maxilla positioned farther back, much smaller grinding teeth

Diagnostic traits of *Orrorin tugenensis* (Senut et al., 2001)

A. General diagnostic traits (see also Box 7.11):
- short upper canines
- M^3s are small and triangular
- P_4 with offset roots and oblique crown
- relatively small dentition for body size
- lesser trochanter of femur medially prominent and with strong muscle insertions

B. Traits distinguishing this species from living and fossil hominids:
- (from *Pan, Gorilla,* and the australopiths generally) "humanlike" morphology of the proximal femur
- (from *Australopithecus*) smaller and mesiodistally shorter cheek teeth, upper canines with a mesial groove
- (from *Ardipithecus*) thicker enamel on grinding teeth, upper canines with a mesial groove

Diagnostic traits of *Ardipithecus kadabba* (Haile-Selassie 2001; Haile-Selassie et al., 2004)

A. General diagnostic traits (see Box 7.10 and the trait list for *Ardipithecus ramidus* that follows)

B. Traits distinguishing this species from living and fossil hominids:
- (from living and fossil apes) tendency for lower canines to be incisiform and show high mesial crown shoulder placement, P_3 with clearly defined anterior fovea
- (from living apes and *Orrorin*) in occlusal view, a more circular outline of upper canine crown
- (from *Ardipithecus ramidus*) sharper lingual cusps on M_3, M^3 with four distinct cusps and squared outline in distal view, P^3 with shallow mesial fovea, P_3 with smaller anterior fovea and more asymmetrical crown outline, crests on upper canine have stronger basal termination

Diagnostic traits of *Ardipithecus ramidus* (White et al., 1994)

A. Traits distinguishing this species from other hominins known in 1994 (see Tables 6.1 and 8.1):
- upper and lower canines larger relative to postcanine teeth
- dm_1 narrow and obliquely elongate, with large protoconid, small metaconid that is distally placed, no anterior fovea, and small, low talonid with little cuspule development

- temporomandibular joint lacks clear articular eminence
- enamel on canines and molars absolutely and relatively thinner
- P^3 more asymmetrical, buccal cusp tall and dominant, and with steep transverse crest posterolingually oriented
- P^3 more asymmetrical, with buccal cusp relatively larger, taller, and more dominant

B. Traits distinguishing this species from living and fossil apes:
- canines more incisiform, with crowns less projecting
- P_3 generally smaller, with weaker mesiobuccal projection of crown base and lacking a functional honing facet
- lower molars generally relatively broader
- foramen magnum anteriorly placed relative to the carotid foramen

Diagnostic traits of *Kenyanthropus platyops* (M. Leakey et al., 2001)

A. General diagnostic traits (see also Box 7.8):
- zygomatic process of maxilla positioned over the premolars and more vertically oriented than the nasal opening
- incisors barely anterior to the bi-canine line
- upper incisor roots nearly equal in size
- upper premolars generally have three roots

B. Traits distinguishing this species from other hominins:
- (from *Ardipithecus ramidus*) buccolingually narrower M^2, molar enamel thicker, deeper glenoid fossa of temporal bone
- (from *Australopithecus afarensis* specifically) transversely flat midface, small acoustic meatus, lack of an occipital–marginal sinus venous system (see Chapter 13)
- (from *Australopithecus africanus* specifically) taller malar region, narrower nasal opening, lack of anterior facial pillars, smaller acoustic meatus
- (from *A. afarensis, A. africanus, A. anamensis,* and *A. garhi*) different lower-face morphology including less subnasal prognathism, nasoalveolar clivus that is sagittally and transversely flat, forwardly positioned zygomatic process of the maxilla, similarly sized upper incisor roots, smaller M^1 and M^2 crowns
- (from *Paranthropus*) smaller molars, thinner enamel, flat (rather than "gutter") nasoalveolar clivus, less subnasal prognathism, stepped nasal opening, malar region taller but narrower, less postorbital constriction
- (from *Homo rudolfensis*) smaller upper molars
- (from *Homo erectus* and later hominans) lacks the set of derived cranial features described by Wood and Collard (1999b)

Diagnostic traits of *Australopithecus afarensis* (Conroy, 1997; Johanson and White, 1979)

General diagnostic traits (see also Box 7.3):
- I^1 wide, I^2 diminutive; both with flexed roots
- permanent canines large, asymmetric, pointed, and projecting slightly above the toothrow
- P_3 with dominant, elongated buccal cusp and usually a small lingual cusp; lacks evidence of sectorial honing characteristic of apes
- relatively small diastemata often present in both upper and lower jaws
- dental arcade generally long, narrow, and with straight sides (not parabolic)
- strong alveolar prognathism with convex clivus

- face includes strong canine juga separated from zygomatic processes by strong depressions
- zygomatic processes are large, with anterior margins located above P^4/M^1 and with inferior margins that flare to front and side
- compound temporonuchal crest on some specimens
- temporomandibular joint is broad and poorly defined
- mandibular ramus broad, but not high
- mandibular corpus rounded and bulbous anteriorly, and relatively deep in larger specimens
- mandibular symphysis slopes strongly to rear
- ilia are low, broad, and show a deep sciatic notch
- large anterior inferior iliac spines
- distinctly oval pelvic girdle that is quite wide both at the level of the iliac crests and the hip joints
- iliac crests (including the anterior superior iliac spines) more laterally flared than in modern humans
- femurs relatively short, but with a long neck
- knees positioned close together near the midline of the body
- patellar groove has a raised lateral lip
- proximal phalanges are longitudinally curved in both hands and feet
- hallux (big toe) is not opposable

Diagnostic traits of *Australopithecus africanus* (Grine, 1993)

A. General diagnostic traits (see also Box 6.3):
- high glabella separated from nasion
- prognathic but flattened nasoalveolar clivus
- anteriorly deep (shelved) palate
- deep glenoid fossa with a distinct articular eminence
- vertically steep tympanic plate
- P_3 bicuspid

B. Traits distinguishing this species from *Australopithecus afarensis:*
- cranium more globular and less pneumatized
- forehead more pronounced
- greater separation of lambda and inion

Diagnostic traits of *Australopithecus anamensis* (M. Leakey et al., 1995)

A. Traits generally distinguishing this species from all other *Australopithecus* (and *Paranthropus*) types (*A. bahrelghazali* and *A. garhi* are excepted here):
- external acoustic meatus is small and has a narrow, elliptical outline
- dental arcade shows toothrows nearly parallel and close together (note: this trait does not distinguish *A. anamensis* and *A. afarensis*)
- mental region of mandible not strongly convex
- mandibular symphysis slopes strongly back and down
- very long, robust canine roots
- distal humeral shaft shows a thick cortex that encloses a small marrow cavity

B. Traits distinguishing this species from *Australopithecus afarensis:*
- less posterior inclination of upper canine root and associated facial skeleton
- lower molars with more sloping buccal sides and upper molars with more sloping lingual sides

- tympanic plate horizontal and lacking defining grooves

C. Traits distinguishing this species from *Ardipithecus ramidus:*
- absolutely and relatively thicker tooth enamel
- upper canine buccal enamel thickens toward the tip
- molars expanded buccolingually
- M_1 and M_2 similar in size
- tympanic tube extends only to the medial edge of the postglenoid process

Diagnostic traits of *Australopithecus bahrelghazali* (Brunet et al., 1996)

A. Traits distinguishing this species from all other hominins known in 1996 (see Tables 6.1 and 8.1):
- mandibular toothrow is parabolic; at the level of P_4 the internal contour is wider than the corpus thickness; symphyseal axis subvertical; corpus of medium height and narrow with a low mental foramen
- anterior teeth large; I_2 and lower C have tall crowns and long roots; lower C also asymmetrical, with long distal cuspule and lingual crest
- lower premolars buccolingually broad with buccal cingula, three entirely distinct roots, and relatively thin enamel
- P_3 bicuspid with a strong metaconid; P_4 molarized with small talonid
- P^3 with three roots and asymmetrical crown

B. Traits distinguishing this species from *Ardipithecus ramidus:*
- enamel thickening at the canine tips
- thicker enamel on premolars

C. Traits distinguishing this species from *Paranthropus:*
- more gracile mandibular corpus
- much larger anterior dentition
- asymmetrical and non-oval P^3

Diagnostic traits of *Australopithecus garhi* (Asfaw et al., 1999)

A. General diagnostic traits (see also Box 7.6):
- U-shaped toothrow with postcanine teeth diverging slightly toward the rear
- canine roots located well lateral to the nasal opening
- zygomatic roots originate above P^4/M^1
- slight degree of premolar molarization

B. Traits distinguishing this species from other hominins:
- (from *Australopithecus afarensis*) smaller incisor-to-postcanine tooth size ratio, larger absolute size of postcanine teeth, more premolar molarization, thicker enamel, dental arcade divergence
- (from *Australopithecus africanus*) presence of maxillary diastemata, absence of anterior pillars in face, nasoalveolar clivus convex
- (from *Paranthropus*) larger canine-to-postcanine tooth size ratio, less premolar molarization, thinner enamel, presence of maxillary diastemata, presence of canine fossa, convex nasoalveolar clivus, absence of facial dishing, less postorbital constriction of cranium
- (from early *Homo*) smaller incisor-to-postcanine tooth size ratio, larger postcanine absolute size, smaller cranial capacity

Diagnostic traits of *Paranthropus aethiopicus* (Grine, 1993)

A. General diagnostic traits (see also Box 7.7):
- "dished" midface (note: this trait distinguishes *P. aethiopicus* from *Ardipithecus, Australopithecus,* and *Homo* but not from the other *Paranthropus* species)
- nasoalveolar clivus that passes smoothly into the nasal floor
- vertically deep and mediolaterally concave tympanic plate
- palate medially thickened and anteriorly shallow
- heart-shaped foramen magnum with a straight anterior margin
- enlarged premolars and molars

B. Traits distinguishing this species from other *Paranthropus* forms (although not from *Australopithecus afarensis*):
- elongate, unflexed cranial base
- marked alveolar prognathism
- shallow glenoid (mandibular) fossa lacking a clearly discernible articular eminence

Diagnostic traits of *Paranthropus boisei* (Grine, 1993)

A. General diagnostic traits (see also Box 7.2):
- "dished" midface (note: this trait distinguishes *P. boisei* from *Ardipithecus, Australopithecus,* and *Homo* but not from the other *Paranthropus* species)
- high hafting of the facial skeleton (note: also found in *P. robustus*)
- high incidence of occipital–marginal sinus rather than transverse sinuses
- absolutely and relatively small incisors and canines
- absolutely and relatively large premolars and molars

B. Traits distinguishing this species from *Paranthropus robustus:*
- greater maxillary depth
- anteriorly deep (shelved) palate
- laterally bowed and "visorlike" zygomatics
- heart-shaped foramen magnum with a straight or posteriorly convex anterior margin
- temporoparietal overlap at asterion
- larger premolars and molars

Diagnostic traits of *Paranthropus robustus* (Grine, 1993)

General diagnostic traits (see also Box 6.3):
- "dished" midface (note: this trait distinguishes *P. robustus* from *Ardipithecus, Australopithecus,* and *Homo* but not from the other *Paranthropus* species)
- high hafting of facial skeleton (note: also found in *P. boisei*)
- low forehead (receding frontal)
- prominent glabella situated below level of supraorbital margin
- flattened nasoalveolar clivus grading smoothly into nasal floor
- anteriorly shallow palate
- deep glenoid fossa with a distinct articular eminence
- vertically deep tympanic plate
- bulbous mastoid region inflated beyond the supramastoid crest
- canines in the same coronal plane as the incisors

- absolutely and (especially) relatively small incisors and canines
- enlarged premolars and molars

Diagnostic traits of *Homo habilis* (Wood, 1992)

A. Traits distinguishing this species (and all other hominans) from *Ardipithecus, Australopithecus,* and *Paranthropus:*
- increased cranial vault thickness
- reduced postorbital constriction (same degree seen in *A. garhi*)
- increased contribution of the occipital bone to cranial sagittal arc length
- increased cranial vault height
- more anteriorly situated foramen magnum
- reduced lower face prognathism
- narrow tooth crowns, particular in the lower premolars
- reduced molar toothrow length

B. Traits distinguishing this species from *Homo rudolfensis:*
- smaller mean brain size
- greater occipital contribution to the sagittal arc
- complex suture pattern of skull
- incipient supraorbital torus
- upper face exceeds midface in breadth
- nasal margins sharp and everted
- zygomatic surface vertical or nearly so
- palate foreshortened
- relatively deep mandibular fossa
- rounded base on body of mandible
- lower premolars and molars show more buccolingual narrowing
- reduced talonid on P_4
- lower premolars mostly single-rooted

C. Traits distinguishing this species from *Homo erectus* and all later hominans:
- elongated anterior basicranium
- mesiodistally elongated M_1 and M_2
- narrow mandibular fossa

Diagnostic traits of *Homo rudolfensis* (Wood, 1992)

A. Traits distinguishing this species from *Ardipithecus, Australopithecus,* and *Paranthropus:* (see the "A" list under *Homo habilis*)

B. Traits distinguishing this species from *Homo habilis:*
- greater mean brain size
- lesser occipital contribution to the sagittal arc
- simple suture pattern of the skull
- supraorbital torus absent
- midface exceeds upper face in breadth
- less everted nasal margins
- zygomatics anteriorly inclined
- large palate
- shallow mandibular fossa
- everted base on body of mandible
- broader lower premolars and molars
- relatively large P_4 talonid
- twin and/or bifid platelike lower premolar roots

C. Traits distinguishing this species from *Homo erectus* and all later hominans: (see the "C" list under *Homo habilis*)

Diagnostic traits of *Homo erectus* (Aiello and Dean, 1990; Conroy, 1997; Rightmire, 1990)

General diagnostic traits (see also Box 10.1):

- brain sizes range between 600 and 1,251 cubic centimeters
- crania long and low in outline, with relatively flat basicranial axis
- pronounced alveolar prognathism
- relatively broad nasal aperture; nasoalveolar clivus is flattened
- large supraorbital tori
- midline keeling of the frontal bone is common; such keeling may continue onto the parietal vault
- parasagittal depressions on either side of the parietal keeling
- marked postorbital constriction
- superior temporal line may produce an angular torus at the parietal mastoid angle
- variable supramastoid crest, prominent in some Indonesian individuals
- transverse torus of the occipital
- zygomatic arch lacks raised articular tubercle
- mandible large and robust, with broad ramus
- mandibular symphysis receding
- thick cranial bones

Diagnostic traits of *Homo heidelbergensis* (Aiello and Dean 1990; Groves, 1989; Rightmire, 1990)

General diagnostic traits (see also Box 12.1):

- brain sizes range between 1,100 and 1,305 cubic centimeters
- wide parietal bones
- upper portion of the occipital is vertical and expanded relative to the nuchal plane; relatively great occipital angulation
- well-developed horizontal supramastoid crest
- barlike articular tubercle
- inferior border of the tympanic plate is thin
- broad frontal bone that recedes strongly
- reduced postorbital constriction
- shortened cranial base
- large supraorbital tori, thickened in the middle and thinning laterally
- external auditory meatus above the level of the glenoid cavity and located between the two posterior branches of the zygomatic root

Diagnostic traits of *Homo neanderthalensis* (Conroy, 1997; Stringer and Gamble, 1993; Stringer et al.,1984; Tattersall, 1995b)

General diagnostic traits (see also Box 14.1):

- brain sizes range between 1,125 and 1,750 cubic centimeters
- skull long and low in profile, with retreating forehead and relatively flat cranial base
- double-arched supraorbital torus characterized by extensive pneumatization
- massive facial skeleton, with midfacial prognathism and a very large nasal opening
- rim of raised bone projecting medially from anterior nasal aperture, forming a secondary internal nasal margin
- cheekbones swept back toward rear of skull
- high, rounded orbits

- pronounced occipital "bun"
- occipital includes suprainiac fossa
- mandibular dentition is forwardly positioned producing a retromolar gap between M_3 and the ramus
- mental foramen under M_1
- broad scapula with strong muscle attachments
- lateral bowing of the radius
- massive head of humerus
- iliac blades show pronounced dorsal rotation
- thin and elongated superior pubic ramus
- femur and tibia robust and thick walled
- short distal limb segments (tibia, radius)

Diagnostic traits of *Homo floresiensis* (P. Brown et al., 2004)

A. General diagnostic traits (see also Box 15.2):
- endocranial volume smaller than or equal to *A. afarensis*
- body height smaller than or equal to *A. afarensis*
- smaller facial height, prognathism, and canine teeth than in either *Australopithecus* or *Paranthropus*
- flexed cranial base
- large canine juga form maxillary pillars
- thicker superior cranial vault bone than *Australopithecus* (but similar to *H. erectus* and *H. sapiens*)
- supraorbital torus over individual orbits (does not form not a continuous bar)
- no evidence of parietal keeling, but some sagittal keeling on the frontal bone
- I^2 smaller than I^1; maxillary diastema possible
- P_3 with relatively large occlusal surface
- coronoid process of mandible higher than condyle
- mandibular symphysis lacks a chin
- ilium with marked lateral flare
- ischial spine not particularly pronounced
- femur with long neck relative to head diameter

Diagnostic traits for *Homo sapiens* (Conroy, 1997; Stringer et al., 1984)

A. General diagnostic traits (see also Box 15.1):
- brain sizes range between 1,000 and 2,000 cubic centimeters
- cranial vault relatively short and high (sharply rising forehead)
- cranial bones reduced in thickness
- weak supraorbital tori
- biparietal breadth greater than or equal to the breadth across the ear region (biauricular breadth)
- occipital region rounded; nuchal area reduced
- reduction/loss of sagittal keeling and parasagittal flattening
- shortened and flexed cranial base
- little facial prognathism (nose may still be large)
- canine fossa present (hollowed cheeks)
- mandible with reduced robusticity and a distinct chin

B. Traits distinguishing this species from *Homo neanderthalensis:*
- cheekbones lack swept-back appearance
- midfacial prognathism lacking
- lower, squarer orbits
- smaller supraorbital tori

- reduced mean brain size
- prominent mastoid processes
- smaller anterior teeth
- hip sockets are less laterally (more ventrally) oriented
- superior pubic ramus shorter and thicker
- postcranial skeleton generally less robust

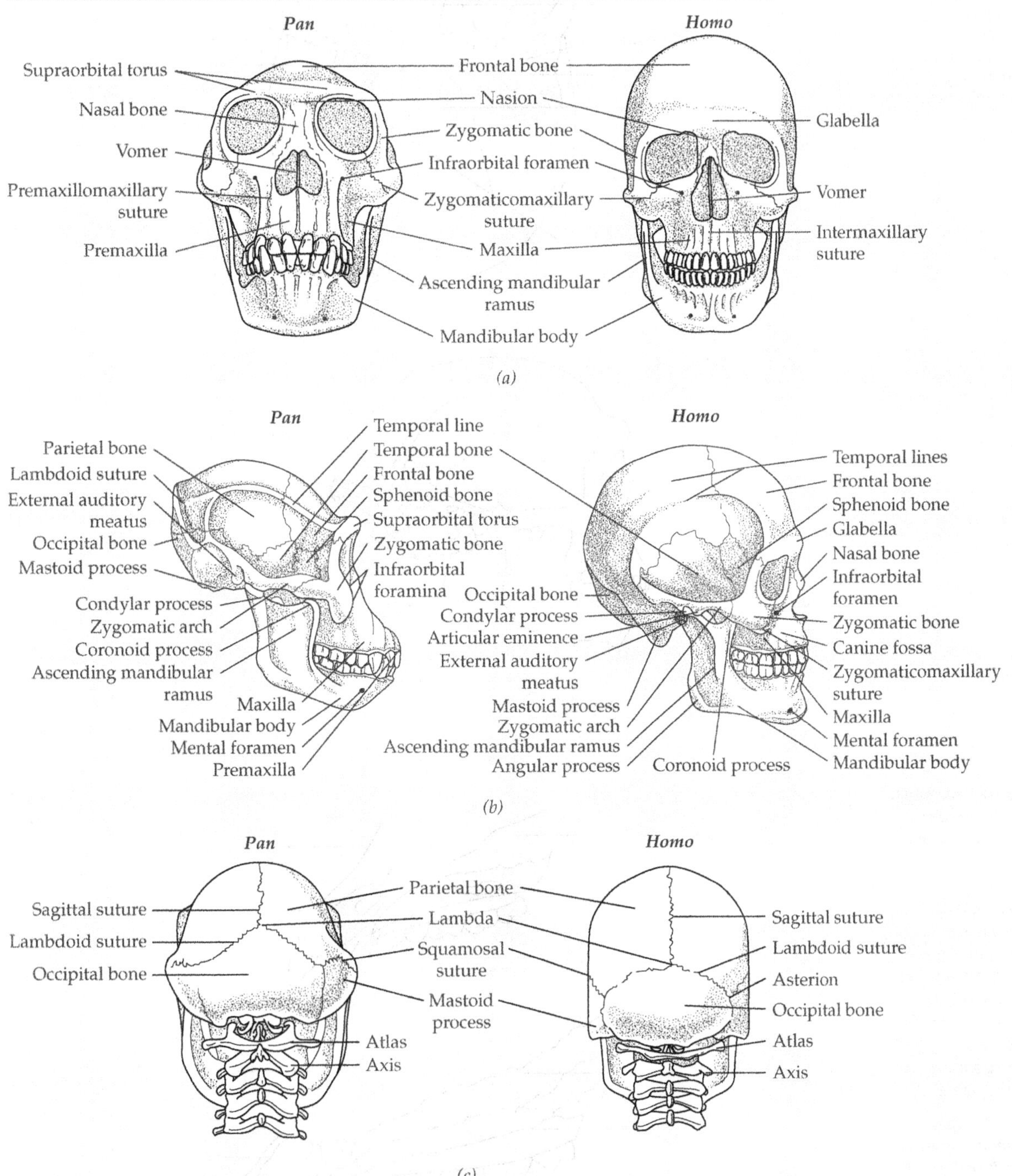

FIGURE A.1

Comparison of the skull in champanzees *(left)* and modern humans *(right)* with the major bones and bony landmarks identified. *(a)* Frontal view. *(b)* Lateral view. *(c)* Posterior view.

Source: From *Reconstructing Human Origins: A Modern Synthesis* by Glenn C. Conroy. Copyright © 1997 by W. W. Norton & Company, Inc. Reprinted by permission of W. W. Norton & Company, Inc.

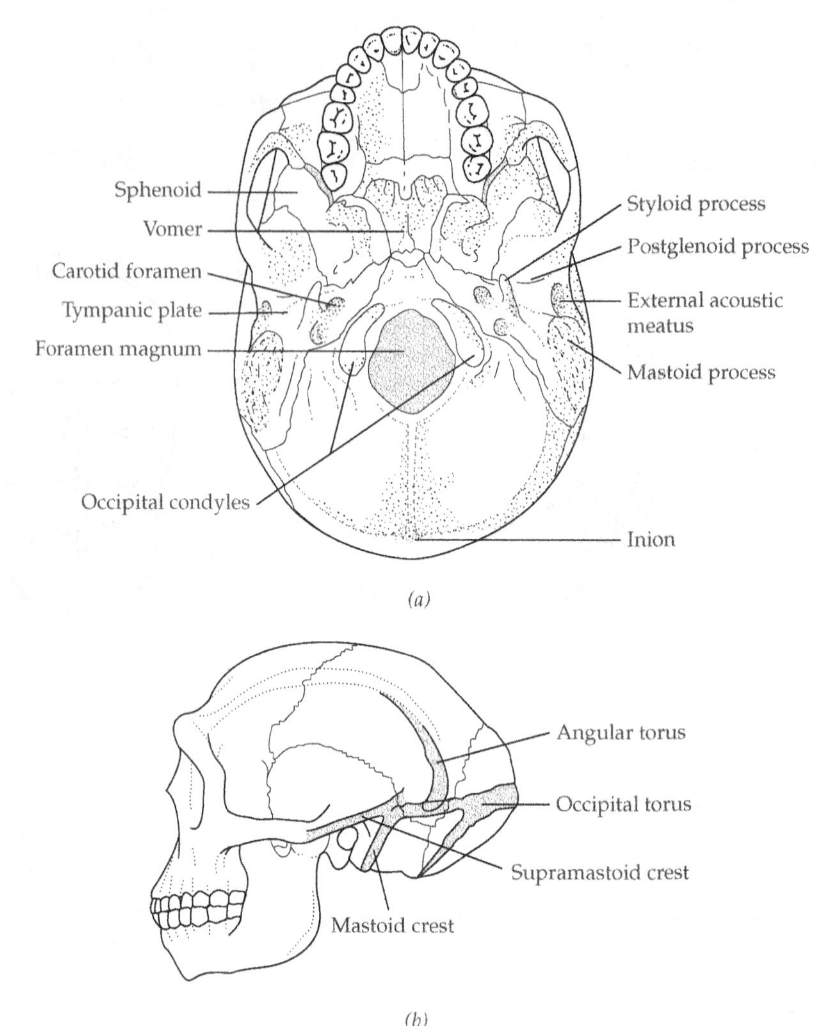

FIGURE A.2
(Top) Selected features of the cranial base of modern humans. *(Bottom)* Reconstructed *Homo erectus* skull showing several bony markings.

Source: From L. Aiello and C. Dean, *An Introduction to Human Evolutionary Anatomy*, Academic Press, 1990. Reprinted by permission of Academic Press, Ltd.

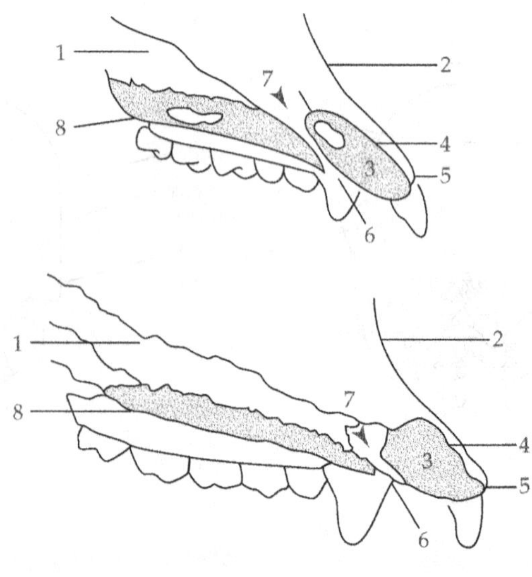

FIGURE A.3
Anatomy of the lower face in two living hominoids. Sagittal sections trhough the premaxilla and palate (shaded areas): *Pan (top)* and *Gorilla (bottom)*. Anatomical parts: 1, vomer; 2, lateral margin of nasal aperture; 3, subnasal alveolar process; 4, nasoalveolar clivus; 5, prosthion; 6, oral incisive fossa; 7 and arrowhead, nasal incisive fossa; 8, hard palate.

Source: From *Reconstructing Human Origins: A Modern Synthesis* by Glenn C. Conroy. Copyright © 1997 by W. W. Norton & Company, Inc. Reprinted by permission of W. W. Norton & Company, Inc.

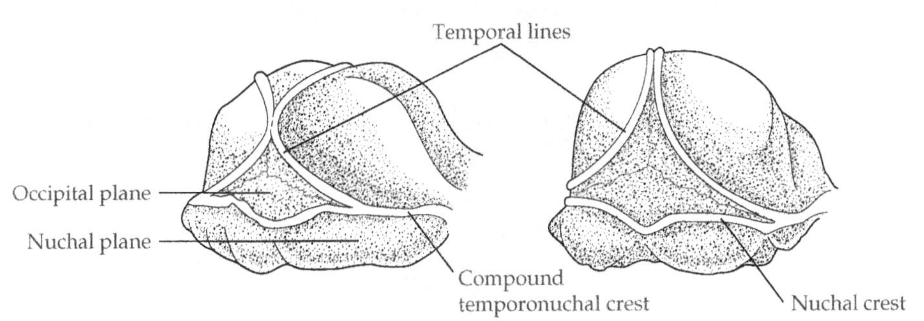

FIGURE A.4
Posterior view of australopith skulls and temporanuchal crest. *Australopithecus afarensis* is shown on the *left* and *A. africanus* on the *right*.

Source: From *Reconstructing Human Origins: A Modern Synthesis* by Glenn C. Conroy. Copyright © 1997 by W. W. Norton & Company, Inc. Reprinted by permission of W. W. Norton & Company, Inc.

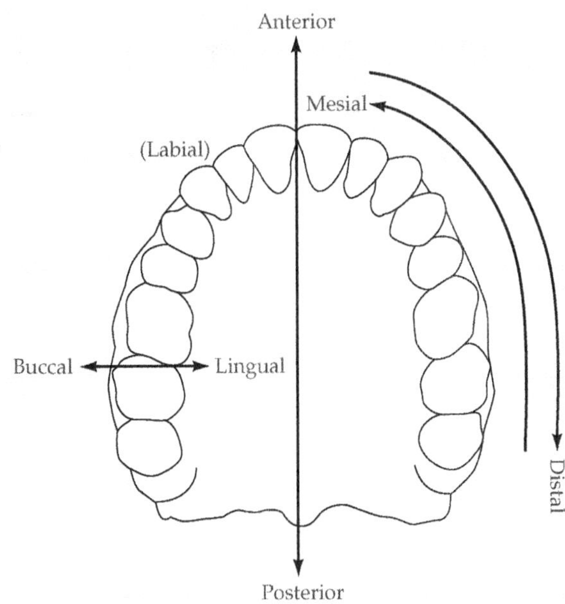

FIGURE A.5
Schematic representation of an upper jaw showing dental terminology for defining position and direction.

Source: Figure redrawn from *Skeleton Keys* by Jeffrey H. Schwartz, Oxford University Press, 1995. Reprinted by permission of the artist John C. Anderton.

FIGURE A.6
Main features of the upper molars *(top)* and lower molars *(bottom)* of hominoids.

Source: Figure redrawn from *Primate Evolution* by Elwyn Simons, Macmillan, 1972. Reprinted by permission of the author.

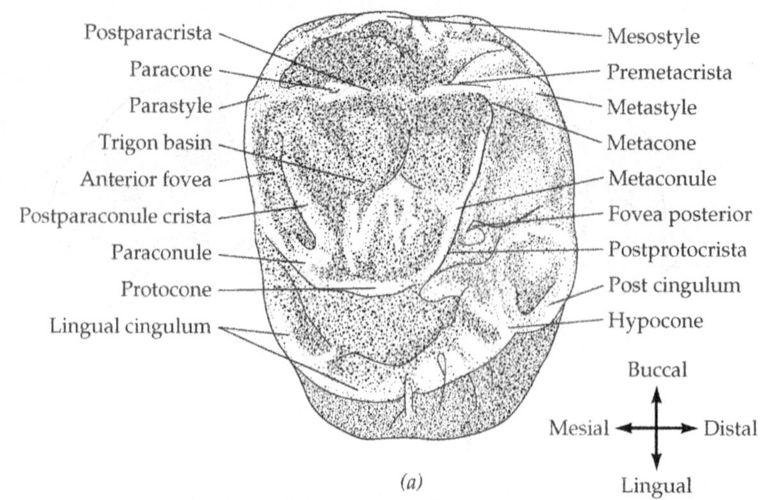

(a)

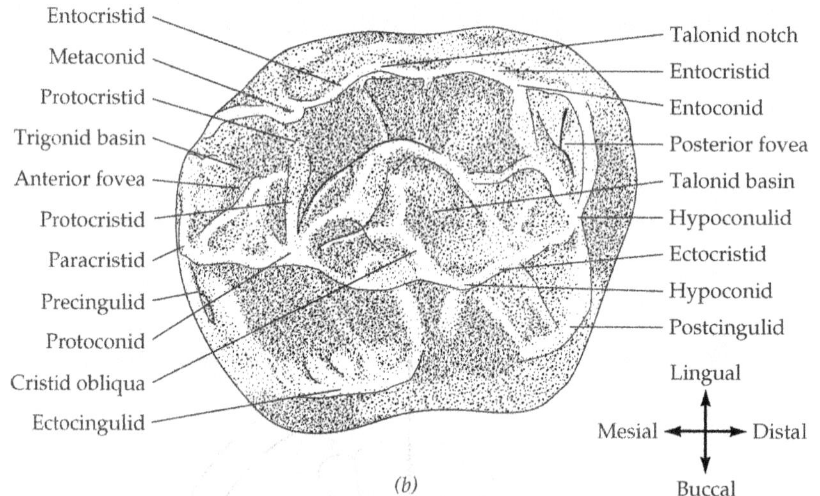

(b)

Glossary

Note: Words in *italics*, except some Latin names and self-explanatory terms, are defined elsewhere in the glossary.

Absolute dating: determining the age in years of *geologic* deposits (and the *fossils* in them). This may be done by examining the chemical composition of rock fragments containing radioactive substances, which decay at known rates. (Compare with *relative dating*.)

Acheulean industry: a stone tool tradition that appeared 1.7 million years ago in Africa.

Adapoidea and Omomyoidea: superfamilies of *Eocene euprimates;* now extinct.

Aegyptopithecus: a basal catarrhine from the Fayum in Africa; dated to the *Oligocene* epoch.

Agglutination: the clumping of *red blood cells* as a result of the reaction of *antibodies* to an *antigen*.

Algeripithecus: an *anthropoid primate* from the early-middle *Eocene* epoch of North Africa.

Alleles: *genes* occupying equivalent positions in paired *chromosomes* yet producing different *phenotypic* effects when they are *homozygous;* alternative states of a gene, originally produced by *mutation*.

Allomothering: typically, care or attention directed toward an infant by a female other than its mother (also called *aunting behavior*).

Allopatric speciation: the production of new *species* through the branching or splitting of existing ones. The process begins with the geographic isolation of one or more *populations* from the bulk of the parent species.

Altiatlasius: once thought to be the oldest known *euprimate fossil;* a *plesiadapiform* from the late *Paleocene* of North Africa.

Altricial: the state of being born helpless and requiring parental care.

Alveolar: referring to the tooth-bearing portion of the jaws.

Amino acids: a group of organic compounds that act as building blocks for *proteins*.

Angular gyrus: the part of the human *cerebral cortex* that allows the information received from different senses to be associated.

Anterior fovea: a *mesially* positioned depression on the surface of a tooth.

Anterior inferior iliac spine: a projection from the *ilium* that serves as an attachment point for certain thigh muscles and also the iliofemoral ligament.

Anthropoid: relating to humans, *apes*, and *monkeys*.

Anthropology: the science of humankind; the systematic study of human evolution, human variability, and human behavior, past and present.

Antibody: a *protein* produced as a defense mechanism to attack a foreign substance invading the body.

Antigens: any organic substances recognized by the body as foreign that stimulate the production of *antibodies*.

Ape: among living animals, a large, tailless, semierect mammal of the order *Primates*. Living types are the *chimpanzee, bonobo, gorilla, gibbon, siamang*, and *orangutan*.

Arboreal: adapted for living in or around trees, as are most *monkeys* and *apes*.

Archaeology: the systematic study of prehistoric human *cultures;* finding and interpreting the cultural products of prehistoric people.

Archaic humans: collectively, *Homo heidelbergensis* and the Neandertals (*Homo neanderthalensis*).

Arcuate fasciculus: a bundle of nerve fibers in the human brain transmitting signals from *Wernicke's area* to *Broca's area*, making possible vocal repetition of words heard and memorized.

Ardipithecus kadabba: an *australopith species* from Ethiopia that dates back to 5.8 to 5.2 million years of age.

Ardipithecus ramidus: an *australopith species* from Ethiopia that dates back to 4.4 million years of age.

Articular eminence: a swelling of the zygomatic arch just anterior to the jaw joint.

Articulation: in anatomy, the joint between two bones; in linguistics, the action of the tongue and lips to form the consonants of *speech*.

Asterion: juncture of the temporal, parietal, and occipital bones.

Artifact: a purposefully formed object.

Assortative mating: the tendency of like to mate with like.

Atlatl: an Aztec name for the spear thrower, a rodlike device used as an extension of the arm that greatly increases both the distance and impact of a throw.

Attractiveness: in *primate* studies, the aspect of female sexuality reflected by attention from males.

Auditory bulla: the bulbous bony development that houses the middle ear region.

Aurignacian: an *Upper Paleolithic*, mainly European tool culture that existed from about 37,000 to 29,000 years ago.

Australopith: a member of the *hominin* subtribe Australopithecina; any representative of the genera *Ardipithecus, Australopithecus, Kenyanthropus, Paranthropus, Orrorin,* and *Sahelanthropus.*

Australopithecus: a *genus* of the tribe Hominini, subtribe Australopithecina; contains five *species: A. afarensis, A. africanus, A. anamensis, A. bahrelghazali,* and *A. garhi.*

Australopithecus aethiopicus: the original name for the megadont *australopith species* now called *Paranthropus aethiopicus.*

Australopithecus afarensis: an *australopith species* that inhabited East Africa from 4.2 to 2.5 million years ago.

Australopithecus africanus: an *australopith species* that inhabited South Africa from 3.5 (4?) to 1.7 million years ago.

Australopithecus anamensis: a *species* of *australopith* that inhabited East Africa from 4.2 to 3.9 million years ago.

Australopithecus bahrelghazali: a *species* of *australopith* known from Chad and dating 3.5 to 3.0 million years ago.

Australopithecus garhi: a *species* of *australopith* from Ethiopia and dating 2.5 million years ago.

Autosome: a *chromosome* other than the *sex chromosomes.*

Axon: processes extending from nerve cell bodies that carry information to other cells.

Balanced polymorphism: the maintenance in a *population* of different *alleles* of a particular *gene* in proportion to the advantages offered by each (e.g., *sickle-cell* and normal *hemoglobin*).

Basal ganglia: subcortical structures located deep within the brain; often connected to the *cerebral cortex* via neural circuits.

Basicranium: base of the skull.

Biface: a tool made by chipping *flakes* off both sides of a core, producing an edge straighter and sharper than those made in earlier cultures, which were chipped on one edge only. A common tool of the *Acheulean industry.*

Bilophodonty: the molar cusp pattern of *Old World monkeys,* featuring four *cusps* arranged in front and rear pairs.

Bioaltruism: behavior that appears to be altruistic but in fact is believed to benefit the animal indirectly by increasing its *inclusive fitness.*

Bioethicist: a person who specializes in exploring the ethical dimensions of biological decisions.

Bipedal: moving erect on the hind limbs only.

Biretia: an early *anthropoid* from Algeria.

Birth canal: the passage through the mother's pelvis by means of which an infant is born.

Blade tools: slender, razor-sharp *flake tools* at least twice as long as they are wide.

Blending inheritance: an outmoded theory stating that offspring receive a combination of all characteristics of each parent through the mixture of their bloods; superseded by Mendelian genetics.

Blood groups: groups of individuals whose blood can be mixed without *agglutination* (e.g., Groups A, B, O, and AB).

Blood plasma: a clear liquid component of blood that carries the *red blood cells, white blood cells,* and *platelets.*

Brachiation: an arboreal locomotor pattern featuring manual swinging from branch to branch.

Branisella boliviana: an *Oligocene platyrrhine monkey* from Bolivia.

Breccia: a lime-cemented jumble of sand, stones, and bones; a common cave fill in South Africa.

Broca's area: a part of the human *cerebral cortex* involved with the hierarchical organization of grammar and the manual combination of objects.

Brow ridge: a continuous ridge of bone in the skull, curving over each eye and connected across the bridge of the nose. An extremely prominent brow ridge is characteristic of the Neandertal people.

Buccal: within the mouth, toward the cheek (see also *lingual*).

Burin: a chisel-like tool used to shape other materials, such as bone, antler, and wood; a tool for making other tools.

Calvaria: a braincase; that is, a skull minus the facial skeleton and lower jaw (plural, *calvariae*).

Canines: pointed teeth in the front of the mouth between the incisors and the premolars. In *monkeys* and *apes,* canines are usually large, projecting beyond the other teeth, and are used for tearing up vegetation and for threats and fights. *Hominin* canines are much smaller.

Canine fossa: concavity in the maxilla just behind the *canine jugum.*

Canine jugum: vertical ridge or bulge in the maxilla caused by a large *canine* root (plural, *juga*).

Carbon 14 (C14): a radioactive form of carbon present in the atmosphere as CO_2 that disintegrates at a predictable rate. The amount of carbon 14 remaining in fossils indicates their age.

Carotid foramen: opening for the carotid artery.

Carpolestidae: a family of *extinct* archaic *primates;* a family of the *semiorder* Plesiadapiformes.

Catarrhines: an infraorder of the *anthropoids* that includes *Old World monkeys, apes,* and *hominids.*

Catastrophism: Georges Cuvier's theory that vast floods and other disasters wiped out ancient life forms again and again throughout the earth's history.

Catopithecus: a particularly well-known *oligopithecine* from the Fayum in Africa.

Cenozoic: geologic era that began about 65 million years ago.

Centrioles: minute granules present in many cells outside the nuclear membrane. The centriole divides in cell division, and the parts separate to form the poles of the spindle.

Cephalic index: a skull measurement sometimes used by *anthropologists;* defined as skull breadth/length x 100.

Cerebral cortex: the gray, wrinkled, outer layer of the brain; largely responsible for memory and, in humans, reasoned behavior and abstract thought; also referred to as the *neocortex.*

Chatelperronian: an *Upper Paleolithic* tool culture of Western Europe; largely contemporaneous with the *Aurignacian culture* (37,000 to 29,000 years BP).

Chiasmata: points where the *chromatids* of a tetrad overlap and segment exchange may occur; *cross-over* points (singular, *chiasma*).

Choppers: small, generally ovoid stones with a few *flakes* removed to produce a partial cutting edge.

Chordata: the *phylum* of animals characterized by the possession of a notochord (a gelatinous dorsal stiffening rod) at some stage of life.

Chromatid: one of the two elements in a duplicated *chromosome.*

Chromosomes: coiled, threadlike structures of *DNA,* bearing the *genes* and found in the nucleus of all plant and animal cells. (See also *meiosis* and *mitosis.*)

Chronospecies: the sort of *species* that are created when an unbroken evolutionary continuum is arbitrarily divided into time-defined units.

Cingulum: shelf of enamel running around the periphery of a tooth (plural, *cingula*).

Clade: members of an evolutionary cluster (e.g., sister *species*) plus their common ancestor.

Cladistic classification: an evolution-based *taxonomy* that gives equal weight to traits and requires *sister groups* to be similarly ranked.

Cladogenesis: branching evolution involving the splitting of a *species* or lineage.

Cladogram: a branching tree diagram displaying evolutionary relationships among organisms.

Class: a *taxonomic* rank in biology. Humans belong to the class *Mammalia.*

Cleaver: an *Acheulean* stone implement with a straight cutting edge at one end; probably used for butchering animal carcasses.

Cline: the gradual change in frequency of a trait or *gene* across a geographic range.

Clivus: see *nasoalveolar clivus.*

Clone: a genetically identical organism asexually reproduced from an ancestral organism.

Close-knee stance: standing with the feet and knees closer together than the hip joints.

Coccyx: the bones at the end of the human and *ape* spine, the remnants of an ancestral tail.

Co-dominant: the term for *alleles* that in *heterozygous* combination produce a *phenotype* distinct from either type of *homozygote.*

Codon: a *nucleotide* triplet that codes for the production of a particular *amino acid* during *protein* production.

Collective phenotype: the set of phenotypic averages and norms that characterize a *population* or *species.*

Colugos: nonprimate *mammals* from Asia known for arboreal gliding; misnamed "flying lemurs."

Condyle: the part of a bone that fits into another bone, forming a movable, hingelike joint, like the part of the lower jaw that bears on the skull.

Consortship: generally, a period of exclusive sexual association and mating between a female and a male.

Conspecifics: members of the same *species.*

Continental drift: a theory that describes the movements of continental land masses throughout the earth's history.

Core area: a portion of the *home range* that is used frequently.

Core tool: an implement made from the core of a rock nodule. (Compare with *flakes.*)

Coronal plane: any plane that divides the body into front and rear portions.

Cranium: the skull without the jaw.

Creationism: the belief that humans and all life forms were specially created by God or some other divine force.

Creation myth: a story describing the origins, usually supernatural, of the earth and life (including humans).

Cretaceous: a period of the *Mesozoic* era, dating 65 to 144 million years ago.

Cro-Magnon: an anatomically modern human living in Europe between 40,000 and 10,000 years ago.

Crossing-over: the exchange of sections between *homologous chromosomes.*

Cultural evolution: changes in human *culture* resulting from the accumulated experience of humankind. Cultural evolution can produce *adaptations* to the environment faster than organic *evolution* can.

Culture: humans' systems of learned behaviors, symbols, customs, beliefs, institutions, artifacts, and technology; characteristic of a group and transmitted by its members to their offspring.

Cusps: conical projections on the biting surfaces of teeth. On the molar teeth of primates these include mainly the metacone, hypocone, protocone, and paracone (upper molars), and the metaconid, hypoconid, hypoconulid, entoconid, and protoconid (lower molars). (See also *molars*).

Débitage: the debris produced during stone tool manufacture.

Deep time: the theory that the earth is billions of years old and thus has a long history of development and change.

Deme: the community of potentially interbreeding individuals at a locality.

Dendrochronology: a dating procedure that involves counting the annual growth rings of trees.

Dental formula: the numbers of incisors, *canines*, premolars, and *molars* in half of the upper and lower toothrows.

Denticulates: stone implements made with toothed or notched edges.

Deoxyribonucleic acid: see *DNA*.

Derived traits: recently evolved characteristics shared by a small number of closely related *species*.

Diastema: a space in the toothrow that accommodates one or more teeth in the opposite jaw when the mouth is closed (plural, diastemata).

Diploid number: the full *chromosome* count in somatic cells (all cells except *gametes*). (Compare with the *haploid* number.)

Direct date: a date on an object itself; for example, a piece of bone may be directly dated by the radiocarbon method.

Directional natural selection: *natural selection* that operates in response to environmental change and produces shifts in the composition of a *population's gene pool* and *collective phenotype*.

Disk-core technique: a *Neandertal* stone-knapping method in which a core is trimmed to disk shape and numerous *flakes* are chipped off; the flakes are then generally retouched.

Distal: farther away from a point of reference; in the jaw, farther away from the anterior midline and toward the back of the mouth (see also *mesial*).

Diurnal: active during the day, as *apes*, *monkeys*, and humans are.

DNA (deoxyribonucleic acid): a chemical substance found in *chromosomes* and *mitochondria* that reproduces itself and carries the *genetic code*.

Dominance hierarchy: the rank structuring of a *primate* group, usually based on winning and losing fights. For some purposes, the ranks within a subset of animals, such as the adult males, may be analyzed separately.

Dominant: in genetics, describes a trait that is expressed in the *phenotype* even when the organism is carrying only one copy of the underlying hereditary material (one copy of the responsible *gene*).

Dorsal: pertaining to the back of an animal or one of its parts; opposite of *ventral*.

Dragon bones: the ancient Chinese term for *fossils* of various sorts that were collected and ground into medicines.

Dryopithecus: an *ape genus* from Europe dating to the mid to late *Miocene* of Europe.

Early *Homo*: general term referring collectively to *Homo habilis* and *Homo rudolfensis*.

Ecological niche: the set of resources and habitats exploited by a *species*.

Ecosystem: ecological system; the interacting community of all the organisms in an area and their physical environment, together with the flow of energy among its components.

Ecotone: an area where two or more ecological zones meet.

Ectotympanic bone: a middle ear bone that supports the eardrum.

Emissary veins: veins that pass through the bones of the skull by means of small openings called *foramina*.

Encephalization quotient (EQ): in mammals, a number expressing observed brain size in a particular species relative to expected brain size calculated from body weight.

Endocast: a *fossilized* cast of the interior of a skull; may reveal much about brain size and shape.

Eocene: the *geologic* epoch extending from 56 to 34 million years BP.

Eosimias: an *anthropoid* from the mid *Eocene* epoch of China.

Epicanthic fold: a fold of skin above the inner border of the eye; characteristic of Asiatic, some Native American, and Khoisan people.

Estrus: the period, usually around ovulation, of sexual *attractiveness* and activity by *primate* and other mammalian females.

Estrus cycle: the interval between periods of sexual *attractiveness* and activity of *primate* females; correlated with ovulation and the *menstrual cycle* but with great flexibility among *catarrhines*.

Ethnic group: a group of people perceived as sharing a common and distinctive *culture*.

Euprimates: a *semiorder* of the *primates* that contains the living *strepsirhines* (lemurs and lorises) and *haplorhines* (*tarsiers, monkeys, apes*, and humans). Also called "primates of a modern aspect."

Evolution: cumulative changes in the average characteristics of a *population* generally thought to occur over many generations. (See also *natural selection*.)

Exons: segments of a *gene's DNA* that code for *protein* production.

External acoustic meatus: auditory tube (ear) opening.

Extinction: the loss of a *species* due to the deaths of all its members.

Family: in human society, generally a unit marked by interdependent subsistence, sexual relationships among adults, and parent–offspring relationships.

Faunal correlation: dating a site by the similarity of its animal *fossils* to those of another site that may carry a reliable *absolute date*.

Female-bonded groups: social groups organized around a set of matrilineal families linked by bonds between the matriarchs.

Female philopatry: when females live and reproduce in their natal group for life.

Femur: the thighbone (plural, *femora*).

Fish gorge: device for catching fish on a line using a moving part that opens at right angles and sticks in the fish's mouth.

Fission-track dating: a method of dating rocks from tracks left by the spontaneous splitting of uranium 238 atoms.

Fitness: an individual's relative degree of success in surviving and reproducing and thus in gaining genetic representation in succeeding generations.

Flake tool: an implement made from a *flake* struck from a stone.

Flakes: sharp-edged fragments struck from a larger stone; may then be used as a cutting tool. (Compare with *core tool.*)

Folivore: as a dietary classification, a *species* that primarily eats leaves and other foliage.

Foramen magnum: the large opening in the cranial base, through which the spinal cord passes to the brain.

Forensic anthropologists: physical *anthropologists* who apply their expertise to matters of law, such as the identification of human remains.

Fossil: the remains of an organism, or direct evidence of its presence, preserved in rock. Generally only the hard parts of animals' teeth and bones are preserved.

Fossil magnetism: naturally occurring property of rocks indicating the polarity of the earth's magnetic field when they were laid down. By a comparison of the polarity of one layer with that of others, the age of a rock can, under certain conditions, be approximated.

Founder effect: the genetic difference between a newly founded, separated *population* and its parent group. The founding population is usually different because its *gene pool* is only a segment of the parent group's.

Fovea: an area of the *haplorhine* retina that allows extremely detailed vision.

Frenulum: a flap of skin that tethers the upper lip to the jaw.

Frontal bone: bone of the *primate* skull that constitutes the forehead and comes down around the eye sockets (orbits).

Frugivore: as a dietary classification, a *species* that primarily eats fruit.

Fusion–fission community: a society that includes several individuals of both sexes and all ages and is characterized by the formation and dissolution of temporary subgroups.

Gametes: reproductive *haploid* sex cells generated by *meiosis,* which fuse with *gametes* of the opposite sex in reproduction; in animals, eggs and sperm.

Gelada: a *species* of terrestrial *monkey* related to *baboons,* found in the mountains of Ethiopia; *Theropithecus gelada.*

Gene: primarily, a functional unit of the *chromosomes* in cell nuclei, which controls the coding and inheritance of *phenotypic* traits; some genes also occur in the *mitochondria.*

Gene flow: the transmission of *genes* between *populations,* which increases the variety of genes available to each and creates or maintains similarities in the genetic makeup of the populations.

Gene frequency: the number of times a gene occurs in proportion to the size of a *population.*

Gene pool: all the *genes* of a *population* at a given time; summing genes within a *species* yields the species' gene pool.

Genetic code: the chemical code based on four *nucleotides, carried by DNA* and *RNA,* which specifies *amino acids* in sequence for *protein* synthesis.

Genetic drift: the genetic changes in *populations* caused by random phenomena rather than by *natural selection.*

Genetic load: the *recessive genes* in a *population* that are harmful when expressed in the rare *homozygous* condition.

Genome: the totality of the *DNA* unique to a particular organism or *species.*

Genotype: the genetic makeup of a plant or animal; the total information contained in all *genes* of the organism. (Compare with *phenotype.*)

Genus: *taxonomic* category composed of a group of *species* that are similar because of common ancestry.

Geology: the study of the earth's physical formation, its nature, and its continuing development.

Glabella: anteriormost point on the frontal bone, usually between the *brow ridges.*

Glenoid fossa: another name for the *mandibular fossa.*

Gluteus medius: one of the muscles of the hip; a lateral stabilizer of the *pelvis* in modern humans.

Gluteus minimus: one of the muscles of the hip; a lateral stabilizer of the *pelvis* in modern humans.

Grades: arbitrarily defined levels of evolutionary development.

Gradualism: the hypothesis that *evolution* has consisted for the most part of gradual, steady change. (Compare with *punctuated equilibrium.*)

Gramnivore: as a dietary classification, a *species* that primarily eats grain and other seeds.

Gravettian: see *Perigordian.*

Group selection: a theoretical model in which *natural selection* is presumed to operate not on the individual animal but on a social group as a unit.

Gummivore: as a dietary classification, a *species* that primarily eats gum.

Gyrification index: a quantitative measure of cortical folding.

Half-life: the time it takes for half of any quantity of a radioactive element to decay to its fission products.

Hamstrings: muscles of the hips and the back of the thigh; thigh extensors.

Hand ax: a bifacially flaked stone implement that characterized the *Acheulean industry.*

Haploid number: the number of *chromosomes* carried by *gametes;* equal to one-half the full count carried by somatic cells. (Compare with *diploid number.*)

Haplorhine: a suborder of the living *primates* that includes the Ceboidea, Cercopitheccoidea, and Hominoidea.

Haplotype: a sequence of linked nucleotides or loci that is exchanged as a block between homologous chromosomes during meiosis.

Harem polygyny: in zoology, a group including one breeding male and multiple females; among humans, one husband and multiple wives and concubines.

Hemispherical asymmetry: the condition in which the two cerebral hemispheres differ in one or more dimensions. In most modern humans, the left hemisphere is somewhat larger than the right.

Hemoglobin: a red *protein* found in *red blood cells* that carries oxygen through the circulatory system of vertebrates and some other animals.

Heritability: a property of *phenotypic* traits; the proportion of a trait's interindividual variance that is due to genetic variance.

Heterodont: having several different types of teeth (incisors, *canines,* etc.), each with a different function.

Heterozygous: having different versions of a *gene (alleles)* for a particular trait. (Compare with *homozygous;* see also *dominant.*)

Heuristic devices: devices that facilitate or stimulate further investigation and thought.

Home base: a place where *hominin* groups gathered for socializing, food sharing, and sleeping.

Home range: the area a *primate* group uses for foraging, sleeping, and so on in a year. (Compare with *territory.*)

Hominan: a member of the subtribe *Hominina;* a member of any *species* belonging to the *genus Homo.*

Hominid: a member of the *primate* family Hominidae; includes all living great apes and living and *fossil hominins.*

Hominina: a subtribe of the tribe Hominini that contains the *genus Homo* and all of its living and *fossil species.*

Hominins: living or fossil members of the *primate* tribe Hominini, which includes *Homo sapiens,* earlier species of the genus *Homo, Ardipithecus, Sahelanthropus, Orrorin, Kenyanthropus, Australopithecus,* and *Paranthropus.*

Hominoid: a *primate* of the superfamily Hominoidea, including all *apes* and humans.

Homo: a *genus* of the tribe Hominini, subtribe Hominina; contains at least six *species: H. habilis, H. rudolfensis, H. erectus, H. heidelbergensis, H. neanderthalensis,* and *H. sapiens.*

Homo antecessor: the proposed new *species* name for certain *fossils* from the site of Gran Dolina, Spain; a taxon not recognized as valid in this book.

Homo erectus: a *hominin species* that inhabited much of the Old World between 1.9(?) million and at least 300,000 years BP; successor to "early *Homo.*"

Homo ergaster: the *species* name given by some *paleoanthropologists* to certain African *fossils* regarded by most workers as early *Homo erectus.*

Homo floresiensis: a *hominan species* that inhabited the Indonesian island of Flores from before 38,000 to 18,000 years BP.

Homo habilis: one of the two *species* of "early *Homo*"; inhabited South and East Africa 2.3 to 1.6 million years ago.

Homo heidelbergensis: the successor to *Homo erectus,* first appearing about 800,000 to 600,000 years BP; ancestral to both *Homo sapiens* and the *Neandertals.*

Homologous: generally, traits that are shared by two or more *taxa* due to descent from a common ancestor.

Homologous chromosomes: *chromosomes* that are similar in shape, size, and sequence of *genes.*

Homo neanderthalensis: a *species* of humans that inhabited Europe and the Middle East from about 350,000 to 27,000 years BP; descended from *Homo heidelbergensis,* the species' common name is usually spelled *Neandertal.*

Homo rudolfensis: one of the two *species* of "early *Homo*"; inhabited East Africa 2.4 to 1.6 million years ago.

Homo sapiens: among living *primates,* the scientific name for modern humans; members of the *species* first appeared about 195,000 years ago.

Homoplasies: trait resemblances between *taxa* due not to common ancestry but to other factors, such as independent adaptation to similar environments.

Homozygous: having identical versions of a *gene (alleles)* for a particular trait. (Compare with *heterozygous.*)

Hybrid speciation: *speciation* through hybridization between two good *species.*

Hyoid: a bone of the throat positioned just above the *larynx* and just below the *mandible;* provides attachment for one of the muscles of the tongue and for certain muscles at the front of the neck.

Hypoglossal canal: an opening in the *occipital bone* just anterior to the *occipital condyle;* allows passage of the hypoglossal nerve to the tongue musculature.

Hyporder: a *taxonomic* rank; a subdivision of a suborder.

Iliac blade: the broad portion of the *ilium,* one of the bones of the *pelvis.*

Iliofemoral ligament: the ligament that prevents backward movement of the trunk at the human hip.

Ilium: the hipbone, part of the *pelvis.*

Inbreeding: mating among related individuals.

Inclusive fitness: the sum total of an organism's individual reproductive success (number of offspring) plus portions of the reproductive success of genetic kin.

Indirect date: a date on material that is associated with the object in question; for example, a human skull may be associated with a particular sedimentary layer that is dated by the K/Ar method to 2 million years BP, thus indirectly dating the skull to 2 million years BP, also.

Infanticide: the killing of infants.

Inion: midline point of the superior nuchal lines.

Insectivore: as a dietary classification, a *species* that primarily eats insects.

Interglacial: a period in which glaciers retreat and the climate warms.

Introns: segments of a gene's *DNA* that do not code for *protein* production (so-called noncoding DNA).

IQ tests: tests that supposedly measure an individual's intelligence quotient. Many consider such tests flawed and of little value, particularly for cross-cultural comparisons.

Iron pyrite: a mineral substance (iron disulfide) that, when struck with flint, makes sparks that will start a fire.

Ischium: one of the bones of the *pelvis.*

Kenyanthropus platyops: an *australopith genus* and *species* from East Africa that dates back to 3.5 to 3.2 million years of age.

Kin selection: the selection of characteristics (and their *genes*) that increase the probability of the survival and reproduction of close relatives.

Knuckle-walking: *quadrupedal* walking on the knuckles of the hands and the soles of the feet, used by bonobos, chimpanzees, and gorillas on the ground.

Lambda: midline juncture of the sagittal and lambdoidal sutures.

Language: the cognitive aspect of human communication, involving symbolic thinking structured by grammar.

Larynx: the voice box; the organ in the throat containing the vocal cords, important in human *speech* production.

Levallois technique: a stone-knapping method in which a core is shaped to allow a *flake* of predetermined size and shape to be detached; originated at least 250,000 years BP.

Life expectancy: the average age at death of individuals born into a particular population.

Limbic system: the emotional brain; a group of structures in the brain that are important in regulating such behavior as eating, drinking, aggression, sexual activity, and expressions of emotion. Proportionately smaller in humans than in other *primates,* it operates below the level of consciousness.

Lingual: in the mouth, toward the tongue (see also *buccal*).

Lithic technology: stone tool technology.

Locus: the position of a nuclear *gene* on a *chromosome;* each locus can carry only one allele of a gene.

Lumbar curve: the forward curvature of the vertebral column in the lower back that helps bring the *hominin* trunk over the hip joints.

Macroevolution: evolutionary change that involves the origin or *extinction* of *species* or higher *taxonomic* groups.

Macromutation: a large and genetically inherited change between parent and offspring.

Magdalenian: an *Upper Paleolithic* culture existing in Western Europe from about 16,500 to 11,000 years BP; produced many *blade* tools and prototype harpoons.

Mammalia: the class of four-legged vertebrates—including humans—having hair or fur, milk glands for suckling their young, and warm blood.

Mandible: the lower jaw.

Mandibular fossa: concave portion of the jaw joint; part of the temporal bone (see *glenoid fossa*).

Mandibular symphysis: the midline connecting the right and left halves of the lower jaw.

Manuports: unmodified stones that could not have occurred naturally at an archaeological site and must have been carried there; how manuports were used is unknown.

Mastoid process: bony projection of the temporal bone posterior to the *external acoustic meatus.*

Mastoid region: the area around the *mastoid process* of the temporal bone.

Matrilineal kinship: kinship traced through the maternal line.

Megadontia: the condition of having enlarged teeth relative to body size.

Meiosis: cell division resulting in the formation of sex cells, each of which will have half the number of chromosomes present in the original cell (the *haploid number*).

Melanocyte: a kind of cell in the skin that produces pigment, giving the skin color.

Menstrual cycle: the interval (generally, monthly) between periods of menstrual bleeding; especially characteristic of *catarrhine* females.

Mental region of mandible: the front, lower edge of the mandibular body.

Mesial: toward the anterior side of a tooth (i.e., toward the midline at the front of the jaw; see also *distal*).

Mesolithic: a *Stone Age* period recognizable at some European sites and characterized by the use of small stone tools called microliths; lasting at most 2,000 years, the Mesolithic followed the *Paleolithic* and preceded the *Neolithic.*

Mesozoic: the geologic era that began about 253 million years ago.

Metaconid: see *cusps.*

Microevolution: evolutionary change within *species; evolution* that affects *populations.*

Microwear: the microscopic pattern of scratches, pits, and polish produced during the use of a stone tool.

Middle Paleolithic: a period of stone tool manufacture in the Old World (mainly Europe, Africa, and Western Asia) that lasted from about 250,000 to 40,000 years BP.

Midfacial prognathism: forward protrusion of the upper jaw, the midface and the nasal regions; characteristic of *Neandertals.*

Miocene: the *geologic* epoch extending from 24 to 5 million years BP.

Mitochondria: granular or rod-shaped bodies in the cytoplasm of cells that function in the metabolism of fat and *proteins.* Probably of bacterial origin.

Molars: grinding teeth, which bear many *cusps. Primate* molars have three to five cusps, depending on the animal; premolars normally have two.

Molecular clocks: a variety of molecular measures for estimating the time of divergence of living *species* from their common ancestor.

Monkey: usually a small or medium-sized, long-tailed arboreal, *quadrupedal,* vegetarian *primate.* The two groups are *New World monkeys* and *Old World monkeys.*

Monogamy: among humans, having only one spouse. (Compare with *polygamy.*)

Monogyny: in zoology, generally having only one mate. (Compare with *polygyny.*)

Monomorphic: both sexes showing the same trait (e.g., similar body size).

Monophyletic: a *clade* with a single common ancestor.

Morotopithecus: a *genus* of *apes* that inhabited East Africa during the early *Miocene.*

Mousterian industry: a *Middle Paleolithic* tool industry from Europe and the Middle East; primarily associated with the *Neandertals.*

Movius line: the geographic dividing line between the *Acheulean* tradition in the West and non-Acheulean *lithic* traditions in Eastern and Southeastern Asia.

mtDNA: genetic material found in the *mitochondria* of cells.

Mutation: generally, a spontaneous change in the chemistry of a *gene* that can alter its *phenotypic* effect. The accumulation of such changes may contribute to *evolution* of a new *species* of animal or plant. (See also *point mutation.*)

Myanmarpithecus: an early *anthropoid* from Myanmar (formerly Burma).

Nasion: midline juncture of the frontonasal and nasal sutures.

Nasoalveolar clivus: anterior edge of the premaxilla.

Natural selection: the principal mechanism of Darwinian *evolutionary* change, by which the individuals best adapted to the environment contribute more offspring to succeeding generations than others do. As more of such individuals' characteristics are incorporated into the *gene pool,* the characteristics of the *population* evolve.

Neandertals: (often spelled Neanderthal) members of the species *Homo neanderthalensis;* archaic humans who lived in Europe and the Middle East between 350,000 and 27,000 years ago.

Neolithic: the New Stone Age; a late stage of stone tool making that began about 10,000 years ago. (See *Stone Age.*)

Neurons: nerve cells; the basic units of the nervous system.

Nocturnal: active during the hours of darkness.

Nuchal area: area of attachment of the muscles of the back of the neck, low on the occipital bone.

Nucleotides: organic compounds, consisting of bases, sugars, and phosphates; found in cells either free or as part of polynucleotide chains.

Occipital bun: a bunlike posterior projection of the occipital bone.

Occipital condyles: pads of bone on the base of the skull that articulate with the uppermost vertebra.

Occipital torus: a ridge running side to side across the occipital bone.

Occlusal plane: the plane lying parallel to the biting surfaces of the teeth.

Occupation level: the land surface occupied by prehistoric *hominins.*

Oldowan tool industry: the earliest known stone-tool *culture,* dating 2.5 million years into the past. The products were very crude stone *choppers* and *flakes.*

Oligocene: the *geologic* epoch extending from 34 to 24 million years BP.

Oligopithecines: late *Eocene anthropoids;* many have been collected from Egypt's Fayum Depression.

Opportunistic mating: mating done whenever and wherever the opportunity presents itself and with whatever partner is available.

Opposable thumb: the ability to hold thumb and index finger together in opposition, giving a *precision grip.*

Optically stimulated luminescence: a method of dating sediments by stimulating them with intense light; such stimulation causes the sediments to release trapped electrons and produce measurable light.

Order: a *taxonomic* rank. Humans belong to the order *Primates.*

Oreopithecus: an *ape genus* from the mid to late *Miocene* in Europe.

Orrorin tugenensis: an *australopith genus* and *species* from western Kenya that dates back to 6 million years of age.

Osteodontokeratic culture: the culture of bone, tooth, and horn tools hypothesized by Raymond Dart for *A. africanus;* now largely dismissed.

Outbreeding: mating among unrelated individuals. (Compare with *inbreeding.*)

Pachyostosis: literally, "thick-boned"; used here to describe the skull bones of *Homo erectus.*

Pair bond: a psychological relationship between mates; thought to be marked by sexual faithfulness.

Palate: the bony plate separating the mouth from the nasal cavity. It is arched in humans and flat in *apes.*

Paleoanthropology: the study of the *fossil* and *cultural* remains and other evidence of humans' extinct ancestors.

Paleocene: the *geologic* epoch extending from 65 to 56 million years BP.

Paleolithic: the Old Stone Age; the earliest stage of stone tool making that began about 2.5 million years ago. (See *Stone Age.*)

Paleomagnetism: magnetism preserved in rock and originally generated by the earth's magnetic field. Past fluctuations in the intensity and direction of this field allow correlation between strata; a form of *relative dating* that can be used for *absolute dating* because the historic pattern of magnetic fluctuations and reversals is known and dated.

Paleontology: the study of the *fossil* remains and biology of organisms that lived in the past.

Paranthropus: a *genus* of the tribe Hominini, subtribe Australopithecina; contains three *species: P. robustus, P. boisei,* and *P. aethiopicus.*

Paranthropus aethiopicus: a megadont *australopith species* that inhabited East Africa 2.7 to 2.3 million years ago.

Paranthropus boisei: a megadont *australopith species;* that lived in East Africa from 2.4 to 1.3 million years ago; also known as *Australopithecus boisei.*

Paranthropus robustus: an *australopith species* that lived in South Africa from 2.0 to 1.0 million years ago; called *Australopithecus robustus* by some authors.

Parapatric speciation: *speciation* among *populations* of sedentary organisms with adjacent geographic ranges.

Parietal mastoid angle: angular connection between the parietal and temporal bones near the *mastoid process.*

Paromomyidae: a family of *extinct* archaic *primates;* a family of the *semiorder* Plesiadapiformes.

Patellar groove: groove separating the femoral condyles, particularly on the ventral aspect of the bone. The lateral lip of the patellar groove is an anterior projection from the lateral condyle that probably functions to prevent dislocation of the kneecap (patella).

Pelvis: a bony structure forming a basinlike ring at the base of the vertebral column with which the legs articulate.

Perigordian: an *Upper Paleolithic* culture of Western Europe, dating 27,000 to 21,000 years BP

Pharynx: the throat above the *larynx.*

Phenetic classification: a *taxonomy* based on physical similarities or differences between *species* or other *taxa.*

Phenotype: the observable characteristics of a plant or an animal; the expression of the *genotype.*

Phonemes: the smallest sound components of *language.*

Phyletic transformation: the conversion (mainly through *natural selection*) of an entire *species* into a new species.

Phylogenetic classification: a *taxonomy* that reflects evolutionary descent and is based on the pattern of primitive and *derived traits;* in traditional evolutionary classifications, traits may be given different weights.

Phylogeny: the evolutionary lineage of organisms; their evolutionary history.

Phylum: a major *taxonomic* rank. Humans are in the phylum *Chordata.*

Piltdown man: a doctored modern human skull and ape jaw that was "discovered" in 1911 and supposed to represent a very primitive human, *Eoanthropus dawsoni,* but exposed as a hoax in 1953.

Pithecanthropus: the original *genus* name given by Eugene Dubois to *fossil* material from Java; now classified as *Homo erectus.*

Platelets: minute blood cells associated with clotting.

Platycephalic: a term describing a skull that is long, low vaulted, and wide.

Platyrrhines: an infraorder of the *anthropoids* that includes the *New World monkeys.*

Pleiotropic genes: *genes* that influence more than one *phenotypic* trait.

Pleistocene: the geologic epoch that lasted from about 1.8 million to 10,000 years ago.

Plesiadapidae: a family of *extinct* archaic *primates;* a family of the *semiorder* Plesiadapiformes.

Plesiadapiformes: a *semiorder* of the *primates* that is now *extinct.* Also called the "archaic primates."

Plesiadapiforms: the common name for *extinct primates* belonging to the *semiorder* Plesiadapiformes.

Pliocene: the *geologic* epoch extending from 5 to 1.8 million years BP.

Plio-Pleistocene: a combination of the last two epochs of the Cenozoic era; the *Pliocene* lasted from 5 to 1.8 million years BP and the *Pleistocene* from 1.8 million to 10,000 years BP.

Point mutation: usually, the substitution of one *nucleotide* in a single *codon* of a *gene* that affects *protein* synthesis and *genotype;* gene *mutation.*

Polygenic traits: traits determined by more than one *gene.*

Polygyny: in zoology, the tendency for a male to have regular sexual access to two or more females.

Polymorphism: the appearance of a *gene* in more than one form among individuals of a *population.*

Population: usually, a local or breeding group; a group in which any two individuals have the potential of mating with each other.

Positive feedback: the process in which a positive change in one component of a system brings about changes in other components, which in turn brings about further positive changes in the first component.

Postcranial: referring to any anatomical feature that is behind the head (in *quadrupeds*) or below the head (in *bipeds*).

Postglenoid process: bony projection that bounds the *mandibular fossa* laterally and posteriorly.

Postorbital bar: a bar of bone running around the outside margin of the orbits of *strepsirhines.*

Potassium-argon dating: *chronometric dating* in which age is determined by measurement of the decay of radioactive potassium 40.

Power grip: a grip involving all fingers of the hand equally, as in grasping a baseball. (Compare with *precision grip.*)

Precision grip: a grip that involves opposing the tip of the thumb to the tips of the other fingers, allowing fine control of small objects. (Compare with *power grip.*)

Prehensile: adapted for grasping.

Primates: an *order* of placental mammals, mostly arboreal, with two suborders: the *strepsirhines* and the *haplorhines.*

Primitive trait: a characteristic inherited from an early ancestor and widely shared among descendants.

Proceptivity: the aspect of female sexuality reflected by inviting copulation.

Proconsul: an *ape* genus from East Africa that lived during the *Miocene* epoch.

Prognathic: having the lower face and jaws projecting in front of the upper parts of the face.

Promiscuous: both females and males having multiple sexual partners.

Prosimians: a suborder used in traditional evolutionary classifications that contained the Lemuroidea, Lorisoidea, and Tarsioidea; not used in this book.

Proteins: molecules composed of chains of *amino acids.*

Protoconid: see *cusps.*

Punctuated equilibrium: the hypothesis that most *species* have long periods *of stasis,* interrupted by episodes of rapid evolutionary change and *speciation* by branching. (Compare with *gradualism.*)

Purgatorius: an *extinct genus* of *plesiadapiform,* dating to about 65 million years ago.

Quadrupedal: moving on four limbs.

Races: divisions of a *species,* usually based on physical or behavioral differences and less well marked than subspecies. Many anthropologists reject the concept of biological races of living humans.

Racism: the assumption of inherent superiority of certain *races* and the consequent discrimination against others.

Ramus: the vertical portion of the *mandible;* as opposed to the mandibular body, which bears the teeth.

Receptivity: the aspect of female sexuality reflected by cooperating in copulation.

Recessive: in genetics, describes a trait that is expressed only when the organism is carrying two copies of the underlying hereditary material (two copies of the responsible *gene*).

Reciprocal altruism: the trading of apparently altruistic acts by different individuals at different times; a variety of *bioaltruism.*

Reconciliation: the act of restoring friendly relations.

Rectus femoris: one of the muscles that flexes the hominin thigh.

Recursion: the production of messages containing imbedded elements that can be understood only in relation to other elements and certain operating rules.

Red blood cells (corpuscles): vertebrate blood cells lacking nuclei and containing *hemoglobin.*

Red ocher: a powdered mineral and earth mixture used as a red pigment.

Relative dating: estimating the ages of *geologic* deposits (and the *fossils* in them) by determining their *stratigraphic* level in relation to that of other deposits whose relative or absolute age is known. (Compare with *absolute dating.*)

Retromolar gap: the space between the lower M3 and the mandibular *ramus:* characteristic of *Neandertals.*

Rhinarium: the moist, hairless nose characteristic of *strepsirhines,* and of most nonprimate mammals.

Ribonucleic acid: see *RNA.*

Ribosomes: cellular organelles that contribute to *protein* synthesis.

Rickets: a pathological condition involving curvature of the bones; caused by insufficient vitamin D.

RNA (ribonucleic acid): a compound found with *DNA* in cell nuclei and chemically close to DNA; transmits *genetic code* from DNA to direct the production of *proteins.* May take two forms: messenger RNA (mRNA) or transfer RNA (tRNA).

Sacrum: the part of the vertebral column that articulates with the *pelvis* and forms the dorsal portion of the pelvic girdle.

Sagittal crest: a ridge of bone running front to rear along the midline of the skull; serves to attach certain jaw muscles. (Compare *sagittal keel.*)

Sagittal keel: a slightly raised ridge running down the midline of a skull; smaller than a *sagittal crest.*

Sagittal suture: the line of union joining the two main side bones of the braincase.

Sahelanthropus tchadensis: an *australopith genus* and *species* from Chad that dates back to 6 to 7 million years of age.

Sangoan: the *Middle Paleolithic* tool industry from East and Central Africa; associated with *Homo heidelbergensis.*

Satellite DNA: tandem repetitions of *DNA* sequences that accumulate at certain locations on *chromosomes* and are usually noncoding.

Savanna: a tropical or subtropical grassland, often with scattered trees (woodland savanna).

Sciatic notch: a deep indentation of the *dorsal* edge of the *hominid ilium.*

Scientific method: the process of developing and testing hypotheses (by attempted falsification) that traditional scientists use to establish the probabilistic validity of their theories.

Scraper: a stone or bone tool for preparing hides and leather, used to scrape the fat and other tissues from the inner surface of the skin.

Secondary altriciality: the phenomenon of an infant's motor skills requiring a lengthy period of postnatal development, as opposed to its sensory systems, which are functional at birth or soon after; characteristic of *H. erectus* and later *hominins.* (See *altricial.*)

Sectorial: literally, "cutting"; refers to the first lower premolar of *apes* and some *monkeys,* which acts as a cutting edge in moving against the upper *canine.*

Semicircular canals: the fluid-filled canals of the inner ear that control balance and coordination.

Semiorder: a subdivision of an *order;* the order *Primates* (fossil and living) contains two semiorders: *Plesiadapiformes* and *Euprimates.*

Serum: the liquid remaining after blood has clotted.

Sex chromosomes: those *chromosomes* that carry *genes* that control gender (femaleness or maleness).

Sex-linked trait: an inherited trait coded on the sex *chromosomes,* and thus having a special distribution related to sex.

Sex swellings: hormone-induced swellings on the hindquarters of certain *primate* females; generally correlated with ovulation.

Sexual dimorphism: characteristic anatomical (and behavioral) differences between the males and females of a *species.*

Sexual selection: a category including intrasexual competition for mates (usually aggressive and among males) and intersexual mate selection (usually of males by females).

Shared derived trait: a characteristic inherited from a relatively recent ancestor and found among a few close *taxa.*

Siamopithecus: a late *Eocene anthropoid* from Thailand.

Sickle-cell anemia: a genetically caused disease that can be fatal, in which the *red blood corpuscles* carry insufficient oxygen.

Sinanthropus pekinensis: the original name given by Davidson Black to ancient *fossils* from Zhoukoudian; now classified as *Homo erectus.*

Sister groups: in *cladistics,* the groups resulting from a dichotomous evolutionary branching event; initially ranked as sister *species,* these groups may change rank because of subsequent branching but must always maintain the same *taxonomic* level.

Sivapithecus: a *genus* of *Miocene apes* that includes *Ramapithecus,* probably ancestral to the *orangutan.*

Sociobiology: science of the biological (especially, genetic) basis of social behavior.

Socioecology: the connection between *species'* ecological relations and their social behaviors; also the study of this connection.

Solutrean: an *Upper Paleolithic* culture existing in western Europe between 21,000 and 16,500 years BP; best known for its laurel-leaf blades.

Speciation: the production of new *species,* either through gradual transformation or the splitting or branching of existing species.

Species: following the biological species concept, a group of interbreeding natural *populations* that are reproductively isolated from other such groups.

Speech: the oral expression of *language,* or spoken language; other expressions include gestural and written language.

Stabilizing natural selection: *natural selection* that operates during periods when the environment is stable and maintains the genetic and phenotypic status quo within a *population.*

Stasis: a period of evolutionary equilibrium or inactivity.

Stereoscopic vision: vision produced by two eyes with overlapping fields, giving a sense of depth and distance; most highly evolved in hunting animals and *primates.*

Stone Age: the earliest period in cultural evolution, from more than 2 million to 5,000 years ago. Recognizable periods are the *Paleolithic,* or Old Stone Age; the *Mesolithic,* or Middle Stone Age; and the *Neolithic,* or New Stone Age.

Stratigraphy: the sequence of geologic strata, or rock layers, formed by materials deposited by water or wind; also the study of this sequence.

Strepsirhines: a suborder of the living *primates* that includes the Lemuroidea and Lorisoidea.

Superior pubic ramus: portion of the pubic bone that runs between the pubic symphysis and the acetabulum.

Suprainiac fossa: a characteristic depression in the occipital bone of *Neandertals.*

Sympathetic hunting magic: the use of rituals and associated artifacts that practitioners believed would help ensure success and safety in the hunt.

Sympatric speciation: *speciation* among *populations* with the same or overlapping geographic ranges.

Syntax: the rules of structure in *language.*

Taiga: the northern coniferous forest bordering the *tundra.*

Talonid: distal, heel-like portion of lower *molars.*

Taphonomy: the scientific study of the conditions under which objects are preserved as *fossils.*

Taxon: a group of organisms at any level of a classification scheme (plural, *taxa*).

Taxonomy: classification of plants or animals according to their relationships and the ordering of these groups into hierarchies. *Taxonomic* levels are ranks within these classifications, e.g., *species* or *genus.*

Temporomandibular joint: jaw joint.

Temporonuchal crest: bony crest running around the posterior and lateral edges of the braincase.

Terrestrial: adapted to living on the ground.

Territory: the area occupied and defended by individuals or groups of animals against *conspecifics.* (Compare with *home range.*)

Thermoluminescence: a method of dating pottery and stone tools by heating them to release trapped electrons; the electrons produce measurable light.

Thorax: the region of the rib cage.

Toothcomb: a dental specialization of *strepsirhines* in which the lower front teeth are closely spaced and forwardly inclined.

Traditional evolutionary classification: a classification scheme that recognizes *grade*-level differences between sister groups.

Trichromatic: referring to the rich color vision produced by having three types of photopigments (molecules that absorb certain wavelengths of light) in the eye.

True breeding (breeding true): the situation in which the members of a genetic strain resemble each other in all important characteristics and show little variability.

Tuff: a rocklike substance formed from volcanic ash.

Tympanic plate: the cranial base surface of the tubular *external acoustic meatus.*

Type specimen: the *fossil* specimen that serves as the basis for identifying all other individuals in a *species;* usually the original specimen to be found.

Uniformitarianism: Charles Lyell's theory that the forces now affecting the earth—water and wind erosion, frost, volcanism—acted in a similar way in the past and that change is always gradual and nondirectional.

Unique derived trait: a characteristic that is a unique evolutionary *adaptation* of a *species.*

Upper Paleolithic: a period of stone tool manufacture in the Old World that lasted from about 40,000 to 10,000 years BP; associated primarily with anatomically modern humans.

Ventral: pertaining to the belly side of an animal or one of its parts; the opposite of *dorsal.*

Vertebrata: a subphylum of the chordates containing all animals with backbones; comprising fishes, amphibians, reptiles, birds, and mammals.

Victoriapithecinae: an *extinct* subfamily of the earliest *catarrhine monkeys.*

Wernicke's area: a part of the human *cerebral cortex* essential in comprehending and producing meaningful *speech.*

White blood cells (leukocytes): vertebrate blood cells lacking *hemoglobin.*

Wide-knee stance: standing with the feet and knees about as far apart as the hip joints.

Xenophobia: a fear or hatred of foreigners.

Y-5 pattern: an arrangement of the *cusps* and grooves of the lower *molars* that is characteristic of *hominoids.*

Zinjanthropus boisei: the original name of the *australopith species* now called *Paranthropus boisei.*

Zygomatic arch: the bony arch running from the cheekbone back to the auditory meatus.

Bibliography

Abbate, Ernesto, Andrea Albianelli, Augusto Azzaroli, Marco Benvenuti, Berhane Tesfamariam, Piero Bruni, Nicola Cipriani, Ronald Clarke, Giovanni Ficcarelli, Roberto Macchiarelli, Giovanni Napoleone, Mauro Papini, Lorenzo Rook, Mario Sagri, Tewelde Medhin Tecle, Danilo Torre, and Igor Villa. "A One-Million-Year-Old *Homo* Cranium from the Danakil (Afar) Depression of Eritrea." *Nature,* 393:458–460, 1998.

Adcock, Gregory, Elizabeth Dennis, Simon Easteal, Gavin Huttley, Lars Jermiin, W. J. Peacock, and Alan Thorne. "Mitochondrial DNA Sequences in Ancient Australians: Implications for Modern Human Origins." *Proceedings of the National Academy of Sciences,* 98:537–542, 2001.

Aiello, Leslie, and Mark Collard. "Our Newest Oldest Ancestor?" *Nature,* 410:526–527, 2001.

Aiello, Leslie, and Christopher Dean. *An Introduction to Human Evolutionary Anatomy.* London, Academic Press, 1990.

Aiello, Leslie, and R. Dunbar. "Neocortex Size, Group Size, and the Evolution of Language." *Current Anthropology,* 34:184–193, 1993.

Aiello, Leslie, and Peter Wheeler. "The Expensive-Tissue Hypothesis." *Current Anthropology,* 36:199–221, 1995.

Alberts, Bruce. "DNA Replication and Recombination." *Nature,* 421:431–435, 2003.

Alexander, R. McNeill. "Human Locomotion." pp. 80–85 in *The Cambridge Encyclopedia of Human Evolution* (Steve Jones, Robert Martin, David Pilbeam, and Sarah Bunney, eds.). Cambridge, Cambridge University Press, 1992.

Alexander, Richard. *Darwinism and Human Affairs.* Seattle, University of Washington Press, 1979.

Alroy, J. "Cope's Rule and the Dynamics of Body Mass Evolution in North American Fossil Mammals." *Science,* 280:731–734, 1998.

Altmann, Jeanne. *Baboon Mothers and Infants.* Cambridge (MA), Harvard University Press, 1980.

Altmann, Stuart (ed.). *Japanese Monkeys: A Collection of Translations.* Atlanta, published by the editor, 1965.

American Sickle Cell Anemia Association. www.ascaa.org.

Andrews, Roy Chapman. *On the Trail of Ancient Man.* New York, G. P. Putnam's Sons, 1926.

Ankel-Simons, Friderun. *A Survey of Living Primates and Their Anatomy.* New York, Macmillan, 1983.

Anonymous. *The Oxford Dictionary of Quotations,* 2nd ed. London, Oxford University Press, 1955.

Antón, Susan. "Evolutionary Significance of Cranial Variation in Asian *Homo erectus.*" *American Journal of Physical Anthropology,* 118:301–323, 2002.

Antón, Susan. "Natural History of *Homo erectus.*" *Yearbook of Physical Anthropology,* 46:126–170, 2003.

Arens, William. *The Man-Eating Myth.* Oxford, Oxford University Press, 1979.

Arsuaga, Juan-Luis. "The First Europeans." *Discovering Archaeology,* 2(5):48–65, 2000.

Arsuaga, Juan-Luis, Ignacio Martínez, Ana Gracia, José-Miguel Carretero, and Eudald Carbonell. "Three New Human Skulls from the Sima de los Huesos Site in Sierra de Atapuerca, Spain." *Nature,* 362:534–537, 1993.

Ascenzi, A., I. Biddittu, P. Cassoli, A. Segre, and E. Segre-Naldini. "A Calvarium of Late *Homo erectus* from Ceprano, Italy." *Journal of Human Evolution,* 31:409–423, 1996.

Aschoff, J., B. Günther, and K. Kramer. *Energiehaushalt und Temperaturregulation.* Munich, Urban and Schwarzenberg, 1971.

Asfaw, Berhane, W. Gilbert, Yonas Beyenbe, William Hart, Paul Renne, Giday WoldeGabriel, Elisabeth Vrba, and Tim White. "Remains of *Homo erectus* from Bouri, Middle Awash, Ethiopia." *Nature,* 416:317–319, 2002.

Asfaw, Berhane, Tim White, Owen Lovejoy, Bruce Latimer, Scott, Simpson, and Gen Suwa. "*Australopithecus garhi:* A New Species of Early Hominid from Ethiopia." *Science,* 284:629–635, 1999.

Ayub, Qasim, Atika Mansoor, Muhammad Ismail, Shagufta Khaliq, Aisha Mohyuddin, Abdul Hameed, Kehkashan Mazhar, Sadia Rehman, Saima Siddiqi, Myrto Papaioannou, Alberto Piazza, Luigi Cavalli-Sforza, and S. Qasim Mehdi. "Reconstruction of Human Evolutionary Tree Using Polymorphic Autosomal Microsatellites." *American Journal of Physical Anthropology,* 122:259–268, 2003.

Baba, Hisao, Fachroel Aziz, Yousuke Kaifu, Gen Suwa, Reiko Kono, and Teuku Jacob. "*Homo erectus* Calvarium from the Pleistocene of Java." *Science,* 299:1384–1388, 2003.

Backwell, Lucinda, and Francesco d'Errico. "Evidence of Termite Foraging by Swartkrans Early Hominids." *Proceedings of the National Academy of Sciences,* 98:1358–1363, 2001.

Bahn, Paul. *The Cambridge Illustrated History of Archaeology.* Cambridge, Cambridge University Press, 1996.

Bahn, Paul. "Cannibalism or Ritual Dismemberment?" p. 330 in *The Cambridge Encyclopedia of Human Evolution* (Steve Jones, Robert Martin, David Pilbeam, and Sarah Bunney, eds.). Cambridge, Cambridge University Press, 1992.

Bahn, Paul. "New Developments in Pleistocene Art." *Evolutionary Anthropology,* 4:204–215, 1995/96.

Balter, Michael. "Paintings in Italian Cave May Be Oldest Yet." *Science,* 290:419–421, 2000.

Balter, Michael. "Scientists Spar over Claims of Earliest Human Ancestor." *Science,* 291:1460–1461, 2001.

Balter, Michael. "Small but Smart? Flores Hominid Shows Signs of Advanced Brain." *Science,* 307:1386–1389, 2005.

Barber, Lynn. *The Heyday of Natural History 1820–1870.* Garden City (NY), Doubleday, 1980.

Bar-Yosef, Ofer. "The Natufian Culture in the Levant, Threshold to the Origins of Agriculture." *Evolutionary Anthropology*, 6:159–177, 1998.

BBC News. "Cave Paintings May Be 'Oldest Yet.'" http://news.bbc.co.uk/1/hi/sci/tech/1000653.stm.

Beach, F. A. "Sexual Attractivity, Proceptivity and Receptivity in Female Mammals." *Hormones and Behavior*, 7:105–138, 1976.

Beard, K. C. "Basal Anthropoids." pp. 133–149 in *The Primate Fossil Record* (Walter Hartwig, ed.). Cambridge, Cambridge University Press, 2002.

Beard, K. C. "East of Eden: Asia as an Important Center of Taxonomic Origination in Mammalian Evolution." *Bulletin of the Carnegie Museum of Natural History*, 34:5–39, 1998.

Beard, K. C., Tao Qi, Mary Dawson, Banyue Wang, and Chuankuei Li. "A Diverse New Primate Fauna from Middle Eocene Fissure-fillings in Southeastern China." *Nature*, 368:604–609, 1994.

Bearder, Simon. "Lorises, Bushbabies, and Tarsiers: Diverse Societies in Solitary Foragers." pp. 11–24 in *Primate Societies* (Barbara Smuts, Dorothy Cheney, Robert Seyfarth, Richard Wrangham, and Thomas Struhsaker, eds.). Chicago, University of Chicago Press, 1987.

Beck, J., D. Richards, R. Edwards, B. Silverman, P. Smart, D. Donahue, S. Hererra-Osterheld, G. Burr, L. Calsoyas, A. Jull, and D. Biddulph. "Extremely Large Variations of Atmospheric 14C Concentration during the Last Glacial Period." *Science*, 292:2453–2458, 2001.

Begun, David. "Planet of the Apes." *Scientific American*, 289(2):74–83, 2003.

Begun, David, and Alan Walker. "The Endocast." pp. 326–358 in *The Nariokotome* Homo erectus *Skeleton* (Alan Walker and Richard Leakey, eds.). Cambridge (MA), Harvard University Press, 1993.

Behrensmeyer, Anna, Nancy Todd, Richard Potts, and Geraldine McBrinn. "Late Pliocene Faunal Turnover in the Turkana Basin, Kenya and Ethiopia." *Science*, 278:1589–1594, 1997.

Bellomo, Randy. "Methods of Determining Early Hominid Behavioral Activities Associated with the Controlled Use of Fire at FxJj 20 Main, Koobi Fora, Kenya." *Journal of Human Evolution*, 27:173–195, 1994.

Benefit, Brenda. "*Victoriapithecus:* The Key to Old World Monkey and Catarrhine Origins." *Evolutionary Anthropology*, 7:155–174, 1999.

Benefit, Brenda, and Monte McCrossin. "Earliest Known Old World Monkey Skull." *Nature*, 388:368–371, 1997.

Benveniste, Raoul, and George Todaro. "Evolution of Type C Viral Genes: Evidence for an Asian Origin of Man." *Nature*, 261:101–108, 1976.

Berger, Lee, Rodrigo Lacruz, and Darryl de Ruiter. "Brief Communication: Revised Age Estimates of *Australopithecus*-Bearing Deposits at Sterkfontein, South Africa." *American Journal of Physical Anthropology*, 119:192–197, 2002.

Berger, Lee, and Phillip Tobias. "A Chimpanzee-Like Tibia from Sterkfontein, South Africa and Its Implications for the Interpretation of Bipedalism in *Australopithecus africanus*." *Journal of Human Evolution*, 30:343–348, 1996.

Bermúdez de Castro, J., J. Arsuaga, E. Carbonell, A. Rosas, I Martínez, and M. Mosquera. "A Hominid from the Lower Pleistocene of Atapuerca, Spain: Possible Ancestor to Neandertals and Modern Humans." *Science*, 276:1392–1395, 1997.

Bermúdez de Castro, J., E. Carbonell, I. Cáceres, J. Díez, Y. Fernández-Jalvo, M. Mosquera, A. Ollé, J. Rodríquez, X. Rodríquez, A. Rosas, J. Rosell, R. Sala, J. Vergés, and J. van der Made. "The TD6 (Aurora Stratum) Hominid Site. Final Remarks and New Questions." *Journal of Human Evolution*, 37:695–700, 1999.

Betzig, Laura (ed.). *Human Nature: A Critical Reader*. New York, Oxford University Press, 1997.

Binford, Lewis, and Chuan Kun Ho. "Taphonomy at a Distance: Zhoukoudian, 'The Cave Home of Beijing Man'?" *Current Anthropology*, 26(4):413–442, 1985.

Binford, Lewis, and Nancy Stone. "Zhoukoudian: A Closer Look." *Current Anthropology*, 27(5):453–475, 1986.

Bischoff, James, Donald Shamp, Arantza Aramburu, Juan Luis Arsuaga, Eudald Carbonell, and J. Bermudez de Castro. "The Sima de los Huesos Hominids Date to beyond U/Th Equilibrium (>350 kyr) and Perhaps to 400–500 kyr: New Radiometric Dates." *Journal of Archaeological Science*, 30:275–280, 2003.

Black, Davidson. "Tertiary Man in Asia: The Choukoutien Discovery." *Nature*, 118:733–734, 1926.

Bloch, Jonathan, and Doug Boyer. "Grasping Primate Origins." *Science*, 298:1606–1610, 2002.

Blumenschine, Robert, Charles Peters, Fidelis Masao, Ronald Clarke, Alan Deino, Richard Hay, Carl Swisher, Ian Stanistreet, Gail Ashley, Lindsay McHenry, Nancy Sikes, Nikolaas van der Merwe, Joanne Tactikos, Amy Cushing, Daniel Deocampo, Jackson Njau, and James Ebert. "Late Pliocene *Homo* and Hominid Land Use from Western Olduvai Gorge, Tanzania." *Science*, 299:1217–1221, 2003.

Boag, Peter, and Peter Grant. "Intense Natural Selection in a Population of Darwin's Finches (*Geospizinae*) in the Galápagos." *Science*, 214:82–85, 1981.

Boaz, Noel, and Russell Ciochon. *Dragon Bone Hill*. Oxford, Oxford University Press, 2004.

Boesch, Christophe. "Is Culture a Golden Barrier between Human and Chimpanzee?" *Evolutionary Anthropology*, 12:82–91, 2003.

Boesch, Christophe, and Hedwige Boesch-Achermann. *The Chimpanzees of the Taï Forest*. Oxford, Oxford University Press, 2000.

Borja, Concepción, Marcos García-Pacheco, Enrique Olivares, Gary Scheuenstuhl, and Jerold Lowenstein. "Immunospecificity of Albumin Detected in 1.6 Million-Year-Old Fossils from Venta Micena in Orce, Granada, Spain." *American Journal of Physical Anthropology*, 103:433–441, 1997.

Boule, Marcellin. *Fossil Men: Elements of Human Palaeontology*. Edinburgh, Oliver and Boyd, 1923.

Bowcock, A., A. Ruiz-Linares, J. Tomfohrde, E. Minch, J. Kidd, and L. Cavalli-Sforza. "High Resolution of Human Evolutionary Trees with Polymorphic Microsatellites." *Nature*, 368:455–457, 1994.

Bower, Bruce. "Wild Chimps Rocked On: Apes Left Unique Record of Stone Tools." www.sciencenews.org. April 11, 2002.

Bowler, James, Harvey Johnston, Jon Olley, John Prescott, Richard Roberts, Wilfred Shawcross, and Nigel Spooner. "New Ages for Human Occupation and Climatic Change at Lake Mungo, Australia." *Nature,* 421:837–840, 2003.

Bowler, Peter. *Theories of Human Evolution.* Baltimore, Johns Hopkins University Press, 1986.

Boyd, W. C. *Genetics and the Races of Man.* Boston, Little, Brown, 1950.

Boysen, Sarah, Valerie Kuhlmeier, Peter Halliday, and Yolanda Halliday. "Tool Use in Captive Gorillas." pp. 179–187 in *The Mentalities of Gorillas and Orangutans* (Sue Taylor Parker, Robert Mitchell, and H. Lyn Miles, eds.). Cambridge, Cambridge University Press, 1999.

Brace, C. Loring. *The Stages of Human Evolution,* 5th ed. Englewood Cliffs (NJ), Prentice Hall, 1995.

Bradley, Daniel, Ronan Loftus, Patrick Cunningham, and David MacHugh. "Genetics and Domestic Cattle Origins." *Evolutionary Anthropology,* 6:79–86, 1998.

Braga, José, and Christophe Boesch. "Further Data about Venous Channels in South African Plio-Pleistocene Hominids." *Journal of Human Evolution,* 33:423–447, 1997.

Brain, C. *The Hunters or The Hunted? An Introduction to African Cave Taphonomy.* Chicago, University of Chicago Press, 1981.

Bräuer, Günter, Yuji Yokoyama, Christophe Falguères, and Emma Mbua. "Modern Human Origins Backdated." *Nature,* 386:337, 1997.

Broom, Robert. *Finding the Missing Link.* London, Watts, 1950.

Broom, Robert. "The Pleistocene Anthropoid Apes of South Africa." *Nature,* 142:377–379, 1938.

Broom, Robert. "Some Notes on the Taungs Skull." *Nature,* 115:560–571, 1925.

Brown, B., A. Walker, C. Ward, and R. Leakey. "New *Australopithecus boisei* Calvaria from East Lake Turkana, Kenya." *American Journal of Physical Anthropology,* 91:137–159, 1993.

Brown, F. H. "Methods of Dating." pp. 179–186 in *The Cambridge Encyclopedia of Human Evolution* (Steve Jones, Robert Martin, David Pilbeam, and Sarah Bunney, eds.). Cambridge, Cambridge University Press, 1992.

Brown, Larry. "Selection in a Population of House Mice Containing Mutant Individuals." *Journal of Mammalogy,* 46:461–465, 1965.

Brown, P., T. Sutikna, M. Morwood, R. Soejono, Jatmiko, E. Wayhu Saptomo, and R. Awe Dur. "A New Small-Bodied Hominin from the Late Pleistocene of Flores, Indonesia." *Nature,* 431:1055–1061, 2004.

Brown, Ryan, and George Armelagos. "Apportionment of Racial Diversity: A Review." *Evolutionary Anthropology,* 10:34–40, 2001.

Browne, Janet. *Charles Darwin: The Power of Place.* New York, Knopf, 2002.

Browne, Janet. *Charles Darwin: Voyaging.* New York, Knopf, 1995.

Brunet, Michel, Alain Beauvilain, Yves Coppens, Emile Heintz, Aladji Moutaye, and David Pilbeam. "*Australopithecus behrelghazali,* Une Nouvelle Espèce d'Hominidé Ancien de al Région de Koro Toro (Tchad)." *C. R. Acad. Sci. Paris,* 322:907–913, 1996.

Brunet, Michel, Alain Beauvilain, Yves Coppens, Emile Heintz, Aladji Moutaye, and David Pilbeam. "The First Australopithecine 2,500 Kilometres West of the Rift Valley (Chad)." *Nature,* 378:273–275, 1995.

Brunet, Michel, Franck Guy, David Pilbeam, Hassane MacKaye, Andossa Likius, Djimdoumalbaye Ahounta, Alain Beauvilains, Cécile Blondel, Hervé Bocherens, Jean-Renaud Boisserie, Louis de Bonis, Yves Coppens, Jean Dejax, Christine Denys, Philippe Duringer, Véra Eisenmann, Gongdibe Fanone, Pierre Fronty, Denis Geraads, Thomas Lehmann, Fabrice Lihoreau, Antoine Louchart, Adoum Mahamat, Gildas Merceron, Guy Mouchelin, Olga Otero, Pablo Campomanes, Marcia Ponce de Leon, Jean-Claude Rage, Michel Sapanet, Mathieu Schuster, Jean Sudre, Pascal Tassy, Xavier Valentin, Patrick Vignaud, Laurent Viriot, Antoine Zazzo, and Christoph Zollikofer. "A New Hominid from the Upper Miocene of Chad, Central Africa." *Nature,* 418:145–151, 2002.

Bunn, Henry. "Comments on Rose and Marshall." *Current Anthropology,* 37:321–323, 1996.

Burenhult, Göran. "Modern People in Africa and Europe." pp. 77–95 in *The First Humans: Human Origins and History to 10,000 BC* (Göran Burenhult, ed.). New York, HarperSanFrancisco, 1993a.

Burenhult, Göran. "Pech-Merle: A 20,000-Year-Old Sanctuary." pp. 112–113 in *The First Humans: Human Origins and History to 10,000 BC* (Göran Burenhult, ed.). New York, HarperSanFrancisco, 1993b.

Burenhult, Göran. "The Venus Figurines." pp. 102–103 in *The First Humans: Human Origins and History to 10,000 BC* (Göran Burenhult, ed.). New York, HarperSanFrancisco, 1993c.

Burkhardt, Frederick, and Sydney Smith (eds.). *The Correspondence of Charles Darwin,* vol. 7. Cambridge, Cambridge UniversityPress, 1991.

CALIB Radiocarbon Calibration. http://radiocarbon.pa.qub.ac.uk/calib/.

Campbell, Bernard. *Human Evolution,* 3rd ed. New York, Aldine, 1985.

Campbell, Bernard. *Humankind Emerging.* Boston, Little, Brown and Company, 1976.

Cann, Rebecca, Mark Stoneking, and Allan Wilson. "Mitochondrial DNA and Human Evolution." *Nature,* 325:31–36, 1987.

Cantalupo, Claudio, and William Hopkins. "Asymmetric Broca's Area in Great Apes." *Nature,* 414:505, 2001.

Caramelli, David, Carles Lalueza-Fox, Cristiano Vernesi, Martina Lari, Antonella Casoli, Francesco Mallegni, Brunetto Chiarelli, Isabelle Dupanloup, Jaume Bertranpetit, Guido Barbujani, and Giorgio Bertorelle. "Evidence for a Genetic Discontinuity between Neandertals and 24,000-Year-Old Anatomically Modern Europeans." *Proceedings of the National Academy of Sciences,* 100:6593–6597, 2003.

Carbonell, E., J. Bermúdez de Castro, J. Arsuaga, J. Díez, A. Rosas, G. Cuenca-Bescós, R. Sala, M. Mosquera, and

X. Rodríquez. "Lower Pleistocene Hominids and Artifacts from Atapuerca-TD6 (Spain)." *Science,* 269:826–830, 1995.

Carroll, Sean. "Genetics and the Making of *Homo sapiens.*" *Nature,* 422:849–857, 2003.

Cartmill, Matt. "New Views on Primate Origins." *Evolutionary Anthropology,* 1:105–111, 1992.

Cartmill, Matt. "Rethinking Primate Origins." *Science,* 184:436–443, 1974.

Cartmill, Matt. *A View to a Death in the Morning.* Cambridge (MA), Harvard University Press, 1993.

Cartmill, Matt, and Katherine Milton. "The Lorisiform Wrist Joint and the Evolution of 'Brachiating' Adaptations in the Hominoidea." *American Journal of Physical Anthropology,* 47:249–272, 1977.

Cavalli-Sforza, Luigi Luca, and Francesco Cavalli-Sforza. *The Great Human Diasporas.* Reading (MA), Addison-Wesley, 1995.

Cela-Conde, Camilo, and Francisco Ayala. "Genera of the Human Lineage." *Proceedings of the National Academy of Sciences,* 100:7684–7689, 2003.

Center for the Study of Chinese Prehistory. www.chinesepre-history.org.

Cheney, Dorothy. "Interactions and Relationships between Groups." pp. 267–281 in *Primate Societies* (Barbara Smuts, Dorothy Cheney, Robert Seyfarth, Richard Wrangham, and Thomas Struhsaker, eds.). Chicago, University of Chicago Press, 1987.

Cheney, Dorothy, and Robert Seyfarth. *How Monkeys See the World.* Chicago, University of Chicago Press, 1990.

Chaimanee, Yaowalak, Varavudh Suteethorn, Jean-Jacques Jaeger, and Stéphane Ducrocq. "A New Late Eocene Anthropoid Primate from Thailand." *Nature,* 385:429–431, 1997.

Chaimanee, Yaowalak, Varavudh Suteethorn, Pratueng Jintasakul, Chavalit Vidthayanon, Bernard Marandat, and Jean-Jacques Jaeger. "A New Orangutan Relative from the Late Miocene of Thailand." *Nature,* 427:439–441, 2004.

Chauvet, Jean-Marie, Eliette Deschamps, and Christian Hillaire. *Dawn of Art: The Chauvet Cave.* New York, Abrams, 1996.

Chu, J., W. Huang, S. Kuang, J. Wang, J. Xu, Z. Chu, Z. Yang, K. Lin, P. Li, M. Wu, Z. Geng, C. Tan, R. Du, and L. Jin. "Genetic Relationship of Populations in China." *Proceedings of the National Academy of Sciences,* 95:11763–11768, 1998.

Churchill, Steven, and Fred Smith. "Makers of the Early Aurignacian of Europe." *Yearbook of Physical Anthropology,* 43:61–115, 2000.

Ciochon, Russell. "The Earliest Asians Yet." *Natural History,* 104(12):51–54, 1995.

Ciochon, Russell, and Gregg Gunnell. "Eocene Primates from Myanmar: Historical Perspectives on the Origin of Anthropoidea." *Evolutionary Anthropology,* 11:156–168, 2002.

Clarke, R. J. "A Corrected Reconstruction and Interpretation of the *Homo erectus* Calvaria from Ceprano, Italy." *Journal of Human Evolution,* 39:433–442, 2000.

Clarke, Ronald, and Phillip Tobias. "Sterkfontein Member 2 Foot Bones of the Oldest South African Hominid." *Science,* 269:521–524, 1995.

Clottes, Jean. "Epilogue: Chauvet Cave Today." pp. 89–128 in *Dawn of Art: The Chauvet Cave* (J.-M. Chauvet, E. Deschamps, and C. Hillaire, eds.). New York, Abrams, 1996.

Coffing, Katherine, Craig Feibel, Meave Leakey, and Alan Walker. "Four-Million-Year-Old Hominids from East Lake Turkana, Kenya." *American Journal of Physical Anthropology,* 93:55–65, 1994.

Conard, Nicholas. "Palaeolithic Ivory Sculptures from Southwestern Germany and the Origins of Figurative Art." *Nature,* 426:830–832, 2003.

Conkey, Margaret. "Humans as Materialists and Symbolists: Image Making in the Upper Paleolithic." pp. 95–118 in *The Origin and Evolution of Humans and Humanness* (D. T. Rasmussen, ed.). Boston, Jones and Bartlett, 1993.

Conroy, Glenn. *Primate Evolution.* New York, W. W. Norton, 1990.

Conroy, Glenn. *Reconstructing Human Origins: A Modern Synthesis.* New York, W. W. Norton, 1997.

Conroy, Glenn, C. Jolly, D. Cramer, and J. Kalb. "Newly Discovered Fossil Hominid Skull from the Afar Depression, Ethiopia." *Nature,* 275:67–70, 1978.

Conroy, Glenn, Martin Pickford, Brigitte Senut, and Pierre Mein. "Diamonds in the Desert: The Discovery of *Otavipithecus namibiensis.*" *Evolutionary Anthropology,* 2: 46–52, 1993.

Conroy, Glenn, G. Weber, H. Seidler, W. Recheis, D. Zur Nedden, and J. Haile Mariam. "Endocranial Capacity of the Bodo Cranium Determined from Three-Dimensional Computed Tomography." *American Journal of Physical Anthropology,* 113:111–118, 2000.

Conroy, Glenn, G. Weber, H. Seidler, P. Tobias, A. Kane, and B. Brunsden. "Endocranial Capacity in an Early Hominid Cranium from Sterkfontein, South Africa." *Science,* 280:1730–1731, 1998.

Coon, Carleton. *The Origin of Races.* New York, Alfred Knopf, 1963.

Coon, Carleton, S. M. Garn, and J. B. Birdsell. *Races: A Study of the Problem of Race Formation in Man.* Springfield (IL), Charles C. Thomas, 1950.

Coppens, Yves. "East Side Story: The Origin of Humankind." *Scientific American,* 270:88–96, 1994.

Coqueugniot, H., J.-J. Hublin, F. Veillon, F. Houët, and T. Jacob. "Early Brain Growth in *Homo erectus* and Implications for Cognitive Ability." *Nature,* 431:299–302, 2004.

Corballis, Michael. *The Lopsided Ape.* New York, Oxford University Press, 1991.

Cosgrove, Richard. "Hunters on the Edge of the Tasmanian Ice." pp. 166–167 in *The First Humans: Human Origins and History to 10,000 BC* (Göran Burenhult, ed.). New York, HarperSanFrancisco, 1993.

Covert, Herbert. "The Earliest Fossil Primates and the Evolution of Prosimians: Introduction." pp. 13–20 in *The Primate Fossil Record* (Walter Hartwig, ed.). Cambridge, Cambridge University Press, 2002.

Covey, Curt. "The Earth's Orbit and the Ice Ages." *Scientific American,* 250(2):58–66, 1984.

Cowen, Richard. *History of Life.* Boston, Blackwell Scientific, 1990.

Currie, Pete. "Muscling in on Hominid Evolution." *Nature,* 428:373–374, 2004.

Cussac Cave. www.bradshawfoundation.com/chauvet/cussac-cave.html.

D'Agnese, Joseph. "Not Out of Africa." *Discover,* 23(8):52–57, 2002.

Dagosto, Marian. "The Origin and Diversification of Anthropoid Primates: Introduction." pp. 125–132 in *The Primate Fossil Record* (Walter Hartwig, ed.). Cambridge, Cambridge University Press, 2002.

Dainton, Mike. "Did Our Ancestors Knuckle-Walk?" *Nature,* 410:324–325, 2001.

Dart, Raymond. "*Australopithecus africanus:* The Man-Ape of South Africa." *Nature,* 115:195–199, 1925.

Dart, Raymond, and Dennis Craig. *Adventures with the Missing Link.* Philadelphia, Institutes Press, 1967.

Darwin, Charles. *The Descent of Man, and Selection in Relation to Sex.* Princeton, Princeton University Press, 1981. (First published in 1871.)

Darwin, Charles. *On the Origin of Species.* Cambridge (MA), Harvard University Press, 1964. (First published in 1859.)

Darwin, Charles. *The Voyage of the* Beagle. Garden City (NY), Doubleday, 1962. (First published in 1839.)

Day, Michael. *Guide to Fossil Man.* Cleveland, World Publishing, 1965.

Day, Michael. "Omo Human Skeletal Remains." *Nature,* 222:1135–1138, 1969.

Deacon, Janette. "South African Rock Art." *Evolutionary Anthropology,* 8:48–63, 1999.

Deacon, Terrence. "Primate Brains and Senses." pp. 109–114 in *The Cambridge Encyclopedia of Human Evolution* (Steve Jones, Robert Martin, David Pilbeam, and Sarah Bunney, eds.). Cambridge, Cambridge University Press, 1992a.

Deacon, Terrence. "The Human Brain." pp. 115–123 in *The Cambridge Encyclopedia of Human Evolution* (Steve Jones, Robert Martin, David Pilbeam, and Sarah Bunney, eds.). Cambridge, Cambridge University Press, 1992b.

Deacon, Terrence. *The Symbolic Species.* New York, W. W. Norton, 1997.

Dean, Christopher, Meave Leakey, Donald Reid, Friedemann Schrenk, Gary Schwartz, Christopher Stringer, and Alan Walker. "Growth Processes in Teeth Distinguish Modern Humans from *Homo erectus* and Earlier Hominins." *Nature,* 414:628–631, 2001.

Deevey, E. S. "The Human Population." *Scientific American,* 203(3):194–204, 1960.

Defleur, Alban, Tim White, Patricia Valensi, Ludovic Slimak, and Évelyne Crégut-Bonnoure. "Neanderthal Cannibalism at Moula-Guercy, Ardèche, France." *Science,* 286:128–131, 1999.

DeGusta, David. "Aubesier 11 Is Not Evidence of Neanderthal Conspecific Care." *Journal of Human Evolution,* 45:91–94, 2003.

de Heinzelin, Jean, J. Desmond Clark, Tim White, William Hart, Paul Renne, Giday WoldeGabriel, Yonas Beyene, and Elizabeth Vrba. "Environment and Behavior of 2.5-Million-Year-Old Bouri Hominids." *Science,* 284:625–629, 1999.

Deino, Alan, Paul Renne, and Carl Swisher, III. "$^{40}Ar/^{39}Ar$ Dating in Paleoanthropology and Archeology." *Evolutionary Anthropology,* 6:63–75, 1998.

Deino, Alan, Lisa Tauxe, Marc Monaghan, and Andrew Hill. "$^{40}Ar/^{39}Ar$ Geochronology and Paleomagnetic Stratigraphy of the Lukeino and Lower Chemeron Formations at Tabarin and Kapcheberek, Tugen Hills, Kenya." *Journal of Human Evolution,* 42:117–140, 2002.

Delgado, Jr., Roberto, and Carel van Schaik. "The Behavioral Ecology and Conservation of the Orangutan (*Pongo pygmaeus*): A Tale of Two Islands." *Evolutionary Anthropology,* 9:201–218, 2000.

Delhanty, Joy. "Human Chromosomes." pp. 274–280 in *The Cambridge Encyclopedia of Human Evolution* (Steve Jones, Robert Martin, David Pilbeam, and Sarah Bunney, eds.). Cambridge, Cambridge University Press, 1992.

Delson, Eric. "Classification of the Primates" pp. xxiii–xxvii in the *Encyclopedia of Human Evolution and Prehistory,* 2nd ed. (E. Delson, I. Tattersall, J. A. Van Couvering, and A. S. Brooks, eds.). New York, Garland, 2000.

Delson, Eric, and I. Tattersall. "Primates." pp. 590–595 in *Encyclopedia of Human Evolution and Prehistory,* 2nd ed. (E. Delson, I. Tattersall, J. Van Couvering, and A. Brooks, eds.). New York, Garland, 2000.

D'Errico, Francesco, Paola Villa, Ana Pinto Llona, and Rosa Ruiz Idarraga. "A Middle Palaeolithic Origin of Music? Using Cave-bear Bone Accumulations to Assess the Divje Babe I Bone "Flute."' *Antiquity,* 72:65–79, 1998.

de Lumley, Henry. "A Paleolithic Camp at Nice." *Scientific American,* 220(5):42–50, 1969.

Desmond, Adrian. *The Ape's Reflexion.* New York, The Dial Press, 1979.

Desmond, Adrian, and James Moore. *Darwin.* New York, W. W. Norton, 1991.

DeVore, Irven, and K. R. L. Hall. "Baboon Ecology." pp. 20–52 in *Primate Behavior: Field Studies of Monkeys and Apes* (Irven DeVore, ed.). New York, Holt, Rinehart and Winston, 1965.

de Waal, Frans. "Apes from Venus: Bonobos and Human Social Evolution." pp. 39–68 in *Tree of Origin* (Frans de Waal, ed.). Cambridge (MA), Harvard University Press, 2001.

de Waal, Frans. *Chimpanzee Politics: Power and Sex among Apes.* New York, Harper and Row, 1982.

de Waal, Frans. *Peacemaking among Primates.* Cambridge (MA), Harvard University Press, 1989.

de Waal, Frans, and Frans Lanting. *Bonobo: The Forgotten Ape.* Berkeley, University of California Press, 1997.

Diamond, Jared. *Collapse: How Societies Choose to Fail or Succeed.* New York, Viking, 2005.

Diamond, Jared. *Guns, Germs, and Steel.* New York, W. W. Norton, 1997.

Diamond, Jared. "The Astonishing Micropygmies." *Science,* 306:2047–2048, 2004.

Dickson, D. B. *The Dawn of Belief.* Tucson, University of Arizona Press, 1990.

Dillehay, Tom. "Palaeoanthropology: Tracking the First Americans." *Nature,* 425:23–24, 2003.

Discovery Channel. *Iceman.* http://dsc.discovery.com/convergence/iceman/iceman.html.

Dixson, Alan. *Primate Sexuality.* Oxford, Oxford University Press, 1998.

Dmanisi. www.dmanisi.org.ge.

Dobzhansky, Theodosius. *Genetics and the Origin of Species.* New York, Columbia University Press, 1937.

Dolhinow, Phyllis. "Play: A Critical Process in the Developmental system." pp. 231–236 in *The Nonhuman Primates* (Phyllis Dolhinow and Agustín Fuentes, eds.). Mountain View (CA), Mayfield Publishing, 1999.

Dolhinow, Phyllis, and Agustín Fuentes (eds.). *The Nonhuman Primates.* Mountain View (CA), Mayfield Publishing, 1999.

Domínguez-Rodrigo, M., and T. Pickering. "Early Hominid Hunting and Scavenging: A Zooarcheological Review." *Evolutionary Anthropology,* 12:275–282, 2003.

Doran, Diane, and Alastair McNeilage. "Gorilla Ecology and Behavior." *Evolutionary Anthropology,* 6:120–131, 1998.

Doran, Diane, and Alastair McNeilage. "Subspecific Variation in Gorilla Behavior: The Influence of Ecological and Social Factors." pp. 123–149 in *Mountain Gorillas* (Martha Robbins, Pascale Sicotte, and Kelly Stewart, eds.). Cambridge, Cambridge University Press, 2001.

Dronkers, Nina. "A New Brain Region for Coordinating Speech Articulation." *Nature,* 384:159–161, 1996.

Duarte, Cidália, Joao Maurício, Paul Pettitt, Pedro Souto, Erik Trinkaus, Hans van der Plicht, and Joao Zilhao. "The Early Upper Paleolithic Human Skeleton from the Abrigo do Lagar Velho (Portugal) and Modern Human Emergence in Iberia." *Proceedings of the National Academy of Sciences,* 96:7604–7609, 1999.

Dubois, Eugene. "*Pithecanthropus erectus*—A Form from the Ancestral Stock of Mankind." pp. 165–175 in *Adam or Ape: A Sourcebook of Discoveries about Early Man* (L. S. B. Leakey, Jack Prost, and Stephanie Prost, eds.). Cambridge (MA), Schenkman, 1971. (Originally published in 1896.)

DuBrul, E., and H. Sicher. *The Adaptive Chin.* Springfield (IL), Charles C. Thomas, 1954.

Duchin, Linda. "The Evolution of Articulate Speech: Comparative Anatomy of the Oral Cavity in *Pan* and *Homo.*" *Journal of Human Evolution,* 19:687–697, 1990.

Ducrocq, Stéphane. "Eocene Primates from Thailand: Are Asian Anthropoideans Related to African Ones." *Evolutionary Anthropology,* 7:97–104, 1998.

Dunbar, R. I. M. "The Price of Being at the Top." *Nature,* 373:22–23, 1995.

Dunbar, R. I. M. "The Social Brain Hypothesis." *Evolutionary Anthropology,* 6:178–190, 1998.

Earth Observatory. http://earthobservatory.nasa.gov.

Eiseley, Loren. *Darwin's Century.* Garden City (NY), Doubleday, 1958.

Eldredge, Niles, and Stephen Jay Gould. "Punctuated Equilibria: An Alternative to Phyletic Gradualism." pp. 82–115 in *Models in Paleobiology* (T. Schopf, ed.). San Francisco, Freeman, Cooper and Company, 1972.

Enstam, Karin, Lynne Isbell, and Thomas de Maar. "Male Demography, Female Mating Behavior, and Infanticide in Wild Patas Monkeys (*Erythrocebus patas*)." *International Journal of Primatology,* 23:85–104, 2002.

Eveleth, Phyllis, and James Tanner. *Worldwide Variation in Human Growth,* 2nd ed. Cambridge, Cambridge University Press, 1990.

Fagan, Brian. *World Prehistory,* 4th ed. New York, Longman, 1999.

Falk, Dean. *Braindance.* New York, Henry Holt, 1992.

Falk, Dean. *Primate Diversity.* New York, W. W. Norton, 2000.

Falk, Dean, John Redmond, Jr., John Guyer, Glenn Conroy, Wolfgang Recheis, Gerhard Weber, and Horst Seidler. "Early Hominid Brain Evolution: A New Look at Old Endocasts." *Journal of Human Evolution,* 38:695–717, 2000.

Feathers, James. "Luminescence Dating and Modern Human Origins." *Evolutionary Anthropology,* 5:25–36, 1996.

Fedigan, Linda. *Primate Paradigms.* Montreal, Eden Press, 1982.

Feibel, Craig. "Tephrostratigraphy and Geological Context in Paleoanthropology." *Evolutionary Anthropology,* 8:87–100, 1999.

Feibel, Craig, and Francis Brown. "Microstratigraphy and Paleoenvironments." pp. 21–39 in *The Nariokotome* Homo erectus *Skeleton* (Alan Walker and Richard Leakey, eds.). Cambridge (MA), Harvard University Press, 1993.

Fleagle, John. *Primate Adaptation and Evolution.* San Diego, Academic Press, 1988.

Fleagle, John, and Marcelo Tejedor. "Early Platyrrhines of Southern South America." pp. 161–173 in *The Primate Fossil Record* (Walter Hartwig, ed.). Cambridge, Cambridge University Press, 2002.

Foley, Robert. "Studying Human Evolution by Analogy." pp. 335–340 in *The Cambridge Encyclopedia of Human Evolution* (Steve Jones, Robert Martin, David Pilbeam, and Sarah Bunney, eds.). Cambridge, Cambridge University Press, 1992.

Foley, Robert, and Marta Mirazón Lahr. "Opinion: Modern Human Origins—Why It's Time to Move On." pp. 249–250 in *Human Evolutionary Genetics: Origins, Peoples and Disease* (M. Jobling, M. Hurles, and C. Tyler-Smith, eds.). New York, Garland, 2004.

Formicola, Vincenzo, and Alexandra Buzhilova. "Double Child Burial from Sungir (Russia): Pathology and Inferences for Upper Paleolithic Funerary Practices." *American Journal of Physical Anthropology,* 124:189–198, 2004.

Fossey, Dian. *Gorillas in the Mist.* Boston, Houghton Mifflin, 1983.

Friday, A. E. "Human Evolution: The Evidence from DNA Sequencing." pp. 316–321 in *The Cambridge Encyclopedia of Human Evolution* (Steve Jones, Robert Martin, David Pilbeam, and Sarah Bunney, eds.). Cambridge, Cambridge University Press, 1992.

Friedberg, Errol. "DNA Damage and Repair." *Nature,* 421:436–440, 2003.

Fruth, Barbara, and Gottfried Hohmann. "How Bonobos Handle Hunts and Harvests: Why Share Food?" pp. 231–243 in *Behavioural Diversity in Chimpanzees and Bonobos* (Christophe Boesch, Gottfried Hohmann, and Linda Marchant, eds.). Cambridge, Cambridge University Press, 2002.

Furuichi, Takeshi, and Chie Hashimoto. "Why Female Bonobos Have a Lower Copulation Rate during Estrus Than Chimpanzees." pp. 156–167 in *Behavioural Diversity in Chimpanzees and Bonobos* (Christophe Boesch,

Gottfried Hohmann, and Linda Marchant, eds.). Cambridge, Cambridge University Press, 2002.

Gabunia, Leo, Susan Antón, David Lordkipanidze, Abesalom Vekua, Antje Justus, and Carl Swisher, III. "Dmanisi and Dispersal." *Evolutionary Anthropology,* 10:158–170, 2001.

Gagneux, P., D. Woodruff, and C. Boesch. "Furtive Mating in Female Chimpanzees." *Nature,* 387:358–359, 1997.

Galik, K., B. Senut, M. Pickford, D. Gommery, J. Treil, A. Kuperavage, and R. Eckhardt. "External and Internal Morphology of the BAR 1002'00 *Orrorin tugenensis* Femur." *Science,* 305:1450–1453, 2004.

Garant, Dany, Loeske Kruuk, Teddy Wilkin, Robin McCleery, and Ben Sheldon. "Evolution Driven by Differential Dispersal Within a Wild Bird Population." *Nature,* 433:60–65, 2005.

Gardner, R. Allen, and Beatrice Gardner. "Teaching Sign Language to a Chimpanzee." *Science,* 165:664–672, 1969.

Garn, Stanley. *Human Races,* 2nd ed. Springfield (IL), Charles C. Thomas, 1965.

Gebo, Daniel, Laura MacLatchy, Robert Kityo, Alan Deino, John Kingston, and David Pilbeam. "A Hominoid Genus from the Early Miocene of Uganda." *Science,* 276:401–404, 1997.

Gee, Henry. "Box of Bones 'Clinches' Identity of Piltdown Palaeontology Hoaxer." *Nature,* 381:261–262, 1996.

Gerloff, Ulrike, Bianka Hartung, Barbara Fruth, Gottfried Hohmann, and Diethard Tautz. "Intracommunity Relationships, Dispersal Pattern and Paternity Success in a Wild Living Community of Bonobos (*Pan paniscus*) Determined from DNA Analysis of Faecal Samples." *Proceedings of the Royal Society, London,* 266:1189–1195, 1999.

Gibbons, Ann. "Great Age Suggested for South African Hominids." *Science,* 300:562, 2003.

Gibbons, Ann. "In Search of the First Hominids." *Science,* 295:1214–1219, 2002.

Gibbons, Ann. "A New Face for Human Ancestors." *Science,* 276:1331–1333, 1997.

Gibbons, Ann. "Oldest Human Femur Wades into Controversy." *Science,* 305:1885, 2004.

Gibbons, Ann. "The Riddle of Coexistence." *Science,* 291:1725–1729, 2001.

Gibson, Greg, and Spencer Muse. *A Primer of Genome Science.* Sunderland (MA), Sinauer Associates, 2002.

Gibson, Kathleen. "Continuity Theories of Human Language Origins Versus the Lieberman Model." *Language and Communication,* 14:97–114, 1994.

Gilad, Yoav, Victor Wiebe, Molly Przeworski, Doron Lanccet, and Svante Pääbo. "Loss of Olfactory Receptor Genes Coincides with the Acquisition of Full Trichromatic Vision in Primates." *PloS Biology,* 2(1):120–125, 2004.

Gill, George. "Does Race Exist? A Proponent's Perspective." *Nova.* www.pbs.org/wgbh/nova/first/gill.html. 2000.

Goodall, Jane. *The Chimpanzees of Gombe: Patterns of Behavior.* Cambridge (MA), Belknap Press (Harvard), 1986.

Goodman, M. "Protein Sequence and Immunological Specificity: Their Role in Phylogenetic Studies of Primates." pp. 219–248 in *Phylogeny of the Primates: A Multidisciplinary Approach* (W. P. Luckett and F. S. Szalay, eds.). New York, Plenum, 1975.

Gore, Rick. "National Geographic Research and Exploration: New Find." *National Geographic,* 202(2):[preface]38–47, 2002.

Gore, Rick. "People Like Us." *National Geographic,* 198(July):91–117, 2000.

Goren-Inbar, Naama, Nira Alperson, Mordechai Kislev, Orit Simchoni, Yoel Melamed, Adi Ben-Nun, and Ella Werker. "Evidence of Hominin Control of Fire at Gesher Benot Ya'aqov, Israel." *Science,* 304:725–727, 2004.

Goss, Charles (ed.). *Gray's Anatomy,* 29th American ed. Philadelphia, Lea & Febiger, 1973.

Gould, Stephen Jay. *Full House.* New York, Harmony Books, 1996.

Gould, Stephen Jay. *The Mismeasure of Man.* New York, W. W. Norton, 1981.

Gould, Stephen Jay. *Time's Arrow Time's Cycle.* Cambridge (MA), Harvard University Press, 1987.

Gouzoules, Harold, Sarah Gouzoules, and Peter Marler. "Vocal Communication: A Vehicle for the Study of Social Relationships." pp. 112–129 in *The Cayo Santiago Macaques* (Richard Rawlins and Matt Kessler, eds.). Albany, State University of New York Press, 1986.

Gouzoules, Sarah, and Harold Gouzoules. "Kinship." pp. 299–305 in *Primate Societies* (Barbara Smuts, Dorothy Cheney, Robert Seyfarth, Richard Wrangham, and Thomas Struhsaker, eds.). Chicago, University of Chicago Press, 1987.

Gowlett, J. "Tools—The Palaeolithic Record." pp. 350–360 in *The Cambridge Encyclopedia of Human Evolution* (Steve Jones, Robert Martin, David Pilbeam, and Sarah Bunney, eds.). Cambridge, Cambridge University Press, 1992.

Graf, Werner, and Pierre-Paul Vidal. "Semicircular Canal Size and Upright Stance Are Not Interrelated." *Journal of Human Evolution,* 30:175–181, 1996.

Gray, J. Patrick. *Primate Sociobiology.* New Haven, HRAF Press, 1985.

Grayson, Donald. *The Establishment of Human Antiquity.* New York, Academic Press, 1983.

Greenfield, Leonard. "Origin of the Human Canine: A New Solution to an Old Enigma." *Yearbook of Physical Anthropology,* 35:153–185, 1992.

Greenfield, Patricia. "Language, Tools and Brain: The Ontogeny and Phylogeny of Hierarchically Organized Sequential Behavior." *Behavioral and Brain Sciences,* 14:531–595, 1991.

Grine, F. E. "Australopithecine Taxonomy and Phylogeny: Historical Background and Recent Interpretation." pp. 198–210 in *The Human Evolution Source Book* (Russell Ciochon and John Fleagle, eds.). Englewood Cliffs (NJ), Prentice Hall, 1993.

Grine, F. E., B. Demes, W. Jungers, and T. M. Cole, III. "Taxonomic Affinity of the Early *Homo* Cranium from Swartkrans, South Africa." *American Journal of Physical Anthropology,* 92:411–426, 1993.

Groves, C. *A Theory of Human and Primate Evolution.* New York, Clarendon Press, 1989.

Gursky, Sharon. "The Behavioral Ecology of the Spectral Tarsier, *Tarsius spectrum.*" *Evolutionary Anthropology,* 11:226–234, 2002.

Haeckel, Ernst. *Natürliche Schöpfungsgeschichte.* 2 vols. Berlin, Georg Reimer, 1868.

Haeusler, Martin, and Henry McHenry. "Body Proportions of *Homo habilis* Reviewed." *Journal of Human Evolution*, 46:433–465, 2004.

Haile-Selasssie, Yohannes. "Late Miocene Hominids from the Middle Awash, Ethiopia." *Nature*, 412:178–181, 2001.

Haile-Selassie, Yohannes, Gen Suwa, and Tim White. "Late Miocene Teeth from Middle Awash, Ethiopia, and Early Hominid Dental Evolution." *Science*, 303:1503–1505, 2004.

Hall, K. R. L., and Irven DeVore. "Baboon Social Behavior." pp. 53–110 in *Primate Behavior: Field Studies of Monkeys and Apes* (Irven DeVore, ed.). New York, Holt, Rinehart and Winston, 1965.

Hall, Roberta, Diana Roy, and David Boling. "Pleistocene Migration Routes into the Americas: Human Biological Adaptations and Environmental Constraints." *Evolutionary Anthropology*, 13:132–144, 2004.

Hamilton, W. D. "The Genetical Theory of Social Behaviour: I and II." *Journal of Theoretical Biology*, 7:1–52, 1964.

Hammer, M. "A Recent Common Ancestry for Human Y Chromosomes." *Nature*, 378:376–378, 1995.

Hammer, M., and S. Zegura. "The Role of the Y Chromosome in Human Evolutionary Studies." *Evolutionary Anthropology*, 5:116–134, 1996.

Haraway, Donna. *Primate Visions*. New York, Routledge, 1989.

Harris, John, and Meave Leakey. "The Faunal Context." pp. 54–60 in *The Nariokotome* Homo erectus *Skeleton* (Alan Walker and Richard Leakey, eds.). Cambridge (MA), Harvard University Press, 1993.

Harrison, G., J. Weiner, J. Tanner, and N. Barnicot. *Human Biology*, 2nd ed. Oxford, Oxford University Press, 1977.

Harrison, T. "Cladistic Concepts and the Species Problem in Hominoid Evolution." pp. 346–371 in *Species, Species Concepts, and Primate Evolution* (W. Kimbel and L. Martin, eds.). New York, Plenum, 1993.

Hartwig-Scherer, Sigrid. "Body Weight Prediction in Early Fossil Hominids: Towards a Taxon-'Independent' Approach." *American Journal of Physical Anthropology*, 92:17–36, 1993.

Harvey, Paul, R. D. Martin, and T. H. Clutton-Brock. "Life Histories in Comparative Perspective." pp. 181–196 in *Primate Societies* (Barbara Smuts, Dorothy Cheney, Robert Seyfarth, Richard Wrangham, and Thomas Struhsaker, eds.). Chicago, University of Chicago Press, 1987.

Hauser, Marc, Noam Chomsky, and W. T. Fitch. "The Faculty of Language: What Is It, Who Has It, and How Did It Evolve?" *Science*, 298:1569–1579, 2002.

Hausfater, Glenn. *Dominance and Reproduction in Baboons* (Papio cynocephalus). In *Contributions to Primatology*, vol. 7. Basel, S. Karger, 1975.

Heape, Walter. "The 'Sexual Season' of Mammals, and the Relation of the 'Pro-Oestrum' to Menstruation." *Quarterly Journal of Microscopical Science*, 44:1–70, 1900.

Henshilwood, Christopher, Francesco d'Errico, Curtis Marean, Richard Milo, and Royden Yates. "An Early Bone Tool Industry from the Middle Stone Age at Blombos Cave, South Africa: Implications for the Origins of Modern Human Behaviour, Symbolism and Language." *Journal of Human Evolution*, 41:631–678, 2001.

Henshilwood, Christopher, Francesco d'Errico, Marian Vanhaeren, Karen van Niekerk, and Zenobia Jacobs. "Middle Stone Age Shell Beads from South Africa." *Science*, 304:404, 2004.

Henshilwood, Christopher, Francesco d'Errico, Royden Yates, Zenobia Jacobs, Chantel Tribolo, Geoff Duller, Norbert Mercier, Judith Sealy, Helene Valladas, Ian Watts, and Ann Wintle. "Emergence of Modern Human Behavior: Middle Stone Age Engravings from South Africa." *Science*, 295:1278–1280, 2002.

Hill, Andrew, Steven Ward, and Barbara Brown. "Anatomy and Age of the Lothagam Mandible." *Journal of Human Evolution*, 22:439–451, 1992.

Hill, W. C. Osman. *Primates: Comparative Anatomy and Taxonomy. II. Haplorhini: Tarsioidea*. New York, Interscience Publishers, 1955.

Hohmann, Gottfried, and Barbara Fruth. "Dynamics in Social Organization of Bonobos (*Pan paniscus*)." pp. 138–150 in *Behavioural Diversity in Chimpanzees and Bonobos* (Christophe Boesch, Gottfried Hohmann, and Linda Marchant, eds.). Cambridge, Cambridge University Press, 2002.

Holden, Constance. "The Origin of Speech." *Science*, 303:1316–1319, 2004.

Holden, Constance. "Race and Medicine." *Science*, 302:594–596, 2003.

Holliday, Trenton. "Postcranial Evidence of Cold Adaptation in European Neandertals." *American Journal of Physical Anthropology*, 104:245–258, 1997.

Hooker, J., D. Russell, and A. Phélizon. "A New Family of Plesiadapiformes (Mammalia) from the Old World Lower Paleogene." *Palaeontology*, 42:377–407, 1999.

Hooton, Earnest. *Up from the Ape*. New York, Macmillan, 1946.

Howell, F. Clark. *Early Man*. New York, Time-Life Books, 1973.

Howell, F. Clark. "Overview of the Pliocene and Earlier Pleistocene of the Lower Omo Basin, Southern Ethiopia." pp. 227–268 in *Human Origins: Louis Leakey and the East African Evidence* (Glynn Isaac and Elizabeth McCown, eds.). Menlo Park (CA), W. A. Benjamin, Inc., 1976.

Howells, W. W. *Getting Here*. Washington, DC, The Compass Press, 1993.

Howells, W. W. "*Homo erectus*—Who, When and Where: A Survey." *Yearbook of Physical Anthropology*, 23:1–23, 1980.

Hrdy, Sarah Blaffer. *The Langurs of Abu*. Cambridge (MA), Harvard University Press, 1977.

Hrdy, Sarah Blaffer. *Mother Nature*. London, Chatto & Windus, 1999.

Hrdy, Sarah Blaffer, and Patricia Whitten. "Patterning of Sexual Activity." pp. 370–384 in *Primate Societies* (Barbara Smuts, Dorothy Cheney, Robert Seyfarth, Richard Wrangham, and Thomas Struhsaker, eds.). Chicago, University of Chicago Press, 1987.

Huang, Wanpo, R. Ciochon, Gu Yumin, R. Larick, Fang Qiren, Henry Schwarcz, Charles Yonge, John de Vos, and William Rink. "Early *Homo* and Associated Artefacts from Asia." *Nature*, 378:275–278, 1995.

Hublin, Jean-Jacques, Fred Spoor, Marc Braun, Frans Zonneveld, and Silvana Condemi. "A Late Neanderthal

Associated with Upper Palaeolithic Artefacts." *Nature,* 381:224–226, 1996.

Huffman, Michael, and Richard Wrangham. "Diversity of Medicinal Plant Use by Chimpanzees in the Wild." pp. 129–148 in *Chimpanzee Cultures* (Richard Wrangham, W. C. McGrew, Frans de Waal, and Paul Heltne, eds.). Cambridge (MA), Harvard University Press, 1994.

Hughes, A., and P. Tobias. "A Fossil Skull Probably of the Genus *Homo* from Sterkfontein, Transvaal." *Nature,* 265: 310–312, 1977.

Hunt, Kevin. "Ecological Morphology of *Australopithecus afarensis:* Traveling Terrestrially, Eating Arboreally." pp. 397–418 in *Primate Locomotion: Recent Advances* (E. Strasser, J. Fleagle, A. Rosenberger, and H. McHenry, eds.). New York, Plenum Press, 1998.

Hurford, James. "The Evolution of Language and Languages." pp. 173–193 in *The Evolution of Culture* (Robin Dunbar, Chris Knight, and Camilla Power, eds.). New Brunswick (NJ), Rutgers University Press, 1999.

Hutchings, W., and L. Brüchert. "Spearthrower Performance: Ethnographic and Experimental Research." *Antiquity,* 71:890–897, 1997.

Huxley, Thomas. *Man's Place in Nature and Other Anthropological Essays.* New York, Appleton, 1915.

IUCN, the World Conservation Union. "Red List of Threatened Species." www.redlist.org. 2004.

Ingman, Max, Henrik Kaessmann, Svante Pääbo, and Ulf Gyllensten. "Mitochondrial Genome Variation and the Origin of Modern Humans." *Nature,* 408:708–713, 2000.

Ingmanson, Ellen. "Tool-Using Behavior in Wild *Pan paniscus:* Social and Ecological Considerations." pp. 190–210 in *Reaching into Thought: The Minds of the Great Apes* (Anne Russon, Kim Bard, and Sue Taylor Parker, eds.). Cambridge, Cambridge University Press, 1996.

International Human Genome Sequencing Consortium. "Finishing the Euchromatic Sequence of the Human Genome." *Nature,* 431:931–945, 2004.

Isaac, G. L. "Aspects of Human Evolution." pp. 509–543 in *Evolution from Molecules to Men* (D. Bendall, ed.). New York, Cambridge University Press, 1983.

Isaac, G. L. "Traces of Pleistocene Hunters: An East African Example." pp. 253–261 in *Man the Hunter* (Richard Lee and Irven DeVore, eds.). Chicago, Aldine-Atherton, 1968.

Isbell, Lynne, and Truman Young. "The Evolution of Bipedalism in Hominids and Reduced Group Size in Chimpanzees: Alternative Responses to Decreasing Resource Availability." *Journal of Human Evolution,* 30:389–397, 1996.

Jablonski, Nina, and George Chaplin. "The Origin of Hominid Bipedalism Re-Examined." *Perspectives in Human Biology, 2/Archaeology in Oceania,* 27:113–119, 1992.

Jablonski, Nina, and George Chaplin. "Skin Deep." *Scientific American,* 287(4):74–81, 2002.

Jacobs, Gerald. "Variations in Primate Color Vision: Mechanisms and Utility." *Evolutionary Anthropology,* 3:196–205, 1994/95.

Jelinek, A. J. "The Lower Paleolithic: Current Evidence and Interpretations." *Annual Review of Anthropology,* 6:11–32, 1977.

Jellema, Lyman, Bruce Latimer, and Alan Walker. "The Rib Cage." pp. 294–325 in *The Nariokotome* Homo erectus *Skeleton* (Alan Walker and Richard Leakey, eds.). Cambridge (MA), Harvard University Press, 1993.

Jenkins, Jr., Everett. *The Creation.* Jefferson (NC), McFarland & Company, 2003.

Jerison, Harry J. *Evolution of the Brain and Intelligence.* New York, Academic Press, 1973.

Jia, Lanpo, and Weiwen Huang. *The Story of Peking Man: From Archaeology to Mystery.* Oxford, Oxford University Press, 1990.

Jobling, Mark, Matthew Hurles, and Chris Tyler-Smith. *Human Evolutionary Genetics: Origins, Peoples & Disease.* New York, Garland, 2004.

Johanson, Donald, and Maitland Edey. *Lucy: The Beginnings of Humankind.* New York, Simon & Schuster, 1981.

Johanson, Donald, and Blake Edgar. *From Lucy to Language.* New York, Simon & Schuster, 1996.

Johanson, Donald, and James Shreeve. *Lucy's Child: The Discovery of a Human Ancestor.* New York, William Morrow and Company, 1989.

Johanson, Donald, and T. White. "A Systematic Assessment of Early African Hominids." *Science,* 203:321–330, 1979.

Johanson, Donald, T. White, and Y. Coppens. "A New Species of the Genus *Australopithecus* (Primates: Hominidae) from the Pliocene of Eastern Africa." *Kirtlandia,* 28:1–14, 1978.

Jolly, Alison. *The Evolution of Primate Behavior,* 2nd ed. New York, Macmillan, 1985.

Jolly, Clifford. "A Proper Study for Mankind: Analogies from the Papionin Monkeys and Their Implications for Human Evolution." *Yearbook of Physical Anthropology,* 44:177–204, 2001.

Jolly, Clifford. "The Seed-Eaters: A New Model of Hominid Differentiation Based on a Baboon Analogy." *Man,* 5(1):5–26, 1970.

Jones, F. Wood. *Arboreal Man.* London, Edward Arnold, 1916.

Jones, Richard. *Human Reproductive Biology.* San Diego, Academic Press, 1991.

Jones, Steve. "The Evolutionary Future of Humankind." pp. 439–445 in *The Cambridge Encyclopedia of Human Evolution* (S. Jones, R. Martin, D. Pilbeam, and S. Bunney, eds.). Cambridge, Cambridge University Press, 1992.

Jungers, William, and Randall Susman. "Body Size and Skeletal Allometry in African Apes." pp. 131–177 in *The Pygmy Chimpanzee* (Randall Susman, ed.). New York, Plenum Press, 1984.

Jurmain, Robert, Harry Nelson, Lynn Kilgore, and Wenda Trevathan. *Introduction to Physical Anthropology,* 7th ed. New York, West/Wadsworth, 1997.

Kano, Takayoshi. "Male Rank Order and Copulation Rate in a Unit-group of Bonobos at Wamba, Zaïre." pp. 135–145 in *Great Ape Societies* (W. C. McGrew, L. Marchant, and T. Nishida, eds.). Cambridge, Cambridge University Press, 1996.

Kappleman, John. "The Attraction of Paleomagnetism." *Evolutionary Anthropology,* 2:89–99, 1993.

Kappelman, John. "The Evolution of Body Mass and Relative Brain Size in Fossil Hominids." *Journal of Human Evolution,* 30:243–276, 1996.

Kappelman, John, Carl Swisher III, John Fleagle, Solomon Yirga, Thomas Bown, and Muligeta Feseha. "Age of *Australopithecus afarensis* from Fejej, Ethiopia." *Journal of Human Evolution,* 30:139–146, 1996.

Kawai, M. "Newly Acquired Pre-Cultural Behavior of the Natural Troop of Japanese Monkeys on Koshima Islet." *Primates,* 6:1–30, 1965.

Kay, Richard, Matt Cartmill, and Michelle Balow. "The Hypoglossal Canal and the Origin of Human Vocal Behavior." *Proceedings of the National Academy of Sciences,* 95:5417–5419, 1998.

Kay, Richard, Callum Ross, and Blythe Williams. "Anthropoid Origins." *Science,* 275:797–804, 1997.

Ke, Y. B. Su, X. Song, D. Lu, L. Chen, H. Li, C. Qi, S. Marzuki, R. Deka, P. Underhill, C. Xiao, M. Shriver, J. Lell, D. Wallace, R. Wells, M. Seielstad, P. Oefner, D. Zhu, J. Jin, W. Huang, R. Chakraborty, Z. Chen, and L. Jin. "African Origin of Modern Humans in East Asia: A Tale of 12,000 Y Chromosomes." *Science,* 292:1151–1153, 2001.

Kehoe, Alice. "Modern Antievolutionism: The Scientific Creationists." pp. 165–185 in *What Darwin Began* (Laurie Godfrey, ed.). Boston, Allyn & Bacon, 1985.

Keith, Arthur. *The Antiquity of Man.* London, Williams and Norgate, 1920.

Keith, Arthur. *An Autobiography.* London, Watts and Company, 1950.

Keith, Arthur. "The Fossil Anthropoid Ape from Taungs." *Nature,* 115:234–235, 1925.

Keith, Arthur. *A New Theory of Human Evolution.* New York, Philosophical Library, 1949.

Kelley, Jay. "Evolution of Apes." pp. 223–230 in *The Cambridge Encyclopedia of Human Evolution* (Steve Jones, Robert Martin, David Pilbeam, and Sarah Bunney, eds.). Cambridge, Cambridge University Press, 1992.

Kelley, Jay. "Neanderthal Teeth Lined Up." *Nature,* 428:904–905, 2004.

Key, Catherine, and Leslie Aiello. "The Evolution of Social Organization." pp. 15–33 in *The Evolution of Culture* (Robin Dunbar, Chris Knight, and Camilla Power, eds.). New Brunswick (NJ), Rutgers University Press, 1999.

Kidd, R., P. O'Higgins, and C. Oxnard. "The OH8 Foot: A Reappraisal of the Functional Morphology of the Hindfoot Utilizing a Multivariate Analysis." *Journal of Human Evolution,* 31:269–291, 1996.

Kimbel, W., R. Walter, D. Johanson, K. Reed, J. Aronson, Z. Assefa, C. Marean, G. Eck, R. Bobe, E. Hovers, Y. Rak, C. Vondra, T. Yemane, D. York, Y. Chen, N. Evensen, and P. Smith. "Late Pliocene *Homo* and Oldowan Tools from the Hadar Formation (Kada Hadar Member), Ethiopia." *Journal of Human Evolution,* 31:549–561, 1996.

King, Mary-Claire, Joan Marks, and Jessica Mandell. "Breast and Ovarian Cancer Risks Due to Inherited Mutations in *BRCA1* and *BRCA2*." *Science,* 302:643–646, 2003.

Kingdon, Jonathan. *Lowly Origin.* Princeton, Princeton University Press, 2003.

Kirk, E. Christopher, Matt Cartmill, Richard Kay, and Pierre Lemelin. "Comment on 'Grasping Primate Origins.'" *Science,* 300:741, 2003.

Klein, Jan, and Naoyuki Takahata. *Where Do We Come From?* Berlin, Springer-Verlag, 2002.

Klein, Richard. "Archaeology and the Evolution of Human Behavior." *Evolutionary Anthropology,* 9:17–36, 2000.

Klein, Richard. *The Human Career.* Chicago, University of Chicago Press, 1989.

Klein, Richard. *The Human Career,* 2nd ed. Chicago, University of Chicago Press, 1999.

Klein, Richard, and Blake Edgar. *The Dawn of Human Culture.* New York, John Wiley and Sons, 2002.

Köhler, Wolfgang. *The Mentality of Apes.* London, Routledge & Kegan Paul Limited, 1927.

Kolata, Gina. "Frequency of AIDS Resistant Gene and Progress of Black Plague from 1347 to 1352." *New York Times,* May 26, 1998.

Kolata, Gina. "Mutant-Gene Study Alters Estimate of Risk to Women." *New York Times,* May 15–16, 1997.

Kordos, László, and David Begun. "Rudabánya: A Late Miocene Subtropical Swamp Deposit with Evidence of the Origin of the African Apes and Humans." *Evolutionary Anthropology,* 11:45–57, 2002.

Krings, Matthias, Anne Stone, Ralf Schmitz, Heike Krainitzki, Mark Stoneking, and Svante Pääbo. "Neandertal DNA Sequences and the Origin of Modern Humans." *Cell,* 90:19–30, 1997.

Krings, Matthias, Cristian Capelli, Frank Tschentscher, Helga Geisert, Sonja Meyer, Arndt von Haeseler, Karl Grossschmidt, Göran Possnert, Maja Paunovic, and Svante Pääbo. "A View of Neandertal Genetic Diversity." *Nature Genetics,* 26:144–146, 2000.

Kullmer, Ottmar, Oliver Sandrock, Rainer Abel, Friedemann Schrenk, Timothy Bromage, and Yusuf Juwayey. "The First *Paranthropus* from the Malawi Rift." *Journal of Human Evolution,* 37:121–127, 1999.

Kuman, Kathleen, and R. J. Clarke. "Stratigraphy, Artefact Industries and Hominid Associations for Sterkfontein, Member 5." *Journal of Human Evolution,* 38:827–847, 2000.

Kummer, Hans. *In Quest of the Sacred Baboon.* Princeton, Princeton University Press, 1995.

Kunzig, Robert. "Learning to Love Neanderthals." *Discover,* 20(8):66–75, 1999.

Kurland, Jeffrey. *Kin Selection in the Japanese Monkey.* In *Contributions to Primatology,* vol. 12. Basel, S. Karger, 1977.

Lahdenperä, Mirkka, Virpi Lummaa, Samuli Helle, Marc Tremblay, and Andrew Russell. "Fitness Benefits of Prolonged Post-Reproductive Lifespan in Women." *Nature,* 428:178–181, 2004.

Lahr, Marta Mirazón. "The Multiregional Model of Modern Human Origins: A Reassessment of Its Morphological Basis." *Journal of Human Evolution,* 26:23–56, 1994.

Lahr, Marta Mirazón, and Robert Foley. "Human Evolution Writ Small." *Nature,* 431:1043–1044, 2004.

Laitman, Jeffrey, and Raymond Heimbuch. "The Basicranium of Plio-Pleistocene Hominids as an Indicator of Their Upper Respiratory Systems." *American Journal of Physical Anthropology,* 59:323–343, 1982.

Laitman, Jeffrey, Raymond Heimbuch, and Edmund Crelin. "The Basicranium of Fossil Hominids as an Indicator of Their Upper Respiratory Systems." *American Journal of Physical Anthropology,* 51:15–34, 1979.

Lamarck, J. B. *Zoological Philosophy (Philosophie Zoologique).* Chicago, University of Chicago Press, 1984. (First published in 1809.)

Landau, Misia. *Narratives of Human Evolution.* New Haven, Yale University Press, 1991.

Larick, Roy, and Russell Ciochon. "The African Emergence and Early Asian Dispersals of the Genus *Homo.*" *American Scientist,* 84:538–551, 1996.

Larson, Edward. *Evolution.* New York, Modern Library, 2004.

Leakey, L. S. B. "A New Fossil Skull from Olduvai." *Nature,* 184:491–493, 1959.

Leakey, L. S. B. *White African.* Cambridge (MA), Schenkman Publishing Company, 1966.

Leakey, L. S. B., P. Tobias, and J. Napier. "A New Species of the Genus *Homo* from Olduvai Gorge." *Nature,* 202:7–9, 1964.

Leakey, Mary. *Olduvai Gorge: Volume 3: Excavations in Beds I and II, 1960–1963.* Cambridge, Cambridge University Press, 1971.

Leakey, Meave, and Alan Walker. "Early Hominid Fossils from Africa." *Scientific American,* 276:74–79, 1997.

Leakey, Meave, Craig Feibel, Ian McDougall, and Alan Walker. "New Four-Million-Year-Old Hominid Species from Kanapoi and Allia Bay, Kenya." *Nature,* 376:565–571, 1995.

Leakey, Meave, Craig Feibel, Ian McDougall, Carol Ward, and Alan Walker. "New Specimens and Confirmation of an Early Age for *Australopithecus anamensis.*" *Nature,* 393:62–66, 1998.

Leakey, Meave, Fred Spoor, Frank Brown, Patrick Gathogo, Christopher Kiarie, Louise Leakey, and Ian McDougall. "New Hominin Genus from Eastern Africa Shows Diverse Middle Pliocene Lineages." *Nature,* 410:433–440, 2001.

Lebel, Serge, and Erik Trinkaus. "Middle Pleistocene Human Remains from the Bau de l'Aubesier." *Journal of Human Evolution,* 43:659–685, 2002.

Le Gros Clark, W. E. *The Antecedents of Man.* Edinburgh, Edinburgh University Press, 1959.

Le Gros Clark, W. E. *The Fossil Evidence for Human Evolution.* Chicago, University of Chicago Press, 1955.

Le Gros Clark, W. E. *Man-Apes or Ape-Men?* New York, Holt, Rinehart and Winston, 1967.

Leighton, Donna. "Gibbons: Territoriality and Monogamy." pp. 135–145 in *Primate Societies* (Barbara Smuts, Dorothy Cheney, Robert Seyfarth, Richard Wrangham, and Thomas Struhsaker, eds.). Chicago, University of Chicago Press, 1987.

Lemonick, Michael, and Andrea Dorfman. "Father of Us All?" *Time,* 160(4):40–47, 2002.

Leonard, Jennifer, Robert Wayne, Jane Wheeler, Raúl Valadez, Sonia Guillén, and Carles Vilá. "Ancient DNA Evidence for Old World Origin of New World Dogs." *Science,* 298:1613–1616, 2002.

Leonard, William, and Marcia Robertson. "Locomotor Economy and the Origin of Bipedality: Reply to Steudel-Numbers." *American Journal of Physical Anthropology,* 116:174–176, 2001.

Leroi-Gourhan, André. *Treasures of Prehistoric Art.* New York, Abrams, 1965.

Levine, Joseph, and David Suzuki. *The Secret of Life.* Boston, WGBH Educational Foundation, 1993.

Lewin, Roger. *Bones of Contention.* New York, Simon & Schuster, 1987.

Lewin, Roger. *Human Evolution: An Illustrated Introduction,* 3rd ed. Cambridge (MA), Blackwell Scientific, 1993.

Lewin, Roger, and Robert Foley. *Principles of Human Evolution,* 2nd ed. Malden (MA), Blackwell Publishing, 2004.

Lewis-Williams, J. *The Rock Art of Southern Africa.* Cambridge, Cambridge University Press, 1983.

Lewontin, R. "The Apportionment of Human Diversity." *Evolutionary Biology,* 6:381–398, 1972.

Li, Tianyuan, and Dennis Etler. "New Middle Pleistocene Hominid Crania from Yunxian in China." *Nature,* 357:404–407, 1992.

Lieberman, Daniel. "Sphenoid Shortening and the Evolution of Modern Human Cranial Shape." *Nature,* 393:158–162, 1998.

Lieberman, Daniel, Brandeis McBratney, and Gail Krovitz. "The Evolution and Development of Cranial Form in *Homo sapiens.*" *Proceedings of the National Academy of Sciences,* 99:1134–1139, 2002.

Lieberman, Daniel, and Robert McCarthy. "The Ontogeny of Cranial Base Angulation in Humans and Chimpanzees and Its Implications for Reconstructing Pharyngeal Dimensions." *Journal of Human Evolution,* 36:487–517, 1999.

Lieberman, Philip. "Human Speech and Language." pp. 134–137 in *The Cambridge Encyclopedia of Human Evolution* (Steve Jones, Robert Martin, David Pilbeam, and Sarah Bunney, eds.). Cambridge, Cambridge University Press, 1992.

Lieberman, Philip. "On the Nature and Evolution of the Neural Bases of Human Language." *Yearbook of Physical Anthropology,* 45:36–62, 2002.

Lindburg, D. G. "The Rhesus Monkey in North India: An Ecological and Behavioral Study." pp. 1–106 in *Primate Behavior: Developments in Field and Laboratory Research,* vol. 2 (Leonard Rosenblum, ed.). New York, Academic Press, 1971.

Littlefield, A., L. Lieberman, and L. Reynolds. "Redefining Race: The Potential Demise of a Concept in Physical Anthropology." *Current Anthropology,* 23:641–655, 1982.

Losos, J. K., K. Warheitt, and T. Schoener. "Adaptive Differentiation Following Experimental Island Colonization in *Anolis* Lizards." *Nature,* 387:70–73, 1997.

Lovejoy, C. O. "Evolution of Human Walking." *Scientific American,* 259:118–125, 1988.

Lovejoy, C. O. "Modeling Human Origins: Are We Sexy Because We're Smart, or Smart Because We're Sexy?" pp. 1–28 in *The Origin and Evolution of Humans and Humanness* (D. Tab Rasmussen, ed.). Boston, Jones and Bartlett, 1993.

Lovejoy, C. O. "The Origin of Man." *Science,* 211:341–350, 1981.

Lovejoy, C. Owen, Kingsbury Heiple, and Richard Meindl. "Did Our Ancestors Knuckle-Walk?" *Nature,* 410:325–326, 2001.

Loy, James. "Estrous Behavior of Free-Ranging Rhesus Monkeys (*Macaca mulatta*)." *Primates,* 12(1):1–31, 1971.

Loy, James. "The Sexual Behavior of African Monkeys and the Question of Estrus." pp. 175–195 in *Comparative*

Behavior of African Monkeys (Evan Zucker, ed.). New York, Alan R. Liss, 1987.

Loy, James, and Calvin Peters. "Mortifying Reflections: Primatology and the Human Disciplines." pp. 3–16 in *Understanding Behavior* (James Loy and Calvin Peters, eds.). New York, Oxford University Press, 1991.

Ludwig, Kenneth, and Paul Renne. "Geochronology on the Paleoanthropological Time Scale." *Evolutionary Anthropology*, 9:101–110, 2000.

MacLarnon, Ann. "The Vertebral Canal." pp. 359–390 in *The Nariokotome* Homo erectus *Skeleton* (Alan Walker and Richard Leakey, eds.). Cambridge (MA), Harvard University Press, 1993.

MacLarnon, Ann, and Gwen Hewitt. "The Evolution of Human Speech: The Role of Enhanced Breathing Control." *American Journal of Physical Anthropology*, 109:341–363, 1999.

MacLarnon, Ann, and Gwen Hewitt. "Increased Breathing Control: Another Factor in the Evolution of Human Language." *Evolutionary Anthropology*, 13:181–197, 2004.

MacLatchy, Laura. "The Oldest Ape." *Evolutionary Anthropology*, 13:90–103, 2004.

Maddox, Brenda. "The Double Helix and the 'Wronged Heroine.'" *Nature*, 421:407–408, 2003.

Makalowski, Wojciech. "Not Junk After All." *Science*, 300:1246–1247, 2003.

Mallegni, Francesco, Emiliano Carnieri, Michelangelo Bisconti, Giandonato Tartarelli, Stefano Ricci, Italo Biddittu, and Aldo Segre. "*Homo cepranensis sp. nov.* and the Evolution of African-European Middle Pleistocene Hominids." *C. R. Palevol* 2:153–159, 2003.

Malthus, Thomas. *An Essay on the Principle of Population*. Oxford, Oxford University Press, 1993. (First published in 1798.)

Manzi, Giorgio. "Human Evolution at the Matuyama-Brunhes Boundary." *Evolutionary Anthropology*, 13:11–24, 2004.

Marean, Curtis, and Zalalem Assefa. "Zooarcheological Evidence for the Faunal Exploitation Behavior of Neandertals and Early Modern Humans." *Evolutionary Anthropology*, 8:22–37, 1999.

Marean, Curtis, and Soo Yeun Kim. "Mousterian Large-Mammal Remains from Kobeh Cave." *Current Anthropology*, 39(Supplement):S79-S113, 1998.

Marshack, Alexander. *The Roots of Civilization*. Mount Kisco (NY), Moyer Bell Limited, 1991.

Martin, Robert A. *Missing Links*. Boston, Jones and Bartlett, 2004.

Martin, Robert D. "Chinese Lantern for Early Primates." *Nature*, 427:22–23, 2004.

Martin, Robert D. "Combing the Primate Record." *Nature*, 422:388–391, 2003.

Martin, Robert D. *Primate Origins and Evolution*. Princeton, Princeton University Press, 1990.

Martínez-Navarro, Bienvenido. "The Skull of Orce: Parietal Bones or Frontal Bones?" *Journal of Human Evolution*, 43:265–270, 2002.

Mayr, Ernst. *The Growth of Biological Thought: Diversity, Evolution, and Inheritance*. Cambridge (MA), Harvard University Press, 1982.

Mayr, Ernst. *One Long Argument*. Cambridge (MA), Harvard University Press, 1991.

Mayr, Ernst. "What Is a Species, and What Is Not?" *Philosophy of Science*, 63:262–277, 1996.

McCrossin, M. L. "New Postcranial Remains of *Kenyapithecus* and Their Implications for Understanding the Origins of Hominoid Terrestriality." Abstract published in *American Journal of Physical Anthropology*, 102(Supplement)24:164, 1997.

McDougall, Ian, Francis Brown, and John Fleagle. "Stratigraphic Placement and Age of Modern Humans from Kibish, Ethiopia." *Nature*, 433:733–736, 2005.

McGrew, W. C. *Chimpanzee Material Culture*. Cambridge, Cambridge University Press, 1992.

McHenry, Henry. "Introduction to the Fossil Record of Human Ancestry." pp. 401–405 in *The Primate Fossil Record* (Walter Hartwig, ed.). Cambridge, Cambridge University Press, 2002.

McHenry, Henry, and Lee Berger. "Body Proportions in *Australopithecus afarensis* and *A. africanus* and the Origin of the Genus *Homo*." *Journal of Human Evolution*, 35:1–22, 1998.

Melnick, Don, and Mary Pearl. "Cercopithecines in Multimale Groups: Genetic Diversity and Population Structure." pp. 121–134 in *Primate Societies* (Barbara Smuts, Dorothy Cheney, Robert Seyfarth, Richard Wrangham, and Thomas Struhsaker, eds.). Chicago, University of Chicago Press, 1987.

Meltzer, David. "Monte Verde and the Pleistocene Peopling of the Americas." *Science*, 276:754–755, 1997.

Meltzer, David. "Pleistocene Peopling of the Americas." *Evolutionary Anthropology*, 1:157–169, 1993.

Mietto, Paolo, Marco Avanzini, and Giuseppe Rolandi. "Human Footprints in Pleistocene Volcanic Ash." *Nature*, 422:133, 2003.

Mitani, John, David Watts, and Martin Muller. "Recent Developments in the Study of Wild Chimpanzee Behavior." *Evolutionary Anthropology*, 11:9–25, 2002.

Mithen, Steven. *The Prehistory of the Mind*. London, Thames and Hudson, 1996.

Mittermeier, Russell, and Dorothy Cheney. "Conservation of Primates and Their Habitats." pp. 477–490 in *Primate Societies* (Barbara Smuts, Dorothy Cheney, Robert Seyfarth, Richard Wrangham, and Thomas Struhsaker, eds.). Chicago, University of Chicago Press, 1987.

Molnar, Stephen. *Human Variation*, 5th ed. Upper Saddle River (NJ), Prentice Hall, 2002.

Montagu, Ashley. *Man's Most Dangerous Myth: The Fallacy of Race*. New York, Columbia University Press, 1945.

Moore, A., G. Hillman, and A. Legge. *Village on the Euphrates*. New York, Oxford University Press, 2000.

Morris, Simon Conway. *Life's Solution*. Cambridge, Cambridge University Press, 2003.

Morwood, M., P. O'Sullivan, F. Aziz, and A. Raza. "Fission-Track Ages of Stone Tools and Fossils on the East Indonesian Island of Flores." *Nature*, 392:173–176, 1998.

Morwood, M., R. Soejono, R. Roberts, T. Sutikna, C. Turney, K. Westaway, W. Rink, J.-X. Zhao, G. van den Bergh, R. Awe Due, D. Hobbs, M. Moore, M. Bird, and L. Fifield. "Archaeology and Age of a New Hominin from

Flores in Eastern Indonesia." *Nature,* 431:1087–1091, 2004.

Moyà-Solà, Salvador, and Meike Köhler. "A *Dryopithecus* Skeleton and the Origins of Great-Ape Locomotion." *Nature,* 379:156–159, 1996.

Moyà-Solà, Salvador, and Meike Köhler. "The Orce Skull: Anatomy of a Mistake." *Journal of Human Evolution,* 33:91–97, 1997.

Moyà-Solà, Salvador, Meike Köhler, David Alba, Isaac Casanovas-Vilar, and Jordi Galindo. "*Pierolapithecus catalaunicus,* a New Middle Miocene Great Ape from Spain." *Science,* 306:1339–1344, 2004.

Mundil, Roland, Kenneth Ludwig, Ian Metcalfe, and Paul Renne. "Age and Timing of the Permian Mass Extinctions: U/Pb Dating of Closed-System Zircons." *Science,* 305:1760–1763, 2004.

Nakatsukasa, Masato, Hiroshi Tsujikawa, Daisuke Shimizu, Tomo Takano, Yutaka Kunimatsu, Yoshihiko Nakano, and Hidemi Ishida. "Definitive Evidence for Tail Loss in *Nacholapithecus,* an East African Miocene Hominoid." *Journal of Human Evolution,* 45:179–186, 2003.

Napier, John R. *The Roots of Mankind.* Washington, DC, Smithsonian Institution Press, 1970.

Napier, John R., and Prue H. Napier. *A Handbook of Living Primates.* London, Academic Press, 1967.

Napier, John R., and Prue H. Napier. *The Natural History of the Primates.* Cambridge (MA), MIT Press, 1985.

Navarro, Arcadi, and Nick Barton. "Chromosomal Speciation and Molecular Divergence—Accelerated Evolution in Rearranged Chromosomes." *Science,* 300:321–324, 2003.

Neisser, Ulric, Gwyneth Boodoo, Thomas Bouchard, Jr., A. Wade Boykin, Nathan Brody, Stephen Ceci, Diane Halpern, John Loehlin, Robert Perloff, Robert Sternberg, and Susana Urbina. "Intelligence: Knowns and Unknowns." *American Psychologist,* 51(2):77–101, 1996.

Neves, Walter, Joseph Powell, and Erik Ozolins. "Modern Human Origins as Seen from the Peripheries." *Journal of Human Evolution,* 37:129–133, 1999.

Ni, Xijun, Yuanqing Wang, Yaoming Hu, and Chuankui Li. "A Euprimate Skull from the Early Eocene of China." *Nature,* 427:65–68, 2004.

Nicolson, Nancy. "Maternal Behavior in Human and Nonhuman Primates." pp. 17–50 in *Understanding Behavior* (James Loy and Calvin Peters, eds.). New York, Oxford University Press, 1991.

Nishida, Toshisada. *The Chimpanzees of the Mahale Mountains.* Tokyo, University of Tokyo Press, 1990.

Nishida, Toshisada, and Mariko Hiraiwa-Hasegawa. "Chimpanzees and Bonobos: Cooperative Relationships among Males." pp. 165–177 in *Primate Societies* (Barbara Smuts, Dorothy Cheney, Robert Seyfarth, Richard Wrangham, and Thomas Struhsaker, eds.). Chicago, University of Chicago Press, 1987.

Nordborg, Magnus. "Opinion: Were Neanderthals and Anatomically Modern Humans Different Species?" p. 264 in *Human Evolutionary Genetics: Origins, Peoples and Disease* (M. Jobling, M. Hurles, and C. Tyler-Smith, eds.). New York, Garland, 2004.

Numbers, Ronald. *The Creationists.* New York, Knopf, 1992.

O'Connell, James, and Jim Allen. "When Did Humans First Arrive in Greater Australia and Why Is It Important to Know?" *Evolutionary Anthropology,* 6:132–146, 1998.

Orel, Vítzslav. *Gregor Mendel: The First Geneticist.* Oxford, Oxford University Press, 1996.

Osborn, H. F. *Men of the Old Stone Age.* New York, Scribner's, 1916.

Otte, Marcel. "On the Suggested Bone Flute from Slovenia." *Current Anthropology,* 41(2):271–272, 2000.

Ovchinnikov, Igor, Anders Götherström, Galina Romanova, Vitaliy Kharitonov, Kerstin Lidén, and William Goodwin. "Molecular Analysis of Neanderthal DNA from the Northern Caucasus." *Nature,* 404:490–493, 2000.

Pääbo, Svante. "The Mosaic That Is Our Genome." *Nature,* 421:409–412, 2003.

Packer, Craig, D. Collins, A. Sindimwo, and J. Goodall. "Reproductive Constraints on Aggressive Competition in Female Baboons." *Nature,* 373:60–63, 1995.

Palmqvist, Paul. "A Critical Re-Evaluation of the Evidence for the Presence of Hominids in Lower Pleistocene Times at Venta Micena, Southern Spain." *Journal of Human Evolution,* 33:83–89, 1997.

Palombit, Ryne. "Dynamic Pair Bonds in Hylobatids: Implications Regarding Monogamous Social Systems." *Behaviour,* 128(1–2):65–101, 1994.

Panger, Melissa, Alison Brooks, Brian Richmond, and Bernard Wood. "Older Than the Oldowan? Rethinking the Emergence of Hominin Tool Use." *Evolutionary Anthropology,* 11:235–245, 2002.

Parish, Amy. "Female Relationships in Bonobos (*Pan paniscus*)." *Human Nature,* 7:61–96, 1996.

Parish, Amy. "Sex and Food Control in the `Uncommon Chimpanzee': How Bonobo Females Overcame a Phylogenetic Legacy of Male Dominance." *Ethology and Sociobiology,* 15:157–179, 1994.

Partridge, T., D. Granger, M. Caffee, and R. Clarke. "Lower Pliocene Hominid Remains from Sterkfontein." *Science,* 300:607–612, 2003.

Pearson, Osbjorn. "Has the Combination of Genetic and Fossil Evidence Solved the Riddle of Modern Human Origins?" *Evolutionary Anthropology,* 13:145–159, 2004.

Pennisi, Elizabeth. "The First Language?" *Science,* 303:1319–1320, 2004.

Pilbeam, David. "Fossils as Dating Indicators." p. 184 in *The Cambridge Encyclopedia of Human Evolution* (S. Jones, R. Martin, D. Pilbeam, and S. Bunney, eds.). Cambridge, Cambridge University Press, 1992.

Pilbeam, David. "Genetic and Morphological Records of the Hominoidea and Hominid Origins: A Synthesis." *Molecular Phylogenetics and Evolution,* 5:155–168, 1996.

Pilbeam, David. *The Ascent of Man.* New York, Macmillan, 1972.

Pinker, Steven. *The Blank Slate.* New York, Viking, 2002.

Pitts, Michael, and Mark Roberts. *Fairweather Eden.* New York, Fromm International, 1998.

Pitulko, V., P. Nikolsky, E. Girya, A. Basilyan, V. Tumskoy, S. Koulakov, S. Astakhov, E. Pavlova, and M. Anisimov. "The Yana RHS Site: Humans in the Arctic Before the Last Glacial Maximum." *Science,* 303:52–56, 2004.

Plavcan, J. Michael, and Jay Kelley. "Evaluating the 'Dual Selection' Hypothesis of Canine Reduction." *American Journal of Physical Anthropology*, 99:379–387, 1996.

Pope, Geoffrey. "Ancient Asia's Cutting Edge." *Natural History*, 102(5):54–59, 1993.

Pope, Geoffrey. "Bamboo and Human Evolution." *Natural History*, 98(10):48–57, 1989.

Population Reference Bureau. www.prb.org.

Potts, Richard. "Archeological Interpretations of Early Hominid Behavior and Ecology." pp. 49–74 in *The Origin and Evolution of Humans and Humanness* (D. T. Rasmussen, ed.). Boston, Jones and Bartlett, 1993.

Potts, Richard. "Home Bases and Early Hominids." *American Scientist*, 72:338–347, 1984.

Potts, Richard. *Humanity's Descent*. New York, William Morrow, 1996.

Potts, Richard, Anna Behrensmeyer, Alan Deino, Peter Ditchfield, and Jennifer Clark. "Small Mid-Pleistocene Hominin Associated with East African Acheulean Technology." *Science*, 305:75–78, 2004.

Price, Peter. *Biological Evolution*. Fort Worth (TX), Saunders College Publishing, 1996.

Pusey, Ann, Jennifer Williams, and Jane Goodall. "The Influence of Dominance Rank on the Reproductive Success of Female Chimpanzees." *Science*, 277:828–831, 1997.

Raby, Peter. *Alfred Russel Wallace: A Life*. Princeton, Princeton University Press, 2001.

Rak, Y. "Australopithecine Taxonomy and Phylogeny in Light of Facial Morphology." *American Journal of Physical Anthropology*, 66:281–287, 1985.

Rasmussen, David Tab. "The Origin of Primates." pp. 5–9 in *The Primate Fossil Record* (Walter Hartwig, ed.). Cambridge, Cambridge University Press, 2002.

Rasmussen, David Tab, and Elwyn Simons. "Paleobiology of the Oligopithecines, the Earliest Known Anthropoid Primates." *International Journal of Primatology*, 13:477–508, 1992.

Raup, David. *Extinction: Bad Genes or Bad Luck?* New York, W. W. Norton, 1991.

Ravosa, Matthew, and Denitsa Savakova. "Euprimate Origins: The Eyes Have It." *Journal of Human Evolution*, 46:355–362, 2004.

Reader, John. *Missing Links: The Hunt for Earliest Man*. London, Penguin Books, 1988.

Reichard, Ulrich. "Extra-Pair Copulations in a Monogamous Gibbon (*Hylobates lar*)." *Ethology*, 100:99–112, 1995.

Relethford, John. "Ancient DNA and the Origin of Modern Humans." *Proceedings of the National Academy of Sciences*, 98:390–391, 2001.

Reno, Philip, Richard Meindl, Melanie McCollum, and C. Owen Lovejoy. "Sexual Dimorphism in *Australopithecus afarensis* Was Similar to That of Modern Humans." *Proceedings of the National Academy of Sciences*, 100:9404–9409, 2003.

Ribnick, Rosalind. "A Short History of Primate Field Studies: Old World Monkeys and Apes." pp. 49–73 in *A History of American Physical Anthropology* (Frank Spencer, ed.). New York, Academic Press, 1982.

Richard, Alison. *Primates in Nature*. New York, Freeman, 1985.

Richards, Michael, Paul Pettitt, Erik Trinkaus, Fred Smith, Maja Paunovic, and Ivor Karavanic. "Neanderthal Diet at Vindija and Neanderthal Predation: The Evidence from Stable Isotopes." *Proceedings of the National Academy of Sciences*, 97:7663–7666, 2000.

Richmond, Brian, David Begun, and David Strait. "Origin of Human Bipedalism: The Knuckle-Walking Hypothesis Revisited." *Yearbook of Physical Anthropology*, 44:70–105, 2001.

Richmond, Brian, and David Strait. "Evidence That Humans Evolved from a Knuckle-Walking Ancestor." *Nature*, 404:382–385, 2000.

Ridley, Mark. *Evolution*, 2nd ed. Cambridge (MA), Blackwell Science, 1996.

Rieseberg, Loren, and Kevin Livingstone. "Chromosomal Speciation in Primates." *Science*, 300:267–268, 2003.

Rightmire, G. P. "Brain Size and Encephalization in Early to Mid-Pleistocene *Homo*." *American Journal of Physical Anthropology*, 124:109–123, 2004.

Rightmire, G. P. *The Evolution of* Homo erectus. Cambridge, Cambridge University Press, 1990.

Rightmire, G. P. "*Homo erectus:* Ancestor or Evolutionary Side Branch?" *Evolutionary Anthropology*, 1:43–49, 1992.

Rightmire, G. P. "The Human Cranium from Bodo, Ethiopia: Evidence for Speciation in the Middle Pleistocene?" *Journal of Human Evolution*, 31:21–39, 1996.

Rightmire, G. P. "Human Evolution in the Middle Pleistocene: The Role of *Homo heidelbergensis*." *Evolutionary Anthropology*, 6:218–227, 1998.

Rilling, James, and Thomas Insel. "The Primate Neocortex in Comparative Perspective Using Magnetic Resonance Imaging." *Journal of Human Evolution*, 37:191–223, 1999.

Roberts, M., C. Stringer, and S. Parfitt. "A Hominid Tibia from Middle Pleistocene Sediments at Boxgrove, UK." *Nature*, 369:311–313, 1994.

Roberts, Richard, Timothy Flannery, Linda Ayliffe, Hiroyuki Yoshida, Jon Olley, Gavin Prideaux, Geoff Laslett, Alexander Baynes, M. Smith, Rhys Jones, and Barton Smith. "New Ages for the Last Australian Megafauna: Continent-Wide Extinction about 46,000 Years Ago." *Science*, 292:1888–1892, 2001.

Robins, A. *Biological Perspectives on Human Pigmentation*. New York, Cambridge University Press, 1991.

Robinson, Bryan. "Limbic Influences on Human Speech." pp. 761–771 in *Origins and Evolution of Language and Speech* (Stevan Harnad, Horst Steklis, and Jane Lancaster, eds.). New York, New York Academy of Sciences, 1976.

Robinson, John G., and Charles Janson. "Capuchins, Squirrel Monkeys, and Atelines: Socioecological Convergence with Old World Primates." pp. 69–82 in *Primate Societies* (Barbara Smuts, Dorothy Cheney, Robert Seyfarth, Richard Wrangham, and Thomas Struhsaker, eds.). Chicago, University of Chicago Press, 1987.

Robinson, John T. *Early Hominid Posture and Locomotion*. Chicago, University of Chicago Press, 1972.

Rodman, Peter, and Henry McHenry. "Bioenergetics and the Origin of Hominid Bipedalism." *American Journal of Physical Anthropology*, 52:103–106, 1980.

Rodman, Peter, and John Mitani. "Orangutans: Sexual Dimorphism in a Solitary Species." pp. 146–154 in

Primate Societies (Barbara Smuts, Dorothy Cheney, Robert Seyfarth, Richard Wrangham, and Thomas Struhsaker, eds.). Chicago, University of Chicago Press, 1987.

Roebroeks, Wil. "Hominid Behaviour and the Earliest Occupation of Europe: An Exploration." *Journal of Human Evolution*, 41:437–461, 2001.

Rogers, L. J., and G. Kaplan. "A New Form of Tool Use by Orang-Utans in Sabah, East Malaysia." *Folia Primatologica*, 63:50–52, 1994.

Rollefson, Gary, and Ilse Köhler-Rollefson. "Early Neolithic Exploitation Patterns in the Levant: Cultural Impact on the Environment." *Population and Environment: A Journal of Interdisciplinary Studies*, 13(4):243–254, 1992.

Ron, Hagai, and Shaul Levi. "When Did Hominids First Leave Africa? New High-Resolution Magneto-stratigraphy from the Erk-el-Ahmar Formation, Israel." *Geology*, 29:887–890, 2001.

Roosevelt, A., M. Lima da Costa, C. Lopes Machado, M. Michab, N. Mercier, H. Valladas, J. Feathers, W. Barnett, M. Imazio da Silveira, A. Henderson, J. Silva, B. Chernoff, D. Reese, J. Holman, N. Toth, and K. Schick. "Paleoindian Cave Dwellers in the Amazon: The Peopling of the Americas." *Science*, 272:373–384, 1996.

Rose, Lisa, and Fiona Marshall. "Meat Eating, Hominid Sociality, and Home Bases Revisited." *Current Anthropology*, 37:307–338, 1996.

Rosenberg, Karen. "The Evolution of Modern Human Childbirth." *Yearbook of Physical Anthropology*, 35:89–124, 1992.

Rosenberg, Noah, Jonathan Pritchard, James Weber, Howard Cann, Kenneth Kidd, Lev Zhivotovsky, and Marcus Feldman. "Genetic Structure of Human Populations." *Science*, 298:2381–2385, 2002.

Ross, Callum, and Maciej Henneberg. "Basicranial Flexion, Relative Brain Size, and Facial Kyphosis in *Homo sapiens* and Some Fossil Hominids." *American Journal of Physical Anthropology*, 98:575–593, 1995.

Rozzi, Fernando, and José Bermudez de Castro. "Surprisingly Rapid Growth in Neanderthals." *Nature*, 428:936–939, 2004.

Ruff, Christopher, and Alan Walker. "Body Size and Body Shape." pp. 234–265 in *The Nariokotome* Homo erectus *Skeleton* (Alan Walker and Richard Leakey, eds.). Cambridge (MA), Harvard University Press, 1993.

Ruff, Christopher, Erik Trinkaus, and Trenton Holliday. "Body Mass and Encephalization in Pleistocene *Homo*." *Nature*, 387:173–176, 1997.

Rumbaugh, Duane, E. Sue Savage-Rumbaugh, and Rose Sevcik. "Biobehavioral Roots of Language." pp. 319–334 in *Chimpanzee Cultures* (Richard Wrangham, W. McGrew, Frans de Waal, and Paul Heltne, eds.). Cambridge (MA), Harvard University Press, 1994.

Sade, Donald Stone. "Determinants of Dominance in a Group of Free-Ranging Rhesus Monkeys." pp. 99–114 in *Social Communication among Primates* (Stuart Altmann, ed.). Chicago, University of Chicago Press, 1967.

Sade, Donald Stone. "Some Aspects of Parent-Offspring and Sibling Relations in a Group of Rhesus Monkeys, with a Discussion of Grooming." *American Journal of Physical Anthropology*, 23:1–18, 1965.

Sargis, Eric. "New Views on Tree Shrews: The Role of Tupaiids in Primate Supraordinal Relationships." *Evolutionary Anthropology*, 13:56–66, 2004.

Sargis, Eric. "Primate Origins Nailed." *Science*, 298:1564–1565, 2002.

Sarich, Vincent. "Immunological Evidence on Primates." pp. 303–306 in *The Cambridge Encyclopedia of Human Evolution* (Steve Jones, Robert Martin, David Pilbeam, and Sarah Bunney, eds.). Cambridge, Cambridge University Press, 1992.

Sarich, Vincent, and Allan Wilson. "Immunological Time Scale for Hominid Evolution." *Science*, 158:1200–1203, 1967a.

Sarich, Vincent, and Allan Wilson. "Rates of Albumin Evolution in Primates." *Proceedings of the National Academy of Sciences*, 58:142–148, 1967b.

Savage-Rumbaugh, Sue, and Roger Lewin. *Kanzi: The Ape at the Brink of the Human Mind*. New York, John Wiley and Sons, 1994.

Savage-Rumbaugh, Sue, Stuart Shanker, and Talbot Taylor. *Apes, Language, and the Human Mind*. New York, Oxford University Press, 1998.

Savolainen, Peter, Ya-ping Zhang, Jing Luo, Joakim Lundeberg, and Thomas Leitner. "Genetic Evidence for an East Asian Origin of Domestic Dogs." *Science*, 298:1610–1613, 2002.

Schick, Kathy, and Nicholas Toth. *Making Silent Stones Speak*. New York, Simon & Schuster, 1993.

Schultz, Adolph. *The Life of Primates*. New York, Universe Books, 1969.

Schultz, Adolph. "The Recent Hominoid Primates." pp. 122–195 in *Perspectives on Human Evolution* (S. L Washburn and P. C. Jay, eds.). New York, Holt, Rinehart and Winston, 1968.

Schwartz, Jeffrey. *Skeleton Keys*. New York, Oxford University Press, 1995.

Schwartz, Jeffrey, and Ian Tattersall. "The Human Chin Revisited: What Is It and Who Has It?" *Journal of Human Evolution*, 38:367–409, 2000.

Schwartz, Robert. "Racial Profiling in Medical Research." *New England Journal of Medicine*, 344:1392–1393, 2001.

Semaw, S., P. Renne, J. Harris, C. Feibel, R. Bernor, N. Fesseha, and K. Mowbray. "2.5-Million-Year-Old Stone Tools from Gona, Ethiopia." *Nature*, 385:333–336, 1997.

Semendeferi, Katerina, and Hanna Damasio. "The Brain and Its Main Anatomical Subdivisions in Living Hominoids Using Magnetic Resonance Imaging." *Journal of Human Evolution*, 38:317–332, 2000.

Semenov, S. *Prehistoric Technology*. New York, Barnes & Noble, 1964.

Senut, Brigitte, Martin Pickford, Dominique Gommery, Pierre Mein, Kiptalam Cheboi, and Yves Coppens. "First Hominid from the Miocene (Lukeino Formation, Kenya)." *Comptes Rendus de l'Académie des Sciences, Paris, Sciences de la Terre et des Planètes* 332:137–144, 2001.

Serendip. http://serendip.brynmawr.edu.

Seyfarth, Robert. "A Model of Social Grooming among Adult Female Monkeys." *Journal of Theoretical Biology*, 65:671–698, 1977.

Shanklin, Eugenia. *Anthropology and Race*. Belmont (CA), Wadsworth, 1994.

Shea, John. "Neandertal and Early Modern Human Behavioral Variability." *Current Anthropology*, 39(Supplement):S45—S78, 1998.

Shea, John. "Neandertals, Competition, and the Origin of Modern Human Behavior in the Levant." *Evolutionary Anthropology*, 12:173–187, 2003.

Shipman, Pat. "Early Hominid Lifestyle: Hunting and Gathering or Foraging and Scavenging?" pp. 31–49 in *Animals and Archaeology*, vol. 1 (J. Clutton-Brock and Caroline Grigson, eds.). Oxford, British Archaeological Association, 1983.

Shipman, Pat. *The Man Who Found the Missing Link*. New York, Simon & Schuster, 2001.

Shreeve, James. "Sunset on the Savanna." *Discover*, 17(7):116–125, 1996.

Sibley, C. G. "DNA-DNA Hybridization in the Study of Primate Evolution." pp. 313–315 in *The Cambridge Encyclopedia of Human Evolution* (Steve Jones, Robert Martin, David Pilbeam, and Sarah Bunney, eds.). Cambridge, Cambridge University Press, 1992.

Sickle Cell Disease. http://sickle.bwh.harvard.edu/menu_sickle.html.

Silcox, Mary. "New Discoveries on the Middle Ear Anatomy of *Ignacius graybullianus* (Paromomyidae, Primates) from Ultra High Resolution X-Ray Computed Tomography." *Journal of Human Evolution*, 44:73–86, 2003.

Silk, Joan, Susan Alberts, and Jeanne Altmann. "Social Bonds of Female Baboons Enhance Infant Survival." *Science*, 302:1231–1234, 2003.

Simons, Elwyn. *Primate Evolution*. New York, Macmillan, 1972.

Simons, Elwyn, "The Fossil History of Primates." pp. 199–208 in *The Cambridge Encyclopedia of Human Evolution*. (Steve Jones, Robert Martin, David Pilbeam, and Sarah Bunney, eds.). Cambridge, Cambridge University Press, 1992.

Simons, Elwyn, and David Tab Rasmussen. "Skull of *Catopithecus browni*, an Early Tertiary Catarrhine." *American Journal of Physical Anthropology*, 100:261–292, 1996.

Singer, Maxine, and Paul Berg. *Genes and Genomes: A Changing Perspective*. Mill Valley (CA), University Science Books, 1991.

Smail, J. Kenneth. "Remembering Malthus: A Preliminary Argument for a Significant Reduction in Global Human Numbers." *American Journal of Physical Anthropology*, 118:292–297, 2002.

Smail, J. Kenneth. "Remembering Malthus II: Establishing Sustainable Population Optimums." *American Journal of Physical Anthropology*, 122:287–294, 2003a.

Smail, J. Kenneth. "Remembering Malthus III: Implementing a Global Population Reduction." *American Journal of Physical Anthropology*, 122:295–300, 2003b.

Small, Meredith. *Female Choices*. Ithaca (NY), Cornell University Press, 1993.

Smith, Fred. "Migrations, Radiations and Continuity: Patterns in the Evolution of Middle and Late Pleistocene Humans." pp. 437–456 in *The Primate Fossil Record* (Walter Hartwig, ed.). Cambridge, Cambridge University Press, 2002.

Smith, G. Elliot. *The Evolution of Man*, 2nd ed. London, Oxford University Press, 1927.

Smith, G. Elliot. "The Fossil Anthropoid Ape from Taungs." *Nature*, 115:235, 1925.

Sober, Elliot, and David S. Wilson. *Unto Others: The Evolution and Psychology of Unselfish Behavior*. Cambridge (MA), Harvard University Press, 1998.

Solecki, Ralph. *Shanidar: The First Flower People*. New York, Knopf, 1971.

Snowdon, Charles. "From Primate Communication to Human Language." pp. 193–227 in *Tree of Origin* (Frans de Waal, ed.). Cambridge (MA), Harvard University Press, 2001.

Spencer, Frank. *Piltdown: A Scientific Forgery*. London, Natural History Museum Publications, 1990.

Sponheimer, Matt, and Julia Lee-Thorp. "Isotopic Evidence for the Diet of an Early Hominid, *Australopithecus africanus*." *Science*, 283:368–370, 1999.

Spoor, Fred, Bernard Wood, and Frans Zonneveld. "Implications of Early Hominid Labyrinthine Morphology for Evolution of Human Bipedal Locomotion." *Nature*, 369:645–648, 1994.

Stanford, Craig. *The Hunting Apes*. Princeton, Princeton University Press, 1999.

Stanford, Craig. "The Hunting Ecology of Wild Chimpanzees: Implications for the Evolutionary Ecology of Pliocene Hominids." *American Anthropologist*, 98(1):96–113, 1996.

Stanford, Craig. "The Social Behavior of Chimpanzees and Bonobos." *Current Anthropology*, 39:399–420, 1998.

Stanford, Craig, John Allen, and Susan Antón. *Biological Anthropology*. Upper Saddle River (NJ), Pearson Prentice Hall, 2006.

Stedman, Hansell, Benjamin Kozyak, Anthony Nelson, Danielle Thesier, Leonard Su, David Low, Charles Bridges, Joseph Shrager, Nancy Minugh-Purvis, and Marilyn Mitchell. "Myosin Gene Mutation Correlates with Anatomical Changes in the Human Lineage." *Nature*, 428:415–418, 2004.

Steklis, H. Dieter, and Netzin Gerald-Steklis. "Status of the Virunga Mountain Gorilla Population." pp. 391–412 in *Mountain Gorillas: Three Decades of Research at Karisoke* (Martha Robbins, Pascale Sicotte, and Kelly Stewart, eds.). Cambridge, Cambridge University Press, 2001.

Stephan, Heinz. "Evolution of Primate Brains: A Comparative Anatomical Investigation." pp. 155–174 in *The Functional and Evolutionary Biology of Primates* (Russell Tuttle, ed.). Chicago, Aldine-Atherton, 1972.

Stephens, J., D. Reich, D. Goldstein, H. Shin, M. Smith, M. Carrington, C. Winkler, G. Huttley, R. Allikmets, L. Schriml, B. Gerrard, M. Malasky, M. Ramos, S. Morlot, M. Tzetis, C. Oddoux, F. di Giovine, G. Nasioulas, D. Chandler, M. Aseev, M. Hanson, L. Kalaydjieva, D. Glavac, P. Gasparini, E. Kanavakis, M. Claustres, M. Kambouris, H. Ostrer, G. Duff, V. Barabov, H. Sibul, A. Metspalu, D. Goldman, N. Martin, D. Duffy, J. Schmidtke, X. Estivill, S. O'Brien, and M. Dean. "Dating the Origin of the CCR5-D32 AIDS-Resistance Allele by the Coalescence of Haplotypes." *American Journal of Human Genetics*, 62:1507–1515, 1998.

Stern, Jr., Jack. "Climbing to the Top: A Personal Memoir of *Australopithecus afarensis*." *Evolutionary Anthropology*, 9:113–133, 2000.

Stern, Jr., Jack, and Randall Susman. "The Locomotor Anatomy of *Australopithecus afarensis*." *American Journal of Physical Anthropology*, 60:279–317, 1983.

Steudel, Karen. "Limb Morphology, Bipedal Gait, and the Energetics of Hominid Locomotion." *American Journal of Physical Anthropology*, 99:345–355, 1996.

Steudel-Numbers, Karen. "Role of Locomotor Economy in the Origin of Bipedal Posture and Gait." *American Journal of Physical Anthropology*, 116:171–173, 2001.

Stewart, Ian. "Real Australopithecines Do Eat Meat." *New Scientist*, 134:17, 1992.

Stewart, Kelly, and Alexander Harcourt. "Gorillas: Variation in Female Relationships." pp. 155–164 in *Primate Societies* (Barbara Smuts, Dorothy Cheney, Robert Seyfarth, Richard Wrangham, and Thomas Struhsaker, eds.). Chicago, University of Chicago Press, 1987.

Stewart, Kelly, Pascale Sicotte, and Martha Robbins. "Mountain Gorillas of the Virungas: A Short History." pp. 1–26 in *Mountain Gorillas: Three Decades of Research at Karisoke* (Martha Robbins, Pascale Sicotte, and Kelly Stewart, eds.). Cambridge, Cambridge University Press, 2001.

Stocking, Jr., George. *Victorian Anthropology*. New York, Free Press, 1987.

Stoneking, Mark. "DNA and Recent Human Evolution." *Evolutionary Anthropology*, 2:60–73, 1993.

Straus, W. L., and A. J. E. Cave. "Pathology and Posture of Neandertal Man." *Quarterly Review of Biology*, 32:348–363, 1957.

Strickberger, Monroe. *Evolution*, 3rd. ed. Boston, Jones and Bartlett, 2000.

Stringer, Christopher. "A Metrical Study of the WLH-50 Calvaria." *Journal of Human Evolution*, 34:327–332, 1998.

Stringer, Christopher, and Clive Gamble. *In Search of the Neanderthals*. New York, Thames and Hudson, 1993.

Stringer, Christopher, J. J. Hublin, and B. Vandermeersch. "The Origin of Anatomically Modern Humans in Western Europe." pp. 51–135 in *The Origins of Modern Humans: A World Survey of the Fossil Evidence* (F. Smith and F. Spencer, eds.). New York, A. R. Liss, 1984.

Struhsaker, Thomas, and Lysa Leland. "Colobines: Infanticide by Adult Males." pp. 83–97 in *Primate Societies* (Barbara Smuts, Dorothy Cheney, Robert Seyfarth, Richard Wrangham, and Thomas Struhsaker, eds.). Chicago, University of Chicago Press, 1987.

Strum, Shirley. *Almost Human*. New York, W. W. Norton, 1987.

Susman, Randall. "Fossil Evidence for Early Hominid Tool Use." *Science*, 265: 1570–1573, 1994.

Sussman, Robert. "Primate Origins and the Evolution of Angiosperms." *American Journal of Primatology*, 23:209–223, 1991.

Suwa, Gen, Berhane Asfaw, Yonas Beyene, Tim White, Shigehiro Katoh, Shinji Nagaoka, Hideo Nakaya, Kazuhiro Uzawa, Paul Renne, and Giday WoldeGabriel. "The First Skull of *Australopithecus boisei*." *Nature*, 389: 489–492, 1997.

Swindler, Daris, and Charles Wood. *An Atlas of Primate Gross Anatomy: Baboon, Chimpanzee, and Man*. Seattle, University of Washington Press, 1973.

Swisher, III, Carl, G. Curtis, T. Jacob, A. Getty, A. Suprijo, and Widiasmoro. "Age of the Earliest Known Hominids in Java, Indonesia." *Science*, 263: 1118–1121, 1994.

Swisher, III, Carl, Garniss Curtis, and Roger Lewin. *Java Man*. New York, Scribner, 2000.

Swisher, III, Carl, W. Rink, S. Antón, H. Schwarcz, G. Curtis, A. Suprijo, and Widiasmoro. "Latest *Homo erectus* of Java: Potential Contemporaneity with *Homo sapiens* in Southeast Asia." *Science*, 274:1870–1874, 1996.

Sykes, Bryan. *The Seven Daughters of Eve*. New York, W. W. Norton, 2001.

Symons, Donald. *The Evolution of Human Sexuality*. Oxford, Oxford University Press, 1979.

Symons, Donald. *Play and Aggression: A Study of Rhesus Monkeys*. New York, Columbia University Press, 1978.

Tanner, James. "Human Growth and Development." pp. 98–105 in *The Cambridge Encyclopedia of Human Evolution* (Steve Jones, Robert Martin, David Pilbeam, and Sarah Bunney, eds.). Cambridge, Cambridge University Press, 1992.

Tattersall, Ian. *The Fossil Trail*. New York, Oxford University Press, 1995a.

Tattersall, Ian. *The Last Neanderthal*. New York, Macmillan, 1995b.

Tattersall, Ian. "Once We Were Not Alone." *Scientific American* (Special Edition), 13(2):20–27, 2003.

Tattersall, Ian, and Jeffrey Schwartz. *Extinct Humans*. New York, Westview Press, 2000.

Tattersall, Ian, and Jeffrey Schwartz. "Hominids and Hybrids: The Place of Neanderthals in Human Evolution." *Proceedings of the National Academy of Sciences*, 96:7117–7119, 1999.

Taub, David, and Patrick Mehlman. "Primate Paternalistic Investment: A Cross-Species View." pp. 51–89 in *Understanding Behavior* (James Loy and Calvin Peters, eds.). New York, Oxford University Press, 1991.

Tavaré, Simon, Charles Marshall, Oliver Will, Christophe Soligo, and Robert D. Martin. "Using the Fossil Record to Estimate the Age of the Last Common Ancestor of Extant Primates." *Nature*, 416:726–729 2002.

Templeton, Alan. "Out of Africa Again and Again." *Nature*, 416:45–51, 2002.

Theunissen, Bert. *Eugène Dubois and the Ape-Man from Java*. Dordrecht, Kluwer Academic Publishers, 1989.

Thieme, Hartmut. "Lower Palaeolithic Hunting Spears from Germany." *Nature*, 385:807–810, 1997.

Thomas, David. *Skull Wars: Kennewick Man, Archaeology, and the Battle for Native American Identity*. New York, HarperCollins, 2000.

Thorne, Alan, and Milford Wolpoff. "The Multiregional Evolution of Humans." *Scientific American* (Special Edition), 13(2):46–53, 2003.

Tobias, P. V. *Hominid Evolution*. New York, Alan R. Liss, 1985.

Toumaï the Human Ancestor. www.cnrsfr/cw/fr/pres/compress/Toumai/Tounaigb/home.html.

Trevathan, Wenda. "Fetal Emergence Patterns in Evolutionary Perspective." *American Anthropologist*, 90:674–681, 1988.

Trevathan, Wenda. *Human Birth: An Evolutionary Perspective.* New York, Aldine de Gruyter, 1987.

Trinkaus, Erik, and Pat Shipman. *The Neandertals.* New York, Knopf, 1993.

Trivers, Robert. *Social Evolution.* Menlo Park (CA), Benjamin/Cummings, 1985.

Turner, II, Christy, and Jacqueline Turner. *Man Corn.* Salt Lake City, University of Utah Press, 1999.

Tutin, Caroline. "Mating Patterns and Reproductive Strategies in a Community of Wild Chimpanzees (*Pan troglodytes schweinfurthii*)." *Behavioral Ecology and Sociobiology,* 6:29–38, 1979.

U.S. Census Bureau. World Population Information. www.census.gov/ipc/www/world.html.

U.S. Gov Info/Resources. "U.S. Life Expectancy Hits All-time High." http://usgovinfo.about.com/cs/census statistic/a/aalifeexpect.htm.

van Schaik, C. P., E. A. Fox, and A. F. Sitompul. "Manufacture and Use of Tools in Wild Sumatran Orangutans." *Naturwissenschaften,* 83:186–188, 1996.

Van Valen, Leigh, and Robert Sloan. "The Earliest Primates." *Science,* 150:743–745, 1965.

Vekua, Abesalom, David Lordkipanidze, G. P. Rightmire, Jordi Agusti, Reid Ferring, Givi Maisuradze, Alexander Mouskhelishvili, Medea Nioradze, Marcia Ponce de Leon, Martha Tappen, Merab Tvalchrelidze, and Christoph Zollikofer. "A New Skull of Early *Homo* from Dmanisi, Georgia." *Science,* 297:85–89, 2002.

Venter, J. C., et al. "The Sequence of the Human Genome." *Science,* 291:1304–1351, 2001.

Verhaegen, Marc, Pierre-François Puech, and Stephen Munro. "Aquarboreal Ancestors?" *TRENDS in Ecology and Evolution,* 17(5):212–217, 2002.

Vignaud, Patrick, Philippe Duringer, Hassane MacKaye, Andossa Likius, Cécile Blondel, Jean-Renaud Boisserie, Louis de Bonis, Véra Eisenmann, Marie-Esther Etienne, Denis Geraads, Franck Guy, Thomas Lehmann, Fabrice Lihoreau, Nievves Lopez-Martinez, Cécile Mourerr-Chauviré, Olga Otero, Jean-Claude Rage, Mathieu Schuster, Laurent Viriot, Antoine Zazzo, and Michel Brunet. "Geology and Palaeontology of the Upper Miocene Toros-Menalla Hominid Locality, Chad." *Nature,* 418:152–155, 2002.

von Koenigswald, G. H. R. *Meeting Prehistoric Man.* New York, Harper & Brothers, 1956.

von Koenigswald, G. H. R., and Franz Weidenreich. "The Relationship between Pithecanthropus and Sinanthropus." *Nature,* 144:926–929, 1939.

Vrba, E. S. "Ecological and Adaptive Changes Associated with Early Hominid Evolution." pp. 63–71 in *Ancestors: The Hard Evidence* (E. Delson, ed.). New York, A. R. Liss, 1985.

Vrba, E. S. "The Pulse That Produced Us." *Natural History,* 102(5):47–51, 1993.

Waddle, Diane. "Matrix Correlation Tests Support a Single Origin for Modern Humans." *Nature,* 368:452–454, 1994.

Wade, Nicholas. "Evolution of Gene Related to Brain's Growth Is Detailed." *New York Times,* January 14, 2004.

Wagner, Günther. "Fission-Track Dating in Paleoanthropology." *Evolutionary Anthropology,* 5:165–171, 1996.

Walker, Alan. "Perspectives on the Nariokotome Discovery." pp. 411–430 in *The Nariokotome* Homo erectus *Skeleton* (Alan Walker and Richard Leakey, eds.). Cambridge (MA), Harvard University Press, 1993a.

Walker, Alan. "The Origin of the Genus *Homo.*" pp. 29–47 in *The Origin and Evolution of Humans and Humanness* (D. T. Rasmussen, ed.). Boston, Jones and Bartlett, 1993b.

Walker, Alan, and Christopher Ruff. "The Reconstruction of the Pelvis." pp. 221–233 in *The Nariokotome* Homo erectus *Skeleton* (Alan Walker and Richard Leakey, eds.). Cambridge (MA), Harvard University Press, 1993.

Walker, Alan, and Richard Leakey (eds.). *The Nariokotome* Homo erectus *Skeleton.* Cambridge (MA), Harvard University Press, 1993.

Walker, Alan, Richard Leakey, J. M. Harris, and F. H. Brown. "2.5 Myr *Australopithecus boisei* from West of Lake Turkana, Kenya." *Nature,* 322: 517–522, 1986.

Wallace, Alfred Russel. *The Malay Archipelago: The Land of the Orang-Utan, and the Bird of Paradise.* New York, Harper & Brother, 1885.

Wallman, Joel. *Aping Language.* Cambridge, Cambridge University Press, 1992.

Walters, Jeffrey. "Transition to Adulthood." pp. 358–369 in *Primate Societies* (Barbara Smuts, Dorothy Cheney, Robert Seyfarth, Richard Wrangham, and Thomas Struhsaker, eds.). Chicago, University of Chicago Press, 1987.

Walters, Jeffrey, and Robert Seyfarth. "Conflict and Cooperation." pp. 306–317 in *Primate Societies* (Barbara Smuts, Dorothy Cheney, Robert Seyfarth, Richard Wrangham, and Thomas Struhsaker, eds.). Chicago, University of Chicago Press, 1987.

Ward, Carol. "Interpreting the Posture and Locomotion of *Australopithecus afarensis:* Where Do We Stand?" *Yearbook of Physical Anthropology,* 45: 185–215, 2002.

Ward, Carol, Meave Leakey, and Alan Walker. "The New Hominid Species *Australopithecus anamensis.*" *Evolutionary Anthropology,* 7:197–205, 1999.

Ward, Steve, Barbara Brown, Andrew Hill, Jay Kelley, and Will Downs. "*Equatorius:* A New Hominoid Genus from the Middle Miocene of Kenya." *Science,* 285:1382–1386, 1999.

Washburn, S. L., and C. S. Lancaster. "The Evolution of Hunting." pp. 293–303 in *Man the Hunter* (Richard Lee and Irven DeVore, eds.). Chicago, Aldine-Atherton, 1968.

Washburn, S. L., and Ruth Moore. *Ape into Man.* Boston, Little, Brown, 1974.

Washburn, Sherwood. "Tools and Human Evolution." *Scientific American,* 203(3):63–75, 1960.

Watts, David. "Social Relationships of Female Mountain Gorillas." pp. 215–240 in *Mountain Gorillas: Three Decades of Research at Karisoke* (Martha Robbins, Pascale Sicotte, and Kelly Stewart, eds.). Cambridge, Cambridge University Press, 2001.

Weaver, Tim. "The Shape of the Neandertal Femur Is Primarily the Consequence of a Hyperpolar Body Form." *Proceedings of the National Academy of Sciences,* 100:6926–6929, 2003.

Weidenreich, Franz. *Apes, Giants and Man.* Chicago, University of Chicago Press, 1946.

Weidenreich, Franz. "The Skull of *Sinanthropus pekinensis:* A Comparative Study on a Primitive Hominid Skull." *Palaeontologia Sinica,* New series D no. 10 (Whole series no. 127). Peking, Geological Survey of China, 1943.

Weiner, J. S. *The Piltdown Forgery.* Oxford, Oxford University Press, 1955.

Weiner, Jonathan. *The Beak of the Finch.* New York, Vintage Books, 1994.

Weiss, Ehud, Wilma Wetterstrom, Dani Nadel, and Ofer Bar-Yosef. "The Broad Spectrum Revisited: Evidence from Plant Remains." *Proceedings of the National Academy of Sciences,* 101:9551–9555, 2004.

Wenke, Robert. *Patterns in Prehistory,* 4th ed. New York, Oxford University Press, 1999.

Wheeler, Peter. "Human Ancestors Walked Tall, Stayed Cool." *Natural History,* 102(8):65–67, 1993.

Wheeler, Peter. "The Influence of Bipedalism on the Energy and Water Budgets of Early Hominids." *Journal of Human Evolution,* 21:117–136, 1991a.

Wheeler, Peter. "The Thermoregulatory Advantages of Hominid Bipedalism in Open Equatorial Environments: The Contribution of Increased Convective Heat Loss and Cutaneous Evaporative Cooling." *Journal of Human Evolution,* 21:107–115, 1991b.

White, Frances. "Activity Budgets, Feeding Behavior, and Habitat Use of Pygmy Chimpanzees at Lomako, Zaire." *American Journal of Primatology,* 26:215–223, 1992a.

White, Frances. "Pygmy Chimpanzee Social Organization: Variation with Party Size and between Study Sites." *American Journal of Primatology,* 26:203–214, 1992b.

White, Frances. "*Pan paniscus* 1973–1996: Twenty-Three Years of Field Research." *Evolutionary Anthropology,* 5:11–17, 1996.

White, J. P., and J. O'Connell. "Australian Prehistory: New Aspects of Antiquity." *Science,* 203:21–28, 1979.

White, Tim. "Earliest Hominids." pp. 407–471 in *The Primate Fossil Record* (Walter Hartwig, ed.). Cambridge, Cambridge University Press, 2002.

White, Tim, Berhane Asfaw, David DeGusta, Henry Gilbert, Gary Richards, Gen Suwa, and F. Clark Howell. "Pleistocene *Homo sapiens* from Middle Awash, Ethiopia." *Nature,* 423:742–747, 2003.

White, Tim, Gen Suwa, and Berhane Asfaw. "*Australopithecus ramidus,* a New Species of Early Hominid from Aramis, Ethiopia." *Nature,* 371:306–312, 1994.

White, Tim, Gen Suwa, and Berhane Asfaw. "*Australopithecus ramidus,* a New Species of Early Hominid from Aramis, Ethiopia." *Nature,* 375:88, 1995.

White, Tim, Gen Suwa, William Hart, Robert Walter, Giday WoldeGabriel, Jean de Heinzelin, J. D. Clark, Berhane Asfaw, and Elizabeth Vrba. "New Discoveries of *Australopithecus* at Maka in Ethiopia." *Nature,* 366:261–265, 1993.

Wilford, John. "Discovery of Flute Suggests Neanderthal Caves Echoed with Music." *New York Times,* October 29, 1996.

Wilford, John. "New Answers to an Old Question: Who Got Here First?" *New York Times,* November 9, 1999.

Williams, George. *The Pony Fish's Glow.* New York, Basic Books, 1997.

Wilson, Edward O. *On Human Nature.* Cambridge (MA), Harvard University Press, 1978.

Wilson, Edward O. *Sociobiology: The New Synthesis.* Cambridge (MA), Harvard University Press, 1975.

WoldeGabriel, Giday, Yohannes Haile-Selassie, Paul Renne, William Hart, Stanley Ambrose, Berhane Asfaw, Grant Heiken, and Tim White. "Geology and Palaeontology of the Late Miocene Middle Awash Valley, Afar Rift, Ethiopia." *Nature,* 412:175–178, 2001.

WoldeGabriel, Giday, Tim White, Gen Suwa, Paul Renne, Jean de Heinzelin, William Hart, and Grant Heiken. "Ecological and Temporal Placement of Early Pliocene Hominids at Aramis, Ethiopia." *Nature,* 371:330–333, 1994.

Wolfe, J., and D. Hopkins. "Climatic Changes Recorded by Tertiary Land Floras in Northwestern North America." pp. 67–76 in *Tertiary Correlations and Climatic Changes in the Pacific* (E. Hatai, ed.). Tokyo, 11th Symp. Pacific Sci. Cong., 1967.

Wolfe, Linda. "Human Evolution and the Sexual Behavior of Female Primates." pp. 121–151 in *Understanding Behavior* (James Loy and Calvin Peters, eds.). New York, Oxford University Press, 1991.

Wolfheim, Jaclyn. *Primates of the World: Distribution, Abundance, and Conservation.* Seattle, University of Washington Press, 1983.

Wolpoff, Milford. *Human Evolution: 1996–1997 Edition.* New York, McGraw-Hill, 1996.

Wolpoff, Milford, Brigitte Senut, Martin Pickford, and John Hawks. "*Sahelanthropus* or '*Sahelpithecus*'?" *Nature,* 419:581–582, 2002.

WonderQuest. www.wonderquest.com.

Wong, Kate. "An Ancestor to Call Our Own." *Scientific American* (Special Edition), 13(2):4–13, 2003.

Wong, Kate. "The Littlest Human." *Scientific American,* 292 (2):56–65, 2005.

Wood, Bernard. "Origin and Evolution of the Genus *Homo.*" *Nature,* 355:783–790, 1992.

Wood, Bernard. "Palaeoanthropology: Hominid Revelations from Chad." *Nature,* 418:133–135, 2002.

Wood, Bernard, and Mark Collard. "The Changing Face of Genus *Homo.*" *Evolutionary Anthropology,* 8:195–207, 1999a.

Wood, Bernard, and Mark Collard. "The Human Genus." *Science,* 284:65–71, 1999b.

Wood, Bernard, and Brian Richmond. "Human Evolution: Taxonomy and Paleobiology." *Journal of Anatomy,* 196:19–60, 2000.

Wood, Bernard, and Alan Turner. "Out of Africa and into Asia." *Nature,* 378:239–240, 1995.

Woodward, A. Smith. "The Fossil Anthropoid Apr from Taungs." *Nature,* 115: 235–236, 1925.

Wrangham, Richard. "Evolution of Social Structure." pp. 282–296 in *Primate Societies* (Barbara Smuts, Dorothy Cheney, Robert Seyfarth, Richard Wrangham, and Thomas Struhsaker, eds.). Chicago, University of Chicago Press, 1987.

Wrangham, Richard, and Jane Goodall. "Chimpanzee Use of Medicinal Leaves." pp. 22–37 in *Understanding Chimpanzees* (Paul Heltne and Linda Marquardt, eds.). Cambridge (MA), Harvard University Press, 1989.

Wrangham, Richard, and Dale Peterson. *Demonic Males.* Boston, Houghton Mifflin, 1996.

Wu, Rukang, and Shenglong Lin. "Peking Man." *Scientific American,* 248(6):86–94, 1983.

World Wildlife Fund. *Living Planet Report 2002.* www.panda.org/news_facts/publications/general/livingplanet/lpr02.cfm.

Wynn, Thomas, and Frederick Coolidge. "The Expert Neandertal Mind." *Journal of Human Evolution,* 46:467–487, 2004.

Wynne-Edwards, V. C. *Animal Dispersion in Relation to Social Behavior.* Edinburgh, Oliver and Boyd, 1962.

Yamagiwa, Juichi, and John Kahekwa. "Dispersal Patterns, Group Structure, and Reproductive Parameters of Eastern Lowland Gorillas at Kahuzi in the Absence of Infanticide." pp. 89–122 in *Mountain Gorillas: Three Decades of Research at Karisoke* (Martha Robbins, Pascale Sicotte, and Kelly Stewart, eds.). Cambridge, Cambridge University Press, 2001.

Yamakoshi, Gen, and Yukimaru Sugiyama. "Pestle-Pounding Behavior of Wild Chimpanzees at Bossou, Guinea: A Newly Observed Tool-Using Behavior." *Primates,* 36:489–500, 1995.

Yerkes, Robert, and Ada Yerkes. *The Great Apes: A Study of Anthropoid Life.* New Haven (CT), Yale University Press, 1929.

Yunxian. www-personal.une.edu.au/~pbrown3/yunxian.html.

Zhang, Jianzhi. "Evolution of the Human *ASPM* Gene, a Major Determinant of Brain Size." *Genetics,* 165:2063–2070, 2003.

Zihlman, Adrienne. "Body Build and Tissue Composition in *Pan paniscus* and *Pan troglodytes,* with Comparisons to Other Hominoids." pp. 179–200 in *The Pygmy Chimpanzee* (Randall Susman, ed.). New York, Plenum Press, 1984.

Zuckerman, S. *The Social Life of Monkeys and Apes.* New York, Harcourt, Brace and Company, 1932.

Credits

Photo Credits

Chapter One

1: Mary Evans Picture Library; 3: The Natural History Museum, London; 4: Wm. Buckland, Reliquiae Diluvianae, 1823; 6: James Hutton, *Theory of the Earth,* 1795; 8: CORBIS; 11 *both,* 16: Bettmann/CORBIS; 20: Courtesy Department Library Services, American Museum of Natural History, photo by Jules Kirschner #311414.

Chapter Two

24: Oscar Miller/SPL/Photo Researchers; 27: Biofoto/Photo Researchers; 46 *top:* Oliver Meckers/Photo Researchers; 46 *bottom:* Photo Researchers.

Chapter Three

58: Gregory Dimijian/Photo Researchers; 66 *top:* Sarah Blaffer Hrdy/Anthro-Photo; 66 *bottom,* 67 *top:* Wildlife Conservation Society; 67 *bottom:* © A. W. Ambler/National Audubon Society/Photo Researchers; 73 *top left:* D. J. Chivers/Anthro-Photo; 73 *top right:* Werner H. Muller/Peter Arnold; 73 *bottom left:* Werner H. Muller/Peter Arnold; 73 *bottom right:* D. J. Chivers/Anthro-Photo; 74 *top left:* Michael Rougier/Getty Images; 74 *top right:* Ralph Mores/Time/Getty Images; 74 *bottom left:* Wildlife Conservation Society; 74 *bottom right:* Richard Wrangham/Anthro-Photo; 76: Fritz Goro; 83 *top left:* Laima Druskis/Photo Researchers; 83 *top right:* Roberta Hershenson/Photo Researchers; 83 *bottom:* Reprinted from *A Handbook of Living Primates,* J. R. Napier and P. H. Napier, Copyright 1967, with permission from Elsevier; 84 *top:* L. V. Bergman/The Bergman Collection.

Chapter Four

90: Tom McHugh/Photo Researchers; 94 *both:* Wildlife Conservation Society; 98 *top left:* Sarah Blaffer Hrdy/Anthro-Photo; 98 *top right:* DeVore/Anthro-Photo; 98 *bottom:* © Walter Gotz, Courtesy of Hans Kummer; 99: DeVore/Anthro-Photo; 103: Joseph Popp/Anthro-Photo; 105: Irven DeVore/Anthro-Photo; 107: Washburn/Anthro-Photo; 111 *top:* David Chivers/Anthro-Photo; 111 *bottom:* Irven DeVore/Anthro-Photo; 113: Robert M. Campbell/National Geographic Image Sales; 115: Hugo Van Lawick/National Geographic Image Sales; 119, 120: Dr. Geza Teleki/Committee for Conservation and Care of Chimpanzees; 121: Alison Hannah; 124: Frans Lanting/Minden Pictures.

Chapter Five

130: Courtesy Department Library Service, American Museum of Natural History Photo C. Chesek (1994) #2A21279; 138: Zoological Society of San Diego: 141 *bottom:* Dr. E. L. Simons/Duke University Primate Center; 145 *top:* The Natural History Museum, London; 147: Ward/Anthro-Photo; 148 *top:* Salvador Moya-Sola.

Chapter Six

160, 163: David L. Brill/Atlanta; 166: Earnest Shirley; 168: William B. Terry, *Early Man;* 171 *top:* Glen Conroy/Washington University Medical School, St. Louis; 171 *bottom:* The Natural History Museum, London; 173 *both,* 174 *both,* 175 *top:* Transvaal Museum, D.C. Panagos; 176: Ronald J. Clarke; 177: Ken MacLeish, *Early Man.*

Chapter Seven

183: Des Bartlett/Photo Researchers; 186: Donald Johanson/Institute of Human Origins; 187 *top:* Bob Campbell/National Geographic Image Sales; 187 *bottom:* Gordan Gaham/National Geographic Image Sales; 188: Des Barlett/Photo Researchers; 189: National Museums of Kenya; 192 *top left:* © David L. Brill/Atlanta; 192 *top right:* Donald Johanson/Institute of Human Origins; 192 *bottom left:* © David L. Brill/Institute of Human Origins; 193 *top:* Institute of Human Origins; 196 *top:* © 1993 David L. Brill; 196 *bottom:* Institute of Human Origins; 199: John Reader/Science Source/Photo Researchers; 202 *all,* 205: National Museums of Kenya; 211: copyright M.P.F.T.

Chapter Eight

221: Courtesy Department Library Service, American Museum of Natural History, Photo by John N. Richards; 224: The Natural History Museum, London; 225 *both:* David L. Brill/Atlanta.

Chapter Nine

239: John Reader/Science Source/Photo Researchers; 252: National Museums of Kenya; 253 *both:* R. Potts; 254 *top:* Kathy D. Schick and Nicholas Toth, CRAFT Research Center, Indiana University (From Schick and Toth, 1993, p. 163); 254 *bottom:* Kathy D. Schick and Nicholas Toth, CRAFT Research Center, Indiana University (From Schick and Toth, 1993, p. 171).

Chapter Ten

262: Courtesy Department Library Services, American Museum of Natural History #335797; 263: From an unpublished manuscript: *Trinil, A Biography of Professor Dr. Eugene Dubois, the Discoverer of Pithecanthropus erectus,* by Dubois's son, Jean M. F. Dubois; 266: Courtesy Department Library Services, American Museum of Natural History, photo by Dr. von Koenigswald #298897; 267 *top:* Courtesy of Rijksmuseum van Natuurlijke Historie, Lieden; 267 *bottom:* From an unpublished manuscript *Trinil, A Biolography of Professor Dr. Eugene Dubois, the Discoverer of Pithecanthropus erectus,* by Dubois's son, Jean M. F. Dubois; 270: Courtesy Department Library Services, American Museum of Natural History, Copied by J. Coxe #336414; 271: Bettmann/CORBIS; 274: Courtesy Department Library Sevices, American Museum of Natural History #333193; 276 *top:* National Museums of Kenya; 276 *bottom:* David L. Brill/Atlanta.

Chapter Eleven

288: Kathy D. Schick and Nicholas Toth, CRAFT Research Center, Indiana University. (From Schick and Toth 1993, p. 236); 293 *all,* 294 *all:* M. Riboud/Magnum Photos; 295: Kathy D. Schick and Nicholas Toth, CRAFT Research Center, Indiana University. (From Schick and Toth 1993, p. 245); 297: Nicholas Toth, CRAFT Research Center, Indiana University, and Giancarlo Ligabue from Ligabue Missions 1986–1990. (From Schick and Toth 1993, p. 277); 299 *left:* DeVore/Anthro-Photo; 300: The Natural History Museum, London.

Chapter Twelve

311, 315 *top:* The Natural History Museum, London; 315 *bottom:* Donald Johanson/Institute of Human Origins; 317: Javier Trueba/Madrid Scientific Films & David L. Brill/Atlanta.

Chapter Thirteen

331: John Reader/SPL/Photo Researchers; 334 *top left:* DeVore/Anthro-Photo; 334 *top center:* Wrangham/ Anthro-Photo; 334 *top right:* DeVore/Anthro-Photo; 334 *bottom all:* eStock Photo; 335 *both:* From *In the Shadow of Man* by Jane van Lawick-Goodall © 1971 by Hugo and Jane van Lawick-Goodall. Reprinted with permission of The Jane Goodall Institute; 336: R. Wrangham/Anthro-Photo; 338: H. S. Terrace/ Anthro-Photo.

Chapter Fourteen

357: © Erik Trinkaus; 360: Rheinisches Landesmuseum Bonn; 362, 363 *top:* Musee de l'Homme; 367: Peabody Museum, Harvard University, Photograph by Hillel Burger; 368: Javier Trueba/Madrid Scientific Films; 371: © Erik Trinkaus; 372: Courtesy Department Library Services, American Museum of Natural History #338383; 378, 379: Ralph S. Solecki; 381: © Alexander Marshack.

Chapter Fifteen

389: Courtesy of Ian Tattersall; 392: Peabody Museum, Harvard University, Photograph by Movius; 393 *both:* The Natural History Museum, London.

Chapter Sixteen

417: © Jean Clottes; 420: Riuchard Jeffrey/Courtesy J. Tixier; 421 *all:* Pierre Boulat/Cosmos; 423: Axel Poignant Archive 424: Courtesy Department Library Services, American Museum of Natural History, Photo J. Kirschner #39686; 426: © Alexander Marshack; 427: Ralph Morse, *Early Man;* 429 *left:* © Alexander Marshack; 431: Courtesy Department Library Services, American Museum of Natural History, Photo Jim Coxe #336871; 432: Courtesy Department Library Services, American Museum of Natural History, Photo Lee Boltin #326474; 433 *top:* G. Shilonsky/Sovfoto /Eastfoto; 433 *bottom:* Novosti Press Agency/Sovfoto/ Eastfoto.

Chapter Seventeen

438: Richard Lord/The Image Works; 445: David Rubinger, Israel; 449 *left:* Smucker/Anthro-Photo; 449 *right:* Betty Press/Woodfin Camp.

Text and Illustration Credits

Chapter One

Fig. 1.10, p. 13: Reprinted by permission of the publisher from *One Long Argument: Charles Darwin and the Genesis of Modern Evolutionary Thought* by Ernst Mayr, p. 72, Cambridge, Mass: Harvard University Press, Copyright © 1991 by Ernst Mayr; Fig. 1.11, p. 14: T. H. Huxley, *Evidence as the Man's Place in Nature,* frontispiece (London, 1863).

Chapter Two

Fig. 2.1, p. 26: Animal cell from *Genes & Genomes* by Maxine Singer and Paul Berg, 1991, p. 4. Reprinted by permission of University Science: 55 D Gate Five Road, Sausalito, CA 94965; Fig. 2.4, p. 30: DNA-RNA from *Genes & Genomes* by M. Singer and P. Berg, 1991, p. 432. Reprinted by permission of University Science: 55 D Gate Five Road, Sausalito, CA 94965; Fig. 2.5, p. 31 *top:* RNA Splicing from Genes & Genomes by M. Singer and P. Berg, 1991, p. 437. Reprinted by permission of University Science: 55 D Gate Five Road, Sausalito, CA 94965; Fig. 2.6, p. 31 *bottom:* Ribosomes Engange mRNA from *Genes & Genomes* by M. Singer and P. Berg, 1991, p. 33. Reprinted by permission of University Science: 55 D Gate Five Road, Sausalito, CA 94965; Fig. 2.7, p. 35: Meisosis from *Genes & Genomes* by M. Singer and P. Berg, 1991, p. 9. Reprinted by permission of University Science: 55 D Gate Five Road, Sausalito, CA 94965; Fig. 2.8, p. 36: Crossing Over from *Genes & Genomes* by M. Singer and P. Berg, 1991, p. 20. Reprinted by permission of University Science: 55 D Gate Five Road, Sausalito, CA 94965; Fig. 2.11, p. 39: Gene Frequency Changes from *Evolution,* 2/e by Mark Ridley, p. 102, © 1996. Reprinted by permission of Blackwell Publishing Ltd.; Fig. 2.12, p. 40: Two Kinds of Selection from *Evolution,* 2/e by Mark Ridley, p. 74, © 1996. Reprinted by permission of Blackwell Publishing Ltd.; Fig. 2.16, p. 51: From *Biological Evolution* 1st edition by PRICE. © 1996. Reprinted with permission of Brooks/Cole, a division of Thomason Learning: www.thomsonrights.com. Fax 800 730-2215.

Chapter Three

Fig. 3.2, p. 64: Primate Distribution Map from *Handbook of Living Primates,* p. 378 by J. Napier and P. Napier, Academic Press, 1967; Fig. 3.7, p. 69 *top:* Comparative skull anatomy from *Physical Anthropology and Archaeology,* 5/e by C. Jolly and S. Plog, 1986. Reprinted by permission of McGraw-Hill Companies; Fig. 3.8, p. 69 *bottom:* Dental Formulae and Teeth from *The Cambridge Encylopedia of Human Evolution,* p. 57 by Steve Jones, Robert Martin, and David Pilbeam, editors, 1992. Reprinted with the permission of Cambridge University Press; Fig. 3.9, p. 70 *top:* Primate, Opossum, Squirrel Hands, p. 24 from *The Cambridge Encylopedia of Human Evolution* by Steve Jones, Robert Martin, and David Pilbeam, editors, 1992. Reprinted with the permission of Cambridge University Press; Fig. 3.13, p. 75 *top:* Reprinted from *Primate Adaptation & Evolution,* J. G. Fleagle, pp. 245–251, Copyright 1988, with permission from Elsevier; Fig. 3.19, p. 84 *bottom:* Based on Swindler & Wood. *An Atlas of Primate Gross Anatomy.* University of Washington Press, 1973; pp. 92–93. Reprinted by permission of the author.

Chapter Four

Fig. 4.2, p. 95: Reprinted from *Primate Adaptation & Evolution,* J. G. Fleagle, p. 57, Copyright 1988, with permission from Elsevier; Fig. 4.8, p. 106: Redrawn from DeVore and Hall (1965); Fig. 4.10, p. 109: From *Primates in Nature* by Alison F Richard, © 1985 by W. H. Freeman and Company, used with permission; Fig. 4.16, p. 117: Chimpanzee and Bonobo Habitats map based on Jane Goodall's *Chimpanzees of Gombe,* Fig. 31, p. 45, © 1986 Harvard University Press. Reprinted with permission of The Jane Goodall Institute.

Chapter Five

Fig. 5.5, p. 136 *top:* Data primarily based on Martin (2004) and Mundil, et al. (2004); Fig. 5.6, p. 136 *bottom:* Robert D. Martin, *Primate Origins and Evolution.* © 1990 R. D. Martin. Reprinted by permission of Princeton University Press; Fig. 5.7, p. 137: Redrawn from Sargis, *Science* 298:1564–1565 (2002). Copyright 2002 AAAS; Fig. 5.9, p. 139: Early Prosimian Skulls, p. 204 from *The Cambridge Encyclopedia of Human*

Evolution by Steve Jones, Robert Martin, and David Pilbeam, editors, 1992. Reprinted with the permission of Cambridge University Press; Fig. 5.13, p. 143: Miocene Ape Fossils Map, p. 224 from *The Cambridge Encylopedia of Human Evolution* by Steve Jones, Robert Martin, and David Pilbeam, editors, 1992. Reprinted with the permission of Cambridge University Press; Fig. 5.15, p. 145 *bottom:* Reprinted from *Primate Adaptation and Evolution,* J. G. Fleagle, p. 369, Copyright 1988, with permission from Elsevier; Fig. 5.16, p. 146: Time Ranges of Extinct Apes, p. 229 from *The Cambridge Encylopedia of Human Evolution* by Steve Jones, Robert Martin, and David Pilbeam, editors, 1992. Reprinted with the permission of Cambridge University Press; Fig. 5.20, p. 149: Redrawn from Begun, 2003. With the permission of the author; Fig. 5.22, p. 151 *bottom:* Redrawn from M. H. Day, *The Fossil History of Man,* 1972. Copyright Oxford University Press; Fig. 5.23, p. 152: Redrawn from *The Antecedents of Man* by W. E. Le Gros Clark, Fig. 69, 1959. Reprinted by permission of Edinburgh University Press; Fig. 5.24, p. 153: Human & Ape Skeleton and Femurs from *An Introduction to Human Evolutionary Anatomy* by L. Aiello and C. Dean, p. 457, © 1990 Academic Press; Fig. 5.24, p. 153: Human & Ape Skeleton and Femurs adapted from *The Life of Primates* by A. H. Schultz, p. 77, 1969, Universe Books; Fig. 5.25, p. 154 *top:* Reprinted from *Atlas der Anatomie des Menschen,* 20th Edition by Sobotta. Reprinted by permission of Urban & Fischer Verlag; Fig. 5.25, p. 154 *top:* Ape and Human Pelvic Girdles from *The Antecedents of Man* by Le Gros Clark, 1962, Edinburgh University Press; Fig. 5.26, p. 154 *bottom:* Ape and Human Center of Gravity from *Introduction to Human Evolutionary Anatomy* by C. Dean and L. Aiello. Academic Press London, 1990; Fig. 5.27, p. 155 *top:* From David Philbeam *The Ascent of Man: An Introduction to Human Evolution.* Published by Allyn & Bacon, Boston, MA. Copyright © 1972 by Pearson Education. Reprinted by permission of the publisher; Fig. 5.27, p. 155 *top:* Reprinted from *Introduction to Human Evolutionary Anatomy,* C. Dean and L. Aiello. Copyright 1990, with permission from Elsevier; Fig. 5.28, p. 155 *bottom:* Reprinted from *An Introduction to Human Evolutionary Anatomy,* L. Aiello and C. Dean, p. 437. Copyright 1990, with permission from Elsevier; Fig. 5.28, p. 155 *bottom:* From David Philbeam *The Ascent of Man: An Introduction to Human Evolution.* Published by Allyn & Bacon, Boston, MA. Copyright © 1972 by Pearson Education. Reprinted by permission of the publisher.

Chapter Six

Fig. 6.14, p. 175 *bottom: Australopithecus africanus* Pelvic Girdle adapted from *Early Hominid Posture and Locomotion* by John T. Robinson, University of Chicago Press, 1972. Reprinted by permission of the author. Fig. 6.17, p. 178: Sterkfontein Stone Choppers. Figure redrawn from *South African Archaeological Bulletin,* Vol. 17, #66, 1962, p. 111; Fig. 6.18, p. 179: From *Reconstructing Human Origins: A Modern Synthesis* by Glenn C. Conroy. Copyright © 1997 by W. W. Norton & Company, Inc. Used by permission of W. W. Norton & Company, Inc.

Chapter Seven

Box 7.1, p. 190: Skulls and Brain Size from *The Antecedents of Man* by W. E. Le Gros Clark, Fig. 69, 1959. Reprinted by permission of Edinburgh University Press; Fig. 7.8, p. 193 *bottom:* © 1981 Luba Dmytryk Gudz/Brill Atlanta; Fig. 7.9, p. 194: Stratigraphic Column from Hadar. Drawn by Bobbie Brown; Fig. 7.12, p. 197: © 1981 Luba Dmytryk Gudz/Brill Atlanta.

Chapter Eight

Fig. 8.3, p. 232 *top:* Department Library Service, American Museum of Natural History & Courtesy of Ian Tattersall; Fig. 8.3, p. 232 *bottom:* Jonathan Kingdon, *Lowly Origin.* © 2003 Princeton University Press. Reprinted by permission of Princeton

University Press; Fig. 8.4, p. 234: Phylogeny redrawn from p. 7687 of C. Cela-Conde, and F. J. Ayala, "Genetics of the Human Lineage" *Proceedings of the National Academy of Sciences.* 100:7684–7689, 2003.

Chapter Nine

Fig. 9.1, p. 243: Hominids Under the Sun by Pete Wheeler from *Natural History,* 102 (8), p. 66, 1993. Reprinted by permission of the author; Fig. 9.3, p. 248: Fetal Heads and Birth Canals from "Evolution of Human Walking" by C. Owen Lovejoy in *Scientific American,* p. 125, November 1988, vol. 259. Reprinted by permission of Carol Donner, the artist.

Chapter Ten

Fig. 10.8, p. 272: Redrawn with permission from original drawings by Janis Cirulis from *Mankind in the Making* by William Howells © 1959, 1967; Fig. 10.13, p. 280 *top:* Homo erectus skulls from *The Cambridge Encylopedia of Human Evolution* by Steve Jones, Robert Martin, and David Pilbeam, editors, 1992. Reprinted with the permission of Cambridge University Press; Fig. 10.13, p. 280 *top:* Reprinted from *Introduction to Human Evolutionary Anatomy,* C. Dean and L. Aiello, p. 437, Copyright 1990, with permission from Elsevier; Fig. 10.14, p. 280 *bottom:* Cladistics Concepts and the Species Problem from T. Harrison in *Species, Species Concepts & Primate Evolution,* R. Kimbel and Martin, eds., 1993. With kind permission of Springer Science and Business Media; Fig. 10.15, p. 283 *left:* Figure adapted from *Atlas der Anatomie des Menschen,* 20th Edition by Sobotta. Reprinted by permission of Urban & Fischer Verlag; Fig. 10.15, p. 283 *right:* Human Vertebra Chart Data from "The Vertebral Canal" by Anne MacLarnon in *The Nariokotome* Homo erectus *Skeleton,* p. 378, by Anne MacLarnon, A. Walker and R. Leakey, eds., Cambridge, Mass:, Harvard University Press, copyright © 1993 by the President and Fellows of Harvard College.

Chapter Eleven

Fig. 11.2, p. 291: Acheulean Artifacts redrawn by R. Freyman and N. Toth from *Olduvai Gorge,* Vol. 3. © 1971 by Mary Leakey. Reprinted by permission of Cambridge University Press; Fig. 11.6, p. 296: Map of Movius Line, p. 352 from *The Cambridge Encylopedia of Human Evolution* by Steve Jones, Robert Martin, and David Pilbeam, editors, 1992. Reprinted with the permission of Joe LeMonnier from *Natural History,* October 1989, p. 50; Fig. 11.10, p. 302: Typical Primate Organ Sizes by L. C. Aiello and P. Wheeler from *Current Anthropology,* 36, no. 2, p. 204, April 1995. Reprinted by permission of University of Chicago Press.

Chapter Twelve

Fig. 12.4, p. 316: Figure redrawn with permission from original drawings by Janis Cirulis from *Mankind in the Making* by William Howells © 1959, 1967; Fig. 12.8, p. 325: Hunting Dependence Chart from *The Cambridge Encylopedia of Human Evolution* by Steve Jones, Robert Martin, and David Pilbeam, editors, 1992. Reprinted with the permission of Cambridge University Press; Fig. 12.10, p. 328: Chimp/Human Split Figure, p. 340 from *The Cambridge Encylopedia of Human Evolution* by Steve Jones, Robert Martin, and David Pilbeam, editors, 1992. Reprinted with the permission of Cambridge University Press.

Chapter Thirteen

Fig. 13.7, p. 344: Figure modified from J. Laitman, R. Heimbuch, and E. Crelin, "The Basicranium of Fossil Hominids as an Indicator of Their Upper Respiratory

Systems." *American Journal of Physical Anthropology,* 51, 1979. Copyright 1979, John Wiley amd Sons, Inc. Reprinted by permission of Wiley-Liss, Inc., a subsidary of John Wiley and Sons, Inc.; Fig. 13.8, p. 346: Reprinted from *Journal of Human Evolution,* Vol. 37, 1999, pp. 191–229, Rilling et al., *"The Primate Neocortex in Comparative Perspective Using Magnetic Resonance Imaging"* Fig. 3, Copyright 1999, with permission from Elsevier; Fig. 13.9, p. 348: Reprinted from *The Primate Neocortex in Comparative Perspective Using Magnetic Resonance Imaging,* Rilling et al., vol. 37, Copyright 1999, with permission from Elsevier and James Rilling; Fig. 13.11, p. 349 *bottom:* Copyright John Wiley and Sons, Inc. Reprinted by permission of Wiley-Liss, Inc., a subsidary of John Wiley and Sons, Inc.; Fig. 13.12, p. 351: Blood Flow Chart adapted from *Braindance,* pp. 134 and 155 by Dean Falk. Copyright © 1992. Reprinted courtesy of Dean Falk; Fig. 13.13, p. 353: Technical Intelligence and Full Cognitive Fluidity from *The Prehistory of the Mind* by Steven Mithen, pp. 145 and 153, 1996. Reprinted by permission of the author and Thames & Hudson, London and New York.

Chapter Fourteen

Fig. 14.4, p. 363: Reconstruction of Neanderthal Skeleton. Courtesy Masson S. A. Editeur, Paris from M. Buole and H. Vallois in *Les Hommes Fossiles,* 1952; Fig. 14.5, p. 365: After Annick Peterson from *In Seach of the Neanderthals* by Christopher Stringer and Clive Gamble. Reprinted by permission of the author and Thames & Hudson, London and New York; Fig. 14.8, p. 370: Skeleton Comparisons from *The Last Neanderthal* by Ian Tattersall, p. 14, 1995. Westview Press, 1999. Courtesy of Ian Tattersall; Fig. 14.11, p. 373: Pleistocene Ice Ages Chart redrawn from "The Earth's Orbit and the Ice Ages" by Curt Covey, *Scientific American,* 250:2. Copyright © Andrew Tomko.

Chapter Fifteen

Fig. 15.5, p. 398 *top:* Aurignacian tools. Figure redrawn by permission from *The Old Stone Age* by Frances Bordes, © 1968 Frances Bordes, Weidenfeld & Nicolson publishers; Fig. 15.6, p. 398 *bottom:* Chatelperronian tools. Figure redrawn by permission from *The Old Stone Age* by Frances Bordes, 1968 Frances Bordes, Weidenfeld & Nicolson publishers; Fig. 15.7, p. 401 *top:* Neanderthal and Modern Human Skulls Compared. Figure redrawn from "The Neadertals" by Erik Trinkaus & William Howells in *Scientific American,* 241:6, 1979. Reprinted by permission of Whitney Powell; Fig. 15.8, p. 401 *bottom:* Redrawn from *In Search of the Neanderthals* by C. B. Stringer and C. Gamble, 1993. Reprinted by permission of Thames & Hudson, London and New York; Fig. 15.9, p. 402: Ian Tattersall: *The Fossil Train,* Oxford University Press, 1995. Courtesy of Ian Tattersall; Fig. 15.11, p. 409: Adapted © 2004 from *Human Evolutionary Genetics: Origins* by Mark Jobling, et al. reproduced by permission of Garland Science/Taylor & Francis Books, Inc.; Fig. 15.12, p. 410: Adapted from J. P. White and J. F. O'Connell, *Science,* 203, 1979. With permission from Science and the authors.

Chapter Seventeen

Fig. 17.5, p. 447: Skin Color Map from *Biological Perspectives on Human Pigmentation,* by A. H. Robins, p. 187, 1991. Reprinted with the permission of Cambridge University Press; Fig. 17.7, p. 450: Mark L. Weiss and Alan E. Mann, *Human Biology and Behavior,* 4th edition, © 1985. Reprinted by permission of Pearson Education, Inc., Upper Saddle River, NJ; Fig.17.8, p. 451: Reprinted with the permission of The Free Press, a Division of Simon & Schuster Adult Publishing Group, from *The Concept of Race* by Ashley Montagu. Copyright © 1964 by Ashley Montagu. All rights reserved; Fig. 17.9, p. 452: From *The Living Races of Man* by Carleton S. Coon and Edward E. Hunt, Jr. Copyright © 1965 by Carleton S. Coon. Used by permission of

Alfred A. Knopf, a division of Random House, Inc.; Fig. 17.10, p. 453: From *The Human Species: An Introduction to Physical Anthropology,* 2/e by Frederick S. Hulse, Copyright © 1963 by Random House, Inc.; Fig. 17.11, p. 457 *top:* Racial Map from *Human Races,* 2/e by S. M. Garn, p. 129, 1965. Courtesy of Charles C. Thomas, Publisher, Ltd., Springfield, Illinois; Fig. 17.12, p. 457 *bottom:* Genetic Diversity Table, from *Genetic Basis of Evolutoinary Change* by Richard C. Lewontin. Copyright © 1974 Columbia University Press. Reprinted with permission of the author; Fig. 17.15, p. 463: Living Planet Report 2004. Published in October 2004 by WWF-World Wide Fund For Nature (formerly World Wildlife Fund), Gland, Switzerland.

Index